GREAT EVENTS FROM HISTORY
NORTH AMERICAN SERIES

GREAT EVENTS FROM HISTORY
NORTH AMERICAN SERIES

Revised Edition

Volume 2
1820 – 1895

Edited by
FRANK N. MAGILL

Associate Editor
JOHN L. LOOS

Managing Editor, Revised Edition
CHRISTINA J. MOOSE

Salem Press, Inc.
Pasadena, California   Englewood Cliffs, N.J.

Editor in Chief: Dawn P. Dawson
Managing Editor: Christina J. Moose
Acquisitions Editor: Mark Rehn
Manuscript Editor: Irene Struthers
Research Supervisor: Jeffry Jensen
Research Assistant: Irene McDermott
Photograph Editor: Valerie Krein
Proofreading Supervisor: Yasmine A. Cordoba
Map Design and Page Layout: James Hutson
Data Entry: William Zimmerman

Library of Congress Cataloging-in-Publication Data

Great events from history : North American series / edited by Frank N. Magill ; associate editor, John L. Loos.
  — Rev. ed.
    p. cm.
  Includes bibliographical references (p.) and index.
  ISBN 0-89356-429-X (set). — ISBN 0-89356-431-1 (vol. 2)
  1. North America—History. 2. United States—History. I. Magill, Frank Northen, 1907-   . II. Loos, John L.
E45.G74   1997
970—dc21

96-39165
CIP

First Printing

CONTENTS

		page
	List of Maps	xxxi
1820's	Free Public School Movement	337
1820's	Social Reform Movement	339
1820	Missouri Compromise	340
1820	Land Act of 1820	343
1821	Mexican War of Independence	344
1821	Santa Fe Trail Opens	346
1823	Hartford Female Seminary Is Founded	348
1823	Jedediah Smith Explores the Far West	350
1823	Monroe Doctrine	352
1824	*Gibbons v. Ogden*	354
1824	U.S. Election of 1824	356
1825	Erie Canal Opens	358
1828	*Cherokee Phoenix* Begins Publication	360
1828	Webster's *American Dictionary of the English Language*	363
1828	Jackson Is Elected President	364
1830	Proslavery Argument	366
1830	Baltimore and Ohio Railroad Begins Operation	368
1830	Webster-Hayne Debate	370
1830	Indian Removal Act	372
1830	Trail of Tears	375
1831	*The Liberator* Begins Publication	377
1831	Cherokee Cases	379
1831	Tocqueville Visits America	381
1831	McCormick Invents the Reaper	383
1831	Nat Turner's Insurrection	385
1832	Jackson vs. the Bank of the United States	387
1832	Nullification Controversy	388
1833	Rise of the Penny Press	391
1833	American Anti-Slavery Society Is Founded	392
1833	Oberlin College Is Established	394
1834	Birth of the Whig Party	396
1835	Texas Revolution	398
1836	Rise of Transcendentalism	399
1837	Rebellions in Canada	401
1837	Mt. Holyoke Seminary Is Founded	403
1839	Amistad Slave Revolt	405
1840's	"Old" Immigration	407
1840	U.S. Election of 1840	408
1841	Upper and Lower Canada Unite	410
1841	Preemption Act	412
1842	*Commonwealth v. Hunt*	414
1842	Frémont's Expeditions	415
1842	Dorr Rebellion	418
1842	Webster-Ashburton Treaty	420
1844	Anti-Irish Riots	422

page

1844 First Telegraph Message 424
1845 Era of the Clipper Ships 426
1846 Howe's Sewing Machine 428
1846 Mormon Migration to Utah 430
1846 Mexican War 432
1846 Oregon Settlement 434
1846 Occupation of California and the Southwest 437
1846 Independent Treasury Is Established 439
1846 Smithsonian Institution Is Founded 440
1846 Surgical Anesthesia Is Safely Demonstrated 442
1847 Taos Rebellion 444
1847 *The North Star* Begins Publication 445
1848 California Gold Rush 448
1848 Treaty of Guadalupe Hidalgo 450
1848 Seneca Falls Convention 452
1849 Chinese Immigration 453
1850 Compromise of 1850 456
1850 Bloody Island Massacre 458
1850 Second Fugitive Slave Law 460
1850 Underground Railroad 462
1851 Akron Woman's Rights Convention 464
1853 Pacific Railroad Surveys 467
1853 National Council of Colored People Is Founded 470
1853 Gadsden Purchase 472
1854 Perry Opens Trade with Japan 474
1854 Kansas-Nebraska Act 476
1854 Birth of the Republican Party 479
1856 Bleeding Kansas 481
1857 First African American University 483
1857 *Dred Scott v. Sandford* 485
1857 New York Infirmary for Indigent Women and Children Opens 487
1857 Cart War 489
1858 Fraser River Gold Rush 491
1858 Lincoln-Douglas Debates 492
1858 First Transatlantic Cable 494
1859 Last Slave Ship Docks at Mobile 496
1859 First Commercial Oil Well 498
1859 John Brown's Raid on Harpers Ferry 499
1860 Pony Express 501
1860 Lincoln Is Elected President 503
1860 Confederate States Secede from the Union 505
1861 Stand Watie Fights for the South 507
1861 Apache Wars 509
1861 Lincoln's Inauguration 511
1861 First Battle of Bull Run 517
1861 Transcontinental Telegraph Is Completed 518
1862 *Monitor* vs. *Virginia* 520
1862 Homestead Act 522
1862 Morrill Land Grant Act 524

page

1862 Great Sioux War 526
1863 Emancipation Proclamation 528
1863 National Bank Acts 530
1863 First National Draft Law 532
1863 Battles of Gettysburg, Vicksburg, and Chattanooga 534
1863 Long Walk of the Navajos 536
1863 Reconstruction 538
1864 Sherman's March to the Sea 541
1864 Sand Creek Massacre 542
1865 Freedmen's Bureau Is Established 544
1865 Surrender at Appomattox and Assassination of Lincoln 545
1865 Vassar College Is Founded 548
1865 New Black Codes 549
1865 Thirteenth Amendment 551
1866 Chisholm Trail Opens 553
1866 Rise of the Ku Klux Klan 555
1866 Civil Rights Act of 1866 558
1866 Race Riots in the South 560
1866 Suffragists Protest the Fourteenth Amendment 561
1866 Bozeman Trail War 563
1867 Office of Education Is Created 565
1867 Purchase of Alaska 567
1867 British North America Act 568
1867 Medicine Lodge Creek Treaty 571
1867 National Grange of the Patrons of Husbandry Forms 572
1868 Impeachment of Andrew Johnson 574
1868 Burlingame Treaty 576
1868 Fourteenth Amendment 577
1868 Washita River Massacre 580
1869 Rise of Woman Suffrage Associations 582
1869 Transcontinental Railroad Is Completed 584
1869 Scandals of the Grant Administration 586
1869 First Riel Rebellion 588
1869 Western States Grant Woman Suffrage 590
1871 Indian Appropriation Act 592
1871 Barnum's Circus Forms 594
1871 Treaty of Washington 596
1872 Great American Bison Slaughter 598
1872 Susan B. Anthony Is Arrested 600
1873 "Crime of 1873" 602
1873 Mackenzie Era in Canada 603
1874 Red River War 605
1874 *Minor v. Happersett* 608
1875 Supreme Court of Canada Is Established 610
1875 Page Law 611
1876 Canada's Indian Act 614
1876 Bell Demonstrates the Telephone 615
1876 Battle of the Little Bighorn 617
1876 Declaration of the Rights of Women 620

page

1877   Hayes Is Elected President 621
1877   Nez Perce Exile 623
1877   Salt Wars 625
1878   Macdonald Returns as Canada's Prime Minister 626
1879   Powell's *Report on the Lands of the Arid Region* 628
1879   Edison Demonstrates the Incandescent Lamp 631
1882   Standard Oil Trust Is Organized 632
1882   Chinese Exclusion Act 634
1882   Rise of the Chinese Six Companies 636
1883   Pendleton Act 638
1883   Brooklyn Bridge Opens 639
1883   Civil Rights Cases 641
1884   U.S. Election of 1884 643
1885   Second Riel Rebellion 646
1886   American Federation of Labor Is Founded 648
1887   Interstate Commerce Act 650
1887   General Allotment Act 652
1889   Hull House Opens 653
1889   First Pan-American Congress 655
1890   Closing of the Frontier 657
1890   Women's Rights Associations Unite 660
1890   Sherman Antitrust Act 662
1890   Mississippi Disfranchisement Laws 664
1890   Battle of Wounded Knee 666
1892   "New" Immigration 668
1892   Yellow Peril Campaign 671
1892   Birth of the People's Party 672
1893   World's Columbian Exposition 674
1894   Pullman Strike 676
1895   Hearst-Pulitzer Circulation War 678
1895   Chinese American Citizens Alliance Is Founded 679

Key Word Index XXVII
Category List XXXVII

LIST OF MAPS

Volume I

Bering Strait Migrations 2
Ancient Civilizations of the Southwest and
   Mesoamerica 10
Mound-Building Cultures and Mound Sites 18
Voyages of Columbus, 1492-1502 24
Major Voyages to the New World After
   Columbus 28
Native Peoples of Eastern North America
   c. 1600 31
Shipwrecks and Wanderings: The Expeditions
   of Narváez and Cabeza de Vaca,
   1528-1536 37
Coronado's Expedition, 1540-1542 43
Frobisher's Voyages, 1576-1578 52
Explorations of Drake, Oñate, and Vizcaíno,
   1579-1602 55
Champlain and French Explorations,
   1603-1616 61
Hudson's Voyage of 1610-1611 66
Settlements of the American Colonies,
   1600-1760 82
Mississippi Valley: The Marquette/Jolliet and
   La Salle Expeditions, 1573-1682 114
Dominion of New England, 1686-1689 124
Voyages to Alaska, 1728-1769 136
Major Battles in the French and Indian War,
   1754-1763 149
Proclamation Line of 1763 158
Quebec Act, 1774 179
Major Sites in the American Revolutionary
   War (includes time line) 186
Territory of the United States in 1783 209
Land Cessions by the States After the
   Revolutionary War, 1783-1802 223
Federalists vs. Antifederalists, 1788 235
Mackenzie's Northwestern Explorations,
   1789-1793 254
Territory of the United States in 1803 279
Western Expeditions of Lewis and Clark
   (1804-1806) and Pike (1806-1807) 288
War of 1812: Battles in the North 307
War of 1812: Battles in the South 308
Territory of the United States in 1819 334

Volume II

Alignment of Free and Slave States After the
   Missouri Compromise, 1821 341
Trails of Tears: Routes of Indian Removal to
   the West After 1830 373
Union of Upper and Lower Canada, 1841 411
Webster-Ashburton Treaty, 1842 421
Territory of the United States in 1846 435
Alignment of Free and Slave States After the
   Compromise of 1850 457
Four Possible Routes: Pacific Railroad
   Surveys, 1853-1855 468
Territory of the United States in 1853 473
Alignment of Free and Slave States After the
   Kansas-Nebraska Act of 1854 477
The Union and the Confederacy 506
The Civil War, 1861-1865
   (includes time line) 514
Pathways to the West, 1840's-1860's 523
Dates of Confederate States' Readmission to
   the Union 539
Trans-Mississippi Railroads and Cattle
   Trails 554
The Dominion of Canada, 1867 569
Indian Wars in the West, 1840's-1890 606
The Riel Rebellions, 1869 and 1885 647
Lands Settled by 1890 658

Volume III

World War I: Western Front, 1918
   (includes time line) 789
World War II: The European Theater
   (includes time line) 922
World War II: The Pacific Theater
   (includes time line) 958
Modern Canada, 1949 990
Korean War, 1950-1953 995

Volume IV

Castro's Cuban Revolution 1026
Modern United States 1036
Vietnam War, 1954-1975 1081
Persian Gulf War, 1991 1253

GREAT EVENTS FROM HISTORY
NORTH AMERICAN SERIES

1820's ■ FREE PUBLIC SCHOOL MOVEMENT:
the birth of the concept of education as a responsibility of a democratic government

DATE: 1820's-1830's
LOCALE: Northeastern, Western, and upper Southern states
CATEGORIES: Cultural and intellectual history; Education; Government and politics
KEY FIGURES:

Henry Barnard (1811-1900), editor of the *American Journal of Education* and commissioner of public schools in Connecticut and Rhode Island

James G. Carter (1795-1849), Massachusetts educational reformer

DeWitt Clinton (1769-1828), governor of New York

Edward Everett (1794-1865), governor of Massachusetts

Horace Mann (1796-1859), secretary of the Massachusetts Board of Education, 1837-1848

Charles Fenton Mercer (1778-1858), Whig politician from Virginia

Thaddeus Stevens (1792-1868), leader of free-school supporters in Pennsylvania House

Calvin Wiley (1819-1887), first superintendent of common schools in North Carolina

SUMMARY OF EVENT. The free public school movement of the late 1820's and the 1830's had its roots in the latter part of the eighteenth century when a number of states had drafted constitutions containing clauses urging public aid to education. Nevertheless, the idea that education was a function of the government of the state rather than of family, church, or philanthropy took hold only gradually. Teaching was generally done by low-paid, untrained young men who regarded it as a temporary occupation. It was not until the early nineteenth century that some states began to enact laws leading to the establishment of public or common schools. Even then, such schools were generally created for, and attended by, pauper children. Moreover, although most states established permanent school funds to supplement local support of schools, few states resorted to direct taxation as a means of financing education.

The free school movement should be understood within the context of Jacksonian democracy and the reform movement of which it was a part. Free public schools were one of many organized efforts for self-improvement which included such other notable developments as the lyceum movement for adult education, lending library societies and associations, literary societies, and debating societies. During the first two or three decades of the nineteenth century, religious and philanthropic institutions were more active than state governments in promoting free public schooling. The Sunday school movement contributed significantly to the growth of interest in public education. Even more important were the efforts of philanthropists working through benevolent societies. The Free School Society of the City of New York, later reorganized as the Public School Society of New York, was typical of such efforts, as was the Philadelphia Society for the Establishment and Support of Charity Schools. Nevertheless, like existing state-supported institutions, these schools were mainly for the benefit of children of the poor.

Not until the late 1820's and the 1830's were demands heard for the establishment of a system of free public schooling open to all. In some of the larger cities, workingmen's parties called upon the state legislatures to establish public schools. Thus the workingmen of Boston declared in 1830 that "the establishment of a liberal system of education, attainable by all, should be among the first efforts of every lawgiver who desires the continuance of our national independence." At the same time, a number of educational reformers, influenced by the social reform movement which swept over the United States in the 1830's and 1840's, began to promote the cause of free public schooling. James G. Carter of Massachusetts wrote newspaper articles and pamphlets suggesting improvements in the educational system of his state; as a member of the Massachusetts House and chairman of the Committee on Education, Carter drafted the bill creating the Massachusetts Board of Education in 1837. Horace Mann, who was named secretary of the board, left a promising legal and political career to dedicate himself to what he called "the supremest welfare of mankind upon the earth." During his twelve years on the board, Mann sustained a concerted campaign on behalf of public education. Largely as a result of efforts by Carter and Mann, Massachusetts led the way in establishing a system of public schooling.

Mann's celebrated "annual reports" were perhaps the single most important factor in bringing the concept of universal free education to the national political agenda. In Mann's 1848 Annual Report, he argued that, "nothing but Universal Education can counterwork this tendency to the domination of capital and the servility of labor." Mann perceived education as "the great equalizer of the conditions of men—the balance wheel of the social machinery. . . . It does better than to disarm the poor of their hostility toward the rich; it prevents being poor." Although Mann's hopes for the impact of education may seem hyperbolic, his leadership on the Board of Education and his Annual Reports resulted in significant and tangible results, including a lengthened school year, increased teacher salaries, the establishment of the first state-supported normal school to train teachers, and an organized state association for public school teachers.

In Connecticut and Rhode Island, Henry Barnard promoted the public school cause. In the South and West, where obstacles to free public schools were greater than in New England, other educational reformers worked to establish systems of public education and to improve facilities and teacher training. Calvin Wiley made North Carolina the center of educational reform in the South. Caleb Mills called for the establishment of a public school system in a series of six annual "addresses" to the Indiana legislature. In neighboring Ohio, Calvin Stowe, a founder of the Western Literary Institute and College of Professional Teachers, contributed to the development of free public schools through his accounts of the Prussian educational system.

The efforts of educational reformers in promoting free schooling were aided by a number of politicians, including governors, such as DeWitt Clinton of New York, Edward Everett and Marcus Morton of Massachusetts, and George Wolf of Pennsylvania. The New York Whig William H. Seward justified state support of common schools on much the same grounds as other internal improvements. In Pennsylvania, Thaddeus Stevens invoked humanitarian and democratic notions in support of a state law supporting public education. Stevens, a young Whig legislator, provided the leadership to pass the 1834 state school law in Pennsylvania that allowed for universal free schools; opposing forces had argued strongly that free education should be provided only for the very poor. Robert Rantoul, Jr., the first Democratic member of the Massachusetts Board of Education, was another spokesman for free schooling. Publicists and editors, such as George Bancroft, William Cullen Bryant, and William Leggett, also lent their voices to the campaign for "universal education."

By 1850, the movement for free public schooling had largely achieved its basic objectives. The principle of public support for common schools was generally accepted throughout the Union. Every state, for example, had by mid-century established some type of permanent school fund. Moreover, every state except Arkansas had experimented with taxation as a means of school support. Taxation was not universally accepted and school tax laws were repealed in some states, but a precedent had been established which would serve as a basis for a unified system of compulsory taxation. Accompanying the principle of public support was the principle of public control of education. By 1850, according to Lawrence Cremin, "the people . . . largely controlled the schools which they had instituted with public funds." Thus the middle of the nineteenth century marked the end of the initial phase of the campaign for free public schooling, during which the essential groundwork was laid, and the beginning of a second phase of expansion and development was made. Despite the tangible advances that occurred during these decades, American free public schools remained in a stage of infancy: There were virtually no compulsory attendance laws; school terms remained relatively short and susceptible to manipulation by the local farming seasons and other factors; the quality and extent of the school curriculum varied widely; teaching methods remained based on rote memorization, and discipline often depended heavily on corporal punishment. Free public education had become the norm only in Massachusetts and selected areas of the North. An 1827 Massachusetts law stipulated that every town of five hundred families or more must create a public high school; this legal provision resulted in more than one hundred Massachusetts public high schools by 1860, yet only two hundred additional public high schools existed in the rest of the country at that time.

For the rest of the nineteenth century and indeed into the twentieth century, the issue of free public schools continued to have opponents as well as supporters. While the supporters might articulate that employers needed literate workers, and social theorists strongly supported the idea that a society founded upon the notion of universal suffrage needed universal public education in order to ensure well-informed voters, there remained critics—including many taxpayers who did not want to educate other people's children—who considered education a private concern. Although the Sunday school movement had helped to publicize the idea of free education, many religious groups wanted to maintain their own schools without public funds and also without public advice and consent in their own specialized curricula.

—*Anne C. Loveland, updated by Richard Sax*

ADDITIONAL READING:

Butts, R. Freeman, and Lawrence A. Cremin. *A History of Education in American Culture*. New York: Henry Holt, 1953. A comprehensive survey of American education, including a dialectical discussion concerning how the free school movement developed from various crosscurrents in educational thought.

Good, Harry G., and James D. Teller. *A History of American Education*. 3d ed. New York: Macmillan, 1973. Chapter 5, "From Private Schools to State Systems," includes a lengthy discussion of the Free School Society (later, the Public School Society) of New York City.

McClellan, B. Edward, and William J. Reese, eds. *The Social History of American Education*. Urbana: University of Illinois Press, 1988. A collection of seventeen essays, arranged chronologically. Michael Katz's article, "The Origins of Public Education: A Reassessment," provides an intellectual context for the free school movement.

Spring, Joel. *The American School, 1642-1990*. 2d ed. New York: Longman, 1990. Spring's informed, though politically slanted, argument shows how the common school movement developed from the premise that education is a panacea for a society with failing families and an oppressive factory culture.

Welter, Rush. *Popular Education and Democratic Thought in America*. New York: Columbia University Press, 1962. Welter argues, especially in chapter 4, that the common school movement benefited greatly from the Democratic Party's commitment to public education.

SEE ALSO: 1785, Beginnings of State Universities; 1802, U.S. Military Academy Is Established; 1820's, Social Reform Movement; 1823, Hartford Female Seminary Is Founded; 1828, Webster's *American Dictionary of the English Language*; 1833, Rise of the Penny Press; 1833, Oberlin College Is Established; 1857, First African American University; 1862, Morrill Land Grant Act; 1865, Vassar College Is Founded; 1867, Office of Education Is Created.

1820's ■ SOCIAL REFORM MOVEMENT: *a wave of religious and philanthropic movements work for humanitarian and democratic reforms, including abolition, temperance, woman suffrage, and access to education*

DATE: 1820's-1850's

LOCALE: Northeastern and Western United States

CATEGORIES: African American history; Civil rights; Education; Religion; Social reform; Women's issues

KEY FIGURES:

Lyman Beecher (1775-1863), patriarch of the Beecher family of reformers

Elihu Burritt (1810-1879), pacifist editor of the *Advocate of Peace and Universal Brotherhood*

Dorothea Lynde Dix (1802-1887), reformer concerned with the treatment of the mentally ill

Charles Fourier (1772-1837), French social theorist whose doctrine of communitarian living was used by many American reformers

Thomas Hopkins Gallaudet (1787-1851), founder of the first free American school for the deaf

William Lloyd Garrison (1805-1879), abolitionist editor of *The Liberator*

Samuel Gridley Howe (1801-1876), founder of the institution that later became known as the Perkins School for the Blind, and husband of writer and reformer Julia Ward Howe

Horace Mann (1796-1859), champion of free public education

Lucretia Coffin Mott (1793-1880), Quaker reformer who organized the Seneca Falls Convention

Theodore Dwight Weld (1803-1895), founder of the American Anti-Slavery Society and organizer of the group "Seventy"

SUMMARY OF EVENT. "In the history of the world the doctrine of Reform had never such scope as at the present hour," declared Ralph Waldo Emerson in 1841. The wave of reform that swept over much of the United States from the 1820's to the 1850's seemed to prove Emerson's theory that the human being is "born . . . to be a Reformer, a Remaker of what man has made; a renouncer of lies; a restorer of truth and good, imitating that great Nature which embosoms us all, and which sleeps no moment on an old past, but every hour repairs herself." In those decades, people enlisted in a variety of causes and crusades, some of which were of a conservative nature, while others challenged basic institutions and beliefs.

The antebellum reform movement was partly a response to economic, social, and political changes following the War of 1812. Such changes provoked feelings of anxiety in the United States, generating anti-Mason, anti-Catholic, and anti-Mormon crusades. However, change also generated a feeling of optimism and confirmed the almost universal faith in progress that characterized early nineteenth century Americans. Reformers came from two groups: religious reformers and the wealthy who felt obligated to help the less fortunate. Evangelical religion played an important role in the origins of the reform movement. The shift from the Calvinistic doctrine of predestination to more democratic teachings that emphasized man's efforts in achieving salvation nourished ideas of perfectionism and millennarianism. Not only could individuals achieve "perfect holiness" but the world itself, as evidenced by the movements of reform, was improving and moving toward the long-awaited thousand-year reign of the Kingdom of God on earth. Besides evangelicalism, the legacy of the Enlightenment and the American Revolution (the natural rights philosophy and the faith in humanity's ability to shape society in accordance with the laws of God and nature) was a stimulus to reform. So was the nineteenth century's romantic conception of the individual. "The power which is at once spring and regulator in all efforts of reform," Emerson wrote, "is the conviction that there is an infinite worthiness in man, which will appear at the call of worth, and that all particular reforms are the removing of some impediment."

Antebellum reformers attacked a variety of evils. Dorothea Dix urged humane treatment for the mentally ill; Thomas Gallaudet and Samuel Gridley Howe founded schools for the deaf and the blind. Prison reform engaged the efforts of some, and a campaign to abolish imprisonment for debt made slow but sure progress in the pre-Civil War period. Horace Mann championed common schools, and free public schooling gradually spread from New England to other parts of the United States. Elihu Burritt, the "learned blacksmith," urged the abolition of war and related evils. Communitarians, inspired by religious or secular principles, withdrew from society to found utopian experiments, such as Oneida, Amana, Hopedale, Ephrata Cloister, and New Harmony. The communitarian teachings of French social theorist Charles Fourier inspired such experiments as Brook Farm, the North American Phalanx of Red Bank, New Jersey, and the Sylvani Phalanx of northeastern Pennsylvania. Lucretia Mott, Elizabeth Cady Stanton, Lucy Stone, and others championed higher education, the suffrage, and legal and property rights for women.

Temperance and abolition were the two most prominent secular crusades of the period. Both of them passed through several phases, moving from gradualism to immediatism and from persuasion to legal coercion. The temperance movement began with an appeal for moderation in the consumption of alcoholic beverages and shifted by the late 1820's to a demand for total abstinence. The Reverend Lyman Beecher's *Six Sermons*, published in 1826, were instrumental in effecting this shift to total abstinence; the "teetotal" position was further popularized in the 1840's by the Washington Temperance Society of reformed "drunkards" (alcoholics) and the children's Cold Water Army. Similarly, the antislavery movement moved from a position favoring gradual emancipation and colonization in the 1820's, to a demand for immediate abolition of the sin of slavery. William Lloyd Garrison's *Liberator* and Theodore Dwight Weld's "Seventy" preached the immediatist doctrine, and it was adopted by the American Anti-Slavery Society, which had been founded in 1833. In the 1840's, some temperance and antislavery reformers, disillusioned by the lack of results from education and moral suasion, turned to politics as a means of achieving their goals. Some abolitionists supported the Liberty and Free-Soil Parties, and later the Republicans, and sought legislation preventing the extension of slavery into the territories. Temperance advocates succeeded in getting statewide prohibition and local option laws passed in a number of states in the early 1850's.

In most cases, the vehicle of reform was the voluntary association. Virtually every movement had a national organization, with state and local auxiliaries, which sponsored speakers, published pamphlets, and generally coordinated efforts in behalf of its cause. Although such societies were often rent by factionalism, they proved remarkably effective in arousing the popular conscience on the moral issues of the day. By 1850, for example, there were almost two thousand antislavery societies with a membership close to 200,000, compared to about five hundred such societies in 1826.

Although most of the reform movements had their largest following in the northeastern and western parts of the United States, their impact was not confined to those sections. Southerners, although hostile to abolitionism and other radical causes, were receptive to pleas for educational and prison reform and for better treatment of the insane and the blind. The temperance crusade made considerable headway in the South. Thus, to a greater or lesser degree, depending on the particular cause, the antebellum social reform movement was a truly national phenomenon.

—Anne C. Loveland, updated by Geralyn Strecker

ADDITIONAL READING:

Foster, Lawrence. *Women, Family, and Utopia: Communal Experiments of the Shakers, the Oneida Community, and the Mormons.* Syracuse, N.Y.: Syracuse University Press, 1991. Intriguing study of religion, sexuality, and women's roles in utopian living.

Griffin, Clifford S. *Their Brothers' Keepers: Moral Stewardship in the United States, 1800-1865.* New Brunswick, N.J.: Rutgers University Press, 1960. Views the antebellum reform movement as an essentially conservative effort by wealthy reformers attempting to preserve social stability, sobriety, and order.

Guarneri, Carl J. *The Utopian Alternative: Fourierism in Nineteenth-Century America.* Ithaca, N.Y.: Cornell University Press, 1991. Evaluates the influence of Charles Fourier's communitarianism on the growth of utopian living in the United States.

Holloway, Mark. *Heavens on Earth: Utopian Communities in America, 1680-1880.* 2d ed. New York: Dover, 1966. Discusses the general characteristics of utopian communities and describes several important examples.

Mandelker, Ira L. *Religion, Society, and Utopia in Nineteenth-Century America.* Amherst: University of Massachusetts Press, 1984. Discusses both the social tensions that caused a need for utopian communities and the internal tensions that caused most of them to fail.

Nye, Russel B. *William Lloyd Garrison and the Humanitarian Reformers.* Boston: Little, Brown, 1955. Explains Garrison's role in the greater humanitarian reform movement, as well as his involvement with abolition groups.

Tyler, Alice Felt. *Freedom's Ferment: Phases of American Social History from the Colonial Period to the Outbreak of the Civil War.* Minneapolis: University of Minnesota Press, 1944. Surveys major reform efforts in context with political, economic, and social conditions in the United States. The conclusions have been challenged by more recent works, but this remains a valuable, comprehensive study of reform.

SEE ALSO: 1790's, Second Great Awakening; 1799, Code of Handsome Lake; 1808, Prophetstown Is Founded; 1814, New Harmony and the Communitarian Movement; 1816, AME Church Is Founded; 1819, Unitarian Church Is Founded; 1820's, Free Public School Movement; 1823, Hartford Female Seminary Is Founded; 1828, *Cherokee Phoenix* Begins Publication; 1828, Webster's *American Dictionary of the English Language*; 1831, *The Liberator* Begins Publication; 1831, Tocqueville Visits America; 1833, American Anti-Slavery Society Is Founded; 1833, Oberlin College Is Established; 1836, Rise of Transcendentalism; 1837, Mt. Holyoke Seminary Is Founded; 1846, Mormon Migration to Utah; 1847, *The North Star* Begins Publication; 1848, Seneca Falls Convention; 1851, Akron Woman's Rights Convention.

1820 ■ MISSOURI COMPROMISE: *a measure that attempts to pacify both Northern and Southern sectional interests by allowing slavery to exist in the southern part of the Louisiana Purchase territory*

DATE: March 3, 1820
LOCALE: Missouri Territory
CATEGORIES: African American history; Civil rights; Laws and acts
KEY FIGURES:
Henry Clay (1777-1852), Speaker of the U.S. House of Representatives
James Tallmadge (1778-1853), representative from New York
John W. Taylor (1784-1854), representative from New York
Jesse Burgess Thomas (1777-1853), senator from Illinois

SUMMARY OF EVENT. Between 1818 and 1819 both the territories of Missouri and Maine petitioned the U.S. Congress to be admitted as new states. The Missouri Territory had been created from the Louisiana Purchase (1803) and was promised constitutional protection. However, Congress could not decide

ALIGNMENT OF FREE AND SLAVE STATES AFTER THE MISSOURI COMPROMISE, 1821

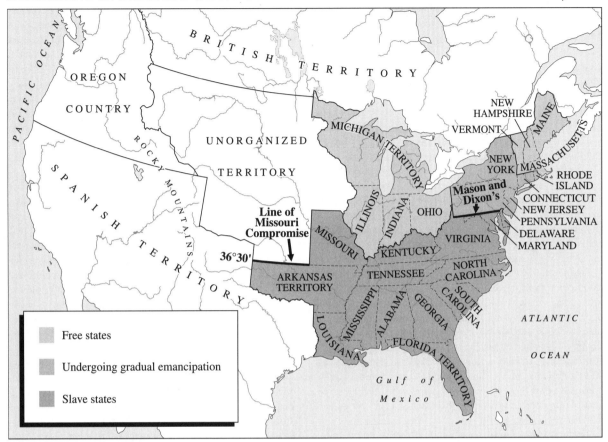

Missouri's application for U.S. statehood threatened the balance between free and slave states and raised the issue of how to handle slavery in the growing Western territories. Finally Congress voted to admit Maine as a free state and Missouri as a slave state and restricted slavery north of 36°30'. This compromise arrangement would stand until 1857, but the seeds of sectional conflict were already sown.

if the right of property applied to the institution of slavery. Should it be allowed in Missouri and the rest of the Louisiana Purchase, or did Congress have the moral responsibility to rectify the issue of slavery that had been avoided since the Constitutional Convention of 1787? It would take three sessions of Congress between 1818 and 1821 before Missouri was fully admitted as a state. The issue of slavery sparked by the ensuing debate spread throughout the country and threatened to cause disunion between the Northern and Southern regions.

At the time Missouri and Maine applied for statehood, the United States consisted of eleven free states and eleven slave states. This political balance had been achieved since 1789 by admitting a slave state and then a free state determined by geographical location and each region's past history with regard to slavery. This arrangement supplied each section with an equal number of senators (two per state) and attempted to equalize representation in the House of Representatives through the three-fifths clause.

The three-fifths clause, added to the final draft of the Constitution, allowed slave states to count each slave as three-fifths of a person to balance their representative power against that of the more densely populated North. Nevertheless, the North had a majority of representatives in Congress (105 to 81). Missouri's admission as a free or slave state therefore became an important issue in the very body that would resolve it. Missouri threatened to extend the influence of the industrial free North in the Senate or provide the majority to the agrarian slaveholding South.

In 1818, Missouri's boundaries were approximately the same as those of today, and the territory was estimated to have 2,000 to 3,000 slaves. Slavery was a historical by-product of prior French and Spanish colonial policies. Missouri reasoned that slavery should be allowed to continue as it had in other territories that had been granted statehood since 1789.

In February, 1819, the House of Representatives responded to this debate by adopting the Tallmadge amendment. Representative James Tallmadge of New York proposed an amendment to the bill allowing Missouri to frame a state constitution. The two clauses in the amendment would restrict the further introduction of slavery into Missouri and provide that all children born to slaves would be free at age twenty-five. Both clauses passed the House. Southern senators were shocked by the bitterness of the debate in the House and the ability of the North to muster votes. They saw the Tallmadge amendment as the first step in eliminating the expansion of slavery. Voting along sectional lines, the Senate rejected both clauses.

Congress adjourned session until December 6, 1819. During this interim, Maine formed a constitution and applied for admission as a free state. Maine had been incorporated into the Massachusetts Bay Colony in 1691 but had started to agitate for separate statehood during and after the War of 1812. Its application for statehood as a free state seemed to provide a possible solution to the Missouri debate that threatened the stability of the young nation. On February 18, 1820, the Senate Judiciary Committee joined the two measures and the Senate passed Maine's and Missouri's applications for statehood but without mentioning slavery. This infuriated Maine which had, as part of Massachusetts, outlawed slavery in 1780. What should have been a routine confirmation of new states became part of the most explosive issue to face the country. Maine would be allowed to separate from Massachusetts and gain statehood as long as Congress approved it by March 4, 1820, or the nine counties would revert back to Massachusetts. Even so, many of Maine's constituency urged that Maine's application fail so that slavery would not spread into Missouri.

Senator J. B. Thomas of Illinois offered a compromise amendment to the Senate bill that would admit Missouri as a slave state with the proviso that the remaining territories in the Louisiana Purchase above 36°30′, Missouri's southern border, would be free of slavery. The Northern-controlled House responded by rejecting this Thomas amendment and passed a proviso prohibiting the further introduction of slavery anywhere. The result was polarization along sectional lines. In turn, the Senate struck out the antislavery provision and added the Thomas amendment. Thus began the final debate over whether slavery would be allowed to expand.

Senator Rufus King of New York continued the debate by stating that Congress, under Article IV, Section 3 of the Constitution, was empowered to exclude slavery from the territory and to make slavery an issue for statehood. "New states *may be* admitted by the Congress into this Union." A precedent had been established under Article IV, Section 3 of the Constitution which forbade slavery in lands above the Ohio River in the Northwest Ordinance of 1787. Therefore, in the minds of many of the Northern congressmen, they should take this opportunity to eliminate slavery from any point west of the Mississippi. In response, Senator William Pickering of Maryland stated that the United States was composed of an equal number of slave states and free states; Missouri should be allowed to determine its own fate.

Missouri responded with anger and frustration, asserting that the issue was not about slavery but rather the issue of state sovereignty. Congress had delayed its admission for years. Missouri, like other states, had the right to choose its property laws. In Missouri as well as the rest of the South, the issue swung from one dealing with slavery to one dealing with property rights and the equality of states within the United States. These issues captured the attention of citizens throughout the country and led to heated debates on all levels. For the first time, slavery was being justified and defended as a good way of life by not only Southern politicians but also the Southern clergy. Would the country be influenced by restrictionists who sought to control this institution, or would states' rights be preserved?

A compromise was eventually reached, between the two houses, in a conference formed to break the deadlock. Speaker of the House Henry Clay of Kentucky stated that he would not support Maine's admission unless Missouri was admitted with no restrictions. The Senate took the House bill and inserted the Thomas amendment. The House under Henry Clay's leadership voted to admit Maine as a free state and Missouri as a slave state and restricted slavery north of 36°30′. It is interesting to note that seven of Maine's nine representatives in the Massachusetts delegation voted against Maine's admission so that their state would not be used to provide a solution to the slavery issue.

Missouri continued to be an issue when it presented a state constitution in November, 1820. As if to get the final word, the Missouri Constitutional Convention had incorporated into its constitution a provision excluding free blacks and mulattoes from the state. This provision incited the antislavery factions in the Senate and House and threatened to destroy the fragile compromise. A "Second Missouri Compromise" was needed which stated that Missouri would not gain admission as a state unless its legislature assured Congress that it would not seek to abridge the rights of citizens. The Missouri legislature agreed to this in June, 1821. On August 10, 1821, President James Monroe admitted Missouri as the twenty-fourth state. After waiting a short time, Missouri's state congress sought to have the last say when it approved statutes forbidding free blacks from entering the state.

The Missouri Compromise would stand for thirty-five years. During that time it served to mark a clear delineation between the growing regional and sectional problems of the North and South and made states' rights the rallying cry for the South until the Civil War.   —*Vincent Michael Thur*

ADDITIONAL READING:

Brown, Richard H. *The Missouri Compromise: Political Statesmanship or Unwise Evasion?* Boston: D. C. Heath, 1964. Contains primary source material showing views of contemporary leaders and varying perspectives of historians.

Clark, Charles E. *Maine: A Bicentennial History.* New York: W. W. Norton, 1977. Condensed overview of Maine history. Index, annotated bibliography, and footnotes.

Commager, Henry Steele, ed. *Documents of American History.* New York: Appleton-Century-Crofts, 1958. Compilation of major American historical documents accompanied by commentary.

Hurt, R. Douglas. *Agriculture and Slavery in Missouri's Little Dixie*. Columbia: University of Missouri Press, 1992. A study of the political and legal impact of the Missouri Compromise during the antebellum era in a seven-county area along the Missouri River.

McPherson, James M. *The Battle Cry of Freedom: The Civil War Era*. Oxford, England: Oxford University Press, 1988. Definitive perspective on the sectional differences leading up to and through the Civil War era. Extensive annotated bibliography, footnotes, and index.

Moore, Glover. *The Missouri Controversy, 1819-1821*. Gloucester, Mass.: Peter Smith, 1967. A significant monograph on the political compromise that signaled nineteenth century sectional controversies during the antebellum era.

Nagel, Paul C. *Missouri: A Bicentennial History*. New York: W. W. Norton, 1977. Condensed overview of Missouri history by a leading historian. Annotated bibliography, footnotes, and index.

Nash, Gary B., ed. *The American People: Creating a Nation and a Society*. 2d ed. New York: Harper & Row, 1990. Overview of American history that places the Missouri Compromise in a national historical context. Index.

SEE ALSO: 1787, Northwest Ordinance; 1803, Louisiana Purchase; 1807, Congress Bans Importation of African Slaves; 1814, Hartford Convention; 1830, Proslavery Argument; 1830, Webster-Hayne Debate; 1850, Compromise of 1850; 1854, Kansas-Nebraska Act; 1854, Birth of the Republican Party; 1856, Bleeding Kansas; 1857, *Dred Scott v. Sandford*; 1858, Lincoln-Douglas Debates; 1859, John Brown's Raid on Harpers Ferry; 1860, Confederate States Secede from the Union.

1820 ■ LAND ACT OF 1820: *the basis for transferring the public domain to individual U.S. citizens for the next two decades*

DATE: April 24, 1820
LOCALE: Washington, D.C.
CATEGORIES: Expansion and land acquisition; Laws and acts
KEY FIGURES:
Thomas Hart Benton (1782-1858), senator from Missouri and a strong advocate of cheap land
Henry Clay (1777-1852), senator from Kentucky who advocated distributing the proceeds of federal land sales to the states
Samuel Augustus Foot (1780-1846), senator from Connecticut who opposed cheap land
Albert Gallatin (1761-1849), secretary of the Treasury, 1801-1814, and organizer of the system of Land Offices

Alexander Hamilton (1755-1804), first secretary of the Treasury and advocate of using the proceeds of land sales to reduce the federal debt
William Henry Harrison (1773-1841), victor over American Indians at Tippecanoe, opening Indiana for Euro-American settlement
Anthony Wayne (1745-1796), Army general who forced American Indians to cede large parts of the Old Northwest to the U.S. government

SUMMARY OF EVENT. The British colonies in North America had been, from the beginning, colonies of settlement. By the time of the Revolutionary War, most of the good agricultural land in the original thirteen colonies had been turned into farms by the settlers, and many were anxious to move west of the Alleghenies, to the area later known as the Old Northwest. The British, in order to ensure the friendship of the natives in that section, had forbidden settlement. With British defeat in the Revolutionary War, the area now belonged to the thirteen colonies, where the pressure to open it to settlement was overwhelming.

In 1785, the Confederation Congress first began deliberations about how to arrange the transfer of land in the Old Northwest, as well as those portions of the Old Southwest, acquired by the 1783 Treaty of Paris with Britain. Several principles were agreed on: Before settlement and transfer of title, the land would have to be ceded by treaty with the Native Americans; the land would have to be surveyed, in square township units, and sale would be by portions of the surveyed townships; and the proceeds of the sale would be used to pay down the federal debt. These principles were embodied in the Ordinance of 1785, which continued to bind the federal government after the adoption of the Constitution in 1789.

In addition to pressure from would-be settlers, the federal government owed obligations to thousands of veterans of the Revolutionary War, who had been promised land grants in lieu of pay during the war. Many of the veterans had received scrip, redeemable in grants from the public domain. As a result, the federal government attempted to begin surveying the land; once at least a modest proportion had been mapped, it could be subdivided into townships and offered for sale. Treaties had been negotiated with some of the native tribes in 1784, 1785, and 1786, in which those tribes ceded much of western New York and western Pennsylvania and large portions of southern Ohio to the United States; the belief prevailed in the Congress that this laid the foundation for surveying and subsequent settlement by Euro-Americans. However, some of the Indians refused to accept the treaties, and battles were fought in the early 1790's between the natives and federal troops. The natives won the first battle, in 1791, but lost in 1794 to a force commanded by General Anthony Wayne at the Battle of Fallen Timbers. Wayne then ravaged the Indian settlements in northern Ohio and forced them to accept the Treaty of Greenville, in 1795, by which they accepted confinement to a reservation in northwestern Ohio and ceded the rest of Ohio, as well as parts of Indiana, Illinois, and a small part of Michigan, to the United

States. In the Old Southwest—which would become the states of Mississippi and Alabama, as well as parts of western Georgia—numerous treaties were concluded with the tribes located there, defining their tribal lands and opening up significant lands for Euro-American settlement, mostly in the southern portions of the area.

Alexander Hamilton, at the Treasury, had begun organizing the system that would administer sales of the land, which, according to the Ordinance of 1785, was to be sold at auction for at least one dollar per acre after being surveyed. Sales were to be administered by the Treasury, and surveying would be supervised by the U.S. geographer (a post abolished in 1796 and replaced by the surveyor general). Surveys were to be of townships in six-mile-square units. In 1796, the price was raised to two dollars per acre, but plots of 640 acres were allowed. However, sales on this scale proved disappointing.

In 1800, William Henry Harrison induced Congress to change the terms of sale. Sales of smaller parcels were allowed, and purchasers were permitted to buy on the installment plan, with payments to be made over a four-year period. Simultaneously, Albert Gallatin, at the Treasury, put in place an organization of land offices located in the areas to be sold; in 1812, these were subordinated to a General Land Office that supervised the local offices, rapidly increasing in number as more land was surveyed and put up for sale. This rearrangement of the system, particularly the inclusion of purchases on credit, laid the basis for a large land boom in the period between 1812 and 1819.

The land boom revealed the weakness of the system created in 1800. Purchases on credit were hard to keep track of, with the limited clerical help in the local land offices and in the General Land Office; and Congress had passed a number of relief acts since 1800, extending the time limits on credit purchases. By 1820, only about a third of the purchase price of the lands recorded as sold had been collected. Federal finances were in perilous shape as a result of the War of 1812, which had raised the federal debt to new heights. Since receipts from land sales, along with tariff receipts, were the only sources of federal income, and as the South opposed any increases in tariff, reform of the sales of public lands was needed.

The Land Act of 1820 abolished credit purchases, requiring full payment in cash. However, the price was reduced from $2 per acre to $1.25 per acre, and those who still owed money on previous credit purchases were given more time to complete payments. Purchasers who still owed money would be allowed to surrender part of the land they had bought to cover the remaining debt due. Although this law dealt with some of the problems in the system of selling off the public domain, it failed to still criticism, for the public lands issue had become deeply enmeshed in sectional politics, which would determine subsequent modifications. *—Nancy M. Gordon*

ADDITIONAL READING:

Carstensen, Vernon, ed. *The Public Lands: Studies in the History of the Public Domain*. Madison: University of Wis-

consin Press, 1963. This book remains a standard source for the most controversial issues associated with the public lands.

Clark, Thomas D., and John D. W. Guice. *Frontiers in Conflict: The Old Southwest, 1795-1830*. Albuquerque: University of New Mexico Press, 1989. An account of the difficulties with the tribes of the Old Southwest and the problems in securing their acceptance of Euro-American settlement.

Gates, Paul W. *History of Public Land Law Development*. Washington, D.C.: Zenger, 1968. This large compendium of information, written for the Public Land Law Review Commission, is the ultimate source of information on the land laws.

North, Douglas C., and Andrew R. Rutten. "The Northwest Ordinance in Historical Perspective." In *Essays on the Economy of the Old Northwest*, edited by David C. Klingaman and Richard K. Vedder. Athens: Ohio University Press, 1987. The most useful of several chapters relating to the disposition of the public domain.

Rohrbough, Malcolm J. *The Land Office Business: The Settlement and Administration of American Public Lands, 1789-1837*. New York: Oxford University Press, 1968. The best detailed history of the operation of the various land offices.

Sword, Wiley. *President Washington's Indian War: The Struggle for the Old Northwest, 1790-1795*. Norman: University of Oklahoma Press, 1985. A detailed account of the conflict with the American Indians to free up the Northwest Territory for Euro-American settlement.

SEE ALSO: 1783, Treaty of Paris; 1785, Ordinance of 1785; 1787, Northwest Ordinance; 1790, Hamilton's *Report on Public Credit*; 1794, Battle of Fallen Timbers; 1803, Louisiana Purchase; 1815, Westward Migration; 1841, Preemption Act.

1821 ■ MEXICAN WAR OF INDEPENDENCE: *the end of Spain's hegemony in North America and the ascendancy of the military in Mexican politics for the next century*

DATE: August 24, 1821-September 28, 1821
LOCALE: New Spain
CATEGORIES: Latino American history; Wars, uprisings, and civil unrest
KEY FIGURES:
Miguel Hidalgo y Costilla (1753-1811), cleric who began the war for independence
Agustín de Iturbide (1783-1824), royalist commander who changed sides, which resulted in Mexico's independence from Spain
José María Morelos y Pavón (1765-1815), cleric who assumed leadership of the independence movement after Hidalgo's execution
Vicente Guerrero Saldana (died 1831), guerrilla chieftain who later became president of Mexico

Guadalupe Victoria (Manuel Félix Adaucto Fernández, 1785-1843), insurgent chieftain who became Mexico's first president

SUMMARY OF EVENT. The beginning of the War of Independence in Mexico is generally dated from El Grito de Dolores, the proclamation of Father Miguel Hidalgo y Costilla in the town of Dolores on September 16, 1810. Certain *criollos* (Spaniards born in the New World) of the intellectual class had been agitating for some time against the Crown in favor of an independent Mexico. When the royal authorities uncovered a plot by Father Hidalgo and his cohorts in Querétaro, Father Hidalgo defied the government openly and headed an insurrection composed of *criollo* liberals, mestizos (Mexican residents of European and African or American Indian descent), and various American Indian groups. His army, which resembled a mob more than a proper military force, won stunning victories initially. Father Hidalgo committed a strategic error, however, by not capitalizing on his momentum to seize the capital, Mexico City. As a result, he was eventually captured, tried by the Inquisition, and executed in 1811.

Following Father Hidalgo's death, leadership of the independence movement fell to another parish priest, the mestizo José María Morelos y Pavón. The *criollos* distrusted the insurgency, especially after Father Morelos began to espouse land redistribution and racial equality. Although much more gifted with military acumen than Father Hidalgo, Morelos resorted to guerrilla warfare because of the small size of his army. His tactics worked. By the spring of 1813, his forces encircled Mexico City. Morelos occupied himself with the political issues of the structure of government after independence. Six months later, royalist forces under General Félix María Calleja del Rey shattered the encircled rebel troops. In the fall of 1815, Morelos was captured. Like Father Hidalgo before him, Morelos was tried, defrocked, and executed.

Only two vestiges of the independence movement remained: the rebel guerrilla forces under chieftain general Guadalupe Victoria (who had changed his name from Manuel Félix Adaucto Fernández), striking from the mountains of Puebla and Veracruz, and a thousand troops in Oaxaca, led by Vicente Guerrero Saldana. By 1819, the viceroy of New Spain reported to King Ferdinand that the insurrection was effectively finished and offered a pardon to the last renegades. Assistance for independence came from an unexpected source—the mother country.

During the exile of the Spanish monarchy during the period of Napoleonic control of Spain, the Central Junta in Cadiz instituted a governing body of elected representatives called the Cortes. The Cortes presided over the writing of Spain's first liberal constitution in 1812, which included some modest anticlerical clauses. Upon his restoration in 1814, Ferdinand VII immediately revoked the constitution, suspended the Cortes, imprisoned or exiled liberal opponents, and prepared an army to crush revolutionary movements in Spanish America. By 1820, Spanish opposition to Ferdinand's reactionism resulted in Colonel Rafael Riego's leading thousands of army troops to force the monarch to accept the Constitution of 1812 and reestablish the Cortes.

The Cortes built upon the foundation of the 1812 constitution to end clerical privileges, reduce the tithe, order the sale of church property, abolish the Inquisition, suppress the monastic order, and expel the Jesuits. The conservative *criollos* in New Spain violently opposed this liberalization. The clergy of New Spain viewed the Constitution and the Cortes as blasphemous, and the wealthy *criollos* relied upon the church for their mortgages. The entire social and economic system of New Spain was threatened: Independence would solve their problem. What was needed was a royalist who could be persuaded to betray the Crown.

Agustín de Iturbide, born to wealthy *criollo* parents, entered the royalist army at a young age and gained the reputation as a formidable, if ruthless, commanding officer against the armies of independence. After the defeat of Morelos, Iturbide's military as well as financial fortune waned. By 1820, after leading a dissolute life in Mexico City, he was penniless and eager for an opportunity to salvage his future. When the viceroy (perhaps upon the advice of the conspiring clerics) chose him to lead twenty-five hundred royalist forces against Vicente Guerrero, Iturbide promptly opened negotiations with the rebel forces to effect independence. Guerrero, although suspicious, agreed to Iturbide's Plan de Iguala, issued on February 12, 1821.

The Plan de Iguala proposed to unite all classes and races under the "three guarantees" which, in reality, served to benefit the *criollos*. First, Mexico would be an independent constitutional monarchy. The crown would be offered to King Ferdinand or another member of European royalty. Second, Roman Catholicism would remain the sole religion, with its clerical privileges left intact. Third, all citizens were to be equal regardless of class or race. The *criollos* especially meant this to apply to their status compared to that of the *peninsulares* (residents of New Spain born in Spain), whom the *criollos* resented because of their privileges. The plan interfered with no property rights. The viceroy, whose replacement from Spain was already en route, resigned after only a few skirmishes.

The new viceroy, Juan O'Donojú, assessed the situation quickly: New Spain was lost. The Treaty of Córdoba, signed by both Iturbide and O'Donojú on August 24, 1821, provided for the peaceful removal of royalist forces and acceptance of most of the terms of the Plan de Iguala. Iturbide had made one important addition to the plan: If no European prince accepted the throne of Mexico, a Mexican could be designated as emperor. On September 27, 1821, Iturbide, at the head of the Army of the Three Guarantees, made his triumphal entry into Mexico City on his thirty-eighth birthday. The next day, Iturbide, as spokesperson for the governing junta, declared Mexico an independent nation.

The independence of Mexico, once the prize possession of the Spanish crown, foreshadowed Spain's decline as a global empire. The independence wars created Mexico's gallery of historical heroes and villains, but they also ushered in a tradition of military intervention to achieve political goals—a legacy from which Mexico has spent much of its national period suffering. For the common people, rural and illiterate, life changed very little as a result of independence. The constant bloodshed that followed throughout the next decade and a half reinforced the powerlessness of peasant Mexicans to change their fate. —*Jodella K. Dyreson*

ADDITIONAL READING:

Anna, Timothy E. *The Mexican Empire of Iturbide*. Lincoln: University of Nebraska Press, 1990. A political history of Mexico at the time of independence, with special emphasis on the statecraft of Agustín de Iturbide. Attempts to alter the traditional villainous view of the emperor by a more sympathetic and complex one.

Bazant, Jan. *A Concise History of Mexico from Hidalgo to Cárdenas, 1805-1940*. Cambridge, England: Cambridge University Press, 1977. A highly quoted narrative history of the formative years of Mexico. Not highly analytical, especially concerning the war for independence, but includes fascinating anecdotes.

Flores Caballero, Romeo. *Counterrevolution: The Role of the Spaniards in the Independence of Mexico, 1804-1838*. Reprint. Translated by Jaime E. Rodriguez O. Lincoln: University of Nebraska Press, 1974. Presents the role of the Spaniards in Mexico as the principal leaders of the colonial economy and the events that resulted in their replacement by the criollos. Refutes the common assumption that the expulsion of the Spaniards after Independence caused the bankruptcy of the Mexican economy.

Meyer, Michael C., and William L. Sherman. *The Course of Mexican History*. 4th ed. New York: Oxford University Press, 1991. A comprehensive, well-balanced history of Mexico. Discusses the impact of events on society, including repercussions of independence for the common folk.

Miller, Robert Ryal. *Mexico: A History*. Norman: University of Oklahoma Press, 1985. Highly readable, concise introduction to Mexican history from pre-Columbian times to the 1980's. Emphasizes the nineteenth century and revolutionary periods.

Robertson, William Spence. *Iturbide of Mexico*. Durham, N.C.: Duke University Press, 1952. A standard biography of Iturbide, based on extensive primary sources in Mexico. Reinforces the traditional portrait of Iturbide as a less-than-admirable figure in Mexican independence. Directly refuted by Anna's study on Iturbide.

Ruiz, Ramón Eduardo. *Triumphs and Tragedy: A History of the Mexican People*. New York: W. W. Norton, 1992. A passionate narrative on Mexican history. Often supplies different perspectives from those of the standard surveys.

SEE ALSO: 1810, El Grito de Delores; 1815, Westward Migration; 1819, Adams-Onís Treaty; 1821, Santa Fe Trail Opens; 1823, Jedediah Smith Explores the Far West; 1835, Texas Revolution; 1846, Mexican War; 1909, Mexican Revolution.

1821 ■ SANTA FE TRAIL OPENS: *the opening of the Southwest to economic exploitation and settlement by the United States prompts conflicts with established Native American and Hispanic populations*

DATE: September, 1821

LOCALE: Southwest

CATEGORIES: Economics; Expansion and land acquisition; Native American history; Transportation

KEY FIGURES:

William Becknell (1790?-1832), trailblazer credited with opening the Santa Fe route for trade purposes

Jacob Fowler (1765-1850) and

Hugh Glenn (1788-1833), traders who sold goods in Santa Fe in 1821

Josiah Gregg (1806-1850), caravan leader in 1831 and author of *Commerce on the Prairies* (1844), a classic account of the Santa Fe trade

Thomas James (1782-1847), St. Louis merchant who engaged in trade on the Santa Fe Trail in 1831

SUMMARY OF EVENT. In the early years of the nineteenth century, Santa Fe was an isolated outpost fifteen hundred miles from the center of Spanish authority in Mexico City. Its inhabitants possessed an abundance of silver, furs, and mules, but they suffered from a lack of fabricated goods. Traders on the Missouri frontier were eager to obtain products from Santa Fe in exchange for inexpensive textiles, cutlery, utensils, and a wide variety of other items. The mutual advantage of trade was obvious, but venturesome traders arriving in Santa Fe between 1804 and 1820 were forcefully reminded that the Spanish Empire was not open to foreigners. Those who failed to heed the warnings had their property confiscated, and a few were imprisoned. The overthrow of the Spanish colonial regime, concluded in 1821, brought an end to Spanish restrictions on commerce in New Mexico, now a northern province of the Republic of Mexico.

The Mexican War of Independence and the Panic of 1819 intensified the need for commerce between the United States and Mexico. For years, Mexico had suffered from currency depletion, as its mineral wealth was shipped to faraway Spain. The revolution, which lasted more than a decade, further weakened the Mexican economy. The Panic of 1819 exacerbated a currency shortage in the western United States. Adventurers hoped to trade durable goods in New Mexico for precious metals, easing their fiscal plight.

In the long run, the conditions that prompted trade did not produce economic equality. Between 1821 and 1846, the Santa Fe Trail, stretching from Independence, Missouri, to Santa Fe, served as a conduit of economic and social change. Mexican officials lacked the personnel to regulate the northern border, so smuggling was rife. North-south trade within Mexico was

Sketch of a wagon train entering Santa Fe, New Mexico, c. 1835 via the Santa Fe Trail. (Courtesy Museum of New Mexico)

reoriented to an east-west trade along the Santa Fe Trail, resulting in a further loss of Mexican wealth. Euro-American merchants married Mexican and Indian women, contributing to the social diversity of the Southwest. Euro-American entrepreneurs displaced many Mexican merchants who earlier had traded in New Mexico.

The initial exchange along the Santa Fe Trail occurred in September, 1821, when William Becknell and his band of thirty men, who had been catching horses near Raton, New Mexico, learned of Mexican independence and proceeded to Santa Fe, where the party exchanged their supplies for silver dollars. The exchange was lucrative: One investor in Becknell's expedition reaped a return of $900 on a $60 investment.

Even before Euro-Americans learned how profitable the Santa Fe trade was, other bands followed Becknell. Thomas James of St. Louis reached Santa Fe in December, 1821, spending the winter there attempting to persuade its citizens to buy his drab cotton fabrics. Another party, led by Jacob Fowler and Hugh Glenn, reached Santa Fe and enjoyed a profitable business. Fowler had first scouted the Sangre de Cristo Moun-

tains to the north and concluded that a gainful fur trade could be developed.

The next spring, William Becknell and a score of men returned to Santa Fe with three wagons of merchandise. Becknell thus gained celebrity as "father of the Santa Fe trade." Knowing that it would be difficult to ascend Raton Pass with heavily laden wagons, Becknell pioneered a new route direct to Santa Fe from the Arkansas River Crossing through the Cimarron Desert, a route known as the Cimarron Cutoff.

Wagons were being used extensively on the trail by 1824, and the number of people and the amount of goods steadily increased each year until 1838, despite many difficulties. Hazards included the problems of conducting a train across treeless plains and waterless desert and the probability of attack by Kiowas and Comanches, who resented being invaded. Upon arriving in Santa Fe, traders had to pay an import tax that sometimes ran as high as 60 percent of the value of their goods. To avoid this tax, traders often resorted to bribery. To counter this chicanery, the Mexican government responded in 1839 with a tax of five hundred dollars per wagon. This measure merely encouraged traders to use larger, often overloaded, wagons. In spite of handicaps and uncertainties, the average wagon train earned a profit of between 10 and 40 percent.

In the total economy of the West, the value of the Santa Fe trade was minimal, averaging only $130,000 a year between 1822 and 1843. The best year was 1841, when the value of goods exchanged reached $450,000. The trade was temporarily stopped by the Mexican government between 1843 and 1844 but was revived during the Mexican War and attained a wartime peak of $1,752,250 in 1846. The business continued after the war, not as an international trade but as a means of supplying United States military forces in the Southwest. Trade was brisk during the Civil War, and the Santa Fe Trail continued to be used for commercial purposes until the railroad era.

This military commerce resulted from the U.S. policy of trying to maintain a permanent American Indian frontier along the western boundary of Missouri and to guarantee the plains region to the tribes, while encouraging and protecting traders who were intruding upon the tribes' domain. Major Stephen Cooper had led a company of thirty traders to Santa Fe in 1823. Two years later, the federal government appropriated thirty thousand dollars to mark the route within the limits of the United States and to seek concessions from the tribes guaranteeing safe passage to the traders. Unfortunately, the markings were made of earthen and stone mounds and were placed upon the little used and longer Mountain Route that ascended the Arkansas River to Bent's Fort near La Junta, Colorado, thence south to Santa Fe, rather than along the Cimarron Cutoff. Fort Leavenworth was established in 1827, principally to guard the trail, but the following year, natives attacked the caravans headed for Santa Fe. Several traders were murdered, others were robbed, wagons were abandoned when the animals drawing them were killed, and at least one party had to walk home. Military escorts were provided at government expense in 1829, 1834, and 1843 to protect the traders as far as the United States boundary. After the Mexican War, further forts were erected, which not only helped to secure trade over the Santa Fe Trail but also served as a market for agricultural products raised in the Southwest.

The Santa Fe trade not only initiated the disintegration of the permanent Indian frontier but also turned the attention of the United States toward the Mexican territory in the Southwest. Reports from traders dispelled the illusion of Mexican military power and demonstrated the ease with which the United States might take over the area. In addition, Santa Fe traders assisted in destroying the concept that the Great Plains were "the Great American Desert."

—*W. Turrentine Jackson, updated by Edward R. Crowther*

ADDITIONAL READING:

Coues, Elliot, ed. *The Journal of Jacob Fowler, 1821-1822.* New York: Frances P. Harper, 1898. The classic work describing how Fowler and Hugh Glenn followed the course of the Arkansas River and secured permission to trap and trade in Mexican territory in 1821.

DeBuys, William. *Enchantment and Exploitation: The Life and Hard Times of a New Mexican Mountain Range.* Albuquerque: University of New Mexico Press, 1985. Details the social and economic changes of the lower Rockies after the opening of trade between Mexico and the United States along the Santa Fe Trail.

Field, Matthew C. *Matt Field on the Santa Fe Trail.* Edited by John E. Sunder. Norman: University of Oklahoma Press, 1960. A vivid memoir of an able journalist who spent the summer of 1839 on the Santa Fe Trail and in the settlements of New Mexico.

Gregg, Kate L. *The Road to Santa Fe.* Albuquerque: University of New Mexico Press, 1952. A definitive account of the survey and marking of the Santa Fe Trail by the U.S. government, 1825-1827. Includes the journals and diaries of George Champlin Sibley and others.

Hall, Thomas D. *Social Change in the Southwest, 1350-1880.* Lawrence: University Press of Kansas, 1989. Details the impact of marriage and commerce on family units in the Rio Grande region.

Magoffin, Susan S. *Down the Santa Fe Trail and into Mexico: The Diary of Susan Shelby Magoffin, 1846-1847.* Edited by Stella M. Drumm. Rev. ed. New Haven, Conn.: Yale University Press, 1962. The account of an observant young woman who accompanied her husband, a veteran Santa Fe trader, to New Mexico and south to Chihuahua City during the Mexican War.

Moorhead, Max L. *New Mexico's Royal Road: Trade and Travel on the Chihuahua Trail.* Norman: University of Oklahoma Press, 1958. A scholarly and interpretive study emphasizing the nature and importance of trade between Santa Fe and Chihuahua City and explaining its relationship to the Santa Fe Trail.

Vestal, Stanley. *The Old Santa Fe Trail.* Boston: Houghton Mifflin, 1939. A popular account that attempts to recapture the experience of those who traveled to Santa Fe.

Young, Otis. *The First Military Escort on the Santa Fe Trail, 1829.* Glendale, Calif.: Arthur H. Clark, 1952. Synthesizes available source materials to describe the attacks made on caravans traversing the Santa Fe Trail in 1828.

SEE ALSO: 1806, Pike's Southwest Explorations; 1815, Westward Migration; 1819, Adams-Onís Treaty; 1820, Land Act of 1820; 1821, Mexican War of Independence; 1823, Jedediah Smith Explores the Far West.

1823 ■ HARTFORD FEMALE SEMINARY IS FOUNDED: *one of the earliest institutions to offer nontraditional studies for women's intellectual development*

DATE: 1823

LOCALE: Hartford, Connecticut

CATEGORIES: Education; Organizations and institutions; Women's issues

KEY FIGURE:

Catharine Esther Beecher (1800-1878), early pioneer in women's education

SUMMARY OF EVENT. Hartford Female Seminary, which Catharine Esther Beecher founded in 1823 and incorporated in 1827, was the second major female seminary to promote the higher education of women, to offer young women a comprehensive education aimed at more than "finishing" them for a successful social life, and ultimately, to invent the profession of teaching and train women in it. It was one of four seminaries contemporary in the area, the others being Emma Willard's in Troy, New York (founded 1821), Zilpah Grant's in Ipswich, Massachusetts (1828), and Mary Lyon's in South Hadley, Massachusetts (1837). Lyon's later became Mt. Holyoke College and Willard's is still in existence.

When Catharine Beecher and her sister Mary opened the seminary in 1823, it was located above a harness shop at the corner of Kinsley and Main Streets in Hartford, Connecticut, and had seven pupils. It soon moved to more spacious quarters in the basement of the North Church. By 1826, the school had nearly one hundred pupils, and Catharine Beecher sought more permanent quarters. Having met Hartford's influential citizens through her family connections, her friendship with writer and former teacher Lydia Sigourney, and her membership in Hartford's First Congregational Church, Beecher appealed to business and religious leaders for subscriptions to her school. They refused. She undertook a religious revival for the daughters and wives of the city's elite families, and then appealed to them, raising $4,850 by selling ninety-seven stock subscriptions to forty-five women at prayer meetings in her home.

A legislative charter was obtained, and by 1827, the seminary had its own building on Pratt Street with a capacity for 150 pupils and eight teachers. Its board of trustees comprised the city's leading religious and financial men. The Honorable Thomas Day was president for twenty years, followed by the Reverend Joel Hawes, who served until 1867.

The building, which was planned by Beecher and architect Daniel Wadsworth, contained a lecture room and six recitation rooms. In 1862, the trustees decided that better facilities were needed and built a large addition containing a gymnasium, several recitation rooms, a music room, and a studio for art classes. The number of pupils increased from 39 to 203 in the period 1861-1868. By 1888, the trustees determined that falling enrollments necessitated closing the school, voted for its dissolution, and sold the building to the Good Will Club for seventeen thousand dollars, of which more than nine thousand dollars was needed to pay off indebtedness.

The dissolution of her school followed by ten years the death of its founder. Catharine Beecher was born September 6, 1800, in East Hampton, Long Island, New York, the first child of the prominent Congregationalist minister, Lyman Beecher, and Roxanna Foote Beecher. The family soon moved to Litchfield, Connecticut, where Catharine attended one of the leading schools for girls, Miss Sarah Pierce's Female Academy.

She also studied music and drawing in Boston. When her mother died in 1816, she helped her Aunt Esther run her father's household until he remarried a year later. She taught briefly in New London, met the young but eminent Yale professor Alexander Fisher and, after some reluctant delay, agreed to marry him. Fisher was drowned in a shipwreck on his way to a one-year tour of European universities, leaving Beecher with a legacy of two thousand dollars and the determination never to marry.

An invitation to spend the winter with Fisher's parents in Franklin, Massachusetts, gave Beecher an opportunity to read Fisher's papers and books on mathematics and natural philosophy (physics). She discovered that her education had not been as rigorous as his, but that she was capable of understanding the topics treated in his materials. She studied algebra, geography, chemistry, and physics. During this period, she also struggled with serious theological concepts, as she tried to reconcile her father's stern religious belief in Fisher's lost spiritual state with her feelings of justice and fairness.

These events, together with the need of a school in Hartford, encouraged her to start the seminary and influenced not only the development of that school but also her numerous writings on the subject of education and women. The seminary, like the three others of the time, had as a goal not only to adapt but also to improve on the curriculum of men's colleges. Beecher believed that women had two, closely intertwined honorable professions: homemaker and teacher. Mothers were teachers and should be trained as such. Beecher viewed homemaking as a profession that, in order to be done well, required scientific and technical training. She and the heads of the other women's seminaries saw a new profession for women, that of the female educator, both inside and outside the home. Beecher also believed that women should teach women. She set up her schools so that the teachers, who were women, would be co-equal with the school administrators (who often were men, at least in the beginning) in the matter of forming policy and curriculum.

Although Beecher spent only a few years at her seminary, it was run according to her philosophies of education. The course of studies included subjects such as drawing, music, and French—subjects that were considered proper for young ladies and enabled them to become accomplished wives for the rising middle class. The curriculum also included subjects that were taught in the men's colleges: geography, rhetoric, ancient history, Euclid's geometry, Abercrombie's mental philosophy, Comstock's philosophy and chemistry, Abercrombie's moral feelings, Comstock's botany, Hedge's logic, Paley's theology, Blake's astronomy, Sullivan's political book, Butler's analogy, and Latin and Greek.

The school was soon divided into primary, junior, and senior classes. The primary division included girls from the ages of six to about twelve years old, who were taught reading, writing, spelling, grammar, composition, and arithmetic. The regular course consisted of five divisions, each with specific courses. A supplementary course was also offered, which was open to students whether or not they had attended the seminary previously. It included extensive courses in music, drawing, and painting, intended for personal accomplishment or teaching. There was also a department of physical culture, reflecting Beecher's lifelong battle against the confining clothing and physical restraints of her period. Here, too, Beecher's struggle between her essentially feminist feelings and her dedication to the customs of her time are evident: The catalog notes that the purpose of physical culture for young ladies is "first, bodily health and its reflex influence on mental ability; next, a graceful, erect and elastic carriage."

Teachers were needed in the new schools in the opening western territories. This need provided jobs for the graduates of the female seminaries and also provided Beecher an opportunity to move west when her father took a pastorate in Cincinnati, Ohio, in 1831. She had some success starting a number of schools, which were essentially normal schools, in Illinois, Wisconsin, and Iowa. Beecher was the founder, in 1847, of the National Board of Popular Education and in 1852, of the American Women's Education Association. She also was the author of a large number of essays, articles, and books.

Beecher's first important educational presentation was in 1829, when she was still at the Hartford Female Seminary. It was part of her continuing effort to raise endowments for her school and to set a pattern of endowments for women's schools, so that their existence would not be so precarious. Beecher correctly foresaw that without endowment, no lasting system of schooling could be maintained. In spite of continued efforts throughout her life, she was never successful. The lack of endowment, the increasing popularity of the public Hartford High School, and the founding of well-endowed colleges for women at Poughkeepsie, New York, Wellesley and Northampton, Massachusetts, and elsewhere, were responsible for the demise of her school.

Beecher was principal of the school until 1831, when she resigned due to ill health and left for Cincinnati with her father. She was replaced temporarily by the Reverend T. H. Gallaudet. In 1832, John P. Brace of Litchfield, nephew of Miss Pierce and head teacher at her school, started a thirteen-year term, with women assistants. From 1845 until the school's closing in 1888, most of the principals were women.

—*Erika E. Pilver*

ADDITIONAL READING:

Boydston, Jeanne, Mary Kelley, and Anne Margolis. *The Limits of Sisterhood: The Beecher Sisters on Women's Rights and Woman's Sphere*. Chapel Hill: University of North Carolina Press, 1988. Letters and other writings of Catharine Beecher, Harriet Beecher Stowe, and Isabella Beecher Hooker. Includes brief but comprehensive and valuable introductions to the book and to each section.

Martin, Jane Roland. *Reclaiming a Conversation: The Ideal of the Educated Woman*. New Haven, Conn.: Yale University Press, 1985. Presents an imaginary conversation with Beecher and philosophers and other educators from other times.

Rugoff, Milton. *The Beechers: An American Family in the Nineteenth Century*. New York: Harper & Row, 1981. Extensive chronological history of Lyman Beecher and his prominent children. Valuable for details of their lives.

Sklar, Kathryn Kish. *Catharine Beecher: A Study in American Domesticity*. New York: W. W. Norton, 1976. Puts Beecher's history, philosophy, and accomplishments into context.

Solomon, Barbara Miller. *In the Company of Educated Women*. New Haven, Conn.: Yale University Press, 1985. Explains the educational settings of, and philosophies about education for, women over time.

SEE ALSO: 1820's, Social Reform Movement; 1833, Oberlin College Is Established; 1837, Mt. Holyoke Seminary Is Founded; 1865, Vassar College Is Founded.

1823 ■ JEDEDIAH SMITH EXPLORES THE FAR WEST: *an American explorer opens both a central and a southern route across the continent to the Pacific Ocean*

DATE: September, 1823-1831
LOCALE: From St. Louis to the Pacific Ocean
CATEGORIES: Expansion and land acquisition; Exploration and discovery; Transportation
KEY FIGURES:

Jedediah Strong Smith (1798-1831), partner in the Rocky Mountain Fur Company and pathfinder to California

William H. Ashley (1778-1838), military officer who sent Smith on his first expedition to the Pacific

Harrison G. Rogers (died 1828), quartermaster of the expedition, who wrote a chronicle of the journey to California

José María de Echeandia (died 1852?), governor of California who demanded that Smith's party leave the province

John McLoughlin (1784-1857), buyer for the Hudson's Bay Company at Fort Vancouver who retrieved and purchased the furs that Smith lost to the natives in southern Oregon

SUMMARY OF EVENT. A native of Chenango County, New York, Jedediah Smith learned to read and write before he and his family moved to St. Louis in 1816. Soon he became interested in fur trapping, beginning his career in Missouri in 1822. Over the next decade, and thirty years before the Treaty of Guadalupe Hidalgo ended the Mexican War and the Southwest was ceded to the United States, Smith would twice traverse the country to open the region to U.S. settlement.

Smith's career shows both entrepreneurship and adventure. His first trek to the Pacific began in 1822, after he had read an advertisement in the *Missouri Gazette and Public Advertiser*. General William H. Ashley had announced plans to hire one hundred men to ascend the Missouri River to work at its headwaters for one to three years. By November, Smith and twelve companions had reached the mouth of the Musselshell River in Blackfoot country. Eight returned east before the winter cut off transportation, while Smith and four others wintered there. The following year, Smith joined an expedition that followed the South Platte River to cross the Continental Divide at what became known as Bridger Pass. From there, they crossed the mountains of northern Colorado, the Great Basin, and the Green River Canyon. Smith continued on to the Pacific.

In 1825, Smith joined forces with Ashley; in 1826, Smith joined with David E. Jackson and William L. Sublette to buy out Ashley and form the Rocky Mountain Fur Company, which grew to be one of the most famous fur-trading companies. They were better trappers and traders than John Jacob Astor's employees, but they also suffered greater losses to Native Americans.

In 1826, loaded with a supply of goods from the East, Smith arrived at the rendezvous of the Rocky Mountain Fur Company located at the Great Salt Lake. His express purpose was to explore the territory both south and west of the lake while his partners conducted the fall hunt. Smith and a party of sixteen men left the Great Salt Lake between August 15 and 22, traveled southwest to the Utah Lake, and then, by way of the Sevier River, crossed a mountain range to the Virgin River. Using this river to guide them, they came upon the Colorado River, crossed to its east bank, and then rode through the Black Mountain country of Arizona for four days before reaching an area occupied by the Mojave tribe. After having rested with the Mojave for more than two weeks, all the while obtaining information about the surrounding territory, the Smith party set out across the Mojave Desert on November 10, 1826; they were guided by two Native Americans who had escaped from a Southern California Spanish mission. Although their exact course for this stage of the journey is unclear, they undoubtedly traveled westward along the earlier Native American trade routes, which were much the same as that followed by the Santa Fe Railroad. They crossed the Sierra Madre range, probably using Cajon Pass, and camped a short distance from the San Gabriel Mission. Thus, Smith's was the first U.S. party to make the overland trip through the Southwest to California.

Although Mexican law forbade their presence in California, Smith and his men were hospitably received by the padres. Governor José María de Echeandia, however, viewed the traders as intruders and purposely delayed answering a letter from Smith requesting permission to journey through the province. After waiting for ten days, Smith went to San Diego to plead with the governor in person. Mollified by this action and the gift of some beaver skins, Echeandia finally agreed not to imprison Smith and his men for violating the border, on condition that they leave California over the route by which they had come. Smith disregarded this condition and led his party (less two men who had succumbed to the charms of mission life in California) back through the Cajon Pass and then either west across the Tejon or north across the Tehachapi Pass into the San Joaquin Valley. Leaving his men to trap beaver, Smith, Silas Gobel, and Robert Evans ascended the middle fork of the Stanislaus River to cross the towering Sierra Nevada. Starting

on May 20, 1827, the three men took eight days to cross the mountains near Ebbetts Pass to the headwaters of the Walker River, which flowed into Walker Lake. Almost nothing is known of Smith's route across the Great Basin, but he probably went east to the vicinity of what is now Ely, Nevada, then northeast to the Great Salt Lake, where he and his associates arrived in June, 1827, after a punishing journey.

After a brief rest, Smith set out with nineteen men on July 13, 1827, to rejoin his hunters in California as he had promised. Traveling the route of the previous year, the party arrived at the Mojave villages, where Native Americans surprised and killed ten of the company; the remainder abandoned most of their belongings and made forced marches across the desert to the San Gabriel Mission. Smith quickly rejoined the hunters he had left in the San Joaquin Valley. The necessity for obtaining food and supplies caused him to travel to the San Jose Mission, where he was arrested and placed in jail and denied access to Governor Echeandia for a time. Although he was finally permitted to talk with Echeandia in Monterey, only the intervention of several U.S. ships' captains prevented Smith's being sent to a Mexican prison. He was forced to post a thirty-thousand-dollar bond to guarantee his departure from California within two months.

From Monterey, Smith's route took him northward to the head of the Sacramento River, then west, probably along the Trinity River to the coast, and northward to the Umpqua River in Oregon. While Smith's party was encamped on this stream, Native Americans attacked them; only Smith and two of his men survived. All the furs were stolen. Among the dead was Harrison G. Rogers, clerk and quartermaster of the expedition. When Smith had returned to the Great Salt Lake the year before, he had left Rogers in charge of the party in the San Joaquin Valley, and Rogers had kept a journal of his experiences.

The three survivors made their way to Fort Vancouver, the Hudson's Bay Company's post on the Columbia River, where Dr. John McLoughlin, the chief factor, gave them aid and sent a party to regain the captured furs, which he subsequently purchased for twenty thousand dollars. The act was a generous one, for Smith had no means of transporting the furs back to the Great Salt Lake. However, McLoughlin exacted a promise that the Rocky Mountain Fur Company would not again penetrate the Northwest. In the spring of 1828, Smith and one companion made their way to Pierre's Hole on the western side of the Teton Mountains, where they rejoined Smith's partners, Jackson and Sublette.

Smith had explored a new route from the Great Salt Lake southwest into California, had made the first crossing of the Sierra, and had opened another route across the Great Basin desert to the Great Salt Lake. In marching to the Columbia River, his men were the first U.S. party to explore the great interior valleys of California. They opened a north-south route and made known California's potential for U.S. traders and settlers. Smith thus became the first U.S. explorer to mark both a central and a southern route across the continent to the Pacific.

In 1830, Smith sold out to the Rocky Mountain Fur Company. The next year, Comanche warriors killed him at a watering hole on the Sante Fe Trail as he was traveling to Taos.

—W. Turrentine Jackson, updated by Duncan R. Jamieson

ADDITIONAL READING:

Dale, Harrison C., ed. *The Ashley-Smith Explorations and the Discovery of a Central Route to the Pacific, 1822-1829.* Rev. ed. Glendale, Calif.: Arthur H. Clark, 1941. First published in 1918, this monograph was for years the standard account of Jedediah Smith's activities. Opened new vistas on the fur trade history and emphasized the interrelationship between trading and exploration.

Morgan, Dale L. *Jedediah Smith and the Opening of the West.* Indianapolis: Bobbs-Merrill, 1953. A biography of Smith and a history of the mountain men and their experiences. Despite a lack of factual information, Morgan dispels some of the myths surrounding Smith's experiences.

Neihardt, John G. *Splendid Wayfaring: The Exploits and Adventures of Jedediah Smith and the Ashley-Henry Men.* Lincoln: University of Nebraska Press, 1970. Analyzes the Ashley-Smith explorations.

Sandoz, Mari. *The Beaver Men.* New York: Hastings House, 1964. An analysis of the place of mountain men, Smith included, in the opening of the West to Euro-Americans.

Smith, Alson J. *Men Against the Mountains: Jedediah Smith and the South West Expedition of 1826-1829.* New York: John Day, 1965. A popular, well-written book, carefully based on the scholarly accounts of Dale, Morgan, and Sullivan.

Terrell, John Upton. *The Six Turnings: Major Changes in the American West.* Glendale, Calif.: Arthur H. Clark, 1968. Places the mountain men in perspective relative to the history of the West.

White, Richard. *"It's Your Misfortune and None of My Own": A History of the American West.* Norman: University of Oklahoma Press, 1991. A scholarly, readable narrative that places Smith in the history of the West.

SEE ALSO: 1769, Rise of the California Missions; 1815, Westward Migration; 1821, Santa Fe Trail Opens; 1842, Frémont's Expeditions; 1846, Mormon Migration to Utah; 1846, Oregon Settlement; 1846, Occupation of California and the Southwest; 1848, California Gold Rush; 1853, Pacific Railroad Surveys.

1823 ■ MONROE DOCTRINE: *the primary articulation of the United States' foreign policy in the Western Hemisphere*

DATE: December 2, 1823
LOCALE: Washington, D.C.
CATEGORIES: Diplomacy and international relations; Latino American history
KEY FIGURES:
John Quincy Adams (1767-1848), Monroe's secretary of state
Alexander I (1777-1825), czar of Russia
Robert Stewart, Viscount Castlereagh (1769-1822), British foreign secretary
George Canning (1770-1827), Castlereagh's successor as foreign secretary
Clemens von Metternich (1773-1859), Austrian chancellor
James Monroe (1758-1831), fifth president of the United States, 1817-1825
Auguste-Jules-Armand-Marie de Polignac (1780-1847), French ambassador to Great Britain
Richard Rush (1780-1859), U.S. minister to Great Britain

SUMMARY OF EVENT. On December 2, 1823, President James Monroe delivered his annual message to the United States Congress. Although most of his remarks concerned domestic matters and largely have been forgotten, his foreign policy declaration became the cornerstone of U.S. policy in the Western Hemisphere. "The American Continents," Monroe declared, "by the free and independent condition which they have assumed and maintain, are henceforth not to be considered as subjects for future colonization by a European power." The president then turned to European colonial policy in the New World:

> With the existing Colonies or dependencies of any European power, we have not interfered, and shall not interfere. But with the Governments who have declared their independence, and maintained it, and whose Independence we have, on great consideration, and on just principles, acknowledged, we could not view any interposition for the purpose of oppressing them, or controlling in any other manner, their destiny, by any European power, in any other light than as the manifestation of an unfriendly disposition towards the United States.

Monroe's message contained three main points outlining the United States' new role as defender of the Western Hemisphere. First, the president announced to Europe that the United States would oppose any attempt to take over any independent country in the Western Hemisphere (the no-transfer principle). Second, he promised that the United States would abstain from European quarrels (non-intervention). Third, Monroe insisted that European states not meddle in the affairs of the New World countries. In other words, Monroe declared that the United States would not take sides in European disputes, but in return, Europe could not tamper with the status quo in the Western Hemisphere.

Monroe's bold message offered no threat to such nations as Great Britain and France. In 1823, the United States lacked the power to enforce its new role in the Western Hemisphere. Fortunately for the United States, Great Britain desired just such a policy as Monroe suggested. The British fleet, not Monroe's declaration, would maintain the independence of Latin America. It was not until 1852 that anyone referred to Monroe's declaration as the Monroe Doctrine, and it was not until the twentieth century that the United States had enough power to insist on international acceptance of the Monroe Doctrine.

Even so, Monroe's words reflected the change in unfriendly

relations between the United States and Great Britain that had led to the War of 1812. The explanation lies in the decisions made at the Congress of Vienna in 1815. Napoleon had been defeated; Prussia, Russia, Austria, France, and Great Britain set out to turn the clock back, through establishing a Quintuple Alliance to undo the damage wrought by Napoleon's ambition. The establishment of the alliance led to the Concert of Europe, which sponsored four congresses between 1818 and 1822. The congresses created the modern system of conference diplomacy, although the various members failed to agree on Europe's future.

Autocratic reactionaries hampered the Quintuple Alliance's effectiveness from the beginning. Czar Alexander I of Russia led the way, convincing the monarchs of Austria and Prussia to join him in the Holy Alliance, which dedicated itself to upholding autocratic rule. Great Britain chose not to join, but continued to be a member of the Quintuple Alliance. As a member of the Quintuple Alliance, Great Britain seemed to support a policy of reestablishing monarchy and opposing revolution. By refusing to join the Holy Alliance, however, the British avoided appearing as the bastion of the conservative reactionaries. When put to the test, Great Britain's actions proved that it favored a system of monarchy and a European balance of power, but not systematic oppression of revolution in others parts of the world.

"Other parts of the world" referred to the newly independent states in the New World. Spain, for one, demanded the return of its New World colonies. In 1820, when Prince Clemens von Metternich, the architect of reaction, suggested that the Concert of Europe had a sacred duty to crush revolution, Great Britain protested. Metternich's proposal would have meant sending an army to Latin America to overthrow the new republics. Great Britain distinguished between a European balance-of-power system, in which revolution would not be permitted, and a colonial empire in the New World where revolution would be allowed to occur. In addition, Spain had monopolized trade with its colonies; only as independent republics could the former colonies maintain a profitable trade with the British.

Alexander I also tried to extend his interests in North America. Through an imperial decree on September 14, 1821, Russia claimed territory on the Pacific coast south to the fifty-first parallel (well into Oregon Country) by insisting that all foreign ships must remain a substantial distance from the coast that far south. Secretary of State John Quincy Adams vigorously opposed the decree, citing the U.S. principle of noncolonization. Russia never enforced the decree.

Viscount Castlereagh, the British foreign secretary, decided that Spanish claims to territory in the New World were less important to Great Britain than profitable trade with Spain's former colonies. Accordingly, the British began devising an arrangement with the United States that would prevent European powers from taking new, or regaining old, colonies in the Western Hemisphere. In August, 1823, George Canning, Castlereagh's successor, suggested to Richard Rush, the U.S. minister to Great Britain, that the two countries jointly declare that they would oppose further colonization of the New World. Rush was reluctant to agree to such a bold move without consulting his own superior, Adams. Canning began a series of discussions with Prince Jules de Polignac, the French ambassador in London, seeking some guarantee that France would not help Spain regain lost colonies in the New World. On October 12, 1823, the ambassador gave Canning the specific assurances he wanted, in a document known as the Polignac Memorandum. France's promise to Great Britain, not the Monroe Doctrine, ended any chance of Spain regaining its colonies in the New World. Unaware of the Polignac Memorandum, Adams advised Monroe against a joint noncolonization declaration with the British. Instead, he suggested that the United States make a unilateral declaration opposing further European colonization in the Western Hemisphere. The resulting declaration came in the president's message to Congress in December, 1823.

Since 1823, Monroe's message has gained much greater significance. During the Civil War, France established a puppet government under Austria's Archduke Maximilian in Mexico. In 1867, by invoking the Monroe Doctrine and threatening invasion, the United States ensured the collapse of Emperor Maximilian's government. In December, 1904, President Theodore Roosevelt added a corollary to the Monroe Doctrine, in which he stated that the United States would not interfere with Latin American nations that conducted their affairs with decency. Should they fail to do so, the United States would then intervene and exercise international police power to ensure the stability of the Western Hemisphere. In 1930, President Herbert Hoover formally repudiated the Roosevelt Corollary by revealing the publication of the Clark Memorandum adjuring any right of the United States to intervene in Latin America. The Monroe Doctrine would thus be applied only as originally intended—to protect Latin America from European intervention.

The United States, however, has found reasons for intervening in the affairs of countries in the Western Hemisphere since 1930. In 1965, President Lyndon Johnson ordered U.S. troops into the Dominican Republic to prevent a takeover of that country by a communist government, although the official justification for that action was the protection of U.S. citizens and property. The same justification was used by President Ronald Reagan in 1983 to invade the small island nation of Grenada. President George Bush, in 1989, used hemispheric stability and his war on drugs to invade Panama and capture Panamanian dictator and alleged drug lord Manuel Noriega.

—*David H. Culbert, updated by William Allison*

ADDITIONAL READING:

Bemis, Samuel Flagg. *The Latin American Policy of the United States: An Historical Interpretation.* New York: Norton Library, 1967. Best account to date of Secretary of State John Quincy Adams' role in forming the Monroe Doctrine.

Donovan, Frank Robert. *Mr. Monroe's Message: The Story of the Monroe Doctrine.* New York: Dodd, Mead, 1963. A narrative history of the formulation of the Monroe Doctrine in the context of the domestic and international situation of the United States at the time.

Hart, Albert Bushnell. *The Foundations of American Foreign Policy.* New York: Da Capo Press, 1970. Discusses the Monroe Doctrine in the context of overall U.S. foreign policy.

May, Ernest R. *The Making of the Monroe Doctrine.* Cambridge, Mass.: The Belknap Press of Harvard University Press, 1975. Stresses the domestic side of the Monroe Doctrine.

Rappaport, Armin, ed. *The Monroe Doctrine.* New York: Holt, Rinehart and Winston, 1964. A solid history of Monroe's message up to the early 1960's.

Ronfeldt, David F. *Rethinking the Monroe Doctrine.* Santa Monica, Calif.: Rand, 1985. Discusses the long-term implications of the Monroe Doctrine.

Smith, Gaddis. *The Last Years of the Monroe Doctrine, 1945-1993.* New York: Hill & Wang, 1994. Attacks the abuse of the Monroe Doctrine by the United States since the end of World War II.

SEE ALSO: 1846, Mexican War; 1889, First Pan-American Congress; 1899, Philippine Insurrection; 1899, Hay's "Open Door Notes"; 1903, Platt Amendment; 1903, Acquisition of the Panama Canal Zone; 1909, Dollar Diplomacy; 1912, Intervention in Nicaragua; 1933, Good Neighbor Policy; 1983, United States Invades Grenada.

1824 ■ GIBBONS V. OGDEN: *the U.S. Supreme Court defines the meaning and scope of the commerce power and coordinates federal and state authority in interstate commerce*

DATE: March 2, 1824
LOCALE: Washington, D.C.
CATEGORIES: Court cases; Economics; Government and politics
KEY FIGURES:
Robert Fulton (1765-1815), inventor and builder of steamboats
Thomas Gibbons (1757-1826), wealthy Georgia lawyer and steamboat company owner
William Johnson (1771-1834), associate justice of the United States
James Kent (1763-1847), chief justice of New York and chancellor of New York
Robert R. Livingston (1746-1813), amateur scientist and speculator in steamboats
John Marshall (1755-1835), chief justice of the United States
Aaron Ogden (1756-1839), entrepreneur, former governor of New Jersey, and steamboat company owner
Daniel Webster (1782-1852), chief attorney for Gibbons
SUMMARY OF EVENT. In order to provide the commercial relations of the United States with a sense of orderliness and

uniformity that had been considerably lacking before 1787, the Constitution of the United States gave Congress the power to "regulate Commerce with foreign Nations, and among the several States, and with the Indian Tribes." Congress almost immediately took advantage of this power in the field of foreign commerce by providing for the regulation of ships and commerce from foreign countries and by enacting the National Coasting Licensing Act in 1793 for the licensing of vessels engaged in coastal trade. The Constitution was silent as to the meaning and scope of the commerce power. It was left to the Supreme Court, thirty years later, to make the first national pronouncement regarding domestic commerce in the case of *Gibbons v. Ogden.*

The catalyst for this decision was the development of the steamboat as an economical means of transportation. This was accomplished in August of 1807, when Robert Fulton and Robert Livingston made a successful voyage up the Hudson River from New York to Albany. In April of 1808, the legislature of the state of New York responded to this success by giving Fulton and Livingston a monopoly to operate steamboats on New York waters for a period of time not to exceed thirty years. All other steam craft were forbidden from navigating New York streams unless licensed by Fulton and Livingston; unlicensed vessels would, if captured, be forfeited to them. A similar grant was obtained from the legislature of Orleans Territory in 1811, thus conferring upon Fulton and Livingston control over the two great ports of the United States, New York City and New Orleans.

The commercial potential of steam transportation was too great to be left to the devices of two men. Rival companies came into being, and a commercial war reminiscent of the old Confederation erupted. New Jersey authorized owners of any boats seized under New York law to capture that state's boats in return. Connecticut would not allow Livingston and Fulton boats to enter her waters. Georgia, Massachusetts, New Hampshire, Vermont, and Ohio enacted "exclusive privilege" statutes for operators of steamboats on their waters. Finally, a number of New York citizens defied the state law and operated unlicensed steam vessels up the Hudson River. Among these was one Thomas Gibbons, possessor of a license granted under the federal Coasting Licensing Act of 1793, operating in competition with a former partner, Aaron Ogden, who had secured exclusive rights from Livingston and Fulton to navigate across the Hudson River between New York and New Jersey. As early as 1812, the New York Court of Errors and Chief Justice James Kent, one of the United States' most prominent jurists, had issued a permanent injunction against intruders on the monopoly. Gibbons persisted in the face of this injunction because of his federal license, and Ogden sought a restraining order in New York Court of Chancery. Kent, who was now chancellor, upheld the monopoly once again, reasoning that a federal coasting license merely conferred national character on a vessel and did not license it to trade, especially in waters restricted by state law. In short, there was no conflict between the act of Congress and the actions of New York

State, for the power to regulate commerce was a concurrent one, existing on both the federal and state levels. Gibbons persisted in appealing to the New York Court of Errors, where Kent's decision was upheld. This set the stage for the final appeal to the United States Supreme Court.

It was expected that the case would be heard during the 1821 term of the court, but for technical reasons it was delayed until February, 1824. The oral arguments lasted four and one-half days that, by all accounts, resulted in a great social and political occasion as well as one of the great moments in U.S. constitutional history. Among the distinguished attorneys presenting the case was Daniel Webster, champion of a strong national government and the best-known orator of his time. Webster opened his argument in sweeping terms by contending that the statutes of New York, and by implication all exclusive grants of others states violated the United States Constitution: "The power of Congress to regulate commerce is complete and entire." Individual states have no concurrent powers in this area; the federal government's domain is exclusive. Webster left no doubt that commerce included navigation. Opposing counsel necessarily wished to limit the notion of commerce to traffic or to the buying and selling of commodities, which would not include navigation. The regulation of New York, he contended, was a matter of internal trade and navigation, the province of the states.

The case before the Court, however, dealt with far more than the conflict between New York State law and a federal coasting licensing act. In the weeks immediately preceding and during the argument in *Gibbons v. Ogden*, Congress was debating whether or not it had the power to build roads and canals, a debate in which the association of slavery with national control over commerce became quickly apparent. If Congress could legislate over matters of internal commerce, it could easily prohibit the slave trade. Furthermore, Marshall's former decisions, particularly in *McCulloch v. Maryland* and *Cohens v. Virginia*, were under fire in Congress, from the president, and in the press. In a sense, the forces arguing the two sides of the case represented national power and the potential for emancipation (some would add those who supported the protective tariff) on the one hand, and, on the other, state sovereignty and the fear of emancipation (with some free trade proponents)—a not altogether logical set of alliances. It was in this context, however, that one month later, on March 2, 1824, John Marshall delivered the decision of the Court.

Typically, the opinion was a broad one, loaded with *dicta* (gratuitous comments or representations), and not typically as nationalistic as expected, or as Webster would have desired. Marshall began by agreeing with Webster's definition of commerce:

> Commerce, undoubtedly, is traffic, but it is something more; it is intercourse. It describes the commercial intercourse between nations, and parts of nations, in all its branches, and is regulated by prescribing rules for carrying on that intercourse. The mind can scarcely conceive a system for regulating commerce between nations, which shall exclude all laws concerning naviga-

tion, which shall be silent on the admission of the vessels of the one nation into the ports of the other and be confined to prescribing rules for the conduct of individuals, in the actual employment of buying and selling, or of barter.

What did the Constitution mean when it said that Congress had the power to regulate such commerce among the several states?

> The word "among" means intermingled with. A thing which is among others is intermingled with them. Commerce among the States cannot stop at the external boundary line of each State, but may be introduced into the interior.

After having laid the logical groundwork for claiming complete and exclusive federal power to regulate such commerce, which was Webster's argument, Marshall then retreated, stating:

> It is not intended to say that these words comprehend that commerce which is completely internal, which is carried on between man and man in a State, or between different parts of the same State, and which does not extend to or affect other States. . . . Comprehensive as the word "among" is, it may very properly be restricted to that commerce which concerns more States than one. . . .

The federal power over commerce was not exclusive, as Webster maintained, although in this instance, the state law was in violation of the federal coasting act. The one concurring opinion in the case given by Justice William Johnson, ironically a Republican appointed by Jefferson, was stronger and more nationalistic than Marshall's. Johnson contended that the power of Congress "must be exclusive; it can reside but in one potentate; and hence, the grant of this power carries with it the whole subject, leaving nothing for the state to act upon." For Marshall, if it was clear that the "acts of New York must yield to the Law of Congress," it was also evident that the "completely internal commerce of a state, then, may be considered as reserved for the state itself." The nationalist chief justice had unwittingly laid the basis for a multitude of legal perplexities by making a distinction between intrastate and interstate commerce (terms he did not use); and it would fall to less subtle judicial minds to interpret this as meaning commerce that does not cross state lines. Lest anyone misunderstand his position on the general enumerated powers of the Congress and on the theory of strict construction of the Constitution adopted by Ogden's counsel and by Chancellor Kent, Marshall concluded his opinion with these words:

> Powerful and ingenious minds, taking, as postulates, that the powers expressly granted to the government of the Union are to be contracted, by construction, into the narrowest possible compass, and that the original powers of the states are retained, if any possible construction will retain them, may, by a course of well digested, but refined metaphysical reasoning, founded on these premises, explain away the construction of our country, and leave it a magnificent structure indeed, to look at, but totally unfit for use. They may so entangle and perplex the understanding, as to obscure principles which were before thought quite plain, and induce doubts where, if the mind were to pursue its own course,

none would be perceived. In such a case, it is peculiarly necessary to recur to safe and fundamental principles. . . .

In other words, the courts should construe the Constitution and the powers of Congress broadly.

In immediate practical terms, Marshall finally had rendered a popular decision. The steamboat monopoly had come to an end, and state fragmentation of commerce was prevented. *Gibbons v. Ogden* was the first great antitrust decision given at a time when monopolies were decidedly unpopular. Lost in the public euphoria over the end of "exclusive grants," save to a few Jeffersonian Republicans, was the fact that Marshall had made the Supreme Court the future arbiter of matters involving congressional power over commerce and intervention into state police and taxing powers. In so doing, he had struck one more blow for a broad view of the Constitution and of national power. Only when steam came to be used for land transportation would the full commercial implications of the Gibbons decision be clear. If, as many maintain, half of the Constitution is the commerce clause (the other half being the due process clause of the Fourteenth Amendment), the *Gibbons v. Ogden* case has been correctly termed the "emancipation proclamation of American commerce."

Marshall's opinion provided the starting point for all subsequent interpretations of the commerce clause. Initially, Marshall's conception was demanded by the needs of a developing nation and an expansive approach to federal authority. The breadth and elastic nature of his definition of commerce, however, justified the extensive commercial enterprises in which the national government has been engaged since, including regulation of new forms of commercial activity brought about by technological changes, inventions, and advances in communications and transportation. In the twentieth century, the commerce power has been used to justify various types of economic legislation (interstate and intrastate), including a presidential wage and price freeze under the Economic Stabilization Act of 1970 and noneconomic matters such as civil rights, kidnapping, and pollution control.

Further refinements of the definition of commerce and the types of activities that it encompasses evolved in a series of cases. Since 1937, the commerce clause has been understood to permit congressional regulation of intrastate activities that have a close and substantial relation to interstate commerce, so that their control is essential for protection from burdens and obstruction. In *United States v. Lopez* (1995), for example, the Supreme Court held that a purely intrastate activity is subject to congressional regulation only if it "substantially affects" interstate commerce. The case dealt with enactment of a 1990 criminal law banning possession of a gun within one thousand feet of a school. According to the Court, such noncommercial enterprise was unrelated to commerce, however broadly it is defined. —*Cecil L. Eubanks, updated by Marcia J. Weiss*

ADDITIONAL READING:

Barron, Jerome A., and C. Thomas Dienes. *Constitutional Law in a Nutshell.* 2d ed. St. Paul, Minn.: West, 1991. A succinct, compact reference on the law for those with a legal or political science background.

Faulkner, Robert K. *The Jurisprudence of John Marshall.* Princeton, N.J.: Princeton University Press, 1968. A comprehensive critique of Marshall's juridical thought. Places *Gibbons v. Ogden* in perspective with regard to Marshall's legal philosophy.

Frantz, John P. "The Reemergence of the Commerce Clause as a Limit on Federal Power: *United States v. Lopez." Harvard Journal of Law and Public Policy* 19, no. 1 (Fall, 1995): 161-174. A scholarly analysis of the *Lopez* case within the framework of the commerce clause, discussing its evolution.

McCloskey, Robert G. *The American Supreme Court.* 2d ed. Revised by Sanford Levinson. Chicago: University of Chicago Press, 1994. A detailed treatment of the Marshall Court. Additional resources are contained in a bibliographical essay.

Newmyer, R. Kent. *The Supreme Court Under Marshall and Taney.* Arlington Heights, Ill.: Harlan Davidson, 1968. Contains detailed information and presents Marshall's philosophy. Places *Gibbons v. Ogden* and the commerce power in historical context.

Pritchett, C. Herman. *Constitutional Law of the Federal System.* Englewood Cliffs, N.J.: Prentice-Hall, 1984. Commentary on the Constitution, placing the rulings in historical and doctrinal context. Includes a chapter on commerce power.

Schwartz, Bernard. *A History of the Supreme Court.* New York: Oxford University Press, 1993. Comprehensive in scope, this scholarly work details the Marshall Court and its influence on U.S. politics and society.

SEE ALSO: 1803, *Marbury v. Madison*; 1807, Voyage of the *Clermont*; 1816, Second Bank of the United States Is Chartered; 1819, *McCulloch v. Maryland*; 1825, Erie Canal Opens; 1832, Nullification Controversy; 1887, Interstate Commerce Act.

1824 ■ U.S. ELECTION OF 1824:
competition among four Republicans results in the splitting of the Republican Party into National Republicans and Democratic Republicans

DATE: December 1, 1824-February 9, 1825
LOCALE: Washington, D.C.
CATEGORY: Government and politics
KEY FIGURES:

John Quincy Adams (1767-1848), secretary of state in the Monroe Administration and sixth president of the United States, 1825-1829

John Caldwell Calhoun (1782-1850), secretary of war in the Monroe Administration and a presidential candidate in 1824 who withdrew

Henry Clay (1777-1852), leading Republican who became secretary of state in the Adams Administration

William Harris Crawford (1772-1834), cabinet member in the Monroe Administration and a presidential candidate in 1824

Andrew Jackson (1767-1845), U.S. military hero and a presidential candidate in 1824

Martin Van Buren (1782-1862), New York politician and leader of the Albany Regency

Daniel Webster (1782-1852), congressman from Massachusetts

Thurlow Weed (1797-1882), newspaper editor from Rochester and a rising politician in New York

SUMMARY OF EVENT. By 1824, the Federalist Party had ceased to exist, and the misnamed Era of Good Feelings was coming to a close. Five men in the Republican Party wanted to succeed the fifth president of the United States, James Monroe. At issue in the minds of some was an impending conflict over slavery that seemed closer as a result of the Missouri Compromise, which "locked in" the states of the slave South to minority status—in the Senate in the short term, and in the House in the longer term. The Missouri Compromise mandated that all territories becoming states above the 36°30′ parallel had to be free states, but that those below the line could be free or slave. Martin Van Buren of New York and William H. Crawford of Georgia had formulated a plan to create a new political party, in which loyalty to the party would be rewarded with political jobs (loosely called the spoils system). A key test of party allegiance would be the willingness of candidates to avoid any discussion of slavery, thus instituting a "gag" on all debate of slavery at the national level.

Crawford was the selection of a rump congressional caucus; his candidacy ended, however, when he suffered a stroke in mid-campaign, temporarily derailing Van Buren's plans for a political party and removing its most logical leader. Crawford had been supported by Monroe and Thomas Jefferson, and claimed to be the only true heir of the Jeffersonian tradition in the race. Born in Virginia and a resident of Georgia, Crawford represented the large plantation interests. He advocated the strict construction of the Constitution and emphasized states' rights.

Of the other four men running for president, Henry Clay of Kentucky put forth the most positive program. With his American System, which involved high protective tariffs and federally supported internal improvements, Clay sought to consolidate the different sections of the country behind him. At the time, Clay had no appreciation of the potential for a mass party such as that entertained by Crawford and Van Buren.

Andrew Jackson of Tennessee was the most popular choice and the nation's premier military hero. He was the only candidate supported outside his own section, appealing not only to the West but also to small farmers in the South and laborers in the East. Much of his popularity came from his reputation as a general—the first general since George Washington to seek the presidency.

John Quincy Adams of Massachusetts, secretary of state in the Monroe Administration, was the choice of conservative New Englanders. Although his statesmanship and personal honesty were admitted by all, his lack of tact and charm and his unwillingness to become involved in the rough-and-tumble of politics prevented him from gaining a popular following.

John C. Calhoun of South Carolina soon withdrew rather than face such formidable opposition for the presidency and became the sole vice presidential candidate.

Without a true modern party structure, complete with primaries and other nominating apparatus, candidates were nominated by the congressional caucuses. The caucus system had picked all presidential candidates prior to 1824, by which time it came under attack for its undemocratic features and for giving Congress too much power. Crawford was the last candidate nominated by the caucus: State legislatures nominated the other candidates, and this new device continued in use until the nominating convention was generally adopted within the next decade.

The greatest difficulty for the nominees was a lack of issues. Even before his stroke, Crawford could not state clearly that the goal of his campaign was to create institutional barriers to stifle debate about a moral issue. All the candidates were for some tariff reform, although Adams termed his tariff policy cautious and Jackson called his judicious. Both Adams and Clay, neo-Federalists, supported the American System, although Adams outstripped Clay in his support of internal improvements. To those issues, Jackson added an attack on the caucus system and supported the right of the people to choose their presidential electors directly.

As there were no real political differences, the contest quickly became one of personalities. There was little campaigning, and most of the excitement was provided by the press. With Crawford's physical infirmity virtually eliminating him, Adams assumed the favorite's position. He was expected to gain from the split in the South and West between Clay and Jackson.

In the election, on December 1, 1824, Jackson received the greatest number of popular votes, but not a majority. The electoral vote count was Jackson, ninety-nine; Adams, eighty-four; Crawford, forty-one; Clay, thirty-seven. As no candidate had received a majority, the choice of the president was passed to the House of Representatives, which would vote by states. Clay was out of the race, for the Constitution stipulated that the House should choose among the three candidates receiving the highest electoral totals.

The choice was between Adams and Jackson, and Clay was in a unique position. As Speaker of the House, he could control many of the votes there, and he was forced to choose between two men, both of whom he heartily disliked. There was only one logical choice for Clay, however, as he considered Jackson unfit for the presidency. On the other hand, as a supporter of the American System—which had arisen out of a need to rebuild the nation after the War of 1812 by assuming certain state debts incurred during the war, establishing a uniform national money supply, and providing tariff protections for budding industries competing with established foreign (mainly British) imports—Clay supported Adams' nationalist public policies. He agreed to meet with Adams to discuss "public affairs," and although both later denied that any deal was made, Clay was able to deliver several states into the Adams camp, notably Clay's own state of Kentucky, whose electors had been instructed to vote for Jackson. In the House election of February, 1825, Adams received thirteen votes to seven for Jackson and four for Crawford.

Rumors of a "corrupt bargain," or deal, between Clay and Adams were rampant. In January, there appeared in the *Philadelphia Columbian Observer* an anonymous letter charging that Clay had sold out to Adams for an appointment as secretary of state. Clay immediately denied the charge and published a card challenging his accuser to a duel. The duel was never fought, nor was any proof of the bargain ever provided. However, one of Adams' first acts as president was to appoint Henry Clay as his secretary of state; thus, according to the Jacksonians, was the "corrupt bargain" consummated. Jackson wrote to one of his supporters, "So you see the Judas of the West has closed the contract and will receive his thirty pieces of silver. . . . Was there ever witnessed such barefaced corruption in any country before?"

Jackson and his supporters believed that he had been cheated out of the presidency because he had refused to bargain with Clay. Jackson, they contended, was the obvious popular choice and should have been named president. Many believed that Congress had been morally bound to elect him. Both Adams and Clay were discredited in many eyes. Jackson resigned his Senate seat and returned to Tennessee, where he was nominated as that state's presidential candidate in 1828. By that time, Van Buren had refocused his party strategy around Jackson, whom he would support in 1828. The election of 1824 actually served to pair a vastly popular candidate with a formidable new political machine run out of Albany: Jackson and Van Buren recognized the power of the press and incorporated "news" papers into political propaganda.

The election of Adams in 1824 terminated the succession of the "Virginia dynasty" in the Republican Party. During Adams' administration, the Jeffersonians split into two wings: the Adams-Clay wing, whose adherents went by the name of National Republicans; and the Jackson wing, whose membership became known as the Democratic Republicans, or simply Democrats. Adams was caught in the middle of this partisan strife, and, unwilling or unable to engage in personal politics, lost popular support and was eventually defeated by Jackson in the campaign of 1828.

—*Cecil L. Eubanks, updated by Larry Schweikart*

ADDITIONAL READING:

Bemis, Samuel F. *John Quincy Adams and the Union*. New York. Alfred A. Knopf, 1956. A diplomatic historian, Bemis emphasizes Adams' diplomacy and suggests that Adams was ordinary.

Brown, Richard H. "The Missouri Crisis, Slavery, and the Politics of Jacksonianism." *South Atlantic Quarterly* 65, no. 1 (Winter, 1966): 55-72. A classic article, asserting that the Jacksonian Party was formed well before the "corrupt bargain" out of fear that the Missouri Compromise would undo the fragile truce that had kept the nation together.

Dangerfield, George. *The Era of Good Feelings*. New York: Harcourt, Brace, & World, 1952. An excellent, traditional summary of the period that examines the Adams Administration in detail and develops interesting portraits of the major participants.

Eaton, Clement. *Henry Clay and the Art of American Politics*. Boston: Little, Brown, 1957. A short biography of Clay that analyzes Clay's decision in 1824, arguing that there was no corrupt bargain.

McCormick, Richard P. *The Second American Party System: Party Formation in the Jacksonian Era*. Chapel Hill: University of North Carolina Press, 1966. Uses statistical analysis of election returns to examine changes in the political party system during this era.

Niven, John. *Martin Van Buren: The Romantic Age of American Politics*. New York: Oxford University Press, 1983. A detailed look at the "little magician," focusing on his political machinations in New York and his contributions to the party structure.

Remini, Robert V. *The Life of Andrew Jackson*. New York. Harper & Row, 1988. A one-volume condensed version of Remini's three-volume biography, against which all others are measured. Highly sympathetic toward "Old Hickory."

SEE ALSO: 1790's, First U.S. Political Parties; 1801, Jefferson Is Elected President; 1812, War of 1812; 1815, Battle of New Orleans; 1816, Second Bank of the United States Is Chartered; 1817, Seminole Wars; 1828, Jackson Is Elected President.

1825 ■ ERIE CANAL OPENS: *providing a waterway from the Great Lakes to the Atlantic, the canal opens commerce to the Old Northwest and changes the lives of all who live along it*

DATE: October 26, 1825
LOCALE: Albany to Buffalo, New York
CATEGORIES: Business and labor; Economics; Science and technology; Transportation
KEY FIGURES:
John Caldwell Calhoun (1782-1850), congressman from South Carolina
DeWitt Clinton (1769-1828), governor of New York, 1817-1821 and 1825-1828
Albert Gallatin (1761-1849), secretary of the Treasury, 1801-1814
William James (1769-1832), Albany businessman who became rich because of the canal

James Madison (1751-1836), fourth president of the United States, 1809-1817

SUMMARY OF EVENT. During the antebellum period, coastal cities in the United States engaged in strenuous competition for the commercial wealth of the expanding West. Before progress could be made in weaving the sections together into a single economic unit, difficulties had to be overcome concerning the accessibility of markets. In 1815, the Old Northwest was without convenient access to the markets of the East Coast. Farmers and merchants were forced to send their products to market by way of the Ohio and Mississippi Rivers to New Orleans and from there to the East Coast.

Farmers in the area of Pittsburgh found it cheaper to ship their goods over this long, circuitous route than to send them overland to Philadelphia or New York, a much shorter distance. Although the federal government had completed the National Road from Cumberland, Maryland, to Wheeling, Virginia, by 1817 it was uneconomical to ship bulky farm produce over this route.

The first major effort to open an economic commercial connection between the West and East occurred in the state of New York, with the construction, between 1817 and 1825, of the 363-mile-long Erie Canal connecting Albany on the Hudson River with Buffalo on Lake Erie. Skeptics at first called the canal Clinton's Ditch after its most consistent advocate, New York governor DeWitt Clinton. Skepticism soon disappeared, however, when the canal had a direct and cumulative effect on the nation in general and the Northwest in particular.

Construction was begun in 1817, with different sections sublet to different contractors. The canal took eight years to build and was considered the construction marvel of its day—some considered it the eighth wonder of the world—yet it was constructed without the aid of a single professional engineer. Most of the canal was hand-dug, aided by horse-, oxen-, or mule-powered scrapers. Malaria and dysentery plagued the workers, most whom were recent immigrants. In 1825, when the Erie Canal opened its waterway, it was four feet deep, had eighteen aqueducts and eighty-three locks, and had a rise of 568 feet from the Hudson River to Lake Erie. Construction costs were more than seven million dollars, but within a few years, toll revenue added more than a million dollars each year to New York coffers.

On October 26, 1825, the canal barge *Seneca Chief* left Buffalo with Governor Clinton and other dignitaries for the opening ride down the canal. As the barge left Buffalo, cannoneers stationed along the way fired relay shots to notify people in New York that the Erie Canal was open. Stopping at most towns along the canal made the first journey a slow one, but on November 4 Clinton stood on the front of his barge and poured a keg of Lake Erie water into the Atlantic, celebrating "the wedding of waters." The canal's opening meant that freight that had cost one hundred dollars per ton to move could now be shipped for six dollars per ton.

During the first decade of its operation, the Erie Canal played a large part in the development of the south shore of Lake Erie. Areas in the northwestern part of New York, now provided with access to markets in New York City, increased in population and productivity. The Erie Canal supplied an all-water route to the northern portions of the Old Northwest and accelerated the growth of these regions. This growing population caused an expansion of production to meet the needs of the immigrants. They, in turn, were able to increase the amount of farm produce available to the East. Their presence also augmented the demand for the importation of Eastern manufactured goods.

Perhaps the most important consequence of "Clinton's Wonder," as it soon came to be known, was the stimulus it gave to other regions, in both the East and the West, to emulate the success of New York by building canals of their own. Ohio in the 1830's, and Indiana and Illinois somewhat later, undertook the construction of canals to join their interiors to the Great Lakes-Erie Canal system. Ohio's canals connected Cincinnati with Toledo and Cleveland. In Indiana, the Wabash and Erie Canal connected Toledo and Terre Haute, while in Illinois, the Illinois and Michigan Canal connected Chicago with the lush lands along the Illinois River. As a consequence of the opening of these waterways, interior arms were opened up and production rose, for farmers now had new routes by which to market their products. The canals also caused many American Indian tribes to be removed to reservations west of the Mississippi River.

The effects of the Erie Canal in the East were equally momentous. The canal solidified the position of New York City as the greatest emporium in the nation. Other Eastern cities, such as Philadelphia and Baltimore, could not afford to sit while New York monopolized the Western trade. If they were to survive as commercial centers, they had to develop their own connections with the West. Thus, Pennsylvania constructed a system of canals and waterways between Philadelphia and Pittsburgh, and followed up with the Pennsylvania Railroad. Baltimore undertook two major improvements: construction of the Baltimore and Ohio Railroad and the Chesapeake and Ohio Canal. Farther to the north, Boston constructed a canal across to Albany, hoping to intercept some of the Western trade.

This vigorous and deadly competition was not without its effects on the established Mississippi River system. Cities functioning as parts of the lake system competed not only with one another but also with cities that formed part of the river system. Toledo and Cleveland were engaged in commercial warfare with Cincinnati and Louisville; St. Louis, especially in the 1850's, felt the impact of the Illinois and Michigan Canal in its struggle with Chicago; and downstream, New Orleans was sensitive to any events that impinged on the trade of St. Louis, Cincinnati, and Louisville.

The railroads added a new dimension to the struggle, and their development overlapped and went beyond the era of the great canals. By the 1850's, the competition initiated by the construction of the Erie Canal had entered a new phase. A struggle involving three transportation systems and a host of cities and towns had evolved. Cities that had pinned their hopes on the canals were bypassed by the railroad. Cities bid with one another, mortgaging their futures for the privilege of being rail hubs. Smaller towns with exalted visions of their economic potential rose and then fell, succumbing to the economic power of more dynamic and luckier competitors.

To keep up with competition from other transportation sources, the Erie Canal was enlarged to a depth of seven feet by 1862. In time, the Champlain, Oswego, and Cayuga-Seneca canals branched off from the Erie, adding canal access to other cities and lakes. This new system of canals was renamed the New York State Canal System. Dredging continued to deepen the canals, and a minimum depth of twelve feet was the norm in the mid-1900's. Plans call for a sixteen-foot depth of water throughout the canal system for the twenty-first century.

—John G. Clark, updated by Russell Hively

ADDITIONAL READING:

Albion, Robert G. *The Rise of New York Port, 1815-1860.* New York: Charles Scribner's Sons, 1939. Evaluates the factors, including the Erie Canal, that led to the commercial leadership of New York City.

Baida, Peter. "The Admirable Three Millions." *American Heritage* 39, no. 5 (July/August, 1988): 16-20. Tells how William James turned sixty thousand dollars into three million dollars, through land investments prior to the completion of the Erie Canal.

Garraty, John A. "101 More Things Every College Graduate Should Know About American History: You Asked for It." *American Heritage* 38, no. 8 (December, 1987): 49-60. A mass of trivia, which reveals that DeWitt Clinton's nickname was Magnus Appollo "because of his large size and impressive appearance."

Goodrich, Carter. *Government Promotion of Canals and Railroads, 1800-1890.* New York: Columbia University Press, 1960. A study of federal, state, and local government aid and encouragement of internal improvements, including an enlightening analysis of state efforts.

Meyer, Balthaser H. *History of Transportation in the United States Before 1860.* Reprint. Washington, D.C.: Peter Smith, 1948. A reference work containing facts and information regarding all the major early road, canal, and railroad developments in the nation.

Shaw, Ronald E. *Erie Water West: A History of the Erie Canal, 1792-1854.* Lexington: University Press of Kentucky, 1966. A complete history of the canal from its conception to completion, and its first twenty-nine years of operation.

Taylor, George R. *The Transportation Revolution, 1815-1860.* Vol. 4 in *The Economic History of the United States.* New York: Holt, Rinehart, and Winston, 1951. Impact that developments in transportation had on the growth of the U.S. economy.

SEE ALSO: 1811, Construction of the National Road; 1815, Westward Migration; 1830, Baltimore and Ohio Railroad Begins Operation.

1828 ■ CHEROKEE PHOENIX BEGINS PUBLICATION: *the first Native American newspaper and the first published in a Native American language*

DATE: February 21, 1828
LOCALE: New Echota, Cherokee Nation, Georgia
CATEGORIES: Communications; Cultural and intellectual history; Native American history; Social reform
KEY FIGURES:
Elias Boudinot (Buck Watie, c. 1803-1839), nephew of Major Ridge and editor of the *Cherokee Phoenix*
John Marshall (1755-1835), chief justice of the United States
John Ridge (c. 1803-1839), Major Ridge's son and lobbyist against removal
Major Ridge (c. 1770-1839), influential Cherokee leader
John Ross (1790-1866), elected principal chief of Cherokees during the removal debate
Sequoyah (1770-1843), Cherokee author of the syllabary that made the written language of the Cherokees possible
Samuel A. Worcester (1798-1859), missionary to the Cherokees

SUMMARY OF EVENT. The *Cherokee Phoenix,* the first Native American newspaper, began on February 21, 1828, as the Cherokee nation created institutions and built its new capital at New Echota in Georgia. Cherokees, who had ceded land in several Southeastern states, remained on a reservation in northwestern Georgia. There they created their own governing institutions following the European model: They wrote a constitution, established a legislature, and built schools and churches.

While Georgia passed laws stripping Cherokees of their rights, the Cherokees used every peaceful means of protest, including the printing press. When the *Cherokee Phoenix* wrote editorials against the laws, Georgians stole the printing press and jailed the staff. Cherokees fought against their removal from Georgia through the press, the courts, and Congress.

Editor Elias Boudinot, a college-educated missionary and clerk of the Cherokee National Council, wrote in both Cherokee and English, hoping the newspaper would help Native Americans to improve both their living conditions and their image in the larger white society. In this era, newspaper editors were often advocates, and political parties or other special interests often subsidized their publications. The *Cherokee Phoenix* received its support from the National Council, white Christian missionaries, and the fund-raising efforts of Boudinot and other Cherokee leaders. Improving a people's image through newspapers was another premise of contemporary journalism, especially among political parties and town boosters. As the First Amendment protected the U.S. press, the Native American press was to be free from restraint, despite its subsidy from the National Council.

The *Cherokee Phoenix* also depended upon the Cherokee language, a writing system for which had been invented by a young Cherokee genius, Sequoyah, a few years earlier. Sequoyah was born around 1770 of a Cherokee mother and a white drifter. He saw that his people were at a disadvantage compared to the whites, who had a printed and written language. With no formal education, this half-breed child grew up to be the only person in history known to have created a written language single-handedly. His eighty-six-character syllabary, using syllables or sounds instead of letters as a basic form, allowed the easy translation of the traditionally oral Cherokee language into written form. Assembling words from these sounds proved easier than doing it from twenty-six letters. White observers were astonished at the speed with which young people learned the language. Cherokee children learned as much language in a few days as English children learned of their language in one or two years. Most of the nation became literate in a matter of months.

In its prospectus, the *Cherokee Phoenix* said the biweekly newspaper would provide laws and public documents of the Cherokee nation; accounts of manners, customs, and the progress of the nation in education, religion, and "the arts of civilized life"; the interesting news of the day; and miscellaneous articles to promote learning among the Cherokees.

The Reverend Samuel Worcester, a Protestant missionary to the Cherokees, provided essential support for the newspaper. Two white printers also accompanied the press, which had to await the manufacture of special type in New England to accommodate Sequoyah's syllabary. The printers set type on the hand press by taking detailed instructions from Worcester instead of learning the language. The printing office also published translations of the Bible into Cherokee. Trying to build an independent state within Georgia, the Cherokees received support from missionaries, Whig Party leaders, and ultimately the U.S. Supreme Court in *Worcester v. Georgia* (1832).

Worcester had refused to sign the loyalty oath that Georgia required of whites working among Native Americans. President Jackson refused to enforce the Court's decision, and Congress had passed the Indian Removal Act of 1830, setting up the process of forcing the Cherokees to move to Indian Territory, now parts of Oklahoma and Kansas. Re-

flecting his missionary-school background, Boudinot editorialized that Cherokees could become civilized and showed a condescending attitude toward Native Americans and other ethnic groups that did not accept Christian assumptions of progress. At first, Boudinot strongly editorialized against removal, despite the growth of individual acts of violence against Cherokees. As a relative of the Ridge family that eventually concluded that getting the best terms for removal was better than resistance, Boudinot signed the removal treaty without approval of the National Council.

Boudinot resisted pressure from Georgians, whose legislature in 1829 stripped Cherokees of their civil rights. Under the

Sequoyah developed the syllabary that made a written Cherokee language possible. As a result, the first newspaper printed in both English and Cherokee, the Cherokee Phoenix, *appeared beginning in 1828.* (Smithsonian Institution Photo No. 991-A)

new laws, whites could commit crimes against Cherokees without punishment, because Cherokees were not allowed to testify against whites in court. Despite a Supreme Court decision supporting them, Jackson refused to intervene. "Full license to our oppressors, and every avenue of justice closed against us," the *Cherokee Phoenix* said. "Yes, this is the bitter cup prepared for us by a republican and religious government—we shall drink it to the very dregs." A year later, the newspaper reported harassment, arrest, and threats of physical harm to its staff members. After the newspaper protested the postmaster's sale of liquor to American Indians to encourage violent incidents, the postmaster retaliated by cutting off the mail.

The move left the *Cherokee Phoenix* without its source of supplies and exchange papers. "This new era," Boudinot wrote, "has not only wrested from us our rights and privileges as a people, but it has closed the channel through which we could formerly obtain our news. By this means the resources of the *Phoenix* are cut off." The newspaper said Native Americans had become more dependent upon sympathetic whites.

The *Cherokee Phoenix* debated basic issues within the Cherokee nation, including acculturation and Christianity. In the paper, national leaders debated how the new government should be organized and how elections should be conducted. While political candidates argued election issues, the newspaper proclaimed the need for national unity. Leaders debated the division of the legislature into two houses and the political system into two parties. The newspaper said all Cherokees must keep "the preservation of ourselves as a free and sovereign people" as their primary goal. The National Council approved a punishment of one hundred lashes against people who formed organizations to foster disunity among the Cherokees.

Violent conflicts between whites and natives became so common that many feared for the safety of Native Americans who remained in the Southeast. Friends seeking to protect Native Americans and enemies seeking to eliminate them came together to remove the Five Civilized Tribes to land west of the Mississippi. Because early voluntary removals had proved so disastrous to the Cherokees and the Choctaws, those remaining in Georgia vowed to remain on their native land. The elected principal chief, John Ross, ordered Boudinot to suppress news of dissention within the National Council over the removal issue; instead, the editor was to present a united front of Cherokee resistance against white encroachment.

The editor resigned in 1832, revealing that he could not manage the paper without a free discussion of such important issues. "I should think it my duty to tell them the whole truth. I cannot tell them that we shall be reinstated in our rights when I have no such hope." Ross appointed his brother-in-law, Elijah Hicks, but Hicks lacked Boudinot's journalistic experience and rhetorical power.

Outside pressure continued. In 1833, the postmaster sent letters to the *Cherokee Phoenix*'s exchanges, stating that the newspaper had been discontinued. The paper's publication became erratic, and in 1834, Hicks suspended publication. His parting editorial asked readers not to give up the fight. "Although our enemies are numerous we are still in the land of the living and the JUDGE of all the earth will impart the means for the salvation of our suffering Nation."

In the fall of 1838, Cherokee men, women, and children were rounded up and forced by the U.S. Cavalry to march from their Georgia home to Indian Territory. Thousands of people suffered and died on the walk that became known as the Trail of Tears. One morning, in June, 1839, a band awaited Boudinot in trees near his new home, under construction. Two men approached him and asked him, as keeper of public medicine, for help. While they walked together, two others joined them. The group then stabbed Boudinot and smashed the former editor's head with a tomahawk six or seven times. They were part of a vigilante organization that held Boudinot and two other members of the Ridge faction responsible for selling Cherokee land, and in revenge carried out their capital punishment. Worcester, with whom Boudinot and his family had been staying, said the killers had cut off his right hand. Boudinot left a wife and six children. Worcester and printer John F. Wheeler, both of whom served prison time in Georgia for their work on the *Cherokee Phoenix*, helped the Cherokees start the *Cherokee Advocate* in 1844 with William P. Ross, the chief's nephew, as editor. It continued free distribution and publication in both Cherokee and English. —*William E. Huntzicker*

ADDITIONAL READING:

Danky, James P., ed. *Native American Periodicals and Newspapers, 1828-1982*. Westport, Conn.: Greenwood Press, 1984. Overview of the history of Native American newspapers.

Luebke, Barbara P. "Elias Boudinot, Indian Editor: Editorial Columns from the *Cherokee Phoenix*." *Journalism History* 6 (1979): 48-51. Discusses Boudinot's conflicts as editor of the *Cherokee Phoenix*.

McLoughlin, William G. *Cherokees and Missionaries, 1789-1839*. New Haven, Conn.: Yale University Press, 1984. Discusses missionary support for the Cherokees.

Mooney, James. *Historical Sketch of the Cherokee*. Chicago: Aldine, 1975. Valuable study by a contemporary who interviewed people involved.

Murphy, James E., and Sharon M. Murphy. *Let My People Know: American Indian Journalism, 1828-1978*. Norman: University of Oklahoma Press, 1981. A history of Native American journalism, with some discussion of the *Cherokee Phoenix*.

Perdue, Theda, ed. *Cherokee Editor: The Writings of Elias Boudinot*. Knoxville: University of Tennessee Press, 1983. Brief biographical introduction to Boudinot, with reproductions of important documents in the history of the *Cherokee Phoenix* and Boudinot's fund-raising.

Riley, Sam G. "The *Cherokee Phoenix*: The Short, Unhappy Life of the First American Indian Newspaper." *Journalism Quarterly* 53, no. 4 (Winter, 1976): 666-671. Discusses Boudinot's editorial dilemmas and political pressure.

SEE ALSO: 1817, Seminole Wars; 1830, Indian Removal Act; 1830, Trail of Tears; 1831, Cherokee Cases.

1828 ∎ Webster's American Dictionary of the English Language: *a key instrument in the movement to assert the United States' cultural independence from Europe*

Date: November, 1828
Locale: New Haven, Connecticut
Category: Cultural and intellectual history
Key figures:

Joel Barlow (1754-1812), a Connecticut Wit whose poetry reflected the movement to create a national literature
Timothy Dwight (1752-1817), president of Yale College and another Connecticut Wit
Samuel Johnson (1709-1784), English lexicographer, whose dictionary had helped to set U.S. standards
Charles Merriam (1803-1880) and
George Merriam (1806-1887), brothers who purchased the rights to publish Webster's dictionary in 1843
Noah Webster (1758-1843), author of *An American Dictionary of the English Language*

Summary of event. Although the United States had achieved political independence from Great Britain in 1783, in many respects the new nation remained a cultural colony of Europe. This influence was particularly evident in "high" culture; literature and the fine arts in the United States were largely derivative and subservient to European, especially British, standards. While it was somewhat predictable that a provincial country would follow the cultural leadership of the metropolitan centers of its mother country, U.S. nationalism after the American Revolution demanded a national culture that would reflect American themes, roots, and ideals. The literary group known as the Connecticut Wits or Hartford Wits, although still imitative of British and continental styles, strained to give the United States a unique and distinguished literature. Nearly half a century later, Ralph Waldo Emerson and other writers continued to call for cultural independence, but despite Walt Whitman's path-breaking poetry in the 1850's, the nature of U.S. cultural relations with Europe was a contentious matter well into the twentieth century. One strong force for and cogent symbol of the recurrent plea for a national culture, however, was the publication by Noah Webster of *An American Dictionary of the English Language* in 1828.

Born in Connecticut in 1758, Webster was graduated from Yale College when he was twenty years of age. As a Yale graduate and member of The Friendly Club in Hartford, he associated with artist John Trumbull, writers Theodore and Timothy Dwight, and other Connecticut Wits. Webster's own early contributions toward elevating American culture were as an educator, a function that his lexicographical career continued on a broader scale. His biographers have regularly accorded him the title Schoolmaster of America or Schoolmaster of the Republic. In this role, he was the author of *A Grammatical Institute of the English Language*, eventually a three-

volume textbook for schoolchildren. The first part of this series became famous as the "Blue-Backed Speller." According to one biographer, no other book, except the Bible, played such a part in unifying the United States. Parts 2 and 3, a grammar and a reader respectively, also did much to mold American self-identity.

Webster's concern with language usage stemmed partly from his conviction that language was an important national bond. He believed that linguistic independence should follow political, with the gradual evolution of a distinct American dialect of English. He was eager to accelerate the process, not only through the sanctioning and encouragement of American usages but also through his advocacy of a reformed American spelling. At one time, adopting a reformed phonetic alphabet seemed to Webster the best way to render the United States culturally independent of Great Britain. He enlisted the support of the venerable statesman Benjamin Franklin in a plan to have the Confederation Congress promulgate the new alphabet. Although Webster came to realize that radical changes could not win support, he remained the advocate of spelling reform, as in the removal of silent or unnecessary letters. His authority did eventually support such minor deviations of American English from the parent tongue as the omission of the *u* in words such as "honour" and "colour." He also defended distinctly American pronunciations and variations. Although Webster lived in rather insular Connecticut, he grasped that the ethnically and racially multicultural populations in the other colonies had infused English with a mixture of indigenous, African, and non-English European vocabulary and sentence structure.

An American Dictionary of the English Language was the logical culmination of Noah Webster's career. Prior to Webster's lexicography, three shorter American dictionaries had appeared, but most people in the United States still depended primarily on British dictionaries, such as Samuel Johnson's famous work. For Webster, however, Johnson's effort was unsatisfactory. Not only did it fail to fit American needs, but also, Webster believed, its author was frequently mistaken in etymology. Webster himself was well-qualified by training and temperament to compile a dictionary. His learning was broad: He had practiced law, written about epidemic diseases, conducted laboratory experiments, and studied business conditions. He delighted in etymological investigations, and learned other languages (eventually more than twenty) to understand the roots and interrelationships of English. He was undoubtedly the United States' first notable comparative philologist. Finally, Webster possessed extraordinary diligence and patience in the compilation and investigation of words.

As a Federalist during much of the period he was preparing the dictionary, Webster had political and social goals for his linguistic reforms. The democratization of politics and society under the Jeffersonians upset him. Believing humans to be intrinsically evil and in need of hierarchical control, Webster, like many other early nineteenth century reformers, longed to establish a "benevolent empire" that would embrace order, sobriety, and other values of an emerging middle class. Language, Webster surmised, would be an important agent in this movement, because words and phraseology modified people's thought patterns and behavior. Although he reveled in Americanisms, Webster worried that the expanding frontier regions, the areas that fueled such language additions, undercut any compact vision of order and would continually support the Jeffersonians. By codifying spelling and grammar and loading his dictionary definitions with his own euphemisms and values, Webster hoped to introduce a purity into U.S. culture that would combat what he perceived as impending chaos. Starting in 1808, when he himself became a convert to the rampant Second Great Awakening and calmed his fears about human depravity, Webster added an evangelical fervor to his vision. Order would still be necessary to fulfill the United States' millennial mission. The dictionary reflected his religious hopes as much as his nationalism.

In 1806, Webster launched his crusade with the publication of a *Compendious Dictionary of the English Language*, whose listings exceeded the number of words in the best English dictionaries by some five thousand. He brought out an abridgment for classroom use the next year. Another two decades remained before two large volumes of *An American Dictionary of the English Language* came from the press in 1828. It listed seventy thousand words (twelve thousand more than the contemporaneous edition of Johnson's dictionary) and included an introduction in which Webster expounded on his ideas about language and etymology. He made use of a preface to assert the parity of American English with the British standard and to defend statesman James Madison, jurist James Kent, writer Washington Irving, and others as authorities equal to the best British masters of the language. Webster's own anti-British attitudes softened over time, but he continued to celebrate American achievements as rivaling those of Europe.

Webster's dictionary soon became the lexicographical benchmark in the United States. After Webster's death in 1843, George and Charles Merriam purchased the publishing rights to his lexicon. Since then, the Merriam-Webster company and others have published many successive editions of the work, from time to time making significant revisions. Still, the name of Noah Webster has remained synonymous with the campaign to validate American English that he began and boosted in the eighteenth and nineteenth centuries.

—*Michael D. Clark, updated by Thomas L. Altherr*

ADDITIONAL READING:

Ellis, Joseph J. *After the Revolution: Profiles of Early American Culture.* New York: W. W. Norton, 1979. The best short introduction to Webster's major contribution to American intellectual independence. Places Webster in the context of postrevolutionary cultural ebullience, along with painter Charles Willson Peale, novelist Hugh Henry Brackenridge, and dramatist William Dunlap.

Moss, Richard J. *Noah Webster.* Boston: Twayne, 1984. Examines Webster's use of linguistics and his role as a literary figure.

Rollins, Richard M. *The Long Journey of Noah Webster.* Philadelphia: University of Pennsylvania Press, 1980. This slim, provocative treatise explores Webster's personal traits as indices of his literary and linguistic endeavors.

Spencer, Benjamin T. *The Quest for Nationality: An American Literary Campaign.* Syracuse, N.Y.: Syracuse University Press, 1957. Webster appears frequently in this study of literary nationalism, which is concerned primarily with the nineteenth century.

Warfel, Harry R. *Noah Webster: Schoolmaster to America.* New York: Macmillan, 1936. A detailed and comprehensive, if overly adulatory, biography of Webster.

Webster, Noah. *Noah Webster: On Being American—Selected Writings, 1783-1828.* Edited by Homer Babbidge. New York: Frederick A. Praeger, 1967. Provides most of the pertinent essays on Webster's linguistic nationalism.

SEE ALSO: 1790's, Second Great Awakening; 1820's, Free Public School Movement; 1820's, Social Reform Movement; 1831, Tocqueville Visits America; 1836, Rise of Transcendentalism.

1828 ■ JACKSON IS ELECTED PRESIDENT:
in the wake of the Missouri Compromise, a new political party system is born, along with the trappings of modern political campaigns

DATE: December 3, 1828
LOCALE: United States
CATEGORY: Government and politics
KEY FIGURES:
John Quincy Adams (1767-1848), sixth president of the United States, 1825-1829
Andrew Jackson (1767-1845), American Indian fighter, "Hero of New Orleans," and seventh president of the United States, 1829-1837
William Harris Crawford (1772-1834) and
Martin Van Buren (1782-1862), co-creators of the party system

SUMMARY OF EVENT. The presidential campaign of 1828 was among the bitterest in U.S. history. It is also one of the most discussed and analyzed, in part because it symbolized a number of practices and trends that were developing in American society. The 1828 contest followed on the heels of the famous "corrupt bargain" election of 1824 and matched the same two major protagonists—John Quincy Adams, the president, and Andrew Jackson. The contest in 1824 also had included William H. Crawford, then secretary of war, and Henry Clay, congressman from Kentucky. When no candidate received a majority in the electoral college, the selection went to the House of Representatives. There, Clay threw his support and electors behind Adams; upon assuming the presidency, Adams named Clay as secretary of state. Jackson and his supporters complained about the "corrupt bargain" that cost Jackson the election and vowed to return in 1828.

More important than the "corrupt bargain," however, was the formation of a new political party system, first conceived in the wake of the Missouri Compromise by the Georgian Crawford and New York politician Martin Van Buren as a way to stifle further political debate over slavery. The Missouri Compromise had built into the process by which territories became states a permanent disadvantage for the slave-holding South: Every northern territory that became a state had to be free, but territories below 36°30′ could be free or slave. Therefore, the South soon would be outvoted in both houses of Congress. Crawford and Van Buren thought they had found a way to demand neutrality of politicians on the issue of slavery through the discipline of a new party system based on political jobs or other party rewards, called "spoils." Individual politicians, from presidential candidates down to local candidates, had an incentive to refrain from taking a position on slavery in return for party support, money, and coverage from the numerous party newspapers.

Crawford's sudden ill health removed him from the 1824 contest too late for Van Buren to find another acceptable candidate to head the new organization. Jackson's popularity made him the perfect vehicle for the Little Magician (as Van Buren was known), and the 1828 election was the appropriate time to debut the new party system. Henry Clay's American System differed little from the policies of the sitting president, Adams. Jackson's campaign focused on the personality of the general, and Adams contrasted Jackson's low-brow, commoner image to his own well-bred, educated, experienced persona.

The contest developed into one of the greatest examples of mudslinging in U.S. political history. No charge, however inaccurate or unfounded, seemed too extreme for the zealous campaigners. Each candidate was the target of vicious slander, as charges of murder, adultery, and pandering were slung back and forth. Adams was portrayed as a monarchist, the darling of the old Federalists, and a profligate spender who presided over a corrupt squadron of insiders and officeholders who lived in undemocratic luxury at the voters' expense. The hoary details of the "corrupt bargain"—that marriage between "the Puritan and the black-leg"—were dredged up repeatedly by the Jacksonians. Jackson fared no better. His enemies portrayed him as a hot-tempered, overly ambitious, would-be tyrant, who had lived in sin with his beloved Rachel, and who appealed to the basest emotions of King Mob.

Changes in the organization of political parties and Van Buren's emphasis on getting out the vote made the outcome a foregone conclusion. Adams' supporters still operated under the assumption that small groups of elites selected the president, while Van Buren's machine understood, and even directed, the new mass politics that had evolved. Several developments made new mass parties practical: Requirements that voters have property had been lifted in most states, allowing far more men to vote than ever before; "newspapers"—little more than political propaganda organs—had expanded greatly

Andrew Jackson, seventh president of the United States. Before ascending to the presidency, Jackson had built a reputation as a military war hero and Indian fighter. His campaign of 1828 presaged politics of the future and a growing division between Southern and Northern states. (Library of Congress)

in number and influence; and the caucus system of selecting candidates or other spokespersons for the parties gave way to the nominating convention. With a popular candidate at the top of the ticket, such as Jackson, who appealed to the newly enfranchised voters, debates over issues were relatively unimportant. The only question was, who could get out the vote? To that end, Van Buren's machine, divided into state, county, city, and precinct suborganizations, easily outclassed the stodgy Adams' campaign apparatus.

Jackson won 647,286 popular and 178 electoral votes to the 508,064 popular and 83 electoral votes of Adams, who carried only the New England section plus New Jersey, Maryland, and Delaware. It was a resounding victory for the general, but it was neither a triumph of democracy over aristocracy nor an economic revolution. Van Buren's spoils system merely replaced Adams' elites with a new group named by Jackson; and with the expansion of the size of government ensured by every election (since it was necessary always to get out more of the vote than one's opponent did), those in power had more power and privilege than ever before. As for an economic revolution, economic gulfs continued to widen during the Jacksonian era.

Van Buren (and Jackson, to a lesser extent) saw the election as ensuring the continuation of the Union by removing the threat of a civil war over slavery. It seemed that voters and candidates could be persuaded to put party loyalty over personal opinions on slavery. That was especially critical in the North, where antislavery sentiments ran high. The new party, called the Democratic Republicans (or simply, Democrats), appeared to be able to contain the debate over slavery by electing candidates who would refuse to deal with it. As one author concluded, the system could survive as long as it could elect "northern men with southern principles." In the process, however, neither Van Buren nor Jackson appreciated the twofold dynamic inherent in the new system, one that increased the scope and authority of the federal government and a second that increased the power of the presidency within that government. In fact, Jackson's presidency produced more vetoes than all six previous administrations put together. The party discipline over slavery could not survive either an antislave president or a Congress dominated by northern men of northern principles, which was exactly what it got in the election of 1860.

—Larry Schweikart

ADDITIONAL READING:

Brown, Richard. "The Missouri Crisis, Slavery, and the Politics of Jacksonianism." *South Atlantic Quarterly* 65, no. 1 (Winter, 1966): 55-72. Shows that the second political party system was conceived as a response to the Missouri Compromise. Maintains that Van Buren and Crawford designed a political organization that would reward party loyalty with jobs, requiring the party faithful to limit or avoid discussion of slavery.

Formisano, Ronald P. *The Transformation of Political Culture: Massachusetts Parties, 1790's-1840's.* New York. Oxford University Press, 1983. Uses Massachusetts as a test case to examine the changes in party organization and structure that led to the evolution of national parties.

McCormick, Richard P. "New Perspectives on Jacksonian Politics." *American Historical Review* 65, no. 2 (January, 1960): 288-301. Uses voter participation statistics to show that the election of 1828 was not a popular revolution and that the true revolution did not occur until 1840, when a Whig was elected.

Marshall, Lynn L. "The Strange Stillbirth of the Whig Party." *American Historical Review* 72, no. 2 (January, 1967): 445-468. A classic study of party organization by the Jacksonians and of the Whigs' ill-fated response. Explains the centralizing tendencies of the spoils system and the nationalization of elections.

Niven, John. *Martin Van Buren: The Romantic Age of American Politics.* New York: Oxford University Press, 1983. A thorough account of the life of the Little Magician, offering a detailed look at Van Buren's political life in New York, although appreciating the role slavery played in national politics.

Remini, Robert V. *The Election of Andrew Jackson.* Philadelphia: J. B. Lippincott, 1963. This concise treatment of the election by a historian sympathetic to Jackson emphasizes the rise of democratic forces and the "common man" over traditional elites.

Schlesinger, Arthur M., Jr. *The Age of Jackson.* Boston: Little, Brown, 1945. A Pulitzer Prize-winning study that views Jackson as a hero. Portrays the election in terms of democratic reaction to elites; more economic in its analysis than Remini's book.

Schweikart, Larry. "Jacksonian Ideology, Currency Control, and 'Central Banking': A Reappraisal." *The Historian* 51, no. 1 (November, 1988): 78-102. Uses Jackson's war on the Bank of the United States to show the effect of the spoils system and the new party organization on the growth of government. Argues that the policies and organizational dynamic of the Jacksonians, regardless of their rhetoric, resulted in greater power accruing to the federal government and to the president in particular.

SEE ALSO: 1790's, First U.S. Political Parties; 1815, Battle of New Orleans; 1816, Second Bank of the United States Is Chartered; 1820, Missouri Compromise; 1824, U.S. Election of 1824; 1830, Proslavery Argument; 1832, Jackson vs. the Bank of the United States; 1834, Birth of the Whig Party; 1840, U.S. Election of 1840.

1830 ■ PROSLAVERY ARGUMENT: *the intellectual bond among Southerners who see slavery as a moral institution, in opposition to Northern abolitionists*

DATE: 1830-1865
LOCALE: The slave states
CATEGORIES: African American history; Economics
KEY FIGURES:
John Caldwell Calhoun (1782-1850), South Carolina politician, political theorist, and U.S. senator
Thomas Roderic Dew (1802-1846), professor of political economy at William and Mary College
George Fitzhugh (1806-1881), Virginia writer and social philosopher
James Henry Hammond (1807-1864), South Carolina lawyer, editor, and U.S. senator
Josiah Nott (1804-1873), physician and author
Thornton Stringfellow (1788-1869), Baptist minister of Culpepper County, Virginia

SUMMARY OF EVENT. In the quarter-century preceding the Civil War, Southerners advanced a wide range of arguments and theories—some old, some new—to justify the institution of chattel slavery. The distinctiveness of proslavery thinking during the years before the Civil War lay less in its content than in its tone or spirit. Defenders of the South's "peculiar institution" were no longer on the defensive; their mood was no longer apologetic. Unlike most of their predecessors, they did not merely tolerate slavery; they defined it as a moral institution and many glorified it. They took the offensive on behalf of slavery partly in response to the attacks of Northern abolitionists. Perhaps the primary objective of their aggressive proslavery campaign was to dispel the doubts of Southerners as to the justice of slavery and to offer compelling proof to nonslaveholders and slaveholders alike that slavery found sanction in religion, science, and morality, forming an essential part of a civilized economic and political order.

Post-1830 proslavery discourse borrowed from a variety of sources, many of which had been used before immediate abolitionism posed a new threat to slavery. Proslavery apologists pointed to the existence of slavery in biblical times and throughout most of history, as well as to the notion of entailment, which blamed the introduction of slavery on the British and predicted social catastrophe should slavery be abolished. These arguments continued to dominate the thinking of most proslavery writers in the 1830's, as evidenced, for example, in Thomas R. Dew's *Review of the Debate in the Virginia Legislature of 1831 and 1832*. Although this was once treated as the first work of the new proslavery discourse, later historians have seen it as the culmination of the earlier, less affirmative phase of proslavery writing in the South. Dew's work, which was widely read, asserted that slavery was a preferred way of compelling efficient labor in the hot states of the lower South, the harbinger of the notions of perpetual slavery developed by later Southern apologists.

Traditionally, historians have understood post-1830 proslavery as a reaction to the publication of William Lloyd Garrison's journal *The Liberator* (1831-1865), which marks the onset of immediate abolitionism, and the fear spawned by Nat Turner's slave rebellion in Southampton County, Virginia. Both events occurred in 1831, but other issues intensified proslavery writing and abolitionist discourse during the 1830's.

Proslavery polemics seem to have escalated along a continuum, rather than suddenly appearing after 1831. Two interrelated themes characterized this escalation of Southern proslavery. The first was a reaction to the abolitionist mail campaign of 1835, in which Northern abolitionists attempted to flood the South with literature arguing that slavery was immoral. In response, Southern ministers and denominations took the lead in denouncing the moral foundations of abolitionists. Virulent antiabolitionism became a major feature— perhaps the single constant—in Southern proslavery. Southerners denounced abolitionism as incendiary, a wanton and dangerous interference with Southern safety. Southerners construed abolitionists as intent upon fomenting rebellion among Southern slaves, and were also infuriated by the "Gag Rule" in Congress, which persuaded Northerners that Southerners would trample on the First Amendment or any other right to preserve slavery.

The second theme involved a defense of slavery more ideological in tone, which blended biblical literalism with conservative social theories, some of which were quite popular among New England Federalists during the early nineteenth century. This strain of thinking challenged industrial economics and modern reform movements, asserting that a stratified social order produced the best society possible. A heavy lace of paternal imagery, which threaded together honor and social responsibility, gave ornamentation to this new proslavery fabric. In the hands of John C. Calhoun, this two-pronged argument proved that slavery was not an evil, as the abolitionists claimed, but "a good—a positive good," "a great blessing to both races," and "the great stay of the Union and our free institutions, and one of the main sources of the unbounded prosperity of the whole."

Typical of thinkers who championed this phase of proslavery writing was Thornton Stringfellow, a Baptist minister of Culpepper County, Virginia, whose *Brief Examination of Scripture Testimony on the Institution of Slavery* argued that slavery enjoyed "the sanction of the Almighty in the Patriarchal Age . . . that its legality was recognized . . . by Jesus Christ in his kingdom; and that it is full of mercy." Godly Southerners, Stringfellow maintained, should withdraw from abolitionists, whose moral notions must originate from some other source than the Bible. In a speech before the U.S. Senate in 1858, James Henry Hammond of South Carolina held that African American slaves provided the "mud-sill" of society, whose labor was necessary but whose mean estate made essential their exclusion from the political process. Slavery was essential to free "that other class which leads progress, civilization and refinement" for more enlightened endeavors. Fortunately, the senator observed, the South had found African Americans perfectly adapted to serve as the "very mud-sill of society and of political government," "a race inferior to her own, but eminently qualified in temper, in vigor, in docility, in capacity to stand the climate, to answer all her purposes."

During the 1850's, other Southern writers embraced more extreme proslavery theories, although these attracted more interest from historians in the twentieth century than from nineteenth century advocates. Henry Hughes, of Port Gibson, Mississippi, drew upon the infant discipline of sociology to buttress his proslavery views. He described slavery as "Ethical Warranteeism," in which the slave labored for a master in return for food, clothing, and shelter. Josiah Nott, of Mobile, Alabama, embraced the theory of polygenesis, holding in *Types of Mankind* that African Americans resulted from a separate creation and were not *Homo sapiens*. Others compared Southern slavery with free labor in the North. In *Sociology of the South* (1854) and *Cannibals All!* (1857), for example, Virginian George Fitzhugh suggested that the Northern states would have to adopt some form of slavery to control the immigrant working classes, or else face moral and social chaos. Free labor, he asserted, produced class warfare in the North, while slavery permitted social harmony in the South. Southern masters had moral obligations toward, and were predisposed to kind treatment of, their slaves; Northern factory owners discarded their laborers at whim.

Most Southerners adhered to the less extreme argument based on the Bible and Plato. The proslavery argument became a justification for the entire Southern way of life, whose culture, social structure, and economy were believed to depend upon the institution of slavery. Its ubiquity helped bind Southerners together and produced the remarkable degree of unity among them in the days following the election of Abraham Lincoln in 1860 and his call for troops in April, 1861. Undoubtedly, the intensity and unanimity with which Southerners defended slavery had much to do with the fact that they had come to identify the system of slavery with Southern society as a whole and with their place in the Union.

—*Anne C. Loveland, updated by Edward R. Crowther*

ADDITIONAL READING:

Faust, Drew Glipin. *The Ideology of Slavery: Proslavery Thought in the Antebellum South, 1830-1860*. Baton Rouge: Louisiana State University Press, 1981. An excellent anthology of proslavery writing, augmented by a thoughtful introductory essay.

Freehling, William W. *The Road to Disunion: Secessionists at Bay, 1776-1854*. New York: Oxford University Press, 1990. Shows clearly the complex uses Southerners made of proslavery thinking and why a degree of intellectual unity was vital in a South divided against itself.

Jenkins, William S. *Pro-Slavery Thought in the Old South*. Chapel Hill: University of North Carolina Press, 1935. The oldest monograph on proslavery thinking, it remains a useful starting point for the study of this phenomenon.

Snay, Mitchell. *Gospel of Disunion: Religion and Separatism in the Antebellum South*. New York: Cambridge University Press, 1993. Illustrates how significant proslavery thinking was in Southern clerical thought and how that created a great degree of intellectual unity in the South.

Tise, Larry E. *Proslavery: A History of the Defense of Slavery in America, 1701-1840*. Athens: University of Georgia Press, 1987. Shows that proslavery thinking existed in both Northern and Southern states, and explains well the subtle shifts in Southern proslavery after 1830.

SEE ALSO: 1820, Missouri Compromise; 1830, Webster-Hayne Debate; 1831, *The Liberator* Begins Publication; 1831, Nat Turner's Insurrection; 1834, Birth of the Whig Party; 1850, Compromise of 1850; 1850, Second Fugitive Slave Law; 1854, Kansas-Nebraska Act; 1856, Bleeding Kansas; 1857, *Dred Scott v. Sandford*.

1830 ■ BALTIMORE AND OHIO RAILROAD BEGINS OPERATION: *the beginning of the railroad era opens the way for rapid westward expansion, flourishing trade, and radical changes from a rural to an increasingly industrial nation*

DATE: January 7, 1830
LOCALE: Baltimore to the Ohio River
CATEGORIES: Business and labor; Economics; Expansion and land acquisition; Science and technology; Transportation

KEY FIGURES:

Charles Carroll (1737-1832), signer of the Declaration of Independence

Peter Cooper (1791-1883), inventor and industrialist who built the early steam locomotive *Tom Thumb*

John Eager Howard (1752-1827), prominent Baltimore resident

Jonathan Knight (1789-1864), mathematician and chief engineer of the railroad

Stephen Harriman Long (1784-1864), army officer who oversaw surveying

Philip Thomas (1776-1861), prosperous Baltimore merchant and promoter of the railroad

Evan Thomas, Philip's brother

SUMMARY OF EVENT. The quickening pace of American life achieved a new momentum in the early national period. The westward movement acquired a national character as New Englanders pushed into the Ohio Valley and Virginians filled up Kentucky and Tennessee. The Eastern seaboard, with its cities and port facilities, turned to the West for its food, and the grain-producing hinterland responded with increased production. New methods of transportation were required to bring the produce of the interior to the coast. Enterprising businessmen, pooling their capital resources, engaged in canal building and railroad construction. Private initiative, in the absence of a consistent government policy of promoting public works, laid the foundation of a national transportation system. This transportation system began with canals, but regions without navigable waterways had to find another method. The railroad provided the answer.

The development of transportation in the early national period took three forms: canals, roads, and railways. Canals, in areas of accessible rivers and lakes, were by far the cheapest. Horsedrawn barges could move heavy bulk commodities inexpensively, and the cost of maintenance was negligible. When the Erie Canal opened in 1825, Buffalo and New York City became entrepôts for Western trade. The Morris Company Canal, under construction from 1824 to 1832, eventually connected New York Harbor to the mouth of the Lehigh River and served to bring Lehigh coal to the seaboard. Other canals were enthusiastically promoted, with the expectation of reaping huge profits from the Western trade. Pennsylvania, smarting from the Erie Canal, constructed the Pennsylvania Portage and Canal System between 1826 and 1840. This elaborate system of cable portages and short canals was a dismal failure. High construction costs and competition from railroads rendered this bold scheme obsolete before it opened.

The construction of roads had a much longer history. The Philadelphia-Lancaster Turnpike, completed in 1794, encouraged road building in other areas. In New England and the middle states, where distances were relatively short, toll roads were constructed feverishly in the 1790's and early 1800's. Still, road transportation was more expensive than canal transportation. High freight costs precluded the movement of bulk commodities, and overland transportation declined rapidly with the rise of canals. By 1821, six hundred miles of new turnpike construction had been authorized, and nearly four thousand miles stood completed. The old National Road, connecting Cumberland, Maryland, and Wheeling, on the Ohio River, fell into neglect after the opening of the Erie Canal. By 1825, the turnpike boom had passed.

The third form of transportation required the assistance of technology. In 1825, the Stockton and Darlington Railroad opened in England. The railroad's potential for the United States quickly was recognized. Within a few years, railroad construction in the United States surpassed that in Great Britain. Shortline railways were first, but with the incorporation of the Baltimore and Ohio Railroad, long-distance rail transportation for goods and passengers became a reality.

Baltimore's decision to sponsor a railway into the interior was, in essence, a manifesto in its struggle with New York City for commercial supremacy. By 1827, Baltimore boasted a population of eighty thousand, of which nearly two-thirds earned their living in commerce or related industries. The completion of the Erie Canal threatened Baltimore's prosperity. Other planned canals, such as the Chesapeake and Ohio Canal, were also a threat to the port of Baltimore. The National Road, which had played a significant role in Baltimore's commercial success, could not compete with New York's all-water route. Hence, the idea of a railroad, an ambitious and fiscally dangerous scheme at best, soon found influential supporters in Baltimore's business community.

Discussion preceded organization. At a dinner party held at the Baltimore home of Colonel John Eager Howard in 1826, the scheme for a railroad linking Baltimore with the Ohio Valley was first discussed. Evan Thomas, an influential member of Baltimore's business elite, who was to become the first president of the new railroad, had just returned from England, where he had viewed the operations of the Stockton and Darlington Railroad. Thomas was enthusiastic about the new enterprise, and he succeeded in arousing the interest of a few business leaders with his vivid descriptions of the English system. Most business leaders, however, remained reticent, and their cautious attitude prevented immediate action. Evan's brother, Philip Thomas, now took up the cause. As a prosperous merchant who felt threatened by New York City's ascendancy, Philip Thomas began pushing the idea at every available gathering. When New York City appeared to be running away with the Western trade, Baltimore's businessmen began to panic. The ideas of the Thomas brothers, so quietly received in 1826, aroused unbridled enthusiasm in the early months of 1827.

On February 2, 1827, at a dinner party held at the home of George Brown, the Thomas brothers presented a discourse on the relative advantages of a railway trade route to the West. Twenty-five businessmen attended this affair, representing a good portion of Baltimore's business elite. After the discourse, a committee was appointed to investigate the feasibility of the scheme. One week later, the committee reported that immediate steps should be taken to construct a railway between the city of Baltimore and a suitable point on the Ohio River. The

report further suggested that a company be formed and a charter of incorporation be obtained from the legislature. Business leaders received the report and took action immediately. A large edition of the report was published in pamphlet form and distributed publicly. News of the plan quickly spread beyond city limits, and throughout the state of Maryland tongues were wagging. When a formal petition for a charter of incorporation was submitted to the Maryland State legislature on February 27, 1827, little opposition was present. The bill for incorporation passed easily the next day, and America's first significant experiment in railroad building was under way.

The charter of the Baltimore and Ohio Railroad Company provided for a capital stock of three million dollars to be raised by the public sale of fifteen thousand shares at one hundred dollars per share. Ten thousand shares were reserved for subscription by the state of Maryland, and five thousand for subscription by the city of Baltimore. When ten thousand shares had been purchased, the corporation would be declared established and all its rights and privileges would take effect immediately. The fiscal organization of the Baltimore and Ohio Railroad transformed the city of Baltimore and the state of Maryland into a private corporation, and the citizens of the state into a public enterprise.

When the stock offer was made, an enthusiastic public responded. Money flowed into the company coffers. Parents took out stock in their children's names, and a wave of speculation swept the state. The stock books were opened on March 20, 1827, at the Farmers Branch Bank in Frederick and the Mechanics Bank in Baltimore. Twelve days later, the books were closed. The Baltimore and Ohio Railroad stock was distributed among twenty-two thousand individuals; nearly every family in the state had a stake in the company. Private enterprise had created a public utility. In effect, the building of the Erie Canal forced the leaders of Baltimore to accept the challenge of an experimental mode of transportation, whereas other cities pursued abortive and costly experiments with canal construction in inappropriate locations.

The actual construction of the line awaited the solution of many engineering problems. Americans were novices in railroad building, but what they lacked in practical experience they more than made up for with energy. The federal government possessed the only repository of engineering knowledge, and the management of the Baltimore and Ohio Railroad raided the government for talent. Colonel Stephen H. Long was recruited from the army, and Jonathan Knight, a well-recognized mathematician, came from the National Road project. Engineers were sent to England to study the British system, and preliminary surveys were made to determine the best route to take. Problems arose, but public impatience goaded the bureaucracy to action.

By the summer of 1828, enough progress had been made to allow a symbolic gesture. The historic significance of America's first long-distance railroad was clearly seen. The citizens of Maryland felt themselves to be upon the threshold of a new era. To ensure a conspicuous place in later history books, the management of the Baltimore and Ohio Railroad sought to commemorate the occasion with the laying of a cornerstone. To perform this symbolic act, they chose Charles Carroll, the last surviving signer of the Declaration of Independence. On July 4, 1828, in a ceremony preceded by parades and speeches, Charles Carroll laid the cornerstone for the United States' first interstate railway.

Two years later, on January 7, 1830, the Baltimore and Ohio Railroad opened its line from Pratt Street through to Carrolton Viaduct for public riding. Four rail cars, pulled by teams of horses, with a total seating capacity of 120 persons, made the first run. While it would be the 1850's before the railroad actually reached Ohio, the thirteen-mile initial line from Baltimore to Ellicott's Mills quickly became a showcase of early U.S. railroading.

Peter Cooper, who owned a Baltimore iron foundry, built the Tom Thumb, a diminutive steam locomotive; in an experimental trial on August 28, 1830, it hauled thirty-six people at speeds up to eighteen miles per hour. The railroad's directors were impressed, and with the help of Baltimore engine builders, the railroad was transformed into a true steam-operated railroad during the 1830's.

As the railroad expanded, the need for technological improvements became evident. Only a year after the railroad began operation, Jonathan Knight, the railroad's chief engineer, said the comfort of the passenger carriages had to be improved by mounting them on springs to improve ride quality. In addition, sheets of timetables, called "Arrangements of Trains," were posted in stations for the edification of travelers. Ridership and freight tonnage increased. Service improvements caused more use. All acted to feed industrial growth. The need for improved railroad equipment spawned support industries to serve it.

The beginning was inauspicious, but the potential for public rail transportation created a railroad mania throughout the nation. Schemes for railroad construction took the public imagination by storm. By 1833, the South Carolina Canal and Railroad Company had completed its line from Charleston to Hamburg, South Carolina. In 1836, the Erie and Kalamazoo Railroad connected Toledo, Ohio, with Adrian Township, in the Michigan Territory. Between 1840 and 1860, an additional twenty-eight thousand miles were added to the nation's railroad system. The growth of railroads allowed the absorption of immigrants both on the coast and in the interior. At the same time, this westward expansion resulted in the displacement of the American Indian population there.

Steam engines of greater efficiency soon replaced the smoking teakettle contraptions of the earlier years, and as horsepower per tonnage increased, freight costs dropped dramatically. What had begun as a private enterprise by Baltimore merchants to save their city became a national institution. The railroad soon came to dominate internal transportation, but more important, the railroad created a need for corporate organization on a large scale. The phenomenal growth of American industry in the second half of the nineteenth century can-

not be understood without reference to the impact of the railroads upon American economic life.

—John G. Clark, updated by Stephen B. Dobrow

ADDITIONAL READING:

Douglas, George H. *All Aboard! The Railroad in American Life*. New York: Paragon House, 1992. Examines how the railroad has shaped the lives of Americans and the communities in which they live.

Faith, Nicholas. *The World the Railways Made*. New York: Carroll & Graf, 1991. Examines the effects of railroads on society on a worldwide basis.

Fishlow, Albert. *American Railroads and the Transformation of the Antebellum Economy*. Cambridge, Mass.: Harvard University Press, 1965. A controversial interpretation of the effect of railroad expansion on the economy of the pre-Civil War United States.

Hornung, Clarence. *Wheels Across America*. New York: A. S. Barnes, 1959. A graphic history of vehicular transportation in North America.

Hungerford, Edward. *The Story of the Baltimore and Ohio Railroad*. 2 vols. New York: G. P. Putnam's Sons, 1928. Traces the history of the Baltimore and Ohio Railroad as an example of corporate institutional growth.

Stover, John F. *American Railroads*. Chicago: University of Chicago Press, 1961. This general history of U.S. railroads places the founding of the Baltimore and Ohio Railroad in historical perspective.

SEE ALSO: 1811, Construction of the National Road; 1815, Westward Migration; 1825, Erie Canal Opens; 1853, Pacific Railroad Surveys; 1869, Transcontinental Railroad Is Completed.

1830 ■ WEBSTER-HAYNE DEBATE: *a crystallization of the difference between the slave and free states in the context of westward expansion*

DATE: January 19-27, 1830
LOCALE: Washington, D.C.
CATEGORIES: African American history; Expansion and land acquisition
KEY FIGURES:
Thomas Hart Benton (1782-1858), senator from Missouri
John Caldwell Calhoun (1782-1850), vice president of the United States under Jackson
Samuel Augustus Foot (1780-1846), senator from Connecticut
Robert Young Hayne (1791-1839), senator from South Carolina, Webster's antagonist
Andrew Jackson (1767-1845), seventh president of the United States, 1829-1837
Daniel Webster (1782-1852), senator from Massachusetts and a great orator

SUMMARY OF EVENT. In December, 1829, Connecticut senator Samuel A. Foot presented a resolution to the United States Senate suggesting the temporary restriction of the sale of public land. Only those lands already surveyed and placed for auction were to be sold. This seemingly inoffensive resolution precipitated America's most famous debate.

A liberal land policy was vital for the continued growth of the West. Thomas Hart Benton, representing the West as a senator from Missouri, jumped to his feet to attack the resolution as a barefaced attempt to keep the emigrant laborer out of the West and to force him to remain in the East as an industrial wage-slave. The endeavor to check the development and prosperity of the West was nothing new, suggested Benton; rather, it was another sign of the hatred of the East toward the West that had so often plagued the forum of national politics. The Missourian ended by saying that the hope of the West lay "in that solid phalanx of the South," which in earlier times had saved that section when in danger.

The Southern political leadership was anxious to make an alliance with the West to secure its support for the slavery issue. The South also was interested in alliance with the West because Southern politicians saw the growing population and economic clout of the North and thought that westward expansion of slaveholding societies would help redress the balance. This was imperative in light of the fact that the Missouri Compromise had unearthed fundamental tensions between the free and slave states. The Southern planter and the Western farmer in alliance could more than offset the Eastern manufacturing interests in controlling the federal government. The hope for such a combination led South Carolina's Senator Robert Y. Hayne to step forward and take up the fight.

Hayne offered Southern support to the West and deftly shifted the argument from land to state sovereignty. If the Eastern proposals were put into effect, said Hayne, the price of land would increase. The income derived from the sale of the higher-priced land would provide a "fund of corruption" that would add to the power of the federal government and correspondingly reduce the independence of the states. Preaching strict constructionist and states' rights views against federal intervention, the South Carolinian declared that "the very life of our system is the independence of the states and there is no evil more to be deprecated than the consolidation of government." In the course of his remarks, Hayne made a bitter attack upon New England and that section's disloyalty during the War of 1812. This incensed Daniel Webster, senator from Massachusetts, who rose to defend his state and section: "Sir . . . I deny that the East has at anytime shown an illiberal policy toward the West." Fearful that he might further alienate the West, Webster ignored Benton and addressed his remarks to Hayne. Attacking the Southerner's views on the consolidation of government, Webster deplored the tendency of some to "habitually speak of the Union in terms of indifference and even disparagement," and then challenged Hayne to meet him on the grounds of states' rights versus national power.

A discussion that had started on the subject of public land policy thus shifted to a debate over the nature and meaning of the federal Union. Both nationalism and state sovereignty were debated by two of their most capable champions. Hayne was an able lawyer, a skilled debater, and a splendid orator. Tall and graceful, with cordial and unaffected manners, he was the epitome of the Southern aristocrat. As the defender of the South and the advocate of that section's doctrines, Hayne stood second only to his mentor and fellow statesman, John C. Calhoun, then the vice president. Webster was the country's greatest orator. Further, he was a man of commanding appearance, with a large head, dark and penetrating eyes, and a deep and resonant voice. It has been said that no man could be as great as Daniel Webster looked. Indeed, his countenance was so overpowering and his oratorical style so effective that even trivial and commonplace statements sounded profound when presented by the "god-like Daniel." Webster brought to his speeches not only a political viewpoint, but a philosophical and conceptual weight that inevitably impressed his listeners.

In an age when political debates were loved by the American people, this battle between two brilliant speakers attracted wide attention. The Senate chamber, a small semicircular room where only forty-eight members sat, was crowded to capacity and the galleries were packed. At one time, so many congressmen came to listen that the House of Representatives could not carry on its normal business.

Hayne answered Webster with a slashing defense of states' rights as it had been outlined by Calhoun. He spoke with logic and eloquence as Calhoun looked down from the Speaker's chair, smiling and occasionally nodding his approval. Hayne's defense was based upon the Virginia and Kentucky Resolves of 1798, and he asserted that each state, while assenting to the federal Constitution, reserved the right to interpret that document within its own borders; that is, the people of any state, if they believed themselves offended, could declare an act of the federal government null and void. Otherwise, Hayne continued, the federal government would have the capacity to "proscribe the limits of its own authority," and this made government without any restriction of its powers. The states and the people would be entirely at the mercy of the federal government.

Webster, in what has been called the greatest speech ever made in the Senate, upheld the doctrine of nationalism. A state could not, he said, annul an act of Congress except "upon the ground of revolution." He believed that the Constitution, as the supreme law of the land, was created by the people, not the states. The primary question, Webster maintained, was not the right of revolution against oppression, but that of determining whose prerogative it was to decide on the constitutionality of the laws. For him there was only one answer: The Constitution was the nation's highest law, and the ultimate appeal lay with the Supreme Court. He ended his endeavor with this peroration:

> When my eyes shall be turned to behold for the last time the sun in heaven, may I not see him shining on the broken and dishonored fragments of a once glorious Union; on states dissevered, discordant, belligerent; on a land rent with civil feuds,

or drenched, it may be, in fraternal blood! Let their last feeble and lingering glance rather behold the glorious ensign of the republic, known and honored throughout the earth, still full high advanced, its arms and trophies streaming in their original lustre, not a strip erased or polluted, nor a single star obscured, bearing for its motto, no such miserable interrogatory as "What is it all worth?" nor those words of delusion and folly, "Liberty first and Union afterwards": but everywhere . . . that other sentiment, dear to every true American heart,—Liberty and Union, now and forever, one and inseparable!

The *Philadelphia Gazette* summed up the result of the debate: "The opposition party generally contend that Mr. Webster overthrew Mr. Hayne; while, on the other hand, the result is triumphantly hailed by the friends of the administration as a decisive victory over the eastern giant." It would be a mistake to see the Webster-Hayne debate solely as part of the buildup to the Civil War; this assumption would be purely the product of historical hindsight. Contemporary observers might well have seen the debate as being between Jacksonian Democrats, with their Southern and Western base, and the emerging Whig Party, which championed national unity above all. Whoever won, the debate clarified the issues and intensified the struggle between states' rights and nationalism. It furnished both North and South with powerful arguments and thus accentuated the ardor with which each defended its cause.

—John H. DeBerry, updated by Nicholas Birns

ADDITIONAL READING:

Baxter, Maurice G. *One and Inseparable: Daniel Webster and the Union.* Cambridge, Mass.: Harvard University Press, 1984. Gives an exposition of Webster's fundamental philosophy of national unity.

Chambers, William Nisbet. *Old Bullion Benton, Senator from the New West: Thomas Hart Benton, 1782-1858.* New York: Russell & Russell, 1970. Examines Benton's role in the debate and also the general question of the West's role in the slavery and states' rights debates.

Current, Richard Nelson. *Daniel Webster and the Rise of National Conservatism.* Boston: Little, Brown, 1955. Places Webster in the context of the rise of the Whig Party and its nationalist ideology.

Petersen, Merrill D. *The Great Triumvirate: Webster, Clay, and Calhoun.* New York: Oxford University Press, 1987. Examines Webster's relations with his legislative colleagues and his pivotal role in the United States' debates about itself; highly recommended.

Smith, Page. *The Nation Comes of Age: A People's History of the Ante-bellum Years.* New York: McGraw-Hill, 1981. Entertaining general history of the period. Asserts the Webster-Hayne debates presaged the Civil War.

SEE ALSO: 1820, Missouri Compromise; 1830, Proslavery Argument; 1831, *The Liberator* Begins Publication; 1831, Nat Turner's Insurrection; 1834, Birth of the Whig Party; 1850, Compromise of 1850; 1850, Second Fugitive Slave Law; 1854, Kansas-Nebraska Act; 1856, Bleeding Kansas; 1857, *Dred Scott v. Sandford*.

1830 ■ INDIAN REMOVAL ACT: *the beginning of forced resettlement of sixty thousand eastern Native Americans to lands west of the Mississippi River*

DATE: May 28, 1830
LOCALE: Georgia and other Southeastern states
CATEGORIES: Expansion and land acquisition; Laws and acts; Native American history
KEY FIGURES:
Elias Boudinot (Buck Watie, c. 1803-1839), nephew of Major Ridge and editor of the *Cherokee Phoenix*
Andrew Jackson (1767-1845), seventh U.S. president, 1829-1837, and advocate of removal
John Marshall (1755-1835), judge who ruled that Georgia could not legislate over the Cherokee nation
John Ridge (c. 1803-1839), son of Major Ridge and a Cherokee leader and lobbyist against removal
Major Ridge (c. 1770-1839), influential Cherokee leader who signed the removal treaty after resisting it for years
John Ross (1790-1866), elected principal chief of the Cherokees during the removal debate
Samuel A. Worcester (1798-1859), missionary to the Cherokees

SUMMARY OF EVENT. Cherokees and other members of the so-called Five Civilized Tribes—Choctaw, Chickasaw, Cherokee, Seminole, and Creek—established independent republics with successful governments. Adapting to their white neighbors, they became farmers, miners, and cattle ranchers. Some had plantations, even owning slaves. They built schools and churches, wrote constitutions, and established independent governments. They learned a bitter lesson: Whites wanted their land, not their assimilation into Euro-American society.

As a local militia leader and politician, Andrew Jackson negotiated the acquisition of fifty million acres of Georgia, Alabama, Tennessee, and Mississippi even before he became president of the United States in 1828. By then, the Cherokees had lost their land outside Georgia, and neighbors had grown increasingly jealous of Cherokee success. For generations, Cherokees had provided a textbook picture of Jefferson's ideal nation of farmers. Sequoyah, a young man of Cherokee and white blood, invented a phonetic alphabet, or syllabary, that enabled almost every member of his nation to become literate within a few months. To hold their remaining land, Cherokees made the sale of any additional land to whites a capital offense.

Yet violent conflicts between whites and natives became so common that many friends and enemies alike advocated removal to protect Cherokees from white citizens who routinely attacked them. In 1817, some Cherokees exchanged land in North Carolina for space in Arkansas. Within two years, six thousand had moved voluntarily, but the move only worsened Cherokee problems. By 1821, the Cherokees were at war with the Osages who had been in Arkansas Territory

TRAILS OF TEARS: ROUTES OF INDIAN REMOVAL TO THE WEST AFTER 1830

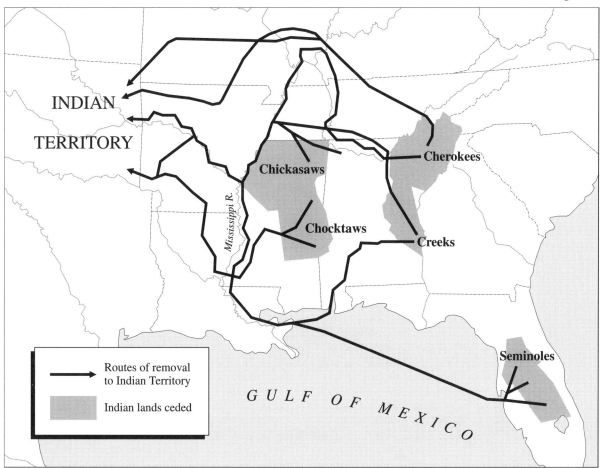

already, and both groups fought whites who continued to move onto their land.

These early voluntary removals proved so disastrous that the Cherokees and Choctaws remaining in Georgia vowed to stay on their native land. Although President James Monroe proposed removal again in 1825, neither Monroe nor his successor, John Quincy Adams, could get the measure through Congress. Only the enthusiasm of President Jackson got removal approved on a close vote in 1830. In 1829, President Jackson admitted that the five republics had made "progress in the arts of civilized life," but he said American Indians occupied land that whites could use. Beyond the Mississippi River lay enough land for Native Americans and their descendants to inhabit without interference "as long as grass grows or water runs in peace and plenty."

Meanwhile, the Georgia legislature extended its power over the Cherokee nation and stripped Native Americans of civil rights. These laws forbade anyone with American Indian blood to testify in court against a white man, annulled contracts between Native Americans and whites, and required an oath of allegiance to Georgia by white people living among American Indians. The laws also prevented Native Americans from holding meetings or digging for gold on their own land.

Instead of going to war, the Cherokees hired two prominent Washington lawyers and went to the U.S. Supreme Court. They lost their first case, challenging Georgia for hanging a Cherokee man convicted under Cherokee law. The second case (*Worcester v. Georgia*) challenged the loyalty oath designed to remove teachers, missionaries, and other whites from the reservation. The Reverend Samuel Worcester and other missionaries among Cherokees refused to sign the loyalty oath, despite public humiliation, abuse, and imprisonment.

Chief Justice John Marshall declared repressive Georgia laws unconstitutional. American Indian nations, Marshall said, were "domestic dependent nations" that could have independent political communities without state restrictions. President Jackson, who had fought American Indians in the South, suggested that Georgia could ignore the Court's decision. The president, not the Court, controlled the army.

Congress also took up Georgia's cause. The Indian Removal Act of 1830 began a process of exchanging Indian lands in the twenty-four existing states for new lands west of the

Mississippi River. In 1834, Congress established Indian Territory, now much of Oklahoma, as a permanent reservation. Major Ridge and his family had been among the strongest opponents of removal, and Cherokee lobbyists, including John Ridge, celebrated their Supreme Court victory in *Worcester.* However, they had thought Whigs in Congress would prevail against Jackson's removal policy.

The federal removal law did not say that Native Americans could be forced to move, but the Ridge family and Cherokee newspaper editor Elias Boudinot began to see the move as necessary to protect Cherokees from increasing violence. Principal Chief John Ross, however, still resisted removal. Believing it in their nation's best interests, the Ridge family signed a removal treaty without approval of the tribal council.

Many natives resisted removal from their ancient homelands. The Alabama Creeks were forcibly removed, some of them in chains. Choctaws were forced out of Mississippi in winter, with no chance to bring provisions against the cold. Some were tricked into getting drunk and signing away their possessions. Others signed away their lands, believing the promises of government officials. Forced marches of Creeks, Choctaws, and Cherokees brought sickness, starvation, and death to thousands of people throughout the 1830's.

The Cherokees faced a special horror. Georgia's repressive laws had created a climate of lawlessness. Whites could steal land, and Cherokees could not testify in court against them. In one notorious case, two white men enjoyed dinner in the home of a family whose father was part Cherokee. In the evening, the parents left temporarily and the guests forced the children and their nurse from the home and set it on fire, destroying the house and all of its contents. The men were arrested, but the judge dismissed the case because all the witnesses were part Cherokee. Only pure-blooded whites were allowed to testify in court.

Finally, Jackson's successor, President Martin Van Buren, ordered General Winfield Scott, with about seven thousand U.S. soldiers and state militia, to begin the forced removal on May 26, 1838. Soldiers quietly surrounded each house to surprise its occupants, according to James Mooney, a researcher who interviewed the participants years later. Under Scott's orders, the troops built stockades to hold people while being prepared for the removal. "From these," Mooney wrote,

> squads of troops were sent to search out with rifle and bayonet every small cabin hidden away in the coves or by the sides of mountain streams, to seize and bring in as prisoners all the occupants, however or wherever they might be found. Families at dinner were startled by the sudden gleam of bayonets in the doorway and rose up to be driven with blows and oaths along the weary miles of trail that led to the stockade.

Men were taken from their fields, children from their play. "In many cases, on turning for one last look as they crossed the ridge, they saw their homes in flames." Some scavengers stole livestock and other valuables, even before the owners were out of sight of their homes. "Systematic hunts were made by the same men for Indian graves, to rob them of the silver pendants and other valuables deposited with the dead." Some sympathetic soldiers allowed one family to feed their chickens one last time, and another to pray quietly in their own language before leaving their home.

Within a week, the troops had rounded up more than seventeen thousand Cherokees and herded them into concentration camps. In June, the first group of about a thousand began the eight-hundred-mile journey. Steamboats took them on the first leg down the Tennessee River. The oppressive heat and cramped conditions fostered disease and caused many deaths. Then the Cherokees walked the last leg of the trip to beyond the western border of Arkansas. Because of the oppressive heat, Cherokee leader John Ross persuaded General Scott to permit them to delay the largest removal until fall. Thus, the largest procession—about thirteen thousand people—started on the long overland march in October, 1838. Most walked or rode horses; they drove 645 wagons.

Dozens of people died of disease, starvation, or exposure on each day of the journey. More than four thousand Cherokees died on the journey that the survivors named the Trail of Tears. The procession reached the Mississippi River opposite Cape Girardeau, Missouri, in the middle of winter. Most had only a single blanket to protect themselves from the winter winds as they waited for the river ice to clear. In March, 1839, they reached their destination in Indian Territory. Many were buried along the road, including Chief John Ross's wife, Quatie Ross, who died after giving up her blanket to a sick child in a sleet-and-snowstorm. Her death left Ross to grieve both his wife and his nation.

In his last message to Congress, President Jackson said he had settled the Native American problem to everyone's satisfaction and saved the race from extinction by placing them "beyond the reach of injury or oppression." Native Americans would now share in "the blessings of civilization" and "the General Government will hereafter watch over them and protect them." Between 1778 and 1871, 370 treaties stipulated land cessions to whites. Jackson ridiculed the idea of making treaties with Native Americans and called the idea of treating American Indians as separate nations an absurd farce.

By the end of June, 1838, Georgians could boast that no Cherokees remained on their soil, except in the stockade. Sixty thousand members of the five republics had been removed beyond the Mississippi River. As many as fifteen thousand men, women, and children died of starvation and disease. The Choctaw had moved in 1832; the Chickasaw in 1832-1834, the Seminole in 1836, and the Creek in 1836-1840. In June, 1839, members of the Ross faction, in revenge for the law that John Ridge signed into effect, murdered John Ridge, Major Ridge, and Elias Boudinot for their signing a removal treaty selling Cherokee land.

—*William E. Huntzicker*

ADDITIONAL READING:

Foreman, Grant. *Indian Removal: The Emigration of the Five Civilized Tribes of Indians.* 2d ed. Norman: University of Oklahoma Press, 1953. The classic and most comprehensive history of removal.

Green, Michael D. *The Politics of Indian Removal: Creek Government in Crisis.* Lincoln: University of Nebraska Press, 1982. Well-researched history of removal as it affected the Creek nation.

Guttmann, Allen. *States' Rights and Indian Removal: "The Cherokee Nation v. the State of Georgia."* Boston: D. C. Heath, 1965. Brief documentary history of the Cherokees' legal struggle to keep their land.

McLoughlin, William G. *Cherokee Renascence in the New Republic.* Princeton, N.J.: Princeton University Press, 1983. Cherokee history up through the removal crisis.

————. *Cherokees and Missionaries, 1789-1839.* New Haven, Conn.: Yale University Press, 1984. Thorough, well-documented history of missionary involvement among the Cherokees in the period leading up to their removal.

Mooney, James. *Historical Sketch of the Cherokee.* Chicago: Aldine, 1975. A valuable study by a contemporary who interviewed people involved.

Moulton, Gary E. *John Ross, Cherokee Chief.* Athens: University of Georgia Press, 1978. Biography of the Cherokee leader at the time of removal.

Remini, Robert V. *The Legacy of Andrew Jackson: Essays on Democracy, Indian Removal, and Slavery.* Baton Rouge: Louisiana State University Press, 1988. The leading biographer of Andrew Jackson reflects on his significance to these issues.

Wallace, Anthony F. C. *The Long, Bitter Trail: Andrew Jackson and the Indians.* New York: Hill & Wang, 1993. Brief overview of the removal policies, the Trail of Tears, and the implications of both for U.S. history.

Wilkins, Thurman. *Cherokee Tragedy: The Ridge Family and the Decimation of a People.* Rev. ed. Norman: University of Oklahoma Press, 1986. Discusses the prominent family of Cherokee leaders.

SEE ALSO: 1817, Seminole Wars; 1828, *Cherokee Phoenix* Begins Publication; 1828, Jackson Is Elected President; 1830, Trail of Tears; 1831, Cherokee Cases.

1830 ■ TRAIL OF TEARS: *the removal to the western Indian Territory of the Five Civilized Tribes is one of the most tragic events of U.S. history*

DATE: May 28, 1830-1842
LOCALE: Southeastern United States
CATEGORIES: Expansion and land acquisition; Native American history
KEY FIGURES:
Levi Colbert (1790?-1834), Chickasaw chief who tried to ease the burden of removal
Menewa (c. 1765-1865), Creek chief who strongly defended his people's rights
Osceola (c. 1804-1838), militant Seminole leader who violently resisted removal

Pushmataha (1764-1824), principal chief of the Choctaws and an able negotiator
John Ross (1790-1866), principal chief and antiremoval leader of the Cherokees

SUMMARY OF EVENT. Soon after 1783, when the Treaty of Paris ended the American Revolution, demands began for the removal of all Native Americans from the southeastern part of the new United States. After a brief renewal of violent resistance, led by warriors like Dragging Canoe of the Cherokees and Alexander McGillivray of the Creeks, most tribes were peaceful but firm in their efforts to remain in their ancestral lands. The exception was the Seminoles in Florida.

Many early treaties were negotiated to persuade these tribes to move west voluntarily. When the desired result was not achieved, Congress passed the Indian Removal Act in 1830, paving the way for forced removal. President Andrew Jackson, an old foe of the southeastern tribes, signed the bill; it became law on May 28, 1830.

The first of these tribes to experience forced removal was the Choctaw of southeastern Mississippi. Preliminary treaties with the Choctaws, whose population was about twenty-three thousand, began with the Treaty of Mount Dexter in 1805. Individual Choctaws had been encouraged to incur debts at government trading posts that were beyond their ability to pay. At Mount Dexter, Choctaw leaders were forced to cede four million acres of their land in return for the cancellation of those debts.

The first exchange of Choctaw land for land in the Indian Territory west of the Mississippi River was approved by the Treaty of Doak's Stand in 1820. Pushmataha, the principal chief and able diplomat of the Choctaws, negotiated this treaty with General Andrew Jackson. However, since white settlers already occupied much of the new Choctaw land, the treaty had little effect.

The Treaty of Dancing Rabbit Creek, signed on September 27, 1830, was the first negotiated under the Indian Removal Act. It provided for the exchange of all Choctaw land for land in the Indian Territory. Choctaw acceptance of this treaty was facilitated by intratribal conflicts and by the duplicity of their self-proclaimed spokesperson, Greenwood Leflore. By the end of 1832, about two-thirds of the Choctaws had emigrated to their new homes. Most others migrated over the next twenty years. A few, including Greenwood Leflore, remained in Mississippi.

The Choctaw removal became a pattern for the removal of the remaining tribes in the Southeast. The next to experience the process were the twenty-three thousand Creeks of eastern Alabama. Led by such chiefs as Menewa, the Creeks bitterly resisted removal. In 1825, Menewa carried out the execution for treason of William McIntosh, a half-breed chief who favored removal.

By 1831, chiefs such as Eneah Micco, although vigorously protesting the invasion of their land by white squatters, realized that only removal could save the Creeks from total destruction. The Treaty of Washington, signed on March 24,

Soon after the passage of the Indian Removal Act of 1830, thousands of Native Americans were transferred west to Indian Territory, in the vicinity of present-day Oklahoma. Forced marches of Creeks, Choctaws, and Cherokees brought sickness, starvation, and death to thousands of people throughout the 1830's. Their path away from their homeland was dubbed the Trail of Tears, depicted in this artist's rendition of 1942 by Robert Lindneux. (Woolaroc Museum, Bartlesville, Oklahoma)

1832, provided for complete removal to the Indian Territory. Although the generous provisions of this treaty soon were ignored, conditions in the Creek Nation became intolerable and they began their sad trek to the west.

Creek migration was interrupted in May, 1836, by reprisal raids against white settlements. This action brought in the U.S. Army, with orders to forcibly remove all Creeks from Alabama. By 1838, the removal was complete. An ironic footnote is that during the course of their removal, several hundred Creek men were impressed into the army for service against their Seminole cousins in Florida.

The least controversial of the Trail of Tears removal was that of the five thousand Chickasaws from the northern parts of Mississippi and Alabama. For thirty years, the government worked to transform the Chickasaws from a hunting society into an agricultural society that would require less land. By 1830, the process seemed complete, but the result had been widespread poverty. It also produced friction between the full-bloods who resisted the process and the part-bloods who favored it.

The Chickasaw removal process was initiated by the Treaty of Pontotoc Creek in 1832. It was agreed that the Chickasaws would move west when suitable land could be obtained. Finding such land was difficult, with the best possibility being part

of the Choctaw domain already established. Levi Colbert, the most prominent of several Chickasaw chiefs, was ill and not present when the Treaty of Pontotoc Creek was signed. He protested the use of coercion by General John Coffee, the leading government negotiator, to get the other chiefs to sign. However, he cooperated with the removal process in order to secure the best possible land and to ease the burden on his people.

Chickasaw removal followed the signing of the Treaty of Doaksville in January, 1837. Land was secured and most of the tribe moved that year. Unlike other tribes, they were able to take most of their possessions with them, and very few died along the way. However, after arrival in the Indian Territory, they faced the typical problems of intertribal conflicts, substandard food, and a smallpox epidemic.

By 1830, about sixteen thousand Cherokees remained on their ancestral lands, by then mostly in northern Georgia and southeastern Tennessee. Their removal, first called the "trail where they cried," is the source of the name Trail of Tears.

The movement to remove the Cherokees began with the signing of the Georgia Compact in 1802, when President Thomas Jefferson agreed to seek reasonable terms for that removal in a peaceful manner. In 1828, when gold was discovered on Cherokee land in Georgia, the process was facilitated, but not on the reasonable terms stipulated by Jefferson. The state of Georgia nullified Cherokee laws and incorporated a large portion of the Cherokee Nation. The Cherokee defense was led by their democratically elected principal chief, John Ross, who took their case to federal court. Although a decision by Chief Justice John Marshall favored the Cherokees, President Jackson refused to enforce it.

A small group of proremoval Cherokees, led by Major Ridge, signed the New Echota Treaty in December, 1835. Following ratification by the U.S. Senate in May, 1836, the entire tribe had two years to move to the Indian Territory. John Ross and the majority protested the treaty and refused to move. Forced removal began in June, 1838. When the journey ended in March, 1839, there were four thousand unmarked graves along the way. About one thousand Cherokees escaped removal by fleeing into the southern Appalachian Mountains. The final tragedy of Cherokee removal was the murder in the Indian Territory of the proremoval leaders who had signed the treaty.

The Seminoles of central Florida, descendants of Creeks who had moved there to escape harassment in the eighteenth century, provide the last chapter in the Trail of Tears. Their population of about six thousand included many African Americans, both freemen and runaway slaves from the Southern states. The desire to cut off that escape route for slaves was part of the incentive for Jackson's invasion and the resulting acquisition of Florida from Spain in 1819 under the Adams-Onís Treaty. The demand to move the Seminoles to the Indian Territory soon followed.

In 1832, an unauthorized group of Seminoles signed the Treaty of Payne's Landing, declaring that all would give up their land and move west. Opposition to the treaty was led by Osceola and Cooacoochee (Wildcat). The result was the Second Seminole War, in 1835. Seminoles captured during that war were immediately deported to the Indian Territory. By 1842, the war was over and the remaining Seminoles slowly migrated west. By 1856, the only Seminoles left in Florida were those in the inaccessible swamps of the Everglades.

The Trail of Tears removals rank among the most tragic episodes in United States history. The policies of three American leaders reveal the changing attitudes on how to best accomplish the removals. After Thomas Jefferson's peaceful persuasion and reasonable terms failed, John C. Calhoun, as secretary of war under President James Monroe, favored educating Native Americans to accept the need for removal. In the end, it was Andrew Jackson's policy of forced removal that completed the distasteful task. —*Glenn L. Swygart*

ADDITIONAL READING:

DeRosier, Arthur. *The Removal of the Choctaw Indians.* Knoxville: University of Tennessee Press, 1970. Discusses removal circumstances. Includes maps and portraits.

Ehle, John. *Trail of Tears: The Rise and Fall of the Cherokee Nation.* New York: Doubleday, 1988. Covers Cherokee history from 1770 to 1840. Details the intratribal conflicts relating to removal policy.

Foreman, Grant. *Indian Removal: The Emigration of the Five Civilized Tribes of Indians.* Norman: University of Oklahoma Press, 1932. Surveys the treaties and leaders of removal. Maps and illustrations.

Gibson, Arrell. *The Chickasaws.* Norman: University of Oklahoma Press, 1971. Puts removal in context with Chickasaw history from the eighteenth century to 1907.

Williams, Jeanne. "The Cherokees." In *Trails of Tears: American Indians Driven from Their Lands.* Dallas: Hendrick-Long, 1992. Puts Cherokee removal in the context of the similar experiences of the Comanche, Cheyenne, Apache, and Navajo.

Wright, J. Leitch. *Creeks and Seminoles: The Destruction and Regeneration of the Muscogulge People.* Lincoln: University of Nebraska Press, 1986. Discusses removal and resettlement in the West. Extensive bibliography.

SEE ALSO: 1817, Seminole Wars; 1819, Adams-Onís Treaty; 1828, *Cherokee Phoenix* Begins Publication; 1831, Cherokee Cases; 1871, Indian Appropriation Act.

1831 ■ THE LIBERATOR BEGINS PUBLICATION: *a major vehicle for advocacy of immediate, in contrast to gradual, abolition of slavery*

DATE: January 1, 1831
LOCALE: Boston, Massachusetts
CATEGORIES: African American history; Communications; Cultural and intellectual history; Social reform
KEY FIGURES:
Maria Weston Chapman (1806-1885), journalist and associate of Garrison
James Forten (1766-1842), African American abolitionist and financial backer of *The Liberator*
William Lloyd Garrison (1805-1879), abolitionist leader
Abraham Lincoln (1809-1865), sixteenth president of the United States, 1861-1865
Benjamin Lundy (1789-1839), Quaker abolitionist
Wendell Phillips (1811-1884), orator and Garrison's associate
Arthur Tappan (1786-1865), first president of the American Anti-Slavery Society
Lewis Tappan (1788-1873), leader of church-oriented abolitionists
Henry C. Wright (1797-1870), Garrison's associate and an advocate of nonresistance

SUMMARY OF EVENT. The initial publication of white abolitionist William Lloyd Garrison's weekly newspaper, *The Liberator*, in Boston, on January 1, 1831, helped to transform the antislavery movement in the United States. It symbolized the beginning of a radical effort to abolish slavery and secure equal rights for African Americans throughout the country.

Garrison and his newspaper were products of the religious revival called the Second Great Awakening, which transformed Protestant theology in the United States. The Awakening engendered moral reform movements in New England and other parts of the North during the early decades of the nineteenth century. Unlike their Calvinist predecessors, those who engaged in moral reform assumed that human beings, by their actions, could create a perfect society and bring about the millennial return of Jesus Christ. In his perception of the sinfulness and criminality of slaveholding, which he believed deprived both slaves and masters of a chance for salvation, Garrison went beyond most of the other reformers of his time.

Garrison was born in Newburyport, Massachusetts, in 1805. Deserted by his seafaring father in 1808, Garrison was raised in poverty by his devout Baptist mother, who instilled in him her strict moral code. At thirteen years of age, he apprenticed with a printer at the *Newburyport Herald*, where he learned the newspaper business. By 1828, he was in Boston as the editor of *The National Philanthropist*, advocating the temperance movement. Garrison also supported what he and others perceived to be the antislavery efforts of the American Colonization Society (ACS), founded in 1817. As the dominant antislavery organization of the 1820's, the ACS advocated the gradual abolition of slavery, combined with the colonization of free black Americans in Africa.

It was Garrison's decision, later in 1828, to join Quaker abolitionist Benjamin Lundy in Baltimore as coeditor of Lundy's weekly newspaper, *The Genius of Universal Emancipation*, that led to *The Liberator* and a more radical antislavery movement. In Baltimore, Garrison observed slavery in practice. Influenced by members of Baltimore's African American community, Garrison came to believe that gradualism would never end the "peculiar institution." African American influences also led Garrison to conclude that the ACS perpetuated a racist assumption that blacks and whites could not live together as equals in the United States.

Garrison's increasing militancy made cooperation with the more conservative Lundy difficult. Garrison's radicalism also led to his imprisonment for libel in the Baltimore jail and to his decision to return to New England to begin his own antislavery newspaper.

In the first issue of *The Liberator*, Garrison proclaimed his conversion to immediate abolitionism. Harshly condemning slaveholders as sinners and thieves, he pointed out that one did not ask sinners to stop sinning gradually or require that thieves gradually stop committing crimes. Christian morality and justice, he insisted, required that slaveholders immediately and unconditionally free their bondspeople.

Garrison was not the first to advocate immediate emancipation. What was significant was his rejection of moderation and his linkage of immediatism with a demand that the rights of the formerly enslaved be recognized in the United States. In his most famous statement, Garrison proclaimed, "I am in earnest—I will not equivocate—I will not excuse—I will not retreat a single inch—AND I WILL BE HEARD."

The initiation of *The Liberator* also is significant for its reflection of biracial cooperation in the antislavery movement. Although Garrison, like other white abolitionists, never entirely escaped the racial prejudices of his time, he and his newspaper enjoyed the strong support of African Americans. Wealthy black abolitionist James Forten of Philadelphia provided crucial financial support to *The Liberator* in its early years. During the same period, Garrison employed black subscription agents, and three-quarters of the newspaper's subscribers were black. In Boston, where white antiabolition sentiment could produce violent confrontations, Garrison enjoyed the physical protection of African Americans.

Meanwhile, Garrison and *The Liberator* played an essential role in the formation of the American Anti-Slavery Society (AASS). Founded in December, 1833, under the leadership of Garrison and New York City businessmen Arthur and Lewis Tappan, the AASS united immediate abolitionists in the United States during most of the 1830's. Reflecting the pacifistic views of Garrison, the Tappans, and others, the society pledged in its Declaration of Sentiments (modeled on the Declaration of Independence) to use peaceful means to bring about the immediate, uncompensated emancipation of all U.S. slaves, without colonization. Promoted by *The Liberator*, dozens of other antislavery newspapers, and thousands of antislavery pamphlets, the AASS grew exponentially. By 1838, it had a membership in the North of approximately one-quarter million and as many as 1,350 local affiliates.

By the late 1830's, however, internal tensions were tearing the AASS apart. The essential problem was that Garrison and his closest New England associates, including Maria Weston Chapman, Wendell Phillips, and Henry C. Wright, had concluded that the spirit of slavery had so permeated the nation that the North—not just the South—had to be fundamentally changed.

Although other abolitionists were reaching similar conclusions in the late 1830's, many of them objected to the specific policies advocated in the columns of *The Liberator* to effect those changes. In particular, an increasingly unorthodox Garrison antagonized church-oriented abolitionists by his wholesale condemnation of organized religion. He also seemed to threaten traditional concepts of patriarchy by his championing of women's rights and, specifically, female equality within the AASS. He appeared to threaten government through his advocacy of nonresistance, the pacifist doctrine that physical force is never justified, even in self-defense or on behalf of law and order. He frustrated those who desired a separate abolitionist political party by condemning political parties as inherently corrupt.

As a result, the abolitionist movement splintered in 1840. Garrison, his New England associates, and a few others across the North retained control of the AASS, but the great majority of abolitionists left the organization. Lewis Tappan began the American and Foreign Anti-Slavery Society, which, until 1855, maintained a church-oriented antislavery campaign. Politically inclined abolitionists organized the Liberty Party. By the 1850's, a majority of non-Garrisonian abolitionists had come to support the Republican Party, which advocated neither immediate abolition nor equal rights for African Americans.

In the 1840's and 1850's, Garrison, in *The Liberator* and elsewhere, continued to promote anticlericalism, women's rights, and nonresistance, as well as immediate emancipation and equal rights for African Americans. Although he and his former AASS colleagues remained in agreement on many points, there was also considerable mutual antagonism. Chances for reconciliation among them diminished in 1842, when Garrison began to call on the people of the North to dissolve the Union. He argued that it was Northern support that kept slavery in existence in the South, implying that, when the North withdrew its support through disunion, the slaves could free themselves. His abolitionist critics responded that disunion was tantamount to the North's exculpating itself from the slavery issue.

When the South, rather than the North, initiated disunion in 1860 and 1861, however, changing circumstances caused Garrison to draw back from some of his more radical positions. He compromised his pacifism and his opposition to party politics by supporting Republican president Abraham Lincoln's war to preserve the Union and free the slaves. When the war ended successfully for the North and slavery was formally abolished, Garrison, old, tired, and seeking vindication, announced that his work was done—although it was clear that black equality had not been achieved with the end of slavery. The last issue of *The Liberator* rolled off its press on December 29, 1865.

—Stanley Harrold

ADDITIONAL READING:

Abzug, Robert H. *Cosmos Crumbling: American Reform and the Religious Imagination.* New York: Oxford University Press, 1994. Demonstrates Garrison's radicalism in the context of early nineteenth century U.S. Protestantism.

Friedman, Lawrence J. *Gregarious Saints: Self and Community in American Abolitionism, 1830-1870.* New York: Cambridge University Press, 1982. A study of relationships among abolitionists. Includes a description of Garrison's circle of abolitionists and his leadership style.

Kraditor, Aileen S. *Means and Ends in American Abolitionism: Garrison and His Critics on Strategy and Tactics, 1834-1850.* New York: Vintage Books, 1970. A probing analysis of Garrison's tactics in comparison with those of other abolitionists.

Merrill, Walter M. *Against Wind and Tide: A Biography of William Lloyd Garrison.* Cambridge, Mass.: Harvard University Press, 1963. The most detailed biography of Garrison to date.

Stewart, James Brewer. *William Lloyd Garrison and the Challenge of Emancipation.* Arlington Heights, Ill.: Harlan Davidson, 1992. A brief biography that explores the personal choices that initiated and maintained Garrison's career as an abolitionist.

Thomas, John L. *The Liberator: William Lloyd Garrison, a Biography.* Boston: Little, Brown, 1963. Portrays Garrison as a romantic individualist who defied authority for psychological reasons.

SEE ALSO: 1830, Proslavery Argument; 1830, Webster-Hayne Debate; 1831, Nat Turner's Insurrection; 1833, American Anti-Slavery Society Is Founded.

1831 ■ CHEROKEE CASES: *two decisions rendered by the U.S. Supreme Court limit the sovereignty of Native American tribes by placing them under federal protection*

DATE: March 18, 1831, and March 3, 1832
LOCALE: Washington, D.C.
CATEGORIES: Court cases; Native American history
KEY FIGURES:
Jeremiah Evarts (1781-1831), missionary and legal expert on Native American affairs
Andrew Jackson (1767-1845), seventh president of the United States, 1829-1837
John Marshall (1755-1835), chief justice of the United States, who rendered the two *Cherokee* decisions
Sequoyah (c. 1770- c. 1843), the Cherokee whose syllabary enabled his people to become literate
Daniel Webster (1782-1852), distinguished lawyer and politician who supported the Cherokees
William Wirt (1772-1834), Cherokee legal counsel and congressman

SUMMARY OF EVENT. In 1823, the U.S. Supreme Court, with John Marshall as chief justice, made the first serious judicial effort to define the relationship between the federal government and Native Americans. The case, concerning disputed land titles, was *Johnson v. McIntosh*. The decision was that the federal government was, in effect, the Native Americans' ultimate landlord and they were the government's tenants. Marshall and the Court majority thus judged the federal government to be responsible for Native American affairs, including the protection of Native American peoples against state actions, which materially affected Native American lives and property.

During a period in which the federal government and the states were locked in disputes about where the Constitution intended ultimate sovereignty to reside and federal authority seemed unsure, Georgia contemplated removing Cherokee and Creek peoples from northern and western portions of the state. To legitimate its plans, Georgia charged that when it had agreed, in 1802, to cede its western land claims to the federal government, the latter had agreed to extinguish Native American titles to those lands and then to return them to the state. The federal government had not done so, and Georgia had been obliged to live since with a Native American state within a state. Land-hungry as a result of expansive pressures from the cotton culture, Georgians themselves initiated steps to remove Native Americans, primarily Cherokees. They denied the relevance of federal treaties with the Cherokees and threatened to use force against federal troops if they were dispatched to protect the tribe. Andrew Jackson's election as president in 1828 accelerated Georgia's actions to begin removal, because Jackson, a veteran Indian fighter who deemed Native Americans "savages," was a proponent of removal.

In December, 1828, the Georgia legislature added Cherokee lands to a number of Georgia counties. Far from being savages, the Cherokees who protested this action had become a successful farming people. Thanks to a syllabary produced by their own Sequoyah, they were literate and produced their own newspaper, the *Cherokee Phoenix*. They instantly assembled a distinguished delegation to appeal to Congress for assistance. This course was applauded by a host of congressmen and public officials—including Daniel Webster and William Wirt—who proclaimed Georgia's legislation unjust, on moral as well as legal grounds. Nevertheless, in December, 1829, Georgia's legislature enacted a comprehensive law that essentially nullified all Cherokee laws. Aggravating the Cherokees' plight, gold was discovered in the following year in western Georgia, and a gold rush flooded their lands with gold seekers, in violation of Cherokee treaties. Under great pressure, Governor George Gilmer claimed the gold as state property and threatened to oust the Cherokees forcibly. Having failed in Georgia's courts, the Cherokees, as a last peaceful resort and encouraged by missionaries such as Jeremiah Evarts and public officials such as Webster and Wirt, appealed to the U.S. Supreme Court under Article III, Section 2 of the Constitution, which gave the Court original jurisdiction in cases brought under treaties or by foreign nations.

In *Cherokee Nation v. Georgia*, Chief Justice Marshall, who had been sympathetic to Cherokee claims but also was aware of Jackson's hostility toward both Native Americans and Marshall's court, dismissed the case. Marshall asserted that the Court lacked the jurisdiction to halt Georgia's sequestration of Cherokee lands. In doing so, he defined the relationship of Cherokees (and, by inference, other Native American tribes) to the federal government as that of a "domestic, dependent nation" rather than a sovereign one.

Marshall modified his decision in 1832, however, when deciding *Worcester v. Georgia*. *Worcester* resulted from a Georgia law enacted in 1831. The law forbade whites from residing on Cherokee lands without a state license; it was aimed primarily at white missionaries who were encouraging Cherokee resistance to removal. Georgia arrested, convicted, and sentenced two unlicensed missionaries, Samuel Worcester and Elizur Butler, whom the American Board of Commissioners for Foreign Missions promptly defended, hiring William Wirt as their counsel. Wirt then was running as a vice presidential candidate for the National Republican Party and as a presidential candidate for the Anti-Masonic Party. Therefore, he hoped for a decision that would embarrass Jackson.

Because the plaintiff in *Worcester* was a white missionary and the defendant the State of Georgia, the Court had clear jurisdiction. Without overruling his *Cherokee Nation* decision, Marshall ruled that the Georgia law was unconstitutional and therefore void, because it violated treaties, as well as the commerce and contract clauses of the Constitution. Furthermore, Marshall declared, Georgia's laws violated the sovereignty of the Cherokee nation, and, in this case, the Court was constrained to define relationships between Native Americans and a state.

Conflict within the Cherokee nation over Indian removal pitted Cherokee against Cherokee. Leader John Ross argued against Indian removal and the Treaty of New Echota, but he finally realized that removal was inevitable. (Smithsonian Institution Photo No. 988-A)

As historians and legal scholars have observed, the Cherokee cases advanced two contradictory descriptions of Native American sovereignty. In *Cherokee Nation v. Georgia*, Marshall delineated the dependent relationship of Native American tribes to the federal government. In *Worcester*, sympathetically stressing historic aspects of Native American independence, nationhood, and foreignness rather than their domestic dependency, he defined the relationship of Native American tribes to the states. Together, these decisions suggested that although Native American tribes lacked sufficient sovereignty to claim political independence and were therefore wards of the federal government, they nevertheless possessed sufficient sovereignty to guard themselves against intrusions by the states, and that it was a federal responsibility to preserve this sovereignty. In subsequent years, these conflicting interpretations were exploited by both the federal government and Native Americans to serve their own purposes.

Marshall's pronouncements were one thing; making them effective was yet another thing. President Jackson who, as chief executive, was the only party capable of enforcing the Court's decision, chose to ignore it. Instead, Jackson threw federal troops into the removal of Cherokees and others of the Five Civilized Tribes to designated Indian Territory beyond the Mississippi. The resulting tragedy became known as the Trail of Tears.   —*Mary E. Virginia*

ADDITIONAL READING:

Deloria, Vine, Jr., and Clifford M. Lytle. *American Indians, American Justice*. Austin: University of Texas Press, 1983. A clearly written study focusing on the development of the Native American judicial system as it existed in the early 1980's. Explains the complexities of Native American legal and political rights as they are understood by the tribes and by the federal government.

_____. *The Nations Within*. New York: Pantheon Books, 1984. Traces the past and weighs the future of Native American sovereignty, from the Doctrine of Discovery through the shift from tribal and federal notions of self-government to self-determination.

Prucha, Francis Paul. *American Indian Treaties*. Berkeley: University of California Press, 1994. Unravels the political anomaly of the treaty system, a system devised according to white perspectives that made the relationships between Native Americans and the federal government unlike the legal and political relationships of any other two peoples.

_____. *The Great Father*. Vol. 1. Lincoln: University of Nebraska Press, 1984. A masterful, detailed analysis of historical relationships—political, economic, and social—between the federal government and Native Americans through cultural changes affecting both groups, from the Revolutionary War to 1980. Chapter 2 discusses the Cherokee cases and American Indian removal.

Satz, Ronald N. *American Indian Policy in the Jacksonian Era*. Lincoln: University of Nebraska Press, 1974. Excellent coverage of the Cherokee cases; also clarifies the complex political climate in which the cases developed around conflicts between the Jackson Administration, Georgia, and the Cherokees.

Williams, Robert A. *The American Indian in Western Legal Thought*. New York: Oxford University Press, 1990. Starting with the thirteenth century notion that the West had a mandate to conquer the earth, this intriguing study explores the laws that evolved to legitimate this mandate, specifically as the mandate was interpreted by Spanish, English, and U.S. laws regarding relations with Native Americans.

SEE ALSO: 1828, *Cherokee Phoenix* Begins Publication; 1830, Indian Removal Act; 1830, Trail of Tears.

1831 ■ TOCQUEVILLE VISITS AMERICA: *a foreign political philosopher offers insights into American democracy, exerting influence on subsequent generations of leaders*

DATE: May 11, 1831-February 20, 1832
LOCALE: United States
CATEGORIES: Cultural and intellectual history; Government and politics

KEY FIGURES:

John Quincy Adams (1767-1848), sixth president of the United States, 1825-1829

Gustave de Beaumont (1802-1866), French magistrate who visited the United States with Tocqueville

Albert Gallatin (1761-1849), former secretary of the Treasury

Samuel Houston (1793-1863), former governor of Tennessee and the husband of a Creek woman

Andrew Jackson (1767-1845), seventh president of the United States, 1829-1837

James Kent (1763-1847), chancellor of the New York Court of Chancery who presented Tocqueville and Beaumont with a copy of his famous *Commentaries on American Law*

Francis Lieber (1800-1872), German refugee who translated the Prison Report for publication in the United States

Francis Lippitt, twenty-two-year-old American in Paris whom Tocqueville employed to translate U.S. pamphlets

Theodore Sedgwick III (1811-1859), American in Paris who aided Tocqueville in his research for *Democracy in America*

Jared Sparks (1789-1866), historian who influenced Tocqueville's view of the United States

Alexis de Tocqueville (1805-1859), French magistrate, political philosopher, and historian

SUMMARY OF EVENT. In May, 1831, two young Frenchmen, Alexis de Tocqueville and Gustave de Beaumont, arrived in the United States. They were magistrates whose official purpose in coming to the New World was to study the U.S. prison system and penal reforms. There was another, more important, motive behind their visit: They had come to observe democracy at first hand. The experience of the French Revolution of 1830 had convinced the two aristocrats, especially Tocqueville, that history was moving toward equality and democratic institutions. A study of the United States, where such conditions already had been reached, would provide an important lesson for the future. As Tocqueville observed, it was not "merely to satisfy a legitimate curiosity that I have examined America; my wish has been to find there instruction by which we may ourselves profit. . . . I confess that, in America, I saw more than America; I sought there the image of democracy itself, with its inclinations, its character, its prejudices, and its passions, in order to learn what we have to fear or to hope from its progress."

Their path, which took them to a number of cities and states, included an exploration of the Michigan wilderness north of Detroit, visits to pioneer cabins, and a steamboat ride down the Mississippi River to New Orleans. Tocqueville not only experienced diverse features of the American landscape but also formed impressions of the different peoples living in American society and the relations between those of different races. Some impressions were more favorable than others. For example, his experiences with Native Americans along his way, including encounters with a group of Iroquois in Buffalo and a group of Choctaw traveling down the Mississippi River to a forced resettlement in Arkansas ordered by President Andrew Jackson, disconcerted him. Believing it was inevitable that the Native American way of life would succumb to the influences and policies introduced to the United States by European immigrants and their descendants, Tocqueville wrote in one of the many notebooks he kept along the way that "the Indian races are melting in the presence of European civilization like snow in the presence of the sun."

Returning to France after a nine-month tour, the men drafted a report on the U.S. prison system and submitted it to their government. Then they commenced their separate analyses of the U.S. system. Beaumont set down his reflections in *Marie: Ou, L'Esclavage aux États-Unis*, a study of race relations in the United States in the form of a novel. Although *Marie* contained many penetrating observations, the fictional approach and somewhat limited scope of the book accounted for its modest reception. Tocqueville's work, a panoramic view of U.S. civilization, won greater recognition and praise.

Democracy in America revealed "the image of democracy"—and of Jacksonian America as well—that Tocqueville had discovered during his travels in the United States. For the young Frenchman, the most striking characteristic of U.S. democracy was "the general equality of condition among people." In Tocqueville's view, equality of condition was "the fundamental fact from which all others seem to be derived, and the central point at which all my observations constantly terminated." *Democracy in America*, issued in two parts, analyzed the effect of this phenomenon on U.S. civilization.

In the first part, published in 1835, Tocqueville analyzed the U.S. political system, describing the workings of township, state, and federal governments, and commenting on the roles of political parties, newspapers, and public associations. The key principle governing the operation of the system, Tocqueville declared, was the principle of the sovereignty of the people, outgrowth of equality of condition. "The people reign in the American political world as the Deity does in the universe," he observed. Among the advantages of democratic government, Tocqueville cited the fact that it "brings the notion of political rights to the level of the humblest citizens." In addition, democratic government creates "an all-pervading and restless activity" that, although it makes for less methodical and skillful public administration than other forms of government, is nevertheless more productive: "if it does fewer things well, it does a greater number of things."

The chief disadvantage of democratic government, in Tocqueville's view, stemmed from the "unlimited power of the majority in the United States." He believed that its effect on public opinion was particularly harmful. Tocqueville's observations on the relations between African Americans and Euro-Americans in Northern states such as Pennsylvania, where slavery was outlawed, helped to contribute to this conclusion. Although their freedom was legally recognized, Tocqueville saw that the force of public opinion concerning African Americans had created conditions under which blacks and whites did not mix as social equals and African Americans

often did not feel comfortable taking part in the political process, although they were legally entitled to participate. His reflections on "the tyranny of the majority," its sources and consequences, constitute one of the major themes of *Democracy in America*.

Tocqueville published the second part of his work in 1840. Here the approach was more philosophical; although he often illustrated his remarks by referring to his experience in the United States, he was concerned primarily with revealing the universal principles of democracy and showing their effect on intellectual and social life. He was less concerned with the politics of democracy than with the culture shaped by widespread equality of condition. In the course of his analysis, Tocqueville pointed out the difficulty of reconciling equality and liberty. Equality of condition nurtured a preference for equality over liberty, he observed. "Democratic communities have a natural taste for freedom," he explained; "left to themselves, they will seek it, cherish it, and view any privation of it with regret. But for equality their passion is ardent, insatiable, incessant, invincible; they call for equality in freedom; and if they cannot obtain that, they still call for equality in slavery." Paradoxically, although liberty was threatened by equality of condition, it nevertheless remained people's best protection: "to combat the evils which equality may produce, there is only one effectual remedy: namely, political freedom," Tocqueville declared. He also emphasized the leveling tendency inherent in democracy. Equality of condition produced a monotonous uniformity of manners and opinions. Under democracy, individualism gave way to conformity. "As the conditions of men become equal among a people," Tocqueville observed, "individuals seem of less and society of greater importance; or rather every citizen, being assimilated to all the rest, is lost in the crowd, and nothing stands conspicuous but the great and imposing image of the people at large. This naturally gives the opinion of the privileges of society and a very humble notion of the rights of individuals; they are ready to admit that the interests of the former are everything and those of the latter nothing."

Tocqueville was one of a number of foreign visitors to the United States in the early nineteenth century. His unbiased yet friendly approach and the accuracy of his observations distinguished him, in the eyes of the people of the United States, from what one contemporary newspaper called "our common herd of travelers." *Democracy in America* exerted a considerable influence on American thought in the nineteenth century, and the twentieth century witnessed a revival of interest in the work. More than one hundred fifty years after its publication, Tocqueville's work still offers valuable and penetrating insights into the nature of U.S. democracy and ranks as one of the classics of political philosophy.

—*Anne C. Loveland, updated by Diane P. Michelfelder*

ADDITIONAL READING:

Hereth, Michael. *Alexis de Tocqueville: Threats to Freedom in Democracy.* Translated by George Bogardus. Durham, N.C.: Duke University Press, 1986. Argues that Tocqueville was not simply interested in describing and commenting on the fundamental principles of democracy, but also was committed to their further development.

Mancini, Matthew. *Alexis de Tocqueville.* New York: Twayne, 1994. A brief but insightful account of Tocqueville's writings. Discusses *Democracy in America* and analyzes Tocqueville's views of Native Americans and slavery.

Pierson, George W. *Tocqueville and Beaumont in America.* New York: Oxford University Press, 1938. A lively, thorough reconstruction of Tocqueville's and Beaumont's visit to the United States, based on published and unpublished sources. In an abridged version of the book, *Tocqueville in America* (Gloucester, Mass.: Peter Smith, 1969), selections concerning women and Native and African Americans were deemphasized as being "matters of lesser interest."

Reeves, Richard. *American Journey: Traveling with Tocqueville in Search of "Democracy in America."* New York: Simon & Schuster, 1982. Retraces Tocqueville's journey across the United States a century and a half later. Engagingly weaves Tocqueville's reflections with commentary on current social conditions in places visited by Reeves and interviews with prominent U.S. citizens.

Schleifer, James T. *The Making of Tocqueville's "Democracy in America."* Chapel Hill: University of North Carolina Press, 1980. An informative, scholarly work that argues that the ideas found in *Democracy in America* took shape from Tocqueville's notes, drafts of his manuscripts, and his readings of works by others, such as the *Federalist* papers.

Tocqueville, Alexis de. *Journey to America.* Rev. ed. Edited by J. P. Mayer and translated by George Lawrence. Garden City, N.Y.: Doubleday, 1971. Presents the fourteen notebooks Tocqueville kept on his tour of the United States to record his interviews and observations, which served as the basis for his reflections in *Democracy in America.*

SEE ALSO: 1790's, First U.S. Political Parties; 1828, Jackson Is Elected President; 1830, Trail of Tears; 1833, Rise of the Penny Press.

1831 ■ McCORMICK INVENTS THE REAPER: *one of the first commercially successful mechanical reapers dramatically reduces the need for labor and makes large-scale wheat production possible*

DATE: Summer, 1831
LOCALE: Walnut Grove, Virginia
CATEGORIES: Economics; Science and technology
KEY FIGURES:
John Deere (1804-1886), manufacturer who introduced the steel plow in 1837
Obed Hussey (1792-1860), inventor of a reaper in 1833
Cyrus Hall McCormick (1809-1884), inventor of a reaper in 1831

John H. Manny (1825-1856), manufacturer of farm implements
A. Y. Moore and
Hiram Moore, developers of the first combine
Jethrow Wood (1774-1834), developer of a cast-iron plow with standardized parts

SUMMARY OF EVENT. In 1830, the total wheat crop in the United States amounted to approximately 40 million bushels. Within nine years, this figure had doubled, and in 1860 it exceeded 170 million bushels. In the 1830's, New York, Pennsylvania, and Virginia were major wheat-producing states, but the center of the wheat-growing area moved steadily westward. In 1839, the Old Northwest produced 31 percent of the nation's crop; in 1849, 37 percent; and in 1859, 46 percent. One reason for the dramatic increase in wheat production was the introduction of mechanized farm equipment, including the McCormick reaper.

During the antebellum period, wheat was the most important cash crop in the Northern agricultural economy, and by 1860 it was the most important cash crop in the United States. Its importance was largely the result of the growth of the domestic economy rather than of the entrance of American grain and flour into European markets. The development of a nationwide transportation system of canals and railroads allowed farmers in formerly isolated regions to participate in the market economy. Crops such as wheat that had been prohibitively expensive to transport by wagon were transported cheaply and easily by rail.

As the domestic economy grew, stimulated by the immigration of large numbers of foreigners after the late 1840's, the demand for wheat and other grains increased proportionately. From 1846 to 1860, prices were fairly high, and farmers throughout the former Northwest Territory (the states of Ohio, Indiana, Illinois, and Wisconsin) expanded their acreage in wheat. With the harvest period short and farm labor scarce, they were unable to produce as much as they wished. Wheat is a crop that progresses from ripe to ruined in about ten days. If not harvested at exactly the right time, the husks open on the stem and the grain rots on the ground. The mechanical reaper went far toward overcoming this bottleneck in production.

Cyrus Hall McCormick is generally credited with the invention of the first reaper containing those essential elements that are still apparent in today's more modern machines. Farmers had long recognized the need for a mechanical reaper. Other inventors in the United States and Great Britain had produced working models of mechanical reapers prior to McCormick's invention, but none had proved commercially successful. In Great Britain, Thomas Brown manufactured and marketed a mechanical reaper before 1820, but sales were slow. Farm labor was still plentiful and cheap, unlike in the United States, and the farms themselves often had small fields that made the use of a machine difficult.

McCormick's experiments took place at the twelve-hundred-acre family farm of Walnut Grove in Virginia's Shenandoah Valley. The problem of a mechanical reaper had intrigued

McCormick's father, Robert. Robert McCormick had attempted to build a reaper a number of times, using tools and materials available in the farm's blacksmith shop, but did not succeed. In 1831, Cyrus McCormick built a reaper that performed successfully. He then set the invention aside for several years to pursue other business interests. It was not until 1834, after a failed attempt to market a hemp-breaking machine invented by his father, that Cyrus resumed work on the reaper and applied for a patent. By 1839, when he placed the first advertisements for the sale of his machine, other reapers already had entered the market. A former sailor from Maine, Obed Hussey, had patented a mechanical reaper in 1833 and had been selling reapers for several years. Hussey was McCormick's first serious competitor. McCormick sold only two reapers in 1840, both of which broke down, so he returned to his workshop to make further improvements in the design. In 1842, he sold six machines; in 1843, twenty-nine.

During this initial period, most of the reapers in use were in the Eastern states, although McCormick's machines had been built in Ohio. McCormick had visited the prairie states, however, and knew that was where the reaper would be in highest demand. Farming, particularly the production of grain crops, was moving west. In 1848, McCormick moved to Chicago and built a factory to manufacture reapers. This location offered several advantages: Transportation was good and getting better with the construction of railroads in Illinois and west of the Mississippi River; Illinois and Wisconsin became the major grain-producing states in the nation by 1860; and the broad, level wheatlands of the West could use machinery more easily than the smaller, hilly, rocky wheatlands of the East. The McCormick establishment in Chicago helped make that city a center for the manufacture of agricultural machinery in the United States. The first full year of manufacture in Chicago, 1849, McCormick's factory produced fifteen hundred reapers. By 1858, sales of the reaper had made McCormick a millionaire.

The mechanical reaper revolutionized grain farming in the United States. Prior to its invention, the methods used in harvesting grain had not changed in thousands of years. The harvest was accomplished with scythes and cradles with a team of rakers and binders following behind. A worker with a scythe or a sickle cut the grain, another worker raked the fallen stalks, and binders gathered the stalks into bundles known as sheaves. The sheaves then were stacked into piles (shocks) to await pick-up by a wagon. It was backbreaking work and resulted in much waste. According to historian of technology Harold Livesay, in 1830 a crew of six laborers—one worker cutting the wheat with the others following behind, raking and binding—could harvest only two acres per day. In the 1840's, the McCormick reaper could handle between ten and fifteen acres per day and required fewer binders following behind. The substantial savings in labor allowed a relatively small workforce to at least triple the acreage harvested.

The reaper had a significant impact prior to and during the Civil War. Reapers sold by McCormick and his strongest competitor, John H. Manny, were common in northern Illinois and southern Wisconsin in the 1850's. One authority estimated that more than seventy thousand reapers and mowers were in operation west of the Appalachians by 1858; by 1860, about 70 percent of the wheat harvested in that area was cut by machine. By 1864, there were 250,000 reapers and mowers in use in the North, enough to provide machines for 75 percent of all Northern farms of more than a hundred acres. A significant number of these machines came from the growing production lines of Cyrus H. McCormick. His profits from sales in 1856 reached three hundred thousand dollars; between 1868 and 1870, annual sales were double what they had been during the war, and the factory on the Chicago River produced eight thousand reapers and mowers for harvest each year.

The mechanization of agriculture and the establishment of Chicago as a center of production came just in time to service the movement of the center of grain production into the trans-Mississippi country. The semiarid prairies of Kansas, Colorado, and Nebraska demanded farming on a large scale. Machinery was necessary. Similarly, the movement of wheat into the bonanza farms of California required machinery. The inventive genius of McCormick, Hussey, Manny, John Deere, and others made it possible to prepare, seed, tend, and harvest thousand-acre wheat farms with relatively small workforces. McCormick did for wheat what Eli Whitney had done for cotton.

—John G. Clark, updated by Nancy Farm Mannikko

ADDITIONAL READING:

Casson, Herbert Newton. *Cyrus Hall McCormick: His Life and Work*. Freeport, N.Y.: Books for Libraries Press, 1971. Definitive biography of McCormick.

Collins, Edward John T. *Sickle to Combine: A Review of Harvesting Techniques from 1800 to the Present Day*. Reading, England: Museum of English Rural Life, 1969. Brief but comprehensive discussion of the evolution of mechanization in agriculture.

Hoseason, David. *Harvesters and Harvesting, 1840-1900*. London: Croom Helm, 1982. Agricultural history focusing on changes in the workforce as farming became more mechanized.

Isern, Thomas D. *Bull Threshers and Bindlestiffs: Harvesting and Threshing on the North American Plains*. Lawrence: University Press of Kansas, 1990. Includes a concise history of the development of harvesting equipment in North America. Highly accessible; clear illustrations.

Livesay, Harold C. *American Made: Men Who Shaped the American Economy*. Boston: Little, Brown, 1979. Contains a concise, lively account of the life of Cyrus McCormick and the company he founded.

Wendel, Charles H. *One Hundred Fifty Years of International Harvester*. Osceola, Wis.: Motorbooks International, 1993. History of the company that McCormick founded, containing descriptions of the various pieces of farm machinery the firm manufactured and sold.

SEE ALSO: 1793, Whitney Invents the Cotton Gin.

1831 ■ NAT TURNER'S INSURRECTION:
a successful slave revolt sends fear through the Southern white community and prompts legislation prohibiting the assembly, education, and movement of plantation slaves

DATE: August 21, 1831
LOCALE: Southampton County, Virginia
CATEGORIES: African American history; Wars, uprisings, and civil unrest
KEY FIGURES:
Cherry Turner, Nat's wife, who held coded maps and lists of the planned insurrection
Nat Turner (1800-1831), African American slave who led an insurrection against the white slave-owners in Southampton County, Virginia

SUMMARY OF EVENT. Although neither the first attempted slave rebellion nor the last during the more than two centuries of African American slavery, Nat Turner's assault against the whites in southeastern Virginia marked the only time a group of black slaves banded together to strike successfully against their white masters. Turner, as far as is known, spent his entire life as a slave in his native Southampton County, where he had been born on October 2, 1800, on the plantation of Benjamin Turner. His mother was probably a native African, who taught him at an early age to believe that he possessed supernatural powers. He was both a mystic and oriented toward religion. In addition to possessing those traits, he could read, and historians have surmised that he learned this skill from the Turner family. Nat became a Christian through the instruction of his grandmother, Bridget, and mostly read the Bible. Perhaps because of his knowledge of the Bible, he became a Baptist preacher. Because of his mysticism, his ability to read, and his activities as a minister, Turner gained considerable influence over his fellow slaves.

Samuel Turner, Benjamin's son, inherited Nat during times of economic depression in Virginia. A newly hired overseer drove the slaves to work harder, and as a consequence, Nat ran away. Although Nat eluded capture for thirty days, he turned himself in to his owner. His return went unpunished, but in the days that followed, Nat saw that his own freedom could not be realized without his people's freedom.

Nat married a slave named Cherry in the early 1820's, and they had three children. Cherry would later conceal coded maps and lists that Turner used in his revolt, which experts have never been able to decode. When Samuel Turner died in 1922, Nat's family was sold to different families. Nat went to a neighboring farm owner, Thomas Moore. He was sold again to Joseph Travis in 1831.

Nat Turner thought of himself as an instrument of God. Between 1825 and 1830, Turner gained respect as a traveling neighborhood preacher. He became deeply religious, fasting and praying in solitude. In his own mind he had been ordained—like the prophets of old—to perform a special mission. He professed that God communicated with him through voices and signs in the heavens. On May 12, 1828, Turner heard a "great noise" and saw "white spirits" and "black spirits" battling. In February, 1831, a certain blueness in the atmosphere—a solar eclipse—persuaded him that God was announcing that the time had come for the slaves to attack their white masters. Turner communicated this message to his band of followers; the rebellion ensued on August 21, when Turner and seven fellow slaves murdered the Travis family. Within twenty-four hours after the rebellion began, the band of rebels numbered seventy-five slaves. In the next two days, an additional fifty-one whites were killed. No evidence exists to indicate that Turner's movement was a part of any larger scheme. One slave, Nat Turner, used the power at his command to attempt to break his shackles and those of his followers.

Turner directed his attack toward the county seat, Jerusalem, and the weapons in its armory; he never made it. The white community responded promptly, and with overpowering force of armed owners and militia, it routed the poorly armed slaves during the second day of the rebellion. Although he eluded capture for six weeks, Turner and all the rebels were either killed or captured and executed. Hundreds of other nonparticipating and innocent slaves were slain as a result of fright in the white community. Turner's court-appointed attorney, Thomas Gray, recorded Turner's "confessions" on November 1, and on November 11, 1831, Turner was hanged. Gray later remarked on Turner's intelligence and knowledge of military tactics.

Although Turner's revolt took place in a relatively isolated section of Virginia, the uprising caused the entire South to tremble. Many white Southerners called for more stringent laws regulating slaves' behavior, such as making it a crime to teach a slave to read or write. Turner's revolt coincided with the blossoming of the abolition movement in the North, for the rebellion occurred in the same year that William Lloyd Garrison began his unremitting assault on the South's "peculiar institution." Although no one has been able to demonstrate that abolitionist activity had any influence at all on Turner, white Southerners were horrified at the seeming coincidence. They described abolitionists as persons who wanted not only to end slavery but also to sponsor a massacre of Southern whites. The white South stood as one against any outside interference with its system.

While white people throughout the South looked anew at slavery, in no place did they look more closely than in Virginia. During the legislative session of 1831-1832, there occurred the most thorough public discussion of slavery in Southern history, prior to 1861. Only four months after Turner's revolt, the legislature appointed a committee to recommend to the state a course of action in dealing with slavery.

Those Virginians opposed to slavery made their case. They argued that slavery was a prime cause of Virginia's economic backwardness; that it injured white manners and morals; and

Artist's rendition of the capture of Nat Turner, leader of the 1831 slave insurrection against white slave owners in Southampton County, Virginia. (Library of Congress)

that, as witnessed by Turner's revolt, it was basically dangerous. While they did talk about abolition as benefiting the
slaves, they primarily maintained that white Virginians would
reap the greatest rewards, for the African Americans, after a
gradual and possibly compensated emancipation, would be
removed from the state. These abolitionists, most of whom
were from western Virginia (modern West Virginia), an area of
few slaves, could not agree on a specific plan to accomplish
their purpose. Slavery's defenders countered by boasting of
Virginia's economic well-being and the good treatment and
contentment of the slaves. Referring to the well-established
belief in the sanctity of private property, they denied that the
legislature had any right to meddle with slave property.

The Virginia legislature decided not to tamper with slavery.
It rebuffed those who wanted to put Virginia on the road to
emancipation. After these debates, white Southerners no longer
seriously considered any alternative to slavery. In the aftermath
of Turner's revolt and Virginia's debate, the South erected a
massive defense of its peculiar institution. That defense permeated Southern politics, religion, literature, and science. Nat
Turner's revolt—the only successful slave uprising in the South—
heralded and confirmed the total Southern commitment to black
slavery. However, Turner left a profound legacy: Slaves would
fight for their freedom. Turner's rebellion has inspired black
activists since, including Marcus Garvey and Malcolm X.

—William J. Cooper, Jr., updated by Marilyn Elizabeth Perry

ADDITIONAL READING:

Bisson, Terry. *Nat Turner*. Los Angeles: Melrose Square, 1988. An easy-to-read account of Nat Turner's life and motivations.

Blassingame, John W. *The Slave Community: Plantation Life in the Antebellum South*. New York: Oxford University Press, 1979. A detailed account of slave culture and community life.

Elkins, Stanley M. *Slavery: A Problem in American Institutional and Intellectual Life*. Chicago: University of Chicago Press, 1959. A major, although controversial, attempt to describe the slave personality.

Gray, Thomas R. *The Confessions of Nat Turner: The Leader of the Late Insurrection in Southampton, Va.* 1831. Reprint. Miami: Mnemosyne, 1969. Contains Turner's own account of his revolt, as given to an official of the court that tried him.

Stampp, Kenneth M. *The Peculiar Institution: Slavery in the Ante-Bellum South*. New York: Alfred A. Knopf, 1956. A classic work on slavery.

Styron, William. *Confessions of Nat Turner*. New York: Random House, 1967. A controversial novel that aimed to show an understanding of Turner's revolt and the institution of slavery but was sharply attacked by African American intellectuals.

Tragle, Henry Irving. *The Southampton Slave Revolt of 1831: A Compilation of Source Material*. Amherst: University of Massachusetts Press, 1971. Reprints primary source material: newspaper accounts, trial records, and other documents written at the time of the revolt.

SEE ALSO: 1831, *The Liberator* Begins Publication; 1839, Amistad Slave Revolt; 1859, John Brown's Raid on Harpers Ferry.

1832 ■ JACKSON VS. THE BANK OF THE UNITED STATES: *the president opposes rechartering the "hydra of corruption" and spurs a period of economic growth and spiraling inflation*

DATE: July 10, 1832
LOCALE: Washington, D.C., and Philadelphia
CATEGORIES: Economics; Government and politics
KEY FIGURES:

Thomas Hart Benton (1782-1858), senator from Missouri
Nicholas Biddle (1786-1844), president of the Second Bank of the United States
Henry Clay (1777-1852), senator from Kentucky and supporter of the bank
William John Duane (1780-1865), secretary of the Treasury in 1833
Andrew Jackson (1767-1845), seventh president of the United States, 1829-1837
David Henshaw (1791-1852), member of Jackson's unofficial Kitchen Cabinet
Louis McLane (1786-1857), secretary of the Treasury, 1831-1833
Roger Brooke Taney (1777-1864), secretary of the Treasury, 1833-1834
Martin Van Buren (1782-1862), governor of New York
Daniel Webster (1782-1852), senator from Massachusetts and supporter of the bank

SUMMARY OF EVENT. If the importance of political events is measured by the intensity of feeling aroused and the vigorous debate engendered among contemporaries, then Andrew Jackson's war against the Second Bank of the United States stands out as one of the critical issues of the antebellum period. It is a fairly simple task to describe the sequence of events that led to the destruction of the bank and to list the personnel on both sides of the struggle. It is extremely difficult, however, to answer the question as to motivation. Why did Jackson unleash such a violent attack? What were the motives of his supporters? Why did Nicholas Biddle, president of the bank, take up the challenge when he did? It is also necessary to consider the net effect of the struggle on the nation.

In 1828, it appeared that the bank had regained general favor throughout the nation. Opposition had not been entirely eliminated, but the success of the bank under Biddle, combined with the vitality of the economy, which was entering into a period of high prosperity, provided antibank elements with little ammunition with which to press their attack. Still, the resentment of interests such as the state bankers existed, awaiting only an opportunity to strike at the national bank. Nor had the memory of the bank's errors during the depression of the early 1820's been entirely erased. Martin Van Buren, governor of New York, had opposed the bank in 1826, and Senator Thomas Hart Benton of Missouri still regarded the institution as a "Monster" and a monopoly that should be destroyed. Such men could do little by themselves, but they were prepared to respond to the call of some more prominent champion of the people against the bank interests. Jackson assumed this role.

Jackson's previous public career as general, planter in Tennessee, judge, senator, speculator, and bank-stock owner provided no foreknowledge of the position that he was to take. When Jackson took office, Biddle, from a well-to-do Philadelphia family, was reasonably sure that he and the president could reach an agreement concerning the bank. Jackson's first annual message to Congress in December, 1829, in which he questioned the constitutionality of the bank while also charging that the bank had failed to establish a uniform and sound currency, and the second message, which treated the bank more harshly, did not demoralize Biddle. That year, Jackson had written Biddle, "I do not dislike your bank any more than all banks. But ever since I read the history of the South Sea Bubble [which had defrauded thousands of eighteenth century British investors] I have been afraid of banks." In 1830, neither Jackson nor Biddle wished to make the bank an issue in the election of 1832. Biddle was persuaded that compromise was possible.

At this point, it appears that the supporters of Jackson and of Biddle convinced the two men that the issue could not be postponed. The bank's charter was valid until 1836, but Senators Henry Clay and Daniel Webster, who performed legal work for the bank, looking to the election of 1832, viewed the bank issue as one that could seriously damage Jackson's chances for reelection. For reasons still not thoroughly explained, Biddle succumbed to their urgings and agreed to apply for recharter prior to the election. Jackson, under the pressure of his antibank advisers, had drifted to a position that made compromise with Biddle unlikely.

A bill for recharter passed the Senate on June 11 and the House on July 3, 1832. Jackson vetoed it on July 10, and the bank's supporters were unable to muster the necessary strength to override the veto. The veto message has been praised and condemned by the advocates and detractors of Jackson. The veto did not deal with the bank as an economic institution but as a vehicle by which the special interests, "the rich and powerful . . . bend the acts of government to their selfish purposes." The bank, according to the president, was irresponsible: It favored the rich against the poor, and it was not compatible with democratic self-government. Jackson seized upon the bank as a symbol of special privileges for the wealthy. He questioned the bank's constitutionality, large number of foreign stockholders, and favoritism for its friends in Congress. He commented, "Many of our rich men have not been content with equal protection and equal benefits, but have besought us to make them richer by act of Congress." The bank became a major issue in the election of 1832, in which Jackson won a convincing victory over Henry Clay.

Jackson considered the election results as a mandate to escalate the war against the bank. Not satisfied that the bank would pass from the scene in 1836, Jackson decided to destroy it at once. In spite of opposition from Congress, Jackson determined to withdraw government deposits from the bank. After dismissing two secretaries of the Treasury who balked at this action, Jackson appointed a third, Roger B. Taney, who suspended the deposits of federal funds in the bank and placed them in various state-chartered banks around the country. The bank reacted to this diminution of its resources by calling in its loans and restricting its credit operations. At this point, Biddle became so obsessed with the threat to the bank that he forgot that the bank had a responsibility to the public. Biddle's policies were more severe than the situation required, but he was determined to demonstrate the power of the bank and thus force its recharter. Jackson had accused the bank of irresponsibility in 1832, and during the period 1834-1836, Biddle's activities substantiated Jackson's charge. The bank lost much support during the last two years of its national charter.

Jackson struck at the bank when the nation could least afford it. The economy was entering a boom cycle. Land sales were mounting rapidly, specie was scarce, credit was overextended, state banks proliferated, their printing presses poured out paper money, and prices rose. Deprived of federal deposits, the Bank of the United States could no longer restrain the manufacture of credit and currency by state banks. Nor could it enter the specie market with strength. While it is impossible to say that the destruction of the Bank of the United States caused the Panic of 1837 and the resultant depression, the severity of both might have been alleviated greatly and the depression shortened had the bank continued to function under a national charter.

—John G. Clark, updated by Joseph Edward Lee

ADDITIONAL READING:

Hammond, Bray. *Banks and Politics in America, from the Revolution to the Civil War*. Princeton, N.J.: Princeton University Press, 1957. Argues that Jackson and the bank's allies were all capitalists, but the Jacksonians favored rapid development while the Bank of the United States was more cautious.

Remini, Robert V. *Andrew Jackson and the Course of American Empire*. 3 vols. New York: Harper & Row, 1977-1984. Provides a thorough background on Jackson, his political rise, and the issues, such as multification, that are identified with the Age of Jackson.

Schlesinger, Arthur M. *The Age of Jackson*. Boston: Little, Brown, 1953. This beautifully written book suggests that Nicholas Biddle personified privilege, and that by attacking the bank, Jackson was championing democracy.

Sharp, James R. *The Jacksonians Versus the Banks: Politics in the States After the Panic of 1837*. New York: Columbia University Press, 1970. Examines the ruinous aftereffects of the demise of the national bank and the rise of untrustworthy state banks.

Watson, Harry L. *Liberty and Power: The Politics of Jacksonian America*. New York: Noonday Press, 1990. Analyzes the political forces that elevated the bank battle to the level of the primary issue in the 1832 presidential campaign.

SEE ALSO: 1790, Hamilton's *Report on Public Credit*; 1816, Second Bank of the United States Is Chartered; 1828, Jackson Is Elected President.

1832 ■ NULLIFICATION CONTROVERSY: *foreshadowing the North-South split of the Union, a state government defies a national tariff*

DATE: November 24, 1832-January 21, 1833
LOCALE: South Carolina
CATEGORIES: Economics; Government and politics
KEY FIGURES:
John Caldwell Calhoun (1782-1850), senator from South Carolina and vice president of the United States
Henry Clay (1777-1852), senator from Kentucky
Robert Young Hayne (1791-1839), governor of South Carolina
Andrew Jackson (1767-1845), seventh president of the United States, 1829-1837
George McDuffie (1790?-1851), South Carolina Nullifier

SUMMARY OF EVENT. By the late 1820's, the Southeastern section of the nation was economically depressed. Most of its fiscal ailments were blamed on the protective Tariff of 1828, which protected the North against competition for its textile goods but limited the South's disposing of its agricultural commodities in the world market. While the South languished, the industrial Northeast flourished. In truth, the soil in the older Southern states was worn out, which meant that the region could not compete on equal terms with the new Gulf states. Leadership in the fight against the tariff fell to South Carolina, where the planter aristocrats enjoyed political power and the relative decline in prosperity was the greatest.

The key to South Carolina's defiance against the tariff was its racial demography and a very conservative political structure, different from that of its slaveholding neighbors. In 1830, South Carolina was the only state with an absolute majority of blacks. Most of them were concentrated on the sea islands and tidal flats south of Charleston. The low-country planters controlled state politics. Very high property qualifications for holding office kept power in the hands of the planter elite. This elite controlled the state legislature, which appointed most officials and therefore had tremendous leverage on public opinion in the state.

A cotton state, South Carolina had experienced a collapse of cotton prices in the Panic of 1819, soil erosion, competition from cotton produced on cheaper, more fertile western lands, and an exodus of its white population. Up-country slaveholders incurred heavy losses when upland cotton prices fell 72 percent by 1829, and they were receptive to the argument of the antitariff advocates, or Nullifiers, which blamed the tariff for their plight. Tariff rates had increased up to 50 percent by 1828, and the Nullifiers argued that these high tariffs caused prices on domestic manufactured goods to rise and potentially limited export markets for agricultural goods. The tariffs penalized one class for the profits of another. Along with the tariff issue, there was the issue of slavery. The leaders of Nullification were rice and sea-island cotton planters whose greater fear was not losing cotton profits but losing control over their African American majority.

South Carolina's most eloquent spokesman was John C. Calhoun, who by the late 1820's had completed his philosophical change from ardent nationalist to states' rights advocate. Calhoun then advocated the ultimate in states' rights thinking— a belief in, and support of, the doctrine of nullification, first stated by Thomas Jefferson and James Madison in the Kentucky and Virginia Resolves of 1798. In 1828, while running as a vice presidential candidate, Calhoun anonymously wrote the "South Carolina Exposition and Protest." This essay was a protest against the Tariff of 1828, known as the Tariff of Abominations by Southerners because of its high protective duties. Calhoun's authorship of this document remained secret, and for four years South Carolina did not act upon it, hoping that President Andrew Jackson would fight for a lower tariff. The "Exposition" and a later paper called "A Disquisition on Government" explained Calhoun's doctrine of nullification.

Contrary to popular belief, Calhoun's theory did not advocate secession; rather, he believed that nullification would prevent the disruption of the Union. Calhoun saw nullification as an antidote to secession. The basic tenets of his argument were that sovereignty was, by its very nature, absolute and indivisible. Each state was sovereign, and the Union was a compact between the states. Each individual state entered into an agreement with the others, and the terms of this covenant went into the Constitution. The Constitution provided for a separation of powers between the states and the federal government, but not a division of sovereignty. Sovereignty was not the sum of a number of governmental powers but the will of the political community, which could not be divided without being destroyed. The states had been sovereign under the Articles of Confederation, and they had not given up their supreme authority when they joined the new Union. Since the Union had been created by the states, and not vice versa, it logically followed that the creator was more powerful than the creature. As the federal government was not supreme, it could exercise only those powers given it by the states, as embodied in the Constitution. Should it exceed these powers, the measures enacted would be unconstitutional.

Who was to be the arbiter of constitutionality? Certainly not the Supreme Court, for it was an instrument of the federal government; and if the federal government were not sovereign, then a branch of that government could not be sovereign. The supreme authority rested solely in the people of the states. When a state believed that a federal law exceeded the delegated powers of Congress, that state could declare the law null and void and prevent its enforcement within its own boundaries. When passing on the constitutionality of a law of the federal government, the state acted through a convention called for the express purpose of considering this question, for this was the only way in which the people of a state could give expression to their sovereign will. This action, however, should be taken only as a last resort to protect its rights. Congress could then counter by offering an amendment authorizing the powers that the state contested. If the amendment were not ratified, the law was to be annulled not only for the state but also for the entire nation. Should it pass, the dissatisfied state would have to yield or secede—it could not remain in the Union without accepting the amendment. Thus, the final arbiter would be the same power that created the Constitution, the people of the states. Calhoun was sure that this would prevent secession, for after three-fourths of the states had spoken against her, rarely would a state secede.

After simmering for four years, the issue of nullification erupted in 1832 over a new tariff. In December, 1831, President Andrew Jackson recommended to Congress a downward revision of the tariff and the elimination of the worst features of the Tariff of Abominations. Such a bill finally was pushed through on July 14, 1832, but the new tariff was not low enough for the Southern planters. Although some of the "abominations" were removed, the general level of the duties was only slightly lower. The greatest reductions were made on noncompetitive manufactured items, and the protective make-up of the tariff hardly had been changed.

By mid-1832, the South Carolina extremists were ready to put the nullification theory into action. Many denounced the Tariff of 1832 as unconstitutional and oppressive to the Southern people. In the subsequent state election that fall, the States' Rights and Unionist parties made the tariff and nullification the chief issues, and when the States' Rights Party elected more than two-thirds of the legislature, it promptly called for a state convention. The convention met in November, 1832, and by a vote of 136 to 26 adopted an Ordinance of Nullification on November 24. Both the Tariffs of 1828 and 1832 were declared null and void. After February 1, 1833, the tariff duties were not to be collected, and should the federal government attempt to collect them forcibly, South Carolina would secede.

Jackson met this challenge in typical fashion. He boldly proclaimed on December 10, 1832, that the Constitution formed a government, not a league, and that the power of a single state to annul a federal law was "incompatible with the existence of the Union, contradicted by the letter of the Constitution, unauthorized by its spirit, inconsistent with every principle on which it was founded, and destructive to the great object for which it was formed." He called nullification an "impractical absurdity" and concluded that "disunion by armed force is treason." This "Proclamation to the People of South Carolina" received the enthusiastic support of nationalists.

While Jackson was bold, he was also conciliatory. In his fourth annual message to Congress, in December, 1832, Jackson promised to press for further reduction of the hated tariffs. This was repeated later the same month when the president issued a proclamation to the people of South Carolina. On January 16, 1833, Jackson sent a message to Congress reviewing the circumstances in South Carolina and recommending measures that would enable him to cope successfully with the situation. Tension mounted as the Senate passed the Force Bill in February. This measure authorized Jackson to use the United States Army and Navy to enforce the federal laws, if necessary.

Fulfilling his promise to see that the tariffs were reduced, Jackson did his best to see that legislation giving him full power to force obedience to the laws was accompanied by bills to reduce the tariffs. While the Force Bill was being debated, Henry Clay brought forward a new compromise tariff bill calling for the gradual reduction of tariff duties over the next ten years. By 1842, the tariff was not to exceed 20 percent. South Carolinians waited anxiously to see what would happen, for it was already apparent that no Southern states were coming to her aid, and she would have to fight it out alone. Calhoun, who had resigned the vice presidency after the passage of the Tariff of 1832 and had been elected immediately to the Senate, objected to the Force Bill but feared that strong opposition might hurt the chances of reconciliation that were presented by the Compromise Tariff. He and Clay worked to push the new tariff bill through Congress, and on March 2, 1833, Jackson signed into law both the Force Bill and the Compromise Tariff of 1833.

Once the Compromise Tariff was passed, South Carolina repealed its Ordinance of Nullification (January 21); however, in a last gesture of defiance, the convention declared the Force Bill null and void. Jackson ignored this final face-saving move on the part of South Carolina, for the Force Bill was irrelevant if the tariff duties were being collected.

Both sides claimed victory. Nationalists declared that the power of the federal government had been upheld by both the president and Congress, while South Carolina asserted that nullification had proved an effective method of sustaining states' rights. However, the failure of any other Southern state to rally to South Carolina's defense showed that the doctrine of nullification was unpopular, and from that time forward, militant Southerners looked to the doctrine of secession as their best redress of grievances.

—John H. DeBerry, updated by Bill Manikas

Additional reading:

Bancroft, Frederic. *Calhoun and the South Carolina Nullification Movement.* Baltimore: The Johns Hopkins University Press, 1928. A brief historical and critical study of Calhoun and the nullification controversy as a political event in Jackson's administration, and of the events leading up to and following it.

Barney, William L. *The Passage of the Republic.* Lexington, Mass.: D. C. Heath, 1987. Discusses the nineteenth century as a conceptual whole, during which time the United States made the transition from the colonial era to the modern nation.

Bedford, Henry F., and H. Trevor Colbourn. *The Americans: A Brief History.* New York: Harcourt Brace Jovanovich, 1976. Chapter 7 discusses the major political issues from 1824 to 1842.

Boucher, Chauncey S. *The Nullification Controversy in South Carolina.* Chicago: University of Chicago Press, 1916. A detailed monograph relating the story of nullification, as found in contemporaneous newspapers, manuscripts, and writings of the participants.

Capers, Gerald M. *John C. Calhoun: Opportunist.* Gainesville: University of Florida Press, 1960. Depicts Calhoun as a Machiavellian politician willing to sacrifice friends, family, and principles to become president.

Coit, Margaret L. *John C. Calhoun.* Boston, Houghton Mifflin, 1950. A Pulitzer Prize-winning biography that presents Calhoun as a statesman and a family man—a farmer at heart, but a politician in practice.

Smith, Page. *The Nation Comes of Age: A People's History of the Ante-bellum Years.* New York: McGraw-Hill, 1981. Chapter 5 emphasizes the themes of slavery and the extension of democracy.

See also: 1816, Second Bank of the United States Is Chartered; 1819, *McCulloch v. Maryland*; 1824, *Gibbons v. Ogden*; 1824, U.S. Election of 1824; 1828, Jackson Is Elected President; 1832, Jackson vs. the Bank of the United States.

1833 ■ RISE OF THE PENNY PRESS: *the birth and proliferation of mass-circulation newspapers that popularize new technologies and consumerism*

DATE: Beginning September 3, 1833
LOCALE: New York City
CATEGORIES: Business and labor; Communications; Cultural and intellectual history; Economics
KEY FIGURES:

James Gordon Bennett (1795-1872), founder and editor or the *New York Herald*, a major *Sun* rival

Benjamin Henry Day (1810-1889), founder and first editor of the *New York Sun*

Richard Adams Locke (1800-1871), *Sun* reporter and author of the "moon hoax" articles

SUMMARY OF EVENT. In the early nineteenth century, literacy was a sign of privilege, denied to many by the restrictions of tradition, custom, and economics. Even in the United States, supposedly the most egalitarian and democratic nation of the Western community, free public education was merely a dream in many sections and communities, and there were only limited reading materials for literate citizens who could not afford to acquire a personal library. Free public libraries were to a large extent unavailable. Newspapers were generally priced beyond the means of potential middle or lower-class purchasers. In fact, the wealthy believed that because they were leaders of society, the press should cater to their interests. Subscription to a newspaper was a sign of status which was associated with the fine clothing, gracious dwellings, expensive carriages, and other appurtenances of the upper class.

The newspapers which served such readers naturally catered to their interests and pretensions. Mercantile and political topics took up most of the space; in fact, many of the journals were devoted exclusively to one or the other of these subjects. However in both mercantile and political areas, the United States was in the throes of change by the early 1830's. The economic world was being revolutionized through rapid technological change. Bringing about improved communication, transportation, and manufacturing technologies, the Industrial Revolution was also spawning a new laboring class that was becoming conscious of its group identity and eager for institutions and leaders that would serve and reflect its interests. In the Democratic Party of Andrew Jackson, many laborers believed that they had found a defender, but while both the Whigs and the Democrats had newspapers that endorsed their general positions, as yet no journals catered to the interests of the working class, whose literacy rate was steadily rising.

It was not, however, only the workers themselves who were aware of this deficiency. The Industrial Revolution had vastly increased the scale of business and manufacturing operations. By 1830 it had precipitated a considerable shift from an individualistic, handicraft, self-sufficient economy toward one in which the individual was dependent upon specialized producers for many of the staples of life. These producers in turn were increasingly aware of their need to reach potential consumers through some form of advertising. The newspaper was an obvious solution; yet in the early 1830's the average circulation of the eleven six-cent dailies published in New York was only about seventeen hundred each. The low circulation was not surprising, since these journals charged between six and ten dollars per year in advance for a subscription—more money than most skilled workers earned in a week. Obviously there was a vast potential audience for aggressive advertisers, and a sizable class of untapped readers and subscribers awaited the person who could or would produce a new, popularly priced and more broadly directed type of journal.

Into this vacuum stepped Benjamin H. Day, a former employee of the *Springfield* (Massachusetts) *Republican* and compositor for the *New York Evening Post*, who, on September 3, 1833, launched the *New York Sun*, the harbinger of a new era of journalism. The *Sun* was the first truly successful one-cent, or penny, newspaper in the United States, but it was not the initial venture along these lines. The *Illustrated Penny Magazine*, published in London, had sold in large quantities in America since 1830, and there had been abortive efforts to found penny papers in Philadelphia, New York, and Boston. Benjamin Day's *Sun* appropriated the techniques utilized by these earlier journals. It was smaller, both in length and in actual page size, than most older newspapers; it cost only a penny per copy; and one did not have to subscribe. The *Sun* was sold on the sidewalks of New York by newsboys despite the indignation of citizens and rivals who charged that the lads were being led into lives of vice and degradation.

The *Sun*'s innovations were not, however, simply in the areas of merchandising, size, or even price. Day brought a new style to journalism: His newspaper was breezy, even flippant, and it ignored politics and purely mercantile concerns in order to concentrate on local color, human interest stories, and sensationalism. Finally, it carried a large volume of advertising, particularly of the "help-wanted" variety; indeed, the rise of advertising coincided with the rise of wide-circulation newspapers. The formula proved most effective. By 1836 the *Sun* had a circulation of some thirty thousand, making it the biggest seller in the United States.

Benjamin Day's sensationalism provoked criticism, but it sold newspapers and brought forth many imitators. Undoubtedly the most significant of these was the project of James Gordon Bennett, who on May 6, 1835, in a Wall Street cellar, established the *New York Herald*, which some scholars regard as "the father of the modern newspaper." Like the *Sun*, Bennett's *Herald* sold for a penny and attracted a mass audience through a heady combination of sensationalism, trivia, local gossip and news, advertisements, and even vulgarity. The *Herald* was, however, more broadly based. As he gained circulation, Bennett also began to publish political essays, foreign commentaries and news, and commercial and financial information. Thus, in a sense, Bennett united the coverage and approach of the "penny press" with the specialized functions of the older "class," party, and mercantile newspapers. By the 1840's and 1850's, the *Herald* was the most aggressive and comprehensive of American journals, and on the eve of the Civil War it had a daily circulation of some sixty thousand, outstripping the *Sun* and leading its other American competitors as well. Furthermore, while it was fashionable to regard Bennett as the *enfant terrible* of American journalism, his influence on other newspapers was profound, since they either aped the *Herald* or consciously reacted against it stylistically.

The *Sun*, the *Herald*, and their many imitators wrought profound changes in American journalism and in the lives of countless American citizens as well. They took the newspaper out of the hands of the privileged few and brought the news and entertainment to an entire social and economic class which the older six-cent daily newspapers had scarcely touched. This was in itself a democratic force, for the common worker was now able to receive information at first hand instead of obtaining a version filtered down through the mercantile and educated classes. Furthermore, politicians and parties could no longer limit themselves to expressions through the "party press." Thus, the penny papers made them somewhat more responsive to their lower- and middle-class constituents. Furthermore, they broadened the concept of "news" through a greater emphasis on sensational items, such as sex and crime, an increase in local coverage, and the inclusion of feature and "human interest" stories. Finally, as they achieved size and power, the penny newspapers fought viciously for circulation, and in the course of their intense competition greatly sped the gathering and publication of news items. In their efforts to "scoop" competitors, the new newspapers used and glamorized the steamboat, the railroad, the telegraph, and other devices which so significantly altered American development. The penny press gave the United States its first genuinely popular journalism and illuminated the path to the future in many areas of American life. —*John H. DeBerry*

ADDITIONAL READING:

Bergmann, Hans. *God in the Street: New York Writing from the Penny Press to Melville*. Philadelphia: Temple University Press, 1995. A history of American writing and intellectual life in the early nineteenth century.

Carlson, Oliver. *The Man Who Made News, James Gordon Bennett*. New York: Duell, Sloan and Pearce, 1942. A detailed account of the journalistic story of the *New York Herald*, as well as of Bennett's life.

Emery, Edwin. *The Press and America: An Interpretive History of Journalism*. 2d ed. Englewood Cliffs, N.J.: Prentice-Hall, 1962. Contains three well-written chapters on the background and development of the penny press and popular journalism.

Lee, James Melvin. *History of American Journalism*. Rev. ed. Garden City, N.Y.: Garden City Publishing, 1923. Although old, this volume contains some interesting information in a chapter entitled "Beginnings of the Penny Press."

Mott, Frank L. *American Journalism: A History, 1690-1960.*

3d ed. New York: Macmillan, 1962. This standard history of American journalism, with an excellent chapter on the penny press of the 1830's.

Nevins, Allan. *The Evening Post: A Century of Journalism.* 1922. Reprint. New York: Russell & Russell, 1968. This history of one of the new "penny" newspapers' older six-cent rivals has an excellent section on the *Sun*, the *Herald*, and the influence of Bennett.

O'Brien, Frank M. *The Story of the Sun, New York: 1833-1928*. 1928. Reprint. New York: Greenwood Press, 1968. A rare account of the *Sun's* establishment, full of anecdotes and trivia, if short on analysis of the paper's importance.

Payne, George Henry. *History of Journalism in the United States*. New York: D. Appleton, 1920. The chapters "Penny Papers and the *New York Sun*" and "James Gordon Bennett and the *Herald*" are still valuable.

Seitz, Don C. *The James Gordon Bennetts, Father and Son: Proprietors of the New York Herald*. Indianapolis: Bobbs-Merrill, 1928. Nine of this colorfully written volume's fifteen chapters are devoted to Bennett.

Trimble, Vance H. *The Astonishing Mr. Scripps: The Turbulent Life of America's Penny Press Lord*. Ames: Iowa State University Press, 1992. A biography of Edward Wyllis Scripps (1854-1926), of the famous Scripps publishing family, which founded numerous newspapers and newspaper leagues.

Weisberger, Bernard A. *The American Newspaperman*. Chicago: University of Chicago Press, 1961. Contains a brief discussion of the penny press, placing it in broad historical perspective.

SEE ALSO: 1824, U.S. Election of 1824.

1833 ■ AMERICAN ANTI-SLAVERY SOCIETY IS FOUNDED: *the union of two centers of radical abolitionism, calling for immediate eradication of slavery*

DATE: December, 1833
LOCALE: Philadelphia, Pennsylvania
CATEGORIES: African American history; Organizations and institutions; Social reform
KEY FIGURES:
James Gillespie Birney (1792-1857), U.S. antislavery leader and presidential candidate for the Liberty Party
Lydia Maria Child (1802-1880), author of numerous antislavery pamphlets and articles
Frederick Douglass (1817?-1895), former slave and the editor of *The North Star*, an abolitionist paper
William Lloyd Garrison (1805-1879), editor of the *Liberator*, an antislavery journal
Benjamin Lundy (1789-1839), editor of the *Genius of Universal Emancipation*, an abolitionist paper
Arthur Tappan (1786-1865), first president of the American Anti-Slavery Society

Lewis Tappan (1788-1873), leader of church-oriented abolitionists

Sojourner Truth (c. 1797-1883), former slave, abolitionist, and a compelling orator

Harriet Tubman (c. 1820-1913), fugitive slave and leading black abolitionist

David Walker (1785-1830), militant Negro abolitionist and author of *Appeal . . . to the Coloured Citizens of the World* (1829)

Theodore Dwight Weld (1803-1895), American Anti- Slavery Society agent

Elizur Wright (1804-1885), one of the founders of the American Anti-Slavery Society

SUMMARY OF EVENT. The tumult of reform and revivalism that swept over the northern and western areas of the United States in the 1830's and 1840's produced a number of voluntary associations and auxiliaries. Perhaps the most important of these was the American Anti-Slavery Society (AASS), founded in December, 1833. Sixty delegates gathered in Philadelphia to form the national organization, electing Arthur Tappan, a wealthy New York businessman, as president. They also approved a Declaration of Sentiments, drawn up by William Lloyd Garrison, Samuel May, and John Greenleaf Whittier, that called for immediate (as opposed to gradual), uncompensated, total abolition of slavery through moral and political action. In signing the declaration, the delegates pledged themselves to "do all that in us lies, consisting with this declaration of our principles, to overthrow the most execrable system of slavery that has ever been witnessed upon earth . . . and to secure to the colored population of the United States, all the rights and privileges which belong to them as men and Americans." Like other reform societies of the day, the American Anti-Slavery Society organized a system of state and local auxiliaries, sent out agents to convert people to its views, and published pamphlets and journals supporting its position. The society grew rapidly; by 1838, it reported approximately 250,000 members and 1,350 auxiliaries.

Before the 1830's, most opponents of slavery advocated moderate methods such as gradual and "compensated" emancipation (which would grant remunerations to former slave owners to compensate them for loss of their slaves) or removal of free African Americans to Liberia, Africa, by the American Colonization Society (ACS), founded in 1817. The formation of a national organization based on the principle of immediatism, or immediate and total emancipation, symbolized the new phase that antislavery agitation entered in the early 1830's—radical, uncompromising, and intensely moralistic. The shift to immediatism was a result of several factors, including the failure of moderate methods; the example of the British, who abolished slavery in the empire in 1833; and, probably most important, evangelical religion. Abolitionists of the 1830's inherited from earlier antislavery reformers the notion that slavery was a sin. This notion, coupled with the contemporaneous evangelical doctrine of immediate repentance, shaped the abolitionist doctrine of immediate emancipation.

Given the influence of evangelical doctrines and methods, it is not surprising that abolitionists emphasized moral suasion over political methods. The demand for immediate emancipation was a purely moral demand: Abolitionists were calling for immediate repentance of the sin of slavery, an action that they believed would necessarily lead to emancipation itself. They hoped to persuade people to emancipate the slaves voluntarily and to form a conviction of guilt as participants in the national sin of slavery. In effect, abolitionists were working for nothing less than a total moral reformation.

The American Anti-Slavery Society represented the union of two centers of radical abolitionism, one in Boston, the other around Cincinnati. William Lloyd Garrison, the key figure among New England abolitionists, began publishing *The Liberator* in 1831 and soon organized the New England Anti-Slavery Society, based on the principle of immediate abolition. While the Garrisonians were galvanizing antislavery sentiment in the Northeast (subsequently aided by the New York Anti-Slavery Society, founded by William Jay, William Goodell, and brothers Lewis and Arthur Tappan in 1834), the West also was shifting from gradualism and colonization to radical abolitionism. In the West, Western Reserve College and Lane Seminary were seedbeds for the doctrine of immediate emancipation. Theodore Dwight Weld, a young man who had been converted to evangelical Christianity by Charles Finney, organized a group of antislavery agents known as the Seventy, who preached the gospel of immediatism throughout the Midwest.

While the leadership of the antislavery movement remained predominantly white, the role of free African Americans as a vital force in its ranks was significant. Prior to 1800, the Free African Society of Philadelphia and black spokespersons such as astronomer Benjamin Banneker and church leader Richard Allen had denounced slavery in the harshest terms. By 1830, there were fifty black-organized antislavery societies, and African Americans contributed to the formation of the American Anti-Slavery Society in 1833. African American orators, especially escaped slaves such as Frederick Douglass and Sojourner Truth, moved large audiences with their impassioned and electrifying oratory. African Americans also helped run the Underground Railroad; Harriet Tubman led more than three hundred blacks to freedom. Generally, African American abolitionists shared the nonviolent philosophy of the Garrisonians, but black anger often flared because of the racism they found within the antislavery ranks. Influenced by tactical and race considerations, white abolitionist leaders such as Garrison and Weld limited their African American counterparts to peripheral roles or excluded them from local organizations. Their discriminatory policies within the AASS glaringly contradicted their egalitarian rhetoric.

The late 1830's marked the high point of the movement for immediate abolition through moral suasion. Abolitionism, like other crusades of the time, was hard hit by the Panic of 1837, which reduced funds and distracted attention away from reform. At the same time, abolitionists faced an internal challenge as the AASS divided into radicals and moderates. One issue causing the split was women's rights. Moderate abolitionists tolerated and even welcomed women in the society, as long as their activities were confined to forming auxiliary societies, raising money, and circulating petitions. They refused, however, the request that women be allowed to speak in public on behalf of abolitionism or to help shape the AASS's policies. They also wanted to prevent abolitionism from being distracted or diluted by involvement with any other secondary reform. At the Anti-Slavery Convention of 1840, Garrison and a group of radical followers used the issue of women's rights to capture the organization for themselves. When they succeeded in appointing a woman to the society's business committee, moderates and conservatives seceded and formed another organization, the American and Foreign Anti-Slavery Society.

The other issue that divided abolitionist ranks was that of political action. Some abolitionists, convinced that political action, not merely moral suasion, was necessary to effect emancipation, formed the Liberty Party in 1840 and nominated James Gillespie Birney for president of the United States. In the 1840's and 1850's, a small group of abolitionists, some of them militant "come-outers" such as Garrison and Wendell Phillips, continued to rely on moral suasion. The majority of abolitionists, however, moved gradually into the political arena, where they became involved in the Free-Soil movement and other aspects of the sectional conflict leading to the Civil War. —*Anne C. Loveland, updated by Sudipta Das*

ADDITIONAL READING:

Abbott, Richard H. *Cotton and Capital: Boston Businessmen and Antislavery Reform, 1854-1868.* Amherst: University of Massachusetts Press, 1991. Examines the activities and ideology of a group of Bostonian businessmen who fostered abolition. Meticulously researched and annotated.

Filler, Louis. *The Crusade Against Slavery, 1830-1860.* New York: Harper & Row, 1960. A comprehensive treatment of the people and groups who made up the antislavery movement and the relation of the movement to other reform activities of the period. Excellent bibliography.

Friedman, Lawrence J. *Gregarious Saints: Self and Community in American Abolitionism, 1830-1870.* New York: Cambridge University Press, 1982. A fresh, challenging analysis of the antislavery movement, written from a psychological perspective and focusing on the first-generation immediatists.

Kraut, Alan M., ed. *Crusaders and Compromisers. Essays on the Relationship of the Antislavery Struggle to the Antebellum Party System.* Westport, Conn.: Greenwood Press, 1983. These essays broke new ground by concentrating on politics, juxtaposing the antislavery crusaders to the national political struggles before the Civil War. An excellent anthology.

McKivigan, John R. *The War Against Proslavery Religion: Abolitionism and the Northern Churches, 1830-1865.* Ithaca, N.Y.: Cornell University Press, 1984. Corrects a number of old interpretations and offers new insights into the impact of antislavery crusaders on Northern churches and major Northeast denominations. Based on primary sources; reflects more recent scholarship.

Perry, Lewis, and Michael Fellman, eds. *Antislavery Reconsidered: New Perspectives on the Abolitionists.* Baton Rouge: Louisiana State University Press, 1979. Fourteen original, thought-provoking essays based on a variety of interpretive and methodological approaches. Attempts to see abolition in the context of the larger society of which it was a part.

Thomas, John L. *The Liberator: William Lloyd Garrison.* Boston: Little, Brown, 1963. In tracing Garrison's career, the author surveys not only the antislavery movement but also the many other reforms in which the well-known editor was engaged.

SEE ALSO: 1787, Free African Society Is Founded; 1831, *The Liberator* Begins Publication; 1831, Nat Turner's Insurrection; 1850, Underground Railroad.

1833 ■ OBERLIN COLLEGE IS ESTABLISHED: the nation's first coeducational institution of higher education and a center of theological training

DATE: December 3, 1833
LOCALE: Lorain County, Ohio
CATEGORIES: Education; Organizations and institutions; Women's issues
KEY FIGURES:
James Bradley, first African American enrolled in the Oberlin system
Antoinette Louisa Brown (1826-1921), pioneer theology graduate of Oberlin
Charles Grandison Finney (1792-1875), celebrated U.S. revivalist, teacher, and later president of the college
John J. Shipherd (1802-1844) and
Philo P. Stewart (1798-1868), cofounders of the community of Oberlin, Ohio, and the Oberlin Collegiate Institute
Charles Stuart (1783-1865), close friend of Weld and largely responsible for Weld's antislavery enthusiasm
Arthur Tappan (1786-1865) and
Lewis Tappan (1788-1873), wealthy New York City merchants who helped finance the Lane Theological Seminary and the Oberlin Collegiate Institute
Theodore Dwight Weld (1803-1895), member of Finney's "holy band" of evangelists

SUMMARY OF EVENT. In 1825, the celebrated Presbyterian revivalist Charles G. Finney appeared in Utica, New York, where he recruited twenty-two-year-old Theodore Weld into his "holy band" of evangelists. Weld, who enrolled in the Oneida Institute in Whitesboro, New York, to prepare for the ministry, also became an exponent of emancipation. Weld's devotion to the antislavery movement was inspired by his close friend, Charles Stuart, a Utica schoolteacher and member of Finney's holy band, who was an avid opponent of slavery.

In 1830, Weld met Arthur and Lewis Tappan, New York City merchants and philanthropists, who were financing Finney's revival movement. Weld sought to persuade them to establish a theological seminary for preparing Finney's converts for the ministry. In 1831, Arthur Tappan agreed to Weld's suggestion and asked him to find a suitable site for the proposed seminary. Weld selected the already established Lane Theological Seminary in Cincinnati, Ohio, which Tappan pledged to endow. He also helped in appointing well-respected scholars to its faculty. Most of the students who enrolled in the school were Finney's converts. The Lane Seminary instantly became a center of debate on the slavery question, as Weld's students demanded immediate emancipation.

Weld's tenure at Lane Seminary proved to be of short duration. Cincinnati was so proximate to the slave area and so dependent on Southern trade that the trustees of the seminary ordered all discussion of the explosive slavery issue to cease immediately. Faced with that administrative injunction, Weld and most of his students who opposed slavery withdrew from the school, establishing their own seminary in Cumminsville, Ohio.

The Reverend John J. Shipherd, a Presbyterian minister, and Philo P. Stewart, who had been a missionary to the Choctaw Indians, had founded the community of Oberlin in Lorain County, Ohio. In 1832, Shipherd and Stewart conceived a plan to establish the community that they hoped would also serve as the site for a theological school. Shipherd wanted such an institution because, as he observed in 1832, "The growing millions of the Mississippi Valley are perishing through want of well-qualified minister and teachers." On December 3, 1833, the Oberlin Collegiate Institute—named in honor of Jean F. Oberlin, an Alsatian clergyman, educator, and philanthropist—opened its doors. The school was founded on Oberlin's "manual labor plan," which had gained popularity at U.S. seminaries in the late 1820's. Strict adherence to a program of manual labor was believed to be a panacea for both the physical and moral ills that threatened students while attending school. Original plans for Oberlin contemplated only a college preparatory program. After consulting with his colleagues, however, Shipherd decided that the college should offer a collegiate curriculum, including a department of theology. He then invited Weld and the "Lane rebels" to join Oberlin.

Moved by the prospect of having, in a single institution, a school for the Lane rebels, a place to educate African Americans, and a platform from which to promote abolition, Tappan financially supported Oberlin, as he had Lane Seminary, saving the school from financial collapse. Weld's students were placed under the tutelage of Charles Finney, who, in 1835, was invited by the trustees of Oberlin to establish the department of theology at the school. The prospects of bringing both the slavery issue and African American students to the school aroused a storm of opposition in the community, leading to six unsuccessful attempts in the Ohio State Legislature to revoke the college's charter. In 1835, Oberlin's trustees, under the threat of losing the Tappans' financial support, approved admission of students "without respect to color" by a margin of one vote. In 1836, James Bradley, an African American, was admitted to the Sheffield Manual Labor Institute, a branch preparatory school established by Oberlin.

From Oberlin's opening in 1835, the trustees approved the admission of women, although initially restricting them to the preparatory program. The event heralded the beginning of collegiate-level coeducation for women in the United States. In September, 1837, Oberlin gained distinction as the first coeducational institution to offer the degree of bachelor of arts to women. Four women who had completed Oberlin's preparatory program were then admitted to the regular curriculum as freshmen. Three of them, Mary Hosford, Mary Kellog, and Caroline Mary Rudd, received bachelor of arts degrees in 1841. "The work of female education," Philo Stewart wrote in 1837, "must be carried on in some form, and in a much more efficient manner than it has hitherto, or our country will go to destruction. For I believe that there is no other way to secure success to our great moral enterprises than to make prevalent the right kind of education for women." Despite Stewart's enthusiasm, however, fewer than six other colleges in the country followed Oberlin's example before the Civil War.

Oberlin restricted women by refusing to allow them to address mixed audiences, thus preventing them from presenting their graduation orations. Admission to the theological seminary also was barred, but, in 1847, Antoinette Brown and Lettice Smith began attending classes in the Theological Institute as "resident graduates pursuing the theological course." Both completed the course. Lettice Smith married, but Antoinette Brown, denied ordination at Oberlin, persisted until she was ordained over the church at South Butler, New York, thus becoming the first woman in the United States ordained to the Christian ministry.

Oberlin's first commencement exercises took place on September 14, 1836, when more than two thousand people witnessed fifteen men graduate from the Theological Institute. In the 1841 commencement, three of the four female students who had entered the freshman class in 1837 received the bachelor of arts degree, along with their nine male classmates. Those three women were the first women in the country to be awarded bachelor's degrees in a collegiate program identical in content to that required of male students pursuing the same degree.

In its first years, the Oberlin Collegiate Institute, formally renamed Oberlin College in 1850, was primarily a religious school. Finney had agreed to teach there in order to train evangelists, and he believed that the conversion of sinners was prerequisite to the millennium that, when attained, would permit other reforms to come about. In his commencement address of 1851, Finney reminded graduates that they had been educated in what he referred to as "God's College." As a member of Oberlin's faculty, and then as president of the school between 1851 and 1866, Finney endeavored to preserve that emphasis. Oberlin emerged from its first years of existence as the nation's first coeducational institution of higher education based on the traditional curriculum, and as a vibrant center of theological training.

—*John G. Clark, updated by Ralph L. Langenheim, Jr.*

ADDITIONAL READING:

Fletcher, Robert S. *A History of Oberlin College from Its Foundation Through the Civil War.* 2 vols. Oberlin, Ohio: Oberlin College Press, 1943. A solid, incisive study of Oberlin's role and place in nineteenth century intellectual life.

Hosford, Frances Juliette. *Father Shipherd's Magna Charta: A Century of Coeducation in Oberlin College.* Boston: Marshall Jones, 1937. Relates accomplishments of various women students and women responsible for educating women at Oberlin.

Lasser, Carol. *Educating Men and Women Together: Coeducation in a Changing World.* Urbana: University of Illinois Press, in conjunction with Oberlin College, 1987. Symposium on coeducation, with many references to Oberlin's influence.

Lasser, Carol, and Marlene Merrill. *Soul Mates: The Oberlin Correspondence of Lucy Stone and Antoinette Brown, 1846-1850.* Oberlin, Ohio: Oberlin College, 1983. Letters between two feminists and abolitionists provide insight regarding Oberlin's influence in these movements.

Tewksbury, Donald G. *The Founding of American Colleges and Universities Before the Civil War with Particular Reference to the Religious Influences Bearing upon the College Movement.* New York: AMS Press, 1965. General survey placing Oberlin's emergence in context.

Woodson, Carter G. *The Education of the Negro Prior to 1861.* New York: Arno Press, 1968. A general survey.

Woody, Thomas. *A History of Women's Education in the United States.* 2 vols. New York: Octagon Books, 1966. A general survey.

SEE ALSO: 1785, Beginnings of State Universities; 1802, U.S. Military Academy Is Established; 1820's, Free Public School Movement; 1820's, Social Reform Movement; 1823, Hartford Female Seminary Is Founded; 1828, Webster's *American Dictionary of the English Language*; 1833, Rise of the Penny Press; 1857, First African American University; 1862, Morrill Land Grant Act; 1865, Vassar College Is Founded; 1867, Office of Education Is Created.

1834 ■ BIRTH OF THE WHIG PARTY: *the strengthening of the two-party system dramatizes sectional divisions that will lead to the Civil War*

DATE: April 14, 1834

LOCALE: United States

CATEGORIES: Government and politics; Organizations and institutions

KEY FIGURES:

John Caldwell Calhoun (1782-1850), vice president of the United States and senator from South Carolina

Henry Clay (1777-1852), senator from Kentucky

William Henry Harrison (1773-1841), military hero and former senator

Andrew Jackson (1767-1845), seventh president of the United States, 1829-1837

Martin Van Buren (1782-1862), eighth president of the United States, 1837-1841

Daniel Webster (1782-1852), senator from Massachusetts

SUMMARY OF EVENT. The emergence of the Whigs as a national party would have moved ahead more rapidly had there been a single overriding issue or outstanding leader to rally around. Since there was neither, the opponents of the Democrats were a hodgepodge of malcontents, an "organized incompatibility" with only one unifying theme: an undying hatred of Andrew Jackson. They disliked the seventh president of the United States, whom they dubbed King Andrew I because of his ostensibly ruthless and dictatorial manner, and they slowly drew together into the Whig Party, the implication being that they opposed tyranny and monarchy, as did the English Whigs. Thus, although the name "Whig" was not official until Henry Clay gave it his stamp of approval in a speech delivered before the Senate on April 14, 1834, it had been in use for approximately two years.

The old Federalists and the National Republicans who opposed Jackson in 1828 were later joined by many who had supported Jackson in that election but had turned against him over divisive questions such as his attack on the Second Bank of the United States and the South Carolina nullification controversy. These desertions were serious jolts to the Democratic Party and strengthened the ranks of a coalescing opposition. This opposition was strongest among the high tariff merchants and manufacturers in the Northeast, wealthy planters in the South, and Western farmers who desired internal improvements.

If there was a common ideological denominator to the Whig Party, it was twofold: support for property rights, and interest in government's capacity to build and improve the nation's institutions. Thus, there was both a conservative and progressive side to the Whig Party. Like the old Federalists, the Whigs tended to represent the financial and business establishment; unlike them, the Whigs understood the impetus toward westward expansion that was seizing the United States in the 1830's. The Whigs became champions of the small businessman, what might later have been called the *petit bourgeois*; their constituency often included entrepreneurs who were in what is now the Midwest and mid-South, who were seeking prosperity and wanted a strong government, friendly to business, to ensure that they got what they sought. The Whig Party did not have the common touch of the Democrats, but neither was it so thoroughly a captive to Southern, slave-holding interests as its counterparts. Indeed, it was out of the Whig Party that the Republican Party, the primary antislavery party, eventually grew. The Whig Party eventually split, over slavery among other things. During its brief existence—less than thirty years—it elected two presidents and maintained the idea that the U.S. party system consisted of two equally strong but ideologically opposed parties, both representing a broad range of interests.

After a time of local building, the new party first tested its national strength in the presidential campaign of 1836. Either Kentucky's Henry Clay, the glamorous "Harry of the West," or Daniel Webster, Massachusetts' eloquent defender of the Union, would have seemed a logical choice to head the ticket. However, their positions on the issues were too well known; in addition, the men were bitter rivals who threatened to split the infant party. Furthermore, many Southern states' rights Whigs looked to John C. Calhoun for leadership. Calhoun joined Clay and Webster in their hatred of Jackson, but he never truly considered himself a Whig. With so many diverse elements, agreement about a candidate or a platform was impossible; consequently, no national nominating convention was held. Instead, Whig strategy was to run several candidates from the different sections of the nation. These candidates included William Henry Harrison of Ohio, who had been a military hero in the Indian wars; Hugh Lawson White of Tennessee, who, it was alleged, had killed a Cherokee chief with his own hands and thus gained credence and acclaim among frontier settlers; and Daniel Webster, the renowned Massachusetts senator and orator. They did not expect that any one of their candidates would receive a majority in the electoral college. However, they hoped to draw enough votes away from the Democratic candidate to prevent him from receiving a majority. The election would then be thrown into the House of Representatives, where a Whig would have a good chance of being chosen.

This multipronged strategy was deemed foolhardy by many at the time and did not augur well for the Whigs' chances in the 1836 election. Leaving nothing to chance, Jackson used his prestige and party organization to win the Democratic nomination for his own vice president, Martin Van Buren, on the first ballot. The Whigs selected Hugh Lawson White of Tennessee, William Henry Harrison of Ohio, and Webster as their standardbearers. The grand strategy backfired, because the Whig candidates split the anti-Jackson vote and enabled the well-disciplined Democrats to put Van Buren in office easily.

The new president inherited a multitude of problems and had been in office only three months when the Panic of 1837 occurred. New York banks suspended specie payments; other banks and businesses began to fail; unemployment rose; and railroads and canals were abandoned as the panic evolved into a lengthy depression. This condition was caused by many things, including Jacksonian financial measures, especially the bank war and the Specie Circular; failure of the wheat crop, ravaged by the Hessian fly; overspeculation in land; and easy credit, which left most Americans in debt. Labor, the backbone of the Democratic Party, suffered heavily, and by late 1837, 90 percent of the Eastern factories were closed. The lingering depression hit the farmers of the South and West hardest, adding stress to their status as debtors.

Van Buren, following the typical political thinking of the day, did little to fight the depression, and his administration ended under a cloud of gloom. Opposition came not only from the Whigs but also from dissident Democrats. The political impact of the depression was immediately apparent as Whig strength rapidly increased.

Voters became Whigs for various reasons. Westerners, caught between their needs and resentments, were badly divided on both the banking and internal improvement issues. Southerners were equally divided between those who, like Calhoun, saw in Van Buren's Independent Treasury sound Democratic policy and those who, like John Tyler of Virginia, still bitterly resented the Democratic administration's attack against nullification. In the Northeast, conservative business interests who called for wider government activity were now more sharply divided from the working groups and farmers than ever before. New political alignments were emerging, and the Democrats, as the party in power, suffered the most from these new developments.

The Whigs showed in the election of 1840 the extent to which they had learned the lessons of popular appeal. When they nominated the old western military hero, William Henry Harrison, rather than Webster or Clay, and placed Tyler, an anti-Jackson Democrat, on the ticket as the vice presidential candidate, the Whigs demonstrated their political sophistication. By proclaiming the true democratic qualities of their candidates—exemplified by such slogans as "Tippecanoe and Tyler Too" and "Log Cabins and Hard Cider"—and refusing to write a platform, they allowed dissatisfied elements in all sections to assume that they would gain their ends. The Whigs' populist campaign led inevitably to some distortions of the truth. Harrison, for instance, was said to have been born in a log cabin, proving his humble origins; in fact, he had been born on a Virginia plantation. The U.S. electorate either did not know this fact or preferred to forget it; they accorded Harrison great popularity. Van Buren, though tainted, was sullenly renominated by the Democrats, and was immediately pictured as an aristocrat of the worst sort by the Whigs. The campaign that developed was all sound and fury, slogan and vituperation. The 1840 campaign, more than any other, may be said to have set the tone for what has come to be seen as the typical U.S. presidential campaign. An emphasis on image and personality rather than ideology and a premium placed on the skillful use of the mass media would from then on be necessary to elect a party candidate president of the United States. Issues were forgotten or ignored as the glamorous Harrison was elected. The rise of the Whigs was now a fact of political life.

—John H. DeBerry, updated by Nicholas Birns

ADDITIONAL READING:

Brown, Thomas. *Politics and Statesmanship: Essays on the American Whig Party*. New York: Columbia University Press, 1985. An important collection that surveys the Whig Party from various informative perspectives.

Carroll, E. Malcolm. *Origins of the Whig Party*. Durham, N.C.: Duke University Press, 1925. Outdated, but much of its material is still useful for research.

Howe, Daniel Walker. *The Political Culture of the American Whigs*. Chicago: University of Chicago Press, 1979. Discusses the ideology and social affiliations of the Whig Party.

McCormick, Richard P. *The Second American Party System*. Chapel Hill: University of North Carolina Press, 1966. Shows how the Whigs fit into the structure of mid-nineteenth century U.S. politics.

Peterson, Merrill D. *The Great Triumvirate: Webster, Clay, and Calhoun*. New York: Oxford University Press, 1987. Examines three important Whig senators of the nineteenth century.

SEE ALSO: 1790's, First U.S. Political Parties; 1790, Hamilton's *Report on Public Credit*; 1816, Second Bank of the United States Is Chartered; 1824, U.S. Election of 1824; 1828, Jackson Is Elected President; 1832, Jackson vs. the Bank of the United States; 1832, Nullification Controversy; 1840, U.S. Election of 1840.

1835 ■ TEXAS REVOLUTION: *after winning independence from Mexico, Texas stays an independent republic for a decade before annexation by the United States*

DATE: June 30, 1835-October 22, 1836
LOCALE: Texas
CATEGORIES: Expansion and land acquisition; Latino American history; Wars, uprisings, and civil unrest
KEY FIGURES:
José Antonio Anvarro (1795-1871), a Tejano jailed by Santa Anna for treason
Stephen Fuller Austin (1793-1836), U.S. *empresario* who obtained large land grants from the Mexican government
Haden Edwards and
Benjamin Edwards, leaders of the abortive Fredonian Republic
Samuel Houston (1793-1863), commander of Texan forces and first president of the Republic of Texas
Manuel Mier y Teran, Mexican general who recommended limiting U.S. influence in Texas
Antonio López de Santa Anna (1794-1876), Mexican general and president of Mexico
William Barret Travis (1809-1836), Texan commander of the Alamo
José de Urrea (1795-1849), general of the Tories from February, 1836, until the end of the war
SUMMARY OF EVENT. The movement of Euro-Americans into Texas is usually dated from 1821, when Spanish authorities granted Moses Austin permission to colonize a large tract of largely unpopulated land. Austin's plea for the grant was based in part upon his claim to Spanish citizenship by reason of his previous residence in Louisiana. Moses Austin's death in Missouri the same year and the creation of an independent Mexico failed to stop the colonization project. Austin's son, Stephen, took over and spent a year in Mexico City persuading the new

authorities that his claim should be accepted. When additional grants were made by the provincial government, Austin's colonization scheme prospered, as did those of other *empresarios* who had received grants. Euro-American settlers from the United States, sometimes accompanied by their slaves, soon represented a large majority of the people of Texas.

Austin and officials of the province of Texas-Coahuila worked in harmony for several years. Slavery was opposed by Mexican officials, but the province of Texas-Coahuila recognized labor contracts that made indentured servants of the slaves. All settlers were required to be Roman Catholics, but they were not required to attend church services. The *empresario* settlers were given such generous terms for acquiring land that they usually sided with the government against people from the United States who were settling illegally in the eastern part of the province. It was with Austin's backing, for example, that the Fredonian Uprising of 1826, led by the brothers Haden and Benjamin Edwards against the government, was put down.

The rapid growth of the Euro-American population in Texas created uneasiness among many Mexican officials. The frequent incidents between Texan and Mexican officials, especially in eastern Texas, were viewed with alarm; the attempts of Presidents John Qunicy Adams and Andrew Jackson to acquire all or part of Texas were greeted with hostility. General Manuel Mier y Teran proposed a plan to save Texas from being overrun by Euro-Americans. Mier y Teran called for placing more Mexican troops in the northern provinces, settling more Mexicans and Europeans in the area, and increasing coastal trade between Texas and the rest of Mexico. The Colonization Law of April 6, 1830, adopted Mier y Teran's suggestions and forbade further immigration from the United States. The plan to attract more Mexicans and increase commerce with Texas failed to materialize, and the limiting of legal immigration from the United States only served to restrict the immigration to illegal settlers who had no vested interest in supporting the Mexican government.

The military occupation of Texas was the only part of the plan that was realized, and it only increased the friction between the government and the settlers. The Texans looked to the presumably liberal revolutionary forces of Antonio López de Santa Anna for relief, and when he came to power, they held a convention at San Felipe in April, 1833, to make plans to petition the new government for the redress of their grievances. Austin was commissioned to present the new government with their requests, including the separation of Texas from Coahuila and a liberalizing of the laws governing immigration and import controls. Austin journeyed to Mexico City, where the Mexican congress agreed to repeal the North American immigration exclusion. Austin, however, was arrested during his return trip on the strength of a letter he had written that appeared to advise the Texans to establish a separate state. He was jailed for two years and could not return to Texas until September 1, 1835.

During Austin's absence, Texas-Coahuila made a number of concessions to the Texans, but Santa Anna's central government was moving to centralize its authority. Although most Texans disapproved of the seizure of the Anahuac Garrison on June 30, 1835, by a group led by William Barret Travis, they were concerned about the apparent intention of the Mexican government to send a greater number of troops to Texas. The Texans responded by calling conventions on August 15 at Columbia and on October 15 at San Felipe. A provisional government was created, although the Texans proclaimed their loyalty to a constitutional Mexican government. An army was created and Austin called for war.

Not all Texans were committed to the call to arms, and opposition increased during the seven-month war. The mainly Irish settlers in the San Patricio region joined forces with the Mexican army and fought against the rebels at Fort Lipantitlán on November 5. Tejanos, or Mexican Texans, were divided in their loyalties: Some were centralists; others supported the rebel forces. Still others tried, largely without success, to remain neutral. This split in allegiances made the Texas revolution a civil war in the truest sense, pitting family member against family member. José Antonio Navarro, a hero to many latter-day Texans, supported the Texas Rebels, while his brother Angel maintained his support for Mexico.

Many Euro-Americans attempted to remain neutral during the spring of 1836. Although they did not support the centralists, many did avoid recruitment into the armed forces. Personal and family protection was their motivating force. Of the few Euro-Americans who did support the centralist cause, most were older and had resided in Texas for more than ten years. There is little evidence that they were very active during the war.

The vast majority of Tejanos who supported the rebel cause were native-born Texans from San Antonio. Their knowledge of the area proved beneficial to the rebels. The effects of the war on Tejanos, however, were devastating. After their homes and farms were ransacked and their supplies used to feed and equip the Texas armies, their initial support for the rebellion faded. Most received no compensation for their sacrifices during the war.

On February 23, 1836, Santa Anna and four thousand troops laid siege to the Alamo. The 187 men inside, mainly newcomers from the United States, held out until March 6, when the garrison, commanded by Travis and including Davy Crockett and James Bowie, was assaulted and wiped out. At Goliad, three hundred defenders under James Fannin surrendered and then were massacred by the Mexican army on March 27.

The delegates who met on March 1, 1836, in Washington, Texas, knew of the siege of the Alamo. Continuing their pattern of following the revolutionary example of the United States, they issued a declaration of independence on March 2 and subsequently adopted a constitution. The siege at the Alamo gave commander-in-chief Sam Houston time to assemble an army. Houston avoided a fight for weeks before surprising Santa Anna's divided army on the west bank of the San Jacinto River near Galveston Bay on April 21, 1836. The Texans defeated twelve hundred Mexicans with their force of

eight hundred. Santa Anna was among the captives. Before being released, Santa Anna pledged himself to secure the independence of Texas, but the Mexican congress disavowed his actions. The Mexican army, however, quickly left Texas and made no serious attempt to regain control. Sam Houston was elected president of the Republic of Texas on October 22, 1836. Houston and most Texans were interested in joining the United States, but for diplomatic and domestic reasons, annexation was not accomplished for almost a decade.

—*Mark A. Plummer, updated by Pamela Hayes-Bohanan*

ADDITIONAL READING:

Fehrenbach, T. R. "The Clash of Cultures," "Revolution," and "Blood and Soil." In *Lone Star: A History of Texas and the Texans.* New York: Wings Books, 1991. Details the story of the *empresarios*, conflicts betweens Euro-Americans and Mexicans in Texas, and the events leading up to the Texas Revolution.

Gaddy, Jerry J., comp. *Texas in Revolt: Contemporary Newspaper Accounts of the Texas Revolution.* Ft. Collins, Colo.: Old Army Press, 1973. Chronological arrangement of newspaper accounts of the revolution from across the country.

Gurasich, Marj. *Benito and the White Dove: A Story of José Antonio Navarro.* Austin, Tex.: Eakin Press, 1989. A fictionalized biography of Navarro and the story of the revolution as told to a young jailer's son.

Lack, Paul D. *The Texas Revolutionary Experience: A Political and Social History, 1835-1836.* College Station: Texas A&M Press, 1992. An account of the various groups that participated in the war, how they responded, and how they were affected.

Nofi, Albert A. *The Alamo and the Texas War of Independence, September 30, 1835 to April 21, 1836.* Conshohocken, Pa.: Combined Books, 1992. Provides detailed information on the various people involved and their roles, strengths, and weaknesses; also details battles.

SEE ALSO: 1821, Mexican War of Independence; 1821, Santa Fe Trail Opens; 1823, Jedediah Smith Explores the Far West; 1828, Jackson Is Elected President; 1842, Frémont's Expeditions; 1846, Mexican War; 1848, Treaty of Guadalupe Hidalgo.1842, Frémont's Expeditions; 1846, Mexican War; 1848, Treaty of Guadalupe Hidalgo.

1836 ■ RISE OF TRANSCENDENTALISM: *the belief that there are truths that transcend proof reflects both a reaction to growing materialism and a confidence in humankind, leading to social experiments and reform movements*

DATE: 1836
LOCALE: New England
CATEGORIES: Cultural and intellectual history; Religion; Social reform

KEY FIGURES:

Amos Bronson Alcott (1799-1888), educational reformer and writer

Orestes Augustus Brownson (1803-1860), editor of the *Boston Quarterly Review*

Ralph Waldo Emerson (1803-1882), former Unitarian minister who became a central figure of the Transcendental movement

Margaret Fuller (1810-1850), editor of *The Dial* and a pioneer crusader for women's rights

Theodore Parker (1810-1860), editor of *The Massachusetts Quarterly Review*

George Ripley (1802-1880), former Unitarian minister and one of the founders of the Transcendental Club

Henry David Thoreau (1817-1862), protégé of Emerson, and author of *Walden* and "Civil Disobedience"

SUMMARY OF EVENT. The Transcendental movement emerged among a small group of intellectuals living in New England. In their lectures and writings, at meetings of the Transcendental Club, which became active in Boston and environs in 1836, and in periodicals such as *The Dial* and *The Western Messenger*, they advanced what their leader, Ralph Waldo Emerson, called the "new views": a synthesis of imported and home-grown notions that produced the distinctive configuration of ideas known as American Transcendentalism.

For the Transcendentalists, the term meant simply that there are truths that go beyond, or transcend, proof. These truths are known to the heart rather than to the mind—are felt emotionally, even though they cannot be proved logically. For example, a doctor can tell whether someone is alive but cannot tell whether it is good to be alive. The Transcendentalists held that most human values lie outside the limits of reason and belong to the realm of instinct or intuition; they are matters of private experience, faith, and conviction.

The Transcendentalists drew on a wide variety of foreign sources, including Platonism and Neoplatonism, German philosophical idealism, Swedenborgianism, the ideas of the French Eclectic school and the English Romantics, and, somewhat later, Confucius' and Buddha's writings. There was no unanimity among them, but most Transcendentalists subscribed to an intuitive idealism, the concept of an organic universe, and a belief in the divinity of the human being. They were antiformalists in religion and literature, and they protested the commercial materialism of nineteenth century America. Although small in number and confined primarily to New England, they represented a significant influence in the history of American thought. Not only did they question prevailing notions about the universe, humankind, and God; they also challenged neoclassical artistic standards, introducing a new aesthetic theory based on the use of symbolism.

Philosophically, American Transcendentalism represented a repudiation of the Lockean philosophy of sensationalism and materialism that had dominated American thought during the eighteenth century and which survived, although in a somewhat modified form, in the Scottish commonsense philosophy of the early nineteenth century. The Transcendentalists elevated intuition over sense experience as a source of knowledge, and they emphasized the superiority of the faculty of "reason" over that of "understanding." Transcendentalist George Ripley explained that Transcendentalists believe in a truth that transcends the sphere of the external sense. In Emerson's words, they "respect the intuitions and . . . give them . . . all authority over our experience."

American Transcendentalism was not primarily a philosophical movement. Although the Transcendentalists argued their case against the dominant culture in the language of philosophy and literature rather than that of theology, they were engaged in a religious demonstration. Just as they repudiated Lockean philosophy, they also rejected its religious equivalent—what Emerson called "the corpse-cold Unitarianism of Brattle Street and Harvard College." The Transcendental movement emerged out of the Unitarian Controversy of the 1830's—a theological debate among Boston Unitarians that focused on the question of miracles, but ultimately extended to such issues as the divinity of Christ, the supernatural interpretation of Christianity, and the organization of the church.

The essence of what opponents called "the latest form of infidelity" may be seen in Emerson's Divinity School Address

Henry David Thoreau was only nineteen at the time that the Transcendentalist club came together. He resided for a time in the home of the movement's leader, Ralph Waldo Emerson, and associated with such Transcendentalists as Margaret Fuller, George Ripley, and Bronson Alcott. Thoreau attempted to act on Transcendentalist doctrines as articulated by Emerson, moving to a hut beside Walden Pond, Concord, for just over a year, and recording his philosophy in Walden *(1854) and his essay on civil disobedience. (Library of Congress)*

of 1838. First, Emerson, a former Unitarian minister, attacked the Unitarian concept of miracles as an interruption of the natural order. "The word Miracle, as pronounced by Christian churches, gives a false impression; it is Monster. It is not one with the falling rain." For Emerson, as for other Transcendentalists, belief in an immanent God eliminated the traditionalism between the natural and the supernatural. Emerson also condemned "historical Christianity," including Unitarianism, because it did not preach the "infinitude of man," and because "the soul is not preached." Christ's message, that God had incarnated himself in humanity, was distorted by later ages, Emerson declared. So was Christ's emphasis on "the eternal revelation in the heart." These two beliefs—that people have divinity within, and that humans have the capacity to apprehend spiritual truth at first hand, by intuition, not mediated by any external authority—formed the heart of Transcendental religion. The immanence of God and the humanity of Jesus also formed a part of the Transcendentalists' creed.

The social philosophy of the Transcendental movement embodied two contrasting outlooks. Some Transcendentalists were led by their belief in the divinity of humankind to espouse an uncompromising individualism. Repudiating the tyranny of the majority, they preached self-culture and self-reliance. Rejecting the demand for conformity to social norms, they argued that each individual must be true to the moral law within. Emerson's "Self-Reliance" (1841) and Henry David Thoreau's "Civil Disobedience" (1849) are the classic expositions of Transcendental individualism and its political and social implications. "Civil Disobedience" was written after Thoreau had been jailed for refusing to pay his poll tax, which he claimed would be used to finance the Mexican War.

Other Transcendentalists emphasized the unity of humankind and stressed cooperation rather than individualism as the key to social improvement. Orestes Brownson, editor of the *Boston Quarterly Review*, represents this side of Transcendentalism. The communitarian experiments at Brook Farm, founded in 1841, and Amos Bronson Alcott's Fruitlands reflected the unifying side of Transcendentalism.

The issue between the two wings of the Transcendental movement was clearly drawn in Emerson's response to an invitation to join the Brook Farm community: "It seems to me a circuitous . . . way of relieving myself of any irksome circumstances, to put on your community the task of my emancipation which I ought to take on myself."

Despite their disagreements as to the proper means of reform, Transcendentalists were united in protesting against such things as slavery, war, and the evils of capitalism. Thus, in its social philosophy, as in its religious and philosophical outlook, the Transcendental movement represented a trenchant critique of the dominant ideology and culture of the antebellum United States.

Transcendentalism has continued to influence American thought. During the 1960's and 1970's, many Transcendentalist ideas were reflected in antiwar protests and the Civil Rights movement. Thoreau's doctrine of passive resistance greatly influenced such social reformers as Mahatma Gandhi and Martin Luther King, Jr.

—*Anne C. Loveland, updated by Russell Hively*

ADDITIONAL READING:

Emerson, Ralph Waldo. *Emerson: Collected Poems and Translations*. New York: Library of America, 1994. This collection of notes and poems is unedited. Includes a detailed chronology and index of Emerson's titles and first lines.

Frothingham, Octavius B. *Transcendentalism in New England: A History*. New York: G. P. Putnam's Sons, 1876. An account of the Transcendental movement written by an insider converted to Transcendentalism under the impact of Theodore Parker's preaching.

Hutchinson, William R. *The Transcendentalist Ministers: Church Reform in the New England Renaissance*. New Haven, Conn.: Yale University Press, 1959. Discusses the major differences between Unitarian ministers during the Transcendental movement. Seventeen Unitarian ministers were in the twenty-six-member Transcendental Club.

Matthiessen, Francis O. *American Renaissance: Art and Expression in the Age of Emerson and Whitman*. New York: Oxford University Press, 1941. Analyzes the writings of Emerson, Thoreau, Hawthorne, Melville, and Whitman and their common "devotion to the possibilities of democracy."

Miller, James E., Jr., et al. "Background American Classic 1840-1870." In *The United States in Literature*. Glenview, Ill.: Scott, Foresman, 1985. Background information in a U.S. literature anthology. Details how Transcendental thought affected the women's rights and abolitionist movements in the 1800's.

Miller, Perry. *The Transcendentalists: An Anthology*. Cambridge, Mass.: Harvard University Press, 1950. Writings of the lesser-known Transcendentalists. The author elaborates on his thesis as to the inherently religious character of the movement.

Whicher, Stephen E. *Freedom and Fate: An Inner Life of Ralph Waldo Emerson*. Philadelphia: University of Pennsylvania Press, 1953. Attempts to reconstruct the inner life of Ralph Waldo Emerson.

SEE ALSO: 1814, New Harmony and the Communitarian Movement; 1819, Unitarian Church Is Founded; 1820's, Free Public School Movement; 1820's, Social Reform Movement.

1837 ■ REBELLIONS IN CANADA: *the citizens of Upper and Lower Canada rebel against colonial government, paving the way for "responsible government"*

DATE: October 23-December 16, 1837

LOCALE: Upper and Lower Canada

CATEGORIES: Canadian history; Native American history; Wars, uprisings, and civil unrest

KEY FIGURES:

Robert Baldwin (1804-1858), moderate reform leader in Upper Canada and son of William Warren Baldwin

William Warren Baldwin (1775-1844), moderate reform leader in Upper Canada

John Colborne (1778-1863), lieutenant governor of Upper Canada, 1826-1835

Charles Duncombe (1792-1867), rebellion leader in London District, Upper Canada

Francis Bond Head (1793-1875), lieutenant governor of Upper Canada, 1835-1837

John George Lambton, Lord Durham (1792-1840), representative of government in Lower and Upper Canada, 1838

William Lyon Mackenzie (1795-1861), editor of the *Constitution* and rebellion leader in Home District, Upper Canada

Louis-Joseph Papineau (1786-1871), leader of the Patriote movement in Lower Canada

John Rolph (1793-1870), moderate reform leader in Upper Canada

John Russell (1792-1878), home secretary of the British government

SUMMARY OF EVENT. The roots of the Rebellions of 1837 in Lower and Upper Canada may be traced to the Constitutional Act of 1791, the framework for the governance of both Canadas. As a response to the American Revolution, the British government wanted to quell any impulses toward democracy in Canada. Both Canadas had an elected Assembly, but both had an appointed Legislative Council (Upper House) and an appointed lieutenant governor. The lieutenant governor also appointed an advisory group, the Executive Council, that influenced the governor's policy making while impeding the work of the elected Assembly. Many members of the Legislative Council were also members of the Executive Council, thus forming the basis for government control by oligarchies in both Lower Canada and Upper Canada. The oligarchy in Lower Canada, the Chateau Clique, was an alliance of clergy, old seigneurial families, and English-speaking merchants in Montreal. Elites of Upper Canada made up the oligarchy called the Family Compact.

With government by oligarchy, political tensions increased during the 1820's and early 1830's. Political unrest coincided with economic difficulties. For several years, agricultural crop yields had been deficient. Increased debt for farmers and price increases for consumers resulted. Adding to the economic instability were the tightening of credit, increasing numbers of bankruptcies, and higher levels of unemployment. This environment spawned reform movements in both Canadas, which led to revolts against the government.

In Lower Canada, in February, 1834, the Assembly, dominated by the reform party, Parti Patriote, under the leadership of Louis-Joseph Papineau, passed the Ninety-two Resolutions detailing Lower Canada's grievances, including the responsibility of the governor to the electorate and election of the legislative council, and submitted them to London. On March 2, 1837, Parliament passed resolutions rejecting the demands made in the Ninety-two Resolutions. Called the Ten Resolutions—or Russell's Resolutions, for Home Secretary Lord John Russell, who presented them to Parliament—they radicalized the Patriotes.

During the summer of 1837, the Patriotes held meetings of armed farmers throughout the countryside. Hearing about these meetings, the government issued warrants for the arrest of the leaders. One center of revolutionary activity was the Richelieu Valley area, to which the leaders had fled after the warrants were issued. A large rally was held at Saint-Charles on October 23. The government responded to the gathering by sending troops. Eight hundred men met the troops at Saint-Denis on November 23 and repulsed them. Two days later, at Saint-Charles, the government won a victory and resistance in the Richelieu Valley abated.

Another area of insurrection in Lower Canada was Two Mountains. Two thousand troops attacked at Saint Eustache on December 14 and killed fifty-eight Patriotes. The troops burned and looted Saint-Benoit two days later. The Patriote movement collapsed. Papineau, disguised as a woman, fled to the United States.

The reform movement in Upper Canada during the early 1830's was made up of several factions. Moderate reformers, such as William Warren Baldwin, his son Robert, and John Rolph, advocated making government responsible to the electorate. Radical reformers such as William Lyon Mackenzie favored the establishment of an elective system of government similar to that of the United States. To this end, Mackenzie investigated the Family Compact and compiled a list of grievances and abuses of power. The tone of the report of the investigation, the Seventh Report on Grievances, alienated Mackenzie from the moderate reform factions. Because the lieutenant governor, Sir John Colborne, did not send the Seventh Report to the Colonial Office, he was dismissed.

The lieutenant governor sent to Upper Canada as Colborne's replacement Sir Francis Bond Head. Head's actions prompted the Executive Council to resign. Head then dissolved the Assembly and called for an election in the colony. Head's participation in the 1836 election campaign aided the Tories and helped defeat the reformers. Longtime members of the Assembly, such as the Baldwins and Rolph, lost their seats.

With the loss of the reformers both from the Assembly and from participation in politics, there was a leadership void in the reform movement, which Mackenzie sought to fill. Mackenzie felt that Russell's Resolutions rejecting the Patriote demands and permitting government to be conducted by executive decree in Lower Canada could be applied to Upper Canada as well. In his newspaper, the *Constitution*, Mackenzie began to discuss similarities in the grievances of Upper Canada and the American colonies before the Revolutionary War. He alluded to the possibility of a rebellion in Upper Canada.

At a meeting in Toronto in August, 1837, a Committee of Vigilance was established. Meetings were scheduled throughout the Home District, as well as in the London District, promoting governmental change. During the fall of 1837, Lieutenant Governor Head, confident that the situation in Upper Canada was stable, sent troops to Lower Canada to aid Sir John Colborne in quelling the civil disturbances there, leaving few troops in Upper Canada. The Home Office had sent Colborne to Lower Canada after replacing him with Head in Upper Canada. Mackenzie realized that the absence of troops was to the advantage of the reform movement. He traveled throughout the Home District speaking at gatherings of disaffected citizens and gained their support for an uprising. December 7, 1837, was set as the date it would occur. The men would gather at Montgomery's Tavern north of Toronto on Yonge Street, march on the capital, and seize control of the government.

The men gathered at Montgomery's Tavern in early December, before plans for provisioning them and staging the insurrection were made. Because they had arrived earlier than the announced date, there was confusion among the leaders. Without a clear plan, the rebels marched south and were met just south of Gallows Hill by a loyalist force hastily put together to guard Toronto. The rebels panicked; many fled. Two days later, Head, assisted by Allan McNabb and some loyalists, drove the remaining rebels from Montgomery's Tavern. Mackenzie crossed the border into the United States on December 11. Two of Mackenzie's men, Samuel Lount and Peter Matthews, were arrested, made examples of, and hanged in April, 1838, for their participation in the rebellion.

Rebels in the London District, under the leadership of Charles Duncombe, did not realize that the Home District rebellion had failed, and they mustered to mount a rebellion on December 13. When it was discovered that loyalists were closing in on them, the London District rebels dispersed. Unmindful of the December 7 proclamation promising amnesty, Duncombe fled to Michigan. The armed rebellions of 1837 ended.

The rebellions of 1837 demonstrated that a majority of the population lacked enthusiasm for following radicals into armed rebellion. The citizenry instead demanded constitutional reforms through British institutions. In May, 1838, the Colonial Office sent John George Lambton, Lord Durham, to the Canadas to investigate the 1837 unrest. His subsequent report called for Upper and Lower Canada to be united and governed by a form of "responsible government"—that is, government whose ministers are entirely responsible to the parliamentary majority, elected by the people. This finally happened in 1848.

—*Mary M. Graham*

ADDITIONAL READING:

Francis, R. Douglas, and Donald B. Smith, eds. *Readings in Canadian History: Pre-Confederation.* 2d ed. Toronto: Holt, Rinehart and Winston of Canada, 1986. Two articles discuss the causes of the rebellions; a third focuses on William Lyon Mackenzie.

McInnes, Edgar. *Canada: A Political and Social History.* 4th ed. Toronto: Holt, Rinehart and Winston of Canada, 1982.

Chapter 10 presents the social, political, and economic context of the rebellion.

Ouellet, Fernand. "The 1837/8 Rebellions in Lower Canada as a Social Phenomenon." In *Pre-Confederation.* Vol. 1 in *Interpreting Canada's Past.* 2d ed. Edited by J. M. Bumsted. Toronto: Oxford University Press, 1993. Describes the political and social situation in Lower Canada leading up to the rebellion.

Read, Colin, and Ronald J. Stagg, eds. *The Rebellion of 1837 in Upper Canada: A Collection of Documents.* Toronto: Champlain Society in Cooperation with the Ontario Heritage Foundation, 1985. Introduction provides details of the causes, events, and aftermath of the rebellion.

Young, Brian, and John Dickinson. *A Short History of Quebec: A Socio-Economic Perspective.* Toronto: Copp Clark Pitman, 1988. Discusses the causes and events of the rebellion in Lower Canada.

SEE ALSO: 1791, Canada's Constitutional Act; 1841, Upper and Lower Canada Unite.

1837 ■ MT. HOLYOKE SEMINARY IS FOUNDED: *an early venture in education for girls that is equal to boys' education and financially accessible to the majority*

DATE: November 8, 1837

LOCALE: South Hadley, Massachusetts

CATEGORIES: Education; Organizations and institutions; Women's issues

KEY FIGURES:

Zilpah Grant (1794-1874), teacher and friend of Mary Lyon

Edward Hitchcock (1793-1864), a young minister

Mary Lyon (1797-1849), founder of Mt. Holyoke Seminary

SUMMARY OF EVENT. Mary Lyon was born on February 8, 1797, in Buckland, Massachusetts, to a farming family. She learned the skills of farm women, such as weaving, making cloth, and cooking, and, beginning at the age of four, also attended school, which was about a mile away from her home. She walked without complaint because school was her greatest delight. In 1802, her father died, and Mary, along with her mother and seven brothers and sisters, ran the farm. When she was seven, however, the school moved to Ashfield, and she began a period of staying with relatives in order to continue attending school, paying them by helping with chores. She would bake, spin, dye, weave, and embroider, as well as take care of the children. Eight years later, Mrs. Lyon decided to remarry and move to Ashfield. Mary stayed on the farm and kept house for her brother Aaron, who paid her a dollar per week for her education.

In 1814, when she was seventeen, Lyon was offered a summer teaching position in the nearby town of Shelburne Falls at a salary of seventy-five cents per week. This first teaching experience was a difficult one, mainly because she did not know how to discipline the students. During the winter months, however, she consulted with experienced teachers to learn their art, and in the summer of 1815, she taught once more at the Shelburne school. During the next few summers, Lyon taught either at Ashfield or at Buckland school, staying with the parents of students, as was the custom of the time.

Still, Lyon longed to further her own education. In 1817, when she was twenty, she heard of a new school opening in Ashfield, called Sanderson Academy. Using all her savings to pay for tuition, she began to study mathematics and astronomy there under Elijah Burritt. She succeeded admirably with her studies, learning the entire Latin grammar, for example, after only a weekend of study. Amanda White became a close friend, and when Lyon did not have funds for the second semester, Amanda's father, Thomas White, persuaded the school board to allow her to stay on free of charge and invited Lyon to live with his family.

When Lyon finished at Sanderson Academy, she moved back to the farm with Aaron and his new wife, Armilla, who by this time had borne three children. Aaron had decided to sell the farm and move to western New York, near Jamestown, and he invited Lyon to move with them. Lyon decided not to go with her brother but to study at Byfield Female Seminary, where she formed a lifelong friendship with Zilpah Grant, a young preceptress (assistant principal) of the school. Simultaneously, Lyon also taught at Sanderson Academy.

During the summer of 1823, Lyon taught at a school in Conway, Massachusetts, where she boarded with a young minister, the Reverend Edward Hitchcock, who was also a geologist, and his wife Orra. The three became fast friends. In 1824, Lyon opened a girls' school in Buckland, which operated during the winter, and spent the summers with Zilpah Grant at the new Adams Female Academy in East Derry, New Hampshire. In 1828, Grant left Adams Academy over a disagreement with the trustees, who wanted to introduce more "feminine" arts, such as dance and music, into the curriculum. Grant then proceeded to open a school in Ipswich, Massachusetts, and invited Lyon to come with her. Although initially reluctant to leave her own school, Lyon eventually decided to become assistant principal and teacher at Grant's school. When Grant became ill, Lyon found herself in charge of the school.

It had been Lyon's lifelong dream to establish a permanent school for women, one endowed in such a way that it would not depend on the whims of temporary trustees. She and Grant had worked toward this goal at Ipswich, but the property was owned by men who did not want to make an endowment but instead wanted a return on their investment. During the summer of 1833, Lyon traveled in New York State, to Troy, Niagara Falls, and Stockton County, where her brother Aaron welcomed her. Thereafter, her life was dedicated to founding her new school. In 1834, she wrote, "My heart has so yearned over the adult female youth in the common walks of life, that it has sometimes seemed as if there was a fire, shut up in my bones." She envisioned a school that was plain, with simple food and labor done by the families of teachers and students. The school would own its own property, its finances handled by trustees who expected no profit. Tuition would be low, allowing even poor women to attend.

Lyon raised the first thousand dollars for the project, going from house to house and town to town, appealing for contributions from old friends such as Thomas White and Edward Hitchcock. Eventually, the residents of ninety-one towns gave a total of twenty-seven thousand dollars. Engaging a group of male trustees, she left them the choice of the school's location; they decided on South Hadley, Massachusetts. Despite controversy over the school's goals—which some denounced as unChristian and unfeminine—it opened in 1837 with eighty students. A nearby mountain, Mt. Holyoke, gave the school its name. As was customary at the time, the students were to live at the school, and they went to work cooking and furnishing their rooms.

Mt. Holyoke Seminary prospered: Enrollment rose, wings were added to the main building, and visiting professors arrived to lecture. Hitchcock lectured on human anatomy using a manikin whose organs could be detached. Teaching methods were experimental for the time. Compositions were written; classes were conducted by topic and discussion, rather than by rote. Academic standards were high, and no one under the age of sixteen was admitted. Tuition was sixty-four dollars per year. One of the more famous pupils at Mt. Holyoke was the poet Emily Dickinson, who wrote to a friend regarding the entrance examinations:

> You cannot imagine how trying they are, because if we cannot go through them in a specified time, we are sent home. . . . I never would endure the suspense which I endured during those three days again for all the treasures of the world.

In February, 1849, after caring for a sick student, Lyon became ill, and on March 5, just after her fifty-second birthday, she died. In 1893, Mt. Holyoke Seminary became Mt. Holyoke College, and one hundred years after that, Mary Lyon was recognized as a member of the Women's Hall of Fame in Seneca Falls, New York. On February 28, 1987, a stamp was issued by the U.S. Post Office in her honor.

—Winifred O. Whelan

ADDITIONAL READING:

Browne, Sheila E. "Daring to Dream: Women Scientists Then and Now." *Mount Holyoke Alumnae Quarterly* 76 (Winter, 1993). This article shows how Mt. Holyoke began a tradition of women scientists and argues that women are more successful in science when they study at women's colleges.

Faragher, John Mack, and Florence Howe, eds. *Women and Higher Education in American History: Essays from the Mount Holyoke College Sesquicentennial Symposia.* New York: W. W. Norton, 1988. Situates Lyon and her philosophy in the history of higher education for women.

Hitchcock, Edward, comp. *The Power of Christian Benevolence Illustrated in the Life and Labors of Mary Lyon.* 9th ed. Northampton, Mass.: Hopkins, Bridgman, 1851. Abridged and enlarged. New York: American Tract Society, 1858. Hitchcock's biography is written from personal knowledge of Lyon's life; contains text from many of her letters.

McFeely, William S. "Mary Lyon: The Life of Her Mind." *Mount Holyoke Alumnae Quarterly* 70 (Winter, 1987). Traces the life of Lyon from the viewpoint of her searching for her goal in life. He emphasizes her belief in what the mind can accomplish.

Rosen, Dorothy. *A Fire in Her Bones: The Story of Mary Lyon*. Minneapolis: Carolrhoda Books, 1995. Classified as juvenile literature, this book presents an accurate and well-written portrayal of Lyon's life.

SEE ALSO: 1823, Hartford Female Seminary Is Founded; 1833, Oberlin College Is Established; 1857, New York Infirmary for Indigent Women and Children Opens; 1865, Vassar College Is Founded.

1839 ■ AMISTAD SLAVE REVOLT:
abolitionists win a victory in the judicial battle that follows an illegal importation of Africans as slaves

DATE: July 1, 1839
LOCALE: Coastal waters between Havana and Puerto Príncipe, Cuba
CATEGORIES: African American history; Diplomacy and international relations; Latino American history; Wars, uprisings, and civil unrest
KEY FIGURES:
John Quincy Adams (1767-1848), former president of the United States, 1797-1801, and advocate for the Africans
Roger Sherman Baldwin (1793-1863), chief counsel for the Africans
Joseph Cinqué (died 1879), charismatic leader of the captive Africans
José Ruiz, Cuban who purchased Africans illegally processed as slaves
Lewis Tappan (1788-1873), abolitionist leader who spearheaded support for the captured Africans
Martin Van Buren (1782-1862), eighth president of the United States, 1837-1841
SUMMARY OF EVENT. The British-Spanish Treaty of 1817 banned African slave trading as of 1820; however, enforcement was not adequate to deter many fortune seekers, and a highly lucrative covert slave trade existed, especially between Africa and Cuba. In April, 1839, a Portuguese slave ship left West Africa bound for Havana filled with more than five hundred illegally purchased Africans, mostly Mendis. After a middle passage that lasted two months and killed approximately one-third of the Africans, the ship anchored offshore of Havana and the surviving human cargo were brought to land after dark. Government officials receiving kickbacks provided paperwork declaring these Africans to be *ladinos*, slaves resid-

ing in Cuba prior to 1820, which would make their sale legal. Within a few days, José Ruiz purchased forty-nine adult male Africans, and Pedro Montes bought four children, three girls and a boy.

The slaves were loaded onto the schooner *Amistad*, which set sail for Puerto Príncipe, a few days' journey away. The Africans, unable to communicate with the Spanish-speaking owners or crew, became convinced that they were to be eaten. On the third night out, the charismatic Joseph Cinqué picked the lock on his iron collar and broke into the cargo hold, where he and others found cane knives. The Africans took over the ship, killing the captain and the cook. The two crew members disappeared, perhaps having jumped overboard. Ruiz, Montes, and Antonio, the captain's slave cabin boy, were spared.

The Africans demanded to be taken to Sierra Leone. For almost two months, Ruiz and Montes pretended to comply; during the day they sailed southeast, occasionally landing to scavenge for food and water, but at night they headed north and northeast, in hopes of finding help. The Africans, knowing nothing about navigation, did not realize they were being duped.

The schooner slowly tacked up the Eastern seaboard of the United States. Often sighted, its now decrepit condition and the many blacks on board aroused suspicion. On a stop to obtain food off the coast of Long Island, the *Amistad* came to the attention of the government brig USS *Washington*, whose captain, Thomas Gedney, ordered the schooner boarded. The thirty-nine surviving slaves, by now almost starved and unable to resist, were taken into custody.

Ruiz and Montes filed suits to have their slave property returned to them; Gedney claimed salvage rights to the *Amistad* and its cargo, including the slaves; the Spanish government demanded the fugitives be handed over to it; U.S. abolitionists clamored for the Africans to be set free. The case was a complicated one: Although African slave trade was banned, slavery in Cuba was legal and Ruiz and Montes had paperwork documenting their ownership. Moreover, there were U.S.-Spanish relations, especially Pinckney's Treaty of 1795, to be considered in determining whether or not the United States should recognize Spanish property rights to the Africans. Precedents from an earlier slaver incident, the *Antelope* case, had to be analyzed also. Perhaps most important, the *Amistad* affair carried grave implications for the slavery issue in the United States—and President Martin Van Buren hoped to avoid that issue in his upcoming reelection campaign, knowing that his success depended on maintaining his coalition of Northern and Southern supporters.

Newspapers across the land kept an interested public informed of the status of the case. For the most part, Northerners were sympathetic toward the Africans, while Southerners felt they should be returned to the Spanish government to be tried for piracy and murder. The affair probably would have been handled quietly and quickly, had not the abolitionists recognized in it the potential to raise the public's awareness of the moral and legal issues at stake in the slavery question. They

Death of Capt. Ferrer, the Captain of the Amistad, July, 1839.

Don Jose Ruiz and Don Pedro Montez, of the Island of Cuba, having purchased fifty-three slaves at Havana, recently imported from Africa, put them on board the Amistad, Capt. Ferrer, in order to transport them to Principe, another port on the Island of Cuba. After being out from Havana about four days, the African captives on board, in order to obtain their freedom, and return to Africa, armed themselves with cane knives, and rose upon the Captain and crew of the vessel. Capt. Ferrer and the cook of the vessel were killed; two of the crew escaped; Ruiz and Montez were made prisoners.

The Amistad Slave Revolt of 1839. The ensuing Supreme Court trial, which was decided in favor of the Africans, excited international interest and advanced the cause of abolitionists. (Library of Congress)

saw in this case an opportunity to argue the principle of natural law, which they felt entitled every person, regardless of color, to liberty. The case also provided them a chance to test the degree to which people of color were protected by the law.

Abolitionists and other opponents of slavery quickly formed the *Amistad* Committee, made up of Simeon Jocelyn, Joshua Leavitt, and Lewis Tappan, to raise money for legal counsel and to appeal to President Van Buren to allow the case to be decided by the United States court system rather than turning the prisoners over to the Spanish government. The committee acquired the legal services of Roger Sherman Baldwin, Seth Staples, and Theodore Sedgwick. They also sought out native Africans who could communicate with the *Amistad* blacks, for so far depositions had been given only by the Spaniards and the cabin boy. Eventually they engaged the services of James Covey, a native African who could speak the Mendi language. Covey was allowed to leave his duties aboard a British cruiser indefinitely in order to serve as interpreter for the Africans.

The legal proceedings began in mid-September, 1839, in the United States Circuit Court convened in Hartford, Connecticut. Amid a complex maze of issues dealing with salvage rights, international law, jurisdiction disputes, and legal definitions of property and personhood, the case worked its way over the next eighteen months from Circuit Court to District Court, back to the Circuit Court and finally to the Supreme Court. The abolitionists made sure that the case stayed before the public, even filing assault and battery and illegal imprisonment suits against Montes and Ruiz on behalf of several of the Africans to generate further attention. The public, although ambivalent in its responses to the legal and moral questions, stayed interested. People flocked to and even paid admission to see the Africans, who were now allowed visitors, outdoor exercise, English lessons, and religious instruction.

The case also excited international interest, and the cause of the abolitionists was substantially aided when Dr. Richard Robert Madden, a British official living in Havana, traveled more than one thousand miles to give a moving and informed deposition concerning the state of the slave trade in Cuba. He spelled out the means and extent of illegal activities and clarified the status of *ladinos*. He also stated that the children on board the *Amistad* were without doubt too young to be pre-1820 Cuban residents, and that he strongly believed that all the *Amistad* captives were *bozales*, newly imported Africans, not *ladinos*.

In January, 1840, Judge Andrew T. Judson of the U.S. District Court of Connecticut ruled that the Africans could not be counted as property in the calculation of salvage value, nor could they legally be held as slaves, because their initial purchase had been illegal. The government appealed the case, and a few months later, Judge Smith Thompson of the U.S. Circuit Court concurred in Judson's decision. The government again appealed, and the case came before the United States Supreme Court in early 1841. John Quincy Adams argued passionately on behalf of the defendants. On March 9, 1841, the Supreme Court also ruled that Africans brought to Cuba illegally were not property, that as illegally held free men they had a right to mutiny, and that they should therefore be released. The Africans, who by now could speak English, spent the next months continuing their religious instruction and going to exhibitions arranged by abolitionists to raise money for their return to Africa. In November, 1841, they sailed to Sierra Leone, accompanied by a small group of New England missionaries.

The *Amistad* decision was a great victory for abolitionists and raised the public's awareness of the slavery issue. The case fed secessionist sentiments in the Southern states but helped opponents of slavery focus on legal attacks against the institution.

—Grace McEntee

ADDITIONAL READING:

The "Amistad" Case: The Most Celebrated Slave Mutiny of the Nineteenth Century. New York: Johnson Reprint, 1968. Contains correspondence between the U.S. and Spanish governments concerning the *Amistad* case, as well as the "Argument of John Quincy Adams, Before the Supreme Court of the United States."

Barber, John Warner. *A History of the Amistad Captives.* New York: Arno Press, 1969. This reprint of an 1840 account of the *Amistad* case contains biographical sketches of the surviving Africans and an account of the trials. Illustrations.

Jones, Howard. *Mutiny on the "Amistad": The Saga of a Slave Revolt and Its Impact on American Abolition, Law, and Diplomacy.* New York: Oxford University Press, 1987. Provides a thorough, scholarly discussion of the incident in its contemporaneous political context. Includes brief analyses of the legal arguments.

Martin, Christopher. *The "Amistad" Affair.* New York: Abelard-Schuman, 1970. A full-length history of the case, including an introduction to the African slave trade and an epilogue that traces the case's surfacings long after 1841.

Owens, William A. *Black Mutiny: The Revolt on the Schooner "Amistad."* Philadelphia: Pilgrim Press, 1968. A dramatized but well-researched rendering of the incident. Dialogue largely taken from primary sources, but often paraphrased. Includes information on the fate of the Africans after the trial that is not found in many studies.

SEE ALSO: 1795, Pinckney's Treaty; 1807, Congress Bans Importation of African Slaves; 1859, Last Slave Ship Docks at Mobile.

1840's ■ "OLD" IMMIGRATION: *in the wake of economic and political upheaval in Europe, more than one million Germans and Irish move to the United States*

DATE: 1840's-1850's
LOCALE: Western Europe and the United States
CATEGORIES: Expansion and land acquisition; Immigration
KEY FIGURES:
John O'Mahoney (1816-1877), Irish-born immigrant who helped found the Irish Republican Brotherhood
William Henry Seward (1801-1872), governor of New York and U.S. senator, who was sympathetic to the immigrants
SUMMARY OF EVENT. The years before the Civil War, during which there was an influx of Germans and Irish into the United States, was one of the most significant periods in U.S. immigration history. Of the 31,500,000 persons counted in the 1840 census, 4,736,000 were of foreign birth. The census also showed that the greatest number of immigrants had come from two countries: 1,611,000 from Ireland and 1,301,000 from Germany (principally from the southwestern states of Würt-temberg, Baden, and Bavaria). The migration, which had gained momentum in the years following the Napoleonic Wars, reached large numbers by the 1840's and grew dramatically in the 1850's, when more than one million Germans and Irish came to the United States. The Crimean War, the Panic of 1857, and the Civil War were among the events that brought an end to this wave of immigration.

When seen in broad perspective, the migration reflected the process of economic and social change that had gathered force in the period of peace after 1815. The rapid increase in the population of Europe served to magnify the evils that the factory system had brought about by displacing old societal patterns and swelling the army of paupers. Of far greater importance at the time, however, was the disruption of life for the agricultural masses. In Ireland, population pressures had led to a continuing subdivision of land and to a structure of paying rent to absentee landowners that amounted to economic persecution. The remarkably fecund potato made this complex system possible, but events would soon uncover its tragic limitations. Dependence on the potato was not as great in southwestern Germany, but the process of subdividing the land there had grown considerably. Moreover, the encumbrance of ancient tithes and dues was compounded by a web of mortgages, as debts were incurred to improve farming practices. In both countries, tenant farmers constituted the bulk of emigrants before the 1840's. Yet their departure, inspired chiefly by the fear of losing status and not by immediate need, revealed that a long-run process of adjustment was in the making.

The potato famine precipitated this process. The blight began in 1845 and assumed devastating proportions by the following year. Untold suffering and death marked the movement of the Irish to the coast, where ship fever took its toll in 1847. Although the potato famine extended to Germany, there was less actual misery in the country. The rumor that the United States was about to close its gates, however, created a situation approaching panic among the many who were desperately seeking to emigrate before it was too late. The great exodus enabled a process of land consolidation to begin; consolidation, in turn, stimulated further emigration after the famine had passed. Repression in the wake of Europe's Revolution of 1848 also added political exiles to the tide of migration from Germany, but their numbers were small. The overwhelming mass of people were driven by economic, rather than political, forces.

Patterns of commerce that had developed between North America and Europe made cheap transportation available and helped to determine the way the newcomers settled in the United States. Irish immigrants came by two major routes. Ships carrying timber from Canada to Ireland made the return trip with cargos of emigrants, most of whom then began the trek southward to New England. Another route lay through Liverpool, where the cotton ships from Southern ports returned to Boston and New York. Once in the new land, the mostly unskilled Irish took whatever jobs were available. It was common for male immigrants to start in canal and railroad construction and then move into the mill towns to take on more permanent work in large urban areas.

Among the unique aspects of Irish immigration in the nineteenth century was that more women emigrated than men; thus, there were more Irish women than men in the United States throughout the century. Although female Irish immigrants have often been stereotyped as maids, they worked in many of the same occupations as other U.S. women in the nineteenth century and were often able to see their daughters move into higher-paying or more prestigious positions, such as that of schoolteacher.

Germans, on the other hand, were unique because of the large number of family groups that emigrated. Approximately two-thirds of the Germans who emigrated came as family groups. The first large group of German Jews came in the 1840's, as thousands fled social and economic persecution in Bavaria. The Germans, like the Irish, came by two basic routes, but greater diffusion and diversity characterized their settlement. Many chose to stay in the East, while others moved westward along the Erie Canal through Buffalo and out to Ohio. By the 1840's, a larger contingent came to New Orleans on the cotton ships from Le Havre. Some remained in the South, notably in Texas, but the majority of German immigrants moved to the valleys of the upper Ohio and Mississippi Rivers. There, as in the East, they brought a range of craft and professional skills into the urban centers. The vast number who settled on the land, meanwhile, generally preferred to buy farms already cleared by earlier settlers.

The reception of the newcomers was somewhat mixed. The abundance of space and the ideal of asylum generally tended to make the reception of immigrants favorable. Persons of influence, such as Governor William H. Seward of New York, added to this positive viewpoint by recognizing the contributions that immigrants had made to the development of the country. Opposition arose on several grounds, however. The influx of immigrants undoubtedly increased the problems of crime, poverty, unemployment, and disease, particularly in large urban areas. Bloc voting and the fear of political radicalism made many fear the newcomers. The different customs of the Irish and Germans, such as German beer gardens and Irish wakes, offended many Americans. The belief that there was a papal plot among Irish and German Catholics to subvert Protestantism and democracy provided the greatest focus to nativist sentiments. In the 1850's, a nativist movement known as the Know-Nothings attempted to harness such feelings; its timing and rapid demise reflected less a fear of foreign influences than the internal tensions engendered by the conflict of slavery and the disruption of the Whig Party. Few people in the United States called for anything more than closing the gate on any undesirable immigrants, and the lengthening of the probationary period of citizenship from five to twenty-one years.

The significance of German and Irish immigration in the two decades prior to the Civil War lies in the cultural diversity they gave to the United States and the assistance they gave to the building of their new country.

—*Major L. Wilson, updated by Judith Boyce DeMark*

ADDITIONAL READING:

Clark, Dennis. *Hibernia America: The Irish and Regional Cultures*. Contributions in Ethnic Studies 14. New York: Greenwood Press, 1986. Discusses the Irish in the United States from the colonial era through the nineteenth century, with emphasis on the push/pull factors of immigration. Comprehensive bibliography.

Diner, Hasia. *Erin's Daughters in America: Irish Immigrant Women in the Nineteenth Century*. Baltimore: The Johns Hopkins University Press, 1983. A well-balanced portrayal of Irish immigrant women, describing their lives in Ireland and their successes and failures in the United States.

Griffin, William D. *A Portrait of the Irish in America*. New York: Charles Scribner's Sons, 1981. Photographic essay of Irish immigration, with detailed captions. Includes an introductory text with many drawings and photographs from the nineteenth century.

Handlin, Oscar. *Boston's Immigrants 1790-1880: A Study in Acculturation*. Cambridge, Mass.: The Belknap Press of Harvard University Press, 1959. A classic of immigrant history, which focuses on one community that contained a large proportion of Irish emigrants.

Levine, Bruce. *The Spirit of 1848: German Immigrants, Labor Conflict, and the Coming of the Civil War*. Urbana: University of Illinois Press, 1992. Discusses the relationship of Germans in Europe and the United States. Compares the Revolutions of 1848 and the American land debates that led to war.

Rippley, LaVern J. *The German-Americans*. Boston: Twayne, 1976. Focuses on Germans in the United States in the nineteenth century. Discusses German American contributions to U.S. culture.

SEE ALSO: 1848, California Gold Rush; 1849, Chinese Immigration.

1840 ■ U.S. Election of 1840: *two truly national parties campaign using tactics that will characterize future U.S. elections*

DATE: December 2, 1840
LOCALE: United States
CATEGORY: Government and politics
KEY FIGURES:
Henry Clay (1777-1852), leading Whig politician
William Henry Harrison (1773-1841), ninth president of the United States, 1841
Andrew Jackson (1767-1845), seventh president of the United States, 1829-1837
Richard Mentor Johnson (1780-1850), vice president of the United States under Van Buren, denied the Democratic nomination in 1840

Thaddeus Stevens (1792-1868), leading anti-Freemason
politician, who supported Harrison

John Tyler (1790-1862), Whig vice presidential candidate
from Virginia who advocated states' rights

Martin Van Buren (1782-1862), eighth president of the
United States, 1837-1941

Thurlow Weed (1797-1882), head of the Whig political
machine in New York

SUMMARY OF EVENT. The presidential election campaign of
1840 marked the beginning of a new era in U.S. politics: For
the first time, two parties that were truly national in scope
competed for the presidency. In every state, politics was now
established on a two-party basis. This campaign also inaugurated the circus carnival atmosphere that was to characterize
presidential elections. It represented the culmination of the
democratic surge of the Jacksonian age. More U.S. citizens—
2.4 million—voted in 1840 than in any previous election.
They represented 78 percent of the electorate, a turnout rarely,
if ever, equaled in a presidential election. Indeed, some historians have commented on the irony of the fact that the first true
expression of the Jacksonian era's mass political parties was to
elect a Whig president.

The Whig Party, which was formed during Andrew Jackson's second administration, was an aggregation of dissimilar
groups. It included the old National Republicans, who had
always been opposed to Jackson, former Anti-Masons, and
many people who had supported Jackson in 1828 but later
turned against him because of his stand on such major issues
as nullification, federal aid to internal improvements, and the
Bank of the United States. Some Democrats became Whigs
because of Jackson's allegedly arbitrary and dictatorial conduct as president.

The Whigs had made their first try for the presidency
against Jackson's designated heir, Martin Van Buren, in 1836.
At that time, the party had no central organization and no
unifying bond except its opposition to Jackson and his party.
Accordingly, it ran three candidates—one in the Northeast,
one in the South, and one in the West—in an effort to take
enough electoral votes away from Van Buren to deny him a
majority and throw the election into the House of Representatives, where one of their men might be chosen. The plan
failed, but the Whig's Western candidate, William Henry Harrison, showed promise as a vote-getter.

For the campaign of 1840, the Whigs were determined to
present a more united front. In an effort to achieve unity
behind one man, they borrowed a technique from the enemy—the national party nominating convention. The first
Whig National Convention met in Harrisburg, Pennsylvania,
in December, 1839. There the delegates and party leaders
turned aside the claims of Henry Clay, the party's leading
figure, because he was too closely identified with the issues
and the bitter partisanship of the Jackson years. They wanted a
man who could appeal to a broad spectrum of voters and who
would alienate few persons because of his past activities.
Harrison became their man. Although he had run four years

earlier, he was not really identified with Jacksonian politics. In
addition, he was a military hero, even if of a lesser magnitude
than Jackson. As Harrison's running mate, the convention
chose John Tyler, a former Democrat from Virginia. To avoid
revealing their lack of agreement on a program, the Whigs
offered the voters no platform, saying only that they would
correct the abuses of the Van Buren Administration. The way
to win, they decided, was to wage a campaign of "passion and
prejudice" and not to concentrate on the issues.

The Democrats held their convention in Baltimore in May,
1840, and renominated Van Buren. The Democratic platform
endorsed states' rights; opposed federal aid to internal improvements, a protective tariff, and the Bank of the United
States; and asserted that the federal government had no right to
interfere with slavery in the states. They refused to renominate
Richard M. Johnson of Kentucky as their vice presidential
candidate because of his questionable personal conduct, although he, in effect, became the party's candidate.

The campaign was an exciting one. As a result of a well-
publicized remark by a Democratic reporter, for the Whigs it
became the "log cabin and hard cider" campaign. The reporter
facetiously suggested that the way to get Harrison out of the
campaign would be to "Give him a barrel of hard cider, and
settle a pension of two thousand a year on him, and . . . he will
sit the remainder of his days in his log cabin by the side of a
'sea coal' fire, and study moral philosophy." The Whigs seized
upon this slur to advertise their candidate as a simple man of
the people, in contrast to the effete, cologne-scented, cham-
pagne-drinking Van Buren. Every Whig rally held throughout
the country had as its focal point a log cabin, and hard cider
was freely dispensed.

Whig leaders cleverly adapted their campaign techniques to
the realities of an expanding suffrage. They sold souvenirs and
employed slogans, mottoes, verses, and songs. They published
many inexpensive newspapers and sent stump speakers to all
parts of the country. They had an elaborate organization that
extended from the national to the local level.

The Democrats' campaign efforts were no match for those
of the Whigs. They questioned Harrison's ability, belittled his
military record, and tried unsuccessfully to get him to commit
himself on important issues. Although his popular majority
was only 150,000 votes, Harrison won by an electoral landslide of 234 to 60 votes.

A third party, the Liberty Party, had participated in the
campaign. It was the first party with an antislavery ideology to
compete in a national election. It attracted little attention and
garnered only seven thousand votes, but its appearance
marked the beginning of the political crusade against slavery,
which was to continue under different party names until it
achieved its goal—the end of chattel slavery.

The Whigs won a hollow victory in 1840. Only one month
after his inauguration, Harrison died, and Vice President Tyler
assumed the presidency. He soon fell into bitter disagreement
with the Whig leaders in Congress, especially over the creation
of a new Bank of the United States. The congressional Whigs

read Tyler out of the party, and a new, more sectional political alignment began to form, the ultimate consequences of which were to threaten the very existence of the Union.

Most ironic, the level of voter turnout in the election exceeded that of any since the creation of the "second American party system." While the elections of the "first American party" period, wherein only propertied adult white males could vote, had very high turnouts, the Jacksonian revolution had not turned out as large a percentage of the vote in 1828, 1832, or 1836 as it did in 1840. Another irony was associated with the election: At the time the Whigs achieved their victory—one of only two in their brief history—their appeal to elite groups made them "stillborn" in the era of modern mass parties. Thus, Harrison won only by being thoroughly un-Whiggish. Finally, the creation of political parties that relied on patronage as a reward for party loyalty ensured that in the long run, the Whigs' position would triumph: Whigs favored a larger role for the federal government—something the Jacksonians supposedly opposed—but the fact that the government grew with each election, regardless of the winning party, vindicated the position of the Whigs. Gradually, the Democrats pinned their entire hopes for avoiding a controversy over slavery on the very institution, the federal government (and especially the presidency), against which they had campaigned for many years.

—*William J. Cooper, Jr., updated by Larry Schweikart*

ADDITIONAL READING:

Gunderson, Robert G. *The Log-Cabin Campaign.* Lexington: University Press of Kentucky, 1957. A traditional account of the campaign of 1840, critical of the Whigs.

McCormick, Richard P. *The Second American Party System: Party Formation in the Jacksonian Era.* Chapel Hill: University of North Carolina Press. 1966. A quantitative study of party formation, highlighted by the revelation that the real crest of Jacksonian democracy did not appear until 1840.

Marshall, Lynn. "The Strange Stillbirth of the Whig Party." *American Historical Review* 72 (January, 1967): 445-468. A classic study of party organization and the internal dynamic toward centralization of political power in the federal government as a result of the spoils system and patronage.

Niven, John. *Martin Van Buren: The Romantic Age of American Politics.* New York: Oxford University Press, 1983. A superb study of the Jacksonians' party strategist, the "Red Fox of Kinderhook."

Remini, Robert V. *The Life of Andrew Jackson.* New York: Harper & Row, 1988. A one-volume condensed version of Remini's three-volume biography, against which all others are measured. Highly sympathetic toward "Old Hickory."

Schlesinger, Arthur M., Jr. *The Age of Jackson.* Boston: Little, Brown, 1945. A Pulitzer Prize-winning book, highly sympathetic to the Jacksonians. Asserts that the era was a time when democracy foamed at its highest point, filled with the entrepreneurial aspirations of a new generation of businesspersons and the political energy of a new wave of enfranchised voters.

SEE ALSO: 1790's, First U.S. Political Parties; 1816, Second Bank of the United States Is Chartered; 1824, U.S. Election of 1824; 1832, Jackson vs. the Bank of the United States; 1834, Birth of the Whig Party.

1841 ■ UPPER AND LOWER CANADA UNITE: *for the first time, Canada exercises the powers of "responsible government"*

DATE: 1841

LOCALE: Canada

CATEGORIES: Canadian history; Government and politics

KEY FIGURES:

Robert Baldwin (1804-1858) and

Francis Hincks (1807-1885), Canadian politicians

George Durham (1792-1840), British official who wrote a crucial report on Canada

Louis Lafontaine (1807-1864), Montreal political leader

John Russell (1792-1878), British colonial secretary

Charles Poulett Thompson, Baron Sydenham (1799-1841), governor of Canada

SUMMARY OF EVENT. After the Canadian Rebellion of 1837, it was clear that some form of self-government would need to be granted to the colony. The British colonial secretary, Lord John Russell, was determined to act upon the recommendations of the 1839 report of Lord Durham, who had been commissioned by the British government to assess conditions in Canada. Russell and Durham shared a common reformist vision for the colonies. Although they certainly wanted Canada to remain under British control, as liberals they wanted Canada to emulate Great Britain and possess some form of responsible government, a term peculiarly associated with the British parliamentary system. In responsible government, ministers are entirely responsible to a parliamentary majority, which has been elected by the people. Responsible government entails the ministers of the government always being accountable to the much broader Parliament. Any time the government loses the Parliament's confidence, the Parliament is dissolved and a new government must be formed.

Russell and Durham thought that responsible government would eliminate the corruption and self-interest rampant in Canadian politics of the day. More important, they hoped it would quell the stirrings of national self-assertiveness manifested in the Rebellion of 1837. What they did not want was full independence for Canada; they wanted the responsible government in Canada to exercise control only over certain fiscal and administrative matters and leave the rest to Great Britain. To carry out this plan, Russell turned to a wealthy Manchester industrialist, Charles Poulett Thompson. Thompson was a self-made man who embodied many of the liberal virtues of individualism and self-reliance. Before embarking to Montreal in 1839, where he was to assume the position of governor of a united province of Canada, Thompson was

UNION OF UPPER AND LOWER CANADA, 1841

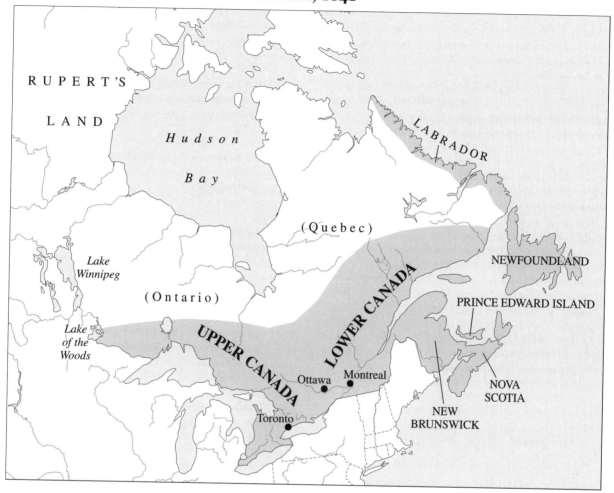

granted the title of Baron Sydenham. It is as "Sydenham" that he is usually known in Canadian historical literature. Sydenham was a talented businessman who, by temperament, was more of an administrator than a nuts-and-bolts politician. His talents were formidable, but they faced a strenuous challenge in a restive Canada.

Sydenham's principal achievement was to preside over Canada's becoming a united province. Until 1841, Canada had been divided into two provinces: Upper Canada and Lower Canada. "Upper" and "Lower" referred to the provinces' relative positions on the St. Lawrence River. Quebec was Lower Canada because it was close to the mouth of the St. Lawrence River. What eventually became known as Ontario was Upper Canada, because it was farther upstream with regard to the river's course. Sydenham's mandate was to reconfigure these two provinces into two divisions of a united province. They were renamed Canada East and Canada West and made subordinate to the provincial government in Montreal. Canada West and Canada East had equal numbers of seats in the legislature, largely so that more populous but

French-speaking Canada East did not dominate the political process. It was hoped that these steps would foster Canadian national unity. Behind this hope was the assumption that the division between English-speaking and French-speaking Canadians could be overcome. Durham's report had recommended the maintenance of the traditional British policy of allowing French Canadians to speak their own language and practice their religion as they wished. However, there was also a tacit supposition that, as Canadian national unity accelerated, the French element would slowly become subordinate to the English. Sydenham had far more contact with English-speaking Montreal merchants who dominated the business life of Quebec than with the French inhabitants of the province. He had little opportunity to hear the grievances and hopes of the latter.

Like most colonial governors coming into a country they had never visited, Sydenham's initiation into his office was rocky. In dealing with the Canadian legislature, he had to contend with a number of determined personalities representing entrenched and vested interests in the Canadas. Like

Sydenham, they were self-made merchants, but they lacked the governor's theoretical commitment to liberalism and free markets. They were mainly concerned with protecting their own stake in the Canadian economy. On the one hand, these Canadian political leaders helped to make up the body politic that Sydenham was supposed to galvanize into fully responsible government. On the other hand, they often frustrated Sydenham's agenda, which was to help unify the country. Their representation of regional interests often undermined Sydenham's policies. Louis Lafontaine was the most prominent Francophone politician of the era; he, along with his colleagues Robert Baldwin and Francis Hincks (both hailing from Ontario), consistently labored to ensure that their constituencies and their economic interests would not be subjected to Sydenham's jurisdiction and sway.

Sydenham was in an anomalous position. As governor, he theoretically was responsible both to the Colonial Office in London and to the Canadian legislature in Montreal. Thus he constantly was pulled between two inherently competing interests, and neither the basis of his authority nor any privileges or limits attached to it were ever fully or satisfactorily defined. Sydenham's government could not be fully responsible, because it was never clear precisely to what organ it was supposed to exercise its responsibility. The insufficiencies of this model were apparent even to Russell and Sydenham, but they held onto it because it was the only way they could bridge all their competing goals. They wanted simultaneously to prepare Canada for self-government and to prevent it from doing anything contrary to the wishes of Great Britain.

Another problem with the operation of Sydenham's government was the governor's own ambiguous status. As governor, he was theoretically the representative of the Crown, that is to say Queen Victoria. In the British constitutional system, the queen or king reigns but does not rule: Parliament exercises actual authority. Sydenham, as the deputy of the Crown, in theory merely should have presided over the political process and left the actual government to ministers. In practice (and in a manner certainly endorsed by Russell), Sydenham essentially acted as his own prime minister. He believed he had to do this or the competing Canadian political interests would not have permitted his program of reform to succeed. Sydenham usually managed to assemble a group in the legislature to support a particular bill he had sponsored, but each group of supporters was different. Lacking a permanent power base, Sydenham had to take whatever votes he could and hope that somehow he would continue to find a way to scrape together a coalition. Even were he able to do this as a matter of course, it would not have provided a stable or consistent form of government. Moreover, Sydenham's greatest political asset—his impartiality and his representation of the state itself and not just a particular political interest—was compromised by the petty lobbying he had to do among the legislature in order to advance his reform program.

The untenability of Sydenham's reform program was clear in the fall of 1841. Sydenham did not live to realize his failure fully: He died that autumn in a riding accident, his life ending at the relatively young age of forty-two. His successor, Sir Charles Bagot, attempted to carry on in Sydenham's stead, but the problems that had overtaken his predecessor remained. Russell's vision of a government that was responsible but not totally so was unstable and self-contradictory. It also stood against the rising currents of Canadian nationalism that were to swell in the next two decades. Sydenham's government did, however, provide the first vision of a united self-ruling Canada, and for that he is an important figure in Canadian political history.   —*Nicholas Birns*

ADDITIONAL READING:

Ajzenstat, Janet. *The Political Thought of Lord Durham.* Montreal: McGill-Queen's University Press, 1988. Explores the theoretical program for colonial government upon which Sydenham attempted to act.

Careless, J. M. S. *The Union of the Canadas.* Toronto: McClelland and Stewart, 1967. A history of the period by a famed Canadian historian. Provides a general overview of the major currents of political life.

Craig, Gerald. *Upper Canada: The Formative Years.* New York: Oxford University Press, 1963. Centers on the English-speaking population and its rising national consciousness.

Greer, Alan, and Ian Radforth. *Colonial Leviathan.* Toronto: University of Toronto Press, 1992. A systematic study of the rise of Canadian nationhood, taking a largely sociohistoric approach.

Raddall, Thomas. *The Path of Destiny.* Garden City, N.Y.: Doubleday, 1957. A popular narrative history covering the period, written by a well-known Canadian novelist.

SEE ALSO: 1837, Rebellions in Canada; 1858, Fraser River Gold Rush; 1867, British North America Act.

1841 ■ PREEMPTION ACT: *the West wins a sectional victory in the drive for free land*

DATE: September 4, 1841
LOCALE: Washington, D.C.
CATEGORIES: Expansion and land acquisition; Laws and acts
KEY FIGURES:
Thomas Hart Benton (1782-1858), Democratic senator from Missouri who led the campaign for preemption
Henry Clay (1777-1852), Whig senator from Kentucky who opposed a liberal land policy
Andrew Jackson (1767-1845), seventh president of the United States, 1829-1837
John Tyler (1790-1862), tenth president of the United States, 1841-1845
Martin Van Buren (1782-1862), eighth president of the United States, 1837-1841

SUMMARY OF EVENT. The passage of the Land Law of 1820 did not terminate the debate over public land policy in the United States. Indeed, the western portion of the United States became more insistent and demanding concerning the liberalization of land laws. With migration feeding the West with a never-ending stream of inhabitants and with numerous Western territories ready for admission to the Union as states, this section of the nation gained political power. As the West grew in influence, the Northeast and the Southeast vied with each other to gain the political support of the West.

Between 1815 and 1850, the political life of the nation became increasingly sectionalized. Each section had a position on the major issues of the day, which included land policy, tariffs, internal improvements, and fiscal policies. These issues assumed more importance as the national debt was paid off, freeing up resources for other purposes.

On most issues, the Northeast and the Southeast were on opposite sides. This allowed the West to embark on protracted negotiations designed to win support for liberalization of land policies in return for support on issues of major significance in the Northeast or Southeast. It was in this context that the West was able to push for its pet objectives, preemption and graduation. This pressure also led to the decision of the Jackson Administration to force the tribes of the Old Southwest—the Cherokees, Creeks, Chickasaws, Choctaws, and Seminoles—to move to new lands west of the Mississippi River. These lands, now the state of Oklahoma, were designated Indian Territory. The forced transfer of these, the Five Civilized Tribes, became the infamous Trail of Tears. Meanwhile, the West pressed for liberalization of the laws governing sale of the public lands.

Graduation was a device whereby the price of land would be reduced proportionate to the time that the land had been on the market unsold. At the end of a specified period of time, unsold land would be turned over to the state in which it was located. Senator Thomas Hart Benton of Missouri introduced such legislation in 1824 and again in 1830, but it was not until 1854 that the Graduation Act was passed; it contributed to the land boom of the mid-1850's.

Preemption meant recognition of the legal right of squatters on the public domain to purchase the land they occupied when it was offered for sale. As early as 1807, with the Intrusion Act, effective preemption was provided retrospectively for squatters on public land; between 1799 and 1830, a number of preemption acts had been passed, but they were all retrospective, of limited duration, and restricted to specific localities. In 1830, Congress passed the first general preemption law, the Preemption Act of 1830, permitting squatters cultivating the land in 1829 to buy up to 160 acres at the minimum price. This kind of legislation proved very difficult to administer, and there were numerous instances of fraud. Nevertheless, several hundred thousand acres of land were sold to settlers under the terms of this law.

What the West wanted, however, was permanent and prospective preemption. Henry Clay and the Whigs preferred distribution, that is, turning over the receipts from sale of the public lands to the states to finance internal improvements. After extensive and complex political maneuverings, a Distribution-Preemption Act passed Congress in September of 1841, with the proviso tacked on that if the tariff rose above 20 percent, distribution would be halted. This occurred in 1842, and distribution was halted, but preemption remained a permanent part of the public land laws of the United States.

The Preemption Act of 1841 recognized that settlement prior to purchase did not constitute trespassing, and that the use of the land for settlement was more important than for raising revenue, although the latter goal had been the original objective of selling off the public lands. Under the law, any adult citizen (or an alien who had declared his intention to become a citizen) who had occupied, cultivated, and erected a dwelling on the public lands could purchase a tract of up to 160 acres at the minimum price. Theoretically, the provision still applied only to surveyed lands; however, squatting on unsurveyed lands increased, and the original settlers, if interested, were normally allowed to benefit from the Preemption Act once the lands were surveyed.

The Preemption Act of 1841 proved to be only a waystation in the process of moving the distribution of public lands to free lands. This principle was incorporated in the Homestead Act of 1862, whose passage then became possible because the South had withdrawn from the Union and the West had the power to achieve its ultimate end, free land for settlers.

—*John G. Clark, updated by Nancy M. Gordon*

ADDITIONAL READING:

Carstensen, Vernon, ed. *The Public Lands: Studies in the History of the Public Domain.* Madison: University of Wisconsin Press, 1968. Contains twenty-three excellent articles on the history of the public lands.

Feller, Daniel. *The Public Lands in Jacksonian Politics.* Madison: University of Wisconsin Press, 1984. A detailed and enlightening examination of the politics of legislating on the public lands.

Gates, Paul W. *History of Public Land Law Development.* Washington, D.C.: Zenger, 1968. Written for the Public Land Law Review Commission, this is the most exhaustive treatment of public land law available.

North, Douglas C., and Andrew B. Rutten. "The Northwest Ordinance in Historical Perspective." In *Essays on the Economy of the Old Northwest,* edited by David C. Klingaman and Richard K. Vedder. Athens: Ohio University Press, 1987. Provides a quick summary of the legislative actions that make up the public land law of the United States.

Rohrbough, Malcolm J. *The Land Office Business: The Settlement and Administration of American Public Lands, 1789-1837.* New York: Oxford University Press, 1968. The inside story of what went on in the Land Offices in which the sales of the public lands were conducted.

SEE ALSO: 1820, Land Act of 1820; 1830, Trail of Tears; 1862, Homestead Act.

1842 ■ Commonwealth v. Hunt: *a legal foundation is laid for the rights of workers to organize and strike*

Date: 1842
Locale: Boston, Massachusetts
Categories: Business and labor; Court cases
Key figures:

Jeremiah Horne, bootmaker who refused to abide by the rules of the Bootmakers' Society

Samuel D. Parker, district attorney and prosecutor in the case of *Commonwealth v. Hunt*

Robert Rantoul, Jr. (1805-1852), counsel for the Boston Journeymen Bootmakers' Society

Lemuel Shaw (1781-1861), chief justice of the Massachusetts Supreme Judicial Court

Peter O. Thatcher, judge of the Boston Municipal Court

Isaac Wait, operator of a shoe manufacturing establishment

Summary of event. Although its impact was not felt for almost three-quarters of a century, the case of *Commonwealth v. Hunt*, decided by the Supreme Judicial Court of Massachusetts in 1842, was a major event in the evolution of the legal status of organized labor. The case dealt with one of the more difficult problems encountered in Anglo-American law: the definition and treatment of combinations of employers or employees (or both) engaged in the restraint of trade.

Analysis of American labor in the nineteenth century had been complicated by the questions of whether the trade union itself was unlawful as an organization or, instead, had become unlawful through the way it was utilized to achieve demands. Answers to those queries were required before any law applying to organized labor could be stated with any degree of certainty. They were provided, for the most part, by the decision of *Commonwealth v. Hunt*, which helped to fix principles by which the rights of labor might be definitely ascertained.

Beginning with the Philadelphia Shoemakers' case in 1806, courts in the United States had followed the lead of English courts and the common-law doctrine of criminal conspiracy by punishing persons seeking to form labor organizations. Precedence for that American decision had been provided by the 1721 English case of *Rex v. Journeyman Tailors of Cambridge*, in which a labor union seeking higher wages for its members was regarded as a criminal conspiracy. In 1800, Parliament assigned criminal penalties for workers entering "any combination to obtain an advance of wages or to lessen or alter the hours of work." This British doctrine was in accord with the generally accepted opinion that the demands of labor organizations would upset the economic laws of supply and demand, artificially increase the price of goods and services, and interfere with the freedom to contract. Ultimately, it was believed, the organization of labor would upset the natural relationship between population and food supply.

Commonwealth v. Hunt tested those concerns in the United States. The case stemmed from the activities and policies of the Boston Journeymen Bootmakers' Society. In 1841, this society sought to establish a "closed shop," a plan whereby employers would hire only those workers who were approved by the society's union and who would agree to follow a strict set of labor rules. Society member Jeremiah Horne violated one of those rules when he agreed to take on extra work without receiving extra pay. The union immediately organized a work stoppage, to continue until Horne either paid a stiff fine for violating union rules or was fired by his employer. Reluctant to lose his employee, Isaac Wait offered to pay the fine for Horne to help him comply. Horne, however, refused to allow payment of the fine; Wait, therefore, was forced to fire him.

Horne later took up the matter with the state prosecutor, district attorney Samuel D. Parker, who presented the case to a grand jury. Parker secured an indictment against the shoemakers' union; the indictment charged that the union had criminally conspired to control Wait's employment practices and had made efforts to bring economic ruin upon Horne, Wait, and other union members. In short, Parker accused the union of attempting to create a closed shop.

The trial was heard in Boston Municipal Court before Judge Peter O. Thatcher. Thatcher ran his courtroom under the assumption that the future welfare of the state and the nation depended upon the jury's assistance in preventing labor unions from gaining recognition in society. Defense counsel Robert Rantoul, Jr., argued that labor organizations were analogous to professional organizations and that the common-law doctrine of criminal conspiracy should be rejected as hostile to American freedom. Thatcher rejected these arguments and suggested to the jury that, as a matter of law, the Boston Journeymen Bootmakers' Society (and, by implication, other labor unions) constituted an unlawful conspiracy. The jury returned a guilty verdict.

When the case was appealed to the Judicial Court, Rantoul's main argument was that the common-law doctrine of criminal conspiracy was not a part of the law of Massachusetts. Once again, Rantoul's line of reasoning was not accepted; however, Chief Justice Lemuel Shaw did provide a legal reinterpretation of the law, providing a foundation upon which to overturn the society's conviction. A conspiracy, said Shaw, must be a combination (of employers and/or employees) united for an unlawful purpose or a combination united to accomplish an innocent purpose by unlawful means. By that standard, Shaw went on to find that a combination united for the purpose of inducing fellow workers to join a given organization and to follow its rules was not unlawful. It was an unwarranted assumption, he reasoned, to conclude that the society would have abused its power. Had it done so, it would have been answerable to the criminal law; but it was not unlawful for workers to have organized, even for the purpose of forming a closed shop to demand higher wages. Moreover, in refusing to work so long as Horne was not discharged, the journeymen had merely been exercising their lawful right to work or not to work. Shaw decided that it was lawful, however, to demand that the individual worker in question be fired, since the union had not relied on force or fraud to expel him, nor had it insisted that his employer violate the provisions of a contract. Finally, Shaw rejected the prosecution's argument that the union was conspiring to impoverish Horne, Wait, and others. He justified his rejection by pointing out that the even-handed, mechanical enforcement of the rule against combinations united to impoverish third parties by indirect means would result in an excessive stifling of open competition, the basic premise of a capitalist society.

Thus, the rule of *Commonwealth v. Hunt* may be stated as follows: While the common law of conspiracy is a part of the Massachusetts common law, the mere formation and operation of a labor organization in the interest of its members does not constitute a criminal conspiracy.

The impact of the decision in *Commonwealth v. Hunt* as legal precedent was sufficiently great, according to some labor historians, to deter the use of the doctrine of criminal conspiracy against unions for some forty years after its implementation. Yet, when the courts revived the doctrine during the 1880's, its effectiveness was soon eclipsed by the more versatile method of securing injunctions against labor organizing activity. The injunction clause, and not the criminal conspiracy doctrine, was used in connection with the Sherman Antitrust Act of 1890 to force the breakup of monopolistic combinations engaged in the restraint of free enterprise. *Commonwealth v. Hunt*, however, remained a piece of pro-labor legislation worthy of veneration by those well disposed to the cause of the worker. Justice Oliver Wendell Holmes, Jr., while serving on the Supreme Judicial Court of Massachusetts, spoke highly of Shaw's reasoning in the influential dissent in *Vegelahn v. Guntner* (1896). *Commonwealth v. Hunt* thus ultimately earned high recognition by becoming associated with Holmes and the cause of labor reform.

—*James J. Bolner, updated by Thomas J. Edward Walker and Cynthia Gwynne Yaudes*

ADDITIONAL READING:

Green, James, and Hugh Carter Donahue. *Boston's Workers: A Labor History.* Boston: Trustees of the Boston Public Library, 1979. A community history that analyzes the significant contributions of Boston's working classes, describing the independent initiatives of community labor organizers. Index, bibliography.

Gregory, Charles O. *Labor and the Law.* New York: W. W. Norton, 1949. Provides a concise summary of *Commonwealth v. Hunt* and its significance for the history of labor law. Index.

Levy, Leonard W. *The Law of the Commonwealth and Chief Justice Shaw: The Evolution of American Law, 1830 to 1860.* Cambridge, Mass.: Harvard University Press, 1957. A "judicial biography" that discusses Shaw's contributions to the law of criminal conspiracy; contains some thought-provoking chapters on Shaw's concept of objectivity. Index, bibliography.

Mason, Alpheus T. *Organized Labor and the Law.* Durham, N.C.: Duke University Press, 1925. Presents the fundamental legal doctrines that have guided the courts of the United States in defining and setting limits upon the rights of organized labor. Index, bibliographical essay.

Tomlins, Christopher L. *The State and the Unions: Labor Relations, Law, and the Organized Labor Movement in America, 1880-1960.* New York: Cambridge University Press, 1985. An institutional history of both unions and the legal regulation of labor organization and activity. Discusses the impact of *Commonwealth v. Hunt* on "modern" labor legislation. Index, bibliography.

SEE ALSO: 1886, American Federation of Labor Is Founded; 1894, Pullman Strike; 1905, Industrial Workers of the World Is Founded; 1911, Triangle Shirtwaist Company Fire; 1935, National Labor Relations Act; 1935, Congress of Industrial Organizations Is Founded; 1955, AFL and CIO Merge.

1842 ■ FRÉMONT'S EXPEDITIONS:
explorations of the West provide the main source of information for settlers from the East

DATE: May, 1842-1854
LOCALE: Trans-Mississippi West
CATEGORIES: Expansion and land acquisition; Exploration and discovery
KEY FIGURES:

John James Abert (1788-1863), chief of the Bureau of Topographical Engineers, Frémont's commanding officer

Christopher "Kit" Carson (1809-1868), Frémont's guide on his Rocky Mountain expeditions

Thomas "Broken Hand" Fitzpatrick (1799-1854), guide on Frémont's second expedition

John Charles Frémont (1813-1890), American explorer and army officer, nicknamed "The Pathfinder"

Alexander "Alexis" Godey (1818-1889), hunter and scout on Frémont's second, third, and possibly fourth expeditions

Lucien Bonaparte Maxwell (1818-1875), friend of Kit Carson who accompanied Frémont on three western expeditions.

Charles Preuss (1803-1854), German scientist and cartographer who accompanied Frémont's first, second, and fourth western expeditions

Joseph R. Walker (1798-1876), guide on Frémont's third expedition

SUMMARY OF EVENT. John Charles Frémont, an officer in the U.S. Army Topographical Engineers and Missouri senator Thomas Hart Benton's son-in-law, led five expeditions into the West between 1842 and 1854. His first began in St. Louis in May, 1842, with Charles Preuss as cartographer and Lucien Bonaparte Maxwell as hunter. On the way up the Missouri River to Chouteau's Landing (now Kansas City), Frémont met Kit Carson, who was to guide him west. Following the Santa Fe Trail to near modern Topeka, Kansas, the expedition then turned northwest to the Platte River near the Grand Island. Moving west along the Oregon Trail to the mouth of the South Platte River (North Platte, Nebraska), Frémont, accompanied

Nicknamed "The Pathfinder," John C. Frémont led five expeditions into the West between 1842 and 1854. His maps and route descriptions formed one of the principal guides to U.S. western migration, and his status as a public hero stimulated western development. (Library of Congress)

by a few companions, followed the South Platte River to Fort St. Vrain (near Greeley, Colorado). He then proceeded north to Fort Laramie, rejoined the main party, and took the Oregon Trail to South Pass. The expedition then traveled north to just beyond modern Pinedale, Wyoming. Here, Frémont climbed what he thought was the highest peak in the Rocky Mountains and dramatically displayed a U.S. flag with a superimposed eagle and arrows. Frémont probably climbed Woodrow Wilson Peak, south of Gannet Peak, which is the highest peak in the Wind River Mountains but not the highest peak in the Rocky Mountains. Frémont then retraced his steps to modern Grand Island, Nebraska, continuing to St. Louis via the Platte and Mississippi Rivers.

Frémont's commanding officer, Colonel John James Abert, then directed him to survey the gap between his 1842 mapping and Commodore Charles Wilkes's 1841 Pacific coast survey. Frémont left St. Louis on May 29, 1843, with Preuss, Maxwell, and Thomas "Broken Hand" Fitzpatrick. In an evasion of orders, they took a twelve-pound mountain howitzer from the St. Louis arsenal. Frémont followed his 1842 route to near modern Topeka, Kansas, but followed the Kansas River westward to the junction of the Republican and Smoky Hill branches (Junction City, Kansas). Frémont thereafter paralleled Republican River to near modern Atwood, Kansas, diverting Fitzpatrick north to the Platte River with the bulk of the party along the way. Leaving the Republican River, he turned northwesterly to the South Platte River, following it to Fort St. Vrain. There he met Alexander Godey and Carson, who had journeyed north from Taos.

Frémont then explored the area between Fort St. Vrain and the Arkansas River. After returning to Fort St. Vrain to meet the main party, Frémont crossed the mountains by way of the Cache de la Poudre River. Fitzpatrick and most of the party went north to Fort Laramie with instructions to rejoin Frémont at Fort Hall (near Fort Hall, Idaho). Frémont intersected the Oregon Trail at a point about twenty miles above the Devils Gate, now submerged by the Pathfinder Reservoir. Frémont then followed the Oregon Trail into the mountains of western Wyoming. At Beer Springs (Soda Springs, Idaho) on the Bear River, he sent Carson north to Fort Hall for supplies, while he traveled south to the Great Salt Lake. Rejoining Fitzpatrick at Fort Hall, he sent some men back to Missouri. Frémont then took the Oregon Trail to the Walla Walla mission, continuing down the Columbia River to The Dalles. Here Frémont left most of his party under Carson, while he traveled by canoe to Fort Vancouver to confer with Hudson Bay Company officials and obtain supplies.

Instead of retracing his route homeward, Frémont proposed to map a new course, across the Great Basin and Rocky Mountains. He hoped to determine whether Klamath Lake was the source of the Sacramento River; locate Mary's Lake somewhere between Great Salt Lake and the Sierra Nevada; and find the Buenaventura River, shown on early maps as flowing from the Rocky Mountains into San Francisco Bay. On November 25, 1843, Frémont started down the Des Chutes River,

reaching the edge of the Great Basin by January, 1884. There food was scarce, and men and animals were near exhaustion. Either because of these difficulties or by design, Frémont abandoned his proposed route, crossing the Sierra Nevada into California. Men became snowblind, native guides deserted, and two men were driven mad on the monthlong trip. The group, abandoning the howitzer, survived on horse and dog meat, eventually arriving at Sutter's Fort (near Sacramento, California).

Heading south to avoid another difficult mountain crossing, Frémont was led by an Indian through a more southerly pass, probably Oak Creek Pass, about five miles south of Tehachapi Pass. Frémont intercepted the Old Spanish Trail below Cajon Pass and followed it to Santa Clara (Utah), where Joseph Walker joined as a guide. Continuing north, they traveled along the Wasatch Mountains to the Great Salt Lake. Frémont then crossed Soldier Summit, skirted the south flank of the Uinta Mountains, and followed the Yampa River across western Colorado. Reaching the Front Range, he turned south through the Parks, intersecting the Arkansas River below the Royal Gorge. He then followed the river to Bent's Fort (between Las Animas and La Junta, Colorado). Leaving the Santa Fe Trail about twenty miles east, Frémont cut north to the Smoky Hill River and proceeded east to modern Kansas City.

In February, 1845, Frémont was ordered to mount a third expedition to the headwaters of the Arkansas and Red Rivers. Upon reaching Bent's Fort, he sent Lieutenant James W. Abert, son of Colonel John J. Abert, down the Canadian and Arkansas Rivers, guided by Fitzpatrick. Accompanied by Carson, Godey, and Walker, Frémont moved up the Arkansas River, skirted the Royal Gorge, crossed Tennessee Pass, followed the White River, crossed the Grand and Green Rivers, and went down the Duchesne and Timpanogos Rivers to the Great Salt Lake. He then crossed the Salt Lake Desert to Pilot Peak, Nevada. At modern Mound Spring, he sent the main party down the Humboldt River under Walker to the Humboldt Sink. He took a small detachment southwest across the Great Basin to Walker's Lake, where the expedition reunited. Frémont then directly crossed the Sierra Nevada to Sutter's Fort, while Walker and the main body marched south through Owen's Valley and crossed Walker Pass to join Frémont in California. There Frémont became involved in the Bear Flag Revolt and Mexican War until January, 1847, when he returned east.

In 1848, after resigning from the army, Frémont obtained private funding for a fourth expedition seeking a pass through the Rocky Mountains along the thirty-eighth parallel. This expedition became snowbound and lost eleven of thirty-three men by starvation and exposure, without finding a pass. Frémont retreated to Taos, New Mexico, reorganized, and continued to California by way of the Gila River.

Frémont's fifth expedition, privately financed, again sought the thirty-eighth parallel railroad route. Leaving Westport (Kansas City), September 20, 1853, with photographer Solomon Nunes Carvalho and topographer-artist F. W. von Egloffstein, Frémont proceeded to Bent's Fort. The men then crossed the Rocky Mountains by Cochetopa Pass, which they reached on

December 15. They crossed the Colorado Plateau to Parowan, Utah, losing one man to cold and hunger. Here Frémont left Carvalho and von Egloffstein and continued across the Great Basin and into California by the headwaters of the Kern River.

Frémont's scientific contribution was slight: Plant collections from the first two expeditions were lost, geological collections were sketchy, and he collected no zoological material. In some cases, it appears that his reports, written after his return, exaggerate and rationalize his actions. However, Frémont's maps and route descriptions became the principal guide to U.S. western migration, and he became a public hero and stimulated western development.

—Ralph L. Langenheim, Jr., based on the original entry by
W. Turrentine Jackson

ADDITIONAL READING:

Egan, Ferol. *Frémont, Explorer for a Restless Nation.* 1977. Reprint. Garden City, N.Y.: Doubleday, 1985. Contains a comprehensive annotated biography.

Frémont, John C. *Memoirs of My Life.* New York: Belford, Clarke & Company, 1887. Frémont's story as he told it.

Goetzmann, William H. *Exploration and Empire: The Explorer and the Scientist in the Winning of the American West.* New York: Alfred A. Knopf, 1966. Describes Frémont's first two western expeditions and evaluates his scientific, geographic, and political significance.

Jackson, Donald, and Mary Lee Spence, eds. *The Expeditions of John Charles Frémont.* 3 vols. Urbana: University of Illinois Press, 1970-1973. Annotated original documents, including Frémont's reports, proceedings of the court martial, and a map portfolio.

Preuss, Charles. *Exploring with Frémont.* Translated and edited by Erwin G. Gudde and Elisabeth K. Gudde. Norman: University of Oklahoma Press, 1958. Interesting perspective of a German scientist who disliked the West and his assignment, and was contemptuous of Frémont.

SEE ALSO: 1804, Lewis and Clark Expedition; 1806, Pike's Southwest Explorations; 1808, American Fur Company Is Chartered; 1810, Astorian Expeditions; 1815, Westward Migration; 1821, Santa Fe Trail Opens; 1823, Jedediah Smith Explores the Far West; 1846, Mormon Migration to Utah; 1846, Oregon Settlement; 1846, Occupation of California and the Southwest; 1848, California Gold Rush; 1853, Pacific Railroad Surveys.

1842 ■ DORR REBELLION: *a major expression of the tensions between property holders and democratic forces during the Jacksonian era*

DATE: May 18, 1842
LOCALE: Rhode Island
CATEGORIES: Business and labor; Civil rights; Wars, uprisings, and civil unrest

KEY FIGURES:

J. A. Brown, president of the Rhode Island Suffrage Association

Thomas Wilson Dorr (1805-1854), lawyer and politician who organized the People's Party

Samuel W. King (1786-1851), governor of the established government in Rhode Island

Seth Luther (1817-1846), radical labor leader identified with the movement for reform after 1840

John Tyler (1790-1862), tenth president of the United States, 1841-1845

SUMMARY OF EVENT. The Dorr Rebellion was the most dramatic effort in the United States before the Civil War to make liberal changes in suffrage and representation. The timing and nature of the drama are best explained by the unique circumstances that existed in Rhode Island. In the aftermath of the American Revolution, there were property qualifications in order to vote in all thirteen of the original colonies. Those who were not property holders of a certain degree (varying from state to state) could not vote. It was the new state of Vermont, admitted in 1791, that was the first to provide for universal male suffrage: that is, permitting all free men more than twenty-one years of age to vote regardless of their level of property ownership. In the waves of democratization that swept over the United States during the Jeffersonian and Jacksonian eras, every state except Rhode Island repealed its property qualification. In the colonial era, Rhode Island had been a hotbed of political and religious toleration, far more liberal than its immediate neighbors. Ironically, the very absence of an established church that had made Rhode Island unique in the 1600's was to impede political reform in the 1800's. Because the reform movement lacked an established church against which to struggle, reformers' efforts to rally popular sentiment to their cause necessarily were limited.

The Rhode Island constitution was based on the Royal Charter of 1663, which limited the right to vote to owners of $134 in land and to their eldest sons. Increasingly out of step with the egalitarian tendencies of the later time, this vestige of the old order became even more undemocratic as the development of industry served, by creating a large class of landless factory workers, to reduce the actual proportion of eligible voters. At the same time, the success enjoyed by conservative elements in blocking all proposals for a reapportionment of legislative seats penalized the manufacturing areas and enhanced the power of the static and declining towns. Change of some sort, however, was certain to come. The examples of reform in other states proved contagious, and the growth of support within Rhode Island cut across social, economic, sectional, and party lines. Seth Luther, a radical labor leader, lent his eloquent voice to the cause. Finally, the cumulative effects of economic depression after 1837 and the leveling spirit of the "log cabin" presidential campaign of William H. Harrison in 1840 gave new urgency and a more radical tone to the demands for change.

The Rhode Island Suffrage Association, founded in 1840,

gave voice to these demands. Professing feelings of despair over securing justice within the existing government, Thomas Wilson Dorr, Dr. J. A. Brown, and other leaders of the organization assumed the high ground of natural rights and appealed directly to the sovereign will of the people. A People's Party was formed and held a convention that wrote the People's Constitution, approved by an overwhelming majority of adult males in December, 1841. The new document provided for the more equitable reapportionment of legislative seats and removed the $134 freehold requirement for voting. This turn of events spurred the charter, or legal, government into action. Under its auspices, the Landholder's Constitution was written. On the vital matter of suffrage, this constitution retained the old property qualification only in the case of foreign-born citizens. Through the influence of the Rhode Island Suffrage Association, however, it was defeated, and the stage was set for a political crisis. Elections were held under the People's Constitution, and on May 3, 1842, "Governor" Dorr and a full slate of officers launched the new "government." The people of Rhode Island then faced the conflicting claims of two authorities.

The crisis did not last long. The new government hesitated to take possession of the state house and other facilities, and the extralegal legislature timidly adjourned after a two-day session. This adjournment enabled Governor Samuel W. King and his council of advisers under the charter government to seize the initiative. Appeals to the nativist, propertied, rural, and Protestant sentiments within the state drew support away from the Dorr regime, as did numerous arrests of Dorr's followers under the Algerine law, which prescribed unusually severe penalties for participating in the new government. Although President John Tyler turned down all requests for federal troops, the official recognition that he gave to the charter government lent to it additional strength. In the face of these moves, further efforts by Dorr proved to be unavailing. He did receive generous expressions of sympathy from key Democratic spokesmen in Washington (where he made a personal appeal) and from Tammany Hall (headquarters of the New York Democrats and of the Society of St. Tammany, an oath-bound society dedicated to championing the enfranchisement of propertyless whites), but no solid support for making good his claims on Rhode Island was forthcoming. On May 18, 1842, and again on June 27, he appeared at the head of a small military force, but each encounter with the state militia ended in a bloodless fiasco.

The sequel to the rebellion was more moderate than many had reason to expect. It is true that martial law, prolonged from the end of June until August 8, led to additional arrests and to one death in an isolated mob action. Life sentences were given to Dorr and five other leaders, but an effective check to the spirit of reaction developed as the rebellion became an issue in state politics. In 1845, Dorr and his associates were pardoned under the terms of a general amnesty act, and in 1851, their civil rights were restored.

Nor could the cause of reform totally be denied. Under the very government that had suppressed the uprising, a new constitution was adopted and put into effect in May, 1843. On balance, the new constitution represented a limited gain for political democracy. It clearly embodied the theory of government by consent, and its provisions generally made the government more relevant to modern needs. The inclusion of a bill of rights supplied another deficiency of the old charter, as did a more careful definition of the separation of powers. The reapportionment of seats for the lower house removed most inequities in the old scheme, although the provision for a maximum of twelve seats for any one town tended to favor the smaller towns over Providence. On the matter of voting rights, the constitution fell short of the ideal of universal manhood suffrage. All native-born citizens with two years of residence were allowed to vote upon the payment of a poll tax of one dollar. By contrast, the $134 property requirement was retained for foreign-born citizens; and since most of these persons were laborers in the manufacturing areas, they were effectively disenfranchised.

Rhode Island, a small state out of the main path of westward development characterizing the United States in the antebellum era, was not typical of U.S. political life in the 1840's. Its entrenched customs and the virulent willingness of its property-owning class to defend their privileges were unusual. Yet contemporary events such as the Anti-Rent War in New York State demonstrated that the social tensions exhibited in the Dorr Rebellion were hardly unique to Rhode Island. The outcome of the Dorr Rebellion was a defeat for democracy only as seen in the narrowest possible terms. In broader terms, it was a symptom of the irresistible currents of democracy that had seized the United States in the nineteenth century. Although the Dorr Rebellion did not succeed in its immediate objectives, eventually it contributed to the gradual realization of the image of the United States as the fully representative democracy promised in the Constitution. Although the Dorr Rebellion was in quest of only universal white male suffrage (most of the rebels, indeed, were quite open and adamant about this), it was, in an oblique way, a part of the struggle that was to culminate twenty years later in the Emancipation Proclamation.   —*Major L. Wilson, updated by Nicholas Birns*

ADDITIONAL READING:

Coleman, Peter J. *The Transformation of Rhode Island, 1790-1860.* Providence, R.I.: Brown University Press, 1963. Discusses social and political conditions in the Rhode Island of the era.

Dennison, George. *The Dorr War: Republicanism on Trial, 1831-1861.* Lexington: University Press of Kentucky, 1976. A narrative and analytical history.

Gettleman, Marvin. *The Dorr Rebellion: A Study in American Radicalism.* New York: Random House, 1973. The most important book to date on the Dorr Rebellion.

Williamson, Chilton. *American Suffrage: From Property to Democracy.* Princeton, N.J.: Princeton University Press, 1960. Chronicles the Dorr Rebellion as part of the expansion of the franchise before the Civil War.

Zinn, Howard. *A People's History of the United States*. New York: Harper & Row, 1980. Discusses the Dorr Rebellion as an episode in the history of U.S. working-class radicalism.

SEE ALSO: 1840, U.S. Election of 1840; 1865, Thirteenth Amendment; 1868, Fourteenth Amendment.

1842 ■ WEBSTER-ASHBURTON TREATY: *the settlement of a U.S.-Canadian boundary dispute sets a precedent for amicable relations between North American neighbors*

DATE: August 9, 1842
LOCALE: Maine-New Brunswick border
CATEGORIES: Canadian history; Diplomacy and international relations; Expansion and land acquisition; Treaties and agreements
KEY FIGURES:
Alexander Baring, Baron Ashburton (1774-1848), special envoy from Great Britain to the United States
Alexander McLeod (1796-1871), Canadian citizen arrested for murder in the *Caroline* affair
Jared Sparks (1789-1866), historian and unofficial lobbyist for Webster
John Tyler (1790-1862), tenth president of the United States, 1841-1845
Daniel Webster (1782-1852), secretary of state
SUMMARY OF EVENT. The Webster-Ashburton Treaty settled a boundary controversy that had irritated Anglo-American relations since the Treaty of Paris had been signed in 1783. This dispute in the Northeast involved sovereignty over portions of northern Maine and the Canadian province of New Brunswick. The area involved was not large, the region was remote and lightly populated, but again and again from 1783 to 1842, conflict between America and Great Britain intruded to prevent some rational settlement of the dispute.

The boundary problem was the result of ignorance about the geography of the northeastern region and of the failure of the negotiators at Paris in 1783 to attach maps to the treaty with the boundary line clearly marked upon them. The treaty language stated that the Maine-New Brunswick boundary was to be the St. Croix River from Passamaquoddy Bay to its source, and then "a line drawn due north, from the source of the St. Croix River, to the Highlands which divide those rivers which empty into the River St. Lawrence from those which fall into the Atlantic Ocean." Unfortunately, British-American surveyors could not agree on which of two streams emptying into Passamaquoddy Bay was the St. Croix River; nor were the highlands described in the treaty identified to the satisfaction of both sides. As a result, until the boundary was definitely fixed, the inhabitants of an area of approximately 7.7 million acres did not know whether they owed allegiance to Canada or to the United States.

Numerous efforts were made to settle the conflict. One provision of Jay's Treaty in 1794 was for a mixed commission to identify the "real" St. Croix River and chart its course. Its findings, which offered a compromise solution to the dispute, were made part of a general convention signed in 1803. Congress refused, however, to consent to this agreement, largely because of the article dealing with the Northwest boundary question involving Oregon. Nothing further was attempted until the negotiations at Ghent in 1814 called to end the War of 1812. There, the British tried hard to win a favorable Canadian boundary settlement because, during the war, they had become aware of the importance of the area for the construction of a projected military highway from Montreal and Quebec to the Maritime Provinces. The United States refused to accede to British demands, and the peace treaty merely created four commissions to mark the entire boundary from the Atlantic to the Lake of the Woods, west of Lake Superior. With regard to the Northeast, the treaty provided that, should the commission fail to agree, the question would be given over to arbitration by a third state.

When the joint commission failed to reach agreement, the king of the Netherlands was asked to arbitrate the matter in 1827. The royal arbitrator proposed to divide the disputed territory almost equally between the two parties. Great Britain was willing to accept this compromise, as was President Andrew Jackson, but the states of Maine and Massachusetts opposed a solution that gave away a large piece of Maine's territory. Jackson submitted the issue to the Senate, which rejected the solution that had been proposed by the king of the Netherlands. Political pressures and concern for national prestige prevented the issue from being resolved for another decade.

The 1830's witnessed numerous incidents related to the boundary issue, which further heightened the tension between the United States and Great Britain. The Canadian insurrection of 1837 elicited great sympathy from Americans along the frontier, and the *Caroline* affair (in which a U.S. citizen, Amos Durfee, was killed on U.S. soil by Canadians assisting British authorities) inflamed opinion against Great Britain throughout the United States. The arrest and trial in 1840 of Alexander McLeod, a Canadian deputy sheriff, for the murder of Durfee, which most historians believe he did not commit, brought anti-British sentiment to a peak and stood in the way of any compromise on the boundary issue. Great Britain threatened war if McLeod was convicted. McLeod was acquitted and the threat passed, but the incident underscored the danger of letting the tension between Great Britain and the United States over Canadian border issues continue to simmer.

More directly related was the so-called Aroostook War—a threatened conflict between Maine and New Brunswick forces in 1839. The fertile Aroostook Valley was, in this period, the scene of incidents of claim-jumping and furious competition for timber and land, and there was increasing violence. The danger of an armed clash was averted through a truce arranged by General Winfield Scott, but the basic problems remained to imperil the peace.

WEBSTER-ASHBURTON TREATY, 1842

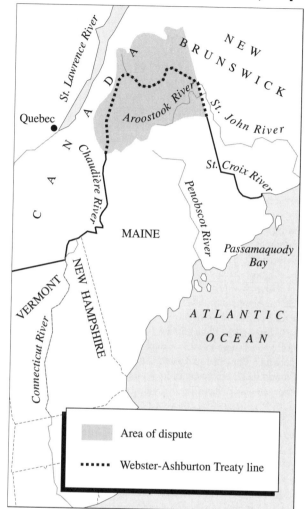

Area of dispute

•••••• Webster-Ashburton Treaty line

The conflict was finally resolved in 1841, soon after Daniel Webster became secretary of state and Baron Ashburton (Alexander Baring), who had married a Philadelphia heiress and had extensive financial interests in the United States, was appointed special envoy for Great Britain with powers to resolve the boundary controversy. Ashburton's appointment signified the new priority placed by the British on Canadian issues. In the aftermath of Lord George Durham's report, which had called attention to Great Britain's previous neglect of the Canadian situation, the British government now was determined to take Canadian matters in hand. Ashburton was instructed to negotiate amicably with the United States and to settle the border issue once and for all. Even before Ashburton's arrival, Webster had announced that the United States would consider a compromise boundary in the Northeast. Webster, as pro-British as any U.S. politician of his era, was convinced that the dispute must be settled. To do so, however, the McLeod case would have to be resolved and the state of

Maine would have to be persuaded to accept a surrender of territory claimed as its own. McLeod was acquitted by a New York jury, but direct intervention by Webster was required to accomplish the second aim.

The negotiation of the Canadian border treaty was a high personal priority for Webster. He saw it as the capstone of his tenure as secretary of state and prolonged his tenure in that office just to negotiate the treaty. William Henry Harrison, the Whig president who had appointed Webster to the State Department, had died in 1841 after only a month in office, leaving the presidency to his vice president, John Tyler, who was a Democrat by party. Most of Harrison's cabinet were Whigs, and most resigned when Tyler showed he had no intention of following Whig policies. Webster, although also a Whig, stayed on because he saw the negotiation of the treaty with Great Britain as a crucial and fundamental diplomatic achievement.

Webster and Ashburton began informal conversations in the autumn of 1841 and made rapid progress. They agreed to "split the difference" over the territory in dispute between Maine and New Brunswick; the United States won the line north of latitude 45° north as the boundary of New York and Vermont; minor adjustments were made in the region of Lake of the Woods in Minnesota and articles dealing with extradition, suppression of the international slave trade, and the *Caroline* affair were drafted.

The objections of Maine and Massachusetts to a compromise settlement, which were overcome only after strenuous efforts, culminated in the payment of $150,000 to each of the two states by the federal government. Jared Sparks, a noted historian, lobbied for the treaty in the Maine legislature, for which he was paid $14,500 by Ashburton. The treaty was signed on August 9, 1842, and was approved by the Senate less than two weeks later.

The Webster-Ashburton Treaty was an important achievement. It removed a source of potential conflict and brought about immediate improvement in Anglo-American relations. Historians agree that settlement of the Oregon controversy would have been exceedingly difficult without use of the Webster-Ashburton Treaty as a precedent. Nevertheless, the negotiations, or more precisely Webster's role in them, are accounted by some as a failure in United States diplomacy. By the treaty's terms, the United States conceded approximately five thousand of the twelve thousand square miles of disputed territory to Great Britain. There now exists strong evidence (much of which was available to Secretary of State Webster, had he wished to uncover it) to support the validity of the original U.S. claims. On the other hand, concessions made by Ashburton in the Lake of the Woods region gave the United States clear title to sixty-five hundred square miles of territory that later revealed valuable deposits of iron ore.

The United States had fought two previous wars against British troops based in Canada. The Webster-Ashburton Treaty did much to ensure that such a circumstance would never happen again. Although Webster was accused of sacrificing more territory to the British than necessary, his flexibility no doubt contributed to British willingness to let the United States have the richest portions of the Oregon Territory only a few years later. Webster and Ashburton did much to guarantee the unprecedented amity and peace that prevailed on the United States-Canadian border in the centuries after their agreement.

—*Theodore A. Wilson, updated by Nicholas Birns*

ADDITIONAL READING:

Bourne, Kenneth. *Britain and the Balance of Power in North America, 1815-1908*. Berkeley: University of California Press, 1967. Adds a valuable perspective, but misleadingly implies that all the diplomatic cards were in Great Britain's hands.

Jones, Howard. *To the Webster-Ashburton Treaty: A Study in Anglo-American Relations, 1783-1843*. Chapel Hill: University of North Carolina Press, 1977. Argues that the treaty ended the animosity between the United States and Great Britain.

Peterson, Merrill D. *The Great Triumvirate: Webster, Clay, and Calhoun*. New York: Oxford University Press, 1987. Sheds light on Webster's motives during the negotiations.

Raddall, Thomas. *The Path of Destiny*. Garden City, N.Y.: Doubleday, 1957. A popular narrative history covering this period in Canadian history.

Stevens, Kenneth R. *Border Diplomacy: The Caroline and McLeod Affairs in Anglo-American-Canadian Relations, 1837-1842*. Tuscaloosa: University of Alabama Press, 1989. The most important book to date on the treaty and its diplomatic background. Gives an account of each side's perspectives during the negotiations.

SEE ALSO: 1783, Treaty of Paris; 1794, Jay's Treaty; 1815, Treaty of Ghent; 1837, Rebellions in Canada; 1841, Upper and Lower Canada Unite; 1846, Oregon Settlement.

1844 ■ ANTI-IRISH RIOTS: *in a period of rising immigration and intercultural friction, nativists riot against Irish-Catholic workers*

DATE: May 6-July 5, 1844
LOCALE: Philadelphia
CATEGORIES: Immigration; Religion; Wars, uprisings, and civil unrest
KEY FIGURES:
George Cadwalader (1803-1879), militia commander
Hugh Clark, political leader of Irish weavers
Francis Kenrick (1796-1863), Catholic bishop of Philadelphia
Samuel Kramer, editor of the *Native American*
Lewis Levin (1808-1860), leader of the American Republican Party
Morton McMichael (1807-1879), Philadelphia police chief

SUMMARY OF EVENT. Rapid population growth, industrialization, and cultural conflict characterized urban America in the 1840's and helped produce bloody anti-Irish riots in Philadelphia's industrial suburbs of Kensington and Southwark in the summer of 1844. Already the second largest U.S. city in 1840, Philadelphia's population grew by more than one-third in the 1840's, from twenty-five thousand people to thirty-six thousand. Irish immigrants, hard-pressed by the Great Famine that had decimated the potato crops in their homeland, stimulated this growth, and made up 10 percent of Philadelphia's population in 1844. Prior to commuter railroads and automobiles, most people lived near their workplace, and cities were densely populated. Low-income newcomers such as the Irish resided in cheap, substandard housing and symbolized the ill effects of disorderly urban growth to longtime Philadelphians.

Lacking in job skills and capital, Irish immigrants filled the bottom rungs in the emerging industrial order's occupational ladder. As its population grew, Philadelphia expanded its involvement in large-scale manufacturing. By 1840, half of Philadelphia's sixteen thousand working adults labored in manufacturing, and 89 percent of the workers in Kensington toiled in industrial trades. American-born whites predominated in such well-paying craft occupations as ship carpenter and ironmaker, leaving low-paying jobs requiring less skill, such as weaving, for Irish newcomers. Perceiving immigrants and African Americans as competitors, many white American workers used violence to drive them from trades and neighborhoods.

In the 1830's, Philadelphia, like other major cities, hosted a strong working-class trade union and political movement. At its height, the General Trades Union of Philadelphia City and County (GTU) included more than ten thousand workers representing more than fifty different trades. Collective action in an 1835 general strike for a ten-hour day succeeded in winning shorter hours and wage hikes in numerous workplaces. GTU activists voted against conservative Whigs opposed to strikes and Catholic immigrants. The Panic of 1837 weakened the GTU and undermined the solidarity of its culturally and occupationally diverse constituency.

In the 1840's, native-born Protestant skilled workers fought for a dwindling supply of jobs and received little help from the financially weakened GTU. Evangelical Protestants from all social classes joined moral reform campaigns for temperance and strict observance of the Sabbath. Temperance and Sabbatarianism symbolized American-born white workers' efforts to survive hard times through personal discipline. Workers made up the majority of temperance societies in industrial suburbs such as Kensington and Southwark. Moral reforms often attacked immigrant cultural institutions, such as the Roman Catholic church and Sunday tavern visits. Economic contraction and moral reform eroded the GTU's bonds of working-class solidarity, which might have prevented ethnic conflict in 1844.

The American Republican Party, dedicated to eliminating the influence of Catholic immigrants in public life, best exploited the anxieties of native-born workers. The party flourished briefly in eastern cities in the mid-1840's, drawing support from American-born workers and middle-class professionals such as Philadelphia's Lewis Levin, a struggling lawyer and aspiring politician from South Carolina. In the spring of 1844, American Republicans campaigned against Catholic voters' attempts to protect their children from Protestant religious instruction in the public schools. Protestant-dominated Philadelphia schools used the King James version of the Bible as a classroom textbook. Objecting that the King James version was not authoritative, Catholics preferred the Douay Bible, which included annotations written by the Vatican. Philadelphia's Catholic bishop, Francis Kenrick, wanted public schools to allow Catholic students to bring their Bibles to class or be exempted from Protestant religious instruction. American Republicans accused Philadelphia Catholics of plotting to remove the Bible from the schools entirely and to have priests take over classrooms.

In April, 1844, American Republicans staged rallies across the city to whip up support for their nativist program. Violence between the Irish and nativists broke out when nativists gathered near Irish neighborhoods. American Republicans scheduled a mass meeting for May 6 in Kensington's third ward, a neighborhood composed mainly of Irish weavers. On May 6, rain drove hundreds of nativists who traveled to the third ward rally to seek cover at the Nanny Goat Market, a covered lot of market stalls. Approximately thirty Irish waited at the market, and one yelled, "Keep the damned natives out of the market house; it don't belong to them. This ground is ours!" Samuel Kramer, editor of the pro-American Republican *Native American* newspaper (named for Anglo-American nativists, not American Indians), tried to finish his speech against the Catholic proposals for the Douay Bible, but Irish hecklers drowned him out. A shoving match escalated into fistfights and gunfire as nativists and Irish battled for control of the market house. Police arrived at dusk and temporarily restored order. Four men died, three of them nativists, and many more were wounded in the fighting.

The next day, nativists massed in Kensington for revenge. The *Native American* ran the headline: "Let Every Man Come Prepared to Defend Himself!" A parade of nativists marched through Kensington under a U.S. flag and a banner declaring, "This is the flag that was trampled underfoot by Irish Papists." Nativist mobs rampaged through Kensington for two more days, burning homes and invading two Catholic churches, where rioters defaced religious objects and looted valuables. Although Sheriff Morton McMichael tried to calm public disorder, police were too few in number to stop the violence. Needing reinforcements, McMichael called on General George Cadwalader, commander of the First Brigade of Pennsylvania state militia, stationed in Philadelphia. On May 10, state troops brought peace to the city and kept it under martial law for a week.

Tension prevailed in June, amid criticism of city officials and militia commanders for failing to prevent violence. American Republicans still had public support, and Catholics worried about more violence. Catholics feared that nativists would use July 4 patriotic celebrations as a pretext to riot. Parishioners at St. Philip's Church in Southwark, just south of Philadelphia, hoarded weapons inside the church in order to defend it. Hearing of the arms cache, on July 5, Levin led thousands of nativists, including volunteer militia with cannons, to St. Philip's to demand the weapons. Stung by earlier criticism, Cadwalader's militia promptly seized the church and ordered nativists away. When the mob refused to move, Cadwalader opened fire and a pitched battle involving cannon and rifle fire ensued for a day and a half. The militia, helped by city police, prevailed in fighting that left two rioters dead and dozens of state troops and civilians wounded.

The American Republican Party campaigned on the riots by attacking reigning politicians as the allies of Irish Catholics and making martyrs of the nativists killed in the riots. In October, Levin and another American Republican won election to the U.S. House of Representatives, and nativists captured several county offices, mostly on the strength of votes from working-class Kensington and Southwark. The American Republicans faded in the late 1840's, but nativists returned in the 1850's under the aegis of the American, or Know-Nothing, Party.

The riots forced Irish Philadelphians to band together as an ethnic group. The most prominent Irish opponent of the mobs was Hugh Clark, a master weaver and ward politician worth more than thirty thousand dollars in 1850. Clark had stridently opposed striking Irish journeymen weavers prior to 1844. Master weavers, some of them Irishmen like Clark, cut journeymen's wages in the wake of the Kensington riot, confident that few non-Irish workers would protest the cuts. Bishop Kenrick urged conciliation and softened his public position on the Bible controversy. American Republican anger at police and militia actions temporarily stalled police reform, but in the 1850's, Philadelphia and other cities established professional police departments to prevent more riots like those of 1844.

—*Frank Towers*

ADDITIONAL READING:

Davis, Susan G. *Parades and Power: Street Theatre in Nineteenth-Century Philadelphia*. Philadelphia: Temple University Press, 1986. Examines public celebrations that frequently turned violent, such as the parade that became a riot in Kensington.

Feldberg, Michael. *The Philadelphia Riots of 1844: A Study of Ethnic Conflict*. Westport, Conn.: Greenwood Press, 1975. The most comprehensive account of the riots.

Knobel, Dale T. *Paddy and the Republic: Ethnicity and Nationality in Antebellum America*. Middletown, Conn.: Wesleyan University Press, 1986. A study of nativistic stereotypes of the Irish that fed the riot.

Lannie, Vincent P., and Bernard C. Diethorn. "For the Honor and Glory of God: The Philadelphia Bible Riots of 1844." *History of Education Quarterly* 8, no. 1 (Spring, 1968): 44-106. Examines the Bible controversy in Philadelphia schools.

Laurie, Bruce. *Working People of Philadelphia, 1800-1850*. Philadelphia: Temple University Press, 1980. Provides background on workers and unions.

Montgomery, David. "The Shuttle and the Cross: Weavers and Artisans in the Kensington Riots of 1844." *Journal of*

Social History 5, no. 4 (Summer, 1972): 411-446. Analyzes the conflict in terms of social class.

Warner, Sam Bass, Jr. *The Private City: Philadelphia in Three Periods of Its Growth.* Philadelphia: University of Pennsylvania Press, 1968. Analyzes the riots in the context of other disturbances and police reform.

SEE ALSO: 1840's, "Old" Immigration.

1844 ■ FIRST TELEGRAPH MESSAGE: *a breakthrough in long-distance communication begins to bind an expanding nation*

DATE: May 24, 1844
LOCALE: New York City
CATEGORIES: Communications; Science and technology
KEY FIGURES:

Leonard D. Gale (1800-1883), Samuel Morse's colleague at New York University, who suggested improvements to the telegraph

Joseph Henry (1797-1878), physician and scientist who claimed to have suggested the principle of the telegraph

Samuel Finley Breese Morse (1791-1872), painter and inventor credited with perfecting the electric telegraph and the Morse code

Francis O. J. "Fog" Smith (1806-1877), congressman from Maine

Alfred Vail (1807-1859), U.S. inventor who improved Morse's instrument

SUMMARY OF EVENT. The invention of the electric telegraph was undoubtedly one of the most significant events in U.S. history, profound in its impact on not only communications but also other aspects of life. It is ironic that this tremendous development was given a major boost by a man who was trained in the art of communication, but communication of an entirely different nature. Samuel F. B. Morse was at the time a highly regarded artist. The improbable details of Morse's career and the origins of the telegraph are the sort from which folktales and legends are born.

Experiments with the magnetic telegraph go back to the eighteenth century in both Europe and the United States, paralleling the discovery and development of electricity. The first major breakthroughs were made by two Englishmen, William F. Cooke and Charles Wheatstone, and one American, Joseph Henry. Wheatstone and Cooke patented a telegraph that worked by electromagnetism in 1837, and their system was dominant in Great Britain until 1870. Henry developed an improved electromagnet and in 1831 devised an apparatus that rang a bell attached to the end of a mile of wire. Samuel Morse was ostensibly unaware of these earlier discoveries at the time he developed his version of the telegraph.

Morse, son of a prominent Massachusetts clergyman, Jedidiah Morse, was graduated from Yale University in 1810 and spent the next several years in England studying art. Although he failed to gain economic security, he became an artistically successful portraitist after his return to the United States in 1815. Morse returned to Europe and travel between 1829 and 1832. Shortly before coming back to America, the direction of his life began to change.

On the eve of his return, Morse saw the Paris semaphore system and was intrigued by its inefficiency and slowness. The possibilities of transmitting messages by electricity began to interest him. He brought a limited amount of earlier experience to this interest. At Yale, he had attended lectures and demonstrations on electricity by Benjamin Silliman and Jeremiah Day, and he had taken courses in electricity given by James Freeman Dana at the New York Athenaeum. However, Morse was ignorant of Joseph Henry's discoveries in electromagnetism and of the various European experiments with electromagnetic needle telegraphs.

During his sea voyage back to the United States in October, 1832, Morse was enthralled by conversations with Dr. Charles Thomas Jackson concerning the electromagnet and other discoveries in electricity. Morse is reported to have commented, "If the presence of electricity can be made visible in any part of the circuit, I see no reason why intelligence may not be transmitted instantaneously by electricity." Morse now supposedly became obsessed with the problem of turning this vision into reality. Financial and artistic disappointments forced Morse to abandon his artistic career and to accept a position as professor of arts and design at the University of the City of New York (later, New York University). Simultaneously, he returned to work on the telegraph. Several of his colleagues were supportive of his endeavors.

By 1836, Morse had devised a crude apparatus that he showed to Leonard Gale, a colleague who was a lecturer in chemistry. Gale made valuable suggestions for improvement of the device, and Morse later received additional recommendations from Alfred Vail and Joseph Henry. In his system, which came to be known as Morse telegraphy, an electric circuit, customarily using an overhead wire and the earth as the other conductor, is set up. An electromagnet in the receiver is activated by alternately making and interrupting the circuit. Audible clicks known as the Morse code provide a fast and reliable system of signaling. Relays eventually were provided to channel the signals over great distances. However, by the time Morse created his version of the telegraph, several of its aspects had already been anticipated in Great Britain, France, and Germany, and Morse's claim to being the inventor were questioned. Subsequently, he was compelled to defend his invention in court.

By 1837, Morse could transmit a message over seventeen hundred feet of wire, and he entered his discovery with the United States Patent Office. Lacking funds, he then appealed to Congress for financial aid, but it was not until 1843 that the body voted thirty thousand dollars for construction of a forty-four mile line between Washington, D.C., and Baltimore, Maryland. On May 24, 1844, this line transmitted the first formal telegraph message, as Morse sent the greeting "What hath God wrought" to Vail in Baltimore. Coupled with the earlier transmission of news emanating from the Whig National Convention and later from that of the Democrats, Morse's demonstration attracted the attention and interest of many congressmen and other citizens. However, the first line was rarely used and fell into disrepair. For several years, development of the telegraph industry was hampered by business problems, litigation, and disputes over patents.

The federal government originally considered operation of the telegraph to be part of the post office, but this scheme was abandoned, and aggressive promoters moved into the field. No other industry, not even the railroads, experienced more rapid growth. Telegraph poles began to dot the landscape as the lines were extended to most major cities east of the Mississippi River. Within a few years, there were fifty telegraph companies in the United States. In 1848, every state east of the Mississippi, except Florida, was connected to the growing network. By the beginning of 1852, more than twenty-three thousand miles of telegraph lines had been built. The system comprised fifty thousand miles by 1861, when San Francisco was reached, signaling the completion of the transcontinental telegraph. The creation of the Western Union Telegraph Company in 1856 standardized and consolidated the system of widely divergent characteristics and practices.

As it expanded, the industry became more sophisticated technologically, and the problem of overcrowded single lines, uninsulated wires with resulting feeble messages, toppling telegraph poles, and flimsy construction were overcome speedily. Improved wire-stringing techniques, the use of appropriate poles to support the wires, the application of insulators, and an improved conductor helped to establish the reliability of the telegraph. By 1860, improvements in synchronizing the sending and receiving apparatuses of the several systems made it possible to send and print as many as sixty words a minute. The telegraph was used by both sides in field operations during the Civil War.

As the lines expanded, so did speed and reliability, and the original hesitancy to use the telegraph disappeared. Newsgathering, business, financial, and transportation interests were revolutionized. The invention became an important factor in the rise of big business because financiers, manufacturers, and tradespeople of all kinds could now communicate directly and instantaneously with distant businesspersons or their representatives. Steamboat operators and shippers benefited from early notification of changes in navigation conditions.

After the Civil War, some railroads began to string out their own telegraph lines to trace the location of trains and to direct traffic. Trains were first dispatched by telegraph in 1851, which greatly increased the speed and safety of railroading. Finally, the invention of the stock ticker—a special type of telegraph— was a major factor in the explosive growth of Wall Street stock market operations during the third quarter of the nineteenth century. The teletype, also an extension of the telegraph, followed in the first quarter of the twentieth century.

In many ways, the telegraph symbolized the advent of a new electrical era in which distances among individuals, businesses, and governments would be drastically reduced. Along with the railroads, the telegraph and its associated inventions—the telephone, the Atlantic cable, the teletype, and others—laid the foundation for a new age of rapid mass communications and globalism. Although the original Morse telegraph apparatus soon became obsolete, Samuel Morse's contribution to its invention and development are widely accepted.

—James E. Fickle, updated by Peter B. Heller

ADDITIONAL READING:

Coe, Lewis. *The Telegraph: A History of Morse's Invention and Its Predecessors in the United States.* Jefferson, N.C.: McFarland, 1993. A onetime telegraph operator puts Morse's invention in perspective. Appendix includes biographical sketches of "Men of the Telegraph" and discusses how some of them felt slighted by Morse's seeming attempt to monopolize credit.

Dickerson, Edward N. *Joseph Henry and the Magnetic Telegraph: An Address Delivered at Princeton College, June 16, 1885.* New York: C. Scribner's Son, 1885. Highlights the contributions of the prominent physicist, who became the first secretary of the Smithsonian, to Morse's version of the telegraph.

Kieve, Jeffrey. *The Electric Telegraph: A Social and Economic History.* Newton Abbot, England: David and Charles, 1973. Emphasizes Great Britain's development of the electric telegraph by William Fothergill Cooke, Charles Wheatstone, and others, with little reference to Samuel Morse. Based exclusively on British official and private sources.

Mabee, Carleton. *The American Leonardo: The Life of Samuel F. B. Morse.* New York: Octagon Books, 1969. The standard biography of the inventor, promoter, businessman, and amateur politician. Discusses the role that Leonard Gale, Alfred Vail, and others played in Morse's work on the electric telegraph.

Marland, E. A. *Early Electrical Communication.* New York: Abelard-Schuman, 1964. A critical assessment of Morse's role in the development of the telegraph and the Morse code. Takes exception to Morse's denial of the contributions of predecessors and contemporaries in the invention.

Morse, Samuel F. B. *Samuel F. B. Morse: His Letters and Journals.* Edited by Edward Morse. 1914. Reprint. Boston: Houghton Mifflin, 1972. Illustrations and details of the frustrations and triumphs experienced by the inventor of the telegraph. Recognizes the assistance that Morse received from contemporaries and the claims to his innovation made by others.

Thompson, Robert L. *Wiring a Continent: The History of the Telegraph Industry in the United States, 1832-1866.* New York: Arno Press, 1972. The first two chapters deal with the beginnings of telegraphy, from 1832-1845. A succinct and objective account.

SEE ALSO: 1858, First Transatlantic Cable; 1860, Pony Express; 1861, Transcontinental Telegraph Is Completed; 1900, Teletype Is Developed.

1845 ■ Era of the Clipper Ships:
booming trade with California, Australia, and China gives rise to fast and beautiful seagoing vessels

Date: 1845-1857
Locale: New England, New York, and California
Categories: Economics; Science and technology; Transportation
Key figures:

John Willis Griffiths (1809-1882), naval architect and designer of the *Rainbow*

Donald McKay (1810-1880), shipbuilder and designer of clippers

Matthew Fontaine Maury (1806-1873), developer of current and wind charts

Nathaniel B. Palmer (1799-1877), commander and designer of clippers

Samuel Hartt Pook (1801-1864), designer and builder of many successful clippers

William H. Webb (1816-1899), outstanding designer of packets and clippers

Summary of event. Although the clipper ship's actual design and construction developed primarily for economic reasons, its relatively rapid decline was a result of the Civil War, the Panic of 1857, and the dramatic development of steam vessels. Because of labor costs and an inability to secure knowledgeable crew members, four- to six-masted, gaft-rigged limber and cargo schooners were built to compete with steamships. The design and building of clippers brought preeminence in naval architecture to the United States and, for a brief time, gave U.S. merchants and entrepreneurs domination of overseas trade, particularly in the southern Pacific and some areas of Asia. The dramatically beautiful lines of the clippers—so named for their ability to "clip along"—and their fantastic speed under great clouds of sail excited the admiration of those who saw them. Thus the years 1845 to 1857, the period during which the clipper ships flourished, has been termed "the clipper ship era."

The creation of speedy, long-range sailing vessels was a product of the great ongoing expansion in world seaborne commerce that took place after 1830. Among the effects of the Industrial Revolution were a concentration of industry, large-scale shipment of raw materials from all over the world, and mass transportation of manufactured goods. More trade meant greater demand for ships, especially large oceangoing vessels. The tonnage of the United States alone increased from 1,191,776 in 1830 to 5,353,868 in 1860. U.S. companies claimed more and more of the carrying trade in the North Atlantic, and eventually the Pacific and elsewhere, because of their packet lines (primarily passenger boats, carrying mail and goods, plying at regular intervals between two designated ports) and the lower shipbuilding costs in the United States.

U.S. companies had proven their abilities in the unique design and construction of larger and larger merchant ships. The next step was to build wooden sailing ships that would combine great speed with large cargo capacity, concepts preceded by the earlier construction of packet ships. Many of the innovations needed for clipper ships required the available types and specific qualities of northeast woods and the tall trees of the northwest forests, the latter being utilized as masts and spars. Consequently, the United States was in a position to take the lead in producing such ships by 1840, largely through the technological leadership of a small number of dedicated and innovative naval architects and builders. In the search for speed, they created perhaps the most beautiful ships ever to carry sail.

Earlier ships designed for the North Atlantic packet service, where speed was highly valued, were the progenitors of the clippers. Previously, oceangoing vessels of any size were relatively squat and heavy in appearance, with rounded bows and deep keels. The desire for speed and the demand for passenger space in the packets stimulated construction of ships of greater length in proportion to width, and vessels with more extreme lines, sharper bow lines, and nearly flat bottoms. Development and construction of such ships commenced in 1821. This form of hull design first appeared on the Hudson River run between New York and Albany, and later in the Dramatic Line ships built in 1836 and 1837. These highly efficient modified packets lowered the record for passage between New York and Liverpool by more than five days.

So-called true clippers borrowed certain improvements from the packets and ideas from other types of vessels, such as the "Baltimore clipper." The latter was characterized by a sharp bow, concave lines, and eventually a more pronounced tumble-home, in which the inward inclination of a vessel's upper sides meant the upper deck was narrower than the main and lower decks. The *Akbar*, built by Samuel Hall of Boston for the China tea trade in 1839, the *Ann McKim* of Baltimore, also constructed in 1839, and several other ships built at about that time contained many of these modifications.

The first vessel with all the features of a clipper was the *Rainbow*, designed by J. W. Griffiths and built by a New York shipyard in 1845. Griffiths, a famous designer and writer on the subject of naval architecture, had advocated in 1841 that the best design would combine the horizontal keel, flat floor, and greater ratio of length to width of the packets with the sharp bows and concave lines of Baltimore-designed vessels. His views proved to be correct, and the *Rainbow*, which was successfully employed in the China trade, where speed was essential, was the prototype clipper ship, although it was smaller and carried less canvas than later clippers. Considerable experimentation took place during the 1840's in an effort to improve on the design of the *Rainbow*.

The golden days of the clipper ships began with the discovery of gold in California and Australia, and the resulting clamor for large, fast passenger vessels to transport the gold seekers to distant lands. Between 1848 and 1854, general prosperity and the continuing need for transportation to Cali-

The huge clipper Great Republic *weighed 4,555 tons and was built in 1853 by Donald McKay. In the 1840's and 1850's, prior to the advent of the steamship, clippers dominated the waves and established the United States as a leader in naval architecture.* (Library of Congress)

fornia, for which fabulous rates could be asked, made the demand for clippers appear inexhaustible. At the rates they commanded, these vessels could pay for themselves in one voyage. Hulls became narrower, bows sharper, and the clippers were given more and more sail. Some clippers carried masts reaching nearly two hundred feet above the deck. Between 1850 and 1853, some 200,000 to 300,000 tons of shipping were engaged in the California trade. Between 1843 and 1853, 270 clipper ships were built in the United States.

The most famous clipper was the aptly named *Flying Cloud*. Designed and built by Donald McKay, the most famous marine architect of the period, and launched in 1851, the *Flying Cloud* was the epitome of the extreme clipper. Two hundred eight feet long, forty feet, eight inches in breadth, and displacing 1,783 tons, she carried almost thirteen thousand running yards of canvas. On her maiden voyage in 1854, the *Flying Cloud* made a one-day run of 374 miles and set a record of eighty-nine days for the trip from Boston to San Francisco, a record that still stood for sailing ships in the 1990's. An ordinary merchant ship took nearly two hundred days for the sixteen-thousand-mile voyage around the Horn. Other clippers startled the public by setting record after record on other routes. By the late 1850's, many U.S. clippers were capable of sailing 250 nautical miles a day. In 1854, the *Champion of the Seas* traveled 465 nautical miles in a single twenty-four-hour period, at an average speed of nearly twenty knots.

Responding to the demand for greater clippers (caused by high building costs and the relative inefficiency of this type of ship), McKay built the huge *Great Republic* (4,555 tons) in 1853. Other large clippers also were constructed, although none so large as the *Great Republic*. The supply of clippers finally outran demand; only on long voyages where speed was at a premium could they compete effectively with slower, higher-capacity merchant vessels. Mounting building costs were also a factor in their decline, so that by 1860, the era of the clipper ships had ended, although some historians, such as Arthur Clark, see the end of the clipper era as coinciding with the opening of the Suez Canal in 1869.

—Theodore A. Wilson, updated by John Alan Ross

ADDITIONAL READING:

Albion, Robert G. *Square-Riggers on Schedule: The New York Sailing Packets to England, France, and Cotton Ports.* Princeton, N.J.: Princeton University Press, 1938. This study of the packet ships that greatly influenced clipper design is a classic in its field.

Chappelle, Howard Irving. *The Baltimore Clipper.* New York: Bonanza Books, 1930. A well-researched account of the origin of clipper ships. Profusely illustrated and indexed.

_____. *The Search for Speed Under Sail: 1700-1855*. New York: W. W. Norton, 1967. Authoritative illustrated text on the development of sailing ships. Profusely illustrated and indexed.

Clark, Arthur H. *The Clipper Ship Era*. New York: G. P. Putnam's Sons, 1910. An informative history of U.S. merchant shipping and the origins of clipper ships, particularly the *Ann McKim* and the *Rainbow*.

McKay, Richard C. *Some Famous Sailing Ships and Their Builder, Donald McKay*. New York: G. P. Putnam's Sons, 1928. This book is typical of the memorial literature on clipper ships and their builders.

Whipple, A. B. C. *The Challenge*. New York: William Morrow, 1987. An informative and well-researched account of the *Challenge* and role of the captain's wife, Eleanor Cressy, as a navigator. Illustrated and indexed.

_____. *The Clipper Ships*. Alexandria, Va.: Time-Life Books, 1980. Well-written history of the technological innovations and descriptions of many people associated with the various socioeconomic activities of clipper ships. Excellent illustrations.

SEE ALSO: 1807, Voyage of the *Clermont*; 1848, California Gold Rush; 1853, Pacific Railroad Surveys; 1860, Pony Express; 1869, Transcontinental Railroad Is Completed.

1846 ■ HOWE'S SEWING MACHINE: *a new device revolutionizes the textile industry and helps turn an agrarian country into an industrial nation*

DATE: 1846

LOCALE: Boston, Massachusetts

CATEGORIES: Business and labor; Economics; Science and technology

KEY FIGURES:

Elias Howe (1819-1867), generally credited as the inventor of the first practical U.S. sewing machine

Walter Hunt (1796-1859), first U.S. sewing machine inventor

Thomas Saint, English cabinet maker and inventor who held the first British patent for a mechanical sewing device, in 1790

Isaac Merrit Singer (1811-1875), developer and mass marketer of U.S. sewing machines

Barthelemy Thimonnier (1793-1859), French inventor of a sewing machine in the late 1820's

Allen Benjamin Wilson (1824-1888), inventor of a sewing machine with four-motion mechanical sewing

SUMMARY OF EVENT. The United States entered the nineteenth century as a small agrarian nation heavily dependent upon others for essential manufactured products. By the end of the century, it had become a rich and powerful country with a diversified economy, well on the way to unquestioned leadership among the world's industrial states. The origins of this evolution are clearly evident in the antebellum period, particularly in the two decades before the Civil War, as a coalescence of historical forces transformed the national economy. New methods of transportation, expanded domestic markets, the westward movement, and the growth of industry contributed to the reshaping of the United States. The development of new labor-saving machinery and the emergence of the factory system were of central importance in making it possible for a small population to spread out over a wide geographical area without a dissipating industrial development.

The Industrial Revolution was spawned in Great Britain, and as in so many other areas of American development, English technology and patterns of industrial production shaped early United States manufacturing efforts. In addition to demonstrating ingenuity in adapting European technology to New World conditions, U.S. inventors gradually began to move toward original breakthroughs that, in turn, built and stimulated new industries. The invention of the sewing machine represented the vitality of U.S. inventiveness and Yankee ingenuity. The spectacular results of the sewing-machine industry characterized the evolution of the U.S. mercantile economy into the age of industrial capitalism.

The development of the sewing machine is a classic example of the old truism that "necessity is the mother of invention," as several men independently developed the basic principles of the sewing machine in response to an obvious need. By the 1830's, Americans had passed beyond the age of a self-sufficient household economy to a point where families depended upon specialized producers for many of their daily needs. As early as 1825, the first ready-to-wear clothing factory manufacturing sailors' suits appeared in the United States. All the work in this operation was done by hand. Soon, many similar factories appeared; clearly, the U.S. market was ready for a sewing machine.

Many people contributed to the development of the sewing machine and the industry it spawned. The earliest record of a mechanical sewing device is a 1790 British patent that was issued to Thomas Saint, an Englishman. The machine is described as a device to sew leather. It is not known if this machine was ever built. In 1830, a French tailor, Barthelemy Thimonnier, patented and built a chainstitch machine that, while not completely satisfactory, did perform sufficiently well for the developer to prosper briefly from the sale of his invention. However, Thimonnier and his machines eventually fell victim to the blows of irate tailors who believed the machine threatened their livelihood, and also to the upheaval of the Revolution of 1848 in France.

During the same period, Walter Hunt, an American living in New York City, developed a lockstitch machine for sewing, stitching, and seaming cloth. Hunt's machine was imperfect but workable. Like Thimonnier's machines, it fell prey to social conditions and hostile beliefs, not technical failure. Believing that his machine would throw many seamstresses out of work, Hunt did not perfect or seek to patent it. He abandoned his project in 1838.

That same year, Elias Howe started on his long quest to construct a machine that could sew. Howe was apprenticed to a Boston builder of precision instruments and, while working in his shop, overheard a conversation between his employer and a customer to the effect that a fortune awaited the man who could develop a practical sewing machine. The poverty-stricken Howe became obsessed with the pursuit of this goal and the attendant wealth. After much experimentation and failure, he finally patented such a machine in 1846. Howe deserves credit for solving some of the most vexing problems in the development of the sewing machine, and particularly for the introduction of the shuttle (the holder of a second thread, known as a bobbin) and the point-eyed needle through which the spooled thread passes. The synchronized movements of the bobbin and needle threads produced a secure lockstitch that could not easily be unraveled.

After securing his patent, Howe made an unsuccessful trip to England to market his sewing machine. Upon returning home in 1849, he discovered a ready market for the sewing machine in the United States. However, many competitors were already in the field, most with machines that infringed upon his patent. Howe spent the remainder of his life trying, unsuccessfully, to protect his patented rights.

Perhaps the ablest of the early inventors was Allen B. Wilson. In 1848, while living in Michigan and unaware of parallel efforts by inventors in the East, Wilson conceived of a sewing machine that included a motion to grip the material and automatically move it forward. Wilson, like Howe, did not receive great monetary reward for his inventions. Unlike Howe, he is not often mentioned, although his inventive genius had a far-reaching effect on the development of the sewing machine.

One of the most important of Howe's competitors was Isaac Merrit Singer, who in 1850 began to market the first really practical sewing machine in the United States. The Singer design proved adaptable to a variety of tasks in both the home and the factory. By 1860, an aggressive sales force of three thousand sold 111,000 sewing machines for both domestic and commercial uses.

With professional seamstresses barely able to eke out a living working eighteen hours a day on slow, laborious hand-stitching, the machine proved to be a vast success in the clothing industry. The garment districts of various cities began to use the machine so extensively that by 1858, in the city of Troy, New York, alone, there were three thousand sewing machines producing shirts and collars. The value of ready-made U.S. clothing production increased from forty million dollars in 1850 to more than seventy million dollars in 1860.

Because the machine could sew through leather, it gradually was adapted to all the sewing phases of shoe production. By 1880, the mechanization and division of labor in the shoe industry was almost complete, and the cost, which had been seventy-five cents with hand labor, was reduced to about three cents per pair. Between 1864 and 1870, the number of shoes produced by machine increased from five million pairs per year to more than twenty-five million; by 1895, it had reached one hundred twenty million. The machine also was used for the production of saddlery and harnesses. Using the "Ameri-can system" of standardized parts pioneered by Eli Whitney, and drawing heavily upon techniques already developed in the small arms and clock industries, factories for the manufacture of sewing machines soon ranked among the country's largest establishments.

The Civil War brought final and dramatic proof of the machine's capabilities and importance to the economy. At the beginning of the conflict, soldiers' uniforms were imported; by 1863, a mechanized domestic industry, concentrated in New York, Boston, Philadelphia, and Cincinnati, was able to clothe the entire Union forces. Similarly, the boot and shoe industry rapidly expanded to meet the wartime emergency. The local newspaper in Lynn, Massachusetts, reported that "buildings for shoe factories are going up in every direction; the hum of machinery is heard on every hand." The demand for boots and shoe-sewing machines was so great that their developer received $750,000 in royalties annually during the war.

The sewing machine, its production, its sale, and the industries it spawned had clearly become big business by the end of the nineteenth century. During the latter half of the nineteenth century, there were more than two hundred sewing machine companies in the United States. While the manufacture of clothing was the principal purpose of the sewing machine, by the year 1900, sewing machines were also used to produce tents, sails, saddles, harnesses, linens, pocketbooks, trunks, banners, flags, and numerous other products, to the aggregate sum of nearly a billion dollars.

The development of the sewing machine was typical of many U.S. industries during that period. Furthermore, it represented the emergence of an industry dominated by the type of specialized entrepreneurs who concentrated on production of a single item or closely related products, and the phasing out of the merchant capitalists with diversified economic life in the late eighteenth and early nineteenth centuries. With this transition, America entered the age of industrial capitalism. Elias Howe and his peers in the invention and manufacture of the sewing machine played a central and significant role in this development.　　　*—James E. Fickle, updated by Sue Bailey*

ADDITIONAL READING:

Cooper, Grace Rogers. *The Invention of the Sewing Machine.* Washington, D.C.: Smithsonian Institution, 1968. Presents the history of the sewing machine. Appendices contain biographical sketches of early inventors, U.S. sewing machine patent list, nineteenth century sewing machine companies, and more.

Davis, Anne Taylor, ed. "Bicentennial." *Daily News Record* (New York), February, 1976. A special edition celebrating the United States bicentennial. Covers the textile industry, including the sewing machine. Sketches, diagrams, and photographs enhance the text.

Fernandez, Nancy Page. "Innovations for Home Dressmaking and the Popularization of Stylish Dresses." *Journal of American Culture* 17, no. 3 (Fall, 1994): 11. Discusses the appearance and spread of dressmakers' drafting systems, paper patterns, and sewing machines in the late 1800's, and their effect on women's dress and roles.

Lyon, Peter. "Isaac Singer and His Wonderful Sewing Machine." *American Heritage* 9, no. 6 (October, 1958): 34-38, 103-109. This colorful account emphasizes Singer's flamboyant private life as well as his contributions to the industry.

Marcial, Gene. "After Several Alterations, Singer Looks Sharp." *Business Week*, no. 3253 (February 24, 1992): 90. Brief discussion of what has happened in the last two decades of the twentieth century to the Singer Sewing Machine Company, founded in the 1800's.

Parton, James. "The History of the Sewing Machine." *Atlantic Monthly* 19 (May, 1867). A contemporaneous account, based on interviews with Elias Howe.

Pursell, Carroll W., Jr. "Machines and Machine Tools, 1830-1880." In *The Emergence of Modern Industrial Society: Earliest Times to 1900*, edited by Melvin Kransberg and Carroll W. Pursell, Jr. Vol. 1 in *Technology in Western Civilization*. New York: Oxford University Press, 1967. Briefly traces the development of the sewing machine. Places the industry's growth in the perspective of general industrial development.

See also: 1790, Slater's Spinning Mill; 1793, Whitney Invents the Cotton Gin.

1846 ■ Mormon Migration to Utah:
masses of ideologically bound settlers blaze a trail in the best-organized westward migration in U.S. history

Date: February 4, 1846-September, 1848
Locale: Great Plains and the Great Basin
Categories: Expansion and land acquisition; Religion; Settlements
Key figures:
Samuel Brannan (1819-1889), Mormon leader who urged Young to bring his followers to California
James Bridger (1804-1881), mountain man who advised the Mormons against going into the Great Basin
William Clayton (1814-1879), who suggested use of an odometer to record the daily distance traveled
Orson Hyde (1805-1878), in charge of the halfway house at Kanesville, Iowa
Hebert C. Kimball (1801-1868),
Edward Martin (1818-1882), and
James G. Willie (1814-1895), who were in charge of the ill-fated fourth and fifth companies of the handcart migration
Orson Pratt (1811-1881) and
Erastus Snow (1818-1888), first two of the advanced party to enter Salt Lake Valley
Parley P. Pratt (1807-1857) and
John Taylor (1808-1887), Mormon leaders who organized companies for the westward march
Willard Richards (1801-1868), first and second counselors in the presidency of the church

Brigham Young (1801-1877), president of the Church of Jesus Christ of Latter-day Saints, who organized and supervised the Mormon migration into the Great Basin

Summary of event. According to Joseph Smith's account, on September 22, 1827, he received a set of gold plates from the angel Moroni on Cumorah, a hill near Palmyra, New York. His translation of the plates, called the Book of Mormon, was published in 1830. On April 6, 1830, in Fayette, New York, Joseph Smith and his associates founded the Church of Jesus Christ of Latter-day Saints, commonly referred to as the Mormons. In order to avert persecution and violence, the Mormons periodically moved en masse to new locations. In 1831, Joseph Smith moved the church headquarters to Kirtland, Ohio. Facing continued persecution, Smith and his followers moved to Missouri in 1838. By 1840, the Mormons had founded the city of Nauvoo, Illinois, which grew rapidly, becoming the state's largest city in 1844, with a population of twenty thousand.

The Mormons aroused antagonism in Illinois because they voted as a unit, they openly drilled their militia (the Nauvoo Legion) for defensive purposes, and some church leaders practiced polygamy. In 1844, Joseph Smith became a candidate for president of the United States, and a non-Mormon newspaper was established to fight Smith. When this newspaper was destroyed, Smith was blamed, arrested, and jailed in Carthage, Illinois. On June 27, 1844, a mob attacked the jail and murdered Joseph Smith and his brother, Hyrum. Continuing hostilities forced the Mormons out of Illinois in 1846. What farms and homes could be sold were sold at ruinous prices, and the proceeds were used to buy wagons, horses, cattle, and supplies.

Brigham Young, who had recently returned from missionary activities in England, was chosen to lead his people. He soon proved to be a hardheaded realist—an organizing genius capable of directing his people in their search for a new Zion. Smith had planned to move his people to the Great Basin in the Rocky Mountains, and Young now put the plan into effect. The evacuation began on February 4, 1846, and during February, approximately sixteen hundred Mormons crossed the Mississippi River on the ice and established temporary quarters in eastern Iowa at Garden Grove, where other Mormons soon joined them. It was here that plans were made for the western trek. A small party was sent ahead to select the route across Iowa, to choose camping places, to build and repair roads, and to construct bridges where necessary. With foresight, they were instructed to build log cabins at strategic sites, to dig wells, plow the land, and plant a crop of corn so that those who followed might be comforted and fed. By the time the vanguard of the expedition reached the Missouri River, in June, 1846, the main party, including the very young and the very old, the ill and the infirm, was ready to start. Their journey was made easier as a result of this careful planning. By fall, nearly twelve thousand Mormons were encamped at Winter Quarters on the west bank of the Missouri River, opposite Council Bluffs, near the site of present Omaha.

Poorly housed and inadequately fed, the emigrants suffered greatly in the bitter cold of the winter months of 1846-1847.

Scurvy and malaria broke out, and more than six hundred persons died before spring. The able-bodied were taught the most effective methods of crossing the Great Plains. Brigham Young had decided that a small, well-organized "pioneer band" led by him would push ahead of the main party, marking the trail and selecting the destination. Determined that the migration to follow should be orderly and efficient, he organized the people into hundreds, fifties, and tens, with a specified leader over each group. Instructions were issued concerning the driving of wagons and stock, the procedure for forming a compact corral at night, and the participation in religious services, including morning and evening prayers and the Sabbath as a day of rest. Young also emphasized the importance of keeping records of the route, the distance traveled each day, and the location of camping places for the benefit of those who were to follow.

The Mormons, because of their desperate need for funds, had hoped to obtain a contract from the United States government to build way stations and stockades along the Oregon Trail as they moved west. However, difficulties with Great Britain in the Northwest were settled by an amicable boundary compromise in 1846, and war came instead with Mexico in the Southwest. The Mormons therefore were called upon to fight rather than to build. By the middle of July, 1846, 549 men, known as the Mormon Battalion, enlisted in the United States Army at Winter Quarters to accompany the Army of the West headed for New Mexico and California.

The Pioneer Band of 148 people, led by Young, set out on April 16, 1847, driving a large herd of livestock and carrying a year's supply of provisions packed into seventy-three wagons. Instead of following the Oregon Trail on the south bank of the Platte River, the Mormons blazed a new route north of the stream, where the banks were higher and the grass more plentiful, because of the limited number of travelers. This route became known as the Mormon Trail. The party arrived at Fort Laramie on June 2, 1847; from that outpost, they arrived at Fort Bridger on July 7, 1847, following the regular Oregon Trail across Wyoming. Along the way, they met Jim Bridger, a mountain man, who warned the emigrants of the mountains and the barren deserts that lay ahead on their proposed route. Bridger urged them to select a more hospitable valley, but the Mormons wanted isolation as well as productive land.

Shortly before they reached the Green River, the party met Samuel Brannan, who had come eastward from California to intercept them and urge Young to colonize on the Pacific coast. Brannan had led a group of Mormons from Nauvoo to New York, where they had chartered a vessel to carry them around Cape Horn to the Pacific coast with all the equipment and supplies for successful colonization. Young turned a deaf ear to Brannan's praises of California and pressed on over the rugged Uinta Range, across the desert, and into the Wasatch Mountains. As the men labored to clear a pathway for the wagon train, Young lay ill in one of the wagons, suffering from mountain fever. When he caught a glimpse of the Salt Lake

Valley from the mountain heights, he announced that this was the place for which he had been looking. Working their way down a defile, now known as Emigration Canyon, the Mormons entered the Salt Lake Valley on July 24, 1847, a day since celebrated as Pioneer Day.

The pioneers immediately went to work damming mountain streams and constructing irrigation canals to flood the land before planting a crop. They built log houses connected by adobe walls to form a rectangular enclosure or fort. One detachment was sent to explore a route to California and to procure cattle and seed grains. The seeds were planted so late in the season that the crops did not have time to mature; the food supplies they had brought with them were desperately limited, and only by careful planning was starvation prevented.

Young started east with a few followers to organize the migration for 1848. Not far from the Great Salt Lake, he met a Mormon company of 1,553. Driving more than thirty-five hundred cattle, sheep, horses, and hogs, this group had followed the route of the Pioneer Band. A few weeks later, there were more than eighteen hundred Mormons on the southern tip of the Great Salt Lake. In September, 1848, Young returned to Utah, bringing with him twenty-five hundred additional emigrants. It was five years, however, before the remainder of the population from Nauvoo reached Salt Lake.

The Perpetual Emigrating Fund Company was started in 1849 to aid poverty-stricken emigrants, chiefly from foreign lands, in making the trip to Salt Lake, with the understanding that they would pay back their loans with interest so that similar loans could be made to future travelers. Between 1856 and 1860, 2,962 immigrants walked all the way to Salt Lake, pulling or pushing 653 handcarts containing their worldly goods. Close to a hundred Mormon communities were established in the Great Basin between 1847 and 1857, proving that cooperative, planned colonization was more effective than individual effort in a hostile physical environment.

—W. Turrentine Jackson, updated by Alvin K. Benson

ADDITIONAL READING:

Bashore, Melvin L. *Mormon Pioneer Companies Crossing the Plains, 1847-1868*. Salt Lake City, Utah: Historical Department, Church of Jesus Christ of Latter-day Saints, 1989. Diaries capture the emigration of the Mormon pioneers, from the first company to the last, including the remarkable handcart companies.

Bringhurst, Newell G. "A New Frontier Sanctuary." In *Brigham Young and the Expanding American Frontier*. Boston: Little, Brown, 1986. Summarizes the Mormon pioneer trek west, emphasizing its importance in colonizing the Western United States.

Kimball, Stanley B., and Violet T. Kimball. *Mormon Trail: Voyage of Discovery*. Las Vegas, Nev.: KC Publications, 1995. Follows the Mormon pioneers along the Mormon Trail, identifying significant history and trail sites and markers.

Knight, Hal, and Stanley B. Kimball. *111 Days to Zion*. Salt Lake City, Utah: Deseret Press, 1979. A day-by-day account of the trek of the first company of the Mormon pioneers from

Winter Quarters to the Salt Lake Valley. Drawing from first-hand diaries, it captures the spirit of the travelers who braved more than a thousand wilderness miles. Detailed maps.

Smith, Joseph Fielding. "The Settlement in the Rocky Mountains." Part 5 in *Essentials in Church History*. 22d ed. Salt Lake City, Utah: Deseret Book Company, 1967. Essential points of Mormon history are portrayed in chronological order. Detailed discussion of the reasons for leaving Illinois, preparations for departure, camp organization and regulations, dangers encountered along the way, the experiences of the Mormon Battalion, and the locating and settling of Salt Lake Valley.

Talbot, Dan. "The Mormon Battalion." In *A Historical Guide to the Mormon Battalion and Butterfield Trail*. Tucson, Ariz.: Westernlore Press, 1992. Maps and summary of the Mormon Battalion trek of more than two thousand miles, including name, company, and rank of each member.

SEE ALSO: 1806, Pike's Southwest Explorations; 1814, New Harmony and the Communitarian Movement; 1815, Westward Migration; 1820's, Social Reform Movement; 1823, Jedediah Smith Explores the Far West; 1846, Mexican War.

1846 ■ MEXICAN WAR: *a boundary dispute provides an opportunity for land-hungry Americans to acquire half of Mexico's territory*

DATE: May 13, 1846-March 10, 1848
LOCALE: Mexico
CATEGORIES: Expansion and land acquisition; Latino American history; Wars, uprisings, and civil unrest
KEY FIGURES:
Pedro María Anaya, interim president of Mexico, 1847
Mariano Aristta (1802-1855), commander of Mexican forces along the Rio Grande when war began
José Joaquín Herrera (1792-1854), acting president of Mexico, 1844-1845
Mariano Paredes y Arrillaga (1797-1849), president of Mexico in 1846
Manuel de la Peña y Peña (1789-1850), president of Mexico, 1848
James Knox Polk (1795-1849), eleventh president of the United States, 1845-1849
Antonio López de Santa Anna (1794-1876), Mexican general and president of Mexico, 1847, 1853-1855
Winfield Scott (1786-1866), commander of the U.S. Army, who led the capture of Mexico City
John Slidell (1793-1871), minister plenipotentiary to Mexico, 1845
Zachary Taylor (1784-1850), commander of the U.S. Army in northern Mexico
Nicholas Philip Trist (1800-1874), special agent appointed to negotiate a treaty with Mexico

John Tyler (1790-1862), tenth president of the United States, 1841-1845

SUMMARY OF EVENT. The United States' annexation of Texas in 1845 precipitated a major crisis in relations between Mexico and the United States. President Andrew Jackson had recognized Texan independence in 1837, but fearing the addition of another slave state to the Union, antislavery forces and Northern Whigs successfully blocked efforts to annex the Texas Republic. In 1843, Antonio López de Santa Anna warned that U.S. annexation of Texas, a province over which Mexico still claimed sovereignty, would be equivalent to declaring war against the Mexican Republic. In April, 1844, Sam Houston, president of the Texas Republic, accepted the United States' offer for annexation, on the condition that United States military and naval protection would be forthcoming as a defense against any Mexican invasion. The Senate, however, rejected the proposed annexation treaty in June.

In May, the Democratic Party convention had nominated an ardent expansionist, James K. Polk, for president, and in its campaign platform the party advocated the annexation of Texas and the acquisition of the whole of Oregon. The Whig Party nominee, Henry Clay, who tried to avoid these expansionist issues, lost the election by a narrow margin. Viewing Polk's victory as a public mandate for Texas annexation, President Tyler recommended that the lame duck Congress by joint resolution offer to annex Texas. A joint resolution required only a simple majority vote of both Houses, whereas a treaty could be ratified only by a two-thirds vote of the Senate. Congress passed the resolution in February, and President Tyler signed it on March 1, 1845, three days before Polk's inauguration. Mexico then broke off diplomatic relations with the United States.

Polk, accepting Tyler's action, came to office with half of his party's foreign policy platform virtually accomplished. Texas formally entered the Union in December, but the explosive Texas question remained to be settled with Mexico. The immediate issue was a boundary dispute, with Polk supporting Texas' questionable claim to the Rio Grande as its southwestern frontier rather than the Nueces River, farther north. In June, Polk ordered Brigadier General Zachary Taylor to move his forces into the disputed area, and by July, Taylor had established a base on the south bank of the Nueces River near Corpus Christi. In November, upon receiving confirmation that the Mexican government was prepared to receive a commissioner to discuss the boundary issue, Polk dispatched John Slidell, a Louisiana politician, to Mexico as minister plenipotentiary. Polk instructed Slidell to discuss three other outstanding issues: the purchase of California, the purchase of New Mexico, and the payment of damages to U.S. nationals for losses incurred in Mexican revolutions. Slidell was authorized to offer twenty-five million dollars for California and five million dollars for New Mexico, and to propose United States assumption of U.S. damage claims against the Mexican government in return for its recognition of the Rio Grande boundary.

Slidell reached Mexico City on December 6. The government of acting president José Joaquín Herrera, in response to growing domestic opposition to negotiations, refused to receive him. On January 13, 1846, the day after Slidell's report of the refusal reached him, Polk ordered Taylor to advance through the disputed territory to the Rio Grande. In late December, the Herrera government had been overthrown, in part because of its alleged lack of firmness toward the United States. The new president, General Mariano Paredes y Arrillaga, reaffirmed Mexico's claim to Texas and pledged himself to defend Mexican territory. On March 12, 1846, replying to Slidell's final inquiry, Paredes, too, refused to receive the U.S. minister.

Slidell reported to Polk in Washington on May 8. The next day, news arrived from Taylor that on April 25, a large Mexican force had crossed the Rio Grande and surrounded a smaller U.S. reconnaissance party; when the U.S. party attempted to break out of the encirclement, eleven of its members were killed and the rest wounded or captured. The cabinet endorsed an immediate request for a declaration of war. In Polk's war message, which he delivered to Congress on May 11, the president reviewed the boundary and claims issues and then concluded: "Mexico has . . . shed American blood upon American soil. . . . War exists . . . by the act of Mexico herself." On May 13, he signed the declaration. Already, Taylor had fought and won the battles of Palo Alto and Resaca de la Palma, and on May 18, he occupied Matamoros.

Polk's strategy was to occupy Mexico's northern provinces, blockade Mexican ports, and conquer New Mexico and California. By September, Taylor's army had taken Monterrey in Northern Mexico, but not without heavy casualties, as the Mexicans battled fiercely to defend their city. By January, 1847, U.S. forces were also victorious in the West and had secured New Mexico and California. Although successful militarily, the strategy failed to bring Mexico to terms, because the United States demanded too much Mexican territory. In order to bring an end to the war, Polk decided to shift the major military effort from the northern periphery to the heart of Mexico. The plan called for Major General Winfield Scott to take Veracruz, march through the mountains, and capture Mexico City.

U.S. forces entered Veracruz on March 29, 1847, following a weeklong land and naval bombardment, and on April 8, Scott's army set out along the National Road for the Valley of Mexico. Paredes had been deposed in August, 1846, and the new Mexican provisional president was General Antonio López de Santa Anna. In September, he had taken an army north to oppose Taylor. The two armies met at Buena Vista in February, 1847, in a hotly contested battle. Both sides would later claim victory. Santa Anna then returned to central Mexico, where he prepared to repulse Scott's invasion.

On April 18, Scott defeated Santa Anna at Cerro Gordo, and on May 15, he reached Puebla, only seventy-five miles from Mexico City. After a ten-week delay waiting for reinforce-

Battle of Chapultepec, September 13, 1847: The walled park of Chapultepec held a military school which Los Niños, the Boy Heroes, defended against U.S. assault as the Americans bore down on the Mexican capital in the last days of the war. (Library of Congress)

ments and hoping to negotiate, Scott resumed the advance, again defeating Santa Anna's forces in bloody encounters at Contreras and Churubusco. Santa Anna retreated to Mexico City, and an armistice was effected to allow the Mexican government to consider U.S. peace proposals delivered by Nicholas P. Trist, who met with a Mexican commission headed by former president José Herrera.

The Mexicans were prepared to surrender Upper California and give up claims to Texas. However, they refused to relinquish New Mexico and demanded an independent buffer state between the Rio Grande and the Nueces River. Finally, the Mexicans demanded that no territory they surrendered should permit slavery, which had been abolished in Mexico. The United States refused such conditions, and the two armies met at Molino del Rey and Chapultepec. The student cadets at the military college gallantly defended Chapultepec, and have entered Mexican folklore as the Boy Heroes.

Scott entered the capital on September 14, 1847. Santa Anna had fled the country, and the interim Mexican president, Pedro María Anaya, informed Trist that he was prepared to negotiate. Negotiations were conducted in February, 1848, with the next acting president, Manuel de la Peña y Peña. The resulting Treaty of Guadalupe Hidalgo, ratified by the Senate on March 10, 1848, ended the war. By the treaty, the U.S.-Mexico boundary was set at the Rio Grande, Gila, and Colorado Rivers, and Mexico relinquished New Mexico and Upper California; in return, the United States paid Mexico $15 million and assumed the $3.25 million in claims of its citizens.

—Jeffrey Kimball, updated by James A. Baer

ADDITIONAL READING:

Bauer, K. Jack. *The Mexican War, 1846-1848*. Lincoln: University of Nebraska Press, 1992. New edition of a thorough account of the politics, diplomacy, and battles of the Mexican War. Several good maps of battlefields and photographs of participants on both sides.

Bergeron, Paul H. *The Presidency of James K. Polk*. Lawrence: University Press of Kansas, 1987. A history of the Polk Administration, which suggests that Polk was less than forthright in his refusal to make public his opinion on Mexico before taking office.

Eisenhower, John S. D. *So Far from God: The U.S. War with Mexico, 1846-1848*. New York: Random House, 1989. Detailed account of the strategy of war and the battles, much of it taken from diaries and journals of the participants.

Langley, Lester D. *America and the Americas: The United States in the Western Hemisphere*. Athens: University of Georgia Press, 1989. Places events of the Mexican War within the ongoing relationship between the United States and all Latin American nations. Raises issues of possible British influence in Texas and the importance of California to Polk.

Singletary, Otis A. *The Mexican War*. Chicago: University of Chicago Press, 1960. Offers a critical analysis of the politics, the fighting, and the individuals in the war with Mexico. Chapter 6 focuses on what the author calls the "Hidden War" of unruly U.S. troops in Mexico.

SEE ALSO: 1821, Mexican War of Independence; 1835, Texas Revolution; 1842, Frémont's Expeditions; 1846, Mormon Migration to Utah; 1846, Occupation of California and the Southwest; 1847, Taos Rebellion; 1848, Treaty of Guadalupe Hidalgo; 1853, Gadsden Purchase.

1846 ■ OREGON SETTLEMENT: *a U.S.-British treaty opens the way to American migration into the Pacific Northwest*

DATE: June 15, 1846
LOCALE: Pacific Northwest
CATEGORIES: Canadian history; Expansion and land acquisition; Exploration and discovery; Settlements
KEY FIGURES:
James Cook (1728-1779), English explorer and navigator
George Hamilton Gordon, Lord Aberdeen (1784-1860), foreign secretary of Great Britain, 1828-1830 and 1841-1846
Alexander Mackenzie (1764?-1820), Canadian fur trader, explorer, and leader of the British North West Company
Richard Pakenham (1782-1868), British minister to the United States, 1845
Robert Peel (1788-1850), prime minister of Great Britain, 1841-1846
James Knox Polk (1795-1849), eleventh president of the United States, 1845-1849
George Vancouver (1757-1798) English navigator who explored the northwest coast and Nootka Sound
Daniel Webster (1782-1852), U.S. secretary of state
SUMMARY OF EVENT. The struggle for possession of the lush Oregon Country was among the most difficult and danger-fraught episodes in American westward expansion. Four powers—Spain, Russia, Great Britain, and the United States—originally held claims to Oregon. Their claims rested on such diverse supports as papal bulls and imperial ukases, but most strongly upon voyages of discovery and exploration between the 1540's and the 1790's. Spanish voyagers had first mapped the California coast in the mid-sixteenth century and first sighted the mouth of the Columbia River in 1775.

Russian claims to the region arose from the voyage to Alaska in 1741 of Vitus Bering, a Danish mariner in the service of Czar Peter the Great. Russian interests followed the fur trade south, and in 1821 the czar issued a ukase extending Russian's sphere of influence as far south as latitude 51° north. British claims dated from Sir Francis Drake's travels off the northern California coast in 1579 during his voyage around the world. Almost two hundred years passed before another Englishman, Captain James Cook, sailed along the coast between the forty-fourth parallel and northern Alaska in 1778 and claimed the region for the British crown. However, the British government ordered Cook not to interfere with previous Spanish claims to the northwest coast but stated they would recog-

TERRITORY OF THE UNITED STATES IN 1846

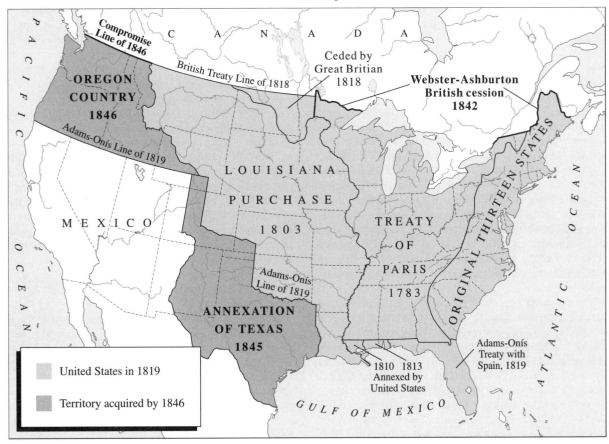

nize claims in the name of George III with consent of the indigenous population and in convenient situations. Fourteen years later, a British expedition, led by George Vancouver, entered the great harbor now named Puget Sound and explored the lower reaches of the Columbia River.

These maritime discoveries gave rise to overland expeditions from central Canada. Alexander Mackenzie, leader of the British North West Company, a fur-trading enterprise based in Montreal, reached the coast in 1793, the first Euro-American to complete a successful overland journey across North America north of Mexico. Others, such as Simon Fraser and David Thompson, of the British Hudson's Bay Company, followed. In the years 1807-1810, Thompson set up a chain of trading posts on the western slope of the Rocky Moutains. These traders quickly expanded their operations into the area north of the Columbia River.

American claims also were founded upon exploration. In 1788-1789, two Boston schooners, the *Columbia* and the *Lady Washington*, traded along the Oregon coast. Captain Robert Gray returned with the *Columbia* in 1791-1792 and sailed into the great river which he named for his vessel some two months before British explorers sighted the river. There is no evidence, however, that either Gray or Vancouver took formal

possession of the region. The United States' claim was bolstered by the Lewis and Clark expedition of 1804-1806. After their epochal trek up the Missouri and across the Continental Divide, Lewis and Clark reached the mouth of the Columbia, spending the winter of 1805-1806 there and formally raising the United States flag over the entire territory. They did not explore north of the Columbia River. The first American settlement, the trading post established at Astoria in 1811, ultimately failed, although it indicated future American interest in Oregon.

Initially, four powers had held claims to the Oregon country by virtue of acts of discovery and exploration, but by 1825, only Great Britain and the United States remained in competition for the region. Spain relinquished its claims north of the forty-second parallel to the United States in the Adams-Onís Treaty of 1819. In 1824, Russia and the United States signed a treaty by which Russia accepted 54°40′ as the southern limit of its territory. A similar arrangement was made the next year between Russia and Great Britain.

By the mid-1820's not only had the struggle for Oregon been limited to the United States and Great Britain, but the area in contention had been defined as the region west of the Rockies between latitude 42° and 54°40′ north. For the next twenty years, efforts were made to reach an acceptable division of this territory. Although both sides were to raise and maintain claims unwarranted by the facts of exploration or settlement, the struggle focused on the Columbia River and the triangular-shaped region between the Columbia and latitude 49° north, including the great harbor of Puget Sound.

Since Great Britain's prime concern was to protect its commercial interests, the British insisted upon sovereignty over the Columbia River south of the 49° to the Pacific Ocean. The United States argued for extension of the 49° line—which already served as the boundary between the United States and Canada east of the Rockies—from the Rockies to the Pacific, and offered the privilege of free navigation of the Columbia River to British subjects. In the 1820's, neither side was willing to make significant concessions, and Oregon remained a contested land. In 1827 the two powers reconfirmed arrangements made in 1818 which provided for joint occupation of the territory and free entry of American and British subjects into Oregon without prejudice to the claims of either power.

For the next fifteen years, Oregon was not the subject of diplomatic negotion between the two nations; however, much was taking place to force resolution of the rival claims. Although immigration of Americans was not to become large until after 1841 (when great numbers of pioneers, possessed by "Oregon fever," came plodding west over the Oregon Trail), the stage was set in the 1830's by the missionary activities of Jason Lee, Marcus Whitman, and others who spread tales of Oregon's rich soil and mild climate. In 1845 alone, some three thousand immigrants reached this promised land, and by the end of that year there were about five thousand Americans in the region south of the Columbia River compared with some seven hundred British (almost all fur trappers and traders) north of the river. It was inevitable that the Americans would clamor for clear title to the land occupied, and that the United States government would respond.

During the Webster-Ashburton negotiations over the Canadian boundary in 1842, Secretary of State Daniel Webster expressed a willingness to concede American claims to most of the territory north of the Columbia River, though retaining the Olympic Peninsula and harbors in Puget Sound. In return, Great Britain was to exert pressure on Mexico to cede California north of the 36° to the United States. The West reacted violently to this proposed "surrender" of Oregon, reflecting the growing importance of that territory as a political issue and its central place in the mysticism of "manifest destiny."

Despite the campaign oratory and slogans of the Democrats in 1844, most Americans were relucant to fight for the Oregon territory north to 54°40′. James K. Polk, eleventh president of the United States, did not consider his election a mandate to occupy the whole of Oregon. Concerned about the implications of London's reaction to American public bravado, the president privately approached Richard Pakenham, British minister to the United States, with an offer to divide Oregon at latitude 49°. Though hardly a great step toward compromise, 49° was much less threatening than 54°40′, since previous administrations had proposed a similar settlement on three occasions. Pakenham committed the grievous error of rejecting the proposal upon his own initiative. Polk, however, now could portray himself as the injured party, and abruptly withdrew the 49° compromise. It was, he said, Great Britain's turn to offer substantial concessions. In his annual message to Congress in December, 1845, Polk stated that the United States was ready to support its claim to the whole of Oregon, basing his position upon the principle of opposition to the establishment of any European "colony or dominion" upon the North American continent. This statement, henceforth, was known as the Polk Corollary to the Monroe Doctrine. In brief, it stated (1) that "the people of this continent alone have the right to decide their own destiny"; (2) that no European power should interfere to prevent the union of the United States with another independent state of the North American continent "because it might disturb the balance of power"; and (3) that "no future European colony or dominion shall with our consent be planted or established on any part of the North American continent."

After four months of debate embittered by sectional and political conflict, Congress, on April 22, 1846, passed a resolution which empowered Polk to terminate the Oregon joint occupation arrangement of 1827 with one year's notice. Thus, when the one-year abrogation period elapsed, the two nations faced open conflict or embarrassing retreat. The Conservative government of Sir Robert Peel in Great Britain, immersed in the struggle over repeal of the Corn Laws, did not desire conflict with the United States. America's preeminent place in British trade also helped to cool British irritation. However, Oregon was a ticklish political issue. Peel's government disbanded in December, 1845, after an aggressive Whig campaign to denounce Tory cowardice regarding Oregon. The Whigs, however, found it impossible to form a new government and promised to observe a truce with the Tories while a settlement of the Oregon crisis was sought.

Lord Aberdeen, foreign secretary of Great Britain, drew up a treaty proposal which reflected almost total acceptance of American demands and suggested a boundary of 49° to the strait of Juan de Fuca if Great Britain could be guaranteed free navigation of the Columbia River. Polk received this proposal offically on June 6, 1846, almost a month after the United States' declaration of war against Mexico. On June 10, he sent the treaty without change to the Senate. Five days later, the Senate had approved and ratified it.

The Oregon settlement was a great diplomatic success for the United States. By more than balancing the concessions offered to the British in the Webster-Ashburton Treaty, the United States gained rich and strategically situated land to which Great Britain possessed stronger claims. This favorable outcome was not primarily Polk's achievement; to a greater extent it was a victory of time and circumstance.

—*Theodore A. Wilson, updated by John Alan Ross*

ADDITIONAL READING:

Cook, Warren L. *Flood Tide of Empire: Spain and the Pacific Northwest, 1543-1819*. New Haven, Conn.: Yale University Press, 1973. Examines the political intrigue, espionage, and national debate in Europe to gain control of the lucrative sea otter pelt areas of the northwest coast.

Galbraith, John S. *The Hudson's Bay Company as an Imperial Factor, 1821-1869*. Berkeley: University of California Press, 1957. A model study of the relations between special economic interests and national foreign policy.

Gough, Barry M. *Distant Dominion: Britain and the Northwest Coast of North America, 1579-1809*. Vancouver: University of British Columbia Press, 1980. A comprehensive study of British motives for exploration of the northwest coast.

Graebner, Norman A. *Empire on the Pacific: A Study in American Continental Expansion*. New York: Ronald Press, 1955. Author argues against "manifest destiny" sentiment for American expansion into Pacfic Northwest and Oregon.

Merk, Frederick. *The Oregon Question: Essays in Anglo-American Diplomacy and Politics*. Cambridge, Mass.: Harvard University Press, 1967. Essays essential to critically examining the many foreign and American myths that influenced the Oregon Treaty of 1846.

Morgan, Murray. *Puget's Sound: A Narrative of the Early Tacoma and the Southern Sound*. Seattle: University of Washington Press, 1979. Review of original journals regarding the Hudson's Bay Company and other early fur traders.

Pethick, Derek. *The Nootka Connection: Europe and the Northwest Coast, 1790-1795*. Vancouver: Douglas & McIntyre, 1980. A comparative study of expanding American, British, Russian, and Spanish exploration and trading interests in the northwest coast region.

Sellers, Charles G. *Continentalists, 1843-1846*. Vol. 2 in *James K. Polk*. Princeton, N.J.: Princeton University Press, 1966. Discusses Polk's role in the settlement of the Oregon question.

SEE ALSO: 1579, Drake Lands in Northern California; 1728, Russian Voyages to Alaska; 1793, Mackenzie Reaches the Arctic Ocean; 1804, Lewis and Clark Expedition; 1808, American Fur Company Is Chartered; 1810, Astorian Expeditions; 1819, Adams-Onís Treaty; 1823, Jedediah Smith Explores the Far West; 1842, Webster-Ashburton Treaty.

1846 ■ OCCUPATION OF CALIFORNIA AND THE SOUTHWEST: *the Army of the West is charged with winning New Mexico and California for the United States*

DATE: June 30, 1846-January 13, 1847
LOCALE: Greater Southwest
CATEGORIES: Expansion and land acquisition; Exploration and discovery; Latino American history; Wars, uprisings, and civil unrest

KEY FIGURES:

Manuel Armijo (1792?-1853), governor of the province of New Mexico
Christopher "Kit" Carson (1809-1868), guide to Frémont
José Castro (1818-1893), commander of Mexican troops in California
Philip St. George Cooke (1809-1895), commander of the Mormon Battalion with the Army of the West
Alexander W. Doniphan (1808-1887), commander of troops marching from Santa Fe to Chihuahua City
William H. Emory (1811-1887), member of the Topographical Engineers, who accompanied Kearny from New Mexico to California
John Charles Frémont (1813-1890), explorer who became involved in the Bear Flag Revolt in California
Archibald H. Gillespie (1812-1873), U.S. Marine Corps officer who brought confidential messages to California from government officials
William B. Ide (1796-1852), leader of the Bear Flag Revolt and president of the California Republic
Stephen Watts Kearny (1794-1848), commander of the Army of the West
James Wiley Magoffin (1799-1868), Santa Fe trader and Army intelligence agent
James Knox Polk (1795-1849), eleventh president of the United States, 1845-1849
Robert Field Stockton (1795-1866), commander of U.S. naval forces in California

SUMMARY OF EVENT. When the United States declared war on Mexico in May, 1846, the military strategy of President James K. Polk and his advisers was to occupy the capitals of the northern Mexican provinces and march on Mexico City itself. Polk hoped the two campaigns would result in a quick end to the war. He assigned the task of winning New Mexico and California to the Army of the West, commanded by Brigadier General Stephen Kearny. In the spring of 1846, Kearny assembled his forces at Fort Leavenworth. Under his command were three hundred regular dragoons and five hundred Mormon youths, led by Lieutenant Colonel Philip St. George Cooke, who had been recruited from their encampment at Council Bluffs, Iowa, where Brigham Young was making plans to move westward to Deseret. Kearny also was accompanied by a regiment of infantry and a train of wagons. Missouri frontiersmen and recruits brought the total personnel under his command to twenty-seven hundred.

On June 30, 1846, this army started for Santa Fe, following the Santa Fe Trail for eight hundred miles, first to Bent's Fort on the Arkansas River and then southward into New Mexico. On the outskirts of Santa Fe, Kearny learned that three thousand Mexicans under the command of Manuel Armijo, the governor of New Mexico, had occupied a strategic canyon through which Kearny's men would have to pass. Rather than risk a military clash, Kearny resorted to diplomacy, sending forward intelligence agent James Magoffin, who, acting on secret instructions from Polk, succeeded in convincing Armijo that he should flee southward. Colonel Juan de Archuleta, Armijo's second-in-command, proved more difficult and would not withdraw the Mexican Army until Kearny promised that he would occupy only part of New Mexico, leaving the rest to Archuleta. Kearny's army then marched into Santa Fe without contest, but disregarding his promise to Archuleta, Kearny issued a proclamation announcing the United States' intention to annex the whole of New Mexico. He promised the residents a democratic government and a code of law, and he named Charles Bent as governor. When settlers in southern New Mexico questioned his actions, Kearny took a detachment down the Rio Grande to ensure the loyalty of Mexican villages.

With the first phase of his campaign completed, Kearny continued his program by separating his army into three forces. One he left behind in New Mexico to hold the province. Another, composed of three hundred volunteers from Missouri under Colonel Alexander Doniphan, went south by way of El Paso to occupy Chihuahua City. Magoffin, sent ahead to ensure a peaceful occupation, was unsuccessful. Doniphan's troops had to fight the Battle of Brazito before occupying El Paso, and they had to drive back a Mexican army of four thousand at Chihuahua City. Kearny had taken the third force of three hundred dragoons out of Santa Fe on September 25, 1846, and headed for California. He was accompanied by Lieutenant William Emory and other officers of the Topographical Engineers, who were making observations on the feasibility of wagon and railroad routes. The expedition moved rapidly down the Rio Grande and then west along the Rio Gila. There it encountered a detachment led by Kit Carson, bringing the news east that California was in the hands of the United States. Assuming that a military campaign would be unnecessary on the coast, Kearny ordered two-thirds of his troops back to Santa Fe and commanded the reluctant Kit Carson, now a lieutenant in the United States Army, to guide him and one hundred dragoons westward.

The division of Kearny's force was fortunate for the interests of the United States, because the detachment returning to New Mexico arrived in time to suppress the Taos Revolt led by the disgruntled Archuleta, in which Governor Bent and other officials had been slain. The revolutionaries took refuge within the adobe church there, and the United States' forces had to storm the walls and kill many Mexican leaders before the revolt came to an end and U.S. authority was restored.

At the same time, the United States extended its authority to California. Before war had been declared between the United States and Mexico, Thomas O. Larkin, the U.S. consul in California, had hoped that he could effect a peaceful transfer of the Mexican province to the United States. Larkin's hopes were dashed, however, by events surrounding John C. Frémont's appearance in California between December, 1845, and June, 1846. Frémont had secured permission from Governor José Castro for his scientific expedition to winter in California on the condition that Frémont avoid coming near any settlements. Frémont's failure to honor the agreement prompted Castro to demand Frémont's departure from California. Avoiding hos-

tilities temporarily, Frémont led his detachment slowly up the Sacramento River Valley until he was overtaken at Klamath Lake by Lieutenant Archibald Gillespie of the U.S. Marines, carrying confidential messages and papers from the U.S. government and from relatives. The exact contents of these communications have remained unknown; however, Frémont thereupon returned to California, despite Castro's order to leave, and made his way to the vicinity of Sonoma. There, in June, he immediately became involved in an uprising of settlers from the United States, a insurrection known as the Bear Flag Revolt, so named for a flag bearing the symbols of a red star and a bear, which the insurgents adopted as their standard.

Frémont's national reputation as a hero in the conquest of California waned when the Bear Flag Revolt was assessed against the efforts of Larkin to secure California peacefully for the United States, and when it was learned that the war with Mexico—which prescribed the U.S. conquest of California—had been declared before the Bear Flag Revolt took place. Critics have censured Frémont for having provocatively endangered relations between the United States and Mexico at a time when Frémont could not have known of the state of war. Historians point out that the Bear Flag Revolt had little importance in the United States' conquest of California, because Commodore John Sloat's first official act of conquest was to sail into Monterey Bay and raise the United States flag over the customs house on July 7, twelve days before Frémont's arrival in Monterey.

Events of the Bear Flag Revolt merged with the conquest by United States forces. The first stage of operations, from July 7 to August 15, 1846, resulted in the temporary occupation of every important settlement in California, including San Francisco, Sutter's Fort, Monterey, and Los Angeles. It was news of this success that Kit Carson was carrying to the east when he met Kearny. Scarcely had Carson departed when a local revolt erupted in Los Angeles on September 22, and the United States troops under Gillespie were forced to retreat to the Pacific port of San Pedro, leaving southern California once again in Mexican hands. Commodore Robert F. Stockton, in charge of U.S. naval forces, left Monterey for the south. Meanwhile, the Mexicans, learning of Kearny's approach to San Diego, had come out to meet him near present-day Escondido, California. In the ensuing Battle of San Pasqual, United States troops were mauled badly but managed to struggle on to San Diego. Kearny then joined Stockton's forces in a successful march into Los Angeles. Frémont, in the meantime, marched down the California coast with deliberation. The Mexican leaders who had violated their paroles made at the time of the first capitulation were afraid of retribution at the hands of Kearny or Stockton, and so sought out Frémont in the mountains north of Los Angeles, where they surrendered at Cahuenga on January 13, 1847.

The conquest of the Southwest was at last complete. A bitter quarrel then ensued between Stockton and Kearny over who was in command in California. Frémont sided with Stockton, but Kearny appealed to Washington, D.C., and received confirmation of his authority. Diplomatic complications delayed the signing of the Treaty of Guadalupe Hidalgo until February, 1848, more than a year after the fighting in the northern Mexican provinces had ceased. As a result of the treaty, the United States acquired all or portions of the future states of California, Nevada, Utah, Colorado, New Mexico, and Arizona. Native Americans and Mexicans passed under the suzerainty of the United States.

—*W. Turrentine Jackson, updated by Edward R. Crowther*

ADDITIONAL READING:

Clarke, Dwight L. *Stephen Watts Kearny: Soldier of the West*. Norman: University of Oklahoma Press, 1961. The definitive biography of Kearny, a leading figure in the conquest of the Southwest.

Eisenhower, John S. D. *So Far from God: The U.S. War with Mexico, 1846-1848*. New York: Random House, 1989. A survey of the Mexican War written for a popular audience.

Harlow, Neal. *California Conquered: The Annexation of a Mexican Province, 1846-1850*. Berkeley: University of California Press, 1982. A thorough treatment of the economic, cultural, and physical conquest of California.

Limerick, Patricia Nelson. *The Legacy of Conquest: The Unbroken Past of the American West*. New York: W. W. Norton, 1987. Argues that the conquest of land by the United States catalyzed social and economic interaction, and fashioned the agenda for ongoing problems between subjugated peoples and the majority society.

Weber, David J. *The Mexican Frontier, 1821-1846: The American Southwest Under Mexico*. Albuquerque: University of New Mexico Press, 1982. An outstanding survey of the social, economic, and diplomatic realities of the old Mexican Cession and California.

SEE ALSO: 1821, Mexican War of Independence; 1821, Santa Fe Trail Opens; 1823, Jedediah Smith Explores the Far West; 1835, Texas Revolution; 1842, Frémont's Expeditions; 1846, Mormon Migration to Utah; 1846, Mexican War; 1847, Taos Rebellion; 1848, California Gold Rush.1846, Mormon Migration to Utah; 1846, Mexican War; 1847, Taos Rebellion; 1848, California Gold Rush.

1846 ■ INDEPENDENT TREASURY IS ESTABLISHED: *management of Treasury funds is removed from state-chartered banks, resulting in a federal means of regulating the monetary system*

DATE: August 6, 1846
LOCALE: Washington, D.C.
CATEGORIES: Economics; Government and politics; Organizations and institutions
KEY FIGURES:
Henry Clay (1777-1852), U.S. congressman from Kentucky
William Fitzhugh Gordon (1787-1858), U.S. congressman from Virginia

James Guthrie (1792-1869), educator, railway promoter, secretary of the Treasury, 1853-1857
Andrew Jackson (1767-1845), seventh president of the United States, 1829-1837
James Knox Polk (1795-1849), eleventh president of the United States, 1845-1849
John Tyler (1790-1862), tenth president of the United States, 1841-1845
Martin Van Buren (1782-1862), eighth president of the United States, 1837-1841

SUMMARY OF EVENT. Creation of the Independent Treasury system, finally achieved in 1846, was the outgrowth of the controversy arising from President Andrew Jackson's refusal to accept recharter of the Second Bank of the United States. In 1833, Jackson and his secretary of the Treasury, Roger B. Taney, determined to withdraw government deposits from the Second Bank and transfer them to state-chartered banks. Since there was a hint of political patronage in this process, the newly selected deposit banks were soon termed the "pet banks." There were few checks on how these banks were to operate.

The years from 1833 to 1836 were a time of economic boom. Gold flowed into the country in payment for cotton exports and foreign investment. The gold entered bank reserves and banks responded by expanding loans, note issues, and deposits. There was a strong upsurge in sales of public lands by the government, bringing a flood of revenues and enabling the government to pay off the national debt. Government deposits expanded rapidly, and in June of 1836, Congress voted to distribute the surplus to the states.

In 1837, however, a deflationary panic occurred, partly in response to the withdrawal of specie from banks to carry out the distribution of the surplus. The Panic of 1837, and the depression that followed, resulted in the failure of numerous banks, including some that held government deposits. More commonly, banks continued to operate but refused to redeem their liabilities in specie. As the economic depression reduced government revenue, the Treasury was hard-pressed by the unavailability of its bank deposits. Furthermore, there was widespread public resentment against the banking system, which was blamed for the panic and depression. The Treasury found itself obliged to make some of its payments using depreciated notes of its deposit banks. An element among the Jacksonian politicians had long held the view that banks' privilege to issue banknote currency should be curbed. This view was reflected in government directives restricting the acceptability of small-denomination banknotes in payments to the government, and in the Specie Circular of July, 1836, which ordered that payments to the government for public-land purchases be made in gold or silver.

However, the Panic of 1837 proved short-lived. Most banks resumed specie payments in the spring of 1838, a process facilitated by continued inflow of gold from overseas. Then, during 1839, deflationary conditions returned. This time, there were heavy gold exports and downward pressure on money and credit, leading to a 30 percent decline in prices between 1839 and 1843. Concern for the Treasury deposits and anti-bank sentiment combined to provide support for creating an Independent Treasury—independent of the banks, that is.

Proposals for an Independent Treasury system began as early as 1834 in Congress, when William F. Gordon, an anti-Jackson Democrat, introduced such a measure to curb the potential political influence involved in relations with the "pet banks." President Martin Van Buren, in a message to a special session of Congress on September 5, 1837, called for a specie currency, criticized the operation of state-chartered banks, and suggested a plan to open Treasury depositories independent of the banks. Congress debated the idea for the next nine years and finally passed the Independent Treasury Act on June 30, 1840, only to repeal it on August 13, 1841. On August 1, 1846, such a system was enacted again. It served as the basis for managing government funds until the inception of the Federal Reserve System in 1914.

The Independent Treasury Act adopted in 1840 reflected the antibank sentiments of Jacksonian Democrats. The election of 1840 shifted power to the Whigs, who repealed the 1840 law before it had much effect. The Independent Treasury was replaced as an issue by the efforts of Henry Clay and the Whigs to charter a new national bank. However, the untimely death of President William Henry Harrison brought John Tyler into the presidency. Tyler, a strong proponent of states' rights, vetoed two bills to create a new national bank. The victory of James K. Polk and the Democratic Party in 1846 allowed the reenactment of the Independent Treasury.

Under the new system, subtreasuries were established in six leading cities, with responsibility for receiving, safeguarding, and paying out government funds. The government's mints (coinage factories) participated in these operations. All government transactions were to be conducted either in gold and silver coin or in Treasury notes. The latter were short-term, interest-bearing securities issued as part of the national debt. Some of them were issued with very low interest rates and were clearly designed to circulate as paper currency, even though they were not technically legal tender. The government now maintained no deposit accounts with banks, nor could it receive checks or banknotes for payments to the government.

Although technically independent of the banks, the Treasury's operations soon displayed substantial influence on banking conditions. At times, government revenues exceeded disbursements, and specie accumulated in the Treasury offices, draining off reserves from the banks and putting banks under pressure to contract loans, with deflationary consequences. At other times, government deficits led to a net flow of specie from Treasury to banks, with expansionary effects that were not always desirable. Ingenious methods were devised by secretaries of the Treasury to try to prevent these operations from causing financial damage. During the early 1850's, for example, boom conditions—arising in part from the California gold discoveries—led to a large increase in specie held in the Treasury. The national debt had increased substantially

since 1836. This gave Secretary of the Treasury James Guthrie the opportunity to buy government securities in the open market. These purchases helped transfer funds from the Treasury to the banks and relieve them from deflationary pressure. Such operations became an important element in Treasury operations during the remainder of the period until to 1914.

The Civil War altered the character of the system. In 1863 and 1864, with the passage of the National Bank Acts, the government adopted a system of chartering local banks, to be called national banks. These were eligible to hold government deposits. Legal-tender government paper currency, the "greenback," was introduced in 1862. Both government and banks went off the specie standard until 1879, so government transactions were conducted with paper money. However, the subtreasuries continued to operate and to influence bank reserves and monetary conditions.

—*Paul B. Trescott*

ADDITIONAL READING:

Hammond, Bray. *Banks and Politics in the United States from the Revolution to the Civil War*. Princeton, N.J.: Princeton University Press, 1957. The breezy narrative gives extensive attention to both the economic and political aspects of the Second Bank and Independent Treasury.

McPaul, John M. *The Politics of Jacksonian Finance*. Ithaca, N.Y.: Cornell University Press, 1972. Shows the origins of the Independent Treasury idea in the conflicting elements among Jackson's political supporters, some favoring relatively unrestricted banking and others opposing all bank operations.

Schlesinger, Arthur M., Jr. *The Age of Jackson*. New York: Mentor Books, 1945. Devotes considerable attention to the financial policies of the 1830's and 1840's. Extremely pro-Jackson and economically naïve; written in a dramatic style.

Taus, Esther Rogoff. *Central Banking Functions of the United States Treasury, 1789-1941*. New York: Columbia University Press, 1943. Although pedestrian, probably the most complete description of the workings of the Independent Treasury system.

Timberlake, Richard H. *Monetary Policy in the United States: An Intellectual and Institutional History*. Chicago: University of Chicago Press. A monetary economist examines the evolution of monetary thinking and policy in the 1830's and 1840's in chapters 4, 5, and 6.

SEE ALSO: 1790, Hamilton's *Report on Public Credit*; 1816, Second Bank of the United States Is Chartered; 1832, Jackson vs. the Bank of the United States; 1834, Birth of the Whig Party; 1863, National Bank Acts.

1846 ■ SMITHSONIAN INSTITUTION IS FOUNDED: *birth of a major repository of the most revered artifacts of U.S. history*

DATE: August 10, 1846
LOCALE: Washington, D.C.
CATEGORIES: Cultural and intellectual history; Organizations and institutions; Science and technology

KEY FIGURES:

John Quincy Adams (1767-1848), sixth president of the United States, 1825-1829

Spencer Fullerton Baird (1823-1887), zoologist, naturalist, and second secretary of the Smithsonian Institution

John C. Calhoun (1782-1850), U.S. congressman and senator from South Carolina

Joseph Henry (1797-1878), U.S. physicist and first secretary of the Smithsonian Institution

James Knox Polk (1795-1849), eleventh president of the United States, 1845-1849

Theodore Roosevelt (1858-1919), twenty-sixth president of the United States, 1901-1909

James Smithson (1765-1829), English chemist and mineralogist

SUMMARY OF EVENT. Storehouse of the nation's treasures, the Smithsonian Institution is one of the most universally appealing attractions of Washington, D.C. Its seven buildings and zoological garden serve both the casual visitor and the serious scholar. Its activities are not limited simply to preserving mementos of the past; the institution also gathers scientific data at installations such as the Smithsonian Astrophysical Observatory in Cambridge, Massachusetts. Smithsonian teams have worked in the United States and overseas, sending back reams of scientific information and many specimens as a part of the institution's effort to widen knowledge of humans and their environment.

The Smithsonian Tropical Research Institute in the former Panama Canal Zone, operated by the Smithsonian Institution on Barro Colorado Island, is the only tropical research station of its type in the Western Hemisphere. The Smithsonian Bureau of American Ethnology, founded in the 1870's, has studied American Indian life in North and South America and the West Indies; it has collected and published information on tribal customs and conditions, excavated burial mounds and preserved their contents, and recorded native songs and stories. A few of the other divisions in the Smithsonian's vast complex include Washington's National Zoological Park; the John F. Kennedy Center for Performing Arts, also in Washington, D.C.; and the Cooper-Hewitt Museum of Decorative Arts and Design in New York City.

Certainly the institution has lived up to the hopes of its founder, the noted English chemist and mineralogist James Smithson. While no one knows precisely what prompted Smithson's generosity to a country he had never seen, there is speculation that the circumstances of his birth gave him an emotional link with a nation dedicated to equality. James Smithson was the illegitimate son of a wealthy farmer, Hugh Smithson, who later became duke of Northumberland. Smithson never acknowledged the existence of his son James. Thus, it was as "James Lewis Macie, Gentleman Commoner" that the young man entered Oxford University in 1782. In 1787, a year after graduation, he was made a fellow of the Royal Society of London for Improving Natural Knowledge. His first scientific paper, presented in 1791, was signed with the surname Macie; his second, delivered November 18, 1802, bore the name James Smithson, Esquire.

Fortunately for the young scientist, his mother was wealthy. On her death, he inherited a sizable fortune, which financed his scientific work and allowed him to live comfortably. A few years before his own death, Smithson drew up an unusual will leaving his money to his nephew with the proviso that, should the nephew die childless, the entire estate was to go "to the United States of America to found at Washington, under the name of the Smithsonian Institution, an establishment for the increase and diffusion of knowledge among men." Smithson died in Genoa, Italy, on June 27, 1829; his nephew died without heirs in 1835; and in September of 1837, the United States inherited $508,318.46

The funds arrived in the United States in 1838, triggering a prolonged and at times impassioned congressional debate about their acceptance and also about the alternatives for increasing and diffusing knowledge. Senator John C. Calhoun of South Carolina vigorously opposed acceptance, on grounds that it was demeaning for the government to act as executor for a citizen. Massachusetts representative John Quincy Adams, the former president, made the acceptance and wise use of the fund a personal crusade. Indeed, Adams truthfully may be considered the U.S. father of the Smithsonian. On August 10, 1846, President James K. Polk signed the bill creating the Smithsonian Institution and authorizing it, in effect, to serve as the national museum, a chemical laboratory, a library, an art gallery, and a site for public lectures. Among its most important early possessions were Smithson's magnificent mineral collection, manuscripts, and other personal property. Congress followed the signing by appropriating money to construct a building "without necessary ornament" to house the institution's offices and activities. In 1847, James Renwick, architect of St. Patrick's Cathedral in New York City, designed the distinctive Smithsonian building, a red-brown freestone structure strongly resembling a Norman castle complete with crenellated towers, spires, and arched windows.

By virtue of the office, the president of the United States is chairman of the Smithsonian Institution's governing body; however, few, except Theodore Roosevelt, have been seriously concerned with the Smithsonian's development. The actual daily direction is in the hands of the secretary, whose position is equivalent to that of head of an independent federal agency. In establishing the qualifications of the secretary, the first Board of Regents in 1846 declared that it must be a person of high character, "capable of advancing science and promoting letters by original research and effort." To fill the post, they selected Joseph Henry of Princeton University, the foremost U.S. physicist of his day. During his thirty-two-year tenure, Henry established the direction the institution was to take. Under his leadership, scientific activities were emphasized, reflecting Henry's professional bias. From some of the projects grew the United States Weather Bureau and the Geological Survey. In another program, original scientific work was published and distributed to libraries in many countries. Despite continuous struggles with Congress for appropriations and a disastrous fire in 1865, which destroyed much of Smithson's collection, the institution prospered.

After Henry's death in 1878, the renowned naturalist Spencer Fullerton Baird became the second secretary. Baird chose to emphasize work in the natural sciences. Smithsonian teams continued their exploratory activities, and Baird instituted a system to allow the exchange of scientific information among nations. He also organized the United States Fish Commission and served as its first commissioner. Such activities thus led to the establishment of the world-famous marine biological station, the Marine Laboratory at Woods Hole, Massachusetts.

The Smithsonian's work has not been limited to scientific areas alone. In the 1920's, both the National Collection of Fine Arts and the Freer Gallery of Oriental Art came under Smithsonian control. In 1937, Andrew Mellon gave the nation his amazing art collection and a fifteen-million-dollar gallery building; it became a bureau of the Smithsonian, although administered by its own board of trustees. Additional buildings and research are planned as the Smithsonian continues to enlarge the functions that James Smithson had presumably willed. This expansion has not come easily, because the returns on Smithson's bequest have to be supplemented annually by Congressional budgetary appropriations. Private endowments and gifts have also provided funding. It would seem that the hopes of its early champions are not in jeopardy, and that the Smithsonian Institution will continue to be a crucible of learning, discovery, and culture.

—*Anne Trotter, updated by Peter B. Heller*

ADDITIONAL READING:

Carmichael, Leonard, and J. C. Long. *James Smithson and the Smithsonian Story*. New York: G. P. Putnam's Sons, 1965. The opening chapters of this well-illustrated book were penned by the senior author, the seventh secretary of the Smithsonian. Shows how the vision of James Smithson was made real by the institution's first secretary, Joseph Henry.

Hafertepe, Kenneth. *America's Castle: The Evolution of the Smithsonian Building and Its Institution, 1840-1878*. Washington, D.C.: Smithsonian Institution, 1984. Focuses on the influence of the first secretary, Joseph Henry, on the early Smithsonian buildings' architecture.

Henry, Joseph. *January, 1844-December, 1846: The Princeton Years*. Vol. 6 in *The Papers of Joseph Henry*, edited by Marc Rothenberg. Washington, D.C.: Smithsonian Institution, 1992. Includes a heavily annotated exchange of correspondence among important individuals involved in the founding of the Smithsonian Institution and the appointment of Joseph Henry as its first secretary.

Jones, Bessie Z. *Lighthouse of the Skies*. Washington, D.C.: Smithsonian Institution, 1965. Discusses the crucial role of John Quincy Adams in pressing for the creation of the Smithsonian Institution.

Oehser, Paul H. *The Smithsonian Institution*. 2d ed. Boulder, Colo.: Westview Press, 1983. Appendix includes the text of the congressional law of August 10, 1846, that created the Smithsonian, and Secretary Joseph Henry's initial program presented to the institution's Board of Regents on December 13, 1847.

Painter, George. "James Smithson's Bequest to the United States: The Smithsonian Institution." *American History Illustrated* 17, no. 1 (March, 1982): 30-35. Discusses why the English scientist, James Smithson, willed his estate to a country that he had never seen.

Watts, J. F. *The Smithsonian*. Introduction by Arthur M. Schlesinger, Jr. New York: Chelsea House, 1987. This brief, illustrated work provides a simply written version of the Smithsonian Institution's origins and evolution.

SEE ALSO: 1893, World's Columbian Exposition; 1897, Library of Congress Building Opens; 1913, Armory Show.

1846 ■ SURGICAL ANESTHESIA IS SAFELY DEMONSTRATED: *a medical advancement saves lives by making formerly painful surgical procedures possible*

DATE: October 16, 1846
LOCALE: Georgia
CATEGORIES: Health and medicine; Science and technology
KEY FIGURES:

Charles Thomas Jackson (1805-1880), eccentric Boston physician and scientist who claimed full credit for Wells's and Morton's work

Crawford Williamson Long (1815-1878), Georgia physician who first used ether in surgery

William Thomas Green Morton (1819-1868), Boston dentist who first demonstrated surgical anesthesia for the public

Horace Wells (1815-1848), Boston dentist who attempted to use nitrous oxide as an anesthetic

SUMMARY OF EVENT. On October 16, 1846, in the Massachusetts General Hospital, William Thomas Green Morton, a Boston dentist, gave the first public demonstration of the successful use of surgical anesthesia. Although surgery had made considerable progress during the previous two centuries as anatomists had gradually delineated the major outlines of gross anatomy, the surgical patient still faced excruciating pain and the virtual certainty of secondary infections. Without anesthetics, the agonies of the patients forced surgeons to operate as quickly as possible, and the shock and pain often proved disastrous. Dreaded diseases, such as hospital gangrene or blood poisoning, often hastened the patient's death. In the 1840's, U.S. ingenuity had solved the problem of anesthesia; control of infection had to await the bacteriological revolution in the last half of the nineteenth century.

Among the many discoveries in the history of medicine, few have provoked so much controversy as that of anesthesia. No fewer than four American claimants to the honor of introducing this benevolent contribution to humanity vied with each other for recognition during their lifetimes. Subsequently, the controversy acquired an international flavor. Simultaneous events in England further blurred the claim to discovery. The argument quickly focused on the superiority of ether versus chloroform. The struggle has since been carried on by historians. The American contest, however, now rests largely between Crawford W. Long, who was the first to use surgical anesthesia, and William Thomas Green Morton, who first publicly demonstrated its use.

By 1840, the stage was set for the advent of anesthesia. Surgeons, as deeply troubled by the agonies of their patients as by the difficult logistics of operating on a screaming, writhing patient, were eager for help. A growing humanitarian spirit, with its acute sensitivity to human suffering, made the public more receptive to innovations. Yet, it was the rapid development of dentistry in America that created a strong demand for some sort of pain reliever. By this time, three anesthetic agents were available: nitrous oxide, sulfuric ether, and chloroform. The exhilarating effects of the first two gases were well known, and "ether frolics" and "laughing gas" parties had become common indoor pastimes. In the course of these parties, it had been observed that individuals under the influence of the gases appeared to feel no pain.

The first professional man to see the significance of these agents in relieving pain was Crawford W. Long, a Georgia physician. He had witnessed the effect of sulfuric ether during ether frolics and determined to try it as an aid to surgery. Between 1842 and 1846, Long performed eight operations using sulfuric ether on human patients. However, he made no effort to publish his work until after Morton's demonstration of the anesthetic properties of ether in 1846.

A Boston dentist, Horace Wells, also experimented with anesthesia. He had observed the results of nitrous oxide during laughing gas parties and decided to see if it could provide the basis for painless extraction of teeth. After several successes, he arranged for a public demonstration of his technique at the Harvard Medical School. Precisely what happened there is unclear. Apparently the nitrous oxide had not taken its full effect on the patient. When Wells began to pull a tooth, the patient let out a terrified yell, and the students began to laugh and hiss. Wells fled, leaving his instruments behind. After this humiliation, he arranged a further demonstration, but this time he gave too large a dose and the patient nearly died. Wells retired in disgrace, giving up all attempts to use nitrous oxide as an anesthetic.

Meanwhile, William Morton, another Boston dentist, was investigating the problem of surgical anesthesia. At the suggestion of Charles Thomas Jackson, a well-known physician, geologist, and chemist, Morton experimented with ether. When he felt confident, Morton persuaded John Collins Warren to allow him to anesthetize one of the famous surgeon's patients. It was Morton's use of anesthesia during this operation in 1846 that introduced anesthesia to the world. Jackson later demanded credit for the discovery, but his claim was rejected by the public and the academic community.

Ironically, misery was the lot of the three persons chiefly responsible for the introduction of anesthesia: Wells committed suicide soon after his unhappy appearance before the Harvard students; Morton sacrificed his career while fighting for recognition as the rightful discoverer of ether as an anesthetic and died a frustrated and bitter man; and Jackson was ultimately committed to an insane asylum. Long escaped the litigation and public quarreling in which Jackson and Morton became embroiled. He survived the Civil War and died a respected and successful practitioner in Georgia. His failure to publish the results of his early experiments deprived him of credit for the discovery of anesthetic surgery, and had he not encountered the publicity given to Morton's successful demonstration in 1846, Long might never have made mention of his work.

News of Morton's demonstration of painless surgery spread rapidly throughout the world, and the use of anesthesia (a name suggested by Oliver Wendell Holmes) for surgical and obstetrical purposes quickly became general. In 1869, an acrimonious debate erupted between English obstetrician Sir James Young Simpson and Jacob Bigelow, a Boston physician. The controversy focused more on whether Simpson had taken more credit than he was due for the discovery of a safe anesthetic than on the superiority of ether over chloroform. As the number of surgical operations increased, so did the incidence of secondary hospital infections; it took another twenty years for the work of the Englishman Lord Joseph Lister in antiseptic, and later aseptic, techniques to alleviate this problem in American hospitals.

As a result of the use of anesthesia, surgery eventually became a healthier and relatively painless procedure for the patient. The successful use of anesthesia also permitted the development of better surgical techniques and a more sophisticated understanding of anatomy. Nevertheless, as knowledge of anesthesia and bacteriology steadily widened, the way was being prepared for making the twentieth century the age of the surgeon.   —*John Duffy, updated by Kathleen Carroll*

Additional reading:

Boland, Frank Kells. *The First Anesthetic: The Story of Crawford Long*. Athens: University of Georgia Press, 1950. This scholarly work leaves little doubt that Long was the first to use ether as an anesthetic.

Duncum, Barbara M. *The Development of Inhalation Anaesthesia with Special Reference to the Years, 1846-1900*. London: Oxford University Press, 1947. The definitive work dealing with the background and controversy over surgical anesthesia, and its later development in the late nineteenth century. Includes a survey of political and social attitudes in various countries during the nineteenth century and illustrates how they influenced the study of anesthesia.

Keys, Thomas E. *The History of Surgical Anesthesia*. New York: Schuman's, 1945. Traces the earliest attempts to relieve pain. Focuses on the broadening of the field of anesthesia in the late nineteenth and early twentieth centuries, including such topics as local, regional, and spinal anesthesia; rectal anesthesia; "twilight sleep"; and other anesthetic techniques.

Ludovici, L. J. *Cone of Oblivion: A Vendetta in Science.* London: Max Parrish, 1961. Centers on the controversies that raged between 1840 and 1860.

MacQuitty, Betty. *The Battle for Oblivion: The Discovery of Anesthesia.* London: George S. Harrap, 1969. Follows Morton's struggle for recognition; includes some beautiful photographs.

Shryock, Richard Harrison. *Medicine and Society in America, 1660-1860.* New York: New York University Press, 1960. This classic general history of U.S. medicine emphasizes the role of U.S. dentistry in the discovery of anesthesia.

Sykes, W. Stanley. *Essays on the First Hundred Years of Anaesthesia.* Edinburgh, Scotland: E. & S. Livingstone, 1960. Includes a rich variety of illustrations and photographs. Establishes the political and social issues that were a part of the Victorian Age and serve as a background to the development of practical anesthetic procedures.

SEE ALSO: 1900, Suppression of Yellow Fever; 1906, Pure Food and Drug Act; 1912, U.S. Public Health Service Is Established; 1952, Development of a Polio Vaccine; 1981, First AIDS Cases Are Reported.

1847 ■ TAOS REBELLION: *resistance by Hispanics and Indians in New Mexico leads to the first revolt against new U.S. authority*

DATE: January 19, 1847
LOCALE: Taos, New Mexico
CATEGORIES: Native American history; Wars, uprisings, and civil unrest
KEY FIGURES:
Charles Bent (1799-1847), prominent trader on the Santa Fe Trail, appointed first U.S. governor of New Mexico by Kearny
Stephen Watts Kearny (1794-1848), colonel who led the Army of the West to New Mexico and California
Sterling Price (1809-1867), commander who took over when Kearny left for California
Tomasito, Taos Indian rebel who was believed to have murdered Bent
Donaciano Vigil (1802-1877), appointed first U.S. lieutenant governor by Kearny
SUMMARY OF EVENT. In the twenty years prior to the outbreak of the Mexican War of 1846, the northern borderlands frontier of Mexico had undergone profound changes. A breakdown in relations with Native Americans, particularly the Apaches and the Comanches, resulted in such an increase in Native American raids that whole sections of the frontier were depopulated of settlers. Unable to institute effective pacification measures, the national government in Mexico City largely abdicated responsibility for frontier defense to the northern Mexican states and territories, a task few had the resources to implement or maintain. At the same time, U.S. influence in the borderlands was

growing. In the province of New Mexico, the opening of the Santa Fe Trail in 1821 increasingly drew north-central Mexico into the economic sphere of the United States; while in Mexican Texas, large-scale U.S. immigration led that area to declare its independence from Mexico in 1835-1836. When the United States annexed Texas in 1845, precipitating the crisis that would lead to war with Mexico, the northern borderlands frontier of Mexico seemed acutely vulnerable to a U.S. takeover.

In Missouri, Colonel Stephen Watts Kearny recruited the so-called Army of the West among enthusiastic frontier supporters of manifest destiny and Missouri merchants eager to expand their Mexican markets. Following the Santa Fe Trail, Kearny and sixteen hundred troops set out first for Bent's Fort, a trading establishment just north of the Arkansas River, then the United States-Mexico border. Charles and William Bent, with their partner Ceran St. Vrain, had established the post in 1833. From it, they had quickly monopolized the fur and American Indian trades of the southern Rockies and Great Plains. They also had expanded into the Santa Fe trade, operating a mercantile outlet in Taos, New Mexico, where Charles Bent had taken up residence after marrying into a prominent New Mexican family. From Bent's Fort, Kearny's forces left for New Mexico, preceded by James Wiley Magoffin, a Santa Fe trader acting as President James Polk's emissary. Arriving in Santa Fe, Magoffin secretly met with New Mexico governor Manuel Armijo and persuaded him that resistance was futile. After making a show of defending the province, Armijo fled southward, allowing U.S. troops to occupy New Mexico. On August 18, 1846, Kearny's forces entered Santa Fe, the capital.

Kearny quickly reassured the sixty thousand inhabitants of New Mexico that U.S. rule would not threaten their persons or possessions. The Kearny Code, in conjunction with the United States Constitution, codified these promises and provided a legal framework for the conquered province. Kearny established a new civil government, naming Charles Bent as governor and Donaciano Vigil of Santa Fe as secretary or lieutenant governor. Soon after, Kearny departed for California to continue the conquest of northern Mexico. Colonel Sterling Price, newly arrived from Missouri with additional troops to garrison the province, took military command.

Kearny's governmental appointments had excluded many of the New Mexico *ricos*, or upper classes, who had formerly controlled the province. Several of his appointees, many of whom had traded for years in New Mexico, held land grants or interests in land grants that had been issued earlier by former governor Armijo. Their new positions of authority gave these appointees the opportunity to expand their New Mexico holdings at the expense of the *ricos*, or so many *ricos* believed. Rumors began circulating throughout the province that the U.S. occupiers wished to register land titles, in preparation for the seizure of the *ricos'* property, and to exact heavy taxes (as a territory of Mexico, New Mexico was exempt from paying national taxes). Moreover, Taos Indians believed that Charles Bent also wished to acquire lands of the Pueblo de Taos. As a result, Tomás Ortiz, Diego Archuleta (formerly Armijo's second-in-command), and possibly Padre Antonio José Martí-nez of Taos, along with other prominent native New Mexicans, began to conspire against U.S. rule, planning an uprising. Lieu-tenant Governor Vigil, learning of the conspiracy, quickly sup-pressed it, but not before news of the planned insurrection had spread to towns and communities in northern New Mexico.

On January 14, 1847, Governor Bent left for Taos (also called Don Fernando de Taos, to differentiate it from the pueblo of same name, only two miles north of the village), ignoring warnings from Vigil that such a journey might be dangerous in the volatile climate following the suppression of the conspir-acy. Bent felt reasonably secure, not only because he had long resided in Taos but also because news of U.S. victories farther south in Chihuahua seemed to preclude the possibility of aid reaching New Mexico from that quarter. On January 19, 1847, however, Taos Indians, led by one Tomasito, joined insurrec-tionists in the village, led by Pablo Montoya. They destroyed U.S. settlers' homes and attacked the residence of Charles Bent. Bent himself was killed and scalped, as were other Americans and Mexican supporters of the new regime. The insurrectionists then burned a nearby distillery at Arroyo Hondo, also operated by a U.S. citizen. Similar uprisings occurred at other northern communities, most notably at Mora, where seven more U.S. settlers, many of them Santa Fe traders, were killed.

When news of these events reached Santa Fe, Colonel Price immediately set out for Taos with 480 men and four artillery pieces, while Vigil took over as provisional governor and issued a proclamation denouncing the rebels. The insurgents, numbering almost two thousand, met Price's forces on Janu-ary 29, 1847, at the village of Cañada, twenty-five miles north of Santa Fe. The U.S. settlers drove the rebels toward the Pueblo de Taos, where they made their stand in the fortress-like church. On February 3, 1847, the battle resumed. Turning their artillery on the church, the U.S. forces breached the walls, forcing the insurgents out. After more fighting, the Taos Indians and their Hispanic allies eventually surrendered, hav-ing suffered losses of 150 persons. U.S. losses were seven killed and forty-seven wounded.

While in custody awaiting trial, Tomasito, believed to have been responsible for Bent's murder, was shot and killed by a U.S. soldier. Pablo Montoya and fourteen others were tried by court-martial and sentenced to death. The New Mexico civil court indicted other conspirators, who were subsequently tried for treason against the United States and executed. President Polk and Secretary of War William L. Marcy later pointed out that the conspirators could not actually have been guilty of treason against the United States, as the United States and Mexico were still at war. Nevertheless, they supported the measures taken to end the uprising and the execution of its principal leaders. Diego Archuleta fled New Mexico before he could be apprehended but later returned, took the oath of allegiance to the United States, and became active in territo-rial politics. Padre Martínez, against whom nothing was ever proven definitely, also escaped indictment and continued his leadership role in northern New Mexico until his death in 1867.

Although peace returned to New Mexico following the uprising, four years of military rule followed. In 1850, the Territory of New Mexico was finally established. Although Anglo-Americans tended to dominate federally appointed po-sitions, the New Mexico *ricos* established firm control over the legislative assembly, largely securing their place in the new order. Other native New Mexicans, however, lost their lands to unscrupulous Anglo-American lawyers who used their knowl-edge of U.S. law and their political connections to undermine land guarantees given in the Treaty of Guadalupe Hidalgo, which ended the Mexican War. The Taos Indians lost much of their former territory during the period of U.S. rule over New Mexico.   —*Joseph C. Jastrzembski*

ADDITIONAL READING:

Crutchfield, James Andrew. *Tragedy at Taos: The Revolt of 1847*. Plano, Tex.: Republic of Texas Press, 1995. First com-prehensive narrative of the events at Taos. Contains valuable appendices concerning the participants, a chronology of events, casualty figures, and other items of interest.

Keleher, William A. *Turmoil in New Mexico, 1846-1868*. Santa Fe, N.Mex.: Rydal Press, 1952. Details the events lead-ing up to the U.S. invasion of New Mexico and the subsequent occupation of the province.

Simmons, Marc. *New Mexico: An Interpretive History*. Al-buquerque: University of New Mexico Press, 1988. Chapter 4 covers the events of the occupation of New Mexico and briefly discusses the Taos Rebellion.

Twitchell, Ralph Emerson. *The History of the Military Oc-cupation of the Territory of New Mexico from 1846 to 1851 by the Government of the United States*. 1909. Reprint. Chicago: Rio Grande Press, 1963. Quotes extensively from government documents; provides biographical sketches of the principal participants.

Weber, David J. *The Mexican Frontier, 1821-1846: The American Southwest Under Mexico*. Albuquerque: University of New Mexico Press, 1982. A comprehensive overview of the Mexican borderlands before the Mexican War. Discusses the economic impact of the Santa Fe Trade, American Indian relations, the church, society, and culture.

SEE ALSO: 1821, Mexican War of Independence; 1821, Santa Fe Trail Opens; 1846, Mexican War; 1846, Occupation of California and the Southwest; 1848, Treaty of Guadalupe Hidalgo; 1853, Gadsden Purchase.

1847 ■ THE NORTH STAR BEGINS PUB-LICATION: *the first of Douglass' news-papers campaigns against slavery and for abolition*

DATE: December 3, 1847
LOCALE: Rochester, New York
CATEGORIES: African American history; Communications; Cultural and intellectual history

KEY FIGURES:

Martin Robison Delaney (1812-1885), coeditor of *The North Star*

Anna Murray Douglass (1813?-1882), Frederick Douglass' first wife

Frederick Douglass (Frederick Augustus Washington Bailey, 1817?-1895), orator, abolitionist, editor, and publisher of *The North Star*

William Lloyd Garrison (1805-1879), abolitionist and early mentor to Douglass

Gerrit Smith (1797-1874), financial backer of several of Douglass' newspapers

Elizabeth Cady Stanton (1815-1902), feminist and social reformer

SUMMARY OF EVENT. When the first issue of *The North Star* appeared on December 3, 1847, critics and readers discovered a newspaper that blended sardonic humor with moral urgency, written in a polished style. Some readers, however, were skeptical of editor Frederick Douglass' sophistication. Fathered by a white man and born to the slave Harriet Bailey in Talbot County, Maryland, Frederick Bailey had worked in bondage as a slave for Thomas Auld, witnessing the horrors of slavery, the brutal beatings, and even murder. In his teens, he had taught himself to read and write from a discarded speller and copybook, and learned public speaking by imitating orations appearing in *The Columbian Orator*, an abolitionist publication. *The Columbian Orator* led to his awareness of the abolitionist movement and influenced his writing style when he later published *The North Star*. Clashing with his master in 1838, Frederick escaped from Baltimore to New York with Anna Murray, a free African American domestic servant. Once married, they settled in New Bedford, Massachusetts, which offered sanctuary. To prevent recapture, Frederick changed his surname to Douglass, in honor of a character in Sir Walter Scott's poem *Lady of the Lake*.

Douglass became active in local abolitionist gatherings, discovering his gift as a compelling speaker who provided firsthand examples of barbaric slavery. He became a favorite on the lecture circuit during the early 1840's; his autobiography, *Narrative of the Life of Frederick Douglass* (1845), sold more than thirty thousand copies over the next five years. Douglass came under the tutelage of the leading abolitionist of the times, William Lloyd Garrison. From Garrison's abolitionist newspaper, *The Liberator*, Douglass no doubt learned much about newspaper operations.

As Douglass' fame increased, so did his risk of capture as an escaped slave. In 1845, he sailed for England, then on to Scotland and Ireland, where he passionately lectured on the inhumane treatment of slaves. His newfound friends, moved by his personal plight, arranged to purchase Douglass' freedom for $711.66. Before returning to the United States in 1847, he also received $2,175 to bankroll his own antislavery newspaper.

When Garrison objected to Douglass' projected newspaper, the two close friends became estranged, then bitter enemies. Douglass believed that the white abolitionists thought him a child to be led, whereas African Americans must lead to gain respect. He held that his newspaper could create that leadership and help increase self-respect among African Americans. Douglass knew of the hazards in starting an African American newspaper, because about one hundred such papers existed in the United States, the first having been started in 1827. He located in Rochester, New York, because it had strong antislavery sentiments and publishing there reduced the competition with *The Liberator* in Boston and the *National Anti-Slavery Standard* in New York City.

On December 3, 1847, the first issue of *The North Star* appeared—a four-page weekly with a subscription cost of two dollars per year, circulation of two to three thousand, and publishing costs of eighty dollars per week at the first print

Orator, editor, and civil rights activist Frederick Douglass published several periodicals in his lifetime, including The North Star, *dedicated to the abolitionist cause and to advancement of African Americans.* (The Associated Publishers, Inc.)

shop owned by an African American. Douglass chose journalist Martin Delaney as coeditor, but the two soon clashed over the issue of "colonization," by which freed slaves would seek a separate homeland in Africa rather than integrate within the United States' white society. When a disgusted Delaney left in 1848 to found a colony in the Niger Valley, in Africa, Douglass became sole editor, vigorously espousing the principles of integration, as he did throughout his life.

In the first issue of *The North Star*, Douglass urged African Americans to become politically active and pledged that his newspaper would aggressively attack slavery, work to free Southern slaves, and promote African American morality and progress. The lead article recounted the convention of "colored people" of 1847, with its primary objectives of abolishing slavery and elevating free African Americans. In subsequent years, *The North Star* dealt with a plethora of burning issues: injustice, inequality, racism, the avoidance of drink and dissipation, the benefits of integrated school systems, the elimination of segregated hotels and railroads, the folly of war and capital punishment, the worth of laborers, the imperative need for racial unity among African Americans, and the unfair voting practices leveled against African Americans in Northern states. *The North Star* came to the defense not only of persecuted African Americans but also of American Indians, the Irish, and other immigrant groups.

From its beginnings, *The North Star* lived up to its masthead: RIGHT IS OF NO SEX—TRUTH IS OF NO COLOR—GOD IS THE FATHER OF US ALL, AND ALL WE ARE BRETHREN. Douglass vigorously supported the women's rights movement, linking enslaved women to the abolition movement itself. At the Seneca Falls Convention in 1848, Douglass was the only one of the thirty-two men attending to speak and vote in favor of Elizabeth Cady Stanton's Declaration of Sentiments, which demanded equality for women. He effectively used *The North Star* to promote Stanton's feminist cause.

Financially, *The North Star* foundered after six months. Douglass mortgaged his house and used his lecture fees to keep the paper going. From time to time, he received financial gifts from Gerrit Smith, a philanthropist, reformer, and wealthy New York landowner. In 1851, the two men agreed to merge the financially troubled *North Star* with Smith's struggling *Liberty Party Paper*. Douglass maintained editorial control over the paper while including political news of the Liberty Party; he broadened his readership to four thousand; and he accepted a comfortable subsidy from Smith. The new effort, *Frederick Douglass' Paper*, appeared in June, 1851, and lasted until 1859. The paper continued Douglass' efforts in regard to abolition, equality, and women's rights. Douglass also dabbled in the Liberty Party campaigns, endorsing Smith and helping him win a seat in Congress. In 1852, Douglass himself became the first African American nominated for vice president on the Equal Rights Party ticket of 1852.

Recurring financial problems forced Douglass to reduce the size and frequency of his paper in 1859. His third effort, *Douglass' Monthly*, circulating in England as well as in the United States, lasted until the middle of the Civil War, 1863. Like the other two papers, *Douglass' Monthly* remained a magnet for African American writers and reformers and framed Douglass' own inimitable style and wit as well. He actively recruited African American soldiers for the war. He viewed Abraham Lincoln as the best hope for his race, pressing for the Emancipation Proclamation that Lincoln delivered in 1863. He proposed land reform, federally financed education, and a national association for African Americans. He believed that interracial marriages would someday eliminate racial hatred.

After the Civil War, Douglass moved to Washington, D.C. There he published the *New National Era*, focusing on the interests of the newly freed African Americans. During that paper's existence (1870-1873), Douglass editorialized on Reconstruction, the rise of mob lynchings in the South, race relations, politics, labor, and education. From 1873 until his death in 1895, Douglass continued to be heard on the lecture circuit and in leading newspapers. A self-made man, rising against great odds from slavery to publisher, race leader, prominent abolitionist, social reformer, and political activist, Douglass is one of the most important African Americans of the nineteenth century and became a powerful symbol in the Civil Rights movement throughout the twentieth century.

—*Richard Whitworth*

ADDITIONAL READING:

Douglass, Frederick. *The Frederick Douglass Papers.* Edited by John W. Blassingame and John R. McKivigan. 5 vols. New Haven, Conn.: Yale University Press, 1979-1992. A reconstruction of Douglass' thoughts and opinions from fragmentary newspapers, such as *The North Star*, and manuscript sources.

Huggins, Nathan I. *Slave and Citizen: The Life of Frederick Douglass.* Boston: Little, Brown, 1980. Analyzes the complexities of abolition ideology. Portrays Douglass as troubled and self-contradictory at times.

Martin, Waldo E. *The Mind of Frederick Douglass.* Chapel Hill: University of North Carolina Press, 1984. Focuses on Douglass' formative years and the reworking of his views on slavery, inequality, and injustice.

Meltzer, Milton, ed. *Frederick Douglass, in His Own Words.* San Diego, Calif.: Harcourt, Brace, 1995. Profiles people surrounding Douglass. Samples articles from *The North Star* and Douglass' other newspapers.

Rogers, William B. *"We Are All Together Now": Frederick Douglass, William Lloyd Garrison, and the Prophetic Tradition.* New York: Garland, 1995. Juxtaposes the values, beliefs, and actions of Douglass and Garrison.

Voss, Frederick S. *Majestic in His Wrath: A Pictorial Life of Frederick Douglass.* Washington, D.C.: Smithsonian Institution Press, 1995. Brings together rare photos and commentary to commemorate the centennial of Douglass' death.

SEE ALSO: 1831, *The Liberator* Begins Publication; 1850, Underground Railroad; 1848, Seneca Falls Convention; 1863, Emancipation Proclamation.

1848 ■ California Gold Rush: *discovery of the precious metal invites a flood of Eastern fortune seekers and global immigrants into the new U.S. territory*

DATE: January 24, 1848-September 4, 1849
LOCALE: Western slope of the Sierra Nevada
CATEGORIES: Expansion and land acquisition; Immigration; Settlements
KEY FIGURES:
Thomas Oliver Larkin (1802-1858), U.S. consul in California
James Wilson Marshall (1810-1855), discoverer of gold on the south fork of the American River
Richard Barnes Mason (1797-1850), military governor of California
John Augustus Sutter (1803-1880), owner of the mill where gold was discovered

SUMMARY OF EVENT. On January 24, 1848, James W. Marshall discovered gold in the terrace of a mill that a group of men were erecting for John A. Sutter on the south fork of the American River. Despite Sutter's efforts to keep the news secret until he could secure and protect the vast estates he had obtained by Mexican land grants, California newspapers revealed the find in March. By May, the rush had started, and San Francisco, Monterey, San Jose, and other California communities were depopulated of men who headed for the streams flowing westward from the Sierra Nevada. During the first working season in the summer of 1848, Californians, joined by a few men from Oregon and Hawaii, searched for the precious metal without competition from the horde of gold seekers who would soon descend on the gold country.

News of the discovery first reached the East in August, when the New York *Herald* published a report; the next month, official word arrived from Thomas O. Larkin, the U.S. consul in Monterey, who was alarmed at the impact of the event. After a tour of the diggings, Richard B. Mason, military governor of California, forwarded a report to Washington, D.C., accompanied by a small box of sample gold. In December, 1848, when President James K. Polk notified Congress of the gold discovery in his annual message, the United States and the whole world realized that earlier reports were true. Gold fever broke out in the eastern United States; thousands made arrangements to go to California in the spring. Some gold seekers planned to migrate and operate independently, while others organized cooperative groups or companies to share expenses, labor, and profits.

Many people living on the eastern seacoast elected to travel to California by sea. Within a month following the president's message, sixty-one ships had left the Atlantic seaports for a voyage of six months around Cape Horn, arriving at their destination in the summer months of 1849. It was possible to shorten the journey by taking a steamship to Chagres, crossing the Isthmus of Panama by land, and boarding another ship at Panama, bound for California, but passages were uncertain,

even the most expensive accommodations were inadequate, and the isthmus was disease-ridden. When this route became overcrowded, some travelers chose a longer crossing through Nicaragua; however, they found greater difficulty obtaining passage on the Pacific side, because the vessels headed north already had been overloaded in Panama.

The largest number of gold seekers went to California overland, a shorter and cheaper trip. Warm weather permitted an early start on a journey across northern Mexico or New Mexico. Texas trails converged on El Paso, from which the adventurers headed west by way of Tucson and the Gila River into southern California, and then northward to regions in the Sierra where gold had been discovered. Santa Fe was another base, at which people arrived from Fort Smith, Arkansas, having ascended the valley of the Canadian River, or having come west from Missouri by way of the Santa Fe Trail. At Santa Fe, some people elected to turn southward down the Rio Grande and west along the Gila River, following the route of Stephen Kearny's Army of the West into California. Others turned north and west in a greater semicircular path, known as the Old Spanish Trail, that went into southern California. The most popular route was the well-known Platte River Trail to the South Pass, then by way of Fort Hall or Salt Lake City to the California Trail, and across Nevada along the banks of the Humboldt River.

The overland migration of 1849 along this route appeared to duplicate that of earlier years, but there were considerable differences. The danger from attacks by Native Americans was minimized because of the number of travelers, and parties were not nearly so likely to lose the route. The heavy traffic exhausted the grass supply needed for animals, however, and water holes along the trail were infected with Asiatic cholera. Suffering was intense, because the immigrants knew nothing about traveling along plains or over mountains. Guides were scarce, and many guidebooks and newspaper accounts were misleading. The trails were marked by the graves of those who had succumbed to cholera, dysentery, or mountain fever. Beyond the South Pass, much of the route was over hot and dusty alkali deserts. In the desert crossing between the sinks of the Humboldt and Carson Rivers, the ground was littered with abandoned wagons and carcasses of dead animals. Many weary immigrants resorted to pack animals or walked across the Sierra Nevada. A relief society in Sacramento financed and delivered medical and food supplies to groups stranded in the desert, saving many lives. Conditions were equally bad in the desert west of the mouth of the Gila River. Those who wandered from the established routes encountered indescribable suffering; one party leaving the Colorado River to strike directly west into California left most of its members in a valley subsequently known as Death Valley.

San Francisco became the metropolis of the gold country, and supply towns grew at the strategic locations of Marysville, Sacramento, and Stockton. Hundreds of mining camps sprang up near the diggings, with picturesque names such as Poker Flat, Hangtown, Red Dog, Hell's Delight, and Whiskey Bar expressing the sentiments of a predominantly male society.

OFF FOR CALIFORNIA.

This contemporary lithograph, published in 1849, lampoons the fever that struck many who participated in the gold rush. California offered the hope of adventure and wealth; for some, it also offered an escape from responsibilities—or worse. (Library of Congress)

Most of the "forty-niners" who migrated to California were young, unmarried, and male. However, thousands of women also made the voyage to California.

So many people came to California that the majority of gold seekers found it necessary to labor long, hard hours to obtain the gold necessary to provide shelter and food. The weak and the defenseless were quickly weeded out. As economic pressures mounted, prejudice against racial and national minorities increased. California mining camps were cosmopolitan, and the Euro-Americans from New England, the South, the Missouri frontier, and elsewhere used various devices to discriminate against such groups as the Chinese, Mexicans, and African Americans. Native-born Euro-Americans constituted almost 80 percent of all the forty-niners. The second largest group was from Mexico and other countries of Latin America. Approximately 7 percent came from Europe and Asia. English and German immigrants were more successful at mining than were the French, most of whom returned to the supply towns and became shopkeepers. To escape the drudgery, miners occasionally spent days of recreation engaged in contests of strength, endurance, and speed to demonstrate their physical prowess. Many found amusement at night in the saloons,

where they gambled at red dog or faro, or in dancehalls with women. Still, the miners were noted for their spontaneous humanitarianism in aiding the distressed.

When the gold rush began, California had a population of fourteen thousand; by the end of 1849, there were an estimated one hundred thousand in the former Mexican province. Exhibiting admirable leadership, some of these men laid plans for the calling of a constitutional convention to meet in September, 1849, to organize a new state seeking admission into the United States.

In the early days, mining in California was highly rewarding—an average miner obtained between ten and fifty dollars a day—but the rate of return declined rapidly as time passed. Nevertheless, until 1865 or thereabouts, an average of almost fifty million dollars of gold per year was mined in California. While the first fortunes were made in the more easily accessible placer deposits, the later fortunes generally were made by mining corporations that could afford the capital and machinery required to work the deeper deposits.

The more than seventy-five thousand people who migrated to California in the hope of earning their fortunes had a tremendously significant effect on American history. The huge influx of people from the East displaced many Native Americans and highlighted racial tensions between the native-born and foreign-born. The notion of "manifest destiny" (a term that had surfaced three years earlier in an article by John L. O'Sullivan appearing in *The United States Magazine and Democratic Review*)—whereby expansionist interests held that it was "the fulfillment of our manifest destiny to overspread the continent allotted by Providence for the free development of our yearly multiplying millions"—had taken hold of the nation. Because of the large numbers of westward-moving fortune seekers, California was admitted as a state in 1850. California miners developed new mining technology that benefited mining in other regions of the country.

—*W. Turrentine Jackson, updated by Judith Boyce DeMark*

ADDITIONAL READING:

Caughey, John W. *Gold Is the Cornerstone.* Berkeley: University of California Press, 1948. A brief overview of several significant facets of the gold rush, including discovery, the rush of the forty-niners, and the significance to California and United States history.

Gordon, Mary M., ed. *Overland to California with the Pioneer Line.* Urbana: University of Illinois Press, 1984. A collection of memories of participants in various land expeditions to California during the 1840's.

Levy, Jo Ann. "Forgotten Forty-Niners." In *American History.* Vol. 1. Guilford, Conn.: Dushkin, 1995. Provides new information on the experiences of women in the California mining camps and surrounding towns.

Paul, Rodman W. *California Gold: The Beginning of Mining in the Far West.* Cambridge, Mass.: Harvard University Press, 1947. Covers several economic and social aspects of the gold rush era, including the impact on California, the contributions of the California miners to mining technology, and the regulation of mining society, particularly the growth of vigilante committees.

Royce, Sarah. *A Frontier Lady: Recollections of the Gold Rush and Early California.* Lincoln: University of Nebraska Press, 1977. A diary that describes the author's experiences as a wife who took part in the California gold rush.

SEE ALSO: 1842, Frémont's Expeditions; 1846, Mexican War; 1846, Occupation of California and the Southwest; 1848, Treaty of Guadalupe Hidalgo; 1849, Chinese Immigration; 1853, Pacific Railroad Surveys; 1858, Fraser River Gold Rush; 1896, Klondike Gold Rush.

1848 ■ TREATY OF GUADALUPE HIDALGO: the conclusion to the Mexican War results in cession of extensive Mexican lands to the United States

DATE: February 2, 1848

LOCALE: Guadalupe Hidalgo, near Mexico City

CATEGORIES: Latino American history; Treaties and agreements

KEY FIGURES:

James Buchanan (1791-1868), U.S. secretary of state

Manuel de la Peña y Peña (1789-1850), president of Mexico

James Knox Polk (1795-1849), eleventh president of the United States, 1845-1849

Antonio López de Santa Anna (1794-1876), general and president of Mexico, 1847, 1853-1855

Winfield Scott (1786-1866) and

Zachary Taylor (1784-1850), U.S. generals

Nicholas Philip Trist (1800-1874), chief clerk of the U.S. Department of State

SUMMARY OF EVENT. The Treaty of Guadalupe Hidalgo, drafted and signed at the Mexican village of Guadalupe Hidalgo, near Mexico City, ended the Mexican War (1846-1848). The war had been prompted partly by hawkish adherents of manifest destiny, a belief in the inevitable expansion of the United States through the whole of North America, although it had nominally erupted over disputed territories shortly after the United States annexed the Republic of Texas in 1845. The specific cause of the war was the dispute over which river— the Rio Bravo del Norte or the Nueces—marked a boundary line between the two countries. War had been declared formally in April of 1846, after Mexican and U.S. troops clashed in the disputed territory between the two rivers.

In Mexico, political turmoil and poor military strategy and preparedness at first led to fairly easy U.S. victories. Successful campaigns in northeastern Mexico by General Zachary Taylor caused the collapse of the Mexican government and the recall from exile of General Antonio López de Santa Anna, who fought a close but losing battle against Taylor at Buena Vista in February of 1847. The tide turned fully against Mexico when General Winfield Scott invaded Mexico at Veracruz and fought his way inland against tough resistance to capture Mexico City. The crucial battle in Scott's march from the sea was fought against Santa Anna at Cerro Gordo on April 18, 1847; even with Santa Anna's defeat, Scott's army had difficulty, and it was not until September 14, 1847, that his troops entered and took control of the Mexican capital.

Santa Anna, threatened with impeachment for his conduct of the war, went once more into exile. In order to take direct command of the Mexican forces, he earlier had named Manuel de la Peña y Peña interim president and eventually had to ask the Peña government for permission to leave Mexico. It was Peña who was forced to agree to the terms of the Treaty of Guadalupe Hidalgo, negotiated under the weakest possible conditions for Mexico. For a payment of $15 million and $3.25 million in claims of Mexican citizens, Mexico ceded to the United States the territories of New Mexico and Upper California. The agreement also established the Mexican-American boundary, which followed the course of the Rio Grande from the Gulf of Mexico to the southern border of New Mexico, west to the Gila and Colorado Rivers, and eventually to a point just south of San Diego on the Pacific Ocean.

The negotiations leading up to the treaty were complex. In April of 1847, President Polk had sent Nicholas P. Trist of the

Department of State to Scott's camp with a secret treaty proposal drafted by James Buchanan, secretary of state. Trist was empowered to consider counterproposals and secure an armistice, which was actually arranged in late August of that same year. Scott had been in secret communication with Santa Anna, who, without the knowledge of the Mexican government, was trying to arrange treaty terms on his own. Santa Anna assured Scott that hostilities could be suspended and a treaty negotiated if and when Scott's army laid siege to Mexico City. Scott had even written a memorandum in which he avowed that he would fight a battle in view of the capital and then "give those in the City an opportunity to save the capital by making a peace."

Scott, with victories at Contreras and Churubusco in August, 1847, had met Santa Anna's conditions. The road to Mexico City was open, and the remnants of Santa Anna's army had been put to disordered flight, taking refuge within the capital. Scott was certain that a peace with a compliant Santa Anna could be quickly negotiated. Santa Anna, however, was as deceitful and crafty as Scott was forthright and naïve. He knew that Scott's army was wracked by disease, declining morale, and logistics problems, and he believed that time was an invisible ally. As his blame-shifting maneuvers made clear, he also wanted to avoid making any treaty concessions that would tarnish his national image. Thus, although a cease-fire was arranged and agreed to, the efforts to draft a mutually acceptable set of terms at the ensuing peace conference proved futile and were probably doomed from the outset. The armistice broke off on September 6, and on September 14 Scott took Mexico City. Santa Anna had already fled.

When it became clear to Buchanan and Polk that Santa Anna was stalling, Polk ordered the recall of Trist, in part to counteract the impression that the United States was anxious to achieve a peace, a view gaining currency among the Mexican people. Trist did not return, however; he stayed on after the futile negotiations broke off and fighting resumed. The war dragged on past the departure of Santa Anna, who met his final defeat at Puebla on October 11. It was abundantly clear that Mexico could not turn the war's tide, and within two months, it sued for peace. Trist, never having returned home, became the chief U.S. negotiator at Guadalupe Hidalgo, where the treaty was finally signed.

The drafted terms, readied by January 24, 1848, more fully realized the territorial ambitions of the United States than the terms that had been discussed during the earlier armistice conference, which had at least left the Texas border question open. However, even from the outset of the earlier negotiations, it had been clear that the United States was determined to annex both Upper California and New Mexico. In the end, Santa Anna's delaying tactics had proved a bit more costly to Mexico.

Because a flawed map was used during the treaty negotiations, the boundaries between Mexico and the United States remained open to interpretation. Surveyors could not agree on the identity of the first branch of the Gila River, one of the important demarcation lines, and the boundary line between Mexico and the United States in the area separating the Gila River and the Rio Grande was not settled. However, both the Rio Grande and the Gila River were established as principal boundaries. Mexico thereby ceded territories south of the Nueces River and all of Upper California from one nautical league south of San Diego to the Northwest Territories. The United States gained all of the Territory of New Mexico, the disputed lands in southern Texas, and Upper California. In consideration for ceding this vast acreage, the United States was to pay only the stipulated $15 million plus the $3.25 million in claims. It was a grand bargain for the expansionist believers in manifest destiny. The treaty terms were quickly accepted by Polk and, with some amendments, ratified by the U.S. Senate on March 10, 1848.

The Treaty of Guadalupe Hidalgo did not immediately end the boundary issue. In 1853, during the administration of Franklin Pierce, the current border between Mexico and the United States was finally set when the United States purchased the Arizona Territory from Mexico in the Gadsden Purchase and described the boundary line between the two countries in the disputed area.

An important provision of that treaty, Article VII, granted U.S. citizenship with full constitutional rights to the Mexicans living in the ceded territories and guaranteed them ownership of their land. However, through the invalidation of Spanish and Mexican land grants, federal courts and the U.S. Congress allowed government agencies, ranchers, land speculators, and business and railroad magnates to gobble up acreage that, by the terms of the treaty, rightly belonged to Mexican Americans. Over two generations, almost twenty million acres of their land was lost to private owners and state and federal agencies.

—John W. Fiero

ADDITIONAL READING:

Brack, Gene M. *Mexico Views Manifest Destiny, 1821-1846: An Essay on the Origins of the Mexican War*. Albuquerque: University of New Mexico Press, 1975. A concise investigation of the growth of anti-American sentiment in Mexico on the path toward hostilities. Good selected bibliography.

Callahan, James M. *American Foreign Policy in Mexican Relations*. New York: Macmillan, 1932. First important study of the United States' Mexican policy. Gives principal attention to continuing problems in the decades after the Treaty of Guadalupe Hidalgo, up through the Díaz era.

McAfee, Ward, and J. Cordell Robinson, comps. *Origins of the Mexican War: A Documentary Source Book*. 2 vols. Salisbury, N.C.: Documentary Publications, 1982. A useful repository of original documents pertaining to the Mexican War. Helpful for research in primary materials.

Pletcher, David M. *The Diplomacy of Annexation: Texas, Oregon, and the Mexican War*. Columbia: University of Missouri Press, 1973. One of the best studies on U.S. expansionism. The section on the Mexican War is regarded as a fair and balanced discussion.

Singletary, Otis A. *The Mexican War*. Chicago: University of Chicago Press, 1960. A concise study of the diplomacy and politics involved in the war, reviewing both the U.S. and

Mexican positions. Not a detailed military history, but examines the relevance of major engagements to the final treaty.

SEE ALSO: 1821, Mexican War of Independence; 1821, Santa Fe Trail Opens; 1835, Texas Revolution; 1846, Mexican War; 1846, Occupation of California and the Southwest; 1847, Taos Rebellion; 1853, Gadsden Purchase.

1848 ■ SENECA FALLS CONVENTION: *the beginning of the women's rights movement and the fight for woman suffrage*

DATE: July 19-20, 1848
LOCALE: Seneca Falls, New York
CATEGORIES: Civil rights; Women's issues
KEY FIGURES:
Frederick Douglass (1817?-1895), former slave, abolitionist, and publisher
Lucretia Coffin Mott (1793-1880), Quaker abolitionist and coconvener of the convention
Elizabeth Cady Stanton (1815-1902), coconvener of the convention and advocate of woman suffrage

SUMMARY OF EVENT. The Women's Rights Convention assembled in Seneca Falls, New York, July 19-20, 1848, is widely held to be the beginning of the women's rights movement in the United States. Organized and led by Elizabeth Cady Stanton and Lucretia Coffin Mott, its attendees approved the Declaration of Sentiments and Resolutions written by Stanton. The ninth of its twelve resolutions, and the only seriously challenged resolution, called for woman suffrage.

The Seneca Falls Convention had its origins in 1840, when Mott and Stanton met in London, England, during the World Anti-Slavery Convention. Mott and her husband, James, active Quakers and supporters of abolition, were delegates to the convention, as was Henry Brewster Stanton, Elizabeth's husband. The convention, perhaps fortuitously for the women's rights movement, determined to exclude women from the floor of delegates. Although Stanton and Mott were upset by this action, their exclusion from the conference provided Stanton with the opportunity for extended conversations with Mott, who was twenty-two years her senior and an experienced and dedicated reformer. They determined that, upon their return to the United States, they would call a convention to consider the status of women.

Eight years passed before their London decision became a reality. In 1848, when Lucretia Mott was visiting in the Seneca Falls region, now home to the Stanton family, the two women met again. Aided by Martha Wright (Mott's sister), Jane Hunt, and Mary McClintock, Mott and Stanton planned the convention, which took place with only one week's preparation. The call to the convention was made in the July 14 issue of the *Seneca Country Courier* and stated that "a Convention to discuss the social, civil and religious condition and rights of women, will be held in the Wesleyan Chapel, at Seneca Falls,

New York, on Wednesday and Thursday, the nineteenth and twentieth of July, current; commencing at 10 o'clock A.M." The announcement went on to inform attendees that the first day would be exclusively for women and the second for the general public.

Having announced the meeting, the organizing committee set about planning the agenda for the two-day convention and drafting a statement of their "sentiments" and the proposed resolutions for the assembly to consider.

The text of the Declaration of Sentiments and Resolutions is a seminal statement of the women's rights movement. It articulates the rationale and the goals of the movement and provides the agenda for its leaders into the twentieth century. Its writing fell primarily to Elizabeth Cady Stanton. Her early education and background in the law made her the natural choice for this task. Born into a well-known, upper-middle-class family, Elizabeth had received an education rare for women of her day. Partly self-educated, relying on books used by her brothers, she gained a grounding in the classics. Later she attended Emma Willard's Female Seminary, benefiting from the best formal education available to women in the 1830's. Returning home from the Willard Seminary, she read law in her father's office, which gave her an initial grounding in the current civil laws and the legal status of women's rights, or more correctly, lack of rights. This background, enhanced by association with the abolitionist movement before and after her marriage, made Stanton the theoretical voice, literally and in print, of the women's movement throughout the latter half of the nineteenth century.

With the declaration written, the planners of the convention awaited the arrival of its attendees. Reports differ on the exact number—some have estimated as many as three hundred—but especially significant is the number of men who arrived: twenty-two, including the abolitionist and publisher Frederick Douglass. The fact that men attended caused the planners to alter their original plan to reserve one day exclusively for women. They also asked James Mott, Lucretia's husband, to chair the session. Lucretia Mott, a well-known and articulate spokesperson and the only previously announced speaker, was joined by a host of well-known, or soon-to-be-well-known, spokespersons on a wide-ranging list of human rights, specifically the rights of women. Mary and Elizabeth McClintock spoke, and Ansel Bascom reported on the consideration of women's rights during the recently adjourned New York Constitutional Convention.

Stanton's speech captured the essence of the convention, stating unequivocally her position and summarizing the views she had been nurturing for several years. As a result, she was launched into a leadership position in the women's rights movement. Her initial statement is an appropriate summary of her thinking:

> I should feel exceedingly diffident to appear before you at this time, never having spoken in public, were I not nerved by a sense of right and duty, nor did I not feel the time had fully come for the question of women's wrongs to be laid before the public,

did I not believe that woman herself must do this work; for woman alone can understand the height, the depth, the length, and the breadth of her own degradation. Man cannot speak for her, because he has been educated to believe that she differs from him so materially, that he cannot judge of her thoughts, feelings, and opinions by his own. Moral beings can only judge of others by themselves. The moment they assume a different nature for any of their own, they utterly fail. . . .

Day two of the convention focused on consideration of the Declaration of Sentiments and Resolutions. The declaration was obviously and consciously modeled on the text and style of the Declaration of Independence. Following the preamble—fifteen examples of men's "absolute tyranny" over women—the declaration insisted that women have "immediate admission to all the rights and privileges which belong to them as citizens of the United States." Twelve resolutions followed. They were unanimously supported and signed by sixty-eight women and thirty-two men. The only resolution that caused serious debate was the ninth, which stated, straightforwardly and unambiguously, that "it is the duty of the women of this country to secure to themselves their sacred right to the elective franchise." For Stanton, this resolution was the key to the accomplishment of all the other goals. She believed that the electorate must be representative of all views and needs if legislatures were to pass laws securing and protecting the rights of all, specifically those ensuring the rights of women. With the help of Frederick Douglass, the noted abolitionist, Stanton was able to secure narrow passage of this resolution, thus becoming the first public voice within the women's rights movement for woman suffrage.

The Seneca Falls Convention of 1848 drew immediate reaction, much of it unfavorable. Douglass continued his support and documented the event in an editorial in his paper, *The North Star*, a week after the convention. Despite criticism, the women's rights movement had begun, and a follow-up session was held in Rochester, New York. Other leaders emerged, various agendas took precedence, and debate continued for many years before woman suffrage finally was realized with the passage of the Nineteenth Amendment in 1920, seventy-two years after Stanton and Douglass had persuaded a reluctant delegation to support it. —*Ann Thompson*

ADDITIONAL READING:

Banner, Lois W. *Elizabeth Cady Stanton: A Radical for Woman's Rights*. Boston: Little, Brown, 1980. An informative, basic biography, providing a highly readable picture of Stanton's life and thought.

Cromwell, Otelia. *Lucretia Mott*. Cambridge, Mass.: Harvard University Press, 1958. Chapter 12 covers the Seneca Falls Convention and is helpful in understanding Mott's role and her positions.

Donovan, Josephine. *Feminist Theory: The Intellectual Traditions of American Feminism*. New York: Frederick Ungar, 1985. Conveys the philosophical and theoretical underpinnings of the women's movement, of which Stanton is recognized as a key theorist.

Du Bois, Ellen Carol, ed. *Elizabeth Cady Stanton, Susan B. Anthony: Correspondence, Writings, Speeches*. New York: Schocken Books, 1981. An excellent source for original texts, with critical commentary provided by W. E. B. Du Bois.

Griffin, Elizabeth. *In Her Own Right: The Life of Elizabeth Cady Stanton*. New York: Oxford University Press, 1984. An excellent biography of Stanton, with a helpful bibliography. Chapter 4 details the Seneca Falls Convention.

Schneir, Miriam, ed. *Feminism: The Essential Historical Writings*. New York: Random House, 1972. Contains a helpful introduction, as well as commentaries on key texts of the women's rights movement.

SEE ALSO: 1776, New Jersey Women Gain the Vote; 1851, Akron Woman's Rights Convention; 1866, Suffragists Protest the Fourteenth Amendment; 1869, Rise of Woman Suffrage Associations; 1869, Western States Grant Woman Suffrage; 1872, Susan B. Anthony Is Arrested; 1876, Declaration of the Rights of Women; 1890, Women's Rights Associations Unite; 1916, National Woman's Party Is Founded; 1920, League of Women Voters Is Founded; 1920, U.S. Women Gain the Vote.

1849 ■ CHINESE IMMIGRATION: *the California gold rush draws thousands of Chinese immigrants, who furnish hard labor and suffer nativist antipathy*

DATE: 1849-1852
LOCALE: San Francisco
CATEGORIES: Asian American history; Immigration
KEY FIGURES:
Tong K. Achick, leader of Four Great Houses
Norman As-sing, merchant and early leader of the Chinese community in San Francisco
John Bigler (1805-1871), governor of California, 1848-1852
George B. Tingley, California state senator

SUMMARY OF EVENT. In 1848, the electrifying news that gold had been discovered in California was carried by every ship sailing from U.S. ports. Spread to every corner of the world, the word soon began to draw adventurers away from family and livelihoods to seek their fortunes in this distant land. In 1849, a tremendous number of pioneers—German, Irish, Scandinavian, Russian, Mexican, and others—streamed into San Francisco, doubling the population of the state within two years. Among these "forty-niners" was one group set apart by race, dress, and language—the Chinese. Drawn to the United States by the promise of golden wealth, the Chinese arrived in ever-increasing numbers, to the growing alarm of California residents.

Almost all the Chinese entering the United States at this time came from the area around Canton, in the southeastern province of Kwangtung. For centuries, Cantonese peasants had made their living as laborers, farmers, and fishermen. During the late 1840's, floods, famines, peasant revolts, and overpopulation forced many to leave their villages and seek work in nearby countries in the South China Sea. When word reached the province of gold mines opening in California, Cantonese were eager to leave their impoverished homeland for the chance of riches just across the Pacific. They were cautious, however—the journey was long, expensive, and uncertain. Only three Chinese made the trip in 1848.

In 1849, the news of larger and richer gold claims in California enticed 325 Cantonese to set sail for San Francisco. Most of these young, unskilled men were sojourners, hoping to prospect for a few years, acquire wealth, and return home. Like other new arrivals in the city, they outfitted themselves with supplies, including sturdy boots in place of their cotton shoes, and set out for the gold-bearing mountains around Sacramento. They often traveled and worked in groups for companionship and protection, taking over low-yielding claims that had been abandoned for more prosperous sites. Through diligence and frugality, honed by generations of mar-

ginal existence in China, they frequently turned abandoned claims into profitable ventures.

Not all Chinese immigrants, however, sought wealth in the gold mines. Some found work in the cities, particularly San Francisco, which offered abundant opportunity for unskilled laborers. Shops, restaurants, liveries, hotels, and other businesses grew desperately short of workers as able-bodied men abandoned their jobs to pan for gold. Chinese—newly arrived immigrants or disheartened miners—began filling these positions as general laborers, carpenters, and cooks. They also assumed jobs normally reserved for women—who were in short supply in this rugged frontier boomtown—such as seamstresses, launderers, and domestics. Their conscientious work style, quiet demeanor, and dependable service made them ideal employees. California businessmen soon began sending advertising notices to Canton, recruiting Chinese workers for their various enterprises.

Successful Chinese miners and workers also began opening

Chinese immigrants began to flood California after the discovery of gold, in the early 1850's. As their numbers increased, their presence was reviled by Euro-American nativists who believed that they were stealing their jobs. Nevertheless, during a period when the nation was expanding there was a great need for labor, and Chinese men did much of the backbreaking work in the mines and in building the transcontinental railroad. (Asian American Studies Library, University of California at Berkeley)

their own businesses in the cities. In addition to equipping miners and supplying mining camps, they established restaurants, hotels, and various small businesses catering to both Chinese and Westerners. Norman As-sing, an English-speaking Chinese man who settled in San Francisco, managed his own candy store, bakery, and a popular restaurant in which he often entertained local politicians and policemen with lavish banquets. In December, 1849, his fellow countrymen elected him as the leader of the first Chinese mutual-aid society in the United States, an organization assisting newly arrived Chinese immigrants. This association filled an important role for the Chinese, who relied greatly on family and village relations for social and economic sufficiency. Through letters and returning sojourners, news of profitable work in the cities and mines reached relatives and friends in Kwangtung. In 1850, approximately 450 more Chinese emigrated to California; the following year, the number jumped to more than 2,700. These new arrivals found assistance and familiar food and lodging in San Francisco's new Chinatown, a district in which Chinese had begun to settle for convenience and safety. After a short period of adjustment, most Chinese immigrants followed their predecessors into the mountains, joining one of the many Chinese mining camps operating around Sacramento. Others remained in the city to work as manual laborers. In general, these early Chinese immigrants worked with exceptional diligence, industry, and enterprise and led a reticent existence in the mining camps and cities.

These positive qualities earned the early Chinese immigrants acceptance among the California business community. Although their waist-length braided hair, blue cotton pants and jackets, and broad-brimmed straw hats set them apart from the rest of the townspeople and "forty-niners," they were warmly welcomed as a valuable and respected segment of the citizenry. A San Francisco judge summed up the early goodwill of Americans toward the Chinese: "Born and reared under different Governments and speaking different tongues, we nevertheless meet here today as brothers. . . . You stand among us in all respects as equals."

That goodwill wore thin as increasing numbers of Chinese arrived in the city. In 1852 alone, more than twenty thousand Chinese landed at San Francisco, bringing the total number of Chinese on the coast to approximately twenty-five thousand. The flood of new arrivals severely taxed the city's resources, particularly in Chinatown, where most settled, at least temporarily. In packed Chinese boardinghouses, one cot was often rented to a number of workers who slept on it on a rotating basis. Overcrowding created sanitation problems, increased crime, and caused higher prices. Abundant cheap labor stimulated competition for unskilled work that, over time, drove down wages. The white settlers' attitude toward the Chinese and Chinatown began to shift from curiosity to contempt.

The attitude of white miners in the gold fields also changed. Prior to 1852, bandits and claim-jumpers had occasionally driven Chinese off successful excavations, but these attacks were generally motivated by greed, not racism. After 1852,

antagonism and violence against Chinese miners increased. In Jacksonville, white miners drove Chinese miners off their claims and out of town. In Chili Gulch, a mob beat a Chinese miner to death. For protection, Chinese banded together in large mining camps, easily recognized by names such as China City, China Creek, China Flat, China Gulch, and China Town.

Under the slogan "California for Americans," nativists began demanding legislation to restrict Chinese laborers and miners. In 1852, the California legislature responded by passing the state's first discriminatory tax law, the Foreign Miners' Tax. This law required all miners who were not citizens of the United States to pay a monthly license fee. Since the Chinese were the largest recognizable group of foreign miners and already were concentrated in easily accessible mining camps, they constituted the majority of those taxed. The same year, California state senator George B. Tingley introduced a bill to eliminate "coolie labor"—contracts made with Chinese laborers for work in California for a set number of years. California governor John Bigler also began a crusade against Chinese immigration on the grounds that it constituted a danger to the welfare of the state. Tong K. Achick, a missionary-schooled, English-speaking Cantonese who emigrated to San Francisco, represented the Chinese position before the California legislature. As leader of the Four Great Houses in San Francisco—forerunner of the famous Six Companies—he argued that these laws unfairly targeted law-abiding Chinese, who were an asset, not a liability, to the state.

The mood in California, however, had changed, and Tong and other Chinese advocates were unable to stop the growing anti-Chinese sentiment. California nativists continued to push for state and national legislation limiting Chinese immigration. Their efforts culminated in the Chinese Exclusion Act of 1882, the first federal legislation restricting immigration to the United States.

—*Daniel J. Meissner*

ADDITIONAL READING:

Barth, Gunther. *Bitter Strength: A History of the Chinese in the United States, 1850-1870.* Cambridge, Mass.: Harvard University Press, 1964. Describes the early years of Chinese immigration, providing a good examination of the development of anti-Chinese sentiment in California.

Bodnar, John. *The Transplanted: A History of Immigrants in Urban America.* Bloomington: Indiana University Press, 1985. Although centering on European immigration, addresses issues common to the Chinese experience, which spurred natives to emigrate to the United States.

Chan, Sucheng. *Asian Americans: An Interpretive History.* Boston: Twayne, 1991. Examines factors influencing Asian emigration and the problems Asians faced in adjusting to the United States.

Coolidge, Mary Roberts. *Chinese Immigration.* New York: Henry Holt, 1909. Comprehensively details Chinese immigration, the rise of anti-Chinese sentiment, and the politics of exclusion.

Miller, Stuart Creighton. *The Unwelcome Immigrant: The American Image of the Chinese, 1795-1882.* Berkeley: University of California Press, 1969. Examines Chinese immigration in terms of coolie labor and the fear that Chinese laborers would undermine labor and revive slavery.

Takaki, Ronald. *Strangers from a Different Shore: A History of Asian Americans.* New York: Penguin Books, 1989. Chapter 3 succinctly examines the early years of Chinese immigration. Other chapters explore the Asian immigrant experience in detail.

SEE ALSO: 1848, California Gold Rush; 1868, Burlingame Treaty; 1875, Page Law; 1882, Chinese Exclusion Act; 1882, Rise of the Chinese Six Companies; 1892, "New" Immigration; 1895, Chinese American Citizens Alliance Is Founded; 1898, *United States v. Wong Kim Ark*; 1899, Hay's "Open Door Notes"; 1917, Immigration Act of 1917; 1924, Immigration Act of 1924; 1943, Magnuson Act.

1850 ■ COMPROMISE OF 1850: *a last national attempt to resolve the question of slavery in the territories brings the nation closer to civil war*

DATE: January 29-September 20, 1850

LOCALE: Washington, D.C.

CATEGORIES: African American history; Expansion and land acquisition; Laws and acts

KEY FIGURES:

John Caldwell Calhoun (1782-1850), senator from South Carolina

Henry Clay (1777-1852), senator from Kentucky

Stephen Arnold Douglas (1813-1861), senator from Illinois

Millard Fillmore (1800-1874), thirteenth president of the United States, 1850-1853

William Seward (1801-1872), congressman from New York

Zachary Taylor (1784-1850), twelfth president of the United States, 1849-1850

Daniel Webster (1782-1852), senator from Massachusetts

David Wilmot (1814-1868), congressman from Pennsylvania

SUMMARY OF EVENT. The United States' acquisition of large land areas following the annexation of Texas in 1845 and the Mexican Cession that followed the Mexican War's end reopened the issue of slavery in the territories for most people in the United States. During the same period, most citizens embraced the idea of manifest destiny and its call for United States' expansion and eventual control of the continent.

Beginning in the 1830's, thousands of settlers officially left the United States when they crossed the Mississippi River, intent on harvesting the Western lands' potential and earning statehood for their new homes. However, the Constitution, while creating a mechanism for the addition of states and acknowledging the right of each state to permit and even encourage slavery within its boundaries, made no mention of slavery's status in future states. Because the power to admit new states lay exclusively with Congress, it could impose any condition it wished, conceivably requiring either the guarantee or abolition of slavery as a condition for admission. The national government had first addressed the issue when the Confederation Congress passed the Northwest Ordinance of 1787. This excluded slavery from the unsettled area north of the Ohio River to the Mississippi River's eastern bank, the edge of the United States' holdings, as a favor to the Chesapeake's tobacco planters, who feared that additional competition would drive down the value of the crops.

The issue reemerged in 1817, when Missouri applied to join the United States as a slave state. The question came before the Congress in 1819, and sectional tensions erupted. Balance between slave and free states existed in the U.S. Senate, which had eleven states each from the free North and the slave-owning South. The North's growing population gave it a decisive advantage in the House of Representatives, so proslave forces committed themselves, at the minimum, to maintaining a balance between the regions in the Senate. At the time, between two thousand and three thousand slaves lived in the Missouri Territory, yet some Northern leaders, such as Rufus King of New York, argued that Congress should require the restriction of slavery before Missouri received statehood.

A temporary solution emerged in 1820, when Senator Henry Clay of Kentucky brokered a solution to the crisis. The Missouri Compromise stipulated that Missouri would be admitted to the Union as a slave state, while Maine, which had petitioned for statehood in late 1819, was admitted as a free state. The compromise also prohibited slavery from the remainder of the Louisiana Purchase in the area north of 36°30′ north latitude, while permitting it south of that line. Between 1820 and 1848, this solution maintained the national peace, as the Senate remained balanced with thirty members representing the free states and an equal number representing the slave states' interests.

The Mexican War disrupted the relative peace. As a consequence of its victory, the United States received millions of acres of land spanning the area from the Continental Divide west to the Pacific Ocean and south from the forty-ninth parallel to Mexico. However, the problems flared even before the war ended, when David Wilmot, a member of the House of Representatives from Pennsylvania, attached an amendment to an appropriations bill. As he conceived it, any territory acquired from Mexico must exclude slavery in perpetuity. Although it failed to win passage, the Wilmot Proviso fueled the smoldering fires of sectionalism, as many assumed that any additional western lands would be governed by the Missouri Compromise.

This idea vanished in 1850. The discovery of gold in California in 1848 brought thousands to the American River Valley, and less than a year later, the young California Republic petitioned the Senate for admission to the Union. Besides disrupting the balance between slave and free states, California straddled the 1820 compromise's line and threw the prior agreements into chaos. In both houses of Congress, the question of slavery became paramount: Southerners rejected any

ALIGNMENT OF FREE AND SLAVE STATES AFTER THE COMPROMISE OF 1850

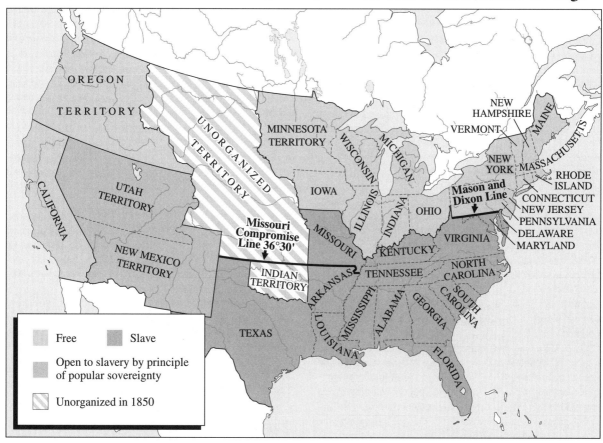

OREGON TERRITORY

UNORGANIZED TERRITORY

MINNESOTA TERRITORY

NEW HAMPSHIRE

VERMONT

MAINE

NEW YORK MASSACHUSETTS

RHODE ISLAND

CALIFORNIA

UTAH TERRITORY

WISCONSIN

MICHIGAN

IOWA

Mason and Dixon Line

CONNECTICUT

NEW JERSEY

PENNSYLVANIA

DELAWARE

MARYLAND

Missouri Compromise Line 36°30'

ILLINOIS

INDIANA

OHIO

VIRGINIA

NEW MEXICO TERRITORY

MISSOURI

KENTUCKY

INDIAN TERRITORY

ARKANSAS

TENNESSEE

NORTH CAROLINA

SOUTH CAROLINA

TEXAS

LOUISIANA

MISSISSIPPI

ALABAMA

GEORGIA

FLORIDA

Legend:
- Free
- Slave
- Open to slavery by principle of popular sovereignty
- Unorganized in 1850

After the Mexican War, the United States acquired vast western tracts. The new land and the California gold rush prompted western migration, raising the issue of slavery in the territories once again, thirty years after the Missouri Compromise. The Compromise of 1850 admitted California as a free state; created the territories of Utah and New Mexico with no restrictions on slavery; fixed the modern Texas boundary; paid Texas for ceding lands for the New Mexico territory; prohibited slave trading in Washington, D.C.; and enacted the Fugitive Slave Act of 1850.

attempt to exclude the practice from the West by nearly unanimous margins, while Free-Soilers from the North rejected the possibility of losing equal economic competition by similar percentages. Left in the middle were some elements of the national Whig Party, which struggled to preserve the Union while remaining a national party itself. The idea of disunion grew, and the failure to achieve a national solution likely would have guaranteed a civil war in 1850. Senator John C. Calhoun of South Carolina, long a firebrand for states' rights, proposed the formation of a sectional party to guarantee the practice of slavery. William Seward, an abolitionist representative from New York, also rejected the possibility of a compromise, citing the immorality of slavery. President Zachary Taylor, the hero of the Mexican War and a Southerner, was also an ardent unionist and supported California's admission as a free state while rejecting the extreme position of persons such as Calhoun.

The first concrete proposal for compromise came from Senator Henry Clay of Kentucky, on January 29, 1850. He introduced a series of five resolutions designed to allow "amicable agreement of all questions in controversy, between the free and slave states, growing out of the subject of slavery." Clay proposed that the California Republic join the United States as a free state; that the rest of the territory acquired in the Mexican Cession be organized without any decision on slavery; that Texas receive monetary compensation in exchange for giving up its claims to parts of contemporary New Mexico; that the slave trade within the District of Columbia be abolished (although the actual practice of slavery would not be affected); and that a more rigorous fugitive slave law be enacted.

The reaction to Clay's proposals reflected the sectional divisions of the day. On February 5 and 6, Clay presented his resolutions and spoke for the Union's preservation. One week later, Mississippi senator Jefferson Davis rejected Clay's proposals, using bitter language that also attacked Northern intentions. John C. Calhoun's last Senate appearance came on March 4, when he was carried into the chamber as Virginia's

James Mason delivered his last speech for him. Calhoun's text rejected compromise on the principle of slavery in the territories and declared that the only way to preserve the Union was for the North to concede the South's equal rights in the territories and for the abolitionists to stop agitating on the slavery question. On March 7, Daniel Webster gave one of his most famous speeches, in which he declared that he spoke "not as a northern man, but as an American." He acknowledged that both sides had just grievances and urged support for Clay's whole plan, calming some tensions with his eloquent plea that the Union be preserved. The abolitionists' position was explained on March 11 by William Seward, who opposed the compromise and cited a higher law than the Constitution, one that rejected the practice of slavery.

In April, the Senate referred Clay's resolutions to a select committee, which the Kentuckian chaired. The committee reported back to the full Senate an Omnibus Bill that contained the substance of the five original resolutions and sparked another four months of debate. Two major stumbling blocks to the compromise disappeared in July, when President Taylor and Calhoun both died. Millard Fillmore, who supported the compromise's ideas, replaced the Mexican War hero Taylor, who had bitterly opposed the Omnibus Bill and had threatened to veto it.

While Clay was vacationing away from Washington, D.C., Stephen A. Douglas broke the Omnibus Bill into five parts and steered them through the Senate, and the House of Representatives followed suit. By September 20, Congress had adopted the five bills that made up the Compromise of 1850.

The efforts of various members of Congress to resolve the crisis of slavery in the territories effectively ended with the efforts in 1850. In 1854, the attempts at balancing the competing interests of the Free-Soil North with the proslave South ended when Senator Douglas proposed that the Kansas and Nebraska areas be organized using the concept of popular sovereignty, such as was used for the areas obtained from Mexico. Congress adopted the Kansas-Nebraska Act that year, triggering a number of serious reactions. Among these was the formation of a national political party dedicated to the idea of an exclusively free-soil policy in the West. The new Republican Party immediately became a force on the national political landscape, and its candidate, John C. Frémont, came within four states of being elected president in 1856. Ultimately, the election of Abraham Lincoln in 1860, a man committed to both the preservation of the Union and the free-soil doctrine, drove the South to secession.

—John G. Clark, updated by E. A. Reed

ADDITIONAL READING:

Collins, Bruce. *The Origins of America's Civil War.* New York: Holmes & Meier, 1981. A review of the individuals, events, and ideas of the period before the war. Examines the opposing ideas and decisions in the antebellum period to find the Civil War's real origins.

Foner, Eric, ed. *Politics and Ideology in the Age of the Civil War.* New York: Oxford University Press, 1980. A thorough analysis of the competing ideas and values during the antebellum period. Traces the political struggles leading up to and through the Civil War.

Holman, Hamilton. *Prologue to Conflict: The Crisis and Compromise of 1850.* New York: W. W. Norton, 1966. One of the most comprehensive examinations of the events surrounding the last major congressional attempt to avoid the war. Presents the national and regional political events that drove the crisis and the individual and cumulative effects.

Potter, David. *The Impending Crisis, 1848-1861.* New York: Harper & Row, 1976. Traces the nation's path to the start of the Civil War, beginning with the emergence of the Free-Soil Party in 1848. Examines the political, economic, and social factors that combined to make war inevitable. The standard scholarly work.

Stampp, Kenneth, ed. *The Causes of the Civil War.* Rev. ed. Englewood Cliffs, N.J.: Prentice-Hall, 1974. A multileveled examination of events, personalities, and ideas. Evaluates the disparate factors at play in the United States in the mid-nineteenth century and evaluates how they contributed to lead the nation into the Civil War.

SEE ALSO: 1820, Missouri Compromise; 1830, Proslavery Argument; 1850, Second Fugitive Slave Law; 1850, Underground Railroad; 1854, Kansas-Nebraska Act; 1856, Bleeding Kansas; 1857, *Dred Scott v. Sandford.*

1850 ■ BLOODY ISLAND MASSACRE: *an early conflict with California Indians illustrates Euro-American attitudes*

DATE: May 6, 1850

LOCALE: Upper Clear Lake, California

CATEGORIES: Latino American history; Wars, uprisings, and civil unrest

KEY FIGURES:

Andrew Kelsey (died 1849), settler and miner killed by Indians

Augustine (fl. 1840-1880), self-identified vaquero foreman at the Kelsey Ranch.

Ben Kelsey, settler, miner, and brother of Andrew

Nathaniel Lyon (1818-1861), commanding officer of the punitive expedition against the Pomo Indians

Charles Stone (died 1849), settler and miner, killed by Indians, and according to one account Kelsey's brother-in-law

SUMMARY OF EVENT. Accounts of the Bloody Island Massacre (sometimes called the Clear Lake Massacre), its cause, and its aftermath are few, brief, and inconsistent. The massacre involved killing of perhaps as many as several hundred Pomo Indians in May, 1850, by U.S. Army troops sent to retaliate for the murder of Charles Stone and Andrew Kelsey in December, 1849. Although many different names apply to the indigenous inhabitants of the area, the name "Pomo" is used throughout extant accounts.

In fall, 1847, the brothers Andrew and Ben Kelsey, Charles Stone, and a man named Shirland bought Salvador Vallejo's land claim, Sixteen Leagues, located west of Clear Lake. Andrew Kelsey and Stone then moved onto the claim and built an adobe house close to the modern town of Kelseyville. According to Augustine, a Pomo "foreman" employed by Kelsey and Stone, about five hundred local Pomos spent two months building the adobe house. For this, the group received the insufficient ration of one steer per day. In the summer of 1848, Stone and Kelsey mustered all the Pomos of the area, selected twenty-six strong, young men, including Augustine, and took them to the Feather River Mines. According to Augustine, the Pomos gathered a bag of gold "as large as a man's arm" for which each was paid with a pair of overalls, a hickory shirt, and a red bandanna. In turn, Kelsey and Stone used the gold to buy Vallejo's cattle, thus establishing themselves as ranchers.

Many reports describe Kelsey and Stone's abuse of the Pomos and resultant conflicts. The ranch apparently was a gathering point for "rough" characters from the mines. During their visits, it was common practice to torture, shoot, and assault Indians "for the sport of it." In addition, Pomos working on the ranch were so poorly fed that they began slaughtering a ranch animal now and then for food. Punishment for this and other infractions included lashing, hanging men up by their hands without food, and death. Pomo women also were "requisitioned" by Kelsey and Stone for sexual purposes. Newspaper accounts and "eyewitness" reports are nearly unanimous in condemning Kelsey and Stone's conduct and many agree that they earned their murders. In contrast, Salvador Vallejo's agents, though by no means softhearted, apparently had no comparable conflicts with the Clear Lake Pomos, who were considered inoffensive and cooperative.

In the spring of 1848, Pomos on the Kelsey-Stone ranch rose up and besieged the two white men in their house. They were unable, however, to force their way in, because Kelsey and Stone had earlier persuaded them to store their weapons in the loft of the building. A friendly Pomo brought word of the siege to Sonoma so Ben Kelsey, accompanied by several others, rode to the ranchers' rescue. Arriving after dark, they found the house darkened and surrounded by what they referred to as a "horde of dancing, shrieking and yelling fiends." After assessing the situation, they charged the mob, making as much noise as possible, but without firing on the Pomos. The tactic scattered the Indians and the rescuers reached the house. Shortly thereafter, the Pomos returned for a palaver. The outcome was a joint expedition of Kelsey, Stone, the rescue party, and the Clear Lake Pomos to the Russian River Valley. There they raided several *rancherias*, where they captured a group of other Pomos, whom they took to Sonoma for distribution as laborers among the settlers of that area.

A second mining expedition organized by Ben Kelsey in the spring of 1849, involving between fifty and one hundred Clear Lake Pomos, found no gold and ended in disaster. After Ben Kelsey sold the expedition's supplies to other prospecting groups for his own profit, the group was stricken with malaria.

Kelsey, himself incapacitated, and the other white people then abandoned the sick, destitute Pomos far from home and in hostile territory. Only three of them managed to return to Clear Lake. The fate of this group further inflamed the Pomos against Stone and Andrew Kelsey.

In the fall of 1849, Andrew Kelsey and Charles Stone were murdered by the Pomos on their ranch. Details regarding the murder and its aftermath differ wildly. In some accounts, Augustine's wife, who had been forced to live with the white men in the absence of her husband, poured water into Kelsey and Stone's loaded weapons the night before the murders, thus disarming the ranchers and opening the way for an assault. In other accounts, Kelsey and Stone were shot from ambush through the windows of the house. In yet another story, Stone was "called out" and shot with arrows, after which Kelsey jumped out of the window and ran into the woods, where he was killed by an old, rock-wielding man. In yet another version, Stone broke out of the house, took refuge in an outbuilding, was dragged out, and had his throat cut. Murder in response to abuse is the only element common to these stories, derived mostly from hearsay accounts, many of which were recorded decades after the event.

On Christmas Day, 1849, Ben Kelsey informed Lieutenant J. W. Davidson at Sonoma, California, of the killings and departed for his brother's ranch with fifteen men. Davidson followed the next day with Lieutenant Wilson of the First Dragoons and twenty-two men. Upon their arrival, Stone's body was found "shockingly mutilated, in a vat and covered with hides." Davidson and Wilson then trailed the Pomos to an island in Clear Lake, which could not be invaded without boats. The Pomos refused to surrender those responsible or to come ashore. Davidson's party then returned to the ranch, found Andrew Kelsey's body in the woods, and buried the two ranchers. Thereafter, they conducted Ben Kelsey and his group out of the valley with Kelsey's cattle. In his report, Davidson stated that all of the Pomos upon the lake were "more or less concerned in this atrocious murder," thus setting the stage for punishing the whole tribe.

On May 6, 1850, a military detachment set out from Benecia, California, under the command of Captain Nathaniel Lyon to "punish" the Pomos. On the advice of Lieutenant Davidson, boats and wagons to carry them were brought to the lake; the first wheeled vehicles ever to enter the region. Part of the force proceeded up the western shore with a howitzer, driving the Pomos ahead of them. The Pomos took refuge at an island at the head of the lake. Meanwhile, the remainder of the force traveled up the lake by boat, taking position on the lake side of the island. Then, the shore party fired the howitzer into the massed Pomos on the island. The panicked Indians ran to the opposite shore only to be greeted by musket fire from the amphibious party. According to Lyon's report, between sixty and "a hundred and upwards" were killed of the supposed four hundred on the island. Details in other accounts differ substantially, but all agree that many Pomos, including women and children, were killed. Furthermore, there is no agreement as to whether any individual Pomos involved in the killing were actually with this group. Thereafter, Lyon, believing that some of those involved in the murders had fled to the Russian River Valley, crossed the divide into that valley and caught a group of Pomos on an island in the Russian River. He reports killing an estimated seventy-five. Peace apparently was arranged by a local, informal treaty in 1850 but in 1851 Colonel R. McKee entered into a treaty with the Pomo. This treaty, however, was not ratified by the United States Senate.

—*Ralph L. Langenheim, Jr.*

ADDITIONAL READING:

Heizer, Robert F., ed. *Collected Documents on the Causes and Events in the Bloody Island Massacre of 1850.* Berkeley, Calif.: Archaeological Research Facility, Department of Anthropology, University of California, 1973. Comprehensively reprints government reports, newspaper accounts, eyewitness accounts, and early reminiscences. Includes Native American accounts.

_____. *The Destruction of the California Indians.* Salt Lake City: Peregrine Press, 1973. A large collection of original documents.

Josephy, Alvin M. *500 Nations: An Illustrated History of North American Indians.* New York: Alfred A. Knopf, 1994. Includes a short account of the Clear Lake Massacre based on narrowly selected sources.

Nabokov, Peter, ed. *Native American Testimony.* Foreword by Vine Deloria, Jr. New York: Viking, 1991. Includes the account of William Benson, chief of the Pomos, born twelve years after the event to a Pomo woman and a settler and raised in the tribe after his father's death.

SEE ALSO: 1848, California Gold Rush.

1850 ■ SECOND FUGITIVE SLAVE LAW: *a law aimed at making the rendition of fugitive slaves from Northern states easier for Southern slaveholders exacerbates tensions between North and South*

DATE: September 18, 1850
LOCALE: Washington, D.C.
CATEGORIES: African American history; Laws and acts
KEY FIGURES:

Salmon Portland Chase (1808-1873), U.S. senator from Ohio
James Murray Mason (1798-1871), principal author of the Second Fugitive Slave Law
William Henry Seward (1801-1872), U.S. senator from New York
Harriet Beecher Stowe (1811-1896), author of *Uncle Tom's Cabin*
Harriet Tubman (c. 1820-1913), slave rescuer
Daniel Webster (1782-1852), U.S. senator from Massachusetts

SUMMARY OF EVENT. The United States Congress passed the Second Fugitive Slave Law in September, 1850, as part of the Compromise of 1850. This compromise, its supporters hoped, would provide a permanent settlement of the long-standing dispute between the North and the South over slavery. The dispute had reached crisis proportions in 1848, after the United States forcefully acquired from Mexico huge territories in the Southwest, which raised the issue of the status of slavery in those territories. Most of the provisions of the Compromise of 1850 dealt with that issue. Southern white spokespersons also insisted that the government do something to prevent slave escapes into the North and to make it easier for masters to reclaim fugitive slaves from there.

Slave escapes had been common long before the United States became an independent country. It was the decision of the Northern states following the Revolutionary War to abolish slavery within their bounds that created a sectional issue. As a result, in 1787, Southern influence brought about the insertion in the U.S. Constitution of a clause providing that slaves escaping from one state to another were not to be freed but returned to their masters.

This clause established the constitutional basis for fugitive slave laws. The first such law, passed by Congress in 1793, allowed masters, on their own, to apprehend escaped slaves in the free states. Although this law provided no legal protection for persons accused of being fugitive slaves, neither did it authorize state or federal assistance for masters attempting to reclaim slaves.

Several events in the 1840's prompted Southern whites to intensify demands for a stronger fugitive slave law. First, the number of slave escapes increased as the slave labor system in the border slave states weakened. Second, a few black and white abolitionists became active in helping slaves escape. Third, Northern states began passing "personal liberty laws" requiring jury trials to determine the status of African Americans accused of being fugitive slaves. Such trials provided protection to those falsely accused and also made it more difficult for masters to reclaim actual escapees.

The Supreme Court addressed this last issue in the case of *Prigg v. Commonwealth of Pennsylvania* (1842). In *Prigg*, the Court ruled that a state could not interfere with the right of a master to recapture slaves. The Court also ruled, however, that, because the power to legislate on the fugitive slave issue was purely national, states were not required to assist in the enforcement of the First Fugitive Slave Law. This ruling allowed for a new series of personal liberty laws that denied masters the support they needed to apprehend alleged slaves. For many Southern whites, who feared that slave escapes were a major threat to the existence of slavery in the border slave states, the fugitive slave law issue loomed as large as the issue of slavery in the territories in the late 1840's. In response to these concerns, Senator James Mason of Virginia proposed the passage of a new and stronger fugitive slave law, on January 3, 1850.

When Mason's much-amended bill became law nine months

later, it appeared to be all that Southern whites demanded. It provided that United States marshals had to assist masters in arresting fugitive slaves and that the marshals could, in turn, summon Northern citizens to help. It provided that United States circuit courts appoint numerous commissioners who were empowered to evaluate the truth of a master's claim and authorize the return of fugitives to a master's state. Accused fugitives were not permitted to testify before the commissioners. The commissioners would receive a fee of ten dollars if they accepted a master's claim and only five dollars if they did not. Anyone who interfered with the apprehension of alleged fugitive slaves or who helped such persons escape was subject

to a fine of up to one thousand dollars and imprisonment for up to six months.

To many Northerners, the new law seemed to be excessively harsh and corrupting. Even Northerners who expressed no opposition to slavery in the South had little enthusiasm for assisting in the rendition of fugitive slaves. The denial to the accused of the right to testify, of the writ of habeas corpus, and of a jury trial appeared to be invitations for the unscrupulous to use the new law to facilitate kidnapping of free African American Northerners. That commissioners were paid more to remand to the South persons accused of being fugitive slaves than to exonerate such persons seemed to be a bribe in

Tensions between free and slave states rose during the 1840's, and Southern white spokespersons insisted that the government do something to prevent their slaves from escaping into the North and to make it easier for masters to reclaim them. As part of the Compromise of 1850, Congress responded with the Second Fugitive Slave Law. These pages from a contemporary account discuss the lengths to which slaves would go to attain their freedom—and the cruel consequences if they were caught. (Library of Congress)

behalf of the putative masters. The official explanation of the different fees—that to send the accused back to the South required more paperwork than to reject a master's claim—seemed a disingenuous excuse to many Northerners. Finally, because the law was retroactive, fugitive slaves who had lived safely in the North for many years were now subject to recapture.

To abolitionists, who opposed the very existence of slavery and encouraged slaves to escape, and to antislavery politicians, who contended that the South was seeking to expand its slave system into the North, the new law was anathema. The law's harshness and its apparent invasion of Northern states' rights led less committed Northerners to oppose it as well. Even as the bill that became the Second Fugitive Slave Law made its way through Congress, antislavery senators Salmon P. Chase of Ohio and William H. Seward of New York attempted, without success, to defeat it or to include in it provisions for jury trials. Antislavery Northerners denounced Senator Daniel Webster of Massachusetts for his March 7, 1850, endorsement of the bill. When it became law on September 18, there were protests throughout the North, although most Northerners acquiesced in its enforcement.

In many instances, however, enforcement was very difficult. As soon as the law went into effect, African Americans escaping from the South went to Canada, beyond the reach of the law. Others who had lived in the North for years took refuge across the Canadian border in times of danger. New personal liberty laws in a number of Northern states—several of which required jury trials—not only protected those falsely charged with being fugitive slaves but, by adding expenses, discouraged masters from pressing claims. Harriet Beecher Stowe's best-selling novel, *Uncle Tom's Cabin*, first published in serial form in 1851-1852, both reflected and encouraged Northern antipathy to the Second Fugitive Slave Law. By portraying slavery as a brutal system and depicting fugitive slaves sympathetically, Stowe aroused an emotional Northern reaction against the law.

Most striking, blacks and whites physically resisted enforcement of the law throughout the 1850's. Shortly after the law went into effect, former slave Harriet Tubman, with the help of black and white abolitionists, began her career of leading bands of slaves out of the South. Meanwhile, in Boston, Massachusetts; Christiana, Pennsylvania; Syracuse, New York; Wellington, Ohio; Milwaukee, Wisconsin; and elsewhere in the North, armed biracial mobs obstructed the enforcement of the act.

While the law was peacefully enforced in large regions of the North, its most important effect was to widen the gulf between the North and South. Many Northerners considered the law to be unconstitutional and an immoral Southern aggression, in behalf of an oppressive institution, upon not only African Americans but also the rights and values of Northern whites. White Southerners, many of whom had predicted that the new Fugitive Slave Law would be ineffective, regarded Northern resistance to it as another sign of antipathy toward

the South and its institutions. What had been designed as part of a compromise to quiet sectional animosities, instead increased those animosities and helped lead the nation into civil war in 1861.

—Stanley Harrold

ADDITIONAL READING:

Brandt, Nat. *The Town That Started the Civil War*. Syracuse, N.Y.: Syracuse University Press, 1990. Analyzes events related to the Oberlin-Wellington fugitive slave rescue of 1859, one of the more famous instances of violent resistance to the Second Fugitive Slave Law.

Campbell, Stanley W. *The Slave Catchers: Enforcement of the Fugitive Slave Law, 1850-1860*. New York: W. W. Norton, 1972. Discusses the background, constitutionality, and Northern reaction to the Second Fugitive Slave Law, as well as its enforcement.

Hamilton, Holman. *Prologue to Conflict: The Crisis and Compromise of 1850*. New York: W. W. Norton, 1964. Places the Second Fugitive Slave Law in the context of a broader discussion of the Compromise of 1850.

Potter, David M. *The Impending Crisis, 1848-1861*. Completed and edited by Don. E. Fehrenbacher. New York: Harper & Row, 1976. A thorough political history of the era during which the Second Fugitive Slave Law was passed and enforced.

Slaughter, Thomas P. *Bloody Dawn: The Christiana Riot and Racial Violence in the Antebellum North*. New York: Oxford University Press, 1991. Places the Christiana riot, one example of violent resistance to the Second Fugitive Slave Law, in the broader context of white racism and African American poverty.

SEE ALSO: 1793, First Fugitive Slave Law; 1820, Missouri Compromise; 1830, Proslavery Argument; 1850, Compromise of 1850; 1850, Underground Railroad; 1854, Kansas-Nebraska Act; 1856, Bleeding Kansas; 1857, *Dred Scott v. Sandford*.

1850 ■ UNDERGROUND RAILROAD:
thousands of slaves are helped to gain freedom with the aid of abolitionists

DATE: Flourished 1850-1860
LOCALE: From the Southern states to Canada
CATEGORIES: African American history; Social reform
KEY FIGURES:

Levi Coffin (1798-1877), a Quaker who helped three thousand fugitive slaves and was called the President of the Underground Railroad

Thomas Garrett (1789-1871), a Quaker abolitionist who sheltered several thousand fugitive slaves over a forty-year period

William Still (1821-1902), a black Philadelphia abolitionist and stationkeeper, an early chronicler of the Underground Railroad

Harriet Tubman (c. 1820-1913), a former slave who became the most famous conductor on the Underground Railroad

SUMMARY OF EVENT. The Underground Railroad was a loose network of secret routes by which fugitive slaves made their way from the Southern slave states north to freedom, often as far as Canada. Parts of the Underground Railroad may have been in place as early as 1786. By 1850, Southern slave owners were claiming enormous loss of slave property to it, although many believe these claims were exaggerated. It is impossible to know how many slaves made their way to freedom—estimates range from sixty thousand to a hundred thousand between 1800 and 1865.

Many slaves reached freedom without the aid of the Underground Railroad, and many, especially those in the Deep South, did not flee north but went instead to Mexico or found refuge with the Seminoles, Cherokees, or other Native American tribes. However, the majority of fugitive slaves escaped from the border states and fled north. Usually, the most dangerous leg of their journey was reaching a station on the underground line; once there, conductors would pass them from site to site toward safety.

It was almost impossible for a runaway slave to reach freedom successfully without assistance. Most slaves had little or no knowledge of geography and fled with only vague notions of where they were headed; most left with no money and few provisions and had to risk asking strangers along the way for food, shelter, and protection from pursuers. For the most part, persons helping runaways performed impulsive acts of compassion and did not consider themselves to be part of a resistance group. In parts of the country, however, the numbers of fugitives coming through were so great that predetermined escape routes, safe houses, and plans of action were organized. In time, some Underground Railroad lines were highly organized, and at least some routes existed in most of the states between the South and Canada.

The two most frequent escape corridors were from Kentucky and Virginia into Ohio and from there north, and up the Eastern Seaboard through New England. Ohio especially was crisscrossed with routes of escape, as were western Pennsylvania and New York, eastern Indiana, and northwestern Illinois. The Middle Atlantic states and New England also had many well-established routes; lines existed west of Ohio and even, to some degree, in the South. After passage of the Fugitive Slave Law of 1850 (the Second Fugitive Slave Law), organized aid to runaways grew, as the threats to free African Americans as well as fugitive slaves increased and more antislavery sympathizers felt the moral obligation to risk civil disobedience.

No one knows when or how the name Underground Railroad began, although legend has it that it was coined after a frustrated slavecatcher swore that the fugitives he was pursuing had disappeared as thoroughly and suddenly as if they had found an underground road. As knowledge of the existence of escape routes spread, so did the railroad terminology, with words such as "conductors," "stations," "stationkeepers," and "lines."

Conductors often used inventive means to transport fugitives safely from station to station. Many were hidden under goods or in secret compartments in wagons. A few, such as Henry "Box" Brown, were actually boxed and shipped by train or boat. At least once, slaves were hidden in carriages forming a fake funeral procession. There were so many routing options along some lines that tracing was difficult. Barns, thickets, attics, spare rooms, woodsheds, smokehouses, and cellars were used as stations. Fugitives often were disguised: A hoe could make a runaway look like a hired-out day laborer; fine clothes could disguise a runaway field hand as a servant of gentlefolk; cross-dressing could keep fugitives from matching descriptions on handbills. Mulattoes could sometimes pass as whites. Perhaps the most famous escape effected through disguise was that of husband and wife William and Ellen Craft, who, with Ellen disguised as a white Southern gentleman and William as her valet, made it from Georgia to Philadelphia, where the Underground Railroad then transported them to safety. Once at a station, fugitives were given shelter, food, clothing, and sometimes money, as well as help in reaching the next stop.

Quakers—mostly of the Hicksite sect—played a large and early role in maintaining the Underground Railroad; in 1797, George Washington complained of Quakers helping one of his slaves escape. Other sects, such as Covenanters and Wesleyan Methodists, also contributed a number of agents. Particular locations, such as Oberlin College in Ohio, became important centers of activity. Women as well as men played active roles, especially in providing food and clothing to fugitives, and women often organized auxiliaries to support the more visible vigilance and abolitionist committees.

The role played by white antislavery sympathizers, although important, has tended to be overemphasized. In Southern states, fellow slaves usually were the source of food and a hiding place for escapees. In border states, free blacks provided the most important help to fugitives, both in all-black settlements and in cities where black abolitionists worked alongside their white counterparts. Many African American churches and vigilance committees extended protection, support, and help in relocation to fugitives who reached the free states.

Whites rarely took the initiative to go south and effect escapes, but a number of former slaves returned to help friends and family flee. The most famous conductor to recruit escapees was the remarkable Harriet Tubman. Having herself escaped from slavery, she made some nineteen daring and successful trips into Southern states to bring out groups of slaves, despite the forty-thousand-dollar bounty on her head. She is credited with personally leading more than three hundred slaves to safety, never losing anyone in her charge, and earned the title "the Moses of her people."

The period of greatest activity for the Underground Railroad was from 1850 to 1860. Among the most active white stationkeepers was Levi Coffin: In thirty-five years of activism in Indiana and Ohio, Coffin helped three thousand fugitive slaves on their way north. Quaker Thomas Garrett of Wilmington, Delaware, aided several thousand fugitives over a forty-year period; he lost all of his property to court fines as a result but refused to cease his work.

Important black members of the Underground Railroad included the Reverend William H. Mitchell of Ohio, who in twelve years provided temporary shelter for thirteen hundred fleeing slaves; Robert Purvis of Philadelphia, Pennsylvania; William Whipper of Columbia, Pennsylvania; Henry Highland Garnet of New York; Lewis Hayden of Boston, Massachusetts; Frederick Douglass of Rochester, New York; and William Wells Brown of Buffalo, New York.

However, most of those who hid, fed, transported, and otherwise aided fugitive slaves have remained anonymous. Likewise, records about the fugitives themselves are scarce. Following the Civil War, several prominent activists published memoirs about their Underground Railroad activities that included accounts of some of the slaves they aided. Black stationkeeper William Still of Philadelphia kept notes on almost seven hundred fugitives he helped, providing valuable statistics. His records indicate that 80 percent of runaways were male and that significant numbers of house servants as well as field hands fled. However, the names and profiles of the vast majority of the thousands of men, women, and children who braved the hazards of flight in desperate bids for freedom remain unknown.

—*Grace McEntee*

ADDITIONAL READING:

Buckmaster, Henrietta. *Let My People Go: The Story of the Underground Railroad and the Growth of the Abolition Movement*. Boston: Beacon Press, 1941. This early history discusses the Underground Railroad within the broader context of the growth of antislavery sentiment.

Coffin, Levi. *Reminiscences of Levi Coffin*. New York: Arno Press, 1968. Coffin's massive memoir remains an important primary source; this work reprints his third edition of 1898. Illustrated.

Gara, Larry. *The Liberty Line: The Legend of the Underground Railroad*. Lexington: University of Kentucky Press, 1961. Corrects Siebert's more romanticized depictions of the Underground Railroad. Counters popular notions that exaggerate the role of white abolitionists and underplay blacks' contributions in helping fugitive slaves.

Quarles, Benjamin. *Black Abolitionists*. New York: Oxford University Press, 1969. Situates the work of free black stationkeepers and conductors within the larger context of overall African American involvement with antislavery efforts.

Siebert, Wilbur H. *The Underground Railroad from Slavery to Freedom*. 1898. Reprint. New York: Arno Press, 1968. This landmark history is the first scholarly study of the Underground Railroad. Although somewhat romanticized and at times too reliant on personal memory, it is a thorough, well-researched examination of much value. Illustrations, maps.

Still, William. *The Underground Railroad*. 1872. Reprint. Chicago: Johnson, 1972. A vast collection of narratives and sketches, focusing on the fugitives' stories. Includes miscellaneous materials by and about "aiders and advisors of the road."

SEE ALSO: 1820, Missouri Compromise; 1830, Proslavery Argument; 1850, Compromise of 1850; 1850, Second Fugitive Slave Law; 1854, Kansas-Nebraska Act; 1856, Bleeding Kansas; 1857, *Dred Scott v. Sandford*.

1851 ■ AKRON WOMAN'S RIGHTS CONVENTION: *the second statewide women's rights convention highlights the connection between the causes of women and abolitionists*

DATE: May 28-29, 1851
LOCALE: Akron, Ohio
CATEGORIES: Civil rights; Social reform; Women's issues
KEY FIGURES:
Betsey Mix Cowles (1810-1876), teacher, school founder, and reformer
Frances Dana Gage (1804-1894), reformer, writer, and lecturer who presided over the convention
Sojourner Truth (c. 1797-1883), evangelist, speaker on abolition and women's rights

SUMMARY OF EVENT. By the late 1840's, the accelerated growth of the United States affected all aspects of life. Territorial expansion to the West and industrial development changed the social fabric as immigrant labor created urban areas and modified gender and class roles. The women's rights movement emerged from this dynamic context. Most of the founding mothers had gained experience in organizing from earlier participation in the temperance, antislavery, moral purity, and health reform movements through their churches and benevolent societies. On July 19, 1848, they came from the surrounding areas to assemble in a Wesleyan chapel in Seneca Falls, New York, to begin the organized women's rights movement. By the end of this first meeting, sixty-eight women and thirty-two men had signed the Declaration of Sentiments, a compilation of gender inequities ending with a series of resolutions to shape the agenda for the coming years.

The movement had able leaders in Susan B. Anthony, a pragmatic, yet intense organizer; theorist Elizabeth Cady Stanton, who lacked mobility because of her large family; Quaker reformer Lucretia Mott; orators Lucy Stone and Ernestine Rose; and many others. Male reformers participated in these early years. When they joined the women at their next meeting in the Quaker community of Salem, Ohio, the women barred the men from vocal participation to raise their awareness of women's plight and won a resolution to secure equal rights for all persons.

The first National Woman's Rights Convention was organized by wealthy reformer Paulina Wright Davis and held October 26 and 27, 1850, in Worcester, Massachusetts. New leaders attending this meeting included Antoinette Brown, who

Sojourner Truth became a voice for both women's rights and the abolitionist cause, as evidenced in her "Ar'n't I a Woman?" speech at the Second Women's Rights Convention at Akron, Ohio, in 1851. Although the connection between women's rights and abolitionism was strong during these years, the women's rights movement would later split over the issue of whether to include abolition in their platform. (The Associated Publishers, Inc.)

became the first ordained female minister; Harriot Hunt, a medical pioneer; and Sojourner Truth, evangelist and abolitionist.

The connection between women's rights and abolitionism was strong during these early years. Arguments against the moral, legal, and social conditions of slavery raised women's awareness of their own restrictions. Societies, newspapers, lyceums, lecture circuits, fairs, and support networks began to include other reforms, including women's right to speak in public on behalf of slaves. Gradually, women broke down barriers and developed skills that would help them develop their own movement for women's rights.

These connections appeared at what is generally called the Second National Woman's Rights Convention, May 28-29, 1851, at Akron, Ohio. (Because of the loose organization through steering committees during the early years of the movement, confusion about titles of conventions abounds. Akron's meeting is also referred to as the Second Statewide Convention or as the Akron Convention. The Worcester, Massachusetts, Convention in October, 1851, also is referred to as the Second National Woman's Rights Convention.) Ohio had the greatest number of antislavery societies of any state in the country in 1840. Ohio had recently adopted a new constitution, which had mobilized both antislavery and women's rights supporters working to shape the new laws. Although the Ohio constitution remained unchanged regarding women, agitation continued throughout the state.

Akron was a midpoint location, drawing leaders from the East and from various pockets of reform in Ohio. The strongest center of support came from Salem, Ohio, the Quaker community in Columbiana County, home of the *Anti-Slavery Bugle*, the newspaper of the Garrisonian Western Anti-Slavery Society. Salem was home for many male and female supporters of women's rights and equality: Jane Elisabeth (Lizzie) Hitchcock and new husband Benjamin Jones, co-editors of the *Anti-Slavery Bugle*; Mary Ann and Oliver Johnson, who succeeded Lizzie and Ben Jones as editors; Emily Robinson; and Lot and Eliza Holmes. Supporter of abolitionism and temperance Martha J. Tilden, wife of a congressman, represented Akron. Teacher and school founder Betsey M. Cowles came from Austinburg, representing Canton. Josephine Sophia White Griffing came from Medina as one of the Western Anti-Slavery Society's most active and effective lecturers. From the southern part of the state came Sarah Ernst, a Cincinnati Garrisonian.

The Akron Woman's Rights Convention tapped Ohio leadership. Frances Dana Gage of McConnelsville, Ohio, a married woman with four young children, was elected president of this convention. Gage's skills as a writer for abolition and temperance had brought her into the reform network that supported women's rights. Although she admitted to never attending a regular business meeting and feeling entirely inexperienced in organizational procedures, her organizational and intellectual skills provided the basis for her leadership. Unlike the other Ohio reformers, who had come from New England to settle the West, Gage was born in Ohio and had married an Ohioan. In her opening speech to the convention, she related how women had struggled alongside men in adapting to the environment. These experiences demonstrated the common needs of women and their shared humanity with men. She traced the false basis in religion and custom giving men predominance over women. She sought with "a loving spirit" to bring men into the movement for women's rights to create "a revolution without armies, without bloodshed" to improve the conditions of society by granting women their rights.

Ohio leaders read letters of support from Paulina W. Davis of Rhode Island, Elizabeth Cady Stanton and Amelia Bloomer of New York, former Oberlin student Lucy Stone, and Geritt Smith. The current status of women was presented in reports. L. Maria Giddings spoke on the common law. Betsey Mix Cowles detailed labor conditions and wages. Pittsburgh's Jane G. Swisshelm related women's sphere to education, a topic also addressed by Emily Robinson.

The reports provided a stage for commentary. Debate ensued, with ministers quoting scripture assigning women a secondary role. They recounted that Jesus had chosen no female apostles, that Eve had caused all the sin in the world, and that John had instructed women to be silent. As the meeting degenerated in this debate, a tall figure emerged from the back of the church hall and requested the right to speak. Many in the crowd responded in the negative, saying women's rights and "nigger's rights" did not mix. Gage, however, had been a strong supporter of the antislavery movement and had great respect for the proposed speaker, Sojourner Truth. Gage assented to the request.

The speech given by Sojourner Truth turned the tide in favor of women's rights. This former New York slave, named Isabella Van Wegener, had experienced a religious conversion and had renamed herself Sojourner Truth as she entered a career as an itinerant preacher and antislavery lecturer. Called the Lybian Sybil by Lydia Maria Child, Truth stood more than six feet tall and had very dark skin, which created a physical presence in any gathering. Although illiterate, Truth was an eloquent orator and had addressed similar crowds in the antislavery lecture circuit and spoken to earlier women's rights conventions at Worcester, Massachusetts, in 1850. Her speech at the Akron Convention was recounted both by Gage and by the *Anti-Slavery Bugle* as "Ar'n't I a Woman?" Truth argued that she had worked as hard as a man, had physical needs similar to those of a man, and deserved the same rights in return. She asked the ministry about the origin of Christ—from God and a woman, with man having no part. When asked about lack of female apostles, she countered with women's roles attending Christ at the crucifixion and mentioned the women to whom he appeared after resurrection. In defense of Eve, she argued that if one woman could turn the world upside down, then women together could correct the world's problems, if given rights.

Accounts of the magical influence of her speech were in agreement that she had provoked respect and admiration and turned the event into a successful women's rights convention. The convention resolved to use the periodical press to shape public sentiments, to use teachers and mothers to shape young minds, to form labor partnerships, and to repeal laws that created different privileges. Caroline Severance reported on the event in the Cleveland newspapers; in May, 1853, she presided over the first annual meeting of the Ohio Woman's Rights Association, which had been founded May 27, 1852, in Ravenna. The Akron Convention reflected the internal contradictions that would increasingly emerge in the growing women's rights movement.

—*Dorothy C. Salem*

ADDITIONAL READING:

Bernhard, Virginia, and Elizabeth Fox-Genovese, eds. *The Birth of American Feminism: The Seneca Falls Woman's Convention of 1848.* St. James, N.Y.: Brandywine Press, 1995. Focuses on the founding convention; also provides information on following meetings.

Buhle, Mari Jo, and Paul Buhle, eds. *The Concise History of Woman Suffrage: Selections from the Classic Work of Stanton, Anthony, Gage, and Harper.* Urbana: University of Illinois Press, 1978. Includes a few primary sources.

Flexner, Eleanor. *Century of Struggle: The Woman's Rights Movement in the United States.* New York: Atheneum, 1973. Still one of the best analyses of the movement for women's rights.

Langley, Winston E., and Vivian C. Fox, eds. *Women's Rights in the United States: A Documentary History.* Westport, Conn.: Greenwood Press, 1994. Provides primary documents and bibliographic information.

Mabee, Carleton. *Sojourner Truth: Slave, Prophet, Legend.* New York: New York University Press, 1993. Provides information about Truth's background and her role in the women's movement.

Stanton, Elizabeth Cady, Susan B. Anthony, and Matilda Joslyn Gage, eds. *History of Woman Suffrage.* 6 vols. New York: Fowler & Wells, 1881-1922. Reprint. New York: Arno Press, 1969. Volume 1 provides some information from Gage's reminiscences on the convention.

Washington, Margaret, ed. *Narrative of Sojourner Truth.* New York: Vintage Books, 1993. A newer edition of Truth's narrative, with an introduction by the editor.

Women's Rights Convention. *Proceedings of the Women's Rights Convention, Held at Akron, Ohio, May 28 and 29, 1851.* Although the original proceedings are in poor condition and must be read with a magnifying glass, they are available on microfiche and offer contemporary insights into the event.

SEE ALSO: 1831, *The Liberator* Begins Publication; 1833, American Anti-Slavery Society Is Founded; 1847, *The North Star* Begins Publication; 1848, Seneca Falls Convention; 1850, Underground Railroad; 1853, National Council of Colored People Is Founded; 1857, New York Infirmary for Indigent Women and Children Opens; 1866, Suffragists Protest the Fourteenth Amendment; 1869, Rise of Woman Suffrage Associations.

1853 ■ PACIFIC RAILROAD SURVEYS: *four survey groups seek routes to the Pacific, identifying numerous paths to the coast*

DATE: March 2, 1853-1857
LOCALE: Trans-Mississippi West
CATEGORIES: Expansion and land acquisition; Exploration and discovery; Transportation
KEY FIGURES:

E. G. Beckwith, explorer of the forty-first parallel route west from Fort Bridger to Salt Lake and California

Thomas Hart Benton (1782-1858), senator from Missouri who championed a route from St. Louis to San Francisco near the thirty-eighth parallel

Jefferson Davis (1808-1899), secretary of war who ordered the surveys

William H. Emory (1811-1887), officer of the Topographical Corps who was in charge of the Office of Exploration and Surveys

John C. Frémont (1813-1890), son-in-law of Benton, politician, explorer, and opportunity-seeker

John W. Gunnison (1812-1853), officer in charge of exploration of the route between the thirty-seventh and thirty-eighth parallels

Theodore Dehone Judah (1828-1863), young engineer from Connecticut who found the best route through the Sierras

Amiel Weeks Whipple (1816-1863), officer in command of the survey along the thirty-fifth parallel

SUMMARY OF EVENT. On March 2, 1853, Congress passed the Pacific Railroad Survey Bill, which authorized the secretary of war, Jefferson Davis, to initiate exploration of possible routes across the trans-Mississippi West to the Pacific Ocean and to report findings to Congress within ten months. This legislation was an attempt to break a political and economic deadlock over the location of the first transcontinental railroad. Davis decided to use officers of the Army Topographical Corps to make the surveys and placed them under Major William H. Emory.

For years, there had been a proposal for a northern railroad route from Lake Michigan to the Columbia River, with a branch to San Francisco. Isaac Stevens, a young Army officer who had just accepted the governorship of Washington Territory, was placed in command of the northern survey, which covered the country between the forty-seventh and forty-eighth parallels. This party was divided into two sections: one group, led by Stevens, ascended the Missouri River to the mouth of the Yellowstone River at Fort Union and explored westward; a second party, led by Captain George B. McClellan, explored eastward from Puget Sound, seeking adequate passes through the Cascade Mountains. Numerous supposedly satisfactory passes across the Continental Divide were located, but no pass over the Cascades was found, because McClellan erroneously thought the snow of Snoqualmie Pass and elsewhere was too deep. Snowdrifts forty feet high could bury railroad workmen's cabins. Nevertheless, in 1853, Stevens

Four Possible Routes: Pacific Railroad Surveys, 1853-1855

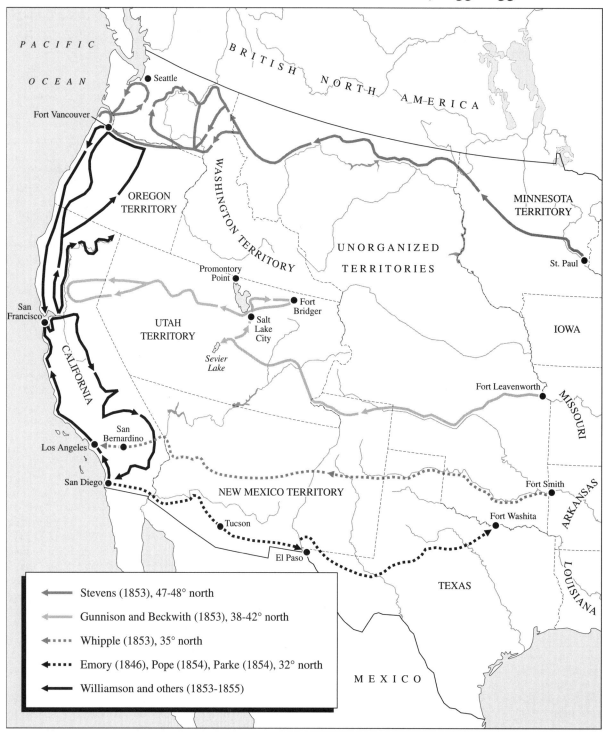

PACIFIC OCEAN

Seattle

Fort Vancouver

BRITISH NORTH AMERICA

OREGON TERRITORY

WASHINGTON TERRITORY

UNORGANIZED TERRITORIES

MINNESOTA TERRITORY

St. Paul

Promontory Point

Fort Bridger

San Francisco

UTAH TERRITORY

Salt Lake City

Sevier Lake

IOWA

CALIFORNIA

Fort Leavenworth

MISSOURI

San Bernardino

Los Angeles

San Diego

Tucson

NEW MEXICO TERRITORY

El Paso

Fort Smith

ARKANSAS

Fort Washita

LOUISIANA

TEXAS

MEXICO

Stevens (1853), 47-48° north

Gunnison and Beckwith (1853), 38-42° north

Whipple (1853), 35° north

Emory (1846), Pope (1854), Parke (1854), 32° north

Williamson and others (1853-1855)

Officers of the U.S. Topographical Corps located at least four accessible routes to the Pacific; however, none of these four routes was precisely followed for the first transcontinental railroad. It took the genius of Theodore Judah to engineer the first workable cut through the Sierras between California's American and Yuba Rivers, making possible the linking of east with west at Promontory Point, Utah, in 1869.

enthusiastically reported that two practical routes through different passes over the Cascade Mountains were available. Citizens around Puget Sound were not convinced, and the legislature of Washington Territory commissioned Frederick West Lander, a civilian engineer, to survey another route from Puget Sound to South Pass.

South of Stevens' survey was a route near the thirty-eighth parallel along a line proposed by Thomas Hart Benton, senator from Missouri, with its starting point at St. Louis and its terminus in San Francisco. In 1848, Benton's son-in-law, John C. Frémont (called "Pathfinder" in a newspaper), had explored a portion of this route, named the Buffalo Trail. In seeking a satisfactory pass through the mountains in southern Utah, he had failed dramatically and disastrously by getting his group trapped twelve thousand feet up in the Rocky Mountains in mid-December. Ten of his men starved or froze to death. When Lieutenant John W. Gunnison subsequently was placed in command of the official survey along the thirty-eighth parallel instead of Frémont, Benton, in disappointment, promoted two privately sponsored explorations along the same route. One, led by Frémont, was accompanied by newspaper reporters to publicize the route.

Gunnison's expedition, including topographer Richard H. Kern and a German botanist, Frederick Creuzefeldt, left Fort Leavenworth in June, 1853, and explored several new routes across the Great Plains. Gunnison was killed in October on the Sevier River in Utah by Paiute Indians. Before his death, he had reported that the railroad route along the thirty-eighth parallel was far inferior to the one along the forty-first parallel that had been used by emigrants in covered wagons. The death of his party closed the Buffalo Trail. Gunnison's was the only one of the four government survey expeditions to end in death.

Central route surveys were resumed the following spring, when Lieutenant E. G. Beckwith moved westward along the forty-first and forty-second parallels. His first responsibility was to reexamine the path traversed in 1850 by Captain Howard Stansbury, from Fort Bridge westward to Salt Lake. Beckwith found two satisfactory routes into the Great Basin through the Weber and Timpanagos Canyons. This route had elevations ranging from nine thousand to twelve thousand feet. Up to this point, contact with American Indian tribes had been peaceful, except with the Paiutes, who seemed to resent the intrusion onto their lands. Authorized to continue the forty-first-parallel survey into California in February, 1854, Beckwith's party followed the customary emigrant route along the Humboldt River across Nevada, but upon reaching the sink of the stream, the party turned north to explore new passes across the Sierra Nevada and was successful in locating two: Madeline Pass and Nobles Pass.

The third party, under Lieutenant Amiel Weeks Whipple, was ordered to explore the thirty-fifth-parallel route via Albuquerque and the Zuñi villages. This route was championed by California senator William H. Gwin, who hoped for a railroad from San Francisco to Albuquerque, from where several branches would go to Independence, Missouri; Fort Smith,

Arkansas; Austin, Texas; and elsewhere. West of Albuquerque, the surveying group examined a route, later adopted by the Atchison, Topeka and Santa Fe Railroad. Whipple traversed the Mojave Desert to the Cajon Pass and crossed over into San Bernardino. He reported that this pass, so long used by traders and emigrants, was practical for railroad construction.

The southern, or thirty-second-parallel, route had already been explored by Emory, first when he was serving the Army of the West in the Mexican War and later as a member of the United States-Mexican Boundary Commission. Emory's survey of the boundary was accepted to bridge the gap from the Pima villages to the Colorado River, and Lieutenant R. S. Williamson was assigned the exploration in California. After extensive examination of the mountains of southern California, Williamson and his associates concluded that Walker Pass, long thought to be the southern gateway into California, was impractical for a railway because of its difficult westward approach. Nearby Tehachapi Pass was found to be superior. John G. Parke recommended a route from the mouth of the Gila River via the San Gorgonio Pass into Los Angeles, rather than a more southerly line to San Diego. From Los Angeles, a railway northward into the San Joaquin Valley could easily cross Tejon Pass. These politically inspired routes were not properly engineered. The government surveys did not address the fact that railroads require grades no steeper than 116 feet to the mile and curves with a minimum three-hundred-foot radius to keep locomotives on track. It took the genius of Theodore Judah to engineer the first workable cut through the Sierras between California's American and Yuba Rivers, making possible the linking of east with west at Promontory Point, Utah, in 1869. The final phase for field operations of the Pacific Railroad surveys was that of Williamson and Lieutenant H. L. Abbott seeking the best routes from California into the Pacific Northwest. They located two practical coastal routes, one to the east and one to the west of the Cascades.

The officers of the Topographical Corps thus located most of the accessible routes through the mountain barrier to the Pacific Slope that were to be followed by modern railroads and highways. Their numerous reports, published in a series of quarto volumes at the direction of Congress in 1857, plainly showed that there was no unsurmountable difficulty in building a railroad to the Pacific. At least four routes were practicable, so instead of settling the sectional deadlock over the proposed route, as originally intended, the surveys stimulated new discussion. However, the surveys had reconnoitered the routes that later were used by the transcontinental railroads.

Each of the survey groups met some of the many Native American tribes indigenous to the areas traversed. Using interpreters who had been captives of these tribes lessened the possibility of social error. Thus, the survey groups met with chiefs on equal terms. Gifts and goods were exchanged, and each could make only good reports of any encounter. Some survey groups made tribal lexicons, some having only twenty-eight words as an entire vocabulary. Whipple's group noted that nearly all the wealthy American Indians of central Oklahoma and western Arkansas had Mexican or African slaves. Lieutenant Whipple, in a letter dated June 30, 1855, to Jefferson Davis, said, "The quiet and peaceful manner in which we passed through the various tribes of Indians, usually hostile toward Americans is a proof of the sound discretion of those officers, and the good discipline of the men composing their command." Only after the intrusion of the wagon trains, the railroads, and white settlements did the Native Americans rise up in arms.

—W. Turrentine Jackson, updated by Norma Crews

ADDITIONAL READING:

Albright, George L. *Official Explorations for Pacific Railroads*. Berkeley: University of California Press, 1921. A compendium based almost totally on government documents. Summarizes plans by Whitney and Benton and the actual surveys. Well arranged.

Ogburn, Charlton. *Railroaders: The Great American Adventure*. Washington, D.C.: National Geographic Society, 1977. Discusses U.S. railroads and the people who built them, ran them, and made their fortunes by owning them.

Robertson, Donald B. *Encyclopedia of Western Railroad History*. Caldwell, Idaho: Caxton Books, 1986. Includes facts on the rise and decline of the railroad in the West, from earliest times.

United States War Dept. *Reports of Explorations and Surveys to Ascertain the Most Practicable and Economical Route for a Railroad from the Mississippi River to the Pacific Ocean*. Washington, D.C.: Government Printing Office, 1855. A comprehensive report, covering all visible aspects, including various tribal vocabularies. Diaries and lithographs bring history to life.

Wheeler, Keith, and the editors of Time-Life Books. *The Railroaders*. New York: Time-Life Books, 1973. Presents interesting facets of the development of the railroad in the United States. Many photographs.

Williams, John H. *A Great and Shining Road: The Epic Story of the Transcontinental Railroad*. New York: Times Books, 1988. Provides a dramatic history of the building of railroads across the United States and discusses what it meant to the states they crossed.

SEE ALSO: 1830, Baltimore and Ohio Railroad Begins Operation; 1861, Transcontinental Telegraph Is Completed; 1869, Transcontinental Railroad Is Completed.

1853 ■ NATIONAL COUNCIL OF COLORED PEOPLE IS FOUNDED: *one of the first groups concerned with the advancement of African Americans and the cause of abolition*

DATE: July 6, 1853
LOCALE: Rochester, New York
CATEGORIES: African American history; Organizations and institutions

KEY FIGURES:
Richard Allen (1760-1831), African American leader and founder of the first Negro Convention
Frederick Douglass (1817?-1895), former slave and founder of *The North Star*

SUMMARY OF EVENT. On Wednesday, July 6, 1853, more than one hundred delegates from around the country assembled in Rochester, New York, for a three-day convention to form the National Council of Colored People. This organization was an outgrowth of a larger movement, the Negro Convention Movement, which had begun almost twenty-three years earlier.

Philadelphia had been the host of the first meeting for the Negro Convention Movement, September 20-24, 1830. Richard Allen formed the convention with the intention of improving the lives of African Americans by raising their social status through education and, possibly, emigration. The convention met many times in many cities, discussing plans for improvement, and the group thrived on the increasing solidarity among its members. It was at one of the convention meetings, in Rochester, New York, that the plan for the National Council of Colored People was adopted. The meeting in Rochester drew many prominent African American leaders, including Frederick Douglass, James McCune Smith, and James Pennington.

A constitution was drawn up for the new organization, and a president and several vice presidents were chosen. There were a total of twenty-two members, divided among four committees. One committee was in charge of public relations and also was responsible for a library and museum of African American people. Another committee was instructed to help develop and direct a manual-labor school. A third supervised the protective unions. The last committee was the business committee, which dealt with the greatest share of the workload. Its role was to assist in the selling of African American products and the employment of African American people, and to act as a resource center for the advancement of African Americans.

At the meeting in 1853, the group also discussed the rampant racial oppression of the African American people, even as they were discussing signs of improvement in society. Members of both the convention and the newly formed National Council of Colored People believed that, in order to increase the rate of improvement of the social status of African Americans, it was necessary to create a new institution for the education of African American youth.

The new institution would be an industrial school that concentrated on agriculture and the mechanical arts. Convention members believed that the education of African American youth would enable them to acquire wealth, intelligence, virtue, and eventually, happiness. On the second day of the convention, the council elected to withdraw from the proposed school plan because of the exclusive nature of the school.

The discussion on the last day of the meeting of the National Council of Colored People focused on the term "colored" in the name of the organization. After much discussion, the organization determined to stay with their original name. In the final hours of the last day of the convention, the council endorsed two seminaries as places for the education of African Americans—McGrawville College and Allegheny City College.

On November 15, 1853, elections were held in several cities to elect delegates for the formation of new state councils that would act in accordance with the National Council of Colored People. The leading delegates would attend the national council meetings as well as their own state council meetings. The first meeting of the National Council of Colored People was held November 23, 1853, in New York. At least one council member each from the states of New York, Connecticut, Rhode Island, and Ohio was missing, but because of the great distance the other council members had traveled, the meeting continued. After proceeding with the meeting, one delegate from Ohio appeared and demanded that all prior proceedings be nullified. This caused great distress among the council members; eventually, the minutes of the meeting were lost, never to be found again. The controversy resulting from the Ohio delegate's demands created a somewhat hostile working environment, which contributed to the short life of the council. Despite the bleak beginnings of the national council, the state councils were operating much more smoothly and with enthusiasm.

In both the national and state councils, the idea of an African American school was revisited. Frederick Douglass defended the school plan unsuccessfully for two years. The country was experiencing an economic depression, which made it hard to fund the school. There also was still concern over the exclusive nature of an African American school. In many ways, the country itself was split on the issue of a separate African American nation, which many emigrationists had proposed. The idea of a separate African American school brought many emotions to the forefront. Integrationists were wary of accepting such a school plan because of the isolation of the school and its students, yet even they saw benefits in an all African American school. Emigrationists considered the proposal and were much more willing to begin work on construction. Amid much opposition, in October, 1855, the convention elected to discontinue plans for the proposed school. The other committees set up by the first national convention and their ambitious plans to assist African Americans in business pursuits and the creation of a library and museum seemed to have stopped on paper. There is no record of any progress having been made toward the goals, nor of the meeting of the members of the committees.

The second meeting of the National Council of Colored People was scheduled for May 24, 1854, in Cleveland, but it was postponed in order to accommodate more delegates. Eventually, only a few delegates were able to attend. Among the members attending, a debate developed over the recognition of Ohio at the national level, creating a deadlock. A suggestion was made to dissolve the organization, and after a close vote, the National Council of Colored People continued to operate. Ohio, however, withdrew its participation.

At the meeting of May 8, 1855, nearly all the delegates were from New York, as most others had declined to participate. The issue of an African American school again was discussed and once again defeated. Another issue was discussed for the first time—emigration to Canada. Although most delegates at the convention were willing to remain in the United States, they expressed trepidation on the matter of the United States Constitution and the issue of slavery. The issue of emigration was the last to be discussed before the close of the final meeting of the National Council of Colored People. The state councils continued to operate and pursue social equality for African Americans for a few years longer, with councils in some states surviving longer than others.

Although the National Council of Colored People lasted for only a few years, its attempts at social reform—tackling such important topics as the education and emigration of African Americans—were significant because they occurred on a national level, bringing recognition to the need for improvement of African American lives.

—*Jeri Kurtzleben*

ADDITIONAL READING:

Bell, Howard Holman. *A Survey of the Negro Convention Movement, 1830-1861.* New York: Arno Press, 1969. Contains substantial information on the Negro Convention Movement, from which the National Council of Colored People was formed.

Blassingame, John W., and John R. McKivigan, eds. *The Frederick Douglass Papers.* Series 1, *Speeches, Debates, and Interviews.* Vol. 2, *1847-1854.* New Haven, Conn.: Yale University Press, 1991. Includes several references to the industrial college proposed at the 1853 meeting in Rochester, New York.

_____. *The Frederick Douglass Papers.* Series 1, *Speeches, Debates, and Interviews.* Vol. 3, *1855-1863.* New Haven, Conn.: Yale University Press, 1991. Includes an interview with President Andrew Johnson, in which the intent of the National Convention is discussed.

_____. *The Frederick Douglass Papers.* Series 1, *Speeches, Debates, and Interviews.* Vol. 4, *1864-1880.* New Haven, Conn.: Yale University Press, 1991. Contains a speech and several pages of notes from the National Council meeting in May, 1855.

Hornsby, Alton, Jr. *Chronology of African-American History.* Detroit, Mich.: Gale Research, 1991. Places the National Council of Colored People in the context of relevant information on its foundation.

Ploski, Harry A., and James Williams, eds. *The Negro Almanac: A Reference Work on the African American.* Detroit, Mich.: Gale Research, 1989. A beginning source of information on the Negro Convention Movement in 1831.

SEE ALSO: 1775, Pennsylvania Society for the Abolition of Slavery Is Founded; 1784, Hall's Masonic Lodge Is Chartered; 1787, Free African Society Is Founded; 1816, AME Church Is Founded; 1820's, Social Reform Movement; 1831, *The Liberator* Begins Publication; 1833, American Anti-Slavery Society Is Founded; 1847, *The North Star* Begins Publication; 1850, Underground Railroad; 1857, First African American University.

1853 ■ GADSDEN PURCHASE: *the United States secures southern New Mexico and Arizona as the last territories within the nation's contiguous boundaries*

DATE: December 31, 1853
LOCALE: Southern New Mexico and Arizona
CATEGORIES: Expansion and land acquisition; Latino American history; Treaties and agreements
KEY FIGURES:
Jefferson Davis (1808-1889), secretary of war and an influential adviser of Pierce
Manuel Diez de Bonilla (1800-1864), Mexican minister of foreign relations and head of its negotiating team
James Gadsden (1788-1858), Pierce's minister to Mexico
William Learned Marcy (1786-1857), secretary of state
Franklin Pierce (1804-1869), fourteenth president of the United States, 1853-1857
Antonio López de Santa Anna (1794-1876), general and president of Mexico, 1847, 1853-1855

SUMMARY OF EVENT. In 1853, the newly elected president, Franklin Pierce, appointed James Gadsden of Charleston, South Carolina, as minister to Mexico. Along with other diplomatic duties, the ambassador's immediate task was to negotiate a treaty with the southern republic. The need for such an arrangement had grown out of imperfections and conflicting interpretations of the 1848 Treaty of Guadalupe Hidalgo, which had formally ended the Mexican War. These problems had severely strained U.S.-Mexican relations, seriously threatening the peace between the two countries.

The major objective in Gadsden's mission, however, was the acquisition of a land cession. The United States desired territory to resolve a potentially explosive dispute arising from the failure of the Mexican-American Boundary Commission to mark satisfactorily the southwestern boundary between the two countries along the Rio Grande after the Mexican War. The disagreement over the border threatened peaceful relations among the mixed Anglo-American Mexican population living in the border area of the Mesilla River Valley. More significant, Gadsden sought additional Mexican territory large enough to facilitate constructing a transcontinental railroad through the Gila River Valley. This was the long-talked-about extreme southern route favored by many prominent Southerners. In many ways, there was no person better fitted for the task than Gadsden.

Gadsden was not an experienced diplomat, but his diverse background had provided him with abilities adequate for the post. His career included military service as a close adviser to former president Andrew Jackson, minor political offices in Florida's territorial government, and an extensive business background as president of the Charleston Railroad Company. He was not widely known outside his native Southern soil, but he was a close acquaintance of Secretary of War Jefferson

Davis, the Mississippi states' rights leader and perhaps Pierce's most influential adviser. Davis and Gadsden shared similar political views: They were both supporters of the expansion of slavery and both were Southern nationalists. Gadsden owed his appointment to Davis.

Perhaps the major factor in Davis' recommendation of Gadsden resulted from a mutual interest in the development of Southern railroads. From his position as president of the Charleston Railroad Company, by 1850 Gadsden had become perhaps the most conspicuous champion of Southern railways and was instrumental in promoting virtually every contemporary venture in the region. Like many railroad supporters of the antebellum period, Davis and Gadsden increasingly came to see the economic and military value of a railroad connecting the two coasts. Such a road would facilitate better defense of the Pacific settlements, but just as important, it would advance the commercial interests of the nation, providing an opportunity to develop better trade and commerce with the Far East.

Both Davis and Gadsden had long believed that the best route for the nation's proposed transcontinental railway lay in the South, but their views were not shared by all Pacific railroad enthusiasts. After the end of the Mexican War and the acquisition of California, the question of building a transcontinental railroad was one of the nation's major political and economic issues, one that divided the country along sectional lines. Several feasible routes came under discussion, including a northern route that proposed cities like Milwaukee or Chicago as the eastern terminals, and a southern route with Mississippi River cities St. Louis, Memphis, Vicksburg, and New Orleans all vying for contention. The terrain and natural barriers might present special engineering and construction problems in some regions, but each route had its champions—people who understood the potential economic benefits that would accrue to proposed eastern terminus cities and the geographical section through which the road would run.

Gadsden advocated a southern route, with Memphis as the eastern terminus on the Mississippi River. Traversing the countryside along the thirty-second-parallel through El Paso, Texas, and the Gila River Valley of northern Mexico, this route had some advantages over its rivals. In particular, Gadsden and supporters boasted over its shorter distance to the coast, a year-round temperate climate, and the absence of formidable natural obstacles that might impede track construction. As secretary of war, Davis sanctioned the thirty-second-parallel route as the most practicable and economical location for the railway. All that lay in the way of making the extreme southern route the most eligible line was U.S. ownership of the entire right-of-way.

Gadsden was instructed not only to resolve the southern boundary dispute but also to purchase a sufficient amount of land to facilitate the southern route. Exactly how much land was sufficient and the price the United States was willing to pay for it were not clear, but Secretary of State William Marcy thought Gadsden could make the purchase for a moderate cost, because the barren region was of little value other than for the railroad.

TERRITORY OF THE UNITED STATES IN 1853

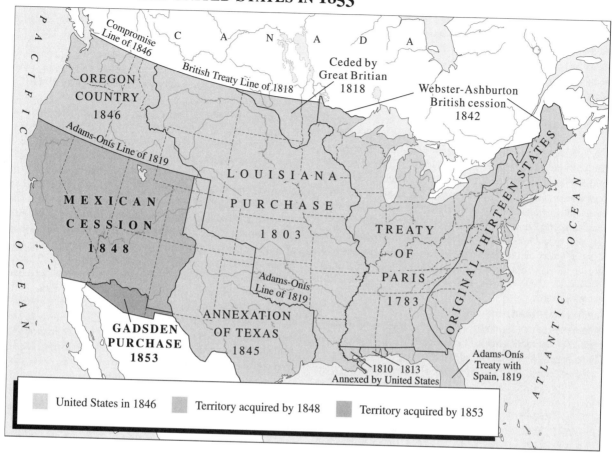

Mexican leaders did not share entirely the U.S. view about the land. Since the end of the Mexican War in 1848, Mexico's attitudes toward its northern neighbor had been marked not only by hostility but also, more significantly, by an inclination to be suspicious of the United States' territorial designs. In the United States, Southern expansionists, desiring to increase slave-holding territory, were noticeably evident; this presence made Mexico, already victimized by U.S. imperialism, even more apprehensive. In the United States, the notion of "manifest destiny" had lost little of its luster, and Mexican officials realized that.

Despite Mexican fears, Gadsden believed that a treaty could be effected. If the United States were willing to pay liberally, he said, an agreement embracing all of the administration's objectives, not just a land purchase, could be achieved. The fact that General Antonio López de Santa Anna, Mexico's president, was governing a country in dire economic straits made Gadsden more optimistic. Justified on the grounds that the United States needed a more defensible natural boundary separating the two nations, Gadsden actually pursued a course of territorial acquisition that far exceeded the need to adjust the boundary and to acquire the coveted railroad route. For fifty million dollars, Gadsden sought 250,000

square miles of Mexican territory, an amount that certainly would have been consistent with the wishes of Jefferson Davis and others who were interested in the expansion of slavery. Santa Anna remained adamant against both Gadsden's personal territorial desires and all but the most minimal demands later advanced by the Pierce Administration; the Mexican people were unwilling to see any further unnecessary dismemberment of their country, and only enough land would be sold for the more limited U.S. purposes.

Complicated by a web of intrigue, chicanery, and blusterism, negotiations ensued for several months. The three-man Mexican negotiating team headed by Minister of Foreign Relations Manuel Diez de Bonilla proved equal to its task; Gadsden failed to achieve all that he or the administration sought. Especially disappointing to him was his inability to purchase two or more border states in order to achieve the desired natural boundary between the two countries. Nevertheless, on December 31, 1853, Gadsden and the other plenipotentiaries assembled at the American Legation Headquarters, where they signed what was to be referred to in the United States as the Gadsden Treaty. The purchase area agreed to in the treaty consisted of fifty-five thousand square miles of territory in southern New Mexico and Arizona. Domestic politics, largely influenced by the sectional issue of slavery, later caused Congress to reduce the cession by approximately nine thousand square miles. The final price tag for the lands covered in the treaty was ten million dollars.

Although Gadsden had failed to accomplish all that either he or the administration had hoped, most people in the United States had reasons to be pleased with the treaty's provisions. The agreement had resolved all the immediate and potentially dangerous issues with Mexico and thus preserved peaceful relations. It also provided for the acquisition of the much-coveted southern route for the Pacific railroad, although because of the regional rivalry, many regarded this feature to be of minimal value. Article VII granted U.S. citizenship with full constitutional rights to the Mexicans living in the ceded territories and guaranteed them ownership of their land—although the courts and Congress allowed government agencies, ranchers, land speculators, and the railroad magnates to take possession of much of their acreage. Except for the purchase of Alaska, the land cession constituted the last major acquisition of territory within the present-day continental boundaries of the United States. —Robert L. Jenkins

ADDITIONAL READING:

Davis, William C. *Jefferson Davis: The Man and His Hour.* New York: HarperPerennial, 1991. Contains some material on Davis' relationship with Gadsden and the treaty.

Faulk, Odie B. *Too Far North, Too Far South.* Los Angeles: Westernlore Press, 1967. A good account of one of the most serious issues necessitating the treaty.

Fogel, Robert W. *Railroads and American Economic Growth.* Baltimore: The Johns Hopkins University Press, 1964. A good introduction to the important issue of railroading in the antebellum period and its role in the expansion of the nation's economy.

Garber, Paul Neff. *The Gadsden Treaty.* Gloucester, Mass.: Peter Smith, 1959. Although dated, this has remained the only comprehensive published study on all aspects of the subject.

Potter, David M. *The Impending Crisis, 1848-1861.* New York: Harper & Row, 1976. Primarily an account of the sectional crisis of the antebellum period, but provides some insight into the role of Gadsden's treaty in the controversy.

SEE ALSO: 1846, Mexican War; 1846, Occupation of California and the Southwest; 1847, Taos Rebellion; 1848, Treaty of Guadalupe Hidalgo.

1854 ■ PERRY OPENS TRADE WITH JAPAN:
an isolationist nation begins to emerge as a significant trading partner

DATE: March 31, 1854
LOCALE: Edo Bay (now Tokyo Bay), Japan
CATEGORIES: Asian American history; Diplomacy and international relations; Economics

KEY FIGURES:
Millard Fillmore (1800-1874), thirteenth president of the United States, 1850-1853
Komei (1821-1867), emperor of Japan, 1846-1867
Hotta Masayoshi (1810-1864), senior councillor to Komei
Tokugawa Nariaki (1800-1860), lord of Mito, Japan
Matthew Calbraith Perry (1794-1858), commander of the U.S. expedition to Japan

SUMMARY OF EVENT. The mission of Commodore Matthew Calbraith Perry to Japan from 1852 to 1854 was dramatic evidence of the United States' increasing interest in eastern Asia. It followed a series of overtures by other Western countries and coincided with a period of significant debate within Japan's ruling class over the prospect of opening the country to outside, particularly Western, influences.

From 1620 until Commodore Perry's squadron sailed into Edo Bay (later called Tokyo Bay), Japan had practiced a policy of rigid isolation and the exclusion of foreigners. In the sixteenth and early seventeenth centuries, Japan's experiences with Western missionaries and traders had been so negative that almost all contact with the outside world was broken off. Only the Dutch, Chinese, and Koreans were allowed to trade through one small port. In the nineteenth century, the desire to develop commercial relations, to exploit Japan's proximity to China, and to satisfy curiosity about Japan caused repeated attempts to open relations with Japan.

Prior to Perry's expedition, several European countries attempted to develop relations with Japan. Between 1771 and 1804, Russian individuals and government representatives made four separate, unsuccessful attempts to open Japan to trade. Japan redoubled its commitment to defend its northern islands against possible Russian advances, and no further interaction took place until Russia again exerted pressure in 1847. England was rebuffed in its 1818 effort to convince Japan to open trade. Following China's defeat in the Opium Wars, Japan was even further resolved to resist foreign influence.

Perry's mission was at least the fourth U.S. effort to open relations with Japan. In 1832, President Andrew Jackson had sent an envoy, Edmund Roberts, to negotiate treaties in East Asia. He concluded treaties with Siam (later known as Thailand) and with the Sultan of Muscat (later part of Oman) but died en route to Japan in 1836. In 1837, the merchant ship USS *Morrison* attempted to land in Japan but was repelled by cannon fire. In 1846, Commodore James Biddle arrived in Japan with the same goal that Edmund Roberts had been unable to achieve, but the Japanese refused to negotiate.

By 1850, the U.S. government was being pressed to open Japan. There was a clamor for the negotiation of a convention to protect U.S. sailors shipwrecked in Japanese waters, and the growing use of steam-powered merchant ships led to the demand for coaling stations. There also was a great desire for new markets in the Far East. In 1852, Millard Fillmore, thirteenth president of the United States, sent another expedition in an attempt to break down Japan's seclusion. He chose Perry as its commander and minister plenipotentiary and gave him broad powers. Perry was assigned five steam warships and four sailing vessels; his instructions were to arrange for commercial relations and to negotiate a treaty.

Perry's expedition left Hampton Roads, Virginia, in November, 1852. Gifts were carried to demonstrate the United States' technological prowess, including a telegraph set and a miniature steam locomotive with cars and track. Eight months later, in 1853, Perry led four ships into Edo Bay. The Japanese, who had never seen steamships before, were greatly impressed. Perry was determined to avoid the mistakes of other Western envoys. Under strict orders to use force only if absolutely necessary, he assumed a confident bearing and insisted on dealing only with the highest officials. At first, representatives of the *bafuku*, or military government, demanded that the ships proceed to Nagasaki, the only port at which Westerners were permitted to have contacts with the Japanese government. Perry refused to be intimidated or to leave Edo Bay until he was assured that the dispatches he carried, including a letter from the president of the United States to the emperor of Japan, would be delivered in the appropriate quarters. When the Japanese finally promised that the emperor would receive the U.S. treaty proposals, Perry steamed away, but not before he informed the emperor's agents that he intended to return in the spring of 1854 with a larger force and with the expectation of a favorable response.

The *bafuku* solicited advice from members of the Japanese ruling class on how to respond to Perry's demands. Seven hundred proposals were submitted, with none offering an ideal solution. A group led by the lord of Mito, Tokugawa Nariaki, advocated resistance to invasion at all costs. The *Rangakusha*, or "masters of Dutch learning" school, which had learned something of the West through Japan's limited connections to the Netherlands, argued that Japan's substantial military capabilities would be no match for Western armies backed by modern industrial technologies. They also believed that Japan would benefit more than it would lose from more exposure to Western ideas and technologies.

While Emperor Komei and his advisers debated what response Japan should make to U.S. overtures, Perry returned to his exploration of the Far East. Believing that the glittering prospects for U.S. trade in the Far East required that the United States gain territorial footholds in the area, he took possession of certain of the Boning Islands, established a coaling station on Okinawa, and cast covetous eyes on Formosa; however, his superiors in Washington repudiated these actions.

In February, 1854, Perry returned to Japan with an impressive squadron of eight warships. The Japanese leaders had decided to deal with the North Americans as the least threatening of the Western powers. Japan was ready to accept, at least in part, the proposals of the United States. Perry exploited his advantage by demanding a treaty similar to the liberal agreement that the United States had negotiated with China in 1844, but the final terms, concluded in the Treaty of Kanagawa, signed on March 31, 1854, were less inclusive. The United

Commodore Matthew Perry, as rendered by a Japanese artist. Perry was the first westerner other than Dutch traders to succeed in opening trade between Japan and the West. (Library of Congress)

States was to be permitted to establish a consulate at Shimoda, a small port on Honshu near Edo Bay, but there was no provision allowing U.S. citizens to take up permanent residence, and U.S. citizens and merchant vessels were allowed to enter only two small ports, Shimoda and Hakodate. Japan bound itself to assist shipwrecked U.S. sailors and return them and their belongings to the proper authorities. The agreement did not provide for the establishment of coaling facilities or for extraterritorial rights for U.S. citizens, but it did contain an article ensuring that the United States would be offered any future concessions that might be offered to other powers. Japan soon reached similar agreements with England, France, Russia, and the Netherlands. The immediate and practical effects of the treaty negotiated by Perry were minimal, and even they were not supported fully by Emperor Komei and his advisers. The treaty prepared the way, however, for a broader commercial treaty that was signed by the emperor's senior councillor, Hotta Masayoshi, in 1858.

—*Theodore A. Wilson, updated by James Hayes-Bohanan*

ADDITIONAL READING:

Fallows, James. "When East Met West: Perry's Mission Accomplished." *Smithsonian* 25, no. 4 (July, 1994): 20-33. Discusses the event as an encounter between Commodore Perry and Masahiro Abe. Gives a history of previous missionary and other contacts in Japan.

Hane, Mikiso. "The Fall of the Tokugawa Bakufu." In *Modern Japan: A Historical Survey.* 2d ed. Boulder, Colo.: Westview Press, 1992. Thorough, readable account of the political debates in Japan over how to respond to Western demands to open trade.

McDougall, Walter A. "Edo 1853." In *Let the Sea Make a Noise: A History of the North Pacific from Magellan to MacArthur.* New York: Basic Books, 1993. Describes Perry's expedition in the context of the overall maritime strategy of the United States.

Morison, Samuel Eliot. *"Old Bruin": Commodore Matthew C. Perry, 1794-1858.* Boston: Little, Brown, 1967. Chapters 20 through 28 of this biography detail contacts with Japan from Perry's perspective.

Morton, W. Scott. "The Winds of Change: The Tokugawa Shogunate: Part II, 1716-1867." In *Japan: Its History and Culture.* New York: McGraw-Hill, 1984. Puts Japan's response to Commodore Perry in a broad social context of Japan's struggle over relations with the Western world.

Preble, George Henry. *The Opening of Japan: A Diary of Discovery in the Far East, 1853-1856.* Edited by Boleslaw Szczesniak. Norman: University of Oklahoma Press, 1962. The diary of Rear Admiral Preble, who served on the USS *Macedonian* as it accompanied Perry's expeditions to Japan, provides detailed observations of the expeditions.

Wiley, Peter Booth, with Korogi Ichiro. *Yankees in the Land of the Gods: Commodore Perry and the Opening of Japan.* New York: Viking, 1990. Description of Commodore Perry's encounter with the Japanese draws on both U.S. and Japanese sources. Maps and illustrations.

SEE ALSO: 1892, Yellow Peril Campaign; 1907, Gentlemen's Agreement; 1913, Alien Land Laws.

1854 ■ KANSAS-NEBRASKA ACT: *the Compromise of 1850 proves temporary when the problem of slavery in the territories reemerges*

DATE: May 30, 1854
LOCALE: Washington, D.C.
CATEGORIES: African American history; Laws and acts
KEY FIGURES:

David Rice Atchison (1807-1886), Whig senator from Missouri

Salmon Portland Chase (1808-1873), Free-Soil Democrat senator from Ohio

Jefferson Davis (1808-1889), secretary of war

Archibald Dixon (1802-1876), Whig senator from Kentucky

Stephen Arnold Douglas (1813-1861), Democratic senator from Illinois

Franklin Pierce (1804-1869), fourteenth president of the United States, 1853-1857

Alexander Hamilton Stephens (1812-1883), Whig congressman from Georgia

Charles Sumner (1811-1874), Whig senator from Massachusetts

SUMMARY OF EVENT. The issue of the expansion of slavery was laid aside only temporarily with the passage of the Compromise of 1850, although the compromise had seemed to be fairly successful in the two or three years immediately following its enactment. Several events kept the compromise in the public eye, including the seizure in the North of African Americans under the provisions of the Second Fugitive Slave Law (1850), the publication of Harriet Beecher Stowe's *Uncle Tom's Cabin* in 1852, and the last of three filibustering expeditions launched from New Orleans in August, 1851, by Venezuelan Narcisco Lopez against Spanish Cuba. Many people in the United States hoped that the slavery issue would disappear, and the economic pressures of life absorbed the attention of most average citizens. Moreover, no prominent politicians had captured the public's imagination. Lackluster, noncontroversial candidates were nominated in the presidential campaign of 1852—Franklin Pierce of New Hampshire for the Democrats and General Winfield Scott for the Whigs. The election, won by Pierce, was no more exciting than the candidates. Evidence of the desire of U.S. voters to maintain the status quo was demonstrated further in the poor showing of John P. Hale of New Hampshire, the standard-bearer of the Free-Soil Party. With the Democrats in control and apparently committed to the Compromise of 1850, the United States seemed destined to at least another four years of relative calm.

The issue of slavery in the federal territories was reopened in January, 1854, when Stephen A. Douglas of Illinois, chair-

ALIGNMENT OF FREE AND SLAVE STATES AFTER THE KANSAS-NEBRASKA ACT OF 1854

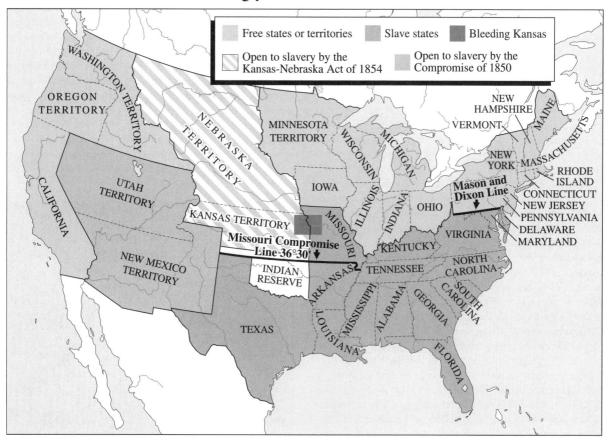

In fashioning legislation to organize the territory of Nebraska, Illinois senator Stephen A. Douglas was pressured by proslavery leadership to amend the final bill so as to repeal the section of the Missouri Compromise prohibiting slavery north of 36°30'. In addition, the territory was divided at the fortieth parallel into the two territories of Kansas and Nebraska. Most Northerners considered the Missouri Compromise to be a sacred pledge; its repeal destroyed the political calm that had been preserved by the Compromise of 1850 and resulted in "Bleeding Kansas," a small civil war that presaged the Civil War of 1861.

man of the Committee on Territories, reported a bill to organize the Platte country west of Iowa and Missouri as the territory of Nebraska. Douglas' main interest was in opening the West to settlement and to the construction of a railroad to the Pacific coast. Douglas did not wish to deal with the slavery question and he (like his soon-to-be nemesis, Abraham Lincoln) doubted that the institution could survive on the Great Plains, but he realized that he needed Southern votes to get the territorial bill through Congress.

In the original form, the bill included a provision, similar to that found in the acts organizing the territories of Utah and New Mexico, that the territory would determine the question of its status as a slave or free state at the time of admission. The clause dealing with slavery was intentionally ambiguous, but it probably would have left in effect—at least during the territorial stage—the provisions of the Missouri Compromise that barred slavery in the Louisiana Purchase territory north of

36°30' north latitude. The ambiguity of the bill bothered Southern political leaders, particularly the rabidly proslavery David R. Atchison of Missouri, president pro tempore of the Senate and acting vice president. Yielding to the pressure of Senator Atchison and other Southern leaders, Douglas and his committee added a section to the bill that permitted the people of the territory, acting through their representatives, to decide whether the territory should be slave or free. This "popular sovereignty" formula for dealing with the slavery question implied the repeal of the Missouri Compromise restriction on slavery.

The proslavery leaders were not satisfied with the implicit abrogation of the Missouri Compromise. As Whig senator Archibald Dixon of Kentucky pointed out, under popular sovereignty, the restriction of slavery would remain in effect until the territorial settlers acted to end it. In the interim, immigration of slaveholders into the territory would be prohibited.

Proslavery leadership forced Douglas to amend the bill further so as to repeal explicitly that section of the Missouri Compromise prohibiting slavery north of 36°30′. In addition, the territory was divided at the fortieth parallel into the two territories of Kansas and Nebraska. Most Northerners considered the Missouri Compromise to be a sacred pledge, and its repeal was quite enough to destroy the relative political calm that had been prevalent in the nation since 1850.

Much more was at work, however. The Missouri Compromise had led to the creation of the political party system, utilized by the Democrats and finally adopted by the Whigs, under which party loyalty was ensured through the disposition of party and government jobs (known as patronage or the spoils system). Under that system, the tensions created by the Missouri Compromise were to be kept under control, for anyone could be controlled by the promise of employment, according to the assumptions of the new party system. The effect of the party system was to increase the size and scope of federal government operations in every election, because to get elected, a candidate had to promise more jobs than his opponent. The result for the slavery interests was that the South, slowly but surely, was being placed in a permanent minority status in the Senate and House. If an antislavery president were elected, the now-powerful federal government could act directly on slavery in the South.

The Kansas-Nebraska Act, especially Douglas' concept of popular sovereignty, offered hope to the South that the dynamic created by the spoils system could be short-circuited. If territories could decide whether or not to permit slavery, then slave interests could flood the new territories with proslavery settlers and vote in slavery, regardless of the attitudes of Congress or the president.

Douglas still had to guide the bill through passage in the face of widespread and violent criticism from the North. The bill was certain of passage in the Senate, although it was the object of impassioned attack by Senators Salmon Chase of Ohio and Charles Sumner of Massachusetts. In the House, however, the issue was doubtful, and it was there that Douglas marshaled the power of the Pierce Administration to force dissident Democrats into line behind the bill. By whip and spur, the Kansas-Nebraska Act was driven through the House by a large sectional vote of 113-100. Nearly all Southern Democrats supported the measure. All forty-five Northern Whigs opposed it, while thirteen of nineteen Southern Whigs, led by Alexander Stephens of Georgia, favored it. The divisiveness of the issue was represented best by the fact that of eighty-six Northern Democrats, forty-two voted against it in spite of patronage and other pressures brought to bear by administration leaders. In doing so, the Democrats showed the utter futility of basing a slavery strategy on the spoils system: Ideology proved stronger than economics, and the idea that the national debate over slavery could be contained with the promise of a few jobs was mortally wounded.

The passage of the Kansas-Nebraska Act had momentous consequences. The act touched off the forces that eventually brought war. It reopened sectional issues and embittered sectional relations by arousing the entire North. It destroyed the Whig Party in the deep South and increased Southern unity and influence in the Democratic Party. It contributed greatly to the demise of the Whig Party in the North and divided the Northern Democrats, inducing many of them to leave the party. Most important, it led to the formation, beginning in 1854, of the Republican Party. That party was founded in diametric opposition to the operating principles of the Democratic Party. Instead of holding that economic self-interest took precedence over ideology, the Republicans held that fundamental beliefs mattered more than temporal, material benefits in the long run. The Republicans thus made slavery—the issue that the Democrats and the Whigs refused to touch—the focal point of their campaigns.

Senator Charles Sumner of Massachusetts vigorously opposed the passage of the Kansas-Nebraska Act, which offered hope to the South that the political spoils system could be short-circuited. If territories could decide whether or not to permit slavery, then slave interests could flood the new territories with proslavery settlers and vote in slavery, regardless of the attitudes of Congress or the president. The act spurred the growing sectionalism that would lead to "Bleeding Kansas" two years later, and eventually a nationwide Civil War. (Library of Congress)

On a personal level, Douglas gained little support in the South and lost an important part of his support in the North. Douglas, misinterpreting Northern sentiment toward this initially innocent piece of legislation, had opened a political Pandora's box. The legislation reflected Douglas' personal views accurately, though. He sincerely disliked slavery, but thought that it was an issue of choice of the slaveholder; therefore, the matter of human bondage was not a moral issue but simply a matter of votes. Douglas could say honestly that he opposed slavery personally, but supported a slaveholder's right to own slaves. Thus, the agony of Douglas and the struggle for Kansas had begun.

—*John C. Gardner, updated by Larry Schweikart*

ADDITIONAL READING:

Gienapp, William E. *The Origins of the Republican Party, 1852-1856*. New York: Oxford University Press, 1987. A seminal book that downplays the role of specific events in the success of the Republican Party and emphasizes the competition between the Know-Nothings and the Republicans. Focuses on the collapse of the Whigs and the nativist movements that reflected mass changes at the state levels.

Holt, Michael. *The Political Crisis of the 1850's*. New York: W. W. Norton, 1978. A thorough treatment of the era, emphasizing the breakdown of the two-party system as a cause of the Civil War. Downplays economic and cultural factors.

Johannsen, Robert W. *Stephen A. Douglas*. New York: Oxford University Press, 1973. The quintessential biography of Douglas.

McPherson, James W. *Battle Cry of Freedom: The Era of the Civil War*. New York: Oxford University Press, 1988. A broad historical narrative, emphasizing slavery and cultural differences as the causes of the Civil War.

Nevins, Allen. *A House Dividing, 1852-1857*. Vol. 2 in *Ordeal of the Union*. New York: Charles Scribner's Sons, 1947. A brilliantly written, classic interpretation of sectional differences as the cause of war. Encompassing people, events, economics, culture, and ideology. The single best starting place for an understanding of the United States in 1854.

Nichols, Roy Franklin. "The Kansas-Nebraska Act: A Century of Historiography." *Mississippi Valley Historical Review* 43 (September, 1956): 187-212. A traditional guide to the historical literature and a concise account of the legislative history and consequences of the act. Posits the "blundering generation" of politicians as the cause of sectional strife.

Wolff, Gerald. *The Kansas-Nebraska Bill: Party, Section, and the Coming of the Civil War*. New York: Revisionist Press, 1977. Another interpretation of the Civil War emphasizing party breakdown, but specific to the Kansas-Nebraska Act.

SEE ALSO: 1820, Missouri Compromise; 1830, Proslavery Argument; 1835, Texas Revolution; 1850, Compromise of 1850; 1850, Second Fugitive Slave Law; 1854, Birth of the Republican Party; 1856, Bleeding Kansas; 1857, *Dred Scott v. Sandford*; 1858, Lincoln-Douglas Debates; 1859, John Brown's Raid on Harpers Ferry; 1860, Lincoln Is Elected President.

1854 ■ BIRTH OF THE REPUBLICAN PARTY:
the new party welded together fragments of Whigs, Know-Nothings, and free-soil interests and presaged the sectionalization that eventually brought civil war

DATE: July 6, 1854

LOCALE: Ripon, Wisconsin

CATEGORIES: Government and politics; Organizations and institutions

KEY FIGURES:

Salmon Portland Chase (1808-1873), senator from Ohio and an early convert to the Republican Party

John Charles Frémont (1813-1890), Republican presidential candidate in 1856

Horace Greeley (1811-1872), editor of the *New York Tribune*, who joined the Republican Party in 1855

John McLean (1785-1861), associate justice of the United States and a candidate for the Republican nomination in 1856

William Henry Seward (1801-1872), senator from New York who converted to the Republican Party in 1855

Thurlow Weed (1797-1882), political boss of New York who joined the Republican Party in 1855

SUMMARY OF EVENT. The development of the United States' political parties went through several stages during the antebellum period of U.S. history. During the Washington Administration, domestic and foreign issues combined to produce the Federalists, led by Alexander Hamilton, and the Democratic-Republicans, under the leadership of Thomas Jefferson. Federalism had its day in the 1790's but lost control of the government in 1800. By 1815, the Federalist Party had disintegrated, leaving the field to the Jeffersonians. For the next two decades, everyone claimed to be a Republican, that is, the heir of Jefferson, and political organizations revolved around powerful personalities such as John Quincy Adams, Henry Clay, and Andrew Jackson. After Jackson narrowly lost his bid for the presidency in 1824, the Republican Party split into two rival camps. President John Quincy Adams and Secretary of State Henry Clay provided the leadership of the National Republicans, while Andrew Jackson, taking the name of the old Jeffersonians, began organization of the Democratic-Republicans, later called the Democratic Party.

Jackson's election in 1828 signaled another development in the evolution of political parties, as opposition to Jackson congealed into the Whig Party. The Democratic-Republican and Whig parties dominated the political stage until the 1850's. During this period of a growing electorate, issues arising out of reformist impulses, expansion, and slavery stimulated the rise of various third parties, such as the Anti-Masons, the Liberty Party, the Free-Soil Party, and the Know-Nothings. The tensions engendered by the sectional controversy assured the dominance, among the third parties, of the antislavery groups. The Whig Party suffered the most from the presence of these minor parties, because its major strength lay in the North, the center of antislavery and free-soil sentiment. The Compromise of 1850 seriously weakened the Whig Party, as did the deaths of Henry Clay and Daniel Webster in 1852. The Kansas-Nebraska Act dealt the Whigs a fatal blow and helped cause the formation of an entirely new political organization—the Republican Party.

The national uproar over the Kansas-Nebraska Act damaged the unity of both the Whigs and the Democrats. By repealing the old Missouri Compromise, which had made 36°30′ north latitude (except for Missouri) the dividing line between slave and free-soil territories in the Louisiana Purchase Territory, the Kansas-Nebraska Act split both the Democrats and the Whigs into groups that either endorsed or condemned the extension of slavery into the territories, thus giving encouragement to the Free-Soilers. Both of the major parties possessed strong free-soil cores. These groups, in opposing the Kansas-Nebraska Act and the efforts of the administrations of Franklin Pierce and James Buchanan to force the admission of Kansas as a slave state, gradually drifted away from their original alignments into loosely knit parties held together by a common opposition to the Democratic policy in Kansas. Protest meetings occurred throughout the country in February and March of 1854. These meetings, encouraged by Free-Soilers, proved to be the first stirrings of a new political party, but the activities of the opponents of the Kansas-Nebraska Act in Ripon, Wisconsin, are generally considered to have launched that party, the Republican Party, into existence.

The events in Ripon came at a meeting held by several Whigs, Free-Soilers, and Democrats in the Congregational Church on February 28, 1854. The meeting had been called by Major Alvan E. Bovay, a prominent Whig who had, in 1852, met with Horace Greeley and discussed the formation of a new party. The group in Ripon passed a resolution stating that if the Kansas-Nebraska bill passed, they would form a new party, to be called the Republican Party. After the passage of the Kansas-Nebraska bill, Major Bovay went from house to house to announce a meeting on March 20, 1854. Of approximately one hundred voters in the village, fifty-three turned out and voted to dissolve the local Whig and Free-Soil organizations. A committee of five was appointed to form the new party.

On July 6, 1854, a formal convention was held in Jackson, Michigan. This convention, held outdoors under the oaks, attracted hundreds of citizens from throughout the state. The convention adopted a platform and nominated a full slate of candidates for state offices. This first Republican convention has given Jackson, Michigan, its claim as the birthplace of the Republican Party. Both Michigan and Wisconsin, forging coalitions, elected their candidates on the state ticket that year. In 1855, the Republicans took control and elected Nathaniel P. Banks of Massachusetts as Speaker of the Thirty-fourth Congress.

The Republicans were not an immediate success. Many Democrats and Whigs who did not favor the Kansas-Nebraska Act were reluctant to break with their established parties. In addition, while Republican popularity was damaged by its association with abolitionism, the Temperance and Know-Nothing parties competed with the Republican Party for public support. The political campaigns of 1854 and 1855 were inordinately confused by the numerous groups entering the fray. Republicans were most successful when they arranged fusion tickets with these other groups. The obvious weakness of the Republicans made their organization less attractive to Whigs, who found themselves politically homeless. The struggle between proslavery and antislavery elements in Kansas again came to the aid of the Republicans, who, of all the anti-Kansas-Nebraska groups, were most persistent in their assaults on the proslavery Democratic policy in Kansas. In 1855, the Republicans won a political victory in Ohio and also gained the support of political boss Thurlow Weed and Senator William H. Seward, former Whigs from New York. With their strength growing rapidly, the Republicans planned to enter a slate in the presidential election of 1856. By that time, the original Free-Soil founders of the party had been reinforced by former Whigs, antislavery Democrats, and former Know-Nothings. All united on the basis of their opposition to the extension of slavery in the territories.

Appreciable support and sympathy for the Republicans were brought about by several factors: a disappointing convention of Republicans and other anti-Nebraskans at Pittsburgh in February, 1856; the sack of Lawrence, Kansas, by a proslavery mob; and the physical assault on Senator Charles Sumner of Massachusetts by Preston Brooks, a representative from South Carolina, in May, 1856. The improvement in Republican hopes guaranteed a lively fight at the Republican National Convention in Philadelphia in June, 1856.

John Charles Frémont, the Western explorer and adventurer, won the presidential nomination and approached the election with some hope of receiving most of the Whig and some of the Know-Nothing votes. For so young a party, the results of the 1856 election were spectacular. James Buchanan, the victorious Democratic candidate, polled 1,838,169 votes to Frémont's 1,335,265. Buchanan received 174 electoral votes, Frémont 114. Beneath those figures lay a poignant political fact—of the nineteen states Buchanan carried in the election, only five were free states. The eleven states that voted for Frémont, however, were all free states. The Democratic and Republican parties were sectional parties as no others had been before them. The South believed it had reason to fear a Republican victory in 1860.

During the four years following 1856, the new party grew rapidly, capturing the House of Representatives, absorbing most Whigs and Know-Nothings, and acquiring a cadre of experienced political leaders. The new party, composed of diverse elements, emphasized free-soil in the territories but successfully disassociated itself from the taint of abolitionism, and attracted support by advocating a homestead bill and old Whig measures such as internal improvements. Their remarkable showing in 1856 justified the optimism with which the

Republicans faced the future. By the same token, the quick growth of the party testified to the ominous sectionalization of politics in the nation. This sectionalization came to the forefront with the outbreak of the Civil War after the election in 1860 of Republican Abraham Lincoln as president of the United States. In this election, the upstart new political party elected a man whom most historians consider the finest president ever to lead the United States of America.

—John C. Gardner, updated by Kay Hively

ADDITIONAL READING:

Crandall, Andrew W. *The Early History of the Republican Party, 1854-1856*. Gloucester, Mass.: P. Smith, 1960. Points out the dissatisfaction that had surfaced in the Whig and Democratic parties, which spawned the formation of the Republican Party.

Cuomo, Mario, and Harold Holzer, eds. *Lincoln on Democracy*. New York: HarperCollins, 1990. A look at Lincoln's views on democracy and how they lined up with those of the new Republican Party.

Foner, Eric. *Free Soil, Free Labor, Free Men: The Ideology of the Republican Party Before the Civil War*. New York: Oxford University Press, 1970. Discusses the idea that the Republican Party was formed over the issue of free labor and the moral tone this set against the use of slave labor in the South.

Holzer, Harold, ed. *The Lincoln-Douglas Debates*. New York: HarperCollins, 1993. The full text of the debates of Abraham Lincoln and Stephen Douglas, which reveals the striking differences between the newly formed Republican Party and the established Democratic Party.

Van Deusen, Glyndon G. *William Henry Seward*. New York: Oxford University Press, 1967. A biography of an early leader in the Republican Party who was an early rival of Abraham Lincoln.

SEE ALSO: 1790's, First U.S. Political Parties; 1824, U.S. Election of 1824; 1828, Jackson Is Elected President; 1831, Tocqueville Visits America; 1834, Birth of the Whig Party; 1840, U.S. Election of 1840; 1850, Compromise of 1850; 1854, Kansas-Nebraska Act; 1856, Bleeding Kansas; 1858, Lincoln-Douglas Debates; 1860, Lincoln Is Elected President.

1856 ■ BLEEDING KANSAS: *a territorial war between free-soil and proslavery elements presages a national civil war*

DATE: May 21, 1856-August 2, 1858
LOCALE: Kansas Territory
CATEGORIES: African American history; Government and politics
KEY FIGURES:

James Buchanan (1791-1868), fifteenth president of the United States, 1857-1861
John Calhoun (1806-1859), surveyor general of Kansas and Nebraska Territories

Stephen Arnold Douglas (1813-1861), senator from Illinois
John White Geary (1819-1873), governor of Kansas Territory, 1856-1857
James Henry Lane (1814-1866), Free-Soil leader in Kansas
Franklin Pierce (1804-1969), fourteenth president of the United States, 1853-1857
Charles Robinson (1818-1894), leader of Free-State Party in Kansas; elected governor by that faction in 1856
Robert John Walker (1801-1869), governor of Kansas Territory, 1857-1858

SUMMARY OF EVENT. The chaos that was Kansas between 1855 and 1858 had a tremendous impact upon the entire nation. The Whig Party disintegrated under the pressure of the slavery controversy, while the Democratic Party split into feuding sectional factions and the Republican Party was born. Politicians suddenly found themselves without political homes. Political reputations were made and unmade when prominent national figures paid the price of their inability to resolve the sectional disputes while facing challenges from rising young men. The United States seemed to be drifting off course, and people wondered about the ultimate fate of a nation that apparently had lost control of its own destiny.

With the opening of Kansas Territory to settlement in 1854, a contest began between groups supporting slavery (mainly persons from Missouri) and settlers from the Northwestern states who were free-soilers in practice, if not ideology. Since the Missourians were closest, they seized control of the territorial government and immediately enacted proslavery legislation. President Franklin Pierce and his successor, James Buchanan of Pennsylvania, accepted the proslavery Kansas government and committed the Democratic Party to the admission of Kansas as a slave state. The numerical dominance of slavery's supporters soon dwindled as settlers from free states found their way into the territory. By September, 1855, there were enough Free-Soilers in Kansas to enable them to repudiate the territorial legislature, organize a Free State Party, and call for a constitutional convention to meet in Topeka. There, in October and November, 1855, a free-state constitution was written. In January, 1856, Governor Charles Robinson and a legislature were elected. Kansas found itself with two governments—one supporting slavery and considered legal by the Democratic administration in Washington, but resting upon a small minority of the population; and the other representing majority opinion in Kansas but condemned as an act of rebellion by President Pierce and Senator Stephen A. Douglas of Illinois.

Douglas' role was of particular interest, as he had drafted the Kansas-Nebraska Act as a way to extend a railroad westward across the territories. Douglas favored the theory of popular sovereignty, meaning "let the people decide." That doctrine, however, was exposed—eventually by Abraham Lincoln in the Lincoln-Douglas debates—as unconstitutional: The will of the people could not be held above constitutionally protected rights. Douglas' bill, however, created an entirely new concern. The North had started to outdistance the South in population, giving it more seats in Congress, and the Missouri Compromise had ensured that the North would have a permanent advantage in the Senate. Southerners started to realize that if the "wrong" presidential candidate came to office, the South would find itself excluded from the power.

Although proslave and free-soil groups moved into Kansas, actual bloodshed remained at a minimum through 1855; nevertheless, the territory quickly came to symbolize the sectional dispute. Anti-Kansas-Nebraska groups composed of former Whigs and dissident Democrats arose and eventually were led by Douglas. Douglas, at the eleventh hour, had come to realize the extent of his unpopularity in the North and to recognize the fraud that the proslavery government in Kansas had propagated.

Violence became commonplace in Kansas through the spring and summer of 1856. Armed free-soil and proslavery parties skirmished along the Wakarusa River south of Lawrence as early as December, 1855; but it was the sack of Lawrence in May, 1856, by a large band of proslavery Border Ruffians from Missouri, that ignited the conflict. Retaliation was demanded: John Brown, the abolitionist crusader, his four sons, and three others struck at Pottawatomie, where they executed five settlers who were reputed to be proslavery. That act of terrorism sparked further retaliation. Early in August, free-soil forces captured the slavery stronghold of Franklin; later that month, free-soilers, led by Brown, repelled an attack by a large party of proslavers at Osawatomie. Guerrilla warfare raged throughout the territory until September, when a temporary armistice was achieved by the arrival of federal troops and a new territorial governor, John W. Geary. However, a solution to the travail of Kansas could come only from Washington, D.C., and it would have to overcome the determination of the Democratic administration and its Southern supporters to bring Kansas into the Union as a slave state. Meeting at Lecompton in January and February, 1857, the proslave territorial legislature called for an election of delegates to a constitutional convention. No provision was made, however, to submit what could only be a proslavery constitution to a popular vote. The measure passed over Governor Geary's veto.

The constitutional convention that met in Lecompton in September, 1857, hammered out a document to the electorate; the proslavery leadership would agree only to submit the document to the people with the choice of accepting it with or without the clause explicitly guaranteeing slavery. However, ample protection for slavery was woven into the fabric of the constitution. Even if the "constitution without slavery" clause had won popular approval, thereby causing slavery to exist "no longer," slaves already in Kansas as property would not be affected. Opponents refused to go to the polls, and the proslavery Lecompton Constitution was approved in December, 1857.

The Free-Soil Party, meanwhile, had captured control of the territorial legislature and had successfully requested the new territorial governor, Frederick P. Stanton, to convene the legislature in order to call for another election. In the new election,

one might vote for or against the entire Lecompton Constitution. On January 4, 1858, the Lecompton Constitution met overwhelming defeat. Kansas was, by that time, free-soil in sentiment, but the Buchanan Administration, which followed Pierce's, saw otherwise. It supported the Lecompton Constitution, which became a test of Democratic Party loyalty. Although Douglas came out against the administration's position, the Senate voted in March, 1858, to admit Kansas under the Lecompton Constitution. Public sentiment in the North opposed such a policy, and the House of Representatives voted to admit Kansas as a state only on the condition that the state constitution be submitted in its entirety to the voters at a carefully controlled election. That proviso, called the Crittenden-Montgomery Amendment, was rejected by the Senate.

Out of the deadlock, a House-Senate conference ensued that proposed the English Bill, a compromise measure designed to save the Buchanan Administration from utter defeat. The bill stipulated that the Lecompton Constitution should be submitted to the people of Kansas again: If approved, the new state would receive a federal land grant; if rejected, statehood would be postponed until the population of the territory reached ninety-three thousand (a contradiction of the process by which all other territories had become states, but the legal requirement to have a representative in Congress). Although Congress passed the bill in May, the voters of Kansas rejected the Lecompton Constitution again, this time by a margin of six to one. In January, 1861, after several Southern states announced secession, Kansas entered the Union as a free state under the Wyandotte Constitution.

For Kansas, the storm ended with the defeat of the Lecompton Constitution in August, 1858; but for Douglas, condemned as a traitor to his party, and for the Democrats, it had just started. Douglas soon met Abraham Lincoln, the Republican nominee for the Senate seat in Illinois, at Ottawa, Illinois, in the first of their historic debates. In another debate, at Freeport, Lincoln, using the Supreme Court's 1857 ruling in the *Dred Scott* case that Congress could make no law prohibiting slavery, queried Douglas as to how he would keep slavery out of a territory using popular sovereignty. Douglas replied that the population could vote to install antislave judges and sheriffs who would not enforce slavery restrictions. That answer was ridiculed as the "Freeport Doctrine" by Southerners, and destroyed any chances Douglas had of carrying the South in the 1860 election. Lincoln, who lost the Senate race to Douglas, captured the presidency in 1860 without a single Southern electoral vote.

The role of the territories in offering the South a means to continue slavery has been subject to considerable analysis. An important factor in the weakened position of the South was the political party—the Democratic Party—that was created specifically to exclude slavery from the national political debate. The Albany-Richmond Axis provided the base of Democratic Party support that tacitly agreed that the party offer presidential candidates who were "Northern men of Southern principles"—in other words, men who could draw the large electoral states of the North but who would not use the power of the federal government to attack slavery. The irony of the Democratic Party was that it acquired party allegiance by granting government jobs—patronage—which, in turn, caused the government to grow larger and more powerful with each election. As a result, by the time the Republicans became a national force, the federal government stood to pose a threat to slavery in the "wrong" hands. Since the Republicans' first principle was the elimination of slavery in the territories, their election posed the threat of placing federal power—by then, far greater than anyone had dreamed it might be in the 1820's—into the hands of a party determined (in Southerners' eyes) to destroy slavery.

Finally, the apparent victory of the Free-Soil elections in Kansas had the immediate effect of convincing railroads that the state would remain free. The *Dred Scott* ruling made that outcome completely uncertain; as a result, the railroad stocks crashed, bringing on the Panic of 1857, which, ironically, advanced the Republican Party's fortunes in the North.

—John G. Clark, updated by Larry Schweikart

ADDITIONAL READING:

Calomiris, Charles W., and Larry Schweikart. "The Panic of 1857: Origins, Transmission, Containment." *Journal of Economic History* 51 (December, 1990): 807-834. Analyzes the relationships between railroad politics in Kansas and the financial markets, especially as the *Dred Scott* decision led to the Panic of 1857.

Gienapp, William E. *The Origins of the Republican Party, 1852-1856.* New York: Oxford University Press, 1987. Emphasizes the rise of the Republican Party as the crucial element in ending the earlier U.S. party system. Argues that the formation of the Republican Party represented a realignment that started with the demise of the Whigs, continued with the rise of the Know-Nothings, and culminated with the events in Kansas that galvanized the disparate elements.

Holt, Michael. *The Political Crisis of the 1850's.* New York: John Wiley & Sons, 1978. Focuses on the transformation of political parties in the 1850's; argues that sectional differences, as expressed in the party dissolution, caused the Civil War. Still the best one-volume study of the period.

McPherson, James K. *Ordeal by Fire.* New York. Alfred A. Knopf, 1982. An excellent single-volume study, essentially part of McPherson's more popular *Battle Cry of Freedom* (1988), that touches on all explanations of the crises, ultimately finding political causes.

Nichols, Roy F. *The Disruption of American Democracy.* New York: Macmillan, 1948. A traditional, yet effective, analysis of the 1850's, emphasizing the destruction of the Democrats as the national party. Does not successfully explain the relationship between patronage, spoils, the growing size of government, and the anxiety that growth caused in the sections.

SEE ALSO: 1820, Missouri Compromise; 1830, Proslavery Argument; 1835, Texas Revolution; 1850, Compromise of 1850; 1850, Second Fugitive Slave Law; 1854, Kansas-Nebraska Act; 1854, Birth of the Republican Party; 1857, *Dred Scott v. Sandford*; 1858, Lincoln-Douglas Debates; 1859,

John Brown's Raid on Harpers Ferry; 1860, Lincoln Is Elected President.

1857 ■ FIRST AFRICAN AMERICAN UNIVERSITY: *the first major institution of higher education for African American youth opens as the Ashmun Institute*

DATE: January 1, 1857
LOCALE: Chester County, Oxford, Pennsylvania
CATEGORIES: African American history; Education
KEY FIGURES:
Jehudi Ashmun (1794-1828), editor who worked for the repatriation of African Americans, and for whom Ashmun Institute was named
Sarah Emlen Cresson Dickey, wife of John Miller Dickey, who helped found the school
John Miller Dickey (1806-1878), founder of Ashmun Institute, now known as Lincoln University
Abraham Lincoln (1809-1865), sixteenth president of the United States, 1861-1865

SUMMARY OF EVENT. Lincoln University originally opened its doors as Ashmun Institute, on January 1, 1857, in Chester County, Oxford, Pennsylvania. The institute's purpose was to give African American youth an opportunity to receive a sound, well-balanced education. Although many people through many decades helped to create the idea of a school devoted to the higher education of African Americans, John Miller Dickey was the man who put the idea to work.

Dickey, the son of a minister and of Scotch-Irish descent, attended Dickinson College in Milton, Pennsylvania. He was graduated in 1824 with a bachelor of arts degree; that fall, he entered the Princeton Theological Seminary to become a Presbyterian minister, following in the footsteps of his many relatives who also were ministers. In 1827, at twenty-one years of age, he was graduated from the seminary and received his first assignment, at the Presbytery of New Castle in Newark, Delaware. In 1829, he received a new assignment in Georgia from the Board of Missions. He found that the slaves in the area listened ardently to his sermons, and he was particularly impressed by their desire to learn.

On June 12, 1834, Dickey married Sarah Emlen Cresson, the daughter of a wealthy Quaker family. The marriage was frowned upon by the Quakers because Dickey was a Presbyterian, a religion that the Quakers thought did not hold the same beliefs as they did. For this marriage, Sarah was rejected from the Quaker meeting; nevertheless, the Quaker religion had helped her to develop and continue her support and concern for African Americans, which she took with her into her marriage to John Dickey.

Many circumstances led to the founding of Ashmun Institute. The past life of Dickey and his wife played an important role in the school's founding. John Miller, Dickey's grandfather, had given money for the education of African American youth in earlier years, and Miller's acquaintance, Benjamin Franklin, also saw the need for an African American school. Both Dickey and his wife had many relatives who were ardently opposed to slavery. Another reason for Dickey's interest, according to him, was the kidnapping of two young African American girls, Rachel and Elizabeth Parker. Although both girls were returned to their home, the incident helped Dickey to realize the inherent inequalities in the lives of the African American youth and the difficulties they experienced because they were not given the same opportunities that other young people enjoyed. The death of Dickey's own child was another factor in his decision to create the institute.

Sometime in 1853, Sarah picked the land on which they would establish an institute for the education of youth of African descent in science, art, and theology. In the same year, John Miller Dickey announced his plans for an African American university, which would be called Ashmun Institute. In order to bring the institute into being, a committee was set up to gather funds and secure the Ashmun Institute's charter through the legislature. By April 29, 1854, the Ashmun Institute Bill was signed by Governor Bigler, allowing for the construction of the new school. Because there were not enough funds to construct the buildings, Dickey used his own money (for which he would later be reimbursed) to finance construction of the president's house and a schoolroom with attached dormitories. By the fall of 1856, the school was nearly ready to open, and the Reverend John Pym Carter was selected as its first president.

Ashmun Institute was named after Jehudi Ashmun, who was born on April 21, 1794, in Champlain, New York. In 1820, four years after graduating from the University of Vermont, he took a job as the editor of *The African Intelligencer*, a magazine devoted to the movement for African emigration to Liberia promoted by the American Colonization Society, an African American organization. Through his involvement in the magazine, Ashmun learned that a conductor was needed for a trip to Liberia to help take slaves back to their homeland. After working for repatriation of African Americans, he died in 1828 after a long illness. In naming their school after him the Dickeys memorialized Ashmun for his outstanding work. The first building of Ashmun Institute was dedicated on December 31, 1856, the fifth anniversary of the kidnapping of Rachel Parker.

Classes at Ashmun Institute began January 1, 1857, with two students, James Ralston Amos and his brother Thomas. The first decades of the institution's operation were rather difficult—funding continued to be a challenge, and the outbreak of the Civil War emptied Ashmun Institute's classroom for a short time. There was concern that the institute would be raided as the war began, but no such instances were reported. After the war, there was a surge in enrollment, and the school began to expand.

Students at the four-year institute received instruction in geography, history, grammar, composition, elocution, and mathematics. They also received instruction in Greek, He-brew, and Latin. In addition, the students learned church theology and history, as well as taking courses in prayer and pulpit exercises. Although scholarship was important, each term the students were also evaluated on their other qualities, including piety, talents, diligence, eloquence, prudence, economy, zeal, health, and influence. The curriculum changed and became even more diversified as the school became more established.

On February 7, 1866, the board of the institute began the process to change the name of the institute to Lincoln University in honor of Abraham Lincoln, who had fought so vehemently for the rights of African Americans and who had helped to free them from slavery throughout the United States. The Pennsylvania legislature approved the change of name, and after April 4, 1866, Ashmun Institute was known as Lincoln University.

There were many notable presidents of the university as it continued to grow and become a respected institution. Isaac Norton Rendall, who was among the great contributors, was president from 1865 until 1905. In 1945, Horace Mann Bond became the first alumnus of Lincoln University to become its president, as well as the first African American to hold the position. He served in the position until 1957.

Lincoln University has remained a predominantly African American school and is proudly recognized as the oldest school with the purpose of educating African American youth. Among the list of graduates are several famous persons, including Langston Hughes, the famous poet and author, in 1929, and Thurgood Marshall, the first African American Supreme Court justice, in 1930.   *—Jeri Kurtzleben*

ADDITIONAL READING:

Blassingame, John W., and John R. McKivigan, eds. *The Frederick Douglass Papers*. Series One. *Speeches, Debates, and Interviews*. Vol. 4, *1864-1880*. New Haven, Conn.: Yale University Press, 1991. Includes a speech in which Douglass discusses Lincoln University as an example; notes for the speech compares Lincoln University to other African American institutions.

Bond, Horace Mann. *Education for Freedom: A History of Lincoln University*. Princeton, N.J.: Princeton University Press, 1976. A major primary source that gives details of the university's beginning and growth. Written by a former president of Lincoln University.

Hill, Leven, ed. *Black American Colleges and Universities*. Detroit, Mich.: Gale Research, 1994. Includes a brief university history, current statistics, and enrollment information.

Hornsby, Alton, Jr. *Chronology of African-American History*. Detroit, Mich.: Gale Research, 1991. Includes a short but descriptive history of Ashmun Institute at its beginning and as it changed to Lincoln University.

Ploski, Harry A., and James Williams, eds. *The African American Almanac: A Reference Work on the African American*. Detroit, Mich.: Gale Research, 1989. Places the founding of the institute among other the African American advances.

SEE ALSO: 1853, National Council of Colored People Is Founded.

1857 ■ DRED SCOTT V. SANDFORD: *the U.S. Supreme Court rules that Congress cannot limit slavery in the territories, nullifying the Missouri Compromise*

DATE: March 6, 1857
LOCALE: Washington, D.C.
CATEGORIES: African American history; Court cases
KEY FIGURES:
Montgomery Blair (1813-1883), Scott's counsel
John Catron (1786-1865),
Benjamin Robbins Curtis (1809-1874), and
John McLean (1785-1861), associate justices
John F. A. Sanford, Scott's owner and the defendant in the case
Dred Scott (c. 1795-1858), African American slave who was the plaintiff in the case
Roger Brooke Taney (1777-1864), chief justice of the United States

SUMMARY OF EVENT. Few decisions of the United States Supreme Court have had the political repercussions of *Dred Scott v. Sandford* (documents of the time misspelled the defendant's name). The decision supplied the infant Republican Party with new issues against the Democrats, already divided by the civil war in Kansas referred to by modern historians as Bleeding Kansas. The decision also was an embarrassment to the Republicans, for in denying the authority of Congress to legislate on slavery in the territories, the ruling destroyed the major platform of the Republican Party. The Court's opinion also damaged, if not destroyed, the practicability of Stephen A. Douglas' doctrine of popular sovereignty; if Congress had no authority to regulate slavery in the territories, neither could territorial legislatures do so, because they were inferior bodies created by Congress. The Court had entered completely into the political issues tearing at the Union, and the reputation of Chief Justice Roger B. Taney was shattered in the North.

Two pertinent questions were raised by the *Dred Scott* case. First, could an African American, whose ancestors were imported into the United States and sold as slaves, become a member of the political community created by the U.S. Constitution and thereby be guaranteed the rights and privileges of a U.S. citizen? Second, does the Constitution consider African Americans as a separate class of persons distinct from the class known as citizens?

Dred Scott was a slave of African descent. In 1834, he was taken by his owner, John Emerson, an army surgeon, to the free state of Illinois and then to Wisconsin Territory, which was free by the provisions of the Missouri Compromise of 1820. Dr. Emerson returned to Missouri with Scott in 1838. After Emerson's death in 1846, Scott sued Mrs. Emerson in the Missouri courts for his freedom, on the grounds of his residence in a free state and later in a free territory. Although he won in the lower court, the state supreme court reversed the

decision in 1852 and declared that Scott was still a slave because of his voluntary return to Missouri. During this litigation, Mrs. Emerson remarried and, under Missouri law, the administration of her first husband's estate passed to her brother, John F. A. Sanford. Because Sanford was a citizen of New York, Scott's lawyer, acting on the grounds that the litigants were residents of different states, sued for Scott's freedom in the United States circuit court in Missouri. The verdict there also went against Scott.

As expected, the case was appealed to the United States Supreme Court, where it was argued in February, 1856, and reargued in January, 1857. At first, the Supreme Court agreed to decide against Scott on the grounds that, under Missouri law as interpreted by its supreme court, he was a slave, despite his residence on free soil. For a variety of reasons, the judges changed their minds and determined to deal with the controversial questions of African American citizenship and congressional power over slavery in the territories. One of the justices confidentially informed President-elect James Buchanan of the Court's intention. Buchanan supported the Court's plan and even persuaded one justice to concur in the majority opinion. The Supreme Court announced its decision two days after Buchanan's inauguration as president.

Although each of the nine justices issued a separate opinion, a majority of the Supreme Court held that African Americans who were descendants of slaves could not belong to the political community created by the Constitution and enjoy the right of federal citizenship; and that the Missouri Compromise of 1820, forbidding slavery in the part of the Louisiana Purchase territory north of 36°30′ north latitude, was unconstitutional. According to the opinion of Chief Justice Taney, African Americans were "beings of an inferior order" who "had no rights which the white man was bound to respect." The significance of Taney's comments is that they established a perception of African Americans that transcended their status as slaves. In considering the issue of equality, Justice Taney did not limit his assessment of African Americans to those who were slaves, but also included African Americans who were free. Taney's opinion raises questions about the extent to which this precept of the inferiority of African Americans helped to establish conditions for the future of race relations in the United States.

Although individual states might grant citizenship to African Americans, state action did not give blacks citizenship under the federal Constitution. Therefore, concluded Taney, "Dred Scott was not a citizen of Missouri within the meaning of the Constitution of the United States, and not entitled as such to sue in its courts." There is considerable evidence that African Americans were not considered citizens and guaranteed rights and privileges by the United States Constitution. One of these rights, the ability to sue, was critical to the opinion of the Court. First, the Constitution granted each of the thirteen states the authority to continue the importation of slaves until 1808. In so doing, the Constitution supported an enterprise that relegated African Americans to the status of

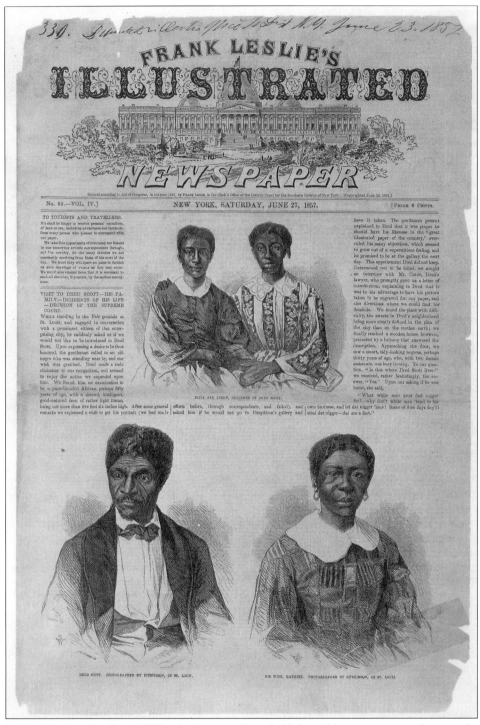

In Dred Scott v. Sandford *(1857), the Supreme Court held that African Americans who were descendants of slaves could not belong to the political community created by the Constitution and enjoy the right of federal citizenship, and that the Missouri Compromise of 1820, forbidding slavery in the part of the Louisiana Purchase territory north of 36°30′ north latitude, was unconstitutional. The case aroused national interest in the sectional debate between North and South, and Scott and his family became objects of celebrity.* (Library of Congress)

chattel. In effect, extending the trading of slaves by the states for more than thirty years after the signing of the Constitution shows that African Americans were not included as a class granted citizenship. The Constitution also indicated that states were to make a commitment to each other to assist slave owners in retaining their property. Because slaves were defined as chattel, this applied directly to them as a class. Finally, the intent of the Constitution to exclude African Americans as citizens was revealed in the congruence between the stated ideas and the conduct that was prescribed. That is, the authors of the Constitution expected the language and the actual practices and conventions during that time period to be consistent.

On the second point, Taney declared that, since slaves were property, under the Fifth Amendment to the Constitution—which prohibited Congress from taking property without due process of law—Congress had only the power and duty to protect the slaveholders' rights. Therefore, the Missouri Compromise law was unconstitutional. This part of Taney's opinion was unnecessary, an *obiter dictum*, for, having decided that no African American could become a citizen within the meaning of the Constitution, there was no need for the Supreme Court to consider the question of whether Congress could exclude slavery from the territories of the United States. The Supreme Court's decision was consistent with earlier decisions regarding slavery. Historically, the Court's opinions had protected slave owners' rights to their property, even when the chattel was slaves.

The two antislavery justices in the Court, John McLean and Benjamin Curtis, wrote dissenting opinions. They stated that before the adoption of the Constitution, free African Americans were citizens of several states and were, therefore, also citizens of the United States. Consequently, the United States circuit court had jurisdiction in the *Dred Scott* case. Because the Constitution gave Congress full power to legislate for the federal territories, it could act as it pleased regarding slavery, as on all other subjects.

The nation reacted strongly to the Supreme Court's decision. The South was delighted, for a majority of the justices had supported the extreme Southern position. All federal territories were now legally opened to slavery, and Congress was obliged to protect the slaveholders' possession of their chattel. The free-soil platform of the Republicans was unconstitutional. The Republicans denounced the decision in the most violent terms, as the product of an incompetent and partisan body. They declared that when they obtained control of the national government, they would change the membership of the Supreme Court and secure reversal of the decision. Northern Democrats, while not attacking the Supreme Court, were discouraged by the decision, for if Congress could not prohibit slavery in any territory, neither could a territorial legislature, a mere creation of Congress. Therefore, popular sovereignty also would cease to be a valid way of deciding whether a federal territory should be slave or free.

The Supreme Court's decision in this case and many subsequent opinions of the Court would have an adverse impact upon African Americans seeking legal rights as citizens of the United States. Moreover, as the first decision since *Marbury v. Madison* (1803) to reverse an act of Congress as unconstitutional, it generated lower esteem for the Court among Northerners, widening the growing rift between North and South.

—*John G. Clark, updated by K. Sue Jewell*

ADDITIONAL READING:

Abraham, Henry J. *Freedom and the Court: Civil Rights and Liberties in the United States.* New York: Oxford University Press, 1967. Focuses on civil rights and liberties for African Americans in the United States.

Bell, Derrick. *Faces at the Bottom of the Well: The Permanence of Racism.* New York: Basic Books, 1992. Employs literary models in addressing the issue of how African Americans experience racial injustice in the judicial system in the United States.

_____. *Race, Racism and American Law.* 2d ed. Boston: Little, Brown, 1980. Presents a comprehensive analysis of U.S. law that asserts that racial inequality is integrated into the legislative and judicial system in the United States.

Jewell, K. Sue. *From Mammy to Miss America and Beyond: Cultural Images and the Shaping of U.S. Social Policy.* New York: Routledge, 1993. Discusses how institutional policies and practices in the United States contribute to social inequality for African Americans in general, and African American women in particular.

Paul, Arnold, ed. *Black Americans and the Supreme Court Since Emancipation: Betrayal or Protection?* New York: Holt, Rinehart and Winston, 1972. Explores various precedent-setting Supreme Court cases that reveal the Court's failure to ensure equal rights for African Americans.

SEE ALSO: 1820, Missouri Compromise; 1830, Proslavery Argument; 1835, Texas Revolution; 1850, Compromise of 1850; 1850, Second Fugitive Slave Law; 1854, Kansas-Nebraska Act; 1854, Birth of the Republican Party; 1856, Bleeding Kansas; 1858, Lincoln-Douglas Debates; 1859, John Brown's Raid on Harpers Ferry; 1860, Lincoln Is Elected President.

1857 ■ NEW YORK INFIRMARY FOR INDIGENT WOMEN AND CHILDREN OPENS: *founded to address the needs of women and children, the infirmary gives birth to the first U.S. nursing school*

DATE: May 12, 1857
LOCALE: New York City
CATEGORIES: Health and medicine; Organizations and institutions; Social reform; Women's issues
KEY FIGURES:
Katharine "Kitty" Barry (1847-1910?), Elizabeth Blackwell's adopted daughter and lifelong companion
Elizabeth Blackwell (1821-1910), first woman of modern times to graduate from an accredited medical school

Emily Blackwell (1826-1910), Elizabeth's sister and partner in efforts to establish services and medical training for women

Marie E. Zakrzewska (1829-1902), one of the infirmary's three founding doctors

Summary of event. In the early 1800's, six children were born to the extraordinary Samuel Blackwell family, in which both sexes were given equal, rigorous educations and male family members were astonished by the treatment of women outside their home. Two of the four Blackwell sisters, Elizabeth and Emily, paved the way for women in medicine in the United States and Europe: Elizabeth became the first woman in the United States to earn a diploma from a medical college, and Emily followed her example five years later.

At a time when women generally were confined by society to the home, the Blackwell girls quietly demanded the same rights to which they had always been entitled in their family. Their father, a minister of the Dissenters congregation, was well known for his stand on issues of basic human rights, including slavery and women's rights. He brought the family from England to the United States in 1832 after his sugar refinery business was lost in a fire. His sons, Henry and Samuel, both married famous suffragists: Henry wed Lucy Stone and signed an agreement allowing her to retain her maiden name; Samuel married Antoinette Brown, an ordained minister. Both brothers were instrumental in helping their sisters financially with their educations and in obtaining support from public figures for their sisters' infirmary and other social and educational projects serving women and children.

After graduating in January, 1849, from Geneva College Medical School in New York (now Hobart and William Smith Colleges), Elizabeth was unable to gain a graduate position in any teaching hospital in the United States. Conditioned to the hardships of fighting for her cause by having had to apply to twenty-nine colleges before Geneva admitted her, she began a fierce campaign to receive the further medical training she needed. Although Elizabeth had excellent references from professors and personal friends who were physicians, the public was extremely reluctant to accept a woman in what was traditionally a male role. She traveled to England and then to France, but in both countries was not accepted as a physician. Unwilling to accept defeat, she entered the famous Paris women's hospital, La Maternité, as a nurse in training. Her experiences there, coupled with her college summer intern experience at the Blockley Almshouse in Philadelphia, made her keenly aware of the lack of attention to proper hygiene. Preventive health measures and the importance of good physical hygiene and sanitation practices became a permanent part of the focus of her medical practice. She also believed that a new dimension would be added to medical practice if women had access to treatment by qualified and caring women physicians.

In 1851, Elizabeth returned to New York eager to begin her medical career. She could not find a landlord who would allow her to hang her professional sign on his building, and she had difficulty persuading patients that she was as capable as any male doctor. Although her finances hardly allowed it, in order to have professional offices, she bought a house at 79 East 15th Street on Tompkins Square in New York City. From home, she began offering part-time free services to women and children of the tenement slums of the lower East Side. Financial hardship and lack of recognition became a way of life as Dr. Blackwell constantly faced the gender prejudices of the public. In 1854, her loneliness led her to adopt a seven-year-old orphan, Katharine Barry, who remained her companion for life and provided an important source of personal and professional support.

Depleting her own funds and those offered by her loyal family, Elizabeth refused to relinquish her goals. Once trust was established, word spread that the sympathetic and determined young woman was an excellent physician, and in her first year, she treated more than two hundred patients. During this time, she also prepared and gave a series of lectures on the principles of good hygiene, and in doing so, attracted the support of a group of Quakers in the city, who sponsored bazaars and gift fairs to raise money for her work.

The desperate need for medical care for the poor prompted her to begin plans for a larger dispensary. She solicited the help of her sister Emily, who had graduated from Western Reserve Medical School in Cleveland. Dr. Marie Zakrzewska, another young woman Elizabeth had encouraged during her training, now also a graduate of Western Reserve, agreed to come and help as well. On May 12, 1857, the three women opened the New York Infirmary for Indigent Women and Children, a hospital where women were cared for completely by women, at 64 Bleeker Street. The three doctors were assisted by the group of Quaker supporters and other women working to raise funds, important New Yorkers such as Horace Greeley of the *New York Tribune*, and reputable doctors who lent their names. The opening address was given by Dr. Henry Ward Beecher, a noted preacher and the brother of Harriet Beecher Stowe. Emily, a skilled surgeon and administrator, was an important force in the daily running of the hospital and was able to carry on whenever necessary in Elizabeth's absence. The next year, the New York legislature granted the infirmary official recognition as well as financial support of one thousand dollars per year.

Elizabeth's plans for the infirmary did not end with treating patients. She had wanted for years to improve and intensify medical training for women, both as nurses and as doctors. Although supporters thought her overly ambitious, in 1858 she opened a nursing school in conjunction with the infirmary, and on April 13, 1864, the New York legislature passed an enabling act for a woman's medical school. In 1866, she realized her dream of a full medical college as she opened the doors to fifteen students.

The only facility of its kind where the needs of women were met by women, the infirmary's success mounted. Growing pains were constant, and by 1860 a new building had been obtained on Second Avenue and 8th Street. The hospital then had an infirmary and a dispensary, where clinical cases were treated on an outpatient basis. A visiting health nurse went to homes to teach rules of sanitation and hygiene in order to advance preventive medicine, an innovation in medical practice of the nineteenth century. The medical college flourished, and in 1874 a mansion at 5 Livingston Place was converted into a hospital in which 7,549 patients were treated during the next year. In 1889, a site nearby was purchased for a six-story building for the college.

In 1898, the Cornell University Medical College agreed to accept women on equal terms with men. Elizabeth concluded that the need for her separate school was diminished and arranged to transfer her students to Cornell, but the New York Infirmary for Indigent Women and Children continued. The infirmary has remained an important institution in New York, not only for its service to its patients but also for what it represents in the pioneering of new territory for women in medical careers and the advancement of the field of public health and preventive medicine in general.

—*Sandra C. McClain*

ADDITIONAL READING:

Baker, Rachel. *The First Woman Doctor: The Story of Elizabeth Blackwell, M.D.* New York: Julian Messner, 1944. A good general biography for young readers. Includes a detailed account of the infirmary's history in chapters eight and nine.

Blackwell, Elizabeth. *Pioneer Work in Opening the Medical Profession to Women.* 1895. Reprint. New York: Schocken Books, 1977. Blackwell's autobiography and her own account of the infirmary history. Includes a bibliography of her other writings.

Flexnor, Eleanor. "The Intellectual Progress of Women, 1860-1875." In *Century of Struggle: The Women's Rights Movement in the United States.* Rev. ed. Cambridge, Mass.: The Belknap Press of Harvard University Press, 1975. Discusses the Blackwells' founding of the infirmary and its history in the context of the women's movement of the nineteenth century.

Lerner, Gerda, ed. *The Female Experience: An American Documentary.* Indianapolis: Bobbs-Merrill, 1977. Contains two excerpts from Elizabeth Blackwell's autobiography and *The First Annual Report of the New York Dispensary for Poor Women and Children*, the forerunner of the infirmary.

Wilson, Dorothy Clarke. *Lone Woman: The Story of Elizabeth Blackwell, the First Woman Doctor.* Boston: Little, Brown, 1970. A good source of information about the infirmary and details of the personalities involved. Excellent bibliography.

SEE ALSO: 1820's, Free Public School Movement; 1820's, Social Reform Movement; 1823, Hartford Female Seminary Is Founded; 1833, Oberlin College Is Established; 1837, Mt. Holyoke Seminary Is Founded; 1848, Seneca Falls Convention; 1851, Akron Woman's Rights Convention; 1865, Vassar College Is Founded.

1857 ■ CART WAR: *a series of armed raids against Tejano cartmen ends a profitable business enterprise and secures Anglo economic ascendancy in Texas*

DATE: August-December, 1857
LOCALE: San Antonio, Texas, and the Texas Gulf coast
CATEGORIES: Latino American history; Wars, uprisings, and civil unrest
KEY FIGURES:
Lewis M. Cass (1782-1866), U.S. secretary of state
Elisha M. Pease, governor of Texas
Manuel Robles y Pezuela, Mexican minister to the United States

SUMMARY OF EVENT. The 1857 Cart War, in which Mexican American cart teamsters in Texas were attacked by masked raiders seeking to destroy their trade, is rooted in the historic tensions between peoples of different ethnicities who resided in Texas. Soon after Euro-Americans began arriving in Spanish (later Mexican) Texas at the beginning of the nineteenth century, racial conflicts intermittently flared into violent encounters. Many whites had inherited negative images of Hispanic peoples from their Western European ancestors' creation of the *Leyendas Negras*, or Black Legend. The Black Legend portrayed the inhabitants of the Iberian peninsula and their descendants as cruel, lazy, vicious, arrogant, and dissolute. Many Europeans believed that intermarriage between Europeans and native peoples produced a "mongrelization" of races. Euro-American migrants into Texas generally regarded people whose backgrounds were Spanish, Mexican, or Native American as inferior.

This attitude of superiority accounts in part for the Texans' war for independence against the Republic of Mexico from 1835 to 1836. Tejanos (Texas residents of Mexican descent, whether born in Mexico, the United States, or the Republic of Texas) became increasingly suspect in the eyes of Anglos (white, English-speaking, non-Mexican Americans), although many Tejanos had fought alongside the Anglo Texans during the war. Following independence, the Republic of Texas systematically began dispossessing Tejanos of their lands, economic livelihoods, and legal rights. East Texas was virtually depopulated of its substantial Tejano presence. One of the few places where Tejanos held any numerical, economic, and political power by the time of statehood in 1845 was the most important settlement in Texas in the nineteenth century, San Antonio.

By 1857, Tejanos monopolized the commercial transportation of food and merchandise between the coast of Texas and the trading center of San Antonio. These *arrieros* (mule and ox drivers) worked with teams of oxen or mules and large carts comprising single pairs of five- to seven-foot wheels of cottonwood puncheons fastened with wooden pins and rawhide straps. The axles were made of a strong wood such as pecan or live oak. Thus, emergency repairs could be made using natural materials that were readily available. The Tejano teamsters' engineering ingenuity, combined with superior teamster skills and low rates, enabled them to operate very profitably. It is estimated that *arrieros* made up almost 60 percent of the Tejano workforce in Texas. A Northern traveler through Texas in 1855-1856, Frederick Law Olmsted, observed, "The Mexican [Tejano] appears to have almost no other business than that of carting goods. Almost the entire transportation of the country is carried on by them with oxen and two-wheeled carts."

In the late summer of 1857, reports began to appear in local newspapers of attacks on Tejano freighting by masked bands of armed men. Ambitious Anglo teamsters had been trying for some time to appropriate the freight business away from the *arrieros*. They were unable to compete with the low rates charged by the already established Tejano commercial ventures, however. Frustrated, they retaliated by first harassing and then assassinating Tejano freighters and by looting and stealing their cargoes. As word spread of the depredations, Anglo communities worried about a race war, and the Tejanos feared an increase in the carnage directed at them. Anglo citizens in Goliad County warned that retaliation by armed Tejanos would provide an excuse for extermination.

Because the killings and thefts were vengeful acts by a particular group against innocent victims, a segment of the Anglo population protested the assaults, although it is unclear whether the Anglos were motivated by humanitarian or economic considerations. Some griped that rates rose when the *arrieros* refused to haul merchandise along dangerous routes. Others feared dire economic consequences for the entire region. Prices had increased 30 percent since the attacks. Alarmed Tejanos left San Antonio in unprecedented numbers. Despite a reported seventy-five murders, government and law authorities were slow to intervene.

Eventually, a committee of citizens from San Antonio was charged with investigating the matter. Some area newspapers called for inquiries also, although they often invoked racist rhetoric in doing so, referring to the Tejanos as a "weak race," "greaser population," and "low in the scale of intelligence."

A combination of factors led to a conclusion of the bloodshed. Military escorts accompanied the Tejano cartmen at the insistence of San Antonio merchants who were losing profits. Communities organized volunteer companies, which operated under lynch-law traditions, to bring about order. International diplomacy even played a role. The Mexican minister to Washington, Manuel Robles y Pezuela, notified U.S. secretary of state Lewis M. Cass on October 14, 1857, that Robles y Pezuela's sources reported that armed bands in Texas were hunting down and murdering Mexicans on the public roads. The entreaty of Robles y Pezuela (and the possible international diplomatic consequences) compelled Secretary Cass to pressure the governor of Texas, Elisha M. Pease, to settle the troubles.

Although the raids ended, no one was ever arrested for participation in the crimes. Many even refused to acknowl-edge the wrongs perpetrated against the Tejano entrepreneurs. In December, 1857, Karnes County citizens condemned the use of military escorts and the actions of the governor. They called the "peon Mexican teamsters . . . intolerable nuisance[s]" who destroyed property. Goliad County citizens expressed similar sentiments.

Ultimately, the perpetrators of the Cart War accomplished their objective. Never again would Tejano freighters dominate commercial shipping in Texas. The *arrieros*, however, had already demonstrated that, in spite of the stifling prejudice directed against them, skill and business acumen could bring them economic success as long as they were allowed to engage in commerce without violent interference by others envious of their success. The economic ascendancy of Anglo Texans would not be challenged by Tejanos until the twentieth century. Standard histories of Texas ignored the Cart War until the 1980's, when prominent Tejano historians such as Arnoldo De León focused attention upon it.   —*Jodella K. Dyreson*

ADDITIONAL READING:

De León, Arnoldo. *The Tejano Community, 1836-1900*. Albuquerque: University of New Mexico Press, 1982. A survey of the inner workings of an ethnic community in nineteenth century Texas, by a leading Chicano historian. Describes the cart trade and its importance to the economies of both San Antonio and the Tejano people.

_____. *They Called Them Greasers: Anglo Attitudes Toward Mexicans in Texas, 1821-1900*. Austin: University of Texas Press, 1983. Thorough account of the incidents based upon primary sources, in particular contemporaneous newspapers. Portrays the Cart War as an example of the pervasive racism practiced and tolerated by Anglos against Tejanos in the nineteenth century.

Matovina, Timothy M. *Tejano Religion and Ethnicity: San Antonio, 1821-1860*. Austin: University of Texas Press, 1995. Examines the interrelationship of religion and ethnicity in one of the major urban areas of the Southwestern borderlands during the transition period prior to the American Civil War, when Anglos wrested political and economic power away from the Tejano community.

Meier, Matt S., and Feliciano Ribera. *Mexican Americans/ American Mexicans: From Conquistadors to Chicanos*. Rev. ed. New York: Hill & Wang, 1993. Standard history survey of people of Mexican descent in the United States. Useful introduction tackles nomenclature considerations; glossary of potentially unfamiliar terms. Places the Cart War in the larger context of patterns of economic intimidation practiced against Mexican Americans in the Southwestern borderlands.

Montejano, David. *Anglos and Mexicans in the Making of Texas, 1836-1986*. Austin: University of Texas Press, 1987. Award-winning history of relations between Anglos and those of Mexican descent in Texas since the winning of Texas independence. Employs sociological models and traditional historical sources to connect early historical experience in the post-Mexican period to twentieth century attitudes. Includes a brief account of the Cart War.

Rocha, Rodolfo. "The Tejanos of Texas." In *Texas: A Ses-quicentennial Celebration*, edited by Donald W. Whisenhunt. Austin, Tex.: Eakin Press, 1984. Brief, blunt overview of the Tejano experience, based on more extensive works.

SEE ALSO: 1835, Texas Revolution; 1846, Mexican War; 1846, Occupation of California and the Southwest; 1847, Taos Rebellion; 1848, Treaty of Guadalupe Hidalgo; 1853, Gadsden Purchase; 1877, Salt Wars.

1858 ■ FRASER RIVER GOLD RUSH: *an influx of prospectors and settlers into western Canada stimulates subsequent development of the interior of British Columbia*

DATE: Spring, 1858
LOCALE: Fraser River Canyon
CATEGORIES: Canadian history; Expansion and land acquisition; Settlements
KEY FIGURES:
James Douglas (1816-1877), governor of British Columbia during the Fraser River gold rush
Frank Laumeister, entrepreneur who brought camels to the Fraser River canyon for purposes of using them as pack animals

SUMMARY OF EVENT. In 1857 much of the Western Hemisphere was in the throes of a great depression known as the Panic of 1857. A significant number of banks, the railroads, and a wide array of businesses had gone bankrupt. As a result of the economic uncertainties created by the depression, coupled with the depletion of gold in California, many Westerners turned to Canada to seek their fortunes. Earlier reports of gold being found in the Thompson River—a tributary of the Fraser River to the north—prompted interest in the Fraser River canyon. On March 23, 1858, at Hill's Bar on the Fraser River ten miles north of Fort Hope, British Columbia, a small group of prospectors from California discovered gold. Their discovery produced a gold rush that rivaled that of the California rush in 1849.

By July of 1858, largely as a result of the discovery of gold at Hill's Bar, several thousand miners had moved into the Fraser River area. By the end of the 1858 season, nearly $2 million had been taken from Hill's Bar. Subsequent discoveries of gold farther north on the Fraser River at Boston's Bar and China Bar caused much excitement among local prospectors, but news of these discoveries beyond the interior of British Columbia and Victoria did not become widespread until February of the following year.

During the summer of 1858, fortune seekers from Vancouver and Victoria began sailing up the Fraser River to Fort Hope and farther upstream to Yale. In July of 1858 a sternwheeler called the *Umatilla* arrived in Yale carrying several thousand miners; the majority of these minors had for some time been working their way north from California. Yale eventually became the major distribution center for prospectors and entrepreneurs who were moving goods in and out of the canyon. Toward the end of 1858 many of the miners who had obtained significant amounts of gold in the initial stages of the Fraser gold rush traveled downstream to Yale to send their earnings to Victoria for safekeeping. In Victoria, the governor of British Columbia, James Douglas, sent a sample of the gold (approximately eight hundred ounces) to San Francisco for minting. Some historians have suggested that in February of 1859 a local San Franciscan merchant, aware of the existence of the Canadian gold at the local mint, leaked information of the source of the gold to the public at a meeting of the San Francisco Volunteer Firemen's Association. Although solid documentation for this particular story has not surfaced, it is certain that by the spring of 1859 the rush was on.

Throughout the early part of 1859 prospectors from California, Oregon, and Washington began to make their way to British Columbia. Many of these fortune seekers traveled by ship, while others made their way overland using existing trails and, in some cases, carving out new ones. By July of 1859 it has been estimated that Yale's population had skyrocketed to more than thirty thousand. Victoria, British Columbia's capital, had already been supporting a growing population of adventurers, but with news of gold having been found farther inland, Victoria's mostly transient population exploded.

By 1866, however, most of the surface gold-bearing deposits had become depleted. As had been the case in California, only those operators who had the capital to organized large-scale operations remained in the gold-mining business. Many of the prospectors remained in Canada and explored tributaries of the northern reaches of the Fraser River system. Although some discoveries of small deposits of gold were recorded, none matched the volume of the initial Fraser River strike.

With the Fraser River gold rush came numerous economic, social, and political changes. For example, at the height of the gold rush Frank Laumeister, an entrepreneur who had not done well at prospecting, brought twenty-one camels from Arizona to the Fraser River country with the goal of charging miners excessive packing fees. One camel, Laumeister often boasted, could pack more than a thousand pounds of goods, nearly three times as much as a mule. This venture came to be known by the miners as the Dromedary Express, despite the fact that Bactrian camels were used.

Perhaps the most significant by-product of the gold rush was the development of British Columbia's infrastructure. Starting in 1861, a small crew of Royal Engineers from England surveyed the Fraser River canyon to lay the foundations for building a road that eventually ran from Yale to Lytton. This road came to be known as the Caribou Wagon Road and to this day is considered a major feat of engineering: In order to carry out the construction, the engineers had to navigate the steep slopes of the Fraser River canyon, building tunnels at several places where the canyon is particularly steep, including a two-thousand-foot tunnel cut out of solid stone near

China Bar. By 1863, most of the eighteen-foot-wide road had been completed in the general vicinity of the southern portion of the Fraser canyon drainage. By 1865 the road was complete, extending more than four hundred miles north, where it linked the Fraser River country with other parts of British Columbia.

Although the gold rush opened the interior of British Columbia for economic growth and prosperity, the entire process did not unfold without problems. From 1858 through to the early 1860's the Fraser Canyon region was largely unregulated by a stable system of law enforcement. Governor Douglas in Victoria had foreseen problems but had not predicted the sheer numbers of people who would settle in British Columbia as a result of the gold rush. Douglas therefore was not adequately prepared to manage such a large influx of people. Conflicts among the miners often broke out, creating a general environment of chaos. When these conflicts occurred it was usually up to local informal leaders to settle these disputes. Often these "foreign judges" had criminal pasts of their own that could, in many cases, be traced to the gold fields of California. Thus, many of their judicial decisions, often sanctioned by showing off their guns, were self-serving and seldom consistent with British/Canadian law. In fact, Governor Douglas referred to the California miners in general as "a specimen of the worst of the population of San Francisco: the very dregs, in fact, of society."

On several occasions Fraser River miners came into direct conflict with local Native Americans over land rights. Some of these conflicts escalated into armed altercations. During the summer of 1858, for example, several miners began cutting into an embankment at a place called Spuzzum (several miles north of Yale). The miners inadvertently uncovered a native burial ground. More interested in gold than in sacred artifacts and with a callous degree of indifference, they tossed aside the burial goods. Several days after the incident, infuriated local natives began taking sniper shots at the miners. The miners quickly formed a vigilante committee of approximately forty men and set out to settle the problem according to their own system of law. Upon hearing that two miners had been killed by Indians near the small community of Lytton, the vigilante committee marched upstream until they encountered a small group of natives at a village site near Spuzzum. A skirmish ensued in which seven natives were killed and the village burned to the ground. Conflicts between the natives and the miners escalated until in the fall of 1858, when the local natives surrendered.

News of these conflicts finally reached Governor Douglas in Victoria. Fearing that the reported outbreaks of hostility might develop into an attempt to annex British Columbia for the United States, Douglas organized several British warships, complete with ready to fight "Blue Coats," and sent this force to Fort Hope. The governor's suspicions were not entirely unwarranted. Reports had reached Victoria concerning the activities of a former California judge named Ned McGowan. McGowan, who also had a criminal record, had been openly encouraging an insurrection against the British crown. Upon the arrival of the warships most of the fighting subsided. McGowan, along with his followers, curtailed their activities. The presence of the British military, coupled with a growing influx of people not directly interested in mining, produced a long period of stability for the Fraser River region.

—*Michael Shaw Findlay*

ADDITIONAL READING:

Elliot, Gordon R. *Barker Quesnel and the Cariboo Gold Rush*. Vancouver: Douglas & McIntyre, 1978. A general history of the Fraser River gold rush including its historical impact on British Columbia.

Gough, Barry M. *Gunboat Frontier: British Maritime Authority and Northwest Coast Indians, 1846-1890*. Vancouver: University of British Columbia Press, 1984. Briefly discusses the initial discovery of gold at Hill's Bar, as well as conflicts between miners and native peoples.

Leduc, Joanne, ed. *Overland from Canada to British Columbia: By Mr. Thomas McMicking of Queenston, Canada West*. Vancouver: University of British Columbia Press, 1981. Anecdotal history that includes several brief accounts of personal experiences of various characters associated with the Fraser River gold rush.

Myers, Jay. *The Fitzhenry and Whiteside Book of Canadian Facts and Dates*. Markham, Ontario: Fitzhenry and Whiteside, 1986. A chronological listing of events and dates for the general history of Canada.

Waldman, Carl, ed. *Atlas of the North American Indian*. New York: Facts On File, 1985. Detailed reference source on Native American history and culture. Includes brief discussion of impact of gold rushes in western North America on indigenous populations.

Watkins, Mel, ed. *Handbook to the Modern World: Canada*. New York: Facts On File, 1993. Details Fraser River gold rush and the eventual economic impact of gold mining on the development of British Columbia.

SEE ALSO: 1793, Mackenzie Reaches the Arctic Ocean; 1846, Oregon Settlement; 1848, California Gold Rush; 1900, Teletype Is Developed.

1858 ■ LINCOLN-DOUGLAS DEBATES: *in a contest for a U.S. Senate seat, two politicians articulate a nation's division over the issue of slavery*

DATE: June 16-October, 1858
LOCALE: Illinois
CATEGORIES: African American history; Government and politics
KEY FIGURES:
James Buchanan (1791-1868), fifteenth president of the United States, 1857-1861, a Democrat who opposed Douglas

Stephen Arnold Douglas (1813-1861), senator from Illinois, a Democrat seeking reelection

William Henry Herndon (1818-1891), personal friend, law partner, and biographer of Lincoln

Abraham Lincoln (1809-1865), Republican candidate for the Senate from Illinois

Lyman Trumbull (1813-1896), Republican senator from Illinois

John Wentworth (1815-1888), Republican editor and owner of the *Chicago Democrat*

SUMMARY OF EVENT. The presidential campaign of 1856 and subsequent Republican successes attested to the strength of the newly formed Republican Party. In the congressional elections of 1858, the Republicans were prepared to capitalize on "Bleeding Kansas" and the *Dred Scott* decision of March, 1857, in order to solidify their position in Congress. Many Republicans were willing to cooperate with those who opposed the Buchanan Administration, including the anti-Nebraska Democrats, Know-Nothings, and former Whigs.

Events in Kansas upset the Democratic Party. Although many Democrats had opposed the Kansas-Nebraska Act from the beginning, others opposed it only after the situation in Kansas deteriorated and the administrations of Franklin Pierce and James Buchanan continued to demand the admission of Kansas as a slave state. It was the proslavery Lecompton Constitution and Buchanan's insistence that Congress admit Kansas under it that caused the party split. Stephen A. Douglas, the author of the Kansas-Nebraska Act, broke with Buchanan to lead the opposition to the admission of Kansas as a slave state, because a majority of the people there wanted it to be free. At the same time, Douglas faced the task of defending his Senate seat against the challenge of the well-organized Republican Party.

Before the adoption of the Seventeenth Amendment in 1913, United States senators were elected by their state's legislature, not by popular vote. A candidate normally did not conduct a statewide campaign for the office, nor did parties seeking to remove an incumbent normally designate an official candidate. The times were not normal, however, and the Republicans in Illinois nominated Abraham Lincoln as their candidate for Douglas' seat. Lincoln then challenged his opponent, Douglas, to a series of debates, and Douglas accepted. Douglas was well aware that his political future was at stake but hoped to turn to his advantage the anti-Lecompton stand that he had taken on the admission of Kansas to statehood. Lincoln, who had served only one term in Congress and who had failed in his bid for the Senate in 1856 to Lyman Trumbull, had nothing to lose by sharing the spotlight with Douglas.

Lincoln and Douglas made a thorough canvass of Illinois in 1858. Lincoln traveled more than forty-five hundred miles and Douglas more than five thousand. Each candidate made about sixty speeches and numerous impromptu appearances mostly from the rear platforms of railroad cars. The speeches and the seven joint debates attracted tens of thousands of listeners and received wide newspaper coverage. Lincoln was transformed into a person of national reputation.

Lincoln was nominated for the Senate seat at the Republican convention in Springfield in June, 1858. In his acceptance speech, delivered June 16, Lincoln included a phrase from the New Testament that was arguably the most radical of his career: "A house divided against itself cannot stand." While not part of the formal debates with Douglas, Lincoln's "House Divided" speech set the tone for the entire campaign. Avoiding any overt statements that he would formally work to end slavery, Lincoln continued to defend his prophecy throughout his campaign; Douglas argued equally vehemently that the nation had always existed "half slave and half free" and could continue to do so.

Douglas replied on July 9 in Chicago to Lincoln's statements; Lincoln again spoke on July 10. The formal debates began in Ottawa, Illinois, on August 21, 1858, before ten thousand people. Douglas spoke first, hammering Lincoln and accusing him and the Republican Party of being a party of abolition. Lincoln, caught unawares by Douglas' ferocity, stumbled through his speech. He would be better prepared at future debates.

The contestants journeyed to Freeport on August 27. This time, Lincoln took the offensive. He trapped Douglas into conceding that the people in a United States territory had the authority to "exclude slavery prior to the formation of a State Constitution," a reply known as the Freeport Doctrine. This placed Douglas at odds with much of the Democratic Party, which had believed the *Dred Scott* decision by the Supreme Court had eliminated such popular sovereignty. The debates moved on to Jonesboro on September 15, Charleston on September 18, Galesburg on October 7, Quincy on October 13, and Alton on October 15.

The strategy of both men was set before the first formal meeting. Lincoln concentrated on Douglas' authorship of the Kansas-Nebraska Act and its repeal of the Missouri Compromise. He charged that Douglas was merely a puppet of the slave-power conspiracy, that popular sovereignty had been buried by the *Dred Scott* decision, and that there was a national conspiracy to legitimize slavery in the free states. Douglas assailed Lincoln as an advocate of African American suffrage and charged him with attempted subversion of the Supreme Court. He accused Lincoln of opposing the *Dred Scott* decision on the grounds that it denied African American citizenship while masking an insidious intention to interfere with the domestic institutions of individual states.

Lincoln was embarrassed by Douglas' effort to associate him with abolitionism. While admitting his opposition to slavery, Lincoln acknowledged his inability to come up with a solution to the problem short of abolition. No less than Douglas, Lincoln believed that African Americans were basically inferior to Euro-Americans, but Lincoln, unlike Douglas, held that slavery was an immoral system inconsistent with the principles and practices of democratic government. Lincoln insisted that the contagion of slavery must be kept out of the new territories. Douglas countered by demanding that the settlers make this decision. Lincoln responded by pointing out that because the *Dred Scott* decision prohibited Congress from legislating about slavery in the territories, territorial legislatures were similarly prohibited, because they had been created by Congress. Douglas, seeking to salvage popular sovereignty, suggested at Freeport that, regardless of the *Dred Scott* decision, the people of a territory could exclude slavery lawfully prior to the formation of a state government, for slavery could not exist without the protection of a slave code enacted by the territorial legislature. At the conclusion of the joint canvass, Lincoln advocated that principles of equality as set forth in the Declaration of Independence be applied to the new territories. Douglas concluded with the statement that the nation could endure forever half slave and half free.

In the November elections, the Republicans swept the North. However, Douglas was reelected in Illinois, despite the Republican state ticket having drawn 125,000 votes to 121,000 for the Douglas Democrats and 5,000 for the Buchanan Democrats. Because United States senators were chosen by state legislatures in 1858, not by popular vote, in the contest for seats in the Illinois legislature, the Democrats bested the Republicans by forty-six seats to forty-one, and Douglas was elected to the Senate.

Despite his defeat, Lincoln had become a national figure, with a reputation for moderation that was attractive to former Whigs. The radical implications of his House Divided prediction had, by then, drifted into the background. Lincoln had more than held his own during the debates with Douglas, a well-known rival and formidable opponent. Lincoln's words, edited as they were in contemporaneous newspapers, grabbed the attention of all who read them. Lincoln was well aware of the importance of public sentiment and would put this knowledge to excellent use the next time he faced Douglas, in the presidential election of 1860.

—John G. Clark, updated by Richard Adler

ADDITIONAL READING:

Angle, Paul M., ed. *Created Equal? The Complete Lincoln-Douglas Debates of 1858*. Chicago: University of Chicago Press, 1958. Among the earlier collections of the debates. Although lacking more accurate transcripts discovered later, it is still an excellent source.

Baringer, William E. *Lincoln's Rise to Power*. Boston: Little, Brown, 1937. The story of Lincoln's rise from a local Illinois politician to national prominence.

Beveridge, Albert J. *Abraham Lincoln, 1809-1858*. 2 vols. Boston: Houghton Mifflin, 1928. Among the best works on Lincoln's career prior to the presidency.

Donald, David Herbert. *Lincoln*. New York: Simon & Schuster, 1995. A definitive study of Lincoln, which includes recently discovered manuscripts from his early years in politics.

Holzer, Harold, ed. *The Lincoln-Douglas Debates: The First Complete, Unexpurgated Text*. New York: Harper-Collins, 1993. A complete collection of the debates, including recently discovered transcripts that update much of the pre-

viously available material. With inclusion of speakers' asides and pauses, presents an excellent dramatization of the talks.

Johannsen, Robert W. *Stephen A. Douglas*. New York: Oxford University Press, 1973. A comprehensive biography and authoritative account of the career of Douglas.

Meyer, Daniel. *Stephen Douglas and the American Union*. Chicago: University of Chicago Press, 1994. A well-researched biography, with particular focus on the slavery issue.

SEE ALSO: 1820, Missouri Compromise; 1830, Proslavery Argument; 1835, Texas Revolution; 1850, Compromise of 1850; 1850, Second Fugitive Slave Law; 1854, Kansas-Nebraska Act; 1854, Birth of the Republican Party; 1856, Bleeding Kansas; 1857, *Dred Scott v. Sandford*; 1859, John Brown's Raid on Harpers Ferry; 1860, Lincoln Is Elected President.

1858 ■ First Transatlantic Cable: *a communications link between North America and Great Britain opens an era of political and economic cooperation*

DATE: August 4, 1858-July 27, 1866
LOCALE: Atlantic Ocean
CATEGORIES: Communications; Science and technology
KEY FIGURES:
Marc Isambard Brunel (1806-1859), industrial architect who designed and constructed the SS *Great Eastern*
Cyrus West Field (1819-1892), principal organizer of the venture to lay a cable across the Atlantic Ocean
Matthew D. Field, engineer who linked Newfoundland and Nova Scotia by telegraphic cable
Matthew Fontaine Maury (1806-1873), oceanographer who surveyed the Atlantic between Newfoundland and Ireland, and developed wind and tide tables
Samuel Finley Breese Morse (1791-1872), inventor of the telegraph

SUMMARY OF EVENT. Among the most important developments of the nineteenth century were the invention of the magnetic telegraph, a simple electrical device that revolutionized the field of communications, and the launching of the SS *Great Eastern*, which made possible the laying of the transatlantic cable. Samuel Morse invented the electric telegraph in 1837; by the mid-1840's, his telegraph had already made possible almost instantaneous communication over long distances. In 1845, Morse secured a congressional appropriation of thirty thousand dollars to set up, between Washington, D.C., and Baltimore, the nation's first telegraph line.

The first successful underwater cable of substantial length was completed in 1850, connecting Dover and Calais by way of the English Channel. That accomplishment inspired similar projects in Scandinavian waters and in the Mediterranean Sea. Frederick N. Gisborne, an English engineer, was the first to conceive the notion of a transatlantic communication cable. In 1854, he encouraged Sir Marc Isambard Brunel to visit New

York to persuade the young businessman Cyrus Field to form a cable company, after being assured by Morse that great distances would not hinder the telegraph's operation. Lieutenant Matthew F. Maury, known as the father of oceanography, had previously surveyed the Atlantic depths between Newfoundland and Ireland and was able to give precise information as to the best route.

The task of promoting capital and organizing a company to carry forward the venture was taken up primarily by Field, who had risen to a junior partnership in a New York wholesale paper business, and in 1841, after the firm declared bankruptcy, established his own company. Within ten years he had amassed a fortune of $250,000, enough to enable him to retire at age thirty-three. His interest in the possibility of a transatlantic cable was stimulated by his meeting, in 1854, with Frederick N. Gisborne, a Canadian promoter; after that meeting, Field organized a company to connect St. John's, Newfoundland, with New York and the Eastern seaboard. A successful telegraphic link would shorten by forty-eight hours the time required to bring European news to the United States. Field then pondered the next step: direct communication with Europe through a twenty-three-hundred-mile-long cable from Newfoundland to Ireland. This project received the support of a group of wealthy businessmen, and in May, 1854, the New York, Newfoundland, and London Electric Telegraph Company was organized and financed by $1.5 million in subscriptions. In the summer of 1856, the company established a telegraph link between Newfoundland and Nova Scotia, under the direction of engineer Matthew D. Field.

In 1856, Cyrus Field went to England to seek the assistance of the British government for his latest project. He was favorably received, and the British promised both ships and funds. Field then was able to obtain similar commitments from the United States government. He immediately set up a joint stock company in England, the Atlantic Telegraph Company, which took over the New York, Newfoundland, and London Telegraph Company's monopoly for the laying of cables. Possessing capital of more than £350,000, and the support of both governments, the Atlantic Cable Company was ready to begin its herculean task. Field commissioned three British companies to make three thousand miles of heavily insulated steel thread cable, which weighed 1,860 pounds per mile.

Field's first attempt at laying the cable began on August 5, 1857, when a flotilla of nine ships sailed from Valentia Bay on the west coast of Ireland. One U.S. ship, the *Niagara*, and one British vessel, the battleship *Agamemnon*, were assigned the difficult task of paying out the cable as the British-American ships moved westward. All went well for six days, but then, 355 miles at sea, the inferior cable snapped in a heavy swell, and the operation had to be abandoned. Experts from the two nations blamed the failure on each other, but Field and his associates remained confident of ultimate triumph.

For the next attempt, in the summer of 1858, it was decided that the two cable ships should meet in mid-ocean, splice the ends of a new line, and each then reverse course. On June 26,

1858, the *Agamemnon* proceeded toward Ireland and the *Niagara* toward Newfoundland. When the ships were some forty miles apart, the cable again broke after six recovery attempts, with the loss of 290 miles of cable. Cyrus Field's company had lost $2.5 million.

Improved equipment was installed, another attempt at splicing was initiated, and the *Agamemnon* and the *Niagara* gingerly steamed away from each other and headed in opposite directions. This time the cable held together and the *Agamemnon* reached Ireland on August 4, 1858. The English directors of the Atlantic Cable Company sent the first message: "Europe and America are united by telegraphic communication." Later that day, President James Buchanan and Queen Victoria exchanged congratulatory remarks, and messages of all sorts were communicated between England and the United States. Most of them expressed the hope that the Atlantic cable would unite the two countries in eternal friendship. After a brief period, however, signals over the cable grew faint and finally gave out completely, after only three hundred messages had been transmitted. The cable failed because of inadequate insulation, but Field was accused of fraud, and his company faced financial collapse for a time. Without conceding defeat, Field continued to promote his idea, but the intervention of the Civil War caused a delay.

In 1864, Field joined with Brunel and secured the now infamous twelve-thousand-ton steamship *Great Eastern*, "the unappeasable whale that ate men and gold." The *Great Eastern*, often referred to as "an elephant spinning a cobweb," was the daily subject for caricatures and malicious press cartoons. By July 14, 1865, however, everything was ready as the *Great Eastern* lay at Sheerness after taking on great spools of the tar-manila-wrapped wire cable from navy hulks down from London. Even the Prince of Wales came aboard and said, "I wish success to the Atlantic Cable," a taped message that took two seconds to travel the 1,395 nautical miles of still-coiled, blemish-free cable. The *Great Eastern*, with fifteen hundred tons of coal and a dead load of twenty-one thousand tons, left her native river with a flotilla of English steamer ships to the accompaniment of fiddles, bagpipes, and cheering crowds.

Initially, the cable was laid at six knots per hour, but the entire operation was fraught with gales, broken cable, and even "flagrant evidence of mischief." On many occasions, long sections of the cable were lost and had to be laboriously retrieved with five-pronged anchors. Each section had to be carefully inspected for flaws, which then required tedious splicing. On August 2, the *Great Eastern* crossed the halfway mark. Then the operation, beset by rumors of sabotage, had to stop until an improved cable could be manufactured and the weaknesses and problems of laying the cable had been eliminated. There were 1,186 miles of trailing cable that was only partially alive. The area was marked with a red sea buoy with a black ball before the *Great Eastern* left.

On July 13, 1866, after Field reorganized the cable company, the *Great Eastern* commenced laying new cable again, joining her new cable to the shore end off Valencia, and completed laying the cable in fourteen days. On Friday, July 27, the final splice was made successfully, after the cable was carried ashore at Hearts Content relay station. On her return voyage, the *Great Eastern* located the red buoy with the black ball, and after grappling thirty times, the lost cable was retrieved. One crew member said, "Only God can know the sensation of this moment." The social, economic, and political effects of the transatlantic cable were almost immediate in both the United States and Great Britain.

—*Theodore A. Wilson, updated by John Alan Ross*

ADDITIONAL READING:

Babcock, F. Lawrence. *Spanning the Atlantic.* New York: Alfred A. Knopf, 1931. A competent account of the efforts to lay an Atlantic cable.

Emmerson, George S. *The Greatest Iron Ship: S.S. Great Eastern.* Newton Abbot, Devon.: David & Charles Limited, 1980. A thorough account of the world's once-largest iron ship, which was converted to lay the first Atlantic cable.

McDonald, Philip B. *A Saga of the Seas: The Story of Cyrus W. Field and the Laying of the First Atlantic Cable.* New York: Wilson-Erickson, 1937. A history relaying the obstacles to and final success of the cable.

Morse, Samuel F. B. *Samuel F. B. Morse, His Letters and Journals.* Edited by Edward Lind Morse. 2 vols. Boston: Houghton Mifflin, 1914. Although incomplete, this edition of Morse's letters and papers is of considerable value.

Thompson, Holland. *The Age of Invention.* New Haven, Conn.: Yale University Press, 1921. Emphasizes social and other effects of technological changes.

Tyler, David B. *Steam Conquers the Atlantic.* New York: Appleton-Century-Crofts, 1939. Places the laying of the Atlantic cable in the wider context of the early years of the transatlantic steamships.

SEE ALSO: 1844, First Telegraph Message; 1860, Pony Express; 1861, Transcontinental Telegraph Is Completed; 1900, Teletype Is Developed.

1859 ■ LAST SLAVE SHIP DOCKS AT MOBILE: *the arrest and prosecution of the* Clotilde *finally ends the illegal slave trade in the United States*

DATE: July, 1859
LOCALE: Mobile Bay, Alabama
CATEGORY: African American history
KEY FIGURES:

Abaky (born 1846?), a surviving African woman
Bill Foster, captain of the *Clotilde*
Gossalow (born 1839), a surviving African man
Timothy Meagher, plantation owner, steamboat captain, and owner of the *Clotilde*

SUMMARY OF EVENT. There are contradictory reports about slavers—ships especially built to transport slaves—during the

period from 1858 to 1861. Historians, however, have managed to piece together an accurate account of the *Clotilde*, the last U.S. slave ship, which smuggled more than a hundred Africans into Alabama.

The slave trade was outlawed by Congress in 1808. This brutal business continued without serious interference, however, until the early 1820's, when federal officials began capturing slavers and freeing their prisoners. Public sentiment, even in the South, did not favor revival of the trade. To annoy Northern antislavery and abolitionist advocates, numerous rumors were spread by slave traders and sympathizers about slavers landing on the southeastern coast. For example, the *New York Daily Tribune* received many letters reporting landings of slavers in Florida and the Carolinas. There were even rumors in the 1860's of a prosperous underground slave-trading company operating in New Orleans. The *Clotilde*'s history, however, has been confirmed by eyewitness accounts and careful reconstruction of events by historians.

Congress had revived laws against slave trading and declared that anyone convicted would be hanged. The United States had been later than almost every other civilized nation in the world in abolishing slave trading. Even New York City, bastion of abolitionists, became a refuge for eighty-five slave ships, many of them built and sent to Africa from that city. Much profit could be made in the $17,000,000-per-year business. According to one account, 15,000 Africans were smuggled to the United States in 1859 alone, the last 117 of whom were brought by the *Clotilde*. In contrast, the British government, after issuing its injunction against the slave trade in the eighteenth century, seized and destroyed 625 slave ships and freed their forty thousand prisoners. In the United States, only the abolitionists consistently confronted the government for its apathy toward slave smuggling.

Timothy Meagher, with brothers Jim and Byrns, masterminded the *Clotilde* project. Timothy, an imposing Irishman known for his adventurous character, was a plantation owner and captain of the steamboat *Roger B. Taney*, which carried passengers, cargo, and mail to and from Montgomery on the Alabama River. Apparently in a lighthearted argument with some passengers on his steamboat, Meagher made a thousand-dollar bet that within a year or two he would bring a ship full of slaves to Mobile Bay without being apprehended by federal officials. Meagher had many years' experience in cruising the Alabama River. He knew his way around every hidden bayou, swamp, canebrake, and sandbar better than anyone else in the South. For his operation, he needed a slave ship. He purchased a lumber schooner called the *Clotilde* for thirty-five thousand dollars in late 1858 and rebuilt it as a 327-ton slaver. He hired his friend Bill Foster, who was experienced in constructing and sailing the old slavers, as skipper.

Foster was to sail to the west coast of Africa and seek King Dahomey's assistance in procuring two hundred young slaves. The *Clotilde* was equipped with a crew, guns, and cutlasses. To control the prisoners, Meagher supplied the ship with iron manacles, rings, and chains. Foster hired his crew from all over the South, enticing them with liquor, money, and promises of adventure. In the dead of night, massive quantities of food, mainly yams and rice, and drinking water were transported to the ship from Meagher's plantation. To give the ship the look of a lumber schooner, some piles of lumber were placed on the deck. Captain Foster hired the infamous King Dahomey and his drunken thugs to raid villages and capture two hundred young, healthy men and women. The attacks must have taken place early one summer morning in May or early June of 1859. King Dahomey's band raided the two peaceful villages of Whinney and Ataka. They burned huts, injured women and children, and tied up more than 170 young Africans by their necks. The captives were forced into the hold of the *Clotilde*.

The return trip was an awful scene of helpless people, racked with convulsions, crammed into dark, damp quarters, lacking adequate food and water. Foster had as many as thirty-nine bodies thrown overboard before arriving back in the United States. The ship returned in July, 1859, and waited in front of Biloxi in the Mississippi Sound. Foster hired a friend's tugboat and in the dead of night, pulled the *Clotilde*, undetected by government vessels present in Mobile Bay, to a prearranged location in the swamps of the Tombigbee River. Meagher was the best man to maneuver the craft in the treacherous bayous. The sick, exhausted Africans were moved quietly to an out-of-the-way plantation belonging to Meagher's friend, John M. Dabney, who hid them in the canebrakes. From there, Meagher took charge of his steamer, the *Roger B. Taney*, and kept Foster and the *Clotilde* crew members hidden aboard her until they reached Montgomery, where they were paid off and whisked to New York City for dispersal.

The slaver *Clotilde* was promptly burned at water's edge as soon as its African cargo had been removed. Meagher made elaborate preparations to throw townsfolk and government officials off the track. The Department of Justice was informed, however, and Meagher was arrested at his plantation and placed on trial in short order. Meagher's trial was a sham. He was released on bond for lack of evidence. His efforts to conceal all signs of the ship and its cargo had paid off, but he had to spend close to $100,000 in lawyers' fees and bribes. The prosecution was delayed, and the secessionists came to his rescue. News of the *Clotilde*'s landing and Meagher's trial was drowned by the presidential campaign and widespread talk of civil war.

Government officials finally learned where the Africans were hidden. They commissioned the steamer *Eclipse* for finding and transferring the Africans to Mobile. Meagher, learning of the government's decision, got the *Eclipse* crew and government passengers drunk, giving him and his men time to move the prisoners to a friend's plantation two hundred miles up the Alabama River.

Meagher's slave-smuggling venture was a financial disaster. He bought the Africans from King Dahomey for $8,460 in gold plus ninety casks of rum and some cases of yard goods. He was able to sell only twenty-five slaves; it is not clear

exactly what happened to the rest. There were reports that Meagher later transferred the others to his plantation near Mobile. Some ended up marrying and living with local blacks in the vicinity. Some were reported to have died of homesickness or other maladies. Many others settled in cabins behind the Meagher plantation house, which was burned in 1905.

In 1906, a journalistic account of the *Clotilde* episode appeared in *Harper's Monthly* magazine. The author, H. M. Byers, had found several soft-spoken Africans who told of having been smuggled aboard the *Clotilde*. They still maintained some of their own culture and language, along with their African gentleness of demeanor. Most of their children were married to local black residents of Mobile and neighboring areas. Byers conducted extensive interviews with two who had endured the journey from Africa to Alabama: an old man named Gossalow, who had a tribal tattoo on his breast, and an old woman named Abaky, who had intricate tribal tattoos on both cheeks. Gossalow and his wife had been stolen from the village of Whinney, and Abaky from the town of Ataka, near King Dahomey's land. They had kept many of their old traditions in their original form with little modification. For example, they still buried their dead in graves filled with oak leaves. They spoke nostalgically of their peaceful West African farms, planted with abundant yams and rice.

The destruction of the *Clotilde* might be said to symbolize the end of one of the most despicable enterprises in modern history and the beginning of the infusion of the vibrant African culture into North American society. —*Chogollah Maroufi*

ADDITIONAL READING:

Byers, H. M. "The Last Slave Ship." *Harper's Monthly Magazine* 53 (1906): 742-746. A sensationalized journalistic version of the episode, but filled with valuable and accurate details. Especially valuable are the author's interviews with two surviving Africans who were smuggled into the United States aboard the *Clotilde*.

Howard, Warren S. "The Elusive Smuggled Slave." In *American Slavers and the Federal Law: 1837-1862*. Berkeley: University of California Press, 1963. Provides various accounts of the *Clotilde*.

Sellers, James Benson. *Slavery in Alabama*. Birmingham: University of Alabama Press, 1950. Conveys the historical and social mood of that period and gives some details of the *Clotilde's* smuggling operation.

Spear, John R. *The American Slave Trade: An Account of Its Origins, Growth and Suppression*. Williamstown, Mass.: Corner House, 1978. A well-researched and thoroughly documented book about the slave trade in general. Chapter 19 provides an account of the *Clotilde* voyage and its aftermath.

Wish, Harvey. "The Revival of the African Slave Trade in the United States, 1859-1860." *Mississippi Valley Historical Review* 27 (1940-1941): 569-588. A comprehensive account of various smuggling operations just before the Civil War.

SEE ALSO: 1807, Congress Bans Importation of African Slaves; 1807, Voyage of the *Clermont*; 1839, Amistad Slave Revolt.

1859 ■ FIRST COMMERCIAL OIL WELL:
the Drake well proves that petroleum can be the basis of a national industry

DATE: August 27, 1859
LOCALE: Titusville, Pennsylvania
CATEGORIES: Business and labor; Economics; Science and technology
KEY FIGURES:
Luther Atwood, Boston chemist who analyzed Pennsylvania crude oil
George Henry Bissell (1821-1884) and
J. G. Eveleth, organizers of the Pennsylvania Rock Oil Company
Francis Beattie Brewer, physician and first promoter of Titusville, Pennsylvania oil
Edwin Laurentine "Colonel" Drake (1819-1880), man who directed drilling of the first commercial oil well in the United States
Samuel M. Kier (1813-1874), early commercial developer of petroleum as a medicine and illuminant
Benjamin Silliman (1779-1864), Yale chemistry professor who proved the commercial value of Pennsylvania crude oil
William A. "Uncle Billy" Smith, salt-well driller and blacksmith hired to drill Drake's well
James M. Townsend, New Haven, Connecticut, banker and principal investor in Seneca Oil Company

SUMMARY OF EVENT. On Sunday afternoon, August 27, 1859, William A. "Uncle Billy" Smith discovered oil in a well that he was drilling for "Colonel" Edwin L. Drake on Oil Creek near Titusville, Pennsylvania. Drake's well was neither the first oil well nor the first drilled well. However, it ignited an "oil boom," raising Pennsylvania production from about 2,000 barrels in 1859 to about 500,000 barrels in 1865. Thereafter, U.S. production quickly expanded, exceeding 80 percent of the world supply from 1865 through 1883.

Petroleum was known and used in the United States long before 1859. Jesuit missionaries first reported oil springs at Cuba, New York, in 1656, and Peter Kalm visited and reported on the Oil Creek springs in 1748. By the eighteenth century, Seneca Indians were trading oil at Niagara. Settlers had begun skimming petroleum from Oil Creek for medicinal purposes after the Revolutionary War. Samuel M. Kier of Pittsburgh, the most significant petroleum producer and marketer before Drake, had begun bottling and selling petroleum from salt wells near Tarentum, Pennsylvania, in about 1847. Approximately three years later, Kier developed a distilling process that made possible the use of petroleum as an illuminant as well as a medicine. His distillate, called carbon oil, came into general use in western Pennsylvania and New York City. Kier established a much larger market for oil and brought that market to the attention of New York entrepreneurs. The price of the product rose steadily because of its scarcity, thus stimulating a search for petroleum.

Interest in the oil found along Oil Creek was revived by Ebenezer Brewer, who sent five gallons to his son, Dr. Francis Beattie Brewer. Francis Brewer gave some of the oil to Dr. Dixi Crosby, dean of the New Hampshire Medical School, and to O. P. Hubbard, professor of chemistry at Dartmouth College. In 1851, Francis Brewer joined his father's lumber firm, timbering at Titusville. Brewer spent considerable time examining oil springs on the company's property, persuading himself that they should be exploited. In 1854, he again visited Dartmouth and met with Albert Crosby, son of Dixi Crosby, who unsuccessfully attempted to organize a stock company to exploit the springs. A few weeks later, Dartmouth alumnus George H. Bissell visited his alma mater. The young New York lawyer saw the sample and was struck by its commercial possibilities as a medicine.

In the summer of 1854, Bissell and his law partner, J. G. Eveleth, sent a representative to examine and report on the Pennsylvania oil property. If the report was favorable, they planned to form a company to acquire the land and exploit its petroleum. The report was favorable, and in September, Dr. Brewer appeared in New York ready to sell and lease part of the oil rights. Bissell and Eveleth, however, decided first to seek advice from some leading New Haven, Connecticut, citizens who they believed were potential investors. The New Haven interests were intrigued but wanted confirmation of the preliminary reports and a scientific study of the oil. Eveleth went to Titusville to inspect the properties. He and Bissell also engaged Luther Atwood, a Boston chemist, and Professor Benjamin Silliman of Yale University to evaluate the oil's economic value.

Eveleth's report was glowing, and on November 10, the deal between Brewer and the partners was concluded. In December, the partners founded the first oil company in the United States, the Pennsylvania Rock Oil Company of New York. Capital was difficult to raise, however, until Silliman presented his report in 1855. Silliman's assurance that at least 50 percent of the crude oil could be recovered as an illuminant of immediate commercial value, and 90 percent as distilled products with marketable promise, greatly reinforced interest in petroleum as a commercial commodity. The New Haven investors, however, because of investor liability under New York law, required that the company reincorporate in Connecticut.

On September 18, 1885, the Pennsylvania Rock Oil Company of Connecticut was organized. A favorable report from an investors' committee that visited Titusville whetted the New Haven businessmen's interest, but continued distrust between the New York and New Haven investors, as well as the Panic of 1857, delayed activity until December, 1857. Then, James M. Townsend, one of the New Haven investors, sent Edwin L. Drake, a thirty-eight-year-old railroad conductor, to make another inspection of the proposed oil field. Drake, a casual acquaintance of Townsend, had no technical experience but was available and could obtain a railroad pass to the Titusville area, thus reducing Townsend's expenses. Drake returned with an optimistic report, and on March 23, 1858, the New Haven investors organized the Seneca Oil Company of

Connecticut. Drake, who was only a minor stockholder, was appointed president and manager. He returned to Titusville in May, 1858, and began trenching to collect oil. Encountering water in a dug well, he decided to drill into bedrock.

Drake then went to the salt-drilling center of Tarentum to secure a driller and began construction of an engine house and derrick at the well site. The driller failed to appear, and work was halted for the winter. In the spring, the driller again did not appear. Apparently, the man thought Drake insane and had agreed to come only to get rid of him. In April, 1859, Drake hired "Uncle Billy" Smith of Saline for $2.50 a day, including the labor of Smith's son. Smith, a salt-well driller, was also a blacksmith able to make drilling tools. Smith worked continuously from May to August without significant result. Townsend, who by now was financing the operation from his own funds, instructed Drake to pay off his outstanding obligations and terminate the project. The well was then sixty-nine feet deep.

On August 26, the bit dropped into a crevice, and drilling was suspended. The next day, Smith went to the well on a routine inspection and saw a dark film floating on the water several feet below the derrick floor. He and his son used an improvised ladle to secure some of the substance, which proved to be oil. When Drake arrived on Monday morning, he rigged an ordinary hand pump to the shaft and soon was pumping up to twenty barrels of crude oil per day. By demonstrating that petroleum could be drilled for and secured in substantial quantities, Drake and Smith ushered in the great western Pennsylvania oil boom and laid the foundation of a giant U.S. industry.

—*James E. Fickle, updated by Ralph L. Langenheim, Jr.*

ADDITIONAL READING:

Clark, J. Stanley. *The Oil Century: From the Drake Well to the Conservation Era.* Norman: University of Oklahoma Press, 1959. Commemorating the petroleum industry's centennial, this book concentrates on the period before 1865.

Giddens, Paul H. *The Birth of the Oil Industry.* New York: Macmillan, 1938. A detailed account of the origin and first ten years of the modern oil industry.

_____. *Early Days of Oil: A Pictorial History of the Beginnings of the Oil Industry in Pennsylvania.* Princeton, N.J.: Princeton University Press, 1948. Photographs and illustrations of life in the oil region.

Knowles, Ruth Sheldon. *The First Pictorial History of the American Oil and Gas Industry, 1859-1983.* Athens: Ohio University Press, 1985. Discussion and photographs of the Drake well and its consequences.

Owens, Edgar Wesley. "The Earliest Oil Industry." In *Trek of the Oil Finders: A History of Petroleum Exploration.* Tulsa, Okla.: American Association of Petroleum Geologists, 1975. A succinct account of the origins of petroleum exploitation and of drilling the Drake well.

Williamson, Harold F., and Arnold R. Daum. *The American Petroleum Industry: The Age of Illumination, 1859-1899.* Evanston, Ill.: Northwestern University Press, 1959. Comprehensive, well-documented history of the early oil industry and drilling of the Drake well.

Yergin, Daniel. "Oil on the Brain: The Beginning." In *The Prize.* New York: Simon & Schuster, 1991. Discusses events leading to the drilling of the Drake well and the immediate consequences of its success.

SEE ALSO: 1882, Standard Oil Trust Is Organized.

1859 ■ JOHN BROWN'S RAID ON HARPERS FERRY: *an attempt by a militant abolitionist to liberate and arm Virginia slaves makes civil war inevitable*

DATE: October 16-18, 1859
LOCALE: Harpers Ferry, Virginia
CATEGORIES: African American history; Civil rights; Wars, uprisings, and civil unrest
KEY FIGURES:

John Brown (1800-1859), militant abolitionist who planned and led the raid on Harpers Ferry

John H. Kagi (1835?-1859), veteran of the antislavery struggle and Brown's chief lieutenant

Robert Edward Lee (1807-1870), Army colonel who led the contingent of Marines that captured Brown and his followers

Franklin Benjamin Sanborn (1831-1917), Massachusetts abolitionist and secretary of the Massachusetts State Kansas Committee

Henry Alexander Wise (1806-1876), governor of Virginia

SUMMARY OF EVENT. John Brown's abortive raid on the federal arsenal at Harpers Ferry, Virginia (now West Virginia), in October, 1859, stands out as a critical episode in the spiraling sequence of events that led Northerners and Southerners into the Civil War in 1861. Brown, long a militant abolitionist, emigrated to Kansas Territory in 1855 with five of his sons to participate in the struggle between proslavery and Free State forces for control of the territory. Their insurrection was in the same spirit as earlier violence perpetrated by abolitionist, Free State militias such as the Border Ruffians following election of a proslavery, territorial legislature in 1854. With a small band of Free State men, Brown helped initiate civil war in Kansas by murdering five allegedly proslavery settlers along Pottawatomie Creek, in May, 1856. Historians would later dub this era "Bleeding Kansas."

Brown's experience in the Kansas civil war convinced him that a conspiracy existed to seize the national territories for slavery. Having long since lost faith in combating slavery by peaceful means, Brown vowed to strike a violent blow at the heart of slavery. An intense Calvinist, Brown had come to believe that he was God's personal instrument to eradicate the inhuman institution. As early as 1857, he had decided to seize a mountain fortress in Virginia with a small guerrilla force and incite a bloody slave rebellion that would overthrow the slave powers throughout the South.

To that end, Brown sought funds and arms from abolitionists in the North. Under the guise of seeking money to continue the Free State fight in Kansas, Brown secured the friendship and financial aid of the Massachusetts State Kansas Committee—a group dedicated to helping the Free-Soil forces in Kansas and elsewhere. The resolute and persuasive Brown won the support of six prominent antislavery figures, who agreed to form a secret Committee of Six to advise him and raise money for his still-secret mission. The Secret Six consisted of a well-educated group of dedicated abolitionists and reformers: Franklin B. Sanborn, a young Concord schoolteacher and secretary of the Massachusetts State Kansas Committee; Thomas Wentworth Higginson, a "disunion abolitionist" and outspoken Unitarian minister; Theodore Parker, a controversial theologian-preacher; Samuel Gridley Howe, a prominent physician and educator; George Luther Stearns, a prosperous merchant and chairman of the Massachusetts State Kansas Committee; and Gerrit Smith, a wealthy New York landowner and reformer.

Throughout the remainder of 1857, the indefatigable Brown trained a small group of adventurers and militant abolitionists in preparation for his mission. In May, 1858, Brown moved on to Chatham, Canada, holding a secret "Constitutional Convention" attended by thirty-four African Americans and twelve whites. There, he outlined his plans to invade Virginia, liberate and arm the slaves, defeat any military force brought against them, organize the African Americans into a government, and force the Southern states to concede emancipation. Under Brown's leadership, the convention approved a constitution for a new state once the slaves were freed, and elected Brown commander in chief with John Kagi, his chief lieutenant, as secretary of war.

Brown's proposed invasion was delayed in 1858, when a disgruntled follower partially betrayed the plans to several prominent politicians. The exposé so frightened the Secret Six that they urged Brown to return to Kansas and create a diversionary operation until rumors of the Virginia plan dissipated. Brown also agreed not to inform the Secret Six of the details of his plans, so that they could not be held responsible in case the

In a mural by John Stuart Curry, located in the state capitol building in Topeka, Kansas, John Brown is depicted as an almost mythic, Moses-like figure leading the raid on Harpers Ferry for the cause of abolition. (National Archives)

invasion failed. In December, 1858, Brown conducted the diversion as planned, by leading a raid into Missouri, liberating eleven slaves, and escorting them to Canada. He then began final preparations for the invasion of Virginia.

Harpers Ferry, situated at the confluence of the Potomac and Shenandoah Rivers in northern Virginia, was the initial target in Brown's plan, because he needed weapons from the federal arsenal to arm the liberated slaves. Brown and three of his men arrived at Harpers Ferry on July 3, 1859, and set up headquarters at the Kennedy farm, seven miles east of Harpers Ferry in Maryland. The rest of Brown's twenty-one young recruits (sixteen whites and five African Americans) slowly trickled in. On the night of October 16, 1859, after several months of refining his plans, Brown led eighteen of his followers in an assault on the arsenal and rifle works at Harpers Ferry. They quickly captured the arsenal, the armory, and a nearby rifle works, and then seized hostages from the townspeople and surrounding countryside.

Fearing a slave insurrection, the armed townspeople gathered in the streets, and church bells tolled the alarm over the countryside. Brown stood his ground, anxiously waiting for the slaves from the countryside to rally to his cause. By 11:00 A.M. the next day, Brown's men—holed up in the small fire-enginehouse of the armory—engaged in a pitched battle with the assembled townspeople, farmers, and militia. By dawn the following morning, a company of horse Marines under the command of Colonel Robert E. Lee took up positions in front of the armory. When Brown refused Lee's summons to surrender unconditionally, the Marines stormed the armory, wounded Brown, and routed his followers. Seventeen people died in the raid; ten of the dead, including two of Brown's sons, were raiders. Five raiders were captured, two were taken prisoner several days later, but five escaped without a trace.

Governor Henry A. Wise of Virginia decided that Brown and his coconspirators should be tried in Virginia rather than by federal authorities, even though their attack had been against federal property. Brown and the captured raiders stood trial at Charles Town, Virginia; on October 31, the jury found them guilty of inciting a slave rebellion, murder, and treason against the state of Virginia. After the trial, in a final attempt to save his life, Brown's lawyers collected affidavits from many of his friends and relatives alleging that Brown suffered from hereditary insanity and monomania. Brown rejected his defense, claiming that he was sane. He knew that he could better serve the abolitionist cause as a martyr, a sentiment shared by Northern abolitionists. Governor Wise agreed that Brown was sane, and on December 2, 1859, John Brown was hanged at Charles Town. Six of his fellow conspirators met a similar fate.

Brown's raid intensified the sectional bitterness that led to the Civil War. Although the vast majority of Northerners condemned the incident as the work of a fanatic, the outraged South, racked by rumors of a slave insurrection, suspected all Northerners of abetting Brown's crime. Republican denials of any link with Brown were of little avail. Northern abolitionists, including the Secret Six, who had been cleared of complicity, gathered by the hundreds throughout the North to honor and acclaim Brown's martyrdom. The South was in no mood to distinguish between the Northern Republicans who wanted to contain slavery and the small group of abolitionists who sought to destroy the institution. The South withdrew even further into a defense of its peculiar institution, stifled internal criticism, and intensified its hatred and suspicion of the "Black Republican" Party. In 1861, Northerners marched to war to the tune of "John Brown's Body"—fulfilling Brown's prophecy that "the crimes of this guilty land will never be purged away; but with Blood."

—Terry L. Seip, updated by Richard Whitworth

ADDITIONAL READING:

Boyer, Richard O. *The Legend of John Brown: A Biography and a History*. New York: Alfred A. Knopf, 1972. A basic reference for scholars. Covers not only the events but also the temper of the era that culminated in the Civil War.

Oates, Stephen B. *Our Fiery Trial: Abraham Lincoln, John Brown, and the Civil War Era*. Amherst: University of Massachusetts Press, 1979. Shows how Lincoln, Brown, and Nat Turner were interconnected in the events that hurled the United States toward civil war.

_____. *To Purge This Land with Blood: A Biography of John Brown*. 2d ed. Amherst: University of Massachusetts Press, 1984. An even handed account of Brown and the events he precipitated, by an eminent historian. Provides maps and pictures of Brown's associates.

Quarles, Benjamin, com. *Blacks on John Brown*. Urbana: University of Illinois Press, 1972. Includes a variety of poems, letters, and reports written by African Americans from 1858 to 1972 about John Brown, including selections by Frederick Douglass, W. E. B. Du Bois, Countee Cullen, and Langston Hughes.

Renehan, Edward J. *The Secret Six: The True Tale of the Men Who Conspired with John Brown*. New York: Crown, 1995. Details the lives of the six unlikely revolutionaries—five aristocratic Bostonians and one moneyed New Yorker—who financed John Brown's bloody raid. Lively reading.

SEE ALSO: 1850, Compromise of 1850; 1854, Kansas-Nebraska Act; 1854, Birth of the Republican Party; 1856, Bleeding Kansas; 1860, Lincoln Is Elected President; 1860, Confederate States Secede from the Union.

1860 ■ PONY EXPRESS: *a horse-and-rider postal delivery service bridges the thousand-mile gap between East and West*

DATE: April 3, 1860-October 26, 1861
LOCALE: Trans-Missouri West
CATEGORIES: Communications; Transportation
KEY FIGURES:
William Frederick "Buffalo Bill" Cody (1846-1917), famous
    Pony Express rider

William B. Dinsmore, president of the Overland Mail
Company, which assumed responsibility for the Pony
Express in July, 1861
William George Fargo (1818-1881), director of the Overland
Mail Company
William McKendree Gwin (1805-1885), senator from
California who proposed the Pony Express
"Pony Bob" Haslam (born 1840?), rider who established a
record by riding 380 miles with only nine hours of rest
William Hepburn Russell (1812-1872),
Alexander Majors (1814-1900), and
William B. Waddell (1807-1872), founders of the Pony
Express

SUMMARY OF EVENT.

WANTED: YOUNG SKINNY WIRY FELLOWS not over eighteen.
Must be expert riders willing to risk death daily. Orphans preferred. WAGES $25 per week. Apply, Central Overland Ex-
press, Alta Bldg., Montgomery St.

This help-wanted advertisement of 1860 may be the most
famous in the world. It drew eighty riders, forty going east and
forty going west, to carry mail for the Pony Express. The
young men were in the saddle at all times, dressed in their
distinctive costume of a gaudy red shirt and blue pants.

The Pony Express was inaugurated on April 3, 1860, when
the first rider left St. Joseph, Missouri; the following day,
another pony headed east from Sacramento, California. The
enterprise was sponsored by Russell, Majors, and Waddell, a
well-known freighting firm that recently had entered the overland mail business by consolidating the various lines along the
central route into a company known as the Central Overland,
California and Pikes Peak Express Company. Intense rivalry
developed with the Butterfield Overland Mail Company,
which had received a government contract to deliver the mails
on a longer southern route from Missouri to San Francisco,
running stages in a great semicircle by way of Fort Smith, El
Paso, Tucson, Yuma, and Los Angeles.

Some historians claim the Pony Express actually began in
1839, when a Swiss adventurer named John Sutter arrived in
Monterey in Upper California. Gold discovered while a saw-
mill was being built at Sutter's fort in February, 1848, caused
a land rush across the United States that coined a new name for
a class of people: forty-niners. By 1860, the U.S. population
on the West Coast had grown to half a million, three hundred
thousand in California alone. Transplanted from parts east,
they craved information, letters, newspapers, books, and
magazines from "the States." They wanted news that was not
a month or two old. Their need for fresh news gave rise to the
Pony Express, a service that could provide ten-day delivery
from St. Joseph, Missouri, to Sacramento, California.

William M. Gwin, a senator from California who supported
all schemes to improve mail service to the Pacific Coast, was
eager to publicize the fact that the central route, favored by
emigrants, was practicable and shorter for mail delivery than

the southern "oxbow" route. He suggested to William H.
Russell of Russell, Majors, and Waddell that Russell's firm
establish a fast express and mail system with men on horse-
back over the central route. Gwin promised to seek congressional reimbursement for the cost of the experiment and
pointed out to Russell that publicity associated with the enterprise would advertise the advantages of the stage route and
might result in lucrative mail contracts.

Financial assistance was not forthcoming from the government, but Russell decided to go ahead; he notified his partners
that he proposed to organize the Pony Express, with relays of
horsemen that would carry the mails between Missouri and
California in ten days. (Russell probably did not realize how
much his proposal resembled a system used by Darius the
Great, King of Persia, 522-486 B.C.)

Alexander Majors and William B. Waddell, Russell's partners, rejected the idea at first but later agreed, although with
reluctance. The public announcement of the creation of the
Pony Express caused great excitement, because Russell agreed
to deliver letters between St. Joseph, Missouri, and Placerville,
California, for five dollars per ounce within ten days, half the
time that it took on the Butterfield route. Russell undertook the
responsibility of establishing 190 way stations between ten
and fifteen miles apart along the route, and he selected the
fleetest horses to be ridden by men noted for their light weight,
physical stamina, and steady nerves. Success depended on
their ability and endurance. The mail, wrapped in oiled silk to
protect it from the weather, was placed in a leather *mochila*
that fit over the saddle. No more than twenty pounds of mail
was carried by a single pony, the number of letters depending
upon the total weight. Among the most famous deliveries west
were a copy of Lincoln's inaugural address and news of the
outbreak of the Civil War.

The Pony Express was organized as a giant relay race, each
rider driving a pony at a gallop between one station and the
next, where another animal would be saddled and waiting.
Only two minutes were allowed to change horses and transfer
the *mochila* before the rider was off to the next station. Each
man had a run of between seventy-five and one hundred miles,
over which he was expected to average nine miles per hour. If
his replacement were not waiting at the end of his run, he was
to ride on, because the mail had to be kept moving night and
day. Eighty riders were in their saddles at all times. The life
was hard and dangerous because of inclement weather and the
possibility of Indian attacks. In emergencies, riders such as
"Buffalo Bill" Cody and "Pony Bob" Haslam made rides of
several hundred miles that brought them great fame.

The pay for Pony Express riders was $125 a month, a good
income for the time. The real test came in the winter of 1860-
1861. Instead of covering the entire distance from Missouri to
California, most trips were confined to the distance between
Fort Kearney, Nebraska, and Fort Churchill, Nevada, the ter-
mini of the telegraph under construction. A schedule of thirteen days was maintained between the ends of the telegraph
lines, with a total of seventeen or eighteen days for the entire

distance between St. Joseph and San Francisco. From the standpoint of drama, romance, and publicity, the Pony Express was an outstanding success.

Although rates were high—it cost approximately thirty-eight dollars to deliver each letter—the number of letters carried increased from 49 to 350 per trip within a year. Nevertheless, Russell, Majors, and Waddell encountered financial difficulties. They lost about a thousand dollars per day on the operation and did not receive payment from the United States government for delivering freight. Losses incurred by the Pony Express alone were estimated at half a million dollars.

In desperation, Russell, with the cooperation of a clerk in the Department of the Interior, appropriated $870,000 in Indian Trust Fund bonds to be used as security for maintaining the firm's credit and borrowing power. Meanwhile, the Overland Mail Company had been forced to abandon its southern route through Texas after that state had joined the Confederacy at the outbreak of the Civil War, and its equipment was moved to the central route. This company was heavily indebted to Wells, Fargo, and Company for funds advanced to outfit and maintain the line. Wells, Fargo directors on the board of the Overland Mail Company forced the retirement of John Butterfield as president and elected William Dinsmore to take his place.

The reorganized company obtained a government contract on March 2, 1861, providing for a daily overland mail and a semiweekly Pony Express on the central route with an annual compensation of one million dollars. Thus, the Pony Express received financial support from the federal government after July 1, 1861, and the responsibility for its operation was transferred to the Overland Mail Company controlled by Wells, Fargo. Russell, Majors, and Waddell were forced into bankruptcy, and the Pony Express was officially discontinued on October 26, 1861, two days after the overland telegraph line was completed.

—*W. Turrentine Jackson, updated by Russell Hively*

ADDITIONAL READING:

Bloss, Roy S. *Pony Express: The Great Gamble.* Berkeley, Calif.: Howell-North Books, 1959. A carefully researched, well-balanced story of the Pony Express.

Chapman, Arthur. *The Pony Express.* New York: G. P. Putnam's Sons, 1932. A well-written, popular account of the history and lore of the Pony Express.

Hafen, LeRoy R. *The Overland Mail, 1848-1869.* Glendale, Calif.: Arthur H. Clark, 1926. This classic work on the subject provides the essential background for understanding the Pony Express in a single chapter.

Limerick, Patricia Nelson. *Legacy of Conquest: The Unbroken Past of the American West.* New York: W. W. Norton, 1987. Contrasts the historical myths and the reality of the American West.

Paul, Rodman W. *The Far West and the Great Plains in Transition 1859-1900.* New York: Harper & Row, 1988. A history of the settlement and development of the American West in the latter half of the nineteenth century.

Settle, Raymond W., and Mary L. Settle. *Saddles and Spurs: The Pony Express Saga.* Harrisburg, Pa.: Stackpole, 1955. Written by authors who have spent a lifetime studying the history of the Russell, Majors, and Waddell Company, for which their ancestors worked.

SEE ALSO: 1861, Transcontinental Telegraph Is Completed; 1869, Transcontinental Railroad Is Completed.

1860 ■ LINCOLN IS ELECTED PRESIDENT: *election of the first modern Republican president of the United States provokes secession of the Southern states from the Union*

DATE: November 6, 1860
LOCALE: United States
CATEGORY: Government and politics
KEY FIGURES:
John Bell (1797-1869), Constitutional Union presidential candidate in the 1860 election
John Cabell Breckinridge (1821-1875), Democratic presidential candidate in the South in the 1860 election
James Buchanan (1791-1868), fifteenth president of the United States, 1857-1861
Stephen Arnold Douglas (1813-1861), Democratic presidential candidate in the North in the 1860 election
Abraham Lincoln (1809-1865), sixteenth president of the United States, 1861-1865

SUMMARY OF EVENT. Members of the recently created Republican Party approached the 1860 election with great enthusiasm. The outgoing Democratic president, James Buchanan, had accomplished little of significance during his term in office, and he chose not to be a candidate for reelection in 1860. Republican candidates had enjoyed success in Northern and Western states in both the 1856 and 1858 elections, and they hoped that an attractive Republican presidential candidate would be victorious in the November, 1860, general election.

The Democrats were in serious trouble. Democratic unity had been shattered under pressures engendered by the Kansas-Nebraska Act, and Democrats could not be certain of victory in any single state in the North in 1860. Democratic candidates who opposed allowing the extension of slavery into newly created states alienated Southern voters, and those Democrats who supported slavery were politically unacceptable in the Northern and Western states. Only in the South was the Democratic Party holding firm, but Democrats throughout the nation recognized that their party could not win behind a Southern candidate. A Northerner was necessary, but the Southern wing of the Democratic Party insisted that the candidate not take a strong position against slavery. No such disunity existed in the Republican Party, which had expressed its opposition to slavery in its 1856 platform. Republicans were jubilant at the impending split of the Democrats and, in order not to throw away this golden opportunity, sought a moderate candidate who would appeal to former Whigs, Northerners, and residents of border and Western states.

Partisan disputes rather than genuine confrontation with national problems had characterized U.S. politics between the end of Andrew Jackson's presidency in 1837 and the election of Abraham Lincoln in 1860. James Buchanan, the incumbent Democratic president from Pennsylvania, had been singularly ineffective in uniting his party, and his animosity toward Senator Stephen A. Douglas from Illinois was obvious to fellow Democrats.

The country was enjoying a healthy economy in 1860. The economic downturn of the mid-1850's, culminating in the Panic of 1857, was now over. By 1860, the United States had achieved a considerable measure of economic integration, and the various regions had grown more dependent on one another. Domestic trade was of far more importance to the national economy than foreign trade. Many Southerners, however, continued to feel that their economic growth would depend largely on cotton production. They also believed that slavery was essential and should be protected, not only in Southern states but also in the territories and recently created states in

Abraham Lincoln, sixteenth president of the United States, whose election to the presidency prompted the secession of the Confederate states, would use the powers of the executive to maintain and fight for the Union in the face of Civil War. (Library of Congress)

the Midwest and West. The economy of the North and the Northwest, however, was no longer totally dependent on cotton and other agricultural products from the South. Northern manufacturing and Northwestern agriculture had achieved sufficient strength to produce adequate capital for further expansion, as was clearly demonstrated during the Civil War. Southern politicians, however, entered the campaign of 1860 as if nothing had changed economically since the 1840's.

During the winter of 1859-1860, Senator William H. Seward of New York appeared to be the leading candidate for the Republican nomination, but several prominent Republicans, including Salmon P. Chase from Ohio, Simon Cameron from Pennsylvania, Edward Bates from Missouri, and the influential newspaper publisher Horace Greeley from New York, argued that Seward, who had a reputation for being a strident orator, might offend too many voters and cost the Republicans such key states as Ohio, Pennsylvania, New York, Missouri, and Massachusetts. Many Republicans therefore mounted a stop-Seward campaign. At the Republican convention in Chicago, in May, 1860, Seward led on the first two ballots. After forty-seven delegates from Pennsylvania changed their votes from Cameron to Lincoln, delegates from many other states also changed their minds, and Abraham Lincoln was nominated on the third ballot. The convention selected Hannibal Hamlin from Maine as the Republican vice presidential candidate.

Unlike the Republicans, the Democrats were terribly divided. At their national nominating convention in Charleston, South Carolina, in April, 1860, Southern delegates demanded the acceptance of the Alabama platform that called for the positive protection by Congress of slavery in the territories. The South was willing to accept Stephen Douglas as the Democratic candidate only if he accepted the Alabama platform. Realizing that Northern and Western voters never would tolerate the spread of slavery into new U.S. territories and states, Douglas refused to support the Alabama platform. The delegations of eight Southern states then withdrew from the convention and called for another convention to meet in Richmond, Virginia. Douglas and his followers adjourned to Baltimore, where he was nominated.

The Southern delegates who met in Richmond intensified the split by nominating a separate ticket, headed by John C. Breckinridge of Kentucky. The Republicans' chances for victory improved even more when certain former Whigs formed the Constitutional Union Party. This party was especially popular in border states. At its convention in Baltimore, the Constitutional Union Party nominated John Bell of Tennessee. The field was a full one, with four candidates seeking the support of the nation. With the splintering of the Democrats, the creation of the Constitutional Union Party, and the unity of the Republicans, the election of Lincoln was almost a certainty.

Although the other candidates traveled extensively during the 1860 campaign, Abraham Lincoln chose to adhere to the tradition of the day and stayed home in Springfield, Illinois.

Until the twentieth century, many presidential candidates felt that it was undignified for a candidate for the highest office to campaign personally. Because there were four candidates, Lincoln simply needed a plurality and not a majority in order to win the electoral votes in Northern, Midwestern, and Eastern states, in which the Republicans had strong support. By remaining in Springfield, Lincoln was able to deliver set speeches affirming his intention of protecting the Constitution and preserving the Union. He did not have to answer unexpected questions from reporters, and he avoided making any blunders during the campaign.

The Republicans swept the North, with Douglas carrying only New Jersey and Missouri. The Bell ticket carried three border states, while Breckinridge received all the electoral votes in the South. By popular vote, Lincoln was a minority president. His 1,866,452 votes compared with a total of 2,815,617 for his opponents. In electoral votes, however, Lincoln received 180, while his opponents received 123. Nearly 70 percent of the voters opposed expansion of slavery into the territories.

The Republicans gained control of the presidency and the House of Representatives, but the Democrats retained control of the Senate. Republican success was attended by dire consequences. News of the election of Lincoln precipitated the secession of South Carolina, followed by the secession of six other Southern states by February, 1861. Outgoing President Buchanan did nothing to stop this illegal secession. The responsibility of preserving the Union fell on Abraham Lincoln, who took his oath of office on March 4, 1861.

—John G. Clark, updated by Edmund J. Campion

ADDITIONAL READING:

Einhorn, Lois J. *Abraham Lincoln, the Orator: Penetrating the Lincoln Legend*. Westport, Conn.: Greenwood Press, 1992. Contains an excellent analysis of the eloquence and effectiveness of such important speeches by Lincoln as the Gettysburg Address and the Cooper Union speech of February 27, 1860.

Lincoln, Abraham. *Lincoln on Democracy*. Edited and introduced by Mario Cuomo and Harold Holzer. New York: HarperCollins, 1990. Reproduces the texts of famous speeches delivered by Abraham Lincoln. Contains several essays on his importance in the preservation of democratic values in the United States.

Oates, Stephen B. *With Malice Toward None: The Life of Abraham Lincoln*. New York: Harper & Row, 1977. A well-documented, reliable biography of Lincoln. Good discussion of his defeat by Stephen Douglas in the 1858 Illinois Senate campaign and his successful campaign for the White House two years later.

Randall, J. G. *Lincoln, the President: Springfield to Gettysburg*. 4 vols. New York: Dodd, Mead, 1945-1955. Good description of Lincoln's career in law and politics, from his years in Springfield until the decisive battle of the Civil War.

Sandburg, Carl. *Abraham Lincoln: The Prairie Years*. 2 vols. New York: Harcourt Brace, 1926. Although now quite old, this two-volume study of Lincoln's career before the White House and Sandburg's four-volume work *Abraham Lincoln: The War Years* (1939) still constitutes one of the most readable biographies of Lincoln.

SEE ALSO: 1854, Birth of the Republican Party; 1858, Lincoln-Douglas Debates; 1861, Lincoln's Inauguration.

1860 ■ CONFEDERATE STATES SECEDE FROM THE UNION: *the beginning of the American Civil War marks one of the darkest periods of the Union's history*

DATE: December 20, 1860
LOCALE: Montgomery, Alabama
CATEGORIES: Government and politics; Wars, uprisings, and civil unrest
KEY FIGURES:

Howell Cobb (1815-1868), president of the convention called to create a Southern republic

Jefferson Davis (1808-1889), president of the Confederate States of America

Robert Barnwell Rhett (1800-1876), leader of South Carolina's secessionist movement

Alexander Hamilton Stephens (1812-1883), vice president of the Confederate States of America

Robert Augustus Toombs (1810-1885), former senator from Georgia who became the first Confederate secretary of state

SUMMARY OF EVENT. On December 20, 1860, the delegates of the Convention of the People of South Carolina voted 160 to 0 to adopt an ordinance of secession dissolving the "union now subsisting between South Carolina and the other States under the name of 'United States of America.'" The South Carolinians, wishing to maintain their radical leadership of the South, had moved quickly to take the initiative in the secession movement. News of Abraham Lincoln's election to the presidency of the United States had reached South Carolina by November 7, and on November 13, the legislature authorized the calling of a state convention. Delegates were quickly chosen in special elections, and the convention met on December 17. Three days later, South Carolina seceded.

Secession was justified, according to members of the 1860 convention, under the ancient "compact theory" of states' rights. According to this concept, individual states were sovereign. They had voluntarily entered into the Union, and they could leave lawfully whenever they chose or whenever they believed the terms of the compact or agreement under which they were united (the Constitution) were violated. This action could be taken by a specially elected state convention representing the sovereign power of a state.

Most Southerners believed that their liberty and their property, particularly their slaves, were threatened by the election victory of a political party composed exclusively of Northerners. The Western territories would, it was assumed, become

THE UNION AND THE CONFEDERACY

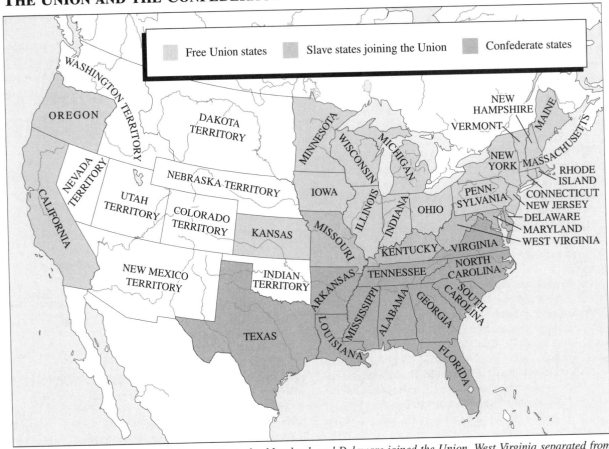

Although originally slave states, Missouri, Kentucky, Maryland, and Delaware joined the Union. West Virginia separated from Virginia at the beginning of the war and joined the Union in 1863.

free states, and the political imbalance would be perpetuated and increased.

The other states of the Deep South shared South Carolina's view that to remain in the Union would be intolerable. In fact, Mississippi was prepared to take the initiative had South Carolina delayed. Starting on January 9, 1861, Mississippi, Florida, and Alabama seceded on successive days. In Georgia, Alexander Stephens, among others, urged a wait-and-see policy, because the Republican government had not yet taken office. Other powerful Georgians, such as Robert Toombs and Howell Cobb, called for separation, and the Georgia convention voted for secession on January 19. Louisiana, where Union sentiment was considerable, adopted an ordinance of secession on January 26. In Texas, the secessionists were opposed by Governor Sam Houston, but a state convention voted to secede on February 1, subject to a popular referendum, which accepted secession three weeks later. Texas was the last of the seven states to secede before Lincoln took office.

Robert Barnwell Rhett, although a "fire-eater" secessionist, saw the necessity of forming a national government for the Southern states. He introduced a resolution at the South Caro-

lina convention calling for another convention to be held in Montgomery, Alabama, for the purpose of forming a Southern Republic. Delegates from South Carolina, Mississippi, Florida, Alabama, Louisiana, and Georgia met in the Alabama capital on February 4, 1861, the Texas delegation arriving later. Cobb, the former Speaker of the United States House of Representatives and secretary of the Treasury, was elected president of the convention. A committee quickly drafted a provisional constitution, which was adopted on February 8, and the Confederate States of America was born.

The provisional constitution provided for the creation of an interim government for one year or until a permanent government should be established. The members of the convention became the provisional Congress and elected Jefferson Davis, of Mississippi, as provisional president, and Alexander Stephens, of Georgia, as provisional vice president. On February 18, 1861, Davis and Stephens were inaugurated, and Davis moved quickly to form a cabinet.

On March 11, the convention unanimously adopted a permanent constitution. It was similar to the U.S. Constitution in that it provided for three branches of the central government, further dividing power between the state governments and the central government. There also were important differences, reflecting both the states' rights principles and the interests of Southern agriculture. State sovereignty was expressly recognized; the president and vice president were elected for six-year terms, with a one-term limitation; the president was allowed to veto individual items in appropriations bills; slavery and the interests of the slaveholders were specifically upheld, including the right to transport slaves from state to state; slavery was established in the territories; participation in the international slave trade was outlawed, as a concession to Britain and France; protective tariffs were forbidden, in recognition of the South's economic role as an exporter of agricultural goods and an importer of manufactured goods; Confederate expenditures for internal improvements were prohibited; and a two-thirds vote of both houses of the Confederate congress was required to pass important appropriations bills.

The new government had hoped that it would be permitted to depart the Union in peace. However, with the firing on Fort Sumter, on April 12-13, 1861, all hopes for voluntary recognition by the Northern government vanished. The firing on Fort Sumter was followed by Lincoln's call for troops from the various states, including those of the upper South. These states were forced to join the Confederacy or participate in the coercion of the states of the Deep South. Although in each state of the upper South there was strong Union sentiment, Virginia, North Carolina, Tennessee, and Arkansas nevertheless joined the Confederacy in April and May. Missouri and Kentucky were divided and were claimed by both the Union and the Confederacy. Maryland and Delaware, the remaining slave states, did not join the Confederacy.

The Confederate Congress welcomed Virginia into the Confederacy by moving its capital to Richmond on July 20, 1861. On November 6, 1861, the first general elections were held under the permanent Constitution. Davis and Stephens were elected president and vice president of the "permanent" Confederacy. The fourth and last sessions of the provisional congress closed in February of 1862, when the new senate and house assembled. On February 22, 1862, Jefferson Davis was inaugurated president for a term of six years. The first congress under the permanent constitution of the Confederacy held four sessions and the second congress held two sessions, with the final adjournment of the body taking place in March, 1865.   —*Mark A. Plummer, updated by Susan M. Taylor*

ADDITIONAL READING:

Coulter, E. Merton. *The Confederate States of America, 1861-1865.* Baton Rouge: Louisiana State University Press, 1950. This large volume concentrates on life behind the lines in the Confederacy, dealing only briefly with the military campaigns of the war.

Davis, William C. *A Government of Our Own: The Making of the Confederacy.* New York: Free Press, 1994. Paints a detailed picture of secession and the creation of the Confederate States of America.

Eaton, Clement. *A History of the Southern Confederacy.* New York: Macmillan, 1954. A well-documented history of the Confederate States of America, including the disaffection of the Southern states and their secession.

Jones, Howard. *The Crisis over British Intervention in the Civil War.* Chapel Hill: University of North Carolina Press, 1992. Discusses the Civil War in detail, adding an international dimension to this period in history.

Roland, Charles P. *The Confederacy.* Chicago: University of Chicago Press, 1960. A comprehensive, easy-to-read history of the creation, rise, and fall of the Confederate States of America.

Thomas, Emory M. *The Confederacy as a Revolutionary Experience.* Columbia: University of South Carolina Press, 1991. Summarizes the major events and problems of the Confederacy; discusses the background of secession and the formation of the government.

Yearns, Wilfred B. *The Confederate Congress.* Athens: University of Georgia Press, 1960. Thorough description of the work of the Confederate Congress, which generally followed the administration's leadership.

SEE ALSO: 1860, Lincoln Is Elected President; 1861, Stand Watie Fights for the South; 1861, Lincoln's Inauguration; 1861, First Battle of Bull Run; 1862, *Monitor* vs. *Virginia*; 1863, Emancipation Proclamation; 1863, Battles of Gettysburg, Vicksburg, and Chattanooga; 1863, Reconstruction; 1864, Sherman's March to the Sea; 1865, Surrender at Appomattox and Assassination of Lincoln.

1861 ■ STAND WATIE FIGHTS FOR THE SOUTH: *a great Native American leads an Indian regiment for the Confederacy and is the last to surrender*

DATE: 1861-1865

LOCALE: Indian Territory, southwest Missouri, western Arkansas

CATEGORIES: Native American history; Wars, uprisings, and civil unrest

KEY FIGURES:

Jefferson Davis (1808-1889), president of the Confederate States of America

John Drew (1796-1865), Confederate Cherokee who led a regiment of full-blooded Cherokees

Ben McCulloch (1811-1862), Confederate Indian Territory commander

Albert Pike (1809-1891), Confederate commander, Department of Indian Territory

John Ross (1790-1866), principal chief of the Cherokee Nation

Stand Watie (1806-1871), Confederate general who led a regiment of mixed-blood American Indians

SUMMARY OF EVENT. With the outbreak of the Civil War in 1861, both the Union and the Confederacy looked toward the

Indian Territory for support. American Indians there, mostly members of the famed Five Civilized Tribes (the Cherokee, Chickasaw, Choctaw, Creek, and Seminole), had connections with the federal government through various agencies, but most also had Southern roots in the Carolinas, Alabama, Kentucky, Georgia, and Tennessee. In March, 1861, Confederate president Jefferson Davis commissioned Albert Pike to visit Indian Territory to seek treaties with the Five Civilized Tribes. It was hoped that a strong Confederate force in Indian Territory would prevent Union sympathizers in Kansas from raiding Texas. Pike's visit with all the tribes in Indian Territory was largely successful. Shortly afterward, General Ben McCulloch raised two American Indian regiments: one led by Colonel John Drew and the other by Colonel Stand Watie. Drew and Watie were bitter enemies, and during much of the war commanders on the western front kept the two Cherokee regiments separated as much as possible. Watie, a mixed-blood Cherokee, had been born in Georgia and was one of the signers of the New Echota Treaty, which sold Cherokee lands in Georgia to the United States government. He was also a prosperous Cherokee landowner and businessman, a brilliant warrior, and a member of an opposition faction within the Cherokee tribe. His signature on the new Echota Treaty put him at odds with the more dominant faction of the Cherokee Nation, led by John Ross.

Watie was a great leader, and even in the face of extreme hardships, especially during the winter months, he kept his regiment together and participated in numerous battles. Although the treaties that had been signed with the Confederacy promised that Indian regiments would not be required to fight outside Indian Territory, Watie's troops also were called to duty in Missouri and Arkansas. Over a four-year span, the old Cherokee warrior and his forces fought at Wilson's Creek, Newtonia, Bird Creek, Pea Ridge, Spavinaw, Fort Wayne, Fort Gibson, Honey Springs, Webber's Falls, Poison Spring, Massard Prairie, and Cabin Creek. Watie's abilities on the battlefield were widely recognized and greatly heralded by both his contemporaries and historians. His greatest skills were gaining and keeping the confidence of his troops and his wily guerrilla tactics. Watie's regiment, without his presence on the field, also fought the Second Battle at Newtonia in Southwest Missouri in 1864. The first Newtonia battle, fought in 1862, is of major historic significance, because it was the only Civil War battle in which American Indians fought on both sides. In most battles, Watie's Confederate Cherokees fought admirably. In a losing cause at the Battle of Pea Ridge in Arkansas, however, they and Colonel Drew's troops were accused of bad conduct because they were too easily routed during the battle and because they allegedly scalped some of the federal casualties. This act, when reported to the upper command of the Confederate Army, created a great embarrassment among officers, most of whom had been trained at such prestigious military academies as West Point, where cadets were taught to be gentlemen as well as warriors. The loss at Pea Ridge was made even greater by the death of General McCulloch, who had

Cherokee general Stand Watie would fight for the South to the bitter end of the Civil War, even after the Southern cause was clearly lost. (Library of Congress)

organized and fought with the Cherokees from the beginning.

Despite the overwhelming support given the Confederacy in 1861, when the tide of war turned in favor of the Union and the Confederacy became unable to supply its forces on the frontier, disenchantment took hold of the leaders of the various tribes. In February, 1863, the Cherokee Council met on Cowskin Prairie in Indian Territory and voted to end its alliance with the Confederacy. Colonel Watie refused to accept the vote and vowed to continue his fight. This created an even deeper split in the Cherokee tribe. Watie's forces and Cherokee civilians with attachments in the South remained loyal to Watie, even establishing a government that they claimed was the legitimate government of the Cherokee Nation. These Southern sympathizers elected Watie as the principal chief. Those now aligned with Union forces recognized John Ross as their chief, although he left Indian Territory and returned to his wife's family in Pennsylvania. At the time of this deepening split, there were about ten thousand Cherokees with Union sympathies and seven thousand supporters of the Confederacy. This situation actually created a civil war within a civil war.

On May 10, 1864, Watie was promoted to the rank of brigadier general, the only American Indian to attain this rank in the Civil War. In the remaining months of the conflict, General Watie fought without reservations for his beloved Confederacy. One of his most spectacular successes was the sinking of the steam-driven ferry *J. R. Williams* on the Arkansas River at Pleasant Bluff and making off with food and clothing for his Cherokee and Creek troopers, breaking a major supply route for Union forces at Fort Gibson. Successful raids on Union supplies kept Watie's forces busy, supplied, and inspired to stay in the fight.

Because the battlefield situation for the Confederacy was growing worse, Watie called all the Cherokee units to his camp on June 24, 1864. At that meeting, the Cherokee Troops, Confederate States of America, resolved to "unanimously re-enlist as soldiers for the war, be it long or short." In September of 1864, Watie masterminded a plan to attack and steal a Union supply-wagon train worth one million dollars. This battle was fought at Cabin Creek in Indian Territory and is said to have been Watie's greatest success. His brilliance and bravery were not enough, however, as the Confederacy was losing battle after battle. On April 9, 1865, General Robert E. Lee surrendered for the Confederacy at Appomattox Courthouse in Virginia. General Watie fought on, hoping to win the battle for the West, but it was not to be. On June 23, 1865, Brigadier General Stand Watie surrendered at Doakesville in Indian Territory, the last Confederate general to lay down his sword.

The contribution made by American Indians in the Civil War was enormous. An estimated 3,500 fought for the Union and 1,018, or more than 28 percent, died while in service to their country. Census figures in the Cherokee Nation showed a population of 21,000 in 1860. By 1867, that number had dropped to 13,566. Approximately one-third of the nation had been lost, either in battle or to hunger and exposure, which were suffered by soldiers and civilians alike. After the war, General Watie became more involved in the political activities of the Cherokee Nation and in resettling his people in the aftermath of the conflict. On September 7, 1871, the great general became ill and was taken to his old home at Honey Creek, where he died on September 9.   —*Kay Hively*

ADDITIONAL READING:

Cunningham, Frank. *General Stand Watie's Confederate Indians*. San Antonio, Tex.: Naylor, 1959. A full account of Stand Watie's efforts during the Civil War and his political life within the Cherokee Nation. Many photographs of that era.

Dale, Edward Everett, and Morris L. Wardell. *History of Oklahoma*. New York: Prentice-Hall, 1948. Contains a thorough chapter on the Civil War in Oklahoma by two outstanding Oklahoma historians.

Gaines, W. Craig. *The Confederate Cherokees: John Drew's Regiment of Mounted Rifles*. Baton Rouge: Louisiana State University Press, 1989. Concentrates on Colonel John Drew's regiment and contrasts it with Stand Watie's more successful regiment.

Josephy, Alvin M., Jr. *Civil War in the American West*. New York: Alfred A. Knopf, 1991. Discusses the Civil War battles that were fought west of the Mississippi River.

Woodworth, S. E. *Jefferson Davis and His Generals: The Failure of Confederate Command in the West*. Lawrence: University Press of Kansas, 1990. Discusses Jefferson's top military men and their leadership on the Western front during the Civil War.

SEE ALSO: 1828, *Cherokee Phoenix* Begins Publication; 1830, Indian Removal Act; 1830, Trail of Tears; 1831, Cherokee Cases; 1860, Confederate States Secede from the Union; 1861, First Battle of Bull Run; 1863, Battles of Gettysburg, Vicksburg, and Chattanooga; 1864, Sherman's March to the Sea; 1865, Surrender at Appomattox and Assassination of Lincoln.

1861 ■ APACHE WARS: *incursion of white settlers into the Southwest leads to armed conflicts with indigenous Chiricahua Apaches*

DATE: February 6, 1861-September 4, 1886
LOCALE: Southwest
CATEGORIES: Native American history; Wars, uprisings, and civil unrest
KEY FIGURES:
George Nicholas Bascom, U.S. Army lieutenant
Cochise, also known as *Goci*, or *His Nose* (c. 1812-1874), principal chief of the eastern Chiricahua
Mangas Coloradus, or *Red Sleeves* (c. 1791-1863), father-in-law to Cochise and an important chief of the eastern Chiricahua
George Cook, commander of the U.S. Army in southern Arizona territory
Charles Gatewood, U.S. Army lieutenant who was instrumental in persuading Geronimo to surrender
Geronimo (c. 1827-1909), shaman and important leader of the western Chiricahua
Nelson Miles (1839-1925), commander of the U.S. Army in Arizona after Cook
Edmond Shirland, generally believed responsible for the death of Mangas Coloradus
SUMMARY OF EVENT. After the signing of the Treaty of Guadalupe Hidalgo in 1848, large portions of northern Mexico were ceded to the United States. As a result of the acquisition of these new lands, numerous white settlers began moving into the newly formed Arizona and New Mexico territories. Much of this region was the traditional range of various Apache groups, particularly numerous bands of Chiricahua, Coyotero, and Mimbreño Apache. Many of these groups practiced raiding, taking goods from others as an extension of their traditional methods of subsistence. Raiding increased in frequency as more white settlers moved into Apache territory.

In 1861, an Apache raiding party (thought to have been Coyotero Apache, not Chiricahua) kidnapped a boy who had been a member of a group of white settlers. The U.S. military reacted quickly by ordering Lieutenant George Bascom to investigate the incident and, if necessary, to take action against the "hostiles" that were thought to have committed the raid. On February 6, 1861, Bascom, possibly as a result of an invitation to the Chiricahua, persuaded Cochise, the principal chief of the eastern Chiricahua, and some of his family and followers, to come in for a peace parley. During the early stages of what has been termed the Bascom affair, Cochise, speaking on behalf of the eastern Chiricahua, tried to convince Bascom that it was not Chiricahua Apache who had conducted the raid. Bascom had Cochise and several of the chief's relatives arrested. Cochise later escaped. Bascom, as an act of reprisal for the kidnapping and Cochise's escape, ordered the execution of the chief's relatives.

Although conflicts between white settlers and Apache groups had occurred before 1861, this incident is generally viewed by historians as the starting point of what has come to be called the Apache Wars. Numerous armed conflicts involving various Apache groups occurred from 1861 to 1886 on both sides of the U.S.-Mexican border. For example, in retaliation for the execution of his relatives, Cochise organized a surprise attack on the Gidding party at Stein's Peak near Doubtful Canyon. Cochise killed nine of the settlers but lost sixty of his warriors in the attack. Numerous battles ensued in the years that followed. In July of 1862, Cochise and his father-in-law Mangas Coloradus and other Chiricahuas were attacked by infantry under the command of "Star Chief Carleton." During the battle, Mangas Coloradus was wounded. Mangas Coloradus survived the wound, but in January of 1863 he was covertly executed and beheaded after he had attempted to surrender and sue for peace with captain Edmond Shirland of the California Volunteers. This sentence was delivered without any official record of a fair trial.

In the year 1865 the Apache wars reached a pinnacle. With the end of the American Civil War the attention of the United States military, along with the bulk of its forces, shifted west to land traditionally occupied by Native American tribal groups. Action taken against the Apache by the Mexican military was also increasing. In late winter of 1865, for example, Mexican Federales from Sonora attacked and killed thirty-nine Apaches. Mexican forces, combined with pressure exerted by U.S. military forces in the American Southwest, caused Cochise and other Apache leaders to remain constantly on the run. In 1866 Cochise was driven by U.S. forces into hiding in Mexico, where he continued to harass white settlers by periodically crossing the border to conduct surprise attacks. These skirmishes continued until October 10, 1872, when Cochise finally signed a truce with the Americans at Cochise's camp in the Dragoon mountains in southern Arizona. Cochise died two years later.

Other Apache leaders, however, refused to abide by the truce of 1872 and continued their attacks on settler groups. Further west Geronimo, a Bedonkohe/Chiricahua shaman from northern Mexico, was fighting his own wars against both Mexican and U.S. forces. By 1861 the U.S. Army was firmly established in southern Arizona. Forts Bowie and Apache had been built to assist the army in protecting the increasing numbers of settlers who continued to enter the Arizona territory. In 1871 the Camp Grant Massacre destroyed an entire Apache camp.

In 1872 General George Cook, who had a reputation among Washington politicians for decisiveness in his dealings with Indian groups, took command of the Southwest operation. From 1872 until 1886 and his dismissal, Cook's career was dominated by attempts to keep Geronimo in check. In 1877 Geronimo, along with family members and other Chiricahuas, was arrested by Cook's men. Geronimo and his people were subsequently resettled on the reservation at San Carlos. Sometimes referred to as "Hell's Forty Acres," San Carlos proved to be an inhospitable environment lacking sufficient water and game for Apache survival. The army, in an attempt to conciliate the Apache, introduced corn agriculture to the reservation. The Chiricahua were traditional hunters and gatherers and attempts at agriculture, especially on arid reservation land, soon failed. Four years later, many Apache—including Geronimo—fled the reservation. From 1881 until his surrender at Skeleton Canyon in 1886, Geronimo fought numerous battles with both U.S. and Mexican forces. He also continued raiding white settlements. During this period of time Geronimo surrendered several times to the U.S. military. Late in the year 1881, for example, Geronimo was recaptured by General George Cook and taken to Fort Apache. Geronimo and his followers were again taken to the reservation. Nothing had changed; the Apache could not make a sufficient living on the reservation, so they eventually fled to Mexico.

In April of 1882 Geronimo returned to San Carlos and conducted a raid. There he killed the chief of police and captured several Mimbreño Apache (former followers of the Apache leader Victorio), whom Geronimo forced to go back to Mexico with him. In May of 1883 Cook decided to pursue Geronimo by taking several units of infantry and cavalry into Mexico. On May 15, after several days of strenuous marching through Mexico's Sierra Madre, Cook attacked the camp of a group of Mimbreño Apache headed by Chato. Although the battle itself was indecisive, it had become evident that the military was not going to give up its pursuit of Geronimo. In the days that followed the battle several chiefs of the Mimbreño Apache, including Chato, Loco, and Nana, surrendered to Cook. In March of 1884 Geronimo, by now a revered Apache leader, surrendered to Cook. This surrender and the subsequent confinement on the reservation, like the others, did not last. Geronimo fled and surrendered two more times.

Historians generally agree that Cook's goal was to secure a lasting peace with Geronimo and other Apaches. Cook's inability to keep Geronimo under the purview of the U.S. government, however, forced military and political leaders in Washington, D.C., to remove Cook from his command. General Nelson Miles was sent to replace Cook. General Miles was not as sympathetic to the plight of the Apache as had been General Cook. General Miles immediately sent out a force of approximately five thousand soldiers to seek out and capture

Geronimo and his small band (estimated to be about twenty-four in number). On September 4, 1886, Geronimo, along with twenty-three members of his band of Chiricahuas (mostly women and children), surrendered for the final time at Skeleton Canyon—about sixty-five miles from Apache Pass, where the first skirmish of the Apache Wars had been fought. After Geronimo's surrender General Miles had all Chiricahuas in the immediate vicinity arrested, including the scouts that had been used by the army to track down Geronimo. Geronimo, his followers, and the former Apache scouts were placed in rail cars and transported east to a reservation in St. Augustine, Florida. With Geronimo's surrender and his removal to Florida, the Apache Wars ended.   —*Michael Shaw Findlay*

ADDITIONAL READING:

Cole, D. C. *The Chiricahua Apache, 1846-1876: From War to Reservation*. Albuquerque: University of New Mexico Press, 1988. A general history of Chiricahua with special attention to cultural conflicts with Euro-Americans.

Griffen, William B. *Apaches at War and Peace: The Janos Presidio, 1750-1858*. Albuquerque: University of New Mexico Press, 1988. Details the emergence of the Mexican presidio system and the subsequent relocation and resettlement of various Apache groups in southern New Mexico, Arizona, and northern Mexico.

————. *Utmost Good Faith: Patterns of Apache-Mexican Hostilities in Northern Chihuahua Border Warfare, 1821-1848*. Albuquerque: University of New Mexico Press, 1989. Summarizes historical accounts of hostilities between the Chiricahua Apache and Mexican military forces in Northern Mexico.

Skimin, Robert. *Apache Autumn*. New York: St. Martin's Press, 1993. A historical novel that describes the Apache Wars.

Stockel, Henrietta H. *Survival of the Spirit: Chiricahua Apaches in Captivity*. Las Vegas: University of Nevada Press. Describes the history of Chiricahua captivity, specifically during the period.

SEE ALSO: 1846, Mexican War; 1847, Taos Rebellion; 1848, Treaty of Guadalupe Hidalgo; 1853, Gadsden Purchase; 1862, Great Sioux War.

1861 ■ LINCOLN'S INAUGURATION: *even as tensions between North and South peak, Lincoln pledges to uphold the Union*

DATE: March 4, 1861
LOCALE: Washington, D.C.
CATEGORY: Government and politics
KEY FIGURES:

Edward Dickinson Baker (1811-1861), senator from Oregon
James Buchanan (1791-1868), fifteenth president of the United States, 1857-1861
Hannibal Hamlin (1809-1891), vice president of the United States

Abraham Lincoln (1809-1865), sixteenth president of the United States, 1861-1865
William Henry Seward (1801-1872), secretary of state
Roger Brooke Taney (1777-1864), chief justice of the United States

SUMMARY OF EVENT. Abraham Lincoln spent the evening of Election Day, November 6, 1860, reading the election returns at the telegraph office in Springfield, Illinois. The next day, he received congratulations on his election to the presidency at his temporary office in the State House. Lincoln remained in Illinois until February 11, 1861, when he began a personal appearance tour en route to the nation's capital. He arrived in Washington, D.C., at 6:00 A.M. on February 23—unannounced, because an assassination attempt was feared.

Lincoln's secretive arrival was symptomatic of the crisis atmosphere that the country experienced between his election and his inauguration. The constitutional provision that allowed a four-month delay in seating the president contributed to the crisis. Lincoln was powerless to take any official action that would quiet the fears of the South and was unwilling to commit himself publicly to a future course of action. Meanwhile, the lame-duck president, James Buchanan, stood by helplessly while seven states of the lower South seceded from the Union and took possession of most of the federal forts in the deep South.

Lincoln believed that it would be wise to remain in Illinois during most of his term as president-elect. Remaining at home would shield him to some extent from office-seekers, and it would enable him to remain silent concerning the crisis, over which he could have little control. He refused to make any statements on the subject, fearing that it would do no good and it might do harm.

Knowing that the situation was tense, Lincoln wanted to do nothing that would force the remaining slave states out of the union, but he also knew that Congress was due to adjourn in mid-April. Between the inauguration and Congress' departure, there was little time to do what might be necessary. What time there was to act with the full government in session could not be taken up with explaining speeches or clarifying positions. The president-elect also was cognizant that there were hotheads on both sides of the issue, North and South, who would seize on any remark, any act, no matter how trivial, to fan the flames of sectional conflict. With his hands tied by the four-month delay and tensions rising, the politically astute Lincoln preferred to wait until he was actually sworn in as president of the United States. Lincoln devoted the time to preparing his own inaugural address and to thinking through his various options, which were few indeed.

President-elect Lincoln also maintained a low profile because he was not certain of his role in the upcoming Republican administration. It would take some time to form his cabinet, which had to include a number of very prominent politicians, such as William Henry Seward and Salmon P. Chase, who were skeptical of Lincoln's administrative abilities and leadership qualities. Lincoln, from Illinois, was a man of the West, and many Eastern Republicans resented his position within the party. Although seven states had seceded before Lincoln left Illinois, he remained steadfast in his decision not to become involved in a public discussion concerning the crisis. Privately, however, he urged his Republican friends in Congress to stand firm against any compromise that might allow the extension of slavery.

The idea of compromise over issues pertaining to slavery was a political tradition. In the spirit of the famed compromiser Henry Clay, Kentucky senator John Jordan Crittenden introduced a measure that would prohibit the extension of slavery in all territory north of the old Missouri Compromise line of 1820 (36°30'). South of the line, slavery would be protected. Furthermore, there would, by federal law, be no interference with the domestic slave trade. A constitutional amendment would be introduced to prohibit any interference with slavery in any state. Southern senators expressed interest in the compromise if the incoming Lincoln Administration would openly endorse it. The argument that passage of the compromise promised to bring the South back into union found support among moderates in the Congress. Lincoln, on the other hand, quietly opposed the Crittenden Compromise because he felt that it would extend slavery into the territories. If the compromise were endorsed by Lincoln and his Republican supporters, the staunch nonextensionists and abolitionists within the Republican Party would be alienated from the new administration even before the president-elect's inauguration.

Lincoln began his journey to the capital on February 11. He made polite speeches before many of the state legislatures and in most of the major cities on his circuitous route. Rumors of attempts to assassinate the president-elect were widespread, but Lincoln refused to change his itinerary through Indiana, Ohio, New York, New Jersey, and Pennsylvania. After repeated warnings from his closest advisers, he did agree to pass unannounced through Baltimore, Maryland, at night, rather than risk an incident in that slave state. In Washington, D.C., during the ten days before his inauguration, he undertook a fatiguing round of conferences and courtesy calls.

March 4 dawned cloudy and raw, but it soon became bright and clear. General Winfield Scott, anticipating the worst, took extreme but unobtrusive measures to protect the president's route to the Capitol. Sharpshooters were placed on the roofs of the buildings, soldiers were spaced along the route, cannons were placed on the Capitol lawn, and the presidential carriage was guarded heavily by an escort detail. Lincoln and Buchanan entered the president's carriage a few minutes after noon for the ride to the Capitol. There, they entered the building through a boarded tunnel. The Senate was called to order, and Lincoln observed as the oath was administered to Hannibal Hamlin as vice president.

A crowd of more than thirty thousand was waiting in front of the portico of the unfinished Capitol building when, at about 1:00 P.M., the presidential party arrived on the platform. Lincoln was introduced by his old friend from Oregon, Sena-

tor Edward D. Baker. Lincoln put on his steel-rimmed spectacles and read his speech, which took about half an hour. Chief Justice Roger B. Taney then administered the oath of office, and the procession to the White House began.

Lincoln's inaugural address dealt exclusively with the secession crisis. Other topics, "about which there is no special anxiety, or excitement," were dismissed. Lincoln began by assuring the Southern states that their property, peace, and personal security were in no danger from the Republican administration. Lincoln took the position, however, that the Union of the States was perpetual. Because he was pledged to uphold the Constitution, he would use "the power confided to me . . . to hold, occupy and possess the property and places belonging to the government and to collect the duties." Lincoln qualified this statement by hinting that he would forgo the enforcement of federal laws "where hostility to the United States, in any interior locality" shall be universal. Lincoln ended his speech by placing the question of civil war in Southern hands. "The government will not assail you. You can have no conflict, without being yourselves the aggressors." He added: "We must not be enemies. Though passion may have strained, it must not break our bonds of affection."

The day after his inaugural, Lincoln was confronted with information that threatened the status quo. Major Robert Anderson, in command of Fort Sumter in the harbor off Charleston, South Carolina, reported that he could hold the fort for only a few weeks, unless he received provisions. Lincoln had to decide quickly whether to send provisions and risk hostilities or do nothing and see the fort, one of the few remaining symbols of federal authority in the South, abandoned. He decided to send provisions. The Confederacy, having been notified of his plans, bombarded the fort before it could be resupplied. The first shot was fired at 4:30 A.M., April 12, 1861. The Civil War had begun.

—*Mark A. Plummer, updated by James J. Cooke*

ADDITIONAL READING:

Baringer, William E. *A House Dividing: Lincoln as President Elect.* Springfield, Ill.: The Abraham Lincoln Association, 1945. This classic work contains a vast amount of important information.

Donald, David Herbert. *Lincoln.* New York: Simon & Schuster, 1995. An insightful biography that explains many of Lincoln's political motivations.

McPherson, James M. *Abraham Lincoln and the Second American Revolution.* New York: Oxford University Press, 1990. A major study of Lincoln and the Civil War as a revolutionary event.

_____. *Battle Cry of Freedom: The Civil War Era.* New York: Oxford University Press, 1988. A carefully crafted, prizewinning analysis of the Civil War.

Nevins, Allan. *Prologue to Civil War, 1859-1861.* Vol. 2 in *The Emergence of Lincoln.* New York: Scribner, 1950. A classic, useful, and detailed study of the coming of hostilities.

SEE ALSO: 1854, Birth of the Republican Party; 1858, Lincoln-Douglas Debates; 1860, Lincoln Is Elected President.

THE AMERICAN CIVIL WAR

Nov. 6, 1860	ABRAHAM LINCOLN'S ELECTION TO THE U.S. PRESIDENCY triggers the secession of South Carolina. *See* **1860, Lincoln Is Elected President.**
Dec. 20, 1860	SOUTH CAROLINA SECEDES FROM THE UNION, followed by Virginia (Apr. 17), Arkansas (May 6), Tennessee (May 7), North Carolina (May 20). West Virginia organizes its own government on June 11 and is admitted to the Union on June 20, 1863. Maryland, Kentucky, and Missouri eventually join the Union after bitter contention. *See* **1860, Confederate States Secede from the Union.**
Apr. 12, 1861	ATTACK ON FORT SUMTER: South Carolina's Palmetto Guard, under command of General P. G. T. Beauregard, opens fire on Fort Sumter following President Lincoln's announcement that he is sending reinforcements to that garrison. The Civil War begins.
Apr. 15, 1861	LINCOLN CALLS FOR MILITIAMEN: Announcing that an "insurrection" exists, Lincoln calls for a volunteer militia of 75,000 men for three months' service.
Apr. 19, 1861	BLOCKADE OF THE SOUTH: Lincoln announces that the United States will blockade the Confederate shore along the Atlantic and Gulf coasts. The declaration tacitly acknowledges existence of a state of war, although the conflict is still officially considered an insurrection. Lincoln asks Robert E. Lee to head the Northern army; Lee, considering his first duty to be to his state, opts to lead the Virginia militia instead.
May 13, 1861	GREAT BRITAIN DECLARES NEUTRALITY: In this announcement, the British recognize the Confederacy as a "belligerent," arousing Union concerns that Great Britain may go a step further and recognize the Confederate States as a sovereign nation.
July 21, 1861	FIRST BATTLE OF BULL RUN: Near Manassas Junction, Virginia, Union general Irvin McDowell and his green Union troops are routed by Southern forces under General Beauregard, reinforced by Joseph E. Johnston and Thomas J. "Stonewall" Jackson. What began as a spectator event, with townspeople packing picnic lunches to eat while watching the conflict, ends in a Northern rout. *See* **1862, First Battle of Bull Run.**
Nov. 8, 1861	*Trent* AFFAIR: The USS *San Jacinto* under Captain Charles Wilkes stops the British steamer *Trent* to take into custody two Confederate envoys to Great Britain, increasing Union-British tensions. After Lord Palmerston dispatches troops to Canada, Secretary of State William H. Seward orders the release of the two Confederates on Dec. 26, evading an international crisis.
Feb. 16, 1862	FALL OF FORT DONELSON: In Tennessee, Confederate troops at Fort Donelson under General Nathan Bedford Forrest surrender to General Ulysses S. Grant. Nashville falls on Feb. 25.
Mar. 6-8, 1862	BATTLE OF PEA RIDGE: Northern victory results in Union control of the bitterly divided state of Missouri.
Mar. 9, 1862	*Monitor* vs. *Virginia*: The South's ship *Virginia* (a rebuilt version of the *Merrimack*) meets the North's *Monitor* in the first battle of two ironclad vessels, revolutionizing naval warfare. The outcome of the battle is considered a draw. *See* **1862, *Monitor* vs. *Virginia*.**
Mar. 17, 1862	MCCLELLAN BEGINS HIS PENINSULAR CAMPAIGN: Failing to move quickly enough for Lincoln, head of the Union forces George B. McClellan is relieved of general command (Mar. 11) and placed in charge of the Army of the Potomac. He ignores Lincoln's orders to move directly against the Confederate capital at Richmond and launches his own campaign up the peninsula between the James and York rivers. Despite advancing within twenty miles of Richmond with superior forces, McClellan waits for reinforcements rather than attack while he has the advantage.
Apr., 1862	CONFEDERATE CONSCRIPTION ACT: Passed by the Confederacy, this draft law arouses controversy, especially because it exempts from the draft anyone who owns twenty or more slaves.
Apr. 6-7, 1862	BATTLE OF SHILOH: In the northern Mississippi River theater, Union forces under Grant and Confederate forces under Albert S. Johnston, after a number of battles for control of the region, clash at Shiloh. The battle is a two-day slaughter that ultimately results in a Southern retreat and Northern exhaustion. Both sides sustain heavy losses totaling approximately 23,000. Johnston is killed, to be replaced by Robert E. Lee.

THE CIVIL WAR, 1861-1865

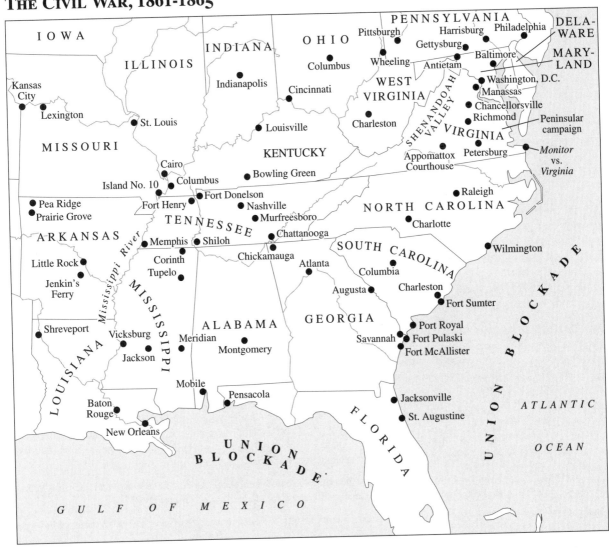

Apr. 28, 1862   FALL OF NEW ORLEANS: Commander of the West Gulf Blockading Squadron David G. Farragut destroys most of the Confederate fleet as he moves up the Mississippi River to bombard New Orleans. Union occupation of New Orleans is overseen by General Benjamin F. Butler, whose dictatorial methods arouse controversy.

May 25, 1862   JACKSON FORCES UNION RETREAT: Confederate general Stonewall Jackson pushes Union troops in the Shenandoah Valley back across the Potomac River and forces Northern states to send militia to defend Washington, D.C.

May 31, 1862   BATTLE OF FAIR OAKS AND SEVEN PINES: McClellan's army, now within five miles of Richmond but forced by rains flooding the Chickahominy River to split into two groups, is attacked by General Joseph E. Johnston. Both sides sustain losses totaling approximately 14,000.

June 26-July 2, 1862   SEVEN DAYS' BATTLE: Confederate general Robert E. Lee resolves to save Richmond, now under Union threat from McClellan. In a string of engagements, Stonewall Jackson and J. E. B. "Jeb" Stuart assist Lee in driving back Union forces despite the North's superior numbers. Casualties for both sides total approximately 25,000. Marks the end of McClellan's peninsular campaign.

July 17, 1862	CONFISCATION ACT: Congress passes legislation that frees slaves whose masters serve in the Confederate Army, but not slaves in the North. Has little practical emancipatory effect, but lays a legal foundation for the Emancipation Proclamation.
Aug. 28-30, 1862	SECOND BATTLE OF BULL RUN: Union commander Henry Halleck sends General John Pope to McClellan's aid near Richmond. Lee, moving to prevent the joining of the two Union forces, sends Stonewall Jackson to attack Pope's troops. The two forces meet at Bull Run, where the South succeeds in driving the North back to Washington, D.C.
Sept. 17, 1862	BATTLE OF ANTIETAM: Near Sharpsburg, Maryland, Union troops under McClellan force a Confederate retreat (under Lee) across the Potomac River. With 24,000 casualties, the day is the war's bloodiest yet.
Sept. 23, 1862	EMANCIPATION PROCLAMATION: Lincoln releases the Emancipation Proclamation to the newspapers. The proclamation states that slaves whose masters are Confederates as of Jan. 1, 1863, will be free as of that date. The announcement adds a second objective to the Union war: liberation of the slaves. In effect, few Southern slaves see immediate emancipation, although Union troops increase by the addition of African Americans to their ranks. *See* **1863, Emancipation Proclamation.**
Dec. 13, 1862	BATTLE OF FREDERICKSBURG: Exasperated by McClellan's procrastinations and refusals to attack, Lincoln has replaced him with Ambrose E. Burnside. With 113,000 Union to 75,000 Confederate troops, Burnside attacks Confederates at Fredericksburg, Virginia, but sustains severe losses. Lincoln replaces Burnside with Joseph Hooker.
Dec. 31, 1862	BATTLE OF MURFREESBORO: Confederate general Braxton Bragg is forced to withdraw from Tennessee by Union general William S. Rosecrans.
Mar. 3, 1863	CONSCRIPTION ACT: Congress passes the first federal draft law. The creation of a national military incites controversy regarding individual and state rights. In New York City (July 13-16), draft riots result in 128 killed—mostly blacks at the hands of Irish American immigrants. *See* **1863, First National Draft Law.**
May 2-4, 1863	BATTLE OF CHANCELLORSVILLE: Lee, holding position below the Rappahannock River since Fredericksburg, is attacked by Hooker. With 60,000 troops to the Union's 130,000, Lee divides his contingent in two, sending Stonewall Jackson through the dense area called the Wilderness to strike one flank of the Union. Results in a Union retreat but costs the South nearly 11,000 casualties—including the death of Stonewall Jackson.
July 1-3, 1863	BATTLE OF GETTYSBURG: Union forces under General George G. Meade rout Confederates under Lee; each side sustains approximately 25,000 casualties. The casualties are the worst yet, but the battle is a turning point: After a string of Southern victories, the North now has the upper hand. *See* **1863, Battles of Gettysburg, Vicksburg, and Chattanooga.**
July 4, 1863	FALL OF VICKSBURG: Union general Ulysses S. Grant takes Vicksburg, on the Mississippi River, from the command of Confederate general J. C. Pemberton after a grueling six-week siege. Secures the Mississippi River for the North. *See* **1863, Battles of Gettysburg, Vicksburg, and Chattanooga.**
Sept. 19-20, 1863	BATTLE OF CHICKAMAUGA CREEK: In northwestern Georgia, Union generals William Rosecrans and George Thomas engage Confederate generals Braxton Bragg and James Longstreet; 38,000 casualties. Union troops retreat to Chattanooga.
Nov. 19, 1863	GETTYSBURG ADDRESS: Lincoln delivers one of the briefest and most memorable speeches in history at the dedication of Gettysburg Cemetery in honor of the Gettysburg dead. Announcing "a new birth of freedom," Lincoln emphasizes the need to preserve a nation "dedicated to the proposition that all men are created equal," implying a new, higher purpose for the war: emancipation as well as preservation of a Union "of the people, by the people, for the people."
Nov. 24-25, 1863	BATTLE OF CHATTANOOGA (LOOKOUT MOUNTAIN AND MISSIONARY RIDGE): Now in command of the western armies, Grant joins forces with Generals William Tecumseh Sherman, Joseph Hooker, and George Thomas to push Confederate general Braxton Bragg south from Tennessee. Bragg is driven off Lookout Mountain but entrenches his troops on Missionary Ridge; Union forces under Thomas then storm the ridge and rout the Southern forces. This victory in the Mississippi region drives a wedge into the South, splitting the Confederacy. *See* **1863, Battles of Gettysburg, Vicksburg, and Chattanooga.**

Dec. 8, 1863	LINCOLN'S RECONSTRUCTION PLAN: Lincoln announces a plan for Reconstruction based on amnesty for Confederates who take a loyalty oath and recognition of Southern states in which 10 percent of the population has taken the oath and in which the state government has accepted emancipation of the slaves. Radical Reconstruction, instituted in 1867, will prove much more painful for the South. *See* **1863, Reconstruction.**
May 5-6, 1864	BATTLE OF THE WILDERNESS: In the thickly overgrown area near the site of the Chancellorsville battle one year before, the first confrontation in an unrelenting month of warfare pits Lee against Grant. The North is routed, and the South sustains heavy losses as well; casualties total about 28,000. Wounded soldiers left in the Wilderness are burned alive in a fire fueled by dead leaves and other debris.
May 8-12, 1864	BATTLE OF SPOTSYLVANIA COURTHOUSE: A five-day exchange of gunfire marks the longest continuous engagement to that time in military history. 20,000 casualties; the South loses Jeb Stuart.
June 1-3, 1864	BATTLE OF COLD HARBOR: Grant, pushing toward Richmond, loses 12,000 men (7,000 in less than ten minutes) and is accused of coldly sending his men into one of the most murderous engagements of the war.
June 15-18, 1864	SIEGE OF PETERSBURG: Grant outwits Lee for the first time, moving south of the James River to Petersburg rather than approaching Richmond from the north. A blunder by one of Grant's generals, however, prevents the Union from taking Petersburg. After Grant sustains heavy losses, troops on both sides settle in for ten months of trench warfare that anticipates World War I. General Burnside's strategy of opening Petersburg by igniting a five-hundred-foot-deep tunnel lined with gunpowder (July 30) creates a huge crater but ultimately fails.
June 27, 1864	BATTLE OF KENNESAW MOUNTAIN: In Georgia, Joseph E. Johnston defeats Union general William Tecumseh Sherman, who has been in charge of the Union's western war while Grant is at Petersburg. Sherman will rally to move toward Atlanta.
July, 1864	CONFEDERATE DRIVE NORTH: General Jubal Early moves into Maryland across the Potomac River, coming within five miles of Washington, D.C. Grant moves forces north from Petersburg to defend the capital, driving Early back into the Shenandoah Valley, where Union general Philip H. Sheridan defeats Early. Sheridan then destroys everything, using the same tactics as Sherman in Georgia.
Sept. 2, 1864	FALL OF ATLANTA: After engaging Confederate general John Bell Hood in July outside Atlanta, Sherman forces the South to evacuate the city. This Union victory breaks the North's despondency over the stagnating siege of Petersburg and helps Lincoln win reelection against unfavorable odds. Sherman will completely destroy Atlanta before leaving it on his march toward Savannah.
Nov. 15, 1864	SHERMAN'S MARCH TO THE SEA: On the principle that defeat of the South requires defeat of civilian supplies and infrastructure as well as troops, Sherman ruthlessly and methodically destroys everything in his path—animals, crops, buildings, equipment—as he moves toward Savannah on Georgia's Atlantic coast. Savannah falls on Dec. 22. *See* **1864, Sherman's March to the Sea.**
Dec. 15-16, 1864	BATTLE OF NASHVILLE: Union forces under Generals John M. Schofield and George H. Thomas destroy Confederate general John Bell Hood's forces and secure Tennessee for the North.
Apr. 9, 1865	LEE'S SURRENDER AT APPOMATTOX COURTHOUSE: Ill-clothed and starving, Confederate forces begin to desert their regiments; civilians too are gasping under the North's chokehold. Despite Confederate president Jefferson Davis' arming of the slaves, the war is coming to a close. Sherman, whose war machine has turned north into the Carolinas, meets Johnston at Bentonville in the final battle of the war (Mar. 19-20). At Richmond, the long siege of Petersburg ends when Grant's persistent battering of Lee finally drives him south into North Carolina. There Grant surrounds him, exacting his surrender on Apr. 9. *See* **1865, Surrender at Appomattox and Assassination of Lincoln.**
Apr. 14, 1865	ASSASSINATION OF LINCOLN: Enraged by Union victory, a Confederate sympathizer, actor John Wilkes Booth, takes advantage of Lincoln's decision to make a rare public excursion to the theater, shooting him at point-blank range as the president and Mary Todd Lincoln are seated in their private box. Lincoln dies the next morning at 7:30 A.M. *See* **1865, Surrender at Appomattox and Assassination of Lincoln.**
Apr. 18, 1865	JOHNSTON SURRENDERS TO SHERMAN: At Raleigh, North Carolina, Johnston surrenders to Sherman under terms similar to those concluded at Appomattox Court House. On May 26, a similar capitulation occurs at New Orleans, following the capture of President Davis in Georgia on May 10. The Civil War is over.

1861 ■ FIRST BATTLE OF BULL RUN: *the first major confrontation of the Civil War results in a victory for the South and a realization of the brutality of battle*

DATE: July 21, 1861
LOCALE: Bull Run Creek, or Manassas Junction, Virginia
CATEGORY: Wars, uprisings, and civil unrest
KEY FIGURES:
Pierre Gustave Toutant Beauregard (1818-1893), commander of Confederate troops near Manassas Junction
Thomas Jonathan "Stonewall" Jackson (1824-1863), Confederate general
Joseph Eggleston Johnston (1807-1891), commander of Confederate troops sent to reinforce Beauregard
Irvin McDowell (1818-1885), commander of Union troops in northern Virginia
James Ewell Brown "Jeb" Stuart (1833-1864), Confederate brigadier general

SUMMARY OF EVENT. The Civil War began April 12, 1861, at Charleston, South Carolina, when Confederate forces fired on Fort Sumter. For three months thereafter, small fights but no major battles occurred from the Atlantic coast west to Missouri. Then, during July, in the vicinity of a watercourse in northern Virginia called Bull Run, Union and Confederate soldiers met in the largest battle ever fought to that time on the North American continent. That great conflict, the First Battle of Manassas, or Bull Run, was the first of many bloody engagements that marked the road between Washington and Richmond, the capitals of the old Union and the new Confederacy.

With the decision, in May, 1861, to make Richmond the infant nation's capital, Confederate leaders began to strengthen their forces in northern Virginia. President Jefferson Davis brought his country's military hero, General Pierre G. T. Beauregard, the conqueror of Fort Sumter, to help direct those forces. These troops could both threaten Washington, D.C., and protect Richmond, from a suitable distance. The Confederates were divided into two main groups: one, under Beauregard, numbering about twenty-four thousand troops, was centered on Manassas Junction, thirty miles southwest of Washington; the other, under General Joseph E. Johnston, numbering about eleven thousand, was situated sixty miles west of Manassas, near Winchester, Virginia.

While the Confederates were establishing themselves in these positions, the North was beginning to build its military machine. After the battle at Fort Sumter, President Abraham Lincoln had issued an initial call for seventy-five thousand volunteers. Across the Union, armies were being formed. Directing this mobilization from Washington, seventy-five-year-old Winfield Scott, veteran of a half-century of military service and general in chief, tried to make order out of chaos. Under Scott, Brigadier General Irvin McDowell was in command of the Union forces stationed across the Potomac River in Virginia. From his headquarters in Arlington House, which had been the home of Robert E. Lee, McDowell strove to weld his raw recruits into an effective fighting force.

General Scott, who had more experience than any other officer in the United States Army, developed a plan for the war known as the Anaconda Plan. According to Scott's strategic concepts, the Union fleet would seize the Ohio and Mississippi Rivers, thereby dividing the Confederacy in two. The Navy would then blockade all major Southern ports, prohibiting exportation of cotton and importation of war material. The South then would be strangled slowly in a vise-like grip (hence the name Anaconda Plan). There would be few casualties, and best of all, a wholesale bloodbath involving Americans would be avoided, making reconciliation easier. Scott, who had worked so well with the Navy in the Mexican War, knew that it would take time to train the flood of volunteers, and the longer combat could be avoided, the better it would be for all concerned. Scott, a soldier, thought in military terms, and he did not have to face the tremendous political pressures that Lincoln was experiencing. Except for the naval blockade, Lincoln rejected Scott's plan in favor of more direct, immediate attacks demanded by his Northern constituency. (Through bitter experience, the Union would eventually gain victory by a process that, in most essentials, resembled Scott's original plan.)

The troops pouring into Washington were totally ignorant of war, and they had not the slightest idea of drill, military discipline, or camp sanitation. Many Northern units wore gray uniforms, and many Southern troops wore blue uniforms. For both sides, there was a bewildering variation in weapons. Some Rebels and Yankees arrived in their camps with antiquated flintlock muskets and obsolete smoothbore muskets. Officers on both sides read the drill manual while putting their troops through the required formations. With many units bringing cooks from the best restaurants in New York or New Orleans, the opposing camps took on the air of summer outings rather than schools for war. Scott knew that these "green" attitudes would spell disaster when the issue was finally joined on the battlefield.

While Scott and McDowell wanted time to organize and train their troops, Northern public opinion demanded action. A clamor arose for a march to Richmond to put down the rebellion in order to teach the Rebels a lesson. President Lincoln also urged offensive movement, for he believed the North had to attack to win. Finally, upon Lincoln's order, McDowell's untried army of about thirty-five thousand moved south toward Beauregard's Confederates. No previous American had ever taken so large an army into battle.

Beauregard, with his army drawn up behind a small stream named Bull Run, knew about McDowell's advance. To reinforce the defending army, the Confederate government ordered General Joseph E. Johnston to come to Beauregard's aid. Johnston began transferring his troops eastward, but before Beauregard could launch his attack, McDowell struck. On the morning of July 21, he ordered his army across Bull Run and hit Beauregard's left flank. His well-planned assault drove the Confederates back in chaos and confusion. The inexperienced troops on both sides fought well, but the Union soldiers steadily forced the Confederates to retreat toward Henry House Hill, the commanding topographical feature on the battlefield. As the advancing Union regiments approached the hill, they ran into elements of Johnston's army. Johnston had used the railroad to transport his soldiers (a first in warfare), which enabled him to move rapidly to make his junction with Beauregard. Just as the Confederate line on Henry House Hill seemed about to break, General Bernard Bee of South Carolina pointed to a Virginia brigade on the crest and shouted to his beleaguered comrades that it was standing like a stone wall against the Union onslaught. General Thomas J. Jackson's stand saved the day for the Confederate troops and earned the general the sobriquet "Stonewall."

With Johnston's fresh troops, the Confederates began advancing. Initially, the Northern units withdrew in an orderly fashion. Suddenly Union units were attacked with great violence by Colonel Jeb Stuart's First Virginia Cavalry. Heat, weariness, and lack of water and food began to take their toll, and the Northern troops began, often with no orders, to withdraw from the field. Officers tried with varying degrees of success to keep the troops on the field, while some took charge of the withdrawing regiments to ensure some semblance of order. When Confederate artillery fire caused the blocking of a key bridge, the retreat became a rout. Caught up in the Union rout were dignitaries from Washington, including congressmen, who had come down to have a Sunday picnic in the countryside and watch the gallant Northern boys "whip the Rebels."

Although the Confederates had defeated their enemy and possessed the battlefield, they could not press their advantage. They were too exhausted and too disorganized to mount a major pursuit and threaten Washington. The Confederates had administered the Union a smashing defeat, yet, like most of the battles that were to follow, this one was indecisive, for it produced neither serious military disadvantage for the North nor advantage for the South. The First Battle of Bull Run was widely celebrated in the South, but it was Lincoln and the North that began a serious training and supply program for their troops. In this, the Union gained a slight advantage from the battle.

Although it would be dwarfed in size and ferocity in the months ahead, this first great battle clearly demonstrated that the North and the South were faced, not with a romantic adventure, but with a real and brutal war.

—*William J. Cooper, Jr., updated by James J. Cooke*

ADDITIONAL READING:

Catton, Bruce. *Mister Lincoln's Army.* Garden City, N.Y.: Doubleday, 1951. A classic, well-written narrative of the start of the Civil War.

Davis, William C. *Battle at Bull Run.* Garden City, N.Y.: Doubleday, 1977. The most detailed account of the battle, filled with personal detail.

_____. *First Blood: Fort Sumter to Bull Run.* Alexandria: Time-Life Books, 1983. Balances campaign history with personal accounts.

Henderson, G. F. *Stonewall Jackson and the American Civil War.* 2 vols. London: Longmans, 1932. Still a classic in the field.

Williams, T. Harry. *P. G. T. Beauregard: Napoleon in Gray.* Baton Rouge: Louisiana State University Press, 1955. Still the major work on Beauregard to date.

SEE ALSO: 1860, Lincoln Is Elected President; 1860, Confederate States Secede from the Union; 1861, Lincoln's Inauguration; 1862, *Monitor* vs. *Virginia*; 1863, Emancipation Proclamation; 1863, First National Draft Law; 1863, Battles of Gettysburg, Vicksburg, and Chattanooga; 1863, Reconstruction; 1864, Sherman's March to the Sea; 1865, Surrender at Appomattox and Assassination of Lincoln.

1861 ■ TRANSCONTINENTAL TELEGRAPH IS COMPLETED: *extension of telegraph wires from the Mississippi River to the West Coast catalyzes communication and trade, tightening the union between East and West*

DATE: October 24, 1861
LOCALE: Western United States
CATEGORIES: Communications; Science and technology
KEY FIGURES:

Edward Creighton (1820-1874), construction superintendent of the Pacific Telegraph Company

Stephen J. Field (1816-1899), chief justice of California, 1859-1863, and associate justice of the U.S. Supreme Court, 1863-1897

Amos Kendall (1789-1869), journalist, public administrator, Morse's business manager, and a major promoter of telegraph service

John Middleton, president of the California State Telegraph Company

Hiram Sibley (1807-1888), president of the Western Union and Missouri Telegraph Company

Jeptha H. Wade (1811-1890), founder of the Overland Telegraph Company

SUMMARY OF EVENT. The significance of the electromagnetic telegraph, successfully demonstrated by Samuel F. B. Morse in 1836 and later made operational by the Washington-Baltimore forty-mile line in 1844, was recognized in the United States west of the Mississippi River only in the early 1850's. During that hiatus, private companies came to see the possibilities inherent in an apparatus able to send messages over long distances by using a code of some kind. At first, however, telegraph companies were organized helter-skelter. Thus, in 1853, the California State Telegraph Company was established to connect San Francisco with Marysville by an indirect line running via San Jose, Stockton, and Sacramento. The prosperity of this line led to the construction of a telegraph line from Sacramento eastward to Placerville, Auburn, Grass Valley, and Nevada City by the Alta Telegraph Company in 1854. Newspaper editors in both San Francisco and Sacramento began to encourage the building of a line southward through the San Joaquin Valley to obtain and relay news brought by the overland stage from the East with the greatest speed possible. By October, 1860, telegraphic communication between San Francisco and Los Angeles had been established. In 1859, the California legislature had pledged six thousand dollars a year to the first telegraph company connecting that state with the East. In anticipation of technical difficulties or a temporary break of the line by bad weather or raids by American Indians, the legislature pledged four thousand dollars for a second line.

In 1858, similar developments were taking place in Missouri, where one company had installed glass insulators on the trees along the banks of the Missouri River and strung wire between them all the way from St. Louis to Kansas City by way of Booneville. Another group of promoters began a line from Memphis to Fort Smith, Arkansas, intending to follow the route of the Butterfield Overland Mail Company, and they encouraged another company to start work eastward from Los Angeles on the same route. To avoid the necessity of procuring and erecting poles, and possibly to prevent disruption of the line by Indians, one impractical promoter thought that the best scheme was to lay the cable along the bottom of the Canadian River between Fort Smith and Santa Fe, New Mexico.

By the mid-1850's, telegraph lines by fledgling companies proliferated and competition between them gave way to profitable mergers as the telegraph was pushed westward. Short, disconnected, decrepit lines were rebuilt and combined into existing networks. The United States government was also taking an active interest in the process. On June 16, 1860, Congress passed the Pacific Telegraph Act, allocating forty thousand dollars a year for ten years to any company stringing a telegraph line from the western boundary of the state of Missouri to San Francisco, with the understanding that the government was to have priority in the use of the line to transmit official messages free of charge. The contract was obtained by the Western Union and Missouri Telegraph Company, which was aggressively represented by Hiram Sibley, its president. In 1856, Sibley had begun consolidating several new companies into the Western Union Company, providing a powerful boost to the completion of the transcontinental telegraph. Edward Creighton, the construction superintendent, spent the entire summer of 1860 in the West surveying and gathering information. Among other actions, he notified the citizens of Denver that, if they wanted the line to run through their community, they would have to buy twenty thousand dollars in company stock. When they refused, he recommended that the telegraph be strung along the regular emigrant trail from Fort Laramie to the South Pass, located in Wyoming.

Meanwhile, Sibley had dispatched Jeptha H. Wade to con-solidate the chaotic telegraph industry in California into the Overland Telegraph Company, with capital of $1,250,000. This company, under the superintendency of James Gamble, was to push a line eastward from Carson City, Nevada, through Ruby Valley, Egan Canyon, and Deep Creek—the route of the Pony Express—to Salt Lake City, Utah. The Missouri and Western Telegraph Company, which operated a telegraph system between St. Louis and Omaha, Nebraska, established the Pacific Telegraph Company to build a line, under the direction of Edward Creighton, from Omaha up the Platte River via Fort Kearney to Fort Laramie, then up the Sweetwater River to South Pass and on to Salt Lake City.

The physical and human difficulties were great. Wires and insulators for the western section had to be shipped from New York to San Francisco via Cape Horn and then hauled eastward over the Sierra Nevada and the deserts beyond. The task of delivering and distributing poles on the treeless plains was monumental. Barrels of water had to be hauled into the desert by teams for the construction crews working in the summer of 1861. The Mormons were reluctant to have the telegraph line built across Utah and were uncooperative in providing timber and workers. The goodwill of the American Indians through whose lands the line was to pass had to be secured. In spite of these obstacles, construction of the line was so well organized and energetically pursued by both Creighton and Gamble that the wires were connected in Salt Lake City on October 24, 1861, much earlier than expected. That evening, Stephen J. Field, chief justice of California and brother of Cyrus W. Field, promoter of the first Transatlantic cable, notified President Abraham Lincoln that the task was completed. Sensing the importance of the event, he stated that the telegraph would bind both East and West to the Union and proclaimed the loyalty of the citizens of the Pacific coast to government of the United States.

The extension of telegraph lines from the Mississippi River to the West Coast had a profound impact on several aspects of American life. Newspapers now came to include "telegraph news." Stockbrokers and businesspersons could move important information at great speed. Railroads became the most valuable partners of the telegraph. For example, railroads agreed to lay telegraph lines along their rights-of-way. They provided office space in depots for telegraphers, employed both by them and by the telegraph company, and provided free transportation to those who repaired telegraph lines. The major telegraph company west of the Mississippi River, Western Union, contracted to transmit messages relating to railroad business free of charge and to give priority to wires concerning the movement of trains. In this way, traffic could be better coordinated and railroad safety increased. In exchange, the railroads offered Western Union a monopoly of protected routes. Thanks to the western telegraph, the North American continent became unmistakably smaller.

—W. Turrentine Jackson, updated by Peter B. Heller

ADDITIONAL READING:

Gabler, Edwin. *The American Telegrapher: A Social His-*

tory, 1860-1900. New Brunswick, N.J.: Rutgers University Press, 1988. Informative historical account of the development of the wiring of the West and the people involved. Illustrated; useful bibliography.

Harlow, Alvin F. *Old Wires and New Waves: The History of the Telegraph, Telephone, and Wireless.* New York: D. Appleton-Century, 1936. Still one of the classics on the subject. Discusses the history of the Western Union Telegraph Company and its leaders. Bibliography, illustrations.

Kendall, Amos. *Autobiography.* New York: Peter Smith, 1971. The life story of one of the leading early advocates of telegraphy includes interesting historical vignettes.

Kranzberg, Melvin, and Carroll W. Pursell, Jr., eds. *The Emergence of Modern Industrial Society, Earliest Times to 1900.* Vol. 1 in *Technology in Western Civilization.* New York: Oxford University Press, 1967. The article on communications provides a brief but pointed summary of the development and impact of the telegraph.

Pursell, Carroll W., Jr., ed. *Technology in America: A History of Individuals and Ideas.* Cambridge, Mass.: MIT Press, 1981. The introduction provides the social context in which vast distances were overcome by railroad and telegraph in the mid-nineteenth century.

Thompson, Robert L. *Wiring a Continent: The History of the Telegraph Industry in the United States, 1832-1866.* Princeton, N.J.: Princeton University Press, 1947. An excellent account of the early years. Highlights the physical achievements and colorful individuals involved, and the impact of the first large-scale major application of electricity through the telegraph.

SEE ALSO: 1844, First Telegraph Message; 1858, First Transatlantic Cable; 1869, Transcontinental Railroad Is Completed; 1876, Bell Demonstrates the Telephone.

1862 ■ MONITOR VS. VIRGINIA: *a battle between ironclad ships marks the beginning of a new era in naval warfare*

DATE: March 9, 1862

LOCALE: Hampton Roads, Virginia

CATEGORIES: Science and technology; Wars, uprisings, and civil unrest

KEY FIGURES:

Franklin Buchanan (1800-1874), commander of the *Virginia*

John Ericsson (1803-1889), Swedish American inventor, designer, and builder of the *Monitor*

Samuel Dana Greene (1840-1884), lieutenant who commanded the *Monitor* after Worden's wounding

Catesby ap Roger Jones (1821-1877), lieutenant commander of the *Virginia* during its battle with the *Monitor*

Stephen Russell Mallory (1813?-1873), Confederate secretary of the navy

Gideon Welles (1802-1878), Union secretary of the navy

John L. Worden (1818-1897), commander of the *Monitor* until wounded in combat with the *Virginia*

SUMMARY OF EVENT. To build a new navy while his new nation was engaged in a war for survival, Confederate secretary of the navy Stephen R. Mallory determined to adapt new technologies. First on his agenda was equipping his navy with ironclad warships. Although both France and England were building such vessels, the Union navy had maintained its faith in wooden frigates, sloops, and gunboats. The new Southern nation, agrarian in outlook and character, had neither the skilled shipbuilding personnel nor the iron-manufacturing industry to lay down a fleet of iron-armored war vessels immediately. Yet Mallory lobbied the Confederate Congress for such new and expensive technology, telling them, "I regard the possession of an iron armored vessel as a matter of the first necessity." The Confederacy could never compete with the U.S. Navy in numbers of vessels, he said; thus, armored ships that could stand up to squadrons of wooden-walled frigates were essential.

Mallory sent agents to England to order ironclads from British and Scottish naval yards, and at home, put naval lieutenant John M. Brooke and naval constructor John L. Porter to work designing an ironclad to be built in the Confederacy. Independently, both developed the same design—the ship's gun deck protected by an armored casemate, its sides sloping inward to ricochet enemy shot. The decks fore and aft of the casemate would ride at water level, and boilers and machinery would be carried below the waterline to further protect them from enemy fire.

Union secretary of the navy Gideon Welles, blessed with a strong fleet of conventional wooden warships, was less inclined toward new technology than were others, such as Swedish-born inventor John Ericsson. Ericsson took a number of recent ideas and combined them into a new and radical ironclad design. Instead of a long casemate housing many guns, his ironclad would mount two huge cannons in a round, revolving turret, set squarely in the center of a flat-decked iron ship.

When the Union navy abandoned its base at Norfolk, Virginia, to the Confederates, it burned and scuttled several war vessels, including the six-year-old steam frigate *Merrimack*. The frigate's hull, the Rebels found, would make a good platform for their casemated ironclad, and the conversion began. When word of it reached President Abraham Lincoln and Secretary Welles, it spurred the Union navy into immediate action on ironclads. The peculiar vessel John Ericsson called the *Monitor* was now a top naval priority.

The Confederates named the ship they built from the remains of the *Merrimack* the CSS *Virginia*. Yet, perhaps because of the alliterative properties of "the *Monitor* and the *Merrimack*," the name of the earlier, U.S. wooden frigate has been used most often to identify the Confederate vessel. Even during the war, Confederate citizens and newspapers referred to the Confederate ironclad *Virginia* as the *Merrimack*.

The race to have an ironclad combat-ready and on the eastern fighting front resulted in a draw. The *Monitor*, built in one hundred days, showed development problems on her trial runs. Her speed was minimal because of a malfunctioning blower, and she would barely answer her helm: She weaved like a drunkard between the shores of Brooklyn and Manhattan. Ericsson fixed these problems, and on March 6, 1862, the *Monitor* left New York bound for Hampton Roads to meet the threat of the *Virginia*.

The Confederates' *Virginia* made her trial run on March 8, steaming toward the U.S. blockading squadron in Hampton Roads. The vessel's commander, Franklin Buchanan, made it a trial by fire, steaming with an untried, ten-gun vessel into the teeth of the enemy's naval might. The *Virginia* rammed and sank the forty-four-gun *Cumberland* and chased aground the fifty-gun *Congress*, the forty-six-gun *Minnesota*, and the forty-six-gun *St. Lawrence*. The *Virginia*'s shells set the *Congress* afire. The Yankees' return fire had no effect on the ironclad.

Burning and aground, the *Congress* surrendered. Confederate gunboats moved in to evacuate wounded sailors from the vessel, drawing small arms fire from U.S. soldiers ashore. Captain Buchanan returned fire from the *Virginia*'s foredeck and was wounded in the thigh. Command of the ironclad passed to his executive officer, Catesby ap R. Jones. With the tide falling, two Union ships destroyed, and two more aground and awaiting execution, Jones avoided grounding the *Virginia* by taking her back to her moorings near Norfolk. The next morning, with the rising tide, the *Virginia* steamed back into the Hampton Roads to finish off the wooden fleet. Unexpectedly, she encountered the *Monitor*, which had arrived during the night. The two immediately locked in combat, the wooden ships all but forgotten.

Carrying only explosive shell (no solid shot) in anticipation of fighting only wooden ships, the *Virginia* was unable to penetrate the *Monitor*'s armor. One of her shells damaged the *Monitor*'s pilot house, however, wounding her captain, Commander John L. Worden. Lieutenant S. Dana Greene assumed command. The *Monitor*'s shot broke some iron plating on the *Virginia* but could not penetrate her armor. For four hours, the two heavyweights fought it out, giving spectators around Hampton Roads a show some thought to be the greatest naval battle of all time.

A falling tide finally forced the deep-draft *Virginia* to break off the engagement and steam for home. She returned to a hero's welcome, but Jones and others aboard were frustrated at having sunk neither the *Monitor* nor the *Minnesota*. In four hours' combat, Jones had developed a great respect for the *Monitor*. "Give me that vessel," he told a friend, "and I will sink this one in twenty minutes." In subsequent days, the *Virginia* was unable to force the *Monitor* to resume the duel. Secretary Welles forbade the *Monitor* the option of renewing the fight unless it were absolutely necessary to save the wooden blockading fleet.

Southerners looked to subsequent Confederate ironclads to break the Union blockade of their port cities. Mallory had thought that the *Virginia* could steam to New York, carrying the war to the north and laying that city under tribute. Buchanan told him that was impossible: The *Virginia* was not seaworthy. (Neither was the *Monitor*. She went down at sea within weeks after the *Virginia* was burned when McClellan's army forced the evacuation of Norfolk.) This quick dashing of Mallory's offensive hopes may have made him more amenable to President Jefferson Davis' idea of fighting a strictly defensive war. Thus, the score and more of Confederate ironclads the *Virginia* spawned stayed mostly on the defensive, successfully holding the ports of Mobile, Savannah, Charleston, and Wilmington, as well as the capital city of Richmond, against the Union Navy. All were taken, like Norfolk, by armies from the rear.

The *Monitor*, too, begat copies. This style of Union ironclad proved superior, with its lighter draft, heavily armored turret, and larger guns, when tried in battle against the Confederate ironclads *Atlanta* and *Tennessee*; and its revolving turret became the standard of the world's navies for the next century.

Armored ships and floating batteries had seen combat before the *Virginia* fought the *Monitor*, but the devastation the *Virginia* wrought on the U.S. wooden ships, and the publicity surrounding the entire Hampton Roads affair, made the contest of the *Virginia* and the *Monitor* the defining moment in the world's move from wood to armor in naval warfare.

—*Maurice K. Melton*

ADDITIONAL READING:

Baxter, James P., III. *The Introduction of the Ironclad Warship*. Cambridge, Mass.: Harvard University Press, 1933. A scholarly analysis of the British, French, and U.S. ironclad programs, including the *Virginia*, the *Monitor*, and other Confederate and Union ironclads.

Brooke, John M., and John L. Porter. "The Plan and Construction of the *Merrimack*." In *Battles and Leaders of the Civil War*, edited by Robert U. Johnson and Clarence C. Buel. Vol. 1. New York: Century, 1887. This and six other articles by participants provide fascinating reading and are invaluable for their insight and detail. As with all participants' accounts, they must be read with a critical eye.

Durkin, Joseph T. *Stephen Russell Mallory: Confederate Navy Chief*. Chapel Hill: University of North Carolina Press, 1954. The standard study of the Confederate secretary of the navy.

Scharf, J. Thomas. *History of the Confederate States Navy*. New York: Rogers & Sherwood, 1887. This giant work by a Confederate midshipman and postwar Baltimore attorney has been the standard work on the Confederate navy for more than a century.

Still, William N., Jr. *Iron Afloat: The Story of the Confederate Armorclads*. Nashville, Tenn.: Vanderbilt University Press, 1971. Reprint. Columbia: University of South Carolina Press, 1985. The standard work on the Confederacy's ironclad warships.

SEE ALSO: 1776, First Test of a Submarine in Warfare; 1807, Voyage of the *Clermont*; 1845, Era of the Clipper Ships.

1862 ■ HOMESTEAD ACT: *response to the demand for land in the West stimulates settlement of vast territories*

DATE: May 20, 1862
LOCALE: Washington, D.C.
CATEGORIES: Expansion and land acquisition; Laws and acts
KEY FIGURES:
Thomas Hart Benton (1782-1858), Democratic senator from
   Missouri and early advocate of homestead legislation
George Henry Evans (1805-1856), labor leader in New York
   and advocate of a liberal land policy
Horace Greeley (1811-1872), editor of the *New York
   Tribune*, reformer, and advocate of homestead legislation
Andrew Johnson (1808-1875), Democratic senator from
   Tennessee who led the fight for homestead legislation
Abraham Lincoln (1809-1865), sixteenth president of the
   United States, 1861-1865

SUMMARY OF EVENT. The United States grew enormously between 1840 and 1860. The continental limits of the nation were reached, with the exception of Alaska, by 1854, through the acquisition of Mexican territory ceded in the Treaty of Guadalupe Hidalgo (1848) and the Gadsden Purchase (1853). The population continued its upward spiral, moving from slightly more than seventeen million in 1840 to more than thirty million in 1860. Canals, steamboats, turnpikes, and railroads knot the nation together into an integrated economic unit. Hundreds of thousands of people crossed the Atlantic to take up residence in the dynamic nation, while other hundreds of thousands moved into the western regions of the country.

The growth of the West was especially marked. While the population of all sections grew, the North and the South experienced less relative growth during these two decades than did the West. The West achieved a position of equality with the older sections during this period and became more insistent in its demands upon the government.

The intensification of sectional antagonisms engendered by the controversy over slavery and its future in the nation fatally obstructed efforts at the national level to provide guidelines and incentives for growth. By the opening of the 1840's, sectional lines had hardened. Southern majorities in Congress consistently blocked legislation called for by the other sections of the country. This was true in debates over the tariff, internal improvements, central banking, and land policy. The West won a significant victory in the debate over the disposition of the public domain with the passage of the Preemption Act of 1841, which gave squatters the right to purchase up to 160 acres of land that they had settled and improved for $1.25 per acre. The next logical step for Westerners was for the government to provide completely free land as a reward for those who settled and developed the region.

The campaign to achieve free land was waged on two fronts. Westerners such as Missouri senator Thomas Hart Benton consistently pushed for such legislation and were joined by increasing numbers of other Westerners committed to the free-soil idea. The slavery controversy erupted vigorously during the Mexican War, with efforts by free-soil Whigs to pass the Wilmot Proviso. It was obvious that the idea of free homesteads would work to the advantage of free-soil groups, by attracting into the newly won territories the more mobile population of the North. Therefore, the Free-Soil Party made homestead legislation part of its platform for the 1848 campaign. By the 1850's, most Northerners accepted the idea that the land should be settled as rapidly as possible in order to bring it into production and to provide a stable population that would serve as a market for the industrial centers in the East. The Eastern-based Land Reform movement, led by George Henry Evans and supported by Horace Greeley and his *New York Tribune*, rounded out the alliance.

The struggle for homestead legislation was waged in Congress during the 1850's. The congressional sessions of 1851, 1852, and 1854 devoted much time to such proposals. Southerners were opposed to the concept and argued that no benefits would accrue to their section. In spite of the leadership of Andrew Johnson of Tennessee, the Senate, dominated by the Southern wing of the Democratic Party, managed to block passage of several bills that passed the House of Representatives. When the Senate finally passed a homestead bill, in 1860, it was vetoed by President James Buchanan. The Republican Party committed itself to this policy and incorporated a homestead plank in its platform of 1860.

The election of Abraham Lincoln in 1860 did not guarantee the passage of homestead legislation, because the South still controlled the Senate. The secession of the Southern states made passage possible. During the special session of Congress in 1861, a bill was introduced into the House and passed in February, 1862. It passed the senate in May and was signed by President Lincoln on May 20.

Under the provisions of the bill, which was to go into effect January 1, 1863, a settler twenty-one years of age or older who was, or intended to become, a citizen and who acted as the head of a household could acquire a tract of acres of surveyed public land free of all but a $10 registration payment. Title to that land went to the settler after five years of continuous residence. Alternatively, after six months, the claimant could purchase the land for $1.25 per acre. Over the years, amendments and extensions of the act made it applicable to forest land and grazing land and enlarged the maximum acreage tract that the settler could acquire.

In 1873, the Timber Culture Act attempted to adjust the original act to more arid Western conditions by allowing the homesteading of an additional 160 acres on which the homesteader agreed to plant at least 40 acres (later reduced to 10 acres) of trees. The Desert Land Act of 1877 allowed Western ranchers to homestead up to a square mile, or 640 acres, of ranch land in certain areas. In the 1930's executive decisions by President Franklin Delano Roosevelt and the Taylor Grazing Act withdrew the remainder of the public domain from private entry. By then, 285 million acres had been homesteaded.

PATHWAYS TO THE WEST, 1840'S-1860'S

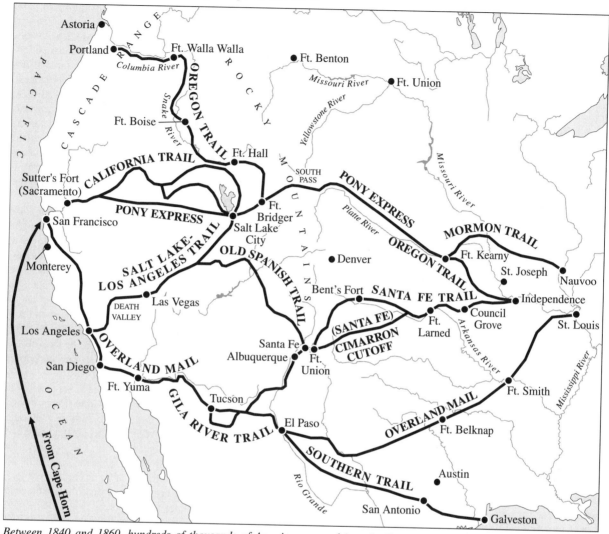

Between 1840 and 1860, hundreds of thousands of Americans moved into the Western regions of the United States, at first in search of wealth during the California gold rush, and later in search of land and a new life. Trails originally carved by explorers such as Meriwether Lewis and William Clark, Zebulon Pike, the Astorians, and the Mormons became the pathways, roads, and railway tracks to the West.

The Homestead Act was not the complete success its supporters hoped it would be. Homesteading was never attractive to the working class and urban poor in the East. There also were many competing forms of federal land distribution, including purchase by speculators, massive land grants to railroads, the sale of dispossessed Native American lands, and Morrill Act lands turned over to states for sale to support public education. Altogether, more than 80 percent of public lands were distributed through means other than homesteading. In addition, fewer than half of the nearly three million homesteaders who filed claims actually "proved up" and acquired title to the land after five years. A "Southern" Homestead Act of 1866, designed to provide land to former slaves,

was especially disappointing. It was never effectively implemented and was strenuously opposed by Southern whites. Despite failures, the Homestead Acts helped several million families to obtain land and settle in the West, and it became an important symbol of the effort to create an egalitarian, middle-class, agrarian society in the United States in the nineteenth century.   —*John G. Clark, updated by Kent Blaser*

ADDITIONAL READING:

Fite, Gilbert C. *The Farmers' Frontier: 1865-1900.* New York: Holt, Rinehart and Winston, 1966. A basic survey with an especially strong treatment of the Homestead Act.

Gates, Paul Wallace. *History of Public Land Law Development.* Washington, D.C.: Government Printing Office, 1968.

Summary of the work of one of the foremost scholars of the Homestead Act and public land law.

Lanza, Michael L. *Agrarianism and Reconstruction Politics: The Southern Homestead Act*. Baton Rouge: Louisiana State University Press, 1990. The only extensive treatment of this neglected aspect of homestead legislation.

Layton, Stanford J. *To No Privileged Class: The Rationalization of Homesteading and Rural Life in the Early Twentieth-Century American West*. Salt Lake City, Utah: Signature Books, 1988. A brief work that focuses on the cultural and intellectual aspects of the homestead movement.

Shannon, Fred A. *The Farmer's Last Frontier: Agriculture, 1860-1897*. New York: Farrar and Rinehart, 1945. An older but detailed and still important standard work.

Stratton, Joanna. *Pioneer Women: Voices from the Kansas Frontier*. New York: Simon & Schuster, 1981. Documents women's perspectives on homesteading.

Tilghman, Wendy B. *The Great Plains Experience*. Lincoln, Nebr.: University of Mid-America, 1981. A companion volume to the documentary series of the same title; one segment, "The Settling of the Plains," chronicles the settlement of Custer County, Nebraska, from 1865 to 1900.

SEE ALSO: 1820, Land Act of 1820; 1841, Preemption Act; 1848, Treaty of Guadalupe Hidalgo; 1853, Gadsden Purchase; 1862, Morrill Land Grant Act.

1862 ■ MORRILL LAND GRANT ACT: *the federal government grants land to states for the establishment of agricultural and engineering colleges, paving the way toward higher education for the masses*

DATE: July 2, 1862
LOCALE: Washington, D.C.
CATEGORIES: Education; Laws and acts
KEY FIGURES:

James Buchanan (1791-1868), fifteenth president of the United States, 1857-1861

Abraham Lincoln (1809-1865), sixteenth president of the United States, 1861-1865

Justin Smith Morrill (1810-1898), congressman and senator from Vermont

SUMMARY OF EVENT. The author and successful promoter of the Morrill Land Grant Act of 1862 was Justin Smith Morrill, congressman from Vermont. Morrill was first elected to national office in 1854 as a Whig. With the demise of that party, Morrill helped to found the Republican Party in Vermont. In the House, Morrill served on both the Committee on Territories and the Committee on Agriculture, and he finally became chairman of the powerful Ways and Means Committee in 1861. Elected to the Senate in 1862, he served there until his death in 1898.

Several attempts to use land revenues to aid the promotion of public education had been made before Morrill's bill. The Ordinance of 1785 provided that the sixteenth section in each township was to be set aside for educational purposes. In 1848, when the Oregon Territory was organized, Section 36 was added to Section 16 in each township for common schools. The Preemption Act of 1841 (known also as the Distribution-Preemption Act) turned over to the states, for internal improvements, one-half million acres. Wisconsin, Alabama, Iowa, and Oregon used the proceeds from the sale of these lands for public schools. Revenues from the Swamp Lands Acts of 1849 and 1850 were applied in many states for the purpose of common education. Beginning as early as the 1840's, a movement made progress in the northeastern states for the establishment of agricultural colleges. In the 1850's, several states petitioned Congress for land to be used for educational purposes.

Morrill was interested in both education and agriculture. He regretted the fact that most existing institutions taught on the classical plan, so farmers, mechanics, and others employed at manual labor were not scientifically trained, and in most cases, they were doomed to the haphazard methods of self-education. In 1856, Morrill introduced a resolution that the Committee on Agriculture investigate the possibility of establishing one or more agricultural schools patterned after West Point and Annapolis. This resolution was not acted upon, but in 1857, Morrill introduced a bill that public lands be donated to the states for the purpose of providing colleges to train students in agricultural and mechanical arts. The land was to be apportioned to each state in a quantity of twenty thousand acres for each senator and representative the state had in Congress, and sixty thousand acres to each territory. Proceeds from the sale of this land were to be used in the state as a perpetual fund, the interest of which was to be appropriated to the support of a college. Within a period of five years after the passage of the bill, a college had to be established. If sufficient land for such a grant were not available in a particular state, that state was to receive an equivalent amount of land scrip that could be used to purchase land elsewhere. This scrip had to be sold to private individuals, who could then choose holdings in the unoccupied areas of any public-land state according to the amount of scrip purchased.

Once the bill was presented to both houses of Congress, much opposition appeared. The South argued that it was inexpedient and unconstitutional, and many of the Western states believed that since the grants were to be made on the basis of population, it differed little from Henry Clay's distribution scheme. Many congressmen from states with large holdings attacked the bill on the grounds that large quantities of land scrip would be issued to the older Eastern states where there was no public domain, and the scrip soon would be acquired by land speculators who would claim large tracts of the best lands in the newer states. This land would then be held until the values had increased, and Western settlement and improvement thus would be retarded. In spite of this opposition, the bill passed both the House and the Senate by narrow margins.

President James Buchanan vetoed the land bill. It was, he said, unconstitutional and deprived the government of the needed revenue from land sales. It would make the state too dependent upon the federal government and would set up colleges in competition with existing institutions. Finally, the federal government could not compel the states to use the funds for the specified purpose if the states chose to do otherwise. A vote was quickly taken in the House to override the veto, but it failed to get the necessary two-thirds vote.

Unwilling to accept defeat, Morrill presented a second bill on December 16, 1861. It was almost identical to the first bill, except that the number of acres was increased to thirty thousand for each representative and senator. President Abraham Lincoln previously had informed Morrill that he would allow such a bill to become law. The issues were practically the same as before; however, in this instance, the representatives from the older Eastern states made a determined effort to force passage of the bill. With the passage of the Homestead Act virtually assured (it was signed into law in May and granted land acreage in 160-acre lots to anyone willing to reside upon it continuously for five years), the Easterners feared that their other chances to secure title to Western lands were materially reduced. President Lincoln signed the bill on July 2, 1862.

The language of the Morrill Land Grant Act that Lincoln signed into law suggested a populist leaning. It provided for at least one college in each state at which studies of agriculture and the "mechanic arts" (engineering) would be available to support both a liberal and practical education of what were termed "the industrial classes," that is, the working class. Morrill no doubt was influenced by the rising democratic social climate in the United States; the growing power of workers and middle and lower managers; the importance of agriculture, industry, and commerce; and the growing body of scientific knowledge. The bill also struck a blow at the traditions of college education inherited from England and Germany that directed higher education to the preparation of well-to-do young men for careers as ministers, lawyers, scientists, college faculty, and high-level civil servants.

The concept of the land-grant college was a major contribution to the wider availability of higher education in the United States. The colleges were readily supported by the states. They made possible public college-level learning at low cost and established research as a legitimate activity of higher education. As a result, agricultural and engineering arts and sciences, as professions, were elevated to positions of academic respectability.

Most of the land-grant colleges received not land but scrip, which they used to purchase public land at $1.25 per acre. Under the terms of the act, eleven states received 1,769,440 acres of land. Public-land states later admitted to the Union received similar grants. Twenty-seven states eventually received scrip instead of land, and almost eight million scrip-acres were issued. The older states, which benefited because of their large populations, were authorized to select their acreage anywhere in the West. New York, for example, selected

forest lands in Wisconsin and prairie lands scattered throughout the western Mississippi River Valley to use its 990,000-acre allotment. In all, the states received 140 million acres through the Morrill Land Grant Act and similar measures. None of this land was given to homesteads, and nearly all of it passed through the hands of speculators on its way to final users.

A second Morrill Land Grant Act was passed in 1890, stipulating that Congress was to make regular appropriations for the further support of land-grant colleges. The 1890 act resulted in the creation of seventeen agricultural and mechanical colleges in the South for African Americans. This act also established the practice of federal grants to institutions of higher education. Appropriations were increased in 1907, 1935, 1952, and 1960. By the 1960's, there was at least one land-grant institution in every state in the Union.

Land-grant institutions have played a special role in developing several fields of study, particularly in agriculture and veterinary medicine. About 75 percent of the bachelor's degrees and 98 percent of the advanced degrees in these subjects are awarded by land-grant colleges. Engineering is another field that has been well developed in land-grant colleges, two-fifths of all such degrees coming from these institutions. Almost 51 percent of degrees in home economics are conferred by land-grant schools. A significant and little-known role is the one played by the land-grant college in military education. Thousands of officers have received their initial military training from these institutions.

Although the initial role of land-grant colleges was to teach the arts of agriculture and engineering. Over the years, as additional funds and needs arose, the institutions directed some of their efforts toward research and bringing the results of that research to the users through extension offices. In many instances, the colleges must not only satisfy the needs of their traditional clientele but also serve the interests of the general public. In addition, land-grant colleges increasingly face the challenges of international competition and environmental sensitivity and awareness.

—John H. DeBerry, updated by Albert C. Jensen

ADDITIONAL READING:

Eddy, Edward D., Jr. *Colleges for Our Land and Time: The Land-Grant Ideas in American Education.* New York: Harper & Row, 1956. A comprehensive treatment of the land-grant movement from its beginning to the middle of the twentieth century.

James, Edmund J. "The Origins of the Land-Grant Act of 1862 (the So-Called Morrill Act) and Some Account of Its Author, Jonathan B. Turner." In *The University Studies* 4, no. 1 (November, 1910): 1-111. This work, published by the University of Illinois, proposes "to prove that Jonathon B. Turner, a onetime professor at Illinois College in Jacksonville, Illinois, was the real father of the so-called Morrill Act of July 2, 1862."

Meyer, James H. *Rethinking the Outlooks of Colleges Whose Roots Have Been in Agriculture.* Berkeley: University of California Press, 1992. Discusses how, since passage of the

Morrill Land Grant Act, agriculture had been challenged to become internationally competitive and environmentally sensitive, as well as economically viable.

_____. "The Stalemate in Food and Agriculture Research, Teaching, and Extension." *Science* 260 (May 14, 1993): 881, 1007. Discusses how the Land Grant Act provided for colleges to teach agriculture and the "mechanic arts," but how this role has had to broaden to meet the demands of agribusiness and the interests of the general public.

Nevins, Allan. *The Origins of the Land-Grant Colleges and State Universities: A Brief Account of the Morrill Act of 1862 and Its Results*. Washington, D.C.: Civil War Centennial Commission, 1962. An excellent brief discussion of the subject by a major historian.

Parker, William Belmont. *The Life and Public Services of Justin Smith Morrill*. Boston: Houghton Mifflin, 1924. This full-scale biography of Morrill traces his career from country storekeeper to powerful senator, with special emphasis on the land-grant acts of 1862 and 1890.

Rasmussen, Wayne D. *Taking the University to the People: Seventy-five Years of Cooperative Extension*. Ames: Iowa State University Press, 1989. Describes the important function of land grant institutions in making available the results of agricultural research directly to the user.

U.S. Department of the Interior. *Survey of the Land-Grant Colleges and Universities*. Directed by Arthur J. Klein, Chief of the Division of Collegiate and Professional Education. Washington, D.C.: Government Printing Office, 1930. A monumental survey of the achievements of land-grant colleges. An excellent historical introduction discusses the genesis of the idea, the adoption of the legislation, and its implementation.

SEE ALSO: 1785, Beginnings of State Universities; 1820, Land Act of 1820; 1841, Preemption Act; 1848, Treaty of Guadalupe Hidalgo; 1853, Gadsden Purchase; 1862, Homestead Act.

1862 ■ GREAT SIOUX WAR: *Minnesota Sioux lose their tribal lands to encroaching white settlers in one of the largest mass slaughters in U.S. history*

DATE: Beginning August 17, 1862
LOCALE: Southern Minnesota
CATEGORIES: Native American history; Wars, uprisings, and civil unrest
KEY FIGURES:
Little Crow, also known as *Taoyateduta* (c. 1820-1863), principal war chief of the Santee Sioux
Little Six, also known as *Shakopee* (died 1865), Santee leader of the "blanket" Sioux, hanged at Fort Snelling
Mankato (c. 1830-1862), Santee chief killed at the Battle of Wood Lake

Andrew J. Myrick (died 1862), Redwood Agency trader
John Pope (1823-1892), administrative commander of the Northwest Department
Alexander Ramsey (1815-1903), governor of Minnesota
Henry H. Sibley (1811-1891), field commander of the Minnesota Militia

SUMMARY OF EVENT. On August 17, 1862, four Santee Sioux men, returning from a fruitless search for food beyond the boundaries of their southern Minnesota reservation, attacked and killed five white settlers near Acton, in Meeker County. Ordinarily, the culprits would have been surrendered to white authorities, but these were no ordinary times. The Sioux of Minnesota were starving. Long-promised annuities were slow in coming, as usual, and doubts about the ability of a nation divided by civil war to fulfill its obligations to an isolated frontier led traders at the Redwood Agency to refuse to open their warehouses until payment in gold arrived from Washington, D.C. Trader Andrew Myrick had advised the starving population to "go home and eat grass, or their own dung." On August 18, a large war party attacked and looted the Redwood Agency and wiped out most of a military expedition from Fort Snelling. Myrick, among the first to fall, was found with his mouth symbolically stuffed with grass. As politicians argued over payment of annuities in paper money or in gold, the Great Sioux War began.

Although the outbreak of hostilities appeared to be local, its causes must be viewed in a national context. The Fort Snelling reserve, established in 1819 near present-day St. Paul, was, until 1851, the only land in Minnesota Territory that did not belong to Native Americans. Nevertheless, thousands of white settlers, in the familiar pattern of national expansion, occupied most of southern Minnesota. In 1851, the Minnesota Sioux negotiated away most of their best hunting grounds in the treaties of Traverse de Sioux and Mendota, and were tricked into signing away most of the promised compensation to pay debts, real and imagined, to traders there. The remaining annuities were slow in coming and insufficient to support the Sioux, and there was no promise of permanent occupancy of the Minnesota reservation. Furthermore, there was no consistent policy regarding American Indians in the United States during the period. Native Americans had no legal recourse against white depredations. Appeals for protection from soldier and civilian alike fell on deaf ears. The quality and abilities of American Indian agents declined as the nation moved toward the Civil War. Resentment smoldered, but several hundred of the approximately seven thousand Sioux in Minnesota cut their hair, donned "white men's" clothes, and took up farming following the 1851 treaties. These "farmer" Sioux received most of the annuities, and a rift developed between them and the traditional, or "blanket," Sioux.

Despite the influx of settlers, the Minnesota frontier had been generally peaceful. The occasional murder of a settler by a native resulted in the miscreant being turned over to white authorities for punishment. In 1857, a group of renegade blanket Sioux slaughtered thirty settlers in northern Iowa and southern Minnesota, causing momentary panic in the area. Led by Chief Little Crow, the Sioux denied responsibility for the outlaws and formed a party to pursue them into Dakota Territory. The effort proved futile, but apparently satisfied white authorities. No punishment for the Spirit Lake Massacre was forthcoming. Annuities were paid on time, and the prestige of the United States declined among the image-conscious Sioux. By 1862, most of Minnesota's white male settlers had left to fight in the Civil War, and the Sioux, confined to a narrow strip of land along the Minnesota River, were facing starvation.

Chief Shakopee and his followers knew the Acton murders would be avenged. Although Chief Little Crow, long a spokesman for the Sioux, had lost prestige when he cut his hair and began farming, he remained the person most able to unify the Sioux. He was reluctant and argued against war. Accused of cowardice, he replied,

> The white men are like the locusts when they fly so thick the sky is like a snowstorm. Yes, they fight among themselves, but if you strike one of them, they all will turn upon you and devour your women and little children . . . you will die like the rabbits when the hungry wolves hunt them in the hard moon.

Nevertheless, he led the Sioux, forlornly hoping to regain his prestige.

The Sioux were inefficient attackers. Most of the inhabitants of the Redwood Agency escaped to spread the alarm at Fort Ridgely. During the first week, far more whites were spared than were killed, many taken prisoner by Little Crow and protected from harm in his camp. Attacks on New Ulm and settlers in Brown and Renville Counties convinced the Sioux that success was imminent. Little Crow knew that Fort Ridgley, which protected the Minnesota River Valley, would have to fall. Meanwhile, panic spread across the Midwest, as politicians from Iowa, Wisconsin, Nebraska, and Dakota Territory petitioned the federal government for troops and leadership. Minnesota governor Alexander Ramsey, who had negotiated the fateful 1851 treaties, appointed his old political rival, former governor Henry H. Sibley, to lead the Minnesota Militia against the Sioux. General John Pope, in disgrace because of his defeat at the Second Battle of Bull Run in Virginia, was assigned to head the new Northwest Department. His policy of pursue and confine would dominate American Indian policy in the trans-Mississippi West for years to come. He directed the Minnesota war from St. Paul.

On August 20 and again on August 22, before Sibley reached Fort Ridgely with a motley crew of raw recruits, Little Crow and Chief Mankato attacked. The fort's cannon was used to devastating effect; only three of the fort's defenders were killed, and both attacks were repelled. The Sioux attacked New Ulm the second time on August 23, but again failed. Several other settlements suffered attacks, but the fate of the now demoralized Sioux was sealed.

By the middle of September, Sibley had formed his sixteen hundred troops into a fighting unit and moved north. On September 23, Sibley defeated several hundred warriors under Chief Mankato, who was killed. As most of the combatants slipped away, Sibley rounded up 400 Sioux, conducted trials, and sentenced 306 to death. President Abraham Lincoln reviewed the records and, refusing to "countenance lynching, within the forms of martial law," commuted most of the sentences. On December 28, 1863, thirty-eight Sioux were hanged on a single scaffold at Mankato, the largest mass execution in U.S. history.

The war was not over. Little Crow was murdered near Hutchinson in 1863; Shakopee was kidnapped in Canada and hanged at Fort Snelling in 1865. The U.S. Army, following General Pope's orders, pursued the Sioux west. Such occasional engagements as the Battle of White Hill, Dakota, in 1863, and the Battle of the Little Bighorn, in Montana Territory in 1876, kept the Sioux moving. The Great Sioux War cost the lives of 413 white civilians, 77 soldiers, and 71 American Indians, counting those 38 hanged at Mankato. There was no treaty, no negotiation to end the war. All Sioux, blanket and farmer, were condemned to lose all but a minuscule piece of their tribal lands in Minnesota, and ultimately, their way of life. The 1890 Battle of Wounded Knee, in which U.S. troops killed almost two hundred Sioux, was the last battle in the American Indian wars.

—*Stephen G. Sylvester*

ADDITIONAL READING:

Anderson, Gary Clayton. *Little Crow: Spokesman for the Sioux.* St. Paul: Minnesota Historical Society Press, 1986. A carefully researched and documented biography of the most important Native American war leader; sympathetic to both Little Crow and the Santee Sioux. Provides a detailed description of the war.

Anderson, Gary Clayton, and Alan R. Woolworth, eds. *Through Dakota Eyes: Narrative Accounts of the Minnesota Indian War of 1862.* St. Paul: Minnesota Historical Press, 1988. Carefully edited, readable first-person accounts of the war, some sympathetic to the blanket Sioux, some to the farmer Sioux who opposed the war.

Blegen, Theodore C. *Minnesota: A History of the State.* St. Paul: University of Minnesota Press, 1975. The standard history of Minnesota. Its chapter on the Sioux War is solid and balanced.

Ellis, Richard N. *General Pope and U.S. Indian Policy.* Albuquerque: University of New Mexico Press, 1970. Ellis' detailed account provides insight into the policy of punishment and containment that grew out of the war.

Lass, William E. *Minnesota: A History.* New York: W. W. Norton, 1977. Chapter 5 is a concise but insightful statement of the war's effect on Minnesota.

Utley, Robert M. *The Indian Frontier of the American West: 1846-1890.* Albuquerque: University of New Mexico Press, 1984. Although the description of the war is brief and simplistic, it places the war in the context of Western policy toward the American Indians.

SEE ALSO: 1861, Apache Wars; 1864, Sand Creek Massacre; 1866, Bozeman Trail War; 1867, Medicine Lodge Creek

Treaty; 1868, Washita River Massacre; 1872, Great American Bison Slaughter; 1874, Red River War; 1876, Battle of the Little Bighorn; 1877, Nez Perce Exile; 1890, Closing of the Frontier; 1890, Battle of Wounded Knee.

1863 ■ EMANCIPATION PROCLAMATION: *in an effort to preserve the Union, President Lincoln declares all slaves in rebel states to be free*

DATE: January 1, 1863
LOCALE: Washington, D.C.
CATEGORY: African American history
KEY FIGURES:

Montgomery Blair (1813-1883), postmaster general who believed that the Emancipation Proclamation would ruin the Lincoln Administration politically

Salmon Portland Chase (1808-1873), secretary of the Treasury, who at first advised a course more moderate than emancipation by presidential proclamation

Horace Greeley (1811-1872), editor of the *New York Tribune* and a strong proponent of emancipation

Abraham Lincoln (1809-1865), sixteenth president of the United States, 1861-1865

William Henry Seward (1801-1872), secretary of state who was principally responsible for the timing of the Emancipation Proclamation

Edwin McMasters Stanton (1814-1869), secretary of war and a staunch advocate of emancipation

Charles Sumner (1811-1874), senator from Massachusetts who influenced Lincoln to emancipate the slaves

SUMMARY OF EVENT. The cabinet met at noon on September 22, 1862. President Abraham Lincoln sought to put the members at ease by reading to them from a book of humorous stories, but soon he came to the business at hand. The president announced that he intended to issue that day an emancipation proclamation. Lincoln stated that, since he had consulted the cabinet on the subject before, he desired no comments from them on this occasion. Then he read the proclamation. As of January 1, 1863, all slaves held in states "in rebellion against the United States" would be forever free.

Lincoln had not reached his decision to proclaim emancipation without much thinking and soul-searching. From his youth, he had opposed slavery on both moral and economic grounds. Yet Lincoln was a practical politician and a pragmatic man. He negotiated the secession crisis always inspired by a desire to preserve the Union. It is fair to say that Lincoln wished to abolish slavery but would translate his wish into action only if abolition would enhance his efforts to attain peace. Because he was a practical man, Lincoln realized that emancipation was only part of the solution to the problem of race relations in the United States. He foresaw the plight of the freed slaves and favored compensated emancipation (emanci-

pation accompanied by compensation for former slave owners) and voluntary colonization for African Americans to soften racial adjustment. Because of the priority Lincoln gave to union, until 1862 he subordinated his convictions and tentative solutions about slavery to the struggle for union. In part, Lincoln hedged on the idea of emancipation so as not to risk the secession of the loyal slave states—Delaware, Kentucky, Maryland, and Missouri—to the Confederacy.

The president did not find it easy to divorce the ideals of union and emancipation. Both abolitionist ideologists and practical men pressed him to expand his administration's war aims to include emancipation and had done so since the Civil War began in 1861. Senator Charles Sumner of Massachusetts carried on a one-man campaign to move Lincoln to action on the question of slavery. Horace Greeley's influential *New York Tribune* criticized the Lincoln Administration for its lack of concern for the moral issue. Delegations of citizens petitioned Lincoln to act against human bondage. Lincoln heard these and other pleas but made no commitment to official action.

Sometime in the late spring of 1862, the president made his decision. The war was not going as well as he wished; emancipation would not hinder the effort and might help. He determined to emancipate the slaves by presidential proclamation. Lincoln still pondered the timing of his momentous step, and so he told no one of his decision. He retreated often from the White House to the telegraph room of the War Department, in search of privacy. Early in June, the president began drafting his proclamation in the telegraph room. He worked slowly and kept his own counsel. Between mid-June and mid-July, Lincoln spoke with a few members of his administration about the step he contemplated.

On July 22, 1862, Lincoln read a draft proclamation to the entire cabinet and asked for comment. Secretary of War Edwin M. Stanton applauded the document and expressed the opinion that emancipation would assist the war effort. Salmon P. Chase, secretary of the Treasury, thought the move too sudden and sweeping. Chase favored emancipation by the military, as areas of the South were occupied by federal troops. Postmaster General Montgomery Blair feared political repercussions in the fall congressional elections and predicted doom for the Republicans should the president carry out his intentions. Secretary of State William H. Seward's comments impressed Lincoln most of all. Seward favored the issuance of an emancipation proclamation but questioned the president's timing. Union troops were then in retreat from Richmond, and George B. McClellan's Peninsular Campaign had proved to be abortive. Emancipation must not seem to be the desperate act of a defeated Union. Lincoln concurred with Seward and waited for a victory.

Victory seemed to be a long time in coming. The Confederates assumed the offensive in the summer of 1862, defeated the federal troops in the Second Battle of Bull Run, and marched into Maryland. On September 17, the Union Army fought the Battle of Antietam, and the Confederates withdrew back across the Potomac River into Virginia. Lincoln decided that this withdrawal of the enemy was success enough, and called in the cabinet on September 22. Northern newspapers announced the proclamation the next day.

The document the president presented to his cabinet and the same day made public was the preliminary Emancipation Proclamation. Although this was intended to affect millions of Southern slaves, plantation owners paid the announcement little heed, declaring that it was a "Yankee trick" that freed slaves outside Northern borders while keeping others enslaved. While Southerners worried that the proclamation might create an atmosphere of rebellion among the slaves, the announcement also strengthened their resolve to defeat the Union armies.

The preliminary proclamation differed in minor respects from the Emancipation Proclamation issued on January 1, 1863, which actually effected emancipation. Perhaps the most significant feature of the document was that it limited emancipation to those states—and portions of states, in the final draft— that were in rebellion. Lincoln limited emancipation in this manner because he based his authority to free the slaves on acts of Congress that provided for the confiscation of rebel property and forbade the military from returning slaves of rebels to their owners. Such authority did not encompass a general emancipation. Also, Lincoln hoped to persuade Congress to act upon the principles of compensation and voluntary colonization in dealing with slaves and slave owners in loyal areas.

Many African American leaders who lived in the North, Frederick Douglass among them, rallied to the cause, urging African Americans to join the Union Army. The Confederacy did not recognize Lincoln's proclamation, and its four million slaves remained in bondage until Union armies were victorious. However, many Southern blacks heeded the call and threw down their tools to escape over Northern borders, and many joined the Union forces. Those slaves already held within Union lines in Tennessee, Louisiana, and Virginia were freed. As the Northern troops marched southward, they liberated African Americans in the towns they defeated.

Doctrinaire abolitionists in the North criticized the president's moderation. Yet on September 22, 1862, Lincoln had taken his stand. The war for union widened into a crusade against slavery. Foreign governments paused in their consideration of aiding the South, but the consensus, as Seward had

In this 1863 sketch, emancipation is idealistically depicted (center round) by political cartoonist Thomas Nast. The freeing of the slaves was anticipated to redress the cruelties and abuses of slavery, shown in the surrounding margins. In fact, the postwar years brought a wave of state laws, called Black Codes, designed to circumvent Reconstruction and cancel African Americans' civil rights. (The Associated Publishers, Inc.)

predicted, was dismissal of the proclamation. Generally, European leaders tried to find fault with it. Nevertheless, Lincoln had ensured the survival of the union and given the slaves hope. In the end, slavery was doomed.

—*Emory M. Thomas, updated by Marilyn Elizabeth Perry*

ADDITIONAL READING:

Franklin, John Hope. *The Emancipation Proclamation.* Garden City, N.Y.: Doubleday, 1963. Analyzes Lincoln's stand on slavery and the political issues of the day.

Lincoln, Abraham. *Lincoln on Democracy.* Edited and introduced by Mario M. Cuomo and Harold Holzer. New York: HarperCollins, 1990. A collection of speeches, letters, notes, and diary entries on the subjects of equality and freedom, written by Lincoln throughout his lifetime.

McPherson, James M. *Abraham Lincoln and the Second American Revolution.* New York: Oxford University Press, 1990. Essays by a renowned historian on the changes wrought by the Civil War.

_____. *The Struggle for Equality: Abolitionists and the Negro in the Civil War and Reconstruction.* Princeton, N.J.: Princeton University Press, 1964. This thoughtful book proposes that the abolitionists were influential in securing emancipation by goading the president to action.

Neely, Mark E., Jr. *The Last Best Hope of Earth: Abraham Lincoln and the Promise of America.* Cambridge, Mass.: Harvard University Press, 1993. A carefully researched analysis of Lincoln as a national leader, emphasizing Lincoln's contributions to preserving the Union.

Quarles, Benjamin. *Lincoln and the Negro.* New York: Oxford University Press, 1962. Treating the Emancipation Proclamation broadly, argues that it was a definite blow for freedom, as Lincoln himself realized.

SEE ALSO: 1850, Compromise of 1850; 1850, Second Fugitive Slave Law; 1850, Underground Railroad; 1860, Confederate States Secede from the Union; 1861, Stand Watie Fights for the South; 1863, First National Draft Law; 1863, Reconstruction; 1865, Surrender at Appomattox and Assassination of Lincoln; 1865, New Black Codes; 1865, Thirteenth Amendment; 1866, Civil Rights Act of 1866; 1868, Fourteenth Amendment.

1863 ■ NATIONAL BANK ACTS: *a measure to finance the Civil War moves control of the United States' banking and monetary system under the auspices of the federal government*

DATE: February 25, 1863-June 3, 1864
LOCALE: Washington, D.C.
CATEGORIES: Economics; Laws and acts
KEY FIGURES:
Salmon Portland Chase (1808-1873), secretary of the Treasury

Jay Cooke (1821-1905), private banker who organized the sale of government bonds during the Civil War
Hugh McCulloch (1808-1895), Indiana banker, first comptroller of the currency
Thaddeus Stevens (1792-1868), Republican congressman from Pennsylvania, opponent of the National Bank Acts

SUMMARY OF EVENT. Of the many crises faced by the federal government in conducting the war against the Confederacy, none was more difficult to resolve than financing the conflict. The government had to obtain revenue to pay for the war and at the same time expand support for the war among members of the financial community. Revenues declined while expenses mounted.

Salmon P. Chase, secretary of the Treasury in Lincoln's first administration, was reluctant to impose an income tax, aware that such taxes generated strong hostility. Chase, a Democrat, had no personal qualms about issuing paper money or about having government control the banks; he was much more interested in what he considered to be the larger issue—successfully prosecuting the war. An income tax was enacted in August, 1861, which commanded 3 percent of incomes exceeding eight hundred dollars per year, and that percentage rose in subsequent years. Nevertheless, taxation could raise only a small part of the income needed to fight the war. Foreign lenders, having recently lost money in the Panic of 1857, did not want to invest in a nation at war. Public confidence in the United States was low, especially after the early Union failures on the battlefield. The banks of the country had suspended specie payments by December, 1861. Lincoln's first administration met that crisis by issuing paper currency.

The first Legal Tender Act of February 25, 1862, authorized the issue of $150 million in national notes, or "greenbacks." Subsequent acts raised the authorized total to $450 million. Since the federal government itself suspended specie payments, refusing to redeem the paper money in gold or silver, the greenbacks were an inconvertible paper money supported only by the credit of the government. More important to war financing, however, was the sale of bonds by the government through the efforts of financier Jay Cooke. He utilized mass-marketing strategies to reach new groups of middle-class investors with great success. Cooke and his associates sold more than $1 billion worth of federal securities. However, during the early days of the war, in 1862 and 1863, when the battlefield success of the Union was in doubt, even Cooke had difficulty selling the bonds.

The government ultimately sold its bond issues because of the relationship between bond purchases and the establishment of the national banking system. Prior to the Civil War, privately owned, state-chartered banks could issue their own money, backed by a specie reserve. The notes of those banks competed in the open market like other commodities, with weaker banks' notes trading at a substantial discount. Critics argued that the nation needed a uniform currency, and that the state banks were unstable. (Similar arguments had been made in the early nineteenth century by those wishing to establish the Bank of the United States.) The latter charge was not true; some systems, especially in the South, proved remarkably solvent and stable during the Panic of 1857, particularly where branch banking was permitted.

Some critics saw a national banking system as a way to link the uniform currency to a banking system that also would provide an outlet for the government's securities. In January, 1863, the Senate started work on such a system. State banks resisted, correctly fearing that a national banking system would have unfair competitive advantages. Thaddeus Stevens, a Republican congressman from Pennsylvania, opposed the new system. Secretary Chase, however, with support from Senator John Sherman of Ohio, pushed the bill through the Senate with a close vote. Stevens blocked the bill in the House for months, but it passed there in February, 1863. Many who voted for the bill opposed the concept in principle, but supported it at the request of Chase, who argued that it was necessary in order to continue the war. Cooke also threw his influence behind the bill.

The act provided for the creation of national banks, which were required to purchase government bonds as a condition of receiving their federal charters. They then were permitted to issue notes up to 90 percent of the market value of the bonds. In an amending act of June, 1864, Congress made provisions for converting state banks into members of the national banking system. Still, state banks resisted, and only the imposition of a federal tax of 10 percent upon state bank notes eliminated state bank competition. That act also ensured that the government would have a monopoly over the creation of money and could inflate at will. National banks were limited to note issues of $300 million, which, along with the greenbacks, became the national currency.

The system suffered from inadequate balance in its distribution of money across the nation—$170 million of the $300 million went to New England and New York—and the national banks proved to have inadequate redemption mechanisms. Demand for money in the West, especially, evolved into a considerable political issue after the Civil War. The laws also prohibited national banks from establishing branches (unless they entered the system with branches) and had other restrictions, including higher capital requirements, than banks with state charters had. On the positive side, only national banks could be chosen as depositories for the Treasury Department's tax revenues, and only national banks could issue notes. States retaliated by lowering their capital requirements, and state banks found that they could avoid the tax on bank notes by using demand deposits to finance their loans and investments, making state bank note issues irrelevant. Over time, the number of state-chartered banks overtook the number of national banks.

The national banking system did not eliminate financial crises or panics. Indeed, the poor redemption mechanisms and the lack of competitive currencies from state banks made panics more likely. Nationwide panics occurred in 1873, 1893,

and 1907, eventually generating calls for reform that led to the creation of the Federal Reserve System in 1913. By 1900, deposits in national banks stood at $2,356 million, while deposits in nonnational banks totaled $3,005 million.

Creation of national banks and the corollary destruction of private note issue had another effect on the nation's banking system. After the Civil War, the South's banking system was devastated, and the prospects for either former Confederates or freedmen receiving federal charters were slim, if not nonexistent. Without national banks in the South, a dearth of capital occurred that retarded the postbellum growth of the region. Moreover, the destruction of competitive note issue by banks eliminated opportunities for the freedmen to create their own sources of capital. Thus, the National Bank Acts discriminated against the newly freed slaves. Whether the Radical Republicans in Congress intended to punish the South or the system accidentally discriminated against the South and West remains a matter of debate.

Another effect, almost surely unintended, was to destabilize the banking system by removing an important market constraint, namely the necessity for banks to maintain specie reserves for their notes. At the same time, the government had to reduce the number of greenbacks in circulation, and from 1865 to 1879, the amount of greenbacks fell. Nevertheless, international factors led to the long-term deflation that the nation experienced from 1865 to almost 1900. That deflation was viewed by farmers and miners as damaging, and helped create groups, such as the Populists, who sought inflation, either through "free silver" or through the renewed issue of greenbacks.

The Populists and others feared that the money power was concentrated in New York, particularly in the hands of New York Jewish bankers. Those fears were incorporated into the Federal Reserve Act, by which twelve Federal Reserve Banks were spread throughout the country. Most people unhappy with the national bank system, however, had failed to note the more serious threat: Note issue was centralized within the federal government in Washington, not with financiers in New York. Consequently, it proved relatively easy to move final authority over the nation's money and banking system to Washington, D.C., during the Great Depression.

—*John G. Clark, updated by Larry Schweikart*

ADDITIONAL READING:

Doti, Lynne Pierson, and Larry Schweikart. *Banking in the American West: From the Gold Rush to Deregulation.* Norman: University of Oklahoma Press, 1991. Discusses the shortages of currency in the West caused by the national banking system. Analyzes the Western pressure for inflationary programs such as "free silver" and greenbacks. Compares branching systems in the West to states with nonbranching systems, describing the former as stronger.

Livingston, James. *Origins of the Federal Reserve System: Money, Class, and Corporate Capitalism, 1890-1913.* Ithaca, N.Y.: Cornell University Press, 1986. Argues that business interests rearranged the banking system to compensate for increases in labor costs. Although an unusual approach, most economists reject this interpretation of the development of banking in the late 1800's.

Schweikart, Larry. *Banking in the American South from the Age of Jackson to Reconstruction*. Baton Rouge: Louisiana State University Press, 1987. Demonstrates that the Southern banking system was healthy on the eve of the Civil War, that branching made it especially competitive, and that the National Bank and Currency Acts particularly hurt the South.

Sharkey, Robert P. *Money, Class, and Party: An Economic Study of Civil War and Reconstruction*. Baltimore: The Johns Hopkins University Press, 1959. Shows that many Democrats supported central banking; reveals splits in the Republican Party over money, mainly along class lines.

Timberlake, Richard H. *The Origins of Central Banking in the United States*. Cambridge, Mass.: Harvard University Press, 1978. Argues that government abused the "necessary and proper" clause to acquire power over note creation and authority over banking. Describes a system of clearinghouses developed in the late 1800's that effectively dealt with the problems caused by the national bank system.

See also: 1790, Hamilton's *Report on Public Credit*; 1816, Second Bank of the United States Is Chartered; 1832, Jackson vs. the Bank of the United States; 1846, Independent Treasury Is Established; 1873, "Crime of 1873"; 1887, Interstate Commerce Act; 1913, Federal Reserve Act.

1863 ■ First National Draft Law: *the United States' first conscription act taps Northern manpower to defeat the South*

Date: March 3, 1863
Locale: Washington, D.C.
Categories: Laws and acts; Wars, uprisings, and civil unrest
Key figures:
James B. Fry, provost-marshal-general of the United States
Abraham Lincoln (1809-1865), sixteenth president of the United States, 1861-1865
Horatio Seymour (1810-1886), governor of New York during the draft riots
Edwin McMasters Stanton (1814-1869), secretary of war
Henry Wilson (1812-1875), chairman of the Senate Committee on Military Affairs

Summary of event. The firing on Fort Sumter on April 12, 1861, came at a time when the regular army numbered only about sixteen thousand officers and troops. The traditional method of increasing the size of the army was to expand the state militias and to form a volunteer emergency national army recruited through the states. The immediate response of President Abraham Lincoln to the firing on Fort Sumter was to call for seventy-five thousand militia volunteers for three months' service. This call was exceeded, and some volunteers were turned away because the expectation was that a show of force would be sufficient to defeat the South. Congress and the president subsequently found it necessary, however, to call for more volunteers. Repeated defeats of the Union Army and the resultant loss of men caused President Lincoln to call for three hundred thousand volunteers in the summer of 1862. The difficulty of obtaining volunteers was soon apparent; bounties were increased and the threat of the draft was invoked. Congress passed the Militia Act of July, 1862, which allowed the states to draft men into the militia and encouraged enlistments. President Lincoln called for another three hundred thousand men to be enrolled into the militia. Although the Militia Act of 1862 gave the federal government power to enroll men in situations where the state machinery was inadequate, the short-term (nine-month maximum) nature of the militia draft and the inequities of the system made it less than satisfactory.

Spurred by the loss of seventy-five thousand men, by news of a conscription law passed by the Confederacy, and by the failure of the states to provide men promptly for the various calls, Congress passed its own Conscription Act on March 3, 1863. Henry Wilson, chairman of the Senate Committee on Military Affairs, was responsible for the introduction of a bill that eventually was passed and labeled "An Act for Enrolling and Calling Out the National Forces and for Other Purposes." This act was the first national draft law in the history of the nation. It called for the creation of the "national forces," which were to consist of all able-bodied male citizens and alien declarants between twenty and forty-five years of age, including African Americans. White opposition to blacks in federal army uniforms noticeably lessened as a result of the draft. In all, more than 168,000 African American recruits were drafted. Certain high officials, medically unfit persons, and hardship cases were exempted. Exemption could also be obtained by paying three hundred dollars or by securing a substitute.

The system was operated by the War Department under the direction of Colonel James B. Fry, provost-marshal-general. Provost-marshals were appointed in districts similar to the congressional districts and enrollments began. Quotas were established and credit was given for enlistments. If the quotas were not met, drawings were held to determine who should be drafted. Small cards were placed in sealed envelopes in a large trunk, and the names were drawn in public by a trustworthy citizen wearing a blindfold. The system of paying three hundred dollars for exemption from service subsequently was abolished, but the privilege of hiring a substitute was continued. The names of more than three million men were gathered, but only about 170,000 were drafted, and 120,000 of those produced substitutes. The primary intent for passage of the law was to speed up voluntary enlistment, and more than one million men enlisted. The chief motivation for these enlistments was probably the threat of the draft.

The draft brought President Lincoln and Secretary of War Edwin McMasters Stanton into conflict with state governors. Those governors who were unenthusiastic about the conduct of the war openly criticized the president and the draft, while governors who favored a more vigorous prosecution of the war often complained that their states had not been given full credit for previous enlistments. Lincoln and Stanton often temporized with the governors by granting postponements or additional credits as the end of the war drew near.

There was considerable resistance to the draft. Pennsylvania, Illinois, Indiana, and Kentucky had considerable problems with enrollment, and draft offices and officers were attacked in those states. The Irish in New York and New Jersey were particularly incensed by the draft, many viewing the conflicts as a rich man's war and a poor man's fight. With fifty-one categories of diseases qualifying men for medical exemption, the system was fraught with medical resistance problems. Surgeons administering medical qualifying exams were confronted by pretended hernias (the most widespread cause of exemption), eye problems caused by applying eye irritants, and pretended deafness. Giving incorrect birth dates, claiming false dependents, and even the enrollment of dead people were other methods of noncompliance. Finally, there were the runaways. Given time to settle their affairs before departing for camp, a considerable number of draftees either relocated or fled to Canada.

With the public generally hostile to the draft, the best way for a community to completely avoid it was to fill the quota with volunteers. Consequently, bounty taxes were implemented to raise revenues to attract foreigners, new immigrants, and the poverty-stricken to enlist. The paying of bounties corrupted the draft system. It produced bounty jumpers who, attracted by lump-sum payments, were willing to jump off trains or boats and escape.

Notorious resistance to the draft instigated the draft riots in New York City. Governor Horatio Seymour's speech of July 4, 1863, attacking the Lincoln Administration for violations of individual liberty, did nothing to decrease the hostility of the New York Irish toward African Americans and the abolitionists. Antidraft rioting, which took place between July 13 and 15, destroyed property and physically harmed many African Americans. Some New York militia units that had been engaged at Gettysburg were hastily ordered back to New York to stop the rioting. Estimates of the casualties in the violence range up to more than one thousand. In spite of the violence, the federal government was determined to enforce the draft with even more fervor.

The Confederacy's calls for volunteers and its national conscription law antedated those of the Union. Jefferson Davis' call for one hundred thousand volunteers came before the firing on Fort Sumter, and the Conscription Act was passed on April 16, 1862, almost a year before similar legislation was passed by the United States. The Confederate act conscripted men from eighteen to thirty-five years of age; later the same

year, it was extended to include those between seventeen and fifty years of age. The Confederate law included a substitute system and a controversial list of exempted persons held to be essential at home. The category that caused the most discussion was that which exempted one slave owner or overseer for each twenty slaves. The Confederate draft was also controversial because it was a national levy; it made no concession to the doctrine of states' rights for which most Southerners claimed to be fighting.

It appears that the Confederacy's early use of a conscription law enabled General Robert E. Lee's armies to continue their general success in the Civil War well into 1863. It was only after the North also began drafting men that President Lincoln could be confident of victory. The North, with a much larger population, was able to sustain its losses and to continue the war indefinitely; the Confederacy could not. Continuance of the draft underscored Northern determination to continue the war to its conclusion. The result was Lee's surrender at Appomattox and the restoration of the Union.

—Mark A. Plummer, updated by Irwin Halfond

ADDITIONAL READING:

Bernstein, Iver Charles. *The New York City Draft Riots: Their Significance for American Society and Politics in the Age of the Civil War.* New York: Oxford University Press, 1990. A detailed, highly readable study of the Civil War's worst draft riot, analyzed within the broader sociopolitical context of Civil War society.

Geary, James W. *We Need Men: The Union Draft in the Civil War.* Dekalb: Illinois University Press, 1991. An extensively footnoted study of the draft law's origins, operation, and effects, containing much statistical demographic data. Based on archival sources.

Kohn, Stephen M. *Jailed for Peace: The History of American Draft Law Violation, 1658-1985.* New York: Praeger, 1987. A thorough study of resistance to compulsory conscription from colonial to recent times, containing an excellent analysis of the first draft law.

Murdock, Eugene C. *One Million Men: The Civil War Draft in the North.* Madison: State Historical Society of Wisconsin, 1971. A scholarly study of how the draft system worked, its shortcomings, the abuses and dodges within the system, and its successes. Detailed, yet readable.

Shannon, Fred A. *The Organization and Administration of the Union Army, 1861-1865.* 1928. Reprint. 2 vols. Gloucester, Mass.: Peter Smith, 1965. A landmark study of the Union Army. Gives considerable attention to inequalities within the conscription system and methods employed to avoid being sent to fight.

SEE ALSO: 1860, Lincoln Is Elected President; 1860, Confederate States Secede from the Union; 1861, Stand Watie Fights for the South; 1861, First Battle of Bull Run; 1863, Emancipation Proclamation; 1863, Battles of Gettysburg, Vicksburg, and Chattanooga; 1864, Sherman's March to the Sea; 1865, Surrender at Appomattox and Assassination of Lincoln.

1863 ■ Battles of Gettysburg, Vicksburg, and Chattanooga: *marking the turning point in the Civil War, these campaigns end the South's offensive capabilities*

Date: July 1, 1863-November 25, 1863

Locale: Gettysburg, Pennsylvania; Vicksburg, Mississippi; Chattanooga, Tennessee

Category: Wars, uprisings, and civil unrest

Key figures:

Braxton Bragg (1817-1870), commander of the Confederate forces at Chattanooga

Ulysses Simpson Grant (1822-1885), commander of the Union forces at Vicksburg and Chattanooga

Joseph Eggleston Johnston (1807-1891), Confederate commander in Mississippi in 1863

Robert Edward Lee (1807-1870), commander of the Confederate Army of Northern Virginia at Gettysburg

George Gordon Meade (1815-1872), commander of the Union Army of the Potomac at Gettysburg

John Clifford Pemberton (1814-1881), commander of the Confederate forces at Vicksburg

William Tecumseh Sherman (1820-1891), Grant's principal subordinate at Vicksburg and Chattanooga

George Henry Thomas (1816-1870), commander of the Union Army of the Cumberland at Chattanooga

Summary of event. Following the First Battle of Bull Run in July, 1861, there was no serious campaigning in the Eastern theater that year. In 1862, George B. McClellan, commander of the Union Army of the Potomac, tried to take Richmond by attacking westward on the peninsula between the York and James Rivers. His campaign failed, and Robert E. Lee, commander of the Confederate Army of Northern Virginia, invaded Maryland. McClellan repulsed him at the Battle of Antietam on September 17. That winter, Ambrose Burnside replaced McClellan and attempted to get at Richmond from the north. Lee stopped Burnside's advance at the Battle of Fredericksburg on December 13. President Abraham Lincoln then put Joseph Hooker in Burnside's place. Early in the spring of 1863, Hooker tried to move around Lee's left flank, but Lee counterattacked and defeated him at Chancellorsville on May 2.

Lee then launched his second invasion of the North, moving in the general direction of Harrisburg, the capital of Pennsylvania. The Army of the Potomac followed, keeping between Lee and the national capital at Washington. On July 1, the two armies came in contact at Gettysburg, a small college town southwest of Harrisburg. George G. Meade, who had just taken command of the Union forces, rushed his men to the town, as did Lee, for what would become the greatest land battle ever fought in the Americas. On the first day, there was fierce fighting on the northern end of the line, where, despite heavy losses (amounting to 80 percent in one brigade), the Union forces held. On

July 2, Lee attacked with his right wing, with similar results.

On July 3, Lee ordered a massive assault on Meade's center, which was fixed on Cemetery Hill. After a planned artillery bombardment of one hour, there ensued an infantry attack of approximately twelve thousand troops under the operational command of Lieutenant General James Longstreet. Longstreet, commanding First Corps and Lee's "Old War Horse," had argued strongly against any fight at Gettysburg and bitterly opposed the attack on July 3. Longstreet had three divisions, the strongest of which was Major General George Pickett's Virginia division. Union artillery and massed infantry fire inflicted casualties of more than 50 percent on the assaulting force and broke up attacking divisions. After an hour of bitter fighting, shattered and dispirited Confederates streamed back from Cemetery Hill. At the same time, east of Gettysburg, General Jeb Stuart's once seemingly invincible Confederate cavalry was soundly defeated. July 3, 1863, was Lee's worst day as commander of the Army of Northern Virginia.

Lee had suffered twenty-eight thousand casualties; Meade, twenty-three thousand. Lee, his army sorely depleted, retired to Virginia. He could now do no more than defend Virginia and hope that the North would abandon its effort to conquer the South, for the Army of Northern Virginia would never again be capable of assuming the offensive.

In the Western theater, meanwhile, the Union was on the offensive. Early in 1862, Ulysses S. Grant had captured Confederate positions at Fort Donelson on the lower Cumberland River and Fort Henry on the Tennessee River. The Confederates fell back to Mississippi, but counterattacked at Shiloh on April 6-7 without success. The Union then took control of all points north of Vicksburg on the Mississippi River. In October, 1862, Grant began an advance down the Mississippi Central Railroad headed for Vicksburg, a fortified city on the Mississippi River. Vicksburg was important because it was on a high bluff, and Confederate artillery there denied passage of the river to the Union boats. While Grant moved along the railroad line with forty thousand men, William T. Sherman, with thirty-two thousand, moved along the river. In December, Confederate cavalry moved into Grant's rear flank and burned his supply dumps at Holly Springs, Mississippi. Grant fell back to bases in Tennessee. Sherman, not realizing that he was unsupported, attacked Vicksburg and suffered heavy casualties.

Grant was determined to take Vicksburg by any means, and during the winter of 1862-1863 he tried to bypass Vicksburg by digging a canal opposite the city. This scheme failed, but Grant did not give up the idea of taking the heavily fortified city. Preparing for a spring campaign, he built up a vast quantity of supplies, most placed on barges, which would be floated downriver. He had decided on a daring campaign to move south of Vicksburg, cross from Louisiana to Mississippi, and then march his army into the heart of Mississippi, taking the capital city of Jackson, which was forty miles east of Vicksburg. Once Jackson was taken and his rear secured, Grant would move on to Vicksburg, attacking from the east. The prepared supply barges that would be offloaded south of Vicksburg would keep Grant's highly mobile army well supplied with ammunition and food. It was a daring plan with many dangers, but taking advantage of surprise, mobility, and a unified command, Grant was confident that he could keep Confederates confused and incapable of massing forces against Grant's smaller army.

On April 30, Grant was on dry ground on the east bank of the Mississippi River. He then began a campaign in which he achieved six victories in seventeen days. Moving north, he defeated two Confederate brigades at Port Gibson on May 1. Continuing his move inland, he headed toward Jackson, the capital of Mississippi and a major railroad center directly east of Vicksburg. With Jackson secure, he would not have to worry about his rear flank when he struck out for Vicksburg. Joseph E. Johnston, Confederate commander in the area, was unable to discover Grant's intentions, and John C. Pemberton, in immediate command at Vicksburg, was equally confused over the Union commander's intentions. The result was that Grant, although far outnumbered in the area (seventy thousand to forty thousand), fought each successive battle with overwhelming superiority. On May 12, one of his three corps defeated a Confederate brigade at Raymond, and two days later, his entire army scattered the six thousand Confederates defending Jackson.

Grant burned the city, destroyed the railroad facilities, and turned west toward Vicksburg. Pemberton finally realized where Grant was and with most of his force, but without help from Johnston, he engaged Grant halfway to Vicksburg at Champion's Hill on May 16. Again, Grant drove the enemy from the field, as he did the next day when Pemberton tried to mount a defense a few miles outside Vicksburg at the Big Black River, where Union troops routed the Confederates, forcing a headlong retreat to the earthworks. Pemberton then withdrew inside his defenses at Vicksburg.

On May 19, Grant and his troops, filled with confidence, assaulted the fortress. The Confederates, safely inside their trenches, easily repulsed the attack. Three days later, Grant tried again, with heavy losses. Grant then realized that he could not take the city by assault and settled into a siege. Reinforcements arriving from the North increased the size of his force to seventy thousand, while abundant supplies allowed his artillery to maintain a constant barrage on the enemy positions. The Confederates were short of supplies. By early July, the citizens were starving, the troops were eating mule meat, and the gunners could fire their artillery pieces only three times a day. On July 3, Pemberton asked Grant for surrender terms. Grant allowed the twenty thousand Confederates to leave Vicksburg upon signing paroles, an agreement not to fight again until properly exchanged. Pemberton accepted. On July 4, Grant raised the Union flag over Vicksburg. With the fall of Port Hudson in Louisiana immediately thereafter, the Mississippi River was in Union hands, and the third of the Confederacy to the west was permanently cut off.

Following his victory, Grant, accompanied by Sherman and his corps, went east to Chattanooga, Tennessee, where a Union Army was under siege. Chattanooga was a railroad center and the largest city in eastern Tennessee, an area noted for its Union sentiments. Braxton Bragg, leading the Confederate forces, had won a victory south of the city at Chickamauga (September 20, 1863), forcing the Union Army to fall back into Chattanooga. Grant arrived in mid-October. After restoring the supply line that Bragg had cut, Grant launched his attack on November 25. He planned to strike Bragg's flanks, with a feint in the center. The troops of George H. Thomas, commander of the Union Army of the Cumberland, made the feint up Missionary Ridge, drove out the Confederates who had been facing them in their trenches, and to the amazement of the Union commanders, continued, without orders, right up the hill to destroy Bragg's line. Bragg lost sixty-seven hundred troops, Grant fifty-eight hundred. Mainly because of good luck, Grant had won another victory. With Vicksburg and Chattanooga firmly in the hands of the Union, the Confederate position in the West had become tenuous at best.

The union strategic and operational victories at Vicksburg and Chattanooga marked the emergence of Ulysses S. Grant as the premier general of the war at that time. Chattanooga confirmed that Grant could win campaigns. In Washington, D.C., Abraham Lincoln, who had dismissed a string of generals and was dissatisfied with Meade's performance after Gettysburg, made Grant the overall commander of Union forces. Leaving Major General William T. Sherman behind in the West, Grant went east to confront and finally defeat Robert E. Lee and the army of Northern Virginia. —*Stephen E. Ambrose, updated by James J. Cooke*

ADDITIONAL READING:

Carter, Samuel, III. *The Final Fortress*. New York: St. Martin's Press, 1980. A well-documented analysis of Grant's Vicksburg campaign.

Cleaves, Freeman. *Meade of Gettysburg*. New York: Morningside Press, 1980. Offers insights into Meade's personality and operational ability.

Cozzens, Peter. *The Shipwreck of Their Hopes: The Battles for Chattanooga*. Urbana: University of Illinois Press, 1994. Explores both Union and Confederate failures at Chattanooga, and explains Grant's highly successful campaign to free the city.

Freeman, Douglas Southall. *R. E. Lee: A Biography*. 4 vols. New York: Charles Scribner's Sons, 1934-1935. The most detailed biography of Lee to date. Pro-Lee, but has an excellent analysis of Lee's campaigns.

Jones, Archer. *Civil War Command and Strategy*. New York: Free Press, 1992. A complete, thoughtful analysis of the war years, with excellent insights into the operational abilities of U. S. Grant.

McFeely, William S. *Grant*. New York: W. W. Norton, 1981. Provides a good analysis of Grant's motivations at Vicksburg and Chattanooga.

SEE ALSO: 1860, Lincoln Is Elected President; 1860, Confederate States Secede from the Union; 1861, Stand Watie Fights for the South; 1861, Lincoln's Inauguration; 1861, First Battle of Bull Run; 1862, *Monitor* vs. *Virginia*; 1863, Emancipation Proclamation; 1863, Reconstruction; 1864, Sherman's March to the Sea; 1865, Surrender at Appomattox and Assassination of Lincoln.

1863 ■ Long Walk of the Navajos:

forced to walk from their ancestral lands to an arid reservation three hundred miles away, the Navajo lose their home and many of their people

DATE: August, 1863-September, 1866
LOCALE: Arizona and New Mexico
CATEGORY: Native American history
KEY FIGURES:
Barboncito (c. 1820-1871), Navajo war chief
James H. Carleton (died 1873), commander of the
    Department of New Mexico
Christopher "Kit" Carson (1809-1868), frontiersman,
    Indian agent, and soldier
Manuelito (c. 1818-1894), Navajo resistance leader and war
    chief
William Tecumseh Sherman (1820-1891), Union general in
    the Civil War

SUMMARY OF EVENT. Perhaps the most significant event in Navajo history occurred during and immediately after the U.S. Civil War, when U.S. Army troops, under the authority of Colonel Christopher "Kit" Carson, methodically raided and subdued the various bands of Navajos who lived between the three rivers (the Colorado, Rio Grande, and San Juan) that encircled the Dinetah, Navajo ancestral lands in present-day Arizona and New Mexico. This event is significant in U.S. history, because it is one of the last major episodes in Carson's public life, one of the earliest federal attempts to pilot an American Indian reservation policy, and the final military conflict between the Navajo people and the U.S. Army.

After Civil War hostilities began in April, 1861, the West was drained of most of its U.S. Army regulars. During the same month, Kit Carson, serving as the Ute Indian agent in Taos, raised the Stars and Stripes in the town plaza, signifying his allegiance to the Union. Carson was commissioned as a colonel in the First New Mexican Volunteers, and there is every indication that he intended to fight against the Confederate Army. However, Colorado volunteers, in the Battle of Valverde on February 21, 1862, drove Confederate forces back from the Rio Grande, and there were no further Confederate incursions in the New Mexico Territory for the balance of the war.

Meanwhile, Brigadier General James H. Carleton, who had assumed the position of commander of the Department of New Mexico in 1861, was obsessed with the idea of resettling the natives of the New Mexico Territory. As U.S. settlers had entered the region in greater numbers after 1846, relations deteriorated as a result of thievery and cultural misunderstanding. Among the Navajo, the *ladrones* (poor in sheep and possessions) usually perpetrated the raids on the settlers, while the *ricos* (comparatively wealthy) suffered the reprisals. Initially, most *ladrones* were of the war party, while the *ricos* were

peace-seeking. However, years of suffering from counter-raids and reprisals drew even the *rico* Navajos into accepting the inevitability of armed conflict with New Mexican settlers.

As late as December, 1862, eighteen Navajo *ricos* traveled to Santa Fe to seek peace with General Carleton. Carleton rebuffed them, preoccupied at the time with exiling the Mescalero Apache to a barren stretch of the Pecos River Valley in eastern New Mexico known as Bosque Redondo ("round grove of trees"). This strategy was the beginning of Carleton's dream of a "Fair Carletonia," peopled with American Indians who would forgo their pagan habits and accept Christianity and a Euro-American lifestyle.

Once the Apaches were resettled, Carleton, in April, 1863, was willing to talk peace with Navajo chiefs Barboncito and Delgadito, but only on his terms: removal to Bosque Redondo or a fight to the death. The Navajo chiefs apparently tried to explain to Carleton that voluntarily leaving their land would violate their deepest religious beliefs, but Carleton would not relent. In June, 1863, Carleton set July 20, 1863, as a deadline: All Navajos should present themselves at Fort Canby or Fort Wingate; those Navajos remaining at large would be considered as hostiles.

Only a handful of Navajos complied with this ultimatum, and Carleton responded by authorizing Colonel Carson to begin scouting expeditions in August, 1863, to capture or kill Navajos, plunder their crops, and seize their livestock. Carson led a number of scouting expeditions and authorized a number of his officers to do the same. Carson also employed Utes as both guides and warriors in hunting the Navajo.

Actual military skirmishes between the First New Mexican Volunteers and the Navajo were rare throughout the remainder of 1863. By the end of the year, Carson reported seventy-eight Navajos killed and forty wounded. Perhaps more significant was that more than five thousand sheep, goats, and mules belonging to the Navajo had been confiscated, and more than seventy-five thousand pounds of wheat were destroyed or seized. The Navajo could hide from the scouting expeditions of volunteers, but they left behind their hogans and rancheros for the troops to plunder and seize. While the Navajo tribe was not decimated by war, Carson's scorched-earth policy laid the foundation for the threat of mass starvation and, therefore, the likelihood of ultimate surrender.

In January, 1864, two scouting parties, one led by Carson and the other by Captain Albert Pfeiffer, left Fort Canby, taking parallel routes through the Canyon de Chelly area north of the fort. Each party exchanged gunshots for the Navajo arrows that rained down on them from the upper reaches of the sheer red sandstone walls and ancient Anasazi ruins where the Navajo ensconced themselves. The entire joint expedition resulted in only twenty-three Navajos being killed, but two hundred Navajos surrendered, and at least two hundred head of livestock were seized. The peach orchards along the canyon floor were also destroyed. Once the troops returned to Fort Canby, great numbers of surrendering Navajos followed. They were starving, freezing, and dying from exposure. Carson's march along the length of the floor of Canyon de Chelly seems to have proven that the Navajo could remain in relative safety along its ledges, but that the troops could destroy their crops and orchards and seize their livestock, thereby leaving them to starve or surrender.

By March, 1864, there were six thousand Navajos at Forts Canby and Wingate, several thousand more than even Carleton had expected. The first of a series of Long Walks commenced at this time. Although the U.S. Army provided a limited number of carts and horses, those conveyances generally carried blankets and provisions rather than people. Most of the Navajo walked the entire three hundred miles, a journey that took anywhere from eighteen to forty days, while Carleton's plans provided for only eight days of government rations for the journey. There was actually a series of Long Walks from Fort Canby to Fort Sumner (Bosque Redondo), although the first, in March, 1864, was the largest. Although there is no Army record of such deeds, many stories in Navajo oral tradition recount atrocities whereby the old or infirm or pregnant who could not keep up were summarily shot by soldiers.

The Navajo never received the full promise of ample food, clothing, and shelter at Bosque Redondo. Carleton planned to make farmers of the hunter-gatherer Navajo, but there was not enough tillable land in arid eastern New Mexico to support more than eight thousand Navajos and the Mescalero Apaches who were already at Fort Sumner. There was not enough grass for the herds of sheep and goats, leading to frequent raids of the government stock by Kiowas and Comanches. The few crops that were raised were attacked by insects and suffered from flood, drought, and hail. Government rations were meager and of poor quality—the flour the Navajo received often was full of bugs—and the food was foreign to the Navajo, who did not consider bacon a satisfactory substitute for beef. In addition, the Navajo had to live in close quarters with the Mescalero Apaches, their old enemies, and there was a bureaucratic war between the War Department and the Department of the Interior. Indian Agent Lorenzo Labadie was ordered not to take charge of the Navajo under the aegis of the Department of the Interior, since technically, they were prisoners of war and should be quartered by the War Department. The Navajo suffered from hunger and cold, while bureaucrats bickered.

Carleton sent Carson to Bosque Redondo later in 1864 to serve as supervisor there, but Carson left in disgust after three months, disappointed and embarrassed at the failure of the federal government to provide the stipulated terms of surrender. Carson resigned his commission and returned to Taos, where he died in 1868.

Individual bands of the Navajo remained in the Dinetah, most notably one led by Manuelito, withstanding famine, military attack, bad weather, and Navajo treachery. Finally, after repeated attacks by Utes and Hopis deputized by the U.S. Army, Manuelito and twenty-three followers surrendered at Fort Wingate on September 1, 1866.

It soon became evident that Carleton's dream of a "Fair Carletonia" was an abject failure. Carleton was relieved of his command in April, 1867, although it was not until April, 1868, that Manuelito, Barboncito, and other Navajo headmen traveled to Washington, D.C., to ask President Andrew Johnson for permission to return to their ancestral lands. Johnson agreed only to establish a peace commission.

The Taylor Peace Commission arrived at Bosque Redondo in May, 1868, with the expectation of offering the Navajo land in Indian territory (now Oklahoma) to the east. Ironically, General William T. Sherman, the architect of his own scorched-earth policy in Georgia several years earlier, was the Taylor Commission member who first became convinced that the Navajo should be allowed instead to return home.

On June 1, 1868, the Treaty Between the United States of America and the Navajo Tribe of Indians was signed, and the westward Long Walk began by the middle of the month. The initial treaty stipulated only 3.5 million acres for the Navajo (the present-day size of the reservation is 15 million acres) but consecrated Canyon de Chelly as sacred ground to be administered solely by the Navajo tribe. Thus, the Navajo returned to their once and future home, after four years in exile. They never again engaged in military conflict with the U.S. Army.

—Richard Sax

Additional reading:

Amsden, Charles. "The Navajo Exile at Bosque Redondo." *New Mexico Historical Review* 8 (1933): 31-50. A dated but still significant article concerning the Navajo on the Bosque Redondo reservation.

Frink, Maurice. *Fort Defiance and the Navajos*. Boulder, Colo.: Pruett, 1968. This text is directed toward a middle school or high school audience. Chapter 7, "Lost Cause, Long Walk," covers the relocations.

Kelly, Lawrence C. *Navajo Roundup: Selected Correspondence of Kit Carson's Expedition Against the Navajo, 1863-1865*. Boulder, Colo.: Pruett, 1970. A collection of personal letters and U.S. Army general orders, especially those of General E. R. S. Canby, Brigadier General James Carleton, and Colonel Kit Carson.

McPherson, Robert S. *The Northern Navajo Frontier, 1860-1900: Expansion Through Adversity*. Albuquerque: University of New Mexico Press, 1988. A well-documented study of the clash of cultures in the Four Corners area.

Trafzer, Clifford. *The Kit Carson Campaign: The Last Great Navajo War*. Norman: University of Oklahoma Press, 1982. The definitive text on the Long Walk of the Navajos. Well researched and thoroughly annotated, although with some turgid language, especially when describing landscape. Three maps and sixty-eight illustrations.

Utley, Robert M. *The Indian Frontier of the American West, 1846-1890*. Albuquerque: University of New Mexico Press, 1984. Chapter 3 includes a good partial discussion of the events leading to the Long Walk.

See also: 1861, Apache Wars; 1862, Great Sioux War; 1864, Sand Creek Massacre; 1866, Bozeman Trail War; 1867, Medicine Lodge Creek Treaty; 1868, Washita River Massacre.

1863 ■ RECONSTRUCTION: *even before the end of the Civil War, the federal government takes steps to rebuild the devastated South*

DATE: December 8, 1863-April 24, 1877
LOCALE: United States
CATEGORIES: African American history; Economics
KEY FIGURES:
Andrew Johnson (1808-1875), seventeenth president of the United States, 1865-1869
Abraham Lincoln (1809-1865), sixteenth president of the United States, 1861-1865
Thaddeus Stevens (1792-1868), congressman and leader of the Radical Republicans in the House of Representatives
Charles Sumner (1811-1874), senator and leader of the Radical Republicans in the Senate

SUMMARY OF EVENT. The end of the Civil War brought on the enormously complex task of reconstructing the nation. The situation in the South was desperate: Its commercial heart had been destroyed and economic paralysis had set in; banks, money, and credit were nonexistent; people in many areas faced actual starvation; institutions such as churches, schools, and city and county governments had ceased to function. Were these seceded and now destitute Southern states to be treated as erring rebels and quickly returned to the Union? Abraham Lincoln, sixteenth president of the United States, consistently maintained that the "seceding" Southern states had, in fact, never left the Union; those Southern states, according to Lincoln, were to be brought back into their "proper relationship" with the federal government; then "safely at home, it would be utterly immaterial whether they had been abroad."

While the war was still in progress, Lincoln had turned his thoughts to the problem of reconciliation and had devised a plan to restore the South with maximum speed and minimum humiliation. The basis of this restoration would be a loyal minority in each state. To create such a body, Lincoln expected to use the presidential pardoning power. He granted amnesty to all ex-Confederates except high civilian and military officials, who would take an oath of loyalty to the United States. When 10 percent of the 1860 electorate in the state took the oath, that state could then set up a new state government, which would then be recognized by the president. Lincoln proclaimed this "ten percent plan" in effect on December 8, 1863.

The more radical members of Congress—led in the House by Thaddeus Stevens of Pennsylvania and in the Senate by Charles Sumner of Massachusetts—were annoyed by the mildness of Lincoln's approach, and they repudiated the state governments of Tennessee, Arkansas, and Louisiana, which had been established under this plan. The electoral votes from these states were not counted in 1864, and their representatives were not seated in Congress. Forced by political necessity to provide an alternative, the Radical Republicans countered Lincoln by passing the Wade-Davis Bill in June, 1864. That measure stipulated that Congress was to put the Reconstruction program into effect. A majority of the number of persons who had voted in 1860, rather than ten percent, was required to swear allegiance before state governments could be established. Other rigid provisions were enumerated. The new state constitutions had to abolish slavery, repudiate the Confederate debt, and disfranchise Confederate military leaders. Prospective voters had to swear an "ironclad oath" of past as well as future loyalty in order to qualify for the franchise. Since the bill was passed an hour before the session of Congress ended, Lincoln, who objected to the harshness of the radical position, permitted the bill to die by pocket veto. The radicals then approved the Wade-Davis Manifesto, which bitterly attacked Lincoln for ostensibly usurping congressional power.

The sentiment behind a program of Radical Reconstruction had been present from the earliest days of the Civil War, but it coalesced around the Wade-Davis Bill, a measure that would have eliminated the Southern ruling class from participation in the political process. This measure came about as a response by Republicans in Congress who resented or eschewed the reconstruction proposals outlined by Lincoln in December, 1863.

Before any action could be taken by either side, Lincoln was assassinated in April, 1865. His death removed from politics a far-sighted statesman of tact and influence and a man well versed in handling recalcitrant congressmen. It elevated Andrew Johnson, a Southern Democrat from Tennessee, to the presidency. Not elected to this highest office, Johnson lacked the respect and gratitude of the nation that Lincoln had gained as the wartime president. Also, Johnson was stubborn and adamant, particularly when he believed his cause to be right. In such a time of crisis, the Tennessean was, perhaps, ill-suited for the presidency.

Although a Southerner and a former slave owner, Johnson was a devoted Unionist. Without calling Congress into session, he put into operation a plan of reconstruction that closely resembled Lincoln's. This, referred to by historians as "Presidential Reconstruction," was not revealed until May 29, 1865. The basic difference between Johnson's and Lincoln's plan was the number of people excluded from the amnesty; Johnson listed a total of fourteen categories of Southerners who were ineligible for pardon. Still, his pardon policy was extremely lenient, and by September of 1865, pardons were being issued "wholesale." In addition, he asked for explicit guarantees: The new state constitutions had to abolish slavery, declare the secession ordinances null and void, and repudiate the Confederate war debt. Majority consent, rather than 10 percent, was implied, but not specified, and the new legislatures were to ratify the Thirteenth Amendment, which abolished slavery. By the time Congress reconvened in December, 1865, all the ex-Confederate states except Texas had fulfilled Johnson's terms, and the president announced to the assembled legislators that Reconstruction was over.

Johnson's plan staggered many Republicans who determined to contest it. Seeking guarantees that the South accepted

DATES OF CONFEDERATE STATES' READMISSION TO THE UNION

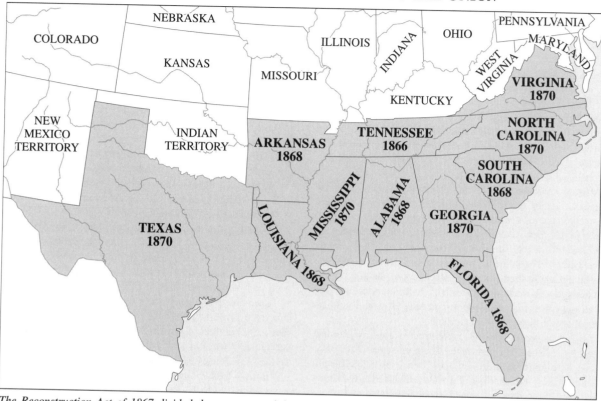

The Reconstruction Act of 1867 divided the ten states of the Deep South into military districts under martial law. An army general overseeing each district was charged with securing a new electorate, enrolling former slaves, and disfranchising former rebels for the purpose of providing for "more efficient government of the rebel states." Thus—over the objections of moderate Republicans and with the aid of sympathetic Democrats—Radical Republicans succeeded in disfranchising former Confederate leaders. Radical Reconstruction also required that the Southern states present acceptable state constitutions to Congress and ratify the Fourteenth Amendment before readmission to the Union would be granted.

the results of the war, the Republicans instead saw that the Southern governments reestablished under the Johnson plan had enacted Black Codes, regulations that had the effect of placing African Americans in a kind of peonage system in Southern society. The Black Codes, in various forms in the Southern states, effectively kept newly freed slaves from voting, getting an education, finding homes, taking advantage of economic opportunities, and gaining equal access to the judicial system. Furthermore, Southern governments had failed to prevent race riots, had elected to office important ex-Confederates such as Alexander H. Stephens, the former vice president of the Confederacy, and generally had given little evidence of a suppliant mood. Politically, the Republicans did not want to jeopardize their position by the rapid return of the Democratic South. Economically, Northern business interests feared Southern opposition to high tariffs and government subsidies, and humanitarians from all sections of the country wanted to see African Americans given political and social equality. Perhaps the most important motivating force was psychological; many Northerners wanted to gloat over their

victory and see some direct evidence of Southern repentance.

After many proposals and counterproposals, the Republicans in Congress proposed the Fourteenth Amendment, which they considered to be a peace treaty. If the South would accept it, the Southern states would be readmitted. The Fourteenth Amendment guaranteed African Americans citizenship, imposed political disabilities upon ex-Confederates, and attempted to compel the former slave states to allow African American suffrage by decreasing their representation in the House of Representatives and the electoral college in the event of disenfranchisement. Given the temper of the North and of Republicans in the spring of 1866, it was an eminently moderate measure. Johnson opposed it, however, and urged the Southern states to reject it. They did, and the measure failed.

On March 2, 1867, Congress passed the first of the Military Reconstruction Acts. This act replaced civil administration with military rule, dividing the South into five military districts whose administrating officers were to take orders from General Ulysses S. Grant rather than from the president. The first duties of these military regimes were to protect persons and property, to create a new electorate based on male suffrage, and to supervise the election of conventions that were to draft new state constitutions. The military governments were also given the right to replace civil officials who had been "fraudulently" elected and to remove "disloyal" members from the state legislatures. The South was now ruled with a firm hand by its military governors. Confederate veterans' organizations and historical societies were suppressed, state and local officials were removed from office, and military tribunals assumed the duties of civil courts when it was found that those courts could not be depended upon to punish violence against African Americans. The army of occupation, consisting of nearly twenty thousand men and aided by an African American militia, enforced military rule; but these forces, deeply resented by the local populace, were kept largely in the background. In general, they were not called out except to supervise elections or to control civil disorders. In each Southern state, the new African American electorate that had been registered by the military helped to choose the conventions that drafted new state constitutions. The new constitutions gave African Americans the right to vote while denying this right to former Confederate leaders. Civil and political equality was also granted to freedmen.

By the summer of 1868, reconstructed governments had been established in seven of the Southern states. After their state legislatures had ratified the Fourteenth and Fifteenth Amendments, the states were formally readmitted to the Union and were allowed to send senators and representatives to Congress. The states of Mississippi, Georgia, Virginia, and Texas were not "reconstructed" until 1870.

This era of "Black Reconstruction" has been greatly misrepresented, for varied and often deceitful reasons, as a time when the South fell prey to uneducated African Americans, opportunistic Northern "carpetbaggers," and a minority of disloyal Southern "scalawags." In reality, however, African Americans never dominated any Southern state government, nor did they ever hold offices in proportion to their numbers within the population. The African Americans elected to office were most often equal in ability to their white predecessors; some, such as Hiram R. Revels, senator from Mississippi, were men of extraordinary talent and ability. Due to a lack of political experience, however, some African American officeholders were manipulated and exploited by avaricious whites. In general, the corruption that characterized several of the state governments in this period was a result of the triumph of white political sophistication and wiles over the political naïveté of the newly elected officeholders.

It is interesting to note that the new African American legislators never did attempt to pass vindictive laws aimed at their former masters. However, no matter what form the new reconstructed governments took, they were bound to be hated by the majority of Southern whites. A program of rebuilding the physical structure of the area—cities, roads, railroads—necessary for economic growth and recovery, resulted in deficit spending characterized by the crushing burden of taxation that was placed on the Southern gentry, plus the graft and bribery that took place on a large scale; such corruption was also common in the North at that time. To answer the threat of this alleged oppression, many Southern whites turned to the formation of secret white supremacist societies such as the Ku Klux Klan and the Knights of the White Camelia. A series of pillages, whippings, and even murders resulted. These actions resulted in the enactment of the Force Acts, or Ku Klux Klan Acts, authorizing the president to suspend *habeas corpus* and to send federal troops to areas that were considered to be the most unruly. By means of this congressional legislation, portions of which were later declared unconstitutional, the first incarnation of the Klan was largely stamped out by 1872 (it would resurface again in the twentieth century).

By 1874 the Democrats had captured control of the House of Representatives, marking the end of Northern Radicalism. The Amnesty Act of 1872 had restored full political rights to the disfranchised ex-Confederates. Factional splits in the Republican Party had been caused by struggles between carpetbaggers and scalawags. African Americans who had been promised "forty acres and a mule" by the Republicans began to desert the party when their hopes failed to materialize. Instead, they would turn to the old master class, in which they had more confidence. These white "redeemer" governments recaptured control of state political machinery between 1869 and 1871 in Tennessee, Virginia, North Carolina, and Georgia, and in 1874 to 1875 in Alabama, Arkansas, Texas, and Mississippi. With the Civil War a more distant memory by this time, the North no longer cared about the freedmen in the South, and shortly after the inauguration of Rutherford B. Hayes in 1877, Reconstruction came to an official end when President Hayes withdrew the last federal troops from Louisiana on April 24 of that year. —*John H. DeBerry, updated by Liesel Ashley Miller*

ADDITIONAL READING:

Anderson, Eric, and Alfred A. Moss, Jr., eds. *The Facts of Reconstruction: Essays in Honor of John Hope Franklin.* Baton Rouge: Louisiana State University Press, 1991. A variety of perspectives on Reconstruction including education, politics, segregation, African American economic Reconstruction, Reconstruction and the Constitution, and the role of violence in Reconstruction.

Burr, Virginia Ingraham, ed. *The Secret Eye: The Journal of Ella Gertrude Clanton Thomas, 1848-1889.* Chapel Hill: University of North Carolina Press, 1990. A personal account of the experiences of an elite, educated, Southern, slave-holding white woman before, during, and after the Civil War. Edited by Thomas' great-granddaughter.

Carter, Dan T. *When the War Was Over: The Failure of Self-Reconstruction in the South, 1865-1867.* Baton Rouge: Louisiana State University Press, 1985. Describes the emergence of leadership in the postwar South, characterizing those in power as "cautious and conservative," responding to emancipation and defeat as best they could.

Foner, Eric. *Reconstruction: America's Unfinished Revolution, 1863-1877.* New York: Harper & Row, 1988. Provides a coherent narrative of how the South and the nation as a whole responded economically, politically, and socially to the end of the Civil War and slavery.

McPherson, James M. *Ordeal by Fire: The Civil War and Reconstruction*. New York: Alfred A. Knopf, 1982. A detailed account of the events leading up to the Civil War, analysis of the military and political battles of the Civil War, and Reconstruction. Photographs, maps.

Smith, Page. *Trial by Fire: A People's History of the Civil War and Reconstruction*. Vol. 5. New York: McGraw-Hill, 1982. A controversial, revisionist interpretation of the Civil War and Reconstruction, Smith's work draws from a variety of sources, including primary accounts from contemporary journals and correspondence.

Sutherland, Daniel E. *The Confederate Carpetbaggers*. Baton Rouge: Louisiana State University Press, 1988. Studies the lives of Southern men and women who left their homes for the North in pursuit of better financial and educational opportunities following the Civil War.

SEE ALSO: 1864, Sherman's March to the Sea; 1865, Freedmen's Bureau Is Established; 1865, Surrender at Appomattox and Assassination of Lincoln; 1865, New Black Codes; 1865, Thirteenth Amendment; 1866, Rise of the Ku Klux Klan; 1866, Civil Rights Act of 1866; 1866, Race Riots in the South; 1868, Impeachment of Andrew Johnson; 1868, Fourteenth Amendment; 1869, Scandals of the Grant Administration; 1877, Hayes Is Elected President; 1883, Civil Rights Cases.

1864 ■ SHERMAN'S MARCH TO THE SEA:
practicing "total war" and demoralization, a Union general carves a path of destruction through Georgia and the Carolinas

DATE: November 15, 1864-April 18, 1865
LOCALE: Georgia and the Carolinas
CATEGORY: Wars, uprisings, and civil unrest
KEY FIGURES:
John Bell Hood (1831-1879), commander of the Confederate Army of Tennessee
Oliver Otis Howard (1830-1909), commander of Sherman's right wing
Joseph Eggleston Johnston (1807-1891), Hood's predecessor
William Tecumseh Sherman (1820-1891), commander of the Union forces
Henry Warner Slocum (1827-1894), commander of Sherman's left wing
SUMMARY OF EVENT. Following his victory at Chattanooga, Ulysses S. Grant went to Washington, D.C., to become the general in chief of the Union army. His successor in the Western theater was William T. Sherman. In the spring of 1864, both generals launched offensives, Grant against Robert E. Lee's Army of Northern Virginia, and Sherman against Joseph E.

Johnston's Army of Tennessee. Grant spent the spring and summer fighting Lee in northern Virginia, suffering heavy casualties but forcing the Confederates to fall back. By fall, the Union forces were besieging Richmond in overwhelming numbers.

Sherman began his campaign on May 7, starting from Chattanooga with a hundred thousand troops and heading toward Atlanta. Johnston, his opponent, had a strength of about sixty-two thousand. Johnston used delaying tactics, refusing to fight a major battle and falling back toward Atlanta. Johnston's use of Fabian tactics exasperated Confederate president Jefferson Davis, who replaced Johnston with John Bell Hood. Despite inferior numbers, Hood attacked Sherman twice, at Peachtree Creek on July 20 and in the Battle of Atlanta on July 22. Hood lost eighty-five hundred soldiers to Sherman's loss of thirty-seven hundred and had to abandon Atlanta. Hood then slipped around Sherman's flank, heading toward the Union supply dumps at Chattanooga and Nashville, Tennessee.

Grant, Union chief of staff Henry Halleck, and President Abraham Lincoln all wanted Sherman to follow Hood and to destroy his army, but instead, Sherman left a comparatively small force under George Thomas at Nashville and prepared to march across Georgia to the Atlantic seaport of Savannah. After burning Atlanta, he began the march on November 15. With Hood moving against Thomas in Nashville (where he eventually lost most of his army in the Battle of Nashville), the Confederates could oppose Sherman's sixty thousand troops with only thirteen thousand soldiers, mostly cavalry. Sherman moved in two wings, brushing all opposition aside. His men lived off the land. "Bummers" went out each morning to the flanks, taking chickens, cows, vegetables, and whatever else they could find. They burned down homes and buildings and destroyed the railroad system. Sherman was determined to see to it that Georgia's civilians realized the horrors of war, and he succeeded. He also wished to cut off Lee's food supply and to encourage desertion in the Army of Northern Virginia, hoping that Confederate soldiers would return to their homes to protect them from his "bummers." As Sherman expressed his philosophy, "Until we can repopulate Georgia, it is useless to occupy it; but the utter destruction of its roads, houses and people will cripple their military resources. . . . I can make the march, and make Georgia howl."

Sherman reached Savannah on December 10. He sent President Lincoln a telegram stating that he wished to offer Savannah as "a Christmas present" to the commander in chief. After refitting his army with supplies brought down from Washington by sea, he marched north into the Carolinas. Again his troops, facing no major opposition, devastated the countryside. The Northern troops were even more severe in South Carolina than they had been in Georgia, since they tended to blame South Carolina, the first state to secede, for the war. As Sherman put it: "We can punish South Carolina as she deserves. . . . I do sincerely believe that the whole United States, North and South, would rejoice to have this army turned loose on South Carolina to devastate that State, in the manner we have done in Georgia." South Carolina's capital city, Columbia, was engulfed in flames in late February.

By late March, 1865, Sherman was in the middle of North Carolina, where his old opponent, Joseph Johnston, had scraped together a small force to resist him. In Virginia, meanwhile, Grant had forced Lee to abandon Richmond and retreat toward western Virginia. By early April, Grant was in close pursuit. Lee, his army almost gone as a result of starvation and desertion, surrendered on April 9 at Appomattox Courthouse, Virginia. By then, the proud Army of Northern Virginia was reduced to a force of 26,700, while Grant had nearly 113,000 troops. Johnston, with the major Confederate Army gone, decided to follow Lee's example, and on April 18 he signed an armistice with Sherman. The Civil War was over. As Sherman, who earlier in his career had directed a Louisiana military school, explained succinctly, "The South bet on the wrong card and lost." His fifty-seven-mile-wide path of destruction demoralized the South's population and, with Grant's military success, helped hasten the war's end. *—Stephen E. Ambrose, updated by Joseph Edward Lee*

ADDITIONAL READING:

Boyd, David F. *General W. T. Sherman as a College President*. Baton Rouge: Ortlieb's Printing House, 1910. Documents Sherman's early service in the South and his fondness for the people of the region.

Chesnut, Mary Boykin. *A Diary from Dixie*. Boston: Houghton Mifflin, 1949. An eyewitness account of the destruction of the South's heartland during Sherman's march.

Davis, Burke. *Sherman's March*. New York: Vintage Books, 1988. This well-written narrative chronicles Sherman's rapid march through Georgia and the Carolinas.

Liddell Hart, Basil Henry. *Sherman: Soldier, Realist, American*. New York: Dodd, Mead, 1929. A dated but still useful biography of Sherman.

Marszalek, John F. *Sherman's Other War: The General and the Civil War Press*. Memphis, Tenn.: Memphis State University Press, 1981. Explores Sherman's rocky relationship with the critical press.

Osborn, Thomas W. *The Fiery Trail*. Knoxville: University of Tennessee Press, 1986. An examination of Sherman's conception of total war.

SEE ALSO: 1863, Reconstruction; 1865, Surrender at Appomattox and Assassination of Lincoln.

1864 ■ SAND CREEK MASSACRE: *the slaughter of Cheyenne women and children by Colorado militia regulars presages the subjugation of Great Plains Indians for the next three decades*

DATE: November 29, 1864
LOCALE: Sand Creek, southeastern Colorado
CATEGORIES: Expansion and land acquisition; Native American history; Wars, uprisings, and civil unrest

KEY FIGURES:
Black Kettle (1803?-1868), chief of the Southern Cheyenne
John M. Chivington (1821-1894), territorial military commander
John Evans (1814-1897), Colorado's territorial governor

SUMMARY OF EVENT. Against the backdrop of the American Civil War, on August 17, 1862, the beleaguered Santee Sioux in Minnesota began an uprising against the continuing encroachment of white settlers. This bloody fighting touched off general warfare the length and breadth of the Great Plains and frightened gold seekers in the new mining settlements of Colorado. Governor John Evans of the new Colorado Territory tried to get Cheyennes and Arapahos to give up their hunting ranges for reservations, but they did not want to leave. In the meantime, white settlers' devastation of the buffalo herds was limiting the tribes' hunting ranges, and regular army troops had moved out to support the Union as a new influx of settlers swept across the plains, seeking fortune and avoiding Civil War service.

Sporadic raids by American Indians made travelers along the California and Santa Fe Trails nervous. White migration and the settlers' practice of decimating buffalo herds merely for their tallow and hides caused concern among the natives, who were hampered further by intertribal warfare, a diminishing food supply, and the scourge of smallpox. On November 10, 1863, Robert North, an illiterate white man of dubious credibility who had lived with the Arapahos, gave a statement to Governor John Evans saying that the Comanches, Apaches, Kiowas, Northern Arapahos, Sioux, and all Cheyennes had pledged to one another to go to war with the settlers in the spring of 1864.

On December 14, 1863, Evans wrote to Secretary of War Edwin Stanton asking for military aid and authority to call out the state militia. The situation remained relatively quiet in the early spring. Cheyennes and Arapahos were fighting the Utes, the Arapahos were feuding with the Kiowas, and the Sioux bided their time. By April, Colonel John M. Chivington's command had begun an aggressive military campaign against American Indians in general and Cheyennes in particular. This campaign provoked a war that lasted well into 1865 and cost the government thirty million dollars.

Chivington, the military commander of Colorado Territory, had had a minor success against Confederate forces in New Mexico in 1862. He was a former Methodist minister who was dubbed the Fighting Parson. Zealous and unscrupulous, he harbored political ambitions. Encouraged by Governor Evans, Chivington used scattered incidents to declare that the Cheyennes were at war, and he sent out soldiers to "burn villages and kill Cheyennes wherever and whenever found." Ominously, he declared that he believed in killing American Indians "little and big."

The tribes struck back. By the summer of 1864, fighting and atrocities on both sides plagued western Kansas and eastern Colorado. In June, Evans, trying to separate peaceful tribes from warlike bands, urged friendly Kiowas and Comanches to report to Fort Larned on the Arkansas River in Kansas and Southern Cheyennes and Arapahos to report to Fort Lyon, 250 miles up the same stream in southeastern Colorado. He ordered the friendly tribes to submit to military authority. A skirmish at Fort Larned rendered this strategy useless, and by August, Evans issued a proclamation calling for indiscriminate killing of American Indians. The natives retaliated by closing the road to Denver, which stopped the mail and caused prices of staples to skyrocket. White settlers mobilized for war.

The Cheyenne chief Black Kettle urgently wanted peace. Accordingly, he and other Cheyenne and Arapaho leaders met with Evans and Chivington at Camp Weld near Denver on September 28, 1864. The talks were confusing, because Evans made the distinction between surrender to the military authorities and securing peace by treaty. The tribal leaders did not understand, and they received no clear promise of peace. Clearly, the settlers were spoiling for a fight. In fact, Chivington had recruited enlistees for his Third Colorado Volunteer Regiment from among mining camp toughs and bums with a promise that they would kill American Indians. The stage was set for a tragedy.

After submitting themselves to military authorities at Fort Lyon in early November, Black Kettle's band of approximately six hundred Indians were sent to make camp to hunt buffalo in the broad, barren valley of Sand Creek, a tributary of the Arkansas River in southeastern Colorado about forty miles north of Fort Lyon. The younger braves having drifted north to listen to the war drums at a council on the Smoky Hill River, Black Kettle's group consisted mostly of old men, women, and children. They were mostly Cheyennes, with a few dozen Arapahos. They believed they were safe.

Chivington's views were unequivocal. He would take no prisoners and "damn any man that was in sympathy with the Indians." After a bitter night march over rolling prairie, Chivington deployed approximately seven hundred men and four howitzers around Black Kettle's village at daybreak on November 29, 1864. In addition to his Third Colorado Volunteer Regiment, Chivington had 175 soldiers of the First Colorado Cavalry and a small contingent of New Mexico infantry.

Mounted troops and foot soldiers swept across the dry creekbed into the Cheyenne camp. Black Kettle ran up a U.S. flag and a white surrender flag over his teepee at the center of the camp. The flags were ignored. Panic ensued as the natives were butchered where they stood. One of the first killed was White Antelope, a seventy-five-year-old man. The Arapaho chief Left Hand fell quickly. Small groups of American Indians fought from sand pits, but most fled in panic. Black Kettle miraculously escaped. Atrocities followed the slaughter.

Eyewitness testimony later recalled, "They [the Indians] were scalped, their brains knocked out; the men used their knives, ripped open women, clubbed little children, knocked them in the head with their guns, beat their brains out, mutilated their bodies in every sense of the word." A Lieutenant Richmond of the notorious Third Colorado shot and scalped three women and five children as they screamed for mercy.

The final tally of American Indian dead ranged from 150 to 500. Three-quarters of those killed were women and children. Chivington's report said of his troops, "All did nobly."

Chivington returned to Denver in triumph, his men brandishing a hundred American Indian scalps. The triumph would be short-lived. A letter from Indian agent S. G. Colley printed in the *Missouri Intelligencer* on January 6, 1865, mentioned the atrocities and stirred public opinion in the states. General Halleck, the Army chief of staff, ordered Chivington investigated, and the district commander, General Curtis, attempted to have him court-martialed. Instead, Chivington mustered out of the service.

Following the massacre, Cheyennes, Arapahos, and Sioux ravaged the South Platte River Valley. They killed approximately fifty whites, burned stage stations, destroyed telegraph lines, and twice sacked the town of Julesburg in northeast Colorado. With the Civil War drawing to a close, on March 3, 1865, a joint resolution of Congress created a joint committee to study the "Indian problem." A shifty and temporary treaty in October, 1865, made peace on the plains but inexplicably contradicted itself and forbade some tribes any legal home. On January 26, 1867, the final report of the joint committee released testimony about the Sand Creek Massacre and traced many American Indian wars to "lawless white men always to be found upon the frontier or boundary lines between savage and civilized life."

The American Indian wars lasted until the closing of the frontier. The constant pressure of whites moving westward across North America had produced constant conflict with the Native Americans. Special circumstances surrounding the Civil War, the Colorado gold rush, and the decline of the buffalo herds led to the tragedy of Sand Creek. The pent-up forces of expansion released in the aftermath of these events ensured that this tragedy would not be an isolated one. Who was "savage" and who "civilized" remains a large historical question.

—Brian G. Tobin

ADDITIONAL READING:

Grinnell, George Bird. *The Fighting Cheyennes*. New York: Charles Scribner's Sons, 1915. Drawing heavily on primary documentation and such venerable authorities as Hubert Howe Bancroft, this detailed account of the Sand Creek events evokes Cheyenne sympathies.

Hoig, Stan. *The Peace Chiefs of the Cheyennes*. Norman: University of Oklahoma Press, 1980. This short work paints the Cheyenne in general, and Black Kettle in particular, as men of peace. Includes many interesting photographs.

Josephy, Alvin M., Jr. *The Indian Heritage of America*. Rev. ed. Boston: Houghton Mifflin, 1991. Examines the clash of cultures in words and illustrations.

Lavender, David. *The Great West*. Boston: Houghton Mifflin, 1985. Suggests that Black Kettle may have been more interested in handouts than in peace.

Utley, Robert M., and Wilcomb B. Washburn. *The Indian Wars*. Boston: Houghton Mifflin, 1985. Puts the Sand Creek Massacre in the context of the times.

See also: 1862, Great Sioux War; 1863, Long Walk of the Navajos; 1866, Bozeman Trail War; 1867, Medicine Lodge Creek Treaty; 1871, Indian Appropriation Act; 1872, Great American Bison Slaughter; 1877, Nez Perce Exile; 1890, Closing of the Frontier; 1890, Battle of Wounded Knee.

1865 ■ Freedmen's Bureau Is Established: *the federal government establishes an agency intended to assist newly freed African Americans in making the transition from slavery to freedom*

Date: March 3, 1865
Locale: Washington, D.C.
Categories: African American history; Organizations and institutions
Key figures:
Oliver Otis Howard (1830-1909), chief commissioner of the Freedmen's Bureau
Andrew Johnson (1808-1875), seventeenth president of the United States, 1865-1869
Thaddeus Stevens (1792-1868), congressman from Pennsylvania who proposed giving forty acres of land to each newly freed adult

Summary of event. On March 3, 1865, Congress created the Freedmen's Bureau, a temporary agency within the War Department. The Freedmen's Bureau, also known as the United States Bureau of Refugees, Freedmen, and Abandoned Lands, was administered by General Oliver Otis Howard from 1865 until it was dismantled by Congress in 1872. The primary objective of the Freedmen's Bureau was to help newly freed African Americans to function as free men, women, and children. In order to achieve this goal, the bureau was expected to assume responsibility for all matters related to the newly freed slaves in the Southern states.

The bureau's mission was an enormous undertaking because of limited resources, political conflicts over Reconstruction policies, and a hostile environment. The work of the bureau was performed by General Howard and a network of assistant commissioners in various states, largely in the South. The Freedmen's Bureau attempted to address many of the needs of the newly freed African Americans, including labor relations, education, landownership, medical care, food distribution, family reunification, legal protection, and legal services within the African American community.

In the area of labor relations, the Freedmen's Bureau dealt with labor-related issues such as transporting and relocating refugees and the newly freed persons for employment, contract and wage disputes, and harsh legislation enacted by some states. Concerning the last issue, many Southern states had passed laws, called Black Codes, that required adult freed men and women to have lawful employment or a business. Otherwise, they would be fined and jailed for vagrancy, and sheriffs would hire them out to anyone who would pay their fine. Given the scarcity of jobs, this policy resulted in former slave owners maintaining rigid control over newly freed African Americans. Another discriminatory law gave the former owners of orphaned African Americans the right to hire them as apprentices rather than placing them with their relatives. Again, this law resulted in the continuation of free labor for many Southerners. The Freedmen's Bureau has been criticized for the failure of its agents to negotiate labor contracts in the interest of the newly freed. The bureau was frequently accused of protecting the rights of the Southern planters, instead.

Obtaining an education was extremely important to the newly freed African Americans. They knew that learning to read and write would enable them to enter into contracts and establish businesses, and would aid them in legal matters. The Freedmen's Bureau provided some support, by providing teachers, schools, and books and by coordinating volunteers. The bureau also made a contribution to the founding of African American colleges and universities. Southern opposition to educating African Americans was a result of the Southerners' fear that education would make African Americans too independent and unwilling to work under the terms established by their former owners. Therefore, Southerners instituted control over the educational administration and classrooms and the entire system. Southern planters used various methods to exert control: frequent changes in administrative personnel, the use of racial stereotypes regarding the intellectual inferiority of African Americans, and educational policy decision making based on paternalism and self-interest. Consequently, educational opportunities were significantly restricted for African American youth.

The newly freed African Americans were eager to acquire property. They demonstrated their interest in owning their own land as individuals and formed associations to purchase large tracts of land. Their sense of family and community was the basis for their strong desire to own land. The Freedmen's Bureau was initially authorized to distribute land that had been confiscated from Southern plantation owners during the Civil War. Specifically, on the sea islands of South Carolina, the bureau was mandated to lease or sell lands that had been confiscated. This land was to be distributed in parcels of forty acres. The decision of Congress to authorize the distribution of land was based on a proposal made by Thaddeus Stevens, the Republican congressman from Pennsylvania. However, President Andrew Johnson acceded to pressure from the rebellious planters to return their lands. The plantation owners were pardoned, and their property rights were restored by President Johnson. Consequently, all land that had been distributed to African Americans was returned to its previous owners. African Americans then were encouraged to sign contracts to work on the land that they once owned. Many refused to comply with this arrangement. Others would not voluntarily leave the property they once owned. When the freed men and women refused to vacate this property, they were evicted.

A medical department was created within the Freedmen's

Bureau. It was to be a temporary service, to ensure that medical services were provided to African Americans until local governments assumed this responsibility. In spite of inadequate resources, the bureau founded forty-five hospitals in fourteen states. Some of the more common problems of the bureau's medical department were inadequately staffed hospitals, medical personnel with little control over health concerns, frequent personnel changes and relocation of hospitals, and lack of funds to purchase food for patients. In spite of these problems, the bureau experienced some success in providing for the medical needs of newly freed African Americans, rendering medical services to large numbers of former slaves, though unable to meet the medical needs of many.

The Freedmen's Bureau also attempted to provide for the social welfare of the freed persons. The agency was noted for rationing food to refugees and former slaves; it assisted families in reuniting with members who had been sold or separated in other ways during slavery.

Protecting the rights of the former slaves was a major task of the Freedmen's Bureau. Republicans believed that African Americans should have the same rights as whites. However, many Southern states enacted Black Codes that severely restricted the civil rights of the freed men, women, and children. These laws, exacting social and economic control over African Americans, represented a new form of slavery. When state legislation prohibited African Americans' equal rights, the bureau attempted to invoke the 1866 Civil Rights Act, which offered African Americans the same legal protections and rights as whites to testify in courts, to own property, to enforce legal contracts, and to sue. The bureau found it extremely difficult to enforce the Civil Rights Act and to prosecute state officials who enforced laws that were discriminatory against African Americans. A shortage of agents and a reluctance among bureau commissioners to challenge local officials contributed to the agency's limited success in enforcing the Civil Rights Act. Finally, the Freedmen's Bureau also established tribunals to address minor legal disputes of African Americans within their own communities. In many instances, freed slaves were able to resolve their own problems. When they could not, they presented their legal concerns to bureau agents.

The task assigned to the Freedmen's Bureau was monumental. The responsibilities of the bureau significantly exceeded the resources and authority granted to it by Congress. The bureau's ability to perform its varied tasks also was impeded by personnel shortages. President Johnson's Reconstruction policies represented another major challenge to the bureau, as they were not always supportive of the bureau's mandate and objectives. Myriad problems associated with the bureau meant that the newly freed men, women, and children were not able to receive the goods and services necessary to gain economic independence. Consequently, they developed extensive self-help networks to address their needs. —*K. Sue Jewell*

ADDITIONAL READING:

Crouch, Barry A. *The Freedmen's Bureau and Black Texans*. Austin: University of Texas Press, 1982. Discusses the Reconstruction era and the Freedmen's Bureau in the state of Texas. Explores how bureau agents performed their tasks in a hostile climate characterized by racial injustices and resistance to change.

Foster, Gaines M. "The Limitations of Federal Health Care for Freedmen, 1862-1868." In *The Freedmen's Bureau and Black Freedom*, edited by Donald G. Nieman. New York: Garland, 1994. Presents a detailed discussion on the medical needs of African Americans following emancipation. Explores the various problems that adversely affected the bureau's ability to deliver medical services to African Americans.

Franklin, John Hope. *From Slavery to Freedom: A History of Negro Americans*. New York: Alfred A. Knopf, 1988. Focuses on the history of people of African descent brought to the United States as slaves. Examines the harsh social and economic conditions that have confronted African Americans and the strategies they used to survive in spite of these societal barriers.

Magdol, Edward. *A Right to the Land: Essays on the Freedmen's Community*. Westport, Conn.: Greenwood Press, 1977. Examines the problems confronting African Americans as freed men, women, and children during Reconstruction. Emphasizes the efforts that African Americans pursued to acquire land and their relentless quest for self-determination.

Westwood, Howard C. "Getting Justice for the Freedmen." In *The Freedmen's Bureau and Black Freedom*, edited by Donald G. Nieman. New York: Garland, 1994. Explores how the Freedmen's Bureau's agents addressed the legal concerns of freed persons during the Reconstruction era.

SEE ALSO: 1863, Reconstruction; 1865, New Black Codes; 1865, Thirteenth Amendment; 1866, Rise of the Ku Klux Klan; 1866, Civil Rights Act of 1866; 1866, Race Riots in the South; 1868, Impeachment of Andrew Johnson; 1868, Fourteenth Amendment.

1865 ■ SURRENDER AT APPOMATTOX AND ASSASSINATION OF LINCOLN: *five days after the South capitulates, President Lincoln is shot at Ford's Theater by a Confederate sympathizer*

DATE: April 9 and 14, 1865

LOCALE: Appomattox Court House, Virginia, and Ford's Theater, Washington, D.C.

CATEGORY: Wars, uprisings, and civil unrest

KEY FIGURES:

John Wilkes Booth (1838-1865), Lincoln's assassin

Ulysses Simpson Grant (1822-1885), general in chief of the victorious Union armies

Andrew Johnson (1808-1875), vice president and successor to Lincoln

Robert Edward Lee (1807-1870), Confederate general who surrendered to Grant on April 9, 1865

Abraham Lincoln (1809-1865), sixteenth president of the
United States, 1861-1865

William Henry Seward (1801-1872), secretary of state

Edwin McMasters Stanton (1814-1869), secretary of war

SUMMARY OF EVENT. The assassination of President Lincoln
occurred only five days after Confederate general Robert E.
Lee surrendered to Union general Ulysses S. Grant at Appomattox Courthouse on April 9, 1865. The other Confederate
armies soon surrendered, and the Civil War came to an end.
Lincoln's body was taken back to Springfield, Illinois, on a
circuitous seventeen-hundred-mile route that retraced his 1861
journey to Washington, D.C.

Lincoln had been the chief architect of the Union victory
that ended the long war. In March, 1864, he called General
Grant to the White House and placed him in overall command
of the Union Armies. Grant then embarked upon a vigorous
campaign aimed at Richmond, engaging Lee's Army of Northern Virginia in two important battles west of Fredricksburg,
Virginia—Wilderness, May 5-7, and Spotsylvania, May 8-9,
1864. Grant suffered heavy casualties but pushed on to Cold
Harbor (June 1-3). There, the Confederates repulsed his attack
which, had it been successful, would have led to the fall of
Richmond. Grant then attempted to outflank Lee by crossing
the James River and driving toward Petersburg, where he
intended to cut vital rail connections. Lee was able to check
Grant's advance short of Petersburg, however, and a nine-
month stalemate ensued.

Meanwhile, General William T. Sherman had completed his
destructive march from Atlanta to the sea at Savannah, Georgia. He then moved northward in a march that was to take him
through South Carolina and North Carolina. All signs pointed
to a Confederate defeat in 1865: The Union blockade was
increasingly effective; Great Britain no longer showed much
sympathy for the Confederacy; the economy of the South was
breaking down under the impact of the war; and Grant continued to receive troop replacements, whereas Lee's troops were
becoming exhausted. A peace conference, which Confederate
president Jefferson Davis had suggested, was held on Febru-

*April 14, 1865: John Wilkes Booth assassinates President Lincoln at Ford's Theater in Washington, D.C. The end of the Civil
War, which had come with Robert E. Lee's surrender to Ulysses S. Grant at Appomattox Courthouse only five days before,
had lifted Lincoln's spirits sufficiently to prompt this rare public appearance. Booth, bitterly disappointed at the Southern
defeat, hoped to renew the South's struggle and further the cause of the Confederacy; his white supremacist sympathies would
prove common among many Southerners during Reconstruction. The president survived the night but never regained consciousness, dying early the next morning. (Library of Congress)*

ary 3, 1865. Confederate vice president Alexander H. Stephens led the delegation from the South, while Lincoln spoke for the Union. Lincoln insisted upon the disbanding of the Confederate forces, but the Confederacy was not then willing to surrender.

In April, 1865, Grant was able to extend Lee's lines to the breaking point, and Lee was forced to evacuated the Confederate capital of Richmond as well as Petersburg. Lee's escape route lay to the west and south; he hoped to join forces with General Joe Johnston in North Carolina, but Grant's forces blocked his escape. Lee, now convinced of the futility of continuing the war, met Grant at the McLean house in Appomattox Courthouse, where he surrendered. Grant, following the spirit of President Lincoln's instructions, agreed to release Lee's officers and men on parole. Lee's troops were allowed to keep their horses, mules, and sidearms and then return home. In short order, the other scattered Confederate armies followed General Lee's lead and began the ordeal of surrender. The last significant group of men under arms, those under the command of General Joseph Johnston, began surrender negotiations with Sherman on April 17. The war had wrought a death toll far greater than anyone could have imagined four years earlier: 360,000 Union soldiers, 260,000 men from the South, and unknown numbers of civilians. The economic havoc would leave the South devastated for a century.

News of Lee's surrender reached Washington the same day it took place, and it was received with great rejoicing. Lincoln made several extemporaneous speeches and one prepared address during the course of the next several days in response to the demands of exuberant crowds. It was Lincoln's view that the South should be welcomed back as brothers to enable healing to begin. In this regard, he was strongly opposed by the Radical Republicans within Congress. It was their view that the South had started the war and should be made to pay. Whether Lincoln might have curbed their hatred remains an unanswered question for history.

At approximately 8:30 P.M. on April 14, President and Mrs. Lincoln, in company with Miss Clara Harris and Major Henry R. Rathbone, entered Ford's Theater to see a performance of *Our American Cousin*. About 10:15 P.M., John Wilkes Booth, a twenty-six-year-old actor who sympathized with the South, slipped into the president's box and fired one shot into the back of Lincoln's head. The president was mortally wounded and died the next morning at 7:22, without ever having regained consciousness. After shooting Lincoln, Booth jumped onto the stage, breaking a small bone in his leg as he landed. From the stage he shouted the motto of Virginia, *Sic semper tyrannis* (thus ever to tyrants). In the confusion, he managed to evade capture in Washington, escaping over the bridge into Virginia. There, his broken leg was set by Dr. Samuel Mudd. It remains unclear whether Mudd was aware of the significance of his patient. Booth was eventually trapped in a tobacco shed near Port Royal, Virginia, on April 26. There Booth died, either by his own hand or from a shot fired by one of the soldiers attempting to arrest him.

Assassination of the president was only one part of a major plot to murder the most important Union officials. Secretary of State William Seward and his sons, Frederick and Augustus, suffered knife wounds at the hands of Lewis Paine, a former Confederate soldier and devotee of Booth. George A. Atzerodt, an alcoholic, was assigned by Booth to kill Vice President Johnson, but he failed to make the attempt. Secretary of War Edwin Stanton took charge of the investigation and ordered the arrest of Paine, Atzerodt, David Herold, Edward Spangler, Samuel Arnold, Michael O'Laughlin, Dr. Samuel Mudd, and Mrs. Mary E. Surratt, owner of the boardinghouse in which the conspirators met. The likelihood is that Mrs. Surratt knew nothing of Booth's plot. However, she was caught up in the passion for revenge that followed Lincoln's murder.

The alleged conspirators were tried before a military commission whose jurisdiction was questionable. The trial lasted from May 10 to June 30, and all the defendants were found guilty. Atzerodt, Paine, Herold, and Surratt were hanged seven days after the trial ended, while Spangler, Arnold, Mudd, and O'Laughlin were sentenced to life imprisonment. Surratt's execution was almost certainly a miscarriage of justice that could not have been carried out if a few weeks or months had been allowed for passions to cool. By contrast, her son John escaped immediate capture and, when tried in 1867, was released after a jury failed to agree on a verdict.

Those sentenced to life imprisonment were pardoned in 1869, with the exception of O'Laughlin, who died of yellow fever at the Dry Tortugas prison off Key West. Dr. Mudd was found guilty as an accessory after the fact, and also sentenced to life imprisonment. However, his heroics during the yellow fever epidemic resulted in a commutation of his sentence, and he also was freed in 1869. Mudd's descendants have continued to argue for his innocence. Former president of the Confederacy Jefferson Davis was taken prisoner soon after Lee's surrender. Although he was indicted for treason and imprisoned two years at Fort Monroe, he never came to trial.

—Mark A. Plummer, updated by Richard Adler

ADDITIONAL READING:

Bishop, Jim. *The Day Lincoln Was Shot*. New York: Harper & Row, 1955. A detailed, hour-by-hour account of the last day in Lincoln's life.

Long, E. B. *The Civil War Day by Day*. New York: Da Capo Press, 1971. A diary of four years of war. While not overly detailed, it provides a chronology of important events throughout the country.

McPherson, James M. *Battle Cry of Freedom*. New York: Oxford University Press, 1988. Arguably the finest one-volume account of the war. Places the war within the perspective of the mid-nineteenth century United States.

Moore, Guy. *The Case of Mrs. Surratt*. Norman: University of Oklahoma Press, 1954. Discusses the role (or lack of it) played by Mrs. Mary Surratt in Lincoln's assassination.

Oates, Stephen B. *With Malice Toward None*. New York: Harper Perennial, 1994. An update of Oates's excellent 1977 biography of Lincoln.

Reck, W. Emerson. *A. Lincoln: His Last Twenty-four Hours.* Columbia: University of South Carolina Press, 1994. A detailed account of Lincoln's last day.

Sandburg, Carl. *Abraham Lincoln.* 2 vols. New York: Harcourt, Brace, 1954. The classic biography of the life of Lincoln.

See also: 1860, Lincoln Is Elected President; 1860, Confederate States Secede from the Union; 1861, Stand Watie Fights for the South; 1861, Lincoln's Inauguration; 1861, First Battle of Bull Run; 1862, *Monitor* vs. *Virginia*; 1863, Emancipation Proclamation; 1863, First National Draft Law; 1863, Battles of Gettysburg, Vicksburg, and Chattanooga; 1863, Reconstruction; 1864, Sherman's March to the Sea; 1868, Impeachment of Andrew Johnson.

1865 ■ Vassar College Is Founded:
the first college for women to offer a full liberal arts curriculum

Date: September 26, 1865
Locale: Poughkeepsie, New York
Categories: Education; Women's issues
Key figures:
Milo Parker Jewett (1808-1882), first president of Vassar
John Howard Raymond (1814-1878), second president of Vassar
Matthew Vassar (1792-1868), a brewer and the founder of Vassar College

Summary of event. When Vassar College opened its doors, a new era began in the higher education of women in the United States. Although many schools for women existed in 1865 and some called themselves colleges, none offered a full college course. Few women's schools offered more than a high school education, and the best existing institution, Mt. Holyoke Seminary, was approximately at the level of a junior college. Oberlin College, Antioch College, and some Western state universities permitted women to take courses, but few women succeeded in meeting the requirements of a bachelor of arts degree. Vassar was unique in offering women an education as rigorous and complete as that offered in the best men's colleges. Its success set a new standard for women's education that other institutions would endeavor to match.

Matthew Vassar, self-made, self-educated, and proud of what he had achieved without formal education, was an unlikely person to found a college for women. Born April 29, 1792, in England, he had come to the United States in 1796 with his parents, who settled in Poughkeepsie, New York, where they operated a brewery. In 1811, Matthew opened his own brewery; thrift and shrewd investments multiplied his wealth. He married in 1813 but had no children. During a trip to Europe in 1845, he was impressed by Thomas Guy's Hospital in London, with its handsome building and monumental statue of the founder; he decided to leave money in his will to build a similar institution in Poughkeepsie.

Vassar showed no interest in higher education for women until after he discussed his hospital plans with Milo P. Jewett, a Baptist minister who, in 1855, took over a school for girls in a building owned by Vassar. Jewett persuaded Vassar that to build and endow "a college for young women which shall be to them what Yale and Harvard are to young men" would create a unique institution that would be a much more memorable monument to his name than any hospital. After some hesitation, Vassar decided to begin the college during his lifetime. In January, 1861, the New York State Legislature passed a charter creating the college, and when the board of trustees met for the first time the next month, Vassar gave them $408,000 (half his estate, with the rest to follow later) to start building. Jewett became the first president of the college, but a falling-out with Vassar led to his resignation in 1864.

During the four years the campus was under construction, Vassar publicized his new institution widely; *Godey's Lady's Book* and *Harper's Weekly* spread the news across the nation. By September, 1865, the great Main Building—modeled after the Tuileries Palace, which Vassar had admired during his tour of France—was ready. Designed to house the entire college, the building contained apartments for president and faculty, rooms for students, classrooms, offices, a library, a large dining room, and an impressive chapel.

John H. Raymond, who succeeded Jewett as president, organized a curriculum fully as rigorous as that of any existing college. When Vassar opened, 353 students between fifteen and twenty-four years of age arrived, but fewer than half were ready to undertake college-level work. Raymond had to establish a preparatory department to bring the others up to grade. Not until 1886 would improvements in U.S. secondary education for women permit Vassar to eliminate the preparatory department.

Matthew Vassar had hoped to hire women as faculty, but except for Maria Mitchell, already world-famous as an astronomer whose discovery of a comet had garnered her a gold medal from the King of Denmark, all the professors were men; women filled the lower ranks. To entice Mitchell, Vassar built an observatory for her on the college grounds, where she chose to live with her father.

Vassar's publicity attracted the attention of critics as well as students. Opponents argued that women were mentally inferior to men and unable to meet male intellectual standards, that they would not be able to stand the physical strain of higher education and would develop brain fever; and that should they manage to survive college, their children would be sickly, if they were able to have children at all. Vassar set out to deflect and disprove all criticism. To protect the health of students, courses in hygiene and physiology were required in the freshman year. A gymnasium with room for a riding school was one of the three original buildings, wide corridors provided room for exercise in winter, and three miles of walkways and riding paths could be used in better weather. To protect the morals of the students, Vassar required them to live under the direct supervision of resident teachers and follow a

NEW BLACK CODES ■ 1865

rigid daily schedule. As alumnae began to succeed in various professions, the college trumpeted their achievements as proof of the ability of women to profit from a rigorous liberal arts education.

Other women's colleges followed Vassar's lead. When Wellesley opened in 1875, only 30 of 314 students were at college level, and the school opened a large preparatory program. Smith College, in the same year, refused to start a preparatory department and attracted only 14 students. By 1885, when Bryn Mawr opened, preparatory departments were no longer necessary, and Bryn Mawr was able to offer graduate degree programs from the start. Mt. Holyoke Seminary added a college-level program and, in 1893, changed its name to Mt. Holyoke College. State universities also responded to Vassar. The University of Wisconsin, which had shunted women into a separate college with more limited and more elementary courses than those available to men, abolished the separate college in 1871.

By the 1890's, the so-called Seven Sister women's colleges—Vassar, Wellesley, Smith, Mt. Holyoke, Bryn Mawr, Radcliffe, and Barnard—were solidly established and able to hire better-educated and more distinguished faculty, many of them women. Gifts from wealthy donors paid for elaborate buildings. Financial aid, however, was limited, and students tended to come from upper-middle-class homes with parents who were professionals or businesspersons. The students came with the full support of their parents and often cited encouragement from fathers as the decisive factor in their decision to go to college.

Separatism, with women in control of all extracurricular life, fostered the development of a women's culture on campus and encouraged a belief in the special mission of educated women. Unlike at coeducational institutions, where men dominated extracurricular activities, students at women's colleges controlled all student life, organizing meetings, politicking among classmates, and handling budgets. Students were prepared to fill leadership roles in national social and political reform movements. Graduates also contributed through volunteer work to school boards and other local institutions. Many graduates became teachers and school administrators; less frequently, they went into medicine, law, or business.

By the 1920's, as the nation became more affluent, the student population changed, showing less interest in reform or preparation for a profession than in enjoying the college experience. Coming from more socially elite and wealthier homes, many of these women had less interest in their studies and little reason to prepare to support themselves. Most now planned to marry and raise a family; few would try for a profession.

In the 1960's, the whole concept of separate education for women came into question, and on women's college campuses the merits of separate education versus coeducation were debated. After lengthy discussion, Vassar turned down an invitation to merge with Yale but, in 1969, decided to become coeducational on its own campus. Radcliffe merged totally

into Harvard. The other five "Sisters" did not become coeducational, although the presence of men on campus became normal under exchange agreements with nearby men's colleges. Proponents of women's colleges insisted on the continuing value of institutions at which women dominated college life. —*Milton Berman*

ADDITIONAL READING:

Gordon, Lynn D. "Vassar College, 1865-1920: Women with Missions." In *Gender and Higher Education in the Progressive Era*. New Haven, Conn.: Yale University Press, 1990. Describes how students and women faculty transformed Matthew Vassar's institution.

Horowitz, Helen Lefkowitz. *Alma Mater: Design and Experience in the Women's Colleges from Their Nineteenth-Century Beginnings to the 1930's*. 2d ed. Amherst: University of Massachusetts Press, 1993. Discusses how the designs chosen for buildings affected college operations and the life of students and faculty.

_____. *Campus Life: Undergraduate Cultures from the End of the Eighteenth Century to the Present*. New York: Alfred A. Knopf, 1987. Discusses how student expectations about college life changed over the centuries. Chapter 4 deals with the experiences of women.

Kendall, Elaine. *"Peculiar Institutions": An Informal History of the Seven Sister Colleges*. New York: G. P. Putnam's Sons, 1976. A witty, anecdotal account of the origins and development of elite Eastern women's colleges.

Newcomer, Mabel. *A Century of Higher Education for American Women*. New York: Harper & Brothers, 1959. Despite its age, this is the standard history of college education for women, with invaluable detail.

Taylor, James Monroe. *Before Vassar Opened: A Contribution to the History of the Higher Education of Women in America*. Boston: Houghton Mifflin, 1914. A scholarly history, by the fourth president of Vassar College, that is the source of all later accounts of the founding of Vassar.

SEE ALSO: 1785, Beginnings of State Universities; 1823, Hartford Female Seminary Is Founded; 1833, Oberlin College Is Established; 1837, Mt. Holyoke Seminary Is Founded.

1865 ■ NEW BLACK CODES: *fearing the effects of the end of slavery, Southern states pass laws to control newly freed African Americans*

DATE: Beginning November 24, 1865
LOCALE: Southern states
CATEGORIES: African American history; Laws and acts
KEY FIGURES:
Benjamin G. Humphreys (1808-1882), governor of Mississippi
Andrew Johnson (1808-1875), seventeenth president of the United States, 1865-1869

Daniel E. Sickles (1819-1914), military commander in South
Carolina

Alfred H. Terry (1827-1890), military commander in Virginia

Lyman Trumbull (1813-1896), senator from Illinois and chair
of the Senate Judiciary Committee

Summary of event. The months immediately following the
end of the U.S. Civil War were a period of great uncertainty.
Wartime president Abraham Lincoln had been killed, and his
successor, Andrew Johnson, was wholly untested. No leadership could be expected from Capitol Hill, since Congress had
gone into a long recess. In the Southern states, a host of
questions required immediate answers; foremost among these
were questions relating to the place of the recently freed slaves
in postwar Southern society. Would the freed slaves continue
to furnish an economical and reliable labor force for Southern
cotton planters? Would the former slaves exact subtle or blatant revenge upon their former masters? Should lawmakers
grant African Americans the vote in the Southern states?
Should the U.S. government give them land? Should the states
pay the cost of a basic education for them? What legal rights
would these five million African Americans enjoy in the postbellum South?

President Johnson developed a lenient plan for Reconstruction, one that called on the Southern states to quickly reorga-
nize their state governments. His only major demands of these
new governments were that they admit that no state had the
right to leave the Union, and that they ratify the Thirteenth
Amendment, which ended slavery. As the new Southern state
legislatures began to meet, their exclusively white members
were most interested in passing laws that would answer some
of the nagging questions about the future place of African
Americans in Southern society. Many legislators believed the
freed slaves would not work unless forced to do so, and they
feared the double specter of an economy without a labor
supply and a huge mass of people who would live on charity
or plunder. In earlier years, laws known as the "slave codes"
had controlled the African American population; some lawmakers now called for a renewal of the slave codes to control
the freed black population.

Mississippi's legislature was the first to take up the question of the rights of, or limitations on, African Americans.
This body met in October, 1865, and quickly fell into arguments over what policies on racial matters should be enacted.
Nearly half of the legislators favored laws that would, in
almost every way, return African Americans to the position
they had occupied in the time of slavery. Mississippi's governor, Benjamin G. Humphreys, intervened and urged lawmakers to ensure certain basic rights to the newly freed slaves.
After Humphreys' intervention, the moderates in the Mississippi legislature had the upper hand and, on November 24,
1865, enacted a bill entitled "An Act to Confer Civil Rights
on Freedmen."

As its title promised, Mississippi's new law did confer
some basic rights on African Americans that they had not
enjoyed as slaves. These rights included the right to sue and be
sued, the right to swear out criminal complaints against others,
the right to purchase or inherit land, the right to marry, and the
right to draw up labor or other contracts. Although the law's
title did speak of conferring civil rights, and a few new rights
were indeed granted, this law—the first of the Black Codes of
the Southern states—was remarkable primarily for the rights it
denied to African Americans. It did give African Americans
the right to own land, but it denied them the right to rent rural
land—thus the legislators sought to perpetuate large gangs of
landless agricultural workers. The act recognized the right to
marry, but it also provided that interracial marriage would be
punished by life imprisonment for both parties. The right to
testify in court was eroded by certain provisions that said the
right to testify did not apply to cases in which both parties in a
lawsuit or criminal case were white, nor to criminal cases in
which the defendant was African American.

Most ominous was the provision that every black citizen in
the state must sign a one-year labor contract by January 1 of
each year and must honor that contract. Should the employee
leave the employer before the end of the year, law enforcement
officers were empowered to return the worker forcibly to his
or her place of employment. In a provision reminiscent of the
old laws that forbade giving help to runaway slaves, this new
law made it a crime to give food, clothing, or shelter to any
African American worker who had left his or her employer
while still under contract. The punishment for helping a runaway was up to two months in jail; for those who helped the
fugitive find work in a state other than Mississippi, the punishment was up to six months in jail. Once again, securing a
stable labor supply for the state was at the forefront of lawmakers' goals.

After Mississippi passed this first Black Code, a flood of
other laws soon followed in Mississippi and the other Southern states. South Carolina's Black Codes forbade African
Americans from pursuing any occupation other than agricultural work, unless the worker paid a prohibitively expensive
fee. Black farm workers there were required by law to work
from sunup to sundown and forbidden from leaving the plantation without the permission of their employer. South Carolina and Mississippi both enacted severe vagrancy laws that
called for the arrest of idle persons, drunkards, gamblers,
wanderers, fighters, people who wasted their pay, circus
hands, actors, and even jugglers. If these persons were African
American, they were to be considered vagrants and fined up to
one hundred dollars and imprisoned. If unable to pay their
fine, their labor would be auctioned off to a white employer,
and their wages used to satisfy the fine.

The Black Codes varied from state to state, but their Northern opponents said they all had the common goal of returning
the freed slaves to a system equivalent to bondage. In some
Southern states, blacks were prohibited from owning guns. In
other states, their assembly in groups was forbidden, or an
evening curfew was imposed. President Johnson, himself a
Southerner, saw little objectionable in the Black Codes, but
many Northerners did. Occupying generals Daniel E. Sickles

in South Carolina and Alfred H. Terry in Virginia overturned all or parts of the Black Codes in their areas, pending action in Congress. In Washington, Senator Lyman Trumbull wrote the Civil Rights Act of 1866, which declared that all persons born in the United States were U.S. citizens, and that all U.S. citizens enjoyed equality before the law. Congress passed this measure over the veto of President Johnson. By 1868, the Fourteenth Amendment brought this same promise of equality before the law into the Constitution itself.

The Black Codes were barely enforced. Overturned by the actions of occupying generals, and later by the U.S. courts, which found them in conflict with the Fourteenth Amendment, they were important chiefly for fueling a conflict in Washington between Johnson's lenient Reconstruction plan and Congress' insistence that the basic rights of African Americans be protected. These codes are also important for their role in bringing about passage of the Fourteenth Amendment. Although African Americans' rights generally were protected between 1866 and 1876, the Southern states found many ways to draft laws that were color-blind on their face, but that could be enforced in a racially biased way. After Reconstruction, few Southern elected officials, and few officeholders nationwide, were very interested in championing African American civil rights.

—Stephen Cresswell

ADDITIONAL READING:

Cohen, William. "Negro Involuntary Servitude in the South, 1865-1940: A Preliminary Analysis." *Journal of Southern History* 42 (February, 1976): 35-50. Discusses the larger picture of black labor and its lack of freedoms, linking the Black Codes to peonage and to the South's convict labor system.

Foner, Eric. *Reconstruction: America's Unfinished Revolution.* New York: Harper & Row, 1988. This massive volume is the basic history of Reconstruction; chapter 5 covers the Black Codes and related events.

Harris, William C. *Presidential Reconstruction in Mississippi.* Baton Rouge: Louisiana State University Press, 1967. Discusses the drafting of Mississippi's Black Codes, which are especially important because they were a model for other Southern state legislatures.

Litwack, Leon F. *Been in the Storm So Long: The Aftermath of Slavery.* New York: Alfred A. Knopf, 1979. Tells the Reconstruction story as much through the eyes of the freed slaves as from the point of view of white government officials.

Wilson, Theodore B. *The Black Codes of the South.* Tuscaloosa: University of Alabama Press, 1965. The only book exclusively devoted to the Black Codes. Provides thoughtful analysis of the meaning of these laws in Southern and African American history.

SEE ALSO: 1804, First Black Codes; 1863, Reconstruction; 1865, Freedmen's Bureau Is Established; 1865, Thirteenth Amendment; 1866, Rise of the Ku Klux Klan; 1866, Civil Rights Act of 1866; 1866, Race Riots in the South; 1868, Fourteenth Amendment; 1883, Civil Rights Cases; 1890, Mississippi Disfranchisement Laws.

1865 ∎ THIRTEENTH AMENDMENT: *the first of the Civil War amendments states that "neither slavery nor involuntary servitude . . . shall exist within the United States"*

DATE: December 18, 1865
LOCALE: Washington, D.C.
CATEGORIES: African American history; Civil rights; Laws and acts
KEY FIGURES:

Frederick Douglass (1817?-1895), abolitionist and orator
William Lloyd Garrison (1805-1879), publisher of *The Liberator* and a founder of the American Anti-Slavery Society
Julia Ward Howe (1819-1910), feminist and abolitionist
Abraham Lincoln (1809-1865), president during the Civil War
Robert Dale Owen (1801-1877), abolitionist whose writings influenced Lincoln
Lucy Stone (1818-1893), abolitionist who fought for universal suffrage

SUMMARY OF EVENT. The antislavery and abolition movements did not begin with the Civil War. As early as 1652, the state of Rhode Island passed antislavery legislation. In 1773, Benjamin Franklin and Dr. Benjamin Rush formed the first abolition society in America. In 1832, the New England Anti-Slavery Society was formed by newspaper editor William Lloyd Garrison, who also helped found the American Anti-Slavery Society in 1833. The Society of Friends, or Quakers, a religious group who settled early in the history of the United States, were very active in the antislavery movement. Their religion forbade the holding of slaves. Quakers primarily settled in the northern part of the country.

In 1807, federal legislation was passed outlawing the importation of slaves after January 1, 1808. However, this did not end the use of slaves in the United States. The writers of the Constitution could not resolve the issue of slavery in America, and so had declared that the slave trade could end by 1808 or anytime later. Eventually, the inability of national leaders to resolve this issue would divide the nation. The Missouri Compromise of 1820 banned slavery in most of the western states and territories. This was overturned by the Supreme Court in 1857, in the famous *Dred Scott* decision.

The split between the states was well in place at this point. Congress, in an attempt to appease pro- and antislavery proponents, adopted five provisions in the Compromise of 1850. The most notable was the Second Fugitive Slave Law, passed in 1851, which provided for slaves who escaped from the South and were found in Northern antislavery states to be returned to slave owners. A great deal of violence erupted over this legislation, which led to the act's repeal on June 28, 1864. This split between the North and the South eventually resulted in the Civil War.

The abolitionist movement had fought throughout the history of the United States for an end to the institution of slavery. Robert Dale Owen, an abolitionist and legislator, struggled for the emancipation of slaves and is thought to have influenced President Abraham Lincoln with his *Policy of Emancipation* (1863), or Emancipation Proclamation. Another radical opponent of slavery was Wendell Phillips, a noted speaker and a graduate of Harvard Law School. He believed that the U.S. Constitution supported slavery and therefore was owed no allegiance by abolitionists. Harriet Tubman was active in the Underground Railroad, which was successful in bringing many slaves into Northern states that would not return them to their owners. John Brown adopted more violent means of expressing his abolitionist sentiment. He raided the federal arsenal at Harpers Ferry, Virginia, and encouraged a slave revolt. He was eventually hanged for his fanaticism. Frederick Douglass was an important abolitionist who played a significant role in the passage toward freedom for the slaves. A runaway slave, he spoke eloquently about the need to redress the wrongs created by slavery.

As Civil War broke out, the movement placed greater pressure on President Lincoln to issue the Emancipation Proclamation. Lincoln had focused a great deal of attention on the issue of slavery during the famous Lincoln-Douglas debates. The Emancipation Proclamation was issued on September 22, 1862, well after the beginning of the Civil War. It announced that in states that had seceded from the union, all slaves would be freed effective January 1, 1863. This proclamation did not free many slaves. It did not apply to states that were part of the Union and was unenforceable in those states involved in the Confederacy. The major function of the Emancipation Proclamation was to announce to all that the Civil War was about slavery.

At the time that the Civil War began, the African American population of the United States consisted of approximately four and a half million people, four million of whom were slaves. White supremacy was the general ideology of both Southerners and Northerners. Slaves were denied such rights as the right to legal marriage, choice of residence, and education, and existed in perpetual servitude. Without significant changes in institutional structures, there was no hope of freedom.

The Thirteenth Amendment was one of three amendments known as the Civil War amendments. The combined purpose of these three amendments was to free the slaves and promote their participation in their country. The Thirteenth Amendment states "neither slavery nor involuntary servitude, except as a punishment for crime whereof the party shall have been duly convicted, shall exist within the United States, or any place subject to their jurisdiction." One of the battles surrounding the Thirteenth Amendment in particular, and all the Civil War amendments in general, concerned the interpretation of the Tenth Amendment. The Tenth Amendment stated that no federal legislation could detract from the power of state government. Those who opposed the Thirteenth Amendment claimed that the right to allow slavery was not specifically denied in the Constitution and therefore fell within the authority of the state.

With the passage of this amendment, the long fight to abolish slavery was over. The amendment was ratified on December 6, 1865, and officially announced on December 18, 1865. For some abolitionists, such as William Lloyd Garrison, the battle had been won: Slavery was ended. Others saw the Thirteenth Amendment as only a beginning.

Frederick Douglass did not have the same high hopes held by Garrison. Douglass believed that slavery would not be abolished until the former slaves acquired the right to vote. The passage of the Civil Rights Act of 1866 did not provide this right. It was not until the passage of the Fourteenth Amendment, in 1868, that citizenship and the rights thereof were guaranteed to "all persons born or naturalized in the United States." Finally, in 1870, former slaves were expressly given the right to vote. Within weeks, the first African American in the U.S. Senate, Hiram R. Revels, took his seat.

On April 15, 1865, President Lincoln died from wounds inflicted by an assassin the night before. Vice President Andrew Johnson took over the reins of the presidency and reconstruction of the nation. Johnson, however, was not highly supportive or sympathetic to the needs of the slaves. Johnson blocked every attempt to extend rights to former slaves. In fact, Johnson vetoed most of the bills that were passed by Congress, only to have his veto overridden by a two-thirds majority of Congress. Impeachment charges eventually ensued, and Johnson was spared by only a one-vote margin. At that point, Johnson withdrew from reconstruction activities and allowed Congress to control the process.

One interesting note is the relationship between the woman suffrage movement and the abolition and black suffrage process. The decision over whether to support the call for the black vote divided the woman suffrage movement. Some believed that a gradual transition, in which first black men received the vote and then all women received the vote, would meet with greater success. Two such women were Lucy Stone and Julia Ward Howe. Others believed that suffrage was "all or nothing," and that women should not forsake their own cause in order to gain the vote for others. Susan B. Anthony and Elizabeth Cady Stanton were opposed to amendments that specifically referred to men and neglected suffrage for women. It was not until the passage of the Nineteenth Amendment in 1920 that women gained the long-sought suffrage.

—Sharon L. Larson

ADDITIONAL READING:

Franklin, John Hope. *From Slavery to Freedom: A History of Negro Americans*. 3d ed. New York: Alfred A. Knopf, 1967. Details the changes undergone by African Americans during the movement toward abolition and after they achieved citizenship.

Furnas, J. C. *The Road to Harpers Ferry*. London: Faber & Faber, 1961. An enlightening discussion of the problems created or observed in the abolitionist movement.

McKissack, Pat, and Fredrick McKissack. *The Civil Rights*

Movement in America from 1865 to the Present. 2d ed. Chicago: Children's Press, 1991. Examines the progression of rights granted since the Civil War.

Owen, Robert Dale. *The Wrong of Slavery, the Right of Emancipation, and the Future of the African Race in the United States.* Philadelphia: J. B. Lippincott, 1864. Writings on the issue of slavery in the United States from an abolitionist of the slave era.

1791 to 1991: The Bill of Rights and Beyond. Washington, D.C.: Commission on the Bicentennial of the U.S. Constitution, 1991. Discusses the history of the Constitution and each of the amendments. The abolitionist movement and passage of the Civil War amendments are discussed in relation to each other.

SEE ALSO: 1850, Compromise of 1850; 1850, Second Fugitive Slave Law; 1850, Underground Railroad; 1857, *Dred Scott v. Sandford*; 1858, Lincoln-Douglas Debates; 1863, Emancipation Proclamation; 1865, Surrender at Appomattox and Assassination of Lincoln; 1866, Civil Rights Act of 1866; 1868, Impeachment of Andrew Johnson; 1868, Fourteenth Amendment.

1866 ■ CHISHOLM TRAIL OPENS: *a trail from the Southwest northward expands cattle markets, opens the Midwest to transport, and closes open ranges*

DATE: 1866
LOCALE: Great Plains
CATEGORIES: Economics; Expansion and land acquisition; Transportation
KEY FIGURES:
Jesse Chisholm (1806?-1868), Scottish-Cherokee trader and guide who pioneered the trail named for him
John Clay (1851-1934), manager and inspector of British-owned ranch properties
James Butler "Wild Bill" Hickok (1837-1876), Abilene marshal who controlled the more lawless elements
Richard King (1825-1885), founder of the King Ranch in southern Texas
Joseph Geating McCoy (1837-1915), Illinois stockman who developed Abilene, Kansas
Charles Russell (1865-1926), artist and chronicler of the West, and ranch life
SUMMARY OF EVENT. At the end of the Civil War, astute and ambitious Texans conceived a plan whereby the numerous herds of longhorn cattle overrunning the southern part of the state could be rounded up and driven north to markets where they would command a higher price. Foremost among these Texans was a former steamboat captain, Richard King, whose original tract of seventy-five thousand acres had been increased to one-half million acres by the time of his death in 1885.

First introduced into California, New Mexico, and Texas by the Spaniards, the scrawny range cattle had been valuable mainly for their hides. For years, small herds had been driven every other year from Texas to New Orleans, St. Louis, or Kansas City by many South Texas Mexican American ranchers. New England shippers frequented Pacific coast ports to gather hides for Eastern tanneries. The Civil War, however, brought many changes to this area. Railroads began pushing westward across the Great Plains; the meat-packing industry was being consolidated by a few leading packers in urban centers such as Kansas City, Omaha, and Chicago, which dominated the national market.

Joseph G. McCoy, an Illinois stockman, assumed the leadership in working out a mutually satisfactory arrangement among the cattleowners, the railroads, and the meatpackers. Cattle worth five dollars a head in Texas were to be driven northward, fattened on the nutritious short grass of the public domain en route, and then delivered to the railhead for shipment to Eastern markets, where they would bring forty to fifty dollars each. McCoy chose Abilene, Kansas, the terminal town on the Kansas Pacific Railroad in 1867, as the initial shipping point. McCoy ordered lumber from Missouri and built stock pens stout enough to hold three thousand restless longhorns. He placed ten-ton scales that could weigh twenty cows at a time. Besides enlarging Abilene with a livery stable, barns, and an office, he also built the Drovers' Cottage, an eight-room hotel.

The Chisholm Trail was the name given to the route by which the cattle were driven northward from southern Texas, entering the Indian Territory at Red River Crossing, and continuing on into Abilene. Jesse Chisholm, a Scottish-Cherokee wagon driver, first marked this trail, which he used to trade buffalo robes with Midwestern tribes. Chisholm, who never raised cattle, knew the need for grass and water on a cattle trail. In 1868, Chisholm died from eating bad bear grease, never completing a trip on the trail named for him. As the railroad moved farther west, alternative routes were made. The Shawnee Trail followed the route of the Chisholm Trail until it veered to Baxter Springs, Kansas. The West Chisholm Trail led into western Kansas and Ellsworth, Kansas. The Panhandle Trail fought its way across the arid mesas of western Texas. The original routes ran from the central part of Indian Territory to the railhead at Ellsworth.

The pressure of farmers taking up homesteads near the railroads forced the cattlemen to relocate their long drives ever farther to the west. Construction of the Atchison, Topeka, and Santa Fe Railroad provided a shorter drive along the Great Western Trail to southwestern Kansas, first to Newton and later to Dodge City, the recognized "cowboy capital" between 1875 and 1885. If the cattle market was overcrowded in Dodge City, some cattleowners drove their herds on northward to meet the Union Pacific. Once Kansas was closed to the cattleowners, ranchers developed the Goodnight-Loving Trail, which ran westward across Texas to the Pecos River country and then northward through eastern New Mexico and Colorado into Wyoming, where there was less competition.

TRANS-MISSISSIPPI RAILROADS AND CATTLE TRAILS

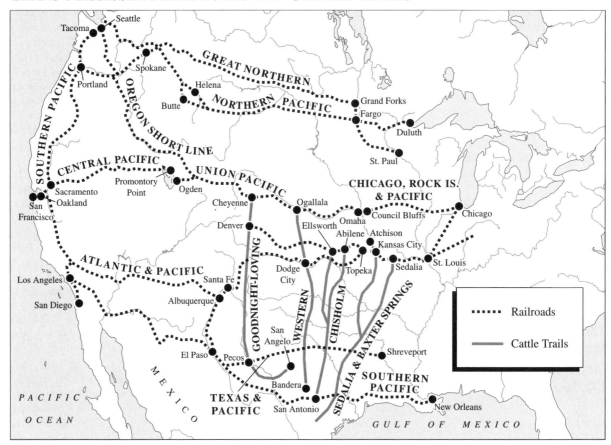

The drives started early in the spring, immediately following the roundup. Usually a herd of twenty-five hundred to three thousand head of cattle was placed in the charge of the trail boss, who hired a dozen cowboys accompanied by a chuckwagon. The cattle were moved along the trail between ten and fifteen miles a day at a pace that would permit them to gain flesh off the rich, nutritious short grass of the Great Plains. Cowboys preferred driving the longhorns. The span of the long horns kept the cattle spaced farther apart, preventing excess body heat and flesh loss. Before leaving on a drive, owners would brand their animals, so separating them at the terminal was simplified. Numerous dangers were encountered along the trail, including American Indian attacks, stampedes, Quantrell's Raiders, jayhawkers, swollen rivers that had to be crossed, and attacks from farmers who did not want the herds crossing their lands and spreading the dreaded Texas fever to their own stock. This fever was caused by ticks, but it was attributed mistakenly to causes ranging from thorny shrubs scratching infected animals to deliberate sabotage.

Despite these hazards, between 1868 and 1871, almost 1.5 million head of cattle were loaded on the trains in the Abilene yards. From 1872 to 1875, Newton, on the Santa Fe line, received 1.5 million animals, and Dodge shipped 1 million of

them to the Eastern markets during the succeeding four years. No business was more widely advertised and romanticized. Tales of cattle kings building large estates and herds, cowboys engaging in the roundups and long drives, lawbreakers congregating in the cowtowns to challenge authority and each other, and sheriffs' and marshals' attempts to maintain law and order were legion.

By 1880, the cattle industry was firmly established throughout the Great Plains. Rumors had circulated about the enormous profits that were available, with estimates running as high as a 40 percent return on capital in a single year. Investors in the East and abroad, primarily in England and Scotland, organized mammoth companies that bought acreage in New Mexico, Texas, and Colorado, totaling eight thousand square miles with herds numbering more than 150,000 head. Between 1881 and 1885, the British invested approximately forty-five million dollars in the cattle business and employed John Clay to oversee their interests. In the process, a mad scramble ensued to obtain land strategically located to control the essential and limited water supply. Some companies resorted to leasing American Indian reservation lands and to enclosing sections of public domain that alternated with those areas that they had purchased from the Western railroads. The aggressive and sometimes illegal activities of the cattle barons made them unpopular with farmers and small ranchers, as well as with the federal government. In an attempt to bring order to the industry, Southern and Great Plains cattleowners organized regional and territorial associations for the purpose of supervising roundups, organizing detective bureaus to prevent cattle rustling, instituting inspection systems to oversee joint shipments of cattle from range to market, and lobbying for political concessions. The collective efforts of these associations led to the creation of the Bureau of Animal Industry by the federal government.

The boom could not last. Northern ranges were overcrowded, and steps were taken to shut off the long drives from Texas. Even so, overproduction caused prices on the domestic market to tumble steadily between 1884 and 1887. To make a bad situation worse, climatic conditions in 1885 and 1886 were disastrous. The summers were hot and dry, reaching 110 degrees. One Fourth of July, there was a hailstorm that killed jackrabbits, yearlings, and antelope, and left cowboys with frozen and scarred faces and hands. In Montana, fifty thousand acres of good grassland burned. In the winter of 1886, three-fourths of some herds were destroyed. In November, a blizzard left snow up to the eaves of cabins. In January, a chinook caused the snow to melt, then on January 28, 1887, the temperatures dropped to fifteen degrees below zero, with winds of sixty miles per hour. More snow fell, isolating men and animals for six weeks. Small animals smothered in the drifts; Texas cattle froze, unaccustomed to severe winters; heartier cattle could not break the ice to get grass. Some animals resorted to eating tar paper off shacks and the wool off the bodies of dead sheep. Charles Russell, the famous Western artist, did his first watercolor, *Waiting for a Chinook*, depicting a humped-up cow circled by wolves, during this winter storm.

The basic economic law of supply and demand on the open range and the whims of the weather dramatized its end. Cattlemen reduced the size of their herds, fenced their ranches, made plans for feeding their animals during the winter months, and concentrated on improved breeding. Even with the number of cattle reduced, the market price did not rise during the 1890's. The industry struggled for survival in the decade of transition. The true story of cowboys and ranches has, over time, evolved into Hollywood fiction for the general populace.

—*W. Turrentine Jackson, updated by Norma Crews*

ADDITIONAL READING:

Adams, Ramon. *The Old-Time Cowhand*. Lincoln: University of Nebraska Press, 1989. A western historian gives insight into the everyday life of cowboys, stressing the differences in geographical locations.

Drago, Harry Sinclair. *Great American Cattle Trails*. New York: Dodd, Mead, 1965. Discusses the development of famous national trails, specifically addressing the business of driving stock.

O'Neal, Bill. *Cattlemen vs. Sheepherders: Five Decades of Violence in the West, 1880-1920*. Austin, Tex.: Eakin Press, 1989. Sheep wars covered a large part of the West, the period

after the drives to shipping points further developed the livestock industry.

Pirtle, Caleb, and Texas Cowboy Artist Association. *XIT, Being a New and Original Exploration, in Art and Words, Into the Life and Times of the American Cowboy*. Birmingham, Ala.: Oxmoor House, 1975. Discusses cowboys, trails, ranchers, and their legacy. Informally written, covering the period when the cattle industry was at its peak. Heavily illustrated, with an extensive bibliography.

SEE ALSO: 1821, Santa Fe Trail Opens; 1823, Jedediah Smith Explores the Far West; 1835, Texas Revolution; 1841, Preemption Act; 1842, Frémont's Expeditions; 1846, Mormon Migration to Utah; 1848, Treaty of Guadalupe Hidalgo; 1853, Pacific Railroad Surveys; 1853, Gadsden Purchase; 1869, Transcontinental Railroad Is Completed.

1866 ■ RISE OF THE KU KLUX KLAN: *a group of white supremacists, disaffected by the outcome of the Civil War, grows into an organization of institutionalized race hatred*

DATE: Beginning 1866
LOCALE: United States
CATEGORIES: African American history; Civil rights; Organizations and institutions
KEY FIGURES:

Edward Young Clarke, ad-man who promoted the Klan during the 1920's

David E. Duke (born 1950), klansman who ran for national office

Nathan B. Forrest (1821-1877), grand wizard of the first Klan

Samuel Green, founder of the Association of Georgia Klans

Ed Jackson (1873-1954), governor of Indiana

Samuel Ralston (1857-1925), senator with Klan connections

William J. Simmons (born 1880), preacher who founded the second Klan

David C. Stephenson (born 1891?), grand dragon in Indiana

James Venable (born 1900), Klan leader

Bill Wilkinson (born 1950), former disciple of Duke and advocate of violence

SUMMARY OF EVENT. With the end of the Civil War in the United States in 1865 and the emancipation of African American slaves in the South, tension arose between old-order Southern whites and Radical Republicans devoted to a strict plan of Reconstruction that required Southern states to repeal their Black Codes and guarantee voting and other civil rights to African Americans. Federal instruments for ensuring African American rights included the Freedmen's Bureau and the Union Leagues. In reaction to the activities of these organizations, white supremacist organizations sprouted in the years immediately following the Civil War: the Knights of the White

Camelia, the White League, the Invisible Circle, the Pale Faces, and the Ku Klux Klan (KKK).

The last of these would eventually lend its name to a confederation of such organizations, but in 1866 it was born in Pulaski, Tennessee, as a fraternal order for white, male, Anglo-Saxon Protestants joined by their opposition to Radical Reconstructionism and an agenda to promote white, Southern dominance. This incarnation of the Klan established many of the weird rituals and violent activities for which the KKK became known throughout its history. They named the South the "invisible empire," with "realms" consisting of the Southern states. A "grand dragon" headed each realm, and the entire "empire" was led by Grand Wizard General Nathan B. Forrest. Positions of leadership were dubbed "giant," "cyclops," "geni," "hydra," "goblin." The white robes and pointed cowls stem from this era as well—donned in the belief that blacks were superstitious and would be intimidated by the menacing, ghostlike appearance of their oppressors, who thus also maintained anonymity while conducting their nefarious nighttime activities. Initially, harassment was planned to keep the people whom these racists considered "uppity Negroes," and those who defended them, "in their place." Such offensive language remains a testament to the bigotry and racism deeply entrenched in white American society and fed upon by the Klan.

Soon the Klan was perpetrating acts of violence, including whippings, house-burnings, kidnappings, and lynchings. As the violence escalated, Forrest disbanded the Klan in 1869, and on May 31, 1870, and April 20, 1871, Congress passed the Ku Klux Klan Acts, or Force Acts, designed to break up the white supremacist groups. John Sherman, speaking in the Senate on March 18, 1871, for the second Force Act, lamented:

> They are secret, oath-bound; they murder, rob, plunder, whip, and scourge; and they commit these crimes, not upon the high and lofty, but upon the lowly, upon the poor, upon the feeble men and women who are utterly defenceless. . . . Where is there an organization against which humanity revolts more than it does against this?

The law passed, although parts of the Force Acts were later ruled unconstitutional by the Supreme Court.

However short-lived the first Klan, it would resurface again in eras of racial tension, often occurring in tandem with peri-

After the Civil War, disappointed white Southerners, angry at the federal government for forcing emancipation and Radical Reconstruction upon their customary caste society, formed the Ku Klux Klan in 1866, initially a society for white males. Klansmen harassed, murdered, and set fire to the homes of African Americans in the name of patriotism and traditional values. (Smithsonian Institution Photo No. 76-14001)

ods marked by xenophobia and anti-immigrant paranoia. It may be no coincidence that the next rise of the Klan presaged the period of the Red Scare (1919-1920) and the Immigration Act of 1921, the first such legislation in the United States to establish immigration quotas on the basis of national origin. In November of 1915, on Stone Mountain, Georgia, a second Ku Klux Klan was founded by preacher William J. Simmons, proclaiming it a "high-class, mystic, social, patriotic" society devoted to defending womanhood, white Protestant values, and "native-born, white, gentile Americans." Such an image of the Klan was perpetrated by the popular 1915 film *Birth of a Nation* (whose original title was *The Klansman*). In it, a lustful African American is shown attempting to attack a white woman, and the Klan, in robes and cowls, rides to the rescue, presenting a positive image of the Klan.

The new Klan cloaked itself as a patriotic organization devoted to preserving traditional American values against enemies in the nation's midst. An upsurge of nationalist fervor swelled the ranks of the Klan, this time far beyond the borders of the South. White men and women both joined to ensure the survival of the white race. This second Klan adopted the rituals and regalia of its predecessor as well as the same anti-black ideology, to which it added anti-Catholic, anti-Semitic, anti-immigrant, anti-birth-control, anti-Darwinist, and anti-Prohibition stances. Promoted by ad-man Edward Y. Clarke, its membership reached approximately 100,000 by 1921 and over the next five years, by some estimates, grew to 5 million, including even members of Congress.

Some Klan observers state that the power of the Klan was worse in the North than in the South: In 1924, an enemy of the Klan, William Allen White, lost a bid for the governorship of Kansas to a Klan sympathizer. Grand Dragon David C. Stephenson, who was known to rule the statehouse in Indiana, helped elect Samuel Ralston, a Klan member, to the Senate in 1922 and influenced voters to elect Ed Jackson as governor (1925-1929). Jackson and Stephenson were later disgraced by investigations into their misuse of funds. Stephenson after kidnapping and raping his secretary, was convicted in 1925 of second-degree murder; she had died during the kidnapping after he had refused to seek medical attention for her when she took poison to force him to get her to authorities.

Stephenson is only one example of the criminal personalities that typified Klan membership. The Klan perpetrated more than five hundred hangings and burnings of African Americans, primarily of men who had broken one of the "racist codes" kept in secret by the Klan. In 1924, forty thousand Klansmen marched down Pennsylvania Avenue in Washington, D.C., sending a message to the federal government that there should be a white, Protestant United States. Finally, the Klan's growing wave of violence alienated many of its members, whose numbers dropped to about 30,000 by 1930.

Klan activities increased again prior to World War II and membership rose toward the 100,000 mark, but in 1944 Congress assessed the organization more than a half million dollars in back taxes, and the Klan dissolved itself to escape. Two

years later, however, Atlanta physician Samuel Green united smaller Klan groups into the Association of Georgia Klans and was soon joined by other reincarnations, such as the Federated Ku Klux Klans, the Original Southern Klans, and the Knights of the Ku Klux Klan. These groups revived the racist agenda and violent methods of previous Klans and during this period were responsible for hundreds of criminal acts. Of equal concern was the Klan's political influence: A governor of Texas was elected with the support of the Klan, and a senator from Maine was similarly elected. Even a Supreme Court justice, Hugo Black, revealed in 1937 that he had been a member of the Ku Klux Klan.

In the 1940's, many states passed laws that revoked Klan charters, and many Southern communities issued regulations against masks. The U.S. Justice Department placed the Klan on its list of subversive elements, and in 1952 the Federal Bureau of Investigation used the Lindbergh law (one of the 1934 Crime Control Acts) against the Klan. Another direct challenge to the principles of the KKK came in the 1960's with the advent of the Civil Rights movement and civil rights legislation. Martin Luther King, Jr., prophesied early in the decade that it would be a "season of suffering." On September 15, 1963, a Klan bomb tore apart the Sixteenth Street Baptist Church in Birmingham, Alabama, killing four young children. Despite the outrage of much of the nation, the violence continued, led by members of the Klan who made a mockery of the courts and the laws that they had broken. Less than a year after the bombing, three civil rights workers were killed in Mississippi, including one African American and two whites from the North involved in voter registration. This infamous event was later documented in the motion picture *Mississippi Burning*. Viola Lee Liuzzo was killed for driving freedom marchers from site to site. Such acts prompted President Lyndon Johnson, in a televised speech in March, 1965, to denounce the Klan as he announced the arrest of four Klansmen for murder.

After the conviction of many of its members in the 1960's, the organization became somewhat dormant, and its roster of members reflected low numbers. Still, as it had in previous periods of dormancy, the Klan refused to die. Busing for integration of public schools in the 1970's engendered Klan opposition in the South and the North. In 1979, in Greensboro, North Carolina, Klan members killed several members of the Communist Party in a daylight battle on an open street. Klan members have patrolled the Mexican border, armed with weapons and citizen-band radios, trying to send illegal aliens back to Mexico. The Klan has been active in suburban California, at times driving out African Americans who attempted to move there. On the Gulf Coast, many boats fly the infamous AKIA flag, an acronym for "A Klansman I Am," a term that dates back to the 1920's. Klan members try to discourage or run out Vietnamese fishers. Klan leaders active since 1970 include James Venable, for whom the Klan became little more than a hobby, and Bill Wilkinson, a former disciple of David Duke. Robert Shelton, long a grand dragon, helped elect two Alabama governors. David Duke, a Klan leader until the late

1980's, decided to run for political office and was elected a congressman from Louisiana despite his well-publicized past associations; in 1991, he ran for governor, almost winning. In the 1980's the Klan stepped up its anti-Semitic activities, planning multiple bombings in Nashville. Klan leaders in the 1990's have trained their members and their children for what they believe is an imminent race war, learning survival skills and weaponry at remote camps throughout the country.

A major blow was struck against the Klan by the Klanwatch Project of the Southern Poverty Law Center, in Montgomery, Alabama, when, in 1984, attorney Morris Dees began pressing civil suits against several Klan members, effectively removing their personal assets, funds received from members, and even buildings owned by the Klan.

Throughout its many generations, the Klan has maintained that it is a patriotic organization, interested in preserving the principles upon which the United States was originally based. However, the Klan's history of violence against African Americans, non-whites in general, and Jews is the most anti-American sentiment conceivable in a republic founded on the principles of tolerance in service of "life, liberty, and the pursuit of happiness."

ADDITIONAL READING:

Bridges, Tyler. *The Rise of David Duke*. Jackson: University Press of Mississippi, 1994. A thorough discussion of a dangerous member of the Klan in the 1990's.

Chalmers, David Mark. *Hooded Americanism: The History of the Ku Klux Klan*. New York: F. Watts, 1981. Considered the bible of books about the Klan, this has seen numerous editions and updatings.

Ezekiel, Raphael. *The Racist Mind: Portraits of American Neo-Nazis and Klansmen*. New York: Viking Press, 1995. Psychological insights into racism. Explores conditions of childhood, education, and other factors in an attempt to explain racist behavior.

Klan: Legacy of Hate. Chicago: Films Incorporated Video, 1982. This excellent if brief documentary provides footage of past and more recent Klan activities.

Randel, William. *The Ku Klux Klan: A Century of Infamy*. Philadelphia: Chilton Books, 1965. An excellent history of origins and events, which also uses a moral perspective.

Stanton, Bill. *Klanwatch: Bringing the Ku Klux Klan to Justice*. New York: Weidenfeld, 1991. The former Klanwatch director explains new initiatives to disable the Klan, most of which have been effective.

Wade, Wyn Draig. *The Fiery Cross: The Ku Klux Klan in America*. New York: Simon & Schuster, 1987. Wade recounts the Klan's history and episodes of violence, revealing its legacy of race hatred.

SEE ALSO: 1859, Last Slave Ship Docks at Mobile; 1863, Emancipation Proclamation; 1863, Reconstruction; 1865, Freedmen's Bureau Is Established; 1865, Surrender at Appomattox and Assassination of Lincoln; 1865, New Black Codes; 1866, Race Riots in the South; 1890, Mississippi Disfranchisement Laws; 1857, *Dred Scott v. Sandford*.

1866 ■ CIVIL RIGHTS ACT OF 1866: *this act joins the Thirteenth Amendment as the first federal legislation to enhance the rights of freed African Americans*

DATE: April 9, 1866
LOCALE: Washington, D.C.
CATEGORIES: African American history; Civil rights; Laws and acts
KEY FIGURES:
Andrew Johnson (1808-1875), president of the United States during Reconstruction
Thaddeus Stevens (1792-1868), antislavery Republican congressman who fought against President Johnson
Charles Sumner (1811-1874), Republican senator opposed to slavery

SUMMARY OF EVENT. At the end of the Civil War lay the long road of Reconstruction. As early as 1863, President Abraham Lincoln had expressed a plan for Reconstruction after the Civil War. These plans required a loyalty oath and acceptance of emancipation from Southern states desiring readmission to the Union. It was not until after Lincoln's assassination that Reconstruction began in earnest.

Andrew Johnson, the seventeenth president of the United States, was vice president at the time of Lincoln's death in 1865. He inherited the problems of rebuilding the country after a lengthy civil war, which had ended in April, 1865. Johnson believed that the responsibility for developing Reconstruction policy should be handled by the president. Johnson's Reconstruction policy provided for a loyalty oath by citizens of states seeking readmission, revocation of the act of secession, abolition of slavery, and repudiation of the Confederate war debt. Several states—including Arkansas, Louisiana, and Tennessee—were readmitted in early 1865 without congressional approval. By the end of 1865, all states had been readmitted except Texas. This Reconstruction plan, however, failed to address the issues associated with the former slaves and their rights.

Congress believed that a debt was owed to the former slaves. The Freedmen's Bureau was created in 1865 as a temporary assistance program to address some of this debt. Food, medicine, schools, and land were made available to freedmen. Early in 1866, Congress passed a new Freedmen's Bureau Act and the first federal Civil Rights Act. Both were vetoed by President Johnson, because he feared that the legislation would extend to people of other races. He asked, "Was it sound to make all these colored people's citizen?" Congress succeeded in quickly overturning these vetoes. In the Senate, J. W. Forney reported that the Senate agreed to pass the vetoed legislation with a two-thirds majority on April 6, 1866. The House of Representatives followed suit on April 9, 1866, the anniversary of the Confederacy's surrender.

During this same time, less positive events were impacting

the freed blacks. The year 1866 brought the founding of the Ku Klux Klan. African Americans were subjected to killings, beatings, and torture. This often occurred to keep them out of the political arena, which offered opportunities for power. Perhaps more detrimental to African Americans was the institutionalized racism of the Black Codes. Black Codes, or Black Laws, were legal enactments developed to regulate the actions and behaviors of freedmen in the South. These codes allowed legal marriage between African Americans, limited rights to testify in court, and limited rights to sue others. The codes also supervised the movements of African Americans in the South, restricted the assembly of unsupervised groups of blacks, forbade intermarriage between people of color and whites, banned African Americans from carrying weapons, restricted African American children to apprenticeships that were nearly slavery, and forced blacks into employment contracts that carried criminal penalties if abandoned. Violation of these codes often resulted in stiffer criminal punishment for African Americans than similar violations did for whites. Southern politicians reinstated by Andrew Johnson's Reconstruction policy were responsible for passage of these codes. It was in this environment that Congress found it necessary to develop legislation to combat the antiblack sentiment.

The Civil Rights Act of 1866 was the first federal law to protect the civil rights of African Americans. Section 1 of this provision established the right of citizenship to all persons born in the United States, without regard to previous servitude. As citizens, African Americans were granted the right to enter into and enforce contracts; inherit, lease, sell, hold, and convey property; give evidence in courts; benefit equally from all laws and ordinances; and be subject to punishments that were the same as given to whites for similar crimes. Section 2 provided for misdemeanor penalties for anyone who deprived another of the rights afforded in section 1. Additional sections dealt with those who were granted the authority to prosecute and enforce this legislation. In order to ensure that this legislation would be enforced, Congress further established acts that were referred to as enforcement acts. Additionally, Congress drafted the Fourteenth Amendment to the Constitution of the United States to protect the freedmen's status.

Historically, the Constitution had been the source of civil liberties for the United States. The first eight amendments to the Constitution provided for a variety of freedoms. The First Amendment granted the freedoms of speech, religion, and assembly, as well as the right to petition the government for the redress of grievances. The Second, Third, and Fourth Amendments provided for a federal militia, the right to own private property, and the right to be protected from unreasonable seizures and searches of private property. The Fifth Amendment provided for the right of due process, ensured that one need not present evidence against oneself, and prevented double jeopardy in court (that is, one cannot be tried for the same offense twice). The Sixth through Eighth Amendments provide for further fair and equitable treatment by the judicial system. The purpose of various civil rights acts has been to extend these rights to all people, particularly those groups for whom these rights were originally withheld, and provide for their enforcement.

Several civil rights acts have been passed in the United States since 1866. The Civil Rights Act of 1871 made it a crime to deny equal protection under the law through duress or force. Civil rights legislation passed in 1875, which guaranteed blacks the right to use public accommodations, was ruled unconstitutional eight years after it was passed. This continued a downhill turn in the rights of African Americans, eventually leading to the Supreme Court's "separate but equal" decision in *Plessy v. Ferguson* (1896). This was the rule until 1954, when the Supreme Court determined that separate but equal was inherently unequal, in *Brown v. Board of Education of Topeka, Kansas*. It was not until 1964, and again in 1968, that any additional civil rights legislation was enacted at the national level. The 1964 and 1968 acts prohibited discrimination in employment, in use of public accommodations such as hotels, and in housing and real estate.

When President Andrew Johnson vetoed civil rights legislation aimed at granting rights to freed blacks, he began a two-year campaign that would end with an impeachment trial. Congressmen became increasingly concerned with Johnson's apparent plan to subvert and sabotage Reconstruction. His appointment of former Confederate leaders who had not vowed allegiance to the Union, his lack of tact in dealing with those with whom he disagreed, his efforts to circumvent Congress and extend presidential powers, and his veto of important civil rights legislation resulted in a special meeting of the House of Representatives on March 2, 1867. Two measures were passed at this special session. One deprived Johnson of his responsibilities as commander in chief of the military; the second deprived him of the right to remove those with whom he disagreed from their cabinet positions. Finally, a resolution was passed to impeach Johnson for alleged violations of these measures. The senate failed to convict Johnson by one vote. However, Johnson was more compliant in the Reconstruction process after this trial.

—*Sharon L. Larson*

ADDITIONAL READING:

Abernathy, M. Glenn. *Civil Liberties Under the Constitution.* 5th ed. Columbia: University of South Carolina Press, 1989. Discusses the Bill of Rights and the historical relevance of civil rights legislation.

Asch, Sidney H. *Civil Rights and Responsibilities Under the Constitution.* New York: Arco, 1968. Analysis of amendments, such as the right-to-vote amendment, in light of ethical questions of the day.

Bardolph, Richard, ed. *The Civil Rights Record: Black Americans and the Law, 1849-1870.* New York: Thomas Crowell, 1970. Presents legal documentation of the African American move toward legal equality.

Blaustein, Albert P., and Robert L. Zangrando, eds. *Civil Rights and the American Negro: A Documentary History.* New York: Trident Press, 1968. Discusses the civil rights legislation that has been passed specifically in relation to the end of slavery.

Chalmers, David M. *Hooded Americanism: The First Century of the Ku Klux Klan.* 3d ed. Durham, N.C.: Duke University Press, 1987. A historical and political examination of the Ku Klux Klan. Lends validity to the discussion of the civil rights and emancipation legislation of the post-Civil War era.

Franklin, John Hope. *From Slavery to Freedom: A History of Negro Americans.* 3d ed. New York: Alfred A. Knopf, 1967. Explores the progress of African Americans through slavery, emancipation, Reconstruction, and the early 1960's Civil Rights movement.

McKissack, Patricia, and Frederick McKissack. *The Civil Rights Movement in America, from 1865-Present.* 2d ed. Chicago: Children's Press, 1991. A discussion of the progress in civil rights since the end of the Civil War and slavery in the United States.

Weinstein, Allen, and Frank Otto Gatell. *Freedom and Crisis: An American History.* 2 vols. New York: Random House, 1978. Volume 2, chapter 24 discusses the dramatic events surrounding Lincoln's assassination, Johnson's impeachment trial, and congressional reconstruction.

See also: 1863, Emancipation Proclamation; 1863, Reconstruction; 1865, Freedmen's Bureau Is Established; 1865, New Black Codes; 1865, Thirteenth Amendment; 1868, Impeachment of Andrew Johnson; 1868, Fourteenth Amendment.

1866 ▪ Race Riots in the South:
economic and social disparities between the races, along with a continuing military presence, lead to violence during Reconstruction

Date: May and July, 1866
Locale: Memphis, Tennessee, and New Orleans, Louisiana
Categories: African American history; Wars, uprisings, and civil unrest
Key figures:
Absalom Baird (1824-1905), military commander of federal troops in New Orleans
Andrew Johnson (1808-1875), seventeenth president of the United States, 1865-1869
Philip H. Sheridan (1831-1888), military governor of Louisiana
George Stoneman (1822-1894), officer in charge of the East Tennessee military district
James Madison Wells (1808-1899), governor of Louisiana, a Union sympathizer

Summary of event. Racial disturbances in Memphis and New Orleans in 1866 were the result of economic, social, and political issues that troubled the nation during Reconstruction. Given the upheaval in the lives of Southerners after the Civil War, the racial disturbances are hardly surprising. In the simplest terms, one of the major tasks of Reconstruction was to assimilate the more than four million former slaves into U.S. society. A more complex view must consider the problems faced by the newly freed African Americans who had to achieve a new identity in a society that had allowed them no control over their own lives. White Southerners had to live with the economic, social, and political consequences of defeat. The military occupation of the South by federal troops after the Civil War angered Southerners, who believed in their right to rebuild and rule their own society without interference from the North. The presence of federal troops (many of them African Americans), an armed citizenry, and the psychological difficulty of accepting the end of the world they had known created explosive conditions that erupted into violence.

The Memphis and New Orleans riots were one result of this upheaval. Soon after the surrender of the Confederate army at Appomattox in April, 1865, legislatures in the South acted to pass a series of Black Codes. These laws were intended to maintain control over the lives of the newly freed African Americans and, in effect, keep them enslaved. For example, harsh vagrancy laws allowed police to arrest black people without cause and force them to work for white employers. President Abraham Lincoln's Emancipation Proclamation, on January 1, 1863, had freed the slaves in the Confederate states. The United States Congress, having abolished slavery throughout the nation with the Thirteenth Amendment to the Constitution in 1865, founded the Freedmen's Bureau to assist the former slaves and was in the process of enacting, over the strong opposition of President Andrew Johnson, a series of Reconstruction Acts intended to repeal the South's Black Codes. President Johnson resisted congressional attempts to admit African Americans to full citizenship, but Congress ultimately overrode his veto and took control of the Reconstruction program in the South.

Many former slaves, rejecting the life they had known on the plantation, moved to the cities of the South. Most African Americans were refugees without any economic resources, competing with Irish and German immigrants for scarce jobs in the war-torn South. Southern white Protestants feared both the immigrants and the African Americans as threats to the social order.

Conditions in Memphis were especially volatile in May, 1866. The city had a reputation as a rowdy river town known for heavy drinking, gambling, prostitution, and fighting. In 1865, the black population of Memphis had increased to between twenty and twenty-five thousand, many of them living in a run-down district near Fort Pickering. The white citizens were alarmed by incendiary newspaper accounts of crime and disorder.

The Memphis police, mostly Irish immigrants, were corrupt and ill-trained and had a record of brutality toward black people. Added to this already explosive mixture was a body of federal troops, four thousand of whom were black soldiers stationed at Fort Pickering waiting to be mustered out of the army. The violence began on April 29, with a street confrontation between black soldiers and white policemen. On May 1, the violence escalated, with fights breaking out between groups of black soldiers and the city police. By May 2, the mob included a number of people from the surrounding countryside as well as white citizens of Memphis. The mob rampaged through the black district, attacking families, raping women, and burning homes. Civil authorities took no steps to curb the disturbance.

After considerable delay, Major General George Stoneman, commanding the federal troops, brought the city under control. The three days of mob violence resulted in the deaths of forty-six African Americans and two white people. An estimated seventy to eighty other people were injured, and some ninety homes of black people, along with several African American churches and schools, were destroyed. African Americans suffered the heaviest casualties. Southern newspapers and civic officials blamed the black soldiers for the outbreak. A committee appointed by Congress, however, attributed the disturbances to the hatred of white people for the "colored race."

While the Memphis riots were the result of local conditions, the New Orleans disturbance of July 30 was caused by state politics and had national significance. Louisiana governor James Madison Wells, a Union sympathizer who needed to consolidate his power over the Confederates in the city and state, supported a plan to reassemble the state constitutional convention that had been disbanded in 1864. This convention, supported by Unionists, planned to gain votes by enfranchising African Americans. The city, sympathetic to Confederate politics, was armed, and the corrupt police force had a record of false arrests and mistreatment of free African Americans. The local newspapers, using highly emotional language, incited the fear of white citizens that African Americans would gain political control.

The commander of the federal troops, General Absalom Baird, should have foreseen the impending violence but apparently ignored the problem. When the delegates to the state convention began to assemble on July 30, fighting broke out between the city police and African American marchers supporting the right to vote. Delegates were dragged from the convention hall and assaulted by people in the street and by the police, who joined in the mob violence. The attacks on African Americans were savage; the wounded were dragged to the city jail and beaten, and the bodies of the dead were mistreated. As the violence escalated, fueled by the drunkenness of the mob, African Americans were dragged from their homes and beaten.

The death toll in the one-day riot included 34 African Americans and 3 white people; approximately 136 people were injured. Although General Baird declared martial law, his action was too late. Several observers, including General Philip H. Sheridan, who was called in to restore order, described the mob violence as a "slaughter." As in the case of the Memphis riots, nearly all the dead and injured were African Americans.

While the Memphis riots were caused by local conditions, the disturbances in New Orleans had state and national political consequences. The Republican Party lost power, paving the way for Democratic control of the state. Precedents for the racial violence that would mark the years of Reconstruction and beyond had been established.   —*Marjorie Podolsky*

ADDITIONAL READING:

Foner, Eric. "The Meaning of Freedom" and "The Making of Radical Reconstruction." In *Reconstruction: America's Unfinished Revolution, 1863-1877.* New York: Harper & Row, 1988. An interpretation of the scholarly history of Reconstruction that combines older views with newer scholarship.

Franklin, John Hope. *Reconstruction: After the Civil War.* Chicago: University of Chicago Press, 1961. Presents a revised view that rejects the carpetbagger stereotype and argues for a more positive representation of African Americans during Reconstruction.

Franklin, John Hope, and Alfred A. Moss, Jr. "The Effort to Attain Peace." In *From Slavery to Freedom: A History of African Americans.* 7th ed. New York: McGraw-Hill, 1994. A widely accepted record of the role of African Americans in U.S. history.

Litwack, Leon F. "How Free Is Free?" In *Been in the Storm So Long: The Aftermath of Slavery.* New York: Vintage Books, 1980. Provides a unique perspective, as it is based on the accounts of former slaves interviewed by the Federal Writers' Project in the 1930's.

Rable, George C. "The Memphis Race Riot" and "New Orleans and the Emergence of Political Violence." In *But There Was No Peace: The Role of Violence in the Politics of Reconstruction.* Athens: University of Georgia Press, 1984. This detailed account of the events in Memphis and New Orleans uses contemporary newspaper articles to bring the story to life and connect the disturbances with similar events in the twentieth century.

Stampp, Kenneth R. "The Tragic Legend of Reconstruction." In *The Era of Reconstruction, 1865-1877.* New York: Alfred A. Knopf, 1969. The author, self-identified as a "revisionist" historian, uses research on race from social scientists to counteract previous historians.

SEE ALSO: 1863, Emancipation Proclamation; 1863, Reconstruction; 1865, Freedmen's Bureau Is Established; 1865, New Black Codes; 1865, Thirteenth Amendment; 1866, Rise of the Ku Klux Klan; 1866, Civil Rights Act of 1866; 1868, Fourteenth Amendment; 1883, Civil Rights Cases; 1890, Mississippi Disfranchisement Laws.

1866 ■ SUFFRAGISTS PROTEST THE FOURTEENTH AMENDMENT: *activists for women's rights and former abolitionists meet to protest the proposed amendment's sexist language*

DATE: May 10, 1866
LOCALE: Church of the Puritans, New York City
CATEGORIES: Communications; Laws and acts; Women's issues

KEY FIGURES:

Susan B. Anthony (1820-1906), teacher and woman suffrage advocate

Julia Ward Howe (1819-1910), writer, lecturer, and social reformer

Lucretia Coffin Mott (1793-1880), president of the convention

Wendell Phillips (1811-1884), abolitionist and orator

Elizabeth Cady Stanton (1815-1902), vice president of the convention

Lucy Stone (1818-1893), speaker and agitator for women's rights

SUMMARY OF EVENT. On Thursday, May 10, 1866, the Eleventh National Woman's Rights Convention was held at the Church of the Puritans, Union Square, New York City, beginning at 10:00 A.M. The convention was called by several prominent activists for women's rights, most notably Elizabeth Cady Stanton. Stanton had been active for many years in abolitionist and reformer circles, working to abolish slavery, bring about labor reform, and secure equal property, labor, and voting rights for women. Many of the participants in the 1866 convention also had participated in the 1848 Women's Rights Convention at Seneca Falls, New York, and most of them were prominent in the movement to secure the rights of African Americans in the aftermath of the Civil War. Almost from the beginning, the battles to abolish slavery and to enfranchise women both legally and socially had gone hand in hand. In 1865, the two goals began to diverge, and this divergence directly prompted the convention of 1866.

In the spring of 1865, the U.S. Congress began considering the Fourteenth Amendment to the Constitution, which specifically stated in Section 2 that if "the right to vote at any election . . . is denied to any male inhabitants . . . or in any way abridged," the representation of such states would be reduced proportionately. The inclusion of the word "male" allowed any state to deny any woman the right to vote without penalty, leaving women no constitutional foundation for their claims to suffrage. As longtime workers for slaves' rights, many women felt particularly betrayed. Elizabeth Cady Stanton was incensed that such a clause would be considered and rallied the support of many followers to combat the implicitly sexist ideals represented by the Fourteenth Amendment.

Other prominent abolitionist leaders disagreed. Horace Greeley, the editor of the *New York Tribune* and one of the country's foremost antislavery leaders, felt that including the idea of the vote for women in the debate over the Fourteenth Amendment would only make the passage of African American voting rights less likely. Likewise, Wendell Phillips, the leader of the American Anti-Slavery Society, felt that woman suffrage would never be approved in the political climate of the day, so it was unwise to endanger the passage of voting rights for male former slaves by linking the two together. Neither of these men seemed moved by Stanton's arguments that half of the former slaves recently freed were women, and that female slaves had been more abused by the slave system—particularly through sexual assault and the selling of their children—than had male slaves.

Therefore, when the convention met in May of 1866, the participants were concerned with woman suffrage and women's rights in general, and specifically with the explicit denial of woman suffrage as expressed in the Fourteenth and Fifteenth Amendments to the Constitution, then under consideration in Congress. The convention listed as its main aim the securing of "equal rights to all American citizens . . . irrespective of race, color, or sex."

As the meeting convened, Elizabeth Cady Stanton was elected president, but she declined, stating that she would prefer the first president to be Lucretia Coffin Mott, so that, in Stanton's words, "The office of President . . . might ever be held sacred in the memory that it had first been filled by one so loved and honored by all." Mott was a longtime worker for universal rights, a famous speaker on the abolitionist circuit, and a well-respected woman by all sides in the suffrage debate; she was elected president by unanimous vote. Although quite old and somewhat enfeebled, Mott agreed to accept the presidency, especially since Stanton, as vice president, would carry out most of the actual duties. Mott praised the movement under way for being broad enough to encompass class, race, and sex, and reminded the participants that progress would

Lucretia Coffin Mott was a longtime worker for universal rights, a famous speaker on the abolitionist circuit, and a well-respected woman by all sides in the suffrage debate. (The Associated Publishers, Inc.)

likely be slow and ultimately would be advanced only by "the few in isolation and ridicule."

Lucretia Mott's presidency of the convention was a brilliant compromise move on Stanton's part to head off differences between two rival groups in the convention's membership, one of which was led by herself and her longtime friend and colleague Susan B. Anthony. Stanton and Anthony were the more radical members of the group, who refused any compromise on the issues of universal suffrage and equality under the law. The other faction, led by Lucy Stone and Julia Ward Howe, was more conservative and willing to compromise on major issues. In later years, these two groups divided even further and worked separately for the passage of the Nineteenth Amendment and other legislation affecting women's rights.

The most significant outcome of the 1866 convention was the drafting and subsequent adoption of an Address to Congress regarding the issues of African American male suffrage and woman suffrage. This document stated the majority opinion of the convention participants, including their belief that "The only tenable ground of representation is universal suffrage, as it is only through universal suffrage that the principle of 'Equal Rights to All' can be realized. All prohibitions based on race, color, sex, property, or education, are violations of the republican idea; and the various qualifications now proposed are but so many plausible pretexts to debar new classes from the ballot-box."

Although the 1866 convention's address was received by Congress, it did not alter the tenor of the debate, and the Fourteenth and Fifteenth Amendments were ratified in 1868 and 1870, respectively. The convention's seeds had been sown, however, and continued to bear fruit. In 1868, Stanton and Anthony founded the Woman Suffrage Association of America, which continued to work on both a state-by-state and a national basis for woman suffrage. This group, later called the National Woman Suffrage Association, also published a journal called *Revolution*, edited by Stanton and Anthony, which supported women's legislative causes. Another group, the American Woman Suffrage Association, worked for suffrage and other rights for women through its own magazine, *The Woman's Journal*, edited by Lucy Stone, Mary Livermore, and Julia Ward Howe.

In August, 1920, the efforts of these and other organizations resulted in the ratification of the Nineteenth Amendment, granting all U.S. women the right to vote in all elections. The 1866 convention had been instrumental in effecting the ratification of universal suffrage laws in the United States, by calling attention to the unfairness of the Fourteenth and Fifteenth Amendments and similar laws that specifically excluded women. The convention also helped organize and inspire former abolitionists to begin a new fight for women's freedom and rights, just as they previously had worked for the rights of former slaves. The ideals expressed in the Address to Congress would later be rediscovered by twentieth century feminists and formed the foundation of the modern movement

for full legal, social, and economic equity for women the world over.

—*Vicki A. Sanders*

ADDITIONAL READING:

Banner, Lois W. *Elizabeth Cady Stanton: A Radical for Woman's Rights*. Boston: Little, Brown, 1980. Describes the atmosphere in which the convention took place and important events growing from it.

Buhle, Mari Jo, and Paul Buhle, eds. *The Concise History of Woman Suffrage: Selections from the Classic Work of Stanton, Anthony, Gage, and Harper*. Urbana: University of Illinois Press, 1978. This shortened form of a six-volume work includes the texts of the call for the convention and the Address to Congress adopted by the convention.

Cromwell, Otelia. *Lucretia Mott*. Cambridge, Mass.: Harvard University Press, 1958. Describes Mott's lifelong work for abolition and women's rights, and explains why she was chosen as the convention's spokesperson.

Hunter College Women's Studies Collective. *Women's Realities, Women's Choices: An Introduction to Women's Studies*. New York: Oxford University Press, 1983. An overview of women's studies, providing information on women's historical and socioeconomic struggles. Situates the convention in its political and social context.

Schneir, Miriam, ed. *Feminism in Our Time: The Essential Writings, World War II to the Present*. New York: Vintage Books, 1994. Contains major writings by most of the participants in the convention; helps establish the historical context in which the convention took place.

SEE ALSO: 1848, Seneca Falls Convention; 1851, Akron Woman's Rights Convention; 1868, Fourteenth Amendment; 1869, Rise of Woman Suffrage Associations; 1869, Western States Grant Woman Suffrage; 1872, Susan B. Anthony Is Arrested; 1874, *Minor v. Happersett*; 1876, Declaration of the Rights of Women; 1890, Women's Rights Associations Unite; 1916, National Woman's Party Is Founded; 1920, League of Women Voters Is Founded; 1920, U.S. Women Gain the Vote.

1866 ■ BOZEMAN TRAIL WAR: *the end of Red Cloud's war opens the door to the U.S. reservation system*

DATE: June 13, 1866-November 6, 1868

LOCALE: Powder River country, Dakota Territory, east of the Bighorn Mountains

CATEGORIES: Native American history; Wars, uprisings, and civil unrest

KEY FIGURES:

John M. Bozeman (1835-1867), settler who laid out the route that started the war

Henry Beebee Carrington (1824-1912), builder and commander of forts on the Bozeman Trail

William Judd Fetterman (c. 1833-1866), army captain killed with his entire command at Fort Kearny

Crazy Horse (c. 1842-1877), key Sioux strategist in the Fetterman battle

Red Cloud (1822-1909), chief opponent to the Bozeman Trail

SUMMARY OF EVENT. In 1862, John M. Bozeman sought a more direct route connecting the newly discovered gold fields around Virginia City, Montana, to the east. Leaving Virginia City, he located a pass that led him to the headwaters of the Yellowstone River, then southeastward along the eastern flank of the Bighorn Mountains, where he traversed the headwaters of the Bighorn, Tongue, and Powder Rivers. Continuing southeast, he intersected the Oregon Trail along the North Platte River seventy miles west of Fort Laramie. This new Bozeman Trail cut directly through the best hunting grounds of the Teton Dakota Sioux—Red Cloud's people.

The Powder River country was a hunter's paradise, home to the great northern bison herd. It had been guaranteed to the Sioux by the Fort Laramie Treaty of 1851, it was the locus of their free-ranging lifestyle, and they meant to keep it. Responding to growing pressure from miners and settlers, however, the government was keenly interested in securing the Bozeman Trail but was uncertain of the best method. Using force to subjugate or exterminate native peoples was a popular idea in the West. Alternatively, an approach based on peace through justice gained support, especially in the East after the Civil War, when humanitarians who previously had been devoted to emancipation and the abolition of slavery turned their attention to the "Indian problem." This East-West rift led to a schizophrenic policy toward American Indians, in which both approaches were tried, often at the same time.

Pursuing force, a string of three forts was built along the Bozeman Trail. Fort Reno was the first, built seventy miles up the Bozeman Trail in late summer of 1865 by General Patrick E. Connor. Best known for slaughtering 273 Paiutes at Bear Creek in 1863, Connor issued the directive to "accept no peace offers and kill any male over twelve." Red Cloud, with Cheyenne and Arapaho allies, mauled Connor's columns; they withdrew, but the fort remained. On July 10 of the following year, Colonel Henry B. Carrington established Fort Phil Kearny forty miles north of Fort Reno at the fork of the Piney Creeks, and in early August, Fort C. F. Smith ninety miles beyond that.

The peace process was tried also. On October 28, 1865, a commission under Governor Newton Edmunds of Dakota Territory announced peace with the Sioux, producing a treaty signed by chiefs already friendly to the settlers. None of the Powder River chiefs signed, as they were all fighting Connor. Red Cloud did go to Fort Laramie the next spring to discuss peace, trade, and Fort Reno. In the middle of peace negotiations, Colonel Carrington arrived at Fort Laramie on June 13, 1866, in a masterpiece of bad timing. He had seven hundred troops, more than two hundred wagons, and orders to build his Bozeman forts. Red Cloud excoriated the commissioner, E. B. Edwards, for already stealing what they were negotiating, and his entire camp was gone the next morning.

Edwards collected some signatures and blithely informed Washington that a satisfactory treaty had been concluded with the Sioux. While Colonel Carrington went on to build his forts, Red Cloud was galvanizing opposition with stunning oratory:

> Hear Ye, Dakotas! . . . before the ashes of the council fire are cold, the Great Father is building his forts among us. You have heard the sound of the white soldier's axe upon the Little Piney. His presence here is an insult and a threat. It is an insult to the spirits of our ancestors. Are we then to give up their sacred graves to be plowed for corn? Dakotas, I am for war!

Recruiting a coalition of three thousand warriors, Red Cloud's war against the Thieves' Road began in earnest.

Within days of their completion, Carrington's forts were under unrelenting guerrilla warfare. In the first five weeks, the colonel reported thirty-three whites killed. By December, ninety-six soldiers and fifty-eight civilians had been killed, many were wounded, and nearly one thousand oxen, cows, mules, and horses had been lost. There were fifty-one separate attacks on Fort Kearny alone.

The worst loss came on December 21, 1866, when the command of Captain William Fetterman was completely annihilated. Having once boasted that he could ride through the whole Sioux nation with eighty good men, Fetterman led exactly eighty soldiers out of Fort Kearny to relieve an embattled party of woodcutters. Disobeying Carrington's orders not to ride out of view of the fort, Fetterman could not resist chasing Crazy Horse, who, acting as a decoy, lured Fetterman into an ambush by two thousand Sioux, Cheyenne, and Arapaho. In the Battle of One Hundred Slain, Fetterman's arrogance had handed the U.S. Army its worst defeat in the Plains Wars.

On August 1, 1867, the Cheyenne attacked hay cutters at Fort Smith, and the next day at Fort Kearny, Red Cloud's Sioux attacked a woodcutters' camp. Although these Hayfield and Wagon Box fights were standoffs, the government began to realize the speciousness of Edmunds' and Taylor's treaties. John Bozeman himself had been caught in 1867 by Blackfoot warriors and killed on his own road.

Major peace initiatives in 1867 were rebuffed by Red Cloud, who persistently refused to sign anything until the forts were gone. Concerned about the cost of a full military campaign and the safety of the new railroads inching westward, Congress decided to concede the Bozeman overland route. Soldiers left Fort Smith on July 29, 1868, Fort Kearny a month later, and Fort Reno a few days after that. Jubilant warriors burned the three forts to the ground, and the Bozeman Trail was closed. On November 6, 1868, Red Cloud signed the Sioux Treaty of 1868 at Fort Laramie. Red Cloud had won his war.

In 1870, Red Cloud and other Sioux were invited to Washington, D.C., to discuss the treaty. Here Red Cloud heard for the first time of provisions calling for permanent settlements on a reservation. Although deeply upset, he was persuaded to make an address at the Cooper Institute in New York City before an audience of social reformers. At noon on June 16, he began with a prayer to the Almighty Spirit, then recited wrongs done to his people, and asked for justice. Praised for its piety, charisma, and sincerity, the speech was an immense success.

His growing influence with the Eastern peace and reform circles allowed Red Cloud to extract future concessions for his people from the government. The treaty articles that had not been explained to him, however, hastened the pace of the Sioux toward becoming "reservation Indians." Still, the success of his implacable opposition to the Bozeman Trail makes his name an appropriate eponym for "Red Cloud's War." —*Gary A. Olson*

ADDITIONAL READING:

Armstrong, Virginia Irving, comp. *I Have Spoken: American History Through the Voices of the Indians*. Chicago: Swallow Press, 1971. Includes three orations by Red Cloud, including the Powder River exhortation (1866) and the complete Cooper Institute speech (1870).

Brown, Dee. "Red Cloud's War." In *Bury My Heart at Wounded Knee*. New York: Holt, Rinehart and Winston, 1970. A good overview of the nineteenth century wars from the Native American point of view.

Hyde, George E. "Red Cloud's War." In *Red Cloud's Folk: A History of the Oglala Sioux Indians*. Rev. ed. Norman: University of Oklahoma Press, 1976. Originally published in 1937 and revised in 1957, this is considered to be a definitive history of the Oglala Sioux. Includes extensive background for the events on the Bozeman Trail. Thirteen illustrations, two maps.

Lazarus, Edward. *Black Hills, White Justice: The Sioux Nation Versus the United States, 1775 to the Present*. New York: HarperCollins, 1991. Includes the full text of the Fort Laramie Treaty of 1868.

McDermott, John D. "Price of Arrogance: The Short and Controversial Life of William Judd Fetterman." *Annals of Wyoming* 63, no. 2 (Spring, 1991): 42-53. A look at Fetterman's character and its fatal consequences.

_____, ed. "Wyoming Scrapbook: Documents Relating to the Fetterman Fight." *Annals of Wyoming* 63, no. 2 (Spring, 1991): 68-72. Gives details of the most significant Army loss in the war.

SEE ALSO: 1862, Great Sioux War; 1864, Sand Creek Massacre; 1867, Medicine Lodge Creek Treaty; 1868, Washita River Massacre; 1871, Indian Appropriation Act; 1872, Great American Bison Slaughter; 1874, Red River War; 1876, Battle of the Little Bighorn; 1877, Nez Perce Exile; 1890, Closing of the Frontier; 1890, Battle of Wounded Knee.

1867 ■ OFFICE OF EDUCATION IS CREATED: *the U.S. government makes a full commitment to public education*

DATE: March 2, 1867
LOCALE: Washington, D.C.
CATEGORIES: Education; Organizations and institutions
KEY FIGURES:
Henry Barnard (1811-1900), educator, journalist, and first U.S. commissioner of education
James Abram Garfield (1831-1881), representative from Ohio

Andrew Johnson (1808-1875), seventeenth president of the United States, 1865-1869
E. E. White (1829-1902), Ohio commissioner of common schools

SUMMARY OF EVENT. On March 2, 1867, President Andrew Johnson signed an act creating a department of education to collect and diffuse "such statistics and facts" concerning the progress and condition of education in the several states and territories as would aid the people of the United States in establishing and maintaining efficient school systems and "promote the cause of education throughout the country." The act provided for the appointment of a commissioner of education charged with reporting annually to Congress the results of investigations and recommendations to carry out the statute's purposes.

The story behind the creation of the United States Department of Education is, in many ways, the story of Henry Barnard, a native of Connecticut, who, when only twenty-six, dedicated himself to the cause of promoting and improving public school education in America. Reasonably well off, Barnard attended both public and private schools in his home state. He was graduated from Yale in 1830, was admitted to the Connecticut bar, and made a grand tour of Europe in 1835. Extensive travel and his own educational experience convinced Barnard that New England's public schools, among America's best, were seriously deficient. In no respect could this country's highly decentralized, ungraded, and miserably taught public institutions compare favorably with the state-controlled, generously supported, and professionally staffed educational systems he had observed in Europe.

Elected to the Connecticut state legislature in 1837, Barnard sponsored two educational reform bills. Both failed, but in 1838 his proposal to create a state Board of Commissioners of Common Schools passed unanimously. The board elected Barnard secretary and defined his duties as follows: (1) to collect by inspection and correspondence all possible information on conditions of the common schools; (2) to propose plans relative to the organization and administration of the schools for consideration by the board and the state legislature; (3) to meet with parents, teachers and administrators in each county; (4) to edit a common school journal, and (5) to promote among the public, in any way possible, interest and information regarding the subject of education.

Seeking comparative data for his report, Barnard wrote several agencies of the federal government soliciting information regarding education in other states. To his amazement, he discovered that no federal office gathered any educational statistics whatsoever. This discovery prompted him to visit Washington, D.C., where he prevailed upon the Van Buren Administration to include a few educational items, particularly regarding illiteracy, in future census questionnaires. Barnard, his friend Horace Mann of Massachusetts, and others interested in common school education used the information so obtained to dramatize the dismal state of American education. Ultimately, they hoped to persuade influential persons, in and out of government, that gathering data on a national scale could contribute substantially to the improvement of public education on the local level.

Their task was not an easy one. Those who favored formal recognition by the national government of common school education and some degree of national responsibility for its promotion disagreed as to the form that recognition should take. Should the federal government establish, support, and administer a comprehensive educational system, as many European nations did, or should it confine itself strictly to collecting and diffusing statistics concerning state and local systems? Even more difficult to overcome than such differences among friends were the objections raised by opponents, who interpreted any plan for federal participation in the educational sphere as an attempt to invade states' rights. Somewhere between these extremes lay the vast majority of Americans. They were either skeptical, apathetic, or unaware that the country had an educational problem.

Henry Barnard probably first proposed the establishment of a special federal agency to collect and disseminate educational information during a speaking tour he made in 1842. In 1845 and again in 1847 he tried without success to interest the trustees of the Smithsonian Institution, just then being organized, in his project. Later, at the National Convention of the Friends of Common Schools meeting in Philadelphia in 1849, Barnard helped to draft a resolution urging congressional action. For the next fifteen years he continued to promote his bureau in lectures, at conventions, and in the pages of his famous *American Journal of Education*.

Illness kept Barnard away from the convention that finally secured the attention of Congress. In February, 1866, at a Washington meeting of the National Association of State and City School Superintendents, Ohio Commissioner of Common Schools E. E. White read a paper advocating the establishment of a national bureau for educational affairs. Joined by the National Teachers' Association, the superintendents voted to present White's proposal to Congress. There it found a sponsor in General James A. Garfield, a Republican representative from Commissioner White's home state of Ohio. On February 14, 1866, Garfield introduced a bill to establish a federal "department of education." The House approved an amended measure on June 19 after a brief speech in which the Ohio congressman cited current illiteracy figures among the American population and reminded his colleagues that the country's political system depended upon an intelligent and informed electorate. Senate approval came early the next year, and on March 2, 1867, President Andrew Johnson signed the bill into law, naming Henry Barnard the first commissioner of the United States Department of Education.

For embittered Andrew Johnson, already hard pressed by a hostile Congress and soon to be the subject of impeachment proceedings, creation of the Department of Education (now the United States Office of Education in the Health, Education and Welfare Department) probably seemed relatively insignificant. For Commissioner Barnard, however, it represented the end of a thirty-year-long battle to achieve national recognition for what he considered the country's most important task: the establishment of "schools good enough for the best and cheap enough for the poorest."   —*Germaine M. Reed*

ADDITIONAL READING:

Annual Report of the United States Commissioner of Education for 1902. Vol. 1. Washington, D.C.: Government Printing Office, 1903. This volume contains two articles dealing with Barnard and his service as commissioner of education. The first, by W. T. Harris, who himself served as commissioner between 1889 and 1906, is entitled "The Establishment of the Office of the Commissioner of Education of the United States and Henry Barnard's Relation to It." The second article, by A. D. Mayo, is "Henry Barnard as First U.S. Commissioner of Education." Both are basic to a detailed study of the circumstances contributing to creation of the agency and the personalities involved.

Blair, Anna Lou. *Henry Barnard, School Administrator*. Minneapolis: Educational Publishers, 1938. A balanced biography of Barnard's career. Blair attempts to place Barnard's life in context with the American public school movement of the nineteenth century.

Kursh, Harry. *The United States Office of Education: A Century of Service*. 1965. Reprint. Westport, Conn.: Greenwood Press, 1977. One chapter is devoted to Barnard and the creation of the agency.

Lee, Gordon Canfield. *The Struggle for Federal Aid, First Phase: A History of the Attempts to Obtain Federal Aid for the Common Schools, 1870-1890*. New York: Teachers College, Columbia University, 1949. Gordon Canfield Lee's slim volume is worth consulting because it places the creation of the Office of Commissioner of Education in perspective.

Lykes, Richard Wayne. *Higher Education and the United States Office of Education, 1867-1953*. Washington, D.C.: Bureau of Postsecondary Education, United States Office of Education, U.S. Government Printing Office, 1975.

Smith, Darrell H. *The Bureau of Education: Its History, Activities, and Organization*. Baltimore: The Johns Hopkins University Press, 1923. Only a few pages deal with the establishment of the Department of Education, but considerable attention is paid to its evolution.

Smith, Theodore C. *The Life and Letters of James Abram Garfield*. 2 vols. New Haven, Conn.: Yale University Press, 1925. The second volume contains a good, if brief, discussion of Representative Garfield's efforts to push the department of education bill through a reluctant Congress and, once the office was established, to protect it from hostile critics who opposed it as unconstitutional, unnecessary, unduly extravagant, and designed simply to employ a "worn-out old man."

Steiner, Bernard C. *Life of Henry Barnard: The First United States Commissioner of Education, 1867-1870*. Washington, D.C.: Government Printing Office, 1919. A scholarly biography of Barnard that is very readable, but somewhat uncritical of its subject. Gives brief treatment to Barnard's career as commissioner.

Warren, Donald R. *To Enforce Education: A Historian of the Founding Years of the United States Office of Education.* Detroit: Wayne State University Press, 1974.

SEE ALSO: 1785, Beginnings of State Universities; 1820's, Free Public School Movement; 1823, Hartford Female Seminary Is Founded; 1828, Webster's *American Dictionary of the English Language*; 1833, Oberlin College Is Established; 1837, Mt. Holyoke Seminary Is Founded; 1846, Smithsonian Institution Is Founded; 1862, Morrill Land Grant Act; 1865, Vassar College Is Founded; 1897, Library of Congress Building Opens.

1867 ■ PURCHASE OF ALASKA: *the United States acquires a vast territory of abundant natural resources and immense strategic importance*

DATE: March 30, 1867
LOCALE: Washington, D.C.
CATEGORIES: Expansion and land acquisition; Treaties and agreements
KEY FIGURES:

Alexander II (1818-1881), Russian czar, who authorized the sale of Russian America

Nathaniel Prentiss Banks (1816-1894), chairman of the House Committee on Foreign Affairs, who led the fight to secure the purchase appropriation

Aleksandr Mikhailovich Gorchakov (1798-1883), Russian foreign minister and chancellor

William Henry Seward (1801-1872), secretary of state, who negotiated the treaty for the U.S. government

Edouard de Stoeckl, Russian minister to the United States, who negotiated the treaty for the Russian government

Charles Sumner (1811-1874), chairman of the Senate Committee on Foreign Relations, who pressed for acceptance of the treaty

Robert John Walker (1801-1869), former U.S. senator and lawyer, who helped secure passage of the appropriation bill

SUMMARY OF EVENT. Unofficial negotiations regarding the sale of Russian America (as Alaska was then called) to the United States were conducted in at least two instances before the Civil War, in 1854 and in 1860. Following the war, the discussion was renewed through the efforts of Baron Edouard de Stoeckl, Russian minister to the United States. Stoeckl believed that the transfer of Russian America was in the best interest of Russia and the future of Russian-United States friendship. Stoeckl received permission to negotiate the sale of Alaska after discussions with Czar Alexander II, Foreign Minister Aleksandr Gorchakov, and other Russian officials during his home leave late in 1866. The minimum price was set at five million dollars. The Russian willingness to sell was apparently motivated by the failure of the Russian American Company, a chartered company organized to exploit Russian America; a fear that the British might take the defenseless territory in the

event of war; and a desire to minimize the possibility of clashes between U.S. and Russian interests in the Pacific.

Secretary of State William H. Seward was an ardent expansionist who was interested in obtaining overseas possessions in the Caribbean and in the Pacific. When Stoeckl returned to Washington in March, 1867, Seward requested U.S. fishing rights in Russian-American territorial waters. When Stoeckl refused, Seward inquired whether Russia would be willing to sell Alaska. Stoeckl responded positively. Seward consulted President Andrew Johnson and the cabinet, which unanimously agreed to open negotiations. Seward's initial bid was five million dollars, but Stoeckl asked twice that amount for the 586,000 square miles of territory. The two agreed on $7 million, but when Stoeckl insisted that the United States take over the Russian American Company, Seward added $200,000 to escape the obligation. Hence the final purchase price was $7.2 million. Stoeckl cabled the details to Foreign Minister Gorchakov, who authorized the signing of the treaty. Stoeckl brought the news to Seward on the evening of March 29 and suggested that the treaty be concluded the next day. Seward was anxious to proceed and wanted to draw up the treaty immediately. The Russian and United States plenipotentiaries summoned their clerks, and the treaty was signed at 4:00 A.M. on March 30, 1867.

A few hours after the signing, President Johnson forwarded the treaty to the Senate for ratification. It initially appeared that the necessary two-thirds vote would not be forthcoming, because Congress and President Johnson had reached an impasse concerning Reconstruction politics. Charles Sumner, chairman of the Senate Foreign Relations Committee, championed the bill, and on April 9, he made an effective three-hour speech that summarized the arguments for the purchase. Later the same day, the Senate gave its approval by a vote of thirty-seven to two. Ratifications were exchanged on June 20.

Most Americans were caught by surprise when the proposed treaty was revealed. There was some hostility and a good deal of criticism expressed. Many newspapers denounced the proposed purchase, calling it "Johnson's Polar Bear Garden," "Seward's Icebox," "Seward's Folly," and "Walrussia," but some New England sea captains and West Coast defenders testified in its favor. Friendship with Russia was also a persuasive reason for accepting the treaty. Many people in the United States had regarded the calling of the Russian fleet at U.S. ports during the Civil War as an act of friendship at a time when England and France appeared hostile toward the cause of the Union. While later research in Russian archives indicates that Russian ships had been dispatched to U.S. ports for strategic reasons, the idea of Russian-American friendship was not entirely illusory.

The formal transfer of Alaska to the United States took place on October 18, 1867, at Sitka, the capital of Russian America on the west coast of Baranof Island, before the agreed price had been paid to Russia. The delay in payment was caused by the failure of the House of Representatives to vote the necessary appropriation. Some members argued that, although the Constitution gave the Senate the exclusive right to approve treaties, it also gave the House the right to originate money bills. These congressmen believed that the House should have been consulted before the treaty was confirmed. Disputes between the executive and legislative branches, which eventually culminated in the impeachment trial of President Johnson, further delayed House action. Both Seward and Stoeckl, however, worked effectively to secure the appropriation. Seward conducted a campaign to educate the newspapers and the public, while Stoeckl retained former senator Robert J. Walker as a lobbyist. Some newspapers and public officials may have received payments for their support of the treaty. Under the management of Seward's friend Nathaniel P. Banks, chairman of the House Committee on Foreign Affairs, the House passed the appropriation bill on July 14, 1868, by a vote of 113 to 43, with 44 abstaining. The Senate concurred on July 17, and the bill became law on July 27. Payment to Russia was finally made on August 1, 1868.

Estimates of the population of Alaska at the time of purchase put the Russian population at about five hundred, the number of Creoles (those of mixed Russian and native descent) at about fifteen hundred, and the number of native Alaskans at between twenty-four and thirty thousand. The Treaty of 1867 permitted inhabitants of Alaska who remained after the Russians departed the option of becoming U.S. citizens within three years, with the exception of "the uncivilized tribes," who would be treated according to the laws that governed "aboriginal tribes" in the United States.

In general, native Alaskans had fared better under Russian rule than they did under initial U.S. rule. The Russians had extended citizenship to the Creoles and allowed some form of tribal government to remain intact among the settled native tribes. Although at first mistreated by the Russian fur traders, who conscripted Aleuts to hunt sea otters, native peoples had begun to gain increasingly benign treatment under the succession of charters that the Russian government granted to the Russian American Company beginning in 1799. The Russians strove to avoid serious conflict with the Alaskan natives during much of the time that Alaska was under Russian rule.

For the first seventeen years of rule by the United States, U.S. policy toward Alaska was one of neglect. Alaska officially became a customs district and was placed under military rule. The War Department dispatched five hundred troops to Sitka and Fort Wrangell under the command of General Jefferson C. Davis. The army was unrestrained in its conduct and introduced a period of general lawlessness into a territory that had enjoyed orderly rule under the Russians. U.S. soldiers introduced disease, alcohol, and firearms to native Alaskans. It was not until the passage of the Organic Act of 1884, which provided limited government for Alaska, that some semblance of civil order was reestablished. The founding of schools and churches by U.S. missionaries in the late nineteenth century, encouraged by Sheldon Jackson, a Presbyterian minister, significantly benefited native Alaskans at a time of neglect by the federal government. The Russian Orthodox Church, which continued to hold the allegiance of native Alaskans after the departure of the Russians, remains the most notable heritage of Russian rule in Alaska.

—Mark A. Plummer, updated by Anne-Marie E. Ferngren

ADDITIONAL READING:

Chevigny, Hector. *Russian America: The Great Alaskan Venture, 1741-1867.* 1965. Reprint. Portland, Oreg.: Binford & Mort, 1979. A comprehensive survey of the Russian period of Alaskan history.

Farrar, Victor J. *The Annexation of Russian America to the United States.* Washington, D.C.: W. F. Roberts, 1937. A brief, standard treatment of the purchase.

Jensen, Ronald J. *The Alaska Purchase and Russian-American Relations.* Seattle: University of Washington Press, 1975. Places the treaty in the larger context of Russian-American relations.

Miller, David Hunter. *The Alaska Treaty.* Kingston, Ontario: Limestone Press, 1981. An important and comprehensive study of the treaty.

Sherwood, Morgan B., ed. *Alaska and Its History.* Seattle: University of Washington Press, 1967. Contains several important articles dealing with the purchase.

Shiels, Archie W. [Archibald Williamson]. *The Purchase of Alaska.* College: University of Alaska Press, 1967. Contains many documents pertaining to the purchase of Alaska.

Van Deusen, Glyndon G. *William Henry Seward.* New York: Oxford University Press, 1967. An outstanding biography of the secretary of state who was the chief proponent of the purchase of Alaska.

SEE ALSO: 1728, Russian Voyages to Alaska; 1790, Nootka Sound Convention; 1959, Alaska and Hawaii Gain Statehood; 1971, Alaska Native Claims Settlement Act; 1974, Construction of the Alaska Pipeline; 1989, *Exxon Valdez* Oil Spill.

1867 ■ BRITISH NORTH AMERICA ACT: *the creation of the Dominion of Canada marks the birth of a new nation*

DATE: July 1, 1867

LOCALE: London, England, and Ottawa, Canada

CATEGORIES: Canadian history; Laws and acts

KEY FIGURES:

George Étienne Cartier (1814-1873), leader of the Quebec delegation immediately before and after the creation of the Canadian confederation

John Alexander Macdonald (1815-1891), first prime minister of Canada

Alexander Mackenzie (1822-1892), second prime minister of Canada

Charles Tupper (1821-1915), influential Nova Scotian, who persuaded delegates from his province to join the Canadian confederation

Queen Victoria (1819-1901), monarch who approved the British North America Act of 1867

THE DOMINION OF CANADA, 1867

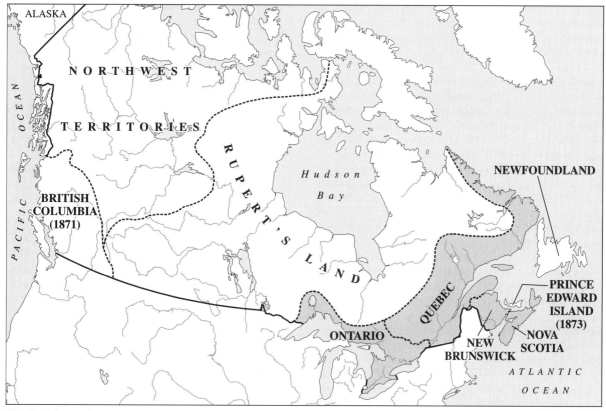

The British North America Act took effect on July 1, 1867. Ontario (formerly Upper Canada), Quebec (formerly Lower Canada), New Brunswick, and Nova Scotia were joined into the Dominion of Canada. British Columbia joined in 1871 and Prince Edward Island in 1873.

SUMMARY OF EVENT. After the British defeat of French forces in the Seven Years' War (1756-1763), the terms of the 1763 Treaty of Paris forced France to yield its former colony, Canada, to Britain. For the first century after the Treaty of Paris, Canada was ruled as a British colony, and almost all important political decisions affecting Canadians were made by the British Parliament in London or by the governor general, who was the Crown's official representative in Canada.

Various British governments saw no reason to change this situation of overt colonial rule from London, until the outbreak of the Civil War in the United States in 1861. Henry Palmerston, the British prime minister from 1859 to 1865, and his chancellor of the Exchequer, William Gladstone, expressed overt support for the Confederates and even considered granting diplomatic recognition to the Confederate government of Jefferson Davis. Moreover, British shipyards built ships for the Confederate navy. These were considered hostile acts in Washington, D.C. The overt distrust between Washington and London became much worse when, in 1861, a U.S. warship stopped the British steamer *Trent* during a trip from Canada to England and removed two Confederate agents, whose goal was to seek active support from England for the Confeder-

ates. This almost provoked a third war between the United States and Great Britain, after the Revolutionary War and the War of 1812.

After the Union victory in the Civil War, the British government realized that the victorious North was extremely angry with Great Britain but still felt positively toward Canadians, who had helped greatly in protecting escaped slaves. Prominent British politicians feared that U.S. forces might invade Canada in retaliation for British support of the Confederates during the Civil War, but believed that no such invasion would take place if Canada became an independent country. U.S. citizens in the North generally wished to maintain good relations with Canada. Thus, it was in Great Britain's self-interest to create, as quickly as possible, an independent form of government in Canada.

The British encouraged two leading Canadian politicians—John A. Macdonald from Ontario (Upper Canada) and George Étienne Cartier from Quebec (Lower Canada)—to propose a political system to unify the various Canadian provinces under a single federal system. The challenge for Macdonald and Cartier was to balance federal and provincial interests while preserving the best elements of the British parliamentary system. The recent experience of the Civil War convinced Macdonald and Cartier that it would be extremely unwise for Canada to grant excessive powers to individual provinces, but they both realized that certain matters needed to be resolved at the provincial level. Unless individual provinces saw economic, social, or political advantages for themselves in a new Canadian union, they would not join the new confederation, as it came to be called. Prince Edward Island, for example, chose not to join the Canadian confederation in 1867, but joined the Dominion of Canada six years later, only when the federal government offered to pay off the large debts the province had incurred as a result of railroad construction on the island.

The negotiations in Canada before the approval of the British North America Act of 1867 took place at conferences held in Charlottetown, on Prince Edward Island, and in Quebec City. It eventually was decided to recommend a legislature with two chambers: a House of Commons with elected members, and a Senate composed of appointed members. The linguistic and religious rights of Canadians were to be protected, and it was specified that either French or English could be used in the Houses of Parliament and in all Canadian courts. The founders of the Canadian confederation granted to the national government the power to regulate trade and commerce, to impose taxes, to control the criminal justice system, to appoint judges, and to overrule decisions rendered by provincial governments. The various provinces were to be responsible for education in their provinces. This section was important because it permitted the French Catholic majority in Quebec to continue subsidizing Catholic schools in Quebec.

Unlike the U.S. Constitution, the British North America Act of 1867 specifically assigned to the federal government, not to the provinces, all powers not especially enumerated in the British North America Act of 1867. The clear intention was to avoid in Canada disagreements about provincial and federal powers similar to the conflicts between federal and state powers that had created so many problems, and even a civil war, in the United States.

The British North America Act of 1867 did not contain a specific bill of rights, but reaffirmed the reality of the unwritten British tradition of protecting basic civil rights. (A specific Charter of Rights and Freedoms was, however, approved by the Canadian Parliament in 1982. Similar to the U.S. Bill of Rights, it also established the equality in law between the French and English languages in Canada.) The British North America Act had restricted the ability of the Canadian Parliament to change its basic provisions without the approval of the British Parliament. In reality, the British government stopped interfering directly in Canadian domestic affairs early in the twentieth century, but the very possibility of British involvement in internal Canadian matters bothered many Canadians, and this requirement was eliminated by the Canada Act of 1982, by which the British government formally recognized Canada's complete independence from Great Britain.

On July 1, 1867, the British North America Act of 1867 took effect, and the confederation of Ontario, Quebec, Nova Scotia, and New Brunswick created the Dominion of Canada. Because of its historical importance, July 1—Canada Day, as it is now known—became the Canadian national holiday. At the suggestion of Queen Victoria herself, John A. Macdonald, who had played the leading role in the creation of the Canadian confederation, was appointed Canada's first prime minister. Macdonald strove to unify Canada both politically and culturally. He was an English-speaking Protestant from Ontario and understood that the unity of Canada required that both major language groups (French and English) and religious groups (Catholic and Protestant) be included at all levels of the federal government. Until his death in 1873, George Étienne Cartier was Macdonald's most important adviser, and most historians feel that the French-speaking Catholic Cartier and the English-speaking Macdonald governed Canada together for the first six years of its independence.

Macdonald's government spent large sums of money to complete the construction of the Canadian Pacific Railway in order to permit travel and trade between eastern and western Canada. During his first six years as prime minister, the Northwest Territories, Manitoba, British Columbia, and Prince Edward Island all joined the Canadian confederation. Although Macdonald served as the leader of the opposition party in the House of Commons from 1873 to 1878, when Alexander Mackenzie served as Canada's prime minister, the years between 1867 and 1891 have generally been called the Macdonald era because of his great influence in creating the modern country of Canada.   —*Edmund J. Campion*

ADDITIONAL READING:

Hutchison, Bruce. *Macdonald to Pearson: The Prime Ministers of Canada*. Don Mills, Ont.: Longmans Canada, 1967. Useful chapters on Macdonald's years of service as prime minister.

Martin, Ged. *Britain and the Origins of Canadian Confederation, 1837-1867*. London: Macmillan, 1995. Excellent analysis of the reasons that Great Britain was so eager to create the Dominion of Canada after the Civil War in the United States.

Smith, Cynthia M., and Jack McLeod, eds. *Sir John A.: An Anecdotal Life of John A. Macdonald*. Toronto: Oxford University Press, 1989. Contains numerous comments on John Macdonald from many different contemporary sources.

Swainson, Donald. *John A. Macdonald: The Man and the Politician*. Toronto: Oxford University Press, 1971. An excellent and well-documented biography of Macdonald.

Taylor, M. Brook, and Doug Owram, eds. *Canadian History: A Reader's Guide*. 2 vols. Toronto: University of Toronto Press, 1994. Presents an excellent analysis of important studies of Canadian politics and society, both before and after the confederation of 1867.

SEE ALSO: 1791, Canada's Constitutional Act; 1837, Rebellions in Canada; 1841, Upper and Lower Canada Unite; 1842, Webster-Ashburton Treaty; 1873, Mackenzie Era in Canada; 1931, Statute of Westminster; 1982, Canada's Constitution Act.

1867 ■ MEDICINE LODGE CREEK TREATY:

tribes of the Great Plains enter an agreement that ultimately results in total submission to the U.S. government

DATE: October 21, 1867

LOCALE: Southwestern Kansas

CATEGORIES: Native American history; Treaties and agreements

KEY FIGURES:

Black Kettle (1803?-1868), leading Cheyenne chief at Medicine Lodge Creek

Roman Nose (c. 1830-1868), Cheyenne warrior who opposed the agreements

Satank, also known as *Sitting Bear* (c. 1801-1871), Kiowa chief and orator at Medicine Lodge Creek

Satanta, also known as *White Bear* (c. 1830-1878), Kiowa chief and orator at Medicine Lodge Creek

Nathaniel G. Taylor (1819-1887), U.S. commissioner of Indian affairs who led the peach commission at Medicine Lodge Creek

Ten Bears (1792-1872), Comanche chief and orator who led peace efforts between the Native Americans and the U.S. government

SUMMARY OF EVENT. For many years, five Native American tribes—the Comanche, the Kiowa, the Kiowa-Apache, the Southern Cheyenne, and the Arapaho—roamed the vast area of the southern Great Plains, following huge buffalo herds. This area became parts of Texas, Oklahoma, New Mexico, Colorado, and Kansas. Northern Cheyenne, Sioux, and other tribes lived a similar life on the northern Great Plains. Warfare was a part of the daily life of these tribes, generally as a result of intertribal rivalries and disputes concerning control of certain sections of the plains. This traditional life began to change when the first Europeans began to arrive on the Great Plains in the sixteenth century. Until the early nineteenth century, however, the changes were limited to the acquisition of steel knives, guns, and other products from European traders. The tribes soon became dependent on these items, but their day-by-day life changed very little.

The dominant leaders of the region were the Comanches, called the Lords of the Southern Plains. Joined by the Kiowas, with whom they established friendly relations about 1790, they controlled the smaller Kiowa-Apache tribe and all land south of the Arkansas River. Their chief rivals north of the Arkansas River were the southern Cheyenne. In 1840, the Comanches and Cheyennes established a fragile peace that also included the Arapaho, the less numerous allies of the Cheyenne. This peace came at the beginning of a decade that would change forever the face of the southern Great Plains. In 1846, the United States annexed Texas. The end of the Mexican War in 1848 added New Mexico, Arizona, and other areas of the Southwest to the United States. For the next half century, the fragile Native American peace of 1840 became a strong bond of brotherhood for the southern plains tribes as they fought to defend themselves and their land against Euro-American settlers, railroads, buffalo hunters, soldiers, and other intruders.

With the acquisition of Texas, the United States inherited a long and bloody conflict between Texans and Comanches, who were described by some as the best light cavalry in the world. The Comanches had long hunted from the Arkansas River to the Rio Grande. In 1821, the government of Mexico began giving land grants in west Texas to settlers from the United States. These settlers immediately challenged the Comanches for control of the area.

The first attempt to confine the Comanches to reservations was a May, 1846, treaty that created two small reservations on the Brazos River. The few Comanches who settled on them soon yearned for the free-spirited life on the vast plains. By 1850, discoveries of precious metals from the southern Rocky Mountains to California were drawing numerous wagon and pack trains through the southern plains. These were soon followed by stagecoach lines and, later, railroads. The increase in traffic was paralleled by increased confrontation with the tribes, who were accustomed to unhindered pursuit of the buffalo.

Between 1846 and 1865, several treaties were signed between the Native Americans of the southern plains and the government of the United States. Lack of confidence, sarcasm, and open contempt on both sides doomed these treaties to failure. The frustration felt by the Native Americans increased when cholera and other diseases carried by Europeans began rapidly decreasing the native populations.

In March of 1863, a party of Native American chiefs from the southern plains went to Washington, D.C., and met with President Abraham Lincoln. Returning home loaded with gifts, these leaders were convinced that coexistence with Euro-Americans was possible. This confidence was hard to maintain after the bloody and unprovoked massacre of Cheyennes at Sand Creek, in Colorado, the following year. Nevertheless, Ten Bears of the Comanche, who had met President Lincoln, Black Kettle of the Cheyenne, who had escaped from Sand Creek, and other chiefs still felt that peace was their best protection and was possible to achieve.

The next effort toward peace was the Little Arkansas Treaty in October, 1865. Representatives of the five southern plains tribes met with U.S. commissioners at the mouth of the Little Arkansas River near Wichita, Kansas. The government wanted to end native American hindrances to movements in and through the plains. The treaty, little more than a stopgap measure, committed the tribes to reservations—the Cheyenne and Arapaho in northern Indian Territory (Oklahoma) and the Comanche, Kiowa, and Kiowa-Apache in western Texas and southwestern Indian Territory. These boundaries were impossible to enforce and did not end the violence, but the treaty set the stage for a more important meeting two years later.

In July, 1867, Congress created a peace commission to establish permanent settlements of grievances between Native Americans and Euro-Americans on the Great Plains. The commission was led by Commissioner of Indian Affairs Nathaniel Taylor and included a senator and three generals. The group chose to meet representatives of the southern plains tribes on the banks of Medicine Lodge Creek in southwestern Kansas. Joining them there were more than four thousand Native Americans representing all five tribes, but not all bands of the tribes. Noticeably absent was the Quahadi, a Comanche band that wanted no peace with the United States government.

The council opened on October 19, 1867, with Senator John B. Henderson giving the opening remarks. Under a large brush arbor, he referred to reservation homes, rich farmland, livestock, churches, and schools for all Native Americans. Although most tribal leaders accepted the promises as positive, the idea of being restricted to reservations covering only a fraction of their beloved Great Plains was sickening. The Kiowa chief Satanta, or White Bear, lamented, "I love to roam over the prairies. There I feel free and happy, but when we settle down we grow pale and die." The Yamparika Comanche chief Ten Bears gave one of the most eloquent statements, declaring, "I was born where there were no inclosures and where everything drew a free breath. I want to die there and not within walls. . . . when I see [soldiers cutting trees and killing buffalo] my heart feels like bursting with sorrow."

In spite of such emotional appeals, Ten Bears and other Comanche chiefs signed the Treaty of Medicine Lodge Creek on October 21, 1867, thereby committing their people to life on the reservation. Black Kettle, with the horrors of the 1864 Sand Creek Massacre fresh in his mind, represented the Cheyenne at the council. He would not sign the treaty until other Cheyenne chiefs arrived on October 26. Although less happy with the treaty than the Comanche and Kiowa leaders, the Cheyenne chiefs signed, primarily to get ammunition for their fall buffalo hunt. The Arapaho chiefs soon did likewise. At the end of the council meeting, Satank rode alone to bid farewell to the Peace Commission. He expressed his desire for peace and declared that the Comanche and the Kiowa no longer wanted to shed the blood of the white man.

The Treaty of Medicine Lodge Creek restricted the five southern plains tribes to reservations in the western half of Indian Territory. However, vague terminology and unwritten promises made the treaty impossible to understand or to enforce. Violence soon erupted on the southern plains. One year after Medicine Lodge Creek, Black Kettle was killed in a confrontation similar to the Sand Creek Massacre, this time on the Washita River in Indian Territory. The violence escalated for several years, then dwindled to isolated incidents before ending at Wounded Knee in 1890.

A poignant illustration of the ultimate effect of the treaty occurred on June 8, 1871, when the seventy-year-old Satank—who along with Satanta and a young war chief named Big Tree had been arrested for attacking a mule train carrying food that the ration-deprived Indians sorely needed—was being transported to Texas to stand trial for murder. Chewing his own wrists in order to slip out of his manacles, Satank then attacked a guard and was shot dead, fulfilling a prophecy that he had uttered only minutes before to fellow prisoners: "Tell them I am dead. . . . I shall never go beyond that tree."—*Glenn L. Swygart*

ADDITIONAL READING:

Brown, Dee. *Bury My Heart at Wounded Knee*. New York: Holt, Rinehart and Winston, 1970. Places the Treaty of Medicine Lodge Creek in the context of Native American history in the western United States.

Grinnell, George Bird. *The Fighting Cheyennes*. 1915. Reprint. Norman: University of Oklahoma Press, 1956. An author who observed the Cheyenne at first hand presents their history up to 1890.

Hagan, William T. *United States-Comanche Relations*. New Haven, Conn.: Yale University Press, 1976. The most complete coverage of the council and treaty at Medicine Lodge Creek.

Josephy, Alvin M., Jr. *500 Nations: An Illustrated History of North American Indians*. New York: Alfred A. Knopf, 1994. A well-illustrated history of North America from its original inhabitants' viewpoint; pages 371-374 cover the treaty, including direct quotations from Indian leaders.

Mooney, James. *Calendar History of the Kiowa Indians*. 1898. Reprint. Washington, D.C.: Smithsonian Institution Press, 1979. Provides a chronology of the tribe.

Rollings, Willard H. *The Comanche*. New York: Chelsea House, 1989. Describes the change in Comanche life after the Medicine Lodge Creek Treaty.

SEE ALSO: 1862, Great Sioux War; 1864, Sand Creek Massacre; 1866, Bozeman Trail War; 1868, Washita River Massacre; 1871, Indian Appropriation Act; 1872, Great American Bison Slaughter; 1874, Red River War; 1876, Battle of the Little Bighorn; 1877, Nez Perce Exile; 1890, Closing of the Frontier; 1890, Battle of Wounded Knee.

1867 ■ NATIONAL GRANGE OF THE PATRONS OF HUSBANDRY FORMS: *the first major organization in the United States to address the social, economic, and educational needs of rural farming populations*

DATE: December 4, 1867
LOCALE: Washington, D.C.
CATEGORIES: Organizations and institutions; Social reform
KEY FIGURES:
Caroline A. Hall (1838-1918), Kelley's niece and secretary
William M. Ireland, founder and the first treasurer of the National Grange
Oliver Hudson Kelley (1826-1913), main organizer of the National Grange movement
William Saunders (1822-1900), first master of the National Grange

SUMMARY OF EVENT. Oliver Hudson Kelley, a federal bureaucrat and former farmer, founded the National Grange of the

Patrons of Husbandry in the late 1860's out of a deep concern for the plight of persons living in rural areas of the United States. He believed that a fraternal organization for farmers and other country folk would contribute to their social and economic well-being. A tour of the Southern states in 1866 confirmed what Kelley had already grasped through his ownership of a farm in Minnesota: Rural life was hardly a paradise. The Jeffersonian vision of the small farm and contented citizen-farmers had crumbled along the more sparsely settled frontier and backwoods areas. Many rural men and women experienced intense isolation, and although they might travel long distances to overcome it, social life and community were difficult to sustain. As a member of the Benton County Agricultural Society, Kelley also had come to understand the harsh economic realities of agriculture and had begun plans to improve the farmers' lot. Whether Kelley expected it or not, the Grange would provide the basis for a widespread agrarian movement for political and economic reform that would rock the major political parties for decades.

In 1867, Kelley left Minnesota to accept a position as a clerk in the Post Office Department in Washington, D.C. There he and William M. Ireland, another clerk who, like Kelley, was a Freemason, began to plan the organization and ritual for a secret society of farmers that would both bind farmers together and advance agriculture. At the suggestion of his niece, Caroline A. Hall, and others, Kelley decided to admit both men and women into the organization. With several other interested government employees, Kelley quickly worked out a constitution. On December 4, 1867, five of the seven men later designated as founders constituted themselves as the National Grange of the Patrons of Husbandry and proceeded to elect officers. William Saunders, a horticulturist in the Agriculture Bureau, became the first Master, but Kelley continued to play the leading role in the organization.

In 1868, Kelley resigned his government position and began promoting the formation of local Granges. He and his team first organized a local chapter, the Potomac Grange, and used it to experiment with the rituals and other organizational aspects. Letters and circulars to farmers around the country, however, elicited only a meager response. Kelley then toured the Midwest, attempting to sell charters at fifteen dollars each for the establishment of local Granges. He met with almost complete failure and was able to continue only by borrowing money and drawing on his wife's small inheritance. Before 1870, only a handful of local Granges had sprung up, mostly in Minnesota and Iowa, and in the next year, only scattered chapters existed in nine states.

Kelley's persistence paid off starting in 1872. The growth rate of the Grange increased sharply. Although only 132 new Granges appeared in 1871, about 1,100, 8,400, and 13,000 formed in the next three years, respectively. Most of the Granges were located in the Midwest, but the network extended into almost every state. Deteriorating economic conditions undoubtedly drove many farmers to seek out organizational remedies. A few months before the Panic of 1873, a farm depression had foreshadowed the national business slowdown. Farmers who may have been looking at the Patrons of Husbandry as a social opportunity now spotted the potential for economic mobilization.

Although the early motivations for the Granges may have been social and educational, local chapters often became involved in business ventures and political affairs. The local and state Granges experienced some success in eliminating or reducing the fees of the middleman in purchasing farm equipment and supplies. In some cases, state organizations appointed agents to deal directly with manufacturers. Montgomery Ward and Company, a Chicago-based retailer, incorporated with the express purpose of trading with the Grangers. Spurred by their success in cooperative buying, many state and local Granges expanded into retailing, manufacturing, and insurance. When the National Grange had amassed a surplus from charter fees, it loaned fifty thousand dollars to state Granges to assist in their expansions. Most of these enterprises eventually failed, however, because farmers lacked experience in selling and manufacturing; some Granges suffered mismanagement, lost membership confidence, and went into bankruptcy. Moreover, manufacturers, wholesalers, and retailers resisted the Granger initiatives. On the whole, however, the movement was successful in forcing down prices, despite limited success in business ventures.

During the 1870's, several farm-state legislatures passed so-called Granger Laws, which placed maximum limits on railroad and warehouse rates. In *Munn v. Illinois* (1877) and similar cases, the U.S. Supreme Court ruled that state rate-fixing was constitutional. The Supreme Court later reversed itself in *Wabash, St. Louis and Pacific Railway Company v. Illinois* (1886), but the pressure from the Granges helped push Congress to create the Interstate Commerce Commission in 1887. Pressing state legislatures to enact maximum rate legislation enhanced the prestige of the Grange movement nationally. Although the constitution of the Grange forbade political activity, state and local granges often were active politically. Other farm-oriented organizations were operating at the same time, sometimes more effectively than the Grange in the political arena, but they lacked the national organization and ready identification of the Grangers. To the American public, the farmer-sponsored legislation concerning railroad rates were Granger Laws.

Despite these perceived political successes, membership in the Grange decreased between 1875 and 1880 almost as rapidly as it had grown from 1872 to 1875. By 1877, membership was down to 411,000 (half the 1875 total), and by 1880, rosters reflected only 124,000 dues-paying members. Ironically, many of the once-attractive features of the Grange became liabilities in the second half of the decade. Rural Americans had found the cooperative features attractive, but when these business endeavors failed, the overall organization lost credibility. Similarly, when political action associated with the Grange movement was successful, the membership grew, but when Granger legislation proved ineffective, many farmers withdrew their support.

After 1880, the Grange continued to function as a social and educational outlet for rural populations, a civic center in small towns, and a bastion of the rural lifestyle in the face of urbanization and modernization. Granger-associated insurance companies remained strong into the next century. Granges also worked closely with the expanded state and federal agricultural extension services. In politics, other farmers' organizations superseded the Granger movement. The Northern, Southern, and Colored Farmers' Alliances of the 1880's became powerful political forces, as did the Populist Party, which hit its peak in the early 1890's. In many ways, these later farmers' organizations were descendants of the National Grange of the Patrons of Husbandry, the first large-scale attempt at agricultural organization in the United States.　—*Mark A. Plummer, updated by Thomas L. Altherr*

ADDITIONAL READING:

Barns, William D. "Oliver Hudson Kelley and the Genesis of the Grange: A Reappraisal." *Agricultural History* 41 (July, 1967): 229-242. Overturns the interpretation that Kelley suddenly conceptualized the Grange in 1867 and established it for mainly social and educational ends.

Buck, Solon J. *The Granger Movement: A Study of Agricultural Organization and Its Political, Economic, and Social Manifestations, 1870-1880.* Lincoln: University of Nebraska Press, 1963. The first serious scholarly history of the Grangers.

Gilman, Rhoda R., and Patricia Smith. "Oliver Hudson Kelley: Minnesota Pioneer, 1849-1868." *Minnesota History* 40 (Fall, 1967): 330-338. Explores Kelley's agricultural experiences prior to leaving Minnesota to start the Grange.

Goodwyn, Lawrence. *Democratic Promise: The Populist Moment in America.* New York: Oxford University Press, 1976. Contrasts the perceived radical strategies of the Farmers' Alliances with the conservative strategies of the Grange.

Nordin, Dennis Sven. *Rich Harvest: A History of the Grange, 1867-1900.* Jackson: University Press of Mississippi, 1974. Argues that Kelley was a reluctant advocate of cooperatives and radical strategies.

Woods, Thomas A. *Knights of the Plow: Oliver H. Kelley and the Origins of the Grange in Republican Ideology.* Ames: Iowa State University Press, 1991. Maintains that Kelley, consistent with his Republican ideology, envisioned the Grange from the outset as a more political and radical organization.

SEE ALSO: 1862, Morrill Land Grant Act; 1867, Office of Education Is Created; 1871, Barnum's Circus Forms; 1887, Interstate Commerce Act; 1892, Birth of the People's Party.

1868 ■ IMPEACHMENT OF ANDREW JOHNSON: *a constitutional crisis pits the powerful legislative branch against an unpopular president*

DATE: February 24-May 26, 1868
LOCALE: Washington, D.C.
CATEGORY: Government and politics

KEY FIGURES:

Salmon Portland Chase (1808-1873), chief justice of the United States
Ulysses Simpson Grant (1822-1885), commanding general of the United States Army
Andrew Johnson (1808-1875), seventeenth president of the United States, 1865-1869
Edwin McMasters Stanton (1814-1869), secretary of war
Thaddeus Stevens (1792-1868), Republican congressman

SUMMARY OF EVENT. When the House of Representatives passed a resolution on February 24, 1868, declaring that President Andrew Johnson should be impeached, no one was surprised. Angry Republicans, especially the radical faction who saw Johnson as the great enemy of their program, had, in January, 1867, put through the House a resolution directing the Judiciary Committee to inquire into Johnson's conduct. The many charges made against the president included an accusation that he had been involved in the Lincoln assassination plot, and although the committee recommended impeachment, the House of Representatives voted it down.

The impeachment campaign arose over Johnson's alleged violation of the Tenure of Office Act passed by Congress on March 2, 1867, and subsequently passed again over the president's veto. This act made the removal of cabinet officers

Fired by his opposition to Reconstruction and his violation of the Tenure of Office Act, Radical Republicans instigated impeachment proceedings against President Andrew Johnson. (Library of Congress)

subject to approval by the Senate. Even supporters of the bill declared that its provisions referred only to cabinet members appointed by a president in office and not to those who had been appointed by his predecessor. Thus, the law should not have applied to cabinet appointees of Lincoln still serving under Johnson in 1867.

The conflict grew out of Johnson's determination to replace Edwin M. Stanton as secretary of war and to test the Constitutionality of the Tenure of Office Act in court. Stanton, a holdover from Lincoln's cabinet whom Johnson considered disloyal, supported the Reconstruction program of Congress, not that of the president. In the summer of 1867, Johnson asked Stanton to resign, but Stanton refused to do so. Johnson thereupon suspended Stanton from office pending concurrence by the Senate, the procedure required by the Tenure of Office Act, and appointed General Ulysses S. Grant as secretary of war *ad interim*. If the Senate did not concur in his action, Johnson planned to take the law to court in order to test its constitutionality. Grant accepted the cabinet post but soon became unhappy because he supported the congressional party and knew that he was its choice for the Republican presidential nomination in 1868. As his discomfort increased, his relations with the president worsened, and historians have debated Grant's integrity, or lack of it, in the episode. When the Senate, as expected, refused to concur in Stanton's ouster, Grant turned the office back to him. Johnson, however, was determined to rid himself of Stanton. General William T. Sherman was invited to take over from Stanton but he refused. At last, the adjutant general of the Army, garrulous old Lorenzo Thomas, agreed to take Stanton's place. On February 21, 1868, Johnson fired Stanton and appointed Thomas. Stanton refused to give up his office, and Thomas would not take it.

At this point, the Radical Republicans in the House saw their chance to strike at Johnson. The House passed by a large majority on February 24 the Covode Resolution, which declared that the president should be impeached. For many, it was a psychological catharsis to bring down the great opponent of Reconstruction and the great sustainer of rebellion. Some powerful legislators, such as Senator Charles Sumner of Massachusetts and Representative Thaddeus Stevens of Pennsylvania, considered Johnson, a Union Democrat originally from North Carolina, to be too allied with Southerners who had only recently laid down their arms. Another motive of the Republicans in Congress was to deal with the real problem of military Reconstruction; in his capacity as chief executive, Johnson had removed generals in the South who had been enthusiastic about military Reconstruction and replaced them with men of his own temper. Congressional Republicans wanted the secretary of war to be someone who supported their own program of Reconstruction; when Johnson moved against Stanton, they felt that they had to stop the president. Impeachment seemed, to many, to be the only way. The House finally passed a resolution consisting of eleven articles; the first nine dealt with the president's alleged violation of the Tenure of Office Act, and the last two charged Johnson with making speeches designed to denigrate Congress and failing to enforce the Reconstruction laws.

After the House had done its work, the Senate had to convict or acquit. The Constitution stipulated a two-thirds majority, which in 1868 meant that the votes of thirty-six senators were necessary for conviction. In early March, with Chief Justice Samuel P. Chase presiding, the senators took the oath to try the president. There was a long debate about whether the Senate sat as a court or as a political party; to Chase, the Constitution clearly indicated that the Senate sat as a court, and he so conducted the proceedings.

On March 30, the trial opened. The prosecution, composed of important Radical Republicans, claimed that Johnson had subverted the will of Congress, the will of the Republican Party, and the will of the people. As the defense duly noted, they made no effort to pin any specific crime on the president. Emphasizing that fact, Johnson's defense counsel argued that Johnson had done nothing to warrant impeachment under the Constitution. Voting took place on May 16; the result was one short of the number needed to convict. Two more votes were taken on May 26, with the same result. Each time the outcome was 35 to 19. Johnson was saved by seven Republicans who supported Reconstruction in Congress but who did not believe there were legal grounds for conviction in this case. Typical of the Republican senators who reluctantly opposed conviction was Kansas' Edmund G. Ross. While no supporter of Johnson, Ross opposed the president's removal from office because he believed the office of the presidency would be seriously damaged if Thaddeus Stevens and Sumner succeeded in their struggle with Johnson.

Thus, President Johnson was acquitted by the narrowest of margins. He served the remainder of his term with little further direct influence on Reconstruction policies. The office of the presidency survived this Constitutional crisis, but the direction of Reconstruction remained firmly in the hands of the leaders of Congress.

—*William J. Cooper, Jr., updated by Joseph Edward Lee*

ADDITIONAL READING:

Beale, Howard K. *The Critical Year: A Study of Andrew Johnson and Reconstruction.* New York: Frederick Ungar, 1958. Clearly explains the positions taken by the executive and legislative branches as the crisis erupted.

Brodie, Fawn M. *Thaddeus Stevens: Scourge of the South.* New York: W. W. Norton, 1959. A well-written biography of Johnson's chief nemesis.

Dewitt, David M. *The Impeachment and Trial of Andrew Johnson.* New York: Russell & Russell, 1903. An old but still useful account of the issues and personalities involved in the impeachment battle.

McKitrick, Eric L. *Andrew Johnson and Reconstruction.* Chicago: University of Chicago Press, 1960. Explores Johnson's view that he, not Congress, should coordinate Reconstruction.

McPherson, James M. *Ordeal By Fire: The Civil War and Reconstruction.* 2d ed. New York: McGraw-Hill, 1992. An analysis of the war and the political intrigue that flourished after Lincoln's assassination.

SEE ALSO: 1863, Reconstruction; 1869, Scandals of the Grant Administration.

1868 ■ BURLINGAME TREATY: *establishes reciprocal rights between China and the United States, including respect for territorial sovereignty and bilateral immigration*

DATE: July 28, 1868
LOCALE: Washington, D.C.
CATEGORIES: Asian American history; Diplomacy and international relations; Immigration; Treaties and agreements
KEY FIGURES:
Anson Burlingame (1820-1870), U.S. minister to China, 1861-1867, appointed in 1868 to head the Chinese delegation to the United States and Europe
I-Hsin, also known as *Prince Kung* (1833-1898), co-regent with the dowager empress of China
William Henry Seward (1801-1872), United States secretary of state
Tz'u-hsi (1835-1908), dowager empress of China
SUMMARY OF EVENT. Formal United States interest in China dates from the thirteen-thousand-mile voyage of the U.S. ship *Empress of China*, under the command of Captain John Green, which departed from New York City on February 22, 1784. The vessel returned from Canton in May, 1785, with tea, silks, and other trade goods of the Orient. Merchants in Philadelphia, Boston, Providence, and New York quickly sought profits in the China trade. By the late 1830's, "Yankee clippers" had shortened the transit time from America's Atlantic ports to Canton from a matter of many months to a mere ninety days.

Political problems, however, hindered commercial relations. The Manchu, or Ch'ing, Dynasty (1644-1912), fearful of Western intentions, restricted trade to one city, Canton, and sharply curtailed the rights of foreigners in China. Chafing at these limits, especially China's refusal to deal with Europeans on terms of equality, caused Great Britain to begin hostilities with the Manchu Dynasty, occasioned by the "unsavory issue" of England's trade in opium with China. The Opium War (1839-1842) resulted in the Treaty of Nanking (August 24, 1842), a triumph for the political and commercial interests of Great Britain in eastern Asia. England obtained the cession of the island of Hong Kong and the opening of four additional cities—Amoy, Ningpo, Foochow, and Shanghai—to British trade. The U.S. government desired similar rights and obtained them in the Treaty of Wanghia (named for a village near Macao) on July 3, 1844; Commissioner Caleb Cushing, although not formally received by China as a minister, was permitted to negotiate this landmark agreement. The United States secured access to the newly opened ports and was extended the right of extraterritoriality; that is, U.S. citizens were to be tried for offenses committed in China under U.S. law by the U.S. consul.

Within the next twenty years, trade with China grew. The United States acquired Washington, Oregon, and California, and, with Pacific ports, had greater access to Chinese markets. The California gold rush (1849) and the construction of the Central Pacific Railroad (completed in 1869), with its need for labor, encouraged Chinese emigration to the United States. Meanwhile, U.S. missionaries, merchants, travelers, and adventurers were arriving in China. Conditions in "the Middle Kingdom," however, were not good. The authority of the central government had been challenged by the anti-Western Taiping Rebellion (1850-1864) and was suppressed only with outside help. Further European incursions into China, epitomized by the Anglo-French War with the Manchus (1854-1858), threatened to curtail U.S. cultural and commercial opportunities in China. If the United States did not act, it would face the prospect of being excluded from China by European imperialism.

Secretary of State William Henry Seward believed that it was time for the United States to have formal representation at the Manchu court. His fortunate choice was Anson Burlingame. Born on November 14, 1820, in rural New York, the son of a "Methodist exhorter," Burlingame had grown up in the Midwest, graduating from the University of Michigan. After attending Harvard Law School, Burlingame went into practice in Boston. With a gift of oratory and exceptional personal charm, Burlingame served in the U.S. House of Representatives (1855-1861) and was a pioneer of the new Republican Party. As a reward for his labor and in recognition of his talents, Burlingame was offered the post of U.S. minister to Austria, but the Habsburgs refused him because of his known sympathies with Louis Kossuth, the Hungarian revolutionary. As a second choice and a compensatory honor, Burlingame was given the assignment to China.

Because the United States was distracted with the Civil War, Burlingame was left on his own and could count on little U.S. military might to support his actions. Acquiring a great admiration for and confidence in the Chinese, Burlingame won the trust and respect of I-Hsin, known as Prince Kung, the co-regent of China with the dowager empress Tz'u-hsi. When Burlingame resigned as the U.S. minister to China, in November, 1867, the Imperial Manchu court asked him to head China's first official delegation to the West. The Burlingame mission toured the United States, being warmly received, and arrived in the United Kingdom as William Gladstone was assuming the prime ministership of that nation. Burlingame's brilliant career was cut short during a subsequent visit to Russia, where he contracted pneumonia, dying in St. Petersburg on February 23, 1870. Few had served their own country so well, and it was said that none had given China a more sincere friendship.

The most outstanding accomplishment of the Burlingame mission was the Burlingame Treaty, signed on July 28, 1868, in Washington, D.C. This document dealt with a variety of issues between China and the United States. The United States pledged itself to respect Chinese sovereignty and territorial integrity, a position in sharp contrast to that of the European powers and one that anticipated the United States' subsequent "open door policy" (1899). The Burlingame Treaty accepted bilateral immigration between China and the United States, and by 1880 there were 105,000 Chinese living in the United States.

By the standards of the 1860's, the Burlingame Treaty was a landmark of fairness and justice. Unfortunately, the United States did not honor its spirit or letter. Anti-immigrant feeling focused on a fear of Chinese "coolie" labor. The infamous Sandlot Riots in San Francisco, in June, 1877, were symptomatic of both the mistreatment of Asian immigrants and the rising sentiment for Asian exclusion. On March 1, 1879, President Rutherford B. Hayes vetoed a congressional bill limiting the number of Chinese passengers on board ships bound for the United States as a violation of the Burlingame Treaty. Hayes did, however, send a mission to China to work for the revision of the Burlingame Treaty. In 1880, China recognized the United States' right to regulate, limit, and suspend, but not absolutely forbid, Chinese immigration.

Two years later, President Chester A. Arthur vetoed a twenty-year suspension of Chinese immigration as being a de facto prohibition, but on May 6, 1882, the Chinese Exclusion Act passed, suspending the importation of Chinese labor for a ten-year period. In 1894, another ten-year exclusion period was enacted; in 1904, exclusion was extended indefinitely. When, on December 17, 1943, Chinese immigration was permitted by an act of Congress, it was within the strict limits of the 1920's quota system, allowing the entrance of only 105 Chinese annually. Not until the mid-twentieth century did the United States depart from an immigration policy centered on ethnic origin, thus allowing the original intent of the Burlingame Treaty to be realized.   —C. George Fry

ADDITIONAL READING:

Dulles, Foster Rhea. *China and America: The Story of Their Relations Since 1784*. Princeton, N.J.: Princeton University Press, 1946. This brief, classic history places the Burlingame Treaty in the broad context of United States-Chinese trade and diplomacy over a period of one hundred fifty years.

Fairbank, John K. *China Perceived: Images and Policies in Chinese-American Relations*. New York: Alfred A. Knopf, 1974. A noted Harvard scholar compares the contrasting sensitivities, traditions, aims, and means of the United States and China as they have affected foreign policy.

Fairbank, John K., Edwin O. Reischauer, and Albert M. Craig. *East Asia: Tradition and Transformation*. Rev. ed. Boston: Houghton Mifflin, 1989. This profusely illustrated and thoroughly documented survey, a standard introduction to the history of Asia's Pacific Rim, illuminates the Chinese situation in 1868.

Miller, Stuart Creighton. *The Unwelcome Immigrant: The American Image of the Chinese, 1785-1882*. Berkeley: University of California Press, 1969. A succinct analysis that explains why the Chinese were the only immigrants other than Africans to be forbidden by law from entering the United States in the nineteenth century.

Mosher, Steven W. *China Misperceived: American Illusions and Chinese Reality*. New York: Basic Books, 1990. This combination of psychohistory and political analysis examines the varied U.S. perceptions of China, ranging from infatuation to hostility. Carefully annotated.

Tsai, Shih-shan Henry. *China and the Overseas Chinese in the United States, 1868-1911*. Fayetteville: University of Arkansas Press, 1983. Well-documented, concise, in-depth study of the key issue between the United States and China in the late nineteenth century: immigration.

SEE ALSO: 1848, California Gold Rush; 1849, Chinese Immigration; 1882, Chinese Exclusion Act; 1882, Rise of the Chinese Six Companies; 1895, Chinese American Citizens Alliance Is Founded; 1898, *United States v. Wong Kim Ark*; 1899, Hay's "Open Door Notes."

1868 ■ FOURTEENTH AMENDMENT: *a definition of citizenship designed for former slaves provides protection against state violations of civil rights*

DATE: July 28, 1868
LOCALE: Washington, D.C.
CATEGORIES: African American history; Civil rights; Laws and acts
KEY FIGURES:
John A. Bingham (1815-1900), Republican congressman and moderate leader
William Pitt Fessenden (1806-1869), Republican senator and prominent moderate
Andrew Johnson (1808-1875), seventeenth president of the United States, 1865-1869
Thaddeus Stevens (1792-1868), Republican congressman and radical leader
Charles Sumner (1811-1874), Republican senator and prominent radical

SUMMARY OF EVENT. The Fourteenth Amendment was part of the plan for Reconstruction formulated by the Republican majority in the Thirty-ninth Congress. Before Congress met in December, 1865, President Andrew Johnson had authorized the restoration of white self-government in the former Confederate states, and the congressmen and senators from those states waited in Washington to be seated in Congress. The state legislatures elected under Johnson's program had met to develop a series of laws called Black Codes, which restricted the rights of the former slaves. While the Republican majority in Congress had no intention of permitting the Johnson approach to Reconstruction to prevail or of seating the unrepentant white Southern representatives, they had no comprehensive

The Fifteenth Amendment, passed in 1870, granted the right to vote regardless of "race, color or previous condition of servitude"; women, however, remained disfranchised. (The Associated Publishers, Inc.)

counterproposal. To gain time and to work out a positive approach, Republicans in the House and the Senate created the Joint Committee of Fifteen on Reconstruction. This committee was composed of six senators and nine representatives.

The Republican majority rejected Johnson's plan because, as the Black Codes demonstrated, the old Confederates could not be trusted to respect the rights of the freedmen. Moreover, the Republicans had no intention of permitting white Southerners, whom they regarded as rebels and traitors, to increase the representation in the House of Representatives of the Southern Democrats. The abolition of slavery had destroyed the old compromise under which five slaves counted as three free persons in apportioning representation in the House and the electoral college, and the Republicans wanted to make sure that the South did not add to its numbers in the House and thus profit from rebellion.

Between December, 1865, and May, 1866, the Republicans attempted to hammer out a program that would accomplish their purposes in the South, unite members of their party in Congress, and appeal to Northern voters. Given the diversity of opinion within the party, this undertaking proved to be difficult. The radicals wanted African American suffrage, permanent political proscription, and confiscation of the property of ex-Confederates. Some maintained they were authorized in these actions by the Thirteenth Amendment, which, they believed, gave Congress the power to abolish the "vestiges of slavery." Moderate Republicans, on the other hand, feared political repercussions from African American suffrage, as such a requirement would result in beginning the Reconstruction process over again. Many moderates also believed that an additional amendment to the Constitution was needed to provide precise authority for Congress to enact civil rights legislation.

From deliberations of the joint committee and debate on the floor of the House came the Fourteenth Amendment. Many Republicans believed that the proposal was in the nature of a peace treaty, although this view was not explicitly stated. If the South accepted the amendment, the Southern states were to be readmitted and their senators and representatives seated in Congress; in other words, Reconstruction would end. Republicans presented a united front during the final vote as a matter of party policy. Because the amendment was an obvious compromise between radicals and moderates, it was too strong for some and too weak for others.

The Fourteenth Amendment became the most important addition to the constitution since the Bill of Rights had been adopted in 1791. It contains five sections:

Section 1, the first constitutional definition of citizenship, states that all persons born or naturalized in the United States are citizens of the United States and of the state in which they reside. It includes limits on the power of states, by providing that no state may abridge the privileges and immunities of citizens, deprive any person of life, liberty, or property without due process of law, or deny to any person within its jurisdiction the equal protection of law. This section was intended to guarantee African Americans the rights of citizenship, al-

though the amendment's framers did not define exactly which rights were included. Nor did they define "state action" to specify whether the term meant only official acts of state government or the actions of individuals functioning privately with state approval.

The courts later interpreted the due process clause to extend the rights of the accused listed in the Bill of Rights, which had applied only to the federal government, to the states. They expanded the notion of equal protection to include other categories, such as sex and disability, as well as race. They also interpreted the word "person" to include legal persons; under this interpretation, corporations found protection from much state regulation.

Section 2 gives a new formula of representation in place of the old three-fifths compromise of the Constitution, under which five slaves were counted as equal to three free persons in determining a state's representation in the House of Representatives and the electoral college. All persons in a state were to be counted for representation, but if a state should disfranchise any of its adult male citizens, except for participation in rebellion or any other crime, the basis of its representation would be reduced proportionally. While not guaranteeing suffrage to African Americans, this provision threatened the South with a loss of representation should black males be denied the vote.

Section 3 declares that no person who has ever taken an oath to support the Constitution (which included all who had been in the military service or held state or national office before 1860) and has then participated in the rebellion can be a senator or representative or hold any civil or military office, national or state. This disability could be removed only by a two-thirds vote of both houses of Congress. This section took away the pardoning power of the president, which congressional Republicans believed Andrew Johnson used too generously.

Section 4 validates the debt of the United States, voids all debts incurred to support rebellion, and invalidates all claims for compensation for emancipated slaves.

Section 5 gives Congress authority to pass legislation to enforce the provisions of the Fourteenth Amendment.

The correspondence and speeches of those who framed the Fourteenth Amendment do not support any theories of economic conspiracy or ulterior motives. The framers desired to protect the former slaves and boost Republicanism in the South by barring old Confederates from returning to Congress and the electoral college with increased voting strength. They hoped to do this without threatening the federal system or unduly upsetting the relationship between the central government and the states. At the same time, Republicans wanted to unify their party and project a popular issue for the approaching electoral contest against Andrew Johnson.

—*William J. Cooper, Jr., updated by Mary Welek Atwell*

ADDITIONAL READING:

Benedict, Michael Les. *A Compromise of Principle: Congressional Republicans and Reconstruction, 1863-1869.* New York: W. W. Norton, 1974. Emphasizes the Republicans' concern that the Fourteenth Amendment maintain the role of the states in the federal system.

Cox, LaWanda, and John H. Cox. *Politics, Principle, and Prejudice: Dilemma of Reconstruction America, 1865-1866.* New York: Free Press, 1963. Posits that civil rights, rather than merely partisan politics, was the central issue during Reconstruction.

Hyman, Harold M., and William Wiecek. *Equal Justice Under Law: Constitutional Development, 1835-1875.* New York: Harper & Row, 1982. Includes a thorough discussion of the Fourteenth Amendment as a logical and necessary extension of the Thirteenth Amendment.

Lively, Donald E. *The Constitution and Race.* New York: Praeger, 1992. Focuses on the association of attitudes toward race and constitutional interpretation. A positive interpretation of the motives of framers of the Fourteenth Amendment.

Nieman, Donald G. *Promises to Keep: African-Americans and the Constitutional Order, 1776 to the Present.* New York: Oxford University Press, 1991. A survey of issues of race and constitutional law that highlights the contributions of African Americans to its development.

Stampp, Kenneth M. *The Era of Reconstruction, 1865-1877.* New York: Alfred A. Knopf, 1965. A classic one-volume study of Reconstruction.

SEE ALSO: 1863, Emancipation Proclamation; 1863, Reconstruction; 1865, Freedmen's Bureau Is Established; 1865, Thirteenth Amendment; 1866, Civil Rights Act of 1866; 1866, Suffragists Protest the Fourteenth Amendment.

1868 ■ Washita River Massacre:
a decisive step in opening the Indian Territory to white settlement

DATE: November 27, 1868
LOCALE: Washita River, Indian Territory
CATEGORIES: Native American history; Wars, uprisings, and civil unrest
KEY FIGURES:
Black Kettle (1803?-1868), Cheyenne chieftain
George Armstrong Custer (1839-1876), commander of the Seventh Cavalry Regiment
Joel H. Elliott, second in command of the Seventh Cavalry Regiment
Philip H. Sheridan (1831-1888), commander of the Department of the Missouri
William Tecumseh Sherman (1820-1891), commander of the Division of the Missouri
Edward W. Wynkoop (born 1836), agent for the Cheyenne and Arapaho tribes

SUMMARY OF EVENT. At dawn on November 27, 1868, troops of the Seventh Regiment of the United States Cavalry, led by Lieutenant Colonel George Armstrong Custer, attacked and massacred a Cheyenne village on the banks of the Washita River in the Indian Territory. In this village of fifty-one lodges were some of the survivors of the 1864 Sand Creek Massacre, including the great Cheyenne chieftain Black Kettle. Custer, having set out on an Indian-hunting expedition and following what he thought was the trail of a large war party, had found the village, located on the south side of the river and surrounded by thick woods. Custer divided his force of seven hundred men into four groups; under cover of darkness, on the night of November 26, he positioned them to the north, south, east, and west of the village. All through the bitterly cold and snowy night, the soldiers waited in absolute silence, without fires, for Custer's signal to attack. Troops G, H, and M, under Major Joel Elliott, were deployed to the north, while troops B and F were south of the village. Troops E and I were down the Washita River, to the right of Elliott's command. Custer, with the regimental band, the color guard, a special sharpshooter company, all the scouts, and troops A, C, D, and K, waited in the center.

Just before dawn, the soldiers crept closer to the village and, at first light, swept down upon the sleeping Cheyennes to the accompaniment of the strains of "Garry Owen," the theme song of the Seventh Cavalry. Custer, on his black stallion, charged through the village and onto a knoll south, from where he watched the fighting. As the Cheyennes ran from their lodges, they were cut down by gunfire or saber, with no quarter given and no distinction made between men, women, or children. Chief Black Kettle and his wife were both shot as they attempted to escape on his pony. Caught entirely by surprise and with few weapons other than bows and arrows, the Cheyennes' only hope was flight—but most were killed by the sharpshooters positioned among the trees. Some did escape by plunging into the icy waters and making their way down the river channel to the Arapaho village of Chief Little Raven. Within a short time, the village fell to the soldiers, who set about killing or capturing those Cheyennes who had taken up defensive positions in the woods.

About 10:00 A.M., Custer noticed that warriors were beginning to gather atop the neighboring hills and, looking for an explanation, questioned one of the female captives. He learned that Black Kettle's village was not the only one on the banks of the Washita River, as he had thought, but was one of many Cheyenne, Arapaho, and Kiowa villages in the area. Shortly after, an officer who had been supervising the roundup of Cheyenne ponies reported that he had seen a very large Arapaho village downriver.

Even so, Custer directed his troops to gather up the spoils of war, which included saddles, buffalo robes, bows and arrows, hatchets, spears, a few revolvers and rifles, all the winter supply of food, most of the Cheyennes' clothing, and all of their lodges. After making an inventory and choosing some personal souvenirs, including one of the lodges, Custer had all the rest burned.

Almost nine hundred of the Cheyennes' horses and mules had now been rounded up. Custer gave the best horses to his officers and scouts, provided mounts for the female captives, then ordered four companies of his men to slaughter the rest of the animals. He had no intention of leaving the horses behind for the warriors and reasoned that taking them along when he left the area would surely provoke attempts by the Cheyennes to recapture them.

In the late afternoon, Custer was informed that Major Elliott, with seventeen men, had chased a small band of fleeing Cheyennes down the river and had not returned. Custer sent out a search party, but no trace of the missing men was found. Custer then called off the search—a decision that added to the growing resentment and anti-Custer sentiments among some of his officers.

As night approached, Custer realized his command was in a precarious position. Besides being burdened with prisoners and their own wounded, his troops were cold and hungry, their mounts were exhausted, and warriors from the other villages had gathered in the surrounding hills. Thus unprepared for further battle, Custer knew that he could not simply retreat toward his supply train, left behind at a safe distance from the fighting, without alerting the warriors to its location and risking that they would reach it first. The stratagem he devised was to convince them that he was advancing downriver to attack again; at the head of his regiment, with band playing, he

traveled east until darkness fell. Seeing this, the warriors hurried back to protect their villages, leaving only a few scouts behind. Custer then reversed back to the battlefield and up the Washita Valley, finally stopping at 2:00 A.M. to camp for the night. The next day, the troops rejoined the supply train and two days later reached Camp Supply, the fort from which Custer had started and at which General Sheridan waited for news of the expedition.

In his official report of the Washita action, Custer stated that 103 Cheyennes had been killed and 53 women and children, some of them wounded, had been taken prisoner. Among the dead were two Cheyenne chieftains, Black Kettle and Little Rock. During the fighting in the village, one officer and three enlisted men of the Seventh Cavalry had been killed. Custer also reported the deaths of Major Elliott and his seventeen men, although at the time he had no actual knowledge of their fate. Their bodies were discovered in the woods by a later expedition.

Opinions differ as to whether Custer's attack upon the Cheyenne was simply another unprovoked massacre such as that at Sand Creek four years earlier. Sherman, Sheridan, and Custer, among others, felt the Washita action was justified because of Cheyenne raids on white settlements along the

At dawn on November 27, 1868, U.S. troops led by George Armstrong Custer attacked and massacred a Cheyenne village on the banks of the Washita River in the Indian Territory. Some felt the Washita action was justified because of raids by Cheyenne warriors on white settlements; others insisted that an entire tribe should not be punished for the acts of a few and noted the United States' failure to meet its obligations under the 1867 Medicine Lodge Creek Treaty. In either case, the massacre marked an escalation in violence as a method of removing Indians to clear the way for white settlement of the Great Plains. (Library of Congress)

Saline and Solomon Rivers in Kansas in August, 1868. During a three-day rampage, two hundred Cheyenne warriors had committed murder and rape and abducted women and children. When Black Kettle and two chiefs of the Arapaho had arrived at Fort Cobb in mid-November, seeking sanctuary and subsistence for their people under the terms of the Medicine Lodge Creek Treaty, they had been refused because General Sheridan now considered both tribes to be hostile after the recent raids. They were told to leave the Indian Territory and warned that troops were in the field.

On the other hand, Indian agent Edward Wynkoop and others insisted that an entire tribe should not be punished for the acts of a few. They further argued that the promises made at Medicine Lodge had led the Cheyenne and Arapaho to expect fair treatment at Fort Cobb, which had not been forthcoming. Furthermore, it has since been established that the trail Custer followed, which he later claimed was that of a Cheyenne war party, actually had been made by Kiowas returning from a raid against the Utes in Colorado.

To place the Washita massacre in historical perspective, scholars point out that the United States Army had failed to subdue the plains tribes in battle on the prairie, and efforts to achieve peace through treaty had been largely unsuccessful. Thus, the invasion of the Indian Territory, of which the Washita massacre was a decisive first step, represented a change of tactics in the United States government's efforts to achieve its ultimate goal: the removal of the plains tribes as an obstacle to white settlement of the Great Plains. —LouAnn Faris Culley

ADDITIONAL READING:

Barnitz, Albert Trovillo Siders, and Jennie Barnitz. *Life in Custer's Cavalry, Diaries and Letters of Albert and Jennie Barnitz, 1867-1868.* Edited by Robert M. Utley. New Haven, Conn.: Yale University Press, 1977. An account of the massacre completed from the writings of one of Custer's troop commanders and his wife.

Brady, Cyrus. *Indian Fights and Fighters.* Lincoln: University of Nebraska Press, 1971. A narrative of the Plains wars, including the Washita massacre. Includes many eyewitness accounts not available elsewhere.

Brill, Charles. *Conquest of the Southern Plains.* Millwood, N.Y.: Kraus Reprint, 1975. A fully illustrated account of all events related to the massacre, with the texts of both Sheridan's and Custer's reports.

Custer, George Armstrong. *My Life on the Plains.* London: The Folio Society, 1963. Contains Custer's account of the events before, during, and after the Washita massacre.

Hoig, Stan. *The Battle of the Washita.* Garden City, N.Y.: Doubleday, 1976. A thoroughly documented account of the Sheridan-Custer campaign. Maps and photographs.

SEE ALSO: 1862, Great Sioux War; 1864, Sand Creek Massacre; 1866, Bozeman Trail War; 1867, Medicine Lodge Creek Treaty; 1871, Indian Appropriation Act; 1872, Great American Bison Slaughter; 1874, Red River War; 1876, Battle of the Little Bighorn; 1877, Nez Perce Exile; 1890, Closing of the Frontier; 1890, Battle of Wounded Knee.

1869 ■ RISE OF WOMAN SUFFRAGE ASSOCIATIONS: *the first organizations devoted to the cause of woman suffrage begin their half-century struggle*

DATE: Beginning May, 1869
LOCALE: New York and Cleveland
CATEGORIES: Civil rights; Organizations and institutions; Women's issues
KEY FIGURES:
Susan B. Anthony (1820-1906) and
Elizabeth Cady Stanton (1815-1902), founders of the National Woman Suffrage Association
Carrie Chapman Catt (1859-1947), twice president of the National American Woman Suffrage Association
Alice Paul (1885-1977), founder of the National Woman's Party
Anna Howard Shaw (1847-1919), suffragist, minister, and medical doctor
Lucy Stone (1818-1893), cofounder of the American Woman Suffrage Association

SUMMARY OF EVENT. The struggle for woman suffrage, marked from start to finish by internal controversy, was first publicly articulated in the United States as a resolution written by Elizabeth Cady Stanton, one of the organizers of the Woman's Rights Convention at Seneca Falls in 1848, and passed at the convention. The early struggle for women's rights paralleled the struggle for the rights of Negroes, as African Americans were then called, and the same people were initially involved in both, forming the Equal Rights Association. At the outbreak of the Civil War, some felt it was more important to work for abolition. Women were told, "This is the Negroes' hour." This split in emphasis resulted in the Thirteenth Amendment to the constitution, emancipating former slaves (1865); the Fourteenth Amendment, guaranteeing equal protection to all persons who were citizens (1868); and the Fifteenth Amendment, granting the franchise regardless of "race, color or previous condition of servitude" (1870) but which, in spite of women's efforts, did not also include "sex" in the wording. Efforts by Stanton and Susan B. Anthony to show that the Fourteenth Amendment included "women" in the word "persons" resulted in a Supreme Court decision in 1874 that it did not.

At the close of a meeting of the Equal Rights Association in New York City, May, 1869, women from nineteen states, led by Stanton and Anthony, formed the National Woman Suffrage Association (NWSA) to work for the emancipation of women through an amendment to the U.S. Constitution. Stanton was the group's president, and Anthony was on the executive committee. Because of a division of opinion on tactics, Lucy Stone, another of the original Seneca Falls organizers, Julia Ward Howe, and others called for another convention in Cleveland, Ohio, November, 1869. They formed the American Woman

Suffrage Association (AWSA), with Henry Ward Beecher as president and Stone as chairman of the executive committee.

The NWSA argued that the federal government was responsible for protecting women from states that denied them suffrage, as the government had protected the rights of black men with the Fourteenth Amendment. Thus, a federal amendment was needed. In addition, the NWSA continued to raise concerns that the movement had begun discussing before the Civil War: equal pay, prostitution, sexual and physical victimization of women and children, and the role of the church in maintaining the oppression of women. Cut off from most former abolitionists, the NWSA consciously reached out to new groups of women. Although attempts to build alliances with working-class women foundered on the deep differences of class, a great deal of interest developed among middle-class professionals. The vote was seen as a tool women could use to gain other rights. The strategies were confrontation and civil disobedience.

The conservative reformers in the AWSA, who later included the Women's Christian Temperance Union, centered their work on obtaining suffrage for women through amendments to individual state constitutions and limited themselves to the one issue of suffrage. The vote was an end in itself. The AWSA appealed mostly to wealthy, educated whites. It believed the vote could be won only by avoiding issues that were irrelevant and calculated to alienate the support of influential sections of the community. It did not organize working women, criticize the churches, or concern itself with the question of divorce.

In 1890, the two organizations united, forming the National American Woman Suffrage Association. Stanton was its president, Anthony the vice president, and Stone the executive committee chair. When Stanton resigned due to advancing age, Anthony was elected her successor, and when she resigned at eighty years of age in 1900, Carrie Chapman Catt became president. Catt was succeeded after four years by the Reverend Dr. Anna Howard Shaw and went on to head the International Woman Suffrage Alliance, but later returned to the helm of NAWSA. The merger put an end to the confrontational tactics of the NWSA. State emphasis won out. The movement's arguments broadened: No longer was suffrage promoted as an equal right, but as a means to clean up corruption and give women the vote to protect their own special interests as mothers concerned for the education of their children, as working women subjected to exploitation without protection, or as the abused wives of drunkards.

Gradually, progress and enthusiasm waned. Between 1870 and 1910, 480 state campaigns resulted in only seventeen referenda in eleven states, only two of which succeeded. In 1913, Alice Paul formed a Congressional Committee within the organization. However, a new schism formed when NAWSA offered Congress a compromise amendment. In 1914, Paul formed the independent Congressional Union for Woman Suffrage, which launched the radical National Woman's Party (NWP) in 1916. The NWP mobilized women through the state organizations to come to Washington for suffrage marches, to picket the White House, and to organize against the Democratic Party and its sitting president, Woodrow Wilson, simply because they were the party in power and had not passed the amendment. In 1918, a Congress with a Republican majority was elected, and President Wilson gave his first address supporting woman suffrage. The NWP kept the pressure on him until he translated his words into action. The Nineteenth Amendment, giving women the vote, as written and submitted by Anthony in 1875, was approved by Congress in 1919 and was ratified in 1920.

Even during the period when suffrage activity was centered in the NAWSA, women in the movement were divided as to methods and philosophy. There was disagreement as to whether emphasis on national or state ratification was best; whether traditional or confrontational methods should be employed; and whether woman suffrage should be the sole issue for which women worked, or if the movement should be put aside for issues such as emancipation and the World War I effort, or combined with all of women's needs. Some historians believe that the presence of dual organizations working for woman suffrage split and weakened the movement; others argue that the duality was positive because it provided a broader base and offered women a choice of conservative or radical feminism.

Since it took supporters fifty years to achieve the goal of a federal amendment, either interpretation may be correct. However, the state-by-state campaign emphasized by the more conservative leaders resulted in political power available to and used by the radical National Woman's Party in the final successful push for ratification. After the Nineteenth Amendment was ratified, the NWP was reorganized to work for equal rights; Alice Paul had the first Equal Rights Amendment introduced into Congress in 1923. The League of Women Voters was organized at the jubilee convention of the NAWSA in 1919. Catt joined this organization, and the schism continued: She thought there was no more need for an organization specifically concerned with women's rights. Both organizations continued to exist in the 1990's, but the League of Women Voters is much better known.

—*Erika E. Pilver*

ADDITIONAL READING:

Berry, Mary Frances. *Why ERA Failed: Politics, Women's Rights, and the Amending Process of the Constitution.* Bloomington: Indiana University Press, 1986. Draws parallels between the earlier fight to win woman suffrage and the struggle to pass the Equal Rights Amendment.

Clinton, Catherine. *The Other Civil War: American Women in the Nineteenth Century.* New York: Hill & Wang, 1984. Provides a comparatively brief, but comprehensive and excellent, treatment.

DuBois, Ellen Carol. *Feminism and Suffrage: The Emergence of an Independent Women's Movement in America, 1848-1869.* Ithaca, N.Y.: Cornell University Press, 1978. Discusses the early years, showing the events that led to the formation of the movement.

Evans, Sara M. *Born for Liberty: A History of Women in America*. New York: Free Press, 1989. A relatively brief treatment, placed in a general context.

Flexner, Eleanor. *Century of Struggle: The Woman's Rights Movement in the United States*. New York: Atheneum, 1970. A detailed history of the struggle, with some attention to the organizations.

Gurko, Miriam. *The Ladies of Seneca Falls: The Birth of the Woman's Rights Movement*. New York: Schocken Books, 1974. Emphasizes the early years and the personalities of the individual leading women.

Katzenstein, Caroline. *Lifting the Curtain: The State and National Woman Suffrage Campaigns in Pennsylvania as I Saw Them*. Philadelphia: Dorrance, 1955. A personal account that includes much national action, as Pennsylvania was one of the active states. Includes letters and other primary source materials not found in other books.

National American Woman Suffrage Association. *Victory: How Women Won It*. New York: H. W. Wilson, 1940. A relatively short account, with useful appendices.

Sinclair, Barbara. *The Women's Movement: Political, Socioeconomic, and Psychological Issues*. 3d ed. New York: Harper & Row, 1983. Succinct treatment of events and issues.

Wagner, Sally. *A Time of Protest: Suffragists Challenge the Republic: 1870-1887*. 2d ed. Carmichael, Calif.: Sky Carrier Press, 1988. Includes direct quotations from resolutions, facsimiles of broadsides, proclamations, and other interesting material.

SEE ALSO: 1848, Seneca Falls Convention; 1851, Akron Woman's Rights Convention; 1866, Suffragists Protest the Fourteenth Amendment; 1869, Western States Grant Woman Suffrage; 1872, Susan B. Anthony Is Arrested; 1874, *Minor v. Happersett*; 1876, Declaration of the Rights of Women; 1890, Women's Rights Associations Unite; 1916, National Woman's Party Is Founded; 1920, League of Women Voters Is Founded; 1920, U.S. Women Gain the Vote.

1869 ■ TRANSCONTINENTAL RAILROAD IS COMPLETED: *the construction of a great iron highway between East and West initiates the decline of the frontier*

DATE: May 10, 1869
LOCALE: Trans-Mississippi West
CATEGORIES: Economics; Science and technology; Transportation
KEY FIGURES:
Oliver Ames (1807-1877) and
Oakes Ames (1804-1873), Boston financiers who controlled the Union Pacific Railroad during the most active period of construction
Charles Crocker (1822-1888), general superintendent of construction of the Central Pacific Railroad

Grenville M. Dodge (1831-1916), army officer responsible for construction of the Union Pacific Railroad when the Civil War ended
Thomas C. Durant (1820-1885), organizer of the Crédit Mobilier for the Union Pacific Railroad
Theodore D. Judah (1826-1863), civil engineer who surveyed possible railroad routes across the Sierra Nevada Mountains
Leland Stanford (1824-1893), governor of California and president of the Central Pacific Railroad

SUMMARY OF EVENT. The desirability of constructing a transcontinental railroad was generally recognized throughout the United States in the 1850's. Many thought the scheme was visionary because of the great distance to be covered, the engineering obstacles to be overcome, and the tremendous outlay of money required for the project. Realistic businessmen knew that government aid would be necessary to complete such a railroad. Politicians, among others, concluded that the nation would be fortunate if financial support could be obtained to build even a single line, and therefore the geographic location of the route became a major sectional consideration. It was believed that this problem could be resolved by the natural topography, and that one route would be found superior to others on the basis of terrain and climate. To find such a route, Congress in 1853 authorized a survey by the U.S. Army Topographical Corps of all the feasible routes to the Pacific Ocean.

The multivolume report of these expeditions revealed that at least four routes seemed practicable for a transcontinental railroad, and two were particularly noteworthy. One of these would connect either St. Louis or Chicago with San Francisco; the other would link New Orleans with Los Angeles. Southerners insisted on the desirability of the latter idea and pointed out that, unlike the northern route, their route did not traverse unorganized territory. The Kansas-Nebraska Act of 1854, which organized these territories, was meant to answer the Southern challenge. However, the question of slavery in the territories, which the Kansas-Nebraska Act aggravated, delayed any decision on a transcontinental railroad route. California residents, however, were impatient with the delay; as a means of placating the agitation there, Congress approved the creation of the Pacific Wagon Road Office to improve the transcontinental wagon roads under the Department of the Interior. With the outbreak of the Civil War, railroad connections with California became a necessity, and, with Southern interests out of the picture, the location of the line was quickly decided upon.

On July 1, 1862, Congress stipulated that two companies should build the first transcontinental railroad. One was the Central Pacific Company, organized a year earlier in California to carry out the construction plans of Theodore D. Judah to cross the Sierra Nevada eastward to tap the rich trade of the Comstock mines of Nevada. The other was the Union Pacific Railroad, which was to build westward from the hundredth meridian to meet the Central Pacific at the California-Nevada

Completion of the transcontinental railroad in 1869 marked a new era of industrialization, trade, and rapid western settlement of the United States. Railroads proliferated during the next half century, as seen in this 1895 photograph of rail construction in the Southwest. (Photo by Mrs. Ella Wormser. Courtesy Museum of New Mexico)

line. Each company was granted a one-hundred-foot right-of-way and five alternate sections of land on each side within ten miles of the railroad. All necessary building supplies could be taken from the public domain. The government agreed to loan the railroad companies, on a first-mortgage basis, sixteen thousand dollars per mile for construction in level country, thirty-two thousand dollars per mile in the foothills, and forty-eight thousand dollars per mile in the mountains. The completion date was set as 1876.

Construction of the Union Pacific began in Omaha in December, 1863, but only forty miles of line were built in 1864 and 1865. The chief problem was one of finance, because private capitalists thought the project too risky an investment, despite generous government loans and land grants. In 1864, Congress came to the aid of the railroad by doubling the size of the land grants and by agreeing to a second mortgage to secure its loans, thus permitting borrowing elsewhere on a first-mortgage basis. The law required that the Union Pacific sell its bonds at par. To resolve this difficulty, Crédit Mobilier of America was organized to handle construction contracts, accepting payment in Union Pacific bonds which it, in turn, placed on the market for whatever they would bring.

Almost all the labor in building the Union Pacific and the Central Pacific was provided by human toilers and draft animals; steam shovels were introduced only at the end of construction. Hence, the railroad was built by armies of men creating whole communities as they moved. Added to this was conflict resulting from the presence on the plains of the Sioux, who had no intention of giving up their lands to the settlers and their iron horse.

The Central Pacific also began construction in 1863, with the aid of the Pacific Railroad Fund raised by a special property tax in California. The state agreed to pay the interest for the following twenty years on the first $1.5 million worth of bonds issued by the company, a total of $2.1 million. Subsidies also were forthcoming from the counties through which the line ran. President Abraham Lincoln decreed that because the Sierra Nevada extended westward into the Sacramento Valley, the railroad promoters could borrow the maximum of forty-eight thousand dollars per mile from the federal government. Construction moved slowly between 1863 and 1867, and the difficult terrain was overcome only by employing seven thousand Chinese, who labored patiently at a rate of thirty to thirty-five dollars per month, with a minimum of equipment.

About nine-tenths of the workforce was Chinese. Many of these laborers had come to California in the wake of the gold rush of 1849, but after they proved to be "wonder workers," the railroad sent agents to China to recruit more.

By the summer of 1867, the crest of the Sierra Nevada was reached and easier downgrades lay ahead. Anticipating this situation, the Central Pacific had obtained from Congress the right to build on across Nevada to meet and connect with the Union Pacific. A race ensued between the two companies, each trying to obtain as much land and government loans as it could.

By 1866, the Union Pacific had reached Fort Kearney, Nebraska. The pace of construction increased the following summer, after a struggle for control of the railroad was resolved between Thomas C. Durant, organizer of the Crédit Mobilier of America, and Oliver and Oakes Ames, Boston financiers. The Chicago and Northwestern Railroad by then had reached Council Bluffs, ending the expensive transportation of rails and supplies up the Missouri River by steamboat.

Army veterans and Irish laborers moved west when the Civil War ended and sought work as construction crews. They were described as first-rate but were a constant source of trouble in their free time. There was a great contrast between these uproarious army veterans and the sober Chinese workers on the Central Pacific. Grenville M. Dodge, an army officer with an aptitude for handling men, assumed responsibility for construction and, when necessary, armed his war veterans to fight off those interfering with construction.

In the spring of 1869, Union Pacific and Central Pacific construction crews came in sight of each other. When the two roads' surveys began to parallel each other, they started building two roadbeds side by side in the hope of obtaining more government aid. Congress intervened and selected Promontory Point in Utah, northwest of Ogden, as the junction of the two lines. The ceremony celebrating the connection of the rails took place there on May 10, 1869, in the presence of railroad officials and distinguished guests. At least a dozen spikes of gold and silver were driven into a polished laurel tie by various speakers, and then the engines came together nose to nose as their whistles blew, bells rang, and the crowd cheered. A war-weary nation had cause to celebrate. Split by secession less than a decade before, the nation now celebrated a new joining.

—*W. Turrentine Jackson, updated by Stephen B. Dobrow*

ADDITIONAL READING:

Douglas, George H. *All Aboard! The Railroad in American Life*. New York: Paragon House, 1992. A social history of railroads in the United States.

Fogel, Robert William. *The Union Pacific Railroad: A Case in Premature Enterprise*. Baltimore: The Johns Hopkins University Press, 1960. Primarily an economic study.

Griswold, Wesley S. *A Work of Giants: Building the First Transcontinental Railroad*. New York: McGraw-Hill, 1962. Concentrates on the actual building of the railroad. Rich in colorful detail and anecdote.

Lewis, Oscar. *The Big Four: The Story of Huntington, Stanford, Hopkins, and Crocker, and of the Building of the Central Pacific*. New York: Alfred A. Knopf, 1938. Contains informal, objective biographies of the builders of the Central Pacific Railroad. Describes early travel and the effects of the railroad monopoly.

McCague, James. *Moguls and Iron Men: The Story of the First Transcontinental Railroad*. New York: Harper & Row, 1964. Discusses the plans and work that were involved in building the first transcontinental railroad.

Mayer, Lynn Rhodes, and Ken Vose. *Makin' Tracks: The Saga of the Transcontinental Railroad*. New York: Barnes & Noble Books, 1995. Tells the story of the transcontinental railroad through illustrations and words of contemporaneous diaries, newspaper accounts, speeches, handbills, reports, and gossip.

Trottman, Nelson S. *History of the Union Pacific: A Financial and Economic Survey*. New York: Ronald Press, 1923. Describes the construction of the Union Pacific Railroad, its financing, its early operation, its failure in 1893 and subsequent reorganization, and its relations with other railroads.

SEE ALSO: 1830, Baltimore and Ohio Railroad Begins Operation; 1853, Pacific Railroad Surveys; 1854, Kansas-Nebraska Act; 1860, Pony Express; 1861, Transcontinental Telegraph Is Completed; 1869, Scandals of the Grant Administration.

1869 ■ SCANDALS OF THE GRANT ADMINISTRATION: *undermining the credibility of the Republican Party and facilitating a Democratic revival, the scandals prompt a movement to reduce political corruption*

DATE: September 24, 1869-1877
LOCALE: United States
CATEGORY: Government and politics
KEY FIGURES:

Oakes Ames (1804-1873), congressman censured for his role in the Crédit Mobilier scandal

Orville E. Babcock (1835-1884), supervisor in the Internal Revenue Service who was implicated in several corrupt schemes

William Worth Belknap (1829-1890), secretary of war in the Grant Administration

George S. Boutwell (1818-1905), secretary of the Treasury

Benjamin Franklin Butler (1818-1893), congressman from Massachusetts and opponent of civil service reform

Abel Rathbone Corbin, Grant's brother-in-law, who was involved in the "Black Friday" gold speculation

Jay Gould (1836-1892) and

James "Jubilee Jim" Fisk (1834-1872), stock speculators

Ulysses Simpson Grant (1822-1885), eighteenth president of the United States, 1869-1877

William Marcy Tweed (1823-1878), political boss of New York City

SUMMARY OF EVENT. During the administration of Ulysses S. Grant, much corruption was exposed at all levels of government—national, state, and local. Even allowing for exaggeration or misrepresentation by the various political opponents, such as Southern conservatives and liberal reformers, or by sensation-mongering journalists and the like, the record of Grant's administration is arguably the worst in U.S. history.

Grant was personally above reproach, but he lacked essential qualities of political leadership. He was a poor judge of character, gathering around him clever politicians with little regard for their moral reputation. His sense of loyalty to his subordinates limited his effectiveness in dealing with their corruption. The way in which he understood the Constitution depreciated the power of the presidency, and in his exercise of the office, he diminished its respect.

Grant's close associates often were involved in acts of doubtful legality. His brother-in-law, Abel Rathbone Corbin, for example, was involved in a scheme with speculators Jay Gould and Jim Fisk to corner the gold market in 1869. To be successful, the manipulators needed assurance that the government would not interfere by selling gold from the Treasury.

Ulysses S. Grant, eighteenth president of the United States. Although personally above reproach, his administration marked a period of growing corruption at all government levels, coinciding with the nation's industrialization, western settlement, and rising technology. (Library of Congress)

When Corbin implied that he had the necessary promise from the president, Gould and Fisk began buying gold with the intention of forcing the price upward and selling at high profits to those who had made commitments payable only in gold. This manipulation led to a stock exchange panic on Black Friday, September 24, 1869. Grant authorized George S. Boutwell, then secretary of the Treasury, to sell government gold to protect business, and the "corner" on the gold was broken. Even so, many brokers went bankrupt because of the actions of Gould and Fisk.

Although the most serious scandals of the Grant Administration were not exposed until after the election of 1872, there was significant opposition within the Republican Party to Grant's renomination. Civil service reformers, opponents of Radical Reconstruction, and party leaders disappointed with their share of federal patronage joined forces in an attempt to deny Grant a second term. When they failed to prevent his renomination by the Republican Party, they formed the Liberal Republican Party and nominated Horace Greeley for president. The Democratic Party also nominated him. Greeley's eccentric behavior and Grant's image as a Civil War hero combined to secure Grant's reelection with an impressive 286 electoral votes out of a possible 352.

Although neither Grant nor his close associates were involved directly, the Republican Party was discredited by the investigation in 1872-1873 of the Crédit Mobilier affair, a scandal that seemed to epitomize the Grant era. Crédit Mobilier was a construction company designated to build the transcontinental railroad for the Union Pacific Company. To ensure the continuation of generous government grants, stock in the Crédit Mobilier was given, or sold at a favorable price, to important politicians, including Grant's two vice presidents, Schuyler Colfax and Henry Wilson, and to many senators and congressmen. The stock paid an annual dividend several times greater than its original cost, as the Crédit Mobilier bilked the Union Pacific and the government of millions of dollars. Congressman Oakes Ames of Massachusetts was censured after a congressional investigation for having been a leader in the scheme, and the episode undermined the reputations of both Congress and the administration.

Suspicions about congressmen's greed were not allayed by the "Salary Grab" Act of March 3, 1873, by which Congress voted itself not only a needed raise but also, through a retroactive clause, a large cash bonus. This act seemed even more inappropriate after the Panic of September 18, 1873. The financial crisis brought on a depression and the repeal of the Salary Grab Act. The Panic of 1873, which was largely precipitated by international financial conditions beyond the control of the Grant Administration, was linked with the corruption of the time in the mind of the public.

Grant's Treasury Department, under William Richardson, carried common corruption to remarkable levels of audacity. John D. Sanborn, a protégé of Benjamin F. Butler, congressman from Massachusetts, was rewarded for campaign contributions with contracts for the collection of delinquent taxes.

His commission was an exorbitant 50 percent. Sanborn even "earned" $213,500 for collecting taxes that would have been paid if he had done nothing.

Among the many scandals of the Grant Administration, none came closer to implicating the president himself than the exposure of the activities of the Whiskey Ring. General John McDonald, an old friend whom Grant had appointed supervisor in the Internal Revenue Service at St. Louis and from whom Grant received political contributions, was indicted in 1875 for having defrauded the government of millions of dollars by conspiring with the distillers to avoid federal taxes. Colonel Orville E. Babcock, Grant's trusted private secretary, was also involved. Grant defended Babcock and allowed him to continue in an official position, although he no longer served as the president's secretary.

Another serious scandal of the Grant Administration implicated Secretary of War William Belknap, who had accepted bribes to keep an Indian post trader in office. Belknap resigned and the House of Representatives impeached him, but the Senate failed to find him guilty because a number of senators believed that they lacked jurisdiction over an officeholder who had resigned.

Much of the corruption of the Grant era was beyond the control of the president. He depended for political support upon the Stalwarts within the Republican Party, a group that included party bosses such as Roscoe Conkling of New York and Oliver Morton of Indiana, whose state organizations dispensed vital federal patronage. State governments, both North and South, were characterized by astounding corruption: Senate seats were sometimes purchased from the members of state legislatures who elected the U.S. senators. Local government was no better. The Tweed Ring of New York City plundered the city of millions of dollars.

An industrial and urban United States was emerging. The transitional character of the era, with its uncertain rules of conduct, encouraged corruption. Hampered by a misguided sense of loyalty, obstinacy, and lack of competence, Grant was unable to cope with the tendencies of his time.

—*Mark A. Plummer, updated by Charles H. O'Brien*

ADDITIONAL READING:

Cashman, Sean Dennis. *America in the Gilded Age: From the Death of Lincoln to the Rise of Theodore Roosevelt.* 3d ed. New York: New York University Press, 1993. A well-rounded, lively account of the economic, social, and political history of the period.

Hesseltine, William B. *Ulysses S. Grant, Politician.* New York: Dodd, Mead, 1935. The standard work on the Grant Administration. It calls him an unfit president but clears him of direct involvement in corruption.

McFeely, William S. *Grant: A Biography.* New York: W. W. Norton, 1981. An authoritative study of Grant as a common man with uncommon ambition. Places the man in his times and deals in detail with the scandals of his administration.

Mandelbaum, Seymour J. *Boss Tweed's New York.* New York: John Wiley & Sons, 1965. Argues that Tweed's purchase of political support and his thievery were expressions of the values and practices of the marketplace, commonly accepted in an era of rapid, unrestrained economic development.

Nevins, Allan. *Hamilton Fish: The Inner History of the Grant Administration.* New York: Dodd, Mead, 1936. Using the voluminous papers of Grant's secretary of state, Nevins has written an illuminating history of the Grant Administration.

Summers, Mark Wahlgren. *The Era of Good Stealings.* New York: Oxford University Press, 1993. A well-documented study of the Grant era that challenges its reputation for common or systemic corruption.

Trefousse, Hans L. *Carl Schurz: A Biography.* Knoxville: University of Tennessee Press, 1982. As senator from Missouri and advocate of civil service reform, Schurz spoke out against the corruption of the Grant Administration. He also was active in the Liberal Republican Party of 1872.

Van Deusen, Glyndon G. *Horace Greeley: Nineteenth Century Crusader.* New York: Hill & Wang, 1964. The last part of this biography deals with the period after the Civil War and the 1872 presidential campaign, in which corruption in the Grant Administration was a major issue.

SEE ALSO: 1868, Impeachment of Andrew Johnson; 1869, Transcontinental Railroad Is Completed; 1873, "Crime of 1873"; 1877, Hayes Is Elected President.

1869 ■ First Riel Rebellion: *westward expansion of Euro-Canadians begins a process of marginalization of the Metis peoples*

DATE: October 11, 1869-July 15, 1870
LOCALE: Red River, Manitoba
CATEGORIES: Native American history; Wars, uprisings, and civil unrest
KEY FIGURES:

John Alexander Macdonald (1815-1891), first prime minister of Canada
William McDougall (1822-1905), Canada's public works minister and first lieutenant governor designee of the Northwest Territories
Andre Nault (1829-1924), member of the provisional government of Assiniboia
Louis-David Riel (1844-1885), leader of the Metis and second president of the government of Assiniboia
Thomas Scott (1846-1870), militant Orangeman hanged for treason by the Metis provisional government

SUMMARY OF EVENT. In the fall of 1869, the Metis living in and around the Red River Valley in present-day Manitoba prevented a party of land surveyors from continuing their work, declared a provisional government, and barred the Canadian prime minister's appointee from taking up his post as territorial governor. This act marked the start of the uprising known as the First Riel, or Red River, Rebellion. The background to the rebellion and Canada's response are complex, and its outcome had important implications for both the Metis and the Dominion of Canada.

The Metis were descendants of French fur traders and American Indian women. Blending elements of both cultures, Metis society flourished on the northern prairies in the late eighteenth and early nineteenth centuries. They were particularly noted for the highly militaristic organization of their twice-annual buffalo hunts.

The latter half of the 1860's was a period of great transition for people living in the British Territories in North America. The Dominion of Canada was created by the British North America Act on July 1, 1867. British Columbia prepared to join the Canadian Confederation, conditioned upon construction of a transcontinental railroad. With the fur trade era at an end, the Hudson's Bay Company prepared to give up its claim to Rupert's Land (that portion of northern Canada whose rivers drain into Hudson Bay) and the Northwest. In order to build the railroad, but also to prevent those lands from becoming part of the United States, Ottawa, under its first prime minister, John A. Macdonald, entered into negotiations to acquire the territories. Canada agreed to pay the Hudson's Bay Company three hundred thousand pounds, and the land transfer was set to occur on December 1, 1869. This was done without consulting the ten thousand Metis and English "halfbreeds" of Red River.

The tensions between French Catholics from Quebec and English Protestants in Ontario—which have continued to this day—affected relations within Red River. Ontario had many new Protestant immigrants in need of land, and Red River, just west of Ontario, seemed the ideal place for them. Although residents of mixed Indian-white ancestry formed more than 80 percent of the population of Red River, there was a great deal of racism directed against them. The French-speaking, Catholic Metis were held in particular disdain by the immigrants from Ontario. The rate at which these new immigrants were arriving suggested to the Metis that they would soon be a minority in the region they had occupied for generations. Finally, several crop failures and the destruction of the buffalo herds had created economic stress among the Metis.

Although the official date of land transfer was several months away, Ottawa sent land surveyors to the Red River in the summer of 1869. Despite Ottawa's promises to respect Metis land tenure, the activities of the surveyors indicated that this would not be the case. The Metis had for many years occupied long, narrow farmsteads extending back from the river. Contrary to this practice, the surveyors delineated square township lots. On October 11, 1869, the surveyors reached the farmstead of Andre Nault. After securing the assistance of eighteen other Metis, Nault forced the surveyors off his land— the first action in the brief Red River Rebellion.

The Metis, under the leadership of Montreal-educated Louis-David Riel, formed the Council of Assiniboia, which one month later declared itself the government of the region. On November 2, the Metis stopped William McDougall, who

had been appointed lieutenant governor of the territory by Prime Minister Macdonald, at the United States border with Assiniboia (the only road into the territory from Ontario) and seized Upper Fort Garry (near present-day Winnipeg). No shots were fired, and the fort's occupants retreated to Lower Fort Garry.

The next move occurred on December 7, 1869, when the Metis seized Lower Fort Garry and arrested approximately fifty white Protestant settlers. Three militant Orangemen among the arrested—John Schultz, Charles Boulton, and Thomas Scott—were tried, convicted of treason, and sentenced to death. Boulton's sentence was commuted, and Schultz escaped to Ontario. Only Scott was hanged, on March 4, 1870. Scott's death made him a martyr and reinforced white Protestant opposition to the French Catholic Metis.

The government of Assiniboia apparently did not plan to remain independent of Canada, but merely wished to guarantee that the rights of the Metis would be respected in an orderly transition of power. Militant Protestants within Ontario urged Ottawa to crush what they viewed as a French Catholic uprising, but Macdonald had no desire to destabilize the delicate balance of power that existed between Protestant Ontario and Catholic Quebec. In January of 1870, Macdonald's government entered into negotiations with Riel's provisional government. Included in the Metis demands were that Assiniboia enter confederation as a province rather than a territory, both French and English were to be the official languages, and high officials were to be bilingual. They also demanded a recognition of the Metis' property rights. In addition, they wanted amnesty for the members of the Metis government.

In May of 1870, the Canadian Parliament passed the Manitoba Act, and the transfer of Rupert's Land from the Hudson's Bay Company to the Dominion of Canada, originally set for the previous December, occurred on July 15, 1870. On the same day, Manitoba became Canada's newest province. While the establishment of the province should have met many of the Metis' demands, in practice it did not. The province was limited to one hundred thousand square miles, Parliament, rather than the Manitoba legislature, retained control of the public lands, and the conveyance of the Metis' land titles was delayed so long that many Metis sold their rights to land speculators and moved farther west. Racism was rampant, and many of the leaders of the Metis government were attacked and murdered. Riel fled to Montana and became a U.S. citizen. Andre Nault was assaulted and left for dead. He fled over the border and was arrested upon his return in 1883.

White Protestant immigrants flooded into Manitoba, so that by 1885, only 7 percent of the population was of mixed ancestry. Although Riel and his followers thought they had ensured a multiethnic society where the Metis could participate as equals, fifteen years after the Manitoba Act, Metis society was in disarray. Poverty and fear of further displacement led the Metis to the Second Riel Rebellion. This time, Cree and Assiniboine Indians—starving because of withheld treaty rations— joined the Metis in their revolt. Riel was summoned from his exile to lead the Metis. Ottawa, fearing a general Indian uprising on the prairies, responded with swift military action rather than negotiation. Riel was arrested, convicted of treason, and hanged on November 16, 1885.

The great Metis society of the prairies was dispersed. Some Metis joined American Indian tribes; others remained largely disenfranchised and impoverished. During the last decades of the twentieth century, Metis have renewed their claims for the lands and rights lost at the time of Canadian confederation.

—*Pamela R. Stern*

ADDITIONAL READING:

Giraud, Marcel. *The Metis in the Canadian West*. Translated by George Woodcock. 2 vols. Lincoln: University of Nebraska Press, 1986. A primary source on the Metis, originally published in French in 1945. Volume 2 deals with the period of the rebellion. Some of the language suggests racial determinism.

McDougall, John. *In the Days of the Red River Rebellion*. Edmonton: University of Alberta Press, 1983. Memoir of a Methodist missionary during the time of the rebellion.

Miller, J. R. *Skyscrapers Hide the Heavens: A History of Indian-White Relations in Canada*. Rev. ed. Toronto: University of Toronto Press, 1991. Chapter 9 deals with the rebellion.

Owram, Doug. *Promise of Eden: The Canadian Expansionist Movement and the Idea of the West, 1856-1900*. Toronto: University of Toronto Press, 1980. Chapter 4 discusses the politics of the Canadian response to the rebellion.

Purich, Donald. *The Metis*. Toronto: James Lorimer, 1988. Highly readable treatment of the Metis. Chapters 3, 4, and 5 deal with the 1869 and 1885 rebellions and their outcomes.

SEE ALSO: 1815, Red River Raids; 1837, Rebellions in Canada; 1867, British North America Act; 1874, Red River War; 1876, Canada's Indian Act; 1885, Second Riel Rebellion.

1869 ■ WESTERN STATES GRANT WOMAN SUFFRAGE: *prior to passage of the Nineteenth Amendment, woman suffrage is granted by several Western states*

DATE: Beginning December, 1869
LOCALE: Primarily Western and Midwestern states
CATEGORIES: Civil rights; Women's issues
KEY FIGURES:
Susan B. Anthony (1820-1906), leader of the National Woman Suffrage Association
Carrie Chapman Catt (1859-1947), founder of the League of Women Voters
Esther Morris (1814-1902), woman suffrage leader in Wyoming and first female justice of the peace
Lucretia Mott (1793-1880) and
Elizabeth Cady Stanton (1815-1902), organizers of the Seneca Falls convention

SUMMARY OF EVENT. Abigail Adams wrote to her husband, John, while he was drafting the Declaration of Independence,

"In the new code of laws which I suppose it will be necessary for you to make, I desire you would remember the ladies." However, the ladies were not remembered. When the Constitution was drafted, there was considerable debate concerning who would be eligible to vote. In the end, the decision about who could vote was left to the individual states to decide. The vote was extended to those in each state qualified to vote for state legislature members. This effectively limited the vote to men.

Elizabeth Cady Stanton and Lucretia Mott organized the Seneca Falls Convention of 1848, the first women's convention organized with the express purpose of improving the position of women through education, suffrage, and more liberal marriage laws. At this meeting, the Declaration of Sentiments was formulated, paralleling the writing of the Declaration of Independence. Woman suffrage was a specific point included in this resolution. Nineteen years later, a territory known for its rugged frontier philosophy granted suffrage to women.

When the Union Pacific Railroad entered Wyoming in 1867, thousands of people poured into the area. Lawlessness abounded, with murders, robberies, holdups, and other criminal activity running rampant. Congress was petitioned for the right to establish a territorial government, and this was approved by Congress and President Andrew Johnson. The government officially was established in the territory of Wyoming in May, 1869.

The first election took place in September, 1869, to select the delegates to the first legislature for Wyoming. Esther Morris, a transplant from the East, had an understanding of woman suffrage issues and had only recently heard a lecture by Susan B. Anthony. With information at hand, she invited twenty of the most influential men in the state to dinner. With clarity of purpose and persuasive skill, she exacted from each of these men a promise to support woman suffrage if elected. Esther Morris later became the first female justice of the peace in the nation. William H. Bright, one of the men present, was elected president of the council when the legislature convened. Bright told his wife, "I have made up my mind that I will do everything in my power to give you the ballot." He soon set about the task of convincing the all-Democrat legislature of the gain associated with presenting a vote for woman suffrage for all the world to see. On November 27, 1869, Bright introduced the suffrage bill. Before the year was out, Wyoming became the first territory to adopt woman suffrage and in 1890, was the first state admitted to the Union with general woman suffrage.

In 1876, as Colorado prepared for statehood at its constitutional convention, the question of woman suffrage was submitted. The amendment, which came up for vote in early 1877, was defeated. Much discussion at that time centered on the dilemma that African Americans had been enfranchised and some indemnity was due the women. The idea of suffrage for women never really died out in Colorado. In 1893, a non-election year, there was new discussion of the women's vote in Colorado. Populists were in control of the Senate and Republicans of the House. Wyoming, directly to the north, had not experienced the problems many had predicted. It was in this

Although women did not receive the right to vote at a federal level until passage of the Nineteenth Amendment in 1920, some states and territories, especially in the West, granted woman suffrage earlier, as seen in this 1888 depiction of women at Wyoming polls, which appeared in Frank Leslie's Illustrated News. (Library of Congress)

climate that a referendum granting the vote to women was proposed. According to the 1876 constitution, women could be granted suffrage if confirmed by referendum. Voters were simply asked to confirm or deny women's right to vote. The measure was confirmed by a margin of more than six thousand votes. Women gathered in front of suffrage headquarters, upon hearing of their victory, started to sing "Praise God from whom all blessings flow." Suffragists left believing that the battle that had been won in Colorado could be won in any Western state.

Earlier, the women of Utah had held the right to vote. In February of 1870, the acting governor of Utah had signed the Act Conferring upon Women of Utah the Elective Franchise in the territory of Utah. This act admitted nearly forty times as many women to the vote as the enfranchisement in Wyoming. However, the road to suffrage for the women of Utah was rocky. In 1887, seventeen years after passage of this act, suffrage for women was withdrawn by congressional action. The legislation, called the Edmunds-Tucker Bill, disfranchised people who were involved in polygamist marriages. Utah was attempting to gain statehood and was deeply embroiled in political issues revolving around the Mormon religious practice of polygyny. Mormon women who had voted were accused of voting the Mormon ticket and therefore not generally supporting the national suffrage movement. It was not until 1896 that the women of Utah could legally vote again. At the time that Utah was admitted to statehood, the constitution, submitted to Congress for review, contained an equal suffrage clause, which was approved by 67 percent of the male voters.

In November, 1896, the voters of Idaho were asked, "Shall Section 2, of Article VI, of the constitution of the state of Idaho be so amended as to extend to women an equal right of suffrage?" When voters went to the polls, the amendment was carried by almost two to one. Elizabeth Ingram, a school-teacher from a small Idaho town, formed the first woman suffrage organization of Idaho in 1893. However, it was the strong involvement of national woman suffrage workers, such as Susan B. Anthony and Carrie Chapman Catt, that was ultimately responsible for passage of women's vote legislation in Idaho.

In 1910, more than eight million women participated in the paid labor force, yet most could not vote in a general election. By the time the Nineteenth Amendment was passed in 1920, granting women the right to vote throughout the United States, many states had already passed woman suffrage legislation. Among these states were: Washington, which granted women the vote in 1910; California, 1911; Oregon, Arizona, and Kansas, 1912; Montana and Nevada, 1914; New York, 1917; and South Dakota, Oklahoma, and Michigan, 1918. Clearly, the West and Midwest dominated the country in advancing the right of women to vote. Numerous other states had approved some woman suffrage. Most Southern states had no statewide enfranchisement of women. The year 1920 was a presidential election year, and for the first time, women across the country were able to participate in the election. —*Sharon L. Larson*

ADDITIONAL READING:

Beeton, Beverly. *Women Vote in the West: The Woman Suffrage Movement, 1869-1896*. New York: Garland, 1986. Provides a thorough discussion of the states that first granted suffrage to women. Gives particular attention to Utah's woman suffrage fight.

The Bill of Rights and Beyond, 1791-1991. Washington, D.C.: Commission of the Bicentennial of the United States Constitution, 1991. Provides a timetable of events leading up to the approval of the Nineteenth Amendment.

Catt, Carrie Chapman, and Nettie Rogers Shuler. *Woman Suffrage and Politics*. New York: Charles Scribner's Sons, 1926. Firsthand information on the fight for woman suffrage, written by a founder of the woman suffrage movement.

Coolidge, Olivia. *Women's Rights: The Suffrage Movement in America, 1848-1920*. New York: E. P. Dutton, 1966. Shows the tone of the early years of the movement and provides a time line of suffrage events.

Gurko, Miriam. *The Ladies of Seneca Falls: The Birth of the Woman's Rights Movement*. New York: Macmillan 1974. An early history, with particular emphasis on Elizabeth Stanton and Lucretia Mott. Contains the wording of the Declaration of Sentiments.

Schneir, Miriam. *Feminism: The Essential Historical Writings*. New York: Random House, 1972. Contains excerpts of writings by well-known suffragists and brief discussions of the history of these women.

SEE ALSO: 1848, Seneca Falls Convention; 1851, Akron Woman's Rights Convention; 1866, Suffragists Protest the Fourteenth Amendment; 1869, Rise of Woman Suffrage Associations; 1872, Susan B. Anthony Is Arrested; 1874, *Minor v. Happersett*; 1876, Declaration of the Rights of Women; 1890, Women's Rights Associations Unite; 1916, National Woman's Party Is Founded; 1920, League of Women Voters Is Founded; 1920, U.S. Women Gain the Vote.

1871 ■ INDIAN APPROPRIATION ACT:
Congress unilaterally determines that Native Americans no longer belong to their own sovereign nations, ending treaty making between U.S. and tribal governments

DATE: March 3, 1871
LOCALE: Washington, D.C.
CATEGORIES: Government and politics; Laws and acts; Native American history
KEY FIGURES:
Felix R. Brunot (1820-1898), head of the Board of Indian Commissioners
Henry Laurens Dawes (1816-1903), congressman from Massachusetts who opposed the treaties

Ulysses Simpson Grant (1822-1885), eighteenth president of
the United States, 1869-1877

Ely Samuel Parker (1828-1895), Seneca leader and Grant's
commissioner of Indian affairs

William Windom (1827-1891), congressman from Minnesota
who supported the treaty system

Richard Yates (1815-1873), senator from Illinois who
opposed the treaty system

SUMMARY OF EVENT. In 1871, Congress voted to end treaty
making with Native American peoples. Since the origins of the
republic, the U.S. government had dealt with tribes by recognizing each one as an independent nation living within the
United States. Hence, ambassadors were sent out from Washington, D.C., to negotiate treaties, and each agreement had to
be ratified by two-thirds of the Senate, as provided in the
Constitution. Chief Justice John Marshall, in *Worcester v.
Georgia* (1832), had determined that this process had to be
followed because each tribe was self-governing and sovereign
in its own territory.

The change took place because many people in the United
States came to believe that the Native American nations no
longer acted like sovereign states. They were too weak, post-
Civil War whites believed, and many had become dependent
on the federal government for their existence. Members of
Congress expressed that view in a series of discussions on
American Indian policy in 1870-1871. In the House of Representatives, the feeling also grew that the House was being
ignored in the development of Indian policy. The only way the
House could influence Native American relations would be by
renouncing the treaty concept. The attack on treaty making
gained strength during the debate over the money to be appropriated for the United States Board of Indian Commissioners.
This agency had been created in 1869 to oversee money
authorized to be spent on Indian programs.

The commissioners' first report suggested major changes in
Indian policy. It called for ending the treaty system and dealing with "uncivilized" native peoples as "wards of the government." Board chair Felix R. Brunot echoed the views of many
U.S. citizens when he declared that it was absurd to treat "a
few thousand savages" as if they were equal with the people
and government of the United States. President Ulysses S.
Grant supported that view, as did his commissioner of Indian
affairs, Ely S. Parker, a member of the Seneca nation. Parker
believed that it was a cruel farce to deal with the tribes as
equals; in his view, most were "helpless and ignorant wards"
of the federal government.

The resentment of members of the House of Representatives at their exclusion from Indian policy making became apparent during debates over treaties negotiated in 1868
and 1869. A May, 1868, agreement with the Osage Nation in
Kansas had ceded eight million acres of land to the government. The land then would be sold to a railroad company for
twenty cents per acre. The House voted unanimously to recommend that the Senate not ratify the treaty because the land
transfer had taken place outside the traditional methods of

selling public property. The Senate responded to the House
plea by rejecting the treaty. Later, however, the land was sold
to the railroad company with the approval of the House.

The House took up the issue of treaty making again in 1869
during a violent debate over the Indian appropriation for 1870.
It provided money for food, clothes, and education for tribe
members living on reservations. The House refused to accept
an increase in funds voted by the Senate. Representatives also
began to question whether native peoples were capable of
signing official treaties with the United States. Most members
attacked the traditional system, although three congressmen
spoke in favor of the treaty process. Representative William
Windom of Minnesota argued that changing the process would
be a breach of faith with the tribes. Revoking the process
would create great confusion among Native Americans and
add to their distrust of the U.S. government.

Representative John J. Logan, Republican of Illinois, responded for the majority, however, by declaring that "the idea
of this Government making treaties with bands of wild and
roving Indians is simply preposterous and ridiculous." Amid
loud cheers and laughter, Logan attacked the character of
native peoples and suggested that they were an inferior race
that should not be treated as equal in status to the people of the
United States. The House refused to approve the appropriation, and the Senate refused to compromise; therefore, no
Indian appropriation bill passed Congress in 1869.

In the debate over the 1871 appropriation, both sides raised
the same arguments. In the Senate, supporters of the treaty
system argued that any change would severely injure any
goodwill native peoples still held toward the U.S. government
system. Senator Richard Yates reiterated the antitreaty sentiment, declaring that the tribes were not civilized and that
making treaties with them had been a mistake. The Senate,
however, passed an appropriation bill and sent it to the House.
While the debate took place, many tribes were waiting for the
money due to them under treaties negotiated in 1868 and 1869.
Unless Congress agreed to an appropriation bill, they would
receive nothing. In a compromise arranged between the two
legislative branches, a sum of two million dollars was appropriated to pay off prior obligations. Debate over the appropriation for the next year bogged down in the House, however.

The Board of Indian Commissioners helped the House position by calling for an end to treaty making and for abrogating
all existing agreements. Only Representative Eugene M. Wilson of Minnesota spoke in favor of continuing the historic
policy. If Native Americans were not protected by treaties,
they would be cheated out of their lands by white speculators and end up with nothing, he argued. Debate in the Senate
and the House seemed far more concerned with constitutional
technicalities than with the welfare of native peoples. Once
more, no bill seemed possible. On the last day of the session,
President Grant urged a compromise, or, he warned, a war
with the tribes was sure to break out. Under this threat, Congress agreed to put aside its differences temporarily and passed
a bill.

When the new Congress opened on January 4, 1871, Representative Henry Dawes of Massachusetts led the call for change. Dawes, who in 1887 would author a major bill in the Senate drastically changing policy toward native peoples, called for a quick program of assimilation in this earlier debate. If natives were to become Americanized—a policy he supported—they should be treated as individuals rather than as members of foreign nations. Native peoples were not and never had been equal to the United States. The House passed a bill denouncing "so-called treaties."

In the Senate, an amendment to delete the words "so-called" before "treaties" led to a vigorous debate. Senator William Stewart of Nevada objected to the amendment. "The whole Indian policy of feeding drunken, worthless, vagabond Indians, giving them money to squander . . . has been a growing disgrace to our country for years." Treaties with "irresponsible tribes" were no treaties at all. Only a few senators agreed with this amendment, however, and "so-called" was eliminated. This angered the House, which refused to accept the Senate version.

Many congressmen and senators were tired of the endless debate and seemed willing to compromise. A conference committee of senators and representatives agreed that past treaties would be accepted or the integrity of the United States would be compromised. It agreed that no more treaties should be negotiated with Native Americans, however. Most conferees agreed that the tribes remaining hardly seemed like legitimate nations, as they were too small, weak, and miserable. The final compromise asserted the validity of prior agreements but provided that in the future, "no Indian nation or tribe within the territory of the United States shall be acknowledged or recognized as an independent nation, tribe, or power with whom the United States may contract by treaty." Both the Senate and the House accepted the compromise, and President Grant signed it into law on March 3, 1871. Treaties would no longer be negotiated with Native American peoples. Native Americans would, instead, become "wards of the state."

—Leslie V. Tischauser

ADDITIONAL READING:

Cohen, Fay G. *Treaties on Trial: The Continuing Controversy Over Northwest Indian Fishing Rights*. Seattle: University of Washington Press, 1986. Shows the continuing importance of treaties and the bitterness still evoked by pre-1871 agreements.

Heizer, Robert F. "Treaties." In *California*. Vol. 8 in *Handbook of North American Indians*. Washington, D.C.: Smithsonian Institution Press, 1978. A brief description of treaty making before 1871.

Jones, Dorothy V. *License for Empire: Colonialism by Treaty in Early America*. Chicago: University of Chicago Press, 1982. Discusses abuses of the system and how native peoples failed to understand the process.

Kvasnicka, Robert M. "United States Indian Treaties and Agreements." In *History of Indian-White Relations*, edited by Wilcomb E. Washburn. Vol. 4 in *Handbook of North American Indians*. Washington, D.C.: Smithsonian Institution Press, 1988. A short discussion of the debate over treaties and how the process was ended.

Prucha, Francis Paul. *American Indian Treaties: The History of a Political Anomaly*. Berkeley: University of California Press, 1994. The full story of treaty making and how it was ended in 1871. Index and list of treaties.

SEE ALSO: 1830, Indian Removal Act; 1830, Trail of Tears; 1831, Cherokee Cases; 1861, Apache Wars; 1862, Great Sioux War; 1863, Long Walk of the Navajos; 1864, Sand Creek Massacre; 1867, Medicine Lodge Creek Treaty; 1868, Washita River Massacre.

1871 ■ BARNUM'S CIRCUS FORMS: *an American institution begins as a traveling show that contributes to a growing national culture*

DATE: April 10, 1871
LOCALE: Brooklyn, New York
CATEGORIES: Cultural and intellectual history; Organizations and institutions
KEY FIGURES:

Philip Astley (1742-1814), innovator of the modern circus in England

James A. Bailey (1847-1906), U.S. circus manager, part owner of The Great London Circus, and later Barnum's partner

Phineas Taylor Barnum (1810-1891), nineteenth century showman

William C. Coup (1837-1895), circus manager who convinced Barnum to form a traveling circus

Joice Heth (c. 1760-1836), female slave who was Barnum's first exhibit

Jenny Lind (1820-1887), Swedish soprano whose American tour Barnum sponsored

John Bill Ricketts (died 1799), promoter who staged the first American circus

Charles Sherwood Stratton, "General Tom Thumb" (1838-1883), dwarf who performed in Barnum's museum and circus

SUMMARY OF EVENT. The Latin word *circus* ("round") was first used by ancient Romans as the name for entertainments held in round arenas. The three elements of the modern circus—a ring, acts, and clowns—were combined first in 1768 by Philip Astley in London. Thomas Pool staged a simple horse and clown show in Philadelphia on August 27, 1785, but John Bill Ricketts staged the first show in the United States called a circus in Philadelphia on April 3, 1793. Ricketts' most famous attraction was "Jack," the white horse George Washington rode in the American Revolution. While the circus in the United States drew from Astley's innovations and the traditions of Europe, certain features were indigenous. At first

American circuses, informative as well as entertaining, featured the menagerie as their central attraction, but they also usually included troupes of acrobats, jugglers, and minstrels. Early circuses in the United States were wholly rural, traveling by horse and wagon fifteen to twenty miles per day between small towns. The traveling tent show provided entertainment for the rural towns as theaters and variety halls did for the cities. The circus parade was adopted as a means of advertisement early in the 1800's, and by the mid-1830's, no fewer than thirty-two shows were touring the country. As cities grew, traveling shows merged with urban horse shows, and in the 1850's, the entertainments often were held in city amphitheaters. However, the city shows lacked the excitement of travel and the allure of the tent.

Perhaps the greatest moment in American circus tradition occurred on April 10, 1871, in Brooklyn, New York, when Phineas T. Barnum invested this ancient tradition with his own spectacular showmanship. Born in Bethel, Connecticut, on July 5, 1810, Barnum had had a variety of occupations before becoming a showman, including editing an abolitionist newspaper. In 1834, he went to New York City and launched his career as a showman by purchasing and exhibiting an African American slave named Joice Heth, whom he claimed was the 161-year-old former nurse of George Washington. The woman, actually eighty years of age at her death, was a perfect example of Barnum's genius at creating public curiosity and excitement; his exploitation of an elderly black woman as a curiosity was also an example of the deeply entrenched racism of the times.

In 1841, Barnum purchased the American Museum (an amalgamation of the old Scudder's Museum and Peale's Museum), located in the center of New York at the corner of Broadway and Ann Streets. The American Museum, to which Barnum devoted most of his career, was an urban forerunner of the grand circus. Before the days of the Metropolitan Museum or the Museum of Natural History, curious travelers found little refuge in New York. In Barnum's establishment they could, for a small admission fee, gaze at stuffed animals from all corners of the world, relics purchased from sea captains returning from Asia and the South Pacific, and a gallery of paintings that Barnum advertised as a national portrait gallery. Most famous for his freaks-of-nature exhibits, Barnum transformed the American Museum into a great cultural sideshow. He exhibited a family of "trained fleas" and a "Feejee" mermaid (the upper half of a monkey sewn to the lower half of a fish), put on the first American Punch and Judy show, and featured concerts and temperance lectures. Just before beginning his European tour in 1843, Barnum met the dwarf Charles Sherwood Stratton, whom he nicknamed General Tom Thumb and hired at a starting weekly salary of three dollars. The American Museum soon became the most popular tourist attraction in New York City.

Barnum's promotion of the American circus was foreshadowed by his sponsorship of Swedish soprano Jenny Lind's enormously successful 1850 singing tour. Soon afterward, Barnum received a shipment of exotic animals, which he

marched up Broadway led by five harnessed pairs of Ceylonese elephants pulling a gaudy gilded chariot. Barnum's Great Asiatic Caravan, Museum, and Menagerie lasted in New York until 1854. Two separate fires destroyed the museum, but each time, Barnum rebuilt.

Barnum had decided to retire in 1870, when William C. Coup, a dedicated young circus manager, talked him into forming the "P. T. Barnum Travelling Exhibition and World's Fair on Wheels," which began its first tour in Brooklyn on April 10, 1871. Coup also suggested transporting the circus by railroad, enabling it to visit larger towns. Huge crowds flocked to Barnum's circus, which showed a profit of more than one million dollars in six months. The circus' popularity soon outgrew its ability to accommodate spectators. Expanding the forty-two-foot-diameter ring would have required retraining all of the animals; so as early as 1872, Barnum added a second ring, and then a third. The three rings were surrounded by a hippodrome track, used for horsemanship and drama. The expanded show traveled by rail in more than sixty cars and could accommodate twenty thousand spectators. Its gross receipts averaged between one and two million dollars each season. Railroads ran excursions to its performances from all nearby points. For rural areas of the United States, it was the great event of the year, with its parade and inevitable advance guard of elephants.

Barnum's circus combined virtually all forms of nineteenth century popular entertainment into one show. Each performance began with the Congress of Nations, a theatrical spectacle in which actors impersonated world leaders and acted out great historical events. These "specs," which typically represented events from ancient history, could last up to thirty minutes and use as many as one thousand actors. One of Barnum's greatest competitors, Adam Forepaugh, Sr., was famous for elaborate spectacles; his reenactment of the American Revolution was greater than any Barnum produced. Further competition came from the rise of Buffalo Bill's Wild West Show, in which actors dressed as cowboys and Indians acted out recent frontier battles. Competition between circuses was so fierce that advertising brigades containing several railroad cars of posters and handbills preceded the circus train itself by as much as a week. Advertisements were often exaggerated and misleading, and circuses not only promoted their own acts, but posted "ratsheets" denouncing their competitors' acts as frauds.

In 1872, Barnum moved the circus to the Hippotheatron on 14th Street in New York, which he hoped would become the show's permanent home. Five weeks later, a fire destroyed all the animals (except two elephants and a giraffe), as well as all the performers' costumes and equipment. Barnum reopened the show by early spring, but suffered great losses. After another fire struck the circus in 1880, Barnum sought a spectacular attraction. At this time, Barnum's closest competitor—James A. Bailey's "The Great London Circus"—featured Columbia, the first baby circus elephant born in captivity. Barnum allegedly offered Bailey $100,000 for it, but Bailey turned down the offer. During the 1881 season, however, the two circuses merged to form Barnum and Bailey's Circus— "The Greatest Show on Earth." Having lived with circus performers most of his life, Bailey organized the show as a traveling village that provided for all of its members' needs.

Perhaps the attraction best associated with Barnum's circus was an enormous African elephant purchased from the London Zoo for ten thousand dollars in 1882. Billed as the world's largest elephant, Jumbo was Barnum's most popular attraction; so popular, in fact, that his name added a new word to the English language. People came from far away to see Jumbo, and spread his name and image throughout North America. The huge success did not last, however. After an Ontario performance on September 15, 1885, Jumbo was killed by a freight train. The circus' financial loss was devastating. Trainers tried to compensate by teaching surviving elephants to carry black hankies in their trunks and wipe their eyes, as if crying. Jumbo's stuffed skin and separately reassembled skeleton traveled with the circus for several years, but never drew the same crowds.

Bailey took over the circus after Barnum's death in 1891. After Bailey's death in 1906, the five Ringling brothers of Baraboo, Wisconsin, bought the show and ran it independently until 1919, when they merged it with their own show to form the Ringling Brothers and Barnum & Bailey Circus. With the development of movies and the growing mobility of cars, trains, and airplanes, the circus' popularity diminished, because people no longer needed the wonders of the world brought to them. By the late twentieth century, the circus played only in the largest cities, performing in sports arenas rather than in the circus tents known as "big tops." Circus World Museum opened in Baraboo, Wisconsin, in 1959.

—Geralyn Strecker

ADDITIONAL READING:

Barnum, P. T. *Barnum's Own Story*. Edited by Waldo R. Brown. New York: Viking, 1927. Reprint. New York: Dover, 1961. Combines and condenses various editions of Barnum's autobiography.

Collins, Matthew. *Barnum's Big Top*. PBS Video, 1991. This documentary combines archival black-and-white movie footage, still photographs, excerpts from letters and journals, and an early audio recording of Barnum's own voice. Describes the growth of Barnum's circus in the larger context of nineteenth century popular culture. A guide for teachers is also available.

Culhane, John. *The American Circus: An Illustrated History*. New York: Henry Holt, 1990. A profusely illustrated history of the American circus that contains much information of Barnum.

Fitzsimons, Raymund. *Barnum in London*. New York: St. Martin's Press, 1970. Biography focusing specifically on Barnum's time in England and how his "Yankee Doodle" character Americanized Great Britain.

Harris, Neil. *Humbug: The Art of P. T. Barnum*. Boston: Little, Brown, 1973. Biography focusing on Barnum's showmanship and business practices.

Saxon, A. H. *P. T. Barnum: The Legend and the Man*. New York: Columbia University Press, 1989. This heavily illustrated scholarly biography offers a critical consideration of Barnum in context with other nineteenth century events.

SEE ALSO: 1867, National Grange of the Patrons of Husbandry Forms; 1872, Great American Bison Slaughter; 1876, Bell Demonstrates the Telephone; 1879, Edison Demonstrates the Incandescent Lamp; 1893, World's Columbian Exposition.

1871 ■ TREATY OF WASHINGTON: *a U.S.-British settlement of differences becomes a milestone in international conciliation*

DATE: May 8, 1871
LOCALE: Washington, D.C., and Geneva, Switzerland
CATEGORIES: Canadian history; Diplomacy and international relations; Treaties and agreements
KEY FIGURES:

Charles Francis Adams (1807-1886), U.S. commissioner to the Geneva arbitration tribunal
Alexander Cockburn (1802-1880), lord chief justice of England and British commissioner to the Geneva arbitration tribunal
Hamilton Fish (1808-1893), U.S. secretary of state
Ulysses Simpson Grant (1822-1885), eighteenth president of the United States, 1869-1877
John Rose (1820-1888), British-Canadian statesman deputized by the British Foreign Office to enter into informal conversations with Fish
Charles Sumner (1811-1874), senator from Massachusetts and chairman of the Senate Foreign Relations Committee

SUMMARY OF EVENT. On February 27, 1871, official Washington shrugged off late-winter dreariness to celebrate the beginning of a momentous gathering of American and British dignitaries. The social festivities that took place did much to dissipate the feelings of bitterness and suspicion that had dominated Anglo-American relations since the Civil War years. The Washington Conference had been called to deal with the *Alabama* claims, the major legacy of Union-British conflict over neutral rights and duties during the Civil War. Proceedings began on a surprisingly cordial note, and within three months the two delegations had reached solutions or provided for later agreement on almost all matters at issue.

Neither side would have believed when the negotiations were first arranged that such an explosive issue as the *Alabama* claims could be resolved with so little difficulty. In the years immediately following the Civil War, Anglo-American relations were dangerously tense. The principal cause was the lasting bitterness of Americans toward what they regarded as Great Britain's shamefully unneutral support of the Confederacy. The British government had on several occasions come perilously close to recognizing Confederate independence, an act tantamount to intervention on the South's behalf. Though that step was not taken, British sympathy for the Confederacy was manifested by toleration of repeated evasions of the Foreign Enlistment Act of 1819, especially that section which prohibited construction in British yards of warships for belligerent powers. The Confederacy hoped to break the blockade and drive Union commerce from the seas by building a navy in Great Britain. The gamble almost succeeded. Confederate warships produced by British shipbuilders sank or seized about 250 Union merchant ships. Three fast commerce destroyers, the *Florida*, the *Shenandoah*, and the notorious *Alabama*, accounted for almost one-fourth of the sinkings. The case of the *Alabama* was so blatant a violation of Great Britain's neutrality that just before her scheduled launching in July, 1862, proceedings were begun to detain the ship. However, the *Alabama* escaped to begin an amazing (and, to the British government, a most embarrassing) career. Although the British soon closed the loopholes in their neutrality laws, the United States government considered that the damage had been done and that Great Britain must be made to pay for its callous disregard of neutral obligations.

During the remainder of the war, Union claims for indemnity arising from depredations committed by the *Alabama* and her sister ships mounted steadily, but the ministry of Lord Palmerston refused to accept responsibility for the Confederate cruisers' activities. American determination to gain satisfaction culminated in the suggestion in 1869 by Senator Charles Sumner, chairman of the Senate Foreign Relations Committee, that Great Britain be made to pay for the damages caused by the Confederate cruisers (estimated at $15 million), the cost of catching them, destruction to the United States merchant marine ($110 million), and (since action by the cruisers had prolonged the war by two full years) an additional $2 billion to cover the cost of war for that period. Sumner's aim was not to bankrupt the British treasury but to force Great Britain to satisfy American demands by the cession of Canada to the United States. London dismissed Sumner's arguments as utter insanity but was forced to note that both President Ulysses S. Grant and his new secretary of state, Hamilton Fish, supported the proposal.

Great Britain decided to negotiate. Fish then adopted a more moderate position, asking for payment of existing claims by Great Britain and an expression of regret. Informal conversations were begun between Fish and Sir John Rose, a British-Canadian statesman and businessman residing in England, whom the British Foreign Office had chosen to convey its interest in pacific settlements of the various disputes. It was soon agreed that a joint commission should be convened to deal with all unresolved issues: the *Alabama* claims, a long-standing conflict over American fishing rights off the Canadian coast, the matter of ownership of the San Juan Islands in Puget Sound, and other minor problems.

The commission, comprising five American and five British representatives, met in Washington from February 27 to May 8, 1871. Buoyed by foxhunting weekends, liberal ministrations of fine liquor, and superb food, the commissioners

agreed without serious difficulty on a fair settlement. Most important was the treaty provision regarding the *Alabama* claims. Great Britain offered regrets for the escape of the *Alabama* and other warships and agreed to submit the claims to binding arbitration. Furthermore, it accepted a definition of rules to govern neutral obligations toward belligerents. Although these regulations were not retroactive, the British were conceding victory to the American position in the forthcoming arbitration proceedings. This Anglo-American agreement was a historic one for the future of neutrality. The treaty also provided for a temporary resolution of the quarrel over fishing privileges, an agreement to submit the question of the San Juan Islands to arbitration, and numerous other economic and territorial agreements. The Washington Treaty was a remarkable accomplishment and had been termed by some as the greatest example of international conciliation ever known. It certainly represented a significant diplomatic victory for the United States.

Arbitration of the *Alabama* claims took place in Geneva, Switzerland, in December, 1871. The discussions nearly collapsed at the outset, for Charles Francis Adams, the United States commissioner, carrying out express instructions from Secretary of State Fish, revived the question (which the British had thought dead and buried) of indirect damages. Fish's motivation was not money, not Canada, but domestic politics. He desired that the tribunal deal with and reject the matter of indirect damages; otherwise, Congress might throw out the treaty. Although the British representative, Sir Alexander Cockburn, lord chief justice of England, was enraged by this tactic, the tribunal exceeded its jurisdiction and ruled out the indirect claims. This act allowed for adjudication of the direct claims. The court found in favor of the United States and awarded damages of $15.5 million.   —*Theodore A. Wilson*

ADDITIONAL READING:

Allen, Harry C. *Great Britain and the United States: A History of Anglo-American Relations, 1783-1952.* New York: St. Martin's Press, 1955. A useful survey of Anglo-American relations.

Boykin, Edward C. *Ghost Ship of the Confederacy: The Story of the Alabama.* New York: Funk and Wagnalls, 1957. Boykin relates the adventures of the *Alabama* in a popularly written study.

Cushing, Caleb. *The Treaty of Washington: Its Negotiation, Execution, and the Discussions Relating Thereto.* New York: Harper & Brothers, 1873. This contemporary analysis of the Washington negotiations is still valuable, especially for understanding the personalities and political issues involved.

Duberman, Martin B. *Charles Francis Adams, 1807-1886.* Boston: Houghton Mifflin, 1961. A comprehensive biography based on exhaustive research in the Adams papers. Describes the crucial role Adams played in the resolution of the Geneva tribunal.

Nevins, Allan. *Hamilton Fish: The Inner History of the Grant Administration.* 2 vols. New York: Dodd, Mead, 1936. A definitive biography which stresses Fish's attentiveness to domestic political factors during his tenure as secretary of state.

Smith, Goldwin A. *The Treaty of Washington, 1871: A Study in Imperial History*. Ithaca, N.Y.: Cornell University Press, 1941. Primarily explores Canada's role in the negotiations over the *Alabama* claims. Also clarifies numerous aspects of the diplomatic engagement.

Winks, Robin W. *Canada and the United States: The Civil War Years*. Baltimore: The Johns Hopkins University Press, 1960. This excellent monograph places in context difficulties between the United States and Canada.

SEE ALSO: 1842, Webster-Ashburton Treaty; 1846, Oregon Settlement; 1867, British North America Act.

1872 ■ GREAT AMERICAN BISON SLAUGHTER: *mass killings of buffalo lead to the near-extinction of the species and destroy the lifeblood of the plains Indians*

DATE: Peaked 1872-1874
LOCALE: American Great Plains
CATEGORIES: Canadian history; Environment; Expansion and land acquisition; Native American history
KEY FIGURES:
William Frederick "Buffalo Bill" Cody (1846-1917), guide and leading bison hunter
George Armstrong Custer (1839-1876), relentless leader of battles to subdue Native Americans
Philip Sheridan (1831-1888), U.S. Army general
William Tecumseh Sherman (1820-1891), U.S. Army leader in the West

SUMMARY OF EVENT. In 1853, the American bison population was estimated at between sixty and seventy million animals. It was reduced to a few thousand in thirty years. The bison's decline was the result of human greed, uncontrolled exploitation, and a United States government policy. Also called the American buffalo, the bison ranged throughout North America from the Rocky Mountains to the Atlantic shoreline and from northern Mexico to southern Canada. Its greatest concentration was on the grasslands of the Great Plains. It was the basis for a total way of life for the Native Americans. The animals provided food, clothing, and shelter. An important part of the nomadic plains tribes' culture was the buffalo-hide tipi, which could be collapsed quickly when the tribe was ready to move on. On the treeless plains, the herds' dried droppings were fuel for the cooking fires.

On the northern Great Plains, where the terrain was rugged, a herd feeding near a cliff would be driven over the precipice by Indian men and boys waving buffalo robes and shouting, an event known as a buffalo jump. The waiting tribe rushed in to butcher as many of the animals as they could. Frequently, many more animals were left dead or dying than could be handled. Contemporaneous writers described the slaughter of from two hundred to two thousand bison in such hunts. However, because of the relatively small population of Native Americans in North America and their primitive weapons, the impact on the bison was slight.

With the end of the Civil War, in April, 1865, army troops traveled west to battle the Cheyenne, Lakota Sioux, and Crow. The army contracted with local settlers to supply the troops with "buffalo beef." Workers constructing the new transcontinental railroad also had to be fed. Contractors included William F. Cody, better known as Buffalo Bill, probably the best-recognized of all the bison killers. Hunters frequently skinned the bison, cut out the tongue, and took only some of the meat, leaving the remainder of the bison to rot on the prairie.

Dressed hides were shipped east as lap robes for winter sleigh and buggy rides or were turned into overcoats. Highly romanticized stories by eastern writers about the exploits of Buffalo Bill and other bison hunters quickly made buffalo robes a status symbol. Demand increased and more bison were slaughtered. Often only the skin was taken, the carcass left to scavengers. Hundreds of thousands of bison were killed each year for food and hides.

Bison also were killed for sport, as it became popular for groups of people to travel to the Great Plains simply to shoot bison. The railroads that linked the East and West cut across the ancient north-south routes of the bison. The seemingly endless herds were an annoyance to the train crews and a temptation to the passengers. When trains were delayed, passengers fired into the massed animals, killing some and wounding many more. The railroads encouraged this, with advertising to induce people to ride their trains.

It is difficult to obtain accurate data on the number of bison slaughtered. Few records were kept and the killing took place over a wide area. In 1872, in western Kansas, approximately two thousand hide hunters were each bringing down about fifteen bison a day. At that rate, hunters were killing thirty thousand bison per day. As soon as the herds in one area were reduced beyond the point of diminishing returns, the hunters moved elsewhere, seeking larger herds. An 1869 report notes that in a good year, about two hundred fifty thousand hides were shipped to the New York market alone. Railroad shipments between 1872 and 1874 totaled 1,378,359 hides.

A peculiarity in the behavior of the bison made them easy targets for hunters. Although bison could be stampeded, hunters in ambush could pick off the animals one by one, because they simply stood as others were shot and dropped in place. Hide hunters called it "a stand." Some of the herd nosed at their fallen comrades and then calmly joined the rest of the animals in grazing. A good hunter could kill seventy-five to one hundred bison per day. One especially skillful hunter, in a bet with his fellows and shooting at a stand from ambush, killed one hundred twenty bison in forty minutes.

The slaughter of the bison was far from a managed or controlled affair. Hunters indiscriminately shot the adults and subadults. Calves were ignored except, possibly, for camp meat. Unweaned, orphaned calves, not yet able to graze the abundant grasses, were left to starve to death. After one particularly large herd was killed, five hundred to one thousand calves wandered off to starve.

The United States government took the position that the still-warring Native Americans could be subdued if the bison were denied to them. The U.S. Army began a program of interdiction of the herds. General Philip Sheridan spoke out strongly in favor of continuing the slaughter of the buffalo "to settle the Indian question." Sheridan's Civil War comrade, General William Sherman, echoed these sentiments. He stated that the only way to force the Native Americans to reservations and turn them into farmers was to clear the prairies of the bison. The government further supported the bison slaughter by providing free ammunition to any buffalo hunter on request.

As early as 1873, fewer and fewer bison were encountered in western Kansas. Hide hunters moved to the northern Great Plains territories and continued the slaughter. The decline spread throughout the range of the bison, and it soon became obvious to most observers that the great herds were gone.

The intensive slaughter for hides was brief, occurring mostly from 1872 to 1874, but the activity extended from 1871 through 1883. Most herds were shot out in about four years, and the hunters then moved on to other areas. Although a few bison survived, undoubtedly the species' numbers had

slipped below that level ecologists call the minimum viable population size. For many animals, more than one male and one female are required to begin a breeding population. The great slaughter left the prairies littered with bison skeletons. For years, farmers could gather a cartload or two of bones and sell them to processors for fertilizer. One bone buyer estimated that from 1884 to 1891, he bought the bones of approximately six million bison skeletons.

Neither the settlers nor the Native Americans could believe that the bison was no more. The settlers thought that the herds had migrated to Canada and would soon return. The Native Americans, drawing on their mythology, believed the animals had returned to a great cavern in the ground to reappear if the right prayers were said and the right supplications were made. The great herds were, however, gone. The impact of the hide hunters' indiscriminate slaughter and the U.S. government's interdiction policy eliminated not only the bison but also the Native American's traditional nomadic way of life. Reluctantly, but with resignation, they became farmers on reservations as the U.S. government had sought. Perhaps the worst blow to the plains Indians was their loss of the religious and cultural relationship with the bison. Their entire civilization and lifeways had been destroyed along with the animals on which they depended.

The indiscriminate killing of thousands of buffalo for sport, at close range from railroad cars, nearly exterminated a native North American species within a single generation during the late nineteenth century. Indians of the Great Plains, whose nomadic lifeways depended on the buffalo, declined dramatically as a result of these animal slaughters. (Library of Congress)

Only a few scattered bison and some in private herds escaped the slaughter. Today, brought together in national parks, preserves, and other protected areas, they have survived and multiplied. —*Albert C. Jensen*

ADDITIONAL READING:

Dary, David A. *The Buffalo Book: The Full Saga of the American Animal.* Chicago: Swallow Press, 1974. Detailed account of bison in North America. Black-and-white photos, index, bibliography.

Foster, John, ed. *Buffalo.* Edmonton, Canada: University of Alberta Press, 1992. A short collection of papers by specialists in ecology and sociology detailing the relationship between the plains Indians and the American bison. Illustrations.

McHugh, Tom. *The Time of the Buffalo.* New York: Alfred A. Knopf, 1972. A factual, readable revision of a professional wildlife biologist's dissertation. Illustrations, index, and detailed bibliography.

Matthews, Anne. *Where the Buffalo Roam.* New York: Grove Weidenfeld, 1992. Describes a plan to restore the Great Plains to their natural condition and the bison to their former numbers. Illustrations and index.

Russell, Don. *The Lives and Legends of Buffalo Bill.* Norman: University of Oklahoma Press, 1960. A detailed examination of the Army scout and bison hunter. Footnotes, extensive bibliography, index, illustrations.

SEE ALSO: 1862, Great Sioux War; 1866, Bozeman Trail War; 1867, Medicine Lodge Creek Treaty; 1868, Washita River Massacre; 1869, Transcontinental Railroad Is Completed; 1871, Indian Appropriation Act; 1874, Red River War.

1872 ■ SUSAN B. ANTHONY IS ARRESTED: *an attempt to vote and have her case heard before the U.S. Supreme Court fails but highlights the cause of woman suffrage*

DATE: November 5, 1872
LOCALE: Rochester, New York
CATEGORIES: Civil rights; Women's issues
KEY FIGURES:
Susan B. Anthony (1820-1906), suffragist and activist for women's rights
Ward Hunt, U.S. associate justice
Henry R. Selden, appeals court judge

SUMMARY OF EVENT. Women activists in the mid-nineteenth century had hoped that with the enfranchisement of blacks would also come enfranchisement for women. Therefore, the Fourteenth and Fifteenth Amendments were severe blows, since their language specifically linked voting with males. Outraged, many women turned their energies with a new urgency toward winning the right vote. The best means to achieve this goal split the women's rights movement. Elizabeth Cady Stanton and Susan B. Anthony founded the National Woman Suffrage Association to work for passage of a Sixteenth Amendment granting women the vote. Lucy Stone organized the American Woman Suffrage Association to work for enfranchisement on a state-by-state basis.

A third line of attack, which crossed organizational lines, was to demonstrate that the Constitution already granted women suffrage. To this end, Victoria Woodhull spoke before the House of Representatives' Judiciary Committee in January, 1871. She pointed out that the Fourteenth and Fifteenth Amendments, despite their linkage of the word "male" to enfranchisement, also guaranteed the vote regardless of "race, color, or previous condition of servitude." She argued that all women belong to a race and are a color, and were therefore guaranteed the right to vote. The Judiciary Committee was not persuaded by Woodhull's argument. Nevertheless, Anthony hoped the presidential election of 1872 could set the stage for another showdown testing the interpretation—and perhaps the constitutionality—of the Fourteenth and Fifteenth Amendments. She and other women determined to attempt to vote in this election, knowing that they would likely not even be allowed to register. Anthony planned, if refused, to file suit against the election registrars and have the matter become one that the courts must decide.

In all, some fifty women from Rochester, New York, tried to register to vote in the 1872 presidential election. Early on voter registration day, Anthony and her three sisters went to their local voter registration site, where Anthony demanded that they be allowed to register. Their right, she explained, was guaranteed both by the Fourteenth Amendment of the U.S. Constitution and by the New York State Constitution. She told the registrars she had sought legal counsel from former Appeals Court judge Henry R. Selden, a respected citizen of Rochester, and he supported her claims. She threatened to sue anyone who turned her away. The women were allowed to register.

On election day, November 5, 1872, Anthony and fifteen other women from her ward voted (Anthony for Republican candidate Ulysses S. Grant). By this time feelings were running so high that none of the other fifty women from Rochester who had registered to vote were allowed to do so. Three weeks later Anthony, the fifteen other women who voted, and two voting inspectors were arrested. When an embarrassed deputy marshal assured her that she could proceed to the district attorney's office without an escort, the fifty-two-year-old Anthony responded, "I prefer to be arrested like anybody else. You may handcuff me as soon as I get my coat and hat."

Anthony had planned to sue any inspector who refused her the right to vote; she had not expected to be arrested herself. She quickly, however, saw the use to which she could put this case. With luck, she could use her trial to bring the case before the Supreme Court and get a national hearing for the cause of woman suffrage.

Anthony's hopes were dashed in this ambition. After two hearings, Anthony had Selden apply for a writ of *habeas corpus*, arguing that the government had no legal right to hold her because no crime had been committed. The court adjourned to consider its response to the writ.

In late January, 1873, a district judge denied the writ and sentenced her to jail until her trial could be held. He placed her bail at $1,000. Anthony promptly stated that she refused to pay bail; Selden, however, insisted on paying. At the time, Anthony did not understand the importance of this act, but she found out minutes after she left court that by paying bail Selden had forfeited all chance of using the writ of *habeas corpus* as a route to the Supreme Court. Selden later said that he understood the legal ramifications but could not bear to have a lady detained in jail. The following day a grand jury indicted Anthony and her trial was set for May 13.

Convinced that she would not get a fair hearing, Anthony spent the time before the trial taking her case to the people. Making speeches at each of the twenty-nine districts in her county, she proclaimed:

> The Declaration of Independence, the United States Constitution, the constitutions of the several States and the organic laws of the Territories, all alike propose to *protect* the people in the exercise of their God-given rights. Not one of them pretends to bestow rights.

When the judge realized what Anthony had done, he ordered the trial moved to Ontario County, saying that it would be impossible to find local jurors unprejudiced by Anthony's speeches. He also delayed the trial until June. Anthony spent the extra time in Ontario County giving the same speeches she had delivered earlier in Monroe County.

The trial opened June 17, 1873, and was presided over in an unorthodox and questionable manner by U.S. associate justice Ward Hunt. When Selden called Anthony to the stand, the prosecution objected, calling Anthony incompetent. Hunt sustained the objection, so Selden spoke as a witness in Anthony's behalf, pointing out, among other things, that as her legal adviser he had counseled Anthony to vote.

At the end of Selden's defense and the district attorney's response, Hunt read his opinion, written *before* the trial began, that "under the 14th amendment, which Miss Anthony claims protects her, she was not protected in a right to vote." The statement concluded with Hunt's order to the jury (despite the fact that such an order clearly violated the law) "to find a verdict of guilty." Selden again objected, but to no avail. His request that the individual jury members be polled was also rejected, as was his request for a new trial.

Hunt then asked the prisoner if she had anything to say. Anthony accused Hunt of having "trampled under foot every vital principle of our government." She continued, "My natural rights, my civil rights, my political rights, my judicial rights, are all alike ignored. Robbed of the fundamental privilege of citizenship, I am degraded from the status of a citizen to that of a subject. . . ." Although ordered to be silent several times, she continued, pointing out that she had been denied a jury of her peers, for as long as women were denied equal rights of citizenship, no man could be her peer; instead, she said, "each and every man [connected with the trial—lawyers, judge, and jury members] was my political superior; hence, in no sense, my peer." Law itself, she insisted, was "all made by men, interpreted by men, administered by men, in favor of men and against women."

When she had finished and sat down, Justice Hunt fined her $100 plus the cost of the prosecution. Anthony retorted, "I will never pay a dollar of your unjust penalty." Had Hunt ordered Anthony held until her fine was paid, she would again have had recourse to the Supreme Court, and considering the blatant disregard of legalities during her hearing Anthony would almost certainly have gained the right to a new trial. But Hunt, knowing this, let her go and never tried to collect the money she owed, ending her hopes of a Supreme Court hearing.

During 1871 and 1872, some 150 women from ten different states and Washington, D.C., attempted to vote. Only a handful were successful in having their ballots counted. Anthony's case, however, was the most publicized and the only one targeted for prosecution, no doubt because of her status as a suffragist leader.

Meanwhile, however, a far less publicized case was making its way to the Supreme Court—that of Virginia Minor, president of the Missouri Woman Suffrage Association. Minor filed suit against a St. Louis, Missouri, registrar who refused to let her register to vote. She argued that states had no right to bar U.S. citizens who were women from voting, as that was to give states power to rescind "the immunities and privileges of American citizenship [which] are National in character. . . ." Her stance that citizenship and the right to vote are synonymous was not upheld by the Supreme Court, which in October, 1874, ruled that citizenship did not necessarily guarantee suffrage. This ruling closed off interpretation as an avenue toward gaining woman's suffrage.

The only routes left for gaining the vote for women were state-by-state legislation or an amendment to the U.S. Constitution. In either case suffragists would have to sway the votes of already enfranchised males—hardly, as Anthony had pointed out, a jury of peers. It would be almost another fifty years before the Nineteenth Amendment was passed in 1920, at last allowing women citizens of the United States the right to vote.

—Grace McEntee

ADDITIONAL READING:

An Account of the Proceedings of the Trial of Susan B. Anthony of the Charge of Illegal Voting, at the Presidential Election in Nov., 1872, and on the Trial of Beverly W. Jones, Edwin T. Marsh and William B. Hall, the Inspectors of Election by Whom Her Vote Was Received. Rochester, N.Y.: Daily Democrat and Chronicle Book Print, 1874. This transcript of the trial is an invaluable primary source.

Anthony, Katharine. *Susan B. Anthony: Her Personal History and Her Era.* Garden City: Doubleday, 1954. A sprightly biography that devotes several pages to the trial.

Barry, Kathleen. *Susan B. Anthony: A Biography of a Sin-*

gular Feminist. New York: Ballantine Books, 1988. This scholarly and sympathetic biography dispels earlier portraits of Anthony as self-serving.

Flexner, Eleanor. *Century of Struggle: The Woman's Rights Movement in the United States*. Cambridge, Mass.: Harvard University Press, 1959. A comprehensive history of the women's rights movement that places specific incidents into the larger historic picture.

Lehman, Godfrey D. "Susan B. Anthony Cast Her Ballot for Ulysses S. Grant." *American Heritage* 37 (1985): 25-31. An engaging and dramatic description that includes often omitted information about public response and the fate of the voting inspectors.

Stanton, Elizabeth Cady, Susan B. Anthony, and Matilda Joslyn Gage, eds. *History of Woman Suffrage*. Vol. 2. New York: Fowler & Wells, 1882. Reprint. New York: Arno Press, 1969. Part of an eleven-volume set, this invaluable primary source is edited by women who worked for women's suffrage for the better part of their long lives, including Anthony and her closest friend and associate, Stanton.

SEE ALSO: 1866, Suffragists Protest the Fourteenth Amendment; 1868, Fourteenth Amendment; 1869, Rise of Woman Suffrage Associations; 1869, Western States Grant Woman Suffrage; 1874, *Minor v. Happersett*; 1876, Declaration of the Rights of Women; 1890, Women's Rights Associations Unite; 1916, National Woman's Party Is Founded; 1920, League of Women Voters Is Founded; 1920, U.S. Women Gain the Vote.

1873 ■ "CRIME OF 1873": *proponents of free silver charge that the 1873 Coinage Act represents a "gold conspiracy"*

DATE: February 12, 1873
LOCALE: Boston, Massachusetts
CATEGORIES: Economics; Government and politics; Laws and acts
KEY FIGURES:
John Jay Knox (1828-1892), comptroller of the currency
Henry Richard Linderman (1825-1879), special assistant to the comptroller of the currency
William Morris Stewart (1827-1909), senator from Nevada
George M. Weston, secretary of the National Monetary Commission

SUMMARY OF EVENT. The "Crime of 1873" was an emotion-laden slogan first used in 1876 by proponents of the free coinage of silver to express hostility toward the Coinage Act, passed on February 12, 1873, which made gold the sole monetary standard, with no provision for the coining of silver dollars. The money controversy, which the shibboleth "Crime of 1873" dramatized, raged between 1865 and 1896 and can best be understood in the context of the nation's antebellum and Civil War monetary policies.

Until the Civil War, the United States functioned under bimetallism—a monetary system based on silver and gold, supplemented by the notes of its banks. The use of the two kinds of specie as money was deemed desirable because there were insufficient quantities of precious metals for the requirements of trade, commerce, and exchange. Under bimetallism, both silver and gold were acceptable for the payment of debts at a rate fixed by the government. The Currency Act of 1834 established a legal ratio between the two metals of sixteen ounces of silver to one ounce of gold (16:1). Under this "mint ratio," the Treasury was obligated to purchase either metal at the established price.

Bimetallism presented a problem, in that the value of silver and gold fluctuated on the world market in response to changes in supply. New supplies of gold from Russia, Australia, and California during the 1840's, for example, caused gold gradually to decline in value. Therefore, silver was undervalued if priced at the mint ratio of 16:1. As predicted by Gresham's law—that higher-valued money is driven out of circulation by cheaper money—silver coins disappeared from circulation, because silver producers preferred to sell their bullion on the world market, where the price was higher than at the mint. By 1853, the market ratio of silver to gold was 15.4:1. In other words, silver producers needed sixteen ounces of silver to exchange for an ounce of gold at the mint, but only 15.4 ounces on the bullion market. Having been out of circulation for years, silver was reduced by Congress in 1853 to a subsidiary metal. Silver remained scarce and undervalued as coin until the 1870's.

Under great pressure to raise money during the Civil War, the government abandoned the specie standard and passed the Legal Tender Acts of 1862, which authorized the printing of fiat money (greenbacks), unsupported by specie but legally acceptable (legal tender) for all debts except interest on government bonds and excise taxes. During the war, the Treasury circulated more than $450 million in greenbacks, which inflated precipitously by 1864. The use of gold became limited primarily to international trade.

When the war ended, the Treasury began urging a program of deflation leading to the eventual retirement of the greenbacks and a return to a specie standard. Resistance in Congress to this hard-money scheme came from a group of soft-money advocates, who opposed a return to specie but differed among themselves over the issue of inflation. Consequently, the Treasury received authority to retire only small quantities of greenbacks. Some soft-money advocates who favored inflation demanded the printing of more greenbacks to be used for payment of the national debt, a proposal that was written into the Democratic Party platform of 1868. By this time, the money controversy had caused factions to grow in the business community (among farmers, bankers, and manufacturers), in geographical regions, and to some extent in political parties, with soft-money supporters generally showing greater strength in the states west of the Appalachians. However, the Greenbackers suffered serious reverses with the passage of the

Public Credit Act of 1869, which pledged payment of the national debt in gold, and the Resumption Act of 1875, which ordered the redemption of greenbacks with gold by 1879.

In the midst of the greenback controversy, John Jay Knox, comptroller of the currency, aided by special assistant Henry Richard Linderman, former director of the mint at Philadelphia, began preparing a revision of the laws dealing with the mints and coinage. One aspect of their work appeared in the Coinage Act of 1873, which discontinued the coinage of silver dollars. The following year, the *Revised Statutes of the United States* demonetized silver by limiting its legal tender function to debts not more than five dollars. Both laws gave belated recognition to the fact that silver had not circulated since the 1840's. At the time, the legislation disturbed no one, not even the silver miners who preferred to sell on the open market. Indeed, Senator William M. Stewart of the silver state of Nevada, who later used the slogan "Crime of '73," failed to oppose either law.

Even as the legislation was passed, however, new mines were opening in the Western states, augmenting the world supply of silver. The market ratio, 15.9:1 in 1873, climbed to 16.1:1 in 1874, and to 16.6:1 by 1875, or about ninety-six cents in gold. As silver prices dropped, mining interests discovered to their dismay that the Currency Act of 1873 blocked the profitable sale of silver to the mint at 16:1. On March 2, 1876, George M. Weston, secretary of the United States Monetary Commission, charged in a letter to the Boston *Globe* that the demonetization of silver was a conspiracy by the creditor class against the people. Weston's letter, which used the word "crime" for the first time, began the controversy over silver. Other advocates of silver took up the charge, demanding the free coinage of silver. Later, Greenbackers and other inflationists, fighting losing battles against resumption, also began supporting silver.

Agitation for the free coinage of silver continued until 1896, when new gold supplies began inducing the price increases that post-Civil War inflationists had desired. Congress, however, previously had passed legislation permitting limited silver coinage. The Bland-Allison Act of 1878 required the Treasury to buy between two and four million ounces of silver per month at the prevailing market price. According to the Sherman Silver Purchase Act of 1890, four million ounces had to be purchased each month. This legislation demonstrated that those who favored silver had far greater strength than the Greenbackers had a decade earlier.

The conspiracy charge against the Currency Act of 1873, which alleged that British financiers plotted to influence Congress, was rejected by most nineteenth century economists and writers. The issue was raised again in 1960 with the discovery of new evidence that seemed to indicate that Linderman foresaw an increase in silver output and, as a monometallist, allegedly plotted to omit silver coinage from the 1873 legislation. Nevertheless, most modern scholarship continues to reject the conspiracy thesis.

—*Merl E. Reed, updated by Charles H. O'Brien*

ADDITIONAL READING:

Barrett, Don Carlos. *The Greenbacks and Resumption of Specie Payments, 1862-1879*. Cambridge, Mass.: Harvard University Press, 1931. This work, which treats the gold standard almost as a moral issue, is still a useful reference.

Friedman, Milton, and Anna J. Schwartz. *A Monetary History of the United States, 1867-1960*. Princeton, N.J.: Princeton University Press, 1963. This massive study by two economists combines economic analysis with economic history. The first three chapters discuss the greenback and silver controversy.

Hixson, William F. *Triumph of the Bankers: Money and Banking in the Eighteenth and Nineteenth Centuries*. Westport, Conn.: Praeger, 1993. Contends that the dominating theme of U.S. monetary history is a perennial conflict between creditors and debtors. Chapters 20 and 21 deal with monetary policy from 1865 to 1896.

Laughlin, J. Laurence. *The History of Bimetallism in the United States*. 4th ed. New York: Greenwood Press, 1968. One of the more scholarly writers in the nineteenth century on the silver issue, Laughlin was a gold supporter; his work still serves as a useful and necessary reference.

Studenski, Paul. *Financial History of the United States*. New York: McGraw-Hill, 1952. This general work contains four chapters on the Civil War and Reconstruction periods that the general reader should find helpful before undertaking more complex studies, such as those by Unger or Friedman and Schwartz.

Timberlake, Richard H. *Monetary Policy in the United States: An Intellectual and Institutional History*. Chicago: University of Chicago Press, 1993. Discusses the evolution of governmental control of the U.S. monetary and banking system. Chapters 10 through 12 discuss the greenback and silver issues.

Unger, Irwin. *The Greenback Era: A Social and Political History of American Finance, 1865-1879*. Princeton, N.J.: Princeton University Press, 1964. An authoritative treatment of the post-Civil War period. Challenges the view of the era as a struggle between embattled farmers and rising capitalists, arguing that it was far more complex and confused.

Weinstein, Allen. *Prelude to Populism: Origins of the Silver Issue, 1867-1878*. New Haven, Conn.: Yale University Press, 1970. Focuses on the politics and social conflicts involved in the first drive to restore silver as a monetary standard.

SEE ALSO: 1863, National Bank Acts; 1869, Scandals of the Grant Administration; 1892, Birth of the People's Party; 1896, McKinley Is Elected President; 1913, Federal Reserve Act.

1873 ■ MACKENZIE ERA IN CANADA: *in Canada's early years of nationhood, Conservative dominance is temporarily interrupted*

DATE: November 5, 1873-October 9, 1878
LOCALE: Ottawa, Dominion of Canada
CATEGORIES: Canadian history; Government and politics

Hugh Allen (1810-1882), Montreal businessman and financier

Frederick Temple Blackwood, Lord Dufferin (1826-1902), governor general of Canada

Edward Blake (1833-1912), former premier of Ontario, minister of finance, 1875-1877, and later Liberal opposition leader

George Brown (1818-1880), Liberal Party founder

George Étienne Cartier (1814-1873), Quebec politician and political ally of Macdonald

John Alexander Macdonald (1815-1891), prime minister, 1867-1873 and 1878-1891

Alexander Mackenzie (1822-1892), prime minister, 1873-1878

SUMMARY OF EVENT. The year 1873 witnessed a dramatic shift of power in Canadian national politics with the fall of Prime Minister John A. Macdonald's government. Canada had become a self-governing dominion of the British crown in 1867, largely as a result of a cooperative effort by bitter political rivals such as Macdonald (a Conservative) and George Brown (a Reformer), who forged a temporary alliance to gain this end. After Quebec, Ontario, and the Maritime Provinces joined in a federal structure and national parliament, this political unity ultimately gave way to partisan party politics. On one side stood the Reformers and "Clear Grits" who established the Liberal Party. Their opponents, the Conservatives or Tories, were headed by Macdonald, a pragmatic Ontario attorney. As party leader, Macdonald attempted to bridge Canadian ethnic, language, and religious divisions through compromise, concessions, and liberal use of patronage to cement political loyalty. The politically astute and charismatic Macdonald put together a diverse combination of Anglo-Protestants, big business, and conservative Catholic French-Canadian nationalists in a truly national party. In contrast, the Liberals were still largely a regional party, with their strongest base, in rural Ontario, consisting of a loose association of provincial rights advocates linked by distrust of powerful central government.

These advantages allowed Macdonald's party to dominate the early years of Canadian political history. The Conservatives advocated strong central government that could defend national interests in competition with the more powerful United States and secure control of the vast but sparsely populated western region. Macdonald governed by promoting ambitious, expensive megaprojects and pork-barrel legislation to keep his coalition of interests unified, appeal to business supporters, and build an economically viable nation. The prime minister's most grandiose and visionary scheme was the construction of a transcontinental railway to create the dominion stretching from sea to sea. This project would unite the sparsely settled and remote West to the rest of Canada, lay the foundation for future immigration and settlement, and promote exploitation of Western natural resources.

Macdonald's strenuous efforts on behalf of this dream brought his downfall. To induce the lightly populated Pacific coast colony of British Columbia into Confederation in 1871, the prime minister made extravagant, expensive, and impossible commitments to begin building the transcontinental railway in two years and to complete the project by 1881. Growing public dissatisfaction was reflected in the 1872 elections, which saw the Liberals nearly destroy the government's majority. After the election, the Liberals came into possession of damning evidence against their foes. Sir Hugh Allen, the head of one of two business syndicates competing for the lucrative government contract to build the Canadian Pacific line, had given the governing party a bribe of $300,000 to aid in the tough election battle and ensure his being granted the contract. George Étienne Cartier, leader of the party organization in Quebec, and Macdonald himself were directly involved in this affair, known as the Pacific Scandal.

As new evidence and public furor mounted, and Macdonald suffered defection from party ranks, Canada's governor general, Lord Dufferin, finally called upon opposition leader Alexander Mackenzie to form a new government on November 5, 1873. When national parliamentary elections were held, the Conservatives were soundly routed as the Liberals received a commanding parliamentary majority of 138 to 67.

Canada's new prime minister was a stubborn, self-made, highly principled, and moralistic Scottish immigrant. Arriving in Upper Canada in 1842, the former stonemason had established himself as a building contractor. Mackenzie became a supporter of George Brown's Reform Party, a Liberal journalist, and eventually a member of the Legislative Assembly of Canada. In 1867, he won a seat in the first Dominion House of Commons and also assumed leadership of the Liberals when Brown gave up this role.

Mackenzie presented a sharp contrast to the convivial and talented, but hard-drinking and morally flawed, Macdonald. Macdonald's successor was a devout Baptist who exuded Victorian piety, an austere, utilitarian outlook, and great earnestness. His nineteenth century liberalism included egalitarian sentiments and a distrust of entrenched class privilege, monopoly, and unchecked institutional power. He also was an advocate of free trade, individual enterprise, thrifty government, and democratic political reforms.

Although Mackenzie applied himself to the task of governing the nation with great diligence and earnestness, he suffered from a combination of bad luck and some personal shortcomings as a leader. One major difficulty was the task of putting together a strong, cooperative cabinet and turning the Liberal Party into a truly national and cohesive organization. It was hard to find experienced and highly qualified Liberals to fill ministerial positions. Quebec was not strongly represented, and the party remained weak in that province. Because only a few cabinet members, such as Edward Blake and Finance Minister Richard Cartwright, were of outstanding quality, much of the burden of debate in Parliament fell upon the prime minister's shoulders. Mackenzie also experienced problems with prominent colleagues such as Blake, the most capable Liberal politician, who thought he was more qualified to head the party and occasionally undermined Mackenzie's authority.

Power had fallen into Mackenzie's lap at an inopportune moment. After the Panic of 1873, Canada, like the United States, had entered a period of economic slump and depression that would persist intermittently for two decades. This situation, although not of his making, made it difficult for Mackenzie to fulfill Macdonald's overly generous contract with British Columbia regarding the railroad connection. The country now had to settle for piecemeal construction of the line as financial considerations permitted.

Another setback for Mackenzie was his failure to obtain a reciprocity agreement with the United States on the lowering of tariffs and customs duties. When this attempt to benefit some groups with lower prices and expanded markets for Canadian products went for naught, as a result of lack of interest in Washington, D.C., the government was left with no economic policy to offer voters in these hard times other than retrenchment.

In spite of these difficulties, the Mackenzie era produced several sound legislative accomplishments. In an effort to reduce electoral fraud and manipulation, which were common occurrences, the government enacted the secret ballot and provided for elections to be held on the same day. Consumer protection laws were passed. The creation of a Supreme Court and the nation's first military academy enhanced Canadian self-rule and lessened dependence on Great Britain. The North West Mounted Police, created by Macdonald in 1873, became firmly established in the West under the new government. In spite of financial constraints, necessary surveying for the transcontinental railway was completed. Mackenzie also pursued government construction of important and difficult sections of the line when private interests were not forthcoming.

The government's electoral mandate came to an end in 1878, and Mackenzie called a national election for September 17. The prime minister hoped the country would reward his hard efforts and record of relatively honest government. However, the unfavorable economic situation and Macdonald's affable and easy manner with audiences enabled him to rebound from the disgrace of the Pacific Scandal. In contrast to the government's tight-fisted economic policy, he championed a vision of prosperity, security, and economic strength through his national policy of protective tariffs, railroad building, and settlement and development of the West. Mackenzie was stunned as the results of 1873 were reversed, resulting in a Conservative parliamentary landslide. The voting public apparently preferred the personable and eloquent, if scandal-tainted, Macdonald to the scrupulously honest but lackluster and plodding Mackenzie. A bitter and disappointed prime minister resigned office on October 9, bringing the short-lived Mackenzie era to a close. Macdonald's Conservatives resumed their dominance until shortly after the old leader's death in the 1890's.

—*David A. Crain*

ADDITIONAL READING:

Foster, Ben. "Mackenzie, Alexander." In *Dictionary of Canadian Biography, 1891-1900*. Vol. 12. Toronto: University of

Toronto Press, 1990. A concise yet thorough and scholarly biographical overview. Discusses Mackenzie's career, personal character, and experience as head of government. Includes bibliographical essay.

Stanley, G. F. G. "The 1870's." In *The Canadians, 1867-1967*, edited by J. M. S. Careless and R. C. Brown. Toronto: Macmillan of Canada, 1967. Overview of the political issues, events, and personalities of this era by a noted Canadian academic.

Thompson, Dale C. *Alexander Mackenzie, Clear Grit*. Toronto: Macmillian of Canada, 1960. A detailed narrative account that does a good job of depicting Mackenzie's problems with matters such as his cabinet, the ethnic issue, and political reform.

Waite, Peter B. *Canada 1874-1896: Arduous Destiny*. Toronto: McClelland & Stewart, 1971. Chapters 2 through 5 provide a readable and colorful account of Canadian national politics in the 1870's, by a prominent Canadian historian.

SEE ALSO: 1867, British North America Act; 1878, Macdonald Returns as Canada's Prime Minister.

1874 ■ RED RIVER WAR: *the U.S. Army defeats three of the West's most formidable Indian tribes, opening large areas of the Southwest to settlement*

DATE: June, 1874-June, 1875
LOCALE: Texas Panhandle, western Indian Territory (Oklahoma), and northwestern Kansas
CATEGORIES: Native American history; Wars, uprisings, and civil unrest
KEY FIGURES:
Gray Beard (died 1875), Cheyenne war chief
Lone Wolf (c. 1820-c. 1879), leader of the Kiowa war faction
Ranald Slidell Mackenzie (1840-1889), commander, Fourth Cavalry
Nelson Appleton Miles (1839-1925), commander, Fifth Infantry
Quanah Parker (c. 1845-1911), Comanche war chief
Philip Henry Sheridan (1831-1888), commander, Military Division of the Missouri
William Tecumseh Sherman (1820-1891), commanding general, United States Army

SUMMARY OF EVENT. Despite good intentions expressed in the 1867 Medicine Lodge Creek Treaty, the southern Great Plains remained a hotbed of hostile Indian activity, lawlessness, and punitive military action. Kiowa and Comanche bands continued to raid into Texas and Mexico, while southern Cheyenne and Arapaho braves still threatened parts of Kansas, often returning to the protection of reservations. The Army, frustrated by restrictions imposed under President Ulysses S. Grant's Quaker Peace Policy, labored to control the volatile situation.

INDIAN WARS IN THE WEST, 1840'S-1890

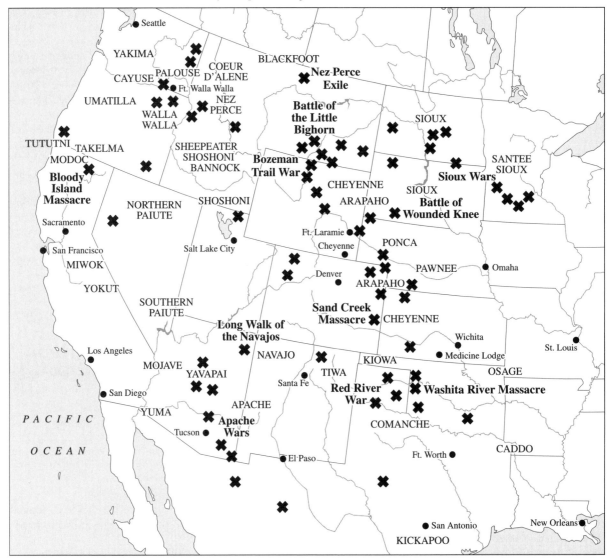

After acquisition of the Oregon Country in 1846 and the Mexican land cessions of 1848 and 1853, white settlers poured into the west, encroaching on ancient Indian lands and disrupting native lifeways by killing buffalo and constructing railroads. Over the next half century, confrontations between white settlers and Native Americans were numerous, as denoted by the x-marked sites above. (Those battles receiving coverage in a separate article in this reference work are also labeled above with the battles' names.)

By 1874, the inadequacies of the reservation system and other outside influences combined to trigger a major tribal uprising. For most members of plains tribes, reservation life and the imposition of Anglo-American values threatened the most basic tenets of their existence, depriving them of freedom, mobility, and dignity. This proved especially problematic for young men, whose status largely depended on demonstrations of bravery in war or prowess on the hunt. Reservation Indians suffered poor food; frequently, promised rations were never delivered. Whiskey traders and horse thieves preyed

on reservations with relative impunity. Most grievous to the American Indians was the wholesale slaughter of the buffalo by hide-hunters and sportsmen who were killing the beasts by the hundreds of thousands, leaving stripped carcasses to litter the prairie. With the arrival of spring, the South Plains erupted in violence, as American Indians left their reservations in large numbers.

On June 27, 1874, several hundred Cheyenne and Comanche warriors attacked a group of twenty-eight buffalo hunters at an old trading post in the Texas Panhandle known as

Adobe Walls. Prominent among the attackers was Quanah Parker, the son of an influential Comanche chief and his captured wife, Cynthia Ann Parker. Despite overwhelming odds, the well-protected buffalo hunters devastated the attackers with high-powered rifles. Although never confirmed, American Indian casualties probably exceeded seventy.

The attack at Adobe Walls signaled the beginning of the Red River War. In July, Lone Wolf's Kiowas assailed a Texas Ranger detachment, Cheyenne warriors struck travel routes in Kansas, and Comanches menaced Texas ranches. As hostile action intensified, the Army received permission to pursue raiders onto previously protected reservations and take offensive action to end the uprising. On July 20, 1874, Commanding General William T. Sherman issued orders initiating a state of war, the prosecution of which fell to Lieutenant General Philip Sheridan, whose massive jurisdiction included the South Plains. Sheridan, like Sherman an advocate of total war, quickly devised the most ambitious campaign yet mounted by the Army against American Indians in the West.

Sheridan's plan called for five independent columns to converge on American Indian camps in the Texas Panhandle, surround them, and punish the Indians to such an extent as to discourage future uprisings. Accordingly, Colonel Nelson Miles marched from Fort Dodge, Kansas, with a large force of cavalry and infantry; Colonel R. S. Mackenzie, with eight companies of cavalry and five infantry companies, moved northward from Fort Concho, Texas; Major William R. Price led a squadron of cavalry eastward from New Mexico; and Lieutenant Colonels John W. Davidson and George P. Buell prepared their commands, comprising several companies of Buffalo Soldiers (African American troopers from the Ninth and Tenth Cavalries), to strike westward from Indian Territory. The total force numbered more than two thousand soldiers and Indian scouts.

In August, Army units moved onto reservations to separate peaceful Indians from the hostile. While almost all Arapahos enrolled as friendly, most Cheyennes refused to submit. Troubles at the Fort Sill agency triggered a confrontation between Davidson's cavalry and a band of Comanches supported by Lone Wolf's Kiowas. Most of these Indians escaped to join hostile factions on the Staked Plains. The Army listed almost five thousand Indians as hostile; of these, roughly twelve hundred were warriors.

A severe drought made water scarce, and late August temperatures reached 110 degrees as Colonel Miles eagerly pushed his men southward. On August 30, near Palo Duro Canyon, the column clashed with Cheyenne warriors, who were soon joined by Kiowas and Comanches. The soldiers prevailed, driving the warriors onto the plains. Miles could not exploit the opportunity, however; supply shortages forced him to retire in search of provisions. The drought gave way to torrential rains and dropping temperatures as Miles linked with Price's column on September 7. Two days later, a band of Kiowas and Comanches assailed a supply train en route to Miles. Following a three-day siege, the American Indians abandoned the effort unrewarded, but the incident complicated the supply crisis.

With Miles temporarily out of action, Mackenzie and his crack Fourth Cavalry Regiment took up the fight. After stockpiling supplies, Mackenzie moved, in miserable conditions, to the rugged canyons of the Caprock escarpment. On September 26, Mackenzie thwarted a Comanche attempt to stampede his horses. Two days later, the crowning achievement of the campaign came as Mackenzie struck a large encampment in Palo Duro Canyon. Following a harrowing descent, wave after wave of cavalry swept across the canyon floor. The soldiers inflicted few casualties but laid waste to the village, burning lodges, badly needed food stocks, and equipment. Mackenzie's troopers completed the devastation by capturing fifteen hundred of the tribe's ponies, a thousand of which the colonel ordered destroyed to prevent their recapture.

Over the next three months, Army units scoured the Texas Panhandle, despite freezing temperatures and intense storms. In November, a detachment from Miles's command destroyed Gray Wolf's Cheyenne camp, recovering Adelaide and Julia German, two of four sisters seized in a Kansas raid. Catherine and Sophia German were released the following spring.

Hungry and demoralized, Indians began to trickle into the reservation by October, but most remained defiant until harsh weather and constant military pressure finally broke their resistance. In late February, 1875, five hundred Kiowas, including Lone Wolf, surrendered. On March 6, eight hundred Cheyennes, among them the elusive Gray Beard, capitulated. In April, sixty Cheyennes bolted from their reservation in an effort to join the Northern Cheyennes; twenty-seven of these, including women and children, were killed by a cavalry detachment at Sappa Creek in northwestern Kansas. On June 2, Quanah Parker and four hundred Comanches—the last organized band—surrendered to Mackenzie at Fort Sill.

After a dubious selection process, seventy-four Indians, ostensibly the leading troublemakers, including Gray Beard and Lone Wolf, were shipped to prison in Florida. Gray Beard was later killed trying to escape; others perished in captivity; but some accepted the benevolent supervision and educational efforts of Lieutenant Richard Pratt. Several Red River War veterans remained with Pratt after their release to assist him in establishing the Carlisle Indian School in 1879.

The Red River War was among the most successful campaigns ever conducted against American Indians. It brought almost complete subjugation to three of the most powerful and revered tribes in North America. It also provided a model for future Army campaigns and boldly confirmed the doctrine of total war. Now less concerned with inflicting casualties, the Army would focus on destroying the American Indians' means and will to resist. Combined with the annihilation of the buffalo, this campaign of eradication made it impossible for American Indians to exist in large numbers outside the reservation. Finally, the campaign's successful completion opened vast areas to white settlement and ranching. —*David Coffey*

ADDITIONAL READING:

Haley, James L. *The Buffalo War: The History of the Red River Indian Uprising of 1874*. Garden City, N.Y.: Doubleday, 1976. Provides substantial background information and military analysis. Maps, illustrations, notes, bibliography, and index.

Hutton, Paul Andrew. *Phil Sheridan and His Army*. Lincoln: University of Nebraska Press, 1985. An expansive study of Sheridan's post-Civil War career, including his role as the Red River War's chief architect. Maps, illustrations, notes, bibliography, and index.

Leckie, William H. *The Buffalo Soldiers: A Narrative of the Negro Cavalry in the West*. Norman: University of Oklahoma Press, 1967. Discusses the considerable role played by African Americans in the frontier Army, devoting an entire chapter to the Red River War. Maps, illustrations, notes, bibliography, and index.

Robinson, Charles M. *Bad Hand: A Biography of General Ranald S. Mackenzie*. Austin, Tex.: State House Press, 1993. A comprehensive study that treats Mackenzie's pivotal role in the Red River War in suitable detail. Maps, illustrations, notes, bibliography, and index.

Utley, Robert M. *Frontier Regulars: The United States Army and the Indian, 1866-1891*. Lincoln: University of Nebraska Press, 1984. An essential study of the frontier Army and the Indian Wars. Includes a chapter on the Red River War and a wealth of other pertinent information. Maps, illustrations, notes, bibliography, and index.

_____. *The Indian Frontier of the American West, 1846-1890*. Albuquerque: University of New Mexico Press, 1984. This authoritative treatment of cultures in conflict includes a discussion of the causes and effects of the Red River War. Maps, illustrations, notes, bibliography, and index.

Wooster, Robert. *Nelson A. Miles and the Twilight of the Frontier Army*. Lincoln: University of Nebraska Press, 1993. Includes a chapter on the controversial soldier's extensive Red River War operations.

SEE ALSO: 1861, Apache Wars; 1862, Great Sioux War; 1863, Long Walk of the Navajos; 1864, Sand Creek Massacre; 1866, Bozeman Trail War; 1867, Medicine Lodge Creek Treaty; 1868, Washita River Massacre; 1871, Indian Appropriation Act; 1872, Great American Bison Slaughter; 1876, Battle of the Little Bighorn; 1887, General Allotment Act; 1890, Closing of the Frontier; 1890, Battle of Wounded Knee.

1874 ■ MINOR V. HAPPERSETT: *the Supreme Court holds that a state can constitutionally forbid a woman to vote, despite her U.S. citizenship*

DATE: October, 1874
LOCALE: Washington, D.C.
CATEGORIES: Civil rights; Court cases; Women's issues

KEY FIGURES:

Susan B. Anthony (1820-1906), U.S. suffragist
Horace Bushnell (1802-1876), author of a book against woman's right to vote
Tennessee Celeste Claflin (1845-1923), author of a polemic in favor of woman's right to vote and sister of Victoria Woodhull
Ralph Waldo Emerson (1803-1882), noted essayist supporting woman's right to vote
Reese Happersett, registrar who refused Virginia Minor permission to register to vote
Virginia Minor (1824-1894), suffragist who brought suit to establish woman's constitutional right to vote
Elizabeth Cady Stanton (1815-1902), U.S. suffragist
Victoria Woodhull (1838-1927), radical suffragist and member of the National Party

SUMMARY OF EVENT. Even before the concerted effort for woman's suffrage in the nineteenth and early twentieth centuries, American women had exercised the right to vote. In January, 1648, Margaret Brent had petitioned the Maryland assembly for permission to vote in their proceedings, and the assembly agreed. The governor of Maryland vetoed the decision, and Brent lodged an official protest. In the same decade, in Rhode Island and New York, women participated in community affairs by voting. In 1776, in New Jersey, all references to gender were omitted from suffrage statutes. During the first fourteen years after the laws were passed, women did not vote, thinking that the laws referred only to men. By 1800, women were voting throughout New Jersey. A legislature composed of all-white, all-male members voted to change the New Jersey law in 1807 so as to include only white, male voters, with the strange argument that allowing women to vote produced a substantial amount of fraud.

During the first half of the nineteenth century, some U.S. women joined with the abolitionist movement in an attempt to blend their search for legal rights for themselves with rights for the slaves. At the time, these women were more concerned with obtaining rights to own property and to enter into contracts than with the right to vote. At these women's first convention in Seneca Falls, New York, in 1848, Elizabeth Cady Stanton did mention as part of the platform that women should have the right to vote, but this right did not become of paramount concern until after the Civil War. At that time, when the slaves were freed and all men were given the right to vote, women were shocked to discover that in spite of all the work that they had done on behalf of the slaves, they had been denied that right. The right to vote thus became the central issue to concerned women for the next seventy years.

Woman's right to vote was an issue that divided the country along race, gender, religious, and political grounds. Among the many men opposed to granting women the right to vote was Horace Bushnell, who wrote *Women's Suffrage; The Reform Against Nature* (1869). In this tract, he argued a traditional nineteenth century position that men and women live in separate spheres, public and private. Men inhabited the public sphere, women, the private. If women entered into the public sphere, the moral nature of current life would be jeopardized. He asserted that it was historic fact, extending back to biblical times, that women were unsuited to any role in the government of countries. Last, he argued that granting suffrage to women would have a negative effect upon married life. Because the man was the accepted head of the household at that time, to grant women the right to vote might threaten this arrangement. Such thinking exemplified that of many men who opposed woman suffrage.

Ralph Waldo Emerson, a noted nineteenth century essayist, disagreed with such thinking. He believed that because all humans are fallible and biased about something, granting women the right to vote would only be correcting the biases. He believed that if one brought together all of the various opinions existing in the country, such a franchise would produce something better.

There were two parties that women could join in their fight for suffrage. One, the American Party, remained a single-issue party. The other, the Nationals, opened itself to other issues, so as to attract wider membership. Among the people it attracted were the sisters Victoria Woodhull and Lady Tennessee Claflin. Woodhull advocated women's rights, in addition to free love, spiritualism, and faith healing, and argued before Congress that women already had the right to vote under the privileges and immunities clause of the Fourteenth Amendment to the Constitution. Claflin wrote a treatise in support of women's suffrage, *Constitutional Equality*. She argued that women and men should not exist in separate spheres, and that if it were feared that the entrance into politics would corrupt women, it was time that women entered into, discovered, and exposed what was so corrupting about politics. She also argued that men's refusal to relinquish their current claims to dominance over women was selfishness on their part.

For a time, both parties published newspapers. In 1869, *The Revolution*, the newspaper of the Nationals, published a set of resolutions that stated, as Woodhull had declared before Congress, that the Constitution already conferred the right to vote upon women because of the privileges and immunities clause. Francis Minor, an attorney from St. Louis, Missouri, wrote the resolution. His wife, Virginia, was president of the Missouri Woman Suffrage Association. When Virginia Minor was turned away from the polls by registrar Reese Happersett in November, 1872, she and Francis, who was required to participate in any legal action his wife might bring, petitioned the courts of St. Louis for damages in the amount of ten thousand dollars.

At the same time that the Minor suit was making its way through the courts, other suffragists were challenging the law. In 1871 and 1872, one hundred fifty women tried to vote in various states throughout the country. Among these was Susan Brownell Anthony, who headed a group of sixteen women in Rochester, New York, in first registering and then voting in the presidential election of 1872. The women did this knowing that they risked being fined up to three hundred dollars and

imprisoned for up to three years. Anthony was not allowed to testify at her trial and was denied the right to a genuine decision by the jury when the judge directed the jury to return a guilty verdict. After the jury returned the verdict, the judge refused to commit Anthony to jail. She therefore lost the right she would have had to appeal her case to the Supreme Court.

The Supreme Court, however, did hear the *Minor* case. It summarily rejected the couple's claims under the Fourteenth Amendment's privileges and immunities clause. The Court held that Mrs. Minor, like all women, was a citizen of the United States, but it dismissed her additional claim that citizenship conveyed upon her the right to vote. This right was not intended as part of the privileges and immunities clause in the Constitution, according to the Court's decision.

The opinion ignored the social factors that were at the root of arguments over whether women should have the vote. These factors, as expressed by Bushnell, Emerson, and Claflin, for example, continued to disturb the country after the *Minor* case was decided and until women achieved suffrage in 1920. The *Minor* case merely indicated to those who were determined to obtain woman suffrage how far they had to go before achieving that right. —*Jennifer Eastman*

ADDITIONAL READING:

Agonito, Rosemary. "Ralph Waldo Emerson." In *History of Ideas on Woman: A Source Book*. New York: G. P. Putnam's Sons, 1977. Emerson, a firm suffragist, believed that the right to vote for women was an inevitable and positive change in society.

Bushnell, Horace. *Women's Suffrage; The Reform Against Nature*. New York: C. Scribner, 1869. Opposes woman suffrage on the grounds that it would undermine women's natural and moral position in society, that is, the private sphere of domesticity.

Claflin, Tennessee C. *Constitutional Equality: A Right of Woman*. New York: Woodhull, Claflin & Co., 1871. This early feminist tract expounded on woman's right to equality and to vote in a world where men and women would share the same life, if men would allow it.

Flexner, Eleanor. *Century of Struggle: The Woman's Rights Movement in the United States*. Cambridge, Mass.: The Belknap Press of Harvard University Press, 1959. A comprehensive study of the women's movements of the nineteenth and early twentieth century, which places the struggle for woman suffrage in a historical context.

Frost-Knappman, Elizabeth, and Kathryn Cullen-DuPont. *Women's Suffrage in America: An Eyewitness History*. New York: Facts On File, 1992. Contains many primary sources concerning woman suffrage, including the *Minor* petition to the lower courts and the later opinion in the *Minor* case by the Supreme Court.

Goldstein, Leslie Friedman. *The Constitutional Rights of Women: Cases in Law and Social Change*. Rev. ed. Madison: University of Wisconsin Press, 1988. Includes little-known commentary on woman suffrage, as well as the Supreme Court opinion in the *Minor* case.

SEE ALSO: 1848, Seneca Falls Convention; 1851, Akron Woman's Rights Convention; 1866, Suffragists Protest the Fourteenth Amendment; 1869, Rise of Woman Suffrage Associations; 1869, Western States Grant Woman Suffrage; 1872, Susan B. Anthony Is Arrested; 1876, Declaration of the Rights of Women; 1890, Women's Rights Associations Unite; 1916, National Woman's Party Is Founded; 1920, League of Women Voters Is Founded; 1920, U.S. Women Gain the Vote.

1875 ■ SUPREME COURT OF CANADA IS ESTABLISHED: *Canada begins to define its judicial independence from Great Britain*

DATE: 1875

LOCALE: Ottawa, Canada

CATEGORIES: Canadian history; Organizations and institutions

KEY FIGURES:

Edward Blake (1833-1912), minister of justice responsible for establishing the Supreme Court

John Alexander Macdonald (1815-1891), advocate of legislative union between Canada and Great Britain and Canada's first prime minister

Alexander Mackenzie (1822-1892), prime minister of Canada, 1873-1878, and leader of the Liberal Party

Oliver Mowat (1820-1903), premier of Ontario

SUMMARY OF EVENT. The Supreme Court of Canada has been the highest court for all legal issues of federal and provincial jurisdiction since 1949. Prior to that, the Judicial Committee of Great Britain's Privy Council was the highest appellate court. The authority of the Judicial Committee rested both on British statute and on royal prerogative. In 1875, Parliament passed a statute, under the Constitution Act of 1867 (formerly called the British North America Act), which established a Supreme Court of Canada. This caused sharp debate among the founders of the Confederation. Specifically, John A. Macdonald argued that the Constitution did not anticipate the creation of such a court.

Many Liberals and Conservatives alike opposed a Supreme Court, fearing the possible consequences for provincial rights. By establishing the Supreme Court, Parliament would be providing itself with a constitutional interpreter. The impartiality of such an interpreter was questioned because the federal government would appoint its members and determine the Court's field of competency.

The Liberal government of Alexander Mackenzie finally persuaded Parliament to vote in favor of a Supreme Court. It argued both the need for standardized Canadian law and the need to provide constitutional interpretation on issues that would affect the evolution of the new federation. An unsuccessful attempt was made by Canadian minister of justice Edward Blake to abolish appeals to the Judicial Committee when the Supreme Court was established. However, the Supreme Court remained bound by the decisions of the Judicial Committee of the Privy Council until 1949.

Appeals in criminal cases were abolished in 1888, a limitation that existed until 1926, when it was held invalid. The Statute of Westminster (1931) gave Canada the authority to reenact this regulation. Arguments against appeals to the Judicial Committee rested on claims that it was demeaning for Canada to be forced to go outside her country for final judicial decisions, that the Privy Council was ill-equipped to consider problems of Canadian federalism, and that the Judicial Committee had misinterpreted the British North America Act in many of its more than 170 judgments.

World War II caused a delay in the move toward completely ending appeals to the Judicial Committee of the Privy Council. In 1949, however, an amendment to the Supreme Court Act transferred ultimate appellate jurisdiction to Canada.

Although the Supreme Court frequently refers to the judgment of the Judicial Committee, it is no longer legally bound to follow those decisions. This allows the Supreme Court greater creativity and flexibility in decision making. On the other hand, it can prove problematic in constitutional matters, given the difficulties that may arise from a disregard for the federalist principles that were firmly established by the Judicial Committee.

The Supreme Court of Canada comprises a chief justice and eight junior justices appointed by the governor-in-council. Members may be selected from among provincial superior court judges or from among those barristers and advocates who have been members of a provincial bar for at least ten years. The Supreme Court Act stipulates that at least three of the judges be appointed from Quebec. Traditionally, three other judges are from Ontario, one from the Maritime Provinces, and two from the western provinces.

Under the Supreme Court Act, the Supreme Court of Canada not only pronounces judgment and advises federal and provincial governments on questions of law and of fact concerning constitutional interpretation, but also is the general court of appeal for criminal cases. The Supreme Court can choose the cases it will hear, with one major exception, called the "reference case." The Court is required to consider and advise on questions referred to it by the federal cabinet or by any provincial cabinet, on any matter that directly concerns the interpretation of the Constitution. This device permits a speedy answer to doubtful constitutional questions without the need to wait until an actual dispute arises. This phenomenon is unique to Canada.

While scholars tend to view the decision of British judges as having a provincial-rights basis, the Supreme Court of Canada strikes most observers as staunchly federalist. In the past, the Supreme Court interpreted the Constitution very liberally, whereas the Judicial Committee of the Privy Council had taken sociopolitical considerations into account in its decision making. The Judicial Committee tended to favor the provinces, and the Supreme Court was, and still is, centralist in nature. The Judicial Committee was more political than juridical, whereas the Supreme Court, until the late twentieth century, strictly adhered to legal interpretations.

The written Constitution has, in the language of politicians, a people's package with a comprehensive list of rights, known as the Canadian Bill of Rights of 1960. This Bill of Rights applied only to federal jurisdictions because the requisite provincial consent was not obtained to make it applicable at the provincial level. It recognizes the rights of individuals to life, liberty, personal security, and enjoyment (not "possession," which is provincial) of property. It protects rights of equality before the law and ensures protection of the law. It protects freedom of religion, speech, assembly, association, and press, as well as legal rights, such as the right to counsel and to a fair hearing. To the extent that it is not superseded by the 1982 Canadian Charter of Rights and Freedoms, the 1960 Bill of Rights remains in effect.

The controversial question of whether the Court must interpret the law and the Constitution in a liberal, textual sense or consider as well social, economic, and political factors continues to be an important issue, especially because of the patriation of the Constitution with its Charter of Rights and Freedoms. The Charter will be whatever the Supreme Court deems it to be, and only a constitutional amendment approved by Parliament and seven provinces, totaling at least 50 percent of the population of all the provinces, may alter a Supreme Court decision.

By a decision in November of 1969, the Supreme Court of Canada put itself in a position to play a new and enlarged role in Canada's political life. In the *Drybones* decision, the Supreme Court rendered inoperative a provision of the Indian Act, basing its judgment on the "equality before the law" clause of the Canadian Bill of Rights. The Court ruled that, if a federal statute cannot be reasonably interpreted and applied without abolishing, limiting, or infringing upon one of the rights or liberties recognized in the Bill of Rights, it is inoperative unless Parliament expressly declares that is is to apply notwithstanding the Bill of Rights. The Court concluded that J. Drybones, who had been found drunk off reserve land in a lobby of a hotel, had been punished because of race under a law whose scope and penalty differ from that for other Canadians.

—*Susan M. Taylor*

ADDITIONAL READING:

Brebner, John Bartlet. *Canada: A Modern History.* Ann Arbor: University of Michigan Press, 1970. Presents the story of Canada's development, written primarily for non-Canadians.

Callwood, June. *Portrait of Canada.* Garden City, N.Y.: Doubleday, 1981. Discusses Canada's economy, constitution, and relationships with Great Britain, France, and the United States.

Creighton, Donald. *Canada's First Century: 1867-1967.* New York: St. Martin's Press, 1970. A comprehensive account of political events and contrasts between the economic growth and erosion of the fundamental national institutions.

_____. *Dominion of the North: A History of Canada.* Toronto: Macmillan of Canada, 1957. Discusses events from the founding of New France through World War II.

Hart, Marjolein C. 't. *The Making of a Bourgeois State: War, Politics, and Finance During the Dutch Revolt.* Manchester, N.Y.: Manchester University Press, 1993. Examines the wars of independence and provides background to the establishment of the Court.

Watkins, Mel. *Canada.* New York: Facts On File, 1993. A thorough overview of Canada, including its judicial system.

SEE ALSO: 1867, British North America Act; 1873, Mackenzie Era in Canada; 1878, Macdonald Returns as Canada's Prime Minister; 1931, Statute of Westminster; 1994, U.S.-North Korea Pact.

1875 ■ PAGE LAW: *designed to prohibit Chinese contract workers and prostitutes from entering the United States, the law eventually excludes Asian women in general*

DATE: February 10, 1875
LOCALE: Washington, D.C.
CATEGORIES: Asian American history; Women's issues
KEY FIGURES:
David Bailey (born c. 1813), U.S. consul general in Hong Kong
H. Sheldon Loring (born 1824), U.S. consul general in Hong Kong after Bailey
John S. Mosby (1833-1916), U.S. consul general in Hong Kong after Loring
Horace F. Page (1833-1890), California congressman

SUMMARY OF EVENT. On February 10, 1875, California congressman Horace F. Page introduced federal legislation designed to prohibit the immigration of Asian female prostitutes into the United States. Officially titled, "An Act Supplementary to the Acts in Relation to Immigration," the Page law evolved into a restriction against vast numbers of Chinese immigrants into the country regardless of whether they were prostitutes. Any person convicted of importing Chinese prostitutes was subject to a maximum prison term of five years and a fine of not more than five thousand dollars. An amendment to the law prohibited individuals from engaging in the "coolie trade": the importation of all illegal Chinese contract laborers. Punishment for this type of violation, however, was much less severe and was much more difficult to effect, given the large numbers of Asian male immigrants at the time. As a consequence of this division of penalties, the law was applied in a most gender-specific manner, effectively deterring the immigration of Asian females into the United States. Within seven years following the implementation of the law, the average number of Chinese female immigrants dropped to one-third of its previous level.

An elaborate bureaucratic network established to carry out the Page law's gender-specific exclusions was a catalyst for the decline in Chinese immigration rates. American consulate offi-

Unionized white workers claimed that Chinese were taking their jobs from them. Measures such as the Page law and, in 1882, the Chinese Exclusion Act were designed to restrict immigration on the basis of nationality. Such political cartoons as this one—appearing in San Francisco, where anti-Chinese sentiment was most intense—depicted Chinese men as evil-looking and brutish. (Asian American Studies Library, University of California at Berkeley)

cials supported by American, Chinese, and British commercial, political, and medical services made up the law's implementation structure. Through intelligence gathering, interrogation, and physical examinations of applicants, the consulate hierarchy ferreted out undesirable applicants for emigration and those suspected of engaging in illegal human trafficking.

This investigative activity evolved well beyond the original intent of the law's authors. Any characteristic or activity that could be linked, even in the most remote sense, to prostitution became grounds for denial to emigrate. Most applications to emigrate came from women from the lower economic strata of society; low economic status therefore became a reason for immigration exclusion. The procedure was a complicated one. Many roadblocks were placed in the way of prospective immigrants. Acquiring permission to emigrate took much time and effort. Passing stringent physical examinations performed by biased health care officials was often impossible. Navigating language barriers through official interviews aimed at evaluating personal character often produced an atmosphere of rigid interrogation, bringing subsequent denial of the right to emigrate. Such a complex system aimed at uncovering fraudulent immigrants placed a hardship upon those wishing to leave China.

Because Hong Kong was the main point of departure for Chinese emigrating to the United States, all required examinations were performed there with a hierarchy of American consulate officials determining immigrant eligibility. In a sense, the Page law actually expanded consulate authority beyond any previous level. Such increased power of the consular general in implementing the law provided an opportunity for possible abuses of power. In 1878, the U.S. consul general in Hong Kong, John Mosby, accused his predecessors of corruption and bribery. According to Mosby, David Bailey and H. Sheldon Loring were guilty of embezzlement. Both men were accused of setting up such an intricate system to process immigration application that bribery soon became the natural way to obtain the necessary permission to do so. Mosby went on to charge that Bailey had amassed thousands of dollars of extra income by regularly charging additional examination fees regardless of whether an exam was performed. Mosby also accused Bailey of falsifying test results and encouraging medical personnel to interrogate applicants in order to deny immigration permission to otherwise legal immigrants.

Most of the allegations of corruption surrounded the fact that monies allotted by the federal government for implementation of the Page law were far below the amount Bailey required to run his administration of it. Given this scenario, the U.S. government scrutinized Bailey's conduct. No indictments came from the official investigation, however, and Bailey, who had previously been promoted to vice consul general in Shanghai, remained in that position. Further examination of Bailey's tenure in Hong Kong has suggested that, if anything, he was an overly aggressive official who made emigration of Chinese women to the United States a top priority of his tenure there rather than an opportunity for profit.

Bailey was replaced in Hong Kong by H. Sheldon Loring. Unlike his predecessor, Loring did not enforce the Page law with as much vigor, allowing a slight, yet insignificant increase in the annual numbers of Chinese immigrants. Nevertheless, Loring did enforce the law in an efficient manner, publicly suggesting that any ship owner who engaged in the illegal transport of women would be dealt with to the fullest extent of the law. Even so, Loring was accused of sharing Bailey's enthusiasm for the unofficial expensive design of the immigration procedure. During Loring's tenure, questions about his character began to surface mostly on account of his past relationships with individuals who engaged in questionable business practices in Asia. By the time that Mosby replaced him, such questions had become more than a nuisance. The new U.S. consul to Hong Kong began to describe his predecessor as a dishonest taker of bribes. Once again, the official dynamics of such charges brought forth an official inquiry from Washington. Like the previous investigation of Bailey, however, this investigation produced no official indictment against Loring. The only blemish concerned an additional fee that Loring had instituted for the procuring of an official landing certificate. As there was precedent for such a fee, Loring, like his predecessor, was exonerated of all charges.

Having decided that his predecessors were indeed corrupt, yet unable to prove it, Mosby pursued enforcement of the Page law with relentless occupation. Keeping a posture that was above accusations of corruption, Mosby personally interviewed each applicant for emigration, oversaw the activities between the consulate and the health examiners, and eliminated the additional charges for the landing permits. In the end, the numbers of Chinese immigrants remained similar to those of Loring and below those of Bailey, with the numbers of Chinese female immigrants continuing to decline. Aside from being free from charges of corruption, Mosby's tenure in office was as authoritative and unilaterally considerate as those of his predecessors.

Regardless of the personalities of the consulate officials in charge of implementing the Page law, the results were the same: the number of Chinese who emigrated to the United States decreased dramatically between the 1875 enactment of the law and the enactment of its successor, the Chinese Exclusion Act of 1882. Furthermore, the law's specific application to Chinese women ensured a large imbalance between numbers of male and female immigrants during the period under consideration. In the long run that imbalance negatively affected Asian American families who had settled in the United States. The barriers that the Page law helped to erect against female Chinese immigrants made a strong nuclear family structure within the Asian American community an immigrant dream rather than a reality.

—*Thomas J. Edward Walker and Cynthia Gwynne Yaudes*

ADDITIONAL READING:

Cheng, Lucie, and Edna Bonacich. *Labor Immigration Under Capitalism.* Berkeley: University of California Press,

1984. Examines the development and intent of political movements among immigrants in the United States before World War II.

Foner, Philip, and Daniel Rosenberg. *Racism, Dissent, and Asian Americans from 1850 to the Present.* Westport, Conn.: Greenwood Press, 1993. A documentary history that traces the political and social segregation of immigrants. Indicates the existence of more than one view among whites, blacks, and others not of Asian descent on the position of Asians in the United States. Extensive historiographical essay, index.

Gordon, Charles, and Harry Rosenfield. *Immigration Law and Procedure.* Albany, N.Y.: Banks Publishers, 1959. An excellent history of immigration and emigration law. Covers the period from the 1830's to the 1950's; sectional discussions of European, African, Chicano, and Asian immigrant experiences. Bibliography, index.

Peffer, George Anthony. "Forbidden Families: Emigration Experience of Chinese Women Under the Page Law, 1875-1882." *Journal of American Ethnic History* 6 (Fall, 1986): 28-46. Solidly documented research article showing the relationship between the Page law and engendered immigration of Chinese during the first seven years of its existence.

Tung, William L. *The Chinese in America: 1820-1973.* Dobbs Ferry, N.Y.: Oceana, 1974. Provides chronological and bibliographical references on changing status of Chinese in American society. Contains good primary source materials.

SEE ALSO: 1842, Dorr Rebellion; 1882, Chinese Exclusion Act; 1882, Rise of the Chinese Six Companies; 1892, "New" Immigration; 1892, Yellow Peril Campaign; 1895, Chinese American Citizens Alliance Is Founded.

1876 ■ CANADA'S INDIAN ACT: *the first comprehensive post-Confederation law to establish Canadian policy toward Native Americans*

DATE: 1876
LOCALE: Canada
CATEGORIES: Canadian history; Laws and acts; Native American history
KEY FIGURES:
Jean Chrétien (born 1934), minister of Indian Affairs and Northern Development during the administration of Prime Minister Pierre Trudeau
Jeannette Lavelle (born 1942), Ojibwa woman who fought the enfranchisement provision of the Indian Act
John Alexander Macdonald (1815-1891), first prime minister of the Dominion of Canada
SUMMARY OF EVENT. The British North America Act of 1867, which created the Dominion of Canada, gave the federal government sole jurisdiction in all issues related to Canadian Indians. This long-held British colonial policy had been established initially in recognition that natives treated in an inconsistent and often unscrupulous manner posed a military threat to British colonies. Even after Indians ceased to be an obstacle to British settlement, the policy was continued with the twin goals of protection and the eventual assimilation of the natives.

With the passage of the Act to Amend and Consolidate the Laws Respecting Indians, better known as the Indian Act of 1876, the government of Prime Minister John A. Macdonald continued the policies established during British colonial rule. As Canada's first prime minister, Macdonald's primary aim was nation-building—to which Canadian Indians, particularly those in the newly acquired prairies, presented an obstacle. With regard to the Indian Act, Macdonald was later quoted as saying, "the great aim of our legislation has been to do away with the tribal system and assimilate the Indian people in all respects with the other inhabitants of the Dominion." Consequently, Canadian Indian policy under Macdonald placed less emphasis on protection and more on assimilation. Ironically, the goals worked at cross purposes. Paternalistic efforts to protect natives emphasized the distinctions between them and the Euro-Canadians, therefore discouraging assimilation. The Indian Act was amended nine times between 1914 and 1930. Nearly every change in the act placed greater restrictions on the activities of Native Canadians.

The Indian Act set out a series of reserved lands that were to be laboratories for training Canadian Indians in the ways of the European settlers. The first reserves were established away from areas of white settlement in an effort to protect Indians from the unsavory elements of Euro-Canadian society. When it became clear that this policy hindered assimilation, new reserves were created near towns populated by whites, in the hopes that natives would learn from their Euro-Canadian neighbors. Another element of the Indian Act provided for the establishment of elected band councils. While these had little power, they were meant to supplant traditional native leadership. The act permitted the superintendent general for Indian Affairs or his agent to remove any elected councilor deemed unfit to serve for reasons of "dishonesty, intemperance, or immorality." The natives of British Columbia were forbidden from engaging in potlatches or any other giveaway feasts, in part, because such ceremonies helped to perpetuate traditional leadership roles. This ban on ceremonies was quickly extended beyond the tribes of British Columbia and the Northwest Coast to nearly all expressions of traditional religion and culture. Canadian Indians also were prohibited from consuming alcohol.

In order to protect tribal lands from sale to non-natives, title to those lands was held by the Crown rather than by the tribes. Reserve lands were exempt from property and estate taxes, and income earned on reserves was exempted from taxation. While these provisions have protected Canadian Indian property from seizure, they also have hindered economic development on the reserves. Because Canadian Indians have been unable to mortgage their lands, it often has been difficult for them to raise capital for development projects. Indian agents, who retained power to make nearly all economic decisions with respect to tribal lands, often resorted to harsh measures (such as withholding relief rations) in efforts to force adoption of Euro-Canadian beliefs and practices.

While many of the provisions of the Indian Act were intended to ease Native Canadians into a Euro-Canadian lifestyle, others were purely racist. In British Columbia, for example, natives had been denied the treaty rights and land tenure provisions afforded natives in much of the rest of Canada. In order to prevent court action to secure those rights, the Indian Act was amended to prohibit fund-raising for the purposes of pursuing land claims.

The Indian Act was significantly revised in 1951 to eliminate much of the blatant discrimination resulting from amendments to the 1876 act. Some discrimination remained, however. One onerous aspect of the Indian Act that was retained codified the category "Indian" as a legal rather than a racial or cultural designation and gave the government the legal power to determine who qualified as an Indian. It also provided that a man could surrender Indian status for himself, his wife, and his children in exchange for Canadian citizenship and a plot of land. Very few natives chose to relinquish their Indian status voluntarily, however. An Indian woman who married a non-Indian or a non-status Indian involuntarily surrendered her own Indian status and benefits, and her children were precluded from claiming Indian status. Non-Indian women who married status Indians, however, became status Indians themselves. This provision of the Indian Act was challenged in 1973 by Jeannette Lavelle, an Ojibwa from Manitoulin Island who had lost her Indian status through marriage. Lavelle based her case on Canada's Charter of Rights and Freedoms. Although Lavelle did not prevail in court, her case and others exposed Canada to condemnation by several international human rights organizations and led to the 1985 passage of Bill C-31, which restored to thousands of Native Canadian women (and their children) the Indian status they had lost through marriage to non-Indians.

The issue of Indian status divides native people as well. While many acknowledge that maintaining a legal status distinct from that of other Canadians creates opportunities for discrimination, others believe that they have inherent aboriginal rights that must be recognized. Despite the flaws and failures of the Indian Act, there has been only one serious attempt to discard it. In 1969, Jean Chrétien, minister of the Department of Indian Affairs and Northern Development, proposed a repeal of the Indian Act. This initiative, which became known as the White Paper, proposed eliminating many of the legal distinctions between natives and non-natives and requiring the provinces to provide the same services to Canadian Indians that they provide to other citizens. Fearing that the provinces would be even more likely to discriminate against natives and that the federal government would abandon its responsibilities for native welfare, many native groups fought the White Paper proposals. They were withdrawn in 1971.

—*Pamela R. Stern*

ADDITIONAL READING:
Dickason, Olive Patricia. *Canada's First Nations: A History of Founding Peoples from Earliest Times.* Norman: University of Oklahoma Press, 1992. Contains several lengthy discussions of the policies generated by the Indian Act.

McMillan, Alan D. *Native Peoples and Cultures of Canada: An Anthropological Overview.* Vancouver: Douglas & McIntyre, 1988. Chapter 12 discusses both the Indian Act and issues related to the status of Canadian Indians.

Satzewich, Vic, and Terry Wotherspoon. *First Nations: Race, Class, and Gender Relations.* Scarborough, Ont.: Nelson Canada, 1993. Contains a thoughtful discussion of the impact of the Indian Act on native women in Canada.

Tennant, Paul. *Aboriginal Peoples and Politics: The Indian Land Question in British Columbia, 1849-1989.* Vancouver: University of British Columbia Press, 1990. A thorough discussion of the history of Canadian Indian policy and relations between Canadian Indians and whites in the province of British Columbia. Several sections deal specifically with the Indian Act.

Tobias, John L. "Protection, Civilization, Assimilation: An Outline History of Canada's Indian Policy." In *Sweet Promises: A Reader on Indian-White Relations in Canada*, edited by J. R. Miller. Toronto: University of Toronto Press, 1991. This article, reprinted from the *Western Canadian Journal of Anthropology*, provides a critical overview of legislation and policy making with regard to Canadian Indians.

SEE ALSO: 1867, British North America Act; 1875, Supreme Court of Canada Is Established.

1876 ■ BELL DEMONSTRATES THE TELEPHONE: *a new era begins as long-distance voice communication surpasses the telegraph in popularity*

DATE: March 10, 1876
LOCALE: Boston, Massachusetts
CATEGORIES: Communications; Science and technology
KEY FIGURES:
Alexander Graham Bell (1847-1922), Scottish-born U.S. inventor
Thomas Alva Edison (1847-1931), U.S. inventor
Hermann Ludwig Ferdinand von Helmholtz (1821-1894), German physiologist, physicist, and anatomist
Johann Philipp Reis (1834-1874), German inventor
Thomas Augustus Watson (1854-1934), Bell's laboratory assistant

SUMMARY OF EVENT. The early interest of Alexander Graham Bell was in the teaching of speech to the deaf, an interest that was the direct result of his father's own work in the area and the influence of his mother, who was hearing-impaired. The elder Bell, like his father before him, devoted himself to the mechanics of sound and is regarded as a pioneer teacher of speech to the deaf. Alexander worked with his father in Edinburgh, Scotland, and after emigrating to the United States, first became a teacher at the Boston School for the Deaf and later became a professor of vocal physiology at Boston University. While at Boston, he improved his knowledge of electricity and continued his study, begun before he came to the United States, of the theories of Hermann von Helmholtz, a German physicist concerned with the mechanical production of sound. In the 1850's, Helmholtz had described the method by which the inner ear responds to differences in pitch, and he had shown that sound quality as recognized by the human ear was a product of a number of overtones that were developed from rapid vibrations over the original sound source.

Bell's invention of the telephone stemmed from his conviction that sound-wave vibrations could be converted into electric current, and that at the other end of the circuit, the current could be reconverted into identical sound waves. Thus, he believed, it would be possible to establish communications that would operate at the speed of light.

Prior to Bell's effort, Philipp Reis, working in Frankfurt, Germany, had developed an apparatus he called a telephone, which could alter an electric current through sound power. His device, which was functioning successfully as a laboratory tool after 1860, reproduced audible sounds, but did not transmit speech. His difficulty, apparently, was a failure to understand that a vibratory mechanism was necessary at both the transmitting and receiving ends of the circuit in order to reproduce the human voice.

In 1874, Bell was able to describe to his father an "electric speaking telephone," but he was not then convinced that the human voice was strong enough to produce the necessary undulating electric current. However, as a result of experiments done the next year, he was able to give his laboratory assistant, Thomas A. Watson, the necessary instructions for building an electromagnetic transmitter and receiver. On March 10, 1876, the first voice communication was made by means of impulses transmitted through wires when Bell, as a result of a laboratory accident, called out to his assistant, "Mr. Watson, please come here. I want you." Watson was on another floor of the building with the receiving apparatus, and distinctly heard this utterance. Bell's success after many experiments in what he called "telephony" came shortly after he began using a liquid transmitter; this discovery secured for Bell full credit for the development of the telephone. He had received a United States patent for his invention just a few days before.

Public demonstrations of the telephone soon followed. The most significant of these took place in June, at the Centennial Exposition in Philadelphia. The telephone was hardly a perfect instrument. For one thing, the liquid transmitter delivered only a feeble electric current and made the instrument cumbersome and sensitive to motion. Even so, it was the most remarkable of all the exhibits at the 1876 exposition. Bell himself demonstrated the device, to the delight of those present, including the Brazilian emperor, Pedro II, who exclaimed when he heard Bell's voice in the receiver: "It talks!" This statement found its way into numerous newspaper headlines, and talk of Bell's invention soon spread throughout the scientific community as well. Back in Boston, Bell and Watson succeeded in holding the first telephone conversation in October of the same year.

Improvements in Bell's early instrument were soon forthcoming; perhaps the most important of those made almost immediately was the carbon granule transmitter credited to Thomas A. Edison. This device transmitted electricity by compressing or expanding the fluctuating air vibrations set up by sound. Once Bell began demonstrating the telephone's ability to carry conversations over telegraph wires, a greater interest in the telephone as a practical means of communication followed. Technical improvements in the telephone led to its commercial development. The first telephone line was installed in 1877. It soon was possible to realize Bell's 1878 prediction that he foresaw the day when a grand system of connecting lines would be established so the people not only could communicate with one another in the same city, but also could communicate over long distances through central receiving and transmitting stations. The direct result of Bell's foresight was the establishment, within about ten years, of the framework of the twentieth century Bell Telephone system.

Although Bell's imagination and scientific understanding led him to further innovations in the years following the invention of the telephone, none were to achieve commercial success. Not long after he invented the telephone, Bell rededicated his energies to his lifelong project of educating the deaf. He began a school for the deaf in Washington, D.C., formed a national society to promote the learning of speech by the hearing-impaired, and was influential in increasing public funding for deaf education in several states. The world, though, chiefly remembers Bell for the remarkable device he made when he was only twenty-nine years of age. On the day of his burial in Scotland, in 1922, telephone service was brought to a halt for one minute in the United States in honor of Bell and his contribution to technology.

—Robert F. Erickson, updated by Diane P. Michelfelder

ADDITIONAL READING:

Bruce, Robert B. *Bell: Alexander Graham Bell and the Conquest of Solitude*. Boston: Little, Brown, 1973. The definitive biography of Bell. Thorough, engaging, and provides a clear, detailed look into the scientific and practical struggles associated with the development of the telephone.

Du Moncel, Theodore. *The Telephone, the Microphone, and the Phonograph*. 1879. Reprint. New York: Arno Press, 1974. Traces the history of the invention of the telephone, with special emphasis on the scientific knowledge involved in its development.

Fischer, Claude S. *America Calling: A Social History of the Telephone to 1940*. Berkeley: University of California Press, 1992. A comprehensive account of the history of the commercial development of the telephone in the United States. Discusses the role of the telephone in changing U.S. social life.

MacKenzie, Catherine. *Alexander Graham Bell: The Man*

Who Contracted Space. Boston: Houghton Mifflin, 1928. An early biography of Bell, based in part on Bell's own recollections of his struggle to invent the telephone, as told to the author.

Ronell, Avital. *The Telephone Book: Technology, Schizophrenia, Electric Speech.* Lincoln: University of Nebraska Press, 1989. The history and significance of the telephone considered from a variety of perspectives, including philosophy, history, literature, and psychoanalysis. Challenging, but valuable for its efforts to connect Bell's interest in deaf communications with his interest in the telephone.

Watson, Thomas A. *Exploring Life.* New York: D. Appleton, 1926. This autobiography of Bell's laboratory assistant provides a vivid account of the invention of the telephone and of the personality of its inventor.

SEE ALSO: 1844, First Telegraph Message; 1858, First Transatlantic Cable; 1861, Transcontinental Telegraph Is Completed; 1879, Edison Demonstrates the Incandescent Lamp; 1900, Teletype Is Developed.

1876 ■ BATTLE OF THE LITTLE BIGHORN: *the end of the Sioux wars marks the destruction of traditional Sioux lifeways*

DATE: June 25, 1876

LOCALE: Southeastern Montana

CATEGORIES: Native American history; Wars, uprisings, and civil unrest

KEY FIGURES:

Frederick W. Benteen (1834-1898), commander of a force at Little Bighorn

George Crook (1828-1890), commander of troops marching from Fort Fetterman

George Armstrong Custer (1839-1876), commander of Seventh Cavalry at Little Bighorn

John Gibbon (1827-1896), commander of troops marching from Fort Ellis

Marcus A. Reno (1835-1889), commander of a force at Little Bighorn

Joseph J. Reynolds (1822-1899), commander of attack at Powder River

Sitting Bull (c. 1831-1890),

Crazy Horse (c. 1841-1877), and

Gall (c. 1840-1894), Sioux leaders at Little Bighorn

Alfred H. Terry (1827-1890), commander of troops marching from Fort Abraham Lincoln

SUMMARY OF EVENT. In 1875, the Sioux—a confederation of seven Native American tribes—had many grievances against the United States. Conditions on their reservations were deplorable, chiefly because of maladministration by the Bureau of Indian Affairs. Supplies promised to the Indians by treaty were inadequate, consisting chiefly of shoddy blankets and food unfit for human consumption. This situation caused many Native Americans to leave their reservations, which resulted in confrontations with miners, cattlemen, and settlers.

The Black Hills gold rush goaded the Sioux into rebellion. The first prospectors invading this area, considered a holy land by the Sioux, had been evicted but were determined to return. When General William T. Sherman ordered Lieutenant Colonel George A. Custer to lead an expedition into the Black Hills in 1874 and report on conditions, a considerable number of gold seekers accompanied Custer's men. The Indian Office tried to purchase Sioux lands and open hunting rights along the Platte River. When negotiations broke down, the area was opened to any miner who wished to enter at his own risk.

By 1875, the Black Hills were overrun with prospectors. Knowing that many young warriors, eager to fight, were leaving their reservations, officials from the Department of the Interior ordered all Sioux to return to their reservations by January 31, 1876, despite prior treaties that permitted the Sioux to hunt on the northern plains. Sioux leaders Sitting Bull (a Hunkpapa), Crazy Horse (an Oglala), and Gall (a Hunkpapa) ignored the order and established an encampment on the Little Bighorn River to the west, which included large numbers of Sioux and Cheyenne followers. The Department of the Interior, viewing these actions as hostile, turned the entire situation over to the United States Army.

Plans were made for a punitive expedition against the Sioux. Troops were to converge upon the enemy in the Bighorn country from three directions: General George Crook was to move northward from Fort Fetterman, located on the North Platte River in Wyoming; Colonel John Gibbon was to march east from Fort Ellis, Montana; and a third column was to head west from Fort Abraham Lincoln at Bismarck, North Dakota, under General Alfred H. Terry, who was to command the campaign. Terry was not eager to undertake the assignment. Custer, in command of the Seventh Cavalry under Terry, had hoped for the command, but he was out of favor with President Ulysses S. Grant. The president had publicly rebuked Custer for testifying at congressional investigations against the secretary of war and the president's brother, who had been engaged in fraudulent Indian trading activities. Aggrieved by this personal attack, Custer sought to regain his prestige by distinguishing himself on the battlefield.

Crook left Fort Fetterman in March, 1876, moving northward toward the rendezvous until he came upon an Indian camp on Powder River that contained about a hundred lodges of Sioux and Cheyenne. Colonel Joseph J. Reynolds, in immediate command of the attack, burned half the village, destroyed much of its food supply and captured its pony herd. Reynolds then unaccountably withdrew his troops from the battle, allowing many Native Americans to escape. When a blizzard developed, the natives reorganized and even regained many of their lost ponies. They then headed eastward to unite with Crazy Horse. The demoralized soldiers returned to Fort Fetterman.

Late in May, Crook moved his force northward a second time and engaged the Sioux on the South Fork of the Rose-

Protesting treaty violations and deplorable conditions on the reservations, Sioux leaders Sitting Bull, Crazy Horse, and Gall established an encampment on the Little Bighorn River in south-eastern Montana in 1876. George Armstrong Custer (above) was defeated and killed in the ensuing battle, but the Sioux victory was short-lived: Relentless pursuit of the Sioux by an enraged U.S. Army ultimately devasted the once great Indian nation. (Library of Congress)

bud River on June 17, 1876. By this time, the Native Americans could no longer tolerate the encroachment of whites. Their anger, coupled with a series of religious dreams of Sitting Bull that depicted a great victory over the white soldiers, fueled their resolve and commitment. One of Sitting Bull's visions during the Sun Dance not only predicted a total victory for the Sioux but also forewarned them not to desecrate the bodies.

The tribal warriors attacked Crook's forces during a mid-morning coffee break. The natives' tactics and tenacious advances astounded and confused Crook's men. Crazy Horse actively participated in the Battle of the Rosebud, while Sitting Bull, whose arms were weakened by his sacrifices of flesh during the Sun Dance, rallied his men and inspired them to action. As a result of the hard-fought battle, Crook's army left the battlefield and he was delayed from joining with Terry and Gibbon. The victorious Native Americans buried their dead and celebrated their triumph for several days. Later they relocated their camp at Greasy Grass (Little Bighorn).

Terry left Fort Abraham Lincoln in May and late in the month joined forces with Gibbon along the Yellowstone River at the mouth of the Powder River. Gibbon reported that his scouts had seen signs of a Native American trail along the Rosebud River. Terry immediately dispatched Custer to follow the natives' path up the Rosebud River. Despite interpretations to the contrary, Custer did not disobey Terry. His standing orders were to engage the enemy in battle when he came in contact with them. Terry had hoped that Custer would not attack until he arrived with the main force, because he wanted time to ascend the river to the Indians' camp and thereby prevent their escape into the Bighorn Mountains. This plan, however, was not realized.

On June 25, 1876, Custer came upon a large encampment of Sioux and Cheyenne spread out along the valley of the Little Bighorn. There were approximately a thousand lodges, containing seven thousand people, of whom two thousand were warriors. Although vastly outnumbered, Custer ordered a charge. Major Marcus A. Reno, leading three troops of cavalry, was sent across the valley floor to attack the natives, while Custer took five troops along the nearby hills in an encircling movement to shut off their retreat. Captain Frederick W. Benteen led three companies to scout the south.

As Reno's troops approached the village, he was met by superior forces, which caused him to dismount and fight on foot. When promised support from Custer did not materialize, Reno retreated to a safer position. Benteen's forces ultimately joined Reno.

Meanwhile, Custer moved along the bluffs overlooking the village. Although there is uncertainty about his exact actions, he attempted to join the attack. However, he was forced to withdraw to higher ground because of overwhelming forces sent against him. The warriors of Sitting Bull, Crazy Horse, and Gall surrounded and killed Custer and his 225 men. Gall later recalled that the battlefield was a dark and gruesome sight and related the effectiveness of the warriors' charges against

Custer's dismounted men. A similar fate would undoubtedly have befallen Reno's command had not General Terry's column arrived.

The Battle of the Little Bighorn, popularly known as "Custer's Last Stand," was a short-lived victory for the Sioux. Despite the destruction of Custer's force, General Terry's campaign, as well as others led by General Nelson A. Miles and Crook, relentlessly pursued the Sioux and Cheyenne. For example, Terry entrapped them in the Tongue River Valley and forced them to surrender and return to the reservation. Crazy Horse was killed at Fort Robinson in 1877. Sitting Bull and his followers escaped to Canada, but starvation forced them to return to the reservation in 1881.

The Native Americans' victory at the Little Bighorn can be attributed to their inspirational leaders, their superior numbers, and their determination to fight. Although Custer must bear major responsibility for the debacle, he was not solely responsible. He certainly underestimated the enemy's numbers and ability to fight. Military attacks on villages usually resulted in the Indians panicking and fleeing, so Custer's orders to attack the village were tactically sound. However, the Indians did not scatter but launched an attack of their own. In addition, Custer's relationship with Reno and Benteen was strained as a result of Custer's inclination to practice favoritism among officers. The Battle of the Little Bighorn had aroused the ire of the United States, as whites sought reasons for the annihilation of Custer's forces. However, the Battle of the Little Bighorn proved ultimately to be a defeat: It ended the freedom and independence that the western Sioux cherished and ushered in the devastating dependence and restraints of the reservation era. —*W. Turrentine Jackson, updated by Sharon K. Wilson and Raymond Wilson*

ADDITIONAL READING:

Carroll, John M., ed. *General Custer and the Battle of the Little Bighorn: The Federal View.* Mattituck, N.J.: J. M. Carroll, 1986. A collection of official documents relating to the battle.

Gray, John S. *Centennial Campaign: The Sioux War of 1876.* Ft. Collins, Colo.: Old Army Press, 1976. Provides the best synthesis of the campaign and battle at Little Bighorn.

Monaghan, Jay. *Custer: The Life of General George Armstrong Custer.* Boston: Little, Brown, 1959. Still the best biography of Custer.

Stewart, Edgar I. *Custer's Luck.* Norman: University of Oklahoma Press, 1955. Explains how Custer's luck in his daring attacks finally ran out at Little Bighorn.

Utley, Robert M. *Cavalier in Buckskin: George Armstrong Custer and the Western Military Frontier.* Norman: University of Oklahoma Press, 1988. Deftly details Custer's complex and contradictory psyche, and analyzes and evaluates his actions at the Little Bighorn.

_____. *The Lance and the Shield: The Life and Times of Sitting Bull.* New York: Henry Holt, 1993. Describes the character of Sitting Bull and his prominent role in the Battle of the Little Bighorn.

SEE ALSO: 1862, Great Sioux War; 1864, Sand Creek Massacre; 1866, Bozeman Trail War; 1872, Great American Bison Slaughter; 1887, General Allotment Act; 1890, Battle of Wounded Knee.

1876 ■ DECLARATION OF THE RIGHTS OF WOMEN: *the National Woman Suffrage Association reminds the United States of its historic obligation to provide equal rights to all citizens*

DATE: July 4, 1876
LOCALE: Philadelphia, Pennsylvania
CATEGORIES: Civil rights; Women's issues
KEY FIGURES:
Susan Brownell Anthony (1820-1906), secretary of the NWSA and editor of the *Revolution*
Matilda Joslyn Gage (1826-1898), vice president of NWSA and contributor to the *Revolution*
Elizabeth Cady Stanton (1815-1902), woman's rights activist, lecturer, and president of the NWSA

SUMMARY OF EVENT. In 1872, a centennial commission was formed to prepare for the 1876 Philadelphia Centennial Exposition. Designed to celebrate one hundred years of U.S. democracy, this exposition would prove to be a monumental and much-publicized affair. More than two hundred buildings were erected, and nearly six million dollars of private, local, state, and federal monies were raised to fund the project.

Although the exposition's organizers reportedly advocated a building for women's exhibits, no funds were allocated. Nevertheless, Elizabeth Duane Gillespie organized the Women's Centennial Committee, whose members sold stock at local bazaars and concerts, raising nearly one hundred thousand dollars to pay for their exhibition. In return, they were promised a display area in the main building of the exposition. Prior to the opening of the centennial, Gillespie's committee was told there was no room available for them. Undaunted, the women raised additional funding to erect a separate women's building. Although the pavilion contained inventions and artwork by women, Elizabeth Cady Stanton, president of the National Woman Suffrage Association (NWSA), opposed the site because it ignored women's challenges to the legal system, particularly those of the suffrage movement.

Determined to represent women's efforts in the suffrage movement, Stanton, Susan B. Anthony, and Matilda Joslyn Gage, as officers of the NWSA, endeavored throughout the centennial's preparations to prepare and issue a declaration of rights for women to counter the scheduled reading of the 1776 Declaration of Independence during the centennial's Fourth of July ceremonies. At the association's headquarters, the officers tirelessly worked sixteen-hour days. In dialogue with Anthony, Stanton and Gage produced the new declaration, including articles of impeachment against the government for its

usurpation of women's rights. Anthony, Stanton, and charter member Lucretia Mott organized a women's convention to be held the same day as the exposition's Fourth of July celebration. Anthony resolved to interrupt the ceremonies at Independence Hall to present a copy of the declaration to Vice President Thomas W. Ferry, who was to officiate the ceremony in President Ulysses S. Grant's absence. Anthony's measure of protest is significant, as a presentation of the Declaration of the Rights of Women ensured that the declaration would be officially recorded as part of the day's events.

Anthony wrote to General Joseph R. Hawley, president of the centennial commission, requesting seats on the platform for NWSA officers in order to show women's representation at the event. Hawley declined. Anthony then secured five press passes from her brother's Kansas newspaper, *The Leavenworth Times*. Noting that the program was to host a visiting party of foreign dignitaries and unwilling to disrupt the scheduled event but adamant about women's representation, Stanton wrote Hawley requesting permission to silently present the women's protest and bill of rights after the reading of the Declaration of Independence. Hawley, fearing the women's declaration would supersede the day's activities, declined the association's second request. Stanton, reportedly angry at the rebuff, refused to participate in Anthony's gesture of protest, choosing instead to wait with Lucretia Mott at the First Unitarian Church, the site of the scheduled convention.

Anthony, Gage, and three officers of the NWSA, Sara Andrews Spencer, Lillie Devereux Blake, and Phoebe W. Couzins, entered Independence Hall armed with press passes and an elaborate roll of parchment that housed the declaration, signed by thirty-one of the most prominent advocates of the suffrage movement. Richard Henry Lee of Virginia was scheduled to read the declaration of 1776, and it was determined that the close of the reading was the appropriate moment for presenting the women's declaration. After Lee's delivery, a hymn was played, muffling the women's approach. Marching to the speaker's stand, the women advanced upon the startled chairman; the foreign dignitaries and military officers before the podium moved to permit the women's arrival. Anthony then presented the declaration to Vice President Ferry, thereby officially registering the document as part of the day's proceedings. Ferry, it is recorded, accepted the declaration without a word and turned pale. The women quickly exited to the musicians' platform on the other side of Independence Hall, handing copies to the outstretched hands of the male audience, while Hawley shouted out "Order, order!" to the cries of the crowd. Foregrounding Washington's statue and the Liberty Bell, Anthony, shaded with an umbrella held by Gage, read to an enthusiastic crowd the NWSA's Declaration of the Rights of Women on July 4, 1876. Stanton was able to envision the latent symbolism of this act, noting with irony that in the same hour, on opposite sides of Independence Hall, men and women expressed their disparate opinions of democracy and its effects.

After receiving an ovation from the assembled crowd, the

association's officers again distributed copies of the document and headed for the convention that was slated to begin at noon. There, in the historic First Unitarian Church, the document was again delivered before a large crowd, this time by Stanton. The reading was followed by speeches regarding various points of the declaration. After five hours, the convention adjourned.

Demystifying the Founding Fathers' documents, which neglected to include women in their rubric of life, liberty, and the pursuit of happiness, the NWSA's declaration revealed men's usurpation of legislative power over women in direct opposition to the principles of democracy. The declaration criticized the introduction of the word "male" into state constitutions, thereby definitively excluding women through terminology and biology; the writ of habeas corpus, which prioritized the marital rights of the husband to the exclusion of the woman's rights; the right to trial by a jury of one's peers, in that the Sixth Amendment did not protect women (the association argued) because women were subject to judges, jurors, and legal counsel who were exclusively men; taxation without representation, given that women were expected to pay taxes but were prohibited from voting; unequal codes for men and women, since (the NWSA argued) the codification of the Bill of Rights enforced unequal laws and punishments according to gender; special legislation for women, because (the association asserted) women's rights had been subject to legislative caprice as laws varied from state to state; representation of women, since by 1876 twenty-four states had been admitted to the Union and not one recognized women's right to self-government; universal manhood suffrage, which the suffrage movement asserted had established a despotism based on biology; and the judiciary of the nation, which opposed the spirit and letter of the Constitution.

Written twenty-eight years after Stanton's Declaration of Sentiments, which ceremoniously opened the first suffrage convention at Seneca Falls in 1848, the 1876 Declaration of the Rights of Women served as a reminder to a nation that was celebrating its achievements over the past century that it still had much to do in the future—grant political enfranchisement to women. —*Michele Mock Murton*

ADDITIONAL READING:

Clinton, Catherine. *The Other Civil War: American Women in the Nineteenth Century*. New York: Hill & Wang, 1984. Details Philadelphia's Centennial Exposition, noting Elizabeth Cady Stanton's opposition to the woman's pavilion because it ignored women's contributions to the legal system.

Griffith, Elisabeth. *In Her Own Right: The Life of Elizabeth Cady Stanton*. New York: Oxford University Press, 1984. Chronicles Stanton's life as a reformer, using her personal correspondence and diary to present additional information regarding the inception of the Declaration of the Rights of Women.

Lutz, Alma. *Created Equal: A Biography of Elizabeth Cady Stanton 1815-1902*. New York: John Day, 1940. Early and insightful biography of Stanton. Provides great detail regard-

ing the Centennial Exposition and the events surrounding the presentation of the women's declaration.

Sherr, Lynn. *Failure Is Impossible: Susan B. Anthony in Her Own Words*. New York: Times Books, 1995. Chronicles, through speeches and letters, Anthony's participation in the NWSA and her crusade for women's rights.

Stanton, Elizabeth Cady. *Eighty Years and More: Reminiscences 1815-1897*. 1898. Introduction by Ellen Carol DuBois. Afterword by Ann D. Gordon. Boston: Northeastern University Press, 1993. Details the motivation behind the creation of the Declaration of the Rights of Women. Unique in that it credits Anthony for her participation in coauthoring the 1876 document.

Stanton, Elizabeth Cady, Susan B. Anthony, and Matilda Joslyn Gage, eds. *History of Woman Suffrage*. Vol. 3. Rochester, N.Y.: Mann, 1886. Chronicles the woman suffrage movement from 1840 to 1885. Offers first-person accounts of the events surrounding the conception and delivery of the Declaration of the Rights of Women. Includes the document in its entirety and newspaper accounts of the event.

SEE ALSO: 1866, Suffragists Protest the Fourteenth Amendment; 1868, Fourteenth Amendment; 1869, Rise of Woman Suffrage Associations; 1869, Western States Grant Woman Suffrage; 1872, Susan B. Anthony Is Arrested; 1874, *Minor v. Happersett*; 1890, Women's Rights Associations Unite; 1916, National Woman's Party Is Founded; 1920, League of Women Voters Is Founded; 1920, U.S. Women Gain the Vote.

1877 ■ HAYES IS ELECTED PRESIDENT: *after a close and hotly disputed election, Hayes assumes the presidency and Reconstruction ends*

DATE: March 2, 1877
LOCALE: United States
CATEGORY: Government and politics
KEY FIGURES:
Rutherford Birchard Hayes (1822-1893), nineteenth president of the United States, 1877-1881
Thomas Alexander Scott (1823-1881), official of the Pennsylvania Railroad
Samuel Jones Tilden (1814-1886), Democratic presidential candidate in 1876

SUMMARY OF EVENT. The Compromise of 1877, the last great compromise between the North and the South, ended Reconstruction. This agreement, which had its antecedents in 1787, 1820, and 1850, came as a direct result of the disputed presidential election of 1876.

The election found the Republicans attempting desperately to retain the presidential power that they had held since their first victory in 1860, but it was no easy task in 1876. The party was rent by feuding between regulars, or Stalwarts, who supported President Ulysses S. Grant, and reformers, who had supported the unsuccessful Liberal Republican candidacy of Horace Greeley in 1872. The Liberal Republicans had quit the party chiefly as a result of the issues of corruption, civil service reform, and Southern policy. In its search for a candidate in 1876, the party, conscious of the danger to its hegemony, steered between Stalwarts and reformers. It finally settled on Rutherford B. Hayes of Ohio, who had risen to the rank of brevet major general in the Union Army and who had served both as a congressman and as governor of Ohio. Hayes was a regular. He had not bolted in 1872, but neither was he a spoilsman, and he had indicated that perhaps the Southern policy needed revision. In his letter accepting the nomination, Hayes espoused reform of civil service and promised Southerners the right to govern themselves without federal interference.

The Democrats believed that 1876 would be their year. They had been out of power since 1860, but their optimism in 1876 was based on political reality. During the 1870's, many Northerners had grown tired of Reconstruction programs and Republican rule; they were eager for change. The existence of the Liberal Republicans in 1872 illustrated that feeling and reflected an underlying racism that had existed among Northerners before the Civil War. Many Northerners were willing to believe stories of the incompetence and corruption of "Negro-Carpetbag" governments because they opposed any Republican government at all, honest or dishonest.

The promise of Reconstruction had failed, too, as a result of racism and economic and class considerations. The Southern Republicans were divided within and from their larger base of support in the North on the basis of class differences. The Republican Party retreated from Southern agrarian reform as it retreated from Northern working-class reform in the 1870's. The immigrant factory worker and the black field hand were both feared as threats to Republican order and individual property rights. Traditional Republican ideology warned against entrusting the propertyless masses with political power. Thus, it was easy for Northerners to accept Democratic charges of corruption in the Republican South and to be unsympathetic to the demands of the Southern poor for economic independence.

Furthermore, Northern Republicans hoped that conciliation with the South would produce a coalition of Northern and Southern conservatives. Many former Whigs and Unionists in the Southern Democratic Party were business-oriented and had little in common with antebellum farmers. They shared the economic and political philosophies of the Northern wing of the Republican Party. During the 1876 electoral crisis, they demanded railroads, manufacturing plants, banks, and internal improvements for the South. The promise of federal funds for their demands gave the South hope that industry and transportation would complement agriculture and produce unparalleled prosperity.

The Democrats therefore were able to capitalize on the Northern eagerness for change. The return of Democratic control in all but three of the former Confederate states helped the party on a national level. In the congressional elections of 1874, the Democrats won a majority of seventy seats in the House of Representatives and almost gained control of the Senate. By 1876, the Democrats were poised to oust the Republicans through their presidential nominee Samuel Tilden, the governor of New York.

The election results were unprecedented. Tilden won a majority of more than 250,000 popular votes, but the count of electoral votes failed to reveal a winner. With 185 electoral votes needed to win, Tilden had 184 undisputed votes, while Hayes had 165. A serious dispute erupted over nineteen electoral votes in the South: eight in Louisiana, seven in South Carolina, and four in Florida. Both parties claimed to have carried the three states, and conflicting sets of returns from each state had been sent to Washington, D.C. There was a minor dispute over one electoral vote from Oregon, but the real battle occurred over the nineteen from the three Southern states.

A grave constitutional problem arose because the Constitution, while stipulating the procedure for counting electoral votes, gave no indication what should be done when more than one set of returns came in from a single state. The Constitution stated that the president of the Senate, in joint session of the House and Senate, should open the electors' certificates and then the votes should be counted, but it did not say who should count them. If the president of the Senate—at this time a Republican—were to count the votes, he would be expected to count the Republican electors' votes that were in dispute; if the Speaker of the House—a Democrat—were to do the counting, he presumably would count the disputed Democratic votes. With no specific guidelines and a politically divided Congress (a Republican Senate and a Democratic House), there was real danger that March 4, Inauguration Day, would arrive before some solution could be reached.

After weeks of uncertainty, on January 29, 1877, Congress established an electoral commission to determine which of the disputed returns should be counted. The commission was to comprise fifteen members: five from the Senate, five from the House, and five from the Supreme Court. There would be seven Democrats, seven Republicans, and one independent—David Davis, an associate justice of the United States. When the Illinois legislature elected Davis to the Senate, his place on the commission went to Associate Justice Joseph P. Bradley, a Republican.

Powerful forces operated to bring about the creation of the commission and agreement on a peaceful settlement. Northern businessmen, Republican and Democratic alike, adamantly opposed any resort to violence. Equally important was the insistence by Southern Democrats that threats of violence were absurd; one war had been enough for them. Tilden adopted an unyielding pacifist stance. Many Southerners, eager for economic largesse for levees, river and harbor improvements, and a Western railroad across Texas, hoped that Hayes would triumph, because his party was disposed to extend government economic aid.

When the commission met on February 9, it soon became apparent that the eight Republicans would stand united and award the presidency to Hayes. The Republican members insisted that the commission could not question the returns but had to accept those certified by the legal authorities in a particular state. Because Republicans controlled Florida, Louisiana, and South Carolina at the time of the election in 1876, all the legally certified returns, in the commission's sense, were for Hayes. Thus the commission allowed Hayes all the disputed votes and declared him the winner.

Many Democrats were unhappy about this decision and threatened to filibuster or otherwise to disrupt the proceedings of Congress in order to prevent the legal election of Hayes. Cooler heads, influenced by the same forces that earlier had stood against violence, prevailed. At last a compromise had been reached, and on March 5, 1877, Rutherford B. Hayes was inaugurated as the nineteenth president of the United States.

—*William J. Cooper, Jr., updated by Bill Manikas*

ADDITIONAL READING:

Barnard, Harry. *Rutherford B. Hayes and His America.* Indianapolis: Bobbs-Merrill, 1954. An extensive biography of the man who became president as a result of the compromise.

Barney, William L. *The Passage of the Republic.* Lexington, Mass.: D. C. Heath, 1987. The status and views of the radicals, whites, and African Americans during Reconstruction are discussed in chapter 7.

Bedford, Henry F., and Trevor Colbourn. *The Americans: A Brief History to 1877.* New York: Harcourt Brace Jovanovich, 1976. Chapter 11 discusses the radical, presidential, and congressional plans of reconstruction and the price paid for Hayes's election.

Davis, Allen F., and Harold D. Woodman. "Reconstruction." In *Conflict and Consensus in Early American History.* 7th ed. Lexington, Mass.: D. C. Heath, 1988. Examines the failure of Reconstruction and the flare-up of Northern racism.

Gerster, Patrick, and Nicholas Cords. *Myth in American History.* Encino, Calif.: Glencoe Press, 1977. Asserts that Reconstruction was not a period of military oppression, and that it furthered the rise of big business.

Patrick, Rembert Wallace. *The Reconstruction of the Nation.* New York: Oxford University Press, 1967. Provides a detailed, interpretive account of Reconstruction. Where necessary, emphasis shifts from the national to the local scene.

Rhodes, James F. *History of the United States from the Compromise of 1850 to the Final Restoration of Home Rule at the South in 1877.* 7 vols. New York: Macmillan, 1893-1906. Volume 7 gives the story of the compromise as seen by the most influential of the nationalist historians.

Richardson, Leon Burr. *William E. Chandler: Republican.* New York: Dodd, Mead, 1940. A detailed biography of the chairman of the Republican National Committee in 1876.

Stampp, Kenneth M. *The Era of Reconstruction, 1865 to 1877.* New York: Alfred A. Knopf, 1965. An excellent one-volume study of Reconstruction.

SEE ALSO: 1863, Reconstruction; 1883, Pendleton Act.

1877 ■ NEZ PERCE EXILE: *Chief Joseph leads his people in retreat for fifteen hundred miles in one of the most remarkable Indian war campaigns of U.S. history*

DATE: June 15-October 5, 1877
LOCALE: Oregon, Idaho, and Montana
CATEGORIES: Native American history; Wars, uprisings, and civil unrest
KEY FIGURES:
Alokut (1842-1877), Joseph the Younger's brother, a tribal war leader
Joseph the Elder (1786-1871), chief of the Wallamwatkins
Joseph the Younger (c. 1832-1904), chief of the Wallamwatkins after his father
Looking Glass (c. 1823-1877), Nez Perce tribal chief and warrior
Oliver O. Howard (1830-1909), U.S. troop commander
SUMMARY OF EVENT. During the nineteenth century, the Nez Perce tribes occupied various areas of the Northwest, including Washington, Idaho, and Oregon. There were five separate groups, each under the leadership of an autonomous chief. One group occupied Oregon territory in the Imnaha and Wallowa Valleys and was under the leadership of Joseph the Elder, or Old Chief Joseph. In 1855, the governor of the Oregon Territory signed a celebrated treaty with him and numerous other Nez Perce leaders, allowing the tribe ownership of all the land in the Imnaha and Wallowa Valleys. The treaty was ratified by the United States Senate.

The treaty of 1855 proved short-lived, however: The Civil War and the discovery of gold at Orofino, Idaho, in 1860, led to an ever-increasing surge of immigration of white settlers into the valleys and territories claimed by the Nez Perce. Because of increasing tensions between the whites and the natives, in 1863 a new treaty was negotiated. The new terms excluded the Imnaha and Wallowa Valleys and other vast areas of land that had been dedicated to the Indians in 1855. The revised treaty was signed by James Reuben and Chief Lawyer, but Chiefs Old Joseph, White Bird, and Looking Glass refused to ratify it. Thus, the treaty was recognized as having treaty Indians and nontreaty Indians.

In 1871, Old Chief Joseph died, leaving the leadership of the Wallamwatkins to his son, the new Chief Joseph, or Joseph the Younger. The continuing influx of white immigrants into the Nez Perce lands caused increasing problems between Indians and whites. In 1876, a commission was appointed to investigate complaints, and it was decided that the nontreaty Nez Perces had no standing and that all groups should go onto designated reservations. In 1877, the U.S. Department of the Interior issued instructions to carry out the commission's recommendations. Preparing for the transition, a council of tribal leaders and U.S. government officials was set to meet on

May 3, 1877. Chief Joseph and his brother, Alokut, represented the Nez Perce, while General Oliver O. Howard represented the U.S. government. The final understanding was that the nontreaty Indians would be on the designated reservations by June 14, 1877.

On June 15, 1877, word was received at Fort Lapwai, Idaho, that the Wallamwatkins had attacked and killed several settlers around Mount Idaho, Idaho. U.S. Army troops were sent from Fort Lapwai to counterattack. On June 17, troops headed into Whitebird Canyon and engaged in a bitter encounter with the Wallamwatkins. The U.S. Army lost thirty-four troops and numerous horses; the Nez Perce, numbering only seventy warriors, had only four wounded in the battle. On July 1, regular troops and Idaho volunteers under Captain Stephen C. Whipple attacked Looking Glass' village. The troops shot, destroyed property, and looted at random. As a result, Looking Glass joined the war effort with Chief Joseph.

By July 13, after numerous skirmishes with General Howard's troops and other soldiers, Chief Joseph led approximately four hundred of his people eastward toward the Lolo Trail in the Bitterroot Mountains. On July 15, Looking Glass urged escape to Montana and proposed joining with the Crow of the plains. Chief Joseph agreed, Looking Glass became supreme war leader, and on July 16, the nontreaty Nez Perces summarily left their homeland.

Chief Joseph and Looking Glass kept track of Howard's position and were able to stall and otherwise frustrate Howard's advance. As a result, the chiefs led the Wallamwatkins through Lolo Trail and into the Missoula area. General Howard subsequently contacted Colonel John Gibbon at Fort Shaw, Montana, and instructed him to take up the pursuit. Gibbon was able to muster 146 men of the Seventh Infantry and 34 civilians.

Chief Joseph and Looking Glass crossed the Continental Divide and encamped their weary followers in the Big Hole Valley, unaware of Colonel Gibbon's pursuit and position. On August 9, Colonel Gibbon's troops made a surprise attack on the Wallamwatkins' camp and engaged in a long and difficult battle. Many Nez Perce lives—mostly of women and children—were lost in the initial confrontation. Chief Joseph and White Bird outflanked Gibbon's troops and led the families to safety, while the warriors under Alokut and Looking Glass split Gibbon's forces. After holding the Army in siege for several days, the warriors eventually broke off the engagement, and the Nez Perce continued their retreat through the Montana territory.

By August 27, Chief Joseph had led the Wallamwatkins into Yellowstone Park, with General Howard and his troops in continuing pursuit. By September 6, Chief Joseph and Looking Glass had made their retreat through the northeast corner of Yellowstone Park. Continuing north, Chief Joseph led his people up through the Snowy Mountains and finally into the northern foothills of the Bear Paw Mountains, an easy day's ride from the Canadian border. Unknown to Chief Joseph, Colonel Nelson A. Miles had been notified by General Howard and was in pursuit from Fort Keogh paralleling Chief Joseph's trail from the north. On September 30, Colonel Miles's troops made a surprise attack on the Wallamwatkins' camp. The fighting during the Bear Paws Battle was intense. The army lost fifty-three men and the Nez Perce lost eighteen warriors, including Alokut, Tulhulhutsut, and Poker Joe. On the night of October 4, General Howard rode into Miles's camp and provided the reinforcements that would ensure a final surrender from Chief Joseph. On October 5, General Howard sent terms of surrender to the Nez Perce. A brief skirmish evolved, and Looking Glass was fired on and killed. Colonel Miles assured Chief Joseph that he and his tribe would be allowed to return home to the Northwest in peace. Feeling that he could do so with honor, Chief Joseph offered one of the most famous surrendering speeches ever documented. Turning to the interpreter, Chief Joseph said:

> Tell General Howard I know what is in his heart. What he told me before, I have in my heart. I am tired of fighting. Our chiefs are killed. Looking Glass is dead. Tulhulhutsut is dead. The old men are all dead. It is the young men who say yes or no. He [Alokut] who led on the young men is dead. My people, some of them, have run away to the hills and have no blankets, no food; no one knows where they are—perhaps freezing to death. I want to have time to look for my children and see how many of them I can find. Maybe I shall find them among the dead. Hear me, my chiefs. I am tired; my heart is sick and sad. From where the sun now stands I will fight no more, forever.

Thus ended the Nez Perce War, one of the most remarkable Indian war campaigns of U.S. history.

Chief Joseph surrendered with 86 men, 148 women and 147 children. The Nez Perces were transported to Fort Keogh for temporary holding. On November 1, despite Colonel Miles's assurances that the tribe would be allowed to return to the Northwest, he was ordered to take his prisoners farther south, to Fort Lincoln, near Bismarck, North Dakota. On November 27, Chief Joseph and his people were moved again (by train) to Fort Leavenworth, Kansas. Kept in unsanitary conditions, plagued by disease and twenty deaths, in July, 1878, Chief Joseph and his people were again moved to the Quapaw Reservation in Kansas territory. By the end of the year, nearly fifty more tribe members had died from disease.

After repeated requests to return to the Northwest, in 1885, eight years after their surrender, the 268 survivors of the nontreaty bands taken into captivity were allowed to return to the Northwest. About half of them were housed at Lapwai, Idaho, and Chief Joseph's Wallowa band was housed at Nespelem on the Colville Reservation in eastern Washington. From the time of his return to the Northwest until his death, September 21, 1904, Chief Joseph attempted in vain to gain permission to return his people to his homeland in the Wallowa Valley in eastern Oregon.

—*John L. Farbo*

ADDITIONAL READING:

Adkison, Norman B. *Indian Braves and Battles with More Nez Perce Lore*. Grangeville, Idaho: Idaho County Free Press,

1967. This brief history chronicles events of the Nez Perce from actual correspondence, journals, and interviews.

_____. *Nez Perce Indian War and Original Stories.* Grangeville, Idaho: Idaho County Free Press, 1966. Another brief chronicle of events of the Nez Perce from actual correspondence, journals, and interviews.

Beal, Merrill D. *I Will Fight No More Forever: Chief Joseph and the Nez Perce War.* Seattle: University of Washington Press, 1963. Detailed history of Chief Joseph and the Nez Perce War.

Chalmers, Harvey, II. *The Last Stand of the Nez Perce.* New York: Twayne, 1962. Detailed history of Chief Joseph and the Nez Perce War.

Gidley, Mick. *Kopet: A Documentary Narrative of Chief Joseph's Last Years.* Seattle: University of Washington Press, 1981. This brief history well documents various photographs, journals, and correspondence.

SEE ALSO: 1846, Oregon Settlement; 1862, Great Sioux War; 1871, Indian Appropriation Act.

1877 ■ SALT WARS: *Anglo-American entrepreneurs enter the trans-Pecos area, disturbing traditional Mexican and Tejano practices*

DATE: September 10-December 17, 1877
LOCALE: Trans-Pecos region of Texas
CATEGORIES: Latino American history; Wars, uprisings, and civil unrest
KEY FIGURES:
Thomas Blair, U.S. Army captain
Louis Cardis (1829-1877), merchant and political leader
Charles H. Howard (died 1877), lawyer and district judge
Richard B. Hubbard, governor of Texas
Ramón Ortiz (1813-1896), priest and pacifist
John Tays, commander of the Texas Rangers

SUMMARY OF EVENT. For years, the people of the trans-Pecos region of Texas and Mexico, also known as the El Paso area, had traveled to the *salinas*, or salt lakes, to get salt. The *salinas* were situated about one hundred miles east of El Paso, in the foothills at the base of Guadalupe Peak. Records indicate that as early as 1800, the inhabitants of the area made regular treks from ranches and villages to gather rock salt. To harvest the salt, people would hand-pick chunks of rock salt from the edges of the *salinas*.

In the late 1860's, Anglo-Americans began moving into this generally Hispanic area, acquiring large landholdings and taking political control. The ensconced Hispanic American population began to lose political and social dominance. Both the Anglos and the Hispanics depended on joint efforts from their Mexican neighbors and the military, who came and went to and from Fort Bliss, to maintain an active economy.

In 1854, Louis Cardis, born in Italy, settled in El Paso, becoming a merchant and contractor who supplied goods to the barracks at Fort Bliss. He spoke Spanish and knew the Mexican character well. His business put him in contact with many people on the border: Anglo-Americans, Mexicans, and Mexican Americans. He became an adviser and friend to many people in the region, although his contacts with the newcomer Anglo-Americans were not as successful. Anglos, seeing commercial opportunities in the area, showed resentment toward the Hispanic population that had long provided the needs of the people of the trans-Pecos. This attitude caused friction between the newly arrived "gringos" and the established Hispanics, a division that formed based on race and political cronyism. The steady immigration of Europeans, Middle Eastern merchants, Confederate War veterans, and others expanded Cardis' business, giving him daily contacts with these diverse groups.

Charles H. Howard, a Missourian who had served in the Confederate Army, came to El Paso in 1872. Howard, a lawyer, was a man of imposing appearance, a powerful physique, determined, rather reckless, and forceful. A Democrat, Howard became a district judge in 1874. Cardis, a Republican, was delegate to the lower house in 1864, attended the Constitutional Convention in 1875, and was elected to the legislature in 1876. As Cardis' political tenure had preceded Howard's arrival in El Paso, a political struggle between these two men ensued. Howard had political position, but not the large, multi-ethnic following of Cardis. Howard saw opportunity in the growth of the region. To take advantage of this opportunity, he enlisted the help of his father-in-law, Major George B. Zimpleman, to acquire title to the salt lakes. Howard then began charging the local residents for harvesting the salt.

This angered the people, who had always taken all the salt they needed, free of charge. As a result, these ordinarily law-abiding people began to take matters into their own hands. They met and made plans to storm the *salinas* and take salt by force. Using his political influence, Judge Howard had two prominent Mexicans in this protest group arrested. The storming of the *salinas* took place on September 10, 1877, at San Elizario, a stagecoach stop and resting spot for the military located midway between El Paso and the *salinas*. The mob was so incensed that they arrested and imprisoned Howard, the district and county judges with him, and then organized their own court to try them. Cardis and Father Ramón Ortiz, the well-known curate of Mission Nuestra Señora de Guadalupe in El Paso del Norte, interceded for the two men, who were released on the condition that they leave the area and never return. Howard signed his abdication with reluctance. He had no intention of yielding the salt lakes.

Howard fled to New Mexico. Four of his friends put up a twelve-thousand-dollar bond that guaranteed Howard would stand by his word and would allow free salt harvesting. From New Mexico, Howard appealed continuously to the Texas legislature and Texas governor R. B. Hubbard to allow him to return to El Paso. His demands included unrestricted control of the salt lakes and military or Texas Ranger intervention in the "race war" and the "invasion from Mexico." Howard created news statewide by publicly accusing Cardis of plotting his assassination.

On October 10, 1877, Howard returned to the trans-Pecos, although he faced death threats if he returned to the region. On that day, in the store of a merchant friend, Cardis had just finished writing a letter to Chico Barela, one of the mob leaders, pleading with him to stop the violence and above all to be lenient with Charles Howard. Cardis placed the letter in his breast pocket and sat talking with two men, when Howard came in carrying a double-barreled shotgun. The merchant asked Howard not to shoot inside his store, but Howard ignored the plea. Cardis was hit in the heart with the second shot. Howard again fled to New Mexico and on October 25, 1877, again asked Governor Hubbard for military intervention in controlling the "mob."

Howard returned to El Paso in early December. The governor had sent twenty Texas Rangers, under the leadership of Lieutenant John B. Tays, who resented having to guard only one man. Howard's overbearing attitude did not help. Meanwhile, Hubbard had called on President Rutherford B. Hayes for assistance, which was granted. Because of slow communications, however, an Army attachment headed by Captain Thomas Blair did not receive the orders in time to arrive with Howard and the Rangers.

On his arrival at San Elizario, on a Monday, Tays found the village full of people who regularly harvested salt, armed and angry. The Texas Rangers took cover and shooting began. By Thursday, there were two dead. Howard's bondsmen and friends, betrayed by Howard, asked him to join them and the Rangers in giving in to the harvesters. This was the only time that Texas Rangers ever surrendered. On December 17, 1877, to avenge Cardis' death and for the free use of the salt lakes, the harvesters and villagers shot Howard and his bondsmen. The bondsmen were shot not because of guilt but because of their association with Howard.

By the time the United States military arrived, four men had been killed, many had been wounded, and the mob had dispersed. Indictments were made, but no one was arrested or brought to trial. A congressional investigation attempted to get the facts, but in the end nothing happened other than that Fort Bliss was reopened.

Eventually, people were allowed again to take salt as they wished. This situation continued until 1891, when the Lone Star Salt Company bought the salt lakes and began processing salt with modern methods. —*Norma Crews*

ADDITIONAL READING:

Metz, Leon. *El Paso Chronicles.* El Paso, Tex.: Mangan Books, 1993. A complete history of the El Paso area from before Christ to modern times. Covers archaeological, political, military, and other aspects of the region.

_____. *Roadside History of Texas.* Missoula, Mont.: Mountain Press, 1994. Includes coverage of little-known Texas historical events.

Sonnichsen, C. L. *The El Paso Salt War, 1877.* El Paso: Texas Western Press, 1961. A detailed study of each of the

events that contributed to the eruption of the Salt War, its climax, and its ending.

_____. *I'll Die Before I'll Run: The Story of the Great Feuds of Texas.* New York: Devin-Adair, 1962. A history of some of the conflicts between individuals and groups from the early 1800's to the 1930's. Illustrations.

Webb, Prescott. *The Texas Rangers.* Boston: Houghton Mifflin, 1935. A history of the Texas Rangers, their beginnings, and their major activities to the mid-1930's.

SEE ALSO: 1835, Texas Revolution; 1846, Mexican War; 1848, Treaty of Guadalupe Hidalgo; 1857, Cart War.

1878 ■ MACDONALD RETURNS AS CANADA'S PRIME MINISTER: *a second administration by the Conservative prime minister aims to protect Canadian enterprises from foreign competition and encourages western settlement*

DATE: 1878

LOCALE: Ottawa, Canada

CATEGORY: Canadian history

KEY FIGURES:

George Étienne Cartier (1814-1873), Conservative minister of defense under Macdonald, 1867-1873

Wilfrid Laurier (1841-1919), Liberal prime minister of Canada, 1896-1911

John Alexander Macdonald (1815-1891), Conservative prime minister of Canada, 1867-1873 and 1878-1891

Alexander Mackenzie (1822-1892), Liberal prime minister of Canada, 1873-1878

Charles Tupper (1821-1915), Conservative prime minister of Canada, 1896

SUMMARY OF EVENT. It is difficult to overestimate the importance of John Macdonald in early Canadian history. Along with his two most influential associates, George Étienne Cartier from Quebec and Charles Tupper from Nova Scotia, Ontarian John Macdonald played a central role in persuading the British government to approve the British North America Act, which ended Canada's colonial status and united the Canadian provinces under a single federal system. Alexander Mackenzie, Tupper, and Cartier created a political system that protected religious freedom, established English and French as the official languages of the new Dominion of Canada, and created a balance between the power of the federal and provincial governments.

On July 1, 1867, the British North America Act of 1867 took effect, and John Macdonald became Canada's first prime minister. Macdonald was an English-speaking Protestant from Ontario, and Cartier was a French-speaking Catholic from Quebec. They both understood that the unity of their new country required that representatives from Canada's major linguistic groups (English and French) and religions (Catholic and Protestant) be included at all levels of government. Although Macdonald was the prime minister, most historians believe that he and Cartier governed Canada together until Cartier's death in 1873. This cooperation contributed to the unity of Canada. A scandal in 1873 that linked certain members of Macdonald's cabinet to bribes paid during the construction of the Canadian Pacific Railway weakened the influence of Macdonald's Conservative Party. Macdonald resigned as prime minister, and he was succeeded by Liberal leader Alexander Mackenzie in November, 1873.

Unfortunately for the honest and hardworking Mackenzie, Canada endured serious economic problems during the mid-1870's, and Canadian voters held him responsible for this depression. In the 1878 general election, John Macdonald promised a new National Policy that would protect Canadian business from unfair competition from U.S. and British companies. John Macdonald and his major adviser, Charles Tupper, argued that unrestricted free trade with the United States and Britain had contributed significantly to the depression of the 1870's (which manifested itself in the United States as the Panic of 1873). This argument proved persuasive with the voters, who returned Macdonald to the office of prime minister. His Conservative Party kept its majority in Parliament until 1896, five years after Macdonald's death, when the Liberals, under Wilfrid Laurier, defeated Prime Minister Charles Tupper and the Conservatives.

Once John Macdonald was again prime minister, the three major aspects of his National Policy were revealed to the public. First, he imposed high tariffs on certain imported goods in order to protect Canadian companies from foreign competition. This did produce the desired effect of ensuring Canadian control over the Canadian economy, but it had the unavoidable side effect of creating inflation, because Canadian manufacturers felt no pressure to keep their prices low, since there was no real competition from other countries. Throughout the 1880's, Canadian voters were willing to accept high prices on products because they felt that low tariffs would have endangered Canadian economic independence by allowing U.S. and British companies to dominate the Canadian market.

A second important element of the National Policy was the completion of the Canadian Pacific Railway, in order to link the eastern provinces to British Columbia. To obtain approval from the House of Commons for the large expenditures required for this massive project, Macdonald and Tupper, his minister of railways and canals, gave overt preference to Canadian construction companies, even if their bids were higher than those received from U.S. or British companies. Macdonald and Tupper presented the nationalistic argument that Canadian economic independence justified the additional expense, and they questioned the patriotism of Edward Blake, the Liberal leader from 1880 to 1887, who had expressed serious doubts about what he considered to be the waste of tax dollars to protect uncompetitive Canadian companies.

After the creation of the Canadian Confederation in 1867, the new Dominion of Canada began expanding westward. Manitoba joined the confederation in 1870, and the following year, British Columbia became a province. Although Alberta and Saskatchewan were still territories and did not become provinces until September 1, 1905, they were an integral part of Canada during the second Macdonald government. Macdonald recognized that it was not sufficient to connect all of Canada physically by completing a transcontinental railroad system. He also had to encourage people to settle in large numbers in the provinces and territories west of Ontario, so that full economic development would be possible in the western part of Canada. He actively encouraged immigration, but he gave overt preference to European immigrants over Asian immigrants and did little to discourage discrimination in British Columbia against Chinese and Japanese immigrants, who nevertheless were responsible for much of the construction of the British Columbia portion of the Canadian Pacific Railway.

Although Macdonald was successful in protecting emerging Canadian companies and in establishing a unified economic system in Canada, he began to pay less attention to the aspirations of the Maritime Provinces and Quebec. Residents in the provinces of Quebec, New Brunswick, Nova Scotia, and Prince Edward Island resented having to pay high prices for products in order to protect manufacturing companies located largely in Ontario and the western provinces, and they did not believe that eastern Canada had benefited significantly from the vast expenditure of tax dollars required for the construction of the Canadian Pacific Railway system. In 1886, the provincial legislature of Nova Scotia seriously considered seceding from the Canadian Confederation. Large numbers of French speakers in Quebec were enraged when John Macdonald approved the execution, in November, 1885, of Louis Riel, a Catholic French Canadian who had revolted against what he perceived to be the terrible mistreatment of French Canadian settlers in Saskatchewan. The hanging of Louis Riel turned him into a martyr among Catholic and French Canadian voters. In hindsight, it appears that if Macdonald had still had an influential French Canadian adviser such as Cartier, who had helped him immensely during the early years of the Canadian Confederation, he would have pardoned Louis Riel and would not have risked alienating French Canadian voters. Growing dissatisfaction in Quebec and the Maritime Provinces with the National Policy of the Conservative Party under Macdonald would contribute greatly to the victory of the Liberal leader Wilfrid Laurier, a Catholic, French-speaking Quebecer, in the general election of 1896.

John Macdonald served as the prime minister of Canada for nineteen years. Although he was highly controversial, even his political opponents appreciated the importance of his central role in transforming Canada from a British colony into an independent country. In an eloquent and sincere eulogy given in the House of Commons on June 8, 1891, only two days after Macdonald's death, the opposition leader, Wilfrid Laurier, described Macdonald as "Canada's most illustrious son, and in every sense Canada's foremost citizen and statesman." The high opinion in which Canadians have held Macdonald, their first prime minister, has not diminished, even though he died more than a century ago. He remains an almost legendary figure in Canadian history.   —Edmund J. Campion

ADDITIONAL READING:

Creighton, Donald. *Canada's First Century: 1867-1967.* Toronto: Macmillan of Canada, 1970. Contains a clear description of the profound changes that occurred in Canada between the creation of Canada in 1867 and Macdonald's death in 1891.

Donaldson, Gordon. *Fifteen Men: Canada's Prime Ministers from Macdonald to Trudeau.* Toronto: Doubleday Canada, 1969. Describes succinctly the nature of John Macdonald's National Policy, which transformed Canada from a collection of provinces into a unified transcontinental nation.

Owram, Douglas, ed. *Canadian History: A Reader's Guide. Confederation to the Present.* Toronto: University of Toronto Press, 1994. Contains an excellent annotated bibliography of historical studies on Macdonald's importance, both to the creation of Canada as an independent country and for his accomplishments as prime minister.

Smith, Cynthia M., and Jack McLeod, eds. *Sir John A: An Anecdotal Life of John A. Macdonald.* Toronto: Oxford University Press, 1989. Despite its subtitle, this book does not merely contain anecdotes about the life of Canada's first prime minister. Includes numerous judicious assessments of Macdonald's career, by both contemporaries and later historians.

Swainson, Donald. *John A. Macdonald: The Man and the Politician.* Toronto: Oxford University Press, 1971. A sympathetic, well-documented biography of Macdonald. Discusses the many political and social problems caused by the implementation of his National Policy.

SEE ALSO: 1867, British North America Act; 1869, First Riel Rebellion; 1873, Mackenzie Era in Canada; 1875, Supreme Court of Canada Is Established; 1876, Canada's Indian Act; 1885, Second Riel Rebellion.

1879 ■ POWELL'S REPORT ON THE LANDS OF THE ARID REGION: *one of the most influential recommendations for government land management and disposition in the Far West*

DATE: 1879

LOCALE: West of the one hundredth meridian

CATEGORIES: Expansion and land acquisition; Exploration and discovery

KEY FIGURES:

Clarence Edward Dutton (1841-1912), geologist responsible for geologic reports on the Grand Canyon and the Colorado Plateau

Grove Karl Gilbert (1843-1918), Powell's chief geologic assistant

Emma Dean Powell (1836-1924), Powell's wife, who accompanied him on several trips

John Wesley Powell (1834-1902), explorer, scientist, promoter, and director of the United States Geological Survey and of the Bureau of Ethnography

Carl Schurz (1829-1906), secretary of the interior and Powell's political ally

William Morris Stewart (1827-1909), senator from Nevada who helped start the Irrigation Survey but later opposed its actions

Almond H. Thompson (1839-1906), Powell's brother-in-law, mapmaker and chief topographer for the Powell surveys

SUMMARY OF EVENT. John Wesley Powell achieved national fame through his pioneering voyage down the Colorado River in 1869. Born in 1834 on a frontier farm in New York, he showed an early interest in education and was introduced to science by a farm neighbor in Ohio. He further developed his scientific interests as a student at colleges in Illinois and Ohio. His career as a schoolteacher and lyceum lecturer was interrupted by the Civil War. A wound received at Shiloh (Pittsburgh Landing) resulted in the amputation of his right arm, after which his wife and first cousin, Emma Dean Powell, accompanied him in the field. Mustered out of the Army, Powell joined Illinois Wesleyan College as a professor of natural history. In 1867, after raising money from various state and federal institutions and private business, he set out on an exploratory trip to the Rocky Mountains. Powell and his wife climbed Pikes Peak and explored the Grand River (now the upper Colorado River) in Colorado. The next year, he returned to climb Longs Peak, explore the White River Valley, and visit Green River, Wyoming. In early spring, 1869, faced by threats of desertion from his crew, Powell had to curb his wife's managerial efforts. She never again accompanied him in the field. During 1869, Powell began collecting artifacts from the Utes, recording Ute legends, and compiling a Ute dictionary. In 1869, Powell descended the Colorado River from Green River, going through the Grand Canyon to the mouth of the Virgin River. Only two days before the trip's end, three discouraged men left the canyon, only to be killed by Paiutes.

July 12, 1870, Congress established the Geographical and Geological Survey of the Rocky Mountain Region, with Powell in charge. Powell's survey spent ten years mapping the Colorado Plateau in Utah and Arizona, publishing reports on natural history and native tribes.

Powell became alarmed by many of his observations and by events elsewhere in the West. Many farmers on the Great Plains, deceived by a series of unusually wet years during the 1860's and early 1870's, settled too far West, beyond the hundredth meridian, where normal rainfall, less than twenty inches per year, was insufficient to grow crops. When the weather cycle turned dry, many farmers were bankrupted and driven from the land. Much agricultural land also was eroded severely by wind and water. In the Rockies, irrigation companies were gaining control over water supplies, and timber cutters were denuding the mountainsides.

As early as 1873, Powell expressed concern about future settlement in the arid West and recommended changing the United States' land classification system. In 1879, he published his *Report on the Lands of the Arid Region of the United States, with a More Detailed Account of the Lands of Utah,* insisting that most of the West was unsuited for settlement and farming as practiced in the humid East. Two-fifths of the United States was arid. He urged closing public lands to entry until they were topographically mapped and classified. Thereafter, the lands were to be distributed to the people according to regulations adapted to Powell's five proposed classes: mineral, coal, pasturage, irrigable, and timber lands. Powell's re-

Boys from the Rosebud Indian Reservation who were shipped to the Carlisle Indian School in Pennsylvania, c. 1880, wearing their school uniforms. The policy of assimilating—essentially Europeanizing—Indian children became more widespread as the Indian Wars destroyed traditional Indian ways of life and forced Native Americans onto reservations. Although the process was conducted with good intentions, its effect was to separate children from their cultural heritage. (National Archives)

port included two proposed laws for organizing irrigation districts and pasturage districts in the western lands. Groups of farmers were to be urged to locate together and form cooperatives, sharing the expense of building dams and ditches to conserve and use water resources. Land units in irrigation districts were to be 80 acres, rather than the accustomed 160. Water rights would inhere in the land, title to the water passing with the land. Powell recommended abandonment of the rectangular system of survey so that irrigable land could be parceled out, giving each person access to water. He proposed organizing grazing units of twenty-five hundred acres, each unit to include water sufficient to irrigate twenty acres of winter hay or farm crops. Settlers would be allowed to file for holdings without charge, but if the water were not utilized within five years, the land and water rights would revert to the public domain. Powell also insisted that riparian rights under English common law, allowing land owners to take all the water they wished from streams crossing or bordering their property, would have to be modified or abrogated in the arid region. Thus, water rights would be limited to the amount required or used on land to be irrigated.

Powell's report described the lands of Utah and their development as directed by the Church of Jesus Christ of the Latter-day Saints (the Mormons) as an example of how his recommendations might be implemented. This part of the report was written by members of Powell's survey: *Irrigable Lands of the Salt Lake Drainage System* by G. K. Gilbert, *Irrigable Lands of the Valley of the Sevier River* by C. E. Dutton, and *Irrigable Lands of That Portion of Utah Drained by the Colorado River and Its Tributaries* by A. H. Thompson. Willis Drummond, Jr., contributed *Land Grants in Aid of Internal Improvements*.

Powell's proposals were unpopular with Westerners. Many small farmers, too impatient to wait on government land reclassification, thought his program closed the door to opportunity. Others thought large land units for grazing favored big cattlemen. His reforms also were opposed by railroads, prospectors and mining companies, cattle associations, land companies, and irrigation companies. Thus, Congress failed to act on Powell's recommendations.

Powell, however, continued efforts to reform land policy in the arid lands. In 1879, he was instrumental in consolidating western geological exploration in the U.S. Geological Survey, which continued the topographic mapping he had recommended. He also organized and became director of the Bureau of Ethnology to study Native American cultures. In 1881, he also became director of the U.S. Geological Survey. In 1887, a decade of drought began, bringing disaster to arid-land farmers and demands for federal irrigation projects. Powell, with the aid of Senator William Stewart of Nevada, secured a congressional resolution in 1888, establishing an Irrigation Survey within the Geological Survey. This resolution also closed entry into most public lands until the irrigable lands had been identified and surveyed. In 1890, however, political opposition drastically reduced funds for the Irrigation Survey. Powell

then retired from the Geological Survey and devoted the remainder of his life to the Bureau of Ethnology, which he served as director for twenty-three years.

More of Powell's 1879 proposals were enacted under conservation-minded administrations in the twentieth century. In 1902, the Newlands Act, creating the Bureau of Reclamation, provided for irrigation districts, dams, and canals more or less according to Powell's 1879 recommendations. The Soil Conservation Service, later the Bureau of Land Management, and the Tennessee Valley Authority, enacted in 1932, incorporate part of Powell's 1879 proposals. Opposition, however, persisted in the 1990's as Republicans called for selling the TVA and Western public lands. —*W. Turrentine Jackson, updated by Ralph L. Langenheim, Jr.*

ADDITIONAL READING:

Darrah, William Culp. *Powell of the Colorado*. Princeton, N.J.: Princeton University Press, 1951. The first and, to date, best full-length biography of John Wesley Powell.

Dellenbaugh, Frederick S. *A Canyon Voyage*. New Haven, Conn.: Yale University Press, 1962. The most complete published narrative of Powell's second expedition along the Colorado River.

Goetzmann, William H. *Exploration and Empire: The Explorer and the Scientist in the Winning of the American West*. New York: Alfred A. Knopf, 1966. A chapter on Powell as an explorer and reformer is included in this Pulitzer Prize–winning book.

Powell, John Wesley. *Report on the Lands of the Arid Region of the United States, with a More Detailed Account of the Lands of Utah*. Edited by Wallace Stegner. Cambridge, Mass.: The Belknap Press of Harvard University Press, 1962. A reprint of the second (1879), corrected edition, with an introduction by the editor.

Stegner, Wallace. *Beyond the Hundredth Meridian: John Wesley Powell and the Second Opening of the West*. Boston: Houghton Mifflin, 1954. This book abounds with special pleading for causes and people, lacks unity, and has a shaky conceptual framework, but is delightful reading and highly informative.

Udall, Stewart L. *The Quiet Crisis and the Next Generation*. Salt Lake City: Peregrine Smith Books, 1988. Discusses Powell's work as part of the conservationist and preservationist movement in the United States.

Watson, Elmo Scott. *The Professor Goes West*. Bloomington: Illinois Wesleyan University Press, 1954. Emphasizes Powell's first Western expedition in 1867 and reprints the reports of expedition member J. C. Hartzell.

SEE ALSO: 1823, Jedediah Smith Explores the Far West; 1842, Frémont's Expeditions; 1846, Mormon Migration to Utah; 1846, Occupation of California and the Southwest; 1848, California Gold Rush; 1853, Pacific Railroad Surveys; 1860, Pony Express; 1861, Transcontinental Telegraph Is Completed; 1862, Homestead Act; 1862, Morrill Land Grant Act; 1866, Chisholm Trail Opens; 1869, Transcontinental Railroad Is Completed; 1890, Closing of the Frontier.

1879 ■ EDISON DEMONSTRATES THE INCANDESCENT LAMP: *a workable electric bulb gives birth to a revolution in lighting and energy*

DATE: October 21, 1879
LOCALE: Menlo Park, New Jersey
CATEGORY: Science and technology
KEY FIGURES:

Charles Batchelor (1845-1910), close aide of Edison
Thomas Alva Edison (1847-1931), versatile U.S. inventor
Moses Gerrish Farmer (1820-1893), early U.S. experimenter with arc lights and incandescent lights
Marshall Lefferts (1821-1876), Western Union executive who sponsored Edison's early inventions
Grosvenor Lowrey, Western Union general counsel, also supportive of Edison's work
John Pierpont Morgan (1837-1913), financier who helped fund Edison's experiments
Francis R. Upton, prominent assistant in Edison's Menlo Park Laboratory

SUMMARY OF EVENT. On October 21, 1879, Thomas A. Edison and five associates at his laboratories in Menlo Park, New Jersey, passed one of the great milestones of modern science—a demonstration of an incandescent lamp that was economical, practical, and durable. The records of that day show that Edison had managed to manufacture an incandescent lamp that burned for thirteen and a half hours. In the excitement of the discovery, notes were incomplete, and there was some talk of a bulb that burned for the unheard-of time of more than forty hours. The light from Edison's first successful lamp gave a feeble, reddish glow, but Edison had set out not merely to invent a new kind of light but rather to revolutionize the science of illumination and to bring electricity within the means of everyone.

The secret of Edison's incandescent lamp is best explained in his patent application (No. 223.898, January 27, 1880): "I have discovered that even a cotton thread, properly carbonized and placed in a sealed glass bulb, exhausted to one-millionth of an atmosphere, offers from one hundred to five hundreds ohms resistance to the passage of current and that it is absolutely stable at a very high temperature." Edison had made an incandescent lamp with a hairlike carbon filament for a burner, having the necessary high resistance and low current, and sealed in a permanent high-vacuum glass to allow the burner to glow without being destroyed by the heat. The importance of Edison's discovery is not that it was the first electric light nor even the first incandescent lamp, but that it was the first electric bulb that could be universally and economically used for domestic lighting, especially as Edison soon managed to "subdivide" the great power generated by dynamos to distribute it to individual users. Still, when he threw the switch at New York's Pearl Street power station in 1882, lighting four

hundred lamps for eighty-five customers, few realized that the inventor had replaced the steam age with the electric age.

Rather, it was only Edison who realized the immense implications of his discovery. A group of Wall Street financiers headed by J. Pierpont Morgan had eagerly bankrolled Edison's first research into electricity but had grown weary of waiting for results. When Edison revealed to them his astonishing success, they balked at following up their investment, fearing that Edison had invented a laboratory toy rather than the modern electric light and power industry that, at Edison's death in 1931, would be valued in the United States alone at fifteen billion dollars. Edison's friend and informal financial adviser, Grosvenor Lowrey, a Western Union attorney who specialized in patents, could get no more funds from Wall Street until Edison made his early success public. The news of Edison's invention did not reach the newspapers until December 21, when the *New York Herald* announced that Edison "makes light without gas or flame, cheaper than oil." The aesthetic importance of Edison's lamp was captured by the *Herald* reporter, who described the effect as a "bright, beautiful light, like the mellow sunset of an Italian autumn."

The triumph of the incandescent lamp was a personal triumph for Edison. His previous success, the invention of the phonograph in 1877, had already brought him fame. In the course of a long career, Edison was responsible for more than a thousand patents, including the invention or improvement of the storage battery, dictaphone, ore separator, electric dynamo, electric locomotive, composition brick, the Sprauge separator, compressing dies, and the Edison Vitascope, a forerunner of the modern movie projector. In pure science, he was responsible for the discovery of the Edison effect, the genesis of modern electronics. The Edison method involved a delegating of authority and working with a number of gifted associates in a well-equipped scientific laboratory. Most of Edison's discoveries were collaborative ventures, but the imagination and the creative impetus were always supplied by Edison himself.

Electricity itself was not new. Sir Humphry Davy had shown the possibility of electric illumination before the Royal Society of London in 1808. After the invention of the dynamo by Michael Faraday in 1831, electricity developed steadily but slowly. At the Philadelphia Centennial Exposition in 1876, Moses G. Farmer demonstrated three large arc lights powered by a primitive transformer. Arc lighting resulted from the oxidation of carbon caused by the flow of current, which created a brilliant blue light. Incandescence relies instead upon heat applied in a vacuum to prevent the heated carbon from melting. The main problems in early incandescence concerned the supply of current and the search for a material that would not melt at a high temperature.

Edison became fascinated by electricity upon seeing Farmer's commercial application of arc lights at Wanamaker's Philadelphia department store in 1878. Edison's genius was not that of pure science; he was always interested in commercial application, and his aim with electricity was not to compete with the arc-light manufacturers but rather to duplicate the success of the gas distributing industry by using electricity. At the time, gas lighting was a major U.S. industry with an income of more than $150 million. New arc lights would threaten only 10 percent of this income. Edison wanted the other 90 percent.

In this endeavor, Edison was, in effect, working from first principles, because most research in electric lighting had been devoted to the arc-light principle. He needed financing, and with confidence and gall in equal proportions, he announced before the fact that he had invented a new and cheap electric light. On October 12, 1878, with W. H. Vanderbilt, Morgan, and several other prominent financiers participating, the Edison Electric Light Company was formed, capitalized with three thousand shares, twenty-five hundred of which were Edison's. The financiers advanced fifty thousand dollars to Edison, who then proceeded to invent the light he had already announced as invented. Edison asserted that it would take only six weeks. The fact that he accomplished his immediate goal in little more than a year was astonishing, but so much publicity had preceded the actual invention that it was some time before it was taken seriously by the public or the financiers, in spite of occasional dramatic interludes, such as the lighting of all of Menlo Park, New Jersey, with the new incandescent lamp. Edison's next obstacle was the demonstration of the practicality of the incandescent lamp in lighting an entire urban area. On December 17,1880, he founded the Edison Electric Illumination Company of New York, which evolved into Consolidated Edison. The laying of mains, the running of generators, and the convincing of a still dubious public took all the inventor's energy. However, his discovery won first prize at the 1881 Paris Electrical Exposition, and soon, patches of light throughout the world's cities announced the arrival of "Edison's lamps." Before he was done, Edison not only had invented a successful incandescent light but also had developed an entire system to generate and distribute electric energy. Credit for bringing electricity to the world is also due to the likes of Alessandro Volta, Sir Humphry Davy, Michael Faraday, and others who had helped the realization of Edison's more dependable, durable, and reliable system.

—*Richard H. Collin, updated by Peter B. Heller*

ADDITIONAL READING:

Baldwin, Neil. *Edison: Inventing the Century.* New York: Hyperion, 1995. This lightly illustrated account, with assistance from scores of individuals, such as Edison family descendants, is commendable for its vignettes and anecdotes. Includes a hundred pages of notes and bibliography.

Clark, Ronald W. *Edison: The Man Who Made the Future.* New York: G. P. Putnam's Sons, 1977. The chapter entitled "The Birth of the Electric Bulb," interesting vignettes, factual material, and attractive halftones recommend this book.

Edison, Thomas A. *Menlo Park: The Early Years, April 1876-December 1877.* Vol. 3 in *The Papers of Thomas A. Edison,* edited by Robert A. Rosenberg et al. Baltimore: The Johns Hopkins University Press, 1994. Includes Edison's early notes on an electric lighting system.

Friedel, Robert D. *Edison's Electric Light: Biography of an Invention.* New Brunswick, N.J.: Rutgers University Press, 1986. A clear explanation of the origins and nature of the electric light bulb, whose genesis was helped by William Wallace's dynamo to generate power.

Josephson, Matthew. *Edison: A Biography.* 1959. Reprint. New York: John Wiley, 1992. This work, written in colorful but accessible language, is nearly encyclopedic in its coverage.

Millard, Andre. "Edison's Laboratory and the Electrical Industry." In *Edison and the Business of Innovation.* Baltimore: The Johns Hopkins University Press, 1990. Places the invention of Edison's high-vacuum incandescent bulb in the broader context of the entire electrical system. A well-researched and illustrated work.

Wachhorst, Wyn. *Thomas Alva Edison: An American Myth.* Cambridge, Mass.: MIT Press, 1981. The few pages devoted to the incandescent lamp, and especially the encyclopedic Edison bibliography, are noteworthy.

SEE ALSO: 1844, First Telegraph Message; 1858, First Transatlantic Cable; 1861, Transcontinental Telegraph Is Completed; 1876, Bell Demonstrates the Telephone.

1882 ■ STANDARD OIL TRUST IS ORGANIZED: *centralized control of a new industry becomes the model for late nineteenth century American business*

DATE: January 2, 1882
LOCALE: Cleveland, Ohio
CATEGORIES: Business and labor; Economics
KEY FIGURES:

Samuel J. Andrews (1817-1906), early Rockefeller partner and inventor of a more efficient refining process
George F. Chester (1813-1897),
Myron R. Keith, and
George H. Vilas (1835-1907), Standard Oil trustees in 1879
Samuel C. T. Dodd (1836-1907), attorney who developed the Standard Oil Trust in 1882
Henry M. Flagler (1830-1913), Rockefeller partner credited with the early development of the trust
John D. Rockefeller (1839-1937), dominant figure in the growth of the Standard Oil Company
William Rockefeller (1841-1922), John's brother, who was also significant in the rise of the Standard Oil Company

SUMMARY OF EVENT. The importance of big business in the U.S. economy was confirmed during the last two decades of the nineteenth century as the United States became one of the world's major industrial powers. The petroleum industry played a leading role in this development and was, in many ways, a harbinger of the new age of U.S. economic supremacy. Although only about thirty years old by 1890, the industry was gigantic—characterized by concentrated ownership in refining and transportation facilities. This concentration had been brought about largely by one dominant organization, the Standard Oil Trust. Formed in 1882, it became the prototype for large-scale U.S. enterprise.

The rise of Standard Oil was brought about largely through the efforts of John D. Rockefeller. A Cleveland bookkeeper whose family fortune would surpass all, Rockefeller has been depicted both as the personification of the Horatio Alger myth of success through hard work and intelligence and as a ruthless, obsessive monster motivated by greed. On one hand, he was regarded as a man of great morality and piety. On the other hand, his businesses operated in a culture of secrecy, duplicity, rebates, drawbacks, and convenient memory loss. Undoubtedly, he had great genius at organization, foresight, considerable administrative talents, and the ability to choose able subordinates.

Starting his career at the age of sixteen years in a small produce firm and later becoming a partner in a grain commission house during the Civil War, Rockefeller sensed the possibilities in the new oil regions of northwestern Pennsylvania but was appalled by the disorder and instability of the new industry. In 1860, one year after Edwin Drake's first successful drilling in Titusville, Pennsylvania, the price of a barrel of oil was twenty dollars. By the end of the next year, it had dropped to ten cents as a result of overproduction. By 1863, Cleveland was linked by rail to the oil fields and Rockefeller invested in a refinery, which soon became the city's largest. After buying out most of his partners, Rockefeller, his brother William, and Samuel Andrews built a second refinery. William moved to New York to develop the Eastern and export trade. Henry M. Flagler became a partner in 1867 and negotiated extremely favorable railroad freight rate arrangements that facilitated the growth of the company.

In 1870, Rockefeller organized the Standard Oil Company (Ohio), which was incorporated as a joint stock company with a capitalization of one million dollars. Rockefeller had begun moving toward vertical integration of his operations. Almost fanatically dedicated to efficiency, he was convinced that destructive and wasteful competition must end if the company were to remain solvent. Therefore, he began acquiring other refineries, first in Cleveland, then in other cities. By the end of 1872, Rockefeller and his associates controlled all the major refineries in Ohio, New York, and Pennsylvania. Over the next decade, the company developed a pipeline system, purchased new oil-bearing lands, acquired extensive oil terminal facilities, and constructed an elaborate and efficient marketing system. By 1879, thirty-seven stockholders of the Standard Oil Company, through the parent, subsidiary, and associated companies, controlled more than 90 percent of U.S. refining capacity.

Operations of the Standard Oil Company and its affiliates developed so rapidly and with such complexity that they soon outgrew the structural framework of the parent company, a situation that distressed and perplexed Rockefeller. The Standard Oil Company (Ohio) was a manufacturing company with multitudinous operations outside the state, despite the fact that it had no legal right to own property or stock beyond the borders of Ohio. It was the nucleus of the richest and most powerful industrial organization in the country and was almost nationwide in scope. However, the expansion had developed in a somewhat haphazard fashion, and the structure lacked coherence and administrative centralization. Between 1873 and 1879, stock in other companies had been acquired in the names of Flagler, William Rockefeller, and others acting as trustees. In 1879, this structure was reorganized and systematized. The trustee device gave the Standard Oil Company a flexible means of expanding beyond the borders of Ohio and, equally important, permitted Rockefeller and his associates to camouflage their activities. Following a strict legal interpretation of the nature of trustees—that they were acting on behalf of stockholders and not of the company per se—Standard Oil Company officials, including Rockefeller himself, denied publicly and under oath that the company owned or controlled certain assets.

By 1879, this informal arrangement clearly had weaknesses that transcended its advantages. If a trustee died, there could be difficult legal problems, and disagreements within the management of the Standard Oil Company could create internal dissension. In 1879, a plan to overcome these dangers was developed, probably by Flagler. All Standard Oil Company properties held in the names of various individuals and all possessions outside Ohio were transferred to three trustees, George H. Vilas, Myron R. Keith, and George F. Chester, who were minor employees at the Cleveland office. Theoretically, these men were to manage the various interests for the exclusive use and benefit of the stockholders of the Standard Oil Company, who would receive profits in the form of dividends proportionate to their holdings. This 1879 plan was legally satisfactory, because all the legal holdings of the Standard Oil Company then were concentrated in the Cleveland office, and the danger of conflict of interest among the trustees was minimized.

Cumbersome and risky, the arrangement did not provide adequate administrative centralization, solve many of the problems of planning and coordinating company activities outside Ohio, or deal with the possibility of double, triple, and even quadruple taxation of the same assets by several states. No provision was made for continuity among the trustees in case of resignations or deaths. There was no method or procedure for the transfer of trust certificates. Finally, Vilas, Chester, and Keith had no real power to control or direct the operations of subordinates, and unity or uniformity was maintained only through cumbersome devices such as occasional meetings of Standard Oil Company leaders in executive committees.

By 1882, these problems were largely solved in a new trust agreement, apparently written by Samuel C. T. Dodd, the chief attorney for the Standard Oil Company, who refined Flagler's idea. Signed on January 2, 1882, the agreement welded separate Standard Oil corporations of various states together by pooling the stock of all. The signatories included the stockholders of the Standard Oil Company, together with Vilas, Chester, and Keith. All properties owned or controlled by the

Standard Oil Company were placed in the hands of nine trustees, including John D. Rockefeller. Each share of Standard Oil Company (Ohio) stock was exchanged for twenty trust certificates at a par value of one hundred dollars each, enabling investors to buy or sell portions of the pool. The trustees were to exercise general supervision over all Standard Oil companies and over other concerns whose stock was held in trust. In effect, a giant new centralized company, the Standard Oil Trust, had been created, although it did not have a legal existence. The new arrangement gave John D. Rockefeller and his associates the administrative flexibility to direct their worldwide activities effectively. By 1885, 70 percent of Standard Oil's business was overseas. The trust produced from wells in Pennsylvania, Texas, and California, and exported to Europe, the Far East and, ironically, the Middle East.

The Standard Oil Trust served as the prototype for other monopolies, until the New Jersey legislature passed a law in 1889 permitting intercorporation stockholding, thereby paving the way for the creation of giant holding companies. One of the first of these would be a successor to the Standard Oil Trust and the target of antimonopoly prosecution, Standard Oil (New Jersey). In a twenty-thousand-word decision rendered in May, 1911, in *Standard Oil Company of New Jersey et al. v. United States*, the Supreme Court gave Standard Oil six months to dismember its empire, thereby leading to the formation of the major U.S. oil companies of the twentieth century.

As the U.S. economy expanded during the nineteenth century, there were numerous endeavors to consolidate businesses. The Standard Oil Trust of 1882 was the most dynamic product of these trends, exemplifying a milestone in the evolutionary chain stretching from primitive pooling agreements to the development of giant holding companies. Through the Standard Oil Trust, Rockefeller, Flagler and Dodd pointed the way toward the complete centralization of giant industries, thus revolutionizing the structure of U.S. business.

—*James E. Fickle, updated by Randall Fegley*

ADDITIONAL READING:

Cochran, Thomas, and William Miller. *The Age of Enterprise: A Social History of Industrial America.* New York: Harper & Row, 1961. A well-written, general treatment of late nineteenth century industrial United States that contains a section on pools, trusts, and corporations.

Hidy, Ralph, and Muriel Hidy. *Pioneering in Big Business, 1882-1911.* Vol. 1 in *History of Standard Oil Company, New Jersey.* New York: Harper & Row, 1955. A detailed study of what would become the most prominent offspring of the Standard Oil Trust.

Kirkland, Edward. *Industry Comes of Age: Business, Labor, and Public Policy, 1860-1897.* New York: Holt, Rinehart & Winston, 1961. A useful survey of late nineteenth century U.S. economic structures and society. Includes an excellent chapter, "The Organization of Production," dealing with combination.

Nevins, Allan. *John D. Rockefeller.* Abridged by William Greenleaf. New York: Charles Scribner's Sons, 1959. A condensed version of Nevins' earlier works on Rockefeller.

_____. *Study in Power: John D. Rockefeller, Industrialist and Philanthropist.* 2 vols. New York: Charles Scribner's Sons, 1953. A comprehensive, well-balanced biography of Rockefeller.

Sampson, Anthony. *The Seven Sisters.* New York: Viking, 1975. Standard Oil features prominently in this well-written history of the world's seven major oil companies, which has been revised several times.

Tarbell, Ida. *The History of the Standard Oil Company.* 2 vols. New York: McClure, Phillips, 1904. This classic polemic reflects the muckraking attitudes of its times.

Williamson, Harold, and Arnold Daum. *The American Petroleum Industry: The Age of Illumination, 1859-1899.* Evanston, Ill.: Northwestern University Press, 1959. This general study of the petroleum industry includes an excellent study on the Standard Oil Trust.

Yergin, Daniel. *The Prize.* New York: Simon & Schuster, 1992. A more recent history of the world petroleum industry.

SEE ALSO: 1859, First Commercial Oil Well; 1890, Sherman Antitrust Act.

1882 ■ CHINESE EXCLUSION ACT: *a new wave of nativist xenophobia generates the first U.S. immigration law to discriminate on the basis of national origin*

DATE: May 9, 1882
LOCALE: Washington, D.C.
CATEGORIES: Asian American history; Immigration; Laws and acts
KEY FIGURES:
James B. Angell (1829-1916), chairman of the U.S. Treaty Commission
Chester Alan Arthur (1830-1886), twenty-first president of the United States, 1881-1885
Henry L. Dawes (1816-1903) and
Joseph R. Hawley (1826-1905), U.S. senators who opposed exclusion
James T. Farley and
John F. Miller (1831-1886), senators from California who were active in the exclusion movement
Denis Kearney (1847-1907), leader of the Workingmen's Party in California and a foe of Chinese immigration
Li Hung-tsao (1820-1897) and
Pao-yun (1807-1891), Chinese plenipotentiaries for treaty negotiations in 1880
SUMMARY OF EVENT. In 1886, the United States dedicated the Statue of Liberty, a monument that stands in symbolic welcome to the "huddled masses" from foreign shores. Yet even as the statue was dedicated, the citizenry had allowed its vision of the country as a refuge for all people to grow dimmer instead of brighter. Four years earlier, in 1882, the United States had taken the first steps to exclude immigrants from China and to restrict

certain classes of immigrants from all foreign countries.

The closing of the door to Chinese immigrants had begun in the early 1850's. Responding to the thousands of Chinese workers who had crossed the Pacific Ocean after 1849 to seek their fortune in the California gold fields, the California state legislature enacted a series of discriminatory laws to discourage settlement and further immigration. The foreign miners' tax of 1852, immigration head tax of 1855, Chinese fishing tax of 1860, and police tax of 1862 imposed discriminatory fines on Chinese laborers, making it difficult for them to continue working in California. By the early 1860's, increased taxation, coupled with the discovery of gold in Australia, reduced the number of Chinese immigrants entering the United States from more than twenty thousand in 1852 to only twenty-seven hundred in 1864.

Precisely at this time, however, a new source of employment was opening for Chinese in the United States. In 1865, the Central Pacific Railroad Company began employing Chinese laborers to lay track for the western portion of the transcontinental railway. Within three years, the company hired ten thousand Chinese workers. The promise of good pay and steady work, far from city taxes and prejudice, again drew Chinese to the United States. Between 1868 and 1870, nearly thirty-five thousand Chinese immigrants passed through San Francisco customs, many directly recruited by U.S. railroad agents in China. With the completion of the transcontinental railroad in 1869, however, these thousands of Chinese laborers returned to the West Coast to seek work. Competition for jobs between Chinese and Euro-American workers in San Francisco and other Pacific coast cities led U.S. workers to intensify their demands for restrictions on Chinese immigration.

Workers in California rallied for stricter control over Chinese immigration. They argued that the growing population and alien customs of the Chinese constituted a threat to basic American institutions. They claimed that Chinese houses and shops were opium dens in which innocent native Californians were debauched. They accused the Chinese of being a race of "coolies" who threatened the wages and dignity of native California labor. In San Francisco, "anti-coolie clubs" and "light hour leagues" organized anti-Chinese demonstrations. Under the leadership of Denis Kearney, a firebrand orator from the sandlots of San Francisco, the Workingmen's Party of California became a potent exclusionist force in state politics and in anti-Chinese riots and demonstrations. Kearney's racist harangues incited workingmen all along the Pacific coast to rise up against the Chinese. Mob violence against the Chinese escalated throughout the 1870's, exemplified by a Los Angeles attack in which a mob of about five hundred assaulted the city's Chinatown, killing a score of its residents.

In the early 1880's, California exclusionists turned the Chinese problem into a national issue, demanding that Congress enact a law that would prohibit Chinese immigration. Party politics gave added weight to the exclusionists' demands on the national level, as both Republicans and Democrats vied for Western constituencies, which they believed to be crucial. In

1879, Congress responded to Western pressure and passed a Chinese exclusion bill. President Rutherford B. Hayes vetoed the measure, because it violated the terms of the Burlingame Treaty of 1868, which permitted unlimited Chinese immigration to the U.S. Chinese plenipotentiaries Li Hung-tsao and

This political cartoon by Thomas Nast shows the tree of American liberty, and the Chinese attempting to cling to it, falling with the weight of anti-Chinese sentiment as manifested in the Chinese Exclusion Act of 1882. (Asian American Studies Library, University of California at Berkeley)

Pao-yun agreed to renegotiate the Burlingame Treaty to include the possibility of limiting Chinese immigration. In 1880, they concluded a treaty with the U.S. representative, James B. Angell, that granted the United States the right to regulate, limit, or suspend the immigration of Chinese laborers, but not absolutely prohibit such immigration.

The Angell treaty opened the door for the creation of federal legislation restricting Chinese immigration. Without delay, California's Senator John F. Miller introduced a bill calling for the suspension of immigration for all Chinese laborers, skilled or unskilled, for a period of twenty years. The Senate heatedly debated the bill. New England senators argued that a founding tenet of the United States—free immigration from all nations for all peoples—was at stake. West Coast senators countered that the future of U.S. laborers was in jeopardy. The bill finally passed the Senate but was vetoed by President Chester A. Arthur because it violated the spirit of the 1880 negotiations with China. Congress immediately drafted another bill, which suspended immigration and naturalization of Chinese laborers, skilled and unskilled, for ten years. On May 9, 1882, President Arthur signed the Chinese Exclusion Act into law. The Exclusion Act was renewed for another ten-year period in 1892, again in 1902, and in 1904 was made permanent. The act was not rescinded until December 17, 1943, during World War II, when it became a source of embarrassment between the two allied nations.

Chinese exclusion initiated a trend toward the passage of increasingly restrictive immigration legislation. President Arthur had signed into law the Immigration Act of 1882, the first general immigration law. This act imposed a tax on every immigrant and prohibited the entry of any convict, "lunatic," "idiot," or person unable to take care of himself or herself without becoming a public charge. Well into the twentieth century, Congress continued to pass legislation limiting the immigration of certain "undesirable" groups.

By 1882, the United States had excluded one nationality and had imposed limitations, however slight, on all potential immigrants. The Chinese question in California had been an explosive one, fueled by racism toward Chinese immigrants who could not and, exclusionists believed, would not assimilate. The interaction of social pressures, economic changes, and opportunistic politics in the United States closed the Pacific door to Chinese laborers. By prohibiting these Chinese from entering the United States, Congress had turned away "huddled masses" even before Emma Lazarus' poetry on the Statue of Liberty had bid them welcome.

—Emory M. Thomas, updated by Daniel J. Meissner

ADDITIONAL READING:

Barth, Gunther. *Bitter Strength: A History of the Chinese in the United States, 1850-1870.* Cambridge, Mass.: Harvard University Press, 1964. Although it does not treat events after 1870, this book is important to an understanding of anti-Chinese sentiment in California.

Chan, Sucheng, ed. *Entry Denied: Exclusion and the Chinese Community in America, 1882-1943.* Philadelphia: Tem-

ple University Press, 1991. Explores the legal ramifications of the Exclusion Act and the act's effects on Chinese who were living in the United States.

Coolidge, Mary Roberts. *Chinese Immigration.* New York: Henry Holt, 1909. A dated but comprehensive book. Argues that the Exclusion Act was necessary to prevent unchecked Chinese immigration from undermining the U.S. economy.

LeMay, Michael C. *From Open Door to Dutch Door: An Analysis of U.S. Immigration Policy Since 1820.* New York: Praeger, 1987. Examines underlying causes of the anti-immigration movement in the United States in response to European and Chinese immigration since 1820.

Miller, Stuart Creighton. *The Unwelcome Immigrant: The American Image of the Chinese, 1785-1882.* Berkeley: University of California Press, 1969. Countering Coolidge's argument of an economic basis for the Exclusion Act, argues that racism was at the root of Californian and U.S. hostility toward Chinese immigrants.

SEE ALSO: 1842, Dorr Rebellion; 1875, Page Law; 1882, Rise of the Chinese Six Companies; 1892, "New" Immigration; 1892, Yellow Peril Campaign; 1895, Chinese American Citizens Alliance Is Founded.

1882 ■ RISE OF THE CHINESE SIX COMPANIES: *rising anti-Asian nativism prompts Chinese immigrants to organize for political representation, social services, and physical protection*

DATE: November 12, 1882
LOCALE: San Francisco, California
CATEGORIES: Asian American history; Immigration
SUMMARY OF EVENT. In the early years of the United States, relations with Imperial China consisted of a small amount of trade in scarce goods. After the second Opium War forced the Chinese emperor to open coastal areas to foreign trade and settlement in 1842, U.S. business interests began to view China as a potential market for exports.

News of the California gold rush of 1848-1849 was the first catalyst for large Chinese emigration across the Pacific to the United States. Many dreamed of streets of gold, but most Chinese emigrants arrived too late to capitalize on the limited riches of gold. Although some did mine for gold, often taking over claims that had been abandoned by miners who had moved on to richer deposits, many others worked as laborers building the transcontinental railroad under dangerous conditions. As more Chinese arrived in the West, some whites began to resent the diligent work habits of the Chinese immigrants and feared that their willingness to work would bring down wages for all workers. Like many other groups of newly arrived immigrants to the United States, many Chinese chose to cling to their native language and customs and live with fellow Chinese immigrants.

The Chinese population in the United States at this time was overwhelmingly male. By 1880, more than one hundred thousand Chinese lived in the western United States, of which only three thousand were women. Because of the preponderance of men, many whites saw the Chinese as transient workers who wanted temporary jobs in the United States to prepare for future marriages after they returned to China. The completion of the railroads and the Panic of 1873 had caused great economic difficulties in the West. Frustrated by political and economic difficulties, many Euro-Americans and elements of organized labor began to blame the Chinese for the lack of jobs and the economic recession. Violence against Chinese in this period was widespread. In October, 1871, crowds of whites burned and looted the Los Angeles Chinatown after two white policemen were killed by Chinese assailants. Nineteen men, women, and children were killed and hundreds injured as angry whites randomly attacked crowds of Chinese.

Hostility toward Chinese immigrants was reflected in the immigration laws of the period. Under intense political pressure from white voters in the West, Congress moved to exclude Chinese and other foreign-born Asians from obtaining citizenship. The 1870 Nationality Act denied the Chinese the possibility of becoming naturalized U.S. citizens, specifying that only foreign-born "free whites" and "African aliens" were eligible for citizenship. In 1878, California convened a constitutional convention to settle what was called the "Chinese problem." The adopted constitution prohibited further Chinese immigration and granted local municipalities the right to exclude Chinese immigrants or confine them to specified areas. California also prohibited Chinese, American Indians, and African Americans from attending public schools.

Chinese immigrants were prohibited from owning property, obtaining business licenses, procuring government jobs, and testifying in any legal proceedings. At the urging of white voters in California, Congress in 1882 passed the first of a number of Chinese exclusion acts that prohibited the entrance of Chinese into the United States. The Supreme Court upheld the exclusion acts, ruling in 1889 that the Chinese were "a race that will not assimilate with us [and] could be excluded when deemed dangerous to peace and security." President Grover Cleveland supported that act and echoed the Court's description of Chinese immigrants' role in American society.

In San Francisco, anti-Chinese laws were supplemented to isolate the large Chinese community. Since the gold rush, San Francisco had been a center for recent immigrants to the United States. Attracted by tales of wealth in San Francisco—*Jinshan*, or "golden mountain"—newly arrived Chinese were forced to settle in the Chinatown area because of local laws and hostility from whites. Local regulations penalized attempts by Chinese merchants to expand by levying special taxes on businesses. There was even a local tax on the long braided hair worn by Chinese men. Segregated by these discriminatory laws, Chinatown began to establish structures to govern and protect its residents. San Francisco's Chinatown, made up primarily of men as a result of the immigration

control acts, had developed a reputation as a center of vice. While most leaders at the time did not encourage assimilation with white society, they did move to control the small criminal element that began to define Chinese society to the non-Chinese residents of San Francisco.

Most of the early Chinese immigrants to San Francisco's Chinatown came from the southern provinces of Guangdong and Fujian. Early on, wealthy merchants in Chinatown had organized around clan groups and district associations in their hometowns in China. By 1854, there were six main associations in Chinatown. The first, formed in 1849, was the Gangzhou Gongsi, named after the district in Guangdong province that was the source of most of its members. The second, the San Yi Gongsi, consisted of immigrants from the administrative districts of Nanhai, Panyu, and Shunde. Immigrants from the districts of Yanging, Xinning, Xinhui, and Kaiping made up the third association, the Si Yi Gongsi. Immigrants from the Xiangshan area formed the fourth association, the Yang He Gongsi. The fifth, the Ren He Gongsi, was made up of the so-called Hakka peoples from Guanxi province.

The formation in 1854 of the sixth association, the Ning Yang Gongsi, marked the informal beginnings of the Chinese Six Companies Association. Formed first as a *kung saw* (public hall), the Six Companies served as a public association for leaders of the major associations in Chinatown to mediate disputes between it members and serve as a representative of the Chinese community as a whole. Newly arrived immigrants from China who were in need of assistance sought out these family or district associations rather than turn to local social service agencies. When business or personal disputes developed between members of different associations, the Six Companies would provide a forum for peaceful mediation of disputes.

The anti-Chinese legislation of the 1880's forced the Six Companies to move toward a more overt role as representatives of Chinese interests in San Francisco. In 1882, the Chinese counsel general in San Francisco, Huang Zunxian, recognized the group as the leading body in Chinatown. The Six Companies moved toward creating a formal representative body within Chinatown to represent Chinese interests. On November 19, 1882, the group formalized its existence by establishing an executive body drawn from members of the existing associations. The Six Companies, formally known as the Chinese Consolidated Benevolent Association (CCBA), adapted some of the representative principles of U.S. political culture. After its reorganization, the office of the president served a specified term and the presidency rotated between member associations that made up the Six Companies.

The CCBA was recognized by the state of California in 1901. At the time, the Six Companies sought to create a body above family clans or associations that would resist the growing anti-Chinese movements in California and the western United States. While it would carry on its role as a mediator in Chinatown, the group now took a more public role in its resistance to anti-Chinese legislation.

After the CCBA's formal establishment in 1882, Chinese diplomats encouraged Chinese communities across the United States, Canada, and South America to establish Chinese Consolidated Benevolent Associations. The Six Companies in San Francisco had limited success in challenging anti-Chinese legislation as violations of the Fourteenth Amendment to the Constitution. The Six Companies supported the 1896 case of *Yue Ting v. Hopkins*, which forced the Supreme Court to overturn San Francisco safety ordinances designed to harass Chinese laundrymen. Anti-Chinese attitudes in San Francisco and across the United States did not diminish after 1900. In 1902, an amendment to extend the Chinese Exclusion Act indefinitely was passed by Congress without debate. China boycotted U.S. goods to protest the legislation.

In the first half of the twentieth century, the Six Companies in San Francisco supported measures to improve the quality of life in Chinatown. In 1905, the Six Companies established a school in Chinatown to teach children Chinese culture and language. In the 1920's, it helped raise funds to construct the Chinese Hospital to serve the Chinatown community. The Six Companies also established block watch programs and night patrols to prevent crime in the Chinatown area. The group still worked to overturn anti-Chinese sentiment and was an increasingly powerful political force, able to deliver votes to local politicians sympathetic to the views of Chinatown citizens.

In 1943, Congress passed an immigration act that repealed the exclusion laws, and barriers to Chinese Americans in the United States began to fall. In California, many Americans of Chinese ancestry moved to white neighborhoods after anti-Chinese laws were overturned. In this period, one of the major activities of the Six Companies was the promotion of the Nationalist government in Taiwan. Because most of the residents of San Francisco's Chinatown had immigrated from mainland China, significant opposition to the historical leadership of the group appeared.

The Six Companies' promotion of social isolation from white society was very divisive in the 1960's. A longtime opponent of federal social programs to aid the poor, the Six Companies eventually embraced government assistance and even administered federal job training programs in the 1970's. As Chinese Americans became more involved in Chinese politics and gained access to higher-paying jobs, participation in Chinatown affairs decreased significantly. The Six Comapnies became less of a force in Chinese American politics on a national scale, but it continued to work from its base in San Francisco. *—Lawrence I. Clark*

ADDITIONAL READING:

Chinn, Thomas W. *Bridging the Pacific: San Francisco Chinatown and Its People*. San Francisco: Chinese Historical Society of America, 1989. A detailed look at San Francisco from its founding to the late 1980's, by the cofounder of the Chinese Historical Association of America. Includes photographs, clan charts, notes on transliteration, business directories, maps, bibliography, and index.

Kinkead, Gwen. *Chinatown: A Portrait of a Closed Society*. New York: HarperCollins, 1992. A valuable resource for observers interested in the inner workings of New York's Chinatown. Provides a detailed portrait of the role of the New York CCBA in its Chinatown.

Nee, Victor, and Brett de Barry Nee. "The Establishment." In *Longtime Californ': A Documentary Study of an American Chinatown*. New York: Pantheon Books, 1973. Examines the founding of the Six Companies and its role in Chinatown in the twentieth century.

SEE ALSO: 1842, Dorr Rebellion; 1875, Page Law; 1882, Chinese Exclusion Act; 1892, "New" Immigration; 1892, Yellow Peril Campaign; 1895, Chinese American Citizens Alliance Is Founded.

1883 ■ PENDLETON ACT: *the civil service system for federal employees replaces the political spoils system*

DATE: January 16, 1883
LOCALE: Washington, D.C.
CATEGORIES: Government and politics; Laws and acts
KEY FIGURES:
Chester Alan Arthur (1830-1886), twenty-first president of the United States, 1881-1885
Dorman Bridgman Eaton (1823-1899), secretary of the National Civil Service Reform League and drafter of the law, who became the first head of the Civil Service Commission
James Abram Garfield (1831-1881), twentieth president of the United states, 1881
Charles Julius Guiteau (1844-1882), disappointed office seeker who shot Garfield
George Hunt Pendleton (1825-1889), Democrat from Ohio who sponsored the act bearing his name

SUMMARY OF EVENT. On July 2, 1881, President James A. Garfield prepared to leave Washington for a vacation in New York State. As the presidential party neared the waiting train, Garfield was shot in the back by Charles J. Guiteau, an unsuccessful aspirant to the office of consult to Paris. He shouted, "I am a Stalwart and Arthur is president now!" Even in an age of widespread graft, Chester A. Arthur, the vice president, had been well known as the head of the New York Customs House, a classically corrupt government agency, and as a spoilsman in Roscoe Conkling's New York Republican political machine. Few expected him to change when he became president at Garfield's death on September 19, but he exhibited an unanticipated coolness toward the Stalwarts (professional machine Republicans) in selecting cabinet replacements and insisted on continuing the prosecution of the "Star Route" mail fraud case. These actions are credited with costing Arthur the presidential nomination in 1884, as well as providing the Democrats with numerous victories in the elections of fall, 1882. As a result, the outgoing Republican Congress was impelled to adopt civil service reform legislation in 1883.

However, a confluence of reasons were responsible, finally, for civil service reform. George Washington, when he was president, initiated the idea that persons of high competence and integrity should be sought to fill public service jobs. This approach resulted in a stable and fairly skilled workforce but contributed to its elite quality. When Andrew Jackson became president in 1829, he operated under the belief that the "common man" had as much right to a government job as the wealthy and that most government jobs could be done by people without special training. He democratized the civil service but also helped justify the spoils system.

By the 1880's, the number of public jobs had greatly increased, and the quality of those serving in them had declined. Several reform attempts failed. The first serious attempt to reform the system was led by Thomas Allen Jenckes, a Republican congressman from Rhode Island. Jenckes was a patent lawyer by profession and also had financial interests in several companies. In both activities he had to rely on the federal mail service, which was inefficient and corrupt. In 1865 he introduced his first civil service reform bill covering all federal agencies, including the post office. His proposal was patterned after the British system and would have covered all federal officials except those appointed by the president with the consent of the Senate. A decade later a number of organized reform groups around the country, concerned first with local and then with national corruption, were formed. A national reform movement was spearheaded by the National Civil Service Reform League, presided over by George William Curtis.

The assassination of Garfield was the spark that lit the smoldering coals not only of the reformers' attempts but also of elected officials' weariness with long lines of people seeking jobs, patronage appointees' weariness with blatant assessments of percentages of their salaries for political party support, and the Republican Congress' assessment that its power might be about to end. Therefore in 1883 the Republican Congress passed an act drafted by Dorman B. Eaton, secretary of the National Civil Service Reform League, and sponsored by Democratic senator George Pendleton of Ohio: the National Civil Service Act, commonly known as the Pendleton Act.

The act had two purposes: to eliminate political influence from administrative agencies and to assure more competent government employees. It established a three-member bipartisan Civil Service Commission appointed by the president with the consent of the Senate for indefinite terms. Eaton became the first chairman of the Civil Service Commission. About ten percent of the government positions were included initially, but other positions, to be designed by the president, could be "covered in"; that is, current patronage appointees could remain in their positions when those positions were included under the act. This provision gave outgoing presidents an incentive to "cover in" increasing numbers of positions over time, which is in fact what happened. The act provided that civil service positions were to be filled through open and competitive examinations; lateral entry was encouraged, and employees were assured tenure regardless of political changes at the tops of the organizations. Employees were also protected against political pressures such as assessments and required participation in campaign activities.

The adoption of a merit system at the federal level was followed immediately by similar adoptions in some of the states. Widespread coverage at the state and local levels was subsequently brought about through requirements attached to most federal grant monies.

Over the years, legislation was added to improve the civil service system. The Classification Act of 1923 established a system for classifying jobs according to qualifications needed to carry them out and tying them to various pay grades, thus providing uniformity throughout the federal system. The Hatch Political Activities Act of 1939 prohibited national civil service workers from taking an active part in politics, and later amendments extended the ban to state and local employees whose programs were financed fully or in part by federal funds. In 1978 the Civil Service Reform Act reassigned the Civil Service Commission's often contradictory functions to two agencies: a new Office of Personnel Management, responsible for policy leadership, and a Merit Systems Protection Board, to handle investigations and appeals. A Senior Executive Service was also established, creating a separate personnel system for the highest-ranking civil service officials in an attempt to provide greater flexibility in assignments and incentives for top senior personnel.   —Anne Trotter, updated by Erika E. Pilver

ADDITIONAL READING:

Cayer, N. Joseph. *Public Personnel Administration in the United States*. New York: St. Martin's Press, 1986. A good survey of the U.S. civil service to date.

Emmerich, Herbert. *Federal Organization and Administrative Management*. University: University of Alabama Press, 1971. A classic in the field, useful for coverage through the 1960's.

Hoogenboom, Ari. *Outlawing the Spoils: A History of the Civil Service Reform Movement, 1865-1883*. Urbana: University of Illinois Press, 1961. Attacks the stereotypes of the "evil" spoilsmen and the "noble" reformers.

Ingraham, Patricia, and Carolyn Ban, eds. *Legislating Bureaucratic Change: The Civil Service Reform Act of 1978*. Albany: State University of New York Press, 1984. An account of the act's provisions and an analysis of their implementation.

SEE ALSO: 1877, Hayes Is Elected President.

1883 ■ BROOKLYN BRIDGE OPENS: *an engineering marvel sets new standards for aesthetic design of utilitarian structures*

DATE: May 24, 1883
LOCALE: New York City
CATEGORY: Science and technology

KEY FIGURES:

James T. Eads (1820-1887), competitor of the Roeblings, who worked with caissons and first became aware of the "bends" sickness

Charles Ellet (1810-1862), former competitor of John in designing suspension bridges

Emily Roebling (1843-1903), Washington Roebling's wife, who assisted him after he was injured

John Augustus Roebling (1806-1869), nineteenth century master designer of suspension bridges

Washington Augustus Roebling (1837-1926), John's son, who directed actual construction of the Brooklyn Bridge

SUMMARY OF EVENT. On May 24, 1883, Chester Alan Arthur, twenty-first president of the United States, and Stephen Grover Cleveland, then governor of New York, together with the mayors of New York and Brooklyn, met with thousands of citizens in attendance to open the majestic Brooklyn Bridge, which was described as the eighth wonder of the world. A marvel of engineering, this suspension bridge seemed to many contemporaries to be a symbol of the American way of life—free, useful, and beautiful. The height of the gothic towers from which hung the great cables and suspenders that supported the roadway was matched only by the tower of Trinity Church in lower Manhattan. The opening of the bridge made it possible to cross the entire continent without once having to use a ferry or get one's feet wet.

The person who envisioned this nineteenth century marvel was John Augustus Roebling, a man whose life in many ways exemplifies the American Dream. Born in the Saxon town of Mülhausen in 1806, he acquired his training in engineering at the Royal Polytechnic Institute in Berlin. While there, he was strongly influenced by the philosopher Friedrich Hegel, who imbued the young man with liberal ideas and the belief that the United States was the land of hope and destiny. Disillusioned with the repressive politics of Germany, Roebling emigrated to the United States with a group of friends in 1831.

They settled in western Pennsylvania, where they established the town of Saxonburg, and most of them became farmers. In 1837, the year he became a naturalized citizen, John Roebling gave up farming to become a state canal surveyor. This work brought him into contact with a new invention that hauled railroad cars and heavy loads up steep inclines by means of a stationary engine and a heavy hemp rope. Noticing that the hemp constantly frayed and threatened to break, Roebling designed a superior rope made from wire and, in 1841, formed a company to manufacture it. The firm provided Saxonburg with a needed industry and the engineer with an income that gave him the financial independence to work only on projects that interested him.

In 1846, Roebling completed his first suspension bridge across the Monongahela River at Pittsburgh. By mid-century he had designed and constructed five others. For more than a decade, his chief rival in the field was Charles Ellet, the first native-born American to receive European training in engi-

neering. Initial competition between the two men had occurred in 1841, when both submitted designs for a suspension bridge across the Schuylkill River at Fairmount. At the last minute, Ellet's proposal was adopted. Although an excellent engineer, Ellet never achieved financial independence because his abrasive temperament cost him numerous contracts. John Roebling eventually won the title Master of the Suspension Bridge in 1854, when Ellet's bridge over the Ohio River at Wheeling collapsed, and his rival was hired to rebuild it. During the 1850's, John Roebling's reputation soared. His bridge over the Niagara River, two miles below the falls, was an advanced structure carrying both railroad tracks and a highway. The hallmarks of his work were utility and grace.

By any standards, Roebling's greatest structure was the Brooklyn Bridge. Not only did he design it, but he also originated the project itself. He conceived the idea of linking New York City and Brooklyn by bridge in 1857 and did the preliminary planning, but he was unable to attract sufficient public support to begin construction. Interest in the project began to revive in 1865, and when during the following winter the East River (a strait connecting New York Bay with Long Island Sound and separating Manhattan from Brooklyn) iced over on several occasions and ferry service was disrupted, irate citizens demanded that something be done. Roebling's plans were finally approved, and a company was commissioned in 1869 to build the bridge. The magnitude of the project was so great that pessimists said it could not be done. The total length of the structure was to be 1,596.6 feet; its 86-foot-wide deck would accommodate two sets of railroad tracks, two electric tram lines, two roadways, and a footpath. Four cables and their accompanying suspenders would have to carry a weight of 18,700 tons.

Work began on January 3, 1870. The chief engineer was a Roebling, but not John. During the previous summer, the inventor had been injured in an accident while selecting the site for the bridge's Brooklyn tower. Despite the amputation of several toes, he contracted tetanus and died.

Directors of the construction company selected John's thirty-two-year-old son to succeed him. Washington Roebling, a graduate of Rensselaer Polytechnic Institute, had worked with his father on several projects, including the great Cincinnati Bridge. He had earned a reputation as a civil engineer in his own right while serving in the Union Army during the Civil War.

Washington Roebling's first task in erecting the Brooklyn Bridge was to build the huge caissons on which the support towers were to rest. Working as much as eighty feet below the surface of the water was hazardous, the greatest danger being from the dreaded caisson disease "the bends." In the first five months of 1872, more than one hundred men were hospitalized with the ailment, and three died. One of the most seriously affected was Roebling himself; he was left crippled, almost mute, and in constant pain for the rest of his life. Unable to inspect work on the bridge personally, he relied upon his memory, a pair of binoculars, and his wife, Emily, who taught herself engineering in order to help him. Month after month he sat by a window watching the construction through binoculars, ordering adjustments as needed and sending messages to the workmen through Emily. The design of the bridge remained faithful to the drawings of John Roebling but included numerous alterations devised by Washington.

With as many as six hundred workmen engaged on the structure, it slowly began to take shape, but costs mounted considerably beyond expectations. In 1878, Roebling announced that he had spent thirteen-and-a-half million dollars, almost twice the amount of the original estimate. For six months, all work stopped until new funds could be raised. In 1881, Roebling almost was fired when he asked for an extra thousand tons of steel to reinforce the decking, and his demand was met only after a fight.

In 1882, Roebling faced the greatest crisis of his professional life. The newly elected mayor of Brooklyn called Roebling's competence into question and was determined to oust him as chief engineer. The unexpressed fear was that, given Roebling's physical infirmity, some of the decisions relating to the bridge were being made by his wife, Emily. Many people questioned the ability of women to deal with technical matters. Emily maintained that she always consulted with her husband before instructions were given to his assistants. She now was determined to save both her husband's reputation and position. She began a letter-writing campaign; she persuaded a key trustee to visit Roebling to ascertain his mental capabilities. Largely as a result of her efforts, the vote for removal failed by two votes. Roebling as chief engineer would see his masterpiece completed.

Eight months later, Roebling sat in his chair by the window to watch the ceremonies as the Brooklyn Bridge was opened to traffic. Celebrations followed. The Roeblings and the suspension structure were vindicated. Clearly, this type of bridge could be used to span great distances. So soundly was the Brooklyn Bridge constructed that no real renovation was necessary until the late 1940's. Equally important was the establishment of the architectural principle that a utilitarian object should be well designed, a concept fully accepted by contemporary architects. In 1964, the Brooklyn Bridge was declared a national monument.

Important as it was, the building of the Brooklyn Bridge was but a detail in a period of great industrial expansion in the United States after the Civil War called the "economic revolution," when the country emerged as a major industrial power. It was a period of corruption, greed, and the creation of great wealth. It was also the period of the political bosses. By the turn of the century, every major city had one. New York was among the first. The Brooklyn Bridge probably never would have been built had it not had the backing of the political bosses of both Brooklyn and New York. By the time William Tweed, New York's political boss, fell from power, the bridge had been declared a "public work" by the state legislature, and despite opposition, the project continued to completion.

—*Anne Trotter, updated by Nis Petersen*

ADDITIONAL READING:
Brooklyn Museum. *The Great East River Bridge, 1883-1983.* New York: Harry N. Abrams, 1983. A commemorative volume on the bridge's centennial. Contains primary source material, such as eyewitness accounts, cartoons, and articles, as well as reproductions of works of art with the bridge as subject.
McCullough, David. *The Great Bridge.* New York: Simon & Schuster, 1972. One of the best all-around accounts of the building of the bridge. Deals with the technical details in an understandable manner, using a mystery writer's ability to build suspense.
Mandelbaum, Seymour J. *Boss Tweed's New York.* Chicago: I. R. Dee, 1990. Often misunderstood, the political bosses and their impact on U.S. political and economic life are being reexamined. This author discusses one of the best-known, most-criticized political bosses and finds much of what he did commendable.
Trachtenberg, Alan. *Brooklyn Bridge, Fact and Symbol.* New York: Oxford University Press, 1965. Fits the building of the bridge into a socioeconomic context, not only as a cultural symbol but also as an indication of the transition of the United States from a rural to an urbanized economy.
Weigold, Marilyn E. *Silent Builder: Emily Warren Roebling and the Brooklyn Bridge.* Port Washington, N.Y.: Associated Faculty Press, 1984. A short but thorough study of Emily Roebling's role in building the bridge. Asserts that she was in full charge at times. Twenty-two relevant photographs.

SEE ALSO: 1869, Transcontinental Railroad Is Completed; 1876, Bell Demonstrates the Telephone; 1879, Edison Demonstrates the Incandescent Lamp; 1854, Kansas-Nebraska Act; 1903, Wright Brothers' First Flight; 1931, Empire State Building Opens.

1883 ■ CIVIL RIGHTS CASES: *the U.S. Supreme Court finds the Civil Rights Act of 1875 unconstitutional*

DATE: October 15, 1883
LOCALE: Washington, D.C.
CATEGORIES: Civil rights; Court cases
KEY FIGURES:
Joseph P. Bradley (1813-1892), U.S. Supreme Court justice who wrote the majority opinion
Robert Brown Elliott (1842-1884), African American U.S. representative from South Carolina
John Marshall Harlan (1833-1911), Supreme Court justice who wrote the dissent
John Mercer Langston (1829-1897), head of the Equal Rights League and a civil rights advocate
Charles Sumner (1811-1874), Republican senator and civil rights advocate
SUMMARY OF EVENT. The Civil Rights Act of 1875 proved to be the last piece of Reconstruction law passed by Congress to

ensure that former slaves and their descendants would not be denied their rights as citizens. Partly as a tribute to Charles Sumner, who had fought tirelessly for civil rights during his lifetime and who had died the previous year, his fellow senators approved the legislation. Sumner had held that the Thirteenth Amendment, in addition to abolishing the institution of slavery, also raised former slaves to a status of legal equality. On that basis, Congress had the power to pass laws that would guarantee African Americans freedom from discriminatory treatment, whether by public authorities or by private individuals. As Congress debated the civil rights bill in the early 1870's, the most visible signs of African Americans' legal inferiority were restrictions and segregation in public facilities. Hotels, inns, theaters, trains, and ships routinely denied accommodations to black patrons.

Anticipating questions about the constitutionality of his proposals, Sumner tied his advocacy of free access to public facilities directly to the abolition of slavery, arguing that because one of the disabilities of slavery was the prohibition against entering public places, the end of slavery should mean freedom to enter the establishments of one's choosing. Restrictions on that freedom based on race constituted a "badge of slavery."

Supporters of the public accommodations law also argued that it could be sustained on Fourteenth Amendment grounds. Representative Robert Brown Elliott insisted that the amendment's equal protection clause required that states secure equality before the law for all citizens as part of their responsibility to advance the common good. He cited the Supreme Court's position in the 1873 *Slaughterhouse* cases that the purpose of the Thirteenth and Fourteenth Amendments was to protect African Americans from those who had formerly enslaved them.

The Republicans had lost their majority in Congress in the 1874 elections. They therefore passed the Civil Rights bill in the lame duck session in early 1875, as a last effort to secure the rights of African Americans before Congress became dominated by Democrats and pro-white Southerners.

The original version of the bill was drafted by African American civil rights activist John Mercer Langston, who gave it to Sumner. As passed, the Civil Rights Act of 1875 included five sections. Section 1 provided for equal access for all Americans to public accommodations and places of amusement. Section 2 defined violations and penalties for violating the equal access provisions. Section 3 gave federal, rather than state, courts jurisdiction in civil rights cases and required that law enforcement agencies cooperate to enforce the law. This section was an attempt to ensure that the act would be enforced and violations prosecuted even in states where local authorities were reluctant to do so. Section 4 forbade racial discrimination in federal or state juries, and Section 5 provided for Supreme Court review of cases arising under the act. An additional provision extending the equal access guarantees to public education was dropped from the bill.

In the year after the passage of the Civil Rights Act, neither Republican Rutherford B. Hayes nor Democrat Samuel Tilden received a majority of the electoral votes. As the outcome of the presidential election remained in doubt, a special commission was appointed to resolve the constitutional crisis. The settlement that allowed Hayes to assume the presidency included an agreement that the federal government would stop trying to enforce civil rights legislation, including the new law passed in 1875. Even so, the law remained on the books until a group of cases, known collectively as the *Civil Rights* cases, came before the Supreme Court in 1883.

The challenges to the law comprised four criminal prosecutions of persons who had excluded African Americans from their hotels or theaters, and a fifth case brought by a black woman who had been excluded from a white railroad car reserved for women. All five cases fell under Sections 1 and 2 of the 1875 law, and the Supreme Court was asked to decide whether these provisions were constitutional under the Thirteenth and Fourteenth Amendments. Could private discrimination be prohibited as one of the "badges of slavery"? Could Congress prevent discrimination by individuals on the grounds that the state was involved when it tolerated or ignored such actions by its citizens?

Justice Joseph Bradley delivered the opinion of the Court. Seven justices joined his opinion; only Justice John Marshall Harlan dissented. Bradley's ruling effectively narrowed the scope of the Fourteenth Amendment to apply only to the official actions of state governments. Congress, he maintained, did not have the power to pass legislation prohibiting discrimination by private individuals. Bradley asserted that such legislation was a "municipal law for the protection of private rights," far beyond the scope of congressional authority. He considered that under the Fourteenth Amendment, Congress' power to ensure that no state deprived a citizen of equal protection of the law meant that Congress could provide relief only after a state agency had acted to deny equal protection. This interpretation of the Fourteenth Amendment left African Americans at the mercy of state governments. Only after a state had acted to deprive them of their civil rights were they allowed to appeal to Congress. As for the acts of individuals that deprived other persons of their rights, the Court's opinion termed such situations "simply a private wrong." The remedy for such discrimination was to bring action in a state court. According to this ruling, private interference, even with the right to hold property, to vote, or to serve as a witness or a juror, could not be prohibited by Congress unless carried out under state authority. Therefore, the case not only limited the federal government in its enforcement of the right to fair access to public accommodations but also curtailed any federal action to ensure access to political rights.

Bradley further denied that the Thirteenth Amendment had any relevance to the case. In the opinion of the Court, "mere discrimination on account of race or color" could not be considered among the badges of slavery. In abolishing slavery, the amendment was not intended to adjust the "social rights" in the community. According to Bradley's opinion, it was time for African Americans to stop being "the special favorite of the laws" and to assume "the rank of a mere citizen." In ruling the Civil Rights Act of 1875 unconstitutional, the Supreme Court advised African Americans that their rights would be protected in the same way as other citizens' rights, by the state governments.

Justice John Marshall Harlan, a former slaveowner, wrote the only dissent in the *Civil Rights* cases. As he would do later in *Plessy v. Ferguson*, Harlan criticized his colleagues for distorting the intent of the Fourteenth Amendment by their narrow definition of state action. He asserted that public establishments were agents of the state, as they operated under state licenses and regulations. Harlan also argued that race had served as a justification for slavery; therefore, racial discrimination surely qualified as a badge of slavery. Emancipation raised the former slaves to the status of freedom and entitled them to the same civil rights as their fellow citizens. The Thirteenth Amendment, in its enforcement clause, gave Congress the power to ensure the enjoyment of those rights, including equal access. Harlan concluded that the constitutional amendments after the Civil War had prohibited any race or class of people from deciding which rights and privileges their fellow citizens could enjoy.

By the majority's narrow definition of state action and of the Fourteenth Amendment's equal protection clause, the Court effectively limited the federal government's power to deal with racial discrimination. Rather than upholding a bold commitment to finishing the transition from slavery to equal citizenship for African Americans, the justices turned back to the traditional separation of powers, opting for a limited definition of congressional authority and deferring to the states to safeguard the welfare of their citizens.

Among those who protested the Court's decision in the *Civil Rights* cases was a group of black lawyers called the Brotherhood of Liberty. They argued that leaving the enforcement of civil rights to the states would be a disaster for African Americans. They criticized Republican federal judges as well as Republican legislators for betraying the purposes of the Reconstruction amendments because of political self-interest. Some black journalists compared the *Civil Rights* cases with the 1857 *Dred Scott* decision, which had denied that any African American could ever be a U.S. citizen.

—*Mary Welek Atwell*

ADDITIONAL READING:

Hyman, Harold M., and William M. Wiecek. *Equal Justice Under Law: Constitutional Development, 1835-1875*. New York: Harper & Row, 1982. Emphasizes issues concerning the Thirteenth Amendment as a source of federal power to enforce civil rights.

Litwack, Leon, and August Meier, eds. *Black Leaders of the Nineteenth Century*. Urbana: University of Illinois Press, 1988. Profiles of prominent African American activists.

Lively, Donald E. *The Constitution and Race*. New York: Praeger, 1992. A careful analysis of constitutional interpretation based on primary sources.

Nelson, William E. *The Fourteenth Amendment: From Political Principle to Judicial Doctrine*. Cambridge, Mass.: Harvard University Press, 1988. A valuable study of the changing application and meaning of the amendment.

SEE ALSO: 1857, *Dred Scott v. Sandford*; 1863, Reconstruction; 1865, Freedmen's Bureau Is Established; 1865, New Black Codes; 1865, Thirteenth Amendment; 1866, Civil Rights Act of 1866; 1868, Fourteenth Amendment; 1896, *Plessy v. Ferguson.*

1884 ■ U.S. ELECTION OF 1884: *the Democratic Party breaks the Republican hold on the presidency*

DATE: November 4, 1884
LOCALE: United States
CATEGORY: Government and politics
KEY FIGURES:
James G. Blaine (1830-1893), former Speaker of the House of Representatives and Republican presidential candidate
Samuel D. Burchard (1812-1891), clergyman whose reference to "rum, Romanism, and rebellion" produced a campaign controversy
Benjamin F. Butler (1818-1893), nominee of the Greenback-Labor Party
Stephen Grover Cleveland (1837-1908), governor of New York and Democratic presidential candidate
John Pierce St. John (1833-1916), nominee of the Prohibition Party
Carl Schurz (1829-1906), Republican reformer whose hatred for Blaine drove him to support Cleveland

SUMMARY OF EVENT. The 1884 presidential contest between James G. Blaine and Grover Cleveland was one of the dirtiest in U.S. history. The parties were evenly split as far as voter loyalties were concerned, and the race turned on the personal character of the two major party nominees. The presidential election was won by Grover Cleveland, a former mayor of Buffalo, New York, and the governor of New York—the first successful Democratic candidate in twenty-four years. The result was close: A shift of six hundred votes in a single state would have reversed the outcome. During a time of electoral stalemate between the parties, such narrow margins in the popular vote were typical. Public excitement in the campaign ran high, and spectacular episodes swayed the electorate throughout the campaign.

When the Republicans met in Chicago on June 3, 1884, to nominate their candidate, the front-runner was the most popular figure of his time, James G. Blaine of Maine. The incumbent president, Chester Alan Arthur, had little support. He had been an adequate president after succeeding the assassinated James A. Garfield in 1881, but the party regulars and the rank and file of the "Grand Old Party" (GOP) preferred the charismatic Blaine. Unfortunately, Blaine also had weaknesses.

This political cartoon by G. Y. Coffin, entitled "Tannhäuser at Chicago: The Grand Tournament of Song for the Presidency,"
records the tenor of the campaign's spectacle and dirty tactics. (Library of Congress)

There were charges that he had used his offices for personal gain. His dealings with an Arkansas railroad while he was Speaker of the House in the 1870's had been recorded in damaging letters now owned by a man named Mulligan. These "Mulligan letters," on which Blaine had written, "Burn this letter when you have read it," dogged him throughout the election.

Blaine's nomination was relatively easy. He was selected on the fourth ballot, and John A. Logan of Illinois became his running mate. For the Republican reformers called Mugwumps (an Indian term meaning "big chief"), Blaine was an impossible choice. Their spokesman, Carl Schurz, said that electing Blaine would have evil results. These discontented Republicans prepared to support the Democratic nominee.

A month later, the Democratic Party met in Chicago. Sensing victory after so many years in the political wilderness, the Democrats had a fresh face in Grover Cleveland. He had gained a reputation in New York as a foe of corrupt politics and an enemy of an activist government. Enemies called him the Veto Governor. Cleveland was a large man, whom his family called Uncle Jumbo. He had quarreled with the New York City political machine, Tammany Hall. Cleveland seemed the clear choice in an era when the Democrats could win the presidency by carrying the solidly Democratic South, New York, and one or two Midwestern states. Cleveland was nominated on the second ballot, and Thomas A. Hendricks of Indiana balanced the ticket as his Midwestern running mate.

The campaign that followed was very dirty. In July, news broke that Cleveland had been involved with a woman named Maria Halpin and that he might be the father of her illegitimate child. Cleveland accepted responsibility for the child and paid for his upbringing. In their rallies, the Republicans tried to capitalize on the episode. Marchers strode behind baby carriages and chanted, "Ma! Ma! Where's My Pa?" Cleveland responded to the allegations by urging his supporters to "Tell the Truth." By admitting what had happened right away, Cleveland defused the scandal.

The Democrats charged Blaine with corruption concerning the Mulligan letters, and further revelations during the campaign added to the force of the allegations. In the giant rallies that they staged, the Democrats shouted together as they walked through the streets of towns and cities:

> Blaine, Blaine, James G. Blaine
> The continental liar from the State of Maine
> *Burn this letter!*

The overall electoral picture in 1884 gave the edge to the Democrats. Their base in the South meant that they had to win fewer Northern states than the Republicans did. The economy had slipped into a mild recession that favored the party out of power. Because the Republicans had been in power so long, accumulated grievances worked against them. As a result of the defection of the Mugwumps, many of the newspapers and magazines in the East that ordinarily favored the Republicans were in the Democratic camp.

In response, the Republicans looked to capitalize on perceived areas of Democratic weakness. Cleveland did not enjoy much support from labor. Accordingly, the Republicans provided money for the Greenback-Labor Party and its presidential candidate, Benjamin F. Butler of Massachusetts. The erratic Butler campaigned with great energy but was not a large element in the outcome of the race.

A source of worry for the Republicans was the Prohibition Party and its standard-bearer, John Pierce St. John. Voters for the "dry" candidate usually came from among former Republicans, and St. John had particular strength in upstate New York, which played a large role in the outcome of the contest.

Blaine became the central focus of the campaign. He wanted to make the protective tariff a major issue, and he stressed economic concerns in his letter accepting the nomination. His record of opposition to Great Britain in foreign affairs also won him support from among Irish American voters. Working against Blaine was Republican disunity. The leader of the GOP in New York, former senator Roscoe Conkling, had a hatred for Blaine dating back to arguments they had had in the House of Representatives during the 1860's. Conkling refused to campaign for Blaine, and that reluctance hurt Republican chances in the key state of New York.

To overcome these obstacles, Blaine decided to embark on a personal campaign swing. Although he was not the first presidential candidate to try this technique, it was an innovation for a major party candidate to woo the electorate directly. Democrats charged that Blaine was lowering the tone of the race for the White House. On the whole, the experiment was successful. Blaine drew large, enthusiastic crowds. The Republicans seemed to be ahead when they carried Maine and Vermont in September, and Ohio went Republican in October. (During this period, not all states voted on the same day.)

The key state was New York: Blaine had to carry it to win. With reports coming in that the Democrats might carve out a victory, the Republican candidate decided to include New York on his speaking schedule. At the end of October, he spent a week in a determined effort to cover the vast expanses of the Empire State. He arrived in New York City on October 28 in a condition of near exhaustion.

On October 29, Blaine met with several hundred Protestant clergymen in his hotel lobby. When the designated speaker was delayed, the group called upon a Presbyterian minister named Samuel Burchard as a substitute. Burchard announced in his remarks that "We are Republicans and don't propose to leave our party and identify ourselves with the party whose antecedents have been rum, Romanism, and rebellion." In his answer, Blaine did not mention Burchard's comment.

The statement caused an uproar, because it attacked Catholicism at a time when Blaine had been wooing the votes of Irish Americans. The Democrats spread the remark as widely as they could, and Republican disavowals were late and ineffective. Another public relations fiasco occurred when Blaine attended a dinner in his honor at Delmonico's restaurant in New York City. The audience was composed of millionaires and business leaders, and the Democrats promptly dubbed it "The Boodle Banquet."

Election day brought further problems for Blaine. In upstate New York, heavy rains kept Republican voters at home in an area where Blaine needed a big turnout. It was soon apparent that the election would be very close. Cleveland had carried the Democratic South, and Blaine had run strongly in the Midwest. The key state was New York, where returns trickled in slowly over several days. In the end, Cleveland won the Empire State by a scant 1,149 votes. The Prohibition ticket had received 25,000 votes, the majority of which would have gone to Blaine under normal circumstances.

Cleveland won the 36 electoral votes of New York, and his total of 219 put him into the White House. Blaine's total was 182 electoral votes. The popular vote was also very close. Cleveland's majority was less than 25,000 ballots. After the election, and in historical accounts since 1884, the episode involving the Reverend Burchard was said to have cost Blaine the election. In fact, Blaine did better than any other Republican might have done. He ran 400,000 votes ahead of James A. Garfield's total in 1880. The real explanation for what happened in 1884 was that, in a Democratic year, Grover Cleveland kept his party united to achieve a narrow victory.

—Lewis L. Gould, based on the original entry by Gustav L. Seligman

ADDITIONAL READING:

Gould, Lewis L. "1884." In *Running for President: The Candidates and Their Images*, edited by Arthur Schlesinger et al. Vol. 1. New York: Simon & Schuster, 1994. A brief account of the 1884 election that incorporates the latest historical scholarship about the outcome of the Blaine-Cleveland race.

Keller, Morton. *Affairs of State: Public Life in Late Nineteenth Century America.* Cambridge, Mass.: The Belknap Press of Harvard University Press, 1977. Useful for understanding how the Blaine-Cleveland contest grew out of the political culture of the late nineteenth century.

McGerr, Michael. *The Decline of Popular Politics: The American North, 1865-1928.* New York: Oxford University Press, 1986. Discusses the election in the context of evolving campaign styles and methods of getting voters to the polls.

Morgan, H. Wayne. *From Hayes to McKinley: National Party Politics, 1877-1896.* Syracuse, N.Y.: Syracuse University Press, 1969. Readable, thorough account that places the 1884 election in the context of the battle between the Republicans and Democrats to secure a national majority.

Welch, Richard. *The Presidencies of Grover Cleveland.* Lawrence: University Press of Kansas, 1988. Discusses how the election of 1884 brought Cleveland to national power and considers the political appeal that took him to the White House.

SEE ALSO: 1877, Hayes Is Elected President; 1892, Birth of the People's Party; 1896, McKinley Is Elected President.

1885 ■ SECOND RIEL REBELLION: *the second Metis rebellion, crushed by government forces, opens the way to settlement of the Canadian prairies by Euro-Canadians*

DATE: March 19, 1885
LOCALE: Saskatchewan
CATEGORIES: Expansion and land acquisition; Native American history; Wars, uprisings, and civil unrest
KEY FIGURES:
Big Bear, also known as *Mistahimaskwa* (1825-1888), Cree chief who sought peace
Leif Crozier (1846-1901), officer of the Royal Canadian Mounted Police
Gabriel Dumont (1837-1906), adjutant general of Riel's army
John Alexander Macdonald (1815-1891), prime minister of Canada
Frederick D. Middleton (1825-1898), British soldier who quelled the rebellion
Poundmaker (1842-1886), Cree chief who joined in rebellion
Louis-David Riel (1844-1885), leader of the Metis
SUMMARY OF EVENT. In 1869-1870, Louis Riel had led a rebellion, in Manitoba against a provincial governor sent out from Ottawa. Riel and his largely French-speaking supporters believed that the governor, William McDougall, represented only the English speakers of Manitoba. After some negotiations, the situation was resolved peacefully, and Manitoba was admitted into the Canadian confederation as a province in which both French and English were official languages. Riel had agreed amicably to go into exile in the United States. A complicated man, Riel belonged to the ethnic group known as the Metis. The Metis (the word denotes "mixture" in French) were part-Native Canadian and part-French. Although they spoke French and were part of Francophone culture, they also had good relations with Native Canadian groups such as the Cree.

By 1885, Riel had become the most controversial figure in Canadian public life. He had run for Parliament from Manitoba and won, but then had been expelled by the legislative body's pro-British majority because they saw his earlier rebellion as treason against the queen. Riel often had been accused of mental instability and spent extended periods of time in a hospital and later a mental asylum during the 1870's. During these years, his religious position, once conventionally Catholic, veered in a maverick direction. Riel began to believe that a North American pope was needed; he proposed this idea to a French bishop of Montreal, who refused to have anything to do with these plans. Riel had left Canada and moved to Montana, where he married a woman from the United States and seemed to forsake his Canadian political ambitions. His absence from the Canadian scene came to a dramatic end in 1883, however, when he returned to the

THE RIEL REBELLIONS, 1869 AND 1885

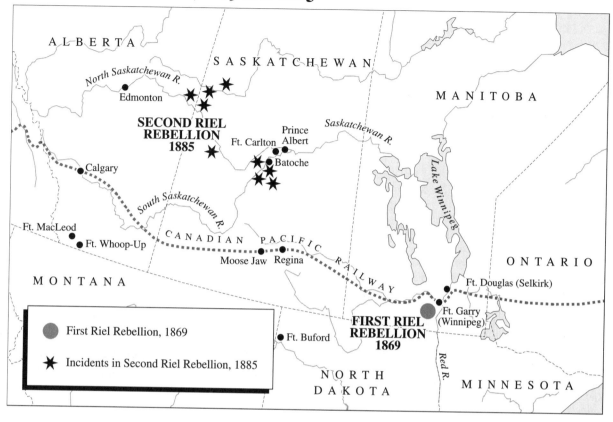

Canadian prairies, this time Saskatchewan, to help the struggling Metis cause.

In July, 1884, Riel arrived in the Metis stronghold of Batoche. He tried to engage in peaceful pro-Metis political activity, but his past and his controversial reputation shadowed these efforts. On March 19, 1885, Riel decided to take the path of direct, violent action when he took control of the main Roman Catholic church in Batoche and mobilized his supporters into military formation, organizing an army led by a capable general, Gabriel Dumont. Riel declared himself governor in opposition to the constituted authorities.

Now the core of Riel's supporters were no longer French Catholics and English-speaking frontier whites (who at this point found Riel much too pronative, and eccentric as well), but Native Canadians. Riel found two crucial allies among the chiefs of the Cree peoples of the plains. These men had very different natures, despite their common ethnic origins. Poundmaker was a determined and vigorous warrior. He was convinced that the only way the native peoples could resist the onslaught of white settlers was through military force. Poundmaker saw that the time for possible action was limited, because the white settlers were rapidly gaining control of the prairie through the efficiency of the Royal Canadian Mounted Police (RCMP) and technological advances, most particularly the Canadian Pacific Railroad. Big Bear, whose Cree name

was Mistahimaskwa, was of a more moderate persuasion than Poundmaker. Big Bear favored negotiations with Euro-Americans in order to safeguard his people's best interests. Although Big Bear never capitulated fully to the violent agenda advocated by Riel and Poundmaker, he did not stand in the way when some of his more extreme followers attacked the villagers of Frog Lake. The leadership skills of Big Bear and Poundmaker formed the backbone of the Northwest rebellion. Riel supplied the vision; they supplied the competence.

Even before the so-called Frog Lake Massacre, the rebellion had begun in earnest. After Riel declared his provisional government on March 19, the RCMP reacted quickly and, led by Superintendent Leif Crozier, within a week had engaged the combined Metis and Indian forces at the village of Duck Lake. The police were forced to retreat, and the Canadian prime minister, Sir John Macdonald, sent in Canadian troops. Aided by the logistical support provided by the railroad, upwards of five thousand troops had arrived in Saskatchewan under the command of General Frederick D. Middleton.

By this time, many of Big Bear's troops had joined Riel and Poundmaker in the rebellion. To government authorities, it seemed as if the entire prairie was in rebellion, although many Native Canadian peoples, especially the populous Blackfoot, remained neutral throughout the conflict. On April 24, Middleton's troops engaged Dumont's in formal battle. The combat ended in stalemate, and Middleton's advance was stymied. Middleton gathered additional troops and, by early May, was approaching Riel's headquarters at Batoche. Middleton devised an effective strategy of having his headquarters remain in a fortified camp south of Batoche while his troops would sortie out during the daytime and attempt to wear down the resistance of the Metis. After several daytime charges of this sort, the Metis were worn down by attrition. On May 15, Riel surrendered himself and Batoche to Middleton. Dumont fled south to Montana.

Poundmaker's resistance against the government had been more effective. It took until May 26 for him to surrender his troops to Middleton at Battleford. Big Bear was never apprehended by the government. After evading capture for more than a month, he voluntarily surrendered to the RCMP at Fort Carlton in early July. Canadian historians have come to see Big Bear as the most far-sighted figure on either side, the only leader who possessed a viable vision of how the prairies could be a place where English speakers, French speakers, and natives could all enjoy autonomy and self-determination.

By mid-July, Riel's trial for treason had begun. Although most French Canadians had turned against Riel because of his religious unorthodoxy and his penchant for violence, now that he was being prosecuted by the English-speaking Macdonald and his government, they once again became Riel's fervent supporters. Riel's lawyers advised him to plead insanity, but Riel decided to speak in his own defense. Riel's explanations of his actions to the jury were possessed of an uncommon lucidity, although there was no hope that the jury, composed largely of English speakers, could be swayed over to Riel's position. Once the jury had found Riel guilty, it was up to Macdonald to decide whether to seek the death penalty. Macdonald considered several factors in making the decision but finally concluded that executing Riel would satisfy the English speakers in Ontario. Despite further medical appeals claiming Riel was insane, the Metis leader was hanged on November 16 in Regina.

Riel became almost an overnight martyr and, whatever the complexities and ambiguities of his life, has remained a metaphor for unexamined possibilities in the Canadian national soul. Big Bear and Poundmaker were given far more lenient sentences, involving only a few years of jail for each; yet both men died before the decade of the 1880's came to a close, and the potential for political resistance on the part of the Native Canadian peoples of the prairies was foreclosed. With the opening of the railroad, the prairie provinces quickly became flooded by white settlers, and by the beginning of the twentieth century they were firmly part of the Canadian body politic.

The Second Riel Rebellion was certainly one of the most dramatic events in nineteenth century Canadian history. Riel's failure, for better or for worse, helped bring into being the Canada that represented the opposite of so much for which he had hoped and struggled. —*Nicholas Birns*

ADDITIONAL READING:

Beal, Bob, and Rod Macleod. *Prairie Fire: The 1885 North-West Rebellion.* Edmonton: Hurtig, 1984. Emphasizes the Native Canadian perspective.

Bowsfield, Hartfield. *Louis Riel: The Rebel and the Hero.* Toronto: Oxford University Press, 1971. A good introductory book.

Flanagan, Thomas. *Riel and the Rebellion: 1885 Reconsidered.* Saskatoon: Western Producer Prairie Books, 1983. Provides a revisionist perspective.

Riel, Louis. *The Collected Writings of Louis Riel.* Edited by George F. G. Stanley. Edmonton: University of Alberta Press, 1985. Shows that Riel was a thinker as well as a political leader.

Siggins, Maggie. *Riel: A Life of Revolution.* Toronto: HarperCollins, 1994. Readable, lively narrative account.

Stanley, George F. G. *The Birth of Western Canada: History of the Riel Rebellions.* Toronto: University of Toronto Press, 1960. Argues that the rebellions were the defining event in western Canadian history.

SEE ALSO: 1815, Red River Raids; 1837, Rebellions in Canada; 1869, First Riel Rebellion; 1874, Red River War; 1876, Canada's Indian Act.

1886 ■ American Federation of Labor Is Founded: *the first effective attempt to organize workers in skilled trades at a national level*

DATE: December 8, 1886
LOCALE: Columbus, Ohio
CATEGORIES: Canadian history; Business and labor; Organizations and institutions
KEY FIGURES:
William H. Foster (born 1947), secretary of the Federation of Organized Trades and Labor Unions of the United States and Canada
Samuel Gompers (1850-1924), first president of the AFL
P. J. McQuire, first secretary of the AFL
Elizabeth Chambers Morgan (born 1850), first woman nominated to a vice presidency of the AFL
Terence V. Powderly (1849-1924), Grand Master Workman of the Knights of Labor during the organization of the AFL
Adolf Strasser, president of the Cigarmakers' International Union and a founder of the AFL

SUMMARY OF EVENT. All indices of industrial production in the United States in the closing decades of the nineteenth century revealed a tremendous rate of growth. Stimulated by the arrival of millions of immigrants, the U.S. population spiraled from fifty million in 1880 to seventy-six million by 1900. With great strides in scientific and technological development, new industries burgeoned with the production of electric lighting equipment, telephones, street railways, adding machines, and typewriters. Older industries consolidated, resulting in the concentration of ownership and control resting increasingly in the hands of relatively few. Trusts, pools, mergers, monopolies, "gentlemen's agreements," and other instruments of consolidation became widespread in the coal-mining, railroad, iron and steel, slaughtering and meatpacking, and oil industries. Intimately associated with this development were such captains of industry as J. P. Morgan, James. J. Hill, and Jay Gould in railroads; Andrew Carnegie in steel; and John D. Rockefeller in oil.

As industries changed and factories grew in size, workers found themselves increasingly distanced from management and from the control of their work. Unorganized workers and even members of many early labor unions were not effective counterweights to these aggregations of wealth and power. Seemingly powerless to press their claims for higher wages, shorter hours, or safe working conditions, various American labor leaders began to think of combining the existing trade unions into a national federation like the British Trades Union Congress (TUC). Like the TUC, this new federation would be able to lobby for legislation, both in Washington, D.C., and in the state capitals. Also like the TUC, it would be composed primarily of craft unions and would allow its constituent members complete autonomy in the operation of their local organizations. These union leaders contended that the first national workers organization, the Noble Order of the Knights of Labor, founded by Philadelphia garment cutter Uriah Stephens in 1869, was unsuited to advance the material interests of skilled workers.

From its initial membership of only nine men, the Noble Order of the Knights of Labor had grown rapidly into a national organization, but faced wide opposition from many segments of society. In response to opposition from the clergy and to avoid being linked with alleged terrorist organizations such as the Molly Maguires, the organization formally abandoned much of its ritualistic secrecy at its 1881 general assembly. Terence Powderly, the newly elected Master Workman, as the Knights called their chief officer, predicted that the new open policies would attract many new members.

For union organizers in the skilled trades, however, the policies of the Knights of Labor were far too impractical. The Knights of Labor promoted the equality of all workers, skilled and unskilled, black and white, male and female. This mixing of occupations in locals, along with the Knights' idealistic involvement in political action and reformist movements, were, they believed, not merely unrealistic but also detrimental to the securing of such immediate bread-and-butter goals as improvements in wages and working conditions. The Knights of Labor believed in organizing workers in assemblies; that is, all the workers in a particular factory or geographic location would be members together. Many craft workers, who believed that their unique skills made them more valuable employees than ordinary laborers, preferred to organize by trade; that is, shoemakers would be in one union and garment cutters in another. At first the Knights of Labor did not oppose the

formation of craft unions, as the leadership believed that workers could benefit from both types of organization. Thus, many members of the Knights of Labor were also active in local trade unions. This spirit of cooperation changed dramatically in the 1880's.

Meeting in Pittsburgh in November, 1881, the national trade unions formed "The Federation of Organized Trades and Labor Unions of the United States and Canada." The federation grew slowly, hindered at first by the economic recession of 1883-1885 and then by defeats in a number of labor disputes. As economic conditions improved, however, membership soared. Yet it was also during these years that the rift between the federation and the Knights of Labor widened, primarily because the leadership of the Knights of Labor opposed striking to secure the eight-hour day. Terence Powderly adamantly opposed the use of a work stoppage to advance workers' causes. Rather than striking, the Knights promoted the use of boycotts to pressure manufacturers into raising wages or improving working conditions. The federation, at its 1884 convention, had adopted a resolution asserting that after May 1, 1886, eight hours should constitute a working day. Appealing to trade unionists, many of the rank-and-file members of the Knights of Labor, and radical socialists, the eight-hour agitation mounted as May, 1886, approached and workers anticipated a nationwide strike to secure this goal.

May, 1886, was a momentous month for the American labor movement. On May 4 in Chicago's Haymarket Square police attempted to disperse a group of workers demonstrating for labor causes when a dynamite bomb was thrown into the crowd. The blast killed seven police officers. In the resulting melee with the crowd, known since as the Haymarket Riot, the police shot and killed a number of demonstrators. More than a hundred people were injured. This bloodshed precipitated a wave of antiradicalism that almost fatally damaged the eight-hour movement. Then a special meeting of the federation convened in Philadelphia. Called by W. H. Foster, the federation's secretary, and by officers of the national unions, including Adolph Strasser of the Cigarmakers' International Union, its purpose was "to protect our respective organizations from the malicious work of an element [in the Knights of Labor] who openly boast that trade unions must be destroyed." The delegates drafted a "treaty" for presentation to the Knights of Labor, who, according to this proposal, should not, except with the consent of the federation, organize trades in which there were unions, and should not intervene in strikes involving federation members. When the Knights of Labor rejected the "treaty" in October, 1886, the trade unions convened another meeting on December 8 for the purpose of drawing "the bonds of unity much closer together between all the trade unions of America" by means of "an American federation or alliance of all national and international trades unions."

At that convention the American Federation of Labor (AFL) was born. Samuel Gompers of the Cigarmakers' International Union was elected the AFL's president, a post he held almost continuously until his death in 1924. By eschewing utopianism and promoting practical objectives, the AFL was able to survive the disastrous strikes of the early 1890's, emerging in 1897 from the great depression of that decade with 265,000 members and uncontested dominance in the American labor movement.

—*William M. Tuttle, updated by Nancy Farm Mannikko*

ADDITIONAL READING:

Fink, Leon. *In Search of the Working Class: Essays in American Labor History and Political Culture.* Urbana: University of Illinois Press, 1994. Collection of articles that provide a good overview of the labor movement.

Foner, Philip S. *Women and the American Labor Movement: From the First Trade Unions to the Present.* New York: Free Press, 1979. Thorough examination of the roles women played in the growth of unions both in the skilled trades and in factories.

Gompers, Samuel. *The Samuel Gompers Papers.* 5 vols. Urbana: University of Illinois Press, 1986. Serious readers in labor history will enjoy reading Gompers' own thoughts on the rise of organized labor.

Laurie, Bruce. *Artisans into Workers: Labor in Nineteenth Century America.* New York: Hill and Wang, 1989. Accessible analysis of the transformation of work in America.

Meltzer, Milton. *Bread and Roses: The Struggle of American Labor, 1865-1915.* New York: Facts On File, 1991. Definitive history of the labor movement in the United States.

Voss, Kim. *The Making of American Exceptionalism: The Knights of Labor and Class Formation in the Nineteenth Century.* Ithaca, N.Y.: Cornell University Press, 1993. Fascinating study of the Knights of Labor.

Yellowitz, Irwin. *Industrialization and the American Labor Movement, 1850-1900.* Port Washington, N.Y.: Kennikat Press, 1977. Examines the relationships between the growth of industry and the growth of organized labor.

SEE ALSO: 1882, Standard Oil Trust Is Organized; 1890, Sherman Antitrust Act; 1894, Pullman Strike; 1902, Anthracite Coal Strike; 1905, Industrial Workers of the World Is Founded; 1935, National Labor Relations Act; 1935, Congress of Industrial Organizations Is Founded; 1938, Fair Labor Standards Act; 1943, Inflation and Labor Unrest; 1955, AFL and CIO Merge.

1887 ■ INTERSTATE COMMERCE ACT:
federal legislation regulates the operation of the railroads

DATE: February 4, 1887
LOCALE: Washington, D.C.
CATEGORIES: Business and labor; Economics; Laws and acts; Transportation
KEY FIGURES:
Stephen Grover Cleveland (1837-1908), twenty-second and twenty-fourth president of the United States

Thomas McIntyre Cooley (1824-1898), first chairman of the Interstate Commerce Commission
Shelby Moore Cullom (1829-1914), senator from Illinois, who advocated regulation of the railroads
John Henninger Reagan (1818-1905), congressman from Texas, who advocated legislation forbidding unfair practices on the railroads
Simon Sterne (1839-1901), chairman of the New York Board of Trade and Transportation, who lobbied strongly for legislation to regulate the railway companies
F. B. Thurber, wholesale grocer in New York who lobbied strongly for regulatory legislation

SUMMARY OF EVENT. By the 1880's, the United States had experienced more than fifty years of railroad expansion. Transcontinental railroad lines tied the nation together, while spurring the growth of industry and agriculture through the rapid transportation of both raw materials and finished goods. During much of this time, government had served as a willing partner to the rapid growth of the railroads. Both national and state governments had provided land for the railroad right-of-way, as well as other subsidies to underwrite the cost of this vital form of transportation. By the end of the Civil War, however, many people in the United States had begun to have second thoughts about the railroads. Although almost no one doubted the need for railroads, many criticized the business practices of the railroad companies. Consumers suffered when railroad companies experienced either too much or too little competition. In regions where one company dominated, that company often took advantage of its monopoly of the market and charged its customers exorbitant fees for necessary services. Where competition was intense, the railroads too often resorted to unfair practices in order to attract and retain the business of large-volume shippers. They reduced rates in some areas to meet competition and raised rates in noncompetitive areas to compensate. They also engaged in such practices as offering rebates or kickbacks to large-volume shippers at the expense of the average consumer. The railroads entered into agreements, often referred to as "pools," among themselves to fix rates at a level higher than the free market permitted. They charged more for a short haul in order to offer special long-haul rates to large shippers. The railroads also were guilty of watering their stock, or overcapitalizing issues, to bilk the investor. These and other practices worked to the advantage of the railroads and a few favored customers. As a result of railroad manipulation of freight charges, it often cost small farmers more to ship their grain than they would receive in payment for it, while large mill owners would receive a discount on the shipment of the finished flour. The unethical business practices thus worked to the detriment of the ordinary shippers, farmers, and the public.

The states responded first to the demands for railroad reform. Many states passed laws that compelled railroads to offer standard rates for all, and many states set up regulatory boards to supervise the practices of the railroad companies. The states, however, could not supervise interstate operations.

Farmers shipping grain from the Dakotas to Minnesota mills or cattle from Texas to Chicago slaughterhouses were not protected by individual state regulations. In addition, the state regulatory laws and boards often created more problems than they solved. Finally, the railroads resisted attempts at state regulation and fought enforcement in the courts. In October, 1886, the Supreme Court (in *Wabash, St. Louis, and Pacific Railway v. Illinois*) held that a state could not regulate commerce that went beyond its boundaries. This meant that any regulation of interstate commerce would have to come from the federal government.

Numerous groups and individuals had long pressed for national legislation to reform the railroads. Organizations of producers, shippers, and merchants demanded an end to practices by which railroad companies took advantage of the need for rail transportation. F. B. Thurber, a New York wholesale grocer, and Simon Sterne, chairman of New York's Board of Trade and Transportation, became active lobbyists. Some of the loudest demands for some system of national regulation began to come from the railroad companies themselves, particularly in the East, where competition was ruthless. Financiers such as Jay Gould recognized that without some reforms, public outrage could lead to harsh regulations in the future.

John H. Reagan, a congressman from Texas and the chairman of the House Committee on Commerce, during the 1870's and early 1880's introduced many bills in Congress that would outlaw specific practices, such as pools, rebates, and price discrimination between long and short hauls. Reagan's approach to the problem was an attempt to clean up the competition among the railroads on the assumption that fair competition was economically healthy for the entire nation. The proposed bills described what would constitute illegal practices but contained no provisions for investigation or regulation. Reagan's attempts to regulate the railroads met with little success until the first administration of President Grover Cleveland.

Cleveland, a Democrat, strongly opposed the growth of government but opposed the idea of government favors to business even more. Following the Supreme Court decision in *Wabash Railroad v. Illinois*, Cleveland urged Congress to take action to regulate the railroads. This time, Congress seemed ready to pass regulatory legislation. Reagan once again introduced a bill in the House of Representatives, while in the Senate, Shelby M. Cullom of Illinois proposed a more far-reaching solution. Cullom's approach, which emerged from extensive committee hearings, embodied a regulatory commission with broad powers to investigate and to bring into court railroad companies whose rates or practices were unfair. Cullom proposed that the federal government take positive action in laying down precisely what constituted unfair tactics and rates. The Reagan and Cullom bills went to a joint committee of the House and the Senate. President Cleveland exerted some influence in favor of Cullom's proposals. From the joint committee emerged the Interstate Commerce Act.

The act followed Reagan's suggestions and prohibited spe-cific abuses, such as long-and short-haul discrimination. It also created the Interstate Commerce Commission (ICC). Under the provisions of the act, the commission would comprise five members whose duty it was to investigate and expose unfair rates and practices among interstate carriers. Congress empowered the commission to take unrepentant railroads into court. After decades of encouraging and subsidizing the railroads, the government had begun to regulate them.

The jubilation of the railroad reformers was short-lived. The courts and the ICC itself seemed determined to frustrate substantive reform. The commission, whose first chairman was Thomas M. Cooley, a professor of law at the University of Michigan, often dealt with the railroads in an extremely conservative manner, and the Supreme Court weakened the commission's powers. Cooley believed in a strict interpretation of the Constitution and was reluctant to expand the power of the federal government. When the railroads chose to dispute the rulings of the ICC, they generally won in court. Of the sixteen cases involving railroads and the ICC that were heard by the Supreme Court between 1887 and 1911, the railroads won fifteen. In the process, the Supreme Court destroyed the commission's power to act against fixing rates, pooling, and long- and short-haul discrimination. Government regulation had been established in theory, but not yet in practice. The Interstate Commerce Act was significant chiefly as a precedent for the genuine economic reform that followed in later years.

—*Emory M. Thomas, updated by Nancy Farm Mannikko*

ADDITIONAL READING:

Cullom, Shelby Moore. *Fifty Years of Public Service: Personal Recollections of Shelby M. Cullom*. New York: Da Capo Press, 1969. A memoir by a politician who lived through some of the most volatile times in U.S. history.

Jones, Alan R. *The Constitutional Conservatism of Thomas McIntyre Cooley: A Study in the History of Ideas*. New York: Garland, 1987. An intellectual history that helps clarify why the ICC accomplished little of substance with Cooley as its chairman.

Neilson, James W. *Shelby M. Cullom: Prairie State Republican*. Urbana: University of Illinois Press, 1962. Biography of one of the prime movers behind the Interstate Commerce Act and its regulatory features.

Reagan, John H. *Memoirs, with Special Reference to Secession and the Civil War*. Edited by Walter Flavius McCaleb. New York: AMS Press, 1978. Originally published in 1906, Reagan's memoirs provide fascinating glimpses into the history of the Confederacy and Gilded Age politics in the United States.

Stone, Richard D. *The Interstate Commerce Commission and the Railroad Industry: A History of Regulatory Policy*. New York: Praeger, 1991. Good, detailed history of the ICC and the growth of both railroads and regulations.

Welch, Richard E. *The Presidencies of Grover Cleveland*. Lawrence: University Press of Kansas, 1988. A thorough examination of the Cleveland presidencies.

SEE ALSO: 1869, Transcontinental Railroad Is Completed.

1887 ■ GENERAL ALLOTMENT ACT: *a policy of alloting land to individual Native Americans in severalty begins to dissolve the tribal nations*

DATE: February 8, 1887
LOCALE: United States
CATEGORIES: Expansion and land acquisition; Laws and acts; Native American history
KEY FIGURES:
Lyman Abbott (1835-1922), editor of the *Christian Union*
Henry Laurens Dawes (1816-1903), senator from Massachusetts
Lewis Henry Morgan (1818-1881), anthropologist
Carl Schurz (1829-1906), reform-minded secretary of the interior, 1877-1881
Henry M. Teller (1830-1914), secretary of the interior, 1882-1885, who argued against allotment
Herbert Welsh (1851-1941), secretary of the Indian Rights Association

SUMMARY OF EVENT. When the General Allotment, or Dawes, Act became law on February 8, 1887, proponents hailed it as the Indian Emancipation Act and Secretary of the Interior L. Q. C. Lamar called it "the most important measure of legislation ever enacted in this country affecting our Indian affairs."

The law dealt primarily with Native American ownership of land. It authorized the president of the United States, through the Office of Indian Affairs in the Department of the Interior, to allot the lands on reservations to individual Native Americans, so that they would hold the land in severalty instead of the tribe's owning the land communally. Each head of a household would receive a quarter-section of land (160 acres); single persons over eighteen years of age and orphans would receive eighty acres; and other persons, forty acres. (In 1891, an amendment to the law equalized the allotments to provide eighty acres for each individual, regardless of age or family status.) The United States government would hold the allotments in trust for twenty-five years, during which time the Native American could not sell or otherwise dispose of his or her land. At the end of that period, he or she would receive full title to it. After the process of dividing up the reservation land for allotments, the federal government could sell the surplus land (often a considerable portion of the reservation) to willing purchasers (most of whom would be Euro-Americans). The money from such sales would go to a fund to benefit Native American education.

The Dawes Act also provided for Native American citizenship. Native Americans who received allotments in severalty or who took up residence apart from their tribe and adopted what Euro-Americans considered civilized ways became citizens of the United States and subject to the laws of the state or territory in which they lived. In 1924, Congress passed the Indian Citizenship Act, granting full citizenship to nearly all Native Americans who were not already citizens, and measures in the late 1940's extended such status to Arizona and New Mexico Native Americans that the 1924 law had missed.

Two groups of Euro-Americans especially welcomed the Dawes Act. Land-hungry settlers who had long cast covetous eyes on the reservation lands—which, to Euro-American thinking, were going to waste because of the lack of productive agricultural practices by Native Americans, whom they considered to be hunters and gatherers—were now able to acquire the lands left over from the allotment process. No doubt, the less scrupulous among the settlers also looked forward to the day when individual Native Americans would receive full title to their land and be able to sell, lease, or otherwise dispose of it. Then pressure, legitimate or not, would likely induce the new owner to part with the acreage.

A second group of Euro-Americans, however, was more influential in securing passage of the Dawes Act. These were the humanitarian reformers of the day, who considered private ownership of land in severalty, U.S. citizenship, education, and consistent codification of laws to be indispensable means for the acculturation of the Native Americans and their eventual assimilation into the mainstream of U.S. society. As ministers from the several Christian denominations, educators, civil servants, politicians, and even a few military personnel, these philanthropists exerted a clout beyond their numbers. Calling themselves the Friends of the Indian, these reformers had been meeting annually since 1869 at the Catskills resort of Lake Mohonk to discuss ways to bring the tribal peoples to what the conveners deemed to be civilization.

Federal politicians had long considered private ownership of land essential to the civilizing process. Thomas Jefferson and the like-minded policymakers of his time had strongly advocated it, and in 1838 the Commissioner of Indian Affairs gave voice to a widespread view when he said, "Unless some system is marked out by which there shall be a separate allotment of land to each individual . . . you will look in vain for any general casting off of savagism. Common property and civilization cannot co-exist."

It was not until the post-Civil War years, when increasing Euro-American pressures on the Native Americans created crisis after crisis, that humanitarians and philanthropists began a concerted drive for "Indian reform." Land in severalty would be the most important factor in breaking up tribalism. The reform groups that were organized—the Board of Indian Commissioners (1869), the Women's National Indian Association (1879), the Indian Rights Association (1882), the Lake Mohonk Conference of Friends of the Indian (1883), and the National Indian Defense Association (1885), to name the most important—all strongly espoused allotment in severalty. Nor were they satisfied with the piecemeal legislation that affected one tribe at a time; the panacea they sought was a general allotment law. Although supporters argued over the speed of implementing allotment, such proponents as Carl Schurz, Herbert Welsh, and the Reverend Lyman Abbott fought energetically for such legislation. They finally won to their cause Senator Henry L. Dawes, chairman of the Senate Committee on Indian Affairs, who successfully shepherded through Congress the measure that bears his name.

Only a few Euro-American voices cried out against the proposal. Congressman Russell Errett of Pennsylvania and a few others protested that the bill was a thinly disguised means of getting at the valuable tribal lands. Senator Henry M. Teller of Colorado argued that the Native Americans did not want to own land in severalty and were not prepared to assume the responsibilities that went with private property and citizenship. He denied the contention of the reformers that private ownership of land would lead to civilization. Albert Meacham, editor of *The Council Fire*, maintained that there was little enthusiasm for severalty among traditionalist Native Americans, and anthropologist Lewis Henry Morgan thought that allotment would result in massive poverty. Presbyterian missionaries apparently were disunited on the subject of allotment, and their views fell by the wayside as the juggernaut of reform plunged ahead.

Native American response to allotment has largely gone unrecorded. The Cherokee, Creek, Chickasaw, Choctaw, Seminole, Sac, Fox, and a few other tribes in Indian Territory, as well as the Seneca in New York, contended that they already mostly owned land individually and won exclusion from the act's operation. By 1906, however, Congress extended allotment to them as well. Most of the complaints came after the act's passage, when Native Americans lost land and found farming difficult under its provisions.

"February 8, 1887," one optimistic spokesman of the Board of Indian Commissioners commented, "may be called the Indian emancipation day." Although much sincere Christian goodwill motivated passage of the Dawes Act, it turned out to be a disaster for Native Americans. The sponsors of the Dawes Act had assumed an unrealistically romantic view of the Native American. People who had had firsthand experience with tribal peoples attempted to prove to the reformers that the "noble savage" had never existed. In 1891, Congress allowed Native Americans to lease their allotments if they were not able to farm for themselves.

The allotments and the leasing moved faster and with less careful discrimination than Dawes and other promoters had intended. Instead of being a measure that turned Native Americans into self-supporting farmers, the act, through the rapid alienation of the Native Americans' lands, meant the loss of the land base on which the tribal peoples' hope for future prosperity depended. Tribal peoples held claim to about 150 million acres of land in 1887. The Dawes Act eventually diverted two-thirds of that acreage out of Native American ownership, down to about forty-eight million acres by 1934. Not until that year, with the passage of the Indian Reorganization Act (the Wheeler-Howard Act, also known as the "Indian New Deal"), did the federal government repeal the Dawes Act and encourage communal forms of ownership again, but by

that time much of the former reservation land was gone as surplus sales, leases, or sales by the individual allottees.

—*Francis P. Prucha, updated by Thomas L. Altherr*

ADDITIONAL READING:

Coleman, Michael C. "Problematic Panacea: Presbyterian Missionaries and the Allotment of Indian Lands in the Late Nineteenth Century." *Pacific Historical Review* 54, no. 2 (1985): 143-159. Shows that the Presbyterians were not united about allotment of tribal lands.

Gibson, Arrell Morgan. "The Centennial Legacy of the General Allotment Act." *Chronicles of Oklahoma* 65, no. 3 (1987): 228-251. Examines the long-range effects of the Dawes Act on Native Americans.

Hoxie, Frederick E. *A Final Promise: The Campaign to Assimilate the Indians, 1880-1920.* Lincoln: University of Nebraska Press, 1984. Interweaves the story of the Dawes Act with the larger assimilationist programs toward Native Americans.

Mintz, Steven, ed. *Native American Voices.* St. James, N.Y.: Brandywine Press, 1995. Contains part of the Dawes Act and a complaint by a Cherokee farmer in 1906.

Prucha, Francis Paul, ed. *Americanizing the American Indians: Writings of the "Friends of the Indian" 1880-1900.* Lincoln: University of Nebraska Press, 1973. Section 2 provides a representative sampling of primary source writings about the Dawes Act.

Washburn, Wilcomb E. *The Assault on Indian Tribalism: The General Allotment Law (Dawes Act) of 1887.* Philadelphia: J. B. Lippincott, 1975. A concise summary of the attitudes that produced the act and its repercussions for Native Americans; contains the full text of the original law.

SEE ALSO: 1867, Medicine Lodge Creek Treaty; 1871, Indian Appropriation Act; 1876, Canada's Indian Act; 1903, *Lone Wolf v. Hitchcock*; 1924, Indian Citizenship Act; 1934, Indian Reorganization Act; 1953, Termination Resolution.

1889 ■ HULL HOUSE OPENS: *two women create one of the first settlement houses, setting the standard for hundreds of subsequent efforts to aid the urban poor*

DATE: September 18, 1889

LOCALE: Chicago's West Side

CATEGORIES: Social reform; Organizations and institutions; Women's issues

KEY FIGURES:

Jane Addams (1860-1935), prominent social reformer and cofounder of Hull House

John Dewey (1859-1952), professor at the University of Chicago

Alice Hamilton (1869-1970), physician who labored under the auspices of Hull House

Florence Kelley (1859-1932), early resident of Hull House

Julia Lathrop (1858-1932), early resident of Hull House
Ellen Gates Starr (1859-1940), cofounder of Hull House
SUMMARY OF EVENT. While traveling in Europe in 1888, Jane Addams and Ellen Gates Starr, close friends who had been classmates at Rockford College in Illinois, pledged to live together in a poor urban neighborhood upon their return to the United States. This decision was prompted in large part by their struggle to find meaning in a world that greatly limited opportunities for women. During the last quarter of the nineteenth century, many of the first generation of college-educated U.S. women rejected women's traditional role as mothers and wives but generally were denied careers in business, law, the ministry, and medicine.

The daughter of a wealthy mill owner and banker, Addams was graduated from college in 1881, then dropped out of medical school, spent two years touring Europe with her stepmother, experienced several bouts of depression, and led a rather aimless life. Starr had been forced to leave Rockford College after one year because of limited family finances. She then taught a variety of subjects at the fashionable Miss Kirkland's School for Girls in Chicago. Like Addams, she was troubled by a sense of futility and searched for direction, a quest that eventually took her from Unitarianism to Episcopalianism to Roman Catholicism. After attending a gory bullfight in Madrid in the spring of 1888, Addams was appalled and ashamed by her lack of disgust with the carnage and resolved to become involved in the lives of suffering people. While en route to the United States, she investigated several reform efforts in London, most notably Toynbee Hall, a social settlement established in 1884.

With Toynbee Hall as their model, Addams and Starr rented an apartment in Chicago in January, 1889, and sought to clarify their goals, raise money for their endeavor, and locate a suitable house. They visited society matrons, leaders of Chicago charities, and clergy; they received pledges of support from the Chicago Women's Club, the Chicago chapter of the Association of Collegiate Alumnae, the head of the Chicago Ethical Society, and the city's most popular minister, Frank Gunsaulus. The directors of the Armour Mission, a nondenominational institution founded in 1886 that sponsored many facilities for the city's poor residents, were especially helpful. Dozens of speeches to clubs, mission boards, and Sunday school classes won Addams and Starr many generous offers of financial support and made them celebrities in the city even before they opened their house.

On September 18, 1889, they moved onto the second floor of the old Hull Mansion, built in 1856 on South Halsted Street on Chicago's West Side. It was surrounded by factories and tenements populated primarily by indigent immigrants. According to Addams, the area had inexpressibly dirty streets, inadequate schools, poor street lighting, miserable paving, unenforced sanitary legislation, and "stables foul beyond description."

Addams and Starr had originally intended simply to live in an impoverished neighborhood and develop cordial relationships with the residents. Their initial plan was to be a presence in the community, both to learn from and to teach their urban neighbors. They hoped that other young, directionless, college-educated women would live with them and find a purpose by interacting with Chicago's poor. Hull House, however, quickly evolved into an institution that furnished a variety of programs and services to those living on the West Side.

Convinced that the influence of the neighborhood's more than two hundred saloons, numerous dance halls, and widespread delinquency could be reduced only by wholesome entertainment and activities, Addams and Starr started clubs for girls and boys, a lending library, music programs, and a social science club. Hull House also provided hot lunches, child care, classes in English, and lectures on art and philosophy. They hung reproductions of great European art in the house, and Starr patiently explained the meaning of these pictures to onlookers. Although their neighbors initially were skeptical, two thousand neighborhood residents soon were visiting the settlement each week.

A gifted group of individuals, including Julia Lathrop, Florence Kelley, and Alice Hamilton, soon joined the Hull House founders. To improve the urban environment, these women campaigned for more effective garbage collection, cleaner streets, public baths, parks, playgrounds, and better schools. By means of their experiences, discussion, debates, publications, and reform activities, they advanced both the theory and practice of social welfare in the United States.

Hull House was not the first settlement house in the United States. That honor belonged to the Neighborhood Guild (later called the University Settlement), founded by Stanton Coit on New York's Lower East Side in 1886. Several months before Hull House opened its doors, two of Coit's associates established College Settlement, also in New York. The roots of these early social settlements were complex. They lay in British Christian socialism, the Social Gospel movement in the United States (an effort of many Protestants to apply biblical social teachings to urban, industrial, economic, and political life), the humanitarian desire to help newly arrived immigrants adjust to life in the United States and the poor to escape indigence, concern for social control, and the rise of sociology as an academic discipline.

Settlements were part of a larger crusade aimed at improving working and living conditions in U.S. cities, which included hundreds of institutional churches, civic organizations, and reform agencies. As more and more people moved into congested urban areas, settlement workers strove to replace the long-standing view of cities as dens of iniquity that should be abolished with a vision of cities as centers of commerce and culture that could be reformed through better housing, sanitation, transportation, employment opportunities, and recreation, and by re-creating a sense of community.

Hull House and other settlements also sprang, in part, from the broader quest of U.S. women to improve themselves and their society. This campaign gave birth to the Women's Christian Temperance Union, the Social Purity League, the General

Federation of Women's Clubs, and numerous other reform and philanthropic organizations. Moreover, settlements both reflected and contributed to the growing belief that poverty was not simply a result of individual flaws and failures but sprang from larger institutional and social forces that society must seek to change.

For several reasons, including the remarkable residents and visitors it attracted, the many facilities it developed, and Addams' zealous efforts to publicize its philosophy and programs, Hull House became the nation's showcase settlement and the prototype for the four hundred other settlements founded during the next two decades. By 1906, only the University of Chicago had more buildings and programs in Chicago than Hull House. Those associated with the settlement made it a center for urban research and social reform. Journalists, scholars, and welfare workers flocked to Hull House to study its success and advance its aims.

In 1895, Addams and others issued *Hull House Maps and Papers*, an in-depth survey of the conditions of the nineteen different nationalities who lived in close proximity to the settlement, which stimulated further research on Chicago and other cities. Much of the settlement's fame, however, stemmed from the national reputation Addams achieved as a result of her many books, articles, and lectures, and her participation in various reform crusades. By the early twentieth century, Addams was considered by many to be the United States' leading lady, widely considered a sage and a saint, a rare exemplar of both practicality and spirituality. —*Gary Scott Smith*

ADDITIONAL READING:

Addams, Jane. *Twenty Years at Hull House*. New York: Macmillan, 1911. A detailed account of the establishment, operation, and philosophy of Hull House. Fifty-one illustrations.

Bryan, Mary Linn McCree, and Allen Davis. *One Hundred Years at Hull-House*. Indianapolis: Indiana University Press, 1990. A compendium of primary sources about Hull House, including numerous photographs.

Carson, Mina. *Settlement Folk: Social Thought and the American Settlement Movement, 1885-1930*. Chicago: University of Chicago Press, 1990. An extensively documented examination of the contribution of U.S. settlement-house workers to the development of social welfare. Provides a historical and ideological context for the work of Hull House.

Davis, Allen. *American Heroine: The Life and Legend of Jane Addams*. New York: Oxford University Press, 1973. A readable appraisal of Addams' work as a reformer and her founding of Hull House. Illustrations and index.

_____. *Spearheads for Reform: The Social Settlements and the Progressive Movement, 1890-1914*. New York: Oxford University Press, 1967. An overview of the origin, guiding principles, activities, and accomplishments of American social settlements during their early years.

Farrell, John C. *Beloved Lady: A History of Jane Addams' Ideas on Reform and Peace*. Baltimore: The Johns Hopkins University Press, 1967. A helpful analysis of the first decade of Hull House.

Levine, Daniel. *Jane Addams and the Liberal Tradition*. Westport, Conn.: Greenwood Press, 1980. A useful discussion of the background, context, daily operations, institutional growth, and community influence of Hull House.

SEE ALSO: 1820's, Social Reform Movement; 1857, New York Infirmary for Indigent Women and Children Opens; 1892, "New" Immigration; 1921, Sheppard-Towner Act.

1889 ■ FIRST PAN-AMERICAN CONGRESS: *a meeting of Western Hemisphere nations sets the precedent for inter-American cooperation and forms the basis of the Organization of American States*

DATE: October, 1889-April, 1890
LOCALE: Washington, D.C.
CATEGORIES: Diplomacy and international relations; Latino American history
KEY FIGURES:
Thomas Francis Bayard (1828-1898), secretary of state under President Grover Cleveland
James Gillespie Blaine (1830-1893), secretary of state when the congress opened, and architect of United States-Latin American relations
Carlos Calvo (1824-1906), Argentine lawyer who wrote extensively defending the sovereignty of Latin American republics
Andrew Carnegie (1835-1919), industrialist and member of the U.S. delegation
Stephen Grover Cleveland (1837-1908), twenty-second (1885-1889) and twenty-fourth (1893-1897) president of the United States
John B. Henderson (1826-1913), head of the U.S. delegation to the congress
Roque Saénz Peña (1851-1914), head of the Argentine delegation to the congress and president of Argentina
Emilio C. Varas, head of the Chilean delegation

SUMMARY OF EVENT. The first Pan-American Congress took place in Washington, D.C., between October, 1889, and April, 1890. The first inter-American meeting to be held in the United States, it was called by Grover Cleveland, twenty-second president of the United States, through invitations sent out by his secretary of state, Thomas F. Bayard. Delegates came from all the states of Latin America that were then independent, except Santo Domingo. When they arrived in Washington, they were met by James G. Blaine, who had succeeded Bayard as secretary of state and who, since 1881, had favored a congress of this nature.

The pan-American ideal included the promotion of closer political, social, and economic bonds between the independent nations of the American continents. It had its roots in a meeting called in Panama by Simón Bolívar in 1826, which had been attended by delegations from Central America, Colombia, Peru, and Mexico. The United States' representatives did not arrive before the end of the conference on July 15, 1826. The conference was a failure, but established a precedent for inter-American cooperation that would follow a "good neighbor" policy advocated by Henry Clay in the 1820's. Subsequent conferences in Lima, Peru, in 1847-1848, in Santiago, Chile, in 1856, and again in Lima in 1865, however, did not include delegations from the United States and reflected the fear on the part of many Latin American nations of U.S. expansionism.

The United States had, by the early 1880's, recovered from the physical wounds of the Civil War, and its financiers were willing to enter the international competition for foreign markets. The country's leaders started to concern themselves with Latin America. That region offered plentiful opportunities for trade and investment. There also was a revival of interest in Central America as a site for a projected interoceanic canal. In March, 1881, Blaine, then secretary of state under President James Garfield, stated that one of the major aims of the Garfield Administration would be the conservation "of such friendly relations with American countries as would lead to a large increase in the export trade of the United States."

Successful trade, however, demands peace and stable governments, and in Latin America there was war and civil disorder. Blaine, who also had a vision of U.S. leadership of American nations, decided that it was his mission to bring peace and stability to Latin America. On November 29, 1881, with the War of the Pacific (1879-1884) being fought between Chile and a Bolivian-Peruvian alliance, Secretary Blaine issued invitations to the Latin American countries to send delegates to a Washington conference in 1882. The announced purpose of the meeting was to find a means of preventing open warfare among American nations. Blaine expected that peace not only would be beneficial to trade but also would lead to a pan-American alliance and give the United States an advantage in securing the rights for an isthmian canal in Panama. Blaine's Latin American policy intended to blend harmoniously pan-Americanism and the Monroe Doctrine. Many Latin American countries were not as confident that those two doctrines were entirely compatible. Chile, fearful that the meeting would impose a settlement in the war, refused to participate, and the meeting was postponed. It was finally held in 1889.

The 1889 invitation to the Washington meeting stated that the conference would deal only with matters of arbitration and trade, and would be consultative in nature rather than policy making. It set the goals of finding peaceful solutions to the problems of the Latin American nations and of considering "questions relating to the improvement of business intercourse and means of direct communication between said countries." It also attempted to "secure more extensive markets for the products of each of the said countries." As a way of demonstrating the economic capabilities of the United States, Blaine arranged for the delegations to be given a six-week railway tour of the country's industrial centers. Delegates traveled to Buffalo, Detroit, Chicago, Pittsburgh, Baltimore, and New York. The United States' interest in opening markets was quickly understood by Latin American delegations to mean increased U.S. business, as the United States' imports of agricultural goods from Latin America exceeded its industrial exports to the region.

The actual discussions at the first Pan-American Congress, as the gathering came to be called, lasted thirteen weeks. Nevertheless, nothing was accomplished on the proposal to establish obligatory arbitration on disputes between American states. The head of the delegation from Chile, Emilio C. Varas, believed that the proposal was the first step in the creation of a permanent court of arbitration, which he feared would be dominated by the host country, and he led the opposition by refusing to discuss the resolution or to vote on it. Also defeated was the United States' proposal to create a customs union in order to attain "trade reciprocity approaching a large scale free trade system."

By the same token, the U.S. delegation rejected a Latin American resolution that would establish, as a basic principle of American international law, that "the nation neither requires nor recognizes any obligations or responsibilities of aliens beyond these established by the Constitution and laws for the native born in the same conditions." The Latin American proposal stemmed from the fact that foreign investors in the area, in cases of conflict, resorted to appeals to their own countries, which often maintained higher standards of protection for individuals. The Latin American delegates, however, felt that this constituted a clear violation of the principle of national sovereignty. They adopted the position of Argentine lawyer Carlos Calvo, who had vigorously defended what he called "indefeasible sovereignty."

Additional areas of interest included port dues, patents and trademarks, extradition, and banking. There were also disagreements. Roque Saénz Peña, head of the Argentine delegation, wanted to maintain an independent policy that did not defer to the United States. One difficult point was a proposal for international arbitration. Chile, especially sensitive to her territorial gains in the War of the Pacific, objected to compulsory arbitration. Secretary Blaine finally attempted to write a compromise statement, but it was never ratified.

On the positive side, considerable progress was made at the meeting in discussing social and cultural matters. The delegates discussed the standardization of sanitary regulations, the building of the intercontinental railroad, and the adoption of uniform weights and measures. Furthermore, the congress agreed to the establishment of the International Bureau of American Republics, and the precedent was set for meetings that have been held from time to time ever since. The congress also created the structure for the Pan-American Union which, housed in a magnificent building donated by Andrew Carnegie, industrialist and a member of the United States delegation, would eventually become the Organization of American States.

—Maurice T. Dominquez, updated by James A. Baer

ADDITIONAL READING:

Bemis, Samuel Flagg. *The American Secretaries of State and Their Diplomacy*. Vol. 8. New York: Cooper Square, 1963. Includes an essay written by Joseph B. Lockey for the original 1928 edition. Chapter 5 discusses Blaine's participation in the Pan-American Congress.

LaFeber, Walter. *The American Search for Opportunity, 1865-1913*. Vol. 2 in *The Cambridge History of American Foreign Relations*. New York: Cambridge University Press, 1993. Pages 74-79 discuss the change from earlier policies reflecting Monroe Doctrine to what Henry Clay had termed a "good neighbor" approach to countries of the Americas.

Langley, Lester D. *America and the Americas: The United States in the Western Hemisphere*. Athens: University of Georgia Press, 1989. Provides an overview of relations between the United States and Latin America, denoting the changes in emphasis over time, including the Monroe Doctrine and the Cold War.

Mecham, J. Lloyd. *A Survey of United States-Latin American Relations*. Boston: Houghton Mifflin, 1965. Chapter 4 treats the concept of pan-Americanism, dividing it into two phases: 1826-1889, during which the United States is excluded; and 1889 to mid-1960's, in which there is hemispheric cooperation.

Pascoe, Elaine. *Neighbors at Odds: U.S. Policy in Latin America*. New York: Franklin Watts, 1990. Reviews relations between the United States and its Latin American neighbors, from the Monroe Doctrine through the Cold War, placing the Pan-American Congress within the framework of gunboat and dollar diplomacy.

SEE ALSO: 1823, Monroe Doctrine; 1898, Spanish-American War; 1903, Acquisition of the Panama Canal Zone; 1912, Intervention in Nicaragua; 1930's, Mass Deportations of Mexicans; 1933, Good Neighbor Policy.

1890 ■ CLOSING OF THE FRONTIER: *the U.S. Census Bureau declares that the American frontier is closed, coinciding with the end of the Indian wars*

DATE: 1890

LOCALE: Great Plains and Far West

CATEGORIES: Expansion and land acquisition; Native American history

SUMMARY OF EVENT. Following the French and Indian War, the victorious British government issued the Proclamation of 1763 and created a frontier line between the Allegheny Mountains and the Mississippi River. This reserved the land to the west "for the moment" to the American Indians, closing it to settlers and land speculators until King George decided what to do with his newly acquired, previously French-dominated territory. U.S. frontiersmen such as Daniel Boone ignored the proclamation and pushed west of the Alleghenies, precipitat-

ing pitched battles with various American Indian tribes, loosely led by the Shawnee chief, Pontiac.

These skirmishes between natives and frontiersmen led Thomas Jefferson to write in the Declaration of Independence that King George had "endeavored to bring on the inhabitants of our frontiers, the merciless Indian Savages, whose known rule of warfare is an undistinguished destruction of all ages, sexes, and conditions." Using these words, Jefferson indelibly linked all American Indian nations to the colonists' definition of frontier.

In 1890, the Census Bureau declared the U.S. frontier closed, based on a definition of "frontier" as an area containing not fewer than two nor more than six persons per square mile and described as "a line between Indians and homesteaders." The director of the Census Bureau in his report stated that "there can hardly be said to be a frontier line."

A young history teacher at the University of Wisconsin, Frederick Jackson Turner, intrigued by the 1890 census, concluded that the closing of the frontier symbolized the end of a great historic movement. He published his thesis in a paper, "The Significance of the Frontier in American History," delivered to the American Historical Association in Chicago in 1893. In this paper, Turner converted the line between American Indians and homesteaders into, in his words, "a meeting point between savagery and civilization," thereby placing his signature on Jefferson's words. Historians of the time took little exception to the word "savages" and dwelt instead upon the appealing thesis of Turner's paper, for it held that U.S. society and institutions were unique, resulting from the existence of "an area of free land, its continuous recession, and the advance of American settlement westward." According to Turner, Europeans had come to America with their cultural baggage, but in the process of adjusting to and ultimately overcoming the primitive environment in which they found themselves, they were transformed into something new— Americans living in an American social setting with distinctly American institutions. This change did not occur all at once as a result of a single meeting by one group of immigrants with a wilderness environment. It was, rather, the result of the repetition of this process on a succession of frontiers over many decades.

Turner noted that there were important differences, as well as similarities, between frontiers. The farming frontier of the Midwest was different from the mining frontier of the Rocky Mountains, and the woodland frontier of the seventeenth and eighteenth centuries was different from the Great Plains frontier of the nineteenth century. At the same time, on virtually all frontiers, the first European immigrants were fur traders and trappers, and they were followed by cattle raisers, pioneer farmers, and government-sponsored explorers. To some areas came miners and ranchers. The process ended with the establishment of villages and towns.

The frontier as an Americanizing influence had several discernible aspects: It transformed European immigrants of diverse cultural backgrounds into a composite nationality; it

LANDS SETTLED BY 1890

Settled

Unsettled

By 1890, when the U.S. Census formally announced the end of the frontier, the American population was approximately sixty-two million, with eight million engaged in agriculture. There were 197,000 miles of railroad track in the United States and almost as many miles of telegraph lines. The year 1890 also saw the Battle of Wounded Knee and the death of Sitting Bull, marking the end of the Indian Wars. Native Americans had ceded all but the most mountainous and inhospitable of their homelands to the U.S. government.

promoted a feeling of nationalism among the people and produced such nation-building events as the Louisiana Purchase; and it promoted democracy not only by encouraging individualism and antipathy toward control but also because on the relative economic equality that existed there. The frontier, according to Turner, exerted an important influence on the persons living there; it produced in its inhabitants a combination of coarseness and strength, acuteness and inquisitiveness, practicality and ingenuity, together with restlessness and optimism. While encouraging individualism, the frontier sometimes also encouraged cooperation, especially in defense against the natives and in seeking help from government in the form of military assistance and favorable economic legislation. Less laudable was the influence of the frontier in promoting laxity in governmental affairs and business dealings, in its general disrespect for law and order accompanied by an impatience with legal processes, and by its attitude of anti-intellectualism. Turner also implied that the frontier alleviated many

social and economic problems inherent in an industrial society and was a safety valve for the discontented.

After a generation of almost universal acceptance, the Turner thesis began to be vigorously attacked in the 1920's, both for what he had said and for what he had failed to say. Historians of a generation then shaped by World War I no longer ignored the exploitation, land thefts, industrialization, lawlessness, and imperialism that had characterized European cultures and that also shaped the United States. Other critics said that Turner had paid no attention to artistic, educational, social, and literary developments; that his terms were ambiguous; that he had failed to test his hypothesis against other frontier experiences; and that his ideas were provincial and some of his statements contradictory. It also was said that Turner had paid no attention to the rise of country towns. In the Great Plains between the 1860's and 1890's, the rise of towns was a direct result of the expansion of railroading in the United States.

Following the Civil War, rights-of-way were granted to the railroads wherever they wanted them. Even American Indian reservations were crisscrossed with tracks. Each railroad right-of-way included miles to either side of the tracks, which the railroads sold to homesteaders for money to lay more track. Railroad stops became towns. Grain, meat, and hides exported East perpetuated the process. By 1890, there were 197,000 miles of railroad track in the United States and almost as many miles of telegraph lines.

In 1860, possibly thirty million bison inhabited the Great Plains. In 1885, five hundred remained on a reserve in Montana. Killing bison made room for cattle and also killed Native Americans. In the 1880's, more than one million Europeans immigrated to the United States. In 1890, in a population of sixty-two million, eight million were engaged in agriculture. The railroads moved ranch and farming products to market.

Some other important information Turner had not taken into account in his thesis included the following: In 1890, six corporations controlled 99 percent of private-sector money. By 1887, the government had substituted agreements for treaties with American Indians. One such agreement granted 160 acres of personal property to American Indian families living on reservations. The General Allotment (Dawes) Act dispersed 32,800 allotments of land to American Indians, covering three million acres, and thus allowed the cession or sale of twenty-eight million acres of "surplus" to white settlers.

Turner defended himself by reminding his detractors that he had never claimed the frontier to be the sole force shaping the United States as a nation. He noted that industrialization, social reform, and imperialism were equally important, but that no reasonable person could deny that three centuries of moving west, during which the U.S. people had conquered three thousand miles of wilderness, had left an imprint on U.S. history and the U.S. character. Still, Turner—in his zeal to describe a U.S. history and culture characterized by faith in democratic institutions, an insistence that class lines should never hinder social mobility, an eagerness to experiment, and a preference for the new over the old—had shaped his notice of the closing of the frontier to his preconceived notions and had ignored the initial conditions by which the frontier was defined by the king and colonists.

In August, 1886, Geronimo surrendered in Arizona. On December 15, 1890, Sitting Bull was murdered by Indian policeman in South Dakota. In the same year, the Wounded Knee Massacre, the last battle between regular army and American Indians, effectively ended thousands of years of indigenous people's domination of North America. "The end of the Indian wars," wrote W. T. Hagan, "marked the conclusion of a long chapter of American history," and it was no coincidence that the year of Wounded Knee was the year the U.S. Census Bureau declared the frontier closed.

—*W. Turrentine Jackson, updated by Glenn Schiffman*

ADDITIONAL READING:

Axelrod, Alan. *Chronicle of the Indian Wars.* New York: Prentice Hall, 1993. This reference work presents a survey of the many conflicts between American Indians and U.S. government military and other officials that led to the end of the Indians' way of life and their assimilation and restriction to reservations.

Billington, Ray Allen. *America's Frontier Heritage.* New York: Holt, Rinehart and Winston, 1966. Billington turns away from Turner's hypothesis and focuses instead on the questions "What was the nature of the frontier experience?" and "What effect has it had on the American character?"

Lewis, Archibald R., and Thomas F. McGann, eds. *The New World Looks at Its History.* Austin: University of Texas Press, 1963. Proceedings of the Second International Congress of Historians of the United States and Mexico, emphasizing the theme of the frontier in history.

Parish, John Carl. *The Persistence of the Westward Movement, and Other Essays.* Berkeley: University of California Press, 1943. Nine essays suggest that the American westward movement was not one but many movements of population. The author examines the forces that brought people to the West, their attempts to reproduce the culture of the East and its necessary modifications, and finally the persistence of the westward movement as a state of mind.

Paxson, Frederic Logan. *When the West Is Gone.* New York: Henry Holt, 1930. Consisting of three lectures delivered at Brown University only a few decades after the closing of the frontier, this brief work analyzes U.S. history from the perspective of the shifting frontier.

Turner, Frederick Jackson. *The Frontier in American History.* New York: Henry Holt, 1920. The classic exposition of the frontier as a shaper of American history, first broached in 1893. Provocative both in its own time and today.

Wise, Jennings C. *The Red Man in the New World Drama.* New York: Macmillan, 1972. An overview of American Indians as they accommodated an ever-encroaching European influx.

Wyman, Walker D., and Clifton B. Kroeber, eds. *The Frontier in Perspective.* Madison: University of Wisconsin Press, 1957. Thirteen lectures delivered at the University of Wisconsin by eminent historians from Canada, Mexico, and the United States on important aspects of the world frontier and the American frontier.

SEE ALSO: 1763, Proclamation of 1763; 1815, Westward Migration; 1820, Land Act of 1820; 1821, Santa Fe Trail Opens; 1823, Jedediah Smith Explores the Far West; 1825, Erie Canal Opens; 1830, Baltimore and Ohio Railroad Begins Operation; 1830, Indian Removal Act; 1830, Trail of Tears; 1835, Texas Revolution; 1842, Frémont's Expeditions; 1846, Mormon Migration to Utah; 1846, Oregon Settlement; 1846, Mexican War; 1848, California Gold Rush; 1853, Pacific Railroad Surveys; 1860, Pony Express; 1861, Apache Wars; 1861, Transcontinental Telegraph Is Completed; 1862, Homestead Act; 1862, Morrill Land Grant Act; 1862, Great Sioux War; 1863, Long Walk of the Navajos; 1866, Chisholm Trail Opens; 1866, Bozeman Trail War; 1867, Medicine Lodge Creek Treaty; 1868, Washita River Massacre; 1869, Transcontinental

Railroad Is Completed; 1872, Great American Bison Slaughter; 1876, Battle of the Little Bighorn; 1879, Powell's *Report on the Lands of the Arid Region*; 1887, General Allotment Act; 1890, Battle of Wounded Knee.

1890 ■ WOMEN'S RIGHTS ASSOCIATIONS UNITE: *the merger of two national women's organizations creates a potent lobby for woman suffrage*

DATE: February 17-18, 1890
LOCALE: Washington, D.C.
CATEGORIES: Organizations and institutions; Women's issues
KEY FIGURES:
Susan B. Anthony (1820-1906) and
Elizabeth Cady Stanton (1815-1902), leaders of the New York-based National Woman Suffrage Association
Lucy Stone (1818-1893), leader of the Boston-based American Woman Suffrage Association
Victoria Claflin Woodhull (1838-1927), radical associate of Stanton

SUMMARY OF EVENT. The men and women who campaigned for women's rights in the nineteenth century usually were involved in other reformist causes. Elizabeth Cady Stanton and Lucretia Mott attended the first World Anti-Slavery Convention in London in 1840; there, women were denied the right to participate. Susan B. Anthony was first involved in the temperance movement; at an 1852 Sons of Temperance meeting in Albany, New York, she was denied the right to speak. By then, Stanton, Mott, and three others had initiated what came to be known as the 1848 Seneca Falls Women's Rights Convention. In the decade prior to the Civil War, feminists made modest gains. Limited protection of a married woman's personal property was legislated in Ohio and New York; increasing numbers of middle-class women were entering the professions. Oberlin College admitted women. Many traditions came under attack. Stanton briefly joined Amelia Bloomer's campaign for women's dress reform and spoke at the 1860 Woman's Rights Convention on the need to reformulate marriage as a civil, not a sacred, contract.

As events led toward the Civil War, the antislavery movement inevitably came to dominate all other reform causes. Basing their argument on Thomas Jefferson and the Declaration of Independence, feminist leaders asserted that both women and African Americans had natural rights. In general, they were in accord with Frederick Douglass, former slave and abolitionist leader, who argued that, if the U.S. Constitution were interpreted literally, it was an antislavery document, and with Victoria Woodhull, radical speaker and editor, who insisted that women already had the legal right to vote.

With the end of the Civil War in 1865 and the proposal of the Fourteenth Amendment to the Constitution, feminists suffered a setback. While the Constitution previously had not defined citizens as male, this amendment did so; for the first time, women were explicitly denied rights as citizens. Previously, they were denied voting rights by state laws alone. With passage of the Fourteenth Amendment, only another amendment could enfranchise them. Like many other abolitionist leaders, Wendell Phillips, elected president of the American Anti-Slavery Society in 1865, argued that women should postpone their own campaign for the vote until rights for African Americans had been constitutionally ensured. Some feminists, such as Lucy Stone, agreed.

By May, 1869, this strategy led to a split among suffragists. The New York group, which became the National Woman Suffrage Association (NWSA), was led by Anthony and Stanton. Stanton was the first NWSA president and remained president for twenty-one years. To establish a short-lived newspaper, *The Revolution*, Anthony and Stanton accepted funds from George Francis Train, a radical Irish American; Train may have been a racist, but his support of organized labor alone would have made him unacceptable to most middle-class reformers. The association with Train offended many members. When the Fifteenth Amendment was proposed, stating that the vote could not be denied on the basis of color, race, or previous servitude, the NWSA urged inclusion of the word "sex." NWSA leaders took a stand on other issues then considered radical, favoring equal pay for equal work and reform of marriage laws, and attempting to draw public attention to the legal and economic plights of housewives, factory workers, prostitutes, and prisoners. The NWSA was open to all, but no man could hold office. NWSA attracted younger women and women from the western frontier, rather than the sheltered ladies of eastern cities.

A Boston-based group, led by Lucy Stone and Henry Blackwell, concentrated on the vote. Founded by Stone, Julia Ward Howe, and Isabella Beecher Hooker, the American Woman Suffrage Association (AWSA) allowed men full participation. Popular preacher Henry Ward Beecher, Isabella Hooker's brother, became the first AWSA president. When a choice had to be made between the causes of woman suffrage and African American suffrage in order to get legislation passed, the Boston group agreed that woman suffrage must wait. The AWSA newspaper was, by comparison with NWSA's, conservative. Mary Livermore, editor of *Woman's Journal*, had left the NWSA because of its radical stance on marriage and dress.

The division was hardened by NWSA's brief acceptance of radical orator Victoria Woodhull. Woodhull, once a spiritualist healer, and her sister, Tennessee Claflin, had become the first female Wall Street brokers. They operated as Woodhull, Claflin & Company and were backed by Cornelius Vanderbilt's money. So long as Vanderbilt money was behind her, Woodhull was treated with respect by the press, but that changed as Vanderbilt's interest waned. In 1870, she began *Woodhull and Claflin's Weekly*, a newspaper that touched on women's issues from hair-dye poisoning to prostitution. In it, she supported her own candidacy for U.S. president, to run in the 1872 elections

The former division between women's groups over whether to combine abolition and woman suffrage agendas was mended in 1890 when the National Woman Suffrage Association and the American Woman Suffrage Association joined forces to become the National American Woman Suffrage Association. (Library of Congress, photo by Barn)

as a third-party candidate. A charismatic orator, Woodhull was accepted, initially, by Stanton and some others in the NWSA. She spoke to large gatherings on such matters as political and civil service corruption, the unequal division of wealth, and the need to unite labor reformers and suffragists. Her most outspoken opponents were from the Boston faction and included Catherine Beecher and Harriet Beecher Stowe (author of *Uncle Tom's Cabin*, 1852), sisters of Henry Ward Beecher. As newspapers focused on details of Woodhull's unconventional personal life, she chose to expose the hypocrisy of her critics by publicly revealing a long-standing affair between Henry Ward Beecher and a married woman member of his congregation. The various scandals alienated many of the New York group from Woodhull; the Boston group was enraged.

For almost two decades, the division between associations remained. Both, probably, had memberships of about ten thousand during this period, while millions of women were drawn into other reformist or self-help movements, including cultural and garden clubs, the Women's National Committee for Law Enforcement, and the Southern Women's Educational Alliance. The largest group was the Women's Christian Temperance Union (WCTU), which had, by 1892, a membership of 150,000; including auxiliaries, its membership was more than 200,000. Frances Willard, WCTU leader, worked with both suffrage associations, seeing woman suffrage as the one route to legislation against alcohol.

Alice Stone Blackwell, Lucy Stone's daughter, was among those who saw the need to unite the two suffrage factions into a single, more effective body. She and Rachel Foster Avery, representing NWSA, were negotiators. The merger took place at a February, 1890, meeting in Washington, D.C. Stanton, then seventy-five years of age, became the first president of the National American Woman Suffrage Association (NAWSA); Anthony and Stone, both seventy-two years of age, served as vice president and executive committee chair, respectively. Stanton resigned as president in 1892, skeptical of the temperance affiliation and the piety and conservativism of the new group; she left to continue her radical attack on organized religion. Publication of her 1895 *Woman's Bible* caused such outrage that NAWSA censured Stanton's work at its 1896 meeting. Stanton was followed as president by Anthony and then by Carrie Chapman Catt, an Iowa superintendent of schools, who was president between 1900 and 1904. A new vigor was given the suffrage movement, however, only by younger women. Harriot Stanton Blatch, Stanton's daughter, returned to the United States in 1907, after having observed radical British suffrage techniques. She organized the first suffrage parades in New York. Catt returned to power in 1915, and, with the younger generation of radicals, led the way to the Nineteenth Amendment in 1920.

—*Betty Richardson*

ADDITIONAL READING:

Barry, Kathleen. *Susan B. Anthony: A Biography of a Singular Feminist.* New York: New York University Press, 1988. A readable scholarly biography, emphasizing Anthony's public life and covering the many issues and divisions of the suffrage movement.

Bordin, Ruth. *Woman and Temperance: The Quest for Power and Liberty, 1873-1900.* Philadelphia: Temple University Press, 1981. Traces the complex relationship between suffrage and the then-more-numerous and powerful forces for temperance, a relationship that led the alcohol industry and drinkers to oppose suffrage.

Flexner, Eleanor. *Century of Struggle: The Woman's Rights Movement in the United States.* Rev. ed. Cambridge, Mass.: The Belknap Press of Harvard University Press, 1975. First published in 1959 and extensively revised in 1975, this remains the best basic survey of women's rights issues from colonial times to 1920.

Griffith, Elisabeth. *In Her Own Right: The Life of Elizabeth Cady Stanton.* New York: Oxford University Press, 1984. The first fully scholarly study of Stanton and her leadership.

Gurko, Miriam. *The Ladies of Seneca Falls: The Birth of the Women's Rights Movement.* New York: Macmillan, 1974. Traces major figures of the women's movement from 1848 through the formation of NAWSA.

Hahn, Emily. *Once upon a Pedestal.* New York: Crowell, 1974. A useful introduction to the subject of women's rights, covering topics from the views of women travelers to birth control and suffrage.

Underhill, Lois Beachy. *The Woman Who Ran for President: The Many Lives of Victoria Woodhull.* Bridgehampton, N.Y.: Bridge Works, 1995. A balanced, scholarly study of the charismatic feminist leader whose scandalous life has caused her to be omitted from or patronized in most early histories.

SEE ALSO: 1848, Seneca Falls Convention; 1866, Suffragists Protest the Fourteenth Amendment; 1868, Fourteenth Amendment; 1869, Rise of Woman Suffrage Associations; 1869, Western States Grant Woman Suffrage; 1872, Susan B. Anthony Is Arrested; 1874, *Minor v. Happersett*; 1876, Declaration of the Rights of Women; 1916, National Woman's Party Is Founded; 1920, League of Women Voters Is Founded; 1920, U.S. Women Gain the Vote.

1890 ■ SHERMAN ANTITRUST ACT: *unfair business monopolies give rise to regulatory legislation*

DATE: July 20, 1890
LOCALE: Washington, D.C.
CATEGORIES: Business and labor; Economics; Laws and acts
KEY FIGURES:
Benjamin Harrison (1833-1901), twenty-third president of the United States, 1889-1893
George Frisbie Hoar (1826-1904), senator from Massachusetts
Richard Olney (1835-1917), attorney general, 1893-1895, and secretary of state, 1895-1897

John Davison Rockefeller (1839-1937), founder and chief executive of Standard Oil Company

John Sherman (1823-1900), senator from Ohio

SUMMARY OF EVENT. The period following the Civil War was one of rapid economic growth and change in the United States. Creation of a nationwide network of railroads gave individual firms a way to serve a nationwide market, enabling them to grow to a large size to improve their efficiency or simply to gain strategic advantages. A conspicuous firm was Standard Oil, led by John D. Rockefeller. The firm was efficient and progressive in developing petroleum refining, but was heavily criticized for such actions as pressuring railroads for preferential rebates and discriminatory price-cutting to intimidate competitors.

Standard Oil effectively controlled the petroleum-refining industry by 1879. In addition to lubricants, its principal product was kerosene, aggressively marketed worldwide as the first cheap and convenient source of artificial light. In 1882, the firm was reorganized in the form of a trust, facilitating the acquisition of competing firms. Although the trust form went out of use soon after, the term "trust" became a common name for aggressive big-business monopolies. Other large combinations were soon formed, so that by 1890, large companies controlled the production of such items as whiskey, sugar, and lead, and dominated the nation's railroads.

Opposition to big-business abuses spread among farmers and in small-business sectors such as the grocery business. Popular concern was fueled by writings such as Edward Bellamy's utopian novel *Looking Backward*, which had sold a million copies within fifteen years after its publication in 1881. Individual states adopted antimonopoly legislation or brought court actions against alleged monopolists. By 1891, eighteen states had adopted some sort of antitrust legislation. Both major political parties adopted vague antimonopoly statements in their platforms for the 1888 election, but neither rushed to submit appropriate legislation at the next congressional session. President Benjamin Harrison was moved to ask for such a statute in his annual message of December, 1889. A bill introduced by Senator John Sherman of Ohio was extensively revised by the Senate Judiciary Committee, under the able guidance of George Hoar and George F. Edmunds. The resulting bill was passed by Congress with virtually no debate and only one opposing vote. President Harrison signed it into law July 20, 1890.

The Sherman Antitrust Act contained three important types of provisions. First, the law outlawed "every contract, combination in the form of trust or otherwise, or conspiracy, in restraint of trade or commerce among the several states or with foreign nations. . . ." This came to be viewed as dealing with "loose combinations" of several firms undertaking joint action. Second, the law made it illegal for any person to monopolize or attempt to monopolize any part of that trade or commerce. This was viewed as dealing with activities of individual large firms. The key terms were not defined, and it remained for lawyers and judges to try to find satisfactory and consistent meanings for them. Third, the law provided for a variety of means of enforcement. The attorney general was empowered to bring criminal or civil court actions against violators. Civil remedies often proved attractive, because the burden of proof was not so difficult to achieve, and the remedies could involve changing industry structure and behavior, not merely applying punishments. In addition, private individuals could sue offending firms for triple the value of their losses.

Between 1890 and 1904, only eighteen suits were filed under the act. Several of these aimed at collusive rate-fixing by railroads, despite their regulated status under the Interstate Commerce Commission. At the time of the Pullman Strike (1894), the courts held that the Sherman Act could be applied to the activities of labor unions. Unions were repeatedly subjected to injunctions and triple-damage suits for strikes, picketing, and boycotts, even after Congress attempted, in the Clayton Act of 1914, to exempt most union activities from antitrust laws.

The Sherman Act's effectiveness was limited severely by the Supreme Court in an 1895 case against the sugar trust, *United States v. E. C. Knight Company*. The ruling defined commerce so narrowly that it excluded almost all forms of interstate enterprise except transportation. The Court was led to make a ruling of this type by the way in which the Justice Department, under Attorney General Richard Olney, framed the case. Collusive behavior among a number of separate firms, however, was not granted such a loophole. In 1899, activities by six producers of cast-iron pipe to agree on contract bids were held illegal in *Addyston Pipe and Steel Co. v. U.S.* These two cases indicated that activities involving several firms were much more likely to be found illegal than the operations of a single-firm monopolist. Perhaps in response, the decade of the 1890's witnessed an unprecedented boom in the formation of giant corporations through mergers and consolidations. The process culminated in the creation of United States Steel Corporation in 1901, capitalized at more than one billion dollars.

Again, public outcry arose. Congress appointed an Industrial Commission in 1899 to consider the trust problem. A preliminary report in 1900 observed that "industrial combinations have become fixtures in our business life. Their power for evil should be destroyed and their means for good preserved." The commission's 1902 report recommended stronger actions against price discrimination. Some large firms were prosecuted successfully. A giant railroad merger was blocked in the *Northern Securities* case of 1904, helping to gain for President Theodore Roosevelt a reputation as a vigorous trust-buster. In 1911, two notorious trusts, Standard Oil and American Tobacco, were convicted of Sherman Act violations. In each case, the convicted firm was ordered to be broken into several separate firms. The Standard Oil settlement made it much easier for new firms to enter petroleum refining, making possible the emergence of such new competitors as Texaco and Gulf Oil. However, prosecution of the ultimate corporate giant, U.S. Steel, was dismissed in 1920.

In 1914, Congress adopted the Clayton Act, which amended the Sherman Act to specify business actions to be prohibited. This outlawed price discrimination, tying and exclusive-dealing contracts, mergers and acquisitions, and interlocking directorships, where these tended to decrease competition or to create a monopoly. The Federal Trade Commission was also established in 1914, charged with preventing unfair methods of competition and helping to enforce the Clayton Act.

Until 1950, Sherman Act prosecutions tended to be relatively effective against collusive actions by separate firms in interstate commerce, situations involving, for example, price-fixing, and agreements to share markets, to boycott suppliers, or to assign market territories. On the other hand, individual firms were left relatively free, even if large and dominant. Treatment of individual large firms shifted somewhat after the government successfully prosecuted the Aluminum Company of America (ALCOA) in 1945. The court agreed with the prosecution that the firm's market share was large enough to constitute a monopoly, and that ALCOA had deliberately undertaken to achieve this monopoly. This case provided a basis for successful antitrust actions against United Shoe Machinery Company in 1954 and against American Telephone and Telegraph (AT&T) in 1982. In the AT&T case, the telephone industry was drastically reorganized. The various regional operating companies became independent, and entry into long-distance phone services was opened up for new competitors. The government's ability to block the formation of giant-firm monopoly was strengthened in 1950, when Congress passed the Celler-Kefauver Antimerger Act, which gave the government stronger authority to block mergers that seemed to threaten to produce monopoly. —*Paul B. Trescott*

ADDITIONAL READING:

Blair, Roger D., and David L. Kaserman. *Antitrust Economics*. Homewood, Ill.: Irwin, 1985. This university textbook puts the Sherman Act into a broad economic context.

Kovaleff, Theodore P., ed. *The Antitrust Impulse: An Economic, Historical, and Legal Analysis*. 2 vols. Armonk, N.Y.: M. E. Sharpe, 1994. Diverse essays reexamine the history and impact of the law.

Letwin, William L. *Law and Economic Policy in America: The Evolution of the Sherman Act*. New York: Random House, 1956. Surveys the background and early application of the law, finding it an unsuccessful experiment.

Thorelli, Hans. *The Federal Antitrust Policy: Origination of an American Tradition*. Baltimore: The Johns Hopkins University Press, 1955. This encyclopedic study focuses on the political and legal background of the Sherman Act, its legislative history, and its early application.

Whitney, Simon N. *Antitrust Policies: American Experience in Twenty Industries*. 2 vols. New York: Twentieth Century Fund, 1958. Excellent case studies give deeper meaning to the law's application.

SEE ALSO: 1882, Standard Oil Trust Is Organized; 1886, American Federation of Labor Is Founded; 1894, Pullman Strike.

1890 ■ MISSISSIPPI DISFRANCHISEMENT LAWS: *state laws effectively eliminate the black vote*

DATE: August, 1890
LOCALE: Jackson, Mississippi
CATEGORIES: African American history; Civil rights; Laws and acts
KEY FIGURES:
Solomon S. Calhoon (1838-1908), lawyer, jurist, and president of the 1890 state constitutional convention
James George (1826-1897), U.S. senator from Mississippi and delegate to the 1890 state constitutional convention
Isaiah T. Montgomery (1847-1923), African American entrepreneur and delegate to the 1890 state constitutional convention
John M. Stone (1830-1900), governor of Mississippi
Edward C. Walthall (1831-1898), U.S. senator from Mississippi

SUMMARY OF EVENT. Mississippi and South Carolina had the largest black populations in the United States. In 1890, fifty-seven of every hundred Mississippians were black. The Fifteenth Amendment to the U.S. Constitution (ratified in 1870) provided that no state could deny the right to vote on account of race; thus, Mississippi had a large black electorate. During the early 1870's, Mississippi voters elected hundreds of black officeholders, including members of Congress, state legislators, sheriffs, county clerks, and justices of the peace. In the mid-1870's, white Democrats launched a counteroffensive, using threats, violence, and fraud to neutralize the African American vote. After 1875, very few blacks held office in Mississippi.

By 1890, many politicians in Mississippi were calling for a convention to write a new constitution for the state. They complained that although only a small number of African Americans were voting, this small number could prove decisive in close elections. Many white leaders feared that black votes could decide close elections and worked toward a new constitution with provisions that effectively would disfranchise black voters. It would be difficult to draft such provisions, however, without running afoul of the Fifteenth Amendment.

The state's two senators illustrated the divisions of opinion that were so widespread among white Mississippians. Senator Edward C. Walthall argued against a constitutional convention, warning that it would only excite political passions for no good purpose. He felt certain there was no way to eliminate black political participation without violating the Fifteenth Amendment, and that if Mississippi made such an attempt, the U.S. government would show new interest in enforcing African American voting rights. On the other hand, Senator James George attacked the old constitution, claiming that it had been drafted by carpetbaggers and ignorant former slaves. George urged that the "best citizens" should now take the opportunity to draft a new state constitution. He warned that black voting could revive unless the state took measures to reduce the black electorate by provisions of the state's highest law.

A bill calling a constitutional convention passed both houses of the state legislature in 1888, but Governor Robert Lowry vetoed it, warning that it was better to accept the state's existing problems than to run the risk of creating new ones by tampering with the state's constitution. Two years later, a similar bill passed both houses of the legislature, and the new governor, John M. Stone, signed the law. Election for delegates was set for July 29, 1890. The voters would elect 134 delegates, 14 of them from the state at large, and the rest apportioned among the counties.

The state's weak Republican Party decided not to field a slate of candidates for at-large delegates. In heavily black Bolivar County, Republicans did offer a local delegate slate with one black and one white candidate. In Jasper County, the white Republican candidate for delegate, F. M. B. "Marsh" Cook, was assassinated while riding alone on a country road. In two black-majority counties, the Democrats allowed white conservative Republicans onto their candidate slates. In several counties, Democrats split into two factions and offered the voters a choice of two Democratic tickets. As it turned out, the constitutional Convention was made up almost exclusively of white Democrats. The membership included only three Republicans, three delegates elected as independents, and one member of an agrarian third party. Only one of the 134 delegates was black: Isaiah T. Montgomery of Bolivar County.

Delegates elected the conservative lawyer Solomon S. Calhoon as president of the convention and immediately set about their work. Convention members had no shortage of ideas on how to limit the suffrage almost exclusively to whites without violating the Fifteenth Amendment. Some suggested that voters must own land, which few African Americans in Mississippi did. Others favored educational tests, since African Americans, only a generation removed from slavery, had had fewer educational opportunities than whites and therefore were often illiterate.

As finally devised, the Mississippi plan for disfranchisement had a number of parts, the most important of which were a literacy test and a poll tax. Under the literacy test, the would-be voter must either be able to read or to explain a part of the state constitution when it was read to him. This latter provision, the so-called "understanding clause," was included as a loophole for illiterate whites. Delegates knew that voting registrars could give easy questions to white applicants and exceedingly difficult ones to African Americans. The poll tax provision stated that a person must pay a poll tax of at least two dollars per year, for at least two years in succession, in order to qualify to vote. The voter would have to pay these taxes well in advance of the election and keep the receipt. The tax was quite burdensome in a state where tenant farmers often earned less than fifty dollars in cash per year. Because Mississippi's African Americans were often tenant farmers, poorer

than their white counterparts, it was thought they would give up the right to vote rather than pay this new tax.

In a notable speech, the black Republican delegate, Isaiah T. Montgomery, announced that he would vote for these new suffrage provisions. He noted that race relations in the state had grown tense and that black political participation in the state had often led whites to react violently. His hope now, Montgomery explained, was that black disfranchisement would improve race relations and as the years passed, perhaps more African Americans would be permitted to vote. The new constitution passed the convention with only eight dissenting votes; it was not submitted to the voters for their ratification.

The new suffrage provisions went into effect just before the 1892 elections. The new voter registration requirements disfranchised the great majority of African Americans in the state; it also resulted in the disfranchisement of about fifty-two thousand whites. The new registration resulted in a list of seventy thousand white voters and only nine thousand African American voters. The predominantly black state Republican Party had won 26 percent of the vote for its presidential candidate in 1888; after the new registration, in 1892, the Republican standard-bearer won less than 3 percent.

Under the Constitution of 1890, Mississippi had an almost exclusively white electorate for three-quarters of a century. This constitution served as a model for other Southern states, which eagerly copied the literacy test, the understanding clause, and the poll tax into their state constitutions. Only after passage of new laws by the U.S. Congress in 1964 and 1965 would African American voters again make their strength felt in Southern elections. —*Stephen Cresswell*

ADDITIONAL READING:

Cresswell, Stephen. *Multiparty Politics in Mississippi, 1877-1902.* Jackson: University Press of Mississippi, 1995. Chapter 4 discusses the drafting of the 1890 constitution and its role in limiting the success of the Republican and Populist parties.

Kirwan, Albert D. *Revolt of the Rednecks: Mississippi Politics, 1876-1925.* Lexington: University Press of Kentucky, 1951. Although dated, this remains the basic political history for the period before, during, and after the state's 1890 Constitutional Convention.

Kousser, J. Morgan. *The Shaping of Southern Politics: Suffrage Restriction and the Establishment of the One-Party South, 1880-1910.* New Haven, Conn.: Yale University Press, 1974. Detailed explanation of how new constitutions in Mississippi and other Southern states led to a homogeneous electorate, essentially a small clique of middle-class whites.

McLemore, Richard Aubrey, ed. *A History of Mississippi.* Hattiesburg: University and College Press of Mississippi, 1973. Chapter 22, written by former governor James P. Coleman, provides a narrative history of the 1890 constitutional convention.

Stone, James H. "A Note on Voter Registration Under the Mississippi Understanding Clause, 1892." *Journal of Southern History* 38 (1972): 293-296. Argues that the understanding clause was not a grossly unfair instrument of racial discrimination, as is often charged. Lays the blame for disfranchisement chiefly on the poll tax.

SEE ALSO: 1863, Reconstruction; 1865, Freedmen's Bureau Is Established; 1865, New Black Codes; 1865, Thirteenth Amendment; 1866, Rise of the Ku Klux Klan; 1866, Civil Rights Act of 1866; 1866, Race Riots in the South; 1868, Fourteenth Amendment; 1883, Civil Rights Cases; 1896, *Plessy v. Ferguson*.

1890 ■ BATTLE OF WOUNDED KNEE: *the last Indian war heralds the close of the American frontier and the end of traditional life for Native Americans*

DATE: December 29, 1890

LOCALE: Wounded Knee Creek, twenty miles east of Pine Ridge, South Dakota

CATEGORIES: Native American history; Wars, uprisings, and civil unrest

KEY FIGURES:

Big Foot (c. 1825-1890), chief of the Minneconjou Sioux

William Frederick "Buffalo Bill" Cody (1846-1917), scout and showman

James W. Forsyth (1835-1906), Seventh Cavalry officer in charge at Wounded Knee

James McLaughlin (1842-1923), agent in charge at the Standing Rock reservation

Nelson Appleton Miles (1839-1925), commander of the Division of the Missouri

Sitting Bull (c. 1831-1890), last great Sioux warrior chief

Wovoka, also known as *Jack Wilson* (c. 1858-1932), Paiute messiah of the Ghost Dance religion

SUMMARY OF EVENT. The Battle of Wounded Knee, on December 29, 1890, was preceded on December 15 by the slaying of Sitting Bull, the last great Sioux warrior chief. His death resulted from an effort to suppress the Ghost Dance religion, which had been begun by Wovoka. Wovoka's admixture of American Indian and Christian beliefs inspired hope in an eventual triumph of the American Indians over the white settlers, who, Wovoka envisioned, would fall through the earth and disappear forever. Although Wovoka preached passivity and patience, some of his zealous disciples carried a slightly more aggressive message, among them a Minneconjou Sioux named Kicking Bear and his brother-in-law, Short Bull. They and other followers of Wovoka introduced the Ghost Dance to the Dakota reservations, including Standing Rock and Pine Ridge.

In an effort to suppress Ghost Dancing, James McLaughlin, the government agent in charge of the Standing Rock reservation, first arrested Kicking Bear, then moved against Sitting Bull, an old adversary and, in McLaughlin's mind, the cynosure of tribal unrest. McLaughlin was convinced that Ghost Dancing could be suppressed only if Sitting Bull were in prison. He called Sitting Bull a fomenter of disturbances, prompting General Nelson A. Miles, U.S. Army Commander of the Missouri Division, to send Buffalo Bill Cody to Standing Rock to persuade the chief to negotiate with Miles. However, McLaughlin complained to Washington and had Cody's mission aborted.

What followed was a fiasco. Forty-three American Indian police, commanded by Lieutenant Bull Head, surrounded Sitting Bull's cabin and ordered him outside. Sitting Bull obeyed, but one of the assembled Ghost Dancers, angered at the arrest, wounded Bull Head with a rifle. Attempting to hit his assailant, Bull Head accidentally shot Sitting Bull at the same time that another American Indian policeman fired a lethal shot through the old chief's head.

When news of Sitting Bull's death reached Big Foot, chief of the Minneconjou at Cherry Creek, he decamped his followers and started a journey toward Pine Ridge, hoping to find protection under Chief Red Cloud. His band consisted of 120 men and 230 women and children. Big Foot himself was ill with pneumonia and had to make the journey in a wagon. On December 28, near Porcupine Creek, the natives encountered troops of the Seventh U.S. Cavalry under the command of Major Samuel Whitside. Although near death, Big Foot arranged a meeting with Whitside, who informed the chief that his orders were to escort the American Indians to Wounded Knee Creek. Big Foot agreed to comply with the major's directions, because Wounded Knee was on the way to Pine Ridge. Whitside then had his men move Big Foot to an Army ambulance to make the trip more comfortable.

The combined trains reached Wounded Knee Creek before nightfall. Whitside saw to their encampment south of his military bivouac. He provided them with rations, some tents, and a surgeon to tend to Big Foot. He also took measures to ensure that none of the American Indians could escape, posting sentinels and setting up rapid-fire Hotchkiss guns in key positions.

During the night, the remaining troops of the Seventh Cavalry arrived, and command of the operation passed from Major Whitside to Colonel James W. Forsyth. The colonel told the junior officer that he had received orders to accompany Big Foot's bands to the Union Pacific Railroad for transport to a military prison in Omaha. The next morning, after issuing hardtack rations to the Indians, Colonel Forsyth ordered them to turn over their weapons. Soldiers stacked up the surrendered arms and ammunition. Not satisfied that all weapons had been turned in, Forsyth sent details to search the tipis. Then the searchers ordered the natives to remove their blankets, which, the soldiers assumed, masked some hidden weapons.

The situation grew tense. The Indians were both humiliated and angry, but they were badly outnumbered and almost all of them had been disarmed. Only the Minneconjou medicine man, Yellow Bird, openly protested. He began Ghost Dance steps and chanted lines from the holy songs that assured the Indians that their Ghost Shirts would not let the soldiers' bullets strike them.

The soldiers found only two rifles during the last search, but one of them belonged to a deaf Sioux brave named Black Coyote, who resisted. Soldiers grabbed him and spun him around, attempting to disarm him, and at that point Black Coyote fired his Winchester, probably by accident. A debacle followed.

The soldiers opened fire on the unarmed Minneconjou at once, slaughtering many of them with repeated volleys from their carbines. Most of the Indians tried to flee, but the Hotchkiss guns opened up on them from their hillside positions. Firing almost a round a second, the soldiers' shots tore into the camp, indiscriminately killing braves, women, and children. The Hotchkiss guns turned the rout into a massacre.

When it was over, Big Foot and more than half of his followers were either dead or seriously wounded. One hundred fifty-three lay dead on the ground, but many of the fatally

Ghost Dance ceremony, c. 1893. The Ghost Dance religion, promulgated by Wovoka (Jack Wilson) as a means of unifying Indians and overcoming white influence, had a militant branch that drew suppressive measures from U.S. officials on the reservations. The resulting battle at Wounded Knee marked the end of the Indian Wars and virtually complete subjugation of the plains tribes. (Smithsonian Institution Photo No. 55296. Photo by James Mooney)

wounded had crawled off to die elsewhere. One estimate claimed that there were barely more than fifty native survivors, only those transported after the massacre. Only twenty-five soldiers were killed, most of them having fallen to friendly fire, not to the Indians.

After the wounded troopers were decamped and sent off toward Pine Ridge, a detail of soldiers rounded up the surviving Indians: four men and forty-seven women and children. Placed in wagons, they also set out for Pine Ridge, leaving their dead to a blizzard that prevented their immediate burial and froze them into grotesque, hoary reminders of the debacle.

An inquiry followed the events at Wounded Knee, prompted by General Miles, who brought charges against Forsyth, but the colonel was exonerated and nothing else came of the investigation. The affair traditionally has been viewed as the last resistance of the Indians to reservation resettlement. It and the death of Sitting Bull, both in 1890, although not singled out, were certainly factors in the conclusions of Frederick Jackson Turner, who claimed in his renowned 1893 thesis that the U.S. frontier had closed in the year of the massacre.

For American Indians, however, the infamous day did not die with the victims. On February 27, 1973, more than two hundred members of the American Indian Movement (AIM) took the reservation site at Wounded Knee by force, proclaiming it the Independent Oglala Sioux Nation and demanding that the federal government make amends for past injustices by reviewing all American Indian treaties and policies. Federal marshals immediately surrounded the group and after two months, coaxed them to surrender with promises of an airing of grievances. For American Indians, Wounded Knee has remained an important symbol of the Euro-American injustice and suppression of their people.   —*John W. Fiero*

ADDITIONAL READING:

Brown, Dee. *Bury My Heart at Wounded Knee: An Indian History of the American West.* New York: Holt, Rinehart & Winston, 1970. A very readable, popular account of the displacement and oppression of the American Indian nations by European settlers, from the beginning to 1890. Includes a helpful but dated bibliography.

Jensen, Richard E., R. Eli Paul, and John E. Carter. *Eyewitness at Wounded Knee.* Lincoln: University of Nebraska Press, 1992. Fine collection of photographs from the Wounded Knee battlefield and related sites, with essays on the American Indian perspective, the Army's role, and the distorted media coverage.

Klein, Christina. " 'Everything of Interest in the Late Pine Ridge War Are Held by Us for Sale': Popular Culture and Wounded Knee." *Western Historical Quarterly* 25 (Spring, 1994): 45-68. Argues that commercial exploitation of Wounded Knee in Cody's Wild West show, photographs, and the dime novel played as significant a role as the military in defeating the Ghost Dancers' dreams of American Indian autonomy. Includes photographs.

Neihardt, John G. *Black Elk Speaks: Being the Life Story of a Holy Man of the Oglala Sioux.* 1932. Reprint. Lincoln: University of Nebraska Press, 1979. This classic work chronicles the spiritual odyssey of Black Elk, a holy man of the Oglala Sioux. Provides important insight into American Indian beliefs and an account of the Wounded Knee massacre.

Utley, Robert M. *Last Days of the Sioux Nation.* New Haven, Conn.: Yale University Press, 1963. A highly regarded, sensitive, evenhanded study that documents the events leading up to Wounded Knee. Contains a chapter on sources, making it invaluable for further study.

Voices from Wounded Knee, 1973. Rooseveltown, N.Y.: Akwesasne Notes, 1974. With edited transcripts of interviews, documents the efforts of the Oglala Sioux to gain national sympathy for the plight of the American Indian by their stand at Wounded Knee Creek in 1973. Includes a chronicle of events from 1868 to 1973 and an account of the 1890 massacre.

SEE ALSO: 1862, Great Sioux War; 1864, Sand Creek Massacre; 1866, Bozeman Trail War; 1871, Indian Appropriation Act; 1872, Great American Bison Slaughter; 1876, Battle of the Little Bighorn; 1890, Closing of the Frontier; 1973, Wounded Knee Occupation.

1892 ■ "New" Immigration: *a new wave of Southern European immigrants meets with nativist resentment and federal controls*

DATE: January 1, 1892-1943
LOCALE: Ellis Island, New York
CATEGORY: Immigration
SUMMARY OF EVENT. In 1808, the United States government purchased Ellis Island from the state of New York for ten thousand dollars. The new federal property, located in New York Harbor about one mile from the southern tip of Manhattan Island, served first as a fort and later as an arsenal. Until 1882, the state of New York had guided the influx of immigration from the old Castle Garden station at the tip of Manhattan. The opening of Ellis Island on January 1, 1892, as the first federal immigration station symbolized a new era for the United States as well as the beginning of the end of free immigration to the New World.

Congress had begun the selective process of excluding undesirable elements among those emigrating to the United States with the passage of the federal Immigration Act in 1882. That measure was designed to prevent the immigration of persons who had criminal records and those who were mentally incompetent or indigent. That same year, Congress also passed the Chinese Exclusion Act (later extended to all Asians) barring an entire nationality from entry as racially undesirable for a period of ten years. In 1904 the act's provisions were extended indefinitely, to be repealed only in 1943.

Most immigrants before the 1890's had come from Northern and Western Europe. In the 1880's a fundamental change occurred. In addition to the traditional immigrants, who shared

Increased immigration from southern and eastern Europe in the late nineteenth and early twentieth centuries provided a flood of new arrivals who were processed through the Ellis Island immigration station in New York Harbor. (Library of Congress)

common language patterns with persons already in the United States, people from Mediterranean and Slavic countries began to arrive in increasing numbers. One may measure the change more dramatically by comparing two peak years in U.S. immigration. In 1882, 87 percent of the 788,000 immigrants came from Northern and Western Europe. In 1907, only 19.3 percent were from Northern and Western Europe, while 80.7 percent came from Southern and Eastern Europe.

A great impetus to immigration was the transportation revolution engendered by the steamship. In 1856, more than 96 percent of U.S. immigrants came aboard sailing ships, on trips that took between one and three months. By 1873, the same percentage came by steamships, which took only ten days. The new steamships were specifically designed for passengers, and while still subject to overcrowding and epidemics, they were a major improvement over the sailing ships. Steamship companies competed for immigrant business and maintained offices in Europe. The Hamburg-Amerika line, for example, had thirty-two hundred U.S. agencies throughout Europe. More than half of the immigrants in 1901 came with prepaid tickets supplied by relatives in the United States.

As the older agricultural economy of Europe was replaced

by an industrial one, many former farmers moved to European cities in search of employment; often unsuccessful in that search, they were easily persuaded to try the New World, where jobs were said to be plentiful. The same railroad-building process that opened the American West to the immigrant made it easier and cheaper for the Europeans to reach their coastal areas and embark for the United States.

Most of the emigration from Southern Europe was occasioned by economic distress. Southern Italy's agriculture was severely affected by competition from Florida in oranges and lemons, as well as by a French tariff against Italian wines. The Italian emigration began with 12,000 in 1880 and reached a peak of nearly 300,000 in 1914. After immigration restriction laws took full effect, Italian immigration fell to 6,203 in 1925.

From Russia and the Slavic areas, emigration was also caused by political and religious problems. Jews fled in reaction to the riots set off by the assassination of Czar Alexander II in 1882, the pogroms of 1881-1882 and 1891, and the 1905-1906 massacres of thousands of Jews. Jewish immigration to the United States began with 5,000 in 1880 and reached a peak of 258,000 in 1907. Some two million Roman Catholic Poles also arrived between 1890 and 1914. In 1925, however,

Origins of European Immigrants to the United States, 1871-1920

Period	Northern and Western Europe	Southern and Eastern Europe
1871-1880	2,127,000	145,000
1881-1890	3,783,000	954,000
1891-1900	1,644,000	1,914,000
1901-1910	1,912,000	6,224,000
1911-1920	2,001,000	2,370,000

Source: Data are from the U.S. Census, 1880-1920.

the Immigration Service recorded only 5,341 entrants from Poland and 3,121 from Russia and the Baltic States.

Two issues caused the greatest concern to American nativists in the 1890's: the tendency of the new immigrants to congregate in the cities, and the fact that they spoke seemingly unassimilable languages. One of the first articulate spokesmen against unrestricted immigration, the Reverend Dr. Josiah Strong, was alarmed by the concentration of foreign peoples in cities. Strong's famous book, *Our Country*, published in 1885, clearly stated what many other U.S. citizens feared: that the new influx of immigrants would create permanent slums and perpetuate poverty.

The urban nature of the settlement was unavoidable. U.S. agriculture was suffering from the same shocks that had disrupted European agriculture, and the populist movement in the country made clear that the myth of utopia in the western United States was no longer believable. Most of the new immigrants were attracted by the pull of U.S. industry and opportunity, and they came to the United States with the express purpose of settling in a city. In addition, new industrial technology had reduced the demand for skilled labor, while the need for unskilled and cheap factory help increased. To add to the social clash between the new and old immigrants, the arrival of a new labor force in great numbers probably allowed some older laborers to move up to more important supervisory and executive positions.

Many new immigrants did not share the optimism and enthusiasm of established Americans. Some tended to be pessimistic and resigned, distrustful of change, and unfamiliar with democratic government after having lived in autocratic situations. At the height of the new immigration occurred the Panic of 1893, followed by a depression that lasted until 1897, which seemed to confirm the fears of persons already settled in the United States that the country and the system were failing. The new immigration, however, was but one of the major social, cultural, and economic changes taking place in the turbulent United States of the 1890's.

In 1907, Congress created the Dillingham Commission to investigate the problems of immigration. Many of the commission's findings reflected the fears of citizens concerning the new immigration and led to the passage of restrictive legislation in the 1920's. Unrestricted immigration ended with the passage of the National Origins Act of 1924, which restricted immigrants in any year to 154,277. Each country's quota could be no more than 2 percent of the number of its natives counted in the 1890 census, a year in which few born in Southern and Eastern Europe were part of the U.S. population.

When Ellis Island closed as a reception center in 1943, few immigrants still arrived by ship, and the Immigration Service could handle all arrivals at Manhattan's docks. When the Atlantic reopened after World War II, planes began to replace ships as vehicles of immigration, and there was no need for Ellis Island. By that time, much of the fear of the "new" immigration had evaporated. Italian, Slavs, and Jews had not remained in permanent slums, mired in perpetual poverty, as Strong had feared, and their descendants had fought side by side with U.S. soldiers of British and German ancestry against the Nazis and the Japanese.

In the 1940's, there was much criticism of the rigidity of the immigration restriction legislation that hampered attempts to deal with the problems of refugees. Not until 1965, however, would the rigid quota system established in 1924 be replaced with a more flexible system. When that reform opened the door to increased entry by Asians and Latin Americans, complaints about the new "new immigrants" began to echo nineteenth century uneasiness about the former "new immigrants."

—Richard H. Collin, updated by Milton Berman

Additional Reading:

Briggs, Vernon M. *Mass Immigration and the National Interest*. Armonk, N.Y.: M. E. Sharpe, 1992. An economist argues that nineteenth and early twentieth century immigration aided the U.S. economy but the post-1965 immigration does not.

Brownstone, David M., Irene M. Franck, and Douglas L. Brownstone, eds. *Island of Hope, Island of Tears*. New York: Penguin Books, 1986. Interviews with elderly people who went through Ellis Island in the early years of the twentieth century provide highly personal accounts of the "new" immigrants. Many photographs.

Daniels, Roger. *Coming to America: A History of Immigration and Ethnicity in American Life*. New York: HarperCollins, 1990. A well-written, scholarly account of U.S. immigration from the colonial period through the 1980's.

Dinnerstein, Leonard, Roger H. Nichols, and David H. Reimers. *Natives and Strangers: Blacks, Indians, and Immigrants in America*. 2d ed. New York: Oxford University Press, 1990. A comparative study of immigrant and minority groups in the United States.

Handlin, Oscar. *The Uprooted*. 2d, enlarged ed. Boston: Little, Brown, 1973. A dramatic narrative focusing on the life experiences of immigrants.

Higham, John. *Strangers in the Land: Patterns of American Nativism, 1860-1925*. New Brunswick, N.J.: Rutgers University Press, 1955. Analyzes the nativist movements that led to the passage of immigration restriction.

Reimers, David M. *Still the Golden Door: The Third World Comes to America*. New York: Columbia University Press,

1985. A study of twentieth century immigration to the United States, primarily after World War II.

SEE ALSO: 1840's, "Old" Immigration; 1882, Chinese Exclusion Act; 1892, Yellow Peril Campaign; 1917, Immigration Act of 1917; 1924, Immigration Act of 1924.

1892 ∎ YELLOW PERIL CAMPAIGN:
anti-Japanese fears have domestic consequences for Japanese American immigrants

DATE: Beginning May 4, 1892
LOCALE: San Francisco, California
CATEGORIES: Asian American history; Diplomacy and international relations; Immigration
KEY FIGURES:
Henry Gage (1852-1924), governor of California
Victor Metcalf (1853-1936), U.S. secretary of commerce
James Phelan (1861-1930), San Francisco mayor in 1900
Theodore Roosevelt (1858-1919), twenty-sixth president of the United States, 1901-1909
Eugene E. Schmitz (1864-1928), San Francisco mayor in 1905
SUMMARY OF EVENT. In 1890, there were only some two thousand Japanese living in America, working mainly as laborers and farmhands in California and the Pacific Northwest. Nevertheless, the use of Japanese to break a labor strike in the coal mines in British Columbia began what was to become a widespread anti-Japanese campaign.

Typical of the political rhetoric that was to become prevalent was a campaign slogan during a political campaign in 1887. A Dr. O'Donnell of San Francisco included the slogan "Japs must go" in his campaign. Although the slogan had little effect on his failed political campaign, it was a sign of things to come.

In 1889, the editor of the *San Francisco Bulletin* began a series of editorials attacking Japanese immigrants and making a case that they were dangerous to white American workers and to American culture. On May 4, 1892, he wrote, "It is now some three years ago that the *Bulletin* first called attention to the influx of Japanese into this state, and stated that in time their immigration threatened to rival that of the Chinese, with dire disaster to laboring interests in California." The *San Francisco Bulletin*'s Yellow Peril campaign helped strengthen the growing anti-Japanese fervor in California. The campaign was not only against Japanese laborers, who they claimed threatened "real" American workers, but also against their perceived threat to American culture. Met with hostility, prejudice, and discrimination, Japanese in many urban areas settled into ethnic enclaves known as Japantowns, where they could feel safe and comfortable among fellow compatriots and secure employment.

On June 14, 1893, the San Francisco Board of Education passed a resolution requiring that all Japanese persons must attend the already segregated Chinese school instead of the regular public schools. Due to Japanese protests, the resolution was rescinded; however, it marked the beginning of legal discrimination against the Japanese in California. In 1894, a treaty between the United States and Japan allowed citizens open immigration, but both governments were given powers to limit excessive immigration. In 1900, due to American protests, Japan began a voluntary program to limit Japanese emigration to the United States.

The Alaska gold rush of 1897-1899 attracted a great number of white laborers, and when the Northern Pacific and Great Northern Railroads worked to build a connecting line from Tacoma and Seattle to the East, extra laborers were needed. The companies turned to Japanese immigrants as workers. Some of these laborers came from Japan and Hawaii. The rapid influx of Japanese laborers created further anti-Asian sentiments and hostility. With the 1882 Chinese Exclusion Act up for renewal in 1902, the anti-Japanese sentiment occurred in the overall context of a growing anti-Asian movement, especially among labor unions and various political groups. In April of 1900, the San Francisco Building Trades Council passed a resolution to support the renewal of the Chinese Exclusion Act and to add the Japanese to this act to "secure this Coast against any further Japanese immigration, and thus forever settle the mooted Mongolian labor problem." The county Republican Party lobbied extensively to get the national Republican Party to adopt a Japanese exclusion plank in their national platform. San Francisco mayor James Phelan and California governor Henry Gage joined the calls for Japanese to be included in the renewal of the Exclusion Act. However, when the exclusion law was extended in 1902, Japanese people were not included.

After the defeat of Russia by Japan in the Russo-Japanese War, a growing fear of Japanese power led to further agitation and political tactics to limit Japanese immigration and influence in America. Whereas Chinese were hated and despised by various politicians, labor leaders, and some regular citizens, Japanese were feared. In 1905, the *San Francisco Chronicle* launched another anti-Japanese campaign, emphasizing the dangers of future immigration. Later, the San Francisco Labor Council, at the urging of Dr. A. E. Ross and with the support of San Francisco mayor Eugene Schmitz, launched boycotts against Japanese merchants and white merchants who employed Japanese workers. Later that year, sixty-seven labor organizations formed the Asiatic Exclusion League (sometimes called the Japanese and Korean Exclusion League), and the American Federation of Labor passed a resolution that the provisions of the Chinese Exclusion Act be extended to include Japanese and Koreans.

In 1906, anti-Asian sentiments continued to grow. San Francisco was struck by a major earthquake in April, and civil unrest increased. Japanese persons and businesses were attacked and looted. On October 11, 1906, the San Francisco School Board ordered that all Japanese, Korean, and Chinese students attend a segregated "Oriental school." (This regulation was later changed to include only older students and those with limited English proficiency.) Japan protested that the school board's action violated the U.S.-Japan treaty of 1894, bringing the San Francisco situation into international focus. To assuage Japan, President Theodore Roosevelt arranged with the school board to rescind its order in exchange for federal action to limit immigration from Japan. In the ensuing U.S.-Japan "Gentlemen's Agreement," Japan promised not to issue passports to laborers planning to settle in the United States and recognized U.S. rights to refuse Japanese immigrants entry into the United States. In an executive order issued on March 14, 1907, Roosevelt implemented an amendment to the Immigration Act of 1907 which allowed the United States to bar entry of any immigrant whose passport was not issued for direct entry into the United States and whose immigration was judged to threaten domestic labor conditions.

Subsequent California legislation, the Heney-Webb bill or Alien Land Act of 1913, attempted to limit Asian interests within the state by prohibiting Asians to own property. Although anti-Japanese sentiments lessened during World War I after Japan joined the Allies in the war against Germany, almost immediately following the war these sentiments resurfaced. The 1917 and 1924 Immigration Acts barred Asian laborers from the United States. In California, a campaign to pass the 1920 Alien Land Act attracted the support of the American Legion and the Native Sons and Daughters of the Golden West.

In an effort to avoid widespread prejudice and discrimination, the Japanese American Citizens League (JACL), founded in 1930 and consisting of second-generation Japanese Americans (Nisei), sought to follow a path of economic success through individual efforts, the cultivation of friendship and understanding between themselves and other Americans, and assimilation into American culture. During the 1930's and 1940's, Nisei were urged by JACL leaders to prove their worth as patriotic Americans by contributing to the economic and social welfare of the United States and to the social life of the nation by living with other citizens in a common community. Their efforts would find a new obstacle in 1941, however, when President Franklin D. Roosevelt issued Executive Order 8802 allowing internment of Japanese Americans in segregated camps. —*Gregory A. Levitt*

ADDITIONAL READING:

Ichihashi, Yamato. *The American Immigration Collection: Japanese in the United States*. 1932. Reprint. New York: Arno Press, 1969. A thorough description of Japanese immigration into the United States with an excellent chapter on anti-Japanese agitation.

McWilliams, Carey. *Prejudice: Japanese-Americans, Symbol of Racial Intolerance*. Boston: Little, Brown, 1944. A dated but excellent account of anti-Japanese American prejudice and discrimination up to World War II.

Takaki, Ronald. *Strangers from a Different Shore: A History of Asian Americans*. Boston: Little, Brown, 1989. An excellent overview of the broader picture of Asian immigration and settlement in the United States.

Wilson, Robert A., and Bill Hosokawa. *East to America: A History of the Japanese in the United States*. New York: William Morrow, 1980. An excellent account of Japanese immigration and settlement in the United States.

SEE ALSO: 1907, Gentlemen's Agreement; 1913, Alien Land Laws; 1942, Censorship and Japanese Internment.

1892 ■ BIRTH OF THE PEOPLE'S PARTY: *agrarian unrest gives rise to grass-roots populism and the national Progressive political movement*

DATE: July 4-5, 1892
LOCALE: Omaha, Nebraska
CATEGORY: Government and politics
KEY FIGURES:

Ignatius Donnelly (1831-1901), leader of the Minnesota Alliance and noted author

James G. Field (1826-1901), Populist vice-presidential candidate in 1892

Leonidas LaFayette Polk (1837-1892), president of the Southern Alliance and editor of the influential *Progressive Farmer*

Thomas Edward Watson (1856-1922), Populist vice-presidential candidate in 1896

James Baird Weaver (1833-1912), Populist presidential candidate in 1892

SUMMARY OF EVENT. Political activists completed the organization of the People's Party of the United States of America, also known as the Populist Party, at the nominating convention held in Omaha, Nebraska, in July, 1892. The formation of a new political party had been discussed for several years in a series of farmer-oriented conventions. Representatives of the powerful Northern and Southern Farmers' Alliances, together with certain labor groups, such as the Knights of Labor, and some smaller organizations of farmers, met at St. Louis in December, 1889, to consider merging and cooperating in political action. At that time they were unable to effect a union of their organizations, but they did discover that many of their political demands were identical. Farmers and workers both agreed that fundamental changes needed to be made in American banking practices, as well as in regulating railroads and in providing for the arbitration of labor disputes.

These political demands were enunciated further at another convention held at Ocala, Florida, in December, 1890. Then at the National Union Conference held in Cincinnati in May, 1891, Ignatius Donnelly, leader of the Minnesota Alliance and a noted author, demanded the immediate formation of a third party; but Leonidas LaFayette Polk, president of the Southern Alliance and editor of the influential *Progressive Farmer*, wrote a letter advising delay. Polk was backed by James B. Weaver from Iowa. A compromise was reached whereby an executive committee was to begin preparations for establishing a new party, but formal organization would be delayed until after a reform convention met in St. Louis in February, 1892. The vast majority of delegates to this convention were representatives of the Farmers' Alliances, but a substantial number of seats were reserved for representatives from certain labor unions. The convention met, heard speeches, adopted a platform, and adjourned. By arrangement, the delegates remained in their seats and reorganized as a political action group. They accepted a motion to appoint a committee to confer with the executive committee which had been appointed at Cincinnati regarding the calling of a national nominating convention. The combined executive committee, in the patriotic mode of the time, adopted plans to authorize 1,776 delegates to meet in a nominating convention on July 4, 1892, in Omaha.

The strength of the People's Party centered in areas where commercial farming of staple crops, such as cotton and wheat, was dominant. These farmers believed that they were at the mercy of monopolies and speculators, and they demanded government legislation regarding the control of money, transportation, and land. The years following the end of the Civil War had proved financially devastating for the nation's farmers as the money supply of the country contracted. The war had contributed to widespread inflation and the depreciation of the value of the dollar. Bankers had pushed for the return to a hard money standard and to holding the supply of money in circulation constant to prevent further inflation. Although the complexities of monetary theory were difficult for people to understand, the result was easily seen: With the supply of money held constant, the more farmers, as a whole, produced, the less each individual farmer would be paid.

By 1892, several previous attempts at forming a third political party had been made. The National Labor Union of 1871, the Greenback Party, and the Union Labor Party had all been inspired by difficulties caused by monetary policies. Each of these parties had appealed to slightly different segments of the population. The People's Party would come the closest to uniting rural farmers with urban labor interests. Still, sectional differences delayed the formation of the party for several years. The Southern Alliance believed that it could capture the Democratic organization, while many Northern Alliance groups wanted to form new parties. The memory of the Civil War remained strong, and Democratic politics had different connotations in different regions. Still, both groups experienced considerable success with their respective strategies in the off-year election of 1890. In the South, four governors and forty-four congressmen who were committed to Alliance principles were elected as Democrats; in the states of the Great Plains, the Populists as an independent party gained the election of two U.S. senators. By 1892, many Southern farmers were disillusioned with the concessions made by the national Democratic Party and were more willing to join a third party movement. The Southern Alliance members were, however, never united on the new strategy. For example, African American farmers who were active in the Southern Alliance had always strenuously opposed cooperating with the Democrats, while white farmers generally supported cooperation.

The 1892 Omaha nominating convention of the People's Party accepted the report of its platform committee. Donnelly's ringing denunciation of the corruption of the two major parties, Congress, the state legislatures, and the bench was adopted as the preamble to the platform. The body of the platform called for an inflated currency (specifically, "free silver," or the unlimited coinage of silver and gold and a "circulating medium" of not less than $50 per capita), a graduated income tax, the establishment of postal savings banks, the nationalization of the railroads, and the prohibition of alien ownership of land. Finally, the committee presented several resolutions that it did not consider as an integral part of the platform. These resolutions included demands for the secret ballot, the initiative and referendum, direct election of senators, and one-term limitations on the presidency. Expression of sympathy for labor and a demand for the restriction of "undesirable immigration" were also included in the attached resolutions.

The majority of the thirteen hundred delegates who attended the Omaha convention probably favored Judge Walter Q. Gresham as their presidential candidate. Gresham would have given a degree of respectability to the new party, and he was believed to be sympathetic to most Populist views. The judge refused to allow his name to be put in nomination, however, and James B. Weaver, an Iowa Alliance leader who had been the Greenbacker presidential candidate in 1880, was nominated on the first ballot. A Southerner was needed to give the ticket balance, and James G. Field, a former Confederate officer from Georgia, was nominated.

In the presidential election of 1892, Grover Cleveland collected 277 electoral votes to 145 for the Republican candidate, Benjamin Harrison; the People's Party garnered only 22, all in the Western states. The Populists polled 1,041,028 popular votes compared to Cleveland's winning total of 5,556,543. In 1894, the Populists increased their combined popular vote to 1,471,600. The presidential election year of 1896 saw the People's Party fuse with the Democratic Party, which had nominated William Jennings Bryan. Bryan, who shared many Populist views, especially in regard to the importance of "free silver," was also nominated by the Populists, although they chose a different vice presidential candidate, Thomas E. Watson, in an attempt to maintain their separate party identity. William McKinley, the Republican candidate, easily defeated the Democratic-Populist ticket. Backed by business interests with deep pockets, the Republicans were able to outspend both the Democrats and the Populists. Standard Oil alone contributed $250,000 to the campaign, an immense sum for that time. Bryan was forced to campaign by commercial carrier, subject to the tight structure of standard railroad timetables, while McKinley enjoyed a private train. It is thus not surprising that the Populists failed to win as a third party and that they failed when they supported Bryan. Their appeal to the American populace was never sufficient to build a strong base for a major party.

—Mark A. Plummer, updated by Nancy Farm Mannikko

ADDITIONAL READING:

Argersinger, Peter H. *The Limits of Agrarian Radicalism: Western Populism and American Politics*. Lawrence: University Press of Kansas, 1995. Intriguing analysis of why rural concerns failed to galvanize the American populace as a whole.

Goodwyn, Lawrence. *The Populist Moment: A Short History of the Agrarian Revolt in America*. New York: Oxford University Press, 1978. A condensed version of Goodwyn's larger work, *Democratic Promise*, intended for a general audience. *Democratic Promise*, a massive scholarly work, is considered the definitive history of the Populist movement.

Griffiths, David B. *Populism in the Western United States*. Lewiston, Idaho: Edwin Mellen Press, 1992. Good discussion of the Populist movement in the Western states.

McMath, Robert C. *American Populism: A Social History, 1877-1898*. New York: Hill and Wang, 1993. An accessible overview of Populism and the People's Party.

Ostler, Jeffrey. *Prairie Populism: The Fate of Agrarian Radicalism in Kansas, Nebraska, and Iowa, 1880-1892*. Lawrence: University Press of Kansas, 1993. Detailed history of Populism in the prairie states.

SEE ALSO: 1863, National Bank Acts; 1867, National Grange of the Patrons of Husbandry Forms; 1869, Scandals of the Grant Administration; 1873, "Crime of 1873"; 1896, McKinley Is Elected President; 1913, Federal Reserve Act.

1893 ■ WORLD'S COLUMBIAN EXPOSITION:
a world's fair displays the technological advances of the nineteenth century and speculates about the future

DATE: May 1-October 30, 1893
LOCALE: Chicago, Illinois
CATEGORIES: Cultural and intellectual history; Science and technology
KEY FIGURES:
Daniel Hudson Burnham (1846-1912), young Chicago architect, chief executive of the fair
Richard Morris Hunt (1827-1895),
Charles Follen McKim (1847-1909), and
Henry Van Brunt (1832-1903), architects who dominated the planning of the fair on classical lines
Frederick Law Olmsted (1822-1903), leading landscape painter who chose Jackson Park as the site for the fair
John Wellborn Root (1850-1891), consulting architect for the fair
Louis Henri Sullivan (1856-1924), leader of the new Chicago school of architecture

SUMMARY OF EVENT. The World's Columbian Exposition, officially named the Chicago World's Fair of 1893, opened its gates on May 1, 1893. By the time it closed on October 30, more than twenty-seven million people had visited the fair, and seventy-seven nations had participated. The fair was one of the few world's fairs to make a profit, returning 14 percent to its astonished stockholders, who had not expected to break even. The effect of the fair upon art, architecture, and urban development in the United States was profound, and its effect upon Europe's recognition of the new United States is difficult to overestimate.

The movement for the World's Columbian Exposition to celebrate the four hundredth anniversary of the landing of Christopher Columbus in America began in 1889 when four cities, Chicago, New York, Washington, and St. Louis, petitioned Congress for the right to stage the fair. Competition was keen. Most of the established cities regarded Chicago as a brash upstart and argued that they had the advantages of denser populations and longer traditions. Chicago, however, pledged ten million dollars, and Congress, convinced of the midwestern city's resolve, voted in 1890 to award to Chicago the World's Columbian Exposition, which was to open in 1893. Banker Lyman Gage was chosen president, and plans for what was to be the famous "Great White City" were begun. A committee of six thousand, the largest ever, planned all aspects of this fair. The site in Chicago was chosen on February 11, 1891, when Frederick Law Olmsted, the great U.S. landscape artist and city planner, chose Jackson Park, an undeveloped stretch of swamp and scrub bounded by Lake Michigan but accessible to the center of Chicago.

The architectural planning of the fair has engendered historical controversy. The distinctive part of the design, the unified architectural planning that made the Great White City a realization of classical architectural forms rather than a celebration of the new Chicago architecture, came about when five Chicago architectural firms asked five outside architects, mainly from New York, to help in designing the fair. John Wellborn Root was the chief architect, but when he died suddenly before the designs were completed, the executive authority passed to Daniel Burnham, one of the younger Chicago architects. Burnham offered no resistance to the New Yorkers, who were at the head of the architectural profession. Richard Hunt, Charles McKim, and Henry Van Brunt were New York architects who took charge of the preparations. They determined that the Middle West should have a display of the best architecture, which in the New Yorkers' eyes did not include the brash new designs of the Western, or Chicago, school.

The Chicago fair was to be a tribute to the dynamic growth of Chicago as a new metropolis and a symbol to the rest of the world that the United States had come of age. The scale of the fair was vast, covering more than six hundred acres. The magnificent Roman classical architecture, which seemed even more miraculous in its juxtaposition with the brash and rough metropolis of Chicago, dominated the entire scene. The Manufacturers Building was 1,687 feet long and 787 feet wide; a ten-story building could have been laid inside it. The Palace of Fine Arts was of equally enormous proportions, covering more than 600,000 square feet. It was the one building that was to remain after the fair was over. Marshall Field, founder of the wholesale and retail firm that bears his name, was asked for one million dollars in order to establish an exhibit of exposition displays in the building. Preservation was not possible, however, as the original materials were meant to be temporary. Field hired Burnham to plan the new building. A material called "staff," invented in France about 1876, was used heavily in the buildings of the Paris Exposition and at the Columbian Fair. Staff was composed of powered gypsum, with alumina, glycerine, and dextrine. It could be molded into any shape, was waterproof, and cost less than one-tenth as much as marble or granite. Sixty-five foreign countries built pavilions. The sixteen leading European and Asian nations constructed lavish buildings, within which they displayed their finest wares. The fair also had the first Ferris wheel ever erected in America. Invented by George Washington Gale Ferris, it was a revolving structure that was 250 feet high, had thirty-six cars, cost fifty cents for a ride of two revolutions, and was filled day and night with riders.

Electricity was still new, and the fair possessed an electrical station that generated three times as much power as was used for the rest of Chicago. There were eight thousand arc lamps and glowworm-sized incandescent lights, the first electric intramural train with a third rail electrically stimulated, and displays of boats of warlike usage. Companies that provided dynamos and other electrical equipment were Edison, Western Electric, and Westinghouse. The Siemens-Halske Company (now Siemens) of Berlin sent a special fifteen-hundred-horsepower plant for incandescent lighting. The Palace of Fine Arts still survives in Chicago as the Museum of Science and Industry; the contemporary artist-sculptor, Augustus Saint-Gaudens, mirrored most public opinion when he asserted that it was the greatest building since Greece's Parthenon.

The World's Columbian Exposition was at the center of the great Chicago cultural outburst and renaissance. The Chicago Symphony, the Public Library, the Art Institute, the Newberry Library, and the University of Chicago all began their development or rebirth in a new form in the same decade. As a national achievement, the fair was even more significant. The Women's Building was designed by a Bostonian, Sophia B. Hayden. There was a Board of Woman Managers and female commissioners worked in the administration of affairs with each state and in every foreign country. The official guide mentions that women exhibitors could compete with men in any department on a common level with men, with "sex not to be recognized or considered." Specific mention is made in the guide that a "young lady of California is exhibiting specimens of wrought-iron work of her own design."

The artificiality of the fair notwithstanding, most people in the United States became aware for the first time that there was such a thing as art in architecture; the large amount of building that followed in the growing American cities was done more carefully and produced better buildings, regardless of style, than would have occurred had the fair not taken place. A new wealthy class had developed in the United States as a result of the profits from U.S. industrialism, and the nouveau riche wished to memorialize themselves by association with what they regarded as the eternal glory of art. The fair was one aspect of this desire; the beginnings of great American art collections was another and more lasting effect. The spirit of upper-class responsibility for American cultural leadership was symbolized and encouraged by the fair. Saint-Gaudens had exclaimed at a meeting of the planners, "This is the greatest meeting of artists since the fifteenth century," and the same feeling was communicated to the American people, who could take pride in an indigenous culture for the first time.

For city planning, the fair was vital. When urban planners saw what planning could do for a section of Chicago swampland, there resulted, among other plans, the imaginative Burnham Chicago Plan of 1909, and the revival of Pierre Charles L'Enfant's plan for Washington, D.C. What followed was an important time for city planning in an increasingly urban United States. The main controversy of the fair revolved around the reactionary classical architecture, but that controversy was relatively unimportant. Tourists and critics visiting Chicago saw the work of the Chicago school of architecture and were impressed by it. The great triumph of the fair was the cultural pride that it instilled in the United States—a pride that was sorely needed in the wake of the Panic of 1893 and the ensuing economic depression. The fair set a standard to live up to, and it pointed the way for future cultural and urban aspirations. By associating themselves with ancient civilizations, Chicago and the United States were suggesting that America was the home of a new, more glorious Renaissance. The fair was as important to rising U.S. nationalism as Frederick Jackson Turner's frontier thesis of U.S. history, which, like the fair, was presented in 1893 in Chicago.

Seventy-four writers, journalists, officials, business leaders, clergy, and others were asked before the opening of the fair to project what the United States would be like in 1993. One music critic forecast that there would be a "telephote" that would provide entertainment at any place of amusement in the city. Their overall answers were more accurate in the technical and economic fields, excluding the auto industry and space travel.   —*Richard H. Collin, updated by Norma Crews*

ADDITIONAL READING:

Columbian Guide Company. *Official Guide to the World's Columbian Exposition*. Chicago: Author, 1893. The official guide to the fair, with prices for everything from baths to boat rides.

Dybwad, G. L., and Joy V. Bliss. *Annotated Bibliography, World's Columbian Exposition, Chicago 1893*. Albuquerque, N.Mex.: Book Stops Here, 1992. Comprehensive bibliography of materials written on the Columbian Exposition.

Goldberg, Vicki. "World's Columbian Exposition, 1893." *Conde Nast Traveler* 29, no. 5 (May, 1994): 126. Describes Chicago in 1893; highlights the first, largest sensations. Features the work of architects Burnham and Sullivan.

Kogan, Herman, and Lloyd Wendt. "That Windy City." In *Chicago: A Pictorial History*. New York: E. P. Dutton, 1958.

Illustrated with historic photographs of the Windy City as it developed and those who did the developing. Presents the positive and negative events in politics and society.

Muccigrosso, Robert. *Celebrating the New World: Chicago's Columbian Exposition of 1893*. Chicago: I. R. Dee, 1993. Presents a layout of the fair; gives detailed information of the buildings, U.S. and foreign; discusses their contents; and highlights inventions that would change the world.

Walter, Dave. *Today Then*. Helena, Mont.: American and World Geography Publishing, 1992. Presents the results of the form filled out by leaders in Chicago area in 1893 on what the United States would be like in 1993.

SEE ALSO: 1846, Smithsonian Institution Is Founded; 1876, Bell Demonstrates the Telephone; 1879, Edison Demonstrates the Incandescent Lamp; 1883, Brooklyn Bridge Opens; 1897, Library of Congress Building Opens; 1913, Armory Show; 1931, Empire State Building Opens.

1894 ■ PULLMAN STRIKE: *a major struggle between management and labor results in federal intervention*

DATE: June 26-July 11, 1894
LOCALE: Pullman, Illinois
CATEGORY: Business and labor
KEY FIGURES:

John Peter Altgeld (1847-1902), governor of Illinois
Stephen Grover Cleveland (1837-1908), twenty-second (1885-1889) and twenty-fourth (1893-1897) president of the United States
Clarence Seward Darrow (1857-1938), special counsel to the American Railway Union
Eugene Victor Debs (1855-1936), president of the American Railway Union
Thomas W. Heathcoate, chairman of the strike committee at Pullman
Richard Olney (1835-1917), U.S. attorney general
John P. Hopkins, mayor of Chicago
George Mortimer Pullman (1831-1897), president of the Pullman Palace Car Company
Edwin Walker, railroad lawyer, special counsel to the General Managers Association, and special federal attorney during the strike

SUMMARY OF EVENT. The Pullman Strike of 1894 was one of the farthest reaching labor-management disputes in United States history. Conducted in the midst of the most catastrophic depression to date, it was the most dramatic of a large number of strikes affecting the nation. The labor upheaval started in Pullman, Illinois, nine miles south of Chicago. What began as a dispute between the Pullman Palace Car Company (PPCC) and three thousand employees developed into a bitter struggle between twenty-four railroads serving Chicago and the American Railway Union (ARU), whose members voted to support their striking brethren in Pullman by boycotting Pullman cars. Before the strike ended, railroad traffic was stopped from Ohio to California, and the federal government had intervened in support of the PPCC and the railroads.

The town of Pullman was already famous. Built in 1880 by George Pullman, the town was widely, although not universally, acclaimed as a unique experiment. It housed all the essentials of life, from food stores to educational and entertainment centers to a multidenominational church. Despite the intentions of its founder, however, it was not a happy place. The preponderance of men among its 8,603 inhabitants indicated a social instability caused partly by George Pullman's refusal to sell homes to his workers. The rents, fixed by Pullman to provide a return of 6 percent, were higher than in nearby towns. There was little democracy in the town government, and the company interfered with elections. As landlord, George Pullman imposed middle-class values that restricted his workers' personal freedom. Among other things, they resented the strict prohibition of alcoholic beverages. Sufficiently concerned with his workers' souls to erect a community church, Pullman rented the structure at fees too high for most religious denominations to pay. Additional grumbling occurred over company charges for utilities. Residents claimed that company spies watched them, and in the plant workers suffered from blacklisting and a policy of granting nearly absolute power to shop foremen.

In the depression of the 1890's, while continuing to pay the usual dividends of 8 percent, the company drastically cut wages. Wage cuts of 30 to 50 percent, without corresponding cuts in already high rents, made it difficult for workers to provide adequate care for their families. In response, the workers formed a grievance committee to discuss their situation with the company. The vice president met with the committee, promising that no reprisals would be taken against workers for voicing their concerns. However, he then proceeded to fire three committee leaders, convincing many workers that a strike remained as the only viable option. By the spring of 1894, desperate workers began flocking to the ARU, which, under the leadership of Eugene V. Debs, had recently won an astounding victory over the Great Northern Railroad. Led by Thomas W. Heathcoate, chairman of the Pullman Strike committee, the emboldened workers decided to strike the PPCC on May 11. A month later, despite Debs's opposition, an ARU convention voted to stop handling Pullman cars after the company ignored efforts to settle the dispute. The union, by detaching Pullman cars from the trains, sought to deplete the revenues of the PPCC and force negotiations. Anticipating trouble with the railroads, Debs tried unsuccessfully to get support from the railroad brotherhoods, which opposed his industrial unionism, and from Samuel Gompers of the American Federation of Labor, who charged Debs with dual unionism. African American railroad workers were less than cooperative. In spite of Debs's urging, African Americans had been barred from ARU membership in a narrowly passed provision to the ARU constitution.

While Pullman workers received support from the ARU, the PPCC found stronger allies in the railroads, already organized into the General Managers Association (GMA), an organization of twenty-four railroad companies operating in or through Chicago. The railroads were determined to honor their contracts with the PPCC, insisting that trains run with Pullman cars attached. Alarmed at the rapid growth of the ARU, they were eager for a chance to crush it. The strike began on June 26, with workers either walking off the job or detaching Pullman cars. Railroad workers in twenty-three states honored the strike, producing a rapid halt in most freight traffic. The GMA retaliated by recruiting strike breakers. Fearing federal intervention, Debs ordered that violence be avoided and offered to operate passenger and mail trains without Pullman cars attached. The railroads refused. By the end of June, fifty thousand workers were idle across two-thirds of the country, and a stalemate had been reached.

From Washington, D.C., the administration of President Grover Cleveland followed the strike with growing alarm, while in Illinois, Chicago Mayor John P. Hopkins and Governor John P. Altgeld, both sympathetic toward the union, kept police and National Guardsmen alerted for possible trouble. With local police ready to preserve law and order but unwilling to break the strike, the GMA worked through subterfuge to involve the federal government. Hoping to create public discontent, the GMA permitted transportation inconveniences, rejected freight shipments, and curtailed passenger service. Meanwhile, Attorney General Richard Olney, a former railroad lawyer, instructed federal district attorneys to punish those stopping the mail. On June 30, Olney hired additional federal marshals, although mail trains continued to run on schedule. Next, he named Edwin Walker, a counsel to the railroads, as special federal attorney. Walker, in effect, assumed command of Justice Department affairs in Chicago.

On July 1, rioting broke out in a Chicago suburb which, together with exaggerated and alarmist newspaper reports of violence, gave Olney an excuse to intervene. On July 2, the federal government secured an injunction against the ARU under the Sherman Antitrust Act, and the next day President Cleveland, ignoring Governor Altgeld, sent in federal troops to protect the United States mails. At the time, local officials had the situation in hand and Altgeld stood ready to use National Guardsmen if needed. The use of the Sherman Antitrust Act against a union, which Congress never intended, was only slightly less startling than the terms of the injunction issued by two federal judges with railroad sympathies. In a sweeping denial of basic rights, the court enjoined union leaders from communicating with their own membership. Had this order been obeyed, it would have destroyed the ARU. On advice of special counsel Clarence Darrow, Debs ignored the injunction, an action for which he later went to jail.

Far from restoring order, the arrival of federal troops led to increased violence on July 5 and 6, when mobs destroyed more than $340,000 of railroad property. Unqualified and hastily deputized federal marshals contributed to the violence.

With the arrest of ARU leaders on conspiracy charges, however, the strike weakened. By July 11, trains were operating in most of the nation, although the strike continued officially for three more weeks.

Apart from property damage, forfeited earnings and wages, and business losses, the strike destroyed the ARU as an effective organization. It introduced new and threatening antilabor weapons, and it led to the eventual dissolution of the model town of Pullman after repeated court suits. Finally, although a presidential commission subsequently absolved the strikers of all responsibility, Debs lost faith in the capitalist system and became a devout convert to socialism, during his six months of incarceration. The strikers were also casualties. Many workers returning to their jobs found out that they had been permanently replaced and blacklisted from future railroad work. The failure of the strike was a major defeat for labor unions in the United States. The ARU had fought an unenviable two-front war against organized management and concerted efforts by the federal government to stop the strike. Few would venture such a battle again. —*Merl E. Reed, updated by Irwin Halfond*

ADDITIONAL READING:

Brommel, Bernard J. *Eugene V. Debs, Spokesman for Labor and Socialism.* Chicago: Kerr, 1978. Based on manuscript sources, this biography provides an excellent overview of Debs's life and his role in the Pullman Strike.

Ginger, Ray. *The Bending Cross: A Biography of Eugene V. Debs.* New Brunswick, N.J.: Rutgers University Press, 1949. Reprint. Kirksville, Mo.: Thomas Jefferson University Press, 1992. Still the most readable and reliable biography of the great labor leader to date. The 1992 reprint offers a new bibliography and pictures.

Lindsey, Almont. *The Pullman Strike.* Chicago: University of Chicago Press, 1942. Although dated and written in dramatic form, this is a good starting point for the background and major events of the Pullman Strike.

Potter, David M. *The Chicago Strike of 1894: Industrial Labor in the Nineteenth Century.* New York: Holt, Rinehart and Winston, 1963. The best overview for the general reader of the forces leading up to and the events of the Pullman Strike.

Smith, Carl S. *Urban Disorder and the Shape of Belief: The Great Chicago Fire, the Haymarket Bomb, and the Model Town of Pullman.* Chicago: University of Chicago Press, 1995. Provides an interesting sociological account of the conditions among the railroad workers that made the Pullman Strike possible, if not inevitable.

Warne, Colston E., ed. *The Pullman Boycott of 1894: The Problem of Federal Intervention.* Boston: D. C. Heath, 1955. Presents views by the major participants and investigative materials by U.S. government agencies.

SEE ALSO: 1882, Standard Oil Trust Is Organized; 1886, American Federation of Labor Is Founded; 1890, Sherman Antitrust Act; 1902, Anthracite Coal Strike; 1905, Industrial Workers of the World Is Founded; 1935, National Labor Relations Act; 1935, Congress of Industrial Organizations Is

Founded; 1938, Fair Labor Standards Act; 1943, Inflation and Labor Unrest; 1955, AFL and CIO Merge.

1895 ■ HEARST-PULITZER CIRCULATION WAR: *rival newspapers vie for mass readership using the devices of a new journalism*

DATE: 1895-1898

LOCALE: New York City

CATEGORIES: Cultural and intellectual history; Diplomacy and international relations; Latino American history

KEY FIGURES:

Richard Harding Davis (1864-1916) and

Karl Decker, Hearst reporters in Cuba

Enrique Dupuy de Lôme (1816-1904), Spanish minister to the United States

Morrill Goddard, chief of Hearst's Sunday edition

William Randolph Hearst (1863-1951), owner of the *New York Journal*

William McKinley (1843-1901), twenty-fifth president of the United States, 1897-1901

Joseph Pulitzer (1847-1911), owner of the *New York World*

Frederic Remington (1861-1909), Hearst's illustrator in Cuba

Valeriano Weyler y Nicolau (1838-1930), commander of Spanish forces in Cuba

SUMMARY OF EVENT. The pattern of modern journalism was established by Joseph Pulitzer. Born in Hungary in 1847, Pulitzer arrived in the United States in 1864 to fight with the Union Army. After the Civil War, the penniless young immigrant journeyed to St. Louis, where, by virtue of his intelligence and hard work, he soon became not only a successful reporter but also a lawyer and crusading politician. Pulitzer served in the Missouri legislature and worked as a reporter on the *St. Louis Post* and the *Westliche Post*, a leading Midwestern German newspaper. In 1876, he purchased the *Post* and the *St. Louis Dispatch*, consolidating them into the *Post-Dispatch*. This venture was such a success that the young publisher turned his attention to the world of New York journalism. In 1883, he purchased the *New York World* from the financier Jay Gould, and in 1887 Pulitzer established the *Evening World*.

It was with the *World* that Pulitzer set the pattern for the "new journalism." Interesting news stories written in a simple, easily comprehended style were presented in a sensational manner to appeal to the widest possible reading audience. The *World* led crusades, such as collecting funds to build the pedestal for the Statue of Liberty, as well as exposés of the white slave traffic, the Louisiana lottery, the ill treatment of immigrants at Ellis Island, and the questionable activities of many large industrial concerns. Stunts also were part of the new journalism. The *World*, for example, sponsored a trip around the world by journalist Nellie Bly, who broke the record of Jules Verne's fictitious Phileas Fogg of *Around the World in Eighty Days* by arriving back in New York after slightly more than seventy-two days. Newspaper illustrations appeared in the *World*, as did high-quality editorials. Pulitzer also conducted imaginative promotional campaigns to increase circulation.

In 1887, a twenty-four-year-old man assumed control of the *San Francisco Examiner*, succeeding his wealthy father. Copying Pulitzer's methods, William Randolph Hearst soon transformed the newspaper into a model of journalistic sensationalism. Like Pulitzer, Hearst was confident that he could become successful in New York City. In 1895, after receiving $7.5 million from the sale of his father's mining stock, Hearst bought the *New York Morning Journal*. The Hearst-Pulitzer circulation war had begun.

Hiring brilliant journalists at any cost, Hearst soon staffed the *Journal* with the nation's brightest talent. The *Journal* carried so many illustrations and so emphasized scandal, crimes, and disaster that its circulation rose dramatically, causing Pulitzer to reduce the price of his morning paper to one cent. In the midst of the 1896 presidential election, Hearst established the *Evening Journal* to compete with Pulitzer's *Evening World*; by the end of 1897, the *Journal*, by continuing to stress sex-and-crime sensationalism, surpassed the *World* in circulation. Competition between Hearst and Pulitzer eventually focused on their Sunday editions, with Hearst finally buying away from the *World* all of its Sunday staff. The chief of Hearst's Sunday edition, Morrill Goddard, pioneered in Sunday sensationalism by developing a panoply of crime, sports, pseudo-scientific articles, "lonely hearts" columns, and above all, a colored supplement of comics known as the *American Humorist*. It was the most popular of these comic characters, the "Yellow Kid," that led to the name "yellow press" to identify the Hearst-Pulitzer brand of sensational journalism.

Some historians have claimed that, had it not been for the Hearst-Pulitzer circulation war, there would have been no Spanish-American War. Although this is a questionable assertion, it is undeniably true that between 1895 and 1898 the *Journal* and the *World* conducted the most emotional campaign of jingoism in the history of U.S. journalism—a campaign that undoubtedly stimulated the fervor of countless people in the United States for war with Spain. Pictures, headlines, and news stories in these newspapers indicted the Spanish for perpetrating atrocities in Cuba. Concentration camps, the mutilation of women and children, and the gruesome activities of the Spanish commander, General Valeriano "the Butcher" Weyler, were daily fare in the *Journal* and the *World*. Initially, the *World*'s correspondents were superior in uncovering or fabricating atrocity stories, but as the competition increased, Hearst dispatched more talent to Cuba. Perhaps the best known of his correspondents were writer Richard Harding Davis and illustrator Frederic Remington, whom Hearst sent to Cuba on his yacht *Vamoose*. Remington is reported to have sent Hearst a telegram that read, "Everything is quiet. There is no trouble here. There will be no war. Wish to return. Remington." To this, Hearst sent the prompt reply, "Please remain. You furnish the pictures and I'll furnish the war. Hearst."

Another of Hearst's reporters, Karl Decker, rescued Evangelica Cisneros, niece of the president of the rebel government, from a prison, smuggled her out of Cuba, and took her to New York and Washington, D.C., where she received a tumultuous welcome, including a meeting with President William McKinley. The *Journal* also printed the "de Lôme letter," in which Enrique Dupuy de Lôme, the Spanish minister to the United States, called President McKinley a "would-be politician." Perhaps the height of the circulation war occurred after the U.S. battleship *Maine* exploded and sank in Havana harbor on February 15, 1898. No guilty party was ever discovered. Yet the *Journal* immediately blamed the Spanish, proclaiming in banner headlines: "Destruction of the Warship *Maine* Was the Work of an Enemy." The *World* also exploited the sinking to inflame the nation's passion for war, and other newspapers joined in the outcry. As the circulations of both the *World* and the *Journal* passed one million, it was evident that other newspapers, such as the Chicago *Tribune*, Chicago *Times-Herald*, Boston *Herald*, and San Francisco *Chronicle* also had begun to appreciate the benefits of the new journalism. The tactics and methods of the Hearst-Pulitzer circulation war have continued to be staples of U.S. journalism ever since.

—*William M. Tuttle, updated by Michael Witkoski*

ADDITIONAL READING:

Littlefield, Roy. *William Randolph Hearst: His Role in American Progressivism*. Lanham, Md.: University Press of America, 1980. One of the Hearst newspapers' greatest claims was that they served as a spokesperson for the common American. The extent to which this was true, and Hearst's use and misuse of that role, is the crux of Littlefield's study.

Mott, Frank Luther. *American Journalism: A History, 1690-1960*. Boston: Houghton Mifflin, 1962. The single most valuable survey to date of U.S. newspapers throughout most of the nation's history. Especially pertinent when it comes to the Hearst-Pulitzer struggle for readership. Contains excellent reproductions of actual pages, which give a true feel for what journalism looked like during the period of the circulation wars.

Robinson, Judith. *The Hearsts: An American Dynasty*. Newark: University of Delaware Press, 1991. Although unique in many ways, William Randolph Hearst had a background and left a legacy. This volume places the Hearst family in the context of American life.

Swanberg, W. A. *Citizen Hearst: A Biography of William Randolph Hearst*. New York: Charles Scribner's Sons, 1961. Although it has been updated by specialized studies in some areas, this work remains the place to start for an understanding of Hearst and his career.

_____. *Pulitzer*. New York: Charles Scribner's Sons, 1967. Presents the basic, indispensable information about Hearst's great rival and one of the major figures in U.S. journalism. Shows the personal nature of the circulation struggle during the period of yellow journalism.

SEE ALSO: 1833, Rise of the Penny Press; 1898, Spanish-American War.

1895 ■ CHINESE AMERICAN CITIZENS ALLIANCE IS FOUNDED: *a major social and political force in the Chinese American community*

DATE: May 21, 1895

LOCALE: San Francisco, California

CATEGORIES: Asian American history; Immigration; Organizations and institutions

SUMMARY OF EVENT. Immigration to the United States by the Chinese began in the mid-nineteenth century. The migration pattern of the Chinese was the same wherever they went: Peasants from rural areas in China migrated to cities looking for work, without securing a sustainable income, and men (mostly young men) left China while their families remained. Their purpose in leaving was twofold: to earn money to send home to their families, and to return to China once they secured sufficient money (around five hundred dollars) to support their families comfortably.

Travel to the United States was beyond the financial capability of most Chinese, so to secure passage to America most Chinese indentured themselves (contracted their labor in advance) to a merchant or a labor agent, a system called the credit-ticket arrangement whereby merchants advanced Chinese money for passage to the United States and kept collecting it for years.

The California gold rush of 1848-1849 had drawn many with its promises of gold-filled streets; in fact, the Chinese name for San Francisco is "Old Gold Mountain." Not all Chinese immigrants, however, willingly left China. Many emigrated because of famine and political and social unrest in Southern China. Others were victims of the so called "Pig Trade," which replaced slavery after it was outlawed following the Civil War. They chose the United States because of exaggerated tales of wealth and opportunity spread by traders and missionaries.

Once the Chinese landed in the United States, labor agents, under the credit-ticket arrangement, gained almost complete domination of their indentured workers and kept them in isolated communities which the agents controlled. These areas became known as Chinatowns. Moreover, many Chinese, not wanting to remain permanently in the United States, had little incentive to assimilate. Their unwillingness or inability to become acculturated into the American "melting pot" became an indictment against all Chinese. Although most Chinese wanted to return to China, many could not secure sufficient money for return passage and never returned to China.

Life in California in the late 1800's was difficult at best for most Chinese. The Chinese communities organized *Hui-Guan* (merchant guilds) that served as welcoming committees, resettlement assistance services, and mutual help societies for newly arrived immigrants. Chinese immigrants were also organized by the Chinese Consolidated Benevolent Association (the Chinese Six Companies), originally agents of Chinese firms in Hong Kong which had established the "coolie trade" to San Francisco. The Six Companies kept traditional Chinese rules, customs, and values as the basis for appropriate behavior, helping protect Chinese from an increasingly anti-Chinese atmosphere.

Anti-Chinese sentiments and violence against Chinese began almost as soon as they arrived in North America. These attitudes existed at the top levels of government and labor unions as well as local citizens. During the mid- to late 1800's, various political parties, including the Know-Nothing Party, the Democratic Party, and the Republican Party, promoted anti-Chinese platforms. During this time, workers' unions organized anti-Chinese activities and anti-Asian sentiments were propagated by newspapers in Western states. In 1871, twenty Chinese in Los Angeles were killed and their homes and businesses looted and burned. In 1877, a similar incident occurred in San Francisco. In Chico, California, five farmers were murdered. Anti-Chinese riots broke out in Denver, Colorado, and in Rock Springs, Wyoming. In 1885, Chinese workers, employed as strikebreakers, were killed at a Wyoming coal mine. Chinese residents in Seattle and Tacoma, Washington, were driven out of town and thirty-one Chinese were robbed and murdered in Snake River, Oregon. In 1905, sixty-seven labor organizations, in order to prevent employers from hiring Asians, formed the Asiatic Exclusion League.

In the early 1890's, the Chinese Six Companies lost face (*mian zi*) when they influenced Chinese not to sign documents required by the Geary Act (1892), an extension of the Chinese Exclusion Act of 1882 which required all Chinese residing in the United States to obtain a certificate of eligibility with a photograph within a year. When the Geary Act was ruled legal, thousands of Chinese Americans became illegal aliens in the United States. Following this disaster, the Tongs, secret societies of criminals that originated in China, used this opportunity to take control of the Chinatowns. The result was a vicious and bloody civil war among Chinese Americans—in which the American police force, for the most part, played a very limited role. Among first-generation Chinese, few actively opposed the rule of the Tongs. Perhaps accustomed to bandits, clan warfare, and warlords in Southern China and imbued with the Daoist spirit of letting things alone, most Chinese did their best to survive without resisting Tong leaders.

Many young American-born (second-generation) Chinese opposed these "old ways" of doing things. They accepted the notion that they were never going to return to China and they wanted to adopt American ways and fit into American culture. These young, second generation Chinese formed the Native Sons of the Golden State in an effort to assimilate into American mainstream culture. The organization's headquarters was located on the second floor of a building at 753 Clay Street in San Francisco. The first officers were The Chen, president; Kun Wu, secretary; and Tai-yung Li, treasurer.

The Native Sons of the Golden State emphasized the importance of naturalization and voters' registration. All members were urged to become American citizens and to vote. The organization also encouraged active participation in the civic affairs of mainstream American life. The leaders thought that some of the anti-Chinese sentiments and discriminatory actions were, in part, due to the traditional attitudes and behaviors of the Chinese immigrants themselves: remaining isolated, not learning English, and not taking part in politics.

As the organization grew, it established chapters in Oakland, Los Angeles, San Diego, Chicago, Portland, Detroit, Pittsburgh, and Boston, eventually changing its name to the Chinese American Citizens Alliance (CACA). In 1913, CACA defeated a California law designed to prevent Chinese from voting. The group fought against the National Origins Act, or Immigration Act of 1924, and sought the right for Chinese males to bring their wives to the United States. CACA helped defeat the Cinch bill of 1925, which attempted to regulate the manufacture and sale of Chinese medicinal products, such as herbs and roots. By promoting numerous social functions— dances, sporting events, dinner parties, and the like—CACA also helped keep Chinese American communities together and moved them toward assimilation. CACA fought against the stereotyped portrayals of Chinese in films, newspapers, and magazines as heathens, drug addicts, or instigators of torture. In 1923, for example, the organization attempted to block publication of a book by Charles R. Shepard, *The Ways of Ah Sin*, depicting negative images of Chinese. CACA has also supported other community organizations, such as Cameron House, Self-Help for the Elderly, and the Chineses Historical Society of America.   —*Gregory A. Levitt*

ADDITIONAL READING:

Chung, Sue Fawn. "The Chinese American Citizens Alliance: An Effort in Assimilation." Los Angeles: University of California, 1965. An unpublished doctoral dissertation, a rare secondary source devoted entirely to the organization.

Daniels, Roger. *Asian America: Chinese and Japanese in the United States Since 1850.* Seattle: University of Washington Press, 1988. Excellent overall account of Asian America that includes a brief description of the Chinese American Citizen Alliance.

Dillon, Richard H. *The Hatchet Men the Story of the Tong Wars in San Francisco Chinatown.* New York: Coward-McCann, 1962. A dated but interesting account of the violence in San Francisco early Chinatown under the rule of the Tongs.

Takaki, Ronald. *Strangers from a Different Shore: A History of Asian Americans.* Boston: Little, Brown, 1989. An account of Asians coming to live in America. Provides some discussion of the Chinese American Citizen Alliance in the 1940's and the late 1980's.

Tsai, Shih-Shan Henry. *The Chinese Experience in America.* Bloomington: Indiana University Press, 1986. Places the movement in context.

SEE ALSO: 1849, Chinese Immigration; 1882, Chinese Exclusion Act; 1882, Rise of the Chinese Six Companies; 1892, Yellow Peril Campaign; 1899, Hay's "Open Door Notes"; 1917, Immigration Act of 1917; 1924, Immigration Act of 1924; 1943, Magnuson Act.

GREAT EVENTS FROM HISTORY
NORTH AMERICAN SERIES

KEY WORD INDEX

Abington School District v. Schempp, 1066

Abolish Slavery, Northeast States, 197

Abolition of Slavery Is Founded, Pennsylvania Society for the, 183

Abscam Affair, 1197

Acquisition of the Panama Canal Zone, 716

Adams-Onís Treaty, 332

Affirmative Action, Expansion of, 1096

AFL and CIO Merge, 1021

AFL-CIO, United Farm Workers Joins with, 1144

Africa, Invasion of North, 941

African American Baptist Church Is Founded, 173

African American Candidate for President, Jackson Becomes First Major, 1220

African American University, First, 483

African Slaves, Congress Bans Importation of, 289

Africans Arrive in Virginia, 68

AIDS Cases Are Reported, First, 1207

Akron Woman's Rights Convention, 464

Alaska, Purchase of, 567

Alaska, Russian Voyages to, 135

Alaska and Hawaii Gain Statehood, 1035

Alaska Native Claims Settlement Act, 1141

Alaska Pipeline, Construction of the, 1167

Albany Congress, 151

Alcatraz Occupation, 1126

Algonquians "Sell" Manhattan Island, 73

Alien and Sedition Acts, 268

Alien Land Laws, 758

Allies Invade Italy, Western, 946

Allotment Act, General, 652

Alta California, Settlement of, 45

AME Church Is Founded, 326

Amendment, Thirteenth, 551

Amendment, Fourteenth, 577

Amendment, Twenty-fourth, 1076

American Anti-Slavery Society Is Founded, 392

American Dictionary of the English Language, Webster's, 363

American Federation of Labor Is Founded, 648

American Fur Company Is Chartered, 295

American in Space, First, 1054

American Indian Religious Freedom Act, 1189

Americans with Disabilities Act, 1251

Amistad Slave Revolt, 405

Anasazi Civilization, 11

Anesthesia Is Safely Demonstrated, Surgical, 442

Anthony Is Arrested, Susan B., 600

Anthracite Coal Strike, 710

Anti-Defamation League Is Founded, 760

Anti-Irish Riots, 422

Anti-Slavery Society Is Founded, American, 392

Antitrust Act, Sherman, 662

Apache Wars, 509

Apollo 11 Lands on the Moon, 1122

Appomattox and Assassination of Lincoln, Surrender at, 545

Arab Oil Embargo and Energy Crisis, 1163

Arctic Ocean, Mackenzie Reaches the, 253

Arid Region, Powell's *Report on the Lands of the*, 628

Armory Show, 753

Arms Reductions, Bush Announces Nuclear, 1255

Arms to Spain, Embargo on, 896

Articles of Confederation, 204

Asian Pacific American Labor Alliance, 1260

Assassination of Lincoln, Surrender at Appomattox and, 545

Assassination of Malcolm X, 1086

Assassination of President Kennedy, 1074

Assassinations of King and Kennedy, 1108

Assembly Line Begins Operation, Ford, 756

Assembly of Virginia, First General, 67

Astorian Expeditions, 299

Astronauts Repair the Hubble Space Telescope, 1281

Atlanta Exposition Address, Booker T. Washington's, 681

Atomic Bombing of Japan, 970

Attica State Prison Riots, 1140

Aztec Empire, 21

Bacon's Rebellion, 117

Bakke, Regents of the University of California v., 1185

Baltimore and Ohio Railroad Begins Operation, 368

Bank Acts, National, 530

Bank of the United States, Jackson vs. the, 387

Bank of the United States Is Chartered, Second, 325

Baptist Church Is Founded, African American, 173

Barnum's Circus Forms, 594

Battle for Leyte Gulf, 959

Battle of Bull Run, First, 517

Battle of Fallen Timbers, 257

Battle of Guadalcanal, 936

Battle of Lexington and Concord, 184

Battle of Midway, 931

Battle of New Orleans, 319

Battle of Oriskany Creek, 199

Battle of Saratoga, 200

Battle of the Bulge, 961

Battle of the Little Bighorn, 617

Battle of the Thames, 311

Battle of Tippecanoe, 304

Battle of Wounded Knee, 666

Battles of Gettysburg, Vicksburg, and Chattanooga, 534

Bay of Pigs Invasion, 1051

Beaver Wars, 88

Beginnings of State Universities, 215

Bell Demonstrates the Telephone, 615

Bennett Era in Canada, 851

Bering Strait Migrations, 1

Berkeley Free Speech Movement, 1083

Berlin Blockade, 984

Bilingual Education Act, 1104

Bill of Rights Is Ratified, U.S., 248

Birth Control League Forms, National, 764

Birth Control Pill, FDA Approves the, 1041

Birth of the People's Party, 672

Birth of the Republican Party, 479

Birth of the Whig Party, 396

Bison Slaughter, Great American, 598

Black Codes, First, 280

Black Codes, New, 549

Black Monday, 885

Black Sox Scandal, 798

Bleeding Kansas, 481

Bloc Québécois Forms, 1249

Bloody Island Massacre, 458
Boat Lift, Mariel, 1199
Bomb Is Detonated, Hydrogen, 1008
Bombed, Oklahoma City Federal Building, 1290
Bombing, World Trade Center, 1274
Bombing of Japan, Atomic, 970
Bombing of Japan, Superfortress, 953
Bombing of Pearl Harbor, 919
Bonus March, 865
Booker T. Washington's Atlanta Exposition Address, 681
Borden Government in Canada, 744
Boston Massacre, 171
Boston Tea Party, 175
Boycott, Montgomery Bus, 1023
Bozeman Trail War, 563
Bracero Program, 938
Brady Handgun Violence Protection Act, 1283
Branch Davidians' Compound Burns, 1276
Brides Act, War, 972
Bridge Opens, Brooklyn, 639
British Conquest of New Netherland, 106
British Navigation Acts, 98
British North America Act, 568
Broken Treaties, Trail of, 1153
Brooklyn Bridge Opens, 639
Brown v. Board of Education, 1015
Brown's Raid on Harpers Ferry, John, 499
Budget and Tax Reform, Reagan's, 1209
Bulge, Battle of the, 961
Bull Run, First Battle of, 517
Burlingame Treaty, 576
Burr's Conspiracy, 284
Bus Boycott, Montgomery, 1023
Bush Announces Nuclear Arms Reductions, 1255
Bush Is Elected President, 1240

Cabeza de Vaca's Expeditions, Narváez's and, 35
Cable Act, 816
Cabot's Voyages, 27
California, Drake Lands in Northern, 54
California, Settlement of Alta, 45
California and the Southwest, Occupation of, 437
California Gold Rush, 448
California Missions, Rise of the, 169
Cambodia, United States Invades, 1129

Campaign, Smith-Hoover, 838
Campbell Becomes Canada's First Woman Prime Minister, 1278
Canada, Bennett Era in, 851
Canada, Borden Government in, 744
Canada, Diefenbaker Era in, 1030
Canada, King Era in, 811
Canada, Laurier Era in, 689
Canada, Mackenzie Era in, 603
Canada, Meighen Era in, 804
Canada, Mulroney Era in, 1221
Canada, Rebellions in, 401
Canada, Trudeau Era in, 1113
Canada Is Established, Supreme Court of, 610
Canada Unite, Upper and Lower, 410
Canada's Citizenship Act, 975
Canada's Constitution Act, 1213
Canada's Constitutional Act, 244
Canada's First Native-Born Governor General, Massey Becomes, 1003
Canada's First Woman Prime Minister, Campbell Becomes, 1278
Canada's Human Rights Act, 1177
Canada's Immigration Act of 1976, 1184
Canada's Indian Act, 614
Canada's Official Languages Act, 1121
Canada's Pay Equity Act, 1231
Canada's Prime Minister, Clark Elected, 1194
Canada's Prime Minister, Macdonald Returns as, 626
Canada's Prime Minister, Pearson Becomes, 1063
Canadian Women Gain the Vote, 785
Carolina Regulator Movements, 165
Carolinas, Settlement of the, 103
Cart War, 489
Carter Is Elected President, 1175
Cartier and Roberval Search for a Northwest Passage, 38
Censorship and Japanese Internment, 927
Challenger Accident, 1225
Champlain's Voyages, 60
Charles Town Is Founded, 107
Charlottetown Accord, Defeat of the, 1263
Chattanooga, Battles of Gettysburg, Vicksburg, and, 534
Cherokee Cases, 379
Cherokee Phoenix Begins Publication, 360
Cherokee War, 154

Chicago Riots, 1115
Children Opens, New York Infirmary for Indigent Women and, 487
China, Rapprochement with, 1145
China Establish Full Diplomatic Relations, United States and, 1190
Chinese American Citizens Alliance Is Founded, 679
Chinese Exclusion Act, 634
Chinese Immigration, 453
Chinese Six Companies, Rise of the, 636
Chisholm Trail Opens, 553
Church Is Established, Episcopal, 230
Church Is Established, Methodist, 167
Church Is Founded, African American Baptist, 173
Church Is Founded, AME, 326
Church Is Founded, Unitarian, 331
CIO Merge, AFL and, 1021
Circus Forms, Barnum's, 594
Citizenship Act, Canada's, 975
Civil Liberties in World War I, Propaganda and, 778
Civil Rights Act, Indian, 1110
Civil Rights Act of 1866, 558
Civil Rights Act of 1960, 1047
Civil Rights Act of 1964, 1077
Civil Rights Act of 1991, 1257
Civil Rights Cases, 641
Civil Rights Restoration Act, 1234
Clark Elected Canada's Prime Minister, 1194
Clermont, Voyage of the, 292
Clinton Is Elected President, 1266
Closing of the Frontier, 657
Code of Handsome Lake, 270
College Is Established, Harvard, 94
College Is Founded, Vassar, 548
Columbus' Voyages, 23
Commerce Act, Interstate, 650
Commercial Oil Well, First, 498
Commercial Radio Broadcasting Begins, 805
Commercial Television, Debut of, 906
Commonwealth, Puerto Rico Becomes a, 1006
Commonwealth v. Hunt, 414
Communitarian Movement, New Harmony and the, 313
Company of New France Is Chartered, 75
Compromise of 1850, 456
Computer, IBM Markets the Personal, 1205

Concord, Battle of Lexington and, 184
Confederate States Secede from the Union, 505
Confederation of the United Colonies of New England, 90
Congress, First Continental, 181
Congress, Indian Delegation Meets with, 189
Congress, Second Continental, 188
Congress Bans Importation of African Slaves, 289
Congress of Industrial Organizations Is Founded, 893
Congress of Racial Equality Is Founded, 930
Connecticut, Settlement of, 81
Conservation Conference, White House, 730
Constitution Act, Canada's, 1213
Constitution Is Adopted, U.S., 224
Constitutional Act, Canada's, 244
Construction of the Alaska Pipeline, 1167
Construction of the National Road, 302
Continental Congress, First, 181
Continental Congress, Second, 188
Coolidge Is Elected President, 828
Cornwallis Surrenders at Yorktown, 206
Coronado's Expedition, 42
Cortés Enters Tenochtitlán, 34
Cotton Gin, Whitney Invents the, 250
Crash, Stock Market, 843
Credit, Hamilton's *Report on Public*, 238
Creek War, 309
"Crime of 1873," 602
Cuban Missile Crisis, 1060
Cuban Revolution, 1025

Dawes Plan, 825
Debate, Webster-Hayne, 370
Debut of Commercial Television, 906
Declaration of Independence, 193
Declaration of the Rights of Women, 620
Defeat of the Charlottetown Accord, 1263
Defeat of the Equal Rights Amendment, 1216
Delano Grape Strike, 1094
Demobilization After World War I, 790
Democracy, Expansion of Direct, 712
Deportations of Mexicans, Mass, 847
Depression, Great, 845

Desegregation Crisis, Little Rock School, 1032
De Soto's Expeditions, 40
Détente with the Soviet Union, 1161
Devaluation of the Dollar, 1138
Development of a Polio Vaccine, 1000
Development of Radar, 876
Dictionary of the English Language, Webster's *American*, 363
Diefenbaker Era in Canada, 1030
Dingley Tariff, 691
Direct Democracy, Expansion of, 712
Disabilities Act, Americans with, 1251
Disarmament Conference, Washington, 812
Disfranchisement Laws, Mississippi, 664
Dollar, Devaluation of the, 1138
Dollar Diplomacy, 732
Dolores, El Grito de, 300
Dominion of New England Forms, 122
Dorr Rebellion, 418
Draft Law, First National, 532
Drake Lands in Northern California, 54
Dred Scott v. Sandford, 485
Drug Act, Pure Food and, 725
Dust Bowl, The, 879

Earthquake, San Francisco, 724
Edison Demonstrates the Incandescent Lamp, 631
Education Is Created, Office of, 565
Eighteen, U.S. Voting Age Is Lowered to, 1136
Eisenhower Doctrine, 1027
Eisenhower Is Elected President, 1010
Elected President, Bush Is, 1240
Elected President, Carter Is, 1175
Elected President, Clinton Is, 1266
Elected President, Coolidge Is, 828
Elected President, Eisenhower Is, 1010
Elected President, Franklin D. Roosevelt Is, 866
Elected President, Hayes Is, 621
Elected President, Jackson Is, 364
Elected President, Jefferson Is, 271
Elected President, Johnson Is, 1085
Elected President, Kennedy Is, 1048
Elected President, Lincoln Is, 503
Elected President, McKinley Is, 687
Elected President, Nixon Is, 1117
Elected President, Reagan Is, 1203
Elected President, Truman Is, 987
Elected President, Wilson Is, 751
Election of 1824, U.S., 356

Election of 1840, U.S., 408
Election of 1884, U.S., 643
El Grito de Dolores, 300
Emancipation Proclamation, 528
Embargo on Arms to Spain, 896
Empire State Building Opens, 857
Employment Act, 974
Energy Crisis, Arab Oil Embargo and, 1163
English Language, Webster's *American Dictionary of the*, 363
Episcopal Church Is Established, 230
Equal Credit Opportunity Act, 1171
Equal Employment Opportunity Act, 1148
Equal Pay Act, 1065
Equal Rights Amendment, Defeat of the, 1216
Equal Rights Amendment, Proposal of the, 820
Era of the Clipper Ships, 426
Erie Canal Opens, 358
Espionage and Sedition Acts, 781
Exclusion Act, Chinese, 634
Executed, Sacco and Vanzetti Are, 836
Executive Order 8802, 917
Expansion of Affirmative Action, 1096
Expansion of Direct Democracy, 712
Exxon Valdez Oil Spill, 1242

Fair Housing Act, 1111
Fair Labor Standards Act, 902
Fallen Timbers, Battle of, 257
Family and Medical Leave Act, 1273
Family Support Act, 1236
Far West, Jedediah Smith Explores the, 350
Farewell Address, Washington's, 263
Farm Workers Joins with AFL-CIO, United, 1144
FDA Approves the Birth Control Pill, 1041
Federal Reserve Act, 762
Federalist Papers Are Published, 227
First African American University, 483
First AIDS Cases Are Reported, 1207
First American in Space, 1054
First Battle of Bull Run, 517
First Black Codes, 280
First Commercial Oil Well, 498
First Continental Congress, 181
First Fugitive Slave Law, 251
First General Assembly of Virginia, 67
First Great Awakening, 137
First Jewish Settlers, 96

First National Draft Law, 532
First Pan-American Congress, 655
First Riel Rebellion, 588
First Telegraph Message, 424
First Test of a Submarine in Warfare, 195
First Transatlantic Cable, 494
First U.S. Political Parties, 234
First Xerographic Photocopy, 904
Fletcher v. Peck, 297
Flight, Lindbergh's Transatlantic, 834
Flight, Wright Brothers' First, 718
Food and Drug Act, Pure, 725
Ford Assembly Line Begins Operation, 756
Formosa Resolution, 1019
Fort Stanwix Treaty, 213
Fourteenth Amendment, 577
Fourteenth Amendment, Suffragists Protest the, 561
Fox Wars, 133
Franco-American Treaties, 202
Franklin D. Roosevelt Is Elected President, 866
Fraser River Gold Rush, 491
Free African Society Is Founded, 219
Free Public School Movement, 337
Free Speech Movement, Berkeley, 1083
Free Trade Agreement, North American, 1279
Freedmen's Bureau Is Established, 544
Freedom of Information Act, 1103
Frémont's Expeditions, 415
French and Indian War, 148
French Explore the Mississippi Valley, 113
Frobisher's Voyages, 51
Frontier, Closing of the, 657
Fugitive Slave Law, First, 251
Fugitive Slave Law, Second, 460

Gadsden Purchase, 472
Gaming Regulatory Act, Indian, 1238
General Agreement on Tariffs and Trade, 1288
General Allotment Act, 652
General Assembly of Virginia, First, 67
Gentlemen's Agreement, 727
Georgia, Settlement of, 140
Germany and Italy Declare War on the United States, 926
Gettysburg, Vicksburg, and Chattanooga, Battles of, 534
Ghent, Treaty of, 321
G.I. Bill, 955

Gibbons v. Ogden, 354
Gideon v. Wainwright, 1062
Gold Rush, California, 448
Gold Rush, Fraser River, 491
Gold Rush, Klondike, 685
Good Neighbor Policy, 868
Governor General, Massey Becomes Canada's First Native-Born, 1003
Grange of the Patrons of Husbandry Forms, National, 572
Grant Administration Scandals, 586
Grape Strike, Delano, 1094
Great American Bison Slaughter, 598
Great Awakening, First, 137
Great Awakening, Second, 236
Great Depression, 845
Great Northern Migration, 742
Great Puritan Migration, 77
Great Sioux War, 526
Gregg v. Georgia, 1173
Grenada, United States Invades, 1218
Griswold v. Connecticut, 1089
Grito de Dolores, El, 300
Guadalcanal, Battle of, 936
Guadalupe Hidalgo, Treaty of, 450
Gulf War, Persian, 1252

Haitian Independence, 245
Half-Way Covenant, 101
Halibut Treaty, 826
Hall's Masonic Lodge Is Chartered, 210
Hamilton's *Report on Public Credit*, 238
Handgun Violence Protection Act, Brady, 1283
Handsome Lake, Code of, 270
Harding Administration, Scandals of the, 809
Harpers Ferry, John Brown's Raid on, 499
Hartford Convention, 316
Hartford Female Seminary Is Founded, 348
Harvard College Is Established, 94
Hawaii Gain Statehood, Alaska and, 1035
Hayes Is Elected President, 621
Hay's "Open Door Notes," 700
Health Service Is Established, U.S. Public, 748
Hearst-Pulitzer Circulation War, 678
Henson Reach the North Pole, Peary and, 738
Hohokam Culture, 7
Homestead Act, 522

Hoover-Stimson Doctrine, 861
Howe's Sewing Machine, 428
HUAC Investigations, 900
Hubble Space Telescope, Astronauts Repair the, 1281
Hudson Bay, Hudson Explores, 65
Hudson Explores Hudson Bay, 65
Hudson's Bay Company Is Chartered, 109
Hull House Opens, 653
Human Genome Project Begins, 1245
Human Rights Act, Canada's, 1177
Hundred Days, The, 870
Hydrogen Bomb Is Detonated, 1008

"I Have a Dream" Speech, King Delivers His, 1068
IBM Markets the Personal Computer, 1205
Immigration, Chinese, 453
Immigration, "New," 668
Immigration, "Old," 407
Immigration Act of 1917, 772
Immigration Act of 1924, 823
Immigration Act of 1976, Canada's, 1184
Immigration and Nationality Act, 1098
Immigration Reform and Control Act, 1227
Impeachment of Andrew Johnson, 574
Inauguration, Lincoln's, 511
Inauguration, Washington's, 228
Incandescent Lamp, Edison Demonstrates the, 631
Independent Treasury Is Established, 439
Indian Act, Canada's, 614
Indian Appropriation Act, 592
Indian Citizenship Act, 822
Indian Civil Rights Act, 1110
Indian Delegation Meets with Congress, 189
Indian Gaming Regulatory Act, 1238
Indian Religious Freedom Act, American, 1189
Indian Removal Act, 372
Indian Reorganization Act, 881
Indian Slave Trade, 111
Indigent Women and Children Opens, New York Infirmary for, 487
Industrial Organizations Is Founded, Congress of, 893
Industrial Recovery Act, National, 874
Industrial Workers of the World Is Founded, 721

INF Treaty Is Signed, 1232
Inflation and Labor Unrest, 942
Insular Cases, 706
Internet, Rise of the, 1293
Internment, Censorship and Japanese, 927
Interstate Commerce Act, 650
Intervention in Nicaragua, 749
Invasion of North Africa, 941
Invention of the Transistor, 981
Iran-Contra Scandal, 1229
Iroquois Confederacy, 29
Islam Is Founded, Nation of, 849
Italy, Western Allies Invade, 946
Italy Declare War on the United States, Germany and, 926

Jackson Becomes First Major African American Candidate for President, 1220
Jackson Is Elected President, 364
Jackson vs. the Bank of the United States, 387
Jamestown Is Founded, 63
Japan, Atomic Bombing of, 970
Japan, Perry Opens Trade with, 474
Japan, Superfortress Bombing of, 953
Japanese American Citizens League Is Founded, 853
Japanese Internment, Censorship and, 927
Jay's Treaty, 259
Jedediah Smith Explores the Far West, 350
Jefferson Is Elected President, 271
Jewish Settlers, First, 96
John Brown's Raid on Harpers Ferry, 499
Johnson, Impeachment of Andrew, 574
Johnson Is Elected President, 1085
Jones Act, 775
Judiciary Act, 232

Kansas, Bleeding, 481
Kansas-Nebraska Act, 476
Kellogg-Briand Pact, 840
Kennedy, Assassination of President, 1074
Kennedy, Assassinations of King and, 1108
Kennedy Is Elected President, 1048
Kent State Massacre, 1131
King, St. Laurent Succeeds, 989
King and Kennedy, Assassinations of, 1108

King Delivers His "I Have a Dream" Speech, 1068
King Era in Canada, 811
King George's War, 146
Klondike Gold Rush, 685
Korean War, 993
Ku Klux Klan, Rise of the, 555

Labor Alliance, Asian Pacific American, 1260
Labor Force, 6.6 Million Women Enter the U.S., 913
Labor Relations Act, National, 887
Labor Standards Act, Fair, 902
Labor Unrest, Inflation and, 942
Lamp, Edison Demonstrates the Incandescent, 631
Land Act of 1820, 343
Land Grant Act, Morrill, 524
Languages Act, Canada's Official, 1121
Last Slave Ship Docks at Mobile, 496
Latin American Citizens Is Founded, League of United, 842
Lau v. Nichols, 1165
Launching of the First Liquid-Fueled Rocket, 832
Laurier Era in Canada, 689
League of United Latin American Citizens Is Founded, 842
League of Women Voters Is Founded, 801
Lend-Lease Act, 915
Lewis and Clark Expedition, 282
Lexington and Concord, Battle of, 184
Leyte Gulf, Battle for, 959
Liberator Begins Publication, *The*, 377
Library of Congress Building Opens, 692
Lincoln, Surrender at Appomattox and Assassination of, 545
Lincoln-Douglas Debates, 492
Lincoln Is Elected President, 503
Lincoln Savings and Loan Declares Bankruptcy, 1243
Lincoln's Inauguration, 511
Lindbergh's Transatlantic Flight, 834
Liquid-Fueled Rocket, Launching of the First, 832
Little Bighorn, Battle of the, 617
Little Rock School Desegregation Crisis, 1032
Little Turtle's War, 241
Lone Wolf v. Hitchcock, 713
Long, Hot Summer, 1101
Long Walk of the Navajos, 536

Lord Dunmore's War, 176
Los Angeles Riots, 1259
Lost Colony of Roanoke, 56
Louisiana Purchase, 278
Love Canal, Toxic Waste at, 1187
Lower Canada Unite, Upper and, 410

MacArthur Confrontation, Truman-, 996
McCarran-Walter Act, 1005
McCarthy Hearings, 999
McCormick Invents the Reaper, 383
McCulloch v. Maryland, 335
Macdonald Returns as Canada's Prime Minister, 626
Mackenzie Era in Canada, 603
Mackenzie Reaches the Arctic Ocean, 253
McKinley Is Elected President, 687
Magnuson Act, 948
Malcolm X, Assassination of, 1086
Manhattan Island, Algonquians "Sell," 73
Manhattan Project, 933
Marbury v. Madison, 275
March to the Sea, Sherman's, 541
Mariel Boat Lift, 1199
Marines in Somalia, U.S., 1268
Maryland Act of Toleration, 92
Masonic Lodge Is Chartered, Hall's, 210
Mass Deportations of Mexicans, 847
Massachusetts Recognizes Slavery, 87
Massey Becomes Canada's First Native-Born Governor General, 1003
Mayan Civilization, 9
Medical Leave Act, Family and, 1273
Medicine Lodge Creek Treaty, 571
Meech Lake Accord Dies, 1247
Meighen Era in Canada, 804
Meredith Registers at "Ole Miss," 1057
Metacom's War, 115
Methodist Church Is Established, 167
Meuse-Argonne Offensive, 787
Mexican Revolution, 739
Mexican War, 432
Mexican War of Independence, 344
Mexicans, Mass Deportations of, 847
Miami Riots, 1201
Midway, Battle of, 931
Migration, Great Northern, 742
Migration, Great Puritan, 77
Migration, Westward, 317
Migration to Utah, Mormon, 430

Migrations, Bering Strait, 1
Military, Rise of Women's Role in the, 1127
Military Academy Is Established, U.S., 274
Minor v. Happersett, 608
Missions, Rise of the California, 169
Mississippi Disfranchisement Laws, 664
Mississippi Valley, French Explore the, 113
Mississippian Culture, 16
Missouri Compromise, 340
Mobile, Last Slave Ship Docks at, 496
Mobilization for World War I, 783
Mobilization for World War II, 907
Mogollon Culture, 15
Monday, Black, 885
Monitor vs. *Virginia*, 520
Monroe Doctrine, 352
Montgomery Bus Boycott, 1023
Moon, Apollo 11 Lands on the, 1122
Mormon Migration to Utah, 430
Morrill Land Grant Act, 524
Mound Builders, Ohio, 5
Mt. Holyoke Seminary Is Founded, 403
Muller v. Oregon, 729
Mulroney Era in Canada, 1221

Narváez's and Cabeza de Vaca's Expeditions, 35
Nat Turner's Insurrection, 385
Nation of Islam Is Founded, 849
National Association for the Advancement of Colored People Is Founded, 734
National Bank Acts, 530
National Birth Control League Forms, 764
National Council of Colored People Is Founded, 470
National Draft Law, First, 532
National Grange of the Patrons of Husbandry Forms, 572
National Industrial Recovery Act, 874
National Labor Relations Act, 887
National Organization for Women Is Founded, 1100
National Park Service Is Created, 771
National Road, Construction of the, 302
National Security Act, 979
National Woman's Party Is Founded, 766
Native Claims Settlement Act, Alaska, 1141

Navajos, Long Walk of the, 536
Navigation Acts, British, 98
Navy, United States Builds a Two-Ocean, 909
Neutrality Acts, 891
New Black Codes, 549
New England, Confederation of the United Colonies of, 90
New England Forms, Dominion of, 122
New France Is Chartered, Company of, 75
New Harmony and the Communitarian Movement, 313
"New" Immigration, 668
New Jersey Women Gain the Vote, 191
New Mexico Expedition, Oñate's, 58
New Netherland, British Conquest of, 106
New Orleans, Battle of, 319
New York City Slave Revolt, 132
New York Infirmary for Indigent Women and Children Opens, 487
Nez Perce Exile, 623
Niagara Movement, 722
Nicaragua, Intervention in, 749
Nixon Is Elected President, 1117
Nixon Resigns, 1169
Nootka Sound Convention, 239
Norse Expeditions, 19
North Africa, Invasion of, 941
North American Free Trade Agreement, 1279
North Atlantic Treaty, 991
North Korea Pact, U.S.-, 1284
North Pole, Peary and Henson Reach the, 738
North Star Begins Publication, *The*, 445
Northeast States Abolish Slavery, 197
Northern Migration, Great, 742
Northwest Ordinance, 221
Northwest Passage, Cartier and Roberval Search for a, 38
Nuclear Arms Reductions, Bush Announces, 1255
Nuclear Test Ban Treaty, 1071
Nullification Controversy, 388

Oberlin College Is Established, 394
Occupation of California and the Southwest, 437
October Crisis, 1133
Office of Education Is Created, 565
Official Languages Act, Canada's, 1121
Ogdensburg Agreement, 912
Ohio Mound Builders, 5

Oil Embargo and Energy Crisis, Arab, 1163
Oil Spill, *Exxon Valdez*, 1242
Oil Trust Is Organized, Standard, 632
Oil Well, First Commercial, 498
Oklahoma City Federal Building Bombed, 1290
"Old" Immigration, 407
"Ole Miss," Meredith Registers at, 1057
Olmec Civilization, 3
Oñate's New Mexico Expedition, 58
"Open Door Notes," Hay's, 700
Operation Overlord, 951
Operation Wetback, 1017
Ordinance of 1785, 216
Oregon Settlement, 434
Organization of American States Is Founded, 983
Oriskany Creek, Battle of, 199
Ottawa Agreements, 864
Overlord, Operation, 951
Ozawa v. United States, 819
Ozone Hole Is Discovered, 1211

Pacific Railroad Surveys, 467
Packing Fight, Supreme Court, 898
Pact, Kellogg-Briand, 840
Page Law, 611
Panama Canal Treaties, 1182
Panama Canal Zone, Acquisition of the, 716
Pan-American Congress, First, 655
Paris, Treaty of, 207
Paxton Boys' Massacres, 160
Pay Equity Act, Canada's, 1231
Peace Corps Is Established, 1050
Pearl Harbor, Bombing of, 919
Pearson Becomes Canada's Prime Minister, 1063
Peary and Henson Reach the North Pole, 738
Pendleton Act, 638
Pennsylvania Is Founded, 121
Pennsylvania Society for the Abolition of Slavery Is Founded, 183
Penny Press, Rise of the, 391
People's Party, Birth of the, 672
Pequot War, 85
Perry Opens Trade with Japan, 474
Pershing Expedition, 768
Persian Gulf War, 1252
Personal Computer, IBM Markets the, 1205
Philippine Insurrection, 698
Photocopy, First Xerographic, 904

Pike's Southwest Explorations, 287
Pilgrims Land at Plymouth, 70
Pinckney's Treaty, 261
Platt Amendment, 715
Plessy v. Ferguson, 683
Plyler v. Doe, 1214
Plymouth, Pilgrims Land at, 70
Polio Vaccine, Development of a, 1000
Political Parties, First U.S., 234
Ponce de León's Voyages, 32
Pontiac's Resistance, 156
Pony Express, 501
Potsdam Conference, 968
Powell's *Report on the Lands of the Arid Region*, 628
Powhatan Confederacy, 48
Powhatan Wars, 72
Preemption Act, 412
Pregnancy Discrimination Act, 1180
President, Bush Is Elected, 1240
President, Carter Is Elected, 1175
President, Clinton Is Elected, 1266
President, Coolidge Is Elected, 828
President, Eisenhower Is Elected, 1010
President, Franklin D. Roosevelt Is Elected, 866
President, Hayes Is Elected, 621
President, Jackson Becomes First Major African American Candidate for, 1220
President, Jackson Is Elected, 364
President, Jefferson Is Elected, 271
President, Johnson Is Elected, 1085
President, Kennedy Is Elected, 1048
President, Lincoln Is Elected, 503
President, McKinley Is Elected, 687
President, Nixon Is Elected, 1117
President, Reagan Is Elected, 1203
President, Theodore Roosevelt Becomes, 708
President, Truman Is Elected, 987
President, Wilson Is Elected, 751
President Kennedy, Assassination of, 1074
Prime Minister, Campbell Becomes Canada's First Woman, 1278
Prime Minister, Clark Elected Canada's, 1194
Prime Minister, Macdonald Returns as Canada's, 626
Prime Minister, Pearson Becomes Canada's, 1063
Prison Riots, Attica State, 1140
Proclamation of 1763, 157
Prohibition, 799

Propaganda and Civil Liberties in World War I, 778
Prophetstown Is Founded, 293
Proposal of the Equal Rights Amendment, 820
Proslavery Argument, 366
Public Health Service Is Established, U.S., 748
Public School Movement, Free, 337
Pueblo Revolt, 118
Puerto Rico Becomes a Commonwealth, 1006
Pulitzer Circulation War, Hearst-, 678
Pullman Strike, 676
Purchase of Alaska, 567
Pure Food and Drug Act, 725
Puritan Migration, Great, 77

Quebec Act, 178
Quebec Sovereignist Movement, 1043
Québécois Forms, Bloc, 1249
Queen Anne's War, 128

Race Riots, Urban, 944
Race Riots in the South, 560
Racial Equality Is Founded, Congress of, 930
Radar, Development of, 876
Radio Broadcasting Begins, Commercial, 805
Railroad Begins Operation, Baltimore and Ohio, 368
Railroad Is Completed, Transcontinental, 584
Railroad Surveys, Pacific, 467
Rapprochement with China, 1145
Reagan Is Elected President, 1203
Reagan's Budget and Tax Reform, 1209
Reaper, McCormick Invents the, 383
Reapportionment Cases, 1056
Rebellions in Canada, 401
Reciprocity Treaty, 895
Reconstruction, 538
Reconstruction Finance Corporation Is Created, 862
Red River Raids, 323
Red River War, 605
Red Scare, 795
Reform Movement, Social, 339
Refugee Relief Act, 1014
Regents of the University of California v. Bakke, 1185
Regulator Movements, Carolina, 165
Religious Freedom Act, American Indian, 1189

Religious Liberty, Virginia Statute of, 218
Removal Act, Indian, 372
Reorganization Act, Indian, 881
Report on Public Credit, Hamilton's, 238
Report on the Lands of the Arid Region, Powell's, 628
Republican Congressional Insurgency, 736
Republican Party, Birth of the, 479
Republican Resurgence, 792
Republicans Return to Congress, 1286
Rhode Island Is Founded, 83
Riel Rebellion, First, 588
Riel Rebellion, Second, 646
Rights of Women, Declaration of the, 620
Riots in the South, Race, 560
Rise of the California Missions, 169
Rise of the Chinese Six Companies, 636
Rise of the Internet, 1293
Rise of the Ku Klux Klan, 555
Rise of the Penny Press, 391
Rise of Transcendentalism, 399
Rise of Woman Suffrage Associations, 582
Rise of Women's Role in the Military, 1127
Roanoke, Lost Colony of, 56
Roberval Search for a Northwest Passage, Cartier and, 38
Rocket, Launching of the First Liquid-Fueled, 832
Roe v. Wade, 1155
Roosevelt Becomes President, Theodore, 708
Roosevelt Is Elected President, Franklin D., 866
Russian Voyages to Alaska, 135

Sacco and Vanzetti Are Executed, 836
St. Augustine Is Founded, 47
St. Laurent Succeeds King, 989
St. Lawrence Seaway Opens, 1039
Salem Witchcraft Trials, 125
SALT II Is Signed, 1195
Salt Wars, 625
San Francisco Earthquake, 724
Sand Creek Massacre, 542
Santa Fe Trail Opens, 346
Saratoga, Battle of, 200
Savings and Loan Declares Bankruptcy, Lincoln, 1243

Scandals, Grant Administration, 586
Scandals of the Harding
    Administration, 809
School Desegregation Crisis, Little
    Rock, 1032
School Movement, Free Public, 337
Scopes Trial, 830
Scott v. Sandford, Dred, 485
Scottsboro Trials, 855
Secede from the Union, Confederate
    States, 505
Second Bank of the United States Is
    Chartered, 325
Second Continental Congress, 188
Second Fugitive Slave Law, 460
Second Great Awakening, 236
Second Riel Rebellion, 646
Sedition Acts, Alien and, 268
Sedition Acts, Espionage and, 781
Seminole Wars, 329
Seneca Falls Convention, 452
Settlement of Alta California, 45
Settlement of Connecticut, 81
Settlement of Georgia, 140
Settlement of the Carolinas, 103
Sewing Machine, Howe's, 428
Sheppard-Towner Act, 814
Sherman Antitrust Act, 662
Sherman's March to the Sea, 541
Sioux War, Great, 526
6.6 Million Women Enter the U.S.
    Labor Force, 913
Sixteenth Amendment, 755
Slater's Spinning Mill, 243
Slave Codes, Virginia, 100
Slave Law, First Fugitive, 251
Slave Revolt, Amistad, 405
Slave Revolt, New York City, 132
Slave Ship Docks at Mobile, Last, 496
Slave Trade, Indian, 111
Slavery, Massachusetts Recognizes, 87
Slavery, Northeast States Abolish, 197
Slavery Is Founded, Pennsylvania
    Society for the Abolition of, 183
Slaves, Congress Bans Importation of
    African, 289
Smith Explores the Far West, Jedediah,
    350
Smith-Hoover Campaign, 838
Smith v. Allwright, 949
Smithsonian Institution Is Founded, 440
Social Reform Movement, 339
Social Security Act, 889
Somalia, U.S. Marines in, 1268
Soto's Expeditions, de, 40

South, Race Riots in the, 560
South, Stand Watie Fights for the, 507
Southern Christian Leadership
    Conference Is Founded, 1029
Southwest, Occupation of California
    and the, 437
Southwest Explorations, Pike's, 287
Sovereignist Movement, Quebec, 1043
Soviet Summit, U.S.-, 1223
Soviet Union, Détente with the, 1161
Space, First American in, 1054
Space Telescope, Astronauts Repair the
    Hubble, 1281
Spaceflights of Voyagers 1 and 2, 1178
Spain, Embargo on Arms to, 896
Spanish-American War, 695
Spinning Mill, Slater's, 243
Stamp Act Crisis, 162
Stand Watie Fights for the South, 507
Standard Oil Trust Is Organized, 632
START II Is Signed, 1271
State Universities, Beginnings of, 215
Statute of Westminster, 859
Stock Market Crash, 843
Stonewall Inn Riots, 1119
Stono Rebellion, 145
Strike, Anthracite Coal, 710
Strike, Pullman, 676
Submarine in Warfare, First Test of a,
    195
Suffrage, Western States Grant Woman,
    590
Suffrage Associations, Rise of Woman,
    582
Suffragists Protest the Fourteenth
    Amendment, 561
Summer, Long, Hot, 1101
Superfortress Bombing of Japan, 953
Suppression of Yellow Fever, 702
Supreme Court of Canada Is
    Established, 610
Supreme Court Packing Fight, 898
Surgical Anesthesia Is Safely
    Demonstrated, 442
Surrender at Appomattox and
    Assassination of Lincoln, 545
Susan B. Anthony Is Arrested, 600
*Swann v. Charlotte-Mecklenburg Board
    of Education*, 1134

Tailhook Scandal, 1262
Taos Rebellion, 444
Tariff, Dingley, 691
Tariffs and Trade, General Agreement
    on, 1288

Tax Reform, Reagan's Budget and,
    1209
Telegraph Is Completed,
    Transcontinental, 518
Telegraph Message, First, 424
Telephone, Bell Demonstrates the, 615
Telescope, Astronauts Repair the
    Hubble Space, 1281
Teletype Is Developed, 704
Television, Debut of Commercial, 906
Tennessee Valley Authority Is
    Established, 872
Tenochtitlán, Cortés Enters, 34
Termination Resolution, 1012
Tet Offensive, 1106
Texas Revolution, 398
Thames, Battle of the, 311
Theodore Roosevelt Becomes
    President, 708
Thirteenth Amendment, 551
Three Mile Island Accident, 1192
Tippecanoe, Battle of, 304
Tocqueville Visits America, 381
Toleration, Maryland Act of, 92
Townshend Crisis, 164
Toxic Waste at Love Canal, 1187
Trade Agreement, North American
    Free, 1279
Trail of Broken Treaties, 1153
Trail of Tears, 375
Transatlantic Cable, First, 494
Transatlantic Flight, Lindbergh's, 834
Transcendentalism, Rise of, 399
Transcontinental Railroad Is
    Completed, 584
Transcontinental Telegraph Is
    Completed, 518
Transistor, Invention of the, 981
Treasury Is Established, Independent,
    439
Treaties, Franco-American, 202
Treaties, Panama Canal, 1182
Treaty, Adams-Onís, 332
Treaty, Burlingame, 576
Treaty, Fort Stanwix, 213
Treaty, Halibut, 826
Treaty, Jay's, 259
Treaty, Medicine Lodge Creek, 571
Treaty, Pinckney's, 261
Treaty, Reciprocity, 895
Treaty, Webster-Ashburton, 420
Treaty of Ghent, 321
Treaty of Guadalupe Hidalgo, 450
Treaty of Paris, 207
Treaty of Versailles, 793

Treaty of Washington, 596
Trial of John Peter Zenger, 142
Triangle Shirtwaist Company Fire, 746
Trudeau Era in Canada, 1113
Truman Doctrine, 977
Truman Is Elected President, 987
Truman-MacArthur Confrontation, 996
Trust Is Organized, Standard Oil, 632
Turner's Insurrection, Nat, 385
Tuscarora War, 130
Twelfth Amendment, 286
Twenty-fourth Amendment, 1076
Two-Ocean Navy, United States Builds
    a, 909
Tydings-McDuffie Act, 877

U-2 Incident, 1045
Underground Railroad, 462
Union, Confederate States Secede from
    the, 505
Unitarian Church Is Founded, 331
United Colonies of New England,
    Confederation of the, 90
United Farm Workers Joins with
    AFL-CIO, 1144
United Nations Charter Convention,
    965
United States and China Establish Full
    Diplomatic Relations, 1190
United States Builds a Two-Ocean
    Navy, 909
United States Enters World War I, 776
United States Invades Cambodia, 1129
United States Invades Grenada, 1218
United States Recognizes Vietnam,
    1291
United States v. Wong Kim Ark, 694
Universal Negro Improvement
    Association Is Established, 780
Universities, Beginnings of State, 215
*University of California v. Bakke,
    Regents of the*, 1185
Upper and Lower Canada Unite, 410
Urban Race Riots, 944
U.S. Bill of Rights Is Ratified, 248
U.S. Constitution Is Adopted, 224
U.S. Election of 1824, 356
U.S. Election of 1840, 408
U.S. Election of 1884, 643
U.S. Marines in Somalia, 1268
U.S. Military Academy Is Established,
    274
U.S.-North Korea Pact, 1284
U.S. Political Parties, First, 234

U.S. Public Health Service Is
    Established, 748
U.S.-Soviet Summit, 1223
U.S. Troops Leave Vietnam, 1159
U.S. Voting Age Is Lowered to
    Eighteen, 1136
U.S. Women Gain the Vote, 807
Utah, Mormon Migration to, 430

V-E day, 967
Vanzetti Are Executed, Sacco and, 836
Vassar College Is Founded, 548
Versailles, Treaty of, 793
Vicksburg, and Chattanooga, Battles of
    Gettysburg, 534
Vietnam, United States Recognizes,
    1291
Vietnam, U.S. Troops Leave, 1159
Vietnam War, 1080
Virginia, Africans Arrive in, 68
Virginia, First General Assembly of, 67
Virginia, Monitor vs., 520
Virginia Slave Codes, 100
Virginia Statute of Religious Liberty,
    218
Vote, Canadian Women Gain the, 785
Vote, New Jersey Women Gain the, 191
Vote, U.S. Women Gain the, 807
Voters Is Founded, League of Women,
    801
Voting Age Is Lowered to Eighteen,
    U.S., 1136
Voting Rights Act, 1091
Voyage of the *Clermont*, 292
Voyagers 1 and 2, Spaceflights of, 1178

Walking Purchase, 143
Walter Act, McCarran-, 1005
War Brides Act, 972
War of 1812, 305
War of Independence, Mexican, 344
Washington, Treaty of, 596
Washington Disarmament Conference,
    812
Washington's Atlanta Exposition
    Address, Booker T., 681
Washington's Farewell Address, 263
Washington's Inauguration, 228
Washita River Massacre, 580
Watergate Affair, 1150
Watie Fights for the South, Stand, 507
Watts Riot, 1092
Webster-Ashburton Treaty, 420
Webster-Hayne Debate, 370

Webster's *American Dictionary of the
    English Language*, 363
West, Jedediah Smith Explores the Far,
    350
West Indian Uprisings, 25
Western Allies Invade Italy, 946
Western States Grant Woman Suffrage,
    590
Westminster, Statute of, 859
Westward Migration, 317
Whig Party, Birth of the, 396
Whiskey Rebellion, 256
White House Conservation
    Conference, 730
Whitney Invents the Cotton Gin, 250
Wilson Is Elected President, 751
Witchcraft Trials, Salem, 125
Woman Prime Minister, Campbell
    Becomes Canada's First, 1278
Woman Suffrage, Western States
    Grant, 590
Woman Suffrage Associations, Rise of,
    582
Woman's Rights Convention, Akron,
    464
Women, Declaration of the Rights of,
    620
Women and Children Opens, New York
    Infirmary for Indigent, 487
Women Enter the U.S. Labor Force, 6.6
    Million, 913
Women Gain the Vote, Canadian, 785
Women Gain the Vote, New Jersey, 191
Women Gain the Vote, U.S., 807
Women Voters Is Founded, League of,
    801
Women's Rights Associations Unite,
    660
Women's Role in the Military, Rise of,
    1127
Wong Kim Ark, United States v., 694
Works Progress Administration Is
    Established, 883
World Trade Center Bombing, 1274
World War I, Demobilization After, 790
World War I, Mobilization for, 783
World War I, Propaganda and Civil
    Liberties in, 778
World War I, United States Enters, 776
World War II, Mobilization for, 907
World's Columbian Exposition, 674
Wounded Knee, Battle of, 666
Wounded Knee Occupation, 1157
Wright Brothers' First Flight, 718

Xerographic Photocopy, First, 904
XYZ Affair, 266

Yalta Conference, 963
Yellow Fever, Suppression of, 702

Yellow Peril Campaign, 671
Yorktown, Cornwallis Surrenders at, 206

Zapotec Civilization, 13
Zenger, Trial of John Peter, 142
Zuñi Rebellion, 79

CATEGORY LIST

NOTE: The entries in this publication are listed below under all categories that apply. The chronological order under each category corresponds to the chronological order of the entries in these volumes.

AFRICAN AMERICAN HISTORY

1619, Africans Arrive in Virginia
1641, Massachusetts Recognizes Slavery
1661, Virginia Slave Codes
1712, New York City Slave Revolt
1739, Stono Rebellion
1773, African American Baptist Church Is Founded
1775, Pennsylvania Society for the Abolition of Slavery Is Founded
1777, Northeast States Abolish Slavery
1784, Hall's Masonic Lodge Is Chartered
1787, Free African Society Is Founded
1787, Northwest Ordinance
1791, Haitian Independence
1793, Whitney Invents the Cotton Gin
1793, First Fugitive Slave Law
1804, First Black Codes
1807, Congress Bans Importation of African Slaves
1816, AME Church Is Founded
1820's, Social Reform Movement
1820, Missouri Compromise
1830, Proslavery Argument
1830, Webster-Hayne Debate
1831, *The Liberator* Begins Publication
1831, Nat Turner's Insurrection
1833, American Anti-Slavery Society Is Founded
1839, Amistad Slave Revolt
1847, *The North Star* Begins Publication
1850, Underground Railroad
1850, Compromise of 1850
1850, Second Fugitive Slave Law
1853, National Council of Colored People Is Founded
1854, Kansas-Nebraska Act
1856, Bleeding Kansas
1857, First African American University
1857, *Dred Scott v. Sandford*
1858, Lincoln-Douglas Debates
1859, Last Slave Ship Docks at Mobile
1859, John Brown's Raid on Harpers Ferry
1863, Emancipation Proclamation
1863, Reconstruction
1865, Freedmen's Bureau Is Established

1865, New Black Codes
1865, Thirteenth Amendment
1866, Rise of the Ku Klux Klan
1866, Civil Rights Act of 1866
1866, Race Riots in the South
1868, Fourteenth Amendment
1890, Mississippi Disfranchisement Laws
1895, Booker T. Washington's Atlanta Exposition Address
1896, *Plessy v. Ferguson*
1909, National Association for the Advancement of Colored People Is Founded
1910, Great Northern Migration
1917, Universal Negro Improvement Association Is Established
1930, Nation of Islam Is Founded
1931, Scottsboro Trials
1941, Executive Order 8802
1942, Congress of Racial Equality Is Founded
1944, *Smith v. Allwright*
1954, *Brown v. Board of Education*
1955, Montgomery Bus Boycott
1957, Southern Christian Leadership Conference Is Founded
1957, Little Rock School Desegregation Crisis
1960, Civil Rights Act of 1960
1962, Meredith Registers at "Ole Miss"
1963, King Delivers His "I Have a Dream" Speech
1964, Civil Rights Act of 1964
1965, Assassination of Malcolm X
1965, Voting Rights Act
1965, Watts Riot
1965, Expansion of Affirmative Action
1967, Long, Hot Summer
1968, Assassinations of King and Kennedy
1968, Fair Housing Act
1971, *Swann v. Charlotte-Mecklenberg Board of Education*
1972, Equal Employment Opportunity Act
1980, Miami Riots
1983, Jackson Becomes First Major African American Candidate for President

ASIAN AMERICAN HISTORY

1849, Chinese Immigration
1854, Perry Opens Trade with Japan
1868, Burlingame Treaty
1875, Page Law
1882, Chinese Exclusion Act
1882, Rise of the Chinese Six Companies
1892, Yellow Peril Campaign
1895, Chinese American Citizens Alliance Is Founded
1898, *United States v. Wong Kim Ark*
1899, Philippine Insurrection
1899, Hay's "Open Door Notes"
1901, Insular Cases
1907, Gentlemen's Agreement
1913, Alien Land Laws
1917, Immigration Act of 1917
1922, *Ozawa v. United States*
1930, Japanese American Citizens League Is Founded
1934, Tydings-McDuffie Act
1942, Censorship and Japanese Internment
1943, Magnuson Act
1959, Alaska and Hawaii Gain Statehood
1968, Bilingual Education Act
1974, *Lau v. Nichols*
1992, Asian Pacific American Labor Alliance

BUSINESS AND LABOR

1790, Slater's Spinning Mill
1793, Whitney Invents the Cotton Gin
1808, American Fur Company Is Chartered
1810, *Fletcher v. Peck*
1825, Erie Canal Opens
1833, Rise of the Penny Press
1842, *Commonwealth v. Hunt*
1842, Dorr Rebellion
1846, Howe's Sewing Machine
1859, First Commercial Oil Well
1882, Standard Oil Trust Is Organized
1886, American Federation of Labor Is Founded
1887, Interstate Commerce Act
1890, Sherman Antitrust Act
1894, Pullman Strike

1897, Dingley Tariff
1902, Anthracite Coal Strike
1905, Industrial Workers of the World Is Founded
1905, Niagara Movement
1906, Pure Food and Drug Act
1907, Gentlemen's Agreement
1908, *Muller v. Oregon*
1910, Great Northern Migration
1911, Triangle Shirtwaist Company Fire
1913, Ford Assembly Line Begins Operation
1913, Alien Land Laws
1917, Mobilization for World War I
1920, Commercial Radio Broadcasting Begins
1929, Stock Market Crash
1929, Great Depression
1930's, Mass Deportations of Mexicans
1930, Baltimore and Ohio Railroad Begins Operation
1932, Reconstruction Finance Corporation Is Created
1933, National Industrial Recovery Act
1935, Works Progress Administration Is Established
1935, National Labor Relations Act
1935, Congress of Industrial Organizations Is Founded
1938, Fair Labor Standards Act
1939, Mobilization for World War II
1941, 6.6 Million Women Enter the U.S. Labor Force
1942, Bracero Program
1943, Inflation and Labor Unrest
1943, Urban Race Riots
1946, Employment Act
1955, AFL and CIO Merge
1959, St. Lawrence Seaway Opens
1965, Delano Grape Strike
1965, Expansion of Affirmative Action
1971, Devaluation of the Dollar
1972, United Farm Workers Joins with AFL-CIO
1978, Pregnancy Discrimination Act
1981, IBM Markets the Personal Computer
1986, Immigration Reform and Control Act
1987, Canada's Pay Equity Act
1989, *Exxon Valdez* Oil Spill
1989, Lincoln Savings and Loan Declares Bankruptcy
1990's, Rise of the Internet

1992, Asian Pacific American Labor Alliance
1993, North American Free Trade Agreement
1994, General Agreement on Tariffs and Trade

CANADIAN HISTORY
A.D. 986, Norse Expeditions
1497, Cabot's Voyages
1534, Cartier and Roberval Search for a Northwest Passage
1576, Frobisher's Voyages
1603, Champlain's Voyages
1610, Hudson Explores Hudson Bay
1627, Company of New France Is Chartered
1670, Hudson's Bay Company Is Chartered
1702, Queen Anne's War
1714, Fox Wars
1754, French and Indian War
1763, Proclamation of 1763
1774, Quebec Act
1790, Nootka Sound Convention
1791, Canada's Constitutional Act
1793, Mackenzie Reaches the Arctic Ocean
1812, War of 1812
1813, Battle of the Thames
1815, Battle of New Orleans
1815, Treaty of Ghent
1815, Red River Raids
1837, Rebellions in Canada
1841, Upper and Lower Canada Unite
1842, Webster-Ashburton Treaty
1846, Oregon Settlement
1858, Fraser River Gold Rush
1867, British North America Act
1871, Treaty of Washington
1872, Great American Bison Slaughter
1873, Mackenzie Era in Canada
1875, Supreme Court of Canada Is Established
1876, Canada's Indian Act
1878, Macdonald Returns as Canada's Prime Minister
1886, American Federation of Labor Is Founded
1896, Klondike Gold Rush
1897, Laurier Era in Canada
1900, Teletype Is Developed
1911, Borden Government in Canada
1917, Canadian Women Gain the Vote
1920, Meighen Era in Canada

1921, King Era in Canada
1924, Halibut Treaty
1930, Bennett Era in Canada
1931, Statute of Westminster
1932, Ottawa Agreements
1936, Reciprocity Treaty
1940, Ogdensburg Agreement
1947, Canada's Citizenship Act
1948, St. Laurent Succeeds King
1952, Massey Becomes Canada's First Native-Born Governor General
1957, Diefenbaker Era in Canada
1959, St. Lawrence Seaway Opens
1960, Quebec Sovereignist Movement
1963, Pearson Becomes Canada's Prime Minister
1968, Trudeau Era in Canada
1969, Canada's Official Languages Act
1970, October Crisis
1977, Canada's Human Rights Act
1978, Canada's Immigration Act of 1976
1979, Clark Elected Canada's Prime Minister
1982, Canada's Constitution Act
1984, Mulroney Era in Canada
1987, Canada's Pay Equity Act
1990, Meech Lake Accord Dies
1990, Bloc Québécois Forms
1992, Defeat of the Charlottetown Accord
1993, Campbell Becomes Canada's First Woman Prime Minister

CIVIL RIGHTS
1734, Trial of John Peter Zenger
1776, New Jersey Women Gain the Vote
1776, Declaration of Independence
1786, Virginia Statute of Religious Liberty
1787, U.S. Constitution Is Adopted
1791, U.S. Bill of Rights Is Ratified
1804, First Black Codes
1820's, Social Reform Movement
1820, Missouri Compromise
1842, Dorr Rebellion
1848, Seneca Falls Convention
1851, Akron Woman's Rights Convention
1859, John Brown's Raid on Harpers Ferry
1865, Thirteenth Amendment
1866, Rise of the Ku Klux Klan
1866, Civil Rights Act of 1866
1868, Fourteenth Amendment

1869, Rise of Woman Suffrage Associations
1869, Western States Grant Woman Suffrage
1872, Susan B. Anthony Is Arrested
1874, *Minor v. Happersett*
1876, Declaration of the Rights of Women
1883, Civil Rights Cases
1890, Mississippi Disfranchisement Laws
1895, Booker T. Washington's Atlanta Exposition Address
1896, *Plessy v. Ferguson*
1898, *United States v. Wong Kim Ark*
1902, Expansion of Direct Democracy
1909, National Association for the Advancement of Colored People Is Founded
1913, Alien Land Laws
1917, Propaganda and Civil Liberties in World War I
1917, Espionage and Sedition Acts
1917, Canadian Women Gain the Vote
1919, Red Scare
1920, U.S. Women Gain the Vote
1922, Cable Act
1923, Proposal of the Equal Rights Amendment
1929, League of United Latin American Citizens Is Founded
1941, Executive Order 8802
1942, Censorship and Japanese Internment
1942, Congress of Racial Equality Is Founded
1944, *Smith v. Allwright*
1951, McCarthy Hearings
1954, *Brown v. Board of Education*
1955, Montgomery Bus Boycott
1957, Southern Christian Leadership Conference Is Founded
1957, Little Rock School Desegregation Crisis
1960, Civil Rights Act of 1960
1962, Meredith Registers at "Ole Miss"
1963, *Gideon v. Wainwright*
1963, Equal Pay Act
1963, King Delivers His "I Have a Dream" Speech
1964, Twenty-fourth Amendment
1964, Civil Rights Act of 1964
1964, Berkeley Free Speech Movement
1965, Assassination of Malcolm X
1965, *Griswold v. Connecticut*
1965, Voting Rights Act

1965, Expansion of Affirmative Action
1967, Long, Hot Summer
1967, Freedom of Information Act
1968, Assassinations of King and Kennedy
1968, Indian Civil Rights Act
1968, Fair Housing Act
1969, Stonewall Inn Riots
1970, Kent State Massacre
1970, October Crisis
1971, *Swann v. Charlotte-Mecklenberg Board of Education*
1971, U.S. Voting Age Is Lowered to Eighteen
1971, Attica State Prison Riots
1972, Equal Employment Opportunity Act
1973, *Roe v. Wade*
1975, Equal Credit Opportunity Act
1976, *Gregg v. Georgia*
1977, Canada's Human Rights Act
1978, Pregnancy Discrimination Act
1978, *Regents of the University of California v. Bakke*
1978, American Indian Religious Freedom Act
1982, *Plyler v. Doe*
1988, Civil Rights Restoration Act
1990, Americans with Disabilities Act
1991, Civil Rights Act of 1991
1993, Family and Medical Leave Act
1993, Branch Davidians' Compound Burns

COMMUNICATIONS
1828, *Cherokee Phoenix* Begins Publication
1831, *The Liberator* Begins Publication
1833, Rise of the Penny Press
1844, First Telegraph Message
1847, *The North Star* Begins Publication
1858, First Transatlantic Cable
1860, Pony Express
1861, Transcontinental Telegraph Is Completed
1866, Suffragists Protest the Fourteenth Amendment
1876, Bell Demonstrates the Telephone
1900, Teletype Is Developed
1939, Debut of Commercial Television
1947, Invention of the Transistor
1981, IBM Markets the Personal Computer
1990's, Rise of the Internet

COURT CASES
1734, Trial of John Peter Zenger
1803, *Marbury v. Madison*
1810, *Fletcher v. Peck*
1819, *McCulloch v. Maryland*
1824, *Gibbons v. Ogden*
1831, Cherokee Cases
1842, *Commonwealth v. Hunt*
1857, *Dred Scott v. Sandford*
1874, *Minor v. Happersett*
1883, Civil Rights Cases
1896, *Plessy v. Ferguson*
1898, *United States v. Wong Kim Ark*
1901, Insular Cases
1903, *Lone Wolf v. Hitchcock*
1908, *Muller v. Oregon*
1922, *Ozawa v. United States*
1925, Scopes Trial
1927, Sacco and Vanzetti Are Executed
1931, Scottsboro Trials
1935, Black Monday
1954, *Brown v. Board of Education*
1962, Reapportionment Cases
1963, *Gideon v. Wainwright*
1963, *Abington School District v. Schempp*
1965, *Griswold v. Connecticut*
1971, *Swann v. Charlotte-Mecklenberg Board of Education*
1973, *Roe v. Wade*
1974, *Lau v. Nichols*
1976, *Gregg v. Georgia*
1978, *Regents of the University of California v. Bakke*
1982, *Plyler v. Doe*

CULTURAL AND INTELLECTUAL HISTORY
1776, Declaration of Independence
1787, *Federalist* Papers Are Published
1820's, Free Public School Movement
1828, *Cherokee Phoenix* Begins Publication
1828, Webster's *American Dictionary of the English Language*
1831, *The Liberator* Begins Publication
1831, Tocqueville Visits America
1833, Rise of the Penny Press
1836, Rise of Transcendentalism
1846, Smithsonian Institution Is Founded
1847, *The North Star* Begins Publication
1871, Barnum's Circus Forms
1893, World's Columbian Exposition

1895, Hearst-Pulitzer Circulation War
1895, Booker T. Washington's Atlanta
    Exposition Address
1897, Library of Congress Building
    Opens
1913, Armory Show
1919, Black Sox Scandal
1920, Commercial Radio Broadcasting
    Begins
1927, Lindbergh's Transatlantic Flight
1939, Debut of Commercial Television
1963, King Delivers His "I Have a
    Dream" Speech
1964, Berkeley Free Speech Movement
1981, IBM Markets the Personal
    Computer
1990's, Rise of the Internet

**DIPLOMACY AND INTER-
    NATIONAL RELATIONS**
1794, Jay's Treaty
1796, Washington's Farewell Address
1797, XYZ Affair
1798, Alien and Sedition Acts
1815, Treaty of Ghent
1823, Monroe Doctrine
1839, Amistad Slave Revolt
1842, Webster-Ashburton Treaty
1854, Perry Opens Trade with Japan
1868, Burlingame Treaty
1871, Treaty of Washington
1889, First Pan-American Congress
1892, Yellow Peril Campaign
1895, Hearst-Pulitzer Circulation War
1899, Hay's "Open Door Notes"
1901, Insular Cases
1903, Platt Amendment
1909, Dollar Diplomacy
1912, Intervention in Nicaragua
1919, Treaty of Versailles
1919, Red Scare
1921, Washington Disarmament
    Conference
1924, Dawes Plan
1928, Kellogg-Briand Pact
1932, Hoover-Stimson Doctrine
1933, Good Neighbor Policy
1935, Neutrality Acts
1936, Reciprocity Treaty
1937, Embargo on Arms to Spain
1940, Ogdensburg Agreement
1941, Lend-Lease Act
1945, Yalta Conference
1945, United Nations Charter
    Convention

1945, Potsdam Conference
1947, Truman Doctrine
1947, National Security Act
1948, Organization of American States
    Is Founded
1948, Berlin Blockade
1949, North Atlantic Treaty
1950, Truman-MacArthur Confrontation
1955, Formosa Resolution
1956, Cuban Revolution
1957, Eisenhower Doctrine
1960, U-2 Incident
1961, Peace Corps Is Established
1961, Bay of Pigs Invasion
1962, Cuban Missile Crisis
1963, Nuclear Test Ban Treaty
1972, Rapprochement with China
1973, U.S. Troops Leave Vietnam
1973, Détente with the Soviet Union
1973, Arab Oil Embargo and Energy
    Crisis
1978, Panama Canal Treaties
1979, United States and China
    Establish Full Diplomatic
    Relations
1979, SALT II Is Signed
1980, Mariel Boat Lift
1983, United States Invades Grenada
1985, U.S.-Soviet Summit
1986, Iran-Contra Scandal
1987, INF Treaty Is Signed
1991, Bush Announces Nuclear Arms
    Reductions
1992, U.S. Marines in Somalia
1993, START II Is Signed
1993, World Trade Center Bombing
1993, North American Free Trade
    Agreement
1994, U.S.-North Korea Pact
1994, General Agreement on Tariffs
    and Trade
1995, United States Recognizes
    Vietnam

ECONOMICS
1627, Company of New France Is
    Chartered
1642, Beaver Wars
1660, British Navigation Acts
1664, British Conquest of New
    Netherland
1670, Hudson's Bay Company Is
    Chartered
1671, Indian Slave Trade
1739, King George's War

1765, Stamp Act Crisis
1767, Townshend Crisis
1773, Boston Tea Party
1790, Hamilton's *Report on Public
    Credit*
1790, Slater's Spinning Mill
1793, Whitney Invents the Cotton Gin
1795, Pinckney's Treaty
1806, Pike's Southwest Explorations
1807, Congress Bans Importation of
    African Slaves
1807, Voyage of the *Clermont*
1808, American Fur Company Is
    Chartered
1810, Astorian Expeditions
1811, Construction of the National Road
1816, Second Bank of the United States
    Is Chartered
1821, Santa Fe Trail Opens
1824, *Gibbons v. Ogden*
1825, Erie Canal Opens
1830, Proslavery Argument
1831, McCormick Invents the Reaper
1832, Jackson vs. the Bank of the
    United States
1832, Nullification Controversy
1833, Rise of the Penny Press
1845, Era of the Clipper Ships
1846, Howe's Sewing Machine
1846, Independent Treasury Is
    Established
1854, Perry Opens Trade with Japan
1859, First Commercial Oil Well
1863, National Bank Acts
1863, Reconstruction
1866, Chisholm Trail Opens
1869, Transcontinental Railroad Is
    Completed
1873, "Crime of 1873"
1882, Standard Oil Trust Is Organized
1887, Interstate Commerce Act
1890, Sherman Antitrust Act
1897, Dingley Tariff
1903, Acquisition of the Panama Canal
    Zone
1906, San Francisco Earthquake
1908, White House Conservation
    Conference
1909, Dollar Diplomacy
1910, Great Northern Migration
1913, Sixteenth Amendment
1913, Ford Assembly Line Begins
    Operation
1913, Alien Land Laws
1913, Federal Reserve Act

1918, Demobilization After World War I
1924, Dawes Plan
1929, Stock Market Crash
1929, Great Depression
1930's, Mass Deportations of Mexicans
1930, Baltimore and Ohio Railroad Begins Operation
1931, Empire State Building Opens
1932, Reconstruction Finance Corporation Is Created
1932, Ottawa Agreements
1932, Bonus March
1933, The Hundred Days
1933, Tennessee Valley Authority Is Established
1933, National Industrial Recovery Act
1934, Tydings-McDuffie Act
1934, The Dust Bowl
1935, Works Progress Administration Is Established
1935, Black Monday
1935, National Labor Relations Act
1935, Social Security Act
1936, Reciprocity Treaty
1939, Mobilization for World War II
1941, 6.6 Million Women Enter the U.S. Labor Force
1942, Bracero Program
1943, Inflation and Labor Unrest
1943, Urban Race Riots
1946, Employment Act
1955, AFL and CIO Merge
1959, St. Lawrence Seaway Opens
1961, Peace Corps Is Established
1967, Long, Hot Summer
1971, Devaluation of the Dollar
1973, Arab Oil Embargo and Energy Crisis
1974, Construction of the Alaska Pipeline
1981, Reagan's Budget and Tax Reform
1988, Indian Gaming Regulatory Act
1989, Lincoln Savings and Loan Declares Bankruptcy
1993, North American Free Trade Agreement
1994, General Agreement on Tariffs and Trade

EDUCATION

1650, Harvard College Is Established
1785, Beginnings of State Universities
1802, U.S. Military Academy Is Established
1820's, Free Public School Movement
1820's, Social Reform Movement
1823, Hartford Female Seminary Is Founded
1833, Oberlin College Is Established
1837, Mt. Holyoke Seminary Is Founded
1857, First African American University
1862, Morrill Land Grant Act
1865, Vassar College Is Founded
1867, Office of Education Is Created
1912, U.S. Public Health Service Is Established
1925, Scopes Trial
1929, League of United Latin American Citizens Is Founded
1944, G.I. Bill
1954, *Brown v. Board of Education*
1957, Little Rock School Desegregation Crisis
1962, Meredith Registers at "Ole Miss"
1963, *Abington School District v. Schempp*
1964, Berkeley Free Speech Movement
1965, Expansion of Affirmative Action
1968, Bilingual Education Act
1971, *Swann v. Charlotte-Mecklenburg Board of Education*
1974, *Lau v. Nichols*
1978, *Regents of the University of California v. Bakke*
1982, *Plyler v. Doe*

ENVIRONMENT

1872, Great American Bison Slaughter
1908, White House Conservation Conference
1916, National Park Service Is Created
1924, Halibut Treaty
1934, The Dust Bowl
1978, Toxic Waste at Love Canal
1979, Three Mile Island Accident
1981, Ozone Hole Is Discovered
1989, *Exxon Valdez* Oil Spill

EXPANSION AND LAND ACQUISITION

1626, Algonquians "Sell" Manhattan Island
1670, Hudson's Bay Company Is Chartered
1673, French Explore the Mississippi Valley
1702, Queen Anne's War
1711, Tuscarora War
1728, Russian Voyages to Alaska
1737, Walking Purchase
1754, French and Indian War
1763, Proclamation of 1763
1763, Paxton Boys' Massacres
1769, Rise of the California Missions
1774, Lord Dunmore's War
1774, Quebec Act
1784, Fort Stanwix Treaty
1785, Ordinance of 1785
1787, Northwest Ordinance
1790, Nootka Sound Convention
1790, Little Turtle's War
1793, Mackenzie Reaches the Arctic Ocean
1794, Battle of Fallen Timbers
1794, Jay's Treaty
1795, Pinckney's Treaty
1803, Louisiana Purchase
1804, Lewis and Clark Expedition
1806, Pike's Southwest Explorations
1808, American Fur Company Is Chartered
1810, *Fletcher v. Peck*
1810, Astorian Expeditions
1811, Construction of the National Road
1813, Creek War
1815, Westward Migration
1819, Adams-Onís Treaty
1820, Land Act of 1820
1821, Santa Fe Trail Opens
1823, Jedediah Smith Explores the Far West
1830, Webster-Hayne Debate
1830, Indian Removal Act
1830, Trail of Tears
1835, Texas Revolution
1840's, "Old" Immigration
1841, Preemption Act
1842, Frémont's Expeditions
1842, Webster-Ashburton Treaty
1846, Mormon Migration to Utah
1846, Mexican War
1846, Oregon Settlement
1846, Occupation of California and the Southwest
1848, California Gold Rush
1850, Compromise of 1850
1853, Pacific Railroad Surveys
1853, Gadsden Purchase
1858, Fraser River Gold Rush
1862, Homestead Act
1864, Sand Creek Massacre
1866, Chisholm Trail Opens
1867, Purchase of Alaska
1872, Great American Bison Slaughter

1879, Powell's *Report on the Lands of the Arid Region*
1885, Second Riel Rebellion
1887, General Allotment Act
1890, Closing of the Frontier
1896, Klondike Gold Rush
1898, Spanish-American War
1899, Philippine Insurrection
1901, Insular Cases
1903, Acquisition of the Panama Canal Zone
1930, Baltimore and Ohio Railroad Begins Operation
1959, Alaska and Hawaii Gain Statehood

EXPLORATION AND DISCOVERY
A.D. 986, Norse Expeditions
1492, Columbus' Voyages
1497, Cabot's Voyages
1513, Ponce de León's Voyages
1519, Cortés Enters Tenochtitlán
1528, Narváez's and Cabeza de Vaca's Expeditions
1534, Cartier and Roberval Search for a Northwest Passage
1539, De Soto's Expeditions
1540, Coronado's Expedition
1542, Settlement of Alta California
1565, St. Augustine Is Founded
1576, Frobisher's Voyages
1579, Drake Lands in Northern California
1603, Champlain's Voyages
1610, Hudson Explores Hudson Bay
1673, French Explore the Mississippi Valley
1728, Russian Voyages to Alaska
1793, Mackenzie Reaches the Arctic Ocean
1804, Lewis and Clark Expedition
1806, Pike's Southwest Explorations
1810, Astorian Expeditions
1823, Jedediah Smith Explores the Far West
1842, Frémont's Expeditions
1846, Oregon Settlement
1846, Occupation of California and the Southwest
1853, Pacific Railroad Surveys
1879, Powell's *Report on the Lands of the Arid Region*
1909, Peary and Henson Reach the North Pole

GOVERNMENT AND POLITICS
1619, First General Assembly of Virginia
1643, Confederation of the United Colonies of New England
1676, Bacon's Rebellion
1686, Dominion of New England Forms
1734, Trial of John Peter Zenger
1754, Albany Congress
1768, Carolina Regulator Movements
1773, Boston Tea Party
1774, First Continental Congress
1775, Second Continental Congress
1776, Declaration of Independence
1781, Articles of Confederation
1787, U.S. Constitution Is Adopted
1787, *Federalist* Papers Are Published
1789, Washington's Inauguration
1789, Judiciary Act
1790's, First U.S. Political Parties
1790, Hamilton's *Report on Public Credit*
1791, Canada's Constitutional Act
1791, U.S. Bill of Rights Is Ratified
1793, Whiskey Rebellion
1796, Washington's Farewell Address
1801, Jefferson Is Elected President
1803, *Marbury v. Madison*
1804, Burr's Conspiracy
1804, Twelfth Amendment
1811, Battle of Tippecanoe
1814, Hartford Convention
1815, Battle of New Orleans
1819, *McCulloch v. Maryland*
1820's, Free Public School Movement
1824, *Gibbons v. Ogden*
1824, U.S. Election of 1824
1828, Jackson Is Elected President
1831, Tocqueville Visits America
1832, Jackson vs. the Bank of the United States
1832, Nullification Controversy
1834, Birth of the Whig Party
1840, U.S. Election of 1840
1841, Upper and Lower Canada Unite
1846, Independent Treasury Is Established
1854, Birth of the Republican Party
1856, Bleeding Kansas
1858, Lincoln-Douglas Debates
1860, Lincoln Is Elected President
1860, Confederate States Secede from the Union
1861, Lincoln's Inauguration
1867, Impeachment of Andrew Johnson

1869, Scandals of the Grant Administration
1871, Indian Appropriation Act
1873, "Crime of 1873"
1873, Mackenzie Era in Canada
1877, Hayes Is Elected President
1884, U.S. Election of 1884
1892, Birth of the People's Party
1896, McKinley Is Elected President
1897, Laurier Era in Canada
1901, Theodore Roosevelt Becomes President
1902, Expansion of Direct Democracy
1909, Republican Congressional Insurgency
1911, Borden Government in Canada
1912, Wilson Is Elected President
1913, Sixteenth Amendment
1915, National Birth Control League Forms
1917, Espionage and Sedition Acts
1917, Mobilization for World War I
1918, Republican Resurgence
1919, Red Scare
1920, Meighen Era in Canada
1921, Scandals of the Harding Administration
1921, King Era in Canada
1924, Coolidge Is Elected President
1927, Sacco and Vanzetti Are Executed
1928, Smith-Hoover Campaign
1930, Bennett Era in Canada
1931, Statute of Westminster
1932, Reconstruction Finance Corporation Is Created
1932, Franklin D. Roosevelt Is Elected President
1933, The Hundred Days
1933, Tennessee Valley Authority Is Established
1937, Supreme Court Packing Fight
1938, HUAC Investigations
1939, Mobilization for World War II
1940, United States Builds a Two-Ocean Navy
1942, Censorship and Japanese Internment
1942, Manhattan Project
1948, Truman Is Elected President
1948, St. Laurent Succeeds King
1951, McCarthy Hearings
1952, Massey Becomes Canada's First Native-Born Governor General
1952, Puerto Rico Becomes a Commonwealth

1952, Eisenhower Is Elected President
1957, Diefenbaker Era in Canada
1960, Quebec Sovereignist
Movement
1960, Kennedy Is Elected President
1961, Peace Corps Is Established
1962, Reapportionment Cases
1963, Pearson Becomes Canada's
Prime Minister
1963, Assassination of President
Kennedy
1964, Twenty-fourth Amendment
1964, Johnson Is Elected President
1968, Assassinations of King and
Kennedy
1968, Trudeau Era in Canada
1968, Chicago Riots
1968, Nixon Is Elected President
1969, Alcatraz Occupation
1972, Rapprochement with China
1972, Watergate Affair
1974, Nixon Resigns
1976, Carter Is Elected President
1979, Clark Elected Canada's Prime
Minister
1980, Abscam Affair
1980, Reagan Is Elected President
1982, Canada's Constitution Act
1983, Jackson Becomes First Major
African American Candidate for
President
1984, Mulroney Era in Canada
1986, Iran-Contra Scandal
1988, Bush Is Elected President
1990, Bloc Québécois Forms
1992, Clinton Is Elected President
1993, Campbell Becomes Canada's
First Woman Prime Minister
1994, Republicans Return to Congress

HEALTH AND MEDICINE
1846, Surgical Anesthesia Is Safely
Demonstrated
1857, New York Infirmary for Indigent
Women and Children Opens
1900, Suppression of Yellow Fever
1912, U.S. Public Health Service Is
Established
1921, Sheppard-Towner Act
1952, Development of a Polio Vaccine
1960, FDA Approves the Birth Control
Pill
1978, Toxic Waste at Love Canal
1981, First AIDS Cases Are Reported
1982, *Plyler v. Doe*

1989, Human Genome Project
1993, Family and Medical Leave Act

IMMIGRATION
1798, Alien and Sedition Acts
1840's, "Old" Immigration
1844, Anti-Irish Riots
1848, California Gold Rush
1849, Chinese Immigration
1868, Burlingame Treaty
1882, Chinese Exclusion Act
1882, Rise of the Chinese Six
Companies
1892, Yellow Peril Campaign
1892, "New" Immigration
1895, Chinese American Citizens
Alliance Is Founded
1898, *United States v. Wong Kim Ark*
1907, Gentlemen's Agreement
1913, Anti-Defamation League Is
Founded
1917, Immigration Act of 1917
1919, Red Scare
1922, Cable Act
1922, *Ozawa v. United States*
1924, Immigration Act of 1924
1927, Sacco and Vanzetti Are Executed
1930's, Mass Deportations of Mexicans
1942, Bracero Program
1943, Magnuson Act
1945, War Brides Act
1952, McCarran-Walter Act
1953, Refugee Relief Act
1954, Operation Wetback
1965, Immigration and Nationality Act
1978, Canada's Immigration Act of
1976
1980, Mariel Boat Lift
1980, Miami Riots
1982, *Plyler v. Doe*
1986, Immigration Reform and Control
Act

JEWISH AMERICAN HISTORY
1654, First Jewish Settlers
1913, Anti-Defamation League Is
Founded

LATINO AMERICAN HISTORY
A.D. 200, Mayan Civilization
A.D. 700, Zapotec Civilization
1428, Aztec Empire
1492, Columbus' Voyages
1519, Cortés Enters Tenochtitlán

1528, Narváez's and Cabeza de Vaca's
Expeditions
1540, Coronado's Expedition
1542, Settlement of Alta California
1598, Oñate's New Mexico Expedition
1632, Zuñi Rebellion
1810, El Grito de Dolores
1819, Adams-Onís Treaty
1821, Mexican War of Independence
1823, Monroe Doctrine
1835, Texas Revolution
1839, Amistad Slave Revolt
1846, Mexican War
1846, Occupation of California and the
Southwest
1848, Treaty of Guadalupe Hidalgo
1850, Bloody Island Massacre
1853, Gadsden Purchase
1857, Cart War
1877, Salt Wars
1889, First Pan-American Congress
1895, Hearst-Pulitzer Circulation War
1898, Spanish-American War
1903, Platt Amendment
1910, Mexican Revolution
1912, Intervention in Nicaragua
1916, Pershing Expedition
1917, Jones Act
1929, League of United Latin American
Citizens Is Founded
1930's, Mass Deportations of Mexicans
1933, Good Neighbor Policy
1942, Bracero Program
1948, Organization of American States
Is Founded
1952, Puerto Rico Becomes a
Commonwealth
1954, Operation Wetback
1956, Cuban Revolution
1962, Cuban Missile Crisis
1965, Delano Grape Strike
1968, Bilingual Education Act
1972, United Farm Workers Joins with
AFL-CIO
1974, *Lau v. Nichols*
1978, Panama Canal Treaties
1980, Mariel Boat Lift
1980, Miami Riots
1983, United States Invades Grenada

LAWS AND ACTS
1641, Massachusetts Recognizes
Slavery
1649, Maryland Act of Toleration
1660, British Navigation Acts

1661, Virginia Slave Codes
1754, Albany Congress
1763, Proclamation of 1763
1765, Stamp Act Crisis
1767, Townshend Crisis
1774, Quebec Act
1781, Articles of Confederation
1785, Ordinance of 1785
1786, Virginia Statute of Religious
    Liberty
1787, Northwest Ordinance
1787, U.S. Constitution Is Adopted
1789, Judiciary Act
1791, Canada's Constitutional Act
1791, U.S. Bill of Rights Is Ratified
1793, First Fugitive Slave Law
1798, Alien and Sedition Acts
1804, First Black Codes
1804, Twelfth Amendment
1820, Missouri Compromise
1820, Land Act of 1820
1830, Indian Removal Act
1841, Preemption Act
1850, Compromise of 1850
1850, Second Fugitive Slave Law
1854, Kansas-Nebraska Act
1862, Homestead Act
1862, Morrill Land Grant Act
1863, National Bank Acts
1863, First National Draft Law
1865, New Black Codes
1865, Thirteenth Amendment
1866, Civil Rights Act of 1866
1866, Suffragists Protest the Fourteenth
    Amendment
1867, British North America Act
1868, Fourteenth Amendment
1871, Indian Appropriation Act
1873, "Crime of 1873"
1876, Canada's Indian Act
1882, Chinese Exclusion Act
1883, Pendleton Act
1887, Interstate Commerce Act
1887, General Allotment Act
1890, Sherman Antitrust Act
1890, Mississippi Disfranchisement
    Laws
1897, Dingley Tariff
1903, Platt Amendment
1906, Pure Food and Drug Act
1909, National Association for the
    Advancement of Colored People
    Is Founded
1913, Federal Reserve Act
1917, Jones Act

1917, Espionage and Sedition Acts
1920, Prohibition
1920, U.S. Women Gain the Vote
1921, Sheppard-Towner Act
1924, Indian Citizenship Act
1924, Immigration Act of 1924
1931, Statute of Westminster
1933, National Industrial Recovery Act
1934, Tydings-McDuffie Act
1934, Indian Reorganization Act
1935, National Labor Relations Act
1935, Social Security Act
1935, Neutrality Acts
1938, Fair Labor Standards Act
1941, Lend-Lease Act
1943, Magnuson Act
1944, G.I. Bill
1945, War Brides Act
1946, Employment Act
1947, Canada's Citizenship Act
1947, National Security Act
1952, McCarran-Walter Act
1953, Termination Resolution
1953, Refugee Relief Act
1960, Civil Rights Act of 1960
1963, Equal Pay Act
1964, Twenty-fourth Amendment
1964, Civil Rights Act of 1964
1965, Voting Rights Act
1965, Immigration and Nationality Act
1967, Freedom of Information Act
1968, Bilingual Education Act
1968, Indian Civil Rights Act
1968, Fair Housing Act
1969, Canada's Official Languages Act
1971, U.S. Voting Age Is Lowered to
    Eighteen
1971, Alaska Native Claims Settlement
    Act
1975, Equal Credit Opportunity Act
1977, Canada's Human Rights Act
1978, Pregnancy Discrimination Act
1978, Canada's Immigration Act of
    1976
1978, American Indian Religious
    Freedom Act
1982, Canada's Constitution Act
1982, Defeat of the Equal Rights
    Amendment
1986, Immigration Reform and Control
    Act
1987, Canada's Pay Equity Act
1988, Civil Rights Restoration Act
1988, Family Support Act
1988, Indian Gaming Regulatory Act

1990, Americans with Disabilities Act
1991, Civil Rights Act of 1991
1993, Family and Medical Leave Act
1994, Brady Handgun Violence
    Protection Act

NATIVE AMERICAN HISTORY
15,000 B.C., Bering Strait Migrations
1500 B.C., Olmec Civilization
700 B.C., Ohio Mound Builders
300 B.C., Hohokam Culture
A.D. 200, Mayan Civilization
A.D. 200, Anasazi Civilization
A.D. 700, Zapotec Civilization
A.D. 750, Mogollon Culture
A.D. 750, Mississippian Culture
1428, Aztec Empire
1495, West Indian Uprisings
1500, Iroquois Confederacy
1513, Ponce de León's Voyages
1519, Cortés Enters Tenochtitlán
1528, Narváez's and Cabeza de Vaca's
    Expeditions
1539, De Soto's Expeditions
1540, Coronado's Expedition
1542, Settlement of Alta California
1565, St. Augustine Is Founded
1570's, Powhatan Confederacy
1598, Oñate's New Mexico Expedition
1622, Powhatan Wars
1626, Algonquians "Sell" Manhattan
    Island
1632, Zuñi Rebellion
1636, Pequot War
1642, Beaver Wars
1671, Indian Slave Trade
1675, Metacom's War
1676, Bacon's Rebellion
1680, Pueblo Revolt
1711, Tuscarora War
1714, Fox Wars
1737, Walking Purchase
1754, French and Indian War
1754, Albany Congress
1759, Cherokee War
1763, Pontiac's Resistance
1763, Proclamation of 1763
1763, Paxton Boys' Massacres
1768, Carolina Regulator Movements
1769, Rise of the California Missions
1774, Lord Dunmore's War
1776, Indian Delegation Meets with
    Congress
1784, Fort Stanwix Treaty
1790, Nootka Sound Convention

1790, Little Turtle's War
1793, Mackenzie Reaches the Arctic Ocean
1794, Battle of Fallen Timbers
1799, Code of Handsome Lake
1808, Prophetstown Is Founded
1810, *Fletcher v. Peck*
1812, War of 1812
1813, Creek War
1813, Battle of the Thames
1815, Westward Migration
1815, Treaty of Ghent
1815, Red River Raids
1817, Seminole Wars
1821, Santa Fe Trail Opens
1828, *Cherokee Phoenix* Begins Publication
1830, Indian Removal Act
1830, Trail of Tears
1831, Cherokee Cases
1837, Rebellions in Canada
1847, Taos Rebellion
1861, Stand Watie Fights for the South
1861, Apache Wars
1862, Great Sioux War
1863, Long Walk of the Navajos
1864, Sand Creek Massacre
1866, Bozeman Trail War
1867, Medicine Lodge Creek Treaty
1868, Washita River Massacre
1869, First Riel Rebellion
1871, Indian Appropriation Act
1872, Great American Bison Slaughter
1874, Red River War
1876, Canada's Indian Act
1876, Battle of the Little Bighorn
1877, Nez Perce Exile
1885, Second Riel Rebellion
1887, General Allotment Act
1890, Closing of the Frontier
1890, Battle of Wounded Knee
1903, *Lone Wolf v. Hitchcock*
1924, Indian Citizenship Act
1934, Indian Reorganization Act
1953, Termination Resolution
1959, Alaska and Hawaii Gain Statehood
1965, Voting Rights Act
1968, Indian Civil Rights Act
1969, Alcatraz Occupation
1971, Alaska Native Claims Settlement Act
1972, Trail of Broken Treaties
1973, Wounded Knee Occupation

1978, American Indian Religious Freedom Act
1988, Indian Gaming Regulatory Act

ORGANIZATIONS AND INSTITUTIONS

1627, Company of New France Is Chartered
1650, Harvard College Is Established
1670, Hudson's Bay Company Is Chartered
1768, Methodist Church Is Established
1775, Pennsylvania Society for the Abolition of Slavery Is Founded
1784, Hall's Masonic Lodge Is Chartered
1785, Beginnings of State Universities
1787, Free African Society Is Founded
1789, Episcopal Church Is Established
1790's, First U.S. Political Parties
1802, U.S. Military Academy Is Established
1816, Second Bank of the United States Is Chartered
1816, AME Church Is Founded
1819, Unitarian Church Is Founded
1823, Hartford Female Seminary Is Founded
1833, American Anti-Slavery Society Is Founded
1833, Oberlin College Is Established
1834, Birth of the Whig Party
1837, Mt. Holyoke Seminary Is Founded
1846, Independent Treasury Is Established
1846, Smithsonian Institution Is Founded
1853, National Council of Colored People Is Founded
1854, Birth of the Republican Party
1857, New York Infirmary for Indigent Women and Children Opens
1865, Freedmen's Bureau Is Established
1866, Rise of the Ku Klux Klan
1867, Office of Education Is Created
1867, National Grange of the Patrons of Husbandry Forms
1869, Rise of Woman Suffrage Associations
1871, Barnum's Circus Forms
1875, Supreme Court of Canada Is Established
1886, American Federation of Labor Is Founded

1889, Hull House Opens
1890, Women's Rights Associations Unite
1895, Chinese American Citizens Alliance Is Founded
1905, Industrial Workers of the World Is Founded
1905, Niagara Movement
1913, Anti-Defamation League Is Founded
1916, National Woman's Party Is Founded
1916, National Park Service Is Created
1917, Universal Negro Improvement Association Is Established
1918, Republican Resurgence
1919, Black Sox Scandal
1920, League of Women Voters Is Founded
1929, League of United Latin American Citizens Is Founded
1930, Nation of Islam Is Founded
1930, Japanese American Citizens League Is Founded
1935, Works Progress Administration Is Established
1935, Congress of Industrial Organizations Is Founded
1942, Congress of Racial Equality Is Founded
1955, AFL and CIO Merge
1957, Southern Christian Leadership Conference Is Founded
1960, Quebec Sovereignist Movement
1966, National Organization for Women Is Founded
1968, Chicago Riots

PREHISTORY AND ANCIENT CULTURES

15,000 B.C., Bering Strait Migrations
1500 B.C., Olmec Civilization
700 B.C., Ohio Mound Builders
300 B.C., Hohokam Culture
A.D. 200, Mayan Civilization
A.D. 200, Anasazi Civilization
A.D. 700, Zapotec Civilization
A.D. 750, Mogollon Culture
A.D. 750, Mississippian Culture
1428, Aztec Empire

RELIGION

1620, Pilgrims Land at Plymouth
1630, Great Puritan Migration
1632, Settlement of Connecticut

1636, Rhode Island Is Founded
1649, Maryland Act of Toleration
1654, First Jewish Settlers
1662, Half-Way Covenant
1681, Pennsylvania Is Founded
1692, Salem Witchcraft Trials
1730's, First Great Awakening
1768, Methodist Church Is Established
1769, Rise of the California Missions
1773, African American Baptist Church Is Founded
1774, Quebec Act
1786, Virginia Statute of Religious Liberty
1789, Episcopal Church Is Established
1790's, Second Great Awakening
1799, Code of Handsome Lake
1816, AME Church Is Founded
1819, Unitarian Church Is Founded
1820's, Social Reform Movement
1836, Rise of Transcendentalism
1844, Anti-Irish Riots
1846, Mormon Migration to Utah
1930, Nation of Islam Is Founded
1963, *Abington School District v. Schempp*
1978, American Indian Religious Freedom Act
1993, Branch Davidians' Compound Burns

SCIENCE AND TECHNOLOGY
1776, First Test of a Submarine in Warfare
1790, Slater's Spinning Mill
1793, Whitney Invents the Cotton Gin
1807, Voyage of the *Clermont*
1825, Erie Canal Opens
1831, McCormick Invents the Reaper
1836, Rise of Transcendentalism
1844, First Telegraph Message
1845, Era of the Clipper Ships
1846, Howe's Sewing Machine
1846, Smithsonian Institution Is Founded
1846, Surgical Anesthesia Is Safely Demonstrated
1858, First Transatlantic Cable
1859, First Commercial Oil Well
1861, Transcontinental Telegraph Is Completed
1862, *Monitor* vs. *Virginia*
1869, Transcontinental Railroad Is Completed
1876, Bell Demonstrates the Telephone

1879, Edison Demonstrates the Incandescent Lamp
1883, Brooklyn Bridge Opens
1893, World's Columbian Exposition
1900, Teletype Is Developed
1903, Acquisition of the Panama Canal Zone
1903, Wright Brothers' First Flight
1913, Ford Assembly Line Begins Operation
1920, Commercial Radio Broadcasting Begins
1926, Launching of the First Liquid-Fueled Rocket
1927, Lindbergh's Transatlantic Flight
1930, Baltimore and Ohio Railroad Begins Operation
1931, Empire State Building Opens
1934, Development of Radar
1938, First Xerographic Photocopy
1939, Debut of Commercial Television
1942, Manhattan Project
1945, Atomic Bombing of Japan
1947, Invention of the Transistor
1952, Development of a Polio Vaccine
1952, Hydrogen Bomb Is Detonated
1959, St. Lawrence Seaway Opens
1960, FDA Approves the Birth Control Pill
1961, First American in Space
1969, Apollo 11 Lands on the Moon
1974, Construction of the Alaska Pipeline
1977, Spaceflights of Voyagers 1 and 2
1978, Toxic Waste at Love Canal
1981, IBM Markets the Personal Computer
1981, Ozone Hole Is Discovered
1986, *Challenger* Accident
1989, Human Genome Project
1990's, Rise of the Internet
1993, Astronauts Repair the Hubble Space Telescope

SETTLEMENTS
1565, St. Augustine Is Founded
1584, Lost Colony of Roanoke
1603, Champlain's Voyages
1607, Jamestown Is Founded
1620, Pilgrims Land at Plymouth
1626, Algonquians "Sell" Manhattan Island
1630, Great Puritan Migration
1632, Settlement of Connecticut

1636, Rhode Island Is Founded
1663, Settlement of the Carolinas
1670, Charles Town Is Founded
1681, Pennsylvania Is Founded
1732, Settlement of Georgia
1808, Prophetstown Is Founded
1814, New Harmony and the Communitarian Movement
1846, Mormon Migration to Utah
1846, Oregon Settlement
1848, California Gold Rush
1858, Fraser River Gold Rush

SOCIAL REFORM
1730's, First Great Awakening
1775, Pennsylvania Society for the Abolition of Slavery Is Founded
1777, Northeast States Abolish Slavery
1787, Free African Society Is Founded
1790's, Second Great Awakening
1808, Prophetstown Is Founded
1814, New Harmony and the Communitarian Movement
1819, Unitarian Church Is Founded
1820's, Social Reform Movement
1828, *Cherokee Phoenix* Begins Publication
1831, *The Liberator* Begins Publication
1833, American Anti-Slavery Society Is Founded
1850, Underground Railroad
1851, Akron Woman's Rights Convention
1857, New York Infirmary for Indigent Women and Children Opens
1867, National Grange of the Patrons of Husbandry Forms
1889, Hull House Opens
1920, Prohibition
1921, Sheppard-Towner Act
1935, Social Security Act
1935, Congress of Industrial Organizations Is Founded
1938, Fair Labor Standards Act
1941, 6.6 Million Women Enter the U.S. Labor Force
1955, Montgomery Bus Boycott
1960, FDA Approves the Birth Control Pill
1963, King Delivers His "I Have a Dream" Speech
1965, Expansion of Affirmative Action
1988, Family Support Act
1993, Family and Medical Leave Act

TRANSPORTATION

1807, Voyage of the *Clermont*
1811, Construction of the National Road
1815, Westward Migration
1821, Santa Fe Trail Opens
1823, Jedediah Smith Explores the Far West
1825, Erie Canal Opens
1845, Era of the Clipper Ships
1853, Pacific Railroad Surveys
1860, Pony Express
1866, Chisholm Trail Opens
1869, Transcontinental Railroad Is Completed
1887, Interstate Commerce Act
1903, Acquisition of the Panama Canal Zone
1903, Wright Brothers' First Flight
1913, Ford Assembly Line Begins Operation
1927, Lindbergh's Transatlantic Flight
1930, Baltimore and Ohio Railroad Begins Operation
1959, St. Lawrence Seaway Opens
1973, Arab Oil Embargo and Energy Crisis
1978, Panama Canal Treaties

TREATIES AND AGREEMENTS

1778, Franco-American Treaties
1783, Treaty of Paris
1784, Fort Stanwix Treaty
1790, Nootka Sound Convention
1794, Jay's Treaty
1795, Pinckney's Treaty
1803, Louisiana Purchase
1815, Treaty of Ghent
1819, Adams-Onís Treaty
1842, Webster-Ashburton Treaty
1848, Treaty of Guadalupe Hidalgo
1853, Gadsden Purchase
1867, Purchase of Alaska
1867, Medicine Lodge Creek Treaty
1868, Burlingame Treaty
1871, Treaty of Washington
1907, Gentlemen's Agreement
1919, Treaty of Versailles
1921, Washington Disarmament Conference
1924, Halibut Treaty
1928, Kellogg-Briand Pact
1932, Ottawa Agreements
1936, Reciprocity Treaty
1940, Ogdensburg Agreement
1942, Bracero Program

1948, Organization of American States Is Founded
1949, North Atlantic Treaty
1978, Panama Canal Treaties
1979, SALT II Is Signed
1987, INF Treaty Is Signed
1993, START II Is Signed
1993, North American Free Trade Agreement
1994, U.S.-North Korea Pact
1994, General Agreement on Tariffs and Trade

WARS, UPRISINGS, AND CIVIL UNREST

1495, West Indian Uprisings
1598, Oñate's New Mexico Expedition
1622, Powhatan Wars
1632, Zuñi Rebellion
1636, Pequot War
1642, Beaver Wars
1664, British Conquest of New Netherland
1675, Metacom's War
1676, Bacon's Rebellion
1680, Pueblo Revolt
1702, Queen Anne's War
1711, Tuscarora War
1712, New York City Slave Revolt
1714, Fox Wars
1739, Stono Rebellion
1739, King George's War
1754, French and Indian War
1759, Cherokee War
1763, Pontiac's Resistance
1763, Paxton Boys' Massacres
1765, Stamp Act Crisis
1767, Townshend Crisis
1768, Carolina Regulator Movements
1770, Boston Massacre
1773, Boston Tea Party
1774, Lord Dunmore's War
1775, Battle of Lexington and Concord
1775, Second Continental Congress
1776, Indian Delegation Meets with Congress
1776, First Test of a Submarine in Warfare
1777, Battle of Oriskany Creek
1777, Battle of Saratoga
1781, Cornwallis Surrenders at Yorktown
1790, Little Turtle's War
1791, Haitian Independence
1793, Whiskey Rebellion

1794, Battle of Fallen Timbers
1797, XYZ Affair
1804, Burr's Conspiracy
1810, El Grito de Dolores
1811, Battle of Tippecanoe
1812, War of 1812
1813, Creek War
1813, Battle of the Thames
1815, Battle of New Orleans
1815, Red River Raids
1817, Seminole Wars
1821, Mexican War of Independence
1831, Nat Turner's Insurrection
1835, Texas Revolution
1837, Rebellions in Canada
1839, Amistad Slave Revolt
1842, Dorr Rebellion
1844, Anti-Irish Riots
1846, Mexican War
1846, Occupation of California and the Southwest
1847, Taos Rebellion
1850, Bloody Island Massacre
1857, Cart War
1859, John Brown's Raid on Harpers Ferry
1860, Confederate States Secede from the Union
1861, Stand Watie Fights for the South
1861, Apache Wars
1861, First Battle of Bull Run
1862, *Monitor* vs. *Virginia*
1862, Great Sioux War
1863, First National Draft Law
1863, Battles of Gettysburg, Vicksburg, and Chattanooga
1864, Sherman's March to the Sea
1864, Sand Creek Massacre
1865, Surrender at Appomattox and Assassination of Lincoln
1866, Race Riots in the South
1866, Bozeman Trail War
1868, Washita River Massacre
1869, First Riel Rebellion
1874, Red River War
1876, Battle of the Little Bighorn
1877, Nez Perce Exile
1877, Salt Wars
1885, Second Riel Rebellion
1890, Battle of Wounded Knee
1898, Spanish-American War
1899, Philippine Insurrection
1910, Mexican Revolution
1912, Intervention in Nicaragua
1916, Pershing Expedition

1917, United States Enters World War I
1917, Propaganda and Civil Liberties in
 World War I
1917, Mobilization for World War I
1918, Meuse-Argonne Offensive
1940, United States Builds a
 Two-Ocean Navy
1941, Lend-Lease Act
1941, Bombing of Pearl Harbor
1941, Germany and Italy Declare War
 on the United States
1942, Battle of Midway
1942, Manhattan Project
1942, Battle of Guadalcanal
1942, Invasion of North Africa
1943, Inflation and Labor Unrest
1943, Urban Race Riots
1943, Western Allies Invade Italy
1944, Operation Overlord
1944, Superfortress Bombing of Japan
1944, Battle for Leyte Gulf
1944, Battle of the Bulge
1945, Yalta Conference
1945, V-E Day
1945, Potsdam Conference
1945, Atomic Bombing of Japan
1950, Korean War
1950, Truman-MacArthur Confrontation
1956, Cuban Revolution
1961, Bay of Pigs Invasion
1962, Cuban Missile Crisis
1964, Vietnam War
1965, Watts Riot
1965, Delano Grape Strike
1967, Long, Hot Summer
1968, Tet Offensive
1968, Chicago Riots
1969, Stonewall Inn Riots
1969, Alcatraz Occupation
1970, United States Invades Cambodia

1970, Kent State Massacre
1970, October Crisis
1971, Attica State Prison Riots
1972, Trail of Broken Treaties
1973, Wounded Knee Occupation
1973, U.S. Troops Leave Vietnam
1980, Miami Riots
1983, United States Invades Grenada
1991, Persian Gulf War
1992, Los Angeles Riots
1993, Branch Davidians' Compound
 Burns
1995, Oklahoma Federal Building
 Bombed

WOMEN'S ISSUES
1692, Salem Witchcraft Trials
1776, New Jersey Women Gain the Vote
1820's, Social Reform Movement
1823, Hartford Female Seminary Is
 Founded
1833, Oberlin College Is Established
1837, Mt. Holyoke Seminary Is
 Founded
1848, Seneca Falls Convention
1851, Akron Woman's Rights
 Convention
1857, New York Infirmary for Indigent
 Women and Children Opens
1865, Vassar College Is Founded
1866, Suffragists Protest the Fourteenth
 Amendment
1869, Rise of Woman Suffrage
 Associations
1869, Western States Grant Woman
 Suffrage
1872, Susan B. Anthony Is Arrested
1874, *Minor v. Happersett*
1875, Page Law

1876, Declaration of the Rights of
 Women
1889, Hull House Opens
1890, Women's Rights Associations
 Unite
1908, *Muller v. Oregon*
1911, Triangle Shirtwaist Company Fire
1915, National Birth Control League
 Forms
1916, National Woman's Party Is
 Founded
1917, Canadian Women Gain the Vote
1920, League of Women Voters Is
 Founded
1920, U.S. Women Gain the Vote
1921, Sheppard-Towner Act
1922, Cable Act
1923, Proposal of the Equal Rights
 Amendment
1941, 6.6 Million Women Enter the
 U.S. Labor Force
1960, FDA Approves the Birth Control
 Pill
1963, Equal Pay Act
1965, *Griswold v. Connecticut*
1966, National Organization for
 Women Is Founded
1970's, Rise of Women's Role in the
 Military
1972, Equal Employment Opportunity
 Act
1973, *Roe v. Wade*
1975, Equal Credit Opportunity Act
1978, Pregnancy Discrimination Act
1982, Defeat of the Equal Rights
 Amendment
1987, Canada's Pay Equity Act
1992, Tailhook Scandal
1993, Campbell Becomes Canada's
 First Woman Prime Minister